WILEY

John Wiley & Sons, Inc.

David L. Kurtz

University of Arkansas

Annotated Instructor's Edition

Boone & Kurtz's
Contemporary
BUSINESS

15TH EDITION

. . . at the speed of business

The 15th edition of *Contemporary Business* is dedicated to my wife, Diane.
She is the best thing that ever happened to me.
—Dave Kurtz

Vice President & Executive Publisher	George Hoffman
Senior Acquisitions Editor	Franny Kelly
Content Editor	Brian Kamins
Production Manager	Dorothy Sinclair
Senior Production Editor	Valerie A. Vargas
Associate Director of Marketing	Amy Scholz
Marketing Manager	Kelly Simmons
Creative Director	Harry Nolan
Senior Designer	Madelyn Lesure
Text Designer	4 Design Group
Cover Designer	Wendy Lai
Production Management Services	Integra
Photo Department Manager	Hilary Newman
Senior Product Designer	Allison Morris
Media Specialist	Elena Santa Maria

This book was set in Janson Text LT Std-Roman 10/13 by MPS Limited, Chennai, India and printed and bound by Quad/Graphics-Versailles. The cover was printed by Quad/Graphics-Versailles..

This book is printed on acid free paper. ∞

Founded in 1807, John Wiley & Sons, Inc. has been a valued source of knowledge and understanding for more than 200 years, helping people around the world meet their needs and fulfill their aspirations. Our company is built on a foundation of principles that include responsibility to the communities we serve and where we live and work. In 2008, we launched a Corporate Citizenship Initiative, a global effort to address the environmental, social, economic, and ethical challenges we face in our business. Among the issues we are addressing are carbon impact, paper specifications and procurement, ethical conduct within our business and among our vendors, and community and charitable support. For more information, please visit our website: www.wiley.com/go/citizenship.

Evaluation copies are provided to qualified academics and professionals for review purposes only, for use in their courses during the next academic year. †These copies are licensed and may not be sold or transferred to a third party. †Upon completion of the review period, please return the evaluation copy to Wiley. †Return instructions and a free of charge return shipping label are available at www.wiley.com/go/returnlabel. Outside of the United States, please contact your local representative.

ISBN-13   978-1-118-43222-8

Printed in the United States of America

10 9 8 7 6 5 4 3 2 1

| About the Author |

During Dave Kurtz's high school days, no one in Salisbury, Maryland, would have mistaken him for a scholar. In fact, he was a mediocre student, so bad that his father steered him toward higher education by finding him a succession of backbreaking summer jobs. Thankfully, most of them have been erased from his memory, but a few linger, including picking peaches, loading watermelons on trucks headed for market, and working as a pipefitter's helper. Unfortunately, these jobs had zero impact on his academic standing. Worse yet for Dave's ego, he was no better than average as a high school athlete in football and track.

But four years at Davis & Elkins College in Elkins, West Virginia, turned him around. Excellent instructors helped get Dave on sound academic footing. His grade point average soared—enough to get him accepted by the graduate business school at the University of Arkansas, where he met Gene Boone. Gene and Dave became longtime co-authors; together they produced more than 50 books. In addition to writing, Dave and Gene were involved in various entrepreneurial ventures.

This long-term partnership ended with Gene's death a few years ago. But, this book will always be Boone & Kurtz's *Contemporary Business*.

If you have any questions or comments about the new 15th edition, Dave can be reached at ProfKurtz@gmail.com.

| Letter to Instructors |

You've come to trust *Contemporary Business* to cover every aspect of the business world with a critical but fair eye. Let's face it: there are best business practices and those we'd never want to repeat. However, both provide learning opportunities. We've always chosen to take a critical look at the way business is being done in the world and help students understand what they need to know in order to have a long and illustrious business career.

Contemporary Business features a full line of teaching resources to provide instructors with a consistent and well-integrated learning system. This hands-on package guides you through the process of active learning with the tools to create an interactive learning environment. With its emphasis on activities and exercises, the package encourages students to take an active role in the course and prepares them for decision-making in a real-world context.

In addition to *WileyPLUS*, our innovative, research-based, online environment for effective teaching and learning, the 15th edition of *Contemporary Business* now includes an Annotated Instructor's Edition. We have annotated the text to include **Lecture Enhancers** and **Classroom Activities** loaded with up-to-the-minute business issues and examples specifically written to enliven classroom discussion and improve learning.

Now more than ever, business moves at a pace that is unparalleled. Our motivation is to help instructors to keep MOVING AT THE SPEED OF BUSINESS. *Contemporary Business* includes the most current information available and the best supplementary package in the business. You'll find that this new edition gets your students excited about the world of business and helps them improve their critical-thinking skills.

John Wiley & Sons is privileged to be working with you and looks forward to helping you achieve your goals in your Introduction to Business course.

Sincerely,

Franny Kelly
Senior Editor

Kelly Simmons
Marketing Manager

| Instructor Teaching Aids |

The *Annotated Instructor's Edition* includes the following instructor's resource material to aid in teaching this course to your students.

rned by an operatin   es a partnership agree-
reduces each par   the other owners.
fessionals, such   ians, use a similar
etters 'PC atta   e the wave of
tely after the
the U.S. con
small busines   y hospitals. On
Amazon.com i

LECTURE ENHANCER
These questions or exercises have been created to spark discussion and thought among your students.

ble taxation characteristic of a traditional corporatio

LECTURE ENHANCER:
Why might a sole proprietorship or partnership firm want to become an LLC?

wned Corporati

tive for creating a corporation is **employee ownership**, in which work-
ck in the company that employs them. The corporate organization stays
stockholders are also employees. At King Arthur Flour, virtually all the

employee ownership
business ownership in which workers buy shares

CLASS ACTIVITY
These activities are designed to stimulate deeper discussion, energize the class, and improve learning through reinforcement and application. Each one centers around a key question which you, as the instructor, provide to the class.

The exercise may be accomplished in the physical classroom using the "blackboard" or in a distance learning mode using a discussion board or chat room as the vehicle for dialogue.

CLASS ACTIVITY:
Ask students to share their ideas of benefits that might result from a merger of two large banks.

merger agreement in which two or more firms combine to form one company.

acquisition agreement in which one firm purchases another.

Merger

just a
merged with
The merger t
computer syster

The terms me
ferent. In a **merger**,
firm purchases the othe
assets, it also takes on any de   oc
or subsidiary from another firm. Not   pts are succ
to buy T-Mobile USA, an acquisition that would have combine

Chapter Walkthrough

How to use the study aids in this book

Chapter 4

Competing in World Markets

Learning Objectives

1. Explain why nations trade.
2. Describe how trade is measured between nations.
3. Identify the barriers to international trade.
4. Discuss reducing barriers to international trade.
5. Explain the decisions to go global.
6. Discuss developing a strategy for international business.

LEARNING OBJECTIVES at the beginning of each chapter give students a framework for learning the specific concepts in the chapter. Each study objective reappears in the margin where the concept is discussed. Students can review the study objectives in the Summary at the end of the chapter.

THE OPENING VIGNETTE helps students picture how the chapter topic relates to the real world of business. References to the Opening Vignette throughout the chapter help students put new ideas in context, organize them, and remember them.

The Marketing Zen Group: From $1,500 to Millions in Five Years

"Young entrepreneurs have to create their own opportunities. This economy needs fresh blood and bold new ideas." That bright attitude is what took The Marketing Zen Group, Shama Kabani's entrepreneurial Web marketing firm, from a one-person start-up in 2009 to a 30-person global firm in two short years.

Kabani, who founded the Dallas-based company at age 24 with $1,500 of her own money, saw an opportunity while still in college to help firms struggling to get up to speed with online marketing and social media. Their needs and Kabani's interests were a match, so she quickly adapted her original idea, which was to start a general consulting firm, and shifted to building a company that takes over Web marketing services for clients. For clients like Arthur Murray Dance Studios and k9cuisine .com, Marketing Zen Group handles everything from setting up a Facebook and Twitter presence to creating interactive Web sites, developing e-mail marketing campaigns, optimizing search engine results, and launching blogs aimed at clients' target markets. Clients have already seen record results from the firm's efforts, in terms of both Web traffic and sales dollars.

Kabani, who has also written a best-selling book about social media marketing, expects her firm to soon reach multimillion-dollar status. She keeps overhead low by using virtual hiring and lets most employees work off-site. Kabani says hiring is different in an entrepreneurial firm. A large corporation can accommodate many different types of employees, but "in a smaller business, passion is a must in every position. Hire people who are driven to do well and see your business succeed." Kabani herself brings the same degree of passion to her work. At the same time, she cautions against multitasking because it "decreases brain power," believes in elevating value over price, and stresses forgiveness and treating your team well. Kabani declares, "Aim for joy."[1]

BusinessEtiquette

How to Ask for a Raise

Do you think you deserve a raise? If so, here are a few tips to guide your next steps.

- *Be prepared.* If your company uses pay ranges for positions, learn where your pay lies on the scale.
- *Gather important data.* Document your accomplishments, including special projects or tasks. Track any positive feedback from others—both clients and co-workers.
- *Know what you want.* A percentage increase? A set dollar amount? ~~extended~~ vacation time? Make your request reasonable and be as specific as possible.
- *Be confident, but not arrogant.* State your case clearly. Your goal is to get your supervisor to consider your request.
- *Ask for details.* If your supervisor turns down your request, ask for specifics about what you need to do in order to qualify for the raise—and when. If possible, ask for a follow-up meeting within a certain period of time, such as two months.
- *Express thanks.* Regardless of the outcome, promptly send an e-mail with thanks for the meeting and politely recap the conversation. If you got the raise, make sure you demonstrate you deserved it. No raise yet? Don't give up. Get back to work and keep on trying.

Sources: Lindsay Olson, "How to Ask for a Raise," http://www.money.usnews.com, accessed February 19, 2012; Samantha Maziarz Christmann, "Asking For More: Don't Be Afraid to Ask for a Raise," *Buffalo News,* March 15, 2010, http://www.buffalonews.com; "How to Negotiate for a Raise—Even in a Bad Economy," *EmploymentDigest.net,* March 4, 2010, http://www.employmentdigest.net; Mary Sevinsky, "Is a Raise in Your Future for 2010?" *CareerRealism.com,* January 15, 2010, http://www.careerealism.com.

THE BUSINESS ETIQUETTE features discuss useful best business practices such as "Minding Your Social Media Manners," and "Managing a Millennial Workforce."

Hit & Miss

The Tiny Nano—A Potential Hit for Tata Mo...

When the Tata Nano arrived in the United States from India, it didn't hit the road, it went on display at the Coope... Design Museum in New York. "As the world's most affordable car, it... design achievement," said a museum director.

Retailing for $2,500 in India, the Nano is also safe and sturdy, and a potential revolution in transportation for millions of Indian families that can't otherwise afford a car. To keep costs low, Tata relied on existing parts and a highly simplified design. "My particular fascination about the Nano is what I refer to as the 'Nano effect' on the rest of the world's vehicle industry," said one research director. He predicts consumers in other countries will want to buy a car at that low price point.

In addition to developing the Nano, the $63-billion Indian conglomerate went on a "Western" shopping spree recently, purchasing the iconic UK luxury car brands Jaguar and Land Rover. The company says that these brands have now become one of the biggest contributors to the firm's overall earnings.

2. Can you think of a... markets of having a s... road?

Sources: Nano Web site, www.tatanano... March 2, 2012; Devang Murthy, "Tata Motors... http://www.topnews.in, February 15, 2012; "Tata N... September 2011," *Auto News India,* http://www.autonewsindia... 15, 2012; Alan Gell, "The World's Cheapest Car: 2011 Tata Nano," *Examiner.com,* http://www.examiner.com, accessed February 15, 2012; Phil Patton, "A Tata Nano Takes Manhattan," *The New York Times,* http://www.nytimes.com, accessed February 12, 2012; April K. Gupta and Haiyan Wang, "Tata Nano: Not Just a Car But Also a Platform," *BusinessWeek,* http://www.businessweek.com, accessed February 15, 2012.

HIT & MISS features appear throughout the text. They highlight various companies and include a discussion of their successes and failures. Students get a quick look at what makes certain companies succeed while others fall short.

Solving an Ethical Controversy

Do Some Bosses Earn Too Much?

Median CEO pay reached $8.4 million recently, up a whopping 35 percent despite the economic downturn felt by others. Enormous pay packages are meant to reward stellar company performance, but this has not always been true. Meanwhile U.S. firms hold a record amount of cash while millions of workers remain unemployed because business investment has dried up, and repeated financial crises have cost shareholders billions in retirement savings.

Is executive pay excessive?

PRO

1. CEO compensation should reflect the overall state of the economy and should be adjusted accordingly.

2. Poor returns to company shareholders do not merit high rewards to those responsible for increasing overall company value.

CON

1. CEOs must take huge personal and professional risks to successfully manage their firms, and they should be well rewarded.

2. High pay ensures that firms attract and keep talented CEOs, especially in difficult times when their skills are needed.

Summary

As CEO pay skyrocketed from 42 times the average U.S. worker's pay to more than 300 times in recent years, Congress handed shareholders new legislation, which allows them to vote "no" on executives' excessive pay. So far, however, "no" votes have only occurred at fewer than 2% of almost 2,000 publicly traded companies.

Sources: "Trends in CEO Pay," www.aflcio.org, accessed January 16, 2012; Susanne Craig, "Deal Book: Wall Street Is Bracing for Dismal 4ᵗʰ Quarter," *The New York Times*, January 7, 2012, www.nytimes.com; Nathaniel Parish Flannery, "Paying for Failure: The Costs of Firing America's Top CEO's," *Forbes*, October 4, 2011, www.forbes.com; Dale Wannen, "How Shareholders Are Battling Excessive Executive Compensation," Triple Pundit.com, June 30, 2011, www.triplepundit.com; John Holyar, "Investor 'Say on Pay' Is a Bust," *Bloomberg BusinessWeek*, June 16, 2011, www.businessweek.com.

Going Green

Labor Unions and Green Construction

The construction industry has nearly unlimited opportunities to make the world greener. One labor union, the Operative Plasterers and Cement Masons International Association (OPCMIA) has already recognized this and is training its members in the use of new green technologies and processes.

The OPCMIA training program, called Green Five, is being incorporated into existing training curricula to reach about 5,400 participants in 70 programs across local chapters, community colleges, vocational/technical schools, and OPCMIA Joint Apprenticeship and Training Centers. The Green Five program trains plasterers and cement masons in the sustainable use and application of concrete, exterior insulation finish systems, and American Clay. The Green Five program includes Green Awareness Training, which deals with energy-efficient building construction in general, addresses the process of energy assessment and retrofitting existing buildings, and provides an overview of environmentally sustainable products and manufacturing processes. Leadership training and "train-the-trainer" courses are offered as well.

Questions for Critical Thinking

1. How does a progressive stance toward green training help secure an important industry role for OPCMIA going forward?

2. Besides construction ... efit f ... train ... and management?

Sources: Marc Lifsher, "Unions Cry Foul Over Green Contracts," *ENR California*, california.construction.com, accessed March 16, 2012; David Bradley, "TR10: Green Concrete," *Technology Review*, May/June 2010, http://www.technologyreview.com, accessed March 16, 2012; "About OPCMIA," OPCMIA Web site, http://www.opcmia.org, accessed March 16, 2012; Gerry Ryan, "The Green Five Program," *Green Labor Journal*, http://green-laborjournal.com, accessed March 16, 2012.

Assessment Check ✓

1. What are the two main production systems?
2. What are the two time-related production processes?

...riven production evaluates ...ection between

...

...on processes are the analytic ...es a raw material to its compo-...ne or more marketable products; ...m, which combines a number of ...oduce finished products; the continu-...which generates finished items over a ...e; and the intermittent production process, ...roducts in short production runs.

of hazardous wastes. Human factors include the area's labor supply, local regulations, taxes, and living conditions.

Assessment Check Answers ✓

4.1 How does an environmental impact study influence the location decision? An environmental impact study influences the location decision because it outlines how transportation, energy use, water and sewer treatment needs, and other factors will affect plants, wildlife, water, air, and other features of the natural environment.

4.2 What human factors are relevant to the location decision? Human factors include an area's labor supply, labor costs, local regulations, taxes, and living conditions.

Business Terms You Need to Know

product 356	brand 364	distribution strategy 368	supply chain 381
product line 359	brand name 364	distribution channels 369	logistics 381
product mix 359	trademark 364	physical distribution 369	vendor-managed
product life cycle 359	brand equity 366	wholesaler 371	inventory 382

Review Questions

1. Classify each of the following business-to-consumer (B2C) and business-to-business (B2B) goods and services. Then choose one and describe how it could be classified as both.
   a. *Runner's World* or *Esquire* magazine
   b. six-pack of apple juice
   c. limousine service

4. What is the difference between a manufacturer's brand and a private brand? What is the difference between a family brand and an individual brand?

5. What are the three stages of brand loyalty? Why is the progression to the last stage so important to marketers?

6. What are the advantages of direct distribution? When is producer most likely to use direct distribution?

Projects and Teamwork Applications

1. On your own or with a classmate, choose one of the following goods or services. Decide whether you want to market it as a consumer product or a business product. Now create a brand name and marketing strategy for your product.
   a. lawnmower repair service
   b. health foods store

   d. music CDs
   e. paper stationery or notecards

3. Where do you do most of your shopping—in stores or online? Choose your favorite retailer and analyze why you like it. Outline your reasons for shopping there, then add two or three suggestions for improvement.

Web Assignments

1. **Product classification.** Visit the Web site of Johnson & Johnson (http://www.jnj.com) and click on "Our Products." Review the material in the chapter on product classification and then classify Johnson & Johnson's vast array of products.

2. **Shopping centers.** The Mall of America in Minnesota is the nation's largest shopping center. Go to the Mall's Web site (http://www.mallofamerica.com) to learn more about it. Make a list of five interesting facts you learned about the Mall of America.

> **BUSINESS TERMS YOU NEED TO KNOW, REVIEW QUESTIONS, PROJECTS AND TEAMWORK APPLICATIONS, AND WEB ASSIGNMENTS** are designed to promote critical thinking skills and provide students with numerous opportunities to practice key concepts.

Marketing Luxury Brands in China

CASE 12.1

If, as currently projected, 55 percent of purchases of luxury brands worldwide are made by Chinese consumers in 2020, it won't surprise Prada. The company already collects 43 percent of its global earnings from China.

As newly wealthy young Chinese consumers embrace a culture of spending, observers see China becoming the world's largest market for high-end watches, leather goods, designer clothing, cosmetics, and perfume. Recently, Chinese luxury-goods shoppers spent more than $16 billion, an increase of about 25 percent over the preceding year, and they often bought abroad, citing lower prices, ⬚tion, and better service in France, Italy, Great ⬚d Switzerland than they find at home.

⬚pending trend is expected to continue, even if at ⬚ace. "People will have more and more cash to ⬚iscretionary items, including luxury goods," said ⬚f Asia-Pacific investment banking at Citigroup. ⬚hat description doesn't include every Chinese ⬚. Unlike their older Western counterparts, who ⬚on homes, cars, and vacations, nearly half of ⬚xury-goods buyers are between 18 and 34.

But "if you have a population of 1.4 billion," says the Citigroup executive, "even 1 percent of that is a very large number."

Questions for Critical Thinking

1. What advice would you give Western luxury brands such as Prada, Burberry, Ferragamo, and Hugo Boss as they focus on Chinese luxury shoppers?

2. What does the luxury-buying trend suggest for Western manufacturers of ordinary consumer goods that want to do business in China?

Sources: Yang Lina, ⬚nese Tourists Spend Record Amounts on Luxury Goods Overseas, ⬚nei fm, February 8, 2012, http://news.brunei .fm; Wang Zhuoqiong, ⬚se Snap Up Luxury Products," ChinaDaily. com, February 7, 20⬚⬚hinadaily.com; Bettina Wassener, "Across Asia, an Engine of ⬚Luxury Firms," *The New York Times*, December 8, 2011, www.ny⬚⬚a Hutzler, "China Offers Quickest Growth in Emerging Mar⬚⬚⬚rands: Luxury Briefing Wealth Summit," LuxuryDaily.com⬚⬚i, www.luxurydaily.com.

Secret Acres: Getting the Word Out

CASE 12.3

No matter how powerful they are, comic book heroes can't get themselves into bookstores—and readers' hands—without a little help. Leon Avelino and Barry Matthews, co-founders of Secret Acres, know that one of the greatest challenges of publishing is getting books onto the shelves and into readers' shopping carts. The task is even more difficult for small publishers—in this case, small publishers of comic books and graphic novels—because they don't have the wide distribution network of major publishers. But Avelino and Matthews, whose authors consider them the superheroes of comicbook publishing, are undaunted. They know what they are trying to achieve and work doggedly to make it happen.

"Distribution is a difficult thing right now," admits Matthews. "The publishing industry is changing and comic books themselves have a different distribution methodology and wholesale methodology than traditional books do." Unlike conventional book shops, comic book shops do not operate on a return basis. Conventional bookstores receive a small discount when they purchase books from a publisher, but then have the option to return any unsold books to the publisher. Comic book shops take a deeper discount but make no returns. Matthews also notes that currently there is only one major distributor of comic books—Diamond Distributors—which has the leverage to dictate much of what happens in the business of comic book distribution.

In addition, Matthews observes that Secret Acres' graphic novels could easily be sold to the general book market, but many general book distributors prefer not to deal with smaller publishers because they simply don't produce enough books to be profitable.

All of that said, Matthews explains that they are learning alternative ways to distribute their books. "Amazon is great," he says. "They make it very easy for smaller publishers. They treat your books as if they are Amazon books, giving them the sheen of being part of a larger retail channel." Amazon does take a significant cut of sales, but Matthews says it's worth it to broaden the distribution of Secret Acres products. Of course, Secret Acres also sells its entire line directly through its Web site, along with some books from other independent authors and publishers. This sales method is the most profitable for Secret Acres. More importantly, it allows Matthews and Avelino to keep closer tabs on their readers.

Matthews explains that because orders are filled on an individual basis, he can slip promotional materials, notices of upcoming events or new books, and tie-ins right into the package of a customer whose preferences he knows. This one-on-one interaction helps in the management of customer relationships.

> **TWO CASES AND ONE VIDEO CASE** at the end of every chapter focus on successful real companies' processes and strategies. Real employees explain real business situations with which they have been faced, bringing key concepts from the chapter to life.

PART 1

GREENSBURG, KS
New Ways to Be a Better Town

Greensburg, Kansas, had been struggling for years. Located along Highway 54, a major trucking route, the town was merely a pit stop for people on their way somewhere else. It did have a few tourist attractions: the Big Well, the world's largest hand-dug well, and a 1,000-pound meteorite that fell from the sky in 2006.

Lonnie McCollum, the town's mayor, had been looking into ways to breathe new life into the town. McCollum wanted to add a little vintage charm to its quaint Main Street, but could not raise the money. And he had launched a campaign to put the "green" back in Greensburg by promoting green building technology. But the idea, which many residents associated with hippies and tree-huggers, did not go over well.

Then everything changed. "My town is gone," announced Town Administrator Steve Hewitt on May 5, 2007, after surveying the damage caused by a devastating tornado. "I believe 95 percent of the homes are gone. Downtown buildings are gone, my home is gone." With a clean slate and 700 homes to replace, Hewitt vowed to rebuild Greensburg using sustainable materials. He believed the town had a unique opportunity to control its environmental impact and reduce operating costs through increased energy efficiency.

"What if we turned this tragedy into something beautiful?" asked resident Dan Wallach in a new business plan he wrote shortly after the disaster. Wallach and his wife had long been interested in sustainable green living. Using their experience in developing nonprofits, the two launched

Greensburg GreenTown, an organization designed to support Greensburg's green building efforts through education, fund-raising, and public relations management.

One of Wallach's favorite new projects was BTI Greensburg, the local John Deere dealership. Owners [...] and Mike Estes had decided to replace their ruined by[...] ing with an energy-efficient, technologically state-of-[...] showroom featuring radiant heat, solar energy[...] ing, and wind power. With corpora[...] Deere, BTI Greensburg wo[...] dealership.

Long-term plans for Gree[...] incubator, to help displaced businesses[...] and bring new businesses to town; a green indu[...] green museum, and green school system; green build[...] codes and zoning restrictions; and a community of gr[...] homes and businesses.

Questions

After viewing the video, answer the following questions:

1. In what ways is the town of Greensburg like any other business?

2. In what ways is the town of Greensburg a socially responsible organization?

3. What might be the effects of the town's new green building guidelines on residents and businesses? On the regional economy?

4. What kind of business is Greensburg GreenTown? How does its structure differ from John Deere's?

THE CONTINUING VIDEO CASE OF GREENSBURG, KS, which falls at the end of each part, shows how business works in the real world. The video cases describe how the town was devastated by a horrific tornado and shows how the people are rebuilding their lives and their town with a little business ingenuity and a lot of persistence.

LAUNCHING YOUR
[management career]

3

LAUNCHING YOUR CAREER is found at the end of each part. This feature gives students a basic understanding of some of the numerous jobs that are part of each function in a business—and the job path that students may take from entry-level positions to high-level management positions in each of these functional areas.

CAREER ASSESSMENT EXERCISES and projects help students gauge their interest in and natural predisposition for certain careers.

Part 3, "Management: [...]ing People to Achieve [...]jectives," covers Chapters [...] which discuss manage[...] and the internal [...]n resource man[...], and labor–[...]; improving [...]mpowerment, [...]nication; and [...]age-

[...]ep [...]managers who [...]e strategies into [...]rs who work [...]ees to create [...]tisfy customers.

Middle management includes positions such as general managers, plant managers, division managers, and regional or branch managers. They are responsible for setting objectives consistent with top management's goals and planning and implementing strategies for achieving those objectives.

Top managers include such positions as chief executive officer (CEO), chief operating officer (COO), chief [...] fficer (CFO), chief informa-[...] (CIO), and executive vice president. Top managers devote most of their time to developing long-range plans, setting a direction for their organization, and inspiring a company's executives and employees to achieve their vision for the company's future. Top managers travel frequently

telecommunications, security, parking, and supplies—without which no organization could operate. On average, administrative service managers earn $84,000 a year.[2]

Construction managers plan, schedule, and coordinate the building of homes, commercial buildings such as offices and stores, and industrial facilities such as manufacturing plants and distribution centers. Unlike administrative service managers, who work in offices, construction managers typically work on building sites with architects, engineers, construction workers, and suppliers. On average, construction managers earn $94,000 a year.[3]

Food service managers run restaurants and services that prepare and offer meals to customers. They

| Sample Syllabus |

BUGB 101
Introduction to Business
Course Syllabus
Dr. Tim Hatten
thatten@mesastate.edu

TEXT

Contemporary Business, 15th edition – Boone/Kurtz

COURSE OBJECTIVE

This course is intended to provide students a broad overview of the complex and dynamic contemporary world of business. The course will illustrate how human resources management, marketing, production, and finance are major functions that work together to help owners, employees, and customers reach their objectives. Global business must operate within economic, social, legal, and political environments. This course will provide a manager's perspective to working with a wide variety of people and situations within these environments. While this is not a course specifically on international business, the business world is becoming more global, therefore the topic is integrated into every section.

COURSE PROCEDURE

As an introductory course to business, MANY theories and principles will be touched upon. Daily lectures, coupled with class discussion and experiential exercises, will be the main focus of each day. Several video cases will be used to substitute for guest speaker/field trip experiences.

TESTING

There will be five tests throughout the term, including the final. You are responsible for ALL the material in the text and class discussion. Tests will be objective and returned the next class period. Everyone has a bad day on occasion and it really bites when one hits on test day. Therefore your lowest test score will be dropped when calculating your final grade.

MAKE-UPS

NONE. If you are unable to come to class on a scheduled test day, that will be the test score to be dropped. Points from in-class activities cannot be made up.

ARTICLES

Current business article abstracts are required in this class. Articles should be recent (within approx. the last year) and pertain to a chapter from your text. You are to find one article per chapter for 10 chapters and place a copy of it with a one-page synopsis. Articles may be from any business newspaper or periodical - such as *The Wall Street Journal*, *Fortune*, or *Inc.* many of which have full-text articles on their website. You also need to learn to use Business Source Premier and Lexis-Nexis Full-Text Indexes via MSC library home page. The due date for articles will be based on the section of the text where the chapters are located. Articles are due the class period before the test over that chapter. We will spend that day before the exam discussing the articles you bring in. I will randomly call upon several of you to "present" articles during these class periods. The purpose of this assignment is for you to familiarize yourself with business periodicals and increase your ability to speak knowledgeably about current business topics and concerns. Articles will be graded for completeness at the end of the semester (all 10 articles w/abstracts) and professional appearance. A template of the form to use for abstracts is included at the end of this syllabus.

WileyPlus EXERCISES

Your text comes with an interactive online environment. We will be completing a number of exercises from this platform. More info on *WileyPLUS* and specific assignments will follow.

STOCK MARKET PROJECT – Optional for extra credit

Have you ever invested in the stock market? You have heard of people who have made a lot of money buying and selling stocks – and many who have lost money the same way! You have the chance to play the market with this game where everyone starts with the same amount of money. But where everyone finishes with, well . . . we'll see.

In this project, you will learn:

- Risks and rewards of investing in the stock market
- How to obtain information and analysis about companies and industries
- How to read and interpret corporate financial and non-financial information
- Different approaches for making the best stock selections – and when to buy the sell them
- How to buy and sell stocks
- How to track the progress of your stocks
- How to stay informed about any news or actions that may affect the value of your stocks.

Rules:

1. On the first day of the game (Feb. 8) you will invest a total of $100,000 (hypothetical) in at least three stocks listed on any U.S. exchange. No transaction fees are charged for the initial transaction.

2. Write a paragraph explaining which six stocks you purchased, at what price, and how many shares of each stock you purchased. Explain *why* you purchased each stock. (10 points possible)

3. Track your stocks three times per week from the week of through the week of. For each of these weeks, list the *closing price in dollars and cents*. Prepare a graph of the closing prices for each stock. (20 points possible)

4. Keep a detailed record of any buy/sell transaction you make. (5 points possible)

5. *On April 26 sell your stock* at that day's Yahoo Finance closing price.

6. Summarize how much money you made/lost. Explain why you think you made any gains/losses, including any factors that affected your stock prices. (15 points possible). Due May 3.

GRADING

There are 650 points possible.

400 from tests,

100 from article abstracts

100 WileyPlus online text exercises

50 from in-class activities

50 extra credit possible for stock market project

Grades are awarded according to the following scale:

A = 650 − 585 total points

B = 584 − 520

$$C = 519 - 455$$

$$D = 454 - 390$$

Unannounced quizzes will be used to determine which direction "borderline" grades should go at the end of the semester.

While I find that most students are eager to contribute to an atmosphere of learning, I do have a few guidelines upon which I insist:

ATTENDANCE AND PARTICIPATION

Punctual attendance is expected of all students. PERIOD. Also, you should miss a class only if absolutely necessary; i.e., you should not feel "entitled" to a certain number of missed classes. You are expected to be prepared for all classes and to participate in them when appropriate.

90% of success is showing up. If you are involved in a school-sponsored activity, you are expected to make arrangements for missed work prior to the absence. With the exception of school-sponsored activities, any make-up work will be at the discretion of the benevolent dictator behind the podium. Attendance is your decision, but I am disinclined to extend extra help in cases where absenteeism is a problem. In my view, absenteeism starts to be a problem when you miss more than one or two classes per semester.

If you need to miss class for some legitimate reason, please do not contact me to find out what we did, or are going to do. You should contact a classmate to find out what we covered. Oh, and please do not call to find out if it is "OK" to miss class.

Please do not be late for class. It is very disrupting to have students coming into class after we have started. If you have a schedule conflict that regularly prevents you from being punctual, please see me.

When preparing for class, read the chapter *before* class. Also read each Opening case and Concluding cases. These cases will be used to spark class discussion.

MISCELLANEOUS

It is your responsibility to read text assignments before the scheduled classes. I recommend that you spend at least two hours preparing for each hour of class time. There is a lot of terminology that will be new to you covered in this course. New terminology takes longer to "soak in" than terms that are already familiar to you. Understanding of these terms is critical for you for your future classes and life.

SCHEDULE (subject to change)

READ EACH CHAPTER AND BE PREPARED TO DISCUSS IN EVERY CLASS

Week 1	Wed	Orientation
	Fri	Chapter 1 The Changing Face of Business
Week 2	Mon	Chapter 1 The Changing Face of Business
	Wed	Chapter 2 Business Ethics and Social Responsibility
	Fri	Chapter 3 Economic Challenges Facing Contemporary Business
Week 3	Mon	Chapter 3 Economic Challenges Facing Contemporary Business
	Wed	Appendix A The Legal Framework for Business
	Fri	Chapter 4 Competing in World Markets

Week 4	Mon	Chapter 4 Competing in World Markets
		start day of extra credit stock market exercise (optional)
	Wed	article day-bring articles that relate to chapters 1–4 & Appendix A - be prepared to present and discuss
	Fri	**EXAM 1 CHAPTERS 1–4, Appendix A**
Week 5	Mon	Chapter 5 Forms of Business Ownership Organization
	Wed	Chapter 5 Forms of Business Ownership Organization
	Fri	Chapter 6 Starting Your Own Business: The Entrepreneurship Alternative
Week 6	Mon	Chapter 6 Starting Your Own Business: The Entrepreneurship Alternative
	Wed	article day - bring articles that relate to chapters 5–6 - be prepared to present and discuss.
	Fri	Catch-up day
Week 7	Mon	**EXAM 2 CHAPTERS 5–7**
	Wed	Chapter 7 Management, Leadership, and the Internal Organization
	Fri	Chapter 7 Management, Leadership, and the Internal Organization
Week 8	Mon	No Class – Spring Break
	Wed	No Class – Spring Break
	Fri	No Class – Spring Break
Week 9	Mon	Chapter 8 Human Resource Management
	Wed	Chapter 8 Human Resource Management
	Fri	Chapter 9 Top Performance Through Empowerment, Teamwork, and Communication
Week 10	Mon	Chapter 9 Top Performance Through Empowerment, Teamwork, and Communication
	Wed	Chapter 10 Production and Operations Management
	Fri	article day-bring articles that relate to chapters 8–11 - be prepared to present and discuss
Week 11	Mon	**EXAM 3 CHAPTERS 8–10**
	Wed	Chapter 11 Customer-Driven Marketing
	Fri	Chapter 11 Customer-Driven Marketing
Week 12	Mon	Chapter 12 Product and Distribution Strategies
	Wed	Chapter 12 Product and Distribution Strategies
	Fri	Chapter 13 Promotion and Pricing Strategies
Week 13	Mon	Chapter 13 Promotion and Pricing Strategies
	Wed	**ENTREPRENEURSHIP DAY**
	Fri	view and analyze Super Bowl commercials
Week 14	Mon	article day-bring articles that relate to chapters 11–13 - be prepared to present and discuss

	Wed	**EXAM 4 CHAPTERS 11–13**
	Fri	Chapter 15 Understanding Accounting and Financial Statements
Week 15	Mon	Chapter 15 Understanding Accounting and Financial Statements
	Wed	Chapter 17 Financial Management
	Fri	Chapter 17 Financial Management
Week 16	Wed	article day-bring articles that relate to chapters 15–17 - be prepared to present and discuss
	Fri	Catch-up Day

FINAL EXAM – Wednesday Week 17 CHAPTERS 15–17

ARTICLE REVIEW FORM (use as template)

Citation: Author, Article title, Publication, Date & Page: _____

_____

_____

Corresponding chapter in Boone&Kurtz: _____

Article abstract (1–2 paragraphs summarizing the MAIN IDEA of the article):

Information and ideas discussed in this article which are also discussed in your textbook or other

readings (cite text chapter and page #):

Your personal thoughts/opinions on the subject/article:

| Preface |

Solutions at the Speed of Business

A part of every business is change; now more than ever, business moves at a pace that is unparalleled. Containing the most important introductory business topics, *Contemporary Business* includes the most current information available and the best supplementary package in the business. You'll find that this new edition gets your students excited about the world of business, helps them improve their critical-thinking skills, and offers you and your students SOLUTIONS AT THE SPEED OF BUSINESS.

SOLUTIONS AT THE SPEED OF BUSINESS . . . FOR INSTRUCTORS. Consistent with recent editions of *Contemporary Business*, the instructor resources are designed to propel the instructor into the classroom with all the materials needed to engage students and help them understand text concepts. As always, all the major teaching materials are contained within the Instructor's Manual, and this new Annotated Instructor's Edition contains Lecture Enhancers and Classroom Activities. The PowerPoint Presentations and Test Bank have also been updated and improved. Greensburg, KS—our continuing case—is highlighted in part videos, plus we've added two other videos: "One Year Later" and "Future Plans." Our Wiley Business End-of-Chapter Video Series showcases companies such as Zipcar, Seventh Generation, New Harvest Coffee Roasters, and Comet Skateboards.

SOLUTIONS AT THE SPEED OF BUSINESS . . . FOR STUDENTS. With contemporary being the operative word, we've added two new videos to update our Greensburg, Kansas video series. As always, every chapter is loaded with up-to-the-minute business issues and examples to enliven classroom discussion and debate, such as how "social entrepreneurs" are making their mark on emerging businesses. Processes, strategies, and procedures are brought to life through videos highlighting real companies and employees, an inventive business model, and collaborative learning exercises. And to further enhance the student learning process, with *WileyPLUS*, instructors and students receive 24/7 access to resources that promote positive learning outcomes. Throughout each study session, students can assess their progress and gain immediate feedback on their strengths and weaknesses so they can be confident they are spending their time effectively.

How Boone & Kurtz Became the Leading Brand in the Market For more than three decades, *Contemporary Business* has provided the latest in content and pedagogy. Our current editions have long been the model for our competitors' *next* editions. Consider Boone & Kurtz's proven record of providing instructors and students with pedagogical firsts:

- *Contemporary Business* was the first introductory business text written specifically for the student—rather than the instructor—featuring a motivational style students readily understood and enjoyed.

- *Contemporary Business* has always been based on marketing research, written the way instructors actually teach the course.

- *Contemporary Business* was the first text to integrate computer applications—and later, Internet assignments—into each chapter.

- *Contemporary Business* was the first business text to offer end-of-chapter video cases as well as end-of-part cases filmed by professional producers.

- *Contemporary Business* was the first to use multimedia technology to integrate all components of the Introduction to Business ancillary program, videos, and PowerPoint CD-ROMs for both instructors and students—enabling instructors to custom-create lively lecture presentations.

Wiley is proud to be publishing a book that has represented the needs of students and instructors so effectively and for so many years. The 15th edition will continue this excellent tradition and will continue to offer students and instructors SOLUTIONS AT THE SPEED OF BUSINESS.

Pedagogy *Contemporary Business* has always employed extensive pedagogy—such as opening vignettes and boxed features—to breathe life into the exciting concepts and issues facing contemporary business. The 15th edition is packed with updates and revisions to key pedagogical features, including:

- Business Etiquette
- Assessment Checks
- Teamwork Exercises
- Self-Quizzes
- Hit & Miss
- Solving an Ethical Controversy
- Going Green

Continuing to Build the Boone & Kurtz Brand Because the business world is constantly changing, the Introduction to Business instructors need a SOLUTION AT THE SPEED OF BUSINESS. Trends, strategies, and practices are evolving, and students must understand how to perform business in today's world. Keeping this in mind, here are just a few of the important business trends and practices we've focused on for this new edition to help move students forward into a great business career.

What Are Learning Styles?

Have you ever repeated something to yourself over and over to help remember it? Or does your best friend ask you to draw a map to someplace where the two of you are planning to meet, rather than just tell her the directions? If so, then you already have an intuitive sense that people learn in different ways, Researchers in learning theory have developed various categories of learning styles. Some people, for example, learn best by reading or writing. Others learn best by using various senses—seeing, hearing, feeling, tasting, or even smelling. When you understand how you learn best, you can make use of learning strategies that will optimize the time you spend studying. To find out what your particular learning style is, www.wiley.com/college/boone and take the learning styles quiz you find there. The quiz will help you determine your primary learning style:

Visual Learner   Haptic Learner   Print Learner   Kinesthetic Learner

Auditory Learner   Olfactory Learner   Interactive Learner

Then, consult the information below and on the following pages for study tips for each learning style.
This information will help you better understand your learning style and how to apply it to the study of business.

Study Tips for Visual Learners

If you are a Visual Learner, you prefer to work with images and diagrams. It is important that you see information.

Visual Learning
- Draw charts/diagrams during lecture.
- Examine textbook figures and graphs.
- Look at images and videos on *WileyPLUS* and other Web sites.
- Pay close attention to charts, drawings, and handouts your instructor uses.
- Underline; use different colors.
- Use symbols, flowcharts, graphs, different arrangements on the page, white spaces.

Visual Reinforcement
- Make flashcards by drawing tables/charts on one side and definition or description on the other side.
- Use art-based worksheets; cover labels on images in text and then rewrite the labels.
- Use colored pencils/markers and colored paper to organize information into types.
- Convert your lecture notes into "page pictures." To do this:
  - Use the visual learning strategies outlined above.

- Reconstruct images in different ways.
- Redraw pages from memory.
- Replace words with symbols and initials.
- Draw diagrams where appropriate.
- Practice turning your visuals back into words.

If visual learning is your weakness: If you are not a Visual Learner but want to improve your visual learning, try re-keying tables/charts from the textbook.

Study Tips for Print Learners

If you are a Print Learner, reading will be important but writing will be much more important.

Print Learning
- Write text lecture notes during lecture.
- Read relevant topics in textbook, especially textbook tables.
- Look at text descriptions in animations and Web sites.
- Use lists and headings.
- Use dictionaries, glossaries, and definitions.
- Read handouts, textbooks, and supplementary library readings.
- Use lecture notes.

Print Reinforcement
- Rewrite your notes from class, and copy classroom handouts in your own handwriting.
- Make your own flashcards.
- Write out essays summarizing lecture notes or textbook topics.
- Develop mnemonics.
- Identify word relationships.
- Create tables with information extracted from textbook or lecture notes.
- Use text based worksheets or crossword puzzles.
- Write out words again and again.
- Reread notes silently.

- Rewrite ideas and principles into other words.
- Turn charts, diagrams, and other illustrations into statements.
- Practice writing exam answers.
- Practice with multiple choice questions.
- Write paragraphs, especially beginnings and endings.
- Write your lists in outline form.
- Arrange your words into hierarchies and points.

If print learning is your weakness: If you are not a Print Learner but want to improve your print learning, try covering labels of figures from the textbook and writing in the labels.

Study Tips for Auditory Learners

If you are an Auditory Learner, then you prefer listening as a way to learn information. Hearing will be very important, and sound helps you focus.

Auditory Learning
- Make audio recordings during lecture.
- Do not skip class; hearing the lecture is essential to understanding.

- Play audio files provided by instructor and textbook.
- Listen to narration of animations.
- Attend lecture and tutorials.
- Discuss topics with students and instructors.

- Explain new ideas to other people.
- Leave spaces in your lecture notes for later recall.
- Describe overheads, pictures, and visuals to somebody who was not in class.

Auditory Reinforcement
- Record yourself reading the notes and listen to the recording
- Write out transcripts of the audio files.
- Summarize information that you have read, speaking out loud.
- Use a recorder to create self-tests.
- Compose "songs" about information.

- Play music during studying to help focus.
- Expand your notes by talking with other and with information from your textbook.
- Read summarized notes out loud.
- Explain your notes to another auditory learner.
- Talk with the instructor.

- Spend time in quiet places recalling the ideas.
- Say your answers out loud.

If auditory teaming is your weakness: If you are not an Auditory Learner but want to improve your auditory learning, try writing out the scripts from pre-recorded lectures.

Study Tips for Interactive Learners

If you are an Interactive Learner, you will want to share your information. A study group will be important.

Interactive Learning
- Ask a lot of questions during lecture or TA review sessions.
- Contact other students, via e-mail or discussion forums, and ask them to explain what they learned.

Interactive Reinforcement
- "Teach" the content to a group of other students.
- Talking to an empty room may seem odd, but it will be effective for you.
- Discuss information with others, making sure that you both ask and answer questions.

- Work in small group discussions, making a verbal and written discussion of what others say.

If interactive learning is your weakness: If you are not an Interactive Learner but want to improve prove your interactive learning, try asking your study partner questions and then repeating them to the instructor.

Study Tips for Haptic Learners

If you are a Haptic Learner, you prefer to work with your hands. It is important to physically manipulate material.

Haptic Learning
- Take blank paper to lecture to draw charts/tables/diagrams.
- Using the textbook, run your fingers along the figures and graphs to get a "feel" for shapes and relationships.

Haptic Reinforcement
- Trace words and pictures on flashcards.
- Perform electronic exercises that involve drag-and-drop activities.
- Alternate between speaking and writing information.
- Observe someone performing a task that you would like to learn.

- Make sure you have freedom of movement while studying.

If haptic learning is your weakness: If you are not a Haptic Learner but want to improve your haptic learning, try spending more time in class working with graphs and tables while speaking or writing down information.

Study Tips for Kinesthetic Learners

If you are a Kinesthetic Learner, it will be important that you involve your body during studying.

Kinesthetic Learning
- Ask permission to get up and move during lecture.
- Participate in role-playing activities in the classroom.
- Use all your senses.
- Go to labs; take field trips.
- Listen to real-life examples.
- Pay attention to applications.
- Use trial-and-error methods.
- Use hands-on approaches.

Kinesthetic Reinforcement
- Make flashcards; place them on the floor, and move your body around them.
- Move while you are teaching the material to others.
- Put examples in your summaries.
- Use case studies and applications to help with principles and abstract concepts.
- Talk about your notes with another kinesthetic person.

- Use pictures and photographs that illustrate an idea.
- Write practice answers.
- Role-play the exam situation.

If kinesthetic learning is your weakness: If you are not a Kinesthetic Learner but want to improve your kinesthetic learning, try moving flash cards to reconstruct graphs and tables, etc.

Study Tips for Olfactory Learners

If you are an Olfactory Learner, you will prefer to use the senses of smell and taste to reinforce learning. This is a rare learning modality.

Olfactory Learning
- During lecture, use different scented markers to identify different types of information.

Olfactory Reinforcement
- Rewrite notes with scented markers.

- If possible, go back to the computer lab to do your studying.
- Burn aromatic candles while studying.
- Try to associate the material that you're studying with a pleasant taste or smell.

If olfactory learning is your weakness: If you are not an Olfactory Learner but want to improve your olfactory learning, try burning an aromatic candle or incense while you study, or eating cookies during study sessions.

LEARNING STYLES SURVEY CHART

Resources	Visual	Print	Auditory	Interactive	Haptic	Kinesthetic
Hit & Miss	✔	✔		✔		
Launching Your Career	✔	✔		✔		
Learning Goals	✔	✔		✔		
Going Green	✔	✔				
Business Etiquette	✔	✔		✔		
Solving an Ethical Controversy	✔	✔				
Assessment Checks	✔	✔		✔		
Review Questions	✔	✔		✔		
Cases	✔	✔		✔		
Project/Teamwork Applications	✔	✔		✔		
Flashcards	✔	✔		✔	✔	✔
Business Terms	✔	✔		✔		
Interactive Quizzes	✔	✔		✔		
Student PowerPoints	✔	✔		✔	✔	
Audio Summary (English/Spanish)	✔	✔	✔	✔	✔	
Animated Figures	✔	✔	✔	✔	✔	
Case Study Animations	✔	✔	✔	✔	✔	✔
E-lectures	✔	✔	✔	✔	✔	
Greensburg, KS Continuing Case	✔	✔	✔	✔	✔	✔
End-of-Chapter Videos	✔	✔	✔	✔	✔	✔
Final Exam Questions	✔	✔		✔		
Quiz Questions	✔	✔		✔		
Pre-lecture Questions	✔	✔		✔		
Post-lecture Questions	✔	✔		✔		
Video Questions	✔	✔	✔	✔		✔
Drop-box Questions	✔	✔		✔		

| Acknowledgements |

Contemporary Business has long benefited from the instructors who have offered their time as reviewers. Comprehensive reviews of the 15th edition and ancillary materials were provided by the following colleagues:

2012 Advisory Board

Kim Goudy – *Central Ohio Technical College*
Kelly Gold – *Fayetteville Tech Community College*
Frank Harber – *Indian River State College*
Lynda Hodge – *Guilford Tech Community College*
Chuck Kitzmiller – *Indian River State College*
Christy Shell – *Houston Community College*
Rudy Soliz – *Houston Community College*
Ted Tedmon – *North Idaho College*
Richard Warner – *Lehigh Carbon Community College*
Janet Seggern – *Lehigh Carbon Community College*
Susan Kendall – *Arapahoe Community College*
Annette Haugen – *Merced Community College*
Joseph Schubert – *Delaware Technical and Community College*
Robin Kelly – *Cuyahoga Community College*
Frank Barber – *Cuyahoga Community College*
Thomas Byrnes – *Wake Tech Community College*
Marian Matthews – *Central New Mexico Community College*
Tom Darling – *Central New Mexico Community College*
Laura Portolese-Dias – *Shoreline Community College*
Mary Gorman – *University of Cincinnati*
Diana Carmel – *Golden West College*
Eileen Kearney – *Montgomery County Community College*
John McCoy – *Suffolk University*
Cathleen Behan – *Northern Virginia Community College*
Donna Waldron – *Manchester Community College*
Thomas Mobley – *Miami University*

2011 Advisory Board

Gil Feiertag – *Columbus State Community College*
Kellie Enrich – *Cuyahoga Community College*
Sal Veas – *Santa Monica College*
Sally Proffitt – *Tarrant County Community College – Northeast*
David Robinson – *University of California – Berkeley*
Rodney Thirion – *Pikes Peak Community College*
Patricia Setlik – *William Rainey Harper College*
Gary Cohen – *University of Maryland*
Janice Feldbauer – *Schoolcraft College*
Linda Hefferin – *Elgin Community College*
Cynthia Miree-Coppin – *Oakland University*
David Oliver – *Edison State College – Lee Campus*
Lisa Zingaro – *Oakton CC – Des Plaines Campus*
Karen Halpern – *South Puget Sound Community College*
Colette Wolfson – *Ivy Tech CC – South Bend*
John Hilston – *Brevard CC – Palm Bay Campus*
John Striebich – *Monroe Community College*
Nathaniel Calloway – *University of Maryland University College*
Jayre Reaves – *Rutgers University*

In Conclusion

I would like to thank Ingrid Benson, Michelle Dellinger, and Cate Rzasa. Their editorial and production efforts on behalf of *Contemporary Business* were terrific.

Let me conclude by noting that this new edition would never have become a reality without the outstanding efforts of the Wiley editorial, production, and marketing teams. Special thanks to George Hoffman, Lisé Johnson, Franny Kelly, Kelly Simmons, Brian Kamins, Melissa Solarz, and Valerie Vargas.

Brief Contents

Contents

PART 2 Starting and Growing Your Business   132

[**Chapter 13**]

Promotion and Pricing Strategies   390

PART 5   Managing Technology and Information   428

[**Chapter 14**]

Using Technology to Manage Information   428

PART 6 Managing Financial Resources 456

[Chapter 16]

Opening Vignette
Community Banks Team Up to
Fight the Megabanks

Going Green
Green Banking at New
Resource Bank

Hit & Miss
Facebook at the IPO
Crossroads

Hit & Miss
How News Lifts—or Sinks—
World Stocks

BusinessEtiquette
What to Do When Your
Credit Gets Pulled

**Solving an Ethical
Controversy**
Are Debit Card Fees
Too High?

[Chapter 17]

Opening Vignette
Andreessen Horowitz: Silicon
Valley's Venture Capital Firm

Hit & Miss
Apptio Calculates the Cost of
Information Technology

Chapter 1

Learning Objectives

[1] Define what is business.

[2] Identify and describe the factors of production.

[3] Describe the private enterprise system.

[4] Identify the six eras in the history of business.

[5] Explain how today's business workforce and the nature of work itself is changing.

[6] Identify the skills and attributes needed for the 21st-century manager.

[7] Outline the characteristics that make a company admired.

The Changing Face of Business

Neustockimages/iStockphoto

Apple and Steve Jobs: Business Leadership as Art

When Apple's visionary founder and leader Steve Jobs passed away on October 5, 2011, at the age of 56, he was widely hailed as someone whose extraordinary career had transformed the world of business. But Apple's unsurpassed string of successful technological innovations had done far more. The Apple II, the Mac, iTunes, the iPod, the iPhone, the MacBook, and the iPad have transformed the music industry, the entertainment industry, the communications industry, and even the world of print.

Despite a 12-year absence from Apple, during which he founded another successful tech firm called NeXT and built Pixar Animation Studios into an Academy Award winner, Jobs brought his revolutionary computer company from humble start-up to unheard-of success. Apple is estimated to be worth nearly $400 billion today and has become one of the most valuable brand names of all time.

Jobs was passionately committed to innovation. His innate understanding of how to make technology transparently simple to use ensured the success of many of Apple's iconic products, including generations of Mac personal computers and the iPod.

These achievements, and their sleek and appealing designs, led many to think of him both as an artist and a business leader. Jobs's unrelenting attention to detail and quest for perfection could also make him a difficult boss at times, but he inspired enormous devotion and loyalty among his employees. Some say he even transformed our idea of leadership, given his ability to inspire others with the same ideals that fueled his own drive to succeed.

Thanks to Apple, products we never knew we needed have become indispensable to our lives. Nothing about the way we write, listen, speak, text, view entertainment, present information, or surf the Internet will ever be the same. How does one company achieve so much?

An extraordinary leader is an obvious advantage, and few observers expect to see another CEO like Steve Jobs any time soon. But many business leaders today are as passionate and inspired, and their firms also seek to innovate and transform. Those companies that correctly assess what customers want, that deliver it at the right time and for the right price, and that keep ahead of the wave of relentless change they face, as Apple has done, will be more likely to succeed.[1]

Overview

Business is the nation's engine for growth. A growing economy—one that produces more goods and services with fewer resources over time—yields income for business owners, their employees, and stockholders. So a country depends on the wealth its businesses generate, from large enterprises such as the Walt Disney Company to tiny online start-ups, and from venerable firms such as 150-year-old jeans maker Levi Strauss & Company to powerhouses such as Google. What all these companies and many others share is a creative approach to meeting society's needs and wants.

Businesses solve our transportation problems by marketing cars, tires, gasoline, and airline tickets. They bring food to our tables by growing, harvesting, processing, packaging, and shipping everything from spring water to cake mix and frozen shrimp. Restaurants buy, prepare, and serve food, and some even deliver. Construction companies build our schools, homes, and hospitals, while real estate firms bring property buyers and sellers together. Clothing manufacturers design, create, import, and deliver our jeans, sports shoes, work uniforms, and party wear. Entertainment for our leisure hours comes from hundreds of firms that create, produce, and distribute films, television shows, video games, books, and music downloads.

To succeed, business firms must know what their customers want so that they can supply it quickly and efficiently. That means

LECTURE ENHANCER: Explain how Google's strategy for the Android operating system brought new innovation to the smart phone market.

they often reflect changes in consumer tastes, such as the growing preference for sports drinks and vitamin-fortified water. But firms can also *lead* in advancing technology and other changes. They have the resources, the know-how, and the financial incentive to bring about new innovations as well as the competition that inevitably follows, as in the case of Apple's iPhone and Google's Android.

You'll see throughout this book that businesses require physical inputs such as auto parts, chemicals, sugar, thread, and electricity, as well as the accumulated knowledge and experience of their managers and employees. Yet they also rely heavily on their own ability to change with the times and with the marketplace. Flexibility is a key to long-term success—and to growth.

In short, business is at the forefront of our economy—and *Contemporary Business* is right there with it. This book explores the strategies that allow companies to grow and compete in today's interactive marketplace, along with the skills that you will need to turn ideas into action for your own success in business. This chapter sets the stage for the entire text by defining business and revealing its role in society. The chapter's discussion illustrates how the private enterprise system encourages competition and innovation while preserving business ethics.

business all profit-seeking activities and enterprises that provide goods and services necessary to an economic system.

profits rewards earned by businesspeople who take the risks involved in blending people, technology, and information to create and market want-satisfying goods and services.

⌈1⌉ What Is Business?

What comes to mind when you hear the word *business*? Do you think of big corporations like ExxonMobil or Boeing? Or does the local deli or shoe store pop into your mind? Maybe you recall your first summer job. The term *business* is a broad, all-inclusive term that can be applied to many kinds of enterprises. Businesses provide the bulk of employment opportunities, as well as the products that people enjoy.

<u>Business</u> consists of all profit-seeking activities and enterprises that provide goods and services necessary to an economic system. Some businesses produce tangible goods, such as automobiles, breakfast cereals, and digital music players; others provide services such as insurance, hair styling, and entertainment ranging from Six Flags theme parks and NFL games to concerts.

Business drives the economic pulse of a nation. It provides the means through which its citizens' standard of living improves. At the heart of every business endeavor is an exchange between a buyer and a seller. A buyer recognizes a need for a good or service and trades money with a seller to obtain that product. The seller participates in the process in hopes of gaining profits—a main ingredient in accomplishing the goals necessary for continuous improvement in the standard of living.

<u>Profits</u> represent rewards earned by businesspeople who take the risks involved in blending people, technology, and information to create and market want-satisfying goods and services. In contrast, accountants think of profits as the difference between a firm's revenues and the expenses it incurs in generating those revenues. More generally,

Antoine Antoniol/Bloomberg/Getty Images, Inc.

A business, such as this cell phone store, survives through the exchange between buyer and seller; in this case, the customer and the salesperson.

however, profits serve as incentives for people to start companies, expand them, and provide consistently high-quality competitive goods and services.

The quest for profits is a central focus of business because without profits, a company could not survive. But businesspeople also recognize their social and ethical responsibilities. To succeed in the long run, companies must deal responsibly with employees, customers, suppliers, competitors, government, and the general public.

Not-for-Profit Organizations

What do Purdue's athletic department, the U.S. Postal Service, the American Red Cross, and your local library have in common? They all are classified as **not-for-profit organizations**, businesslike establishments that have primary objectives other than returning profits to their owners. These organizations play important roles in society by placing public service above profits, although it is important to understand that these organizations need to raise money so that they can operate and achieve their social goals. Not-for-profit organizations operate in both the private and public sectors. Private-sector not-for-profits include museums, libraries, trade associations, and charitable and religious organizations. Government agencies, political parties, and labor unions, all of which are part of the public sector, are also classified as not-for-profit organizations.

Not-for-profit organizations are a substantial part of the U.S. economy. Currently, more than 1.5 million nonprofit organizations are registered with the Internal Revenue Service in the United States, in categories ranging from arts and culture to science and technology.[2] These organizations control more than $2.6 trillion in assets and employ more people than the federal government and all 50 state governments combined.[3] In addition, millions of volunteers work for them in unpaid positions. Not-for-profits secure funding from private sources, including donations, and from government sources. They are commonly exempt from federal, state, and local taxes.

Although they focus on goals other than generating profits, managers of not-for-profit organizations face many of the same challenges as executives of profit-seeking businesses. Without funding, they cannot do research, obtain raw materials, or provide services. St. Jude Children's Research Hospital's pediatric treatment and research facility in Memphis treats nearly 5,000 children a year for catastrophic diseases, mainly cancer, immune system problems, and infectious and genetic disorders. Patients come from all 50 states and all over the world and are accepted without regard to the family's ability to pay. To provide top-quality care and to support its research in gene therapy, chemotherapy, bone marrow transplantation, and the psychological effects of illness, among many other critical areas, St. Jude relies on contributions, with some assistance from federal grants.[4]

Other not-for-profits mobilize their resources to respond to emergencies. When the massive earthquake and tsunami hit Japan in 2011, it left vast amounts of people throughout the country without shelter, food, and drinking water. The Red Cross took immediate action to provide medical care and relief assistance.[5]

LECTURE ENHANCER: Explain a possible objective of a not-for-profit organization.

not-for-profit organizations businesslike establishments that have primary objectives other than returning profits to their owners.

LECTURE ENHANCER: Name examples of private-sector not-for-profit organizations.

LECTURE ENHANCER: Name examples of public-sector not-for-profit organizations.

LECTURE ENHANCER: What possible risks do not-for-profits face if they choose to sell merchandise or to share advertising with a business in order to raise funds?

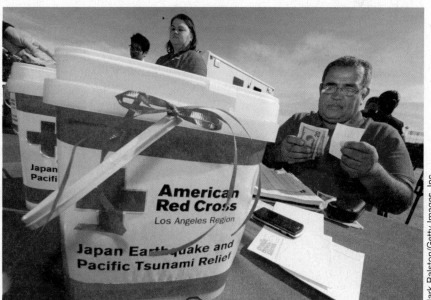

Mark Ralston/Getty Images, Inc.

■ The Red Cross mobilizes its efforts to respond to the earthquake disaster relief in Japan.

LECTURE ENHANCER:
Name a not-for-profit
organization that sells
merchandise or has a profit-
generating arm.

Assessment Check ✔

1. What activity lies at the heart of every business endeavor?

2. What are the primary objectives of a not-for-profit organization?

factors of production four basic inputs: natural resources, capital, human resources, and entrepreneurship.

natural resources all production inputs that are useful in their natural states, including agricultural land, building sites, forests, and mineral deposits.

capital includes technology, tools, information, and physical facilities.

LECTURE ENHANCER:
Name one factor of production and its method of payment. Think of a business in which this factor plays a major part.

LECTURE ENHANCER:
Provide an example of a business that recently upgraded or updated some form of its capital.

Some not-for-profits sell merchandise or set up profit-generating arms to provide goods and services for which people are willing and able to pay. College bookstores sell everything from sweatshirts to coffee mugs with school logos imprinted on them, while the Sierra Club and the Appalachian Mountain Club both have full-fledged publishing programs. The Lance Armstrong Foundation has sold more than 40 million yellow LiveStrong wristbands as well as sports gear and accessories for men, women, and children in the United States and abroad, with the money earmarked to fight cancer and support patients and families.[6] Handling merchandising programs like these, as well as launching other fund-raising campaigns, requires managers of not-for-profit organizations to develop effective business skills and experience. Consequently, many of the concepts discussed in this book apply to not-for-profit organizations as well as to profit-oriented firms.

[2] Factors of Production

An economic system requires certain inputs for successful operation. Economists use the term **factors of production** to refer to the four basic inputs: natural resources, capital, human resources, and entrepreneurship. Table 1.1 identifies each of these inputs and the type of payment received by firms and individuals who supply them.

Natural resources include all production inputs that are useful in their natural states, including agricultural land, building sites, forests, and mineral deposits. One of the largest wind farms in the world, the Roscoe Wind Complex near Roscoe, Texas, generates enough power to support almost a quarter-million homes. Natural resources are the basic inputs required in any economic system.

Capital, another key resource, includes technology, tools, information, and physical facilities. *Technology* is a broad term that refers to such machinery and equipment as computers and software, telecommunications, and inventions designed to improve production. Information, frequently improved by technological innovations, is another critical factor because both managers and operating employees require accurate, timely information for effective performance of their assigned tasks. Technology plays an important role in the success of many businesses. Sometimes technology results in a new product, such as hybrid autos that run on a combination of gasoline and electricity. Most of the major car companies have introduced hybrid models in recent years.

Technology often helps a company improve its own products. Recently Amazon announced that a licensing agreement with Viacom will allow subscribers to Amazon Prime

TABLE 1.1 **Factors of Production and Their Factor Payments**

FACTOR OF PRODUCTION	CORRESPONDING FACTOR PAYMENT
Natural resources	Rent
Capital	Interest
Human resources	Wages
Entrepreneurship	Profit

to stream shows from Viacom's TV channels, such as MTV, Comedy Central, Spike, TV Land, and Logo. Using Prime Instant Video, Amazon Prime members can stream thousands of episodes—unlimited, without commercials, and instant—on any of more than 300 different personal devices, including Kindle Fire.[7]

And sometimes firms rely on technology to help move and track their products more efficiently. The delivery firm UPS has partnered with the Red Cross to launch emergency logistics teams in several U.S. cities. UPS emergency coordinators in each city will gather expert volunteers, ensure that supplies reach disaster areas, and provide storage space.[8]

To remain competitive, a firm needs to continually acquire, maintain, and upgrade its capital, and businesses need money for that purpose. A company's funds may come from owner-investments, profits plowed back into the business, or loans extended by others. Money then goes to work building factories; purchasing raw materials and component parts; and hiring, training, and compensating workers. People and firms that supply capital receive factor payments in the form of interest.

<u>Human resources</u> represent another critical input in every economic system. Human resources include anyone who works, from the chief executive officer (CEO) of a huge corporation to a self-employed writer or editor. This category encompasses both the physical labor and the intellectual inputs contributed by workers. Companies rely on their employees as a valued source of ideas and innovation, as well as physical effort. Some companies solicit employee ideas through traditional means, such as an online "suggestion box" or in staff meetings. Others encourage creative thinking during company-sponsored hiking or rafting trips or during social gatherings. Effective, well-trained human resources provide a significant competitive edge because competitors cannot easily match another company's talented, motivated employees in the way they can buy the same computer system or purchase the same grade of natural resources.

human resources
include anyone who works, including both the physical labor and the intellectual inputs contributed by workers.

Plesea Petre/iStockphoto

Competent, effective human resources can be a company's best asset. Providing benefits to those employees to keep them is in a company's best interest, as software provider SAS has proven.

entrepreneurship
willingness to take risks
to create and operate a
business.

Assessment Check ☑

1. Identify the four basic inputs to an economic system.

2. List four types of capital.

LECTURE ENHANCER:
Name two of Walmart's competitors.

private enterprise system economic system that rewards firms for their ability to identify and serve the needs and demands of customers.

capitalism economic system that rewards firms for their ability to perceive and serve the needs and demands of consumers; also called the private enterprise system.

competition battle among businesses for consumer acceptance.

competitive differentiation unique combination of organizational abilities, products, and approaches that sets a company apart from competitors in the minds of customers.

LECTURE ENHANCER:
How does Walmart differentiate itself among its competitors?

Hiring and keeping the right people matters, as we'll see later in the case at the end of this chapter. Google employees feel they have a great place to work, partly because of the sense of mission—and the perks—the company provides.[9]

Entrepreneurship is the willingness to take risks to create and operate a business. An entrepreneur is someone who sees a potentially profitable opportunity and then devises a plan to achieve success in the marketplace and earn those profits. By age 20, Jessica Mah was CEO of inDinero, a Web site that helps small businesses keep track of their money. Mah had "noticed that anything that touches money is much harder for entrepreneurs than it should be," so she took a risk and started a firm designed to help them.[10]

U.S. businesses operate within an economic system called the *private enterprise system*. The next section looks at the private enterprise system, including competition, private property, and the entrepreneurship alternative.

⌐3⌐ The Private Enterprise System

No business operates in a vacuum. All operate within a larger economic system that determines how goods and services are produced, distributed, and consumed in a society. The type of economic system employed in a society also determines patterns of resource use. Some economic systems, such as communism, feature strict controls on business ownership, profits, and resources to accomplish government goals.

In the United States, businesses function within the **private enterprise system**, an economic system that rewards firms for their ability to identify and serve the needs and demands of customers. The private enterprise system minimizes government interference in economic activity. Businesses that are adept at satisfying customers gain access to necessary factors of production and earn profits.

Another name for the private enterprise system is **capitalism**. Adam Smith, often identified as the father of capitalism, first described the concept in his book *The Wealth of Nations*, published in 1776. Smith believed that an economy is best regulated by the "invisible hand" of **competition**, the battle among businesses for consumer acceptance. Smith thought that competition among firms would lead to consumers' receiving the best possible products and prices because less efficient producers would gradually be driven from the marketplace.

The invisible hand concept is a basic premise of the private enterprise system. In the United States, competition regulates much of economic life. To compete successfully, each firm must find a basis for **competitive differentiation**, the unique combination of organizational abilities, products, and approaches that sets a company apart from competitors in the minds of customers. Businesses operating in a private enterprise system face a critical task of keeping up with changing marketplace conditions. Firms that fail to adjust to shifts in consumer preferences or ignore the actions of competitors leave themselves open to failure. Apple and Microsoft have long been known for their rivalry, despite the fact that on occasion they have teamed up in alliances. For instance, Microsoft recently teamed up with Apple and Oracle in an effort to thwart Android phone makers from using patented technology.[11]

Another of Microsoft's competitors, Google, launched Chrome in an effort to compete in the Web browser market; see the "Hit & Miss" feature.

Hit & Miss

Microsoft and Google Square Off on the Web

Google took a big step into Microsoft-dominated territory with its introduction of home and office tools such as Gmail and Google Docs, and especially with its own operating system, Chrome OS, to challenge Microsoft's long-running Windows series. Google even has a Web browser, also called Chrome, to compete with Microsoft's entrenched Internet Explorer, while Microsoft challenges Google's dominance in Internet searches with its new search engine, Bing.

Google has long supported Web-based applications, as opposed to the desktop applications that have been Microsoft's specialty, but Microsoft is fighting back. It's creating browser-based versions of its desktop Office products including Word, Excel, and PowerPoint to compete with Google's cloud-computing tools. Microsoft's applications, often known for growing by adding more and more features in each new generation, will have to match Google's successful focus on speed and ease of use. Google has used these characteristics to promote a great user experience with its PC products, an advantage it hopes to import into the business applications market. "We want to spoil people like heck in their personal lives," says Google's vice president of product management. "Then when they go to work, they should be asking the question, 'Why are things so hard?'"

Google credits some of its success to its design teams' unwillingness to settle for the status quo. That restlessness means shortfalls in any Google product's performance may be short-lived. Google Docs, for instance, can't yet match Microsoft Word's editing and page layout features, while Google Spreadsheets offers limited performance and scaling capabilities.

Google is so determined to solve such problems, however, that it's helping to shape the creation of the World Wide Web's new HTML5 language, the standard for structuring and presenting content on Web pages and Web-based documents. "We view the Web as a platform," says Google's enterprise product management director. "We don't view it as a companion to the desktop. . . . We want the vast majority of users of Microsoft Office to be able to easily switch to Google Docs."

Critical Thinking Questions

1. What feature or features do you think Google has identified as its basis for competitive differentiation?

2. Some companies are considering using Google's Android operating system for their tablet PCs and netbooks. How would you expect Microsoft to react if Google succeeds in entering the market for desktop applications in this way?

Sources: Carl Brooks, "Online Office App Wars: Microsoft vs. Google vs. IBM," *SearchCloudComputing.com*, accessed February 12, 2012, http://searchcloudcomputing .techtarget.com; M. Merrill, "Microsoft Bing, Google Compete with Health Maps," *Healthcare IT News*, www.healthcareitnews.com, June 2, 2010; Thomas Claburn, "Microsoft Web Apps Will Force Google's Hand," *InformationWeek*, www.informationweek.com, April 10, 2010; Nick Bilton, "A Big-Picture Look at Google, Microsoft, Apple and Yahoo," *The New York Times*, www.nytimes.com, January 22, 2010.

Throughout this book, our discussion focuses on the tools and methods that 21st-century businesses apply to compete and differentiate their goods and services. We also discuss many of the ways in which market changes will affect business and the private enterprise system in the years ahead.

Basic Rights in the Private Enterprise System

For capitalism to operate effectively, people living in a private enterprise economy must have certain rights. As shown in Figure 1.1, these include the rights to private property, profits, freedom of choice, and competition.

The right to **private property** is the most basic freedom under the private enterprise system. Every participant has the right to own, use, buy, sell, and bequeath most forms of property, including land, buildings, machinery, equipment, patents on inventions, individual possessions, and intangible properties.

The private enterprise system also guarantees business owners the right to all profits—after taxes—they earn through their activities. Although a business is not assured

LECTURE ENHANCER:
Choose one of the four rights under the private enterprise system. Give an example of how this right allows freedom to a business.

private property most basic freedom under the private enterprise system; the right to own, use, buy, sell, and bequeath land, buildings, machinery, equipment, patents, individual possessions, and various intangible kinds of property.

FIGURE
1.1

Basic Rights within a Private Enterprise System

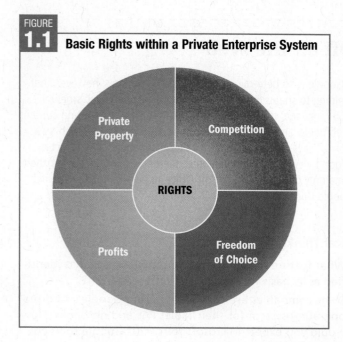

of earning a profit, its owner is legally and ethically entitled to any income it generates in excess of costs.

Freedom of choice means that a private enterprise system relies on the potential for citizens to choose their own employment, purchases, and investments. They can change jobs, negotiate wages, join labor unions, and choose among many different brands of goods and services. A private enterprise economy maximizes individual prosperity by providing alternatives. Other economic systems sometimes limit freedom of choice to accomplish government goals, such as increasing industrial production of certain items or military strength.

The private enterprise system also permits fair competition by allowing the public to set rules for competitive activity. For this reason, the U.S. government has passed laws to prohibit "cutthroat" competition—excessively aggressive competitive practices designed to eliminate competition. It also has established ground rules that outlaw price discrimination, fraud in financial markets, and deceptive advertising and packaging.[12]

The Entrepreneurship Alternative

entrepreneur person who seeks a profitable opportunity and takes the necessary risks to set up and operate a business.

The entrepreneurial spirit beats at the heart of private enterprise. An **entrepreneur** is a risk taker in the private enterprise system. You hear about entrepreneurs all the time—two college students starting a software business in their dorm room or a mom who invents a better baby carrier. Many times their success is modest but, once in a while, the risk pays off in huge profits. Individuals who recognize marketplace opportunities are free to use their capital, time, and talents to pursue those opportunities for profit. The willingness of individuals to start new ventures drives economic growth and keeps pressure on existing companies to continue to satisfy customers. If no one were willing to take economic risks, the private enterprise system wouldn't exist.

LECTURE ENHANCER:
Give a hypothetical example of what government goals might be more easily achieved by limiting a citizen's freedom to choose their own employment.

By almost any measure, the entrepreneurial spirit fuels growth in the U.S. economy. Of all the businesses operating in the United States, about one in seven firms started operations during the past year. These newly formed businesses are also the source of many of the nation's new jobs. Every year, they create more than one of every five new jobs in the economy. These companies are a significant source of employment or self-employment. Of the 27.5 million U.S. small businesses currently in operation, more than 21 million consist of self-employed people without any employees. Almost 8.5 million U.S. employees currently work for a business with fewer than 20 employees.[13] Does starting a business require higher education? Not necessarily, although it can help. Figure 1.2 presents the results of a survey of small-business owners, which shows that about 24 percent of all respondents had graduated from college, and 19 percent had postgraduate degrees.

LECTURE ENHANCER:
Explain how cable companies have become a target of fair-competition laws.

Besides creating jobs and selling products, entrepreneurship provides the benefits of innovation. In contrast to more established firms, start-up companies tend to innovate most in fields of technology that are new and uncrowded with competitors, making new products available to businesses and consumers. Because small companies are more flexible, they can make changes to products and processes more quickly than larger corporations. Entrepreneurs often find new ways to use natural resources, technology, and other factors of production. Often, they do this because they have to—they may not have enough money to build an expensive prototype or launch a nationwide ad campaign.

CLASS ACTIVITY:
Ask how many class members (or their family members) work in a company with fewer than 20 employees.

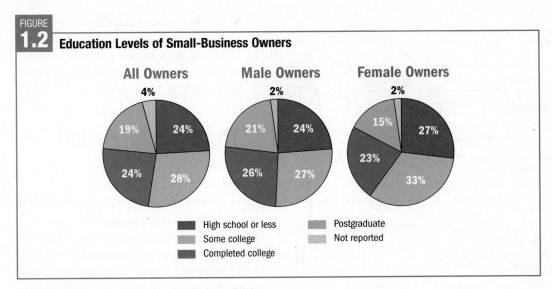

FIGURE 1.2 Education Levels of Small-Business Owners

All Owners
- 4%
- 24%
- 19%
- 24%
- 28%

Male Owners
- 2%
- 24%
- 21%
- 26%
- 27%

Female Owners
- 2%
- 27%
- 15%
- 23%
- 33%

- High school or less
- Some college
- Completed college
- Postgraduate
- Not reported

Note: Numbers may not total to 100 percent due to rounding.

Source: Data from "Survey of Business Owners (SBO): Owner's Education Levels at Start-Up, Purchase, or Acquisition of the Business," U.S. Census Bureau, http://www.census.gov, accessed January 24, 2012.

Sometimes an entrepreneur may innovate by simply tweaking an existing idea. When Carrie Ferrence and Jacqueline Gjurgevich were attending Bainbridge Graduate Institute on Bainbridge Island in Washington State, they noticed that many of the surrounding neighborhoods were "food deserts," lacking stores that sold fresh, locally grown produce and other basic necessities. They founded Stockbox Grocers, which converts old shipping containers into little food stores. The company won a small grant and raised additional funds through Kickstarter. The first StockBox grocery store soon opened in Seattle. Carrie Ferrence says, "It's a tough job market, and you have really few instances in your life to do something that you really love. It's not that this is the alternative. It's the new Plan A."[14]

Entrepreneurship is also important to existing companies in a private enterprise system. More and more, large firms are recognizing the value of entrepreneurial thinking among their employees, hoping to benefit from enhanced flexibility, improved innovation, and new market opportunities. eBay has used mobile technology to reinvent itself and its business customers—many of whom are entrepreneurs. Using augmented reality—which allows such activities as virtually "trying on" clothes via smart phone—eBay sellers have extended their reach to consumers' hands even when they aren't thinking about a purchase. Mobile commerce will allow eBay to do business everywhere—without brick-and-mortar outlets."[15]

As the next section explains, entrepreneurs have played a vital role in the history of U.S. business. They have helped create new industries, developed successful new business methods, and improved U.S. standing in global competition.

LECTURE ENHANCER:
Why are smaller companies more likely to find innovative ways to use the factors of production?

Assessment Check ✓

1. What is an alternative term for *private enterprise system*?

2. What is the most basic freedom under the private enterprise system?

3. What is an entrepreneur?

4 Six Eras in the History of Business

In the roughly 400 years since the first European settlements appeared on the North American continent, amazing changes have occurred in the size, focus, and goals of U.S. businesses. As Figure 1.3 indicates, U.S. business history is divided into six distinct time periods: (1) the Colonial period, (2) the Industrial Revolution, (3) the age of industrial entrepreneurs,

FIGURE 1.3 Six Eras in Business History

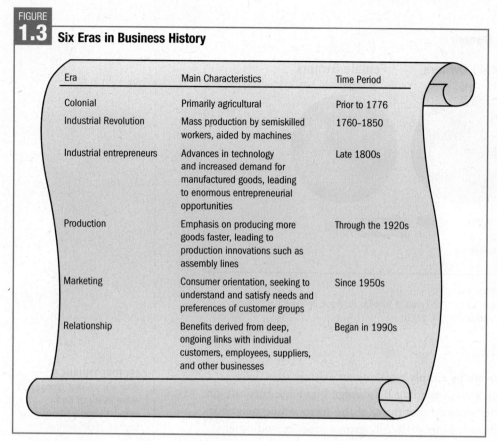

Era	Main Characteristics	Time Period
Colonial	Primarily agricultural	Prior to 1776
Industrial Revolution	Mass production by semiskilled workers, aided by machines	1760-1850
Industrial entrepreneurs	Advances in technology and increased demand for manufactured goods, leading to enormous entrepreneurial opportunities	Late 1800s
Production	Emphasis on producing more goods faster, leading to production innovations such as assembly lines	Through the 1920s
Marketing	Consumer orientation, seeking to understand and satisfy needs and preferences of customer groups	Since 1950s
Relationship	Benefits derived from deep, ongoing links with individual customers, employees, suppliers, and other businesses	Began in 1990s

CLASS ACTIVITY:
Ask students to provide examples of people today who currently earn their income by the making of crafts.

CLASS ACTIVITY:
Lead a discussion to identify the oldest companies in the local area or state that continue their operations.

(4) the production era, (5) the marketing era, and (6) the relationship era. The next sections describe how events in each of these time periods have influenced U.S. business practices.

The Colonial Period

Colonial society emphasized rural and agricultural production. Colonial towns were small compared to European cities, and they functioned as marketplaces for farmers and craftspeople. The economic focus of the nation centered on rural areas, because prosperity depended on the output of farms, orchards, and the like. The success or failure of crops influenced every aspect of the economy.

Colonists depended on England for manufactured items as well as financial backing for their infant industries. Even after the Revolutionary War (1776–1783), the United States maintained close economic ties with England. British investors continued to provide much of the financing for developing the U.S. business system, and this financial influence continued well into the 19th century.

The Industrial Revolution

The Industrial Revolution began in England around 1750. It moved business operations from an emphasis on independent, skilled workers who specialized in building products one by one to a factory system that mass-produced items by bringing together large numbers of semiskilled workers. The factories profited from the savings created by large-scale production, bolstered by increasing support from machines over time. As businesses grew, they could often purchase raw materials more cheaply in larger lots than before. Specialization of labor, limiting each worker to a few specific tasks in the production process, also improved production efficiency.

Influenced by these events in England, business in the United States began a time of rapid industrialization. Agriculture became mechanized, and factories sprang up in cities. During the mid-1800s, the pace of the revolution was increased as newly built railroad systems provided fast, economical transportation. In California, for example, the combination of railroad construction and the gold rush fueled a tremendous demand for construction.

The Age of Industrial Entrepreneurs

Building on the opportunities created by the Industrial Revolution, entrepreneurship increased in the United States. Henry Engelhard Steinway of Seesen, Germany, built his first piano by hand in his kitchen in 1825 as a wedding present for his bride. In 1850, the family emigrated to New York, where Henry and his sons opened their first factory in Manhattan in 1853. Over the next 30 years, they made innovations that led to the modern piano. Through an apprenticeship system, the Steinways transmitted their skills to the following generations. Steinway pianos have long been world famous for their beautiful tone, top-quality materials and workmanship, and durability. Now known as Steinway Musical Instruments, the company still builds its pianos by hand in its factory in Astoria, New York, under the same master-apprentice system that Henry and his sons began. Building each piano takes nearly a year from start to finish. In response to 21st-century demands, the company has launched Etude, an app for the iPad that displays sheet music the user can play on an on-screen piano keyboard. [16]

Inventors created a virtually endless array of commercially useful products and new production methods. Many of them are famous today:

- Eli Whitney introduced the concept of interchangeable parts, an idea that would later facilitate mass production on a previously impossible scale.

- Robert McCormick designed a horse-drawn reaper that reduced the labor involved in harvesting wheat. His son, Cyrus McCormick, saw the commercial potential of the reaper and launched a business to build and sell the machine. By 1902, the company was producing 35 percent of the nation's farm machinery.

- Cornelius Vanderbilt (railroads), J. P. Morgan (banking), and Andrew Carnegie (steel), among others, took advantage of the enormous opportunities waiting for anyone willing to take the risk of starting a new business.

Steinway has built pianos for home use and for artists from John Lennon to Billy Joel.

The entrepreneurial spirit of this golden age in business did much to advance the U.S. business system and raise the country's overall standard of living. That market transformation, in turn, created new demand for manufactured goods.

The Production Era

As demand for manufactured goods continued to increase through the 1920s, businesses focused even greater attention on the activities involved in producing those goods. Work became increasingly specialized, and huge, labor-intensive factories dominated U.S. business. Assembly lines, introduced by Henry Ford, became commonplace in major industries. Business owners turned over their responsibilities to a new class of managers trained in operating established companies. Their activities emphasized efforts to produce even more goods through quicker methods.

During the production era, business focused attention on internal processes rather than external influences. Marketing was almost an afterthought, designed solely to distribute items generated by production activities. Little attention was paid to consumer wants or needs. Instead, businesses tended to make decisions about what the market would get. If you wanted to buy a Ford Model T automobile, your color choice was black—the only color produced by the company.

The Marketing Era

The Great Depression of the early 1930s changed the shape of U.S. business yet again. As incomes nosedived, businesses could no longer automatically count on selling everything they produced. Managers began to pay more attention to the markets for their goods and services, and sales and advertising took on new importance. During this period, selling was often synonymous with marketing.

LECTURE ENHANCER: Compare the options available to buyers of a Ford automobile today compared to during the production era.

Demand for all kinds of consumer goods exploded after World War II. After nearly five years of doing without new automobiles, appliances, and other items, consumers were buying again. At the same time, however, competition also heated up. Soon businesses began to think of marketing as more than just selling; they envisioned a process of determining what consumers wanted and needed and then designing products to satisfy those needs. In short, they developed a **consumer orientation**.

Businesses began to analyze consumer desires before beginning actual production. Consumer choices skyrocketed. Automobiles came in a wide variety of colors and styles, and car buyers could choose among them. Companies also discovered the need to distinguish their goods and services from those of competitors. **Branding**—the process of creating an identity in consumers' minds for a good, service, or company—is an important marketing tool. A **brand** can be a name, term, sign, symbol, design, or some combination that identifies the products of one firm and differentiates them from competitors' offerings.

Branding can go a long way toward creating value for a firm by providing recognition and a positive association between a company and its products. Some of the world's most famous—and enduring—brands include Coca-Cola, IBM, Microsoft, Google, GE, McDonald's, Intel, and Apple.[17]

The marketing era has had a tremendous effect on the way business is conducted today. Even the smallest business owners recognize the importance of understanding what customers want and the reasons they buy.

The Relationship Era

As business continues in the 21st century, a significant change is taking place in the ways companies interact with customers. Since the Industrial Revolution, most businesses have concentrated on building and promoting products in the hope that enough customers will buy them to cover costs and earn acceptable profits, an approach called **transaction management**.

In contrast, in the **relationship era**, businesses are taking a different, longer-term approach to their interactions with customers. Firms now seek ways to actively nurture customer loyalty by carefully managing every interaction. They earn enormous paybacks for their efforts. A company that retains customers over the long haul reduces its advertising and sales costs. Because customer spending tends to accelerate over time, revenues also grow. Companies with long-term customers often can avoid costly reliance on price discounts to attract new business, and they find that many new buyers come from loyal customer referrals.

Business owners gain several advantages by developing ongoing relationships with customers. Because it is much less expensive to serve existing customers than to find new ones, businesses that develop long-term customer relationships can reduce their overall costs. Long-term relationships with customers enable businesses to improve their understanding of what customers want and prefer from the company. As a result, businesses enhance their chances of sustaining real advantages through competitive differentiation.

The relationship era is an age of connections—between businesses and customers, employers and employees, technology and manufacturing, and even separate companies. The world economy is increasingly interconnected, as businesses expand beyond their national boundaries. In this new environment, techniques for managing networks of people, businesses, information, and technology are critically important to contemporary business success. As you begin your own career, you will soon see how important relationships are, including your online presence; see the "Business Etiquette" feature for suggestions on presenting yourself in a positive way through social networking.

Managing Relationships through Technology

Increasingly, businesses focus on **relationship management**, the collection of activities that build and maintain ongoing, mutually beneficial ties with customers and other parties. At its core, relationship management involves gathering knowledge of customer needs and preferences and applying that understanding to get as close to the customer as possible. Many of these activities are based on **technology**, or the business application of knowledge based on scientific discoveries, inventions, and innovations. In managing relationships with customers, technology most often takes the form of communication, via the Internet and cell phone.

Blogs are growing more influential as a link between companies and their customers, and more companies are beginning to take advantage of their directness. Some that are connecting with customers in a positive way through their company blogs are Starbucks, Whole Foods Market, Patagonia, and Southwest Airlines.[18]

Strategic Alliances

Businesses are also finding that they must form partnerships with other organizations to take full advantage of available opportunities. One form of partnership between organizations is a **strategic alliance**, a partnership formed to create a competitive advantage for the businesses involved.

E-business has created a whole new type of strategic alliance. A firm whose entire business is conducted online, such as Amazon or Overstock.com, may team up with traditional retailers that contribute their expertise in buying the right amount of the right merchandise, as well as their knowledge of distribution. Through its Amazon Services branch, Amazon.com, the world's largest e-commerce firm, has formed strategic alliances with retailers to facilitate technology services, merchandising, customer service, and order fulfillment. Name-brand retailers offer their products via Amazon's retail site, backed by over 26 million square feet in its fulfillment sites located around the world. In a recent Customers Choice survey, Amazon has the best customer service among U.S. firms.[19]

---

relationship management collection of activities that build and maintain ongoing, mutually beneficial ties with customers and other parties.

technology business application of knowledge based on scientific discoveries, inventions, and innovations.

strategic alliance partnership formed to create a competitive advantage for the businesses involved; in international business, a business strategy in which a company finds a partner in the country where it wants to do business.

LECTURE ENHANCER:
Give an example of a current e-business strategic alliance.

The Green Advantage

Another way of building relationships is to incorporate issues that your customers care about into your business. As environmental concerns continue to influence consumers' choices of everything from yogurt to clothing to cars, many observers say the question about "going green" is no longer whether, but how. The need to develop environmentally friendly products and processes is becoming a major new force in business today.

Companies in every industry are researching ways to save energy, cut emissions and pollution, reduce waste, and, not incidentally, save money and increase profits as well. King & King Architects of Syracuse, New York, a member of the Green Building Council, recently relocated to a 48,000-square-foot warehouse. A grant from the New York State Energy Research and Development Authority (NYSERDA) enabled King & King to install energy-improved, high-efficiency windows, heating and cooling, ventilation, and insulation. These and many other improvements will save the company the equivalent amount of electricity consumed by 24 single-family homes per year—and won the company a High Performance Building Plaque from NYSERDA.[20]

Energy is among the biggest costs for most firms, and carbon-based fuels such as coal are responsible for most of the additional carbon dioxide in the atmosphere. Many companies have begun to address this issue, none perhaps with more flair than Greensulate, a small business in New York city that insulates rooftops with beautiful meadows of lavender, native grasses, and a hardy plant called sedum. The firm's efforts to date have eliminated more than 3,000 pounds of carbon from the atmosphere.[21] Clean solar energy is coming into its own and may soon be more viable and more widely available. SolarCity, a California installer of rooftop solar cells, is having trouble keeping up with growing demand.[22]

Some "green" initiatives can themselves be costly for firms, especially if the company's business model doesn't work. This was the case with Solyndra, maker of solar panels. Despite a large federal loan, Solyndra's innovative, yet high-priced products became increasingly uncompetitive in the marketplace, which caused the company to file bankruptcy and close its doors.[23] In contrast, Sungevity, a green company profiled in Chapter 6, had a better result.

Josef Becker/iStockphoto

Many companies have begun to address the energy issue. SolarCity provides clean solar energy by installing rooftop solar cells on houses.

Each new era in U.S. business history has forced managers to reexamine the tools and techniques they formerly used to compete. Tomorrow's managers will need creativity and vision to stay on top of rapidly changing technology and to manage complex relationships in the global business world of the fast-paced 21st century. As green operations become more cost-effective, and consumers and shareholders demand more responsive management, few firms will choose to be left behind.

5 Today's Business Workforce

A skilled and knowledgeable workforce is an essential resource for keeping pace with the accelerating rate of change in today's business world. Employers need reliable workers who are dedicated to fostering strong ties with customers and partners. They must build workforces capable of efficient, high-quality production needed to compete in global markets. Savvy business leaders also realize that the brainpower of employees plays a vital role in a firm's ability to stay on top of new technologies and innovations. In short, a first-class workforce can be the foundation of a firm's competitive differentiation, providing important advantages over competing businesses. See how two entrepreneurs came up with a unique idea for businesses to save paper in the workplace in the "Going Green" feature.

Changes in the Workforce

Companies now face several trends that challenge their skills for managing and developing human resources. Those challenges include aging of the population and a shrinking labor pool, growing diversity of the workforce, the changing nature of work, the need for flexibility and mobility, and the use of collaboration to innovate.

Aging of the Population and Shrinking Labor Pool By 2030, the number of U.S. workers 65 or older will reach 72 million—double what it is today—and many of them will soon retire from the workforce, taking their experience and expertise with them. As Table 1.2 shows, the U.S. population as a whole is trending older. Yet today, many members of the Baby Boom generation, the huge number of people born between 1946 and 1964, are still hitting the peaks of their careers. At the same time, members of so-called Generation X (born from 1965 to 1981) and Generation Y (born from 1982 to 2005) are building their careers, so employers are finding more generations in the workforce simultaneously than ever before. This broad age diversity brings management challenges with it, such as accommodating a variety of work-life styles, changing expectations of work, and varying levels of technological expertise. Still, despite the widening age spectrum of the workforce, some economists predict the U.S. labor pool could soon fall short by as many as 10 million people as the Baby Boomers retire.

More sophisticated technology has intensified the hiring challenge by requiring workers to have ever more advanced skills. Although the number of college-educated workers has doubled in the past 20 years, the demand is still greater than the supply. Because of these changes, companies are increasingly seeking—and finding—talent at the extreme ends of the working-age spectrum. Teenagers are entering the workforce sooner, and some seniors are staying longer—or seeking new careers after retiring from their primary careers. Many older workers work part-time or flexible hours. Meanwhile, for those older employees who do retire, employers must administer a variety of retirement planning and disability programs and insurance benefits.

Assessment Check ☑

1. What was the Industrial Revolution?
2. During which era was the idea of branding developed?
3. What is the difference between transaction management and relationship management?

CLASS ACTIVITY:
Ask students which businesses might benefit or suffer from America's aging population.

LECTURE ENHANCER:
What unique skills might each generation bring to the workplace?

Save Paper, Save the Planet

You've probably printed plenty of documents and Web pages that resulted in wasted space, poor formatting, and extra pages, but two young entrepreneurs from the University of Illinois have done something about it. PrintEco, a software startup, is the brain child of Arpan Shah and Tom Patterson, who devised a program that formats print jobs down to the smallest number of pages and eliminates wasted space and unwanted Web ads, images, and other information.

PrintEco's plug-in software offers users the option of printing as usual or the space-saving PrintEco way. There are versions for Microsoft Word, Excel, PowerPoint, Internet Explorer, Firefox, and the Mac operating system. A professional version also offers a Web-based dashboard called PrintEco Analytics, which helps users track the financial and environmental cost of their print jobs. As the company's Web page says, users will save money and time—"not to mention, you can help the environment."

PrintEco has already attracted much attention in its young life. The company recently won a competition for entrepreneurial ventures in clean technology at the annual Opportunity Green conference in California. Given that the prize was $30,000 worth of marketing services, you can probably expect to hear a lot more about PrintEco in the near future.

Questions for Critical Thinking

1. What do you think PrintEco will need to do to remain a viable business?
2. What market forces are likely to help PrintEco succeed?

Sources: Company Web site, www.printecosoftware.com, accessed January 9, 2012; Michael Parrish DuDell, "Opportunity Green and the Value of Collaboration," *Ecomagination,* November 18, 2011, www.ecomagination.com; Candace Lombardi, "PrintEco's Streamlined Print Jobs Available in Firefox," Cnet.com, July 20, 2011, http://news.cnet.com.

TABLE

1.2 Aging of the U.S. Population

AGE	2010	2020	2025
16–64	203 million	214 million	218 million
	66% of total	63% of total	61% of total
65 and older	40 million	55 million	64 million
	13% of total	16% of total	18% of total
Median	37 years	38 years	38.5 years

Source: U.S. Census Bureau, "Resident Population Projections by Sex and Age: 2010 to 2050," *Statistical Abstract of the United States,* http://www.census.gov, accessed January 24, 2012.

diversity blending individuals of different genders, ethnic backgrounds, cultures, religions, ages, and physical and mental abilities.

Increasingly Diverse Workforce The U.S. workforce is growing more diverse, in age and in every other way as well. The two fastest-growing ethnic populations in the United States are Hispanics and people of Asian origin. By the year 2050, the number of Hispanics in the U.S. will grow from a current 35 million to 102 million, or 24 percent of the total population. The Asian population will increase from 10 million to 33 million, or 8 percent of the total U.S. population.[24] Considering that minority groups will make up half the total U.S. population by the year 2050, managers must learn to work effectively with diverse ethnic groups, cultures, and lifestyles to develop and retain a superior workforce for their company.

Diversity, blending individuals of different genders, ethnic backgrounds, cultures, religions, ages, and physical and mental abilities, can enhance a firm's chances of success. Some of the firms that made the top 10 in a recent list of "Top 50 Companies for Diversity" were also leaders and innovators in their industries, including Kaiser Permanente, Sodexo,

PricewaterhouseCoopers, AT&T, Ernst & Young, Johnson & Johnson, IBM, Deloitte, Kraft Foods, and Colgate-Palmolive.[25] Several studies have shown that diverse employee teams and workforces tend to perform tasks more effectively and develop better solutions to business problems than homogeneous employee groups. This result is due in part to the varied perspectives and experiences that foster innovation and creativity in multicultural teams.

Practical managers also know that attention to diversity issues can help them avoid damaging legal battles. Losing a discrimination lawsuit can be very costly.[26]

Outsourcing and the Changing Nature of Work

Not only is the U.S. workforce changing, but so is the very nature of work. Manufacturing used to account for most of U.S. annual output, but the balance has now shifted to services such as financial management and communications. This means firms must rely heavily on well-trained service workers with knowledge, technical skills, the ability to communicate and deal with people, and a talent for creative thinking. The Internet has made possible another business tool for staffing flexibility—**outsourcing**, using outside vendors to produce goods or fulfill services and functions that previously were handled in house. In the best situation, outsourcing allows a firm to reduce costs and concentrate its resources on the things it does best while gaining access to expertise it may not have. But outsourcing also creates its own challenges, such as differences in language or culture.

Offshoring is the relocation of business processes to lower-cost locations overseas. This can include both production and services. In recent years, China has emerged as a dominant location for production offshoring for many firms, while India has become the key player in offshoring services. Some U.S. companies are now structured so that entire divisions or functions are developed and staffed overseas—the jobs were never in the United States to start with. Another trend in some industries is **nearshoring**, outsourcing production or services to nations near a firm's home base.

Flexibility and Mobility

Younger workers in particular are looking for something other than the work-comes-first lifestyle exemplified by the Baby Boom generation. But workers of all ages are exploring different work arrangements, such as telecommuting from remote locations and sharing jobs with two or more employees. Employers are also hiring growing numbers of temporary and part-time employees, some of whom are less interested in advancing up the career ladder and more interested in using and developing their skills. While the cubicle-filled office will likely never become entirely obsolete, technology makes productive networking and virtual team efforts possible by allowing people to work where they choose and easily share knowledge, a sense of purpose or mission, and a free flow of ideas across any geographical distance or time zone.

Managers of such far-flung workforces need to build and earn their trust, in order to retain valued employees and to ensure that all members are acting ethically and contributing their share without the day-to-day supervision of a more conventional work environment. These managers, and their employees, need to be flexible and responsive to change while work, technology, and the relationships between them continue to evolve.

Innovation through Collaboration

Some observers also see a trend toward more collaborative work in the future, as opposed to individuals working alone. Businesses using teamwork hope to build a creative environment where all members contribute their knowledge and skills to solve problems or seize opportunities.

The old relationship between employers and employees was pretty simple: workers arrived at a certain hour, did their jobs, and went home every day at the same time.

CLASS ACTIVITY: Obtain the students' experiences in working in teams with diverse membership. What were the benefits and difficulties the teams encountered?

outsourcing using outside vendors to produce goods or fulfill services and functions that were previously handled in-house or in-country.

offshoring relocation of business processes to lower-cost locations overseas.

nearshoring outsourcing production or services to locations near a firm's home base.

CLASS ACTIVITY: Survey your class to see how many students work on a flexible or part-time basis.

Assessment Check ☑

1. Define *outsourcing, offshoring,* and *nearshoring.*
2. Describe the importance of collaboration and employee partnership.

vision the ability to perceive marketplace needs and what an organization must do to satisfy them.

critical thinking ability to analyze and assess information to pinpoint problems or opportunities.

Companies rarely laid off workers, and employees rarely left for a job at another firm. But all that—and more—has changed. Employees are no longer likely to remain with a single company throughout their entire careers and do not necessarily expect lifetime loyalty from the companies they work for. They do not expect to give that loyalty either. Instead, they build their own careers however and wherever they can. These changes mean that many firms now recognize the value of a partnership with employees that encourages creative thinking and problem solving and that rewards risk taking and innovation.

6 ▪ The 21st-Century Manager

Today's companies look for managers who are intelligent, highly motivated people with the ability to create and sustain a vision of how an organization can succeed. The 21st-century manager must also apply critical-thinking skills and creativity to business challenges and lead change.

Importance of Vision

To thrive in the 21st century, businesspeople need **vision**, the ability to perceive marketplace needs and what an organization must do to satisfy them. Nannu Nobis, co-founder and CEO of Nobis Engineering, is recognized for his firm's environmental work as well as its efforts to convert its own business operations to the highest standards of sustainability. Nobis Engineering—which employs only 100 people and has several offices in the Northeast—recently won prestigious major contracts with the Army Corps of Engineers and EPA valued at $40 million. When the firm expanded to meet client needs, Nobis authorized $5 million to renovate a 20,000-square-foot historic mill building according to the U.S. Green Building Council LEED process. Nobis Engineering employees are rewarded for carpooling and reducing energy use in other ways as well. So far, Nobis Engineering has reduced its carbon emissions by more than 13,000 pounds. "You have to walk the walk," Nannu Nobis says. "Our clients take this [sustainability] seriously and are proud to be with a firm that takes it seriously."[27] Another company with a definite vision is Costco. See the profile of its outgoing CEO in the "Hit & Miss" box.

Importance of Critical Thinking and Creativity

Critical thinking and creativity are essential characteristics of the 21st-century workforce. Today's businesspeople need to look at a wide variety of situations, draw connections among disparate information, and develop future-oriented solutions. This need applies not only to top executives, but to mid-level managers and entry-level workers as well.

Critical thinking is the ability to analyze and assess information to pinpoint problems or opportunities. The critical-thinking process includes activities such as determining the authenticity, accuracy, and

Nobis Engineering employees carpool to save money and reduce energy usage in an effort to promote sustainability.

Costco's Jim Sinegal: "A Classy Guy"

Jim Sinegal, 75, recently retired as CEO of Costco, the giant warehouse retailer he helped found in 1983. Under his management, Costco grew into the third-largest U.S. retailer, worth about $100 billion in annual sales with nearly 600 stores in nine countries.

Sinegal is a living example of Costco's highly principled, employee- and customer-friendly policies. Never an elitist, he chose a hallway office furnished with a cheap folding table and cloth bulletin board. In keeping with his open-door philosophy, the office doesn't even have a door. Sinegal often wears one of Costco's popular $17 dress shirts to work and has been known to give his cell phone number to a reporter rather than protect himself with layers of staff.

By offering above-average pay and a range of generous benefits, Sinegal has kept employee turnover astonishingly low and made Costco a place where employees find a real sense of teamwork, compassion, and community. He takes pride in having visited every one of the company's stores around the world every year, yet despite all the travel that requires, he still berates himself if he can't immediately recall the first name of everyone who works in the headquarters office. As one of the company's vice presidents says, Sinegal is a "classy guy."

Questions for Critical Thinking

1. What do you think Jim Sinegal's vision for Costco was?
2. How did Sinegal's leadership demonstrate that vision to customers and employees?

Sources: David W. Fuller, Tim Talevich, and Brenda Shecter, "The Empire Built on Values," *The Costco Connection,* January 2012, pp. 24-27; Karlee Weinmann, "What Costco CEO James Sinegal Can Teach You about Management," *American Express OPEN Forum,* December 27, 2011, www.openforum.com; Carol Tice, "What Entrepreneurs Can Learn from Costco's CEO," *Entrepreneur,* December 2, 2011, www.entrepreneur.com/blog; Ann Zimmerman, "Costco CEO to Step Down," *The Wall Street Journal,* September 2, 2011, http://online.wsj.com.

---

worth of information, knowledge, and arguments. It involves looking beneath the surface for deeper meaning and connections that can help identify critical issues and solutions. Without critical thinking, a firm may encounter serious problems.

Creativity is the capacity to develop novel solutions to perceived organizational problems. Although most people think of it in relation to writers, artists, musicians, and inventors, that is a very limited definition. In business, creativity refers to the ability to see better and different ways of doing business. A computer engineer who solves a glitch in a software program is executing a creative act.

> **creativity** capacity to develop novel solutions to perceived organizational problems.

Sometimes a crisis calls for creative leadership. Captain Chesley Sullenberger, who famously guided US Airways Flight 1549 to a safe landing in New York's Hudson River, had to make immediate and critical decisions when both his engines quit after hitting birds upon take-off. His passengers' and crew members' lives—and lives on the ground—depended on his quick thinking and years of training. As the jet lost thrust in both engines and drifted at low speed and low altitude over one of the most densely populated areas in the world, Sullenberger faced the challenge of his life. But with quick thinking he managed a safe emergency landing in the Hudson. Speaking at Purdue University's recent commencement ceremonies, Sullenberger told the graduates, that his mission has always been, "make the next flight better than the last one." [28]

With some practice and mental exercise, you can cultivate your own ability to think creatively. Here are some exercises and guidelines:

- In a group, brainstorm by listing ideas as they come to mind. Build on other people's ideas, but don't criticize them. Wait until later to evaluate and organize the ideas.

- Think about how to make familiar concepts unfamiliar. A glue that doesn't stick very well? That's the basis for 3M's popular Post-it® notes.

- Plan ways to rearrange your thinking with simple questions such as, "What features can we leave out?" or by imagining what it feels like to be the customer.

CLASS ACTIVITY:
Lead a class brainstorming discussion asking students for a name for a new oil and lubrication business that also will sell coffee and snacks while customers wait in a comfortable lounge area.

- Cultivate curiosity, openness, risk, and energy as you meet people and encounter new situations. View these encounters as opportunities to learn.

- Treat failures as additional opportunities to learn.

- Get regular physical exercise. When you work out, your brain releases endorphins, and these chemicals stimulate creative thinking.

- Pay attention to your dreams and daydreams. You might find that you already know the answer to a problem.

Creativity and critical thinking must go beyond generating new ideas, however. They must lead to action. In addition to creating an environment in which employees can nurture ideas, managers must give them opportunities to take risks and try new solutions.

Ability to Lead Change

Today's business leaders must guide their employees and organizations through the changes brought about by technology, marketplace demands, and global competition. Managers must be skilled at recognizing employee strengths and motivating people to move toward common goals as members of a team. Throughout this book, real-world examples demonstrate how companies have initiated sweeping change initiatives. Most, if not all, have been led by managers comfortable with the tough decisions that today's fluctuating conditions require.

Factors that require organizational change can come from both external and internal sources; successful managers must be aware of both. External forces might include feedback from customers, developments in the international marketplace, economic trends, and new technologies. Internal factors might arise from new company goals, emerging employee needs, labor union demands, or production problems.

Assessment Check ☑

1. Why is vision an important managerial quality?
2. What is the difference between creativity and critical thinking?

[7] # What Makes a Company Admired?

Who is your hero? Is it someone who has achieved great feats in sports, government, entertainment, or business? Why do you admire the person? Does he or she run a company, earn a lot of money, or give back to the community and society? Every year, business magazines and organizations publish lists of companies that they consider to be "most admired." Companies, like individuals, may be admired for many reasons. Most people would mention solid profits, stable growth, a safe and challenging work environment, high-quality goods and services, and business ethics and social responsibility. *Business ethics* refers to the standards of conduct and moral values involving decisions made in the work environment. *Social responsibility* is a management philosophy that includes contributing resources to the community, preserving the natural environment, and developing or participating in nonprofit programs designed to promote the well-being of the general public. You'll find business ethics and social responsibility examples throughout this book, as well as a deeper exploration of these topics in Chapter 2. For businesses to behave ethically and responsibly, their employees need to have strong moral compasses that guide them. The "Solving an Ethical Controversy" feature demonstrates some of the challenges of defining what is ethical.

As you read this text, you'll be able to make up your mind about why companies should—or should not—be admired. *Fortune* publishes two lists of most-admired companies

LECTURE ENHANCER:
Are there any factors or characteristics that you feel have been left out of the most-admired list?

Solving an Ethical Controversy

Can Fair Trade Be Ethical and Flexible?

Fair Trade USA (FTUSA), the U.S. national fair trade organization, recently rocked the $6 billion fair trade world by splitting from the parent organization, the Fairtrade Labeling Organization (FLO). FTUSA will now set its own ethical standards, certifying coffee, cocoa, and fruit from large plantations employing seasonal workers, as well as from the small, FLO-approved cooperative farms practicing democratic management and ethical treatment of employees. Some fear the split will undermine the fair trade movement.

Can fair trade practices extend to larger producers that don't fit the model of small-farm, participative management?

PRO

1. Paul Rice, head of Fair Trade USA, says his decision to include larger farms will double sales of fair trade goods, benefiting more producers and raising consumer awareness.

2. FTUSA promises to model its plantation standards after FLO's. "We are after results," says Rice. "We want to get things done."

CON

1. Some opponents of Rice's decision have vowed to boycott FTUSA participants such as Green Mountain Coffee, saying the new standards will be lower and will undermine fair trade values.

2. Under the new standards, chocolate bars can carry the FTUSA label if the cocoa is approved even if the sugar is not. Critics call that compromise "unacceptable."

Summary

The success of fair trade ultimately lies with consumers. Will they be confused by two different labeling systems and different standards?

Sources: Twilight Greenaway, "Fair Trade Lite: Fair Trade USA Moves Away from Worker Co-Ops," *Grist*, December 2, 2011, www.grist.org; "An American Rebel Roils Ethical Commerce," *Bloomberg Businessweek*, November 7–13, 2011, pp. 15–16; "Fractures in Fair Trade: Fair Trade USA Leaves Fairtrade Labeling Organization," *Fair Trade Vancouver*, September 25, 2011, www.fairtradevancouver.ca/blog.

---

each year, one for U.S.–based firms and one for the world. The list is compiled from surveys and other research conducted by the Hay Group, a global human resources and organizational consulting firm. Criteria for making the list include innovation, people management, use of corporate assets, social responsibility, quality of management, and quality of products and services.[29] Table 1.3 lists the top 10 "Most Admired Companies" for a recent year.

TABLE

1.3 *Fortune's* Top Ten Most Admired Companies

1 Apple	**5** Procter & Gamble	**9** Microsoft
2 Google	**6** Coca-Cola	**10** McDonald's
3 Berkshire Hathaway	**7** Amazon.com	
4 Southwest Airlines	**8** FedEx	

Source: "World's Most Admired Companies 2011," *Fortune*, http://money.cnn.com, accessed February 11, 2012. Copyright 2010 by Time, Inc. Used by permission and protected by the copyright laws of the United States. The printing, copying redistribution, or retransmission of the material without express permission is prohibited.

Assessment Check ☑

1. Define *business ethics* and *social responsibility*.

2. Identify three criteria used to judge whether a company might be considered admirable.

What's Ahead

As business speeds along in the 21st century, new technologies, population shifts, and shrinking global barriers are altering the world at a frantic pace. Businesspeople are catalysts for many of these changes, creating new opportunities for individuals who are prepared to take action. Studying contemporary business will help you prepare for the future.

Throughout this book, you'll be exposed to the real-life stories of many businesspeople. You'll learn about the range of business careers available and the daily decisions, tasks, and challenges that they face. By the end of the course, you'll understand how marketing, production, accounting, finance, and management work together to provide competitive advantages for firms. This knowledge can help you become a more capable employee and enhance your career potential.

Now that this chapter has introduced some basic terms and issues in the business world of the 21st century, Chapter 2 takes a detailed look at the ethical and social responsibility issues facing contemporary business. Chapter 3 deals with economic challenges, and Chapter 4 focuses on the difficulties and opportunities faced by firms competing in world markets.

Summary of Learning Objectives

[1] Define what is business.

Business consists of all profit-seeking activities that provide goods and services necessary to an economic system. Not-for-profit organizations are business-like establishments whose primary objectives involve social, political, governmental, educational, or similar functions—instead of profits.

Assessment Check Answers ✅

1.1 What activity lies at the heart of every business endeavor? At the heart of every business endeavor is an exchange between a buyer and a seller.

1.2 What are the primary objectives of a not-for-profit organization? Not-for-profit organizations place public service above profits, although they need to raise money in order to operate and achieve their social goals.

[2] Identify and describe the factors of production.

The factors of production consist of four basic inputs: natural resources, capital, human resources, and entrepreneurship. Natural resources include all productive inputs that are useful in their natural states. Capital includes technology, tools, information, and physical facilities. Human resources include anyone who works for the firm. Entrepreneurship is the willingness to take risks to create and operate a business.

Assessment Check Answers ✅

2.1 Identify the four basic inputs to an economic system. The four basic inputs are natural resources, capital, human resources, and entrepreneurship.

2.2 List four types of capital. Four types of capital are technology, tools, information, and physical facilities.

[3] Describe the private enterprise system.

The private enterprise system is an economic system that rewards firms for their ability to perceive and serve the needs and demands of consumers. Competition in the private enterprise system ensures success for firms that satisfy consumer demands. Citizens in a private enterprise economy enjoy the rights to private property, profits, freedom of choice, and competition. Entrepreneurship drives economic growth.

Assessment Check Answers ✅

3.1 What is an alternative term for *private enterprise system*? Capitalism is an alternative word for private enterprise system.

3.2 What is the most basic freedom under the private enterprise system? The most basic freedom is the right to private property.

3.3 What is an entrepreneur? An entrepreneur is a risk taker who is willing to start, own, and operate a business.

4 Identify the six eras in the history of business.

The six historical eras are the Colonial period, the Industrial Revolution, the age of industrial entrepreneurs, the production era, the marketing era, and the relationship era. In the Colonial period, businesses were small and rural, emphasizing agricultural production. The Industrial Revolution brought factories and mass production to business. The age of industrial entrepreneurs built on the Industrial Revolution through an expansion in the number and size of firms. The production era focused on the growth of factory operations through assembly lines and other efficient internal processes. During and following the Great Depression, businesses concentrated on finding markets for their products through advertising and selling, giving rise to the marketing era. In the relationship era, businesspeople focused on developing and sustaining long-term relationships with customers and other businesses. Technology promotes innovation and communication, while alliances create a competitive advantage through partnerships. Concern for the environment also helps build strong relationships with customers.

Assessment Check Answers ✅

4.1 What was the Industrial Revolution? The Industrial Revolution began around 1750 in England and moved business operations from an emphasis on independent, skilled workers to a factory system that mass-produced items.

4.2 During which era was the idea of branding developed? The idea of branding began in the marketing era.

4.3 What is the difference between transaction management and relationship management? Transaction management is an approach that focuses on building, promoting, and selling enough products to cover costs and earn profits. Relationship management is the collection of activities that build and maintain ongoing ties with customers and other parties.

5 Explain how today's business workforce and the nature of work itself is changing.

The workforce is changing in several significant ways: (1) it is aging and the labor pool is shrinking, and (2) it is becoming increasingly diverse. The nature of work has shifted toward services and a focus on information. More firms now rely on outsourcing, offshoring, and nearshoring to produce goods or fulfill services and functions that were previously handled in-house or in-country. In addition, today's workplaces are becoming increasingly flexible, allowing employees to work from different locations. And companies are fostering innovation through teamwork and collaboration.

Assessment Check Answers ✅

5.1 Define *outsourcing*, *offshoring*, and *nearshoring*. Outsourcing involves using outside vendors to produce goods or fulfill services and functions that were once handled in house. Offshoring is the relocation of business processes to lower-cost locations overseas. Nearshoring is the outsourcing of production or services to nations near a firm's home base.

5.2 Describe the importance of collaboration and employee partnership. Businesses are increasingly focusing on collaboration, rather than on individuals working alone. No longer do employees just put in their time at a job they hold their entire career. The new employer–employee partnership encourages teamwork and creative thinking, problem solving, and innovation. Managers are trained to listen to and respect employees.

6 Identify the skills and attributes needed for the 21st-century manager.

Today's managers need vision, the ability to perceive marketplace needs and the way their firm can satisfy them. Critical-thinking skills and creativity allow managers to pinpoint problems and opportunities and plan novel solutions. Finally, managers are dealing with rapid change, and they need skills to help lead their organizations through shifts in external and internal conditions.

Assessment Check Answers ✅

6.1 Why is vision an important managerial quality? Managerial vision allows a firm to innovate and adapt to meet changes in the marketplace.

6.2 What is the difference between creativity and critical thinking? Critical thinking is the ability to analyze and assess information to pinpoint problems or opportunities. Creativity is the capacity to develop novel solutions to perceived organizational problems.

7 Outline the characteristics that make a company admired.

A company is usually admired for its solid profits, stable growth, a safe and challenging work environment, high-quality goods and services, and business ethics and social responsibility.

Assessment Check Answers ✅

7.1 Define *business ethics* and *social responsibility*. Business ethics refers to the standards of conduct and moral values involving decisions made in the work environment. Social responsibility is a management philosophy that includes contributing resources to the community, preserving the natural environment, and developing or participating in nonprofit programs designed to promote the well-being of the general public.

7.2 Identify three criteria used to judge whether a company might be considered admirable. Criteria in judging whether companies are admirable include three of the following: solid profits, stable growth, a safe and challenging work environment, high-quality goods and services, and business ethics and social responsibility.

Business Terms You Need to Know

business 4	competition 8	technology 15
profits 4	competitive differentiation 8	strategic alliance 15
not-for-profit organizations 5	private property 9	diversity 18
factors of production 6	entrepreneur 10	outsourcing 19
natural resources 6	consumer orientation 14	offshoring 19
capital 6	branding 14	nearshoring 19
human resources 7	brand 14	vision 20
entrepreneurship 8	transaction management 14	critical thinking 20
private enterprise system 8	relationship era 14	creativity 21
capitalism 8	relationship management 15	

Review Questions

1. Why is business so important to a country's economy?

2. In what ways are not-for-profit organizations a substantial part of the U.S. economy? What unique challenges do not-for-profits face?

3. Identify and describe the four basic inputs that make up factors of production. Give an example of each factor of production that an auto manufacturer might use.

4. What is a private enterprise system? What four rights are critical to the operation of capitalism? Why would capitalism function poorly in a society that does not ensure these rights for its citizens?

5. In what ways is entrepreneurship vital to the private enterprise system?

6. Identify the six eras of business in the United States. How did business change during each era?

7. Describe the focus of the most recent era of U.S. business. How is this different from previous eras?

8. Define *partnership* and *strategic alliance*. How might a motorcycle dealer and a local radio station benefit from an alliance?

9. Identify the major changes in the workforce that will affect the way managers build a world-class workforce in the 21st century. Why is brainpower so important?

10. Identify four qualities that managers of the 21st century must have. Why are these qualities important in a competitive business environment?

Projects and Teamwork Applications

1. The entrepreneurial spirit fuels growth in the U.S. economy. Choose a company that interests you—one you have worked for or dealt with as a customer—and read about the company in the library or visit its Web site. Learn what you can about the company's early history: Who founded it and why? Is the founder still with the organization? Do you think the founder's original vision is still embraced by the company? If not, how has the vision changed?

2. Brands distinguish one company's goods or services from those of its competitors. Each company you purchase from hopes that you will become loyal to its brand. Some well-known brands are Burger King, Coca-Cola, Hilton, and Old Navy. Choose a type of good or service you use regularly and identify the major brands associated with it. Are you loyal to a particular brand? Why or why not?

3. More and more businesses are forming strategic alliances to become more competitive. Sometimes, businesses pair up with not-for-profit organizations in a relationship that is beneficial to both. Choose a company whose goods or services interest you, such as Patagonia, FedEx, Kellogg, or Costco. On your own or with a classmate, research the firm on the Internet to learn about its alliances with not-for-profit organizations. Then describe one of the alliances, including goals and benefits to both parties. Create a presentation for your class.

4. This chapter describes how the nature of the workforce is changing: the population is aging, the labor pool is shrinking, the workforce is becoming more diverse, the nature of work is changing, the workplace is becoming more flexible and mobile, and employers are fostering innovation and collaboration among their employees. Form teams of two to three students. Select a company and research how that company is responding to changes in the workforce. When you have completed your research, be prepared to present it to your class. Choose one of the following companies or select your own: State Farm Insurance, Archer Daniels Midland, Office Depot, Marriott, or Dell.

5. Many successful companies today use technology to help them improve their relationship management. Suppose a major supermarket chain's management team has asked you to assess its use of technology for this purpose. On your own or with a classmate, visit one or two local supermarkets and also explore their corporate Web sites. Note the ways in which firms in this industry already use technology to connect with their customers, and list at least three ideas for new ways or improvements to existing ones. Present your findings to the class as if they were the management team.

■ Web Assignments

1. **Using search engines**. Gathering information is one of the most popular applications of the Web. Using two of the major search engines, such as Google and Firefox, search the Web for information pertaining to brand and relationship management. Sort through your results—you're likely to gets thousands of hits—and identify the three most useful. What did you learn from this experience regarding the use of a search engine?

   http://www.google.com

   http://www.mozilla.org/en-US/firefox/new/

2. **Companies and not-for-profits**. In addition to companies, virtually all not-for-profit organizations have Web sites. Four Web sites are listed below, two for companies (Alcoa and Sony) and two for not-for-profits (Cleveland Clinic and National Audubon Society). What is the purpose of each Web site? What type of information is available? How are the sites similar? How are they different?

   http://www.alcoa.com

   http://www.sony.com

   http://www.clevelandclinic.org

   http://www.audubon.org

3. **Characteristics of U.S. workforce**. Visit the Web site listed below. It is the home page for the *Statistical Abstract of the United States*. Published annually by the U.S. Census Bureau, the *Statistical Abstract* is a good source of basic demographic and economic data. Click on "Labor Force, Employment, and Earnings." Use the relevant data tables to prepare a brief profile of the U.S. workforce (gender, age, educational level, and so forth). How is this profile expected to change over the next 10 to 20 years?

   http://www.census.gov/compendia/statab/

Note: Internet Web addresses change frequently. If you don't find the exact sites listed, you may need to access the organization's home page and search from there or use a search engine such as Firefox or Google.

SAS Is Still a Great Place to Work

CASE 1.1

The employee benefits and perks at SAS, a privately held business software company in Raleigh, North Carolina, are truly amazing. The company's 300-acre campus houses a gym, weight room, meditation garden, sauna, and Olympic-size swimming pool. But just in case any of the complex's 4,200 employees fall ill, there's a fully staffed free health care center.

The company offers free or subsidized exercise and health programs from Zumba to yoga to smoking cessation. There are two subsidized daycare centers and a summer camp. Job sharing, telecommuting, and domestic-partner benefits for same-sex couples are offered. Other on-site perks include dry cleaning, car detailing, and income tax preparation. One of the three subsidized cafeterias has a piano player who takes requests, and employees can grab take-out for the family at day's end. They can prepare their own snacks in one of the many kitchens—or choose one of the free daily snacks.

Jim Goodnight, the company's only CEO in its 34 years, believes treating employees well is simply good business. With revenues that recently topped $2.3 billion despite a global recession, it appears he's right. One of *Fortune's* best companies to work for in each of the past 13 years, SAS recently earned the top spot. "People do work hard here, because they're motivated to take care of a company that takes care of them," says a communications employee.

At 2 percent, turnover among the 11,000 SAS employees worldwide is well below the industry average. The company receives about 100 résumés for every open position. A typical workweek is 35 hours. Many employees make their own schedules; no one counts sick days. Average tenure is ten years.

Among the 17,000 customers worldwide for SAS's data-mining software are IBM, Microsoft, insurance and pharmaceutical firms, universities, the Census Bureau, and professional baseball teams. Goodnight spends much of his time on the road meeting these customers, though he sometimes admits he would rather be programming. But he's well aware of where the real value of the company lies. "My chief assets drive out the gate every day," he says. "My job is to make sure they come back."

Questions for Critical Thinking

1. Explain how flexible and family-friendly policies have played a role in SAS's success.
2. What kind of relationship does SAS seem to have with its employees? With its customers?

Sources: "100 Best Companies to Work For: #1 SAS," CNNMoney .com, http://money.cnn.com, accessed January 24, 2012; David A. Kaplan, "SAS: A New No. 1 Best Employer," CNNMoney.com, January 22, 2010, http://money.cnn.com; Stefan Stern, "A Good Day for Dr. Goodnight and SAS," Financial Times, January 22, 2010, http://blogs.ft.com; Rick Smith, "'We're Hiring' Sign Remains Out at SAS for 2010," wral Tech Wire, January 21, 2010, http://wraltechwire.com.

CASE 1.2 — Nordstrom Rides High

Nordstrom, the high-end clothing retailer headquartered in Seattle, recently marked its twenty-seventh consecutive month of sales growth as annual sales reached nearly $10 billion and market share grew despite the company's aversion to price markdowns. Competitors such as Saks, Macy's, and Gap struggled during the same period, stumped by slowed consumer spending during the recent economic slump.

Nordstrom, founded in 1901 and still family-run, boasts 117 full-line stores and more than 100 Nordstrom Racks outlets. It has high expectations for its burgeoning online operations and has begun expanding overseas, but cautiously, to nearby Canada. A few key elements have always differentiated the chain. Perhaps the best known is its commitment to outstanding customer service, which some say the company practically invented. Regularly ranked near the top in customer satisfaction surveys, the company rewards its sales associates for their attention to customers with generous pay and a tradition of promoting from within. It also provides superior sales tools, such as

an unrivaled new inventory system that allows salespeople to quickly find what customers want. The system changed the way the store's buyers worked, but the results were worth it.

"We're not trying to make a buck and move on to the next thing," says Peter Nordstrom, in charge of merchandise. "This is our life. We do not want to be the generation who screws it up."

Questions for Critical Thinking

1. How does Nordstrom differentiate itself from other clothing retailers?
2. What makes Nordstrom salespeople stay with the company?

Sources: "Nordstrom Comps Rise Again," Yahoo! Finance, January 6, 2012, http://finance.yahoo.com; "Nordstrom: Major of Future Sales Growth Will Be Online," *RIS News*, November 15, 2011, http://risnews .edgl.com; Cotten Timberlake, "How Nordstrom Bests Its Retail Rivals," *Bloomberg Businessweek*, August 11, 2011, www.businessweek.com.

CASE 1.3 — New Harvest Coffee Roasters Brews Up Fresh Business

If you're one of those people for whom the scent of freshly roasted coffee is irresistible, you have something in common with Rik Kleinfeldt. Kleinfeldt, the co-founder and president of New Harvest Coffee Roasters, is a self-proclaimed coffee fanatic. He dwells on the aroma and

flavor of coffee. He measures the freshness of roasted coffee in hours and days, instead of weeks and months. Kleinfeldt started New Harvest Coffee Roasters 10 years ago as a way to pay homage to fresh coffee and build a business around it.

Kleinfeldt observes Starbucks's tremendous success at creating gathering places for people to enjoy coffee and tea—as well as baked goods—in a relaxed social atmosphere. But he also notes with humor that, although cafes and coffee bars were thriving a decade ago, these popular hang-outs "weren't really about coffee. They were about smoothies and cookies. I thought, maybe it's time to get back to basics and roast some coffee." Kleinfeldt recalls that friends and colleagues—fellow coffee fans—felt the same way. He believed that he had a basis to start a business. "We're coffee people," he explains. "There is a like-minded group of people."

Kleinfeldt also points out that the movement toward locally grown or produced foods has been a big help in establishing and building support for his business. "The idea of local coffee starts with the local roaster," he explains. Although the coffee beans themselves are grown elsewhere—mostly on farms in Costa Rica—they are roasted at New Harvest's facility in Rhode Island, where the company is based. "Freshness is a huge factor" in a good cup of coffee, says Kleinfeldt. "Once it's roasted, it's good for about two to twelve days, which is a good incentive to buy local."

Buying local is exactly what retailers and coffee shops such as Blue State Coffee do, creating a collaborative relationship with New Harvest. Alex Payson, COO of Blue State Coffee—a thriving shop in Rhode Island—observes that most of his customers live within a five or ten-minute walk from his business. Blue State customers are educated about the coffee they drink. "They want to *know*," says Payson smiling. "We connect with our coffee farmers. Our customers ask about the story *behind* our coffee," including farming practices and working conditions. Payson and his colleagues from New Harvest have traveled together to some of the coffee farms in Costa Rica that grow the beans they purchase. In fact, loyal customers can view the progress of such trips on New Harvest's Facebook page.

Relationships with companies like Blue State Coffee as well as with consumers are the basis for New Harvest's growth as a business. "We need strategic alliances," says Rik Kleinfeldt. "Blue State is a great example of that. They buy into what we're doing and we support what they are doing. They collaborate with us—what's good for Blue State is also good for New Harvest." Blue State educates its customers and employees about the benefits of buying from a local firm like New Harvest, which in turn works with certified organic, free trade growers. When

Blue State's workers are able to discuss their products knowledgeably with customers—including where and how they are grown, harvested and roasted—a relationship is developed.

Sharing activities, comments, news, and anecdotes with customers, retailers, and coffee shops through social media such as Facebook and Twitter allows New Harvest to broaden its base without spending more on marketing and advertising. These connections also put a personal face on the company and allow New Harvest to gain important knowledge about the views and preferences of its customers. In addition, they provide valuable opportunities to showcase some of the company's work in the community as well as its support for organizations such as the Rainforest Alliance and New England GreenStart.

"Our mission is to be the leader in our region in developing the palate and expectations of coffee drinkers, in order to create a permanent market for the coffee produced by passionate and skilled growers," states the New Harvest Web site. For Rik Kleinfeldt's company and customers, coffee is much more than a hot cup of joe in the morning. Coffee—organically grown, freshly roasted, and served locally—represents a sustainable way to do business.

Questions for Critical Thinking

1. Give examples of each of the four factors of production that New Harvest must rely on to be a successful operation. How does each contribute to the firm's success?

2. Visit New Harvest's Facebook page. Note specific examples of the ways in which the firm is using social media to manage its relationships.

3. Rik Kleinfeldt notes the importance of strategic alliances with firms like Blue State Coffee. Describe how you think New Harvest benefits from alliances with not-for-profit organizations such as Rainforest Alliance, New England GreenStart, and Rhode Island PBS.

4. New Harvest builds much of its reputation on its efforts toward environmental sustainability. How does this reputation affect its relationship with consumers?

Sources: New Harvest Web site, http://www.newharvestcoffee.com, accessed January 24, 2012; Blue State Coffee Web site, http://www.bluestatecoffee.com, accessed January 24, 2012.

Chapter 2

Learning Objectives

[1] Explain the concern for ethical and societal issues.

[2] Describe the contemporary ethical environment.

[3] Discuss how organizations shape ethical conduct.

[4] Describe how businesses can act responsibly to satisfy society.

[5] Explain the ethical responsibilities of businesses to investors and the financial community.

Business Ethics and Social Responsibility

loops7/iStockphoto

PepsiCo's Chickpeas to Relieve World Hunger

When you think of PepsiCo, the maker of Pepsi, Fritos, Gatorade, and scores of other profitable food products, you probably don't think of the humble chickpea. Yet PepsiCo and chickpeas are linked in a powerful new partnership, inspired by Ethiopia's prime minister, that the company hopes will not only improve its own profits and bolster its growing global nutrition business, but also boost Ethiopia's economy and help alleviate world hunger.

PepsiCo, with annual revenues of about $60 billion, recently announced that it will be working with the United Nations World Food Program and the U.S. Agency for International Development (USAID) to increase the production of chickpeas in Ethiopia. Chickpeas are an important ingredient in PepsiCo's hummus and other products, and they are also a nourishing source of protein that is more sustainable than meat with far lower risks of heart disease or diabetes. Demand for them is increasing around the world. About 100,000 small Ethiopian farmers currently grow the crop, and it is on their efforts that the new partnership will focus.

PepsiCo plans to provide the farmers with better seeds and irrigation methods so they can grow two crops a year instead of one. The hope is that chickpeas can thus become a major export crop for Ethiopia, improving the farmers' lives and communities by increasing their income. PepsiCo itself will be the biggest customer for the newly doubled yield, which will more than meet what it needs as a raw ingredient for its own food products. So, with its partners, PepsiCo will help ensure that some of the extra production is used to produce a wholesome, ready-to-eat food called Wawa Mum that the World Food Program has already used to reduce famine's effects in Pakistan. The humanitarian agency has been looking for additional sources of chickpeas to alleviate hunger around the developing world, especially among the very young, and this partnership will go a long way toward helping it extend its efforts.

Dubbed Enterprise EthioPEA, the three-way chickpea partnership shows PepsiCo's commitment to corporate social responsibility in action. The company's senior vice president of global health and agriculture policy says, "not only will we be helping to alleviate famine and malnutrition, but we will also ensure that local farmers will get more work and guaranteed income while enabling our long-term growth, innovation, and relevance among customers."[1]

Overview

PepsiCo's work with small farmers in Ethiopia demonstrates how collaboration between business and other groups can bring about change and make a difference in society. Many companies—large and small—are concerned with issues such as poverty and world hunger. Seeking answers to such problems sometimes requires a company to forgo short-term profits for a few in favor of longer-term gains for many. It may also involve creating mutually beneficial solutions, as PepsiCo has done.

Although most organizations strive to combine ethical behavior with profitable operation, some have struggled to overcome major ethical lapses in recent years. Ethical failures in a number of large or well-known firms led to lawsuits against firms. The image of the CEO—and of business in general—suffered as the evening news carried reports of executives pocketing millions of dollars in compensation while their companies floundered.

But sometimes bad news is a prelude to good news. In the wake of such stories, companies have renewed their efforts to conduct themselves in an ethical manner and one that reflects a responsibility to society, to consumers, and to the environment. Recently, the Federal Sentencing Commission expanded and strengthened its guidelines for ethics compliance programs, and more and more firms began to pay attention to formulating more explicit standards and procedures for ethical behavior. Companies also began to recognize the enormous impact of setting a good rather than a bad example. Today you are likely to hear about the goodwill that companies such as Target Corporation, Ford Motor Company, and Starbucks generate when they give back to their communities through youth reading programs, raise awareness about water scarcity, recycling or energy conservation, or seek to pay better prices to suppliers.

As we discussed in Chapter 1, the underlying aim of business is to serve customers at a profit. But most companies today try to do more than that, looking for ways to give back to customers, society, and the environment. Sometimes they face difficult questions in the process. When does a company's self-interest conflict with society's and customers' well-being? And must the goal of seeking profits conflict with upholding ethical standards? In response to the second question, a growing number of businesses of all sizes are answering no.

[1]

Concern for Ethical and Societal Issues

An organization that wants to prosper over the long term is well advised to consider **business ethics**, the standards of conduct and moral values governing actions and decisions in the work environment. Businesses also must take into account a wide range of social issues, including how a decision will affect the environment, employees, and customers. These issues are at the heart of *social responsibility*, whose primary objective is the enhancement of society's welfare through philosophies, policies, procedures, and actions. In short, businesses must find the proper balance between doing what is right and doing what is profitable. Home Depot has developed a sophisticated system through which certain goods—such as gas cans, generators, plywood, flashlights, and batteries—are stocked in specific distribution locations so they are readily available for shipment to areas that need them in the event of a natural disaster. Using its supply chain effectively not only benefits society, it boosts Home Depot's bottom line.[2]

In business, as in life, deciding what is right or wrong in a given situation does not always involve a clear-cut choice. Firms have many responsibilities—to customers, to employees, to investors, and to society as a whole. Sometimes conflicts arise in trying to serve the different needs of these separate constituencies. The ethical values of executives and individual employees at all levels can influence the decisions and actions a business takes. Throughout your own career, you will encounter many situations in which you will need to weigh right and wrong before making a decision or taking action. So we begin our discussion of business ethics by focusing on individual ethics.

Business ethics are also shaped by the ethical climate within an organization. Codes of conduct and ethical standards play increasingly significant roles in businesses in which doing the right thing is both supported and applauded. This chapter demonstrates how a firm can create a framework to encourage—and even demand— high standards of ethical behavior and social responsibility from its employees. The chapter also considers the complex question of what business owes to society and how societal forces mold the actions of businesses. Finally, it examines the influence of business ethics and social responsibility on global business.

You will encounter many decisions in your career. How you choose to handle them will shape your ethical values.

StigurKarlsson/iStockphoto

The Contemporary Ethical Environment

Assessment Check ☑

1. To whom do businesses have responsibilities?

2. If a firm is meeting all its responsibilities to others, why do ethical conflicts arise?

LECTURE ENHANCER:
Can you think of a recent example where a company may have acted unethically?

LECTURE ENHANCER:
Do you find these results surprising or unexpected?

Business ethics are now in the spotlight as never before. Companies realize that they have to work harder to earn the trust of the general public, and many have taken on the challenge as if their very survival depends on it. This movement toward *corporate social responsibility* should benefit all—consumers, investors, the environment, and the companies themselves.

Most business owners and managers have built and maintained enduring companies without breaking the rules. One example of a firm with a long-standing commitment to ethical practice is Johnson & Johnson, the giant multinational manufacturer of health care products. The most admired pharmaceutical maker and the ninth-most-admired company in the world, according to *Fortune*, Johnson & Johnson has abided by the same basic code of ethics, its well-known credo, for more than 50 years. The credo, reproduced in Figure 2.1, remains the ethical standard against which the company's employees periodically evaluate how well their firm is performing. Management is pledged to address any lapses that are reported. This pledge was recently put to the test when the company recalled several popular drugs, including Tylenol, Benadryl, and Sudafed, when it learned that equipment at one of its manufacturing plants had not been cleaned properly.[3]

Many companies are conscious of how ethical standards can translate into concern for the environment. Recently, Walmart announced a plan to pursue three sustainability goals:

1. to use only renewable energy sources,

2. to recycle all of its waste, and

3. to sell products that "sustain people and the environment," according to Matt Kistler, the company's senior vice president for sustainability.

The company conducted a survey of its suppliers on their sustainability practices as a first step in developing a "sustainability index" to help its customers assess the impact—on the environment and on society—of products in its stores.[4]

In its latest National Business Ethics Survey, the Ethics Resource Center found that workplace misconduct appears to be at an all-time low, with more employees willing to report such behavior when they witness it. However, workers also said that although ethical cultures were stronger, some felt more pressure to cut corners to save money and get the job done, particularly in a difficult economy.[5]

FIGURE 2.1 **Johnson & Johnson Credo**

Our Credo

We believe our first responsibility is to the doctors, nurses and patients, to mothers and fathers and all others who use our products and services. In meeting their needs everything we do must be of high quality. We must constantly strive to reduce our costs in order to maintain reasonable prices. Customers' orders must be serviced promptly and accurately. Our suppliers and distributors must have an opportunity to make a fair profit.

We are responsible to our employees, the men and women who work with us throughout the world. Everyone must be considered as an individual. We must respect their dignity and recognize their merit. They must have a sense of security in their jobs. Compensation must be fair and adequate, and working conditions clean, orderly and safe. We must be mindful of ways to help our employees fulfill their family responsibilities. Employees must feel free to make suggestions and complaints. There must be equal opportunity for employment, development and advancement for those qualified. We must provide competent management, and their actions must be just and ethical.

We are responsible to the communities in which we live and work and to the world community as well. We must be good citizens—support good works and charities and bear our fair share of taxes. We must encourage civic improvements and better health and education. We must maintain in good order the property we are privileged to use, protecting the environment and natural resources.

Our final responsibility is to our stockholders. Business must make a sound profit. We must experiment with new ideas. Research must be carried on, innovative programs developed and mistakes paid for. New equipment must be purchased, new facilities provided and new products launched. Reserves must be created to provide for adverse times. When we operate according to these principles, the stockholders should realize a fair return.

Source: "Our Company Credo," Johnson & Johnson Web site, http://www.jnj .com, accessed February 15, 2012, © Johnson & Johnson.

LECTURE ENHANCER:
Why might some company leaders believe that lowering the company's ethical standards would help it survive the recession?

LECTURE ENHANCER:
Share an example of a company that uses corporate philanthropy to highlight its social responsibility.

The **Sarbanes-Oxley Act of 2002** established new rules and regulations for securities trading and accounting practices. Companies are now required to publish their code of ethics, if they have one, and inform the public of any changes made to it. The law may actually motivate even more firms to develop written codes and guidelines for ethical business behavior. The federal government also created the U.S. Sentencing Commission to institutionalize ethics compliance programs that would establish high ethical standards and end corporate misconduct. The requirements for such programs are shown in Table 2.1.

The current ethical environment of business also includes the appointment of new corporate officers specifically charged with deterring wrongdoing and ensuring that ethical standards are met. Ethics compliance officers, whose numbers are rapidly rising, are responsible for conducting employee training programs that help spot potential fraud and abuse within the firm, investigating sexual harassment and discrimination charges, and monitoring any potential conflicts of interest. But practicing corporate social responsibility is more than just monitoring behavior. Many companies now adopt a three-pronged approach to ethics and social responsibility:

1. engaging in traditional corporate philanthropy, which involves giving to worthy causes

2. anticipating and managing risks

3. identifying opportunities to create value by doing the right thing.[6]

TABLE 2.1 Minimum Requirements for Ethics Compliance Programs

Compliance standards and procedures. Establish standards and procedures, such as codes of ethics and identification of areas of risk, capable of reducing misconduct or criminal activities.
High-level personnel responsibility. Assign high-level personnel, such as boards of directors and top executives, the overall responsibility to actively lead and oversee ethics compliance programs.
Due care in assignments. Avoid delegating authority to individuals with a propensity for misconduct or illegal activities.
Communication of standards and procedures. Communicate ethical requirements to high-level officials and other employees through ethics training programs or publications that explain in practical terms what is required.
Establishment of monitoring and auditing systems and reporting system. Monitor and review ethical compliance systems, and establish a reporting system employees can use to notify the organization of misconduct without fear of retribution.
Enforcement of standards through appropriate mechanisms. Consistently enforce ethical codes, including employee discipline.
Appropriate responses to the offense. Take reasonable steps to respond to the offense and to prevent and detect further violations.
Self-reporting. Report misconduct to the appropriate government agency.
Applicable industry practice or standards. Follow government regulations and industry standards.

Sources: "An Overview of the United States Sentencing Commission and the Federal Sentencing Guidelines," Ethics and Policy Integration Centre, http://www.epic-online.net; "The Relationship between Law and Ethics, and the Significance of the Federal Sentencing Guidelines for Organizations," Ethics and Policy Integration Centre, http://www.ethicaledge.com; U.S. Sentencing Commission, "Sentencing Commission Toughens Requirements for Corporate Compliance and Ethics Programs," USSC news release, http://www.ussc.gov.

Individuals Make a Difference

In today's business environment, individuals can make the difference in ethical expectations and behavior. As executives, managers, and employees demonstrate their personal ethical principles—or lack of ethical principles—the expectations and actions of those who work for and with them can change.

What is the current status of individual business ethics in the United States? Although ethical behavior can be difficult to track or define in all circumstances, evidence suggests that some individuals do act unethically or illegally on the job. The National Business Ethics Survey identifies such behaviors as putting one's own interests ahead of the organization, abuse of company resources, misreporting hours worked, Internet abuse, and safety violations, among others.[7]

Technology seems to have expanded the range and impact of unethical behavior. For example, anyone with computer access to data has the potential to steal or manipulate the data or to shut down the system, even from a remote location. Banks, insurance companies, and other financial institutions are often targeted for such attacks. The Identity Theft Resource Center recently reported nearly 5 million customer records were exposed in one health insurer's data breach alone.[8] While some might shrug these occurrences away, in fact they have an impact on how investors, customers, and the general public view a firm. It is difficult to rebuild a tarnished image, and long-term customers may be lost.

Nearly every employee, at every level, wrestles with ethical questions at some point or another. Some rationalize questionable behavior by saying, "Everybody's doing it." Others act unethically because they feel pressured in their jobs or have to meet performance quotas. Yet some avoid unethical acts that don't mesh with their personal values and morals. To help you understand the differences in the ways individuals arrive at ethical choices, the next section focuses on how personal ethics and morals develop.

LECTURE ENHANCER:
How might one individual affect overall ethical behavior in the workplace?

LECTURE ENHANCER:
Have you ever been challenged by an ethical question as a student?

Development of Individual Ethics

Individuals typically develop ethical standards in the three stages shown in Figure 2.2: the preconventional, conventional, and postconventional stages. In stage 1, the preconventional stage, individuals primarily consider their own needs and desires in making decisions. They obey external rules only because they are afraid of punishment or hope to receive rewards if they comply.

In stage 2, the conventional stage, individuals are aware of and act in response to their duty to others, including their obligations to their family members, co-workers, and organizations. The expectations of these groups influence how they choose between what is acceptable and unacceptable in certain situations. Self-interest, however, continues to play a role in decisions.

Stage 3, the postconventional stage, represents the highest level of ethical and moral behavior. The individual is able to move beyond mere self-interest and duty and take the larger needs of society into account as well. He or she has developed personal ethical principles for determining what is right and can apply those principles in a wide variety of situations. One issue that you may face at work is an ethically compromised situation; the "Business Etiquette" feature lists some tips for relying on basic etiquette to help you steer clear.

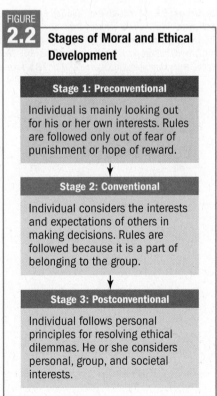

FIGURE 2.2 Stages of Moral and Ethical Development

Stage 1: Preconventional

Individual is mainly looking out for his or her own interests. Rules are followed only out of fear of punishment or hope of reward.

Stage 2: Conventional

Individual considers the interests and expectations of others in making decisions. Rules are followed because it is a part of belonging to the group.

Stage 3: Postconventional

Individual follows personal principles for resolving ethical dilemmas. He or she considers personal, group, and societal interests.

Business Etiquette 101

You might be surprised to discover how easy it is to make an ethical slip at work. If you've mastered the fundamentals of business etiquette, however, you'll have a good ethical foundation for making good decisions in tough situations. Here are some guidelines:

- *Stay focused on your business purpose.* If you develop a close personal relationship with a client or supplier, you may risk a conflict of interest.

- *Don't abuse privileges.* It's tempting to use sick days or personal days for mini-vacations, but if your company distinguishes between these breaks, you should too.

- *Live your values.* Few people are brought up to be untrustworthy. Even if no one knows about it, an unethical choice that betrays your personal values weakens your self-respect and reduces your contribution to the workplace.

- *Don't depend on excuses.* If you're constantly making excuses for your behavior, what does that say about your behavior?

- *Monitor your online behavior.* Never post anything online you wouldn't want to see on the news tomorrow.

- *Don't steal.* Using your work computer for personal tasks like shopping and social networking is just as much theft of company resources as is taking home office supplies.

- *Treat others as you would be treated.* This rule never fails to point the way to ethical behavior and decisions you can be proud of.

Sources: Susan M. Heathfield, "Did You Bring Your Ethics to Work Today?" About.com Human Resources, http://humanresources.about.com, accessed January 10, 2012; Lydia Ramsey, "The Top Twelve Business Etiquette Tips for Social Media," BusinessKnowHow, accessed January 10, 2012, http://www.businessknowhow.com; Dan Schawbel, "Peggy Post on Workplace Etiquette," http://www.forbes.com/sites/danschawbel/2011/12/15, accessed January 10, 2012.

An individual's stage in moral and ethical development is determined by a huge number of factors. Experiences help shape responses to different situations. A person's family, educational, cultural, and religious backgrounds can also play a role, as can the environment within the firm. Individuals can also have different styles of deciding ethical dilemmas, no matter what their stage of moral development.

To help you understand and prepare for the ethical dilemmas you may confront in your career, let's take a closer look at some of the factors involved in solving ethical questions on the job.

On-the-Job Ethical Dilemmas

In the fast-paced world of business, you will sometimes be called on to weigh the ethics of decisions that can affect not just your own future but possibly the future of your fellow workers, your company, and its customers. As already noted, it's not always easy to distinguish between what is right and wrong in many business situations, especially when the needs and concerns of various parties conflict. In the recent past, some CEOs (or their companies) who were accused of wrongdoing simply claimed that they had no idea crimes were being committed, but today's top executives are making a greater effort to be informed of all activities taking place in their firms.

Some clothing retailers donate unworn, unsold garments to charities such as clothing banks. Others, like Sweden-based H&M, destroy and dispose of unsold merchandise. H&M's practice came to the attention of a student in New York City. When her offer to help put H&M in contact with aid organizations went unanswered, the student contacted *The New York Times*, which published a story detailing how H&M—among other retailers—routinely mutilated unsold garments before discarding them to render them unsalable by street vendors or other black-market sellers. The story prompted H&M management to stop destroying unsold clothing. In response, H&M introduced its "Waste" line: garments made of leftover pieces and fabric scraps. The new line promotes recycling and helps reduce textile waste.[9]

Businesses may sometimes refuse to purchase goods or services from a particular country because of rights abuses by the government of that country. The diamond industry has been plagued with such issues. For a number of years, an international ban prohibited the trade of diamonds from the Marange fields of Zimbabwe because of abuses against the workers in those mines. Although the ban was recently lifted, nations and human rights organizations have pledged to keep track of Zimbabwe's government.[10]

Solving ethical dilemmas is not easy. In many cases, each possible decision can have both unpleasant consequences and positive benefits that must be evaluated. The ethical issues that confront manufacturers with unsold merchandise are just one example of many different types of ethical questions encountered in the workplace. Figure 2.3 identifies four of the most common ethical challenges that businesspeople face: conflict of interest, honesty and integrity, loyalty versus truth, and whistle-blowing.

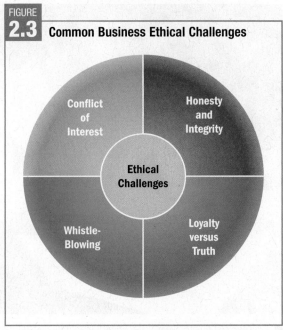

FIGURE 2.3 Common Business Ethical Challenges

Conflict of Interest
A <u>conflict of interest</u> occurs when a businessperson is faced with a situation in which an action benefiting one person or group has the potential to harm another. Conflicts of interest may pose ethical challenges when they involve the businessperson's own interests and those of someone to whom he or she has a duty or when they involve two parties to whom the businessperson has a duty. Lawyers, business consultants, or advertising agencies would face a conflict of interest if they represented two competing companies: a strategy that would most benefit one of the client companies might harm the other client. Handling the situation responsibly would be possible, but it would also be difficult. A conflict may also exist between someone's personal interests and those of an organization or its customers. An offer of gifts or bribes for special treatment creates a situation in which the buyer, but not necessarily the company, may benefit personally.

A conflict of interest may also occur when one person holds two or more similar jobs in two different workplaces. Ethical ways to handle conflicts of interest include (1) avoiding them and (2) disclosing them. Some companies have policies against taking on clients who are competitors of existing clients. Most businesses and government agencies have written policies prohibiting employees from accepting gifts or specifying a maximum gift value. Or a member of a board of directors or committee might abstain from voting on a decision in which he or she has a personal interest. In other situations, people state their potential conflict of interest so that the people affected can decide whether to get information or help they need from another source instead.

Honesty and Integrity
Employers highly value honesty and integrity. An employee who is honest can be counted on to tell the truth. An employee with **integrity** goes beyond truthfulness. Having integrity means adhering to deeply felt ethical principles in business situations. It includes doing what you say you will do and accepting responsibility for mistakes. Behaving with honesty and integrity inspires trust, and as a result, it can help build long-term relationships with customers, employers, suppliers, and the public. Employees, in turn, want their managers and the company as a whole to treat them honestly and with integrity.

conflict of interest situation in which an employee must choose between a business's welfare and personal gain.

CLASS ACTIVITY:
Ask students if they think accepting Super Bowl tickets and trip expenses from a potential major supplier might affect their decision making as a buyer of that company's products.

integrity adhering to deeply felt ethical principles in business situations.

LECTURE ENHANCER:
Think of a hypothetical situation where the honesty and integrity of an employee might help to inspire a customer's trust in the company.

Employers and employees value honesty and integrity, but what should happen when employees misuse Internet privileges for personal purposes?

Unfortunately, violations of honesty and integrity are all too common. Some people misrepresent their academic credentials and previous work experience on their résumés or job applications. Although it may seem tempting to embellish a résumé in a competitive job market, the act shows a lack of honesty and integrity—and eventually it will catch up with you. A recent news report details how a college football coach resigned after information on his biography was questioned.[11]

Others steal from their employers by taking home supplies or products without permission or by carrying out personal business during the time they are being paid to work. For example, Internet misuse during the work day is increasing. Employees use the Internet for personal shopping, e-mail, gaming, and social networking. This misuse costs U.S. companies an estimated $85 billion annually in lost productivity.[12] While the occurrence of such activity varies widely—and employers may feel more strongly about cracking down on some activities than others—most agree that Internet misuse is a problem. Some have resorted to electronic monitoring and surveillance. Compliance with laws regarding the privacy and security of client information is another major reason given for the continuing increase in such monitoring.

Loyalty versus Truth Businesspeople expect their employees to be loyal and to act in the best interests of the company. But when the truth about a company is not favorable, an ethical conflict can arise. Individuals may have to decide between loyalty to the company and truthfulness in business relationships. People resolve such dilemmas in various ways. Some place the highest value on loyalty, even at the expense of truth. Others avoid volunteering negative information but answer truthfully if someone asks them a specific question. People may emphasize truthfulness and actively disclose negative information, especially if the cost of silence is high, as in the case of operating a malfunctioning aircraft or selling tainted food items.

Whistle-Blowing When an individual encounters unethical or illegal actions at work, that person must decide what action to take. Sometimes it is possible to resolve the problem by working through channels within the organization. If that fails, the person should weigh the potential damages to the greater public good. If the damage is significant, a person may conclude that the only solution is to blow the whistle. **Whistle-blowing** is an employee's disclosure to company officials, government authorities, or the media of illegal, immoral, or unethical practices.

A whistle-blower must weigh a number of issues in deciding whether to come forward. Resolving an ethical problem within the organization can be more effective, assuming higher-level managers cooperate. A company that values ethics will try to correct a problem; staying at a company that does not value ethics may not be worthwhile. In some cases, however, people resort to whistle-blowing because they believe the unethical behavior is causing significant damage that outweighs the risk that the company will retaliate against the whistle-blower. Those risks have been real in some cases.

CLASS ACTIVITY: Obtain examples of workplace situations in which students struggled with whether their employer was misrepresenting important product information.

whistle-blowing
employee's disclosure to company officials, government authorities, or the media of illegal, immoral, or unethical practices committed by an organization.

State and federal laws protect whistle-blowers in certain situations, such as reports of discrimination, and the Sarbanes-Oxley Act of 2002 now requires that firms in the private sector provide procedures for anonymous reporting of accusations of fraud. Under the act, anyone who retaliates against an employee for taking concerns of unlawful conduct to a public official can be prosecuted. In addition, whistle-blowers can seek protection under the False Claims Act, under which they can file a lawsuit on behalf of the government if they believe that a company has somehow defrauded the government. Charges against health care companies for fraudulent billing for Medicare or Medicaid are examples of this type of lawsuit.

Despite these protections, whistle-blowing has its risks. When employee Hector Aldana reported safety concerns to his supervisor and the human resources director at Virgin America Airlines, his worries fell on deaf ears. After making numerous attempts to alert management officials, Aldana warned that he would have to contact the FAA. Aldana was immediately fired. Within a short time, he was not only jobless but also bankrupt and homeless. When later asked if the current whistle-blowing laws protected him, Aldana replied with an emphatic "no."[13]

Obviously, whistle-blowing and other ethical issues arise relatively infrequently in firms with strong organizational climates of ethical behavior. The next section examines how a business can develop an environment that discourages unethical behavior among individuals.

LECTURE ENHANCER: Discuss whether the companies for which students work have policies in place to protect whistle-blowers and provide a clear pathway for reporting questionable incidents.

Assessment Check ☑

1. What role can an ethics compliance officer play in a firm?
2. What factors influence the ethical environment of a business?

[3] # How Organizations Shape Ethical Conduct

No individual makes decisions in a vacuum. Choices are strongly influenced by the standards of conduct established within the organizations where people work. Most ethical lapses in business reflect the values of the firms' corporate cultures.

As shown in Figure 2.4, development of a corporate culture to support business ethics happens on four levels:

1. ethical awareness,
2. ethical reasoning,
3. ethical action, and
4. ethical leadership.

If any of these four factors is missing, the ethical climate in an organization will weaken.

Ethical Awareness

The foundation of an ethical climate is ethical awareness. As we have already seen, ethical dilemmas occur frequently in the workplace. So employees need help in identifying ethical problems when they occur. Workers also need guidance about how the firm expects them to respond.

FIGURE 2.4 **Structure of an Ethical Environment**

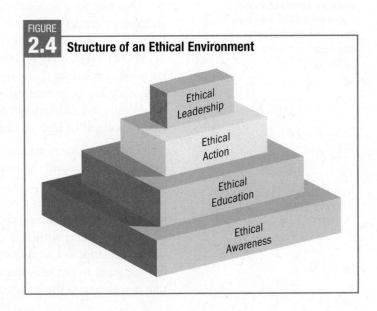

Ethical Leadership

Ethical Action

Ethical Education

Ethical Awareness

Solving an Ethical Controversy

Are Businesses Protecting Themselves from Social Media Abuse?

A recent survey of 120 multinational firms found that while 76 percent use social networking for business, nearly half lack social networking policies. It's probably not surprising, then, that 43 percent have experienced employee misuse of these sites, and nearly one in three has been forced to take disciplinary action. About a quarter of the firms block employee access to social networks, and another quarter permit access at work but monitor it. Should firms also restrict what employees do online in their off-hours?

Should firms control employees' off-duty use of social networks?

PRO

1. An Ethics Resource Center survey shows nearly half of U.S. employees observed a legal or ethical lapse at work, to which the use of social media "appears to be contributing."

2. Employees increasingly believe employees must be expected to properly represent the organization at all times, including at home and online.

CON

1. Some states have laws that protect employees engaged in legal recreational activities when they're not working, which may be construed to include accessing social networks.

2. Companies should hire people they can trust to govern their own behavior.

Summary

This question will continue to be debated. Meanwhile, regardless of the path they choose, companies should hire people they trust; discourage employees from developing personal relationships with clients, bosses, or subordinates; issue clear guidelines for posting company information; and act promptly on any inappropriate employee posts.

Sources: Chat Brooks, "Social Media Contributes to Ethical Lapses at Work," BusinessNewsDaily.com, accessed January 10, 2012, http://www.businessnewsdaily.com; "Charting the Industry: When Social Networking Gets Personal," *PR News,* August 8, 2011, www.prnews.com; "More Than 75 Percent of Businesses Use Social Media, Nearly Half Do Not Have Social Networking Policies," Proskauer company press release, July 14, 2011, http://www.proskauer.com.

---

code of conduct formal statement that defines how an organization expects its employees to resolve ethical issues.

One way for a firm to provide this support is to develop a **code of conduct**, a formal statement that defines how the organization expects employees to resolve ethical questions. Johnson & Johnson's credo, presented earlier, is such a code. At the most basic level, a code of conduct may simply specify ground rules for acceptable behavior, such as identifying the laws and regulations that employees must obey. Other companies use their codes of conduct to identify key corporate values and provide frameworks that guide employees as they resolve moral and ethical dilemmas. Some companies use these to guide employees' online behavior, as the "Solving an Ethical Controversy" box suggests.

The aerospace giant Lockheed Martin, headquartered in Bethesda, Maryland, and with branch offices around the world, has issued a code of conduct to define its values and help employees put them into practice. The code of conduct emphasizes "maintaining a culture of integrity" and defines three basic core values: "Do what's right; respect others; perform with excellence." All employees at every level are expected to treat fellow employees, suppliers, and customers with dignity and respect and to comply with environmental, health, and safety regulations. The code reminds leaders that their language and behavior must not put or even seem to put pressure on subordinates that might induce them to perform in a way that is contrary to the standards set forth in the code. The code also outlines procedures for reporting violations to a local company ethics officer, promising confidentiality and nonretaliation for problems reported in good faith. Lockheed Martin issues a copy of this code of conduct to each employee and also posts it (in 17 languages) on its Web site.[14]

Other firms incorporate similar codes in their policy manuals or mission statements; some issue a code of conduct or statement of values in the form of a small card that employees and managers can carry with them. Harley-Davidson has developed a brief code of ethics that employees can apply both at work and in their personal lives.

CLASS ACTIVITY:
Survey the class to see how many students work for companies that enforce a code of ethics.

Ethical Education

Although a code of conduct can provide an overall framework, it cannot detail a solution for every ethical situation. Some ethical questions have black-and-white answers, but others do not. Businesses must provide the tools employees need to evaluate the options and arrive at suitable decisions.

Many firms have either instituted their own ethics training programs or hired organizations such as SAI Global, which provides outsourced ethics and compliance programs to businesses. Among other services, SAI Global hosts employee reporting services with an anonymous hotline and an ethics case management system. It also helps companies develop appropriate ethics codes with training customized to each company's needs, including specialized online, interactive training systems.[15]

Many authorities debate whether ethics can be taught, but training can give employees the chance to practice applying ethical values to hypothetical situations before they face real-world situations. Similar strategies are being used in many business school ethics programs, where case studies and practical scenarios work best. Convicted white-collar criminal Walter Pavlo, a former employee at telecommunications firm MCI, speaks at colleges and universities about his experiences in the firm and prison. Pavlo, who along with other MCI associates stashed money in offshore accounts, speaks about his actions in an effort to warn students of the consequences of cheating.

Ethical Action

Codes of conduct and ethics training help employees recognize and reason through ethical problems. In addition, firms must provide structures and approaches that allow decisions to be turned into ethical actions. Texas Instruments gives its employees a reference card to help them make ethical decisions on the job. The size of a standard business card, it lists the following guidelines:

- Is the action legal?
- Does it comply with our values?
- If you do it, will you feel bad?
- How will it look in the newspaper?
- If you know it's wrong, don't do it!
- If you're not sure, ask.
- Keep asking until you get an answer.

CLASS ACTIVITY:
Ask students if they can think of any examples where an action may be legal but unethical.

Goals set for the business as a whole and for individual departments and employees can affect ethical behavior. A firm whose managers set unrealistic goals for employee performance may find an increase in cheating, lying, and other misdeeds, as employees attempt to protect themselves. In today's Internet economy, the high value placed on speed can create a climate in which ethical behavior is sometimes challenged. Ethical decisions often require careful and quiet thought, a challenging task in today's fast-paced business world.

Some companies encourage ethical action by providing support for employees faced with dilemmas. One common tool is an employee hotline, a telephone number that employees can call, often anonymously, for advice or to report unethical behavior they have witnessed. Ethics compliance officers, as mentioned previously, can guide employees through ethical minefields.

Ethical Leadership

CLASS ACTIVITY:
Ask students for examples of leaders who "walked the talk" and provided strong ethical leadership.

stakeholders customers, investors, employees, and public affected by or with an interest in a company.

Assessment Check ✔

1. What is the preconventional stage in the development of ethical standards?

2. How can loyalty and truth come into conflict for an employee?

3. How does ethical leadership contribute to ethical standards throughout a company?

social responsibility business's consideration of society's well-being and consumer satisfaction, in addition to profits.

Executives must not only talk about ethical behavior but also demonstrate it in their actions. This requires employees to be personally committed to the company's core values and be willing to base their actions on them. The recent recession exposed executive-level misdeeds that damaged or even destroyed entire organizations and wiped out people's life savings. In the aftermath, some organizations and business leaders have made a commitment to demonstrate ethical leadership and increased social responsibility.

Recently the owner of several juice bars paid her employees to take work shifts where their only job was to perform random acts of kindness—acts that would brighten someone else's day. The "22 Days of Kindness" program was a huge success not only among the company employees but also among members of the community. After the kindness campaign was featured in the local media, the business owner was flooded with applications from people who wanted to work for her company.[16]

Unfortunately, not all organizations are able to build a solid framework of business ethics. Because the damage from ethical misconduct can powerfully affect a firm's **stakeholders**— customers, investors, employees, and the public—pressure is exerted on businesses to act in acceptable ways. But when businesses fail, the law must step in to enforce good business practices. Many of the laws that affect specific industries or individuals are described in other chapters in this book. For example, legislation affecting international business operations is discussed in Chapter 4. Laws designed to assist small businesses are examined in Chapter 5.

Laws related to labor unions are described in Chapter 8. Legislation related to banking and the securities markets is discussed in Chapters 16 and 17. Finally, for an examination of the legal and governmental forces designed to safeguard society's interests when businesses fail at self-regulation, see Appendix A, "Business Law."

[4]

Acting Responsibly to Satisfy Society

A second major issue affecting business is the question of social responsibility. In a general sense, **social responsibility** is management's acceptance of the obligation to consider profit, consumer satisfaction, and societal well-being of equal value in evaluating the firm's performance. It is the recognition that business must be concerned with the qualitative dimensions of consumer, employee, and societal benefits, as well as the quantitative measures

Going Green

Starbucks Re-Designs Its Stores. Now, What About the Cup?

Coffee-selling giant Starbucks has announced plans to design new and remodel existing stores to reduce environmental impact.

The massive project is part of Starbucks's efforts to reposition itself along with a commitment to conserving water and energy, recycling where possible, and using "green" construction methods.

The company has already put some of its energy- and water-conservation goals into practice. The next challenge is those ubiquitous disposable cups. About 3 billion Starbucks paper cups are thrown in the trash each year. Starbucks is determined to change that. The firm launched an outside design contest, looking for innovative ways to solve the problem. And the company has partnered with Georgia Pacific paper mill to recycle some of the cups into Starbucks napkins. The goal is to have a 100-percent recyclable cup by 2015. Meanwhile, customers are helping out: Some are already toting their own reusable travel mugs into Starbucks for a fill-up.

Questions for Critical Thinking

1. How do Starbucks's new plans for its stores reflect its sense of social responsibility?

2. How has Starbucks reached out to customers and the community in order to reach its sustainability goals? Why is this an important step for the business?

Sources: Company Web site, http://www.starbucks.com, accessed February 15, 2012; Anya Kamenetz, "What Are You Going to Do About This Damn Cup?" *Fast Company*, November 2010, pp. 116–120, 174–175; "Starbucks Recycling Cups at Chicago, Seattle Stores," *Environmental Leader*, June 29, 2010, http://www.environmentalleader.com.

of sales and profits, by which business performance is traditionally measured. Businesses may exercise social responsibility because such behavior is required by law, because it enhances the company's image, or because management believes it is the ethical course of action. The "Going Green" feature discusses the efforts of Starbucks to implement environmentally sound practices.

Historically, a company's social performance has been measured by its contribution to the overall economy and the employment opportunities it provides. Variables such as total wages paid often indicate social performance. Although profits and employment remain important, today many factors contribute to an assessment of a firm's social performance, including providing equal employment opportunities; respecting the cultural diversity of employees; responding to environmental concerns; providing a safe, healthy workplace; and producing high-quality products that are safe to use.

A business is also judged by its interactions with the community. To demonstrate their social responsibility, many corporations highlight charitable contributions and community service in their annual reports and on their Web sites. The Mercadien Group, a business and accounting firm based in Princeton, New Jersey, participates with the U.S. Marine Corps in the nationwide Toys for Tots program. The company's office is the official drop-off site for the program, and employees at all levels take part.[17]

Firms such as Full Circle Coupons are based almost entirely on the premise of social responsibility. Full Circle is an Internet-based business that allows subscribers to log on to its Web site, choose a fundraiser or charity they want to support, and print out discount coupons for local

> LECTURE ENHANCER:
> Provide an example of a business in your local area that makes environmental concerns a priority.

Businesses are judged by their interactions with the surrounding community, including employees volunteering at charitable events.

Steve Debenport/iStockphoto

FIGURE
2.5

Business's Social Responsibilities

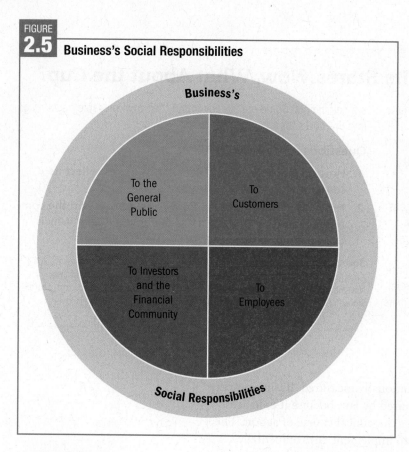

Business's

To the General Public

To Customers

To Investors and the Financial Community

To Employees

Social Responsibilities

social audits formal procedure that identifies and evaluates all company activities that relate to social issues such as conservation, employment practices, environmental protection, and philanthropy.

businesses. Full Circle then donates half the annual subscriber fee of $25 to charity. Owners Martha and Brett Bogart believe they have found a business opportunity that not only generates a profit, but automatically gives back to the community.[18]

Some firms measure social performance by conducting **social audits**, formal procedures that identify and evaluate all company activities that relate to social issues such as conservation, employment practices, environmental protection, and philanthropy. The social audit informs management about how well the company is performing in these areas. Based on this information, management may revise current programs or develop new ones.

Outside groups may conduct their own evaluations of businesses. Various environmental, religious, and public-interest groups have created standards of corporate performance. Reports on many of these evaluations are available to the general public. The New York–based Council on Economic Priorities is one such group. Other groups publicize their evaluations and include critiques of the social responsibility performance of firms.

As Figure 2.5 shows, the social responsibilities of business can be classified according to its relationships to the general public, customers, employees, and investors and other members of the financial community. Many of these relationships extend beyond national borders.

Responsibilities to the General Public

The responsibilities of business to the general public include dealing with public health issues, protecting the environment, and developing the quality of the workforce. Many would argue that businesses also have responsibilities to support charitable and social causes and organizations that work toward the greater public good. In other words, they should support the communities in which they earn profits. Such efforts are called *corporate philanthropy*.

Public-Health Issues One of the most complex issues facing business as it addresses its ethical and social responsibilities to the general public is public health. Central to the public-health debate is the question of what businesses should do about dangerous products such as tobacco and alcohol. Tobacco products represent a major health risk, contributing to heart disease, stroke, and cancer among smokers. Families and co-workers of smokers share this danger as well, as their exposure to secondhand smoke increases their risks for cancer, asthma, and respiratory infections. Many cities have not only banned smoking in public places, but also commercial businesses such as restaurants. Several states, including Arkansas, California, Louisiana, and Maine, have bans on smoking in cars when children under the age of 18 are present, depending on the specific state's law.[19]

Heart disease, diabetes, and obesity have become major public health issues as the rates of these three conditions have been rising. More than 5 million American children between the ages of 6 and 17 are said to be overweight. Three-quarters of obese teenagers will become obese adults at risk for diabetes and heart disease. Jared Fogle became famous for losing 245 pounds over a two-year period through exercise and a diet that included SUBWAY sandwiches. He has since set up the Jared Foundation with the goal of fighting childhood obesity by encouraging children to develop healthy diet and exercise habits. Spreading his message through speaking tours, grants to schools, and programs for children and their families, Fogle says, "My goal is to help children avoid the physical and emotional hardships I went through living with obesity." SUBWAY's Web site lists the nutritional values of its menu items and sources of diet and nutrition advice. The Web site also features a linked page supporting the Jared Foundation and its mission.[20]

Substance abuse is another serious public health problem worldwide. Revelations of the use of illegal steroids by many athletes, particularly in professional baseball, highlight the difficulty of devising accurate tests for performance-enhancing and muscle-building drugs and fairly evaluating the results. Many of the drugs in question are so similar to compounds naturally present in the body that identification is extremely difficult. Recently baseball player Ryan Braun had a positive drug-test ruling (and possible 50-game suspension) overturned.[21] With regard to drug testing, athletes' individual rights to privacy have been questioned, particularly due to their widespread influence on youthful fans. Steroid use is on the rise among high school athletes, despite the publicity about the dangers of such drugs. Tougher penalties for professional players who fail drug tests are being formulated.

To do their part to aid the general public, some businesses collaborate with urban neighborhoods to set up community gardens as a way of showing kids how to eat healthy.

CLASS ACTIVITY:
Can students think of any examples of businesses that have portrayed or distorted their food products or beverages as "healthy" when, in fact, they are not?

Protecting the Environment Businesses impact the environment in a variety of ways—through the energy they consume, the waste they produce, the natural resources they use, and more. Today, many businesses have built goals into their corporate philosophy for taking steps toward protecting the environment. Some have even launched sustainability initiatives—operating in such a way that the firm not only minimizes its impact on the environment, but actually regenerates or replaces used resources. Procter & Gamble and Kaiser Permanente maintain sustainability assessments of their suppliers, rating them on energy and water use, recycling, waste production, greenhouse gases produced, and other factors. Both organizations expect suppliers to meet green standards—or risk losing them as customers.[22]

For many managers, finding ways to minimize pollution and other environmental damage caused by their products or operating processes has become an important economic and legal issue as well as a social one. When General Motors unveiled the Chevrolet Volt, the new car generated a lot of buzz because it is entirely electric. After its battery runs down, a gasoline engine powers an on-board generator that recharges the battery. Despite Volt's "greenness," its sales figures haven't reached GM's expectations, possibly because of the car's sticker price.[23]

Despite the efforts of companies like Procter & Gamble, Kaiser Permanente, General Motors, and thousands of others, production and manufacturing methods still leave behind large quantities of waste materials that can further pollute the air, water, and soil. Some products themselves, such as electronics that contain lead and mercury, are difficult to recycle or reuse—although scientists and engineers are finding ways to do this. In other instances, the action (or lack of action) on the part of a firm results in an environmental

Pacific Biodiesel Recycles Oil from French Fries to Fuel

Robert King founded King Diesel on the island of Maui in Hawaii. The company used conventional diesel fuel to run the generators at the Central Maui Landfill, but King became concerned at the large amounts of used cooking oil being dumped. He contacted Daryl Reece at the University of Idaho. Reece helped develop a process that successfully converted used restaurant oils into biodiesel fuel. Together they founded Pacific Biodiesel, using biodiesel to run the generators at the landfill in one of America's first commercially viable, community-based biodiesel plants. Today Pacific Biodiesel and its associated companies produce and sell biodiesel fuel and design, build, and support biodiesel plants around the country.

Biodegradable and nontoxic, biodiesel fuel can be used in any diesel engine. It is produced from renewable resources such as cooking oil and soybean oil. Biodiesel significantly cuts down on many pollutants and reduces dependence on foreign oil. In addition, the company has pledged not to import any oil—such as soybean oil from South America or palm oil from Southeast Asia—for its product, nor does it export biodiesel outside the United States.

On Maui, restaurants pay haulers to take their used cooking oil to the landfill. The haulers pay the county of Oahu for the right to dump garbage at waste facilities. Pacific Biodiesel's facility at the landfill is rent free. The haulers' fees cover most of the county's payment to Pacific Biodiesel for processing the waste. Shipping this waste off island would be much more expensive; recycling it prolongs the useful life of the landfills and guarantees a local source of energy. On Maui alone, Pacific Biodiesel recycles about 200,000 gallons of oil and grease each year.

Recently Pacific Biodiesel announced it will be supplying biodiesel fuel to the emergency power plant to be located at the Honolulu Airport. The company was selected by Hawaiian Electric Company to be the biodiesel fuel provider.

Questions for Critical Thinking

1. How might Pacific Biodiesel spread the message that recycling is good business as well as good for the environment? How might it reach out to other industries?

2. How does Pacific Biodiesel fulfill its responsibilities to the general public?

Sources: Company Web site, http://www.biodiesel.com, accessed March 8, 2012; Alan Yonan, Jr., "Biodiesel Will Fuel Honolulu Airport Power Plant," *Star Advertiser*, August 3, 2011, http://www.staradvertiser.com; "Official Pacific Biodiesel, Inc. Position on Imported Oil," December 3, 2010, http://www.biodiesel.com.

---

disaster, as in the case of the 2010 explosion and large-scale spill from BP's offshore drilling rig in the Gulf of Mexico. The months-long spill not only affected the ocean and coastal environments, but also the lives of residents and local economies.[24] Despite the difficulty, however, companies are finding that they can be environmentally friendly and profitable, too. Another solution to the problems of pollutants is **recycling**—reprocessing used materials for reuse. Recycling can sometimes provide much of the raw material that manufacturers need, thereby conserving the world's natural resources and reducing the need for landfills. The "Hit & Miss" feature describes a company with a creative twist on recycling, turning used restaurant oil and grease into clean, biodegradable biodiesel fuel.

According to the Environmental Protection Agency, discarded electronic items now make up as much as 40 percent of the lead in landfills in the United States. The Institute of Scrap Recycling Industries estimates that about 2.8 billion pounds of electronic equipment were recycled in a recent year.[25] Firms such as Best Buy are trying to make it easier for consumers to recycle their unwanted electronics, no matter where they bought them. Free of charge, consumers can drop off ink and toner cartridges, rechargeable batteries, and cables, wires, cords, and other small items in kiosks at store entrances. Best Buy also accepts larger items for recycling, such as PCs, VCRs, DVD players, TVs, and computer monitors, and offers Best Buy gift cards for gently used consumer electronics. Other retailers such as Target and Apple offer recycling and trade-in programs, while service providers such as AT&T and Verizon provide drop-off locations for phones and other equipment. Not-for-profit organizations have joined the effort as well. Goodwill Industries recently partnered with Dell Computer to make it easier for consumers to donate their old computer equipment.[26]

recycling reprocessing of used materials for reuse.

LECTURE ENHANCER: Discuss how students have disposed of their old computers or related equipment.

Many consumers have favorable impressions of environmentally conscious businesses. To target these customers, companies often use **green marketing**, a marketing strategy that promotes environmentally safe products and production methods. A business cannot simply claim that its goods or services are environmentally friendly, however. The Federal Trade Commission (FTC) has issued guidelines for businesses to follow in making environmental claims. A firm must be able to prove that any environmental claim made about a product has been substantiated with reliable scientific evidence. In addition, as shown in Figure 2.6, the FTC has given specific directions about how various environmental terms may be used in advertising and marketing.

Other environmental issues—such as finding renewable sources of clean energy and developing **sustainable** agriculture—are the focus of many firms' efforts. Sun Microsystems founder Vinod Khosla works with a group of entrepreneurs and investors in Silicon Valley to develop a new generation of energy.[27] Solar energy, geothermal energy, biodiesel, and wind power are just a few of the renewable sources of energy being developed by entrepreneurs, large energy firms, and small engineering companies.

Mars Incorporated, the maker of Dove Chocolate and other candies, has committed to using only sustainably grown cocoa in all of its chocolate products by 2020. Its Dove dark chocolate line represents the first of its products to be made with the cocoa.[28]

Developing the Quality of the Workforce
In the past, a nation's wealth has often been based on its money, production equipment, and natural resources. A country's true wealth, however, lies in its people. An educated, skilled workforce provides the intellectual know-how required to develop new technology, improve productivity, and compete in the global marketplace. It is becoming increasingly clear that to remain competitive, U.S. business must assume more responsibility for enhancing the quality of its workforce, including encouraging diversity of all kinds.

In developed economies like that of the United States, many new jobs require college-educated workers. With demand high for workers with advanced skills, the difference

Nathan Gleave/iStockphoto

Recycling can help companies do their part to protect the environment. Best Buy stores will take your old TVs, DVD players, computers, cell phones, and other electronic devices to avoid having them end up in landfills.

green marketing a marketing strategy that promotes environmentally safe products and production methods.

sustainable the capacity to endure in ecology.

LECTURE ENHANCER:
Can you think of a product that uses green marketing?

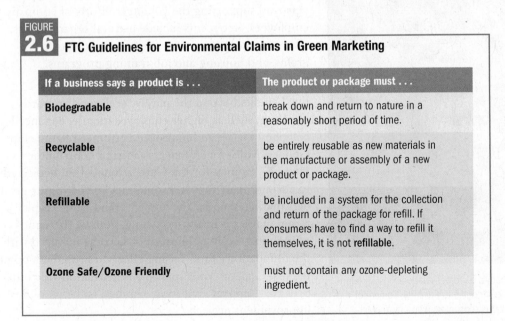

FIGURE
2.6 FTC Guidelines for Environmental Claims in Green Marketing

If a business says a product is . . .	The product or package must . . .
Biodegradable	break down and return to nature in a reasonably short period of time.
Recyclable	be entirely reusable as new materials in the manufacture or assembly of a new product or package.
Refillable	be included in a system for the collection and return of the package for refill. If consumers have to find a way to refill it themselves, it is not **refillable**.
Ozone Safe/Ozone Friendly	must not contain any ozone-depleting ingredient.

between the highest-paid and lowest-paid workers has been increasing. Education plays an important role in earnings, despite success stories of those who dropped out of college or high school to start businesses. Workers with a college degree earn an average of $1,300 a week, whereas those with some high school but no diploma earn less than $500.[29] Businesses must encourage students to stay in school, continue their education, and sharpen their skills. Cheerios supports Spoonfuls of Stories, a national program to encourage young children and their parents to read together by distributing more than 50 million books in specially marked cereal boxes. The company has also contributed more than $3.5 million to First Book, a not-for-profit that gives children from low-income families the chance to own their first new books.[30]

Organizations also face enormous responsibilities for helping women, members of various cultural groups, returning military veterans, and those who are physically challenged to contribute fully to the economy. Failure to do so is not only a waste of more than half the nation's workforce but also devastating to a firm's public image. Some socially responsible firms also encourage diversity in their business suppliers. Retail giant JCPenney's Partnership Program is designed to foster relationships with minority- and women-owned businesses— an effort the company has worked at for more than 30 years.

Through a commitment to developing employee diversity, Walmart's president and CEO Mike Duke recently reiterated the company's emphasis on inclusion. "There isn't a single part of our business that can't benefit from people of all backgrounds contributing different skills, different ideas, and different points of view," said Duke. One area that Duke believes is crucial for Walmart to focus on is the advancement of women in the company worldwide.[31]

LECTURE ENHANCER:
What is one way in which a company could improve the quality of its workforce?

corporate philanthropy
effort of an organization to make a contribution to the communities in which it earns profits.

Corporate Philanthropy As Chapter 1 pointed out, not-for-profit organizations play an important role in society by serving the public good. They provide the human resources that enhance the quality of life in communities around the world. To fulfill this mission, many not-for-profit organizations rely on financial contributions from the business community. Firms respond by donating billions of dollars each year to not-for-profit organizations. This **corporate philanthropy** includes cash contributions, donations of equipment and products, and supporting the volunteer efforts of company employees. Recipients include cultural organizations, adopt-a-school programs, neighborhood sports programs, and housing and job training programs.

Corporate philanthropy can have many positive benefits beyond the purely "feel-good" rewards of giving, such as higher employee morale, enhanced company image, and improved customer relationships. General Mills, for instance, is a major contributor to Susan G. Komen for the Cure, a foundation dedicated to curing breast cancer, through its line of yogurt products marketed under the Yoplait brand name. Yoplait's target market is health-conscious women, the same group most likely to know of or become involved with the foundation's fund-raising efforts. Through its other brands, General Mills sponsors other nationwide initiatives that support education, families, and community improvement projects.[32]

Richard B. Levine/NewsCom

Corporate philanthropy can enhance a company's customer relationships. Through sales of its Yoplait yogurt line, General Mills contributes to Susan G. Komen for the Cure, a charity important to the health-conscious consumers who buy Yoplait.

Companies often seek to align their marketing efforts with their charitable giving. Many contribute to the Olympics and create advertising that features the company's sponsorship. This is known as *cause-related marketing*. In a recent survey, nearly nine out of ten young people said they believed companies had a duty to support social causes, and nearly seven in eight said they would switch brands in order to reward a company that did so. Consumers are often willing to pay even more for a product, such as Newman's Own salad dressings and salsa, because they know the proceeds are going to a good cause.

Another form of corporate philanthropy is volunteerism. In their roles as corporate citizens, thousands of businesses encourage their employees to contribute their efforts to projects as diverse as Habitat for Humanity, the Red Cross, and the Humane Society. In addition to making tangible contributions to the well-being of fellow citizens, such programs generate considerable public support and goodwill for the companies and their employees. In some cases, the volunteer efforts occur mostly during off-hours for employees. In other instances, firms permit their workforces to volunteer during regular working hours. Sometimes volunteers with special skills are indispensable. After the 2011 devastating earthquake and tsunami in Japan, FedEx committed $1 million in cash and transportation and logistics expertise from its own workforce to aid in the relief effort.[33]

Responsibilities to Customers

Businesspeople share a social and ethical responsibility to treat their customers fairly and act in a manner that is not harmful to them. **Consumerism**—the public demand that a business consider the wants and needs of its customers in making decisions—has gained widespread acceptance. Consumerism is based on the belief that consumers have certain rights. A frequently quoted statement of consumer rights was made by President John F. Kennedy in 1962. Figure 2.7 summarizes those consumer rights. Numerous state and federal laws have been implemented since then to protect the rights.

The Right to Be Safe Contemporary businesspeople must recognize obligations, both moral and legal, to ensure the safe operation of their products. Consumers should feel assured that the products they purchase will not cause injuries in normal use. **Product liability** refers to the responsibility of manufacturers for injuries and damages caused by their products. Items that lead to injuries, either directly or indirectly, can have disastrous consequences for their makers.

Many companies put their products through rigorous testing to avoid safety problems. Still, testing alone cannot foresee every eventuality. Companies must try to consider all possibilities and provide adequate warning of potential dangers. When a product does pose a threat to customer safety, a responsible manufacturer responds quickly to either correct the problem or recall the dangerous product. Although we take for granted that our food—and our pets' food—is safe, sometimes contamination leaks in, which can cause illness or even death. Recently a concern about salmonella, a microorganism that produces dangerous infections, caused Nestlé Purina PetCare Company to issue a voluntary recall of two of its dry cat foods—Cat Chow Naturals and Friskies Grillers Blend. No illnesses or deaths were reported, but the company wanted to be certain its products were safe for pets to consume.[34]

consumerism public demand that a business consider the wants and needs of its customers in making decisions.

product liability the responsibility of manufacturers for injuries and damages caused by their products.

LECTURE ENHANCER: What is a company ethically required to do if it discovers one of its products may not be safe?

FIGURE
2.7 **Consumer Rights as Proposed by President Kennedy**

Right to Be Heard

Right to Be Safe

Consumer Rights

Right to Choose

Right to Be Informed

The Right to Be Informed Consumers should have access to enough education and product information to make responsible buying decisions. In their efforts to promote and sell their goods and services, companies can easily neglect consumers' right to be fully informed. False or misleading advertising is a violation of the Wheeler-Lea Act, a federal law enacted in 1938. The FTC and other federal and state agencies have established rules and regulations that govern advertising truthfulness. These rules prohibit businesses from making unsubstantiated claims about the performance or superiority of their merchandise. They also require businesses to avoid misleading consumers. Businesses that fail to comply face scrutiny from the FTC and consumer protection organizations. In advertising the PowerBalance wristband, its maker claimed the product improved strength, balance, and flexibility. Before long, the product had even attracted the attention of professional athletes and celebrities around the globe. Recently, however, the company admitted it had made misleading claims. After settling one $57 million claim and facing several class-action lawsuits, PowerBalance filed for bankruptcy protection.[35]

The Food and Drug Administration (FDA), which sets standards for advertising conducted by drug manufacturers, eased restrictions for prescription drug advertising on television. In print ads, drug makers are required to spell out potential side effects and the proper uses of prescription drugs. Because of the requirement to disclose this information, prescription drug television advertising was limited. Now, however, the FDA says drug ads on radio and television can directly promote a prescription drug's benefits if they provide a quick way for consumers to learn about side effects, such as displaying a toll-free number or Internet address.

The responsibility of business to preserve consumers' right to be informed extends beyond avoiding misleading advertising. All communications with customers—from salespeople's comments to warranties and invoices—must be controlled to clearly and accurately inform customers. Most packaged-goods firms, personal-computer makers, and other makers of products bought for personal use by consumers include toll-free customer service numbers on their product labels so that consumers can get answers to questions about a product.

To protect their customers and avoid claims of insufficient disclosure, businesses often include warnings on products. As Figure 2.8 shows, sometimes these warnings go far beyond what a reasonable consumer would expect. Others are downright funny.

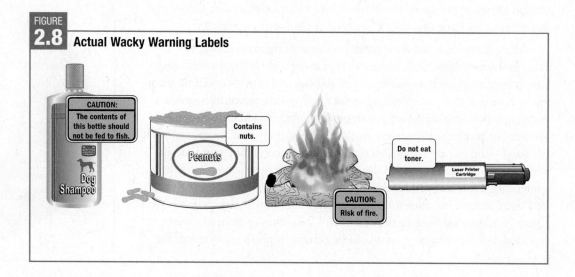

FIGURE 2.8 Actual Wacky Warning Labels

CAUTION: The contents of this bottle should not be fed to fish.
Dog Shampoo

Contains nuts.
Peanuts

CAUTION: Risk of fire.

Do not eat toner.
Laser Printer Cartridge

The Right to Choose Consumers should have the right to choose which goods and services they need and want to purchase. Socially responsible firms attempt to preserve this right, even if they reduce their own sales and profits in the process. Brand-name drug makers have recently gone on the defensive in a battle being waged by state governments, insurance companies, consumer groups, unions, and major employers such as General Motors and Verizon. These groups want to force down the rising price of prescription drugs by ensuring that consumers have the right and the opportunity to select cheaper generic brands.

The Right to Be Heard Consumers should be able to express legitimate complaints to appropriate parties. Many companies expend considerable effort to ensure full hearings for consumer complaints. The auction Web site eBay assists buyers and sellers who believe they were victimized in transactions conducted through the site, deploying employees to work with users and law enforcement agencies to combat fraud. The company has strict guidelines for buyers and sellers and rules for leaving feedback about a buyer or seller. For example, buyers must operate within a list of acceptable goods for sale and may not offer such items as alcohol, pornography, drugs, counterfeit currency, or artifacts from cave formations, graves, or Native American sites. The protection of copyrights is also an important part of eBay's policy.[36]

Responsibilities to Employees

Companies that can attract skilled and knowledgeable employees are better able to meet the challenges of competing globally. In return, businesses have wide-ranging responsibilities to their employees, both here and abroad. These include workplace safety, quality-of-life issues, ensuring equal opportunity on the job, avoiding age discrimination, and preventing sexual harassment and sexism.

CLASS ACTIVITY:
Ask students if they have ever observed a workplace safety issue at work.

Workplace Safety A century ago, few businesses paid much attention to the safety of their workers. In fact, most business owners viewed employees as mere cogs in the production process. Workers—many of whom were young children—toiled in frequently dangerous conditions. In 1911, a fire at the Triangle Shirtwaist Factory in New York City killed 146 people, mostly young girls. Contributing to the massive loss of life were the sweatshop working conditions at the factory, including overcrowding, blocked exits, and a lack of fire escapes. This horrifying tragedy forced businesses to begin to recognize their responsibility for their workers' safety.

The safety and health of workers on the job is now an important business responsibility. The Occupational Safety and Health Administration (OSHA) is the main federal regulatory force in setting workplace safety and health standards. These mandates range from broad guidelines on storing hazardous materials to specific standards for worker safety in industries such as

Laurentiu Iordache/iStockphoto

Workplace safety is an important business responsibility. In potentially dangerous areas, workers are required to wear safety equipment, including hard hats and protective eyewear.

Hit & Miss

Finding Work–Life Balance for the Sandwich Generation

Consider some hard facts:

- More than 25 percent of U.S. families provide care for parents or other elders.
- These workers account for $34 billion a year in lost productivity.
- More than 25 percent of U.S. parents borrow to help their children financially, sometimes delaying retirement.
- Half of all working mothers and 30 percent of fathers stay home to care for ailing children.

No wonder the so-called sandwich generation, full-time employees caring for elders and children, feels squeezed. One employer, however, knows how to help them balance work and family. That's Denver-based Johnson Storage & Moving Co., a family-owned business with 225 employees, founded in 1900 and operating 24 hours a day in five states. In 1995, the company's owner, Jim Johnson, had a revelation: "I felt the best solution is to allow our workers to do their jobs from their home offices and still be eligible for all company benefits."

Says employee Lori Tubaya, Johnson's "custom-fit policies have benefited five generations of my family!" she says. "And I am eternally grateful."

Questions for Critical Thinking

1. Do you agree with Jim Johnson that satisfied employees are important? Why or why not?
2. What might prevent some companies from offering programs like Johnson's?

Sources: Kathryn Britton, "The Sandwich Generation: Looking Both Ways," *Positive Psychology News Daily*, February 15, 2012, http://positivepsychologynews.com; Kimberly Lankford, "The Sandwich Generation: Caught in the Middle," *Kiplinger's Personal Finance*, November 2011, www.kiplinger.com; "Work-Life Balance for Caregivers No Longer a Struggle at Denver-Based Transportation Company," PR Newswire, August 27, 2011, www.prnewswire.com; "Members of the Sandwich Generation Have Resources to Deal with Challenges," Interim Healthcare, July 14, 2011, www.interimhealthcare.com; Lori Tubaya, "Helping the 'Dagwood Sandwich' Generation," MomsRising blog, February 9, 2011, www.momsrising.org/blog; Michelle Noerhren, "Sandwich Generation in a Pickle?" *Working Mother* blogs, January 24, 2011, www.workingmother.com.

---

construction, manufacturing, and mining. OSHA tracks and investigates workplace accidents and has the authority to fine employers who are found liable for injuries and deaths that occur on the job.

One unsettling fact is that as many as 70 teens die every year in the United States as a result of work injuries. Most of these fatalities occur because of unsafe equipment, inadequate safety training, and dangerous work that is illegal or inappropriate for youth. OSHA is taking steps to educate employers and teen workers about safety, health, and a positive work environment. The OSHA Web site has a special section for teens with the answers to most frequently asked questions about such issues as wages, labor standards, harassment issues, and safety at work. In addition, the U.S. Department of Labor's YouthRules! initiative is designed to further educate and empower young workers. The YouthRules! Web page offers information and activities for teens, parents, educators, and employers.[37]

Quality-of-Life Issues Balancing work and family is becoming harder for many employees. They find themselves squeezed between working long hours and handling child-care problems, caring for elderly parents, and solving other family crises. A *sandwich generation* of households, those caring for two generations—their children and their aging parents—has arisen. As the population ages, the share of American households providing some type of care to a relative or friend age 50 or older has grown dramatically in the early years of the 21st century. See the accompanying Hit & Miss box for more insight about the sandwich generation.

As married women spend more time working outside the home, they have fewer hours per week to spend on family. However, working mothers aren't the only employees juggling work with life's other demands. Childless couples, single people, and men all express

LECTURE ENHANCER:
How do you think firms should handle absenteeism?

frustration at the pressures of balancing work with family and personal needs. To help with the work–life balance, some employers are offering flexible work schedules so that parents can meet the needs of their children (or aging parents) as well as their jobs. *Working Mother* magazine offers up its list of 100 best companies to work for offering work–life balance. Criteria for selection include the option to telecommute, flexible scheduling, job sharing, and access to childcare. Some of the magazine's top choices are Bank of America, Deloitte, Discovery Communications, General Mills, and IBM.[38] Increasingly, women are starting their own businesses so they can set their own hours and goals.

Some companies have come up with truly innovative ways to deal with work schedules, including paid time off for vacation or illness. At some of its locations, IBM has done away with prescribed vacation time altogether—the focus is on results. Employees have an informal agreement with their supervisors about when they will be out of the office, based on their ability to complete their work on schedule. The number of days they take off is not tracked; instead vacation time is considered open ended. But the catch is, the work has to be done. Perhaps surprisingly, the firm found that employees put in just as many hours, if not more, under the new program.[39]

Another solution has been to offer **family leave** to employees who need to deal with family matters. Under the Family and Medical Leave Act of 1993, employers with 50 or more employees must provide unpaid leave annually for any employee who wants time off for the birth or adoption of a child; to become a foster parent; or to care for a seriously ill relative, spouse, or self if he or she has a serious health condition or injury. The law requires employers to grant up to 12 weeks of leave each year, and leave may be taken intermittently as medical conditions make necessary. This unpaid leave also applies to an employee who has a serious illness. Workers must meet certain eligibility requirements. Employers must continue to provide health benefits during the leave and guarantee that employees will return to equivalent jobs. The issue of who is entitled to health benefits can also create a dilemma as companies struggle to balance the needs of their employees against the staggering costs of health care.

family leave the Family and Medical Leave Act of 1993 states that employers with 50 or more employees must provide unpaid leave up to 12 weeks annually for any employee who wants time off for the birth or adoption of a child, to become a foster parent, or to care for a seriously ill relative, spouse, or self if he or she has a serious health condition or injury.

Ensuring Equal Opportunity on the Job Businesspeople face many challenges managing an increasingly diverse workforce in the 21st century. Technological advances are expanding the ways people with physical disabilities can contribute in the workplace. Businesses also need to find ways to responsibly recruit and manage older workers and workers with varying lifestyles. In addition, beginning with Lotus Development in 1982, companies have begun to extend benefits equally to employees, regardless of sexual orientation. In particular, that means the company offers benefits such as health insurance to unmarried domestic partners if it offers them to spouses of married couples. More than half of *Fortune* 500 companies currently offer domestic-partner benefits to their employees.[40]

To a great extent, efforts at managing diversity are regulated by law. The Civil Rights Act (1964) outlawed many kinds of discriminatory practices, and Title VII of the act specifically prohibits **discrimination**—biased treatment of a job candidate or employee—in the workplace. As shown in Table 2.2, other nondiscrimination laws include the Equal Pay Act (1963), the Age Discrimination in Employment Act (1967), the Equal Employment Opportunity Act (1972), the Pregnancy Discrimination Act (1978), the Civil Rights Act of 1991, and numerous executive orders. The Americans with Disabilities Act (1990) protects the rights of physically challenged people. The Vietnam Era Veterans Readjustment Act (1974) protects the employment of veterans of the Vietnam War. The Genetic Information Nondiscrimination Act (2008) prohibits discrimination on the basis of genetic tests or the medical history of an individual or that individual's family.

discrimination biased treatment of a job candidate or employee.

2.2 Laws Designed to Ensure Equal Opportunity

LAW	KEY PROVISIONS
Title VII of the Civil Rights Act of 1964 (as amended by the Equal Employment Opportunity Act of 1972)	Prohibits discrimination in hiring, promotion, compensation, training, or dismissal on the basis of race, color, religion, sex, or national origin.
Age Discrimination in Employment Act of 1967 (as amended)	Prohibits discrimination in employment against anyone age 40 or older in hiring, promotion, compensation, training, or dismissal.
Equal Pay Act of 1963	Requires equal pay for men and women working for the same firm in jobs that require equal skill, effort, and responsibility.
Vocational Rehabilitation Act of 1973	Requires government contractors and subcontractors to take affirmative action to employ and promote qualified disabled workers. Coverage now extends to all federal employees. Coverage has been broadened by the passage of similar laws in more than 20 states and, through court rulings, to include people with communicable diseases, including AIDS.
Vietnam Era Veterans Readjustment Act of 1974	Requires government contractors and subcontractors to take affirmative action to employ and retain disabled veterans. Coverage now extends to all federal employees and has been broadened by the passage of similar laws in more than 20 states.
Pregnancy Discrimination Act of 1978	Requires employers to treat pregnant women and new mothers the same as other employees for all employment-related purposes, including receipt of benefits under company benefit programs.
Americans with Disabilities Act of 1990	Makes discrimination against the disabled illegal in public accommodations, transportation, and telecommunications; stiffens employer penalties for intentional discrimination on the basis of an employee's disability.
Civil Rights Act of 1991	Makes it easier for workers to sue their employers for alleged discrimination. Enables victims of sexual discrimination to collect punitive damages; includes employment decisions and on-the-job issues such as sexual harassment, unfair promotions, and unfair dismissal. The employer must prove that it did not engage in discrimination.
Family and Medical Leave Act of 1993	Requires all businesses with 50 or more employees to provide up to 12 weeks of unpaid leave annually to employees who have had a child or are adopting a child, are becoming foster parents, are caring for a seriously ill relative or spouse, or are themselves seriously ill. Workers must meet certain eligibility requirements.
Uniformed Services Employment and Reemployment Rights Act of 1994	Prohibits employers from denying employment benefits on the basis of employees' membership in or obligation to serve in the uniformed services and protects the rights of veterans, reservists, and National Guard members to reclaim their jobs after being absent due to military service or training.
Genetic Information Nondiscrimination Act of 2008	Prohibits employers from discriminating against employees or applicants on the basis of genetic information, including genetic tests of an individual or family member or an individual's personal or family medical history.

Equal Employment Opportunity Commission (EEOC) this commission was created to increase job opportunities for women and minorities and to help end discrimination based on race, color, religion, disability, gender, or national origin in any personnel action.

The **Equal Employment Opportunity Commission (EEOC)** was created to increase job opportunities for women and minorities and to help end discrimination based on race, color, religion, disability, gender, or national origin in any personnel action. To enforce fair-employment laws, it investigates charges of discrimination and harassment and files suit against violators. The EEOC can also help employers set up programs to increase job opportunities for women, minorities, people with disabilities, and people in other protected categories.

Fair treatment of employees is more than a matter of complying with EEOC regulations, however. All employees want to be treated with respect. A minority employee who misses out on a plum assignment may miss out on the big raise that goes with it. As the employee's salary grows more slowly, managers may eventually begin to use the size of the salary as an indicator that the employee contributes less to the organization. While in the past the EEOC has focused on this type of individual situation, currently it is addressing what it terms *systemic discrimination*, which it defines as "a pattern or practice, policy and/or class cases where the alleged discrimination has a broad impact on an industry, profession, company, or geographic location." A systemic discrimination charge usually becomes a class-action suit, which costs considerably more to defend than an individual lawsuit. So firms are examining their employment practices carefully to make sure they are not open to discrimination charges.[41] Chapter 9 takes a closer look at diversity and employment discrimination issues as part of a discussion of human resource management.

Age Discrimination With the average age of U.S. workers steadily rising, more than half the workforce is projected to be age 40 or older in a few years. Yet some employers find it less expensive to hire and retain younger workers, who generally have lower medical bills as well as lower salary and benefits packages. At the same time, many older workers have training and skills that younger workers have yet to acquire. The Age Discrimination in Employment Act of 1967 (ADEA) protects individuals who are age 40 or older, prohibiting discrimination on the basis of age and denial of benefits to older employees.

Ruling in a lawsuit brought under the ADEA, the Supreme Court determined that employers can be held liable for age discrimination against older workers even if they intended no harm. At the same time, the court allowed employers to use "reasonable" factors, such as cost cutting, to defend business practices that might have more severe impacts on older than on younger workers. However, a recent Court ruling shifted the burden of proof onto employees seeking to prove that age discrimination was a factor in their demotion or dismissal.[42]

Legal issues aside, employers might do well to consider not only the experience that older workers bring to the workplace but also their enthusiasm. Many surveys report that older workers who remain on the job by choice—not because they are forced to do so for economic reasons—are often happy with their employment. But other studies show that aging Baby Boomers are increasingly dissatisfied with the workplace due to the falling value of their retirement investments and diminishing options such as relocation. Still, employees with decades of work experience can be a valuable asset to any firm.[43]

In all cases, employers need to plan ahead for the aging of the workforce, finding ways to retain accumulated business wisdom, prepare for the demand for health services, and be ready for growth in the industries that serve seniors. The 55-and-older age group is projected to comprise nearly 37 percent of the population by the end of this decade, whereas the 35-to-44 age group will decrease to about 16 percent. These numbers signify a coming shift in the workforce, as well as in the goods and services needed.[44]

Employers are responsible for avoiding age discrimination in the workplace. As the average age of workers rises, employers will benefit from the older generation's knowledge.

Gregg Matthews/The New York Times/Redux Pictures

Sexual Harassment and Sexism

Every employer has a responsibility to ensure that all workers are treated fairly and are safe from sexual harassment. **Sexual harassment** refers to unwelcome and inappropriate actions of a sexual nature in the workplace. It is a form of sex discrimination that violates the Civil Rights Act of 1964, which gives both men and women the right to file lawsuits for intentional sexual harassment. About 11,000 sexual harassment complaints are filed with the EEOC each year, of which about 16 percent are filed by men.[45] Thousands of other cases are either handled internally by companies or never reported.

Two types of sexual harassment exist. The first type occurs when an employee is pressured to comply with unwelcome advances and requests for sexual favors in return for job security, promotions, and raises. The second type results from a hostile work environment in which an employee feels hassled or degraded because of unwelcome flirting, lewd comments, or obscene jokes. The courts have ruled that allowing sexually oriented materials in the workplace can create a hostile atmosphere that interferes with an employee's ability to do the job. Employers are also legally responsible to protect employees from sexual harassment by customers and clients. The EEOC's Web site informs employers and employees of criteria for identifying sexual harassment and how it should be handled in the workplace.

Preventing sexual harassment can be difficult because it involves regulating the conduct of individual employees. Sometimes victims, especially young employees, are intimidated or unaware of their rights, but the EEOC has set up a Youth@Work program (http://www.eeoc.gov/youth) to ensure that young workers can learn about the various types of discrimination and ways to avoid them.

The cost in settlements or fines can be enormous. So, in addition to ethical and legal reasons, it makes good business sense for firms to prevent this kind of behavior from happening. To avoid sexual harassment problems, many firms have established policies and employee education programs aimed at preventing such violations. An effective harassment prevention program should include the following measures:

- Issue a specific policy statement prohibiting sexual harassment.
- Develop a complaint procedure for employees to follow.
- Create a work atmosphere that encourages sexually harassed staffers to come forward.
- Investigate and resolve complaints quickly and take disciplinary action against harassers.

Unless all these components are supported by top management, sexual harassment is difficult to eliminate.

Sexual harassment is often part of the broader problem of **sexism**—discrimination against members of either sex, but primarily affecting women. One important sexism issue is equal pay for equal work.

Lilly Ledbetter was near retirement when she found out that for a considerable length of time, men at her management level had been getting paid more than she had been. But the Supreme Court threw out her case because she did not sue within the statute of limitations—that is, within 180 days of the first instance of a lower paycheck. Recently the statute of limitations was extended in these types of cases.[46]

U.S. Census statistics show that overall, women still earn 77 cents for every $1 earned by men. The number drops to 68 cents for African American women and 58 cents for Hispanic women. Education, occupation, work hours, and other factors don't seem to affect the gap, which remains unexplained other than the penalty of gender.[47] In some extreme cases,

sexual harassment unwelcome and inappropriate actions of a sexual nature in the workplace.

CLASS ACTIVITY: Ask students to provide recent examples of sexual harassment.

sexism discrimination against members of either sex, but primarily affecting women.

differences in pay and advancement can become the basis for sex discrimination suits, which, like sexual harassment suits, can be costly and time consuming to settle. As in all business practices, it is better to act legally and ethically in the first place.

5   Responsibilities to Investors and the Financial Community

Although a fundamental goal of any business is to make a profit for its shareholders, investors and the financial community demand that businesses behave ethically and legally. When firms fail in this responsibility, thousands of investors and consumers can suffer.

State and federal government agencies are responsible for protecting investors from financial misdeeds. At the federal level, the Securities and Exchange Commission (SEC) investigates suspicions of unethical or illegal behavior by publicly traded firms. It investigates accusations that a business is using faulty accounting practices to inaccurately portray its financial resources and profits to investors. Regulation FD (Fair Disclosure) is an SEC rule that requires publicly traded companies to announce major information to the general public, rather than first disclosing the information to selected major investors. The agency also operates an Office of Internet Enforcement to target fraud in online trading and online sales of stock by unlicensed sellers. Recall that the Sarbanes-Oxley Act of 2002 also protects investors from unethical accounting practices. Chapter 17 discusses securities trading practices further.

What's Ahead

The decisions and actions of businesspeople are often influenced by outside forces such as the legal environment and society's expectations about business responsibility. Firms also are affected by the economic environments in which they operate. The next chapter discusses the broad economic issues that influence businesses around the world. Our discussion will focus on how factors such as supply and demand, unemployment, inflation, and government monetary policies pose both challenges and opportunities for firms seeking to compete in the global marketplace.

Assessment Check

1. What is meant by social responsibility, and why do firms exercise it?

2. What is green marketing?

3. What are the four main consumer rights?

LECTURE ENHANCER: What might be some consequences for investors if a business does not act ethically or legally?

Assessment Check

1. Why do firms need to do more than just earn a profit?

2. What is the role of the Securities and Exchange Commission?

Summary of Learning Objectives

1   **Explain the concern for ethical and societal issues.**
Business ethics refers to the standards of conduct and moral values that businesspeople rely on to guide their actions and decisions in the workplace. Businesspeople must take a wide range of social issues into account when making decisions. Social responsibility refers to management's acceptance of the obligation to place a significant value on profit, consumer satisfaction, and societal well-being in evaluating the firm's performance.

Assessment Check Answers

1.1 To whom do businesses have responsibilities? Businesses are responsible to customers, employees, investors, and society.

1.2 If a firm is meeting all its responsibilities to others, why do ethical conflicts arise? Ethical conflicts arise because business must balance doing what is right and doing what is profitable.

2 Describe the contemporary ethical environment.

Among the many factors shaping individual ethics are personal experience, peer pressure, and organizational culture. Individual ethics are also influenced by family, cultural, and religious standards. Additionally, the culture of the organization where a person works can be a factor.

Assessment Check Answers

2.1 What role can an ethics compliance officer play in a firm? Ethics compliance officers are charged with deterring wrongdoing and ensuring that ethical standards are met.

2.2 What factors influence the ethical environment of a business? Individual ethics and technology influence the ethical environment of a business.

3 Discuss how organizations shape ethical conduct.

In the preconventional stage, individuals primarily consider their own needs and desires in making decisions. In the conventional stage, individuals are aware of and respond to their duty to others. In the postconventional stage, the individual can move beyond self-interest and duty to include consideration of the needs of society. Conflicts of interest occur when a businessperson is faced with a situation in which an action benefiting one person has the potential to harm another, as when the person's own interests conflict with those of a customer. Honesty and integrity are valued qualities that engender trust, but a person's immediate self-interest may seem to require violating these principles. Loyalty to an employer sometimes conflicts with truthfulness. Whistle-blowing is a possible response to misconduct in the workplace, but the personal costs of doing so may be high. Employees are strongly influenced by the standards of conduct established and supported within the organizations where they work. Businesses can help shape ethical behavior by developing codes of conduct that define their expectations. Organizations can also use this training to develop employees' ethics awareness and reasoning. Executives must also demonstrate ethical behavior in their decisions and actions to provide ethical leadership.

Assessment Check Answers

3.1 What is the preconventional stage in the development of ethical standards? In the preconventional stage, the individual looks out for his or her own interests and follows rules out of fear of punishment or hope of reward.

3.2 How can loyalty and truth come into conflict for an employee? Truth and loyalty can come into conflict when the truth about a company or situation is unfavorable.

3.3 How does ethical leadership contribute to ethical standards throughout a company? Employees more readily commit to the company's core values when they see that leaders and managers behave ethically.

4 Describe how businesses can act responsibly to satisfy society.

Today's businesses are expected to weigh their qualitative impact on consumers and society, in addition to their quantitative economic contributions such as sales, employment levels, and profits. One measure is their compliance with labor and consumer protection laws and their charitable contributions. Another measure some businesses take is to conduct social audits. Public-interest groups also create standards and measure companies' performance relative to those standards. The responsibilities of business to the general public include protecting the public health and the environment and developing the quality of the workforce. Additionally, many would argue that businesses have a social responsibility to support charitable and social causes in the communities in which they earn profits. Business also must treat customers fairly and protect consumers, upholding their rights to be safe, to be informed, to choose, and to be heard. Businesses have wide-ranging responsibilities to their workers. They should make sure that the workplace is safe, address quality-of-life issues, ensure equal opportunity, and prevent sexual harassment and other forms of discrimination.

Assessment Check Answers

4.1 What is meant by social responsibility, and why do firms exercise it? Social responsibility is management's acceptance of its obligation to consider profit, consumer satisfaction, and societal well-being to be of significant value when evaluating the firm's performance. Businesses demonstrate social responsibility because it enhances the company's image, or because management believes it is the right thing to do.

4.2 What is green marketing? Green marketing is a marketing strategy that promotes environmentally safe products and production methods.

4.3 What are the four main consumer rights? The four main consumer rights are the right to be safe, to be informed, to choose, and to be heard.

5 Explain the ethical responsibilities of businesses to investors and the financial community.

Investors and the financial community demand that businesses behave ethically as well as legally in handling their financial transactions. Businesses must be honest in reporting their profits and financial performance to avoid misleading investors. The Securities and Exchange

Commission is the federal agency responsible for investigating suspicions that publicly traded firms have engaged in unethical or illegal financial behavior.

Assessment Check Answers ✔️

5.1 Why do firms need to do more than just earn a profit? Firms need to do more than just earn a profit because they should behave in an ethical manner and because investors and shareholders demand such behavior.

5.2 What is the role of the Securities and Exchange Commission? Among other functions, the Securities and Exchange Commission investigates suspicions of unethical or illegal behavior by publicly traded firms.

■ Business Terms You Need to Know

business ethics 32	code of conduct 40	sustainable 47	Equal Employment
Sarbanes-Oxley Act of	stakeholders 42	corporate philanthropy 48	Opportunity Commission
2002 34	social responsibility 42	consumerism 49	(EEOC) 54
conflict of interest 37	social audits 44	product liability 49	sexual harassment 56
integrity 37	recycling 46	family leave 53	sexism 56
whistle-blowing 38	green marketing 47	discrimination 53	

■ Review Questions

1. What do the terms *business ethics* and *social responsibility* mean? Why are they important components of a firm's overall philosophy in conducting business?

2. In what ways do individuals make a difference in a firm's commitment to ethics? Describe the three stages in which an individual develops ethical standards.

3. What type of ethical dilemma does each of the following illustrate? (A situation might involve more than one dilemma.)

    a. Due to the breakup with a client, an advertising agency suddenly finds itself representing rival companies.

    b. A newly hired employee learns that the office manager plays computer games on company time.

    c. An employee is asked to destroy documents that implicate his or her firm in widespread pollution.

    d. A company spokesperson agrees to give a press conference that puts a positive spin on his or her firm's use of sweatshop labor.

4. Describe how ethical leadership contributes to the development of each of the other levels of ethical standards in a corporation.

5. In what ways do firms demonstrate their social responsibility?

6. What are the four major areas in which businesses have responsibilities to the general public? In what ways can meeting these responsibilities give a firm a competitive edge?

7. Identify and describe the four basic rights that consumerism tries to protect. How has consumerism improved the contemporary business environment? What challenges has it created for businesses?

8. What are the five major areas in which companies have responsibilities to their employees? What types of changes in society are now affecting these responsibilities?

9. Identify which Equal Opportunity law (or laws) protects workers in the following categories:

    a. an employee who must care for an elderly parent

    b. a National Guard member who is returning from deployment overseas

    c. a job applicant who is HIV positive

    d. a person who is over 40 years old

    e. a woman who has been sexually harassed on the job

    f. a woman with a family history of breast cancer

10. How does a company demonstrate its responsibility to investors and the financial community?

■ Projects and Teamwork Applications

1. Write your own personal code of ethics. Create standards for your behavior at school, in personal relationships, and on the job. Then assess how well you meet your own standards and revise them if necessary.

2. On your own or with a classmate, visit the Web site of one of the following firms, or choose another that interests you. On the basis of what you can learn about the company from the site, construct a chart or figure that illustrates examples

of the firm's ethical awareness, ethical education, ethical actions, and ethical leadership. Present your findings to class.

a. Sun Microsystems

b. NFL, NHL, NBA, MLB, MLS (or any major professional sports league)

c. Hewlett-Packard

d. Aetna

e. Irving Oil

f. Costco

g. IKEA

3. Now take the company you studied for question 2 (or choose another one) and conduct a social audit on that firm. Do

your findings match the firm's culture of ethics? If there are any differences, what are they and why might they occur?

4. On your own or with a classmate, go online, flip through a magazine, or surf television channels to identify a firm that is engaged in green marketing. If you see a commercial on television, go to the firm's Web site to learn more about the product or process advertised. Does the firm make claims that comply with the FTC guidelines? Present your findings in class.

5. As a consumer, you have come to expect a certain level of responsibility toward you on the part of companies with which you do business. Describe a situation in which you felt that a company did not recognize your rights as a consumer. How did you handle the situation? How did the company handle it? What was the final outcome?

Web Assignments

1. **Ethical standards**. Go to the Web site listed below. It summarizes the ethical standards for all employees and suppliers of John Deere and Company. Review the material and then write a brief report relating Deere's ethical standards to the material on corporate ethics discussed in the chapter. In addition, consider how Deere's ethical standards are integrated with the firm's overall global citizenship efforts.

http://www.deere.com/wps/dcom/en_US/corporate/our_company/citizenship/citizenship_landing.page

2. **Starting a career**. Each year *BusinessWeek* magazine rates the best companies to begin a career. Visit the *BusinessWeek* Web site and review the most recent list. What criteria did

BusinessWeek use when building this list? What role does ethics and social responsibility play?

http://www.businessweek.com

3. **Social responsibility**. Athletic footwear manufacturer New Balance is one of the few companies in its industry that still manufactures products in the United States. Go to the Web site listed below and learn more about the firm's commitment to U.S. manufacturing. Prepare a report that relates this commitment to the firm's other core values.

http://www.newbalance.com/company/

Note: Internet Web addresses change frequently. If you don't find the exact sites listed, you may need to access the organization's home page and search from there or use a search engine such as Bing or Google.

CASE 2.1

Hilton Joins the Global Soap Project

"When living as a refugee in Kenya, I realized soap was hard to come by, even completely nonexistent sometimes. . . . People were suffering from illness simply because they couldn't wash their hands." This experience motivated Derreck Kayongo to found the Global Soap Project, an initiative to provide bars of soap for developing countries, where even schools, hospitals, and health clinics can lack such basic supplies.

A highly effective and inexpensive way to prevent diarrheal diseases, infections, and pneumonia, hand washing can save millions of lives every year. In North America alone, nearly

3 million bars of hotel soap are discarded every day after minimal use. Kayongo's idea was to recycle them into new bars and distribute them to those in need. In its first three years, the Global Soap Project sent more than 25 tons of soap to 20 vulnerable countries, relying on volunteers, non-profit organizations, and non-governmental organizations (NGOs) to get things off the ground.

Now the project has been joined by Hilton Worldwide. The hotel company promises to donate more than 1 million new bars of soap and will invest $1.3 million in the project, along with its own operational expertise to help it expand.

Questions for Critical Thinking

1. One observer notes that the Global Soap Project appears to be a good fit with Hilton's existing sustainability efforts. Why might that be true of a hotel chain?
2. Which organization will benefit more from their partnership, the Global Soap Project or Hilton? Why?

Sources: Organization website, www.globalsoap.org, accessed January 10, 2012; Raz Godelnik, "A Soap Opera at Hilton Hotels," Triple Pundit. com, November 10, 2011, www.triplepundit.com; organization press release, "Hilton Worldwide Announces Partnership with the Global Soap Project," November 9, 2011, www.globalsoap.org; "Hilton Worldwide Collaborates with the Global Soap Project to Recycle used Soap," Hotel Interactive.com, November 9, 2011, www.hotelinteractive.com.

Greener Shipping—At Sea and in Port

CASE 2.2

For years, environmentalists have advocated slower driving and slower flying as ways to save fuel and cut down on greenhouse-gas emissions. This principle also applies at sea. With the price of oil rising, container shipping giant Maersk Line decided to take action.

With more than 500 vessels, Copenhagen-based Maersk is the world's largest shipper. Hundreds of its vessels now sail at 12 knots—a speed known in the industry as "super slow steaming"—instead of the standard speed of 24 or 25 knots. Super slow steaming cuts daily fuel consumption by nearly two-thirds and saves $5,000 an hour. Maersk ships have also lowered their interior lighting and substituted rolls of paper towels for paper napkins in their dining salons.

Shipping containers have also gone green. Whether empty or full, conventional steel containers are heavy and occupy the same amount of space even when empty. Dutch manufacturer Cargoshell devised a container that, when empty, collapses in less than half a minute to one-quarter its full size. Cargoshells can be stacked more compactly than steel containers. While steel containers usually have outward-opening doors that take up an entire side panel, the Cargoshell door simply rolls up or down. Made of fiber-reinforced composite materials, Cargoshells weigh 25 percent less than steel containers and need no paint because they don't corrode. The composites are good insulators, too: important for temperature control. Manufacturing Cargoshells generates less carbon dioxide than manufacturing steel containers.

The ports where cargo ships arrive and depart are crowded with vehicles emitting diesel exhaust—a possible carcinogen—into the atmosphere. To reduce exposure, the U.S. Environmental Protection Agency (EPA) initiated a voluntary, incentive-based program to encourage ports and truck fleet owners to reduce emissions. In an unlikely alliance, the Teamsters have joined forces with environmental groups to persuade the Port of Los Angeles to ban older trucks and to require trucking companies buy newer, cleaner-running rigs.

Taken together, these measures go a long way toward the greening of the shipping industry.

Questions for Critical Thinking

1. How do Maersk and Cargoshell carry out their responsibilities to society?
2. Many of the goods you buy and use are imported from overseas and sold more cheaply than if they were made in the United States. But do they have hidden, nonmonetary costs? Use the information in this case as a guide.

Sources: Maersk Web site, http://www.maersk.com, accessed February 15, 2012; Cargoshell Web site, http://www .cargoshell.com, accessed February 15, 2012; Clean Ports USA, U.S. Environmental Protection Agency, http://epa.gov, accessed February 15, 2012; Steven Greenhouse, "Clearing the Air at American Ports," *The New York Times*, February 26, 2010, http://www.nytimes.com; "Maersk Cuts Fuel Use, Emissions 30% by Slowing Down," *Environmental Leader*, February 18, 2010, http://www.environmentalleader.com; Elisabeth Rosenthal, "Slow and Steady Across the Sea Aids Profit and the Environment," *The New York Times*, February 17, 2010, http://www.nytimes.com; John W. Miller, "Maersk: Container Ship Cuts Costs to Stay Afloat," Polaris Institute, February 2010, http://www.polarisinstitute .org; Jace Shoemaker-Galloway, "Cargoshell Collapsible Shipping Containers: A Greener and Flatter Way to Transport Goods," *Triple Pundit*, February 5, 2010, http://www.triplepundit.com.

Seventh Generation: Beyond Paper and Plastic

Seventh Generation was founded in Vermont twenty years ago on the premise that there's a better way to do business, one that protects both the planet and the people. The company's name is derived from the Great Law of the Iroquois, which mandates that "In every deliberation, we must consider the impact of our decision on the next seven generations." Co-founder and executive chairman Jeffrey Hollender takes this mandate literally.

Hollender refers to himself as "chief protagonist" of Seventh Generation. For two decades, he has campaigned for environmentally responsible consumer products, manufacturing processes, and operations at Seventh Generation. In addition, he campaigns outside the company to raise awareness about the importance of consumerism in preservation of the environment.

Hollender admits to watershed moments in his own life that have led him to redirect his company. When his young son had a particularly severe asthma attack, the doctor told Hollender that the best way to controls his son's asthma was to control his environment—in particular, his household environment. Hollender recognized the enormity of this statement and took it on as a corporate challenge. EPA research had already revealed that the air in the average home is two to five times more polluted than outdoor air. "I realized then that Seventh Generation had a lot more to offer than protecting the outdoor environment, and it became the turning point for the company." If Seventh Generation could offer a broad spectrum of household products that did not contribute to indoor pollution—but performed cleaning and other tasks as effectively as products containing toxic chemicals—the company could achieve an entirely new level of corporate responsibility.

Senior chemist Cara Bondi describes the challenge she and her colleagues faced. "Prior to the last decade, companies would try to put out green products but they didn't really do the job," which resulted in these products failing in the marketplace. If they weren't effective at cleaning laundry or dishes, appealing to consumers' consciences wouldn't help. "If you expect someone to transition from a traditional cleaning product to green cleaning products, you need to have the performance that they expect," she explains. "It was a problem that needed to be addressed. We wanted to be able to give consumers a solution that was authentic and sustaining." In recent years, scientists have been able to isolate more naturally derived ingredients that are equal to chemically based ingredients. Now consumers must be re-educated about these products and convinced to give them another try. One such product has been developed by Seventh Generation in partnership with another firm, CleanWell. It is a disinfectant made from the garden herb thyme. The new product actually kills bacteria on surfaces without the use of toxic chemicals.

As chief executive, Hollender must consider his company as a whole organization—not just a chemistry lab. "When you think about sustainability and responsibility, you have to take a holistic approach," he notes. "You have to look at everything in your supply chain and the life cycle of the product." Hollender emphasizes that a socially responsible firm must consider every input and output, including raw materials, harvesting, manufacturing processes, warehousing, sales, and ultimate use—whether the consumer uses up the product, reuses or recycles it, or throws it away. Hollender describes how, in examining Seventh Generation's inputs and outputs, company researchers discovered that the single most energy-wasting feature of its soap products was the fact that they required hot water to perform effectively. So the firm's team reformulated them to function in cold water.

Seventh Generation continues to develop new and better products. The firm's Web site is filled with information on sustainability, including the blog "Ask the Science Man," where consumers can ask just about any question—such as how to find nontoxic nail polish. And though Hollender's involvement in day-to-day operations is reduced as he takes his message to a nationwide audience, he remains committed to his company's corporate responsibility. "Few businesses are willing to talk about their failures," he says. "But it's that level of transparency that will build deep loyalty with the consumer." Hollender is determined to build a loyalty that will last at least seven generations.

Questions for Critical Thinking

1. What might be some ethical issues faced by Seventh Generation managers, researchers, and employees?

2. What steps might Hollender take to ensure that ethical leadership continues as he spends more time away from Seventh Generation?

3. Give examples of ways in which Seventh Generation fulfills its social responsibilities in each of the four categories: to the general

public; to customers; to investors; and to employees.

4. Visit the Seventh Generation Web site at http://www.seventhgeneration.com and read more about the firm's community involvement. Discuss the company's efforts. Do they match well with the Great Law of the Iroquois?

Sources: Seventh Generation Web site, http://www.seventh generation.com, accessed February 15, 2012; CleanWell Web site, http://www.cleanwelltoday.com, accessed February 15, 2012; "Seventh Generation and Walmart Announce Strategic Partnership," *Market Wire*, July 26, 2010, http://www.marketwire.com; Danielle Sacks, "Jeffrey Hollender: Seventh Generation, Triple Bottom Line Entrepreneur," *Fast Company.com*, February 2, 2010, http://www.fastcompany.com.

Learning Objectives

[1] Discuss microeconomics and explain the forces of demand and supply.

[2] Describe macroeconomics and the issues for the entire economy.

[3] Identify how to evaluate economic performance.

[4] Discuss managing the economy's performance.

[5] Describe the global economic challenges of the 21st century.

Chapter 3

Economic Challenges Facing Contemporary Business

Laura GangiPond/iStockphoto

Boomerang Kids Come Home to Roost

In the new economic reality facing U.S. workers, many parents can't afford to retire because they're unexpectedly stretching resources to support grown children forced to return home because of a lack of employment opportunities. But ironically, by staying in the workforce, these parents may be filling the jobs younger workers need.

Employment rates for young U.S. adults are so low that a record 6 million people between 25 and 34 now live with their parents. The National Endowment for Financial Education (NEFE) reports nearly 6 in 10 parents give financial assistance to grown non-student children. (AARP puts this figure at 7 in 10.) Fully 26 percent took on extra debt in the process, and 20 percent postponed major financial events such as retiring or purchasing a home.

One divorced mom in Florida is helping support three daughters. Two are college graduates in their 20s with thousands of dollars in educational loans and only part-time employment. Because it costs her about $600 to support them, the mom cannot afford homeowners or health insurance. "If the economy remains weak," says NEFE's president, "you may see more parents sacrificing their financial health for their struggling adult offspring." Having raised their children to believe they could achieve anything, parents living with "boomerang" kids are wondering what went wrong. Was it the financial crisis, the global recession, large-scale job outsourcing, or all of the above?[1]

Overview

When we examine the exchanges that companies and societies make as a whole, we are focusing on the *economic systems* operating in different nations. These systems reflect the combination of policies and choices a nation makes to allocate resources among its citizens. Countries vary in the ways they allocate scarce resources.

__Economics__, which analyzes the choices people and governments make in allocating scarce resources, affects each of us, because everyone is involved in producing, distributing, or simply consuming goods and services. In fact, your life is affected by economics every day. Whether you buy tickets to a NASCAR race or decide to stay home and watch TV instead, you are making an economic choice. Understanding how the activities of one industry affect those of other industries, and how they relate in the overall economic status of a country, is an important part of understanding economics.

The choices you make actually may be international in scope. If you are in the market for a new car, you might visit several dealers in a row on the same street—Ford, Chrysler, Honda, Hyundai, and General Motors. You might decide on Hyundai—a Korean firm—but your car might very well be manufactured in the United States, using parts from all over the world. Although firms sometimes emphasize the American origin of their products in order to appeal to consumers' desire to support the U.S. economy, many items are made of components from a variety of nations.

Businesses and not-for-profit organizations also make economic decisions when they choose how to use human and natural resources; invest in equipment, machinery, and buildings; and form partnerships with other firms. Economists refer to the study of small economic units, such as individual consumers, families, and businesses, as __microeconomics__.

The study of a country's overall economic issues is called **macroeconomics** (*macro* means "large"). Macroeconomics addresses such issues as how an economy uses its resources and how government policies affect people's standards of living. The substitution of ethanol for gasoline or biodiesel for diesel fuel has macroeconomic consequences—affecting many parts of the U.S. economy and suppliers around the

economics social science that analyzes the choices people and governments make in allocating scarce resources.

microeconomics study of small economic units, such as individual consumers, families, and businesses.

macroeconomics study of a nation's overall economic issues, such as how an economy maintains and allocates resources and how a government's policies affect the standards of living of its citizens.

LECTURE ENHANCER: How do microeconomic issues impact macroeconomics?

world. Macroeconomics examines not just the economic policies of individual nations, but the ways in which those individual policies affect the overall world economy. Because so much business is conducted around the world, a law enacted in one country can easily affect a transaction that takes place in another country. Although macroeconomic issues have a broad scope, they help shape the decisions that individuals, families, and businesses make every day.

This chapter introduces economic theory and the economic challenges facing individuals, businesses, and governments in the global marketplace. We begin with the microeconomic concepts of supply and demand and their effect on the prices people pay for goods and services. Next we explain the various types of economic systems, along with tools for comparing and evaluating their performance. Then we examine the ways in which governments seek to manage economies to create stable business environments in their countries. The final section in the chapter looks at some of the driving economic forces currently affecting people's lives.

[1] Microeconomics: The Forces of Demand and Supply

Think about your own economic activities. You shop for groceries, subscribe to a cell phone service, pay college tuition, fill your car's tank with gas. Now think about your family's economic activities. When you were growing up, your parents might have owned a home or rented an apartment. You might have taken a family vacation. Your parents may have shopped at discount clubs or at local stores. Each of these choices relates to the study of microeconomics. They also help determine both the prices of goods and services and the amounts sold. Information about these activities is vital to companies because their survival and ability to grow depends on selling enough products priced high enough to cover costs and earn profits. The same information is important to consumers who must make purchase decisions based on prices and the availability of the goods and services they need.

At the heart of every business endeavor is an exchange between a buyer and a seller. The buyer recognizes that he or she needs or wants a particular good or service—whether it's a hamburger or a haircut—and is willing to pay a seller for it. The seller requires the exchange in order to earn a profit and stay in business. So the exchange process involves both demand and supply. **Demand** refers to the willingness and ability of buyers to purchase goods and services at different prices. The other side of the exchange process is **supply**, the amount of goods and services for sale at different prices. Understanding the factors that determine demand and supply, as well as how the two interact, can help you understand many actions and decisions of individuals, businesses, and government. This section takes a closer look at these concepts.

Factors Driving Demand

For most of us, economics amounts to a balance between what we want and what we can afford. Because of this dilemma, each person must choose how much money to save and how much to spend. We must also decide among all the goods and services competing for our attention. Suppose you wanted to purchase a smart phone. You'd have to choose from a variety of brands and models. You'd also have to

You shop for groceries, subscribe to a cell phone service, pay college tuition, fill your car's tank with gas. Each of these choices relates to the study of microeconomics. They also help determine the prices of goods and services and the amounts sold.

decide where you wanted to go to buy one. After shopping around, you might decide you didn't want a smart phone at all. Instead, you might purchase something else, or save your money.

Demand is driven by a number of factors that influence how people decide to spend their money, including price. It can be driven by consumer preferences. It may also be driven by outside circumstances or larger economic events. During the recent recession, the video game industry—including portable players and consoles, software, and associated items—experienced an 8 percent decline in sales during one year. However, video games such as Kingdoms of Amalur: Reckoning and Final Fantasy XIII have enjoyed sales of more than 150,000 units a year.[2]

Demand can also increase the availability of certain types of Web sites and services. Recognizing the enormous popularity of Google's YouTube, and believing the demand would grow, networks NBC and Fox teamed up to launch an online video site, which provides programming from different entertainment companies. The site, called Hulu.com, offers full-length movies and television shows. Recently, Hulu began offering its own original TV series, *Battleground*. Hulu Plus is now available on the Xbox 360, PlayStation 3, and the Nintendo Wii.[3]

In general, as the price of a good or service goes up, people buy smaller amounts. In other words, as price rises, the quantity demanded declines. At lower prices, consumers are generally willing to buy more of a good. A **demand curve** is a graph of the amount of a product that buyers will purchase at different prices. Demand curves typically slope downward, meaning that lower and lower prices attract larger and larger purchases.

Gasoline provides a classic example of how demand curves work. The left side of Figure 3.1 shows a possible demand curve for the total amount of gasoline that people will purchase at different prices. The prices shown may not reflect the actual price in your location at this particular time, but they still demonstrate the concept. When gasoline is priced at $3.76 a gallon, drivers may fill up their tanks once or twice a week. At $4.06 a gallon, many of them start economizing. They may combine errands or carpool to work. So the quantity of gasoline demanded at $4.06 a gallon is lower than the amount demanded at $3.76 a gallon. The opposite happens at $3.36 a gallon. More gasoline is sold at $3.36 a gallon than at $3.76 a gallon, as people opt to run more errands or take a weekend trip. However, as mentioned earlier, other factors may cause consumers to accept higher prices anyway. They may have made vacation plans in advance and do not want to cancel them. Or they may be required to drive to work every day.

Economists make a clear distinction between changes in the quantity demanded at various prices and changes in overall demand. A change in quantity demanded, such as the change that occurs at different gasoline prices, is simply movement along the demand curve. A change in overall demand, on the other hand, results in an entirely new demand curve. Businesses are constantly trying to make predictions about both kinds of demand, and a miscalculation can cause problems. In the case of gasoline, which is derived from crude oil, many factors come into play. For the foreseeable future, we will still depend on fossil fuels until we develop alternative fuel sources. In the long run, many people hope that the investment in and development of alternative energy sources such as shale oil, biodiesel, wind, and solar power may level off the demand for oil. Another issue is the U.S. economy. When a downturn occurs, so does the demand for oil and other goods. But disruptions in energy sources have the opposite effect; international tensions in oil-rich nations or extreme weather that takes refineries offline increase the demand for the oil that is available.[4]

Demand is driven by consumer tastes and preferences as well as by economic conditions. Consumers tend to fill up their gas tanks more frequently when the per-gallon price is low.

demand curve graph of the amount of a product that buyers will purchase at different prices.

FIGURE
3.1

Demand Curves for Gasoline

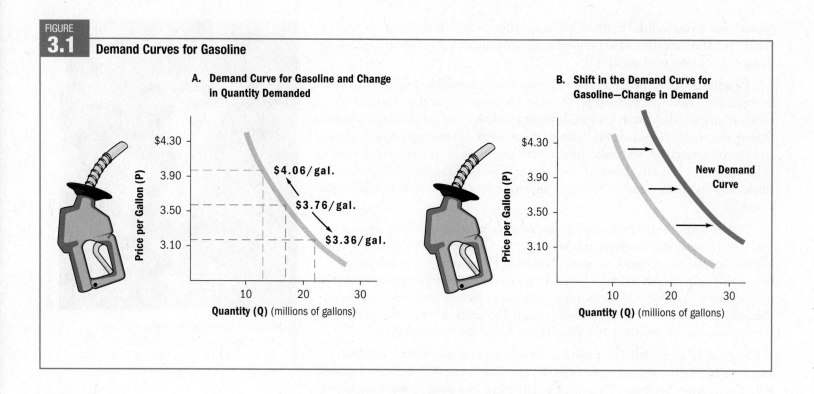

A. Demand Curve for Gasoline and Change in Quantity Demanded

$4.30
$4.06/gal.
3.90
$3.76/gal.
3.50
$3.36/gal.
3.10

Price per Gallon (P)

10   20   30

Quantity (Q) (millions of gallons)

B. Shift in the Demand Curve for Gasoline—Change in Demand

$4.30
New Demand Curve
3.90
3.50
3.10

Price per Gallon (P)

10   20   30

Quantity (Q) (millions of gallons)

We can illustrate how the increased demand for gasoline worldwide has created a new demand curve, as shown in Figure 3.1. The new demand curve shifts to the right of the old demand curve, indicating that overall demand has increased at every price. A demand curve can also shift to the left when the demand for a good or service drops. However, the demand curve still has the same shape.

Although price is the underlying cause of movement along a demand curve, many factors can combine to determine the overall demand for a product—that is, the shape and position of the demand curve. These influences include customer preferences and incomes, the prices of substitute and complementary items, the number of buyers in a market, and the strength of their optimism regarding the future. Changes in any of these factors produce a new demand curve.

Changes in household income also change demand. As consumers have more money to spend, firms can sell more products at every price. This means the demand curve has shifted to the right. When income shrinks, nearly everyone suffers, and the demand curve shifts to the left. With the recent decline in new housing and home improvement, Home Depot and Lowe's experienced a drop in demand. Meanwhile, discount retailers such as Walmart and Walgreens experienced an increase in sales, so their demand curve shifted to the right.[5] Table 3.1 describes how a demand curve is likely to respond to each of these changes.

For a business to succeed, management must carefully monitor the factors that may affect demand for the goods and services it hopes to sell. Costco has free sampling stations throughout its stores where customers can try small portions of various foods prepared on site. This practice encourages customers to buy something in the department where they are sampling.

FACTOR	DEMAND CURVE SHIFTS	
	TO THE RIGHT *IF:*	**TO THE LEFT *IF:***
Customer preferences	Increase	Decrease
Number of buyers	Increase	Decrease
Buyers' incomes	Increase	Decrease
Prices of substitute goods	Increase	Decrease
Prices of complementary goods	Decrease	Increase
Future expectations become more	Optimistic	Pessimistic

Factors Driving Supply

Important economic factors also affect supply, the willingness and ability of firms to provide goods and services at different prices. Just as consumers must decide about how to spend their money, businesses must decide what products to sell, and how.

Sellers would prefer to charge higher prices for their products. A **supply curve** shows the relationship between different prices and the quantities that sellers will offer for sale, regardless of demand. Movement along the supply curve is the opposite of movement along the demand curve. So as price rises, the quantity that sellers are willing to supply also rises. At progressively lower prices, the quantity supplied decreases. In Figure 3.2, a possible supply curve for gasoline shows that increasing prices for gasoline should bring increasing supplies to market.

supply curve graph that shows the relationship between different prices and the quantities that sellers will offer for sale, regardless of demand.

Businesses need certain inputs to operate effectively in producing their output. As discussed in Chapter 1, these *factors of production* include natural resources, capital, human resources, and entrepreneurship. Natural resources include land, building sites, forests, and mineral deposits. Capital refers to resources such as technology, tools, information, physical facilities, and financial capabilities. Human resources include the physical labor and intellectual inputs contributed by employees. Entrepreneurship is the willingness to take risks to create and operate a business. Factors of production play a central role in determining the overall supply of goods and services.

A change in the cost or availability of any of these inputs can shift the entire supply curve, either increasing or decreasing the amount available at every price. If the cost of land increases, a firm might not be able to

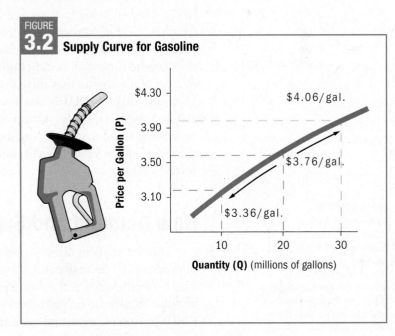

FIGURE

3.2 **Supply Curve for Gasoline**

$4.30 · 3.90 · 3.50 · 3.10

$4.06/gal.

$3.76/gal.

$3.36/gal.

Price per Gallon (P)

10 · 20 · 30

Quantity (Q) (millions of gallons)

⌐3.2¬ Expected Shifts in Supply Curves

FACTOR	SUPPLY CURVE SHIFTS	
	TO THE RIGHT *IF:*	TO THE LEFT *IF:*
Costs of inputs	Decrease	Increase
Costs of technologies	Decrease	Increase
Taxes	Decrease	Increase
Number of suppliers	Increase	Decrease

purchase a site for a more efficient manufacturing plant, which would lower production levels, shifting the supply curve to the left. But if the company finds a way to speed up the production process, allowing it to turn out more products with less labor, the change reduces the overall cost of the finished products, which shifts the supply curve to the right.

Table 3.2 summarizes how changes in various factors can affect the supply curve. Sometimes forces of nature can affect the supply curve. During a record-breaking freeze one recent January, a significant percentage of Florida's citrus crop, including oranges and lemons, was severely damaged. Because the fruit could not be harvested and shipped, supply dropped. The U.S. Department of Agriculture recently raised its estimate for Florida's orange crop by more than a million boxes. A healthy blooming season and plenty of rain brought an increase over the previous season's harvest.[6]

The worldwide fishing industry has often experienced such shifts in the supply curve. In the United States, tourists and locals who were accustomed to an abundance of seafood from the Gulf of Mexico were unable to enjoy their favorite catch during the months after the 2010 BP oil spill. Fishermen and restaurant owners experienced economic hardship first because they couldn't obtain the shrimp and fish, then because they could not overcome the stigma that the catch might be contaminated. Meanwhile, across the globe, Vietnam's shrimp industry was booming, hitting a record high of $2 billion for shrimp exports, including to the shrimp-starved United States. However, the supply curve may be shifting again. Estimates for the most recent Gulf harvest indicate that although white shrimp numbers probably will remain low, the brown-shrimp harvest may be the best in several years.[7]

How Demand and Supply Interact

Separate shifts in demand and supply have obvious effects on prices and the availability of products. In the real world, changes do not alternatively affect demand and supply. Several factors often change at the same time—and they keep changing. Sometimes such changes in multiple factors cause contradictory pressures on prices and quantities. In other cases, the final direction of prices and quantities reflects the factor that has changed the most. Demand and supply can affect employment as well as products.

CLASS ACTIVITY:
Discuss with students how ticket prices could fluctuate depending on which teams are playing. For example, if your favorite team is playing the Yankees, ticket prices for those games could be higher than if your favorite team were playing the Mariners.

Figure 3.3 shows the interaction of both supply and demand curves for gasoline on a single graph. Notice that the two curves intersect at *P*. The law of supply and demand states that prices (*P*) are set by the intersection of the supply and demand curves. The point where the two curves meet identifies the **equilibrium price**, the prevailing market price at which you can buy an item.

If the actual market price differs from the equilibrium price, buyers and sellers tend to make economic choices that restore the equilibrium level. Investors always seem to return to gold as a safe haven for their money. According to economists, consumers who are intent on buying jewelry most likely will do so, but they may buy more or fewer pieces as the price of gold changes over time. The price of gold fluctuated during the recent Greek debt crisis. Once the European Union worked out a first and then a second bailout package for the country, gold prices moved higher. Other factors can have the opposite effect on gold prices. Economists suggest that the price of gold may drop as the U.S economy begins to recover and the dollar becomes stronger against other world currencies.[8]

In other situations, suppliers react to market forces by reducing prices. For a number of years, fast-food chains such as McDonald's and Wendy's have attracted customers by offering everyday value menus and coupons. The recent economic downturn and the accompanying high unemployment rate have meant that people are more likely to eat at home or purchase fast-food value meals rather than choose to dine at a more expensive, sit-down eatery. So the chains experienced a drop in profits. Competition among the chains, already strong, could grow even fiercer, depending on the length of the economic recovery.[9] Included in that competition is the success of the Smashburger chain, as the "Hit & Miss" feature discusses.

As pointed out earlier, the forces of demand and supply can be affected by a variety of factors. One important variable is the larger economic environment. The next section explains how macroeconomics and economic systems influence market forces and, ultimately, demand, supply, and prices.

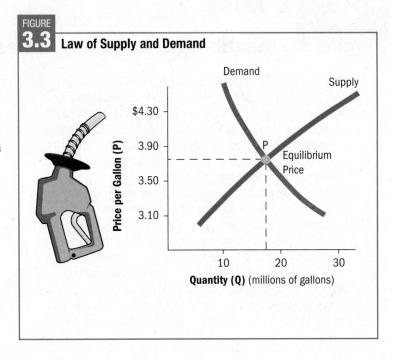

FIGURE 3.3 Law of Supply and Demand

equilibrium price prevailing market price at which you can buy an item.

Assessment Check ✓

1. Define microeconomics and macroeconomics.
2. Explain demand and supply curves.
3. How do factors of production influence the overall supply of goods and services?

Macroeconomics: Issues for the Entire Economy

Every country faces decisions about how to best use the four basic factors of production. Each nation's policies and choices help determine its economic system. But the political, social, and legal environments differ in every country. So no two countries have exactly the same economic system. In general, however, these systems can be classified into three categories: private enterprise systems; planned economies; or combinations of the two, referred to as mixed economies. As business becomes an increasingly global undertaking, it is important to understand the primary features of the various economic systems operating around the world.

Hit & Miss

Smashburger Is, Well, a Smash Hit

Does the world have enough hamburger restaurants? Not according to Tom Ryan, founder of Smashburger, the latest restaurant sensation. With almost 150 U.S. company-owned and franchise locations opened in four years, 450 more in the works, and $54 million in annual revenue, the *Fortune* 500 Denver-based chain is on a roll and plans to launch six international locations. Says CEO David Prokupek, "I don't see the need to wait to bring this brand to the world."

Smashburger stands out by paying attention to the right details. "We custom design different burgers, different side items, different shakes, different local craft beers to really become every city's favorite place," says Prokupek. The Smashburger experience is thus fast, affordable, and distinctive. In addition to burgers that are literally smashed onto a buttered grill, the chain offers salads, chicken sandwiches, flash-fried vegetables, a variety of buns, and unusual toppings such as avocado and garlic mushrooms, chipotle mayo, and spicy brown mustard. To keep service levels high, the company pays above-minimum wages, adds bonuses, and rewards cooks for speed and accuracy, "a real 'wow' factor," according to one franchisee.

"We overinvest in the things that matter most," says Prokupek. And it seems to be working. Forbes recently named Smashburger the top Most Promising American Company.

Questions for Critical Thinking

1. Is Smashburger investing in the right things? What are they?
2. Smashburger's prices are competitive with other "fast casual" chains. Is this a sustainable strategy given its mission?

Sources: "Smashburger Lands on Elite List," *QSR Magazine*, accessed January 11, 2012, www.qsrmagazine.com; "10 Growth Strategies from Inc. 500 CEO's, *Inc.*, accessed January 11, 2012, www.inc.com; J. J. Colao, "Meet America's Most Promising Company: Smashburger," *Forbes*, November 30, 2011, http://www.forbes.com.

LECTURE ENHANCER:
How might a nation's cultural practices influence its economic system?

LECTURE ENHANCER:
How is a business rewarded in the private enterprise system?

LECTURE ENHANCER:
Share a specific example of each type of competition.

pure competition market structure in which large numbers of buyers and sellers exchange homogeneous products and no single participant has a significant influence on price.

Capitalism: The Private Enterprise System and Competition

Most industrialized nations operate economies based on the *private enterprise system*, also known as *capitalism* or a *market economy*. A private enterprise system rewards businesses for meeting the needs and demands of consumers. Government tends to favor a hands-off attitude toward controlling business ownership, profits, and resource allocations. Instead, competition regulates economic life, creating opportunities and challenges that businesspeople must handle to succeed.

The relative competitiveness of a particular industry is an important consideration for every firm because it determines the ease and cost of doing business within that industry. Four basic types of competition take shape in a private enterprise system: pure competition, monopolistic competition, oligopoly, and monopoly. Table 3.3 highlights the main differences among these types of competition.

Pure competition is a market structure, like that of small-scale agriculture or fishing, in which large numbers of buyers and sellers exchange homogeneous products and no single participant has a significant influence on price. Instead, prices are set by the market as the forces of supply and demand interact. Firms can easily enter or leave a purely competitive market because no single company dominates. Also, in pure competition, buyers see little difference between the goods and services offered by competitors.

The fishing industry is a good example of pure competition. As weather and ocean conditions affect seafood supplies, the prices for this commodity rise or fall according to the laws of supply and demand. The clams and mussels that one fishing boat gathers off the coast of New England are virtually identical to those gathered by others. The region's notorious "red tide" of algae sometimes contaminates part of the season's supply of shellfish just when summer tourists want them the most—and prices skyrocket.

Types of Competition

	TYPES OF COMPETITION			
CHARACTERISTICS	**PURE COMPETITION**	**MONOPOLISTIC COMPETITION**	**OLIGOPOLY**	**MONOPOLY**
Number of competitors	Many	Few to many	Few	No direct competition
Ease of entry into industry by new firms	Easy	Somewhat difficult	Difficult	Regulated by government
Similarity of goods or services offered by competing firms	Similar	Different	Similar or different	No directly competing products
Control over price by individual firms	None	Some	Some	Considerable in a pure monopoly; little in a regulated monopoly
Examples	Small-scale farmer in Indiana	Local fitness center	Boeing Aircraft	Rawlings Sporting Goods, exclusive supplier of major-league baseballs

Monopolistic competition is a market structure, like that for retailing, in which large numbers of buyers and sellers exchange differentiated (heterogeneous) products, so each participant has some control over price. Sellers can differentiate their products from competing offerings on the basis of price, quality, or other features. In an industry that features monopolistic competition, it is relatively easy for a firm to begin or stop selling a good or service. The success of one seller often attracts new competitors to such a market. Individual firms also have some control over how their goods and services are priced.

One example of monopolistic competition is the market for pet food. Consumers can choose from private-label (store brands such as Walmart's Ol'Roy) and brand-name products such as Purina in bags, boxes, and cans. Producers of pet food and the stores that sell it have wide latitude in setting prices. Consumers can choose the store or brand with the lowest prices, or sellers can convince them that a more expensive offering, for example the Fromm brand, is worth more because it offers better nutrition, more convenience, or other benefits.

> **monopolistic competition** market structure in which large numbers of buyers and sellers exchange heterogeneous products so each participant has some control over price.

mikeuk/iStockphoto

Fishing is a good example of pure competition. Because seafood gathered by one boat is virtually identical to that gathered by others, the price rises and falls with changes in supply and demand. For example, whenever a poisonous "red tide" of algae infests the fishing areas, the supply of fresh seafood plummets and the price skyrockets.

An **oligopoly** is a market situation in which relatively few sellers compete and high start-up costs form barriers to keep out new competitors. In some oligopolistic industries, such as paper and steel, competitors offer similar products. In others, such as aircraft and automobiles, they sell different models and features. The huge investment required to enter an oligopoly market tends to discourage new competitors. The limited number of sellers also enhances the control these firms exercise over price. Competing products in an oligopoly usually sell for very similar prices because substantial price competition would reduce profits for all firms in the industry. So a price cut by one firm in an oligopoly will typically be met by its competitors. However, prices can vary from one market to another, as from one country to another.

| Microsoft and Google are expanding into each other's territory. Microsoft launched its own cloud-based products suite to compete with Google Enterprise, which includes Gmail and Google Docs.

oligopoly market situation in which relatively few sellers compete and high start-up costs form barriers to keep out new competitors.

monopoly market situation in which a single seller dominates trade in a good or service for which buyers can find no close substitutes.

The final type of market structure is a **monopoly**, in which a single seller dominates trade in a good or service for which buyers can find no close substitutes. A pure monopoly occurs when a firm possesses unique characteristics so important to competition in its industry that they form barriers to prevent entry by would-be competitors. After presiding in their respective areas over what many called monopolies, Microsoft and Google are expanding into each other's territory. Microsoft launched Bing to compete with Google Search. Google countered with Google Chrome OS, aimed at MS Windows. Microsoft also launched Microsoft 365, an online suite of cloud-based applications such as Microsoft Office, Microsoft SharePoint Online, and Microsoft Exchange Online. Microsoft 365 is designed to compete directly with Google Enterprise, which includes Gmail, Google Docs, Google Calendar, and other products.[10]

Many firms create short-term monopolies when research breakthroughs permit them to receive exclusive patents on new products. In the pharmaceuticals industry, drug giants such as Merck and Pfizer invest billions in research and development programs. When the research leads to successful new drugs, the companies can enjoy the benefits of their patents: the ability to set prices without fear of competitors undercutting them. Once the patent expires, generic substitutes enter the market, driving down prices.

Because a monopoly market lacks the benefits of competition, many governments regulate monopolies. Besides issuing patents and limiting their life, the U.S. government prohibits most pure monopolies through antitrust legislation such as the Sherman Act and the Clayton Act. The U.S. government has applied these laws against monopoly behavior by Microsoft and by disallowing proposed mergers of large companies in some industries. In other cases, the government permits certain monopolies in exchange for regulating their activities.

regulated monopolies market situation in which a local, state, or federal government grants exclusive rights in a certain market to a single firm.

With **regulated monopolies**, a local, state, or federal government grants exclusive rights in a certain market to a single firm. Pricing decisions—particularly rate-increase requests—are subject to control by regulatory authorities such as state public service commissions. An example is the delivery of first-class mail, a monopoly held by the U.S. Postal Service. The USPS is a self-supporting corporation wholly owned by the federal government. Its postal rates are set by a postal commission and approved by a board of governors.

During the 1980s and 1990s, the U.S. government trended away from regulated monopolies and toward deregulation. Regulated monopolies that have been deregulated include long-distance and local telephone service, cable television, cell phones, and electric utilities. The idea is to improve customer service and reduce prices for customers through increased competition. In contrast, the FCC's restrictions preventing a single company from owning TV stations, newspapers, and other media in the same market have been recently upheld. Not surprisingly, the National Association of Broadcasters has petitioned the U.S. Supreme Court to undo the FCC's restrictions.[11]

LECTURE ENHANCER:
Name an industry or business that has been a target for deregulation.

Planned Economies: Socialism and Communism

In a **planned economy**, government controls determine business ownership, profits, and resource allocation to accomplish government goals rather than those set by individual firms. Two forms of planned economies are communism and socialism.

Socialism is characterized by government ownership and operation of major industries such as communications. Socialists argues that major industries are too important to a society to be left in private hands and that government-owned businesses can serve the public's interest better than private firms. However, socialism allows private ownership in industries considered less crucial to social welfare, such as retail shops, restaurants, and certain types of manufacturing facilities. Scandinavian countries such as Denmark, Sweden, and Finland have many socialist features in their societies, as do some African nations and India.

The writings of Karl Marx in the mid-1800s formed the basis of communist theory. Marx believed that private enterprise economies created unfair conditions and led to worker exploitation because business owners controlled most of society's resources and reaped most of the economy's rewards. Instead, he suggested an economic system called **communism**, in which all property would be shared equally by the people of a community under the direction of a strong central government. Marx believed that elimination of private ownership of property and businesses would ensure the emergence of a classless society that would benefit all. Each individual would contribute to the nation's overall economic success, and resources would be distributed according to each person's needs. Under communism, the central government owns the means of production, and the people work for state-owned enterprises. The government determines what people can buy because it dictates what is produced in the nation's factories and farms.

Several nations adopted communist-like economic systems during the early 20th century in an effort to correct abuses they believed occurred in their existing systems. In practice, however, the new governments typically gave less freedom of choice in regard to jobs and purchases and might be best described as totalitarian socialism. These nations often made mistakes in allocating resources to compete in the growing global marketplace. Government-owned monopolies often suffer from inefficiency.

Consider the former Soviet Union, where large government bureaucracies controlled nearly every aspect of daily life. Shortages became chronic because producers had little or no incentive to satisfy customers. The quality of goods and services also suffered for the same reason. When Mikhail Gorbachev became the last president of the dying Soviet Union, he tried to improve the quality of Soviet-made products. Effectively shut out of trading in the global marketplace and caught up in a treasury-depleting arms race with the United States,

planned economy economic system in which government controls determine business ownership, profits, and resource allocation to accomplish government goals rather than those set by individual firms.

socialism economic system characterized by government ownership and operation of major industries such as communications.

communism economic system in which all property would be shared equally by the people of a community under the direction of a strong central government.

LECTURE ENHANCER:
What might be a likely drawback to contributing and distributing resources according to each person's needs and abilities?

the Soviet Union faced severe financial problems. Eventually, these events led to the collapse of Soviet communism and the breakup of the Soviet Union itself.

Today, communist-like systems exist in just a few countries, such as North Korea. By contrast, the People's Republic of China has shifted toward a more market-oriented economy. The national government has given local government and individual plant managers more say in business decisions and has permitted some private businesses. Households now have more control over agriculture, in contrast to the collectivized farms introduced during an earlier era. In addition, Western products such as McDonald's restaurants and Coca-Cola soft drinks are now part of Chinese consumers' lives, and Chinese workers manufacture products for export to other countries.

Mixed Market Economies

mixed market economies economic system that draws from both types of economies, to different degrees.

Private enterprise systems and planned economies adopt basically opposite approaches to operating economies. In reality, though, many countries operate **mixed market economies**, economic systems that draw from both types of economies, to different degrees. In nations generally considered to have a private enterprise economy, government-owned firms frequently operate alongside private enterprises. In the United States, programs such as Medicare are government run.

LECTURE ENHANCER:
What are the key societal benefits of a mixed market economy?

France has blended socialist and free enterprise policies for hundreds of years. The nation's energy production, public transportation, and defense industries are run as nationalized industries, controlled by the government. Meanwhile, a market economy operates in other industries. Over the past two decades, the French government has loosened its reins on state-owned companies, inviting both competition and private investment into industries previously operated as government monopolies.

privatization conversion of government-owned and operated companies into privately held businesses.

The proportions of private and public enterprise can vary widely in mixed economies, and the mix frequently changes. Dozens of countries have converted government-owned and operated companies into privately held businesses in a trend known as **privatization**. Even the United States has seen proposals to privatize everything from the postal service to Social Security.

CLASS ACTIVITY:
Discuss how important incentives are to students, and whether they might leave their homes to pursue higher incentives elsewhere.

Governments may privatize state-owned enterprises in an effort to raise funds and improve their economies. The objective is to cut costs and run the operation more efficiently. For most of its existence, Air Canada was a state-owned airline. But in 1989 the airline became fully privatized, and in 2000 the firm acquired Canadian Airlines International, becoming the world's tenth-largest international air carrier. Air Canada now maintains an extensive global network, with destinations in the United States, Europe, the Middle East, Asia, Australia, the Caribbean, Mexico, and South America.[12] Table 3.4 compares the alternative economic systems on the basis of ownership and management of enterprises, rights to profits, employee rights, and worker incentives.

Assessment Check ✓

1. What is the difference between pure competition and monopolistic competition?

2. On which economic system is the U.S. economy based?

3. What is privatization?

┌─┐
│3│
└─┘
Evaluating Economic Performance

Ideally, an economic system should provide two important benefits for its citizens: a stable business environment and sustained growth. In a stable business environment, the overall supply of needed goods and services is aligned with the overall demand for these items. No wild fluctuations in price or availability make economic decisions complicated. Consumers

TABLE
3.4 ## Comparison of Alternative Economic Systems

SYSTEM FEATURES	CAPITALISM (PRIVATE ENTERPRISE)	PLANNED ECONOMIES		
		COMMUNISM	SOCIALISM	MIXED ECONOMY
Ownership of enterprises	Businesses are owned privately, often by large numbers of people. Minimal government ownership leaves production in private hands.	Government owns the means of production with few exceptions, such as small plots of land.	Government owns basic industries, but private owners operate some small enterprises.	A strong private sector blends with public enterprises.
Management of enterprises	Enterprises are managed by owners or their representatives, with minimal government interference.	Centralized management controls all state enterprises in line with three- to five-year plans. Planning now is being decentralized.	Significant government planning pervades socialist nations. State enterprises are managed directly by government bureaucrats.	Management of the private sector resembles that under capitalism. Professionals may also manage state enterprises.
Rights to profits	Entrepreneurs and investors are entitled to all profits (minus taxes) that their firms earn.	Profits are not allowed under communism.	Only the private sector of a socialist economy generates profits.	Entrepreneurs and investors are entitled to private-sector profits, although they often must pay high taxes. State enterprises are also expected to produce returns.
Rights of employees	The rights to choose one's occupation and to join a labor union have long been recognized.	Employee rights are limited in exchange for promised protection against unemployment.	Workers may choose their occupations and join labor unions, but the government influences career decisions for many people.	Workers may choose jobs and labor union membership. Unions often become quite strong.
Worker incentives	Considerable incentives motivate people to perform at their highest levels.	Incentives are emerging in communist countries.	Incentives usually are limited in state enterprises but do motivate workers in the private sector.	Capitalist-style incentives operate in the private sector. More limited incentives influence public-sector activities.

and businesses not only have access to ample supplies of desired products at affordable prices but also have money to buy the items they demand.

Growth is another important economic goal. An ideal economy incorporates steady change directed toward continually expanding the amount of goods and services produced from the nation's resources. Growth leads to expanded job opportunities, improved wages, and a rising standard of living.

Flattening the Business Cycle

A nation's economy tends to flow through various stages of a business cycle: prosperity, recession, depression, and recovery. No "true" economic depressions have occurred in the United States since the 1930s, and some economists believe that society is capable of preventing future depressions through effective economic policies. Consequently, they expect recessions to give way to periods of economic recovery. The "Going Green" feature discusses how one U.S. community is exploring the development of alternative sources of energy that will create new jobs to stimulate the economy.

Going Green

Raleigh Hosts a Smart Grid

Smart-grid technology involves digitally enabled electrical grids that gather, distribute, and act on information about electrical usage in a specific area. It not only holds out the promise of cleaner, cheaper, and more efficient electronic delivery of power for U.S. homes, cars, and businesses; someday it could even allow consumers to generate their own energy and sell surplus capacity to utility companies. Imagine making money from your energy use instead of paying for it.

Raleigh, North Carolina, is one of the country's major smart-grid development hubs. North Carolina State University (NCSU) hosts the multi-university FREEDM Center (for Future Renewable Electric Energy, Delivery, and Management), funded by the National Science Foundation, which is helping develop a digital "smart transformer" that MIT's *Technology Review* calls one of the world's 10 most important emerging technologies.

About 50 technology firms are in partnership with FREEDM, including ABB, Siemens, Eaton, Tantalus Solutions, and Intel, and the project employs about 3,000 people in the area. The U.S. government has provided billions of dollars to fund FREEDM and similar projects around the country, to develop the new technology and make it operational on a large scale. New hardware, software, meters, and controls will be required, and utility companies will need to sign on in numbers.

But the Raleigh team is optimistic. According to FREEDM's director, NCSU professor Alex Huang, smart-grid technology is about five years ahead of its time with the Raleigh experience: "We are pushing electronics into the power grid."

Questions for Critical Thinking

1. Do you think the government's investment in clean energy through initiatives such as FREEDM will pay off? Why or why not?

2. What are some of the benefits the FREEDM Center brings to the local Raleigh economy?

Sources: FREEDM Systems Center, http://freedm.ncsu.edu, accessed February 29, 2012; Venessa Wong, "Raleigh's Smart Grid Bid," *Bloomberg BusinessWeek*, October 13, 2011, www.businessweek.com; David H. Freeman, "Smart Transformers," *Technology Review*, May/June 2011, www.technologyreview.com; John Murawski, "NCSU Takes Leading Role in Developing Smart Grid," *News & Observer*, June 20, 2011, www.newsobserver.com.

Both business decisions and consumer buying patterns differ at each stage of the business cycle. In periods of economic prosperity, unemployment remains low, consumer confidence about the future leads to more purchases, and businesses expand—by hiring more employees, investing in new technology, and making similar purchases—to take advantage of new opportunities.

As recent events show, during a **recession**—a cyclical economic contraction that lasts for six months or longer—consumers frequently postpone major purchases and shift buying patterns toward basic, functional products carrying low prices. Businesses mirror these changes in the marketplace by slowing production, postponing expansion plans, reducing inventories, and often cutting the size of their workforces. During recessions, people facing layoffs and depletions of household savings become much more conservative in their spending, postponing luxury purchases and vacations. They often turn to lower-priced retailers such as Dollar Tree and Dollar General for the goods they need. And they have sold cars, jewelry, and stocks to make ends meet. They have also sold everything from old books to artwork to kitchenware on eBay.

If an economic slowdown continues in a downward spiral over an extended period of time, the economy falls into depression. Many Americans have grown up hearing stories about their great-grandparents who lived through the Great Depression of the 1930s, when food and other basic necessities were scarce and jobs were rare.

In the recovery stage of the business cycle, the economy emerges from recession and consumer spending picks up steam. Even though businesses often continue to rely on part-time and other temporary workers during the early stages of a recovery, unemployment begins to decline as business activity accelerates and firms seek additional workers to meet growing production demands. Gradually, the concerns of recession begin to disappear, and consumers start eating out at restaurants, booking vacations, and purchasing new cars again.

recession cyclical economic contraction that lasts for six months or longer.

CLASS ACTIVITY:
Survey the class to see how many have purchased more store brand items at the grocery or drugstores where they shop, as a result of softer economic conditions.

LECTURE ENHANCER:
How can we determine which phase of the business cycle an economy is in at a certain time?

Productivity and the Nation's Gross Domestic Product

An important concern for every economy is **productivity**, the relationship between the goods and services produced in a nation each year and the inputs needed to produce them. In general, as productivity rises, so does an economy's growth and the wealth of its citizens. In a recession, productivity stalls or even declines.

Productivity describes the relationship between the number of units produced and the number of human and other production inputs necessary to produce them. Productivity is a ratio of output to input. When a constant amount of inputs generates increased outputs, an increase in productivity occurs.

Total productivity considers all inputs necessary to produce a specific amount of outputs. Stated in equation form, it can be written as follows:

During a recession, consumers may shift buying patterns toward basic, functional products carrying low prices. People facing layoffs and depletions of household savings become much more conservative in their spending and often sell cars, jewelry, and stocks to make ends meet.

$$\text{Total Productivity} = \frac{\text{Output (goods or services produced)}}{\text{Input (human/natural resources, capital)}}$$

Many productivity ratios focus on only one of the inputs in the equation: labor productivity or output per labor-hour. An increase in labor productivity means that the same amount of work produces more goods and services than before. Many of the gains in U.S. productivity can be attributed to technology.

Productivity is a widely recognized measure of a company's efficiency. In turn, the total productivity of a nation's businesses has become a measure of its economic strength and standard of living. Economists refer to this measure as a country's **gross domestic product (GDP)**—the sum of all goods and services produced within its boundaries. The GDP is based on the per-capita output of a country—in other words, total national output divided by the number of citizens. As Figure 3.4 shows, only the European Union—which contains 27 member nations and has an estimated GDP of $15.4 trillion—has a GDP higher than that of the United States.[13] In the United States, GDP is tracked by the Bureau of Economic Analysis (BEA), a division of the U.S. Department of Commerce. Current updates and historical data on the GDP are available at the BEA's Web site (http://www.bea.gov).

Price-Level Changes

Another important indicator of an economy's stability is the general level of prices. For the past 100 years, economic decision makers concerned themselves with **inflation**, rising prices caused by a combination of excess consumer demand and increases in the costs of raw materials, component parts, human resources, and other factors of production. The **core inflation rate** is the inflation rate of an economy after energy and food prices are removed. This measure is often an accurate prediction of the inflation rate that consumers, businesses, and other organizations can expect to experience during the near future.

Excess consumer demand generates what is known as demand-pull inflation while increases in the costs of factors of production generates cost-push inflation. America's most

productivity relationship between the number of units produced and the number of human and other production inputs necessary to produce them.

gross domestic product (GDP) sum of all goods and services produced within a country's boundaries during a specific time period, such as a year.

LECTURE ENHANCER: How does inflation benefit wealthier individuals?

inflation economic situation characterized by rising prices caused by a combination of excess consumer demand and increases in the costs of raw materials, component parts, human resources, and other factors of production.

core inflation rate inflation rate of an economy after energy and food prices are removed.

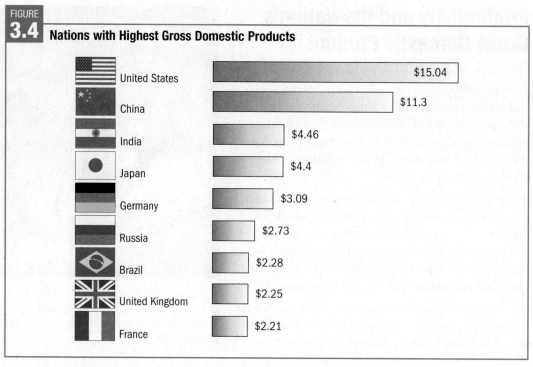

FIGURE 3.4 Nations with Highest Gross Domestic Products

Nation	GDP
United States	$15.04
China	$11.3
India	$4.46
Japan	$4.4
Germany	$3.09
Russia	$2.73
Brazil	$2.28
United Kingdom	$2.25
France	$2.21

Source: *World Factbook*, Central Intelligence Agency, https://www.cia.gov, accessed February 23, 2012.

hyperinflation economic situation characterized by soaring prices.

severe inflationary period during the last half of the 20th century peaked in 1980, when general price levels jumped almost 14 percent in a single year. In extreme cases, an economy may experience **hyperinflation**—an economic situation characterized by soaring prices. This situation has occurred in Argentina, as well as in countries that once formed the Soviet Union (for example, Belarus).

Inflation devalues money as persistent price increases reduce the amount of goods and services people can purchase with a given amount of money. This is bad news for people whose earnings do not keep up with inflation, who live on fixed incomes, or who have most of their wealth in investments paying a fixed rate of interest. Inflation can be good news for people whose income is rising or those with debts at a fixed rate of interest. A homeowner with a fixed-rate mortgage during inflationary times is paying off that debt with money that is worth less and less each year. However, despite the changes in the stock and housing markets, the number of U.S. households with a net worth of at least $1 million grew 8 percent in one recent year to reach 8.4 million. The number of households worth $5 million or more increased 8 percent to 1.06 million.[14]

When increased productivity keeps prices steady, it can have a major positive impact on an economy. In a low-inflation environment, businesses can make long-range plans without the constant worry of sudden inflationary shocks. Low interest rates encourage firms to invest in research and development and capital improvements, both of which are likely to produce productivity gains. Consumers can purchase growing stocks of goods and services with the same amount of money, and low interest rates encourage major acquisitions such as new homes and autos. But there are concerns. The fluctuating cost of oil—which is used to produce many goods—is a continuing issue. Businesses need to raise prices to cover their costs. Also, smaller firms have gone out of business or have been merged with larger companies, reducing the amount of competition and increasing the purchasing power of the larger corporations. Business owners continue to keep a watchful eye on signs of inflation.

The opposite situation—**deflation**—occurs when prices continue to fall. In Japan, where deflation has been a reality for several years, shoppers pay less for a variety of products ranging from groceries to homes. While this situation may sound ideal to consumers, it can weaken the economy. For instance, industries such as housing and auto manufacturing need to maintain strong prices in order to support all the related businesses that depend on them.

Measuring Price Level Changes In the United States, the government tracks changes in price levels with the **Consumer Price Index (CPI)**, which measures the monthly average change in prices of goods and services. The federal Bureau of Labor Statistics (BLS) calculates the CPI monthly based on prices of a "market basket," a compilation of the goods and services most commonly purchased by urban consumers. Figure 3.5 shows the categories included in the CPI market basket. Each month, BLS

Lya Cattel/iStockphoto

When increased productivity keeps prices steady, it can have a major positive impact on an economy. Low interest rates encourage firms to invest in capital improvements—such as building a new company headquarters or expanding its existing space—which are likely to produce productivity gains.

deflation opposite of inflation, occurs when prices continue to fall.

Consumer Price Index (CPI) measurement of the monthly average change in prices of goods and services.

CLASS ACTIVITY:
Ask students which goods or services they think have risen and declined the most in price in the past few years.

LECTURE ENHANCER:
Think of an example of each type of unemployment.

FIGURE 3.5

Contents of the CPI Market Basket

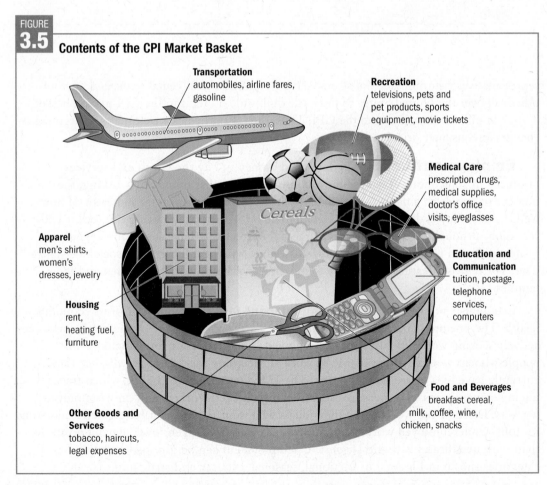

Transportation
automobiles, airline fares, gasoline

Recreation
televisions, pets and pet products, sports equipment, movie tickets

Medical Care
prescription drugs, medical supplies, doctor's office visits, eyeglasses

Apparel
men's shirts, women's dresses, jewelry

Education and Communication
tuition, postage, telephone services, computers

Housing
rent, heating fuel, furniture

Food and Beverages
breakfast cereal, milk, coffee, wine, chicken, snacks

Other Goods and Services
tobacco, haircuts, legal expenses

Cereals

Source: Information from Bureau of Labor Statistics, "Consumer Price Indexes: Frequently Asked Questions," http://www.bls.gov/cpi, accessed February 23, 2012.

Microloans Aid Women's Businesses

Almost half of American workers are women, including working mothers. Regardless of income, all saw their economic status deteriorate during the recent recession and a recent survey found that more than half of working mothers live below the poverty line.

In response to the demands of childcare and earning a living, many women have started their own businesses. After a career in the fashion industry, Tory Burch, herself a working mother, launched a successful shoe design company and later established the Tory Burch Foundation. Her research revealed grim statistics: The majority of poor people in the United States are women. Having a child is one of the leading reasons a woman's income falls below the cost of living. Thus, single mothers are in the greatest danger of poverty.

Inspired by microlenders in the developing world, Burch formed a partnership with ACCION USA, an American microlender. At $500 to $50,000, ACCION USA's loans are somewhat larger than those in developing nations, but many have the same purpose: "to economically empower women." Their clients are more likely to be rejected by traditional banks, so these microloans are essential to their success. Forty percent are women, and more than 80 percent are members of minority groups. ACCION USA reports that more than 90 percent of these microloans have been repaid.

Burch remarks that financing women's companies is more than social responsibility, it's good business and good for the economy. "Women are the hardest hit by the economy," says Burch. "And they repay their loans more often than not."

Questions for Critical Thinking

1. Why might having a baby cause a single mother's income to fall?

2. Why do you think that the payback rate on microloans is so high?

Sources: Tory Burch Foundation, http://www.toryburchfoundation.org, accessed February 23, 2012; "Tory Burch Foundation, National Women's Business Week and a Free CD," *The Clothes Whisperer*, http://www.theclotheswhisperer.co.uk, accessed February 23, 2012; Marshall Heyman, "Fashion Designer Shares the Wealth," *The Wall Street Journal*, http://online.wsj.com, accessed February 23, 2012.

---

representatives visit thousands of stores, service establishments, rental units, and doctors' offices all over the United States to price the multitude of items in the CPI market basket. They compile the data to create the CPI. Thus, the CPI provides a running measurement of changes in consumer prices.

Employment Levels People need money to buy the goods and services produced in an economy. Because most consumers earn that money by working, the number of people in a nation who currently have jobs is an important indicator of how well the economy is doing. In general, employment has dropped during the recent U.S. recession, although it recently began to rebound. Areas that have seen gains include professional and technical services, as well as education, health care, and social assistance.[15] The "Hit & Miss" feature discusses a foundation that helps working women and their families.

unemployment rate percentage of the total workforce actively seeking work but currently unemployed.

Economists refer to a nation's **unemployment rate** as an indicator of its economic health. The unemployment rate is usually expressed as a percentage of the total workforce actively seeking work but currently unemployed. The total labor force includes all people who are willing and available to work at the going market wage, whether they currently have jobs or are seeking work. The U.S. Department of Labor, which tracks unemployment rates, also measures so-called discouraged workers and underemployed workers. Discouraged workers are individuals who want to work but have given up looking for jobs. Underemployed workers are individuals who have taken lower-paying positions than their qualifications would suggest. Unemployment can be grouped into the four categories shown in Figure 3.6: frictional, seasonal, cyclical, and structural.

FIGURE
3.6

Four Types of Unemployment

Frictional Unemployment
· Temporarily not working
· Looking for a job
Example: New graduates entering the workforce

Seasonal Unemployment
· Not working during some months
· Not looking for a job
Example: Farm workers needed only when a crop is in season

Structural Unemployment
· Not working due to no demand for skills
· May be retraining for a new job
Example: Assembly line employees whose jobs are now done by robots

Cyclical Unemployment
· Not working due to economic slowdown
· Looking for a job
Example: Executives laid off during corporate downsizing or recessionary periods

Frictional unemployment is experienced by members of the workforce who are temporarily not working but are looking for jobs. This pool of potential workers includes new graduates, people who have left jobs for any reason and are looking for other employment, and former workers who have decided to return to the labor force. **Seasonal unemployment** is the joblessness of people in a seasonal industry. Construction workers, farm laborers, fishing boat operators, and landscape employees may contend with bouts of seasonal unemployment when wintry conditions make work unavailable.

Cyclical unemployment includes people who are out of work because of a cyclical contraction in the economy. During periods of economic expansion, overall employment is likely to rise, but as growth slows and a recession begins, unemployment levels commonly rise. At such times, even workers with good job skills may face temporary unemployment. Workers in high-tech industries, air travel, and manufacturing have all faced unemployment during economic contraction.

Structural unemployment applies to people who remain unemployed for long periods of time, often with little hope of finding new jobs like their old ones. This situation may arise because these workers lack the necessary skills for available jobs or because the skills they have are no longer in demand. For instance, technological developments have increased the demand for people with computer-related skills but have created structural unemployment among many types of manual laborers or workers who may have been injured and unable to return to work.

frictional unemployment applies to members of the workforce who are temporarily not working but are looking for jobs.

seasonal unemployment joblessness of workers in a seasonal industry.

cyclical unemployment people who are out of work because of a cyclical contraction in the economy.

structural unemployment people who remain unemployed for long periods of time, often with little hope of finding new jobs like their old ones.

Assessment Check ☑

1. Describe the four stages of the business cycle.
2. What are some measures that economists use to determine the health of an economy?

4

Managing the Economy's Performance

monetary policy government actions to increase or decrease the money supply and change banking requirements and interest rates to influence bankers' willingness to make loans.

expansionary monetary policy government actions to increase the money supply in an effort to cut the cost of borrowing, which encourages business decision makers to make new investments, in turn stimulating employment and economic growth.

restrictive monetary policy government actions to reduce the money supply to curb rising prices, overexpansion, and concerns about overly rapid economic growth.

fiscal policy government spending and taxation decisions designed to control inflation, reduce unemployment, improve the general welfare of citizens, and encourage economic growth.

Government can use both monetary policy and fiscal policy in its efforts to fight unemployment, increase business and consumer spending, and reduce the length and severity of economic recessions. For instance, the Federal Reserve System can increase or reduce interest rates, and the federal government can enact tax cuts and rebates, or propose other reforms.

Monetary Policy

A common method of influencing economic activity is **monetary policy**, government actions to increase or decrease the money supply and change banking requirements and interest rates to influence spending by altering bankers' willingness to make loans. An **expansionary monetary policy** increases the money supply in an effort to cut the cost of borrowing, which encourages business decision makers to make new investments, in turn stimulating employment and economic growth. By contrast, a **restrictive monetary policy** reduces the money supply to curb rising prices, overexpansion, and concerns about overly rapid economic growth.

In the United States, the Federal Reserve System ("the Fed") is responsible for formulating and implementing the nation's monetary policy. It is headed by a chairman and board of governors, all of whom are nominated by the president. The current chairman is Ben Bernanke, who also serves as chairman of the Federal Open Market Committee, the Fed's main agency for monetary policy making. All national banks must be members of this system and keep some percentage of their checking and savings funds on deposit at the Fed.

The Fed's board of governors uses a number of tools to regulate the economy. By changing the required percentage of checking and savings accounts that banks must deposit with the Fed, the governors can expand or shrink funds available to lend. The Fed also lends money to member banks, which in turn make loans at higher interest rates to business and individual borrowers. By changing the interest rates charged to commercial banks, the Fed affects the interest rates charged to borrowers and, consequently, their willingness to borrow.

The Federal Reserve uses a number of tools to regulate the economy. The Fed lends money to member banks, which in turn make loans to businesses and individual borrowers.

Uschools University Images/iStockphoto

Fiscal Policy

Governments also influence economic activities by making decisions about taxes and spending. Through revenues and expenses, the government implements **fiscal policy**. This is the second technique that officials use to control inflation, reduce unemployment, improve the general standard of living, and encourage economic growth. Increased taxes may restrict economic activities, while lower taxes and increased government spending usually boost spending and profits, cut unemployment rates, and fuel economic expansion. Recently, in an effort to stimulate investment and spending,

Solving an Ethical Controversy

Student Loans: Forgive and Forget?

The government recently announced plans to help federal student loan borrowers by limiting monthly repayments and forgiving unpaid debt after 20 years. But only some of the millions with tuition debts will qualify. Others may still struggle to repay loans that have actually snowballed over the years, while penalties, fees, and interest accumulate and legal actions loom. With both federal and private student loan defaults rising, a SignOn.org petition proposes forgiving the student loans of *all* U.S. borrowers.

Should lenders forgive all outstanding student loans?

PRO

1. Universal forgiveness would release millions of dollars into the hands of consumers who need it most.

2. Canceling these debts would lower financial barriers to college and encourage more students to seek higher education that can qualify them for better jobs.

CON

1. College graduates enjoy higher lifetime incomes than other employees; they need loan forgiveness less than most.

2. A better way to stimulate the economy is to make smaller cash transfers to a larger group of people, such as the 15 percent of the population living in poverty.

Summary

The U.S. Department of Education says federal student loan defaults rose to almost 9 percent in fiscal year 2009. It is stepping up efforts to protect students from unscrupulous lenders and institutions with low-quality programs that don't improve students' employment prospects.

Sources: Robert Applebaum, "Want a Real Economic Stimulus and Jobs Plan? Forgive Student Loan Debt!" Signon.org, accessed January 11, 2012, http://signon.org; "Consequences of Default," Adventures in Education, accessed January 11, 2012, www.aie.org; Justin Wolfers, "Forgive Student Loans? Worst Idea Ever," Freakonomics.com, November 19, 2011, www.freakonomics.com; Laura Rowley, "Decades Later, Student Loan Default Still Haunts Borrower," Daily Finance.com, November 8, 2011, www.dailyfinance.com; Tamar Lewin, "Student Loan Default Rates Rise Sharply in Past Year," *The New York Times,* September 12, 2011, www.nytimes.com.

---

the U.S. federal government reduced the amount of payroll taxes withheld from employees and paid by them and their employers for Social Security and Medicare. Some now propose forgiving student loans as a way to invigorate the economy, as the "Solving an Ethical Controversy" feature explains.

International Fiscal Policy Nations in the industrial world, including the United States, are currently struggling to find ways to help developing nations modernize their economies. One proposal is to forgive the debts of some of these countries, particularly those in Africa, to stimulate their economies to grow. But not all fiscal experts agree with this idea. They suggest that any debt forgiveness should come with certain conditions so that these countries can build their own fiscal policies. Countries should encourage and allow citizens to own property, lower their tax rates, avoid devaluing their currencies, lay a path for new businesses to start, and reduce trade barriers. In addition, they must improve agriculture, education, and health care so their citizens can begin to set and reach financial goals. The World Bank is an organization that offers such programs as low-interest loans and interest-free credit and grants to developing countries. The World Bank has been involved in helping Japan and Haiti recover from recent catastrophic earthquakes.[16]

budget organization's plan for how it will raise and spend money during a given period of time.

budget deficit situation in which the government spends more than the amount of money it raises through taxes.

national debt money owed by government to individuals, businesses, and government agencies who purchase Treasury bills, Treasury notes, and Treasury bonds sold to cover expenditures.

budget surplus excess funding that occurs when government spends less than the amount of funds raised through taxes and fees.

balanced budget situation in which total revenues raised by taxes equal the total proposed spending for the year.

Assessment Check ◢

1. What is the difference between an expansionary monetary policy and a restrictive monetary policy?

2. What are the three primary sources of government funds?

3. Does a balanced budget erase the federal debt?

The Federal Budget Each year, the president proposes a **budget** for the federal government, a plan for how it will raise and spend money during the coming year, and presents it to Congress for approval. A typical federal budget proposal undergoes months of deliberation and many modifications before receiving approval. The federal budget includes a number of different spending categories, ranging from defense and Social Security to interest payments on the national debt. The decisions about what to include in the budget have a direct effect on various sectors of the economy. During a recession, the federal government may approve increased spending on interstate highway repairs to improve transportation and increase employment in the construction industry. During prosperity, the government may allocate more money for scientific research toward medical breakthroughs.

The primary sources of government funds to cover the costs of the annual budget are taxes, fees, and borrowing. Both the overall amount of these funds and their specific combination have major effects on the economic well-being of the nation. One way governments raise money is to impose taxes on sales, income, and other sources. But increasing taxes leaves people and businesses with less money to spend. This might reduce inflation, but overly high taxes can also slow economic growth. Governments then try to balance taxes to give people necessary services without slowing economic growth.

Taxes don't always generate enough funds to cover every spending project the government hopes to undertake. When the government spends more than the amount of money it raises through taxes, it creates a **budget deficit**. To cover the deficit, the U.S. government borrows money by selling Treasury bills, Treasury notes, and Treasury bonds to investors. All of this borrowing makes up the **national debt**. If the government takes in more money than it spends, it is said to have a **budget surplus**. A **balanced budget** means total revenues raised by taxes equal the total proposed spending for the year.

Achieving a balanced budget—or even a budget surplus—does not erase the national debt. U.S. legislators continually debate how to use revenues to reduce its debt. Most families want to wipe out debt—from credit cards, automobile purchases, and college, to name a few sources. To put the national debt into personal perspective, with roughly 312 million U.S. citizens, each one owes about $49,380 as his or her share.[17]

But for the federal government, the decision is more complex. When the government raises money by selling Treasury bills, it makes safe investments available to investors worldwide. If foreign investors cannot buy Treasury notes, they might turn to other countries, reducing the amount of money flowing into the United States. U.S. government debt has also been used as a basis for pricing riskier investments. If the government issues less debt, the interest rates it commands are higher, raising the overall cost of debt to private borrowers. In addition, the government uses the funds from borrowing, at least in part, to invest in such public services as education and scientific research.

5 ▸ Global Economic Challenges of the 21st Century

Businesses face a number of important economic challenges in the 21st century. As the economies of countries around the globe become increasingly interconnected, governments and businesses must compete throughout the world. Although no one can predict the future, both governments and businesses will likely need to meet several challenges to maintain their global competitiveness. Table 3.5 identifies five key challenges: (1) the economic impact of the continuing threat of international terrorism, (2) the shift to a global information economy, (3) the aging of the world's population, (4) the growth of China and India, and (5) efforts to enhance the competitiveness of every country's workforce.

No country is an economic island in today's global economy. Not only is an ever-increasing stream of goods and services crossing national borders, but a growing number of businesses have become true multinational firms, operating manufacturing plants and other facilities around the world. Even small firms can take advantage of the global workforce, if they are savvy about applying technology and understanding cultural differences. See the "Business Etiquette" feature for some tips.

As global trade and investments grow, events in one nation can reverberate around the globe. But despite the risks of world trade, global expansion can offer huge opportunities to U.S. firms. With U.S. residents accounting for just over 1 in every 22 of the world's nearly 7 billion people, growth-oriented American companies cannot afford to ignore the world market.[18] U.S. businesses also benefit from the lower labor costs in other parts of the world, and some are finding successful niches importing goods and services provided by foreign firms. Still, it is extremely important for U.S. firms to keep close track of the foreign firms that supply their products. A number of U.S. companies have tried having their

LECTURE ENHANCER:
What are some drawbacks to this type of worldwide economic interdependency?

TABLE
3.5 **Global Economic Challenges**

CHALLENGE	FACTS AND EXAMPLES
International terrorism	Assistance in locating and detaining known terrorists. Cooperation in modifying banking laws in most nations in an effort to cut off funds to terrorist organizations. Concerns over potential nuclear threats from Iran.
Shift to a global information economy	Half of all American workers hold jobs in information technology or in industries that intensively use information technology, goods, and services. Software industry in India employs 2.8 million people. There are now more than 2 billion Internet users worldwide.
Aging of the world's population	Median age of the U.S. population is 37 plus, and by 2030, more than 70 million Americans will be age 65 or older—twice the number in 2000. This will increase demands for health care, retirement benefits, and other support services, putting budgetary pressure on governments. As Baby Boomers, now reaching their early 60s, begin to retire, businesses around the globe will need to find ways to replace their workplace skills.
Growth of India and China straining commodity prices	China and India now make up more than one-third of the world's population. China's economic growth has been in the industrial sector, and India's focused more in services. Both countries are now consumers of oil and other commodities, affecting prices.
Enhancing competitiveness of every country's workforce	Leaner organizations (with fewer supervisors) require employees with the skills to control, combine, and supervise work operations.

Sources: Occupational Employment Statistics, Bureau of Labor Statistics, http://www.bls.gov, accessed February 24, 2012; Neha Thirani, "Fast Growth for India's Outsourcing Industry Despite Weak Global Economy, *New York Times*, February 24, 2012, http://india.blogs.nytimes.com; International Telecommunication Union, "Measuring the Information Society 2011," Executive Summary, http://www.itu.int, accessed February 24, 2012; Lindsay M. Howden and Julie A. Meyer, "Age and Sex Composition: 2010," 2010 Census Briefs, http://www.census.gov, accessed February 24, 2012; U.S. Census Bureau, U.S. Population Projections, http://www.census.gov, accessed February 24, 2012; Carl Haub and O. P. Sharma, "India Releases Latest Census Results, Showing Population Catching Up to China," Population Reference Bureau, April 22, 2011, http://www.prb.org.

BusinessEtiquette

Dealing with the Global Workforce

The new global workforce, or "Work 3.0," offers 24/7 access to "the best people no matter where they are in the world," says Gary Swart, CEO of oDesk, a freelancers' website. Key to success is being able to "work with those people as if they're in the room with you."

Here are some tips for finding and working with global employees:

1 Judge language skills wisely. If you need someone to interact with customers, superb command of written and verbal English is a must. If you need a tech worker, don't be put off by slightly less fluency.

2 Set up formal rules for keeping touch with employees you can't see, and make sure everyone adheres to them.

3 Make your expectations clear, and communicate them to all, as often as necessary.

4 Connect time zones to your needs. If you depend on meetings and real-time collaboration, choose remote workers with whom your workday overlaps.

5 To simplify compensation, identify your top candidates and weigh what they can offer *you* and focus less on what their competitors halfway across the world might earn.

6 If you need to train employees, customize your program to their culture. Find out what motivates them and how they can best learn.

Sources: Yanawan Saguanasataya Hurlbut, "Best Practices for Managing Remote Offices," uSamp Blog, http://blog.Usamp.com, accessed February 29, 2012; Darrell Etherington, "Work 3.0 Is Just Getting Underway, Says oDesk's Gary Swart," Gigaom.com, December 8, 2011, http://gigaom.com; Alison Green, "How to Manage Remote Employees," The Quick Base Blog, November 17, 2011, http://quickbase.intuit.com; "How to Leverage the Global Workforce: 5 Quick Tips," ODeskblog, April 13, 2011, www.odesk.com; "Modern Workforce: Managing Remote Workers," Working Girl, February 12, 2011, http://li-workgirl.blogspot.com.

Assessment Check ✔

1. Why is virtually no country an economic island these days?

2. Describe two ways in which global expansion can benefit a U.S. firm.

goods manufactured in China because production costs are significantly lower than they would be in the United States. But there have been so many product recalls of Chinese-made goods during the past several years—ranging from toys and pet food to construction drywall and drinking glasses—that the U.S. Consumer Products Safety Commission (CPSC) has opened an office in Beijing. The goal is to provide the CPSC with closer observation and better communication between U.S. and Chinese firms about manufacturing standards.[19]

U.S. firms must also develop strategies for competing with each other and with foreign firms to meet the needs and wants of consumers overseas. In the huge and fragmented beverage industry, experts predict that the Japanese and Chinese markets for healthy soft drinks, including juice-based and tea-based drinks, will grow significantly over the next few years.[20]

What's Ahead

Global competition is a key factor in today's economy. In Chapter 4, we focus on the global dimensions of business. We cover basic concepts of doing business internationally and examine how nations can position themselves to benefit from the global economy. Then we describe the specific methods used by individual businesses to expand beyond their national borders and compete successfully in the global marketplace.

Summary of Learning Objectives

[1] **Discuss microeconomics and explain the forces of demand and supply.**

Microeconomics is the study of economic behavior among individual consumers, families, and businesses whose collective behavior in the marketplace determines the quantity of goods and services demanded and supplied at different prices. Macroeconomics is the study of the broader economic picture and how an economic system maintains and allocates its resources; it focuses on how a government's monetary and fiscal policies affect the overall operation of an economic system.

Demand is the willingness and ability of buyers to purchase goods and services at different prices. Factors that drive demand for a good or service include customer preferences, the number of buyers and their incomes, the prices of substitute goods, the prices of complementary goods, and consumer expectations about the future. Supply is the willingness and ability of businesses to offer products for sale at different prices. Supply is determined by the cost of inputs and technology resources, taxes, and the number of suppliers operating in the market.

Assessment Check Answers ☑

1.1 Define microeconomics and macroeconomics.
Microeconomics is the study of economic behavior among individual consumers, families, and businesses whose collective behavior in the marketplace determines the quantity of goods and services demanded and supplied at different prices. *Macroeconomics* is the study of the broader economic picture and how an economic system maintains and allocates its resources.

1.2 Explain demand and supply curves. A demand curve is a graph of the amount of a product that buyers will purchase at different prices. A supply curve shows the relationship between different prices and the quantities that sellers will offer for sale, regardless of demand.

1.3 How do factors of production influence the overall supply of goods and services? A change in the cost or availability of any of the inputs considered to be factors of production can shift the entire supply curve, either increasing or decreasing the amount available at every price.

[2] **Describe macroeconomics and the issues for the entire economy.**

Four basic models characterize competition in a private enterprise system: pure competition, monopolistic competition, oligopoly, and monopoly. Pure competition is a market structure, like that in small-scale agriculture, in which large numbers of buyers and sellers exchange homogeneous products and no single participant has a significant influence on price. Monopolistic competition is a market structure, like that of retailing, in which large numbers of buyers and sellers exchange differentiated products, so each participant has some control over price. Oligopolies are market situations, like those in the steel and airline industries, in which relatively few sellers compete and high start-up costs form barriers to keep out new competitors. In a monopoly, one seller dominates trade in a good or service, for which buyers can find no close substitutes.

The major economic systems are private enterprise economy, planned economy (such as communism or socialism), and mixed market economy. In a private enterprise system, individuals and private businesses pursue their own interests—including investment decisions and profits—without undue governmental restriction. In a planned economy, the government exerts stronger control over business ownership, profits, and resources to accomplish governmental and societal—rather than individual—goals. Socialism, one type of planned economic system, is characterized by government ownership and operation of all major industries. Communism is an economic system with limited private property; goods are owned in common, and factors of production and production decisions are controlled by the state. A mixed market economy blends government ownership and private enterprise, combining characteristics of both planned and private enterprise economies.

Assessment Check Answers ☑

2.1 What is the difference between pure competition and monopolistic competition? Pure competition is a market structure in which large numbers of buyers and sellers exchange homogeneous products. Monopolistic competition is a market structure in which large numbers of buyers and sellers exchange differentiated products.

2.2 On which economic system is the U.S. economy based? The U.S. economy is based on the private enterprise system.

2.3 What is privatization? Privatization is the conversion of government-owned and operated agencies into privately held businesses.

[3] **Identify how to evaluate economic performance.**
The four stages are prosperity, recession, depression, and recovery. Prosperity is characterized by low unemployment and strong consumer confidence. In a recession, consumers often postpone major purchases, layoffs occur, and household savings may be depleted. A depression occurs when an economic slowdown continues in a downward spiral over a long period of time. During recovery, consumer spending begins to increase and business activity accelerates, leading to an increased number of jobs.

As productivity rises, so do an economy's growth and the wealth of its citizens. In a recession, productivity stalls or possibly declines. Changes in general price levels—inflation or deflation—are important indicators of an economy's general stability. The U.S. government measures price-level changes by the Consumer Price Index. A nation's unemployment rate is an indicator of both overall stability and growth.

The unemployment rate shows, as a percentage of the total labor force, the number of people actively seeking employment who are unable to find jobs.

Assessment Check Answers ✅

3.1 Describe the four stages of the business cycle. The four stages are prosperity, recession, depression, and recovery. Prosperity is characterized by low unemployment and strong consumer confidence. Recession may include consumers postponing major purchases, layoffs, and decreased household savings. A depression occurs when an economic slowdown continues in a downward spiral over a long period of time. In recovery, consumer spending increases and business activity accelerates.

3.2 What are some measures that economists use to determine the health of an economy? Gross domestic product (GDP), general level of prices, core inflation rate, the Consumer Price Index, and the unemployment rate are all measures used to determine the health of an economy.

⌐4⌐ Discuss managing the economy's performance.

Monetary policy encompasses a government's efforts to control the size of the nation's money supply. Various methods of increasing or decreasing the overall money supply affect interest rates and therefore affect borrowing and investment decisions. By changing the size of the money supply, government can encourage growth or control inflation. Fiscal policy involves decisions regarding government revenues and expenditures. Changes in government spending affect economic growth and employment levels in the private sector. However, a government must also raise money, through taxes or borrowing, to finance its expenditures. Because tax payments are funds that might otherwise have been spent by individuals and businesses, any taxation changes also affect the overall economy.

Assessment Check Answers ✅

4.1 What is the difference between an expansionary monetary policy and a restrictive monetary policy? An expansionary monetary policy increases the money supply in an effort to cut the cost of borrowing. A restrictive monetary policy reduces the money supply to curb rising prices, overexpansion, and concerns about overly rapid economic growth.

4.2 What are the three primary sources of government funds? The U.S. government acquires funds through taxes, fees, and borrowing.

4.3 Does a balanced budget erase the federal debt? No, a balanced budget does not erase the national debt; it just doesn't increase it.

⌐5⌐ Describe the global economic challenges of the 21st century.

Businesses face five key challenges in the 21st century: (1) the threat of international terrorism; (2) the shift to a global information economy; (3) the aging of the world's population; (4) the growth of India and China, which compete for resources; and (5) efforts to enhance the competitiveness of every country's workforce.

Assessment Check Answers ✅

5.1 Why is virtually no country an economic island these days? No business or country is an economic island because many goods and services travel across national borders. Companies now are becoming multinational firms.

5.2 Describe two ways in which global expansion can benefit a U.S. firm. A firm can benefit from global expansion by attracting more customers and using less expensive labor and production to produce goods and services.

■ Business Terms You Need to Know

economics 65	monopoly 74	inflation 79	monetary policy 84
microeconomics 65	regulated monopoly 74	core inflation rate 79	expansionary monetary policy 84
macroeconomics 65	planned economy 75	hyperinflation 80	
demand 66	socialism 75	deflation 81	restrictive monetary policy 84
supply 66	communism 75	Consumer Price Index (CPI) 81	fiscal policy 84
demand curve 67	mixed market economy 76	unemployment rate 82	budget 86
supply curve 69	privatization 76	frictional unemployment 83	budget deficit 86
equilibrium price 71	recession 78	seasonal unemployment 83	national debt 86
pure competition 72	productivity 79	cyclical unemployment 83	budget surplus 86
monopolistic competition 73	gross domestic product (GDP) 79	structural unemployment 83	balanced budget 86
oligopoly 74			

Review Questions

1. How does microeconomics affect business? How does macroeconomics affect business? Why is it important for businesspeople to understand the fundamentals of each?

2. Draw supply and demand graphs that estimate what will happen to demand, supply, and the equilibrium price of coffee if these events occur:

   a. Widely reported medical studies suggest that coffee drinkers are less likely to develop certain diseases.

   b. The cost of manufacturing paper cups increases.

   c. The state imposes a new tax on takeout beverages.

   d. The biggest coffee chain leaves the area.

3. Describe the four different types of competition in the private enterprise system. In which type of competition would each of the following businesses be likely to engage?

   a. large drug stores chain

   b. small yoga studio

   c. steel mill

   d. large farm whose major crop is corn

   e. Microsoft

4. Distinguish between the two types of planned economies. What factors do you think keep them from flourishing in today's economic environment?

5. What are the four stages of the business cycle? In which stage do you believe the U.S. economy is now? Why?

6. What is the gross domestic product? What is its relationship to productivity?

7. What are the effects of inflation on an economy? What are the effects of deflation? How does the Consumer Price Index work?

8. What does a nation's unemployment rate indicate? Describe what type of unemployment you think each of the following illustrates:

   a. discharged armed forces veteran

   b. bus driver who has been laid off due to cuts in his or her city's transit budget

   c. worker who was injured on the job and must start a new career

   d. lifeguard

   e. dental hygienist who has quit one job and is looking for another

9. Explain the difference between monetary policy and fiscal policy. How does the government raise funds to cover the costs of its annual budget?

10. What is the difference between the budget deficit and the national debt? What are the benefits of paying down the national debt? What might be the negative effects?

Projects and Teamwork Applications

1. Describe a situation in which you have had to make an economic choice in an attempt to balance your wants with limited means. What factors influenced your decision?

2. Choose one of the following products and describe the different factors that you think might affect its supply and demand.

   a. UGG boots

   b. Kindle

   c. Miles by Discover credit card

   d. newly created name-brand drug

   e. Detroit Lions football tickets

3. Go online to research one of the following government agencies—its responsibilities, its budget, and the like. Then make the case for privatizing it:

   a. Veterans Administration

   b. Bureau of the Census

   c. Smithsonian Institution

   d. Transportation Security Administration

   e. Social Security

4. Some businesses automatically experience seasonal unemployment. More and more, however, owners of these businesses are making efforts to increase demand—and employment—during the off season. Choose a classmate to be your business partner, and together select one of the following businesses. Create a plan for developing business and keeping employees for a season during which your business does not customarily operate:

   a. children's summer camp

   b. ski lodge

   c. inn located near a beach resort

   d. house painting service

   e. greenhouse

5. On your own or with a classmate, go online to research the economy of one of the following countries. Learn what you can about the type of economy the country has, its major

industries, and its competitive issues. (Note which industries or services are privatized and which are government owned.) Take notes on unemployment rates, monetary policies, and fiscal policies. Present your findings to the class.

a. China

b. New Zealand

c. India

d. Denmark

e. Mexico

f. Canada

g. Chile

Web Assignments

1. **Credit-card regulations**. Several new federal regulations governing credit cards went into effect recently. Visit the Web site listed here and click on "New Credit Card Rules." After reviewing these rules, prepare a brief report highlighting the most significant changes.

1. http://federalreserve.gov/creditcard/

Unemployment. In the United States, the Bureau of Labor Statistics (BLS) compiles and publishes data on unemployment. Go to the BLS Web site (http://www.bls.gov) and click on "Unemployment" (under "Subject Areas"). Read through the most recent report and answer the following questions:

a. What is the current unemployment rate in the United States? How does it compare with those of other developed countries?

b. Which state has the highest unemployment rate? Which state has the lowest unemployment rate?

c. What is the underemployment rate?

3. **Gross domestic product**. Visit the Web site of the Bureau of Economic Analysis (http://www.bea.gov) and access the most recent statistics on the U.S. GDP. Prepare a brief report. What is the current GDP? What is the difference between real and nominal GDP? What are the individual components that make up GDP?

Note: Internet Web addresses change frequently. If you don't find the exact sites listed, you may need to access the organization's home page and search from there or use a search engine such as Bing or Google.

CASE 3.1   Nuclear Energy: Making a Comeback?

In a recent State of the Union address, the president called for more clean-energy jobs, with expansion of nuclear power. Although no nuclear plants have been built in the United States for many years, the 104 currently operating plants generate almost 20 percent of America's electricity. Wind and solar energy together generate less than 5 percent.

An alloy of enriched uranium powers nuclear reactors. Uranium, a metal, can be found in rocks and even seawater as well as in ore deposits in the earth. With 24 percent, Australia has the largest supply overall, but Kazakhstan recently declared that it had surpassed Australia's output. Canada has less than 10 percent of the world's supply but has the highest concentration of top-quality ore. Worldwide, about 67,000 tons of uranium are used each year. At current demand, that supply is expected to last about 70 years. The World Nuclear Association (WNA) predicts that nuclear reactor capacity will increase by about 27 percent in the next decade and that the demand for uranium will grow by 33 percent.

Eventually the demand for uranium will be greater than the supply that can be mined economically. Some analysts believe that the world will run out of uranium sooner rather than later.

Environmentalists object to destructive mining techniques and fear the exploitation of indigenous Australians. A lack of infrastructure and a shortage of experienced workers drive up uranium-processing costs. A still-unsolved and crucial problem is how to manage safe, long-term storage of spent nuclear rods, which continue to emit radioactivity.

The World Nuclear Association disagrees. First, not all uranium deposits have been discovered. Since 1975, the number of known deposits has tripled. The WNA predicts that at *current* rates of usage, known supplies will last 200 years rather than 70 or 80.

Second, the end of the Cold War also meant the end of the nuclear arms race between the United States and the USSR (now Russia). Nuclear warheads contain high-quality enriched uranium. Utility companies and governments also have uranium stockpiles.

Third, researchers are working to make enrichment facilities and reactors more energy efficient.

Fourth, uranium can be recycled from spent nuclear fuel rods and from tailings (uranium left over from the enrichment process). Other sources, such as phosphates and seawater, could become economically viable in the future.

The 2011 catastrophic earthquake and tsunami in Japan damaged a major nuclear power plant, which leaked harmful levels of radiation. Nevertheless, the U.S. president defended nuclear energy, insisting that American nuclear power plants are vigilantly regulated. Recently, the U.S. Nuclear Regulatory Commission granted permits for two nuclear power plants in Georgia.

Questions for Critical Thinking

1. What factors do you think will affect the supply and demand curve for nuclear energy?
2. Describe what type of competition you predict will arise in the nuclear energy industry.

Sources: Matthew L. Wald, "Federal Regulators Approve Two Nuclear Reactors in Georgia," *New York Times*, http://www.nytimes.com, accessed February 24, 2012; Associated Press, "Obama Defends Nuclear Energy," MSNBC.com, http://www.msnbc.msn.com, accessed February 24, 2012; Barack Obama, State of the Union address, January 27, 2010, http://www.whitehouse.gov; "Is Nuclear Power the Future? Obama Calls for More Plants," *USA Today*, January 26, 2010, http://usatoday.com; "The Nuclear Reactor—How They Are Constructed," Virtual Nuclear Tourist, http://www.nucleartourist.com, accessed February 4, 2010; Toni Johnson, "Global Uranium Supply and Demand," Council on Foreign Relations, January 14, 2010, http://www.cfr.org.

Smart Phones: Recession Proof and Growing

CASE 3.2

The ascent of the smart phone has been one of the most revolutionary developments in electronics. Among the many models available are the Nokia N900, the Apple iPhone, Research in Motion's BlackBerry, the Palm Treo, and the Motorola Droid, with others in the works. Microsoft is planning to launch smart phone software to rival Apple's.

Despite the recent recession, smart phones have remained wildly popular in the United States and abroad. The numbers are staggering, with 53 million smart phones shipped worldwide in a recent quarter. Nokia led the global market with almost 40 percent of market share. The BlackBerry was second, with just over 20 percent. The iPhone was third, with over 16 percent. Other smart phones had a combined market share of just over 24 percent.

Competition among the smart phones will almost certainly remain strong and is likely to become stronger. Two influential factors are coverage and applications.

The Droid from Motorola is giving the iPhone a run for its money. The Droid runs on the Verizon network, whereas AT&T had exclusive rights to the iPhone. Verizon has wider network coverage than AT&T, but AT&T allows iPhone users to multitask on one handset. At present, prospective buyers must choose between quality of coverage and multitasking. Recently Apple released the iPhone 4s, which can run on the Verizon network.

In applications, or "apps," the iPhone leads in number of app developers, number of apps, and number of people who have downloaded those apps. Applications number in the hundreds of thousands; Apple alone has 75,000. Most are free; others (about 18 percent) cost just a few dollars. Apps range from weather to games to music to news. A typical user downloads 20 apps, with games far in the lead. Apple recently celebrated its one-billionth iPhone download.

Here are some predictions for the smart phone industry:

- Some analysts forecast that sales of smart phones will soon increase four-fold, and fees for smart phone apps in the United States alone will increase ten-fold to $4.2 billion.

- Smart phones will account for an increasing share of the mobile phone market.
- As we have seen, application stores will experience a boom.
- Location-based services, which already include GPS, will increase. Advertisers may be able to have pop-up ads on the maps you download.

Questions for Critical Thinking

1. How has the rapid development of technology affected competition in the mobile phone industry?

2. How does this technology affect supply and demand in the mobile phone industry?

Sources: Leah Yamshon, "Report: Apple's iPhone 4 Was Most Purchased Smartphone in 2011," IDG News Service, February 23, 2012, http://news.idg.no; Richard Waters, "Microsoft to Promote Smartphone Software," *Financial Times*, January 8, 2012, http://www.ft.com;Apple Web site, http://www.apple.com, accessed June 21, 2011; Amazon Web site, http://www.amazon.com, accessed June 21, 2011; Barnes & Noble Web site, http://barnesandnoble.com, accessed June 21, 2011; Marguerite Reardon, "Microsoft Readies Smartphone Assault on Apple," *cnet news*, February 9, 2010, http://news.cnet.com; "Smart phones Leading the Handset Industry Out of Recession," *Mobile Entertainment*, February 1, 2010, http://www.mobile-ent.biz.

CASE 3.3 Secret Acres: Selling Comics Is Serious Business

Just about everyone remembers a favorite comic book from childhood—whether it was *Spiderman, Tin Tin*, or even *Garfield*. Leon Avelino and Barry Matthews readily acknowledge that they are kids in grown-up bodies with real day jobs (Avelino works for *Sports Illustrated* and Matthews is an accountant for an e-commerce firm) who happen to love comic books and their latest incarnation, graphic novels. Their love for comics in all forms—along with the desire to start their own business—led them to found Secret Acres, a comic book and graphic novel publisher based in New York City. In addition to publishing several works from up-and-coming authors (they have eight books on their list so far), the Secret Acres duo sells books from independent distributors.

Acknowledging that Secret Acres faces many economic challenges if it's going to hang on and eventually succeed, Matthews observes, "Every decision we make, we know what the outcome is going to be because it's all small and it's very close to us." Right now, Secret Acres can use its small size to build relationships with its customers. "We are able, because we're small, to produce a very specific kind of comic book, a specific kind of graphic novel, that appeals to a specific audience," explains Matthews. "I love that. We have a lot of control over what we do and we're not doing anything specifically to turn a buck." That said, the accountant in Matthews knows that in order to stay in business, Secret Acres must sell enough books to push unit costs down, keeping production expenses and prices as low as possible.

Matthews also refers to relationships with book stores, which are personal because he and Avelino do all the communicating themselves. "When you have a small group of stores you are selling from, you have to collect from them on a one-to-one basis," says Matthews. Sometimes the relationship becomes awkward when Matthews or Avelino has to remind a book store owner personally of an unpaid balance.

Another challenge facing the duo is the uncertain future of the print publishing market. The introduction of e-readers such as Amazon's Kindle and Barnes & Noble's Nook creates a new delivery system for printed work. While the e-reader hasn't created the sensation among consumers that its manufacturers had hoped (some competing models have already disappeared from the marketplace), online delivery of printed matter is alive and well—and it's likely that some form of e-reader will eventually catch on. "Publishers are nervous because no one knows how popular e-readers will be in the long run," says Matthews.

Another phenomenon that has taken hold over the last decade is the graphic novel, the fiction genre that combines comic book techniques with the longer, more complex structure of a novel. Graphic novels are particularly popular among teens and college students, but they have received serious attention from the literary world. Some college courses are now taught around the graphic novel, and the American Library Association publishes a list of recommended graphic novels for teens each year. A firm like Secret Acres could capitalize on a literary trend that continues to gain ground.

Matthews and Avelino haven't quit their day jobs yet. They know it will be awhile before they can call themselves full-time publishers. But they love the comic book business and they are willing to wait for the good times they believe are ahead. "We have faith in the fact that if these books find the right audience, they'll do fine," says Avelino. "I'm OK with being patient. We need to keep going long enough to build a back list that is self-supporting." And Secret Acres already has a following among comic fans—their secret is out.

Questions for Critical Thinking

1. What steps might Matthews and Avelino take to create demand for their books? How must a small business like Secret Acres balance supply with demand?

2. How might Secret Acres make the most of an economy that is recovering slowly? What advantages and disadvantages might the firm have over a large publishing company?

3. How would you categorize the competition that Secret Acres faces?

4. Do you think Secret Acres should pursue online distribution through e-readers and other delivery systems? Why or why not?

Sources: Secret Acres Web site, http://www.secretacres.com, accessed February 23, 2012; "Great Graphic Novels for Teens," *Young Adult Library Services Association*, http://www.ala.org/yalsa, accessed February 23, 2012; Harry McCracken, "E-Readers May Be Dead, But They're Not Going Away Yet," *PC World*, August 17, 2010, http://www.pcworld.com.

Learning Objectives

1 Explain why nations trade.

2 Describe how trade is measured between nations.

3 Identify the barriers to international trade.

4 Discuss reducing barriers to international trade.

5 Explain the decisions to go global.

6 Discuss developing a strategy for international business.

Chapter 4

Competing in World Markets

Kaveh Kazemi/Getty Images, Inc.

Fiat Takes Over Chrysler in Global Expansion

After a government-sponsored bankruptcy, Chrysler was purchased in stages by Italian automaker Fiat. Under Sergio Marchionne, CEO of both firms, the merger looks like "the closest thing to a truly symbiotic relationship that the industry has ever seen," said one industry analyst.

While Chrysler's earlier partnership with Germany's Daimler-Benz dissolved in failure, some call Marchionne's efficient melding of Chrysler and Fiat a potential template for future global partnerships in the auto industry. Marchionne told the press that company executives are making all decisions together as one management team.

Chrysler's latest products seem to confirm that things are working well. With plans for the two firms to produce a combined 6 million cars by 2014, Marchionne has started with a new fuel-efficient compact Dodge Dart, based on the chassis and technology of Fiat's storied Alfa Romero, and the Maserati Kubang, a high-end Fiat SUV based on Chrysler's Jeep Grand Cherokee.

The Dodge Dart will be made in the United States, and Marchionne decided to build the Kubang in the Detroit area, saying that such a corporate decision shatters the myth about the type of cars and trucks U.S. automakers are capable of making. And the company passed another financial hurdle recently when it announced its first profitable year since 2005. Marchionne's executives juggle responsibilities that straddle the globe and corporate organization charts. One question he hasn't answered is where the new headquarters will be: Italy, the United States, or some third location. "All options are open," he says.[1]

Overview

Consider for a moment how many products you used today that came from outside the United States. Maybe you drank Brazilian coffee with your breakfast, wore clothes manufactured in Honduras or Malaysia, drove to class in a German or Japanese car fueled by gasoline refined from Canadian crude oil, and watched a movie on a television set assembled in Mexico for a Japanese company such as Sony. A fellow student in Germany may be wearing Zara jeans, using a Samsung cell phone, and drinking Pepsi.

U.S. and foreign companies alike recognize the importance of international trade to their future success. Economic interdependence is increasing throughout the world as companies seek additional markets for their goods and services and the most cost-effective locations for production facilities. No longer can businesses rely only on domestic sales. Today, foreign sales are essential to U.S. manufacturing, agricultural, and service firms as sources of new markets and profit opportunities. Foreign companies also frequently look to the United States when they seek new markets.

Thousands of products cross national borders every day. The computers that U.S. manufacturers sell in Canada are **exports**, domestically produced goods and services sold in markets in other countries. **Imports** are foreign-made products purchased by domestic consumers. Together, U.S. exports and imports make up about a quarter of the U.S. gross domestic product (GDP). The United States is fourth in the world among exporting nations, with exports exceeding $1.5 trillion and annual imports of more than $2.3 trillion. That total amount is more than double the nation's imports and exports of just a decade ago.[2]

Transactions that cross national boundaries may expose a company to an additional

exports domestically produced goods and services sold in markets in other countries.

imports foreign-made products purchased by domestic consumers.

set of factors such as new social and cultural practices, economic and political environments, and legal restrictions.

This chapter travels through the world of international business to see how both large and small companies approach globalization. First, we consider the reasons nations trade, the importance and characteristics of the global marketplace, and the ways nations measure international trade. Then we examine barriers to international trade that arise from cultural and environmental differences. To reduce these barriers, countries turn to organizations that promote global business. Finally, we look at the strategies firms implement for entering foreign markets and the way they develop international business strategies.

Why Nations Trade

As domestic markets mature and sales growth slows, companies in every industry recognize the increasing importance of efforts to develop business in other countries. Walmart operates stores in Mexico, Boeing sells jetliners in Asia, and soccer fans in Britain watch their teams being bought by U.S. billionaires. These are only a few of the thousands of U.S. companies taking advantage of large populations, substantial resources, and rising standards of living abroad that boost foreign interest in their goods and services. Likewise, the U.S. market, with the world's greatest purchasing power, attracts thousands of foreign companies to its shores.

LECTURE ENHANCER:
What are some risks associated with global economic interdependence?

International trade is vital to a nation and its businesses because it boosts economic growth by providing a market for its products and access to needed resources. Companies can expand their markets, seek growth opportunities in other nations, and make their production and distribution systems more efficient. They also reduce their dependence on the economies of their home nations.

International Sources of Factors of Production

Business decisions to operate abroad depend on the availability, price, and quality of labor, natural resources, capital, and entrepreneurship—the basic factors of production—in the foreign country. Indian colleges and universities produce thousands of highly qualified computer scientists and engineers each year. To take advantage of this talent, many U.S. computer software and hardware firms have set up operations in India, and many others are outsourcing information technology and customer service jobs there.

CLASS ACTIVITY:
Ask students to provide examples of goods they have purchased which were made in other countries.

Trading with other countries also allows a company to spread risk because different nations may be at different stages of the business cycle or in different phases of development. If demand falls off in one country, the company may still enjoy strong demand in other nations. Companies such as Kellogg's and IKEA have long used international sales to offset lower domestic demand.

Size of the International Marketplace

In addition to human and natural resources, entrepreneurship, and capital, companies are attracted to international business by the sheer size of the global marketplace. Only one in six of the world's 7 billion people live in a relatively well-developed country. The share of the world's population in the less developed countries will increase over the coming years because more developed nations have lower birthrates. But the U.S. Census Bureau says the global birthrate is slowing overall, and the average woman in today's world bears half as many children as her counterpart did 35 years ago.[3]

As developing nations expand their involvement in global business, the potential for reaching new groups of customers dramatically increases. Firms looking for new revenue are inevitably attracted to giant markets such as China and India, with respective populations of about 1.3 billion and 1.2 billion. However, people alone are not enough to create a market. Consumer demand also requires purchasing power. As Table 4.1 shows, population size is no guarantee of economic prosperity. Of the 10 most populous countries, only the United States appears on the list of those with the highest per-capita GDPs.

Although people in the developing nations have lower per-capita incomes than those in the highly developed economies of North America and western Europe, their huge populations do represent lucrative markets. Even when the higher-income segments are only a small percentage of the entire country's population, their sheer numbers may still represent significant and growing markets.

Also, many developing countries have typically posted high growth rates of annual GDP. The U.S. GDP generally averages between 2 and 4 percent growth per year. By contrast, GDP growth in less developed countries was much greater—China's GDP growth rate averaged nearly 10 percent over a recent three-year period, and India's averaged 7.6 percent.[4] These markets represent opportunities for global businesses, even though their per-capita incomes lag behind those in more developed countries. Many firms are establishing operations in these and other developing countries to position themselves to benefit

CLASS ACTIVITY:
Global companies are aggressively pursuing establishing new markets in the so-called BRIC countries (Brazil, Russia, India, and China). Ask students why this is occurring.

TABLE
4.1

The World's Top 10 Nations Based on Population and Wealth

COUNTRY	POPULATION (IN MILLIONS)	COUNTRY	PER-CAPITA GDP (IN U.S. DOLLARS, 2011 ESTIMATES)
China	1,343	Qatar	$102,700
India	1,205	Luxembourg	$84,700
United States	313	Singapore	$59,900
Indonesia	248	Norway	$53,300
Brazil	205	Brunei	$49,400
Pakistan	190	Hong Kong	$49,300
Nigeria	170	United Arab Emirates	$48,500
Bangladesh	161	United States	$48,100
Russia	138	Switzerland	$43,400
Japan	126	Netherlands	$42,300

Source: *World Factbook*, https://www.cia.gov, accessed March 23, 2012.

FIGURE 4.1

Top 10 Trading Partners with the United States

Country	Total U.S. Imports and Exports per Month
Canada	$49 billion
China	$43
Mexico	$38
Japan	$17
Germany	$13
United Kingdom	$10
South Korea	$8
Brazil	$6.8
Saudi Arabia	$6.6
Netherlands	$6

Source: Data from U.S. Census Bureau, "Top Ten Countries with Which the U.S. Trades," http://www .census.gov/foreign-trade/top/dst/current/balance.html, accessed February 15, 2012.

from local sales driven by expanding economies and rising standards of living. Walmart is one of those companies. As the largest retail firm in the world, Walmart employs 2.2 million workers worldwide. Walmart International is growing fast, with more than 5,300 stores and 740,000 employees in 27 countries as far-ranging as Lesotho and Swaziland in Africa. More than 90 percent of Walmart's overseas stores operate under a local banner.[5]

The United States trades with many other nations. As Figure 4.1 shows, the top five are Canada, China, Mexico, Japan, and Germany. With the United Kingdom, South Korea, Brazil, Saudi Arabia, and the Netherlands, they represent nearly two-thirds of U.S. imports and exports every year.[6] Foreign trade is such an important part of the U.S. economy that it makes up a large portion of the business activity in many of the country's individual states as well. Texas exports more than $206 billion of goods annually, and California exports more than $143 billion. Other big exporting states include Florida, Illinois, New York, and Washington.[7]

LECTURE ENHANCER:
Choose one of these nations and discuss the goods and services that might be involved with U.S. trade.

Absolute and Comparative Advantage

Few countries can produce all the goods and services their people need. For centuries, trading has been the way that countries can meet the demand. If a country focuses on producing what it does best, it can export surplus domestic output and buy foreign products that it lacks or cannot efficiently produce. The potential for foreign sales of a particular item depends largely on whether the country has an absolute advantage or a comparative advantage.

A country has an *absolute advantage* in making a product for which it can maintain a monopoly or that it can produce at a lower cost than any competitor. For centuries, China enjoyed an absolute advantage in silk production. The fabric was woven from fibers recovered from silkworm cocoons, making it a prized raw material in high-quality clothing. Demand among Europeans for silk led to establishment of the famous Silk Road, a 5,000-mile link between Rome and the ancient Chinese capital city of Xian.

Absolute advantages are rare these days. But some countries manage to approximate absolute advantages in some products. Climate differences can give some nations or regions an advantage in growing certain plants. Saffron, perhaps the world's most expensive spice at as much as $500 per ounce, is the stigma of a flowering plant in the crocus family. It is native to the Mediterranean, Asia Minor, and India. Today, however, saffron is cultivated primarily in Spain, India, and Iran, where the plant thrives in the soil and climate. Attempts to grow saffron commercially in other parts of the world have generally been unsuccessful.[8]

A nation can develop a *comparative advantage* if it can supply its products more efficiently and at a lower price than it can supply other goods, compared with the outputs of other countries. China is profiting from its comparative advantage in producing textiles. On the other hand, ensuring that its people are well educated is another way a nation can develop a comparative advantage in skilled human resources. India offers the services of its educated tech workers at a lower wage. But sometimes these strategies backfire. Recently U.S. firms have pulled back from manufacturing or locating customer service operations overseas because of consumer complaints about quality.

To boost its longstanding advantage in research and innovation as global competition increases, IBM formed global research laboratories with other companies, universities, and governments as widespread as Saudi Arabia, Switzerland, China, Taiwan, India, and Ireland. Most recently, Australia was added to the list, with the first IBM lab combining research and development in a single organization. The lab focuses on smarter natural resource and disaster management.[9]

A country can develop a comparative advantage if it supplies its products more efficiently and at a lower price than it supplies other goods. China enjoys a comparative advantage in producing textiles.

HAIBO BI/Getty Images, Inc.

Assessment Check ☑

1. Why do nations trade?

2. Cite some measures of the size of the international marketplace.

3. How does a nation acquire a comparative advantage?

2

Measuring Trade between Nations

Clearly, engaging in international trade provides tremendous competitive advantages to both the countries and individual companies involved. But how do we measure global business activity? To understand what the trade inflows and outflows mean for a country, we need to examine the concepts of balance of trade and balance of payments. Another important factor is currency exchange rates for each country.

A nation's **balance of trade** is the difference between its exports and imports. If a country exports more than it imports, it achieves a positive balance of trade, called a *trade surplus*. If it imports more than it exports, it produces a negative balance of trade, called a *trade deficit*. The United States has run a trade deficit every year since 1976. Despite being one of the world's top exporters, the United States has an even greater appetite for foreign-made goods, which creates a trade deficit.

A nation's balance of trade plays a central role in determining its **balance of payments**—the overall flow of money into or out of a country. Other factors also affect the balance of payments, including overseas loans and borrowing, international investments, profits from such investments, and foreign aid payments. To calculate a nation's balance of payments, subtract the monetary outflows from the monetary inflows. A positive balance of payments, or a *balance-of-payments surplus*, means more money has moved into a country than out of it. A negative balance of payments, or *balance-of-payments deficit*, means more money has gone out of the country than entered it.

balance of trade difference between a nation's exports and imports.

balance of payments overall flow of money into or out of a country.

Major U.S. Exports and Imports

The United States, with combined exports and imports of about $3.8 trillion, leads the world in the international trade of goods and services. As listed in Table 4.2, the leading categories of goods exchanged by U.S. exporters and importers range from machinery and vehicles to crude oil and chemicals. Strong U.S. demand for imported goods is partly a reflection of the nation's prosperity and diversity.

Although the United States imports more goods than it exports, the opposite is true for services. U.S. exporters sell more than $600 billion in services annually. Much of that money comes from travel and tourism—money spent by foreign nationals visiting the United States.[10] The increase in that figure is especially significant because the dollar has declined and continues to fluctuate in terms of foreign currencies in recent years. U.S. service exports also include business and technical services such as engineering, financial services, computing, legal services, and entertainment, as well as royalties and licensing fees. Major service exporters include Citibank, Walt Disney, Allstate Insurance, and Federal Express, as well as retailers such as McDonald's and Starbucks.

Businesses in many foreign countries want the expertise of U.S. financial and business professionals. Accountants are in high demand in Russia, China, the Netherlands, and Australia—Sydney has become one of Asia's biggest financial centers. Entertainment is another major growth area for U.S. service exports. The Walt Disney Company already has theme parks in Europe and Asia, and is now building Shanghai Disney Resort, a multi-billion-dollar park in China.[11]

With annual imports of more than $2.3 trillion, the United States is by far the world's leading importer. American tastes for foreign-made goods for everything from clothing to consumer electronics show up as huge trade deficits with the consumer-goods–exporting nations of China and Japan.

TABLE
4.2 Top 10 U.S. Merchandise Exports and Imports

EXPORTS	AMOUNT (IN BILLIONS)	IMPORTS	AMOUNT (IN BILLIONS)
Agricultural commodities	$115.82	Crude oil	$260.1
Vehicles	88.1	Vehicles	178.9
Mineral fuel	80.5	Televisions, VCRs	137.3
Electrical machinery	77.0	Electrical machinery	119.6
Petroleum preparations	53.5	Automated data processing equipment	113.5
General industrial machinery	51.8	Agricultural commodities	82.0
Specialized industrial machinery	46.8	Clothing	78.5
Scientific instruments	44.3	Petroleum preparations	67.4
Chemicals—plastics	42.0	Chemicals—medicinal	65.2
Chemicals—medicinal	41.9	General industrial machinery	60.4

Source: U.S. Census Bureau, "U.S. Exports and General Imports by Selected SITC Commodity Groups," *Statistical Abstract of the United States: 2012*, http://www.census.gov, accessed February 15, 2012.

Exchange Rates

A nation's exchange rate is the value of one nation's currency relative to the currencies of other countries. **Exchange rate** is the rate at which its currency can be exchanged for the currencies of other nations. It is important to learn how foreign exchange works because we live in a global community and the value of currency is an important economic thermometer for every country. Each currency's exchange rate is usually quoted in terms of another currency, such as the number of Mexican pesos needed to purchase one U.S. dollar. Roughly 13 pesos are needed to exchange for a U.S. dollar. A Canadian dollar can be exchanged for approximately $1 in the United States. The euro, the currency used in most of the European Union (EU) member countries, has made considerable moves in exchange value during its few years in circulation. European consumers and businesses now use the euro to pay bills by check, credit card, or bank transfer. Euro coins and notes are also used in many EU-member countries.

Foreign exchange rates are influenced by a number of factors, including domestic economic and political conditions, central bank intervention, balance-of-payments position, and speculation over future currency values. Currency values fluctuate, or "float," depending on the supply and demand for each currency in the international market. In this system of *floating exchange rates*, currency traders create a market for the world's currencies based on each country's relative trade and investment prospects. In theory, this market permits exchange rates to vary freely according to supply and demand. In practice, exchange rates do not float in total freedom. National governments often intervene in currency markets to adjust their exchange rates.

Nations influence exchange rates in other ways as well. They may form currency blocs by linking their exchange rates to each other. Many governments practice protectionist policies that seek to guard their economies against trade imbalances. For instance, nations sometimes take deliberate action to devalue their currencies as a way to increase exports and stimulate foreign investment. **Devaluation** describes a drop in a currency's value relative to other currencies or to a fixed standard. In Brazil, a currency devaluation made investing in that country relatively cheap, so the devaluation was followed by a flood of foreign investment. Pillsbury bought Brazil's Brisco, which makes a local staple, *pao de queijo*, a cheese bread formed into rolls and served with morning coffee. Other foreign companies invested in Brazil's construction, tourism, banking, communications, and other industries.

For an individual business, the impact of currency devaluation depends on where that business buys its materials and where it sells its products. Business transactions are usually conducted in the currency of the particular region in which they take place. When business is conducted in Japan, transactions are likely to be in yen. In the United Kingdom, transactions are in pounds. With the adoption of the euro in the EU, the number of currencies in that region has been reduced. At present, the EU-member countries using the euro include Austria, Belgium, Cyprus, Estonia, Finland, France, Germany, Greece, Ireland, Italy, Luxembourg, Malta, the Netherlands, Portugal, Slovakia, Slovenia, and Spain. Other countries' currencies

exchange rate the rate at which a nation's currency can be exchanged for the currencies of other nations.

devaluation drop in a currency's value relative to other currencies or to a fixed standard.

A currency devaluation in Brazil made investing in the country relatively cheap. Foreign companies poured money into many of Brazil's industries, including tourism, construction, banking, and communications.

John Wang/Photodisc/Getty Images, Inc.

include the British pound, Australian dollar, the Indian rupee, the Brazilian real, the Mexican peso, the Taiwanese dollar, and the South African rand.

Exchange rate changes can quickly create—or wipe out—a competitive advantage, so they are important factors in decisions about whether to invest abroad. In Europe, a declining dollar means that a price of 10 euros is worth more, so companies are pressured to lower prices. At the same time, if the dollar falls it makes European vacations less affordable for U.S. tourists because their dollars are worth less relative to the euro.

On the Internet you can find currency converters to calculate conversions and help you understand the spending power of a U.S. dollar in other countries.

Currencies that owners can easily convert into other currencies are called *hard currencies*. Examples include the euro, the U.S. dollar, and the Japanese yen. The Russian ruble and many central European currencies are considered soft currencies because they cannot be readily converted. Exporters trading with these countries sometimes prefer to barter, accepting payment in oil, timber, or other commodities that they can resell for hard-currency payments.

The foreign currency market is the largest financial market in the world, with a daily volume of about $4 trillion in U.S. dollars.[12] This is about 10 times the size of all the world's stock markets combined, so the foreign exchange market is the most liquid and efficient financial market in the world.

Assessment Check ✓

1. Compare balance of trade and balance of payments.
2. Explain the function of an exchange rate.
3. What happens when a currency is devalued?

CLASS ACTIVITY:
Ask students who are from other countries or who have traveled internationally about the differences they have seen in the way products such as Coca Cola or McDonald's are offered around the world.

LECTURE ENHANCER:
Choose one of the four barriers shown and discuss how it affects trade between the United States and another country.

Barriers to International Trade

All businesses encounter barriers in their operations, whether they sell only to local customers or trade in international markets. Countries such as Australia and New Zealand regulate the hours and days retailers may be open. In addition to complying with a variety of laws and different currencies, international companies may also have to reformulate their products to accommodate different tastes in new locations. By focusing on cookie products that Chinese consumers like, Kraft Foods quadrupled its revenues in China in a four-year period. The next frontier: the Chinese breakfast market.[13]

In addition to social and cultural differences, companies engaged in international business face economic barriers as well as legal and political ones. Some of the hurdles shown in Figure 4.2 are easily breached, but others require major changes in a company's business strategy. To successfully compete in global markets, companies and their managers must understand not only how these barriers affect international trade but also how to overcome them.

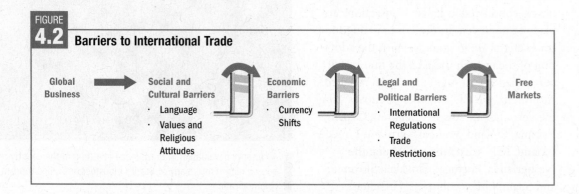

FIGURE 4.2 **Barriers to International Trade**

Social and Cultural Differences

The social and cultural differences among nations range from language and customs to educational background and religious holidays. Understanding and respecting these differences are critical to pave the way for international business success. Businesspeople with knowledge of host countries' cultures, languages, social values, and religious attitudes and practices are well equipped for the marketplace and the negotiating table. Sensitivity to such elements as local attitudes, forms of address, and expectations regarding dress, body language, and timeliness also helps them win customers and achieve their business objectives. The "Business Etiquette" feature offers suggestions for understanding the Japanese culture.

Language English is the second most widely spoken language in the world, followed by Spanish, Hindi, Arabic, and Bengali. Only Mandarin Chinese is more commonly used. Understanding a business colleague's primary language may prove to be the difference between closing an international business transaction and losing the sale to someone else. Company representatives operating in foreign markets must not only choose correct and appropriate words but also must translate words correctly to convey the intended meanings. Firms may also need to rename products or rewrite slogans for foreign markets.

Potential communication barriers include more than mistranslation. Companies may present messages through inappropriate media, overlook local customs and regulations, or ignore differences in taste. One U.S. executive recently lost a deal in China by giving the prospective client a set of four antique clocks wrapped in white paper. Unfortunately, the number four and the Chinese word for clock are similar to the word "death," while white is the traditional color for funerals.[14] Cultural sensitivity is especially critical in cyberspace. Web site developers must be aware that visitors to a site may come from anywhere in the world. Some icons that seem friendly to U.S. Internet users may shock people from other countries. A person making a high-five hand gesture would be insulting people in Greece; the same is true of making a circle with the thumb and index

BusinessEtiquette

Tips for Understanding Japanese Culture

Japan's 127 million people live in a fairly small area and tend to be reserved and introverted; their culture emphasizes conformity more than in the United States. Their literacy rate is nearly 100 percent; 95 percent of the population has completed high school. Here are some tips for respecting Japanese culture that can help you in your global business dealings.

- Dress to impress. Casual wear is not appropriate in work situations.
- Because shoes are often removed indoors in Japan, choose slip-on styles that are easy to get on and off.
- Remember that in Japan a smile can legitimately mean many things, including anger, sorrow, or embarrassment.
- Keep in mind that the Japanese don't make frequent eye contact and are comfortable with silence.
- Remember to give and receive business cards with both hands. Show respect for a business card you are given by examining it carefully.
- Always wrap gifts. In Japan it's safest to have the store wrap your gifts to ensure the paper and other details are appropriate. White, for instance, symbolizes death.
- Keep in mind that the Japanese prefer not saying no and may say yes when they mean otherwise.

Sources: World Population Review, "Population of Japan 2012," www.worldpopulationreview .com, accessed March 2, 2012; "Japanese Etiquette," *Cultural Savvy.com*, www.culturalsavvy.com, accessed February 24, 2011; "Japan," *Cyborlink.com*, www.cyborlink.com, accessed February 24, 2011; Emily Maltby, "Expanding Abroad? Avoid Cultural Gaffes," *The Wall Street Journal*, January 19, 2010, p. B5.

LECTURE ENHANCER:
Can you think of a specific issue, tradition, or social norm within another culture that an American should be particularly sensitive to when doing business within that culture?

finger in Brazil, a thumbs-up sign in Egypt, and a two-fingered peace sign with the back of the hand facing out in Great Britain.

Gift-giving traditions employ the language of symbolism. For example, in Latin America, knives and scissors should not be given as gifts because they represent the severing of friendship. Flowers are generally acceptable, but Mexicans use yellow flowers in their Day of the Dead festivities, so they are associated with death.

Values and Religious Attitudes Even though today's world is shrinking in many ways, people in different countries do not necessarily share the same values or religious attitudes. Marked differences remain in workers' attitudes from country to country, for instance.

U.S. society places a higher value on business efficiency and low unemployment than European society, where employee benefits are more valued. The U.S. government does not regulate vacation time, and employees typically receive no paid vacation during their first year of employment, then two weeks' vacation, and eventually up to three or four weeks if they stay with the same employer for many years. In contrast, the EU mandates a minimum paid vacation of four weeks per year, and most Europeans get five or six weeks. In these countries, a U.S. company that opens a manufacturing plant would not be able to hire any local employees without offering vacations in line with a nation's business practices.

U.S. culture values national unity, with tolerance of regional differences. The United States is viewed as a national market with a single economy. European countries that are part of the 27-member EU are trying to create a similar marketplace. However, many resist the idea of being European citizens first and British, Danish, or Dutch citizens second. British consumers differ from Italians in important ways, and U.S. companies that fail to recognize this variation will run into problems with brand acceptance.

Religion plays an important role in every society, so businesspeople must also cultivate sensitivity to the dominant religions in countries where they operate. Understanding religious cycles and the timing of major holidays can help prevent embarrassing moments when scheduling meetings, trade shows, conferences, or events such as the opening of a new manufacturing plant. People doing business in Saudi Arabia must take into account Islam's month-long observance of Ramadan, when work ends at noon. Friday is the Muslim formal day of worship, so the Saudi workweek runs from Saturday through Thursday. Also, many Muslims abstain from alcohol and consider pork unclean, so gifts of pigskin or liquor would be offensive.

Economic Differences

Business opportunities are flourishing in densely populated countries such as China and India, as local consumers eagerly buy Western products. Although such prospects might tempt American firms, managers must first consider the economic factors involved in doing business in these markets. A country's size, per-capita income, and stage of economic development are among the economic factors to consider when evaluating it as a candidate for an international business venture. Tata, for instance, has an eye on Western auto buyers, even as it markets its low-budget Nano car for the home market in India. See the "Hit & Miss" feature for details.

Infrastructure Along with other economic measures, businesses should consider a country's infrastructure basic systems of communication, transportation, and energy facilities in a country. **Infrastructure** refers to basic systems of communication (telecommunications, television, radio, and print media), transportation (roads and highways, railroads, and airports), and energy facilities (power plants and gas and electric utilities). The Internet and technology use can also be considered part of infrastructure.

Hit & Miss

The Tiny Nano—A Potential Hit for Tata Motors

When the Tata Nano arrived in the United States from India, it didn't hit the road, it went on display at the Cooper-Hewitt National Design Museum in New York. "As the world's most affordable car, it is a design achievement," said a museum director.

Retailing for $2,500 in India, the Nano is also safe and sturdy, and a potential revolution in transportation for millions of Indian families that can't otherwise afford a car. To keep costs low, Tata relied on existing parts and a highly simplified design. "My particular fascination about the Nano is what I refer to as the 'Nano effect' on the rest of the world's vehicle industry," said one research director. He predicts consumers in other countries will want to buy a car at that low price point.

In addition to developing the Nano, the $63-billion Indian conglomerate went on a "Western" shopping spree recently, purchasing the iconic UK luxury car brands Jaguar and Land Rover. The company says that these brands have now become one of the biggest contributors to the firm's overall earnings.

Questions for Critical Thinking

1. Do you think Tata's goal of making transportation affordable in developing countries is realistic? Why?

2. Can you think of any disadvantages for low-income markets of having a sudden influx of cars on the road?

Sources: Nano Web site, www.tatanano.inservices.tatamotors.com, accessed March 2, 2012; Devang Murthy, "Tata Motors Global Sales Rise 21 Percent," http://www.topnews.in, February 15, 2012; "Tata Nano Diesel May Launch by September 2011," *Auto News India*, http://www.autonewsindia.info, accessed February 15, 2012; Alan Gell, "The World's Cheapest Car: 2011 Tata Nano," *Examiner.com*, http://www.examiner.com, accessed February 15, 2012; Phil Patton, "A Tata Nano Takes Manhattan," *The New York Times*, http://www.nytimes.com, accessed February 12, 2012; April K. Gupta and Haiyan Wang, "Tata Nano: Not Just a Car But Also a Platform," *BusinessWeek*, http://www.businessweek.com, accessed February 15, 2012.

Financial systems provide a type of infrastructure for businesses. In the United States, buyers have widespread access to checks, credit cards, and debit cards, as well as electronic systems for processing those forms of payment. In many African countries, such as Ethiopia, local businesses do not accept credit cards, so travelers to the capital city, Addis Ababa, are warned to bring plenty of cash and traveler's checks.

Currency Conversion and Shifts Despite growing similarities in infrastructure, businesses crossing national borders encounter basic economic differences: national currencies. Foreign currency fluctuations may present added problems for global businesses. As explained earlier in the chapter, the values of the world's major currencies fluctuate—sometimes drastically—in relation to each other. Rapid and unexpected currency shifts can make pricing in local currencies difficult. Shifts in exchange rates can also influence the attractiveness of various business decisions. A devalued currency may make a nation less desirable as an export destination because of reduced demand in that market. However, devaluation can make the nation desirable as an investment opportunity because investments there will be a bargain in terms of the investor's currency.

Political and Legal Differences

Like social, cultural, and economic differences, legal and political differences in host countries can pose barriers to international trade. To compete in today's world marketplace, managers involved in international business must be well versed in legislation that affects their industries. Some countries impose general trade restrictions. Others have established detailed rules that regulate how foreign companies can operate.

Political Climate An important factor in any international business investment is the stability of the political climate. The political structures of many nations promote stability similar to that in the United States. Other nations, such as Indonesia, Congo, and Bosnia, feature quite different—and frequently changing—structures. Host nations often pass laws designed to protect their own interests, sometimes at the expense of foreign businesses.

CLASS ACTIVITY: Discuss the recent difficulties Google has faced doing business in China.

After a revolt overthrew long-time Libyan dictator Muammar Gaddafi, a period of uncertainty followed. Many foreign entities doing business in Libya became concerned about what the revolution would mean for the continued operation of their businesses in the war-torn country. However, Libya's Transitional National Council—the interim governing body—declared that it would honor the contracts and arrangements instituted under the previous regime.[15]

Legal Environment When conducting business internationally, managers must be familiar with three dimensions of the legal environment: U.S. law, international regulations, and the laws of the countries in which they plan to trade. Some laws protect the rights of foreign companies to compete in the United States. Others dictate actions allowed for U.S. companies doing business in foreign countries.

The *Foreign Corrupt Practices Act* forbids U.S. companies from bribing foreign officials, political candidates, or government representatives. Although the law has been in effect since 1977, in the past few years the U.S. government has increased its enforcement, including major proceedings in the pharmaceutical, medical device, and financial industries. The United States, United Kingdom, France, Germany, and 36 other countries have signed the Organization for Economic Cooperation and Development Anti-Bribery Convention.

Still, corruption continues to be an international problem. Its pervasiveness, combined with U.S. prohibitions, creates a difficult obstacle for U.S. businesspeople who want to do business in many foreign countries. Chinese pay *huilu*; Russians rely on *vzyatka*. In the Middle East, palms are greased with *baksheesh*. Figure 4.3 compares 179 countries based

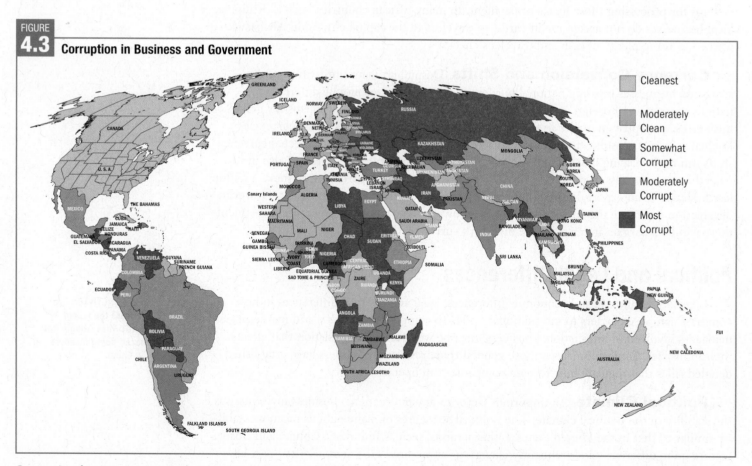

FIGURE 4.3 Corruption in Business and Government

Cleanest
Moderately Clean
Somewhat Corrupt
Moderately Corrupt
Most Corrupt

Source: Data from Transparency International, "Annual Corruption Perceptions Index," http://www.transparency.org, accessed February 15, 2012.

Going Green

Canon Aids Global Reforestation Program

Forests are home to some 300 million people around the globe, about 60 million of whom depend almost entirely on forest habitats for their survival. Nearly 2 million people worldwide make their living from forests in some way, and those numbers don't begin to describe the plant and animal species that flourish in forest habitats.

Canon, the $45 billion global digital imaging company, is stepping in to help reforesting efforts around the world. Its Canon Forestry Program has planted more than 100,000 trees so far, not only in U.S. locations such as Wisconsin and South Carolina in partnership with the Arbor Day Foundation, but also in Vietnam, where reforestation can help reduce the deadly impact of floods as well as help remove harmful carbon dioxide from the air.

An Arbor Day Foundation manager said, "These trees will provide cleaner air and water, habitat for wildlife, and beauty for everyone to enjoy for years to come. By planting trees, Canon USA is demonstrating their commitment to helping the environment for this and future generations."

Questions for Critical Thinking

1. Where else in the world do you think Canon could take an active role in reforestation?

2. Canon USA also plants trees in response to consumers' purchase of its environmentally conscious "Generation Green" brand products. Do you think this strategy would work globally? Why or why not?

Sources: "2011/2012 Canon Social & Cultural Support Activities," company Web site, accessed January 16, 2012, www.canon.com; "Canon Vietnam Continues Reforestation Project," company Web site, accessed January 16, 2012, www.canon.com; "What Does FAO Do?: Forestry," Organization Web site, Food and Agriculture Organization of the United Nations, accessed January 16, 2012, www.fao.org; "Canon USA Plants More than 78,000 Trees in South Carolina and Wisconsin Through the Arbor Day Foundation," Business Wire, December 16, 2011, www.marketwatch.com.

---

on surveys of perceived corruption. This Corruption Perceptions Index is computed by Transparency International, a Berlin-based organization that rates the degree of corruption observed by businesspeople and the general public.

The growth of online business has introduced new elements to the legal climate of international business. Patents, brand names, trademarks, copyrights, and other intellectual property are difficult to police, given the availability of information on the Internet. However, some countries are adopting laws to protect information obtained by electronic contacts. Malaysia imposes stiff fines and long jail terms on those convicted of illegally accessing computers and using information that passes through them.

International Regulations To regulate international commerce, the United States and many other countries have ratified treaties and signed agreements that dictate the conduct of international business and protect some of its activities. The United States has entered into many *friendship, commerce, and navigation treaties* with other nations. Such treaties address many aspects of international business relations, including the right to conduct business in the treaty partner's domestic market. Other international business agreements involve product standards, patents, trademarks, reciprocal tax policies, export controls, international air travel, and international communications. Some international efforts to protect the environment are voluntary, such as Canon's reforestation project. See the "Going Green" feature for the story.

When Congress granted China full trade relations with the United States, China agreed to lower trade barriers, including subsidies that held down the prices of food exports, restrictions on where foreign law firms can open offices, and taxes charged on imported goods. In exchange for China's promise to halve these taxes, called *tariffs*, the United States granted Chinese businesses equal access to U.S. markets enjoyed by most other countries.

Many types of regulations affect the actions of managers doing business in international markets. Not only must worldwide producers and marketers maintain required minimum quality levels for all the countries in which they operate, but they must comply

LECTURE ENHANCER: Which countries seem to have the most corruption?

with numerous specific local regulations. Britain prevents advertisers from encouraging children to engage in such unhealthy behavior as overeating or replacing regular meals with candy and snack foods. Malaysia's Censorship Board prohibits nudity and profanity on TV. Germany and France allow publishers to set prices that retailers charge for their books.

Italian clothing manufacturers have long enjoyed high status for their fabrics and workmanship. However, they believed they were being victimized by a lax labeling system when international clothing designers bought cheaper fabric in China or Bulgaria, had the garments cut in countries with lower labor costs, then sent them to Italy for final sewing. There, they tacked on the prestigious "Made in Italy" label and charged a high price for the goods. The Italian manufacturers pushed for a law requiring that two of the four stages of clothing production must take place in Italy in order to earn the "Made in Italy" label.[16]

Types of Trade Restrictions

tariffs taxes, surcharges, or duties on foreign products.

Trade restrictions such as taxes on imports and complicated administrative procedures create additional barriers to international business. They may limit consumer choices while increasing the costs of foreign-made products. Trade restrictions are also imposed to protect citizens' security, health, and jobs. A government may limit exports of strategic and defense-related goods to unfriendly countries to protect its security, ban imports of insecticide-contaminated farm products to protect health, and restrict imports to protect domestic jobs in the importing country.

Other restrictions are imposed to promote trade with certain countries. Still others protect countries from unfair competition. Regardless of the political reasons for trade restrictions, most take the form of tariffs. In addition to tariffs, governments impose a number of non-tariff—or administrative—barriers. These include quotas, embargoes, and exchange controls.

Tariffs Taxes, surcharges, or duties on foreign products are referred to as <u>tariffs</u>. Governments may assess two types of tariffs—revenue and protective tariffs—both of which make imports more expensive for domestic buyers. Revenue tariffs generate income for the government. Upon returning home, U.S. leisure travelers who are out of the country more than 48 hours and who bring back goods purchased abroad may pay import taxes on the goods' value depending on the country of origin. This duty goes directly to the U.S. Treasury. The sole purpose of a protective tariff is to raise the retail price of imported products to match or exceed the prices of similar products manufactured in the home country. In other words, protective tariffs seek to limit imports and level the playing field for local competitors.

Of course, tariffs create a disadvantage to companies that want to export to the countries imposing the tariffs. In addition, governments do not always agree on the reasons behind protective tariffs so they do not always have the desired effect. The United States imposes a tariff on foreign competitors accused of selling products at lower prices in the United States than U.S. manufacturers charge. The government passed a bill giving the money from these tariffs directly to U.S. plaintiff companies, instead of to the Treasury as in the past. The European Union complies with the Information Technology Agreement (ITA) by eliminating all tariffs on imported electronics goods such as computers and computer parts, flat-panel screens, and fax machines.[17]

More severe than a quota, an embargo imposes a total ban on importing a specified product or even a total halt to trading with a particular country. One result of the United States' long-standing trade embargo with Cuba is the lack of new cars in the country—as you can see in this Cuban neighborhood.

Non-tariff Barriers Non-tariff, or administrative, trade barriers restrict imports in more subtle ways than tariffs. These measures may take such forms as quotas on imports, restrictive standards for imports, and export subsidies. Because many countries have recently substantially reduced tariffs or eliminated them entirely, they increasingly use non-tariff barriers to control flows of imported products.

Quotas limit the amounts of particular products that countries can import during specified time periods. Limits may be set as quantities, such as number of cars or bushels of wheat, or as values, such as dollars' worth of cigarettes. Governments regularly set quotas for agricultural products and sometimes for imported automobiles. The United States, for example, sets a quota on imports of sugar. Imports under the quota amount are subject to a lower tariff than shipments above the quota. Sugar and related products imported at the higher rate may enter the country in unlimited quantities, however.[18]

Quotas help prevent **dumping**. In one form of dumping, a company sells products abroad at prices below its cost of production. In another, a company exports a large quantity of a product at a lower price than the same product in the home market and drives down the price of the domestic product. Dumping benefits domestic consumers in the importing market, but it hurts domestic producers. It also allows companies to gain quick entry to foreign markets.

More severe than a quota, an **embargo** imposes a total ban on importing a specified product or even a total halt to trading with a particular country. The United States has a long-standing trade embargo with Cuba. Embargo durations can vary to accommodate changes in foreign policy.

Another form of administrative trade restriction is **exchange control**. Imposed through a central bank or government agency, exchange controls affect both exporters and importers. Firms that gain foreign currencies through exporting are required to sell them to the central bank or another agency. Importers must buy foreign currencies to pay for their purchases from the same agency. The exchange control authority can then allocate, expand, or restrict foreign exchange in accordance with national policy.

[4]
Reducing Barriers to International Trade

Although tariffs and administrative barriers still restrict trade, overall the world is moving toward free trade. Several types of organizations ease barriers to international trade, including groups that monitor trade policies and practices and institutions that offer monetary assistance. Another type of federation designed to ease trade barriers is the multinational economic community, such as the European Union. This section looks at the roles these organizations play.

Organizations Promoting International Trade

For the 60-plus years of its existence, the **General Agreement on Tariffs and Trade (GATT)**, an international trade accord, sponsored a series of negotiations, called rounds, which substantially reduced worldwide tariffs and other barriers. Major industrialized nations founded the multinational organization in 1947 to work toward reducing tariffs and

quota limit set on the amounts of particular products that countries can import during specified time periods.

dumping selling products abroad at prices below production costs or below typical prices in the home market to capture market share from domestic competitors.

embargo total ban on importing specific products or a total halt to trading with a particular country.

exchange control restriction on importation of certain products or against certain companies to reduce trade and expenditures of foreign currency.

Assessment Check ✓

1. How might values and attitudes form a barrier to trade, and how can they be overcome?

2. What is a tariff? What is its purpose?

3. Why is dumping a problem for companies marketing goods internationally?

General Agreement on Tariffs and Trade (GATT) international trade accord that substantially reduced worldwide tariffs and other trade barriers.

relaxing import quotas. The last set of completed negotiations—the Uruguay Round—cut average tariffs by one-third, in excess of $700 billion; reduced farm subsidies; and improved protection for copyright and patent holders. In addition, international trading rules now apply to various service industries. Finally, the new agreement established the **World Trade Organization (WTO)** to succeed GATT. This organization includes representatives from 153 countries.

World Trade Organization

Since 1995, the WTO has monitored GATT agreements among the member nations, mediated disputes, and continued the effort to reduce trade barriers throughout the world. Unlike provisions in GATT, the WTO's decisions are binding on parties involved in disputes.

The WTO has grown more controversial in recent years as it issues decisions that have implications for working conditions and the environment in member nations. Concerns have been expressed that the WTO's focus on lowering trade barriers encourages businesses to keep costs down through practices that may increase pollution and human rights abuses. Particularly worrisome is the fact that the organization's member countries must agree on policies, and developing countries tend not to be eager to lose their low-cost advantage by enacting stricter labor and environmental laws. Other critics claim that if well-funded U.S. firms such as fast-food chains, entertainment companies, and Internet retailers can freely enter foreign markets, they will wipe out smaller foreign businesses serving the distinct tastes and practices of other countries' cultures.

Trade unions in developed nations complain that the WTO's support of free trade makes it easier to export manufacturing jobs to low-wage countries. But many small and midsize firms have benefited from the WTO's reduction of trade barriers and lowering of the cost of trade. They currently make up 97 percent of all firms that export goods and services, according to the Department of Commerce.

The most recent round of WTO talks was called the *Doha Round* after the city in Qatar where it began. After several years, discussion continues on ways to improve global agricultural trade and trade among developing countries, with the goal of reducing domestic price supports, eliminating export subsidies, and improving market access for goods. Such changes could help farmers in developing countries compete in the global marketplace.[19]

World Bank

Shortly after the end of World War II, industrialized nations formed an organization to lend money to less developed and developing countries. The **World Bank** primarily funds projects that build or expand nations' infrastructure such as transportation, education, and medical systems and facilities. The World Bank and other development banks provide the largest source of advice and assistance to developing nations. Often, in exchange for granting loans, the World Bank imposes requirements intended to build the economies of borrower nations.

The World Bank has been criticized for making loans with conditions that ultimately hurt the borrower nations. When developing nations are required to balance government budgets, they are sometimes forced to cut vital social programs. Critics also say that the World Bank should consider the impact of its loans on the environment and working conditions.

International Monetary Fund

Established a year after the World Bank, the **International Monetary Fund (IMF)** was created to promote trade through financial cooperation and, in the process, eliminate barriers. The IMF makes short-term loans to member nations that are unable to meet their expenses. It operates as a lender of last resort for troubled nations. In exchange for these emergency loans, IMF lenders frequently require significant commitments from the borrowing nations to address the problems that led to the crises. These steps may include curtailing imports or even devaluing currencies. Throughout its existence, the IMF has worked to prevent financial crises by warning the international business community when countries encounter problems meeting their financial obligations. Often, the IMF lends to countries to keep them from defaulting on prior debts and to prevent economic crises in particular countries from spreading to other nations.

However, some countries owe far more money than they can ever hope to repay, and the debt payments make it impossible for their governments to deliver desperately needed services to their citizens. Following a devastating earthquake in Haiti, the G7 countries (the world's most industrialized nations including the United States, Canada, France, and Brazil) promised to cancel any remaining debt owed them by Haiti. The World Bank not only pledged financial support as Haiti struggled to get back on its feet but also waived payment on Haiti's debt for five years while it sought a way to cancel the remaining debt.[20]

International Economic Communities

International economic communities reduce trade barriers and promote regional economic integration. In the simplest approach, countries may establish a *free-trade area* in which they trade freely among themselves without tariffs or trade restrictions. Each maintains its own tariffs for trade outside this area. A *customs union* sets up a free-trade area and specifies a uniform tariff structure for members' trade with nonmember nations. In a *common market*, or economic union, members go beyond a customs union and try to bring all of their trade rules into agreement.

One example of a free-trade area is the **North American Free Trade Agreement (NAFTA)** enacted by the United States, Canada, and Mexico. Other examples of regional trading blocs include the MERCOSUR customs union (joining Brazil, Argentina, Paraguay, Uruguay, Chile, and Bolivia) and the 10-country Association of South East Asian Nations (ASEAN).

North American Free Trade Agreement (NAFTA) agreement among the United States, Canada, and Mexico to break down tariffs and trade restrictions.

NAFTA

NAFTA became effective in 1994, creating the world's largest free-trade zone with the United States, Canada, and Mexico. With a combined population of more than 463 million and a total GDP of more than $18 trillion, North America represents one of the world's most attractive markets. The United States—the single largest market—dominates North America's business environment. Although fewer than 1 person in 20 lives in the United States, the nation's more than $15 trillion GDP represents about one-fourth of total world output.[21]

Canada is far less densely populated but has achieved a similar level of economic development. In fact, Canada's economy has been growing at a faster rate than the U.S. economy in recent years. More than two-thirds of Canada's GDP is generated in the services sector, and three of every four Canadian workers are engaged in service occupations. The country's per-capita GDP places Canada among the top nations in terms of its people's spending power. Canada's economy is fueled by trade with the United States, and its home markets are strong as well. The United States and Canada are each other's biggest trading partners. About 75 percent of Canada's exports and about 50 percent of its imports are to or from the United States.[22] U.S. business is also attracted by Canada's human resources. For instance, all major U.S. automakers have large production facilities in Canada.

With NAFTA allowing free trade for the United States, Canada, and Mexico, the amount of goods and services traded is healthy for Canada's economy as well as the United States.

Mexico is moving from developing nation to industrial nation status, thanks largely to NAFTA. Mexico's trade with the United States and Canada has tripled since the signing of NAFTA, although 18 percent of the country's 115 million people live below the poverty line and per-capita income is about a quarter that of the United States. But Mexico's border with the United States is busy with a nearly endless stream of traffic transporting goods from Mexican factories into the United States. The United States is Mexico's largest trading partner by far, accounting for about 75 percent of total exports and 60 percent of all Mexico's imports.[23]

By eliminating all trade barriers and investment restrictions among the United States, Canada, and Mexico over a 15-year period, NAFTA opened more doors for free trade. The agreement also eased regulations governing services, such as banking, and established uniform legal requirements for protection of intellectual property. The three nations can now trade with one another without tariffs or other trade barriers, simplifying shipments of goods across the partners' borders. Standardized customs and uniform labeling regulations create economic efficiencies and smooth import and export procedures. Trade among the partners has increased steadily, more than doubling since NAFTA took effect.

CAFTA-DR

The **Central America–Dominican Republic Free Trade Agreement (CAFTA-DR)** created a free-trade area among the United States, Costa Rica, the Dominican Republic (the DR of the title), El Salvador, Guatemala, Honduras, and Nicaragua. The agreement—the first of its kind between the United States and these smaller developing economies—ends tariffs on the nearly $40 billion in products traded between the United States and its Latin American neighbors. Agricultural producers such as corn, soybean, and dairy farmers stand to gain under the relaxed trade rules. Overall, CAFTA-DR's effects have increased both exports and imports substantially, much as NAFTA did.[24]

European Union

Perhaps the best-known example of a common market is the **European Union (EU)**. The EU combines 27 countries, over 503 million people, and a total GDP of roughly $15.39 trillion to form a huge common market. Figure 4.4 shows the member countries. Current candidates for membership are Croatia, Iceland, Montenegro, Turkey, and the former Yugoslav Republic of Macedonia.[25]

The EU's goals include promoting economic and social progress, introducing European citizenship as a complement to national citizenship, and giving the EU a significant role in international affairs. To achieve its goal of a borderless Europe, the EU is removing barriers to free trade among its members. This highly complex process involves standardizing

Central America–Dominican Republic Free Trade Agreement (CAFTA-DR) agreement among the United States, Costa Rica, the Dominican Republic, El Salvador, Guatemala, Honduras, and Nicaragua to reduce tariffs and trade restrictions.

European Union (EU) 27-nation European economic alliance.

LECTURE ENHANCER: What are some concerns that member countries might have regarding new countries joining the EU?

Roger Lecuyer/iStockphoto

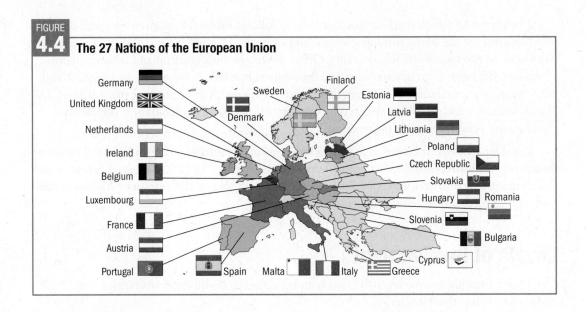

FIGURE 4.4 The 27 Nations of the European Union

Germany
United Kingdom
Netherlands
Ireland
Belgium
Luxembourg
France
Austria
Portugal
Sweden
Denmark
Spain
Malta
Finland
Estonia
Latvia
Lithuania
Poland
Czech Republic
Slovakia
Hungary
Slovenia
Italy
Greece
Cyprus
Bulgaria
Romania

business regulations and requirements, standardizing import duties and taxes, and eliminating customs checks so that companies can transport goods from England to Italy or Poland as easily as from New York to Boston.

Unifying standards and laws can contribute to economic growth. But just as NAFTA sparked fears in the United States about free trade with Mexico, some people in western Europe worried that opening trade with such countries as Poland, Hungary, and the Czech Republic would cause jobs to flow eastward to lower-wage economies.

The EU also introduced the euro to replace currencies such as the French franc and Italian lira. For the 17 member-states that have adopted the euro, potential benefits include eliminating the economic costs of currency exchange and simplifying price comparisons. Businesses and their customers now make check and credit card transactions in euros and use euro notes and coins in making cash purchases.

5 Going Global

While expanding into overseas markets can increase profits and marketing opportunities, it also introduces new complexities to a firm's business operations. Before deciding to go global, a company faces a number of key decisions, beginning with the following:

- determining which foreign market(s) to enter
- analyzing the expenditures required to enter a new market
- deciding the best way to organize the overseas operations.

These issues vary in importance depending on the level of involvement a company chooses. Education and employee training in the host country would be much more important for an electronics manufacturer building an Asian factory than for a firm that is simply planning to export American-made products.

CLASS ACTIVITY:
Lead a discussion of the factors contributing to the recent tension between the more prosperous European countries and the so-called PIIGS (Portugal, Italy, Ireland, Greece, Spain) members of the EU.

Assessment Check ☑

1. What international trade organization succeeded GATT, and what is its goal?

2. Compare and contrast the goals of the World Bank and the International Monetary Fund.

3. What are the goals of the European Union, and how do they promote international trade?

LECTURE ENHANCER:
Looking at Table 4.3, which
site do you think would be
the most objective?

The choice of which markets to enter usually follows extensive research focusing on local demand for the firm's products, availability of needed resources, and ability of the local workforce to produce world-class quality. Other factors include existing and potential competition, tariff rates, currency stability, and investment barriers. A variety of government and other sources are available to facilitate this research process. A good starting place is the CIA's *World Factbook*, which contains country-by-country information on geography, population, government, economy, and infrastructure.

U.S. Department of Commerce counselors working at district offices offer a full range of international business advice, including computerized market data and names of business and government contacts in dozens of countries. As Table 4.3 shows, the Internet provides access to many resources for international trade information.

Levels of Involvement

After a firm has completed its research and decided to do business overseas, it can choose one or more strategies:

- exporting or importing

- entering into contractual agreements such as franchising, licensing, and subcontracting deals

- direct investment in the foreign market through acquisitions, joint ventures, or establishment of an overseas division.

TABLE 4.3 International Trade Research Resources on the Internet

WEB SITE AND ADDRESS	GENERAL DESCRIPTION
Europages http://www.europages.com	Directory of and links to Europe's top 500,000 companies in 33 European countries
World Trade Organization http://www.wto.org	Details on the trade policies of various governments
CIA *World Factbook* https://www.cia.gov/cia/library/publications/the-world-factbook	Basic facts about the world's nations, from geography to economic conditions
STAT-USA http://www.stat-usa.gov	Extensive trade and economic data, information about trends, daily intelligence reports, and background data (access requires paid subscription to the service)
U.S. Commercial Service http://trade.gov/cs	Information about Commerce Department counseling services, trade events, and U.S. export regulations
U.S. Business Advisor http://www.SBA.gov	One-stop access to a range of federal government information, services, and transactions
U.S. State Department http://www.travel.state.gov/travel/cis_pa_tw/tw/tw_1764.html	Listing of the State Department's latest travel warnings about conditions that may affect safety abroad, supplemented by the list of consulate addresses and country information

Although the company's risk increases with the level of its involvement, so does its overall control of all aspects of producing and selling its goods or services.

For Jeffery Adler, it was an offer too good to refuse. His California-based business, Dlush Beverage Joints, a small chain of shops that served fruit smoothies, tea, and baked goods was paid a visit one day by several members of the wealthy Alghanim family from Kuwait. The Alghanims liked the experience so much they proposed a sweet business deal to Adler and his firm: Alghanim Sons Group would become the Persian Gulf franchisees of Dlush. Alghanim now has a 20-year franchise agreement to develop an unlimited number of Dlush stores in six countries throughout the region. Adler receives a percentage of the stores' revenues and a steady income, and the Dlush brand had an immediate international presence.[26]

Zazzle, on the other hand, has worked to develop an international presence via the Internet. The California company offers specialized t-shirts, mugs, hats, and other such items. Zazzle has tailored its business to each specific country by building individual Web sites (in different languages) for 17 countries and offering shipping to another 70. Michael Karns, head of Zazzle's international development, keeps a close watch on all aspects of the company's overseas e-commerce.[27]

Importers and Exporters When a firm brings in goods produced abroad to sell domestically, it is an importer. Conversely, companies are exporters when they produce—or purchase—goods at home and sell them in overseas markets. An importing or exporting strategy provides the most basic level of international involvement, with the least risk and control.

Jeffery Adler, head of Dlush Beverage Joints, joined with Alghanim Sons Group, from Kuwait, to expand his business into the Persian Gulf.

Exports are frequently handled by special intermediaries called export trading companies. These firms search out competitively priced local merchandise and then resell it abroad at prices high enough to cover expenses and earn profits. When a retail chain such as Dallas-based Pier 1 Imports wants to purchase West African products for its store shelves, it may contact an export trading company operating in a country such as Ghana. The local firm is responsible for monitoring quality, packaging the order for transatlantic shipment, arranging transportation, and arranging for completion of customs paperwork and other steps required to move the product from Ghana to the United States.

Firms engage in exporting of two types: indirect and direct. A company engages in *indirect exporting* when it manufactures a product, such as an electronic component, that becomes part of another product sold in foreign markets. The second method, *direct exporting*, occurs when a company seeks to sell its products in markets outside its own country. Often the first step for companies entering foreign markets, direct exporting is the most common form of international business. Firms that succeed at this may then move to other strategies. Crops are imported and exported globally.

In addition to reaching foreign markets by dealing with export trading companies, exporters may choose two other alternatives: export management companies and offset agreements. Rather than simply relying on an export trading company to assist in foreign markets, an exporting firm may turn to an *export management company* for advice and expertise. These international specialists help the exporter complete paperwork, make contacts with local buyers, and comply with local laws governing labeling, product safety, and performance testing. At the same time, the exporting firm retains much more control than would be possible with an export trading company.

An *offset agreement* matches a small business with a major international firm. It basically makes the small firm a subcontractor to the larger one. Such an entry strategy helps a new exporter by allowing it to share in the larger company's international expertise. The small firm also benefits in such important areas as international transaction documents and financing, while the larger company benefits from the local expertise and capabilities of its smaller partner.

Countertrade A sizable share of international trade involves payments made in the form of local products, not currency. This system of international bartering agreements is called **countertrade**.

A common reason for resorting to international barter is inadequate access to needed foreign currency. To complete an international sales agreement, the seller may agree to accept part or all of the purchase cost in merchandise rather than currency. Because the seller may decide to locate a buyer for the bartered goods before completing the transaction, a number of international buyers and sellers frequently join together in a single agreement.

Countertrade may often be a firm's only opportunity to enter a particular market. Many developing countries simply cannot obtain enough credit or financial assistance to afford the imports that their people want. Countries with heavy debt burdens also resort to countertrade. Russian buyers, whose currency is often less acceptable to foreign traders than the stronger currencies of countries such as the United States, Great Britain, Japan, and EU countries, may resort to trading local products ranging from crude oil to diamonds to vodka as payments for purchases from foreign companies unwilling to accept Russian rubles. Still, other countries such as China may restrict imports. Under such circumstances, countertrade may be the only practical way to win government approval to import needed products.

Contractual Agreements Once a company, large or small, gains some experience in international sales, it may decide to enter into contractual agreements with local parties. These arrangements can include franchising, foreign licensing, and subcontracting.

franchise contractual agreement in which a franchisee gains the right to produce and/or sell the franchisor's products under that company's brand name if they agree to certain operating requirements.

Franchising Common among U.S. companies, franchising can work well for companies seeking to expand into international markets, too. A **franchise**, as described in detail in Chapter 5, is a contractual agreement in which a wholesaler or retailer (the franchisee) gains the right to sell the franchisor's products under that company's brand name if it agrees to the related operating requirements. The franchisee can also receive marketing, management, and business services from the franchisor. While these arrangements are common among leading fast-food brands such as McDonald's and KFC, other kinds of service providers also often look to franchising as an international marketplace option.

Domino's Pizza has expanded to more than 9,000 stores in more than 60 international markets around the world. Its largest international market is in Mexico, but wherever it operates, the company fine-tunes its menus to meet local tastes with such specialties as barbecued chicken in the Bahamas, black bean sauce in Guatemala, squid in Japan, and chorizo in Mexico.[28]

Foreign Licensing In a **foreign licensing agreement**, one firm allows another to produce or sell its product, or use its trademark, patent, or manufacturing processes, in a specific geographical area. In return, the firm gets a royalty or other compensation.

Licensing can be advantageous for a small manufacturer eager to launch a well-known product overseas. Not only does it get a proven product from another market, but little or no investment is required to begin operating. The arrangement can also allow entry into a market otherwise closed to imports due to government restrictions. Sometimes a licensing agreement can ensure product freshness by allowing manufacturing to take place in the local market. Morinaga, a Japanese food manufacturer, holds licenses to produce Lipton teas, Kraft cheeses, and Sunkist fruit drinks and desserts in Japan.[29]

Subcontracting The third type of contractual agreement, **subcontracting**, involves hiring local companies to produce, distribute, or sell goods or services. This move allows a foreign firm to take advantage of the subcontractor's expertise in local culture, contacts, and regulations. Subcontracting works equally well for mail-order companies, which can farm out order fulfillment and customer service functions to local businesses. Manufacturers practice subcontracting to save money on import duties and labor costs, and businesses go this route to market products best sold by locals in a given country. Some firms, such as Maryland-based Pacific Bridge Medical, help medical manufacturers find reliable subcontractors and parts suppliers in Asia.

A key disadvantage of subcontracting is that companies cannot always control their subcontractors' business practices. Several major U.S. companies have been embarrassed by reports that their subcontractors used child labor to manufacture clothing.

Offshoring While it is not generally considered a way of initiating business internationally, *offshoring*, or the relocation of business processes to a lower-cost location overseas, has become a widespread practice. China has emerged as the preferred destination for production offshoring and India for services offshoring. Many business leaders argue, in favor of offshoring, that global firms must keep their costs as low as possible to remain competitive. But the apparent link between jobs sent overseas and jobs lost at home has made the practice controversial. Legislatures of various states have tried to slow the tide of offshoring through new laws, but many observers believe the real goal should be to improve corporate research and development efforts in the United States.

Offshoring shows no signs of slowing down, but it is changing, particularly for manufacturers. Mexico, India, and Vietnam are now the countries with the lowest manufacturing costs. Not surprisingly, maintaining flexibility by offshoring to a few different low-cost locations may be U.S. firms' lowest-risk strategy for the future. According to some analysts, if India's currency (the rupee) strengthens against the dollar, U.S. firms could shift some work to other countries, such as Vietnam. If transportation costs begin to rise, U.S. firms could move more work to Mexico.[30]

International Direct Investment Investing directly in production and marketing operations in a foreign country is the ultimate level of global involvement. Over time, a firm may become successful at conducting business in other countries through exporting and contractual agreements. Its managers may then decide to establish manufacturing facilities in those countries, open branch offices, or buy ownership interests in local companies. Because of its focus on offering consumer deals for local businesses, Groupon must invest directly in its operations overseas. See the "Hit & Miss" feature for a description of Groupon's ups and downs in foreign markets.

foreign licensing agreement international agreement in which one firm allows another to produce or sell its product, or use its trademark, patent, or manufacturing processes, in a specific geographical area in return for royalties or other compensation.

subcontracting international agreement that involves hiring local companies to produce, distribute, or sell goods or services in a specific country or geographical region.

CLASS ACTIVITY:
What countries are likely attracting little international direct investment because of political instability, crime, war, or disease?

Groupon's Goal: Spread Deals Around the World

Groupon, the Chicago-based online coupon company, has been called one of the world's hottest Internet start-ups. In its first two years, the firm developed the Internet's largest ad network and rebuffed Google's $6 billion buyout offer. Its GenX CEO Andrew Mason is considered a business superstar because of his innovative—yet simple—way of connecting buyers and sellers.

Groupon—for group coupon—works by numbers: If enough buyers sign up online for its daily coupon deal, the deal is activated. Different deals are available to its 33 million active users.

But despite the buzz, Groupon has stumbled a few times in establishing itself globally. In Japan, Groupon offered a deal for the delivery of *osechi*, a traditional New Year's meal requiring painstaking preparation and meticulous presentation. Because the local restaurant was overwhelmed by the volume of orders, many *osechi* meals arrived late and damaged, at a price consumers did not feel was worthwhile. Mason immediately apologized and promised to rebuild Groupon's reputation in Japan.

In China, Groupon has been criticized for hiring employees away from Chinese competitors; the Chinese market is jammed with about 1,000 group-buying sites, making market entry a challenge. Going forward, Groupon must take on rapidly growing competition from Europe to South America to Asia. In some cases, Groupon has already bought out the competition. Mason is unafraid of these challenges. Nor is he afraid to admit his company's mistakes—as he did in Japan—and learn from them.

Questions for Critical Thinking

1. Why should Groupon establish itself locally in each market it serves?

2. Besides apologizing, what steps might Mason and Groupon take to rebuild its image in Japan? What lessons might be learned from this as the company seeks to gain ground in China?

Sources: Company Web site, http://www.groupon.com, accessed March 2, 2012; Douglas MacMillan, "Groupon Adds 'Thumbs Up' Feedback in revamp of Web site," *Bloomberg Businessweek*, February 12, 2012; Michael Kan, "Chinese Group-Buying Sites Fight Groupon's Alleged Poaching," *PC World*, January 26, 2011, http://www.pcworld.com; "Google to Launch Groupon Competitor," *Mashable*, January 20, 2011, http://mashable .com; "Groupon Apologizes to Customers in Japan," *Associated Press*, January 17, 2011, http://www1.cw.56.com.

In an *acquisition*, a company purchases another existing firm in the host country. An acquisition permits a largely domestic business operation to gain an international presence very quickly. Polaris Industries Inc., a U.S. firm, recently acquired Swissauto Powersports, a Swiss designer of high-performance engines for recreational and racing vehicles. The two companies had a long history of partnering together, but the acquisition will brighten Polaris's international profile. It "directly supports our stated objectives to be the best in powersports and a global market leader," said Polaris's CEO.[31]

joint venture partnership between companies formed for a specific undertaking.

Joint ventures allow companies to share risks, costs, profits, and management responsibilities with one or more host country nationals. By setting up an *overseas division*, a company can conduct a significant amount of its business overseas. This strategy differs from that of a multinational company in that a firm with overseas divisions remains primarily a domestic organization with international operations. Matsushita established Panasonic Automotive Systems Asia Pacific to develop and sell new technology products in India, Thailand, Indonesia, Malaysia, the Philippines, and Vietnam.

From Multinational Corporation to Global Business

multinational corporation (MNC) firm with significant operations and marketing activities outside its home country.

A **multinational corporation (MNC)** is an organization with significant foreign operations. As Table 4.4 shows, firms headquartered in the United States make up half the list of the world's largest multinationals. Brazil, China, the Netherlands, and the United Kingdom make up the other half. Note that the two top industries are banking and oil and gas.

Many U.S. multinationals, including Nike and Walmart, have expanded their overseas operations because they believe that domestic markets are peaking and foreign markets offer greater sales and profit potential. Other MNCs are making substantial investments in

TABLE 4.4

The World's Top 10 Leading Companies (Based on a Combined Ranking for Sales, Profits, Assets, and Market Value)

RANK	COMPANY	INDUSTRY	COUNTRY OF ORIGIN
1	Exxon Mobil	Oil & Gas	United States
2	JPMorgan Chase	Banking	United States
3	General Electric	Conglomerate	United States
4	Royal Dutch Shell	Oil & Gas	Netherlands
5	ICBC	Banking	China
6	HSBC Holdings	Banking	United Kingdom
7	PetroChina	Oil & Gas	China
8	Berkshire Hathaway	Conglomerate	United States
9	Wells Fargo	Banking	United States
10	Petrobras-Petróleo Brasil	Oil & Gas	Brazil

Source: "The World's Biggest Companies," http://www.forbes.com/global2000, accessed May 2, 2012.

developing countries in part because these countries provide low-cost labor compared with the United States and western Europe. In addition, many MNCs are locating high-tech facilities in countries with large numbers of technical school graduates.

6 Developing a Strategy for International Business

In developing a framework in which to conduct international business, managers must first evaluate their corporate objectives, organizational strengths and weaknesses, and strategies for product development and marketing. They can choose to combine these elements in either a global strategy or a multidomestic strategy.

Global Business Strategies

In a **global business** (or *standardization*) **strategy**, a firm sells the same product in essentially the same manner throughout the world. Many companies simply modify their domestic business strategies by translating promotional brochures and product-use instructions into the languages of the host nations.

A global marketing perspective can be appropriate for some goods and services and certain market segments that are common to many nations. The approach works for products with nearly universal appeal, for luxury items such as jewelry and for commodities like chemicals and metals. Alcoa, for instance, is the world's biggest producers of aluminum for markets that

global business strategy offering a standardized, worldwide product and selling it in essentially the same manner throughout a firm's domestic and foreign markets.

Solving an Ethical Controversy

Bribery or the Cost of Doing Business?

Roughly translated, *guanxi* is the Chinese word for relationships and involves making business connections with local companies and officials. Some say *guanxi* is a local custom and a generally accepted business practice, while others say it is a form of bribery to extort money from companies anxious to do business in that country.

Should foreign companies practice *guanxi* when doing business in China?

PRO

1. Building mutually beneficial relationships with connected networks of local businesses and government officials provides foreign companies with strategic advantages.

2. The concept of *guanxi* is a local custom, and companies and officials expect foreign companies to seek their advice and expertise to navigate the complicated business environment in China.

CON

1. The concept of *guanxi* is another word for doing whatever it takes (no matter the cost) to make headway in the Chinese business marketplace.

2. Although they are doing business in a foreign land, U.S. companies must abide by the Foreign Corrupt Practices Act, federal legislation that prohibits the exchange of money for obtaining or retaining business.

Summary

Competing in world markets includes understanding local customs and business practices of the countries in which a company plans to operate. At the same time, however, companies must base their business strategy on solid business and ethical foundations. Regardless of the legal implications in the United States, business officials must know how to operate financially and ethically in any business situation.

Sources: Aruna Viswanatha, "U.S. Corporations Beg Clarity on Anti-Bribery Law," February 21, 2012, http://www.reuters.com; "Avon Bribery Scandal in China, Not Really a Big Deal," China Lawyer in Shanghai (blog), accessed February 13, 2012; Kelly Baldwin, "Guanxi: The Ethics of Chinese Business Relationships," http://myportfolio.usc.edu, accessed February 11, 2012; David Wolf, "Business Ethics and Culture Clashes in China," July 2, 2011, http://siliconhutong.com.

LECTURE ENHANCER:
Give an example of a U.S. company that uses a multidomestic business strategy.

multidomestic business strategy developing and marketing products to serve different needs and tastes of separate national markets.

Assessment Check ✓

1. What is a global business strategy? What are its advantages?

2. What is a multidomestic business strategy? What are its advantages?

include aerospace, automotive, building and construction, consumer electronics, packaging, and commercial transportation. Because in many applications aluminum's strength and light weight mean there are no good substitutes for it, the company forecasts a long-term increase in global demand, especially in China, India, Russia, the Middle East, and Latin America. It also views itself as committed to a global strategy that incorporates the highest ethical and sustainability practices. Recently Alcoa was awarded the top spot for its use of basic resources by the annual Covalence Ethical Rankings, a prestigious international survey that ranks the ethical performance of multinational companies.[32] Regardless of global business strategies, companies need to be aware of cultural and business customs in the countries in which they do business and whether certain behaviors are accepted as "Solving an Ethical Controversy" discusses.

Multidomestic Business Strategies

Under a **multidomestic business** (or *adaptation*) **strategy**, the firm treats each national market in a different way. It develops products and marketing strategies that appeal to the customs, tastes, and buying habits of particular national markets. Companies that neglect the global nature of the Internet can unwittingly cause problems for potential customers by failing to adapt their strategy. European consumers, for instance, were at first hesitant to adopt online ordering of products ranging from books to railroad tickets. But in recent years, Internet use in western Europe has grown dramatically. Companies as diverse as the European divisions of Amazon.com; Egg PLC of London, an online financial services company; and the French national railroad have seen the numbers of visitors to their Web sites climb, along with Internet revenues.

melhi/iStockphoto

Internet users in western Europe are no longer as concerned making purchases for such items as railroad tickets online. As this businessperson enjoys the ability to work on the train, he may be purchasing his return ticket through his online connection.

What's Ahead

Examples in this chapter indicate that businesses of all sizes are relying on world trade. Chapter 5 examines the special advantages and challenges that small-business owners encounter. In addition, a critical decision facing any new business is the choice of the most appropriate form of business ownership. Chapter 5 also examines the major ownership structures—sole proprietorship, partnership, and corporation—and assesses the pros and cons of each. The chapter closes with a discussion of recent trends affecting business ownership, such as the growing impact of franchising and business consolidations through mergers and acquisitions.

Summary of Learning Objectives

1 Explain why nations trade.

The United States is both the world's largest importer and the largest exporter, although less than 5 percent of the world's population lives within its borders. With the increasing globalization of the world's economies, the international marketplace offers tremendous opportunities for U.S. and foreign businesses to expand into new markets for their goods and services. Doing business globally provides new sources of materials and labor. Trading with other countries also reduces a company's dependence on economic conditions in its home market. Countries that encourage international trade enjoy higher levels of economic activity, employment, and wages than those that restrict it.

Nations usually benefit if they specialize in producing certain goods or services. A country has an absolute advantage if it holds a monopoly or produces a good or service at a lower cost than other nations. It has a comparative advantage if it can supply a particular product more efficiently or at a lower cost than it can produce other items.

Assessment Check Answers ✓

1.1 Why do nations trade? Nations trade because trading boosts economic growth by providing a market for products and access to needed resources. This makes production and distribution systems more efficient and reduces dependence on the economy of the domestic market.

1.2 Cite some measures of the size of the international marketplace. Although developing countries have lower per-capita incomes than developed nations in North America and western Europe, their populations are large and growing. China's population is about 1.3 billion and India's is roughly 1.2 billion.

1.3 How does a nation acquire a comparative advantage? Comparative advantage exists when a nation can supply a product more efficiently and at a lower price than it can supply other goods, compared with the outputs of other countries.

2 Describe how trade is measured.

Countries measure the level of international trade by comparing exports and imports and then calculating whether a trade surplus or a deficit exists. This is the balance of trade, which represents the difference between exports and imports. The term *balance of payments* refers to the overall flow of money into or out of a country, including overseas loans and borrowing, international investments, and profits from such investments. An exchange rate is the value of a nation's currency relative to the currency of another nation. Currency values typically fluctuate, or "float," relative to the supply and demand for specific currencies in the world market. When the value of the dollar falls compared with other currencies, the cost paid by foreign businesses and households for U.S. products declines, and demand for exports may rise. An increase in the value of the dollar raises the prices of U.S. products sold abroad, but it reduces the prices of foreign products sold in the United States.

Assessment Check Answers

2.1 Compare balance of trade and balance of payments. Balance of trade is the difference between exports and imports; balance of payments is the overall flow of money into or out of a country.

2.2 Explain the function of an exchange rate. A nation's exchange rate is the rate at which its currency can be exchanged for the currencies of other nations to make it easier for them to trade with one another.

2.3 What happens when a currency is devalued? Devaluation describes a fall in a currency's value relative to other currencies or to a fixed standard.

3 Identify the barriers to international trade.

Businesses face several obstacles in the global marketplace. Companies must be sensitive to social and cultural differences, such as languages, values, and religions, when operating in other countries. Economic differences include standard-of-living variations and levels of infrastructure development. Legal and political barriers are among the most difficult to judge. Each country sets its own laws regulating business practices. Trade restrictions such as tariffs and administrative barriers also present obstacles to international business.

Assessment Check Answers

3.1 How might values and attitudes form a barrier to trade, and how can they be overcome? Marked differences in values and attitudes, such as religious attitudes, can form barriers between traditionally capitalist countries and those adapting new capitalist systems. Many of these can be overcome by learning about and respecting such differences.

3.2 What is a tariff? What is its purpose? A tariff is a surcharge or duty charged on foreign products. Its purpose is to protect domestic producers of those items.

3.3 Why is dumping a problem for companies marketing goods internationally? Dumping is selling products abroad at prices below the cost of production or exporting products at a lower price than charged in the home market. It drives the cost of products sharply down in the market where they are dumped, thus hurting the domestic producers of those products.

4 Discuss reducing barriers to international trade.

Many international organizations seek to promote international trade by reducing barriers among nations. Examples include the World Trade Organization, the World Bank, and the International Monetary Fund. Multinational economic communities create partnerships to remove barriers to the flow of goods, capital, and people across the borders of members. Three such economic agreements are the North American Free Trade Agreement, CAFTA-DR, and the European Union.

Assessment Check Answers

4.1 What international trade organization succeeded GATT, and what is its goal? The World Trade Organization (WTO) succeeded GATT with the goal of monitoring GATT agreements, mediating disputes, and continuing the effort to reduce trade barriers throughout the world.

4.2 Compare and contrast the goals of the World Bank and the International Monetary Fund. The World Bank funds projects that build or expand nations' infrastructure such as transportation, education, and health systems and facilities. The International Monetary Fund makes short-term loans to member nations that are unable to meet their budgets. The fund operates as a lender of last resort.

4.3 What are the goals of the European Union, and how do they promote international trade? The European Union's goals include promoting economic and social progress, introducing European citizenship as a complement to national citizenship, and giving the EU a significant role in international affairs. Unifying standards and laws is expected to contribute to international trade and economic growth.

5 Explain the decisions to go global.

Exporting and importing, the first level of involvement in international business, involves the lowest degree of both risk and control. Companies may rely on export trading or management companies to help distribute their products. Contractual agreements such as franchising, foreign licensing, and subcontracting offer additional options. Franchising and licensing are especially appropriate for services. Companies may also choose local subcontractors to produce goods for local sales. International direct investment in production and marketing facilities provides the highest degree of control but also the greatest risk. Firms make direct investments by acquiring foreign companies or facilities, forming joint ventures with local firms and setting up their own overseas divisions.

Assessment Check Answers ☑

5.1 Name three possible strategies for beginning overseas business operations. Strategies are exporting or importing; contractual agreements such as franchising, licensing, or subcontracting; and making direct investments in foreign markets through acquisition, joint venture, or establishment of an overseas division.

5.2 What is countertrade? Countertrade consists of payments made in the form of local products, not currency.

5.3 Compare and contrast licensing and subcontracting. In a foreign licensing agreement, one firm allows another to produce or sell its product or use its trademark, patent, or manufacturing process in a specific geographical area in return for royalty payments or other compensation. In subcontracting, a firm hires local companies abroad to produce, distribute, or sell its goods and services.

5.4 Describe joint ventures. Joint ventures allow companies to share risks, costs, profits, and management responsibilities with one or more host-country nationals.

⌐6⌐ Discuss developing a strategy for international business.
A company that adopts a global (or standardization) strategy develops a single, standardized product and marketing strategy for implementation throughout the world. The firm sells the same product in essentially the same manner in all countries in which it operates. Under a multidomestic (or adaptation) strategy, the firm develops a different treatment for each foreign market. It develops products and marketing strategies that appeal to the customs, tastes, and buying habits of particular nations.

Assessment Check Answers ☑

6.1 What is a global business strategy? What are its advantages? A global business strategy specifies a standardized competitive strategy in which the firm sells the same product in essentially the same manner throughout the world. It works well for goods and services that are common to many nations and allows the firm to market them without making significant changes.

6.2 What is a multidomestic business strategy? What are its advantages? A multidomestic business strategy allows the firm to treat each foreign market in a different way to appeal to the customs, tastes, and buying habits of particular national markets. It allows the firm to customize its marketing appeals for individual cultures or areas.

■ Business Terms You Need to Know

exports 97	exchange control 111	European Union (EU) 114
imports 97	General Agreement on Tariffs	countertrade 118
balance of trade 101	and Trade (GATT) 111	franchise 118
balance of payments 101	World Trade Organization (WTO) 112	foreign licensing agreement 119
exchange rate 103	World Bank 112	subcontracting 119
devaluation 103	International Monetary Fund (IMF) 112	joint venture 120
infrastructure 106	North American Free Trade	multinational corporation (MNC) 120
tariffs 110	Agreement (NAFTA) 113	global business strategy 121
quotas 111	Central America–Dominican Republic	multidomestic business strategy 122
dumping 111	Free Trade Agreement	
embargo 111	(CAFTA-DR) 114	

■ Review Questions

1. How does a business decide whether to trade with a foreign country? What are the key factors for participating in the information economy on a global basis?

2. Why are developing countries such as China and India becoming important international markets?

3. What is the difference between absolute advantage and comparative advantage? Give an example of each.

4. Can a nation have a favorable balance of trade and an unfavorable balance of payments? Why or why not?

5. Identify several potential barriers to communication when a company attempts to conduct business in another country. How might these be overcome?

6. Identify and describe briefly the three dimensions of the legal environment for global business.

7. What are the major nontariff restrictions affecting international business? Describe the difference between tariff and nontariff restrictions.

8. What is NAFTA? How does it work?

9. How has the EU helped trade among European businesses?

10. What are the key choices a company must make before reaching the final decision to go global?

Projects and Teamwork Applications

1. When Britain transferred Hong Kong to China in 1997, China agreed to grant Hong Kong a high degree of autonomy as a capitalist economy for 50 years. Do you think this agreement is holding up? Why or why not? Consider China's economy, population, infrastructure, and other factors in your answer.

2. The tremendous growth of online business has introduced new elements to the legal climate of international business. Patents, brand names, copyrights, and trademarks are difficult to monitor because of the boundaryless nature of the Internet. What steps could businesses take to protect their trademarks and brands in this environment? Come up with at least five suggestions, and compare your list with those of your classmates.

3. The WTO monitors GATT agreements, mediates disputes, and continues the effort to reduce trade barriers throughout the world. However, widespread concerns have been expressed that the WTO's focus on lowering trade barriers may encourage businesses to keep costs down through practices that may lead to pollution and human rights abuses. Others argue that human rights should not be linked to international business. Do you think environmental and human rights issues should be linked to trade? Why or why not?

4. Describe briefly the EU and its goals. What are the pros and cons of the EU? Do you predict that the European alliance will hold up over the next 20 years? Why or why not?

5. Use the most recent edition of "The *Fortune* Global 500," which usually is published in *Fortune* magazine in July, or go to *Fortune's* online version at http://money.cnn.com/magazines/fortune/global500, to answer the following questions.

   a. On what is the Global 500 ranking based (e.g., profits, number of employees, revenues)?

   b. Among the world's 10 largest corporations, list the countries in which they are based.

   c. Identify the top-ranked company, along with its Global 500 ranking and country, for the following industry classifications: Food and Drug Stores; Industrial and Farm Equipment; Petroleum Refining; Utilities: Gas and Electric; Telecommunications; Pharmaceuticals.

Web Assignments

1. **WTO**. Visit the Web site of the World Trade Organization (http://www.wto.org). Research two current trade disputes. Which countries and products are involved? What, if anything, do the two disputes have in common? What procedures does the WTO follow in resolving trade disputes between member countries?

2. **EU**. Europa.eu is the Web portal for the European Union. Go to the following Web site (http://europa.eu/index_en.htm) and answer the following questions:

   a. What are the steps a country must take to become a member of the EU?

   b. How many EU members have adopted the euro? Which countries will be adopting the euro over the next few years?

   c. What is the combined GDP of EU members? Which EU member has the largest GDP? Which has the smallest GDP?

3. **Nestlé**. Nestlé is one of the world's largest global corporations. Visit the firm's Web site (http://www.nestle.com). Where is the company headquartered? What are some of its best-known brands? Are these brands sold in specific countries or are they sold worldwide? Make a list of three of four issues Nestlé faces as a global corporation.

Note: Internet Web addresses change frequently. If you do not find the exact sites listed, you may need to access the organization's or company's home page and search from there or use a search engine such as Bing or Google.

CASE 4.1   Apple Navigates China

Stung by accusations that its supply chain in China violates safety rules and worker rights, Apple Inc. recently released its annual supplier audit report and for the first time named the more than 150 companies that supply 97 percent of its product parts. According to the report, nearly a third violated Apple's wage and benefits standards.

Seventeen relied on involuntary labor, 112 used unsafe handling for dangerous chemicals, and 5 hired underage workers.

Critics in Asia and the West have long cited unsafe conditions and hazardous materials used by Chinese suppliers that build the iPhone, iPad, iPod, and other

Mac products. Reports of deadly accidents, pollution, improper waste handling, falsified records, seven-day workweeks, forced overtime, worker injuries, and even suicides have dogged the company, often centering on Chinese factories managed by the Foxconn Technology Group.

Even customers can find themselves at risk. The recent planned launch of the iPhone 4S in China was halted before a single phone was sold. As thousands of would-be buyers lined up to await the opening of Apple stories in Beijing and Shanghai, it was clear there would not be enough phones to go around. The crowds grew violent and police were called to disperse them.

CEO Tim Cook says the company "will learn some things for the future and change some things," citing safety as of the "upmost importance" to Apple.

Questions for Critical Thinking

1. Workers at Apple's Chinese suppliers often accept low wages, minimal benefits, and dormitory housing. Should Apple improve their situation or find other suppliers? What effects will such changes have on Apple's products?

2. Do you think reports of unsafe working conditions among its suppliers have hurt Apple's reputation? Why or why not?

Sources: Charles Huhigg and David Barboza, "In China, Human Costs Are Built into an iPad," *The New York Times,* January 25, 2012, www.nytimes.com; Adam Satariano, "Apple Lists Parts Suppliers for First Time, Discloses Violations," *Bloomberg Businessweek,* January 15, 2012, www.businessweek.com; Jessica E. Vascellaro and Owen Fletcher, "Apple Navigates China Maze," *The Wall Street Journal,* January 14, 2012, http://online.wsj.com; Philip Elmer-DeWitt, "Overwhelmed by Crushing Demand, Apple Halts Friday's iPhone 4S Launch in China," CNN Money, January 13, 2012, http://tech.fortune.cnn.com.

TOMS Shoes Takes One Step at a Time

CASE 4.2

On a trip to Argentina, a young U.S. entrepreneur named Blake Mycoskie saw firsthand how a simple pair of shoes, beyond the means of many of the world's poor, could provide everything from the ability to attend school to protection from life-threatening infections. Moved by the experience, Mycoskie had a striking insight: that a revenue-based business was more likely than a charity to sustain itself over the long term. And so TOMS Shoes was born.

TOMS Shoes, which stands for "tomorrow's shoes," makes simple, lightweight, but stylish shoes with a unique business model called One for One. For every pair it sells, TOMS gives a pair of shoes away to a child in need somewhere in the world.

To those who have difficulty understanding his business model, Mycoskie tells this story: "I got to meet Bill Gates. And he said, 'You know, 50 percent of the infectious diseases in the world can be prevented by two things. Toilets and shoes. So, keep doing what you're doing.'"

TOMS' current focus is on preventing a debilitating soil-borne disease, common in Ethiopia, which attacks the lymphatic system. Simply wearing shoes prevents its transmission. Donated shoes are also helping to prevent hookworm in Guatemala. And children who wear shoes can more readily walk to school.

Mycoskie, who recently gave away most of his possessions to live on a small sailboat docked on the California coast, keeps his entrepreneurial hand in everything the company does. With only 50 full-time employees and a crew of enthusiastic volunteers, TOMS recently turned its first profit, in a year in which it also gave away 300,000 pairs of shoes. "It turns out doing the things you enjoy and having fun with them often create the best message."

Questions for Critical Thinking

1. Do you think TOMS's One for One business model is sustainable in the long term? Why or why not?

2. Mycoskie says his customers provide "the best type of marketing you can have" because when asked about their footwear, "they say, 'When I bought this pair of shoes, a child got a pair.'" What lesson do you think other socially responsible firms can learn from TOMS's business practices?

Sources: Company Web site, http://www.toms.com, accessed February 12, 2012; Tamara Schweitzer, "The Way I Work," *Inc.,* http://www.inc.com, accessed February 12, 2012; Kellie Doligale, "Good for the Sole: Toms Founder Set to Visit UK," *The Kentucky Kernel* (University of Kentucky at Lexington), http://kykernel.com, accessed February 12, 2012; Daniel Seberg, "Giving Kids Their First Pair of Shoes," CBS News, http://www.cbsnews.com, accessed February 12, 2012; Karen Leo and Lindsay Goldwert, "TOMS Shoes Saving Lives, One Sole at a Time," *ABC News,* http://www.abcnews.com, accessed February 12, 2012; Shannon Cook, "These Shoes Help Others Get a Step Up," *CNN.com,* http://www.cnn.com, accessed February 12, 2012.

When you peel a potato or run your pizza cutter through to cut a slice, it's likely that you only notice the tool you are using if it doesn't work—if it sticks or snags, gouges the potato or tears the pizza crust. The team at Smart Design doesn't mind not being noticed. They operate quietly behind the scenes, developing a wide range of designs for products made and sold by companies around the world. They come up with designs that make everything from toothbrushes to automobiles function better in human hands. Smart Design engineers developed the popular OXO Good Grips line of kitchen utensils as well as the SmartGauge instrument cluster for the Ford Fusion Hybrid.

"Smart Design is about designing products for people in their everyday life," explains Richard Whitehall, vice president of industrial design for Smart Design. "There are little things you might see in a product that you'd think, 'I wish I'd thought of that—it's a great idea.' " Sometimes it's the simplest or smallest detail in the engineering of a product that makes a difference in whether consumers will continue to use the product or purchase it again. Smart Design tries to make products that work well universally for a wide range of people in different situations. This is where the global challenge comes in—differences in cultural preferences, product use, language, and other factors can make universal product development difficult. But Smart Design has offices in the U.S. and abroad, with testing locations in Europe and Asia, and employees representing more than 20 different countries.

Ted Booth, director of interactive design says, "Interactive design is anything with a 'chip' in it. I can't imagine approaching interactive design without a global perspective." Booth explains how Smart Design develops the design for a mobile phone. "The way people use it varies from country to country," he notes. "So what might look like a new feature in one country is really old hat in another." Booth observes that it is very common for consumers in Finland and South Korea to pay for most goods and services from their mobile phones, whereas this is not a common practice among U.S. consumers. Some of this practice is driven by industry standards, but much of it has to do with cultural expectations. "It's important to have a global perspective [in design] so you know the trends in other countries. You need to design and shape the experience to hit the market and bring something new to the market, but also adapt to individual markets," concludes Booth.

Booth describes his company's work on the "Q" control for HP—a single navigation controller that can be used across all HP products, ranging from TV remotes to printers to cameras. Smart Design tested the Q control in the United States, Germany, Spain, and South Korea. Researchers discovered that, while a few local adaptations were necessary, there was one universal preference among all consumers: everyone needed a "back" button in order to go forward. Booth explains that there is a universal need for people to know that there is an escape, undo—or back—for every function in order for users to feel comfortable completing an interactive task.

Smart Design has an impressive list of worldwide clients, including Ford, Bell Canada, ESPN, World Kitchen, Microsoft, Samsung, and Kellogg's, among many others. The firm has won many accolades, including nationally recognized design awards. But Smart Design remains focused on the details. The firm recently developed the Reach Wondergrip children's toothbrush for Johnson & Johnson when it became apparent that traditional children's toothbrushes were just scaled down from the adult models. Kids couldn't hold them easily and were less likely to brush their teeth. The new Wondergrip children's model changed the industry standard for children's toothbrushes—and brushing habits. Smart Design also developed a women's sports watch for Nike—based on needs and preferences of women runners. And there's that line of kitchen tools that make food preparation and cooking just a little bit easier and more fun.

Richard Whitehall, who actually began his career working for a firm that manufactured mountaineering gear, describes the importance of design in every product used by consumers. "We were trying to think of a situation people were in and trying to design a product in a way that people from different countries—whether they were stuck in the Alps or on a boat—could use in all these different situations." Whether you are climbing a mountain in Switzerland or cutting your pizza in Boston, you want your gear to work flawlessly—and that is the goal of Smart Design.

Questions for Critical Thinking

1. Ted Booth and Richard Whitehall mention some of the cultural barriers that Smart Design faces in developing products for worldwide use. Give examples of other barriers the firm might face in international trade.

2. Describe what you believe would be the best level of involvement for Smart Design to have when doing business in Europe. Remember to take into consideration the impact of the European Union on business transactions.

3. Smart Design already has a presence in South Korea. How might the firm best approach developing products for the market in India? In China?

4. Do you believe it is possible to develop truly universal products? Why or why not?

Sources: Smart Design Web site, http://www.smartdesignworldwide.com, accessed February 12, 2012; "National Design Awards," *Cooper-Hewitt, National Design Museum,* http://www.nationaldesignawards.org, accessed February 12, 2012; Alissa Walker, "Biomimicry Challenge: For IBM, Smart Design Draws Water Inspiration from Ecosystems," *Fast Company.com,* http://www.fastcompany.com, accessed February 12, 2012.

KANSAS

Saline River
Smoky Hill River
Salina
en City
Greensburg
Wichita

PART 1

GREENSBURG, KS

New Ways to Be a Better Town

Greensburg, Kansas, had been struggling for years. Located along Highway 54, a major trucking route, the town was merely a pit stop for people on their way somewhere else. It did have a few tourist attractions: the Big Well, the world's largest hand-dug well, and a 1,000-pound meteorite that fell from the sky in 2006.

Lonnie McCollum, the town's mayor, had been looking into ways to breathe new life into the town. McCollum wanted to add a little vintage charm to its quaint Main Street, but could not raise the money. And he had launched a campaign to put the "green" back in Greensburg by promoting green building technology. But the idea, which many residents associated with hippies and tree-huggers, did not go over well.

Then everything changed. "My town is gone," announced Town Administrator Steve Hewitt on May 5, 2007, after surveying the damage caused by a devastating tornado. "I believe 95 percent of the homes are gone. Downtown buildings are gone, my home is gone." With a clean slate and 700 homes to replace, Hewitt vowed to rebuild Greensburg using sustainable materials. He believed the town had a unique opportunity to control its environmental impact and reduce operating costs through increased energy efficiency.

"What if we turned this tragedy into something beautiful?" asked resident Dan Wallach in a new business plan he wrote shortly after the disaster. Wallach and his wife had long been interested in sustainable green living. Using their experience in developing nonprofits, the two launched Greensburg GreenTown, an organization designed to support Greensburg's green building efforts through education, fund-raising, and public relations management.

One of Wallach's favorite new projects was BTI Greensburg, the local John Deere dealership. Owners Kelly and Mike Estes had decided to replace their ruined building with an energy-efficient, technologically state-of-the-art showroom featuring radiant heat, solar energy, passive cooling, and wind power. With corporate support from John Deere, BTI Greensburg would become a flagship green dealership.

Long-term plans for Greensburg include a business incubator, to help displaced businesses get back on their feet and bring new businesses to town; a green industrial park, green museum, and green school system; green building codes and zoning restrictions; and a community of green homes and businesses.

Questions

After viewing the video, answer the following questions:

1. In what ways is the town of Greensburg like any other business?
2. In what ways is the town of Greensburg a socially responsible organization?
3. What might be the effects of the town's new green building guidelines on residents and businesses? On the regional economy?
4. What kind of business is Greensburg GreenTown? How does its structure differ from John Deere's?

LAUNCHING YOUR
[Global Business
and Economics Career]

In Part 1, "Business in a Global Environment," you learned about the background and current issues driving contemporary business. The part includes four chapters covering such issues as the changing face of business, business ethics and social responsibility, economic challenges facing contemporary business, and competing in world markets. Business has always been an exciting career field, whether you choose to start your own company, work at a local business, or set your sights on a position with a multinational corporation. But today's environment is especially attractive because businesses are expanding their horizons to compete in a global economy—and they need dedicated and talented people to help them accomplish their goals. In fact, professional and business service jobs are found in some of the fastest-growing industries in the U.S. economy and are projected to grow during this decade.[1] So now is the time to explore several different career options that can lead you to your dream job. Each part in this text profiles the many opportunities available in business. Here are a few related to Chapters 1 through 4.

If you're good at math and are interested in how societies and companies function, then maybe a career as an *economist* is in your future. Economists study how resources are allocated, conduct research by collecting and analyzing data, monitor economic trends, and develop forecasts. They look into such vital areas as the cost of energy, foreign trade and exchange between countries, the effect of taxes, and employment levels—both from a big-picture national or global viewpoint and from the perspective of individual businesses. Economists work for corporations to help them run more efficiently, for consulting firms to offer special expertise, or for government agencies to oversee economic decision making. Typically, advanced degrees are needed to climb to top-level positions. Economists typically earn about $90,830 per year.[2]

Or perhaps you are interested in global business. Companies increasingly search the world for the best employees, supplies, and markets. So you could work in the United States for a foreign-based firm such as Nokia or Toyota; abroad in Australia, Asia, Europe, or Latin America for a U.S.-based firm such as Microsoft; or with overseas co-workers via computer networks to develop new products for a firm such as General Electric. With technology and telecommunications, distance is no longer a barrier to conducting business. Global business careers exist in all the areas you'll be reading about in this text—business ownership, management, marketing, technology, and finance.

Global business leaders are not born but made—so how can you start on that career path? Here are the three areas that businesses consider when selecting employees for overseas assignment:

- *competence*—including technical knowledge, language skills, leadership ability, experience, and past performance

- *adaptability*—including interest in overseas work, communication and other personal skills, empathy for other cultures, and appreciation for varied management styles and work environments

- *personal characteristics*—level of education, experience, and social compatibility with the host country.[3]

Solid experience in your field or company ranks at the top of the list of needed skills. Firms want to send employees who have expertise in their business and loyalty to the firm to represent them overseas. Those who obtain their master's of business administration (MBA) degree are reaping rewards financially: In a recent year, the average median base salary for MBA graduates hit $94,500.[4] Companies are reluctant to send new graduates abroad immediately. Instead, they invest in training to orient employees to the new assignment.

Knowledge of and interest in other languages and cultures is the second-highest priority.

Businesspeople need to function smoothly in another society, so they are selected based on their familiarity with other languages and cultures. Because China is a business hot spot, some people have become fluent in Mandarin Chinese to boost their career prospects. Also, some school systems are offering Chinese language classes in addition to their standard offerings of Spanish, French, German, and Russian.

Finally, employees are evaluated on their personal characteristics to be certain that they will fit well in their new country. A person's talent is still foremost in making assignments, but executives with cross-cultural skills are in high demand.

Career Assessment Exercises in Economics and Global Business

1. With the ups and downs in the U.S. economy, economists have been highlighted in the news. The head of the Federal Reserve, Ben Bernanke, has been managing the country's general financial condition. To get an idea of the role economists play in a federal government agency, research Bernanke's background and qualifications. Now make a list of your own skills. Where is there a match of your skills to his? What do you need to change? How can you improve your skill set?

2. To see the effect of the global economy in your community, go to a major retailer. Look at the number of different countries represented in the products on the shelves. Compare your list with those of your classmates to see who found the most countries and what goods those countries provided. Go online to research the career opportunities at the retailer's Web site.

3. To learn more about other countries, do research online for a country in which you are interested. Here are some sources that may be useful:

   - *The World Factbook*, published by the Central Intelligence Agency, https://www.cia.gov/library/ publications/the-world-factbook/. This publication, updated yearly, contains a wealth of information about countries—geography and climate, population statistics, cultural and political information, transportation and communications methods, and economic data.

   - *BusinessWeek* magazine, http://www.businessweek.com. The Web site has links to Asia and Europe, where you can explore breaking news or information on global companies.

   - Online news sites Yahoo! News and Google News, http://news.yahoo.com and http://news.google.com. Both of these online news sites have links to global business news. The Yahoo! site has a link for "Business" and then "Global Economy." The Google site has a "Business" link and then lists sites for many countries and many languages.

   Write a one-page summary of what you found. Make a list of abilities you would need to function well as a businessperson in that country. Concentrate on the areas of competence, adaptability, and personal characteristics. How might you formulate a plan to gain those skills?

Learning Objectives

[1] Discuss why most businesses are small businesses.

[2] Determine the contributions of small businesses to the economy.

[3] Discuss why small businesses fail.

[4] Describe the features of a successful business plan.

[5] Identify the available assistance for small businesses.

[6] Explain franchising.

[7] Outline the forms of private business ownership.

[8] Describe public and collective ownership of business.

[9] Discuss organizing a corporation.

[10] Explain what happens when businesses join forces.

Chapter 5

Forms of Business Ownership and Organization

mangostock/iStockphoto

Snagajob's Success Hooks Investors

When Shawn Boyer tried to help a friend find an internship online in 1999, he didn't know he would soon be the founder and CEO of a fast-growing company, or the winner of a couple of prestigious business awards. Finding no Web sites for part-time or hourly job seekers at that time, Boyer set up a job board to serve them and called it Snagajob.com. A few years later the board had become a full-service online job-search company, offering job opportunities, networking, and advice to a loyal community of more than 30 million hourly workers, most between 18 and 32. Snagajob provides workforce solutions to employers as well.

The U.S. Small Business Administration named Boyer its National Small Business Person of the Year, and his Virginia-based company continued to grow, relocating, adding employees, and developing a casual culture with employee benefits such as paternity leave, backup child care, gym membership, and paid resort vacations to celebrate 5- and 10-year employment anniversaries. Snagajob recently attracted $27 million in investment money from a venture capital firm to help it keep expanding, "especially the sales team," says Boyer. It's a good thing the company was recently named the Best Small Company to Work For in America, too. Having recently grown from 150 to 300 employees, it is rapidly on its way to becoming a mid-sized firm.[1]

Overview

Do you hope to work for a big company or a small one? Do you plan to start your own business? If you're thinking about striking out on your own, you're not alone. On any given day in the United States, more people are in the process of starting a new business than getting married or having a baby. But before you enter the business world—as an employee or an owner—you need to understand the industry in which a company operates, as well as the size and framework of the firm's organization. For example, Snagajob.com is a small but fast-growing business that could spawn a whole new industry. It's important to remember that most larger businesses—like Ford and Apple—began as small businesses.

Several variables affect the way a business is organized, including how easily it can be set up, access to financing, tolerance of financial risk, and strengths and weaknesses that exist in competing firms, as well as the strengths and weaknesses of your firm.

This chapter begins by focusing on small-business ownership, including the advantages and disadvantages of small-business ventures, the contributions of small business to the economy, and the reasons small businesses fail. The chapter examines the services provided by the U.S. government's Small Business Administration, the role of women and minorities in small business, and alternatives for small businesses such as franchising.

The chapter then moves on to an overview of the forms of private business ownership—sole proprietorships, partnerships, and corporations. In addition, the features of businesses owned by employees and families, as well as not-for-profit organizations, are discussed. Public and collective ownership are examined. The chapter concludes with an explanation of structures and operations typical of larger companies and a review of the major types of business alliances.

LECTURE ENHANCER:
Poll students to find out how many of them work for small businesses. How many of those businesses are expanding?

Most Businesses Are Small Businesses

Although many people associate the term *business* with corporate giants such as Walmart, 3M, and ExxonMobil, 99.7 percent of all U.S. companies are considered small businesses. These firms have generated 65 percent of new jobs over the past two decades and employ half of all private-sector (nongovernment) workers.[2] Small business is also the launching pad for new ideas and products. They hire 43 percent of high-tech workers such as scientists, engineers, and computer programmers, who devote their time to developing new goods and services.[3]

What Is a Small Business?

How can you tell a small business from a large one? The Small Business Administration (SBA), the federal agency most directly involved with this sector of the economy, defines a **small business** as an "independent business having fewer than 500 employees." However, those bidding for government contracts or applying for government assistance may vary in size according to industry. For example, small manufacturers fall in the 500-worker range, whereas wholesalers must employ fewer than 100. Retailers may generate up to $7 million in annual sales and still be considered small businesses, while farms or other agricultural businesses are designated small if they generate less than $750,000 annually.[4]

While Will Curran was studying at Arizona State University, he also became the CEO and president of Arizona Pro DJs, which provides everything from security to lights to music for teen events. Will's love of music and entertaining audiences got him deejaying while he was still in high school. Now Arizona Pro DJs, which earned $116,000 in a recent year, has 24 employees, so the government classifies it as a small business.[5]

Because government agencies offer benefits designed to help small businesses compete with larger firms, small-business owners want to determine whether their companies meet the standards for small-business designation. If it qualifies, a company may be eligible for government loans or for government purchasing programs that encourage proposals from smaller suppliers. With assistance like this, Arizona Pro DJs might eventually expand to other areas of the country and become a larger business.

Typical Small-Business Ventures

Small businesses have always competed against each other as well as against some of the world's largest organizations. ModCloth, an online clothing, accessories, and home furnishings retailer founded by the husband-and-wife team Eric and Susan Koger, does both. Launched while the owners were still in college, the business, which is located in Pittsburgh, offers trendy fashions by more than 700 independent designers. The company reaches out to consumers via Twitter, Facebook, and a company blog. It also invites customers to rate possible inventory through its Be the Buyer link. Because of these relationships, ModCloth can compete against other clothing e-tailers of any size.[6]

There has been a steady erosion of small businesses in some industries as larger firms have bought out small independent businesses and replaced them with larger operations. The number of independent home improvement stores has fallen dramatically as Lowe's and other national discounters have increased the size and number of their stores. But as Table 5.1 reveals, the businesses least likely to be gobbled up are those that sell personalized services, rely on certain locations, and keep their overhead costs low.

Photo courtesy Will Curran

Will Curran started Arizona Pro DJs while a student at Arizona State University. The small business provides everything from security to lights to music for teen entertainment events.

TABLE
5.1

Business Sectors Most Dominated and Least Dominated by Small Firms

MOST LIKELY TO BE A SMALL FIRM	FEWER THAN 20 WORKERS
Home builders	97%
Florists	97%
Hair salons	96%
Auto repair	96%
Funeral homes	94%

LEAST LIKELY TO BE A SMALL FIRM	FEWER THAN 20 WORKERS
Hospitals	14%
Nursing homes	23%
Paper mills	33%
Electric utilities	38%
Oil pipelines	38%

Source: U.S. Census Bureau, "Number of Firms, Number of Establishments, Employment, and Annual Payroll by Employment Size of the Enterprise for the United States, All Industries," http://www.census.gov, accessed March 5, 2012.

LECTURE ENHANCER:
Can you think of a local small business that provides customized personal services?

Nonfarming-related small firms create more than half the nation's gross domestic product (GDP). In the past, many of these businesses focused on retailing or a service industry such as insurance. More recently, however, small firms have carved out an important niche for themselves: providing busy consumers with customized services that range from pet-sitting to personal shopping. These businesses cater to the needs of individual customers in a way that big firms can't.

As Figure 5.1 shows, small businesses provide most jobs in the construction, agricultural services, wholesale trade, services, and retail trade industries. Retailing to the consumer is another important industry for small firms. Retailing giants such as Amazon and Macy's may be the best-known firms, but smaller stores and Web sites outnumber them. And these small firms can be very successful, as the owners of ModCloth illustrate, often because they can keep their overhead expenses low.

Small business also plays a significant role in agriculture. Although most farm acreage is in the hands of large corporate farms, most U.S. farms are owned by individual farmers or families, not partners or shareholders.[7] The family farm is a classic example of a small-business operation. It is independently owned and operated, with a limited number of employees, including family members. Cider Hill Farm in Massachusetts is one such farm. Three generations of the Cook family operate the farm together—it produces fruit and vegetables, including a wide variety of cooking and eating apples from its orchards and honey from its on-site beehives. In addition, Cider Hill makes its own fresh cider and cider doughnuts every day and operates a well-stocked country store on the property. During growing season, the farm hosts field trips for schools, offers hay rides, and creates a corn maze in

FIGURE
5.1

Major Industries Dominated by Small Businesses

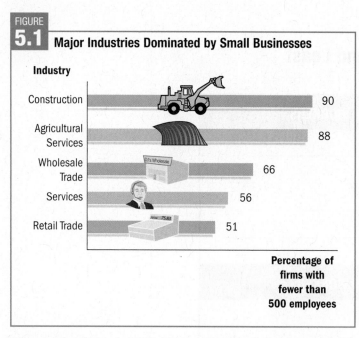

Industry

Construction	90
Agricultural Services	88
Wholesale Trade	66
Services	56
Retail Trade	51

Percentage of firms with fewer than 500 employees

Source: Office of Advocacy, U.S. Small Business Administration, "Small Business Profile: United States," http://www.sba.gov/advocacy, accessed March 6, 2012.

home-based business
firm operated from the residence of the business owner.

LECTURE ENHANCER:
What type of business owner might be the most attracted to creating a home-based business?

CLASS ACTIVITY:
Discuss the possible advantages and disadvantages of working at home.

Assessment Check ✓

1. How does the Small Business Administration (SBA) define *small business*?

2. In what industries do small businesses play a significant role?

its fields. All of these activities contribute to the income of the farm. The Cooks are also dedicated to environmentally friendly farming technologies. Cider Hill operates three wind turbines and uses solar cells to help power its buildings.[8]

Fifty-two percent of small businesses in the United States are **home-based businesses**—firms operated from the residence of the business owner. There are about 16 million such businesses in the United States.[9] People who operate home-based firms often do so because this type of work allows them more control over their business as well as their personal time. Whether you're a morning person or a night owl, in many cases you can structure your business hours accordingly. Access to the Internet and availability of communications devices such as the iPhone and other smart phone technology makes it convenient to run a home-based business. Freedom from overhead costs such as leasing office or warehouse space is another major attraction of home-based businesses. Drawbacks include isolation and less visibility to customers—except, of course, if your customers visit you online. In that case, they don't care where your office is located.

Many small-business start-ups are more competitive because of the Internet. The Internet doesn't guarantee success—there are so many Web sites that a small firm needs to find ways to make its online presence effective. But establishing a Web site is generally less expensive than opening a retail store and reaches a broader spectrum of potential customers. The Connecticut-based eBeanstalk.com is an online toy store. How does this small business compete with the likes of online giants such as Amazon and Toys 'R' Us? The company specializes in learning toys that "help plant the seeds that help children grow." Two teams of experts (including 700 moms) hired by eBeanstalk evaluate more than 10,000 toys from manufacturers, to narrow the selection down to around 600 of what they consider to be the best learning toys. That group may shrink even further. Only the selected toys are included on the site. Consumers appreciate this screening process, knowing they can go straight to eBeanstalk for the toys they want.[10]

American business history is filled with inspirational stories of great inventors who launched companies in barns, garages, warehouses, and attics. For visionaries such as Apple Computer founders Steve Jobs and Steve Wozniak, the logical option for transforming their technical idea into a commercial reality was to begin work in a family garage. The impact of today's entrepreneurs, including home-based businesses, is discussed in more depth in Chapter 6.

⌜2⌟ Contributions of Small Business to the Economy

Small businesses form the core of the U.S. economy. Businesses with fewer than 500 employees generate more than half the nation's gross domestic product (GDP). These companies account for $65 billion in exports, shipping more than 13 percent of all exported goods overseas each year.[11] Small firms are credited with U.S. competitiveness in a number of global markets.[12]

Creating New Jobs

Small businesses make tremendous contributions to the U.S. economy and to society as a whole. One impressive contribution is the number of new jobs created each year by small businesses. While it varies from year to year, on average two of every three new jobs are created by companies with fewer than 500 employees.[13] A significant share of these jobs are created by the smallest companies, those with four or fewer employees. Several provisions of the 2010 Small Business Jobs Act may help give a further boost to these job numbers by raising the dollar amount of small business loans available to companies.[14]

Small businesses also contribute to the economy by hiring workers who traditionally have had difficulty finding jobs at larger firms, such as military veterans returning to the workforce, former welfare recipients, and workers with various challenges. The Small Business Administration provides incentives for companies to hire these types of workers.

Even if you never plan to start your own company, you will probably work for a small business at some point in your career, particularly at the beginning. Small firms often hire the youngest workers. Table 5.2 illustrates some of the newest jobs within both traditional and new industries, many of which can be found in small businesses.

LECTURE ENHANCER:
Have you ever worked for a small business?

Creating New Industries

Small firms give businesspeople the opportunity and outlet for developing new ideas. Sometimes these new ideas become entirely new industries. Many of today's largest and most successful firms, such as Whole Foods, Google, and Amazon, began as small businesses. Facebook co-founders Mark Zuckerberg, Dustin Moskovitz, Chris Hughes, and Eduardo Saverin launched their new business from their college dorm room. Within a few years, Facebook had logged more than 500 million active users, positioned itself as a leader in the new industry of social networking, and prompted others to start their own businesses.[15]

New industries are sometimes created when small businesses adapt to provide needed services to a larger corporate community. Corporate downsizing has created a demand for

TABLE 5.2 New Job Opportunities for Small Businesses

INDUSTRY	JOBS
Green energy and construction	Wind-farm engineers; solar installers and technicians; green-collar specialists and consultants; green construction specialists
Healthcare	Home health care specialists; informatics specialists (workers cross-trained in healthcare and technology)
Self-improvement	Yoga instructors and studio managers; spa managers; nutrition specialists
Education technology	Tech and trade school teachers and administrators; creators of online education materials; specialists in software and hardware for use in schools
Other growing industries	Temporary staffing agencies; repair services; fast-casual dining

Sources: Jason Del Ray and Tamara Schweitzer, "Best Industries for Starting a Business Right Now," *Inc.*, http://www.inc.com, accessed March 2, 2012; "11 Big Ideas to Watch in 2011," *Inc.*, http://www.inc.com, accessed March 2, 2012; U.S. Small Business Administration, "Small Business Jobs Act of 2010," http://www.sba.gov, accessed March 2, 2012.

New industries can be created when small businesses adapt to shifts in consumer interests and preferences. ThinkEco wants to make it easier for consumers to save money and energy.

Assessment Check ✓

1. What are the three key ways in which small businesses contribute to the economy?

2. How are new industries formed?

other businesses to perform activities previously handled by in-house employees. These support businesses may become an industry themselves. The need for wireless communication devices and services to support businesses has resulted in a proliferation of small businesses to fill this niche.

New industries can be created when small businesses adapt to shifts in consumer interests and preferences. For example, the idea of offering accessories for men—dubbed "mancessories" by marketers—has taken root in the U.S. economy, with small businesses at the forefront selling goods ranging from shapewear for bellies to bacon-flavored toothpicks. Web sites and newsletters such as Style Flavors that feature such products report accelerating growth.[16]

Finally, new industries may be created when both the business world and consumers recognize a need for change. The recent emphasis on environmental responsibility—ranging from recycling and reuse of goods to reducing the amount of energy consumed—has fostered a whole new industry of green goods and services, many produced by small companies. ThinkEco is a small firm that has created a device that regulates outlet power, allowing its business customers to save as much as 20 percent on their energy bills. ClearEdge Power, based in Hillsboro, Oregon, offers a fuel-cell power energy system that is particularly effective for other small businesses, such as boutique hotels and restaurants.[17]

Innovation

Small businesses are adept at developing new and improved goods and services. Innovation is often the entire reason for the founding of a new business. In a typical year, small firms develop twice as many product innovations per employee as larger firms. They also produce more than 16 times more patents per employee than larger firms.[18]

Key 20th-century innovations developed by small businesses include the airplane, the personal computer, soft contact lenses, and the zipper. Innovations that already drive small businesses in the 21st century include those that fall into the social networking, security, and green energy industries. The "Business Etiquette" feature offers tips for using online social networking successfully.

⌈3⌋ Why Small Businesses Fail

Small businesses play a huge role in the U.S. economy. But one of the reasons they are so successful is also the reason they may fail—their founders are willing to take a risk. Some of the most common shortcomings that plague a small firm include management inexperience, inadequate financing, and the challenge of meeting government regulations.

As Figure 5.2 shows, 7 out of every 10 new businesses survive at least two years. About 50 percent make it to the five-year mark. But by the tenth year, 82 percent will have closed.[19] Let's look a little more closely at why this happens.

Management Shortcomings

One of the most common causes of small-business failure is the shortcomings of management. These may include lack of people skills, inadequate knowledge of finance, inability to track inventory or sales, poor assessment of the competition, or simply the lack of time to do everything required. Whereas large firms often have the resources to recruit specialists in areas such as marketing and finance, the owner of a small business often winds up wearing too many hats at once.

This could result in bad decision making, which could end in the firm's failure. Krispy Kreme was once a small business that expanded too fast. The company's near failure had nothing to do with the quality of its doughnuts. Instead, as the company grew bigger, so did its debt. In addition, consumers turned their taste buds toward more healthful snacks and break-fast foods produced by competitors. Now under new management, operating at a leaner size, and rolling out strategies such as new offerings and upgraded packaging for its grocery-store products, the firm is recovering.[20]

Owners of small businesses can increase their chances of success if they become educated in the principles of business; know the industry in which they intend to operate; develop good interpersonal skills; understand their own limitations; hire motivated employees; and seek professional advice on issues such as finance, regulations, and other legal matters.[21]

Inadequate Financing

Money is the foundation of any business. Every business—large or small—needs a certain amount of financing in order to operate, thrive, and grow. Another leading problem of small businesses is inadequate financing. First-time business owners often assume that their firms will generate enough funds from their initial sales to finance continuing operations. But building a business takes time. Products need to be developed, employees have to be hired, a Web site must be constructed, distribution strategy has to be determined, office or retail

BusinessEtiquette

How to Use Social Networking in Your Job Search

During one recent year, networking sites such as LinkedIn registered about 1 million new users per month. Here are a few simple tips from the pros to help you stand out from all the other job-seekers who have discovered the benefits of social networking.

- *Research a network before jumping in.* Some networks, such as Facebook, exist mostly to connect friends with each other. Others, such as LinkedIn, have a stronger employment focus. Twitter attracts both types of users. To adopt the right approach—and make the most of a site—learn something about it before you log on.

- *Complete your online profile.* Help prospective employers by filling out your online profile. Update your bio as frequently as possible and provide a link to your own blog or Web page. Don't mix business and personal information in one account or profile. Post an accurate photo of yourself.

- *Share information.* Be willing to share information about companies or career opportunities with like-minded job seekers. You can help an online recruiter find the right person—even if it's not you.

- *Search for people.* Find companies that interest you, then try to make connections with friends, family members, classmates, alumni—anyone who might be able to help you establish contact. A specific job might not be available, but a personal connection could help you when that job does open up.

- *Respect privacy.* Just as you only want to present certain information about yourself online, respect the privacy of potential employers and colleagues. Abide by the privacy settings of your social networking site.

Sources: DeLynn Senna, "Recruiters Reveal Pet Peeves About Job Seekers," *Yahoo! Hot Jobs*, http://www.monster.com, accessed March 6, 2012; Daer Glista, "Etiquette Tips for Social Networking," *EzineMark.com*, http://business.ezinemark.com, accessed March 2, 2012; Lydia Ramsay, "Social Networking Etiquette Tips," http://mts.typepad.com/blog, accessed March 2, 2012.

LECTURE ENHANCER:
Why might small-business managers be more prone to these shortcomings than those in larger companies?

FIGURE 5.2 Rate of Business Failures

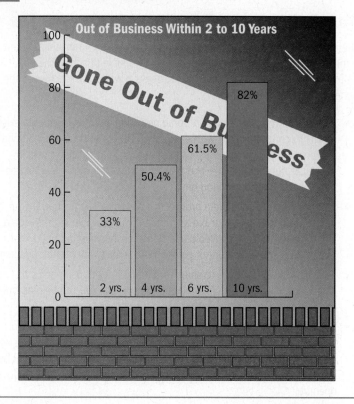

Out of Business Within 2 to 10 Years

Gone Out of Business

	2 yrs.	4 yrs.	6 yrs.	10 yrs.
	33%	50.4%	61.5%	82%

Source: Office of Advocacy, U.S. Small Business Administration, "Frequently Asked Questions: Advocacy Small Business Statistics and Research," http://www.sba.gov, accessed March 3, 2012.

LECTURE ENHANCER:
How might a smaller company that cannot offer a competitive salary or benefits package still attract and keep quality employees?

Ann Dickerson and her husband, Bill Zack, took a unique cookie idea and turned it into a successful business.

space might have to be secured, and so forth. Most small businesses—even those with minimal start-up costs—sometimes don't turn a profit for months or even years.[22]

Although there are stories about business founders starting firms with just a few hundred dollars loaned by a friend or with a cash advance from a credit card, commercial banks and other financial institutions are the largest lenders to small businesses, accounting for 58 percent of total traditional credit to small firms. This type of financing includes credit lines and loans for nonresidential mortgages, vehicles, specialized equipment, and leases.[23]

Figure 5.3 shows that despite their relatively high interest rates, credit cards do remain an important source of financing for small businesses. The heaviest users of credit cards for business financing are firms with fewer than 10 employees. Inadequate financing can compound management shortcomings by making it more difficult for small businesses to attract and keep talented people. Typically, a big company can offer a better benefits package and a higher salary.

With less money to spend on employees, marketing, inventory, and other business costs, successful small companies need to be creative. Ann Dickerson and her husband, Bill Zack, of Signal Mountain, Tennessee, are both former sports journalists. They decided to combine their love of sports with their love of cooking to embark on a new career. Using FDA-approved printer technology and food coloring, their Chattanooga Cookie Company produces cookies that resemble baseball cards, other sports images, company logos, and even works of art. Dickerson says, "I think people like that they can customize them. They can put whatever they ask for on it, even their own face." The cookies—made by hand—come in either sugar, chocolate brownie, coconut, and chocolate chip flavors. "We worked for a year on the recipe and the icing to make them taste as good as they look," Dickerson says. The minimum customized order of two dozen cookies takes about three days to produce; orders of 5,000 cookies or more need a lead time of five days. The company plans on introducing more flavors soon and hopes to buy more machinery, with the goal of mass-producing the cookies and shipping them nationwide.[24]

Government Regulation

Small-business owners cite their struggle to comply with government regulations as one of the biggest challenges they face. Some firms fold because of this burden alone. Paperwork costs account for billions of small-business dollars each year. A large company can better cope with requirements for forms and reports. Larger firms often find that it makes economic sense to hire or contract with specialists in specific types of regulation, such as employment law and workplace safety regulations. By contrast, small businesses often struggle to absorb the costs of government paperwork because of their more limited staff and budgets. The smallest firms—those with fewer than 20 employees—spend 45 percent more per employee than larger firms just to comply with federal regulations.[25]

Recognizing the burden of regulation on small businesses, Congress sometimes exempts the smallest companies from certain regulations. For example, small businesses with 49 or fewer employees are exempt from the Family and Medical Leave Act, which gives employees up to 12 weeks of unpaid leave each year to take care of a newborn child, adopt a child, or care for a family member who has serious health problems.[26] Most small-business owners comply with employment and other laws, believing that such compliance is ethically correct and fosters better employee relations than trying to determine which regulations don't apply to a small business.

Taxes are another burdensome expense for a small business. In addition to local, state, and federal income taxes, employers must pay taxes covering workers' compensation insurance, Social Security payments, and unemployment benefits. Although large companies have similar expenses, they generally have more resources to cover them. But there are also tax incentives designed to help small businesses. These incentives cover a broad range including tax credits for use of biodiesel and renewable fuels, increased research activities, pension plan start-up, and access for individuals with disabilities.[27]

FIGURE 5.3

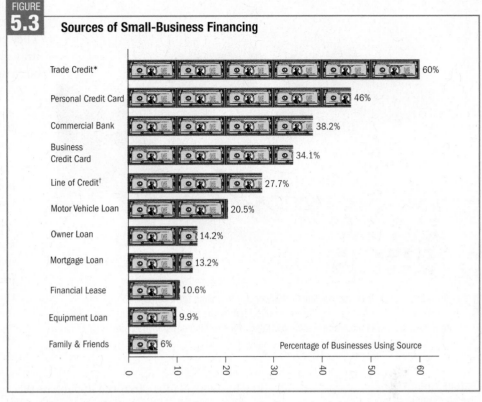

Sources of Small-Business Financing

- Trade Credit* — 60%
- Personal Credit Card — 46%
- Commercial Bank — 38.2%
- Business Credit Card — 34.1%
- Line of Credit† — 27.7%
- Motor Vehicle Loan — 20.5%
- Owner Loan — 14.2%
- Mortgage Loan — 13.2%
- Financial Lease — 10.6%
- Equipment Loan — 9.9%
- Family & Friends — 6%

Percentage of Businesses Using Source

*Trade credit is purchasing goods or equipment from a supplier who finances the purchase by delaying the date of payment for those goods.
†A line of credit is an agreement between a bank and a borrower, indicating the maximum amount of credit the bank will extend to the borrower.

Note: Total exceeds 100 percent because businesses typically use more than one source of financing.

Sources: Small Business Administration, Office of Advocacy, "Financing Patterns of Small Firms," http://www.sba .gov/advocacy, March 3, 2012; Susan Coleman, "Free and Costly Trade Credit: A Comparison of Small Firms," Academy of Entrepreneurial Finance, http://www.google.com, accessed March 3, 2012.

[4] The Business Plan: A Foundation for Success

Large or small, every business needs a plan in order to succeed. While there are tales of firms launched from an idea scribbled on a napkin at a restaurant or sketched out on graph paper in a dorm room, the idea must be backed by a solid plan in order to become reality. A **business plan** is a written document that provides an orderly statement of a company's goals, the methods by which it intends to achieve these goals, and the standards by which it will measure its achievements. The business plan is often the document that secures financing for a firm and creates a framework for the organization.

Assessment Check ☑

1. What percentage of small businesses remain in operation five years after starting? Ten years?

2. What are the three main causes of small-business failure?

business plan written document that provides an orderly statement of a company's goals, methods, and standards.

The business plan is often the document that secures financing for a company and creates a framework for the organization. Business plans identify the firm's missions and goals. They create measurable standards and outline a strategy for reaching company objectives.

Business plans give the organization a sense of purpose. They identify the firm's mission and goals. They create measurable standards and outline a strategy for reaching company objectives. A typical business plan includes the following sections:

- an *executive summary* that briefly answers the who, what, where, when, why, and how questions for the business

- an *introduction* that includes a general statement of the concept, purpose, and objectives of the proposed business

- separate *financial* and *marketing sections* that describe the firm's target market and marketing plan as well as detailed financial forecasts of the need for funds and when the firm is expected to break even—the level of sales at which revenues equal costs

- *résumés of principals*—especially in plans written to obtain financing.

The business plan is often the document that secures financing for a firm and creates a framework for the organization. Business plans identify the firm's mission and goals. They create measurable standards and outline a strategy for reaching company objectives.

Within this structure, an effective business plan contains the written soul of a firm. A good plan addresses the following issues:

- *The company's mission and the vision of its founders.* Look at the home page of any firm's Web site and you will find its mission. At the Web site for TOMS Shoes, visitors learn that "With every pair purchased, TOMS will give a pair of new shoes to a child in need. One for one." Thanks to its customers, TOMS has distributed more than 1 million pairs of new shoes to children in need around the world.[28] This simple declaration states why the company was founded and what it intends to accomplish.

- *An outline of what makes the company unique.* Why start a business that's just like hundreds of others? An effective business plan describes what distinguishes the firm and its products from the rest of the pack. TOMS Shoes illustrates a unique business model with its one-for-one donation program.

- *The customers.* A business plan identifies who the firm's customers will be and how it will serve their needs.

- *The competition.* A business plan addresses its existing and potential competitors as legitimate entities, with a strategy for creating superior or unique offerings. Studying the competition can provide valuable information about what works and what doesn't in the marketplace.

- *Financial evaluation of the industry and market conditions.* This knowledge helps develop a credible financial forecast and budget.

- *Assessment of the risks.* Every business undertaking involves risks. A solid business plan acknowledges these and outlines a strategy for dealing with them.[29]

Whether a firm's intention is to revolutionize an entire industry on a global scale or improve the lives of children by providing them with shoes, the business plan is a major factor in its success. For more detailed information on how to write a business plan, see Appendix D, "Developing a Business Plan."

5 Assistance for Small Businesses

An important part of organizing a small business is financing its activities. Once a business plan has been created, various sources can be tapped for loans and other types of financing. These include government agencies as well as private investors.

Small Business Administration

Small businesses can benefit from using the resources provided by the **Small Business Administration (SBA)**. The SBA is the principal government agency concerned with helping small U.S. firms, and it is the advocate for small businesses within the federal government. Several thousand employees staff the SBA's Washington headquarters and its 1,800 regional and field offices.[30] The SBA's mission statement declares that "Small business is critical to our economic recovery and strength, to building America's future, and to helping the United States compete in today's global marketplace."[31]

Financial Assistance from the SBA Contrary to popular belief, the SBA seldom provides direct business loans. Nor does it provide outright grants to start or expand small businesses.[32] Instead, the SBA *guarantees* small-business loans made by private lenders, including banks and other institutions. To qualify for an SBA-backed loan, borrowers must be "unable to secure conventional commercial financing on reasonable terms and be a 'small business' as defined by SBA size standards."[33] Direct SBA loans are available in only a few special situations, such as natural disaster recovery and energy conservation or development programs. Under the 2009 Recovery Act, the SBA temporarily eliminated specific loan fees and raised the guarantee level on some of its loans.[34] The 2010 Small Business Jobs Act was also intended to make more capital available to entrepreneurs and small business owners.

The SBA also guarantees **microloans** of up to $35,000 to start-ups and other very small firms. The average loan is $13,000, with a maximum term of six years.[35] Microloans may be used to buy equipment or operate a business but not to buy real estate or pay off other loans. These loans are available from nonprofit organizations located in most states. Other sources of microloans include the federal Economic Development Administration, some state governments, and certain private lenders, such as credit unions and community development groups. The most frequent suppliers of credit to small firms are banks.

Small-business loans are also available through SBA-licensed organizations called *Small Business Investment Companies (SBICs)*, which are run by experienced venture capitalists. SBICs use their own capital, supplemented with government loans, to invest in small businesses. Like banks, SBICs are profit-making enterprises, but they are likely to be more flexible than banks in their lending decisions. Large companies that used SBIC financing when they were small start-ups include Apple, Federal Express, and Staples.

Other Specialized Assistance Although government purchases represent a huge market, small companies have difficulty competing for this business with giant firms,

Assessment Check ☑

1. What are the five main sections of a business plan?
2. Why is an effective business plan important to the success of a firm?

Small Business Administration (SBA) principal government agency concerned with helping small U.S. firms.

microloans small-business loans often used to buy equipment or operate a business.

which employ specialists to handle the volumes of paperwork involved in preparing proposals and completing bid applications. Today, many government procurement programs set aside portions of government spending for small companies; an additional SBA role is to help small firms secure these contracts. With set-aside programs for small businesses, up to 23 percent of certain government contracts are designated for small businesses.

Every federal agency with buying authority must maintain an Office of Small and Disadvantaged Business Utilization to ensure that small businesses receive a reasonable portion of government procurement contracts. To help connect small businesses with government agencies, the SBA's Web site offers Central Contractor Registration, which includes a search engine for finding business opportunities as well as a chance for small businesses to provide information about themselves. Set-aside programs are also common in the private sector, particularly among major corporations.

Small Business Investment Companies (SBICs) are for-profit businesses licensed by the Small Business Administration. Using their own capital, SBICs provide loans to small businesses. FedEx used SBIC financing when it was a small start-up company.

In addition to help with financing and government procurement, the SBA delivers a variety of other services to small businesses. It provides information and advice through toll-free telephone numbers and its Web site, http://www.sba.gov. Through its Small Business Training Network, the SBA offers free online courses; sponsors inexpensive training courses on topics such as taxes, networking, and start-ups in cities and towns throughout the nation; and provides a free online library of more than 200 SBA publications and additional business resources. Business owners can find local resources by logging on to the SBA Web site and searching for SBA partners in their region. Local resource partners include small-business development centers, women's business centers, U.S. export assistance centers, and veterans business outreach centers.[36]

Local Assistance for Small Businesses

In conjunction with the federal government or on their own, state and local governments often have programs in place to help small businesses get established and grow. One such region is Washington State's Thurston County. The Thurston County Economic Development Council was founded more than 29 years ago with the mission of "creating a vital and sustainable economy throughout our County that supports the livelihood and values of our residents."[37] The Thurston County EDC provides information and assistance in business planning, licenses and registrations, taxes, and employment considerations. In addition, the council works to connect local businesses with each other and with industry experts, create marketing messages that attract new businesses and customers, and ensure that Thurston County plays an important role in the region's economy.[38] Organizations like the Thurston County EDC offer important resources and links for small businesses around the country.

business incubator
local programs designed to provide low-cost shared business facilities to small start-up ventures.

Business Incubators Some community agencies interested in encouraging business development have implemented a concept called a **business incubator** to provide

RiverNorthPhotography/iStockphoto

Turning Technologies Creates High-Tech Jobs

Turning Technologies, founded in Youngstown, Ohio, has enjoyed breathtaking growth and brought dozens of new jobs to a city with 18 percent unemployment that is haunted by the decline of its old steel mills. Turning has already been called the fastest growing privately held software company in the United States. The firm boasts more than 6,500 clients, and more than a million people use its audience-response products.

Audience-response systems are the wireless keypads that spectators use on TV game shows to register their opinions or answers to questions. Teachers from kindergarten through college also use Turning's audience-response technology. Instructors can ask questions in class using other programs; have students key in answers—anonymously or not—using their remotes; and instantly collate the responses to see how many students answered correctly. Says a school principal about applications of the Turning program, "We have some teachers who are working hard to find the many avenues they can go beyond. You're really only limited by your creativity." Government agencies and nonprofit organizations also use the systems for their training programs.

Most of Turning's 200 employees are young Ohioans who enjoy some of the same benefits as their Silicon Valley counterparts. The firm takes pride in being the kind of success story people have long thought "doesn't happen here."

The bottom line? Good products that are affordable, easy to use, and well marketed can help small companies become engines of growth and job creators.

Questions for Critical Thinking

1. Why might a company such as Turning Technologies locate outside the high-tech hotspots where most firms are? List some possible advantages and disadvantages to that strategy.

2. What should a company like Turning Technologies do if, as it grows, it needs to hire people with technical experience or skills that are hard to find in a depressed area?

Sources: Company Web site, http://www.turningtechnologies.com, accessed March 6, 2012; Anthony Ponce and Shawna Prince, "Classrooms Evolve Beyond Chalkboards, No. 2 Pencils," *NBC Chicago*, http://www.nbcchicago.com/news, accessed March 6, 2012; "Turning Technologies Releases New Polling Tools," *Successful Meetings*, http://www.successfulmeetings.com, accessed March 6, 2012.

low-cost shared business facilities to small start-up ventures. See the "Hit and Miss" feature to read about Turning Technologies' incubator experience. A typical incubator might section off space in an abandoned plant and rent it to various small firms. Tenants often share clerical staff, computers, and other business services. The objective is that, after a few months or years, the fledgling business will be ready to move out and operate on its own.

More than 1,400 business incubator programs operate in the United States, with about 7,000 worldwide. Ninety-four percent are run by not-for-profit organizations focused on economic development. Nearly half of all incubators focus on new technology businesses, and more than half operate in urban areas.[39]

Private Investors

A small business may start with cash from a personal savings account or a loan from a family member. But small-business owners soon begin to look for greater sums of money in order to continue operating and eventually grow. They may want to continue with assistance from private investors. **Venture capital**—money invested in the small business by another business firm or group of individuals in exchange for an ownership share—can give the small business a boost. The National Venture Capital Association reports venture capitalists expect to focus on information technology in general, focusing on consumer Internet and digital media, cloud computing, and mobile/telecom. These investors are tough in their requirements for a solid business plan and expect small-business owners to run lean operations.[40]

LECTURE ENHANCER:
Why would venture capitalists have tougher requirements for a business plan than a bank?

venture capital money invested in a business by another business firm or group of individuals in exchange for an ownership share.

Small-Business Opportunities for Women and Minorities

In the United States today, more than 10 million firms are owned by women, employing more than 13 million workers and generating nearly $2 trillion in sales. In fact, 40 percent of all privately held companies are owned by women. Further, nearly 2 million businesses are owned by women from minority groups, employing 1.2 million people and generating $165 billion in annual revenues.[41]

Women, like men, have a variety of reasons for starting their own companies. Some have a unique business idea that they want to bring to life. Others decide to strike out on their own when they lose their jobs or become frustrated with the bureaucracies in large companies. Jamie Arundell Latshaw served in the U.S. Army for eight years, eventually becoming an officer. While in the Middle East, she saw the need for soldiers to learn about the people and customs of the lands where they would be stationed. When she left the service, she founded Lexicon Consulting. Hired by the Department of Defense and other government agencies, the company helps soldiers learn about foreign cultures before they are deployed, by hiring professional actors and native-speaking immigrants to conduct intensive, realistic training.[42]

Ted S. Warren/AP/Wide World Photos

Jamie Arundell Latshaw, a veteran of the U.S. Army, founded Lexicon Consulting, which helps soldiers learn about foreign countries and customs before they are deployed.

In other cases, women leave large corporations when they feel blocked from opportunities for advancement. Sometimes this occurs because they hit the so-called glass ceiling. Because women are more likely than men to be the primary caregivers in their families, some may seek self-employment as a way to achieve flexible working hours so they can spend more time with their families.

Many nationwide business assistance programs are geared toward women-owned firms. Among the programs offered by the Small Business Administration are the Contract Assistance for Women Business Owners program, which teaches women how to market to the federal government, and the Women's Network for Entrepreneurial Training, which matches experienced businesswomen with women trying to get started. Organizations such as the Center for Women's Business Research provide information, contacts, and other resources as well.

Business ownership is also an important opportunity for America's racial and ethnic minorities. In recent years, the growth in the number of businesses owned by African Americans, Hispanics, and Asian Americans has far outpaced the growth in the number of U.S. businesses overall. Figure 5.4 shows the percentages of minority ownership in major industries. The relatively strong presence of minorities in the services and retail industries is especially significant because these industries contain the greatest number of businesses.

The Small Business Administration has programs targeted to minority-owned small businesses. One is the Mentor-Protégé Program, which pairs an established, financially healthy business with a small minority-owned business. Through the program, the protégé firm gains technical and financial assistance as well as subcontract support.[43]

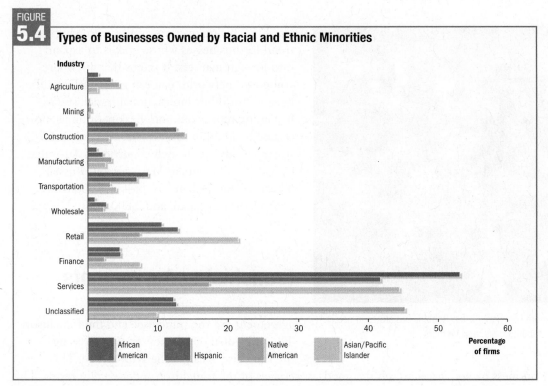

FIGURE 5.4 Types of Businesses Owned by Racial and Ethnic Minorities

Legend: African American, Hispanic, Native American, Asian/Pacific Islander

Industry: Agriculture, Mining, Construction, Manufacturing, Transportation, Wholesale, Retail, Finance, Services, Unclassified

Percentage of firms (x-axis: 0, 10, 20, 30, 40, 50, 60)

Source: Data from Office of Advocacy, U.S. Small Business Administration, "Minorities in Business," http://www.sba.gov/advocacy, accessed March 5, 2012.

Assessment Check ✓

1. What are the various ways the SBA helps small businesses?

2. What are business incubators?

3. Why are small businesses good opportunities for women and minorities?

6 Franchising

Franchising combines large and small businesses into a single entity and is a major factor in the growth of small businesses. **Franchising** is a contractual business arrangement between a manufacturer or another supplier and a dealer such as a restaurant operator or a retailer. The contract specifies the methods by which the dealer markets the product of the supplier. Franchises can involve both goods and services, such as food and wait staff.

Starting a small, independent company can be a risky, time-consuming endeavor, but franchising can reduce the amount of time and effort needed to expand. The parent company has already developed and tested the concept, and the brand is often familiar to prospective customers.

franchising contractual business arrangement between a manufacturer or other supplier, and a dealer such as a restaurant operator or retailer.

The Franchising Sector

Franchised businesses are a huge part of the U.S. economy, accounting for over 9 million jobs in the U.S. workforce. The International Franchise Association reported that franchising is responsible for over 800,000 businesses at a gross value of over $8 billion. The business sectors currently experiencing the most growth are quick-service restaurants, retail food, and personal and business services.[44]

Franchising overseas is also a growing trend for businesses whose goal is to expand into foreign markets. It seems that anywhere you go in the world, you can get a McDonald's burger. But other international franchises are becoming more common. Baskin-Robbins, now owned by Dunkin' Brands, has more than 6,700 stores worldwide in such countries as Australia, Canada, China, Japan, Malaysia, and Russia. There are more than 850 Baskin-Robbins ice cream stores in Japan, and 2,800 in the United States.[45]

International franchises are becoming more common. Baskin-Robbins has stores in nearly 50 countries including Australia, China, Japan, Russia, and Vietnam.

Franchising Agreements

The two principals in a franchising agreement are the franchisee and the franchisor. The individual or business firm purchasing the franchise is called the **franchisee**. This business owner agrees to sell the goods or services of the franchisor under certain terms. The **franchisor** is the firm whose products are sold by the franchisee. For example, McDonald's Corp. is a franchisor. Your local McDonald's restaurant owner is a franchisee.

Franchise agreements can be complex. They involve an initial purchase fee plus agreed-on start-up costs. Because the franchisee is representing the franchisor's brand, the franchisor usually stipulates the purchase of certain ingredients or equipment, pricing, and marketing efforts. The total start-up cost for a SUBWAY franchise may be as low as $78,600.[46] In contrast, McDonald's is one of the more expensive franchises—total start-up costs can run more than $1 million. For this reason, businesspeople interested in purchasing a more expensive franchise often group together.

Benefits and Problems of Franchising

Like any other type of business arrangement, franchising has its benefits and drawbacks. Benefits for the franchisor include opportunities for expansion that might not otherwise be available. A franchised business can move into new geographic locations, including those overseas, at less expense and with the advantages of employing local workers and businesspeople who have intimate knowledge of local preferences. A good franchisor can manage a much larger and more complex business—with fewer direct employees—than could be handled without the franchise option. In most cases, franchisees will be highly attentive to the management of their franchises because of their stake as business owners. If the business is run efficiently, the franchisor will probably experience a greater return on investment than if the firm were run entirely as a company-owned chain of retail shops, restaurants, or service establishments.

Finally, a successful franchisor can usually negotiate better deals on ingredients, supplies, even real estate, because of its financial strength. This clout also benefits the franchisees if the savings are passed along to them.[47]

franchisee individual or business firm purchasing a franchise.

franchisor firm whose products are sold to customers by the franchisee.

LECTURE ENHANCER:
What might be the advantages for a franchise to expand into foreign markets?

LECTURE ENHANCER:
Are you a loyal customer of any franchise?

Franchising can be the quickest way to become a business owner. Some people contend that it's also the least risky. Franchisees have the benefit of name recognition—Papa John's, LA Fitness, Great Clips, and Days Inn—that usually includes a loyal following of customers. The management system of the franchisor has already been established and a performance record is readily available. In addition, franchisors provide a wide range of support to franchisees, including financing, assistance in obtaining a location, business training, supplies, and marketing tools.[48]

Franchisees themselves say they are drawn to the idea of franchising because it combines the freedom of business ownership with the support of a large company. Like other small-business owners, franchisees want to make their own business decisions and determine their own work hours. And they want to have more control over the amount of wealth they can possibly accumulate, as opposed to what they might earn in a salaried job. In an economic slowdown, franchisees might very well be executives who have been laid off during a downsizing or reorganization effort by previous employers. These are highly trained and motivated businesspeople looking for a way to restart their careers.[49] Sometimes the ideas or successes of individual franchisees can benefit the entire company, as was the case with SUBWAY, described in the "Hit & Miss" feature.

Franchising can have its downside—for both franchisors and franchisees. For the franchisor, if its franchisees fail in any way, that failure reflects on the brand as well as the bottom line. The same holds true for the franchisee: a firm that is mismanaged at the top level can spell doom for the smaller business owners who are actually running the individual units. Krispy Kreme, mentioned earlier, is an example of a franchised company that stumbled due to overexpansion. When a firm initially decides to offer franchise opportunities, the company overall may lose money for several years. Of course, in offering franchise opportunities, the franchisor—often the founder of what was once a small business—loses absolute control over every aspect of the business. This uncertainty can make the process of selecting the right franchisees to carry out the company's mission a difficult one.[50]

CLASS ACTIVITY:
Ask students how they might research a frozen yogurt franchise opportunity.

The franchisee faces an outlay of cash in the form of an initial investment, franchise fees, supplies, maintenance, leases, and the like. The most expensive franchises generally are those that involve hotels and resorts, which can run in the millions.[51] For this reason, it is not unusual for groups of businesspeople to purchase a franchise (or several franchise locations).[52] Payments to the franchisor can add to the burden of keeping the business afloat until the owner begins to earn a profit. Choosing a low-cost start up such as Heaven's Best might be a good alternative. Heaven's Best is a cleaning company that specializes in carpet and upholstery for both businesses and residences. The firm offers top-quality methods, equipment, and products along with training, brand awareness, and marketing tools. Businesspeople can purchase a franchise for an investment of as little as $25,000.[53] But it is important for franchisees always to evaluate carefully how much profit they can make once their cost obligations are met.

Because franchises are so closely linked to their brand, franchisors and franchisees must work well together to maintain standards of quality in their goods and services. If customers are unhappy with their experience at one franchise location, they might avoid stopping at another one several miles away, even if the second one is owned and operated by someone else. This is especially true where food is involved. The discovery of tainted meat or produce at one franchise restaurant can cause panic to spread throughout the entire chain. A potential franchisee would be wise to thoroughly research the financial performance and reputation of the franchisor, using resources such as other franchisees and the Federal Trade Commission.

LECTURE ENHANCER:
As a customer, have you ever refused to shop at one franchise location due to poor service or quality of goods at another location?

One Small Franchise Produces One Big Idea

With more than 36,000 sandwich restaurants in 98 countries, SUBWAY is the single largest fast-food chain in the world. SUBWAY is made up of many franchises, and sometimes one franchisee's idea can change the entire organization.

Stuart Frankel is one such franchisee, and his idea was simple: on weekends, charge a special price of $5 for a footlong SUBWAY sandwich. After pressing hard, Frankel and two other local Florida SUBWAY franchisees got the OK from corporate headquarters, even though this was a price decrease of about $1 per sandwich. From there, a chain reaction began.

"I like round numbers," quipped Frankel about the $5 price. SUBWAY customers liked the number too. Meanwhile, SUBWAY's corporate marketing team pushed the $5 promotion nationwide. When the initial four-week promotion was done, marketing executives extended it to seven weeks and then indefinitely, with several sandwich choices.

Demand for the $5 footlongs was so great that franchise owners couldn't get enough bread, turkey, ham, or tuna. "The whole thing took on a life of its own," notes Jeff Moody, CEO of SUBWAY's advertising arm.

Stuart Frankel struck a chord with consumers who were looking for ways to enjoy themselves and stretch each dollar at the same time. "There are only a few times when a chain has been able to scramble up the whole industry, and this is one of them," notes restaurant consultant Jeffrey T. Davis. "It's huge." Sometimes a small idea is really big.

Questions for Critical Thinking

1. Why do you think Stuart Frankel's idea was so successful with consumers? Would it have been as successful during different economic circumstances? Why or why not?

2. A franchise company is only as good as its franchisees. And a franchisee's success is based in part on the decisions and support of corporate leadership. If the $5 footlong promotion had failed, how do you think the outcome would have affected Frankel's franchise business? How might it have affected SUBWAY?

Sources: Company Web site, http://www.subway.com, accessed March 5, 2012; "2012 Franchise 500," *Entrepreneur,* http://www.entrepreneur.com, accessed March 5, 2012; Kim Peterson, "Subway Becomes World's Largest Restaurant Chain," MSN Money, http://money.msn.com, accessed March 5, 2012; "SUBWAY Shows Off Outfits Made from Restaurant Chain's Recycled Packaging," http://www.subway.com, accessed March 5, 2012; "$5 Footlong Subs Are an Every Day Value at SUBWAY Restaurants," http://www.subway.com, accessed March 5, 2012.

Assessment Check ☑

1. What is the difference between a franchisor and a franchisee?

2. What are the benefits to both parties of franchising?

3. What are the potential drawbacks of franchising for both parties?

Some franchisees have found the franchising agreement to be too confining. As the saying goes, you can't add a tuna salad sandwich to the menu at McDonald's no matter how many stores you own. The agreements are usually fairly strict, and that generally helps to maintain the integrity of the brand. Toward this end, some franchise companies control promotional activities, select the site location, or even become involved in hiring decisions. But these activities may seem overly restrictive to some franchisees, especially those seeking independence and autonomy.

Restrictions can also cost franchisees more than they feel is fair. The National Franchise Association, a group that represents more than 80 percent of Burger King's U.S. franchisees, sued the hamburger company for forcing its members to offer consumers a $1 double cheeseburger on its menu, complying with the company's promotional efforts. While the $1 burger offering may seem like a great way to attract and serve hungry consumers, BK franchisees claimed that the promotion cost them a loss of at least 10 cents per burger. In other words, it cost most franchises $1.10 to make and serve a cheeseburger for which they had to charge $1. However, a judge dismissed the lawsuit, siding with Burger King.[54]

7 Forms of Private Business Ownership

Regardless of its size, every business is organized according to one of three categories of legal structure: sole proprietorship, partnership, or corporation. As Figure 5.5 shows, sole proprietorships are the most common form of business ownership, accounting for more than

70 percent of all firms in the United States. Although far fewer firms are organized as corporations, the revenues earned by these companies are 19 times greater than those earned by sole proprietorships.

Each legal structure offers unique advantages and disadvantages. But because there is no universal formula for every situation, some business owners prefer to organize their companies further as S corporations, limited-liability partnerships, and limited-liability companies. In some cases, corporations are owned by their employees.

In addition to the three main legal structures, several other options for ownership exist. These include employee-owned businesses, family-owned businesses, and not-for-profit organizations.

Sole Proprietorships

The most common form of business ownership, the **sole proprietorship** is also the oldest and the simplest. In a sole proprietorship, no legal distinction separates the sole proprietor's status as an individual from his or her status as a business owner. Although sole proprietorships are common in a variety of industries, they are concentrated primarily among small businesses such as repair shops, small retail stores, and service providers such as plumbers, hair stylists, and photographers.

Sole proprietorships offer some unique advantages. Because such businesses involve a single owner, they are easy to form *and* dissolve. A sole proprietorship gives the owner maximum management flexibility, along with the right to all profits after payment of business-related bills and taxes. A highly motivated owner of a sole proprietorship directly reaps the benefits of his or her hard work.

Minimal legal requirements simplify entering and exiting a sole proprietorship. The owner registers the business or trade name—to guarantee that two firms do not use the same name—and takes out any necessary licenses. Local governments require certain licenses for businesses such as restaurants, motels or hotels, and retail stores. In addition, some occupational licenses require business owners to obtain specific insurance such as liability coverage.

Sole proprietorships are also easy to dissolve. This advantage is particularly important to temporary or seasonal businesses that set up for a limited period of time. It's also helpful if the owner needs or wants to close the business for any reason—say, to relocate or to accept a full-time position with a larger firm.

Management flexibility is another advantage of a sole proprietorship. The owner can make decisions without reporting to a manager, take quick action, and keep trade secrets. A sole proprietorship always bears the individual stamp or flair of its owner, whether it's a certain way of styling hair or the way a store window is decorated.

The greatest disadvantage of the sole proprietorship is the owner's personal financial liability for all debts of the business. Also, the business must operate with financial resources limited to the owner's personal funds and money that he or she can borrow. Such financing limitations can keep the business from expanding.

Another disadvantage is that the owner must wear many hats, handling a wide range of management and operational responsibilities. He or she may not have expertise in every area, which may inhibit the firm's growth or even cause the firm damage. In addition, sole

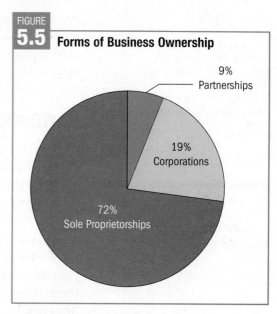

FIGURE 5.5 **Forms of Business Ownership**

9% Partnerships

19% Corporations

72% Sole Proprietorships

Source: Data from U.S. Census Bureau, "Business Enterprise: Sole Proprietorships, Partnerships, Corporations, Table 744," *2012 Statistical Abstract,* http://www.uscensus.gov, accessed March 5, 2012.

sole proprietorship business ownership in which there is no legal distinction between the sole proprietor's status as an individual and his or her status as a business owner.

LECTURE ENHANCER: Why do you think sole proprietorships are the most common type of business ownership?

CLASS ACTIVITY:
Ask class members to offer
a type of business (say,
painting, landscaping, or
pet grooming) and then ask
them to provide examples
of injuries, accidents, or
damage that might occur in
that business.

partnership association
of two or more persons
who operate a business
as co-owners by voluntary
legal agreement.

proprietors may face a higher chance of being audited by the Internal Revenue Service than other types of business owners. Finally, a sole proprietorship usually lacks long-term continuity because a change in personal circumstances or finances can terminate the business on short notice.

Partnerships

Another option for organizing a business is to form a partnership. The Uniform Partnership Act, which regulates this ownership form in most states, defines a **partnership** as an association of two or more persons who operate a business as co-owners by voluntary legal agreement. Many small businesses begin as partnerships between co-founders.

Partnerships are easy to form. All the partners need to do is register the business name and obtain any necessary licenses. Having a partner generally means greater financial capability and someone to share in the tasks and decision making of a business. It's even better if one partner has a particular skill such as design, while the other has a knack for financials.

Most partnerships have the disadvantage of being exposed to unlimited financial liability. Each partner bears full responsibility for the debts of the firm, and each is legally liable for the actions of the other partners. If the firm fails and is left with debt—no matter who is at fault—every partner is responsible for those debts. If one partner defaults, the others are responsible for the firm's debts, even if it means dipping into personal funds. To avoid these problems, many firms establish a limited-liability partnership, which limits the liability of partners to the value of their interests in the company.

Breaking up a partnership is more complicated than dissolving a sole proprietorship. Rather than simply withdrawing funds from the bank, the partner who wants out may need to find someone to buy his or her interest in the firm. The death of a partner also threatens the survival of a partnership. A new partnership must be formed, and the estate of the deceased is entitled to a share of the firm's value. To ease the financial strains of such events, business planners often recommend life insurance coverage for each partner, combined with a buy–sell agreement. The insurance proceeds can be used to repay the deceased partner's heirs and allow the surviving partner to retain control of the business. Because partnerships are vulnerable to personal conflicts that can quickly escalate, it's important for partners to choose each other carefully—not just because they are best friends—and try to plan for the future.

Corporations

corporation legal organization with assets and liabilities separate from those of its owner(s).

A **corporation** is a legal organization with assets and liabilities separate from those of its owner(s). A corporation can be a large or small business. It can be Ford Motor Corp. or a local auto repair shop.

Corporate ownership offers considerable advantages. Because a corporation is a separate legal entity, its stockholders have only limited financial risk. If the firm fails, they lose only the money they have invested. This applies to the firm's managers and executives as well. Because they are not the sole proprietors or partners in the business, their personal savings are not at risk if the company folds or goes bankrupt. This protection also extends to legal risk. Class-action suits involving automakers, drug manufacturers, and food producers are filed against the companies, not the owners of those companies. Although companies such as BP recently experienced class-action suits, their employees and stockholders were not required to pay the settlements from their own bank accounts.[55]

Corporations offer other advantages. They gain access to expanded financial capabilities based on the opportunity to offer direct outside investments such as stock sales. A large corporation can legally generate internal financing for many projects by transferring money from one part of the corporation to another.

One major disadvantage for a corporation is the double taxation of corporate earnings. After a corporation pays federal, state, and local income taxes on its profits, its owners (stockholders) also pay personal taxes on any distributions of those profits they receive from the corporation in the form of dividends.

S Corporations and Limited Liability Corporations To avoid double taxation of business income while minimizing financial liability for their owners, many smaller firms (those with fewer than 100 stockholders) organize as **S corporations**. These companies can elect to pay federal income taxes as partnerships while retaining the liability limitations typical of corporations. S corporations are taxed only once. Unlike regular corporations, S corporations do not pay corporate taxes on their profits. Instead, the untaxed profits of S corporations are paid directly as dividends to shareholders, who then pay the individual tax rate. This tax advantage has resulted in a tremendous increase in the number of S corporations. Consequently, the IRS closely monitors S corporations because some businesses don't meet the legal requirements to form S corporations.[56]

Business owners may also form **limited-liability companies (LLCs)** to secure the corporate advantage of limited liability while avoiding the double taxation characteristic of corporations. An LLC combines the pass-through taxation of a partnership or sole proprietorship with the limited liability of a corporation.

An LLC is governed by an operating agreement that resembles a partnership agreement, except that it reduces each partner's liability for the actions of the other owners. Corporations of professionals, such as lawyers, accountants, and physicians, use a similar approach, with the letters *PC* attached to the business name. LLCs appear to be the wave of the future. Immediately after the first LLC law was passed, most major CPA (certified public accountant) firms in the U.S. converted to LLC status. Today you'll see the LLC or PC designation attached to small businesses ranging from bowling alleys to veterinary hospitals. On a much larger scale, Amazon.com is also an LLC.

Employee-Owned Corporations

Another alternative for creating a corporation is **employee ownership**, in which workers buy shares of stock in the company that employs them. The corporate organization stays the same, but most stockholders are also employees. At King Arthur Flour, virtually all the employees are owners and committed to a sustainable environment. See the "Going Green" feature to learn more.

The popularity of this form of corporation is growing. The number of employee ownership plans has increased dramatically. Today about 20 percent of all employees of for-profit companies report owning stock in their companies; approximately 25 million Americans own employer stock through *employee stock ownership plans (ESOPs)*, options, stock purchase plans, 401(k) plans, and other plans.

Several trends underlie the rise in employee ownership. One is that employees want to share in whatever profit their company earns. Another is that company executives want

King Arthur Flour: Employee-Owned and Green

King Arthur Flour was founded in Vermont in 1790, where it still serves bakers, supermarkets, and consumers coast to coast with top-selling unbleached, all-purpose, whole wheat, white, and organic flours. Since 1996 King Arthur has also been 100 percent employee-owned, giving every employee a stake in reducing the environmental impact of doing business.

King Arthur's employee-managers have replaced light fixtures (saving 65,000 kilowatts of electricity a year), installed energy-efficient appliances, and adopted easy-to-use office recycling plans. Food scraps from its bakery and café feed local farm animals and coffee grounds are composted. Green Seal–certified cleaning products are purchased in bulk to fill reusable containers. Recycled computer paper, non-toxic machine lubricants, and biodegradable pallet wrap are standard. To reduce air pollution, idling is prohibited in the parking lot, carpoolers get priority parking, and bicycles and helmets are provided for the 1.5 mile trip between the company's buildings.

King Arthur is proud to be a certified B Corporation, which holds itself to higher social, environmental legal, and sustainability standards and aims "to redefine success in business."

Questions for Critical Thinking

1. Do you think having a stake in the company's success motivates employees to conserve energy and resources? Why or why not?

2. What can private or publicly owned firms learn from King Arthur's green efforts?

Sources: Company Web site, King Arthur Flour, www.kingarthurflour.com, accessed January 16, 2012; organization Web site, Certified B Corporation, www.bcorporation .net, accessed January 16, 2012; organization Web site, The National Center for Employee Ownership, www.nceo.org, accessed January 16, 2012.

CLASS ACTIVITY:
Ask students: What are the potential benefits and risks of employee ownership?

employees to care deeply about their firm's success and contribute their best effort. These firms remain committed to this kind of involvement and compensation for their workers. Because human resources are so essential to the success of a modern business, employers want to build their employees' commitment to the organization. However, managers also admit that often employees below the executive level are not as informed about the programs as they should be, and their companies could do a better job of educating employees at all levels.[57] Some of the country's most successful public corporations, including Procter & Gamble, Lowe's, and Southwest Airlines, have embraced employee ownership and watched their stock values hold up better than those of other companies.

LECTURE ENHANCER:
Think of a family-owned business. What is your impression of the owner(s)?

Family-Owned Businesses

Family-owned firms are considered by many to be the backbone of American business. The Waltons and the Fords are viewed as pioneers because each of these firms—Walmart and Ford Motor Corp.—was once a small, family-owned company. Family-owned firms come in a variety of sizes and legal structures. But because of the complex nature of family relationships, family-owned firms experience some unique challenges.

CLASS ACTIVITY:
Lead a class discussion about the pros and cons of working with and owning a business with family members.

Whether a family-owned business is structured as a partnership, limited liability corporation, or traditional corporation, its members must make decisions regarding succession, marriages and divorces, compensation, hierarchy and authority, shareholder control, and the like. Whereas some family members may prefer a loose structure—perhaps not even putting certain agreements in writing—experienced businesspeople caution that failing to choose the right legal structure for a family-owned firm can doom the business from the start. "For family-owned businesses, especially those with multi-generational owners, lack of a formal structure is a frequent cause of turmoil and legal disputes which often result in very contentious litigation and, ultimately, the dissolution of the business," asserts one expert in family businesses.[58]

Succession is a major benefit—and drawback—to family-owned firms. On the one hand, a clearly documented plan for succession from one generation to the next is a huge source of security for the firm's continuity. But lack of legal planning, or situations in which succession is challenged, can cause chaos. In fact, only a small percentage of family-owned businesses survive into the second or third generation.

A small family firm that has managed to thrive for five generations is Squamscot Beverages. Originally called Connermade, the company was founded in 1883 when William H. Conner began producing his own "tonic" beverage—a spruce beer that came in glass bottles with porcelain-and-wire stoppers. Conner ran the company until his son Alfred took over in 1911. Alfred remained in charge until 1948, when he handed the reins to his own son, Alfred Jr. Today, Tom Conner and his son Dan manage most aspects of running the firm, which is still headquartered on the family's rural property in New Hampshire. Squamscot Beverages produces soda drinks in a variety of flavors, including birch beer, cola, cream, orange, grape, and ginger ale. Bottles are distributed to small grocery outlets, or customers can visit the bottling plant to select whichever flavors they want. Recently the company sent its first shipment of soda to California and is considering further expanding its distribution. "We have made it through the Great Depression," notes Dan Conner. "We made it through the early '80s housing crunch. We're always going to be here."[59] The Conners are not as famous or as wealthy as the Waltons or Fords, but the chance of their business surviving through future generations is strong.

Family-owned companies are considered by many to be the backbone of American business. Walmart's Walton family started its business with Walton's 5-10 store.

Jb Reed/Bloomberg/Getty Images, Inc.

Not-for-Profit Corporations

The same business concepts that apply to commercial companies also apply to **not-for-profit corporations**—organizations whose goals do not include pursuing a profit. About 1.5 million not-for-profits operate in the United States, including charitable groups, social-welfare organizations, government agencies, and religious congregations. This sector also includes museums, libraries, hospitals, conservation groups, private schools, and the like.

Most states set out separate legal provisions for organizational structures and operations of not-for-profit corporations. These organizations do not issue stock certificates, because they pay no dividends to owners, and ownership rarely changes. They are also exempt from paying income taxes. However, they must meet very strict regulations in order to maintain their not-for-profit status.

City Year Inc. is a not-for-profit organization that supports community service efforts by young people in their late teens and early twenties. Headquartered in Boston, City Year has a number of programs in which volunteers can participate. Its signature program, the City Year Youth Corps, invites 1,750 volunteers between the ages of 17 and 24 to commit to a year of full-time community service in activities such as mentoring and tutoring inner-city school children, helping to restore and reclaim public spaces, and staffing youth summer camps. The organization also partners with for-profit corporations such as Timberland, Comcast, and Pepsi to fund and implement its efforts.[60]

not-for-profit corporation organization whose goals do not include pursuing a profit.

Assessment Check ✔

1. What are the key differences between sole proprietorships and partnerships?

2. What is a corporation?

3. What is the main distinction of a not-for-profit corporation?

Public and Collective Ownership of Business

Though most businesses in the United States are owned by the private sector, some firms are actually owned by local, state, or the federal government. Alaskan Railroad Corp., East Alabama Medical Center, Washington State Ferries, and the Iowa Lottery are all government-owned businesses.[61]

In another type of ownership structure, groups of customers may collectively own a company. Recreational Equipment Inc. (REI) is a collectively owned retailer that sells outdoor gear and apparel. Finally, groups of smaller firms may collectively own a larger organization. Both of these collective ownership structures are also referred to as cooperatives.

Public (Government) Ownership

One alternative to private ownership is some form of *public ownership*, in which a unit or agency of government owns and operates an organization. In the United States, local governments often own parking structures and water systems. The Pennsylvania Turnpike Authority operates a vital highway link across the Keystone State. The federal government operates Hoover Dam in Nevada to provide electricity over a large region.

LECTURE ENHANCER: Can you think of an example of public ownership in your state?

Sometimes public ownership results when private investors are unwilling to invest in a high-risk project—or find that operating an important service is simply unprofitable. The National Railroad Passenger Corporation—better known as Amtrak—is a for-profit corporation that operates intercity passenger rail service in 46 states and the District of Columbia. Congress created Amtrak in the Rail Passenger Service Act of 1970, thereby removing from private railroads the obligation of transporting passengers, because passenger rail travel was generally unprofitable. In exchange, the private railroads granted Amtrak access to their existing tracks at a low cost. The Amtrak board of directors is made up of seven voting members appointed for five-year terms by the president of the United States.[62]

Collective (Cooperative) Ownership

Collective ownership establishes an organization referred to as a *cooperative* (or *co-op*), whose owners join forces to operate all or part of the activities in their firm or industry. Currently, there are about 100 million people worldwide employed by cooperatives.[63] Cooperatives allow small businesses to pool their resources on purchases, marketing, equipment, distribution, and the like. Discount savings can be split among members. Cooperatives can share equipment and expertise. During difficult economic times, members find a variety of ways to support each other.

Assessment Check ✓

1. What is public ownership?

2. What is collective ownership? Where are cooperatives typically found, and what benefits do they provide small businesses?

Cooperatives are frequently found among agricultural businesses. Cabot Creamery is a cooperative of 1,500 small dairy farms spread throughout New England and upstate New York. Cabot is owned and operated by its members—farmers and their families. In addition, Cabot works with other cooperatives around the country to produce and distribute high-quality cheese, butter, and other dairy products.[64]

9

Organizing a Corporation

A corporation is a legal structure, but it also requires a certain organizational structure that is more complex than the structure of a sole proprietorship or a partnership. This is why people often think of a corporation as a large entity, even though it does not have to be a specific size.

Types of Corporations

Corporations fall into three categories: domestic, foreign, and alien. A firm is considered a *domestic corporation* in the state where it is incorporated. When a company does business in states other than the one where it has filed incorporation papers, it is registered as a *foreign corporation* in each of those states. A firm incorporated in one nation that operates in another is known as an *alien corporation* where it operates. Many firms—particularly large corporations with operations scattered around the world—may operate under all three of these designations.

Where and How Businesses Incorporate

Businesses owners who want to incorporate must decide where to locate their headquarters and follow the correct procedure for submitting the legal document that establishes the corporation.

Where to Incorporate Deciding where to incorporate—and establish headquarters—may be based on a number of factors. Most businesses want to be near their customers. Real estate prices as well as services such as public transportation and communications networks are other variables. Access to a good labor pool is another reason for choosing a location. Online businesses such as Amazon.com and eBay don't need to worry about positioning themselves near their customers, but they should consider the local labor pool.

Although most small- and medium-sized businesses are incorporated in the states in which they operate, a U.S. firm can actually incorporate in any state it chooses. The founders of large corporations, or of those that will do business nationwide, often compare the benefits—such as tax incentives—provided by each state. Some states are considered to be more "business friendly" than others. Delaware is one of the easiest states in which to incorporate.

The Corporate Charter Each state has a specific procedure for incorporating a business. Most states require at least three *incorporators*—the individuals who create the corporation. In addition, the new corporation must select a name that is different from names used by other businesses. Figure 5.6 lists the 10 elements that most states require for chartering a corporation.

FIGURE
5.6 Traditional Articles of Incorporation

- Name and Address of the Corporation
- Corporate Objectives
- Type and Amount of Stock to Issue
- Expected Life of the Corporation
- Financial Capital at the Time of Incorporation
- Provisions for Transferring Shares of Stock among Owners
- Provisions for Regulating Internal Corporate Affairs
- Address of the Business Office Registered with the State of Incorporation
- Names and Addresses of the Initial Board of Directors
- Names and Addresses of the Incorporators

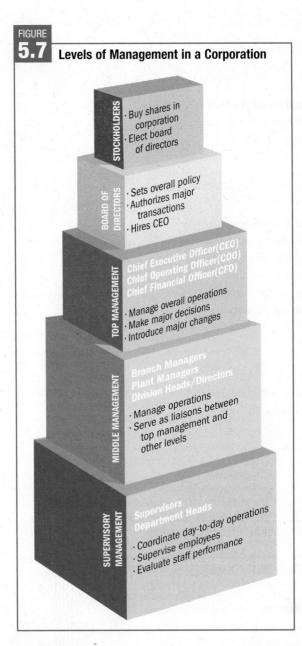

FIGURE 5.7 Levels of Management in a Corporation

STOCKHOLDERS
· Buy shares in corporation
· Elect board of directors

BOARD OF DIRECTORS
· Sets overall policy
· Authorizes major transactions
· Hires CEO

TOP MANAGEMENT
Chief Executive Officer(CEO)
Chief Operating Officer(COO)
Chief Financial Officer(CFO)
· Manage overall operations
· Make major decisions
· Introduce major changes

MIDDLE MANAGEMENT
Branch Managers
Plant Managers
Division Heads/Directors
· Manage operations
· Serve as liaisons between top management and other levels

SUPERVISORY MANAGEMENT
Supervisors
Department Heads
· Coordinate day-to-day operations
· Supervise employees
· Evaluate staff performance

stockholders owners of a corporation due to their purchase of stock in the corporation.

preferred stock shares that give owners limited voting rights, and the right to receive dividends or assets before owners of common stock.

common stock shares that give owners voting rights but only residual claims to the firm's assets and income distributions.

board of directors governing body of a corporation.

The information provided in the articles of incorporation forms the basis on which a state grants a *corporate charter*, which is the legal document that formally establishes a corporation. After securing the charter, the owners prepare the company's bylaws, which describe the rules and procedures for its operation.

Corporate Management

Regardless of its size, every corporation has levels of management and ownership. Figure 5.7 illustrates those that are typical—although a smaller firm might not contain all five of these. These levels range from stockholders down to supervisory management.

Stock Ownership and Stockholder Rights At the top of Figure 5.7 are **stockholders**. They buy shares of stock in the corporation, becoming part owners of it. Some companies, such as family businesses, are owned by relatively few stockholders, and the stock is generally unavailable to outsiders. In such a firm, known as a *closed* or *closely held corporation*, the stockholders also control and manage all of the company's activities. S.C. Johnson & Son is one such firm.

In contrast, an open corporation, also called a *publicly held corporation*, sells stock to the general public, establishing diversified ownership and often leading to a broader scope of operations than those of a closed corporation. Publicly held corporations usually hold annual stockholders' meetings. During these meetings, managers report on corporate activities, and stockholders vote on any decisions that require their approval, including elections of officers. Walmart holds the nation's largest stockholder meeting at the University of Arkansas Bud Walton Arena. Approximately 16,000 people attend. In addition to standard shareholder business, the Walmart meeting has featured celebrities and entertainers such as Tim McGraw and Faith Hill, Queen Latifah, Scotty McCreery, and Will Smith.

Stockholders' role in the corporation depends on the class of stock they own. Shares are usually classified as common or preferred stock. Although owners of **preferred stock** have limited voting rights, they are entitled to receive dividends before holders of common stock. If the corporation is dissolved, they have first claims on assets, once debtors are repaid. Owners of **common stock** have voting rights but only residual claims on the firm's assets, which means they are last to receive any income distributions. Because one share is typically worth only one vote, small stockholders generally have little influence on corporate management actions.

Board of Directors Stockholders elect a **board of directors**—the governing body of a corporation. The board sets overall policy, authorizes major transactions involving the corporation, and hires the chief executive officer (CEO). Most boards include both inside directors (corporate executives) and outside directors—people who are not otherwise employed by the organization. Sometimes the corporation's top executive also chairs the

Solving an Ethical Controversy

Do Some Bosses Earn Too Much?

Median CEO pay reached $8.4 million recently, up a whopping 35 percent despite the economic downturn felt by others. Enormous pay packages are meant to reward stellar company performance, but this has not always been true. Meanwhile U.S. firms hold a record amount of cash while millions of workers remain unemployed because business investment has dried up, and repeated financial crises have cost shareholders billions in retirement savings.

Is executive pay excessive?

PRO

1. CEO compensation should reflect the overall state of the economy and should be adjusted accordingly.

2. Poor returns to company shareholders do not merit high rewards to those responsible for increasing overall company value.

CON

1. CEOs must take huge personal and professional risks to successfully manage their firms, and they should be well rewarded.

2. High pay ensures that firms attract and keep talented CEOs, especially in difficult times when their skills are needed.

Summary

As CEO pay skyrocketed from 42 times the average U.S. worker's pay to more than 300 times in recent years, Congress handed shareholders new legislation, which allows them to vote "no" on executives' excessive pay. So far, however, "no" votes have only occurred at fewer than 2% of almost 2,000 publicly traded companies.

Sources: "Trends in CEO Pay," www.aflcio.org, accessed January 16, 2012; Susanne Craig, "Deal Book: Wall Street Is Bracing for Dismal 4th Quarter," *The New York Times*, January 7, 2012, www.nytimes.com; Nathaniel Parish Flannery, "Paying for Failure: The Costs of Firing America's Top CEO's," *Forbes*, October 4, 2011, www.forbes.com; Dale Wannen, "How Shareholders Are Battling Excessive Executive Compensation," Triple Pundit.com, June 30, 2011, www.triplepundit.com; John Holyar, "Investor 'Say on Pay' Is a Bust," *Bloomberg BusinessWeek*, June 16, 2011, www.businessweek.com.

---

board. Generally, outside directors are also stockholders, so they have a financial stake in the company's performance.

Corporate Officers and Managers The CEO and other members of top management, such as the chief operating officer (COO), chief financial officer (CFO), and the chief information officer (CIO), make most major corporate decisions. Managers at the next level down the hierarchy, middle management, handle the ongoing operational functions of the company. At the first tier of management, supervisory personnel coordinate day-to-day operations, assign specific tasks to employees, and evaluate job performance.

Today's CEOs and CFOs are bound by stricter regulations than in the past. They must verify in writing the accuracy of their firm's financial statements, and the process for nominating candidates for the board has become more complex. In short, more checks and balances are in place for the governance of corporations. A continuing controversy surrounds the rising pay levels of CEOs, however; see the "Solving an Ethical Controversy" feature.

Assessment Check ✓

1. What are the two key elements of the incorporation process?

2. Identify the five main levels of corporate ownership and management.

10 When Businesses Join Forces

Today's business environment contains many complex relationships among businesses as well as not-for-profit organizations. Two firms may team up to develop a product or co-market products. One company may buy out another. Large corporations may split into smaller units. The list of alliances is a varied as the organizations themselves, but the major trends in corporate ownership include mergers and acquisitions and joint ventures.

Mergers and Acquisitions (M&A)

In recent years, mergers and acquisitions among U.S. corporations have hit an all-time high. Airlines, financial institutions, telecommunications companies, and media corporations are just a few of the types of businesses that have merged into giants. Recently, Continental Airlines merged with United Airlines to form one company, which will be known as United Airlines. The merger took time to complete, not least because the two carriers had to combine their computer systems. Together, the airlines form the largest carrier in the world.[65]

The terms *merger* and *acquisition* are often used interchangeably, but their meanings are different. In a **merger**, two or more firms combine to form one company. In an **acquisition**, one firm purchases the other. This means that not only does the buyer acquire the firm's property and assets, it also takes on any debt obligations. Acquisitions also occur when one firm buys a division or subsidiary from another firm. Not all such attempts are successful. Recently, AT&T attempted to buy T-Mobile USA, an acquisition that would have combined the second- and fourth-largest American wireless companies. The government filed a lawsuit to block the deal, which it said would be a violation of antitrust law and substantially lessen competition. Because of the high fees AT&T would have to pay T-Mobile's parent company if the deal fell through, AT&T decided to fight the government's claim. In the end, AT&T gave up its attempt to buy the smaller company and instead negotiated an agreement with T-Mobile on roaming charges for phone users.[66]

Mergers can be classified as vertical, horizontal, or conglomerate. A **vertical merger** combines firms operating at different levels in the production and marketing process—the combination of a manufacturer and a large retailer, for instance. A vertical merger pursues one of two primary goals: (1) to ensure adequate flows of raw materials and supplies needed for a firm's products or (2) to increase distribution. Software giant Microsoft is well known for acquiring small firms that have developed products with strong market potential, such as Teleo, a provider of voice over Internet protocol (VoIP) software and services that can be used to make phone calls via the Internet.

A **horizontal merger** joins firms in the same industry. This is done for the purpose of diversification, increasing customer bases, cutting costs, or expanding product lines. This type of merger is particularly popular in the auto and health care industries. Volkswagen now owns the Porsche brand, while CVS Caremark recently purchased another firm's Medicaid prescription business.

A **conglomerate merger** combines unrelated firms. The most common reasons for a conglomerate merger are to diversify, spur sales growth, or spend a cash surplus that might otherwise make the firm a tempting target for a takeover effort. Conglomerate mergers may join firms in totally unrelated industries. General Electric is well known for its conglomerate mergers—including its ownership of health care services and household appliances. Experts debate whether conglomerate mergers are beneficial. The usual argument in favor of such mergers is that a company can use its management expertise to succeed in a variety of industries. But the obvious drawback is that a huge conglomerate can spread its resources too thin to be dominant in any one market.

CLASS ACTIVITY:
Ask students to share their ideas of benefits that might result from a merger of two large banks.

merger agreement in which two or more firms combine to form one company.

acquisition agreement in which one firm purchases another.

vertical merger merger that combines firms operating at different levels in the production and marketing process.

horizontal merger merger that joins firms in the same industry for the purpose of diversification, increasing customer bases, cutting costs, or expanding product lines.

conglomerate merger merger that combines unrelated firms, usually with the goal of diversification, spurring sales growth, or spending a cash surplus in order to avoid a takeover attempt.

Joint Ventures: Specialized Partnerships

A **joint venture** is a partnership between companies formed for a specific undertaking. Sometimes a company enters into a joint venture with a local firm, sharing the operation's costs, risks, management, and profits with its local partner. This is particularly common when a firm wants to enter into business in a foreign market. DreamWorks Animation recently entered a joint venture with three Chinese firms. The four companies will invest $330 million in a new company, Oriental DreamWorks. Based in Shanghai, the new venture will specialize in family films.[67]

Joint ventures between for-profit firms and not-for-profit organizations are becoming more and more common. These partnerships provide great benefits for both parties. Not-for-profit organizations receive the funding, marketing exposure, and sometimes manpower they might not otherwise generate. City Year, mentioned earlier, enjoys these benefits from partnerships with Timberland, Pepsi, and Comcast along with other firms such as Starbucks and Sears. Recently, Starbucks partnered with City Year Miami and Rebuilding Together Miami Dade to repair a veteran's home in appreciation for his military service. The effort was made possible as part of Sears' Operation Rebuild for Heroes at Home program.[68]

joint venture partnership between companies formed for a specific undertaking.

Assessment Check ✓

1. Distinguish between a merger and an acquisition.
2. What are the different kinds of mergers?
3. What is a joint venture?

LECTURE ENHANCER: Can you think of an example of a joint venture between a commercial firm and a not-for-profit organization?

Courtesy City Year Miami

Joint ventures between for-profit firms and not-for-profit organizations provide great benefits for both parties. Starbucks partnered with City Year Miami and Rebuilding Together Miami Dade to repair a veteran's home in appreciation for his military service, as part of Sears' Operation Rebuild for Heroes at Home program.

What's Ahead

The next chapter focuses on the driving forces behind the formation of new businesses: entrepreneurs. It examines the differences between a small-business owner and an entrepreneur and identifies certain personality traits typical of entrepreneurs. The chapter also details the process of launching a new venture, including identifying opportunities, locating needed financing, and turning good ideas into successful businesses. Finally, the chapter explores a method for infusing the entrepreneurial spirit into established businesses—intrapreneurship.

Summary of Learning Objectives

1 **Discuss why most businesses are small businesses.**

A small business is an independently owned business having fewer than 500 employees. Generally it is not dominant in its field and meets industry-specific size standards for income or number of employees. A business is classified as large when it exceeds these specifications.

Assessment Check Answers ✔

1.1 How does the Small Business Administration (SBA) define *small business?* A small business is defined as an independent business having fewer than 500 employees. However, those bidding for government contracts or applying for government assistance may vary in size according to industry.

1.2 In what industries do small businesses play a significant role? Small businesses provide most jobs in construction, agriculture, wholesale trade, services, and retail trade. In addition, home-based businesses make up 52 percent of American small businesses.

2 **Determine the contributions of small businesses to the economy.**

Small businesses create new jobs and new industries. They often hire workers who traditionally have had difficulty finding employment at larger firms. Small firms give people the opportunity and outlet for developing new ideas, which can turn into entirely new industries. Small businesses also develop new and improved goods and services.

Assessment Check Answers ✔

2.1 What are the three key ways in which small businesses contribute to the economy? Small businesses create new jobs and new industries, and provide innovation.

2.2 How are new industries formed? New industries are formed when small businesses adapt to shifts in consumer interests and preferences. Innovation and new technology can play a significant role. In addition, new industries may be created when both the business world and consumers recognize a need for change.

3 **Discuss why small businesses fail.**

About 7 of every 10 new (small) businesses survive at least two years. But by the tenth year, 82 percent have closed. Failure is often attributed to management shortcomings, inadequate financing, and difficulty meeting government regulations.

Assessment Check Answers ✔

3.1 What percentage of small businesses remain in operation five years after starting? Ten years? About 50 percent are in business after five years; about 82 percent have folded by the 10-year mark.

3.2 What are the three main causes of small-business failure? The three main causes of small-business failure are

management shortcomings, inadequate financing, and difficulty complying with government regulations.

4 **Describe the features of a successful business plan.**

A complete business plan contains an executive summary, an introduction, financial and marketing sections, and résumés of the business principals. Within this structure, an effective business plan includes the company's mission, an outline of what makes the company unique, identification of customers and competitors, financial evaluation of the industry and market, and an assessment of the risks.

Assessment Check Answers ✔

4.1 What are the five main sections of a business plan? The five sections are the executive summary, introduction, financial section, marketing section, and résumés of principals.

4.2 Why is an effective business plan important to the success of a firm? The business plan puts in writing all the reasons the firm can be successful. It contains the written soul of the firm. It is the document that secures financing and creates a framework for the organization.

5 **Identify the available assistance for small businesses.**

The SBA guarantees loans made by private lenders, including microloans and those funded by Small Business Investment Companies. It offers training and information resources, so business owners can improve their odds of success. The SBA also provides specific support for businesses owned by women and minorities. State and local governments also have programs designed to help small businesses get established and grow. Venture capitalists are firms that invest in small businesses in return for an ownership stake.

Assessment Check Answers ✔

5.1 What are the various ways the SBA helps small businesses? The SBA guarantees business loans; helps small businesses compete for government set-aside programs; and provides business information, advice, and training to owners of small businesses. It also advocates for small-business interests within the federal government.

5.2 What are business incubators? Business incubators are programs organized by community agencies that provide such services as rental space, clerical staff, and office equipment in an effort to help small businesses get started.

5.3 Why are small businesses good opportunities for women and minorities? Many women feel they can achieve more as small-business owners and can balance family and work more easily if they own their own firms. Minority business owners can receive special assistance from programs such as the SBA's Mentor-Protégé program.

6 **Explain franchising.**

A franchisor is a large firm that permits a small-business owner (franchisee) to sell its products under its brand name, in return for a fee. Benefits to the franchisor include opportunities for expansion and greater profits. Benefits to the franchisee include name recognition, quick start-up, support from the franchisor, and the freedom of small-business ownership.

Assessment Check Answers ☑

6.1 What is the difference between a franchisor and a franchisee? A franchisor permits a small-business owner (franchisee) to market and sell its products under its brand name, in return for a fee.

6.2 What are the benefits to both parties of franchising? Benefits to the franchisor include opportunities for expansion and greater profits. Benefits to the franchisee include name recognition, quick start-up, support from the franchisor, and the freedom of small-business ownership.

6.3 What are the potential drawbacks of franchising for both parties? The drawbacks for the franchisor include mismanagement and failure on the part of any of its franchisees, overexpansion, and loss of absolute control over the business. Drawbacks for the franchisee include an initial outlay of expenses, problems due to failure on the part of the franchisor or other franchisees, and restrictive franchise agreements.

⌐7⌐ Outline the forms of private business ownership.

A sole proprietorship is owned and operated by one person. While sole proprietorships are easy to set up and offer great operating flexibility, the owner remains personally liable for all of the firm's debts and legal settlements. In a partnership, two or more individuals share responsibility for owning and running the business. Partnerships are relatively easy to set up, but they do not offer protection from liability. When a business is set up as a corporation, it becomes a separate legal entity. Investors receive shares of stock in the firm. Owners have no legal and financial liability beyond their individual investments. In an employee-owned business, most stockholders are also employees. Family-owned businesses may be structured legally in any of these three ways but face unique challenges, including succession and complex relationships. The legal structure of a not-for-profit corporation stipulates that its goals do not include earning a profit.

Assessment Check Answers ☑

7.1 What are the key differences between sole proprietorships and partnerships? Sole proprietorships and partnerships expose their owners to unlimited financial liability from their businesses. Sole proprietorships are more flexible and easier to dissolve than partnerships. Partnerships involve shared work load and decision making, whereas sole proprietorships are entirely the responsibility of one business owner.

7.2 What is a corporation? A corporation is a legal organization with assets and liabilities separate from those of its owners. A corporation can be a large or small business.

7.3 What is the main distinction of a not-for-profit corporation? A not-for-profit organization is set up legally so that its goals do not include pursuing a profit. Most states set out specific legal provisions for organizational structures and operations of not-for-profit corporations. They are exempt from paying income taxes.

⌐8⌐ Describe public and collective ownership of business.

Public ownership occurs when a unit or agency of government owns and operates an organization. Collective ownership establishes an organization referred to as a cooperative, whose owners join forces to operate all or part of the functions in their firm or industry.

Assessment Check Answers ☑

8.1 What is public ownership? Public ownership occurs when a unit or agency of government owns and operates an organization.

8.2 What is collective ownership? Where are cooperatives typically found, and what benefits do they provide small businesses? Collective ownership establishes an organization referred to as a cooperative (co-op), whose owners join forces to operate all or part of the functions in their firm or industry. Cooperatives are frequently found among agricultural businesses. They can also occur in retail. Cooperatives allow small firms to pool their resources, share equipment and expertise, and help each other through difficult times.

⌐9⌐ Discuss organizing a corporation.

There are three types of corporations: domestic, foreign, and alien. Stockholders, or shareholders, own a corporation. In return for their financial investments, they receive shares of stock in the company. Stockholders elect a board of directors, who set overall policy. The board hires the chief executive officer (CEO), who then hires managers.

Assessment Check Answers ☑

9.1 What are the two key elements of the incorporation process? The two key elements are where to incorporate and the corporate charter.

9.2 Identify the five main levels of corporate ownership and management. The five levels are: stockholders, board of directors, top management, middle management, and supervisory management.

⌐10⌐ Explain what happens when businesses join forces.

In a merger, two or more firms combine to form one company. A vertical merger combines firms operating at different levels in the production and marketing process. A horizontal merger joins firms in the same industry. A conglomerate merger combines unrelated firms. An acquisition occurs when one firm purchases another. A joint venture is a partnership between companies formed for a specific undertaking.

Assessment Check Answers ✔️

10.1 Distinguish between a merger and an acquisition. In a merger, two or more firms combine to form one company. In an acquisition, one firm purchases the property and assumes the obligations of another. Acquisitions also occur when one firm buys a division or subsidiary from another firm.

10.2 What are the different kinds of mergers? Mergers can be classified as vertical, horizontal, or conglomerate.

10.3 What is a joint venture? A joint venture is a partnership between organizations formed for a specific undertaking.

◼ Business Terms You Need to Know

small business 134	franchisor 148	preferred stock 158
home-based business 136	sole proprietorship 151	common stock 158
business plan 141	partnership 152	board of directors 158
Small Business Administration (SBA) 143	corporation 152	merger 160
microloans 143	S corporations 153	acquisition 160
business incubator 144	limited-liability corporation (LLC) 153	vertical merger 160
venture capital 145	employee ownership 153	horizontal merger 160
franchising 147	not-for-profit corporation 155	conglomerate merger 160
franchisee 148	stockholders 158	joint venture 161

◼ Review Questions

1. Describe how a small business might use innovation to create new jobs.

2. Why do so many small businesses fail before they reach their tenth year?

3. What are the benefits of developing and writing an effective business plan?

4. What is the Small Business Administration? How does it assist small companies, financially and in other specialized ways?

5. Describe how local governments and business incubators help small firms get established and grow.

6. Why are so many small-business owners attracted to franchising? Under what circumstances might it be better to start an entirely new business instead of purchasing a franchise?

7. What are the benefits and drawbacks to traditional corporate structure? How do S corporations and limited liability corporations enhance the corporate legal structure?

8. Cooperatives appear frequently in agriculture. Describe another industry in which you think collective ownership would be beneficial, and explain why.

9. In a proprietorship and in partnerships the owners and the managers of the business are the same people. How are ownership and management separated in corporations?

10. How might a joint venture between a commercial firm and a not-for-profit organization help both achieve their goals?

◼ Projects and Teamwork Applications

1. Research a large firm to find out more about its beginnings as a small business. Who founded the company? Does the firm still produce its original offerings, or has it moved entirely away from them?

2. Go to the Web site Entrepreneur.com and research information on franchises. Choose one that interests you and evaluate the information about its start-up requirements.

Would you consider a partnership in your franchise with someone you know? Why or why not? Present your findings in class.

3. Brainstorm a small-business idea. Research the industry and major competition online. Draft a business plan. Include your decision on whether your firm will be a sole proprietorship or a partnership.

4. Identify an organization—such as Americorps or the United States Postal Service—that is owned by a unit or agency of government. Imagine that you have been hired by that agency as a consultant to decide whether the organization should remain publicly owned. Research its successes and failures, and write a memo explaining your conclusion.

5. Identify a business and a not-for-profit organization that could form a joint venture beneficial to both. Draft a written proposal for this venture.

■ Web Assignments

1. **Small-business successes.** Visit the Web site at http://www.entrepreneur.com/startingabusiness/successstories/index.html. Scroll through the titles of success stories and choose one that interests you. Read the feature and prepare a brief report answering these questions:

   a. What does the firm do?

   b. Where did the idea originate?

   c. What expertise does the owner have?

   d. How did the business begin?

   e. Who are its competitors?

2. **Great small workplaces.** Winning Workplaces is a not-for-profit organization that is committed to "helping small and midsize organizations create high-performance workplaces." Visit the organization's Web site at http://www.winningworkplaces.com and read at least two postings or articles there that interest you. Summarize the articles and explain how they help fulfill the Winning Workplaces' mission of helping small businesses succeed.

3. **Family-business tips for success.** Go to the Web site for *Family Business Magazine* at http://www.familybusinessmagazine.com and click on the feature article. Read the piece to learn about a particular family-owned business. Alternatively, choose a family-owned business such as S.C. Johnson (large) or Cider Hill Farm (small) and visit the firm's Web site to learn how the company has grown over the years and achieved success.

Note: Internet Web addresses change frequently. If you do not find the exact sites listed, you may need to access the organization's or company's home page and search from there.

Ideeli Gives Members (and Suppliers) Daily Deals   CASE 5.1

If you like to shop online and love a bargain, you may already be among the 4.5 million members of Ideeli.com, a flash-sale Web site whose revenue has grown more than 40,000 percent (that's not a typo) since 2007.

Every day at noon, Ideeli unveils over a dozen new, members-only sales of high-fashion clothing for men, women, and children, along with home furnishings and travel. Items move fast and sales end quickly, but joining the site is easy and discounts can reach 80 percent off retail. The New York City–based company recently took the number-one spot on *Inc.* magazine's list of top 500 firms, earning almost $80 million in revenue.

Ideeli members obviously love surprises and great deals, but what attracts more than 1,000 suppliers to Ideeli's Web site? It's the ability to either speedily unload excess inventory or find new markets for up-and-coming brands, with reduced prices sheltered behind the members-only shopping concept. "Membership helps protect the brand," says one industry expert. "You can't find a sale on Prada or whatever just by Googling. It's behind a wall."

While flash-shopping has already been popular in Europe for a decade, CEO Paul Hurley feels it still has room to grow. "Ideeli is really a lab for what retail is going to become."

Questions for Critical Thinking

1. Do you agree with Paul Hurley that future retailers will adopt his site's flash-sale model? Why or why not?

2. What effect does the membership requirement have on the way the company operates?

Sources: Company Web site, www.ideeli.com, accessed January 16, 2012; Feifei Sun, "Flash Fashion 101: How to Make the most of Gilt, Rue La La and Other Sale Sites," *Time*, December 1, 2011, http://moneyland.time.com; Allison Fass, "Ideeli's HR Chief on How to Hire Well," *Inc.*, October 17, 2011, www.inc.com; Leigh Buchanan, "The Fastest-Growing Private Company of 2011," *Inc.*, August 23, 2011, www.inc.com.

Small Meets Big: Patagonia and Walmart Join Forces for the Environment

When Yvon Chouinard started rock climbing as a teenager, he never dreamed his passion would lead to the ownership of two companies and a lifelong passion for preserving the planet. But 55 years later, the climber-businessperson has joined forces with Walmart—a seemingly unlikely partner—to spread the word that sustainability is cool.

Chouinard founded Chouinard Equipment to make safer, more environmentally friendly equipment for rock climbers and mountaineers. He didn't like the way previous generations of climbers had destroyed mountain environments. Patagonia, founded in 1972, offered the "soft" side of the outdoors—specialized clothing, boots, packs, luggage, and other gear. From the very beginning, Chouinard and his design team worked hard to develop products whose materials and manufacturing processes were eco-friendly. "The reason I am in business is I want to protect what I love," Chouinard explains. "I used to spend 250 days a year sleeping on the ground. I've climbed on every continent. I'm old enough to have seen the destruction."

In fact, in the mid-1990s Chouinard discovered that the cotton Patagonia was using for many of its garments came from industrial farms that used toxic chemicals. His response was swift and definite. He gave his company just 18 months to change completely to organic cotton. Chouinard has also been successful at persuading other businesses to go green.

For the past few years, Chouinard's team has been working with Walmart to develop a sustainability index for its products, sharing valuable information that Patagonia has gained over the years. Walmart is 1,300 times as large as Patagonia, but Patagonia has knowledge and experience that Walmart can use to reinvent itself as an environmentally responsible firm. Chouinard doesn't mind sharing with a company that has such a monumental impact on the marketplace as well as the planet. And Walmart officials are eager to learn. The company plans to post scorecards in its stores, rating products on eco-friendliness and social impact. And it is developing a system to give preference to suppliers who comply with these steps. At one conference of Walmart buyers and executives, Chouinard pointed out that Walmart's use of little LED lights in its stores—which seem to use minimal energy—actually requires 19 plants in California to power them. At this statement, a Walmart buyer stood in the audience and shouted, "We're going to get rid of those!"

Questions for Critical Thinking

1. The alliance between Patagonia and Walmart is an excellent example of a smaller business and a huge firm working together to achieve an objective. Do you think the same results would be possible if Walmart acquired Patagonia? Why or why not?

2. Walmart is learning from Patagonia. But what might Patagonia learn from Walmart?

Sources: "What We Do," Patagonia Web site, http://www.patagonia .com, accessed March 6, 2012; "Patagonia," in "*Inc.* Top Workplaces 2010," http://www.inc.com, accessed March 6, 2012; Monte Burke, "Walmart, Patagonia, Team to Green Business," *Forbes,* http://www.forbes .com, accessed March 6, 2012.

Seventh Generation Cleans Up with Consumer Products

Seventh Generation isn't as old as its company name suggests. In fact, the firm has been in business for a bit more than two decades, merely allowing time for a second generation of employees to move the company's mission forward. But the firm is focused clearly on the future—seven generations in the future, to be precise. Seventh Generation's mission is based on the Great Law of the Iroquois, which states: "In every deliberation, we must consider the impact of our decision on the next seven generations." With that in mind, the company manufactures and sells household products carefully designed and produced to leave as little impact on the natural environment as possible.

Jeffrey Hollender, Seventh Generation's co-founder, is passionate about the planet. "This is a moment in time that we may not have again," he says of the company's efforts to educate consumers about the impact of the products they buy and use—and its alternative offerings.

It's true that Seventh Generation is now a large enough company that Hollender can speak with a voice heard by media, legislators, and the general public. But it wasn't always this way. "We started in 1988 selling energy products like compact fluorescent light bulbs (CFLs) that cost about $28 a piece," recalls Hollender. His company operated out of a single room in Vermont with half a dozen employees. At first, most consumers were reluctant to pay the high price for CFLs or the firm's organic bedding and cleaning products. But Hollender and his staff remained committed. "We basically sold products we needed to live a more responsible, natural lifestyle," explains Hollender.

Despite the company's small size, word about its fresh ideas in household cleaning and energy use spread quickly, despite the fact that many people thought Seventh Generation was a nonprofit organization. "We grew a lot the first three years," says Hollender. "We went from $100,000 to $1 million to $8 million in sales—then we crashed, we hit a wall." Seventh Generation experienced the growing pains that nearly every small business goes through. Hollender admits that the most difficult aspect of growth was realizing it had happened too fast. He cut his own salary, but the decision that caused Hollender the most pain was the layoffs necessary to keep the firm running. "Letting someone go because we had failed to be financially viable enough to employ them, that's my failing," he asserts. "Letting people go has to be the absolute last resort."

But the firm regained its balance and began to grow again with a new sense of purpose. Recently, Seventh Generation is nearing $200 million in sales, with its laundry detergent and diapers as its top-selling products. This figure that allows the company to hire experts in research and development, build stronger relationships with suppliers and customers, engage in business practices that promote sustainability, and market products that fulfill its promise to reduce human impact on the natural environment. "Growth brings credibility," observes Dave Rappaport, Seventh Generation's director of corporate consciousness.

Hollender agrees. "Our size allows a platform to influence the way business is done in America," he comments. Hollender, who turned the job of CEO over to Chuck Maniscalco, now uses his clout to spend more time on not-for-profit environmental initiatives such as the Sustainability Institute.

In addition, Seventh Generation has entered into a strategic partnership with retail giant Walmart to offer environmentally friendly products at more than 1,500 of its stores nationwide as well as on Walmart.com. As part of the alliance, Walmart stores will now carry a range of Seventh Generation's cleaning products, including its best-selling laundry detergent, dish soap, and cleaning spray. An expanded array of products, including baby diapers and wipes, are offered on Walmart.com. CEO Maniscalco is enthusiastic about the partnership. "Seventh Generation and Walmart are committed to helping people learn about natural alternatives and ways to protect themselves and their families," he remarked recently.

Jeffrey Hollender notes that Seventh Generation's work is far from finished. "We need to become a business that is all good rather than less bad," he states. When the company reaches that point, he predicts, its growth could have no limits.

Questions for Critical Thinking

1. Describe specific contributions that you believe Seventh Generation makes to the economy.

2. Given the high failure rate of small businesses, why do you think Seventh Generation has survived?

3. Seventh Generation is a privately held company. Create a chart showing possible benefits and pitfalls for the company if its management decided to sell stock to the general public.

4. Seventh Generation has entered into a strategic partnership with Walmart. Do you think this partnership will be a successful match for both parties? Why or why not?

Sources: Company Web site, http://www.seventhgeneration.com, accessed March 6, 2012; Ronnie Ribitzky, "7 Facts About Seventh Generation," *Portfolio.com*, http://www.portfolio.com, accessed March 6, 2012; "Seventh Generation and Walmart Announce Strategic Partnership," *MarketWire*, July 26, 2010, http://www.marketwire.com; Danielle Sacks, "Jeffrey Hollender: Seventh Generation, Triple Bottom Line Entrepreneur," *Fast Company.com*, February 2, 2010, http://fastcompany.com.

Learning Objectives

1. Define what is an entrepreneur.
2. Identify the different categories of entrepreneurs.
3. Explain why people choose entrepreneurship as a career path.
4. Discuss the environment for entrepreneurs.
5. Identify the characteristics of entrepreneurs.
6. Summarize the process of starting a new venture.
7. Explain intrapreneurship.

Chapter 6

Starting Your Own Business: The Entrepreneurship Alternative

The Marketing Zen Group: From $1,500 to Millions in Five Years

"Young entrepreneurs have to create their own opportunities. This economy needs fresh blood and bold new ideas." That forthright attitude is what took The Marketing Zen Group, Shama Kabani's entrepreneurial Web marketing firm, from a one-person start-up in 2009 to a 30-person global firm in two short years.

Kabani, who founded the Dallas-based company at age 24 with $1,500 of her own money, saw an opportunity while still in college to help firms struggling to get up to speed with online marketing and social media. Their needs and Kabani's interests were a match, so she quickly adapted her original idea, which was to start a general consulting firm, and shifted to building a company that takes over Web marketing services for clients. For clients like Arthur Murray Dance Studios and k9cuisine.com, Marketing Zen Group handles everything from setting up a Facebook and Twitter presence to creating interactive Web sites, developing e-mail marketing campaigns, optimizing search engine results, and launching blogs aimed at clients' target markets. Clients have already seen record results from the firm's efforts, in terms of both Web traffic and sales dollars.

Kabani, who has also written a best-selling book about social media marketing, expects her firm to soon reach multimillion-dollar status. She keeps overhead low by using virtual hiring and lets most employees work off-site. Kabani says hiring is different in an entrepreneurial firm. A large corporation can accommodate many different types of employees, but "in a smaller business, passion is a must in every position. Hire people who are driven to do well and see your business succeed." Kabani herself brings the same degree of passion to her work. At the same time, she cautions against multitasking because it "decreases brain power," believes in elevating value over price, and stresses forgiveness and treating your team well. Kabani declares, "Aim for joy."[1]

Overview

You think you want to start and run your own company. Like Shama Kabani, you've got a great idea for a new business. Maybe you even dream of achieving fame and fortune. If you've been bitten by the entrepreneurial bug, you're not alone. More than ever, people like you, your classmates, and your friends are choosing the path of entrepreneurship.

How do you become an entrepreneur? Experts advise aspiring entrepreneurs to learn as much as possible about business by completing academic programs such as the one in which you are currently enrolled and by gaining practical experience by working part- or full-time for businesses. In addition, you can obtain valuable insights about the pleasures and pitfalls of entrepreneurship by reading newspaper and magazine articles and biographies of successful entrepreneurs. These sources will help you learn how entrepreneurs handle the challenges of starting their businesses. For advice on how to launch and grow a new venture, turn to magazines such as *Entrepreneur*, *Forbes*, *Fast Company*, *Success*, *Black Enterprise*, *Hispanic*, and *Inc*. Entrepreneurship associations such as the Association of African-American Women Business Owners and the Entrepreneurs' Organization also provide valuable assistance. Finally, any aspiring entrepreneur should visit these Web sites:

- U.S. Chamber of Commerce (http://www.uschamber.com)

- Entrepreneur.com (http://www.entrepreneur.com)

- Kauffman Foundation (http://www.kauffman.org)

- The Small Business Administration (http://www.sba.gov)

- *The Wall Street Journal* Small Business (http://online.wsj.com/small-business)

In this chapter, we focus on pathways for entering the world of entrepreneurship, describing the activities, the different kinds of small business owners, and the reason a growing number of people choose to be entrepreneurs. It discusses the business environment in which business owners work, the characteristics that help them succeed, and the ways they start new ventures. The chapter ends with a discussion of methods by which large companies try to incorporate the entrepreneurial spirit.

[1]

What Is an Entrepreneur?

An **entrepreneur** is a risk taker in the private enterprise system, a person who seeks a profitable opportunity and takes the necessary risks to set up and operate a business. Consider Sam Walton, Walmart's founder, who started by franchising a few small Ben Franklin variety stores and then opened his own Walton Five and Dime stores. Today, Walmart has grown into a multibillion-dollar global business that is the largest company on earth.

Entrepreneurs differ from many small-business owners. Although many small-business owners possess the same drive, creative energy, and desire to succeed, what makes entrepreneurs different is that one of their major goals is expansion and growth. (Many small-business owners prefer to keep their businesses small.) Sam Walton wasn't satisfied with just one successful Ben Franklin franchise, so he purchased others. And when that wasn't enough, he started and grew his own stores. Entrepreneurs combine their ideas and drive with money, employees, and other resources to create a business that fills a market need. That entrepreneurial role can make something significant out of a small beginning. Walmart, the company that Sam Walton started, reported net sales in excess of $411 billion for one recent year.[2]

Entrepreneurs also differ from managers. Managers are employees who direct the efforts of others to achieve an organization's goals. Owners of some small start-up firms serve as owner-managers to implement their plans for their businesses and to offset human resource limitations at their fledgling companies. Entrepreneurs may also perform a managerial role, but their overriding responsibility is to use the resources of their organizations—employees, money, equipment, and facilities—to accomplish their goals. When Bobbie Weiner found herself divorced and struggling for cash, she signed up for a special-effects makeup course, hoping that she could acquire some new skills and support herself working in the movie industry. Her hard work has resulted in a successful business. She realized that specialized makeup is needed by many categories of people—actors, the military, Halloween revelers, sports fans, and funeral directors. After doing a few makeup jobs on horror films, Weiner was recruited to work on the blockbuster *Titanic*. That led to a rush of other movies, a contract with the military for camouflage paint, worldwide requests from funeral homes, and her own product line, called Bloody Mary. Although Weiner is now worth millions and employs 250 people at her company, Bobbie Weiner Enterprises in Fort Worth, Texas, she is still very much in charge of the firm's mission, goals, and image.[3]

Studies have identified certain personality traits and behaviors common to entrepreneurs that differ from those required for managerial success. One of these traits is the willingness to assume the risks involved in starting a new venture. Some, like Bobbie Weiner, take that risk out of necessity—they've left or lost previous jobs or simply need a way to generate cash. Others want a challenge or a different quality of life. Entrepreneurial characteristics are examined in detail in a later section of this chapter.

Assessment Check ☑

1. What tools do entrepreneurs use to create a new business?

2. How do entrepreneurs differ from managers?

2

Categories of Entrepreneurs

LECTURE ENHANCER:
Think of a hypothetical example for each type of entrepreneur.

Entrepreneurs apply their talents in different situations. These differences can be classified into distinct categories: classic entrepreneurs, serial entrepreneurs, and social entrepreneurs.

Classic entrepreneurs identify business opportunities and allocate available resources to tap those markets. Dana Hood is a classic entrepreneur. She recognized that dog owners want special attention for their pets when they leave those animals in the care of others. She also knew that pet owners spent $3.4 billion for boarding and daycare centers during one recent year. So, when she founded her daycare center for dogs in Denver, she made certain that her services stood out from the average kennel. At For the Love of Dog, Hood and her staff offer customized services such as grooming and anesthesia–free teeth cleaning, a treadmill, swimming pools, and water misters to cool off her customers' pets during hot weather. In addition, pet owners can purchase high-end organic foods and treats, beds and toys, as well as other retail goods. [4]

While a classic entrepreneur starts a new company by identifying a business opportunity and allocating resources to tap a new market, **serial entrepreneurs** start one business, run it, and then start and run additional businesses in succession. Elon Musk, the founder of such businesses as PayPal, Tesla Motors, and SpaceX, is a serial entrepreneur. Jessica Herrin is also a serial entrepreneur. When Herrin graduated from college with an economics degree, she joined a software start-up firm where she got hooked on the idea of "unlimited potential." At age 24, Herrin co-founded WeddingChannel.com in Los Angeles, which grew within a few years to 100 employees and $21 million in revenues. When her firm was purchased by The Knot, Herrin went on to start Stella & Dot, a high-quality fashion jewelry business sold by more than 12,000 independent representatives at parties and online. Already, Stella & Dot has hit $104 million in revenues, and the jewelry has been featured in business and fashion press—and perhaps more importantly, on celebrities. "I want to build a company that is the next great global brand that changes the lives of women around the world," asserts Herrin. [5]

classic entrepreneur
person who identifies a business opportunity and allocates available resources to tap that market.

serial entrepreneur
person who starts one business, runs it, and then starts and runs additional businesses in succession.

Courtesy Stella & Dot

After selling WeddingChannel.com to The Knot, serial entrepreneur Jessica Herrin founded Stella & Dot, a high-quality jewelry business that has topped more than $100 million in revenues.

Some entrepreneurs focus on solving society's challenges through their businesses. **Social entrepreneurs** recognize a societal problem and use business principles to develop innovative solutions. Social entrepreneurs are pioneers of innovations that benefit humanity. When Samuel Kaymen moved his family to New Hampshire seeking a more rural lifestyle, little did he know that would be the start of a business that eventually would be known for its socially and environmentally responsible approach. A diabetic, Kaymen experimented with making homemade yogurt with no added sugar and sold the product to local health food stores. This was the humble beginnings of Stonyfield Farm, which today is a hugely successful company and a model for social entrepreneurs. In addition to producing the healthiest organic yogurt available, the company established a "Profits for the Planet" program that commits 10 percent of its annual profits to people and organizations working to restore and protect the environment. Stonyfield is also known for using its yogurt lids—millions of them each week—to promote causes, organizations, and environmental initiatives. [6]

[3] Reasons to Choose Entrepreneurship as a Career Path

If you want to run your own business someday, you'll have plenty of company. During one recent year, about 565,000 new businesses were created each month in the United States, with the construction and service industries experiencing the highest rates of activity.[7]

The past few decades have witnessed a heightened interest in entrepreneurial careers, spurred in part by publicity celebrating the successes of entrepreneurs such as Michael Dell, who launched what would become computer giant Dell following his freshman year at the University of Texas; Oprah Winfrey, who parlayed her career as a reporter into the media-production empire Harpo; and Bill Gates, who left Harvard to start Microsoft with friend Paul Allen.

People choose to become entrepreneurs for many different reasons. Some are motivated by dissatisfaction with the traditional work world—they want a more flexible schedule or freedom to make all the decisions. Others launch businesses to fill a gap in goods or services that they could use themselves. Still others start their own firms out of financial necessity, like Bobbie Weiner did with her makeup business. Carol Craig is another such entrepreneur. Craig was a flight officer and computer engineer, specializing in anti-submarine and subsurface warfare for the U.S. Navy. When unsuccessful knee surgery left her with a disabled veteran discharge, she was forced to reevaluate her career plans. She followed her husband, a Navy pilot, around to military posts and discovered that there was greater need for her after all—as a civilian consultant. So she founded Craig Technologies, now headquartered in Florida, which provides system engineering, software development, project management, courseware and training applications, modeling and simulation, database and information technology services to the federal government and other commercial entities. In one decade, the firm has grown from one employee—Carol Craig—to 285 employees and $28 million in revenue. Although Craig didn't plan this to be her career, she says, "I was never afraid of trying new things. I'm an accidental entrepreneur."[8]

Photo by Cathy Heinz(www.cathyheinz.com), provided courtesy of CarolCraig

Former Naval flight officer Carol Craig considers herself an accidental entrepreneur. After being discharged as a disabled veteran, Craig started a technology company that provides avionic software development and project management to various clients.

As pointed out in Figure 6.1, people become entrepreneurs for one or more of four major reasons: a desire to be their own boss, succeed financially, attain job security, and improve their quality of life. Each of these reasons is described in more detail in the following sections.

Being Your Own Boss

The freedom to make all the decisions—being your own boss—is one of the biggest lures of entrepreneurship. After 20 years of working in the fitness industry, Peter Taunton wanted out of the big-box health club scene. But he wasn't finished with fitness. He decided to create a different kind of gym, one for average people who prefer to work out without wearing Spandex shorts or being bombarded by loud music and big-screen TVs. Taunton founded Taunton's Snap Fitness—small, neighborhood-oriented fitness clubs based on affordability, convenience, and cleanliness—headquartered in Chanhassen, Minnesota. Snap Fitness clubs—there are now nearly 2,000 franchised locations—are smaller than the average gym but are open 24 hours a day. They feature up-to-date cardio and training equipment, but that's about all. There are no childcare facilities or smoothie bars, no pools or racquetball courts. This means that the cost of membership falls way below the national average. Taunton likes the fact that he had the authority to put his dreams into action. And his customers seem to agree with his decisions. "People see us, I think, as a breath of fresh air," Taunton observes.[9]

Being your own boss generally means getting to make all the important decisions. It also means engaging in much—if not all—of the communication related to your business, including customers, suppliers, distributors, retailers, and the like. The "Business Etiquette" feature offers tips for professional-style communication—even if you're on the run and using your thumbs.

Financial Success

Entrepreneurs are wealth creators. Many start their ventures with the specific goal of becoming rich—or at least financially successful. Often they believe they have an idea for a superior product and they want to be the first to bring it to market, reaping the financial rewards as a result. Entrepreneurs believe they won't achieve their greatest success by working for someone else, and they're generally right. Of course, the downside is that when they fail, they don't have the cushion of employment.

John Vechey recalls growing up without luxuries. "I bond with anyone who has ever eaten government cheese," he quips. While in college, Vechey and a friend developed an online game called ARC that the pair eventually sold to Sierra for $100,000. Next, with Jason Kapalka and Brian Fiete, Vechey co-founded Seattle-based PopCap, developing such popular games as Bejeweled and Plants vs. Zombies on the premise that online games should be simple and fun for everyone. Believing they still had more to accomplish, the trio turned down a $60 million offer for their company. Their gamble paid off: Video game publisher Electronic Arts recently bought PopCap in a deal worth as much as $1.3 billion.[10]

FIGURE 6.1 Why People Become Entrepreneurs

Desire to Be One's Own Boss

Desire to Succeed Financially

Desire for Job Security

Desire for an Improved Quality of Life

CLASS ACTIVITY:
Discuss the unique stresses and challenges being your own boss might present.

Communicating Electronically

Most entrepreneurs rely heavily on electronic communication to reach the people in their network. They're on the run; busy multitasking. Although you may be adept with your smart phone, it's wise to review a few tips about messaging.

- Don't write in all caps. It makes your message look as if you're yelling at the recipient.

- Avoid subject lines like "Important—Please Read." Such e-mails end up in the spam folder, unread. Instead, use short, descriptive subject lines that help your recipient know what the message is about—for example, "Review of Tuesday's Meeting."

- Don't use slang or shorthand like "LOL," "ru," and "L8." Also avoid smiley or sad-face icons.

- Be friendly but not overly familiar. Never include jokes in a business e-mail or text message.

- Keep it brief. Short messages are more helpful than long ones. If more discussion is necessary, conclude saying you'll follow up with a phone call.

- Remember: Computers and phones are like tape recorders. Messages can be saved—and could come back to haunt you. Never include personal messages within professional ones, and refrain from comments that could damage your company's image or the reputation of others.

Sources: Mark Grossman, "Email Etiquette Is Important," *Grossman Law Group*, http://www.ecomputerlaw.com, accessed February 5, 2012; "Business Email Etiquette: What You Should Know BEFORE You Hit Send," http://www.evancarmichael.com/Women-Entrepreneurs, accessed February 5, 2012; Karl Stolley and Allen Brizee, "Email Etiquette," *Purdue Owl*, http://owl.english.purdue.edu, accessed February 5, 2012; Nina Kaufman, "Making It Legal," *Entrepreneur.com*, http://legal.entrepreneur.com, accessed February 5, 2012.

LECTURE ENHANCER: Why do many people choose entrepreneurship when considering job security?

lifestyle entrepreneur person who starts a business to gain flexibility in work hours and control over his or her life.

Job Security

Although the demand for skilled employees remains high in many industries, working for a company, even a *Fortune* 500 firm, is no guarantee of job security. In fact, over the past ten years, large companies sought efficiency by downsizing and eliminated more jobs than they created. As a result, a growing number of American workers—both first-time job seekers and laid-off long-term employees—are deciding to create their own job security by starting their own businesses. While running your own business doesn't guarantee job security, the U.S. Small Business Administration has found that most newly created jobs come from small businesses, with a significant share of those jobs coming from new companies.[11]

As economies around the world are changing, workers are discovering the benefits of entrepreneurship compared to employment by big firms. In China, where entire industries, such as banking, steel, and telecommunications, are government-owned, young businesspeople are starting their own small firms. There are nearly 500 million people under the age of 30 in China, and their role models are Bill Gates and Michael Dell, reports an entrepreneurship professor at the Europe International Business School in Shanghai.[12]

Quality of Life

Entrepreneurship is an attractive career option for people seeking to improve their quality of life. Starting a business gives the founder independence and some freedom to decide when, where, and how to work. A **lifestyle entrepreneur** is a person who starts a business to gain flexibility in work hours and control over his or her life. But this does *not* mean working fewer hours or with less intensity. Generally it is the opposite—people who start their own businesses often work longer and harder than ever before, at least in the beginning. But they enjoy the satisfaction of success, both materially and in the way they live their lives.

Dan Abrams wanted it all—wealth and the freedom to do the things he loves. An avid backcountry skier, Abrams faced a serious problem: On just about every strenuous run, he was ripping the seams on his ski pants and jackets. "Fortunately, the manufacturers who made that stuff were good about honoring their warranties," acknowledges Abrams. But Abrams wondered, why not make clothes that could withstand the rigors of the backcountry? So Abrams and his friend Greg Steen borrowed $38,000 on their credit cards and launched Flylow Gear in Denver, Colorado, starting with durable new t-shirts. Then they added triple-stitched ski pants and sold out their entire first production run. Flylow's revenues are on course to break $1 million soon. Abrams and Steen are still skiing. "I could build a $1 million company or ski 100 days a year," says Abrams. "I choose to do both and have it all."[13]

Assessment Check ✅

1. What are the four main reasons people choose to become entrepreneurs?

2. What factors affect the entrepreneur's job security?

4 · The Environment for Entrepreneurs

Are you ready to start your own company? Do some research about the environment in which you will be conducting business. There are several important overall factors to consider. There's the economy—whether it is lagging or booming, you may find opportunities. Consider where you want to locate your business. Currently, the states with the highest rate of entrepreneurial activity are Nevada, Georgia, California, Louisiana, and Colorado. And the metropolitan area with the highest rate of activity is Los Angeles.[14]

Overall, the general attitude toward entrepreneurs in the United States is positive. In addition to favorable public attitudes toward entrepreneurs and the growing number of financing options, several other factors—identified in Figure 6.2—also support and expand opportunities for entrepreneurs: globalization, education, information technology, and demographic and economic trends. Each of these factors is discussed in the following sections.

LECTURE ENHANCER: What factors may have contributed to the increased globalization of entrepreneurship?

Globalization

The rapid globalization of business has created many opportunities for entrepreneurs. Entrepreneurs market their products abroad and hire international talent. Among the fastest-growing small U.S. companies, almost two of every five have international sales. Despite her location in Wisconsin, Margaret Maggard sells her yoga-inspired, handmade jewelry—called Bhati Beads—all over the world. The jewelry, which often features hand-carved beads strung on a hand-dyed silk cord, has been showcased on models in magazines ranging from *Lucky* and *Newsweek* to the European fashion magazine *Grazia*.[15]

Growth in entrepreneurship is a worldwide phenomenon. The role of entrepreneurs is growing in most industrialized and newly industrialized nations, as well as in the emerging free-market countries in central and eastern Europe. However, as shown in Figure 6.3, the level of entrepreneurship varies considerably. In factor-driven economies—that is, in countries such as Bangladesh or Jamaica that compete based on unskilled labor and natural resources—on average, more than 10 percent of adults are starting or managing a new business. In countries whose economies are driven by innovation—such as Hong Kong and the United States—the average rate of entrepreneurship is much lower: less than 4 percent.[16]

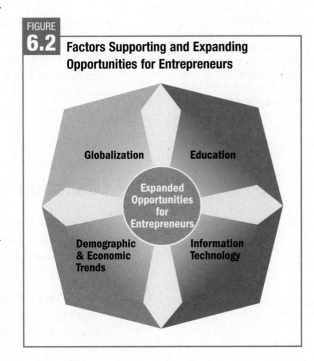

FIGURE 6.2 Factors Supporting and Expanding Opportunities for Entrepreneurs

Globalization

Education

Expanded Opportunities for Entrepreneurs

Demographic & Economic Trends

Information Technology

FIGURE 6.3 Levels of Entrepreneurial Activity in Various Countries

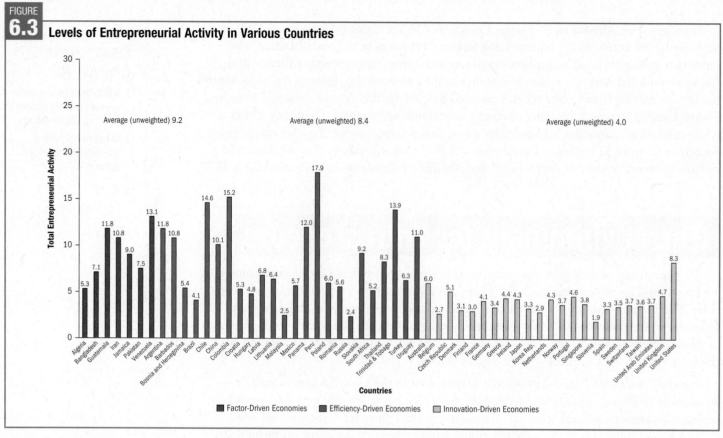

Source: Niels Bosma, Sander Wennekers, and José Ernesto Amorós, "2011 Extended Report: Entrepreneurs and Entrepreneurial Employees Across the Globe," *Global Entrepreneurship Monitor*, 2011, p. 20.

CLASS ACTIVITY:
Use the Web site www
.alibaba.com and lead
a discussion of the
opportunity it offers
entrepreneurs for the global
marketing and purchasing
of an incredible array of
goods and parts for almost
any imaginable business.

Organizations worldwide recognize the importance of developing the next generation of entrepreneurs. Global Entrepreneurship Week (GEW) is one way of reaching out to students as well as recent graduates to encourage entrepreneurship. Founded by the Kauffman Organization and Enterprise UK, the recent week-long GEW held 95,000 events in more than 100 countries for nearly 20 million participants. More than 24,000 companies and organizations planned youth-oriented business events in countries ranging from the United States to South Africa.[17]

Education

The past two decades have brought tremendous growth in the number of educational opportunities for would-be entrepreneurs. Today, more than 100 U.S. universities offer full-fledged majors in entrepreneurship, dozens of others offer an emphasis in entrepreneurship, and hundreds more offer one or two courses in how to start a business.

In addition to traditional classroom experience, a number of schools offer opportunities to intern with a start-up or actually work toward launching a company. The Entrepreneurship and Innovation Group at Northeastern University in Boston, which is staffed by professors who are entrepreneurs themselves, provides students with the chance to work in entrepreneurial settings in a variety of industries including retail, commercial real estate development, financial services, health care, and high-growth technology.[18]

Besides schools, many organizations have sprouted up in recent years to teach entrepreneurship to young people. The Kauffman Center for Entrepreneurial Leadership in Kansas City, Missouri, offers training programs for learners from kindergarten through community college. The center's EntrePrep summer program, which is taught in conjunction with local colleges and universities, teaches high school juniors how to start and manage a company. Students in Free Enterprise (SIFE) is a worldwide not-for-profit organization in which college students, working with faculty advisors, teach grade school and high school students and other community members the value of private enterprise and entrepreneurship.[19] The Association of Collegiate Entrepreneurs has chapters on many college campuses in the United States and Canada.

You don't have to major in business to become an entrepreneur, but students who do major in entrepreneurship or take entrepreneurship courses are three times more likely to start their own business or help someone else start a business.[20] In fact, you don't have to wait for graduation to launch your first start-up, and your business idea doesn't have to change the world. Ge Wang did finish college before starting his business, but he never intended to be an entrepreneur. Wang was a music professor who had earned a bit of notoriety by creating the first orchestra composed entirely of mobile phones. One of Wang's students, Jeff Smith, had started a small tech company before returning to teaching. When Smith met Wang he thought, "This dude is going to change music." So Wang began to create iPhone apps for Smith's new venture, including Sonic Lighter and Ocarina (which turns an iPhone into a flute and has sold more than 3 million downloads). More recent creations are Magic Piano and Glee karaoke. "We want to make apps that make people feel less inhibited—to play music by accident," explains Wang. "There's a little creativity in everyone. We just think we need to nudge them."[21]

Information Technology

The explosion in information technology (IT) has provided one of the biggest boosts for entrepreneurs. As computer and communications technologies have merged and dropped dramatically in cost, entrepreneurs have gained tools that help them compete with large companies. Information technology helps entrepreneurs work quickly and efficiently, provide immediate and attentive customer service, increase sales, and project professional images. In fact, technology has leveled the playing field to the point that, with the use of smartphones and other wireless devices, along with instant Web distribution, a dorm-room innovator can compete with a much larger firm. Technology has also assisted in the tremendous increase of *homepreneurs*—entrepreneurs who run home-based businesses. These successful ventures are described in the "Hit & Miss" feature.

Social networking has further transformed the business environment for entrepreneurs. According to a recent study, more than 90 percent of successful companies now use at least one social media tool. One entrepreneur who embraces the full impact of social media on his business is Adam Kidron, who runs an upscale, health-conscious burger joint in New York City, called 4food. Customers "design" their own burgers on one of the iPads in the

CLASS ACTIVITY:
Survey the class to see how many students have taken at least one specialized course focusing on entrepreneurship.

LECTURE ENHANCER:
What role does education play in encouraging students to start new businesses?

Businesses Based at Home Are Booming

Suppose you've been laid off or you just had a baby. Working from home may seem like the ideal solution. Until recently, home-based businesses lacked credibility. But that's changed. Today, more than 6.6 million home-based businesses contribute at least half of their owners' household income.

Technology has made homepreneurship possible. Some homepreneur businesses are entirely tech-based, such as Web development. Stephen Labuda, president of Agency3, is a former programmer for Deutsche Bank, a large international banking firm. He built Web sites on the side for several years before he quit his job and made Agency3 his full-time, home-based career in Boston. The firm's revenues are now in the millions and Labuda has about half a dozen employees.

Other homepreneurs use technology to operate their business. When Michael and Mary Ferrari retired, they formed UnusualThreads .com, selling designer fashions over the Internet. Working the site part time, they earn enough money to augment their savings and still have time to travel.

Questions for Critical Thinking

1. Could a home-based business succeed without the heavy use of information technology? Why or why not?

2. Outline your own idea for a home-based business that would rely on technology.

Sources: Kate Lister and Tom Harnish, "The State of Telework in the U.S.: How Individuals, Business, and Government Benefit," *Telework Research Network*, www .smallbizlabs.com/homepreneurs, accessed February 5, 2012; Steven Berglas, "Wake-up Call for Newly Hatched Entrepreneurs," http://www.forbes.com, accessed February 5, 2012; Carol Tice, "Homepreneur Winners Keep Growing Despite Downturn," http://blog .entrpreneur.com, accessed February 5, 2012; John Tozzi, "The Rise of the Homepreneur," *BusinessWeek*, http://www.businessweek.com, accessed February 5, 2012.

---

restaurant or on their home computers or smart phones. Then they save the burger recipe to 4food's database. They can go further by posting their creation on Twitter or Facebook, or they can create their own YouTube commercial about it.[22]

Demographic and Economic Trends

Who might be starting a business alongside you? Immigrants to the United States are the most likely to start their own businesses, as well as those between the ages of 55 and 64.[23] As Baby Boomers continue to age and control a large share of wealth in this country, the trend can only be expected to continue. Older entrepreneurs will also have access to their retirement funds and home equity for financing. Many Boomers also plan to work after retirement from traditional jobs or careers, either because they want to or in order to boost income and savings.

As mentioned earlier, college students are jumping on the entrepreneurial wagon in greater numbers, too. Alfonso Olvera started RailTronix while a student at the University of Houston. RailTronix is a Web-based software system that helps rail shippers in the oil industry track their shipments in real time. RailTronix produced $250,000 in revenues in its first year. Now Olvera is developing a similar system for the grain industry.[24]

Demographic trends—including the aging of the U.S. population, the growth of ethnic groups, and the predominance of two-income families—create opportunities for entrepreneurs. Convenience products for busy parents, foods that cater to ethnic preferences, and services designed specifically for older consumers all enjoy opportunities

LECTURE ENHANCER:
Share an example of a successful business that was started by a student.

for success. And as the economy fluctuates, entrepreneurs who are flexible enough to adapt quickly stand the best chance for success. Bobby Flam, owner of Jumbo's Restaurant in Miami, has kept his restaurant in the same location for 44 years despite hurricanes, riots, economic downturns, and the flight of other business. "I stayed because I wanted to be an example that business could succeed here," says Flam. He admits that not much has changed. Flam never turns away someone who is hungry and feeds an average of 10 homeless people a day. He also helps new local entrepreneurs get started in the neighborhood—and enjoys regular visits by sports stars from the Miami Heat and Miami Dolphins.[25]

Assessment Check ✔

1. To what extent is entrepreneurship possible in different countries, and what opportunities does globalization create for today's entrepreneurs?

2. Identify the educational factors that help expand current opportunities for entrepreneurs.

3. Describe current demographic trends that suggest new goods and services for entrepreneurial businesses.

5 Characteristics of Entrepreneurs

People who strike out on their own are pioneers in their own right. They aren't satisfied with the status quo and want to achieve certain goals on their own terms. Successful entrepreneurs are often likely to have had parents who were entrepreneurs—or dreams of starting their own business. They also tend to possess specific personality traits. Researchers who study successful entrepreneurs report that they are more likely to be curious, passionate, self-motivated, honest, courageous, and flexible. The eight traits summarized in Figure 6.4 are especially important for people who want to succeed as entrepreneurs.

Vision

Entrepreneurs generally begin with a *vision*—an overall idea for how to make their business idea a success. Then they pursue that vision with relentless passion. Bill Gates and Paul Allen launched Microsoft with the vision of a computer on every desk and in every home, all running Microsoft software. Their vision helped Microsoft become the world's largest marketer of computer software. It guided the company and provided clear direction for employees as Microsoft grew, adapted, and prospered in an industry characterized by tremendous technological change.

Arguably, every invention from the light bulb to the cell phone originated from a person with vision—someone who viewed the world in a slightly different way. Sometimes inventions have occurred out of necessity or even a mistake. True entrepreneurs know how to turn these situations into opportunities. It's well known that penicillin was created by accident; so was champagne. The heating potential for microwaves was discovered by their inventor while working on another project. Play-Doh was intended to be a cleaning product and Velcro was created by a hunter who noticed that burrs stuck to his socks as he walked through the wilderness.[26]

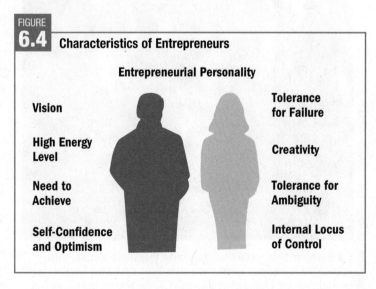

FIGURE 6.4 Characteristics of Entrepreneurs

Entrepreneurial Personality

Vision

High Energy Level

Need to Achieve

Self-Confidence and Optimism

Tolerance for Failure

Creativity

Tolerance for Ambiguity

Internal Locus of Control

High Energy Level

LECTURE ENHANCER:
What are some personal-life issues that might hinder an entrepreneur's success?

Entrepreneurs work long and hard to realize their visions. Many entrepreneurs work full-time at their regular day jobs and spend weeknights and weekends launching their start-ups. Many entrepreneurs work alone or with a very small staff, which means that they often wear most—if not all—of the hats required to get the business going, filling design, marketing, sales, and financial roles. Most entrepreneurs spend at least 70 hours a week on their new business, which can affect their other job (if they have one) and the quality of their personal life—at least in the beginning.[27] Thus, they need a high level of energy in order to succeed.

Need to Achieve

Entrepreneurs work hard because they want to excel. Their strong competitive drive helps them enjoy the challenge of reaching difficult goals and promotes dedication to personal success. A poll conducted by About.com showed Oprah Winfrey as the most admired entrepreneur among adults. The first African American woman billionaire, Winfrey has built an empire stretching from television to magazines to radio. Her own words best illustrate her strong drive: "I don't think of myself as a poor, deprived ghetto girl who made good. I think of myself as somebody who from an early age knew I was responsible for myself, and had to make good."[28]

CLASS ACTIVITY:
Ask students why optimism is an important trait for potential entrepreneurs.

Self-Confidence and Optimism

Entrepreneurs believe in their ability to succeed and they instill their optimism in others. Often their optimism resembles fearlessness in the face of difficult odds. They see opportunities where others see danger lurking. Robbie Vitrano is one such entrepreneur. Owner of Trumpet, a marketing agency based in New Orleans, Vitrano refuses to give up on the small businesses that were wiped out in Hurricane Katrina. Several years after other types of aid have disappeared, Vitrano continues to support his business neighbors—believing that his investment will pay off in the revitalization of the city. Trumpet is now headquartered in the Icehouse, a 12,000-square-foot commercial real estate development in a building that once lay under water. The Icehouse is home to 10 small business and start-ups, organizations that otherwise would have been left without office space. Elsewhere in town, Vitrano jump-started Naked Pizza, which has become so popular that Vitrano sells franchises.[29]

©Richard Drew/AP/Wide World Photos

Entrepreneurs often succeed simply because they won't give up. When sales of Bobbi Brown's cosmetics line stalled, she moved the company to a new location and revamped its advertising. In the process, she successfully differentiated her company from the competition.

Tolerance for Failure

Entrepreneurs often succeed by sheer will and the ability to try and try again when others would give up. They also view setbacks and failures as learning experiences and are not easily discouraged or disappointed when things don't go as planned.

Solving an Ethical Controversy

Entrepreneurs and Ethics: It's Good Business

It's easy to get caught up in the excitement when launching a business, and while it might seem harmless to be overly optimistic or vague about details, experts warn against a lack of transparency. Not only might your venture fall flat as a result, but failure may have ethical or legal ramifications.

Should every business have a code of ethics?

PRO

1. A code of ethics reflects who your organization is, what you stand for, and how others can expect you to behave.

2. A code of ethics is a necessity today. Without it, businesses risk serious legal exposure.

CON

1. Not every entrepreneurial enterprise needs a formal code of ethics. What's important is conveying integrity about how you do business.

2. Accounts of ethics scandals are overblown in the media. In fact, the majority of entrepreneurs conduct their business ethically. A code of ethics won't make a bad person good, nor will the lack of one turn a good person bad.

Summary

Although it's time-consuming to create a formal code of ethics, business experts strongly recommend having one. Entrepreneurs face many challenges and, sometimes, a few failures; but none should be a failure of ethics.

Sources: "Business Ethics," Small Business Administration, http://www.sba.gov, accessed February 2, 2012; Carter McNamara, "Complete Guide to Ethics Management," *Management Help*, http://www.managementhelp.org, accessed February 2, 2012; Chris MacDonald, "Considerations for Writing a Code of Ethics," *Streetwise Small Business Book of Lists*, accessed February 2, 2012; Josh Spiro, "How To Write a Code of Ethics for Business," *Inc.com*, http://www.inc.com, accessed February 2, 2012; Don Knauss, "The Role of Business Ethics in Relationships with Customers," http://www.forbes.com, accessed February 2, 2012.

Bobbi Brown built a big name in the cosmetics industry. Estée Lauder bought her company and Brown stayed on in an active role. The brand faced some setbacks after its acquisition and sales went flat, but Brown never gave up. She met with the CEO, who said the problem was that the cosmetics were not setting themselves apart from the competition. Brown took the criticism in stride, learned from the setback, and decided to change the culture of the company. She moved out of the GM building to a loft in the SoHo section of Manhattan, made advertising photographs more editorial, and approached the cosmetics business as if it were a magazine. The company's numbers vastly improved and eventually hit half a billion dollars.[30]

When things go well, it's easy to take personal credit. But when poor business decisions result in failure, it's a bit more difficult. Truly successful entrepreneurs are willing to take responsibility for their mistakes. That is why an important part of launching any new business is establishing a code of ethics, as discussed in the "Solving an Ethical Controversy" feature.

Creativity

Entrepreneurs typically conceive new ideas for goods and services, and they devise innovative ways to overcome difficult problems and situations. If we look at the top entrepreneurs in the world, we can see that creativity is the common denominator. *Inc.* magazine presents an annual list of the 500 top small businesses, most of which were started by entrepreneurs. The word *solution* is one of the most common to appear in the names of these companies.

Some entrepreneurs find creative solutions to problems; others find creative ways to accomplish a task or provide a service. Still others create entirely new products. Jeff and Karen Lubbers started a sustainable farm—instead of buying groceries with unknown or potentially toxic ingredients—in order to address their young daughter's serious health issues. Today, the thriving Michigan farm offers grass-fed beef and lamb, whey- and corn-fed pork, artisan cheeses, and fresh baked goods. Lubbers Farm also hosts educational workshops and offers a cow-share leasing program.[31]

When his grandmother died, college student Curtis Funk got the idea to record the proceedings and memories of funerals onto CDs and sell them to families through funeral homes. Families of deceased loved ones appreciated the CDs so much that Funk's company, Utah-based FuneralRecording.com, provides live streaming audio and video, transcripts, CDs, and other services. The firm also offers updates through Twitter, under the name "funeraltech."[32]

Tolerance for Ambiguity

Entrepreneurs take in stride the uncertainties associated with launching a venture. Dealing with unexpected events is the norm for most entrepreneurs. Tolerance for ambiguity is different from the love of risk taking that many people associate with entrepreneurship. Successful entrepreneurship is a far cry from gambling because entrepreneurs look for strategies that they believe have a good chance of success, and they quickly make adjustments when a strategy isn't working. An important way entrepreneurs manage ambiguity is by staying close to customers so that they can adjust their offerings to customer desires. One such entrepreneur is Kevin Mitnick. In the mid-1990s, Mitnick was arrested by the FBI for computer hacking and served five years in prison. After his release, Mitnick founded Mitnick Security Consulting, a computer security consultancy. Today, Mitnick is often asked to speak on security issues to government officials and business owners. [33]

Internal Locus of Control

Entrepreneurs have an internal locus of control, which means they believe that they control their own destinies. You won't find entrepreneurs blaming others or outside events for their successes or failures—they own it all.

Diagnosed with a degenerative illness at age 6, Ralph Braun was confined to a wheelchair by the time he was 14. College became too difficult for Braun to navigate in his traditional wheelchair, so he decided to design his own transportation. Within about four months, he had built his first scooter. Braun later redesigned the interior of his van and created a wheelchair lift. Braun's increased mobility attracted the attention of the disabled community and he began to receive requests for scooters, wheelchair-enabled vans, wheelchair lifts, and other products that aid the wheelchair-bound. Indiana-based Braun Corporation has about 650 employees and manufactures a full line of mobility products.[34]

After reading this summary of typical personality traits, maybe you're wondering if you have what it takes to become an entrepreneur. Take the test in Figure 6.5 to find out. Your results may help you determine whether you would succeed in starting your own company.

LECTURE ENHANCER:
What type of ambiguity might an entrepreneur face in the fashion retail industry?

Assessment Check ✅

1. What is meant by an entrepreneur's vision?

2. Why is it important for an entrepreneur to have a high energy level and a strong need for achievement?

3. How do entrepreneurs generally feel about the possibility of failure?

FIGURE 6.5 Quiz for Small Business Success

Choose the answer you think is best for each question. There are no "wrong" answers.

1. What is the key to business success:
   a. business knowledge
   b. market awareness
   c. hands on management
   d. sufficient capital
   e. hard work

2. If a relative ever asks me for advice about starting a business I will tell them to:
   a. work for someone else in the field first
   b. write a business plan
   c. study marketing
   d. give up the idea
   e. learn about budgeting

3. Which is the largest potential trouble spot:
   a. too much growth
   b. too little growth
   c. too fast growth
   d. too slow growth
   e. sporadic growth

4. I trust: (select as many as apply)
   a. nobody
   b. myself
   c. my partner
   d. a few key employees
   e. my customers

5. I am unhappy when my employees are:
   a. late
   b. unhappy
   c. abrupt with customers
   d. resigning
   e. less dedicated than me

6. My customers are: (select as many as apply)
   a. always right
   b. too fussy
   c. demanding
   d. worth listening to
   e. dumb

7. Rank these in order of importance for small-business marketing success:
   a. word-of-mouth
   b. advertising
   c. signs
   d. location
   e. community events

8. When it comes to money I am:
   a. careful
   b. too carefree
   c. emotional
   d. shrewd
   e. hardnosed

9. Financially my firm:
   a. has trouble with cash-flow
   b. has a good line of credit
   c. is financed totally by receipt—no credit
   d. is making better profits this year than last
   e. knows exactly where it is all the time

10. In hiring people:
    a. I take far too long
    b. I look for the cheapest person
    c. personality is more Important than experience
    d. I look for the best person, and am willing to pay
    e. I only hire at the trainee level

11. With my employees:
    a. I treat everybody the same
    b. I try to talk privately to everybody once a week
    c. To whatever extent possible I tailor assignments to personalities
    d. I encourage them to talk to me about the business
    e. I try to work alongside them whenever possible

12. The real key to business success is:
    a. hard work and perseverance
    b. fine products and service
    c. advertising
    d. knowing the fundamentals of business
    e. employees

13. Competition is:
    a. dumb
    b. smart
    c. cunning
    d. everywhere
    e. a constant threat

14. The best competitive advantage is:
    a. experience
    b. understanding what the market wants
    c. confidence
    d. conducting a business ethically
    e. a detailed plan

15. I keep:
    a. careful financial records
    b. in touch with my customers
    c. in touch with my employees
    d. trying new techniques
    e. wanting to retire

16. My dream is:
    a. to grow the business until someone else can run it
    b. to work until I drop
    c. to give up these headaches and have more fun at work
    d. to try another business
    e. to take a vacation

17. I think business plans are:
    a. for the birds
    b. nice but not necessary
    c. something I can do with my accountant
    d. useful and informative
    e. essential—wouldn't do business without them

18. What makes a terrific entrepreneur?
    a. creativity
    b. discipline
    c. consumer orientation
    d. technical proficiency
    e. flexibility

19. What does a business need most?
    a. money
    b. market research
    c. help
    d. time
    e. a solid business plan

20. What is essential to marketing?
    a. "a sixth sense"
    b. market research
    c. customer awareness
    d. experience
    e. testing

Source: U.S. Small Business Administration, "Quiz for Small Business Success," accessed February 27, 2012, at www.ltbn.com/biz_quiz.htm.

Starting a New Venture

The examples of entrepreneurs presented so far have introduced many ways to start a business. This section discusses the process of choosing an idea for a new venture and transforming the idea into a working business.

Selecting a Business Idea

In choosing an idea for your business, the two most important considerations are (1) finding something you love to do and are good at doing, and (2) determining whether your idea can satisfy a need in the marketplace. People willingly work hard doing something they love, and the experience will bring personal fulfillment. The old adages "Do what makes you happy" and "Be true to yourself" are the best guidelines for deciding on a business idea.

LECTURE ENHANCER:
Why is it important that both of these criteria be considered before starting a business?

Success also depends on customers, so would-be entrepreneurs must also be sure that the idea they choose has interest in the marketplace. The most successful entrepreneurs tend to operate in industries in which a great deal of change is taking place and in which customers have difficulty pinpointing their precise needs. These industries allow entrepreneurs to capitalize on their strengths, such as creativity, hard work, and tolerance of ambiguity, to build customer relationships. Nevertheless, examples of outstanding entrepreneurial success occur in every industry. Whether you want to build a business based on your grandmother's cookie recipes or know that you have a better idea for tax-preparation software, you are more likely to succeed if you ask yourself the right questions from the beginning.

Consider the following guidelines as you think about your business ideas:

- List your interests and abilities. Include your values and beliefs, your goals and dreams, things you like and dislike doing, and your job experiences.

- Make another list of the types of businesses that match your interests and abilities.

- Read newspapers and business and consumer magazines to learn about demographic and economic trends that identify future needs for products that no one yet offers.

- Carefully evaluate existing goods and services, looking for ways you can improve them.

- Decide on a business that matches what you want and offers profit potential.

- Conduct marketing research to determine whether your business idea will attract enough customers to earn a profit.

- Learn as much as you can about the industry in which your new venture will operate, your merchandise or service, and your competitors. Read surveys that project growth in various industries.

Many entrepreneurs who start new businesses invent new products or processes. When that happens, the inventor–entrepreneur needs to protect the rights to his or her invention by securing a patent. The U.S. Patent and Trademark Office's Web site (http://www.uspto.gov) provides information about this process, along with forms to apply for a patent. Inventors can also apply for a patent online. The same suggestions apply to entrepreneurs who are interested in copyright protection for their product names or processes. The U.S. Copyright Office's Web site (http://www.copyright.com) provides information about this process, along with forms to apply for copyright protection.

Other entrepreneurial firms come up with innovative ways to build new markets, as the young California solar energy company Sungevity is doing. See the "Going Green" box for the story.

Buying an Existing Business Some entrepreneurs prefer to buy established businesses rather than assume the risks of starting new ones. Buying an existing business brings many advantages: employees are already in place to serve established customers and deal with familiar suppliers, the good or service is known in the marketplace, and the necessary permits and licenses have already been secured. Getting financing for an existing business also is easier than it is for most start-ups. Some sellers may even help the buyers by providing financing and offering to serve as consultants. Most people want to buy a healthy business so that they can build on its success, but an experienced entrepreneur might purchase a struggling business with the intent of turning it around. There are many resources for

Going Green

Sungevity Follows the Sun

If you're considering solar power, a young California company called Sungevity has a solution for you.

Sungevity was recently named "Innovator of the Year" by the PBS television program *Planet Forward*. The firm's vision, that "everyone should be able to go solar," is supported by its innovative business model intended to make solar energy affordable: In addition to selling them, Sungevity also leases solar panels that it owns, installs, and maintains for a monthly fee. Customers' electricity bills go down, along with their consumption of nonrenewable fossil fuels. Using satellite images of roofs and measures of sun intensity, Sungevity can also offer customers accurate online price quotes, via home computer or at Lowe's stores.

The fastest-growing residential solar company in the United States, Sungevity currently operates in eight states, including California (where most customers immediately save 15 percent a month). Major financing through Citigroup will help it continue to grow. "The incentives to go green and have more solar energy are very strong and very positive,"

says the company's chief financial officer. "I think being in 20 states in three years is within the realm of reason."

Questions for Critical Thinking

1. What innovative Sungevity strategies might appeal to middle-class buyers?

2. What are some advantages to Sungevity's online price quote system?

Sources: Company Web site, www.sungevity.com, accessed January 13, 2012; Martin LaMonica, "Sungevity Socks Away Cash for Solar Leasing," CNET News, August 15, 2011, http://news.cnet.com; Eric Brown, "The Future of Solar: Danny Kennedy of Sungevity," EcoTuesday, July 5, 2011, www.ecotuesday.com/blog; Osha Gray Davidson, "Lowe's and Sungevity Announce Solar Partnership," *Forbes*, May 15, 2011, www.forbes.com. "PBS Program Planet Forward Awards Sungevity as Its "Innovator of the Year," PR Newswire, April 13, 2011, www.prnewswire.com.

---

entrepreneurs who are considering the purchase of a business, ranging from information provided by government agencies such as the Small Business Administration to Web sites listing actual companies for sale.

Buying a Franchise Like buying an established business, buying a franchise offers a less risky way to begin a business than starting an entirely new firm. But franchising, which was discussed in detail in Chapter 5, still involves risks, and it is wise to do thorough research before taking the plunge. While there are a multitude of franchises from which to choose, one area that is experiencing tremendous growth is firms whose goods and services are targeted for children and their parents. These businesses offer everything from photography to tutoring to security.

Creating a Business Plan

In the past, many entrepreneurs launched their ventures without creating formal business plans. Although planning is an integral part of managing in contemporary business, entrepreneurs typically seize opportunities as they arise and change course as necessary. Flexibility seems to be the key to business start-ups, especially in rapidly changing markets. But because of the risks inherent in starting a business, it has become apparent that at least some planning is not only advisable but necessary, particularly if an entrepreneur is seeking funds from outside sources.

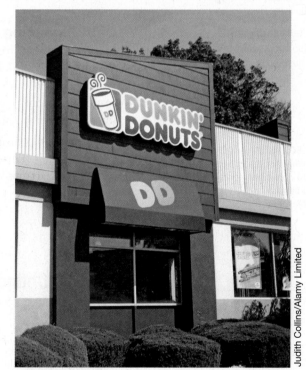

Judith Collins/Alamy Limited

Buying a franchise, such as a Dunkin' Donuts store, offers entrepreneurs a less risky way to begin a business than starting an entirely new firm.

CLASS ACTIVITY: Discuss the benefits of developing a business plan, even if funds are already available.

Before Shez Zamrudeen opened her own high-fashion boutique called Deen, she built a business plan. A major part of Zamrudeen's plan involved finding a way to distinguish her shop from many others in her New Jersey area. She decided to place her flagship store in New Jersey's Powerhouse Arts District in Jersey City—complete with original art work decorating the walls. When the recession hit, Zamrudeen was undaunted. "I had to adjust my current business plan and long-term goals," she admits. "I had to be smarter and more careful with my inventory." But Zamrudeen says she still plans to achieve all her business goals within the next five to ten years.[35]

Chapter 5 and Appendix D discuss business plans in more detail. The Internet also offers a variety of resources for creating business plans. Table 6.1 lists some of these online resources.

Finding Financing

seed capital initial funding used to launch a company.

CLASS ACTIVITY:
Lead a discussion of possible pitfalls of having friends or family invest in your business.

debt financing borrowed funds that entrepreneurs must repay.

LECTURE ENHANCER:
What are the drawbacks to depending upon debt financing to start a business?

A key issue in any business plan is financing. Requirements for **seed capital**, funds used to launch a company, depend on the nature of the business. They can range as high as several million—say, for the purchase of a McDonald's franchise in a lucrative area—or as low as $1,000 for Web site design. Many entrepreneurs rely on personal savings or loans from business associates, family members, or even friends for start-up funds. Table 6.2 lists the common sources of start-up capital.

Debt Financing When entrepreneurs use **debt financing**, they borrow money that they must repay. Loans from banks, finance companies, credit card companies, and family or friends are all sources of debt financing. Although some entrepreneurs charge business expenses to personal credit cards because they are relatively easy to obtain, high interest rates make this source of funding expensive, and the Small Business Administration (SBA) recommends finding alternative methods of funding.

Many banks turn down requests for loans to fund start-ups, fearful of the high risk such ventures entail. This has been particularly true over the past several years. Only a small percentage of start-ups raise seed capital through bank loans, although some new firms can get

TABLE
└ 6.1 ┘ Online Resources for Preparing a Business Plan

AllBusiness.com http://www.allbusiness.com	The "Business Advice" page provides links to examples, templates, and tips for writing a plan.
Inc. http://www.inc.com	Under "Departments," click "How-To-Guides" and then "Writing a Business Plan," which links to 150+ articles about how to write a business plan.
Kauffman eVenturing http://www.kauffman.org/eventuring	The "Explore Topics" section has links to information and resources for researching and writing a plan, as well as presenting it to lenders or investors.
MoreBusiness.com http://www.morebusiness.com	To see a sample plan, select "Business & Marketing Plans" from the list of templates.

TABLE 6.2 Funding Used by Entrepreneurs for Start-ups

SOURCE	PERCENTAGE OF ENTREPRENEURS*
Self-financing	82%
Loans from family, friends, or business associates	22%
Bank loans	18%
Lines of credit	18%
Venture capital	8%
SBA or other government funds	4%

*Percentages do not total 100 because entrepreneurs often use multiple sources to finance start-ups.

Source: "Entrepreneurial America: A Comprehensive Look at Today's Fastest-Growing Private Companies," *Inc., The Handbook of the American Entrepreneur,* http://www.inc.com, accessed February 8, 2012.

SBA-backed loans, as discussed in Chapter 5. Applying for a bank loan requires careful preparation. Bank loan officers want to see a business plan and will evaluate the entrepreneur's credit history. Because a start-up has not yet established a business credit history, banks often base lending decisions on evaluations of entrepreneurs' personal credit histories. Banks are more willing to make loans to entrepreneurs who have been in business for a while, show a profit on rising revenues, and need funds to finance expansion. Some entrepreneurs have found that local community banks are more interested in their loan applications than are the major national banks.

Even entrepreneurs who have previously received funding from banks—and have maintained a good relationship with their lenders—have experienced a credit crunch in recent years. After several years in business, entrepreneur Kevin Semcken learned his bank would no longer fund his $2.5 million line of credit. A line of credit is an approved loan that a business can borrow from when funds are needed. Without that money Semcken's firm, Colorado-based Able Planet, could not buy the raw materials or manufacture its products—headsets, headphones, and assistive listening devices for people with hearing issues. Large retailers such as Costco and Walmart had already placed orders; Semcken reevaluated his business plan and found alternative funding.[36]

Equity Financing To secure **equity financing**, entrepreneurs exchange a share of ownership in their company for money supplied by one or more investors. Entrepreneurs invest their own money along with funds supplied by other people and firms that become co-owners of the start-ups. An entrepreneur does not have to repay equity funds. Rather, the investors share in the success of the business. Sources of equity financing include family and friends, business partners, venture capital firms, and private investors. Able Planet's CEO Kevin Semcken was able to secure equity funding.[37]

Teaming up with a partner who has funds to invest may benefit an entrepreneur with a good idea and skills but little or no money. Investors may also have business experience, which they will be eager to share because the company's prosperity will benefit them. Like

equity financing funds invested in new ventures in exchange for part ownership.

borrowing, however, equity financing has its drawbacks. One is that investment partners may not agree on the future direction of the business, and in the case of partnerships, if they cannot resolve disputes, one partner may have to buy out the other to keep operating.

Some entrepreneurs find creative ways to obtain equity financing. Gavin McClurg did that when he came up with a timeshare business model for his start-up. His venture, called Offshore Odysseys, is actually a multi-year sailing expedition aboard a $1.2 million catamaran named *Discovery* that sails the world. Investors buy timeshare segments for between $20,000 and $30,000, during which they might snorkel near the Equator, kite surf off Fiji, or paraglide above Tahiti. Shareholders may purchase more than one segment and trade their time with other members. Annual fees cover the firm's operating expenses as well as food and beverages on the trip.[38]

Jody Mac Donald Photography

Some entrepreneurs find creative ways to obtain equity financing. Gavin McClurg's venture, Offshore Odysseys, is a sailing expedition aboard a catamaran named *Discovery*. Investors buy timeshare segments for between $20,000 and $30,000 on the journey, during which they might swim, snorkel, kite surf, or paraglide in beautiful, remote parts of the world.

venture capitalists
business organizations or groups of individuals that invest in early-stage, high-potential growth companies.

Venture capitalists are business organizations or groups of private individuals that invest in early-stage, high-potential growth companies. Venture capitalists typically back companies in high technology industries such as biotechnology. In exchange for taking a risk with their own funds, these investors expect high rates of return, along with a stake in the company. Typical terms for accepting venture capital include agreement on how much the company is worth, how much stock both the investors and the founders will retain, control of the company's board, payment of dividends, and the period of time during which the founders are prohibited from "shopping" for additional investors.[39] Venture capitalists require a combination of extremely rare qualities, such as innovative technology, potential for rapid growth, a well-developed business model, and an impressive management team.

Angel investors, wealthy individuals who invest money directly in new ventures in exchange for equity, are a larger source of investment capital for start-up firms. In contrast to venture capitalists, angels focus primarily on new ventures. Many angel investors are successful entrepreneurs who want to help aspiring business owners through the familiar difficulties of launching their businesses. Angel investors back a wide variety of new ventures. Because most entrepreneurs have trouble finding wealthy private investors, angel networks are formed to match business angels with start-ups in need of capital.

The Small Business Administration's Active Capital provides online listings to connect would-be angels with small businesses seeking financing. Venture capitalists that focus on women include Isabella Capital (http://www.fundisabella.com) and Springboard Enterprises (http://springboardenterprises.org). Those interested in minority-owned business include, for example, the U.S. Hispanic Chamber of Commerce (http://www.ushcc.com).

angel investors wealthy individuals who invest money directly in new ventures in exchange for equity.

Government Support for New Ventures

Federal, state, and local governments support new ventures in a number of ways, as discussed in Chapter 5. The Small Business Administration (SBA), state and local agencies, and business incubators all offer information, resources, and sometimes access to financing for entrepreneurs.

Another way to encourage entrepreneurship is through *enterprise zones*, specific geographic areas designated for economic revitalization. Enterprise zones encourage investment, often in distressed areas, by offering tax advantages and incentives to businesses locating within the boundaries of the zone. The state of Florida, for example, has 56 enterprise zones and allows a business located within urban zones to take tax credits for 20 or 30 percent of wages paid to new employees who reside within the urban enterprise zone. Colorado has 16 zones, while Ohio has more than 360 active zones.

Government legislation can also encourage investment in the U.S. economy. The Immigration Act of 1990 (IMMACT 90) recognizes the growing globalization of business. It contains a provision that sets aside visas for immigrants wishing to invest money in a new venture in a *targeted employment area*—a rural area or an area that has experienced an unemployment rate of at least 150 percent of the national average. In addition, IMMACT 90 enables more experts in the fields such as science, engineering, and computer programming to be hired by U.S. firms.[40]

LECTURE ENHANCER:
What are some advantages to starting a business in an enterprise zone?

Assessment Check ☑

1. What are the two most important considerations in choosing an idea for a new business?
2. What is the difference between debt financing and equity financing?
3. What is seed capital?

7 ## Intrapreneurship

Established companies try to retain the entrepreneurial spirit by encouraging **intrapreneurship**, the process of promoting innovation within their organizational structures. Today's fast-changing business climate compels established firms to innovate continually to maintain their competitive advantages. Another form of intrapreneurship is a

intrapreneurship process of promoting innovation within the structure of an existing organization.

Hit & Miss

Intrapreneurship Brings Truvia from the Woods to the Tabletop

"When I first tasted this," says Zanna McFerson about the leaf of the stevia plant, "I knew there had to be something we could do with it." An intrapreneur at the $108 billion food giant Cargill, McFerson was charged with finding a new sugar substitute to enter a $3.3 billion global consumer market dominated by Splenda, Sweet'N Low, and Equal. The market for processed foods was an even larger target.

McFerson's insight—that a plant-based sweetener had more market appeal than a chemical from a corporate lab—was compelling. Today, Truvia, a zero-calorie product made from stevia and more than 200 times sweeter than sugar, is the second-largest seller in the table-top sweetener market. It's also an ingredient in a growing list of products from Kraft and Coca-Cola, including Sprite Green, Vitaminwater Zero, and YoCrunch yogurt.

McFerson and her team worked on the top-secret project, backed by a $100 million budget, in a basement room with blacked-out windows in a lonely building in the woods. Truvia was protected by code names and discussed in meetings held off-site and on

weekends. Research to process and stabilize it, and testing to ensure it was safe and to acquire FDA approval, took three years. Now Cargill is growing its own stevia plants in South America and McFerson is back in her windowed office enjoying Truvia's 55 percent annual growth.

Questions for Critical Thinking

1. What did Truvia's development have in common with a typical entrepreneurial venture?

2. Could an individual entrepreneur have developed the stevia plant into a successful FDA-approved product for the consumer and commercial markets? Why or why not?

Sources: Anne Marie Chaker, "Bracing for the Fake Sugar Rush," *The Wall Street Journal,* January 4, 2012, http://online.wsj.com; Ben Paynter, "Truvia's Test: Can Diet Sweeteners Go Natural?" *Fast Company,* April 25, 2011, www.fastcompany.com; Jenna Goudreau, "Names You Need To Know: Truvia," *Forbes,* May 4, 2011, www.forbes.com.

---

skunkworks project initiated by an employee who conceives an idea, convinces top management of its potential, and then recruits human and other resources from within the company to turn the idea into a commercial project.

LECTURE ENHANCER: What is another possible reason for companies to support intrapreneurship rather than discourage it among employees?

Assessment Check ✔

1. Why would large companies support intrapreneurship?

2. What is a skunkworks?

skunkworks, a project initiated by an employee who conceives an idea, convinces top management of its potential, and then recruits human and other resources from within the company to turn that idea into a commercial project.

Many companies encourage intrapreneurship—30 percent of large firms now allocate funds toward intrapreneurship.[41] 3M is a firm that has long been known for its innovative products. Ranging from Post-It Notes and Scotch Tape to Nutri-Dog Chews and Thinsulate insulation, there are more than 55,000 3M products either on store shelves or embedded in other firms' goods.[42]

Coming up with the ideas for these products, developing them, and testing them before bringing them to market takes time and resources. Former 3M CEO George Buckley believes that the only way to do this is to allocate both time and money in support of intra-praneurship. Despite the recent recession, Buckley maintained $1 billion for research and development. 3M allows its researchers to devote 15 percent of their time to pursue their own ideas. One recent successful product that resulted from this is the first electronic stetho-scope with Bluetooth technology. The company also awards annual Genesis Grants, worth up to $100,000, to 3M scientists for research.[43]

Another company that has supported intrapreneurial efforts to innovate is food giant Cargill, which created the plant-based sweetener Truvia under wraps, as told in the "Hit & Miss" box.

What's Ahead

In upcoming chapters, we look at other trends that are reshaping the business world of the 21st century. For example, in the next part of *Contemporary Business* we explore the critical issues of how companies organize, lead, and manage their work processes; manage and motivate their employees; empower their employees through teamwork and enhanced communication; handle labor and workplace disputes; and create and produce world-class goods and services.

Summary of Learning Objectives

1 Define what is an entrepreneur.

Unlike many small-business owners, entrepreneurs typically own and run their businesses with the goal of building significant firms that create wealth and add jobs. Entrepreneurs are visionaries. They identify opportunities and take the initiative to gather the resources they need to start their businesses quickly. Both managers and entrepreneurs use the resources of their companies to achieve the goals of those organizations.

Assessment Check Answers ✔

1.1 What tools do entrepreneurs use to create a new business? Entrepreneurs combine their ideas and drive with money, employees, and other resources to create a business that fills a market need.

1.2 How do entrepreneurs differ from managers? Managers direct the efforts of others to achieve an organization's goals. The drive and impatience that entrepreneurs have to make their companies successful may hurt their ability to manage.

2 Identify the different categories of entrepreneurs.

A classic entrepreneur identifies a business opportunity and allocates available resources to tap that market. A serial entrepreneur starts one business, runs it, and then starts and runs additional businesses in succession. A social entrepreneur uses business principles to solve social problems.

Assessment Check Answers ✔

2.1 What do classic entrepreneurs and social entrepreneurs have in common? They both identify opportunities and allocate resources to pioneer new innovations.

2.2 Is a social entrepreneur simply a philanthropist? A philanthropist generally promotes human welfare through charitable donations, while a social entrepreneur pioneers new ways to advance social causes and thus enhance social welfare.

3 Explain why people choose entrepreneurship as a career path.

There are many reasons people choose to become entrepreneurs. Some reasons are desire to be one's own boss, desire to achieve financial success, desire for job security, and desire to improve one's quality of life.

Assessment Check Answers ✔

3.1 What are the four main reasons people choose to become entrepreneurs? People generally choose to become entrepreneurs because they want to be their own boss, they believe they will achieve greater financial success, they believe they have more control over job security, and they want to enhance their quality of life.

3.2 What factors affect the entrepreneur's job security? An entrepreneur's job security depends on the decisions of customers and investors and on the cooperation and commitment of the entrepreneur's own employees.

4 Discuss the environment for entrepreneurs.

A favorable public perception, availability of financing, the falling cost and widespread availability of information technology, globalization, entrepreneurship education, and changing demographic and economic trends all contribute to a fertile environment for people to start new ventures.

Assessment Check Answers ✔

4.1 To what extent is entrepreneurship possible in different countries, and what opportunities does globalization create for today's entrepreneurs? In some countries, as many as one-tenth of the adults are starting or managing a new business. As for globalization opportunities, entrepreneurs market their products abroad and hire international talent. Among the fastest-growing small U.S. companies, almost two of every five have international sales.

4.2 Identify the educational factors that help expand current opportunities for entrepreneurs. More than 100 U.S.

universities offer majors in entrepreneurship, dozens of others offer an entrepreneurship emphasis, and hundreds more offer courses in how to start a business. Also, organizations such as the Kauffman Center for Entrepreneurial Leadership, EntrePrep, and Students in Free Enterprise encourage and teach entrepreneurship.

4.3 Describe current demographic trends that suggest new goods and services for entrepreneurial businesses. The aging of the U.S. population, the emergence of Hispanics as the nation's largest ethnic group, and the growth of two-income families are creating opportunities for entrepreneurs to market new goods and services.

⌈5⌋ Identify the characteristics of entrepreneurs.

Successful entrepreneurs share several typical traits, including vision, high energy levels, the need to achieve, self-confidence and optimism, tolerance for failure, creativity, tolerance for ambiguity, and an internal locus of control.

Assessment Check Answers ✔

5.1 What is meant by an entrepreneur's vision? Entrepreneurs begin with a vision, an overall idea for how to make their business idea a success, and then passionately pursue it.

5.2 Why is it important for an entrepreneur to have a high energy level and a strong need for achievement? Because start-up companies typically have a small staff and struggle to raise enough capital, the entrepreneur has to make up the difference by working long hours. A strong need for achievement helps entrepreneurs enjoy the challenge of reaching difficult goals and promotes dedication to personal success.

5.3 How do entrepreneurs generally feel about the possibility of failure? They view failure as a learning experience and are not easily discouraged or disappointed when things don't go as planned.

⌈6⌋ Summarize the process of starting a new venture.

Entrepreneurs must select an idea for their business, develop a business plan, obtain financing, and organize the resources they need to operate their start-ups.

Assessment Check Answers ✔

6.1 What are the two most important considerations in choosing an idea for a new business? Two important considerations are finding something you love to do and are good at doing and determining whether your idea can satisfy a need in the marketplace.

6.2 What is the difference between debt financing and equity financing? Debt financing is money borrowed that must be repaid. Equity financing is an exchange of ownership shares in their company for money supplied by one or more investors.

6.3 What is seed capital? Seed capital is the money that is used to start a company.

⌈7⌋ Explain intrapreneurship.

Organizations encourage intrapreneurial activity within the company in a variety of ways, including hiring practices, dedicated programs such as skunkworks, access to resources, and wide latitude to innovate within established firms.

Assessment Check Answers ✔

7.1 Why would large companies support intrapreneurship? Large firms support intrapreneurship to retain an entrepreneurial spirit and to promote innovation and change.

7.2 What is a skunkworks? A skunkworks project is initiated by an employee who conceives an idea and then recruits resources from within the company to turn that idea into a commercial product.

▨ Business Terms You Need to Know

entrepreneur 170	lifestyle entrepreneur 174	venture capitalists 188
classic entrepreneur 171	seed capital 186	angel investors 189
serial entrepreneur 171	debt financing 186	intrapreneurship 189
social entrepreneur 172	equity financing 187	skunkworks 190

▨ Review Questions

1. Identify the three categories of entrepreneurs. How are they different from each other? How might an entrepreneur fall into more than one category?

2. People often become entrepreneurs because they want to be their own boss and be in control of most or all of the major decisions related to their business. How might this relate to

potential financial success? If there are downsides, what might they be?

3. How have globalization and information technology created new opportunities for entrepreneurs? Describe current demographic trends that suggest new goods and services for entrepreneurial businesses.

4. Identify the eight characteristics that are attributed to successful entrepreneurs. Which trait or traits do you believe are the most important for success? Why? Are there any traits that you think might actually contribute to potential failure? If so, which ones—and why?

5. When selecting a business idea, why is the advice to "do what makes you happy" and "be true to yourself" so important?

6. Suppose an entrepreneur is considering buying an existing business or franchise. Which of the eight

7. Imagine that you and a partner are planning to launch a business that sells backpacks, briefcases, and soft luggage made out of recycled materials. You'll need seed capital for your venture. Outline how you would use that seed capital.

8. Describe the two main types of financing that entrepreneurs may seek for their businesses. What are the risks and benefits involved with each?

9. What is an enterprise zone? Describe what types of businesses might benefit from opening in such a zone—and how their success might be interconnected.

10. What is intrapreneurship? How does it differ from entrepreneurship?

Projects and Teamwork Applications

1. Interview an entrepreneur—you can do this in person, by e-mail, or on the phone. The person can be a local shop or restaurant owner, a hair salon owner, a pet groomer, a consultant—any field is fine. Find out why that person decided to become an entrepreneur. Ask whether his or her viewpoint has changed since starting a business. Decide whether the person is a classic, serial, or social entrepreneur. Present your findings to the class.

2. Certain demographic trends can represent opportunities for entrepreneurs—the aging of the U.S. population, the increasing diversity of the U.S. population, the growth in population of some states, and the predominance of two-income families, to name a few. On your own or with a classmate, choose a demographic trend and brainstorm for business ideas that could capitalize on the trend. Create a poster or PowerPoint presentation to present your idea—and its relationship to the trend—to your class.

3. Review the eight characteristics of successful entrepreneurs. Which characteristics do you possess? Do you think you would be a good entrepreneur? Why or why not? Create an

outline of the traits you believe are your strengths—and those that might be your weaknesses.

4. Many entrepreneurs turn a hobby or area of interest into a business idea. Others get their ideas from situations or daily problems for which they believe they have a solution—or a better solution than those already offered. Think about an area of personal interest—or a problem you think you could solve with a new good or service—and create the first part of a potential business plan, the introduction to your new company and its offerings. Then outline briefly the kind of financing you think would work best for your business and the steps you would take to secure the funds.

5. Enterprise zones are designed to revitalize economically distressed areas. Choose an area with which you are familiar—it may be as close as a local neighborhood or as far away as a city in which you might like to live someday. Do some online research about the area. Then outline your own plan for an enterprise zone—including businesses that you think would do well in the area, jobs that might be created, and other factors.

Web Assignments

1. **Tools for entrepreneurs.** American Express has established what it calls "Open Forum" to allow entrepreneurs and small business owners to communicate with one another and share ideas. Visit the Open Forum Web site and review the available material. Prepare a short report on how Open Forum could help an entrepreneur start and grow a business.

http://www.openforum.com/

2. **Venture capitalists.** Venture capital firms are an important source of financing for entrepreneurs. Most actively solicit funding proposals. Go to the Web site cited here to learn more about venture capital. What are some of the famous

businesses that were originally financed by venture capitalists?

http://www.nvca.org/

3. **Getting started.** Visit the Web site of *Entrepreneur* magazine and click on "Startups." How should you go about researching a business idea? What are the steps involved in getting a product to market?

http://www.entrepreneur.com

Note: Internet Web addresses change frequently. If you don't find the exact sites listed, you may need to access the organization's home page and search from there or use a search engine such as Bing or Google.

CASE 6.1

Glassybaby Does "One Thing Really Well"

When cancer patient Lee Rhodes was unexpectedly soothed by a simple candle, a business was born. Today, Glassybaby produces hand-blown votive candles that require four glassblowers and a 24-hour process to make. Coming in 450 colors, they sell for $40 to $44 each, and sales are expected to top $6 million.

As integral to Glassybaby as its Seattle glass-blowing studios, which are open to customers, is its commitment to donate 7 percent of revenues to help cancer patients cover noninsured expenses. Rhodes has given more than $650,000 to 100 different organizations and hopes to increase that percentage to 10 percent.

Despite suggestions to expand her product line, Rhodes (now healthy) is keeping the business simple. "There's something to be said for sticking to what you're good at," she says. "We make one thing really, really well."

Glassybaby's only stumble so far has been disappointing sales from its New York store. The company inadvertently chose a little-visited location and also failed to realize that New Yorkers, who walk far more than Seattle dwellers, would be reluctant to buy the one-pound candles in any quantity because they were too heavy to carry

home. Without a glass-blowing studio, the New York store couldn't wow customers with artisanship either. "We need to sell the story as well as the product," says Rhodes, who plans to relocate the store, open a studio in New York, and offer same-day delivery.

Questions for Critical Thinking

1. Rhodes says she wasn't intending to start a business. Which qualities of a successful entrepreneur does Rhodes probably have?

2. If you were an entrepreneur like Rhodes, would you expand Glassybaby's product line? Why or why not?

Sources: Company Web site, http://www.glassybaby.com, accessed February 2, 2012; Carolyn Horowitz, "Meet the Entrepreneur of 2011 Award Winners," *Entrepreneur,* December 21, 2011, www.entrepreneur .com; Gwen Moran, "From Cancer Patient to Successful Beacon of Hope," Second Act.com, October 25, 2011, www.secondact.com; Blythe Lawrence, "Glassybaby Founder Lee Rhodes Was Inspired by Adversity," *The Seattle Times,* October 9, 2011, http://seattletimes.nwsource.com; Julie Weed, "How Glassybaby Is Trying To Win Over New Yorkers," *The New York Times,* October 5, 2011, www.nytimes.com; Julie Weed, "Seattle Firm Struggles in the Biggest Market," *The New York Times,* September 28, 2011, www.nytimes.com.

CASE 6.2

Small Businesses Are Big into Social Networking

One of the biggest challenges for entrepreneurs is getting the word out about their new venture. Perhaps that's why entrepreneurs have embraced social media as a communication tool.

If used skillfully, many believe, social media can help level the playing field between small businesses and their giant competitors. David avRutick, co-owner of Folbot, a small kayak retailer, claims that without Twitter, he wouldn't have as many sales as he does. "You can't buy that kind of exposure," avRutick says.

Folbot competes against such household names as L.L. Bean and Cabela's—there's no way the smaller company could challenge the larger ones without widespread interactive communication. However, critics point out that social media sites vary widely in their value to small businesses. "The hype right now exceeds

the reality," observes Larry Chiagouris, a professor of marketing at Pace University's Lubin School of Business.

Despite the fact that the use of social media by firms with fewer than 100 employees doubled in one recent year, only 22 percent of those who responded to a separate survey reported a direct increase in profits as a result of social media use, while half said they broke even on the investment. Others caution that social media networking eats up valuable time, particularly for entrepreneurs whose day is chock-full of tasks ranging from design to distribution and manufacturing to marketing. Most entrepreneurs support the use of social media, but with moderation. Chris Lindland, owner of Cordarounds.com, an online clothing retailer, advises patience. "My business has been visited millions of times, but I haven't made millions of sales," he comments. But he believes patience pays off.

Questions for Critical Thinking

1. How will social networking change the business environment for entrepreneurs?
2. How might entrepreneurs use social media to secure financing?

Sources: Ross Kimarovsky, "10 Small Business Social Media Marketing Tips," *Mashable.com*, http://mashable.com, accessed February 6, 2012; Kasey Wehrum, "Is Social Media Worth Your Time?" http://www.inc.com, accessed February 6, 2012; Sarah E. Needleman, "Entrepreneurs Question Value of Social Media," *The Wall Street Journal*, http://online.wsj.com, accessed February 6, 2012; Paul Frederic, "Smart Social Networking for Your Small Business," http://www.forbes.com, accessed February 6, 2012; Claire Cain Miller, "Yelp Will Let Businesses Respond to Web Reviews," http://www.nytimes.com, accessed February 6, 2012.

Comet Skateboards: It's a Smooth Ride

CASE 6.3

Jason Salfi loves skateboarding. This is how many small businesses begin. The founder has a passion for something—whether it's cooking or surfing or creating video games—and wants to turn it into a business. In Salfi's case, it's skateboarding. The company, now in business for more than a decade, is Comet Skateboards. After Salfi graduated from college, he lived on a boat off the coast of California for a while and partnered with a friend tinkering around with skateboards, which the pair sold to other skateboard fans among their circle of friends. Salfi desired something more. He wanted to find a better way to manufacture skateboards as well as the means to support his newly started family. "Back then, skateboards were made with seven layers of maple and sprayed with a lacquer based coating," he recalls. "Skateboards were accounting for 35 to 40 percent of the natural maple being harvested each year." Salfi loved skateboarding, but he didn't like the way boards were made. He believed that a skateboard could be built with more environmentally sustainable processes and materials. "I wanted to start a company that would make an impression on people and build an awareness around the use of natural resources," Salfi says.

Not long after he established Comet Skateboards, Salfi moved his company and his family back east to Ithaca, New York, where he partnered with e2e Materials, another small start-up. The firm specializes in regionally sourced bio-composite materials; they manufacture their own soy-based resin and bio-composites that Salfi describes as "incredibly strong *and* biodegradable." The formula was exactly what Salfi was looking for. He set up shop and hired several employees, including Bob Rossi, who is head of Web development for Comet as well as president of the Green Resource Hub, an organization that focuses on finding ways for businesses to practice sustainability.

Rossi is impressed with Salfi's total commitment to finding the best way to manufacture his products, even if it means moving cross country. "To move your business into

the opportunity, to create a greener product, that is pretty impressive to me," observes Rossi. "There's a lot of greenwashing out there," says Rossi. He knows the difference. Comet goes much farther than simply purchasing e2e's materials; the firm has adopted a closed-loop manufacturing process, which means that it reduces or eliminates waste by examining the life cycle of all the materials used in its manufacturing process.

It might seem as if Salfi and Rossi aren't cut from the same cloth as the previous generation of skateboarders—they're busy doing good things for the environment and for their community instead of rolling along the fringes of society like the bad boys of original skateboarding. But Salfi remains true to his skateboarding heritage (Rossi admits to being new to the sport). Comet boards have names such as The Voodoo Doll and Shred City, and are built for specialists who prefer downhill or free riding. Riders are invited to contribute ideas for the shapes, graphics, and names of new boards. Comet, which has found a way to actually increase profit potential by using green materials, receives kudos from business bloggers as well as diehard boarding bloggers. It appears that Salfi has found a way to blend doing good with doing good business—in a sport that was once considered far out of the mainstream.

Salfi hopes that Comet Skateboards will ultimately serve as an example of a small business that can make a big difference—while making products that provide fun. "We look at everything we do through the lens of how we can create a model that people can replicate in the future," he says. Salfi observes proudly that although Comet has only been in Ithaca for a few years, so far the company has a 100-percent retention rate of employees. He wants Comet to be a company that is known for its positive working environment, a place where people can develop long-term careers.

"We know that in the grand scheme of things, we're a small company, but through the many means of getting the message out—the Internet, video, music, and photography—we can actually have a broad footprint and make the idea of sustainability and social justice appealing to a broader market," predicts Salfi. While the bottom line—turning a profit—is vital to Comet's survival and growth, Salfi believes that this new way of doing business is more important in the long run. "We like to think we're creating a blueprint for the kind of company that will be around for 100 or 200 years," he muses. Then the skateboarder emerges. With a grin Salfi adds, "At the end of the day we're making skateboards, and we don't want to bum anybody out."

Questions for Critical Thinking

1. In which category (or categories) would you place Jason Salfi as an entrepreneur? Why? Give examples.

2. Salfi notes that the use of information technology—part of the environment for entrepreneurs—can help Comet Skateboards reach a broader audience. Can you identify any demographic and economic trends that might provide opportunities for Comet Skateboard's growth as a business?

3. Which of the traditional characteristics of entrepreneurs do you believe best describe Jason Salfi? Why?

4. As Comet Skateboards reaches the next level of growth, where might the firm have the best chance of obtaining further financing? Why?

Sources: Comet Skateboards Web site, http://www.cometskateboards .com, accessed February 27, 2012; "GOOD Products," Halogen TV, http://www.halogentv.com, accessed March 4, 2011; Nadia Hosni, "Triple Bottom Line: Comet Skateboards," *Tonic*, April 27, 2010, http://www.tonic.com.

GREENSBURG, KS

Greensburg: A Great Place to Start

Ashley Petty started taking massage therapy classes while studying for her business degree. After graduating, she worked for several years as a massage therapist, until the spa where she worked closed. Petty was job hunting when the tornado hit her hometown of Greensburg, Kansas. Watching volunteers, residents, and relief workers exhaust themselves cleaning up the devastated town, she saw an opportunity. She would return home to start her own spa in Greensburg.

It was definitely a risky venture—the last thing she would have expected to find in Greensburg before the storm. Armed with a business plan she had written in college, Petty drove to town hall and applied for one of the temporary trailers that were brought in to house displaced businesses. She got her trailer—a 1970s singlewide, complete with imitation wood paneling, stinky carpet, and a leaky roof. Not exactly the luxe spa she had envisioned in her business plan, but a good enough start. With a fresh coat of paint, some scented candles, and new drapes, she opened Elements Therapeutic Massage and Day Spa.

Petty had expected that her spa would be a hard sell. The storm had destroyed the town's communications, so traditional advertising was out. To build a client base, Petty turned to word of mouth. She went to town meetings, talked to old friends, met with volunteers from all over the country. Still, months went by and she still had barely enough clients to pay her expenses.

Winter hit. It was cold, the ancient furnace ran constantly, drafts blew in the new curtains, and rain soaked the freshly steamed carpet. Elements was the last place anyone would want to go to escape the stress of rebuilding—even Petty couldn't stand to be there. Under normal circumstances, she would have considered more extensive capital improvements, but the trailer was only temporary and she was out of money.

At one town meeting, green architecture firm BNIM presented a plan for the new Downtown Greensburg, including a business incubator to sustain old businesses and promote new ones. Traditionally, a business incubator is reserved for start-ups, but in Greensburg, once-successful businesses needed help getting back on their feet. The incubator would be housed in a totally energy-efficient retail/office building with space for approximately 10 new businesses. The rent would be reasonable, and the utility costs next to nothing. Petty jumped at the chance to apply for a place in the building.

Questions

After viewing the video, answer the following questions:

1. What major challenges does Ashley Petty face in starting her business?
2. How will Greensburg's business incubator stimulate economic development?
3. What are some of the challenges Greensburg faces in recruiting new businesses? What incentives would you offer to encourage new business development there?
4. Would you start a new business in Greensburg? Why or why not?

LAUNCHING YOUR
[Entrepreneurial Career]

In Part 2, "Starting and Growing Your Business," you learned about the many ways that business owners have achieved their dreams of owning their own company and being their own boss. The part's two chapters introduced you to the wide variety of entrepreneurial or small businesses; the forms they can take—sole proprietorship, partnership, or corporation—and the reasons that some new ventures succeed and others fail. You learned that entrepreneurs are visionaries who build firms that create wealth and that they share traits such as vision and creativity, high energy, optimism, a strong need to achieve, and a tolerance for failure. By now you might be wondering how you can make all this information work for you. Here are some career ideas and opportunities in the small-business and e-business areas.

First, whatever field attracts you as a future business owner, try to acquire experience by working for someone else in the industry initially. The information and skills you pick up will be invaluable when you start out on your own. Lack of experience is often cited as a leading reason for small-business failure.[1]

Next, look for a good fit between your own skills, abilities, and characteristics and a market need or niche. For instance, the U.S. Department of Labor reports that opportunities in many healthcare fields are rising with the nation's increased demand for health services.[2] As the population of older people rises, and as young families find themselves increasingly pressed for time, the need for childcare and elder services will also increase—and so will the opportunities for new businesses in those areas. So keep your eyes on trends to find ideas that you can use or adapt.

Another way to look for market needs is to talk to current customers or business associates. When the owner of Michigan-based Moon Valley Rustic Furniture wanted to retire, he went to see Rick Detkowski, who was in the real estate business. The owner intended to offer the buildings to Detkowski and close the business down. But the real estate agent, who owned several pieces of Moon Valley furniture himself, instead decided to buy, not just the buildings, but the furniture business, too. Before the sale was completed—and to determine whether he could run Moon Valley profitably—Detkowski talked with existing customers and furniture dealers, who had been hoping for years that the company would expand its line of sturdy cedar and pine items from the traditional summer lawn furniture into more innovative designs. Further research showed that the general environmental trend among consumers was boosting demand for rustic furniture. So Detkowski took the plunge and is now in the furniture manufacturing business. He has expanded the company's product lines and reorganized the factory floor for more efficiency—and cost savings.[3]

Are you intrigued by the idea of being your own boss but worried about risking your savings to get a completely new and untried business off the ground? Then owning a franchise, such as Quiznos or Dunkin' Donuts, might be for you. The Small Business Administration advises aspiring entrepreneurs that while franchising can be less risky than starting a new business from scratch, it still requires hard work and sacrifice. In addition, you need to completely understand both the resources to which you'll be entitled and the responsibilities you'll assume under the franchise agreement. Again, filling a market need is important for success. To find more information about franchising, access the Federal Trade Commission's consumer guide to buying a franchise at http://www.ftc.gov/bcp/edu/pubs/consumer/invest/inv05.shtm.

Are you skilled in a particular area of business, technology, or science? The consulting industry will be a rapidly growing area for several years, according to the Bureau of Labor Statistics.[4] Consulting firms offer their expertise to clients in private, government, not-for-profit, and even foreign business operations. Business consultants influence clients' decisions in marketing, finance, manufacturing, information systems, e-business, human resources, and many other areas including corporate strategy and organization. Technology consultants support businesses in all fields, with services ranging from setting up a secure Web site or training employees in the use of new software to managing an off-site help desk or planning for disaster recovery. Science consulting firms find plenty of work in the field of environmental consulting, helping businesses deal with pollution clean up and control, habitat protection, and compliance with government's environmental regulations and standards.

But perhaps none of these areas appeal to you quite so much as tinkering with gears and machinery or with computer graphics and code. If you think you have the insight and creativity to invent something completely new, you need to make sure you're informed about patents, trademarks, and copyright laws to protect your ideas. Each area offers different protections for your work, and none will guarantee success. Here again, hard work, persistence, and a little bit of luck will help you succeed.

Career Assessment Exercises in Entrepreneurship and Business Ownership

1. Find out whether you have what it takes to be an entrepreneur. Review the material on the SBA's Web site http://www.sba .gov/smallbusinessplanner/index. html. or take the Brigham Young University's Entrepreneurial Test at http://marriottschool.byu.edu/ cfe/startingout/test.cfm. Answer the questions there. After you've finished, use the scoring guides to determine how ready you are to strike out on your own. What weak areas did your results disclose? What can you do to strengthen them?

2. Find an independent business or franchise in your area, and make an appointment to talk to the owner about his or her start-up experience. Prepare a list of questions for a 10- to 15-minute interview, and remember to ask about details such as the number of hours worked per week, approximate start-up costs, goals of the business, available resources, lessons learned since opening, and rewards of owning the business. How different are the owner's answers from what you expected?

3. Search online for information about how to file for a patent, trademark, or copyright. A good starting point is http://www.uspto .gov. Assume you have an invention you want to protect. Find out which forms are required; the necessary fees; how much time is typically needed to complete the legal steps; and what rights and protections you will gain.

Learning Objectives

[1] Define *management*.

[2] Explain the role of setting a vision and ethical standards for the firm.

[3] Summarize the importance of planning.

[4] Describe the strategic planning process.

[5] Discuss managers as decision makers.

[6] Evaluate managers as leaders.

[7] Discuss corporate culture.

[8] Identify organizational structures.

Chapter 7

Management, Leadership, and the Internal Organization

RelaxFoto.de/iStockphoto

Wegmans Food Markets Still a Great Place to Work

If a company has spent 15 consecutive years on *Fortune's* list of 100 Best Companies to Work For and consistently ranks in the top five, credit must go to its top management team for creating a culture and policies that foster a great work environment. If that company is Wegmans Food Markets, the 79-store family-owned grocery chain based in Rochester, New York, CEO Danny Wegman probably explains it best: "I really believe if you help others, give credit to others, and live with humility, you are a success," he told University of Rochester graduates recently. "Is success what others think about you? I believe success is how you feel about yourself."

Wegman and his management team can feel pretty good about what they've accomplished. While turnover among the 42,000 employees is already low, the $6.2 billion company constantly adds new employee benefits, such as a 24-hour health hotline introduced recently. Employees already enjoy job sharing, compressed workweeks, subsidized gym membership, domestic-partner benefits, and free stop-smoking programs. In fact more than 2,000 workers have enrolled in the stop-smoking program over the past few years.

Giving back to its employees and surrounding communities is also high on the company's list. Since its start back in 1984, the Wegmans scholarship program has awarded more than $80 million in scholarships to more than 25,000 employees. And recently the company gave more than 16 million pounds of food to local food banks.

More than 200,000 people apply for fewer than 900 job openings a year at Wegmans. The company emphasizes making the right hires, but as CEO Wegman knows, management sets the direction. "Make the people you work with successful," he says. "They will make you a superstar."[1]

Overview

When asked about their professional objectives, many students say, "I want to be a manager." You may think that the role of a manager is basically being the boss. But in today's business world, companies are looking for much more than bosses. They want managers who understand technology, can adapt quickly to change, can skillfully motivate employees, and realize the importance of satisfying customers. Managers who can master those skills will continue to be in great demand because their commitment strongly affects their firms' performance. And Danny Wegman's management of his family's grocery chain has ensured the prosperity of the firm, still going strong after almost 80 years.

This chapter begins by examining how successful organizations use management to turn visions into reality. It describes the levels of management, the skills that managers need, and the functions that managers perform. The chapter explains how the first of these functions, planning, helps managers meet the challenges of a rapidly changing business environment and develop strategies that guide a company's future. Other sections of the chapter explore the types of decisions that managers make, the role of managers as leaders, and the importance of corporate culture. The chapter concludes by examining the second function of management—organizing.

What Is Management?

Management is the process of achieving organizational objectives through people and other resources. The manager's job is to combine human and technical resources in the best way possible to achieve the company's goals.

Management principles and concepts apply to not-for-profit organizations as well as profit-seeking firms. A city mayor, the president of the Appalachian Mountain Club, and a superintendent of schools all perform the managerial functions described later in this chapter. Management happens at many levels, from that of the manager of a family-owned restaurant to a national sales manager for a major manufacturer.

The Management Hierarchy

Your local supermarket works through a fairly simple organization that consists of a store manager, several assistant or department managers, and employees who may range from baggers to cashiers to stock clerks. However, if your supermarket is part of a regional or national chain, there will be corporate managers above the store manager. The Stop & Shop Supermarket Company has more than 350 supermarkets located from New Hampshire to New Jersey. It is headquartered in Massachusetts. Within each store there are managers for everything from the meat department to human resources. But at Stop & Shop headquarters, you'll find top-level managers for such functions as finance, consumer affairs, real estate, information technology, sales and operations, and pharmacy among others.[2]

All of these people are managers because they combine human and other resources to achieve company objectives. Their jobs differ, however, because they work at different levels of the organization.

A firm's management usually has three levels: top, middle, and supervisory. These levels of management form a management hierarchy, as shown in Figure 7.1. The hierarchy is the traditional structure found in most organizations. Managers at each level perform different activities.

The highest level of management is *top management*. Top managers include such positions as chief executive officer (CEO), chief financial officer (CFO), and executive vice president. Top managers devote most of their time to developing long-range plans for their organizations. They make decisions such as whether to introduce new products, purchase other companies, or enter new geographical markets. Top managers set a direction for their organization and inspire the company's executives and employees to achieve their vision for the company's future.

The job isn't easy. Many top managers must steer their firms through the storms of an economic downturn, a slump in sales, a quality crisis, and the like. Sometimes the storm involves selling a big dream to investors, stockholders, and managers during a economic downturn. Laura Ipsen, senior vice president and general manager of the Smart Grid Business Unit of Cisco, has met with this challenge. Her idea for San Jose–based Cisco is to create a new energy ecosystem for the

FIGURE 7.1 The Management Hierarchy

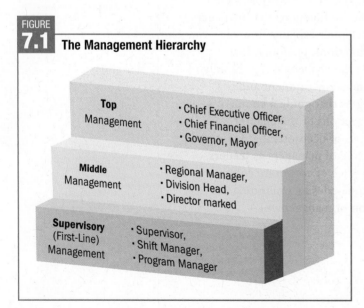

Top Management	• Chief Executive Officer, • Chief Financial Officer, • Governor, Mayor
Middle Management	• Regional Manager, • Division Head, • Director marked
Supervisory (First-Line) Management	• Supervisor, • Shift Manager, • Program Manager

21st century. If she's successful, Ipsen's firm could claim a significant share of what is predicted to be a $100-billion smart-grid market. It's not easy to convince all parties that the gamble is a wise one when the future isn't clear. "My job is like having to put together a 1,000-piece puzzle," says Ipsen, "but I don't have the box top with the picture of what it looks like, and some pieces are missing."[3]

Middle management, the second tier in the management hierarchy, includes positions such as general managers, plant managers, division managers, and unit managers. Middle managers' attention focuses on specific operations, products, or customer groups within an organization. They are responsible for developing detailed plans and procedures to implement the firm's strategic plans. If top management decided to broaden the distribution of a product, a sales manager would be responsible for determining the number of sales personnel required. Middle managers are responsible for targeting the products and customers who are the source of the sales and profit growth expected by their CEOs. To achieve these goals, middle managers might budget money for product development, identify new uses for existing products, and improve the ways they train and motivate salespeople. Because they are more familiar with day-to-day operations than CEOs, middle managers often come up with new ways to increase sales or solve company problems.

Supervisory management, or first-line management, includes positions such as supervisor, section chief, and team leader. These managers are directly responsible for assigning nonmanagerial employees to specific jobs and evaluating their performance. Managers at this first level of the hierarchy work directly with the employees who produce and sell the firm's goods and services. They are responsible for implementing middle managers' plans by motivating workers to accomplish daily, weekly, and monthly goals. A recent survey by the marketing research firm Temkin Group rated customer service at U.S. companies. All of the top-ranked firms have first-line managers who implement the firms' strategies to provide superior customer service. Amazon.com, Kohl's Department Stores, and Costco all have in common first-line managers who see that customer service is a top priority among its employees.[4]

Kohl's Department Stores ranks in the top tier of the Temkin Group's annual top customer-service providing companies. First-line managers make sure that customer service is a priority for all employees.

CLASS ACTIVITY:
Discuss the varying types of stress at each level of management and the contributing factors.

CLASS ACTIVITY:
Lead a discussion on whether recently promoted supervisors can remain friends with people whom they now supervise.

Skills Needed for Managerial Success

Managers at every level in the management hierarchy must exercise three basic types of skills: technical, human, and conceptual. All managers must acquire these skills in varying proportions, although the importance of each skill changes at different management levels.

Technical skills are the manager's ability to understand and use the techniques, knowledge, and tools and equipment of a specific discipline or department. Technical skills are especially important for first-line managers and become less important at higher levels of the management hierarchy. But most top executives started out as technical experts. The résumé of a vice president for information systems probably lists experience as a computer analyst and that of a vice president for marketing usually shows a background in sales. Many firms, including Home Depot and Dell have increased training programs for first-line managers to boost technical skills and worker productivity. Cold Stone Creamery, which operates

LECTURE ENHANCER:
What might happen if a
manager lacks technical
skills?

LECTURE ENHANCER:
What might happen if a
manager lacks human skills?

LECTURE ENHANCER:
What might happen if a
manager lacks conceptual
skills?

LECTURE ENHANCER:
Which of these functions do
you consider to be the most
important? Why?

planning process of
anticipating future events
and conditions and deter-
mining courses of action
for achieving organizational
objectives.

franchises for its premium ice-cream stores nationwide, carefully trains managers and crew members in the art of preparing its specialty ice cream for hungry customers. "We don't interview potential crew members, we *audition* them," says the company.[5]

Human skills are interpersonal skills that enable managers to work effectively with and through people. Human skills include the ability to communicate with, motivate, and lead employees to complete assigned activities. Managers need human skills to interact with people both inside and outside the organization. It would be tough for a manager to succeed without such skills, even though they must be adapted to different forms—for instance, mastering and communicating effectively with staff through e-mail, cell phones, videoconferencing, and text messaging, all of which are widely used in today's offices. As you can imagine, it is important for managers of Cold Stone Creamery ice-cream stores to have excellent human skills not only with customers but also with employees.

Conceptual skills determine a manager's ability to see the organization as a unified whole and to understand how each part of the overall organization interacts with other parts. These skills involve an ability to see the big picture by acquiring, analyzing, and interpreting information. Conceptual skills are especially important for top-level managers, who must develop long-range plans for the future direction of their organizations. After selling his own company, LinkExchange, to Microsoft for $265 million, Tony Hsieh joined Zappos as an advisor and eventually became its CEO. Hsieh's conceptual skills helped Zappos to grow sales to more than $1 billion annually while at the same time winning accolades for being an excellent place to work. Recently, Hsieh helped engineer the sale of Zappos to Amazon in a deal worth $1.2 billion.[6]

Managerial Functions

In the course of a typical day, managers spend time meeting and talking with people, reading, thinking, and sending text or e-mail messages. As they perform all these activities, managers are carrying out four basic functions: planning, organizing, directing, and controlling. Planning activities lay the groundwork, and the other functions are aimed at carrying out the plans.

Planning Planning is the process of anticipating future events and conditions and determining courses of actions for achieving organizational objectives. Effective planning helps a business focus its vision, avoid costly mistakes, and seize opportunities. Planning should be flexible and responsive to changes in the business environment, and should involve managers from all levels of the organization. As global competition intensifies, technology expands, and the speed at which firms bring new innovations to market increases, planning for the future becomes even more critical. For example, a CEO and other top-level managers need to plan for succession—those who will follow in their footsteps. Some CEOs resist this kind of planning, fearing that doing so might shorten their time at the helm of a company. But management experts encourage planning ahead for the next generation of management, in order to keep the company's position in the marketplace strong.[7]

Business mogul Warren Buffet is now in his 80s and showing few signs of slowing down. But it's clear that someone (or several people) must be in place to take the reins of his huge diversified company, Berkshire Hathaway, which has significant holdings in businesses ranging from Geico Insurance to Helzberg Diamonds to NetJets. Recently Buffet tapped Todd Combs, who is half Buffett's age, as an investment manager and potential successor to manage Berkshire's $100 billion investment portfolio, which includes holdings in American Express, the Coca-Cola Company, Procter & Gamble, and other major firms. But no one has yet been named to succeed Buffet as Berkshire's CEO.[8]

Organizing Once plans have been developed, the next step in the management process typically is organizing—the process of blending human and material resources through a formal structure of tasks and authority; arranging work, dividing tasks among employees, and coordinating them to ensure implementation of plans and accomplishment of objectives. Organizing involves classifying and dividing work into manageable units with a logical structure. Managers staff the organization with the best possible employees for each job. Sometimes the organizing function requires studying a company's existing structure and determining whether to restructure it in order to operate more efficiently, cost effectively, or sustainably.

Directing Once an organization has been established, managers focus on directing, or guiding and motivating employees to accomplish organizational objectives. Directing might include training (or retraining), setting up schedules, delegating certain tasks, and monitoring progress. To fulfill the objective of reducing the office electricity bill, an office manager might have incandescent light bulbs replaced by compact fluorescents, ask employees to turn off the lights when they leave a room or use occupancy sensors, and direct the IT staff to program all the office computer screens to turn off after 10 or 15 minutes of inactivity.[9]

Often when managers take time to listen to their employees, the manager gains insight and the employee gets a motivational boost. Fashion designer Eileen Fisher says, "Share information and your own ideas. Be present. Be accessible. Listen."[10]

Controlling The controlling function evaluates an organization's performance against its objectives. Controlling assesses the success of the planning function and provides feedback for future rounds of planning.

The four basic steps in controlling are to establish performance standards, monitor actual performance, compare actual performance with established standards, and make corrections if necessary. Under the provisions of the Sarbanes-Oxley Act, for example, CEOs and CFOs must monitor the performance of the firm's accounting staff more closely than typically had been done in the past. They must personally attest to the truth of financial reports filed with the Securities and Exchange Commission.

[2]

Setting a Vision and Ethical Standards for the Firm

A business begins with a vision, its founder's perception of marketplace needs and the ways a firm can satisfy them. Vision serves as the target for a firm's actions, helping direct the company toward opportunities and differentiating it from its competitors. While she was still in high school, Charlie Javice observed that a 5-year-old's birthday party at the movies cost $200—the same amount as a microloan in a developing country. Together with her brother Elie and two friends, she started PoverUP, a networking Web site with the goal of enabling "socially minded students learn, connect, and invest in microfinance and social businesses" around the world.[11]

organizing process of blending human and material resources through a formal structure of tasks and authority; arranging work, dividing tasks among employees, and coordinating them to ensure implementation of plans and accomplishment of objectives.

directing guiding and motivating employees to accomplish organizational objectives.

LECTURE ENHANCER: Discuss the difference between directing and controlling.

controlling function of evaluating an organization's performance against its objectives.

Assessment Check ✓

1. What is management?

2. How do the jobs of top managers, middle managers, and supervisory managers differ?

3. What is the relationship between the manager's planning and controlling functions?

vision perception of marketplace needs and the ways a firm can satisfy them.

After observing the cost of a child's birthday party, Charlie Javice, her brother and two friends started PoverUP, a networking Web site for socially minded students to learn, connect, and invest in microfinance and social businesses around the world.

Since its inception, PoverUP has started working with other microlenders in the United States and abroad. Recently, *Inc.* magazine named it one of America's Coolest College Start-Ups.[12]

A company's vision must be focused and yet flexible enough to adapt to changes in the business environment. Also critical to a firm's long-term relationship with its customers, suppliers, and the general public are the ethical standards that top management sets. Sometimes ethical standards are set in compliance with industry or federal regulations, such as safety or quality standards. Sometimes new standards are set in response to unethical actions by managers, such as the financial accounting activities that resulted in the Sarbanes-Oxley Act. Currently, firms are taking a closer look at large compensation packages received by their CEOs and other top executives. Due to public outcry, compensation committees are reevaluating their criteria for salaries, bonuses, and other benefits.[13]

The ethical tone that a top management team establishes can reap monetary as well as nonmonetary rewards. Setting a high ethical standard does not merely restrain employees from doing wrong, but it encourages, motivates, and inspires them to achieve goals they never thought possible. Such satisfaction creates a more productive, stable workforce—one that can create a long-term competitive advantage for the organization. In practice, ethical decisions are not always clear-cut, and managers must make difficult decisions. Sometimes a firm operates in a country where standards differ from those in the United States. In other situations, a manager might have to make an ethical decision that undermines profits or even causes people to lose their jobs. And while it's tempting to think that a large firm—by virtue of its size—will have a harder time adopting ethical practices than a small firm, consider the retail giant Best Buy, which recently earned recognition for its ethical standards. Named one of the World's Most Ethical Companies by the Ethisphere Institute, the Minneapolis-based Best Buy consistently demonstrates high standards in a number of areas.

Alex Brigham, executive director of the New York–based Ethisphere Institute, observes the connection between ethics and good business. He said Best Buy's ethical environment "shows a clear understanding that operating under the highest standards for business behavior goes beyond goodwill and 'lip-service' and is linked to performance and profitability."[14]

Sometimes taking an ethical stand can actually cost a firm in lost revenues and other support. When Google announced a reversal of its original stance on censorship in China—essentially shutting down operations there and rerouting traffic to an uncensored site in Hong Kong—not only did the company lose business, it found itself standing eerily alone on the issue. Sometimes, however, firms' actions raise more ethical questions than they answer, as the example in the "Solving an Ethical Controversy" feature shows.

Assessment Check ✔

1. What is meant by a vision for the firm?
2. Why is it important for a top executive to set high ethical standards?

[3] Importance of Planning

Although some firms manage to launch without a clear strategic plan, they won't last long if they don't map out a future. Facebook's founder Mark Zuckerberg says that he didn't have a major plan for the site at the beginning. But Facebook's nearly global reach—and membership of more than 800 million—means that Zuckerberg must plan the firm's next moves in order to outrun competitors and avoid major stumbles. Currently Zuckerberg is studying the Chinese market. Although Facebook is currently blocked in China, 20 percent of the company's app developers live there. "We now have Chinese-language help pages for developers, and we are working on giving them better support," says David Lim of Facebook's mobile developer relations division. "Developers in mainland China are important to us."[15]

Solving an Ethical Controversy

MF Global: Where Did Customers' Money Go?

MF Global Holdings, a brokerage firm and derivatives trader, began its slide toward bankruptcy in late 2011 when Wall Street ratings agencies lost confidence in its heavy purchases of risky European debt. When the dust cleared a few weeks later, some of the $6 billion the firm was supposed to manage for its clients was missing. About $5.3 billion has since been found, but despite Congressional hearings into what went wrong—met with claims of ignorance by former CEO Jon Corzine—some $1.2 billion in customers' money is still unaccounted for, and some fear it may never be recovered.

Should senior management be legally responsible for clients' money losses?

PRO

1. When management knowingly takes unwarranted risk—or breaks the law—executives should make good on resulting customer losses.

2. If managers deliberately profit from lack of oversight, they are culpable and should pay customers for losses.

CON

1. If customers are exposed to illegal risks, it is regulators, not managers, who aren't doing their jobs.

2. Customers who can't afford big losses shouldn't be in high-risk markets.

Summary

Investigations continue. Some fear MF Global might have illegally borrowed from customer accounts and either lost it on bad investments or used it to repay bank loans. Or it may have used a regulatory loophole to send the money to one of its less-regulated subsidiaries.

Sources: "Much of Missing MF Global Money Might Never be Found, Officials Think," Chicago Business.com, January 30, 2012; www.chicagobusiness.com; Zeke Faux and Phil Mattingly, "MF Global Told S&P 'Never Been Stronger' a Week Before Failure," Bloomberg Businessweek, January 30, 2012, www.businessweek.com; Alain Sherter, "Burned MF Global Customers May Be Out of Luck," CBS News.com, January 30, 2012, www.cbsnews.com; "Jon Corzine (MF Global Holdings)," *The New York Times,* accessed January 30, 2012; Alain Sherter, "Corzine Invokes 'Sergeant Schultz' Defense on Missing MF Global Money," CBS News.com, December 8, 2011, www.cbsnews.com; Michael W. Peregrine, "Another View: MF Global's Corporate Governance Lesson," *The New York Times,* December 16, 2011, www.nytimes.com; Sarah N. Lynch, "MF Global's Corzine: I Did Not Intend to Break the Rules," Reuters, December 8, 2011, www.reuters.com.

Types of Planning

Planning can be categorized by scope and breadth. Some plans are very broad and long range, whereas others are short range and very narrow, affecting selected parts of the organization rather than the company as a whole. Planning can be divided into the following categories: strategic, tactical, operational, and contingency, with each step including more specific information than the last. From the mission statement (described in the next section) to objectives to specific plans, each phase must fit into a comprehensive planning framework. The framework also must include narrow, functional plans aimed at individual employees and work areas relevant to individual tasks. These plans must fit within the firm's overall planning framework and help it reach objectives and achieve its mission.

Strategic Planning The most far-reaching level of planning is *strategic planning*—the process of determining the primary objectives of an organization and then acting and allocating resources to achieve those objectives. Generally, strategic planning is undertaken by top executives in a company. As part of its strategy of using company

LECTURE ENHANCER: Which type of planning do you consider to be the most important? Why?

As an example of strategic planning, Staples is using its company resources to raise environmental awareness, and develop and improve products through its annual Staples Global EcoEasy Challenge competition for college students.

resources to raise environmental awareness—and develop or improve products—Staples sponsors its annual Staples Global EcoEasy Challenge, a competition in which college students develop new products or redesign existing ones in an innovative approach to sustainability.[16]

Tactical Planning *Tactical planning* involves implementing the activities specified by strategic plans. Tactical plans guide the current and near-term activities required to implement overall strategies. The Staples Global EcoEasy Challenge is a tactic that reflects strategic planning around environmentally responsible products. Another tactic for the same strategy is Staples' development of its EcoEasy and Sustainable Earth product lines. The company's Web site declares, "As a company, we continue to review and modify the criteria used to identify EcoEasy products to ensure that they are based on sound science, are credible and reflect the current state of the industry."[17]

Operational Planning *Operational planning* creates the detailed standards that guide implementation of tactical plans. This activity involves choosing specific work targets and assigning employees and teams to carry out plans. Unlike strategic planning, which focuses on the organization as a whole, operational planning deals with developing and implementing tactics in specific functional areas. Operational planning related to the Staples EcoEasy Challenge might include identifying competition categories such as creating a product using eco-innovative materials; selecting judges; setting deadlines; reviewing contestant applications; and the like.

Contingency Planning Planning cannot foresee every possibility. Major accidents, natural disasters, and rapid economic downturns can throw even the best-laid plans into chaos. To handle the possibility of business disruption from events of this nature, many firms use *contingency planning*, which allows them to resume operations as quickly and as smoothly as possible after a crisis while openly communicating with the public about what happened. This planning activity involves two components: business continuation and public communication. Many firms have developed management strategies to speed recovery from accidents such as loss of data, breaches of security, product failures, and natural disasters such as floods or fire. If a major disaster or business disruption occurs, a company's contingency plan usually designates a chain of command for crisis management, assigning specific functions to particular managers and employees in an emergency. But crisis more often occurs on a less global scale. For example, a product delivery might go astray, a key person might be sick and unable to attend an important customer meeting, or the power might go out for a day. These instances require contingency planning as well.

Recently the Chevy Volt, a hybrid vehicle, developed problems with fires in crash tests. Chevy's parent company, GM, prepared a contingency plan just in case further problems

TABLE 7.1 Planning at Different Management Levels

PRIMARY TYPE OF PLANNING	MANAGERIAL LEVEL	EXAMPLES
Strategic	Top management	Organizational objectives, fundamental strategies, long-term plans
Tactical	Middle management	Quarterly and semiannual plans, departmental policies and procedures
Operational	Supervisory management	Daily and weekly plans, rules, and procedures for each department
Contingency	Primarily top management, but all levels contribute	Ongoing plans for actions and communications in an emergency

occurred with the Volt. The plan includes advertisements that will refer people to a Web site or a similar source of information on the Volt's safety. Meanwhile, the company has reinforced some structural elements of the cars so that fires are less likely.[18]

Planning at Different Organizational Levels

Although managers spend some time on planning virtually every day, the total time spent and the type of planning done differ according to the level of management. As Table 7.1 points out, top managers, including a firm's board of directors and CEO, spend a great deal of time on long-range planning, while middle-level managers and supervisors focus on short-term, tactical, and operational planning. Employees at all levels can benefit themselves and their company by making plans to meet their own specific goals.

[4] The Strategic Planning Process

Strategic planning often makes the difference between an organization's success and failure. Strategic planning has formed the basis of many fundamental management decisions. Successful strategic planners typically follow the six steps shown in Figure 7.2: defining a mission, assessing the organization's competitive position, setting organizational objectives, creating strategies for competitive differentiation, implementing the strategy, and evaluating the results and refining the plan.

Defining the Organization's Mission

The first step in strategic planning is to translate the firm's vision into a **mission statement**. A mission statement is a written explanation of an organization's business intentions and aims. It is an enduring statement of a firm's purpose, possibly highlighting the scope of operations, the market it seeks to serve, and the ways it will attempt to set itself apart from competitors. A mission statement guides the actions of employees and publicizes the company's reasons for existence.

FIGURE
7.2 **Steps in the Strategic Planning Process**

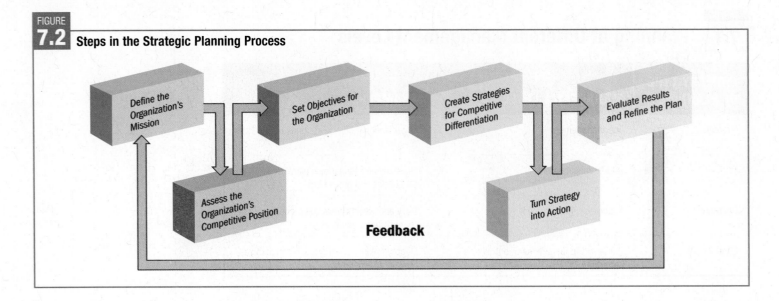

Mission statements can be short or long:

- Starbucks: "To inspire and nurture the human spirit—one person, one cup and one neighborhood at a time."

- Disney: "We create happiness by providing the finest in entertainment for people of all ages, everywhere."

- Nike: "To bring inspiration and innovation to every athlete in the world."

- Sony: "To experience the joy of advancing and applying technology for the benefit of the public."

A good mission statement states the firm's purpose for being in business and its overall goal. The most effective mission statements are memorable as well. The "Going Green" feature describes the mission of Johnson & Johnson, a global manufacturer of pharmaceuticals and health care products.

Assessing Your Competitive Position

Once a mission statement has been created, the next step in the planning process is to determine the firm's current—or potential—position in the marketplace. The company's founder or top managers evaluate the factors that may help it grow or could cause it to fail. A frequently used tool in this phase of strategic planning is the **SWOT analysis**. SWOT is an acronym for *strengths*, *weaknesses*, *opportunities*, and *threats*. By systematically evaluating all four of these factors, a firm can then develop the best strategies for gaining a competitive advantage. The framework for a SWOT analysis appears in Figure 7.3.

To evaluate a firm's strengths and weaknesses, its managers may examine each functional area such as finance, marketing, information technology, and human resources. Or they might evaluate strengths and weaknesses of each office, plant, or store. Entrepreneurs may focus on the individual skills and experience they bring to a new business.

For Starbucks, a key strength is consumers' positive image of the company's brand, which gets them to stand in line to pay premium prices for coffee. That positive image comes from Starbucks's being one of the best 100 companies to work for in the United States, according to *Fortune*, and from its socially responsible corporate policies.

CLASS ACTIVITY:
Lead a class discussion to develop a mission for a new business specializing in baking and selling cupcakes.

SWOT analysis SWOT is an acronym for *strengths, weaknesses, opportunities,* and *threats.* By systematically evaluating all four of these factors, a firm can then develop the best strategies for gaining a competitive advantage.

LECTURE ENHANCER:
How often do you think a company should conduct a SWOT analysis? Why?

Johnson & Johnson: Caring for the World

In its company statement of values, Johnson & Johnson promises, "We must maintain in good order the property we are privileged to use, protecting the environment and natural resources." Johnson & Johnson makes consumer products such as Band-Aids, Listerine, and Johnson's Baby Lotion, as well as medical devices and prescription drugs. Doing so can result in a giant carbon footprint made by manufacturing emissions, chemicals in products and processes, and a tremendous use of energy. Yet Johnson & Johnson has put strategies in place to reach its environmental goals.

The firm sets new long-term goals every five years, under its "Healthy Planet" program, for example, using direct purchase of low-impact hydro and wind power, on-site solar power and landfill gas, and purchasing renewable energy certificates. Johnson & Johnson also operates the largest fleet of hybrid vehicles owned by any corporation in the world.

Part of the "Healthy Planet" program also involves being truthful about green advertising and being specific about sustainability measures. The company is the second-largest producer of solar panels in the United States, and it has received the Leadership in Energy and Environmental Design (LEED) Gold certification for its Spring House research facility in Pennsylvania.

None of these goals could be achieved without support from Johnson & Johnson's leadership. Chairman William Weldon writes, "More than ever, we know that caring for the health and well-being of people is not only an outstanding business but a mission that truly touches lives."

Questions for Critical Thinking

1. What role does the CEO's leadership play in accomplishing Johnson & Johnson's green goals?

2. How does the company's mission relate to sustainability?

Sources: Michael Christel, "J&J's New Lean, Green Lab to Be Key R&D Hub," PharmaLive, http://blog.rddirections.com, accessed March 12, 2012; company Web site, http://www.jnj.com, accessed March 12, 2012; "To Our Shareholders," Annual Report, http://www.investor.jnj.com, accessed March 12, 2012; "Partner Profile," Green Power Partnership, http://www.epa.gov, accessed March 12, 2012.

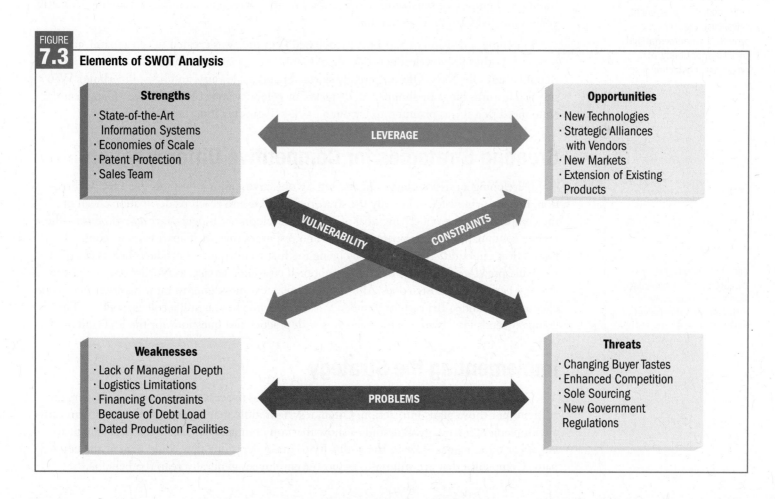

FIGURE 7.3 Elements of SWOT Analysis

Strengths
- State-of-the-Art Information Systems
- Economies of Scale
- Patent Protection
- Sales Team

Opportunities
- New Technologies
- Strategic Alliances with Vendors
- New Markets
- Extension of Existing Products

LEVERAGE

VULNERABILITY

CONSTRAINTS

Weaknesses
- Lack of Managerial Depth
- Logistics Limitations
- Financing Constraints Because of Debt Load
- Dated Production Facilities

Threats
- Changing Buyer Tastes
- Enhanced Competition
- Sole Sourcing
- New Government Regulations

PROBLEMS

CLASS ACTIVITY:
Ask students to discuss and
develop their SWOT list for
the college.

The company's strategic plans have included various ways to build on Starbucks's strong brand loyalty by attaching it to new products and expanding into new markets. The expansion efforts have included creating a Music WiFi Community on its Web site; offering bottled Frappuccino drinks in grocery stores; and opening thousands of Starbucks outlets in Europe, Asia, and the Middle East. Weaknesses include saturating some markets with too many stores and not paying attention to store design. Starbucks eventually addressed these weaknesses by closing some stores and redesigning others.[19]

SWOT analysis continues with an attempt to define the major opportunities and threats the firm is likely to face. Threats might include an economic recession—during which consumers are not willing to pay a premium for products—or a change in federal regulations. Starbucks addressed the threat of an economic downturn by beginning to offer less-expensive, instant coffee in stores such as Costco and Target. Opportunities include such phenomena as the growth of social media. So Starbucks added links to Facebook and Twitter from its Web site.[20]

A SWOT analysis isn't carved in stone. Strengths and weaknesses, like opportunities and threats, may shift over time. A strength may eventually become a weakness and a threat may turn into an opportunity. But the analysis gives managers a place to start.

Setting Objectives for the Organization

objectives guideposts by
which managers define the
organization's desired performance in such areas as
new-product development,
sales, customer service,
growth, environmental and
social responsibility, and
employee satisfaction.

The next step in planning is to develop objectives for the firm. **Objectives** set guideposts by which managers define the organization's desired performance in such areas as new-product development, sales, customer service, growth, environmental and social responsibility, and employee satisfaction. While the mission statement identifies a company's overall goals, objectives are more concrete.

Piperlime, a division of San Francisco–based Gap Inc., was created to sell apparel, accessories, and other fashion products outside of Gap's traditional line, which also includes Banana Republic and Old Navy. Offering trendy skirts, top, boots, jewelry, and bags, Piperlime's Web site also features blogs by shoppers and "picks" by celebrity stylist Rachel Zoe.[21] Gap recently announced that it was planning to try out a brick-and-mortar Piperlime store.[22]

Creating Strategies for Competitive Differentiation

LECTURE ENHANCER:
Discuss specific companies
that have successfully
differentiated themselves
within their markets.

Developing a mission statement and setting objectives point a business in a specific direction. But the firm needs to identify the strategies it will use to reach its destination ahead of the competition. The underlying goal of strategy development is *competitive differentiation*—the unique combination of a company's abilities and resources that set it apart from its competitors. A firm might differentiate itself by being the first to introduce a product such as the iPad to a widespread market; or by offering exceptional customer service, as Nordstrom does; or by offering bargains, as Costco does. After using mobile text messaging to tutor his sister in organic chemistry, Breanden Beneschott founded SmsPREP while he was still a college student. The company sends its subscribers text messages with practice test questions for the SAT and ACT.[23]

Implementing the Strategy

Once the first four phases of the strategic planning process are complete, managers are ready to put those plans into action. Often, it's the middle managers or supervisors who actually implement a strategy. But studies show that top company officials are still reluctant to empower these managers with the authority to make decisions that could benefit the company. Companies that are willing to empower employees generally reap the benefits.[24]

When Tony Hsieh, the CEO of Zappos, decided to sell the company to Amazon, he wanted to keep in place the customer-service strategies that had made Zappos a success. Among these strategies is hiring people who want to "create fun and a little weirdness." Unlike most other companies, Zappos sets no time limit on how long customer service reps speak with customers; the chief goal is to empathize and take care of each customer's needs. The company values excellent customer service over the number of calls taken by its customer service staff.[25]

Zappos values customer service and empowers its employees to take care of each customer's needs.

Ethan Miller/Getty Images, Inc.

Monitoring and Adapting Strategic Plans

The final step in the strategic planning process is to monitor and adapt plans when the actual performance fails to meet goals. Monitoring involves securing feedback about performance. Managers might compare actual sales against forecasts; compile information from surveys; listen to complaints from the customer hot line; interview employees who are involved; and review reports prepared by production, finance, marketing, or other company units. If an Internet advertisement doesn't result in enough response or sales, managers might evaluate whether to continue the advertisement, change it, or discontinue it. If a retailer observes customers buying more jeans when they are displayed near the front door, likely the display area will stay near the door—and perhaps be enlarged. Ongoing use of such tools as SWOT analysis and forecasting can help managers adapt their objectives and functional plans as changes occur.

Assessment Check ✓

1. What is the purpose of a mission statement?
2. Which of the firm's characteristics does a SWOT analysis compare?
3. How do managers use objectives?

5 Managers as Decision Makers

Managers make decisions every day, whether it involves shutting down a manufacturing plant or adding grilled cheese sandwiches to a lunch menu. **Decision making** is the process of recognizing a problem or opportunity, evaluating alternative solutions, selecting and implementing an alternative, and assessing the results. Managers make two basic kinds of decisions: programmed decisions and nonprogrammed decisions.

decision making process of recognizing a problem or opportunity, evaluating alternative solutions, selecting and implementing an alternative, and assessing the results.

Programmed and Nonprogrammed Decisions

A *programmed decision* involves simple, common, and frequently occurring problems for which solutions have already been determined. Examples of programmed decisions include reordering office supplies, renewing a lease, and referring to an established discount for bulk orders. Programmed decisions are made in advance—the firm sets rules, policies, and procedures for managers and employees to follow on a routine basis. Programmed decisions actually save managers time and companies money because new decisions don't have to be made each time the situation arises.

Credit: TOBIAS SCHWARZ/Reuters/Landov LLC

A *nonprogrammed decision* involves a complex and unique problem or opportunity with important consequences for the organization. Examples of nonprogrammed decisions include entering a new market, deleting a product from the line, or developing a new product. Apple's decision to develop and launch the iPad was a nonprogrammed decision that involved research and development, finances, technology, production, and marketing. Decisions were made about everything from what kinds of apps and accessories the iPad would offer to how much the new device would cost consumers.[26]

The introduction of the iPad was a nonprogrammed decision made by Apple involving a complex and unique opportunity with important consequences for the company.

How Managers Make Decisions

In a narrow sense, decision making involves choosing among two or more alternatives, with the chosen alternative becoming the decision. In a broader sense, decision making involves a systematic, step-by-step process that helps managers make effective choices. This process begins when someone recognizes a problem or opportunity, develops possible courses of action, evaluates the alternatives, selects and implements one of them, and assesses the outcome. It's important to keep in mind that managers are *human* decision makers, and while they can follow the decision-making process step-by-step as shown in Figure 7.4, the outcome of their decisions depends on many factors, including the accuracy of their information and the experience, creativity, and wisdom of the person.

Making good decisions is never easy. A decision might hurt or help the sales of a product; it might offend or disappoint a customer or co-worker; it might affect the manager's own career or reputation. Managers' decisions can have complex legal and ethical dimensions. *CRO Magazine* publishes an annual list of the "100 Best Corporate Citizens." These companies make decisions that are ethical, environmentally responsible, fair toward employees, and accountable to local communities and that provide responsible goods and services to customers and a healthy return to investors. These organizations prove that good corporate citizenship is good behavior. The top 10 corporate citizens named one recent year were Johnson Controls, Campbell Soup, IBM, Bristol-Myers Squibb, Mattel, 3M, Accenture, Kimberly-Clark, Hewlett-Packard, and Nike.[27]

Assessment Check ✔

1. Distinguish between programmed and non-programmed decisions.
2. What are the steps in the decision-making process?

FIGURE 7.4 Steps in the Decision-Making Process

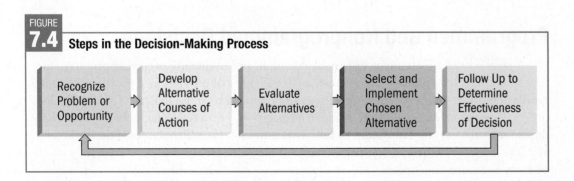

Recognize Problem or Opportunity → Develop Alternative Courses of Action → Evaluate Alternatives → Select and Implement Chosen Alternative → Follow Up to Determine Effectiveness of Decision

IBM's First Female CEO Says Hello

In a smooth, well-planned management transition, IBM's first female chief executive took on her new role in early 2012. A 30-year veteran of the company based in Armonk, New York, Ginni Rometty brings her long experience in sales, business services, corporate acquisitions, and strategic management to the top position at the storied $100 billion firm that hired her as a sales engineer and then groomed her for one top assignment after another.

"I learned to always take on things I'd never done before," Rometty says of her IBM career. And her predecessor and mentor Sam Palmisano said, "She is more than a superb operational executive. With every leadership role, she has strengthened our ability to integrate IBM's capabilities with clients."

Having helped create IBM's current five-year plan as head of sales, marketing, and strategy, Rometty isn't expected to radically change the 100-year-old firm's direction. Profits are at their highest level since 1915, and the company is looking to expand in markets such as cloud computing and analytics.

But there's at least one way in which this "serious, no-nonsense thinker" has already broken the mold. To reach out to IBM's thousands of employees, Rometty, who doesn't use Facebook or Twitter, chose not to use the usual group e-mail but rather an engaging, informal video in which she talked frankly about her priorities for the company in the near future.

Questions for Critical Thinking

1. What advantages do you think Rometty brings to the CEO position?
2. Do you think being female will help or hinder her in the top job? Why?

Sources: Robert McMillan, "Ginni Rometty Says Hello to IBM (Without E-Mail)," Wired.com, January 5, 2012, www.wired.com; Carol Hymowitz and Sarah Frier, "IBM's Rometty Breaks Ground as Company's First Female Leader," *Bloomberg Businessweek,* October 26, 2011, www.businessweek.com; Scott Martin, "IBM Taps First Woman CEO to Succeed Palmisano," *USA Today,* October 25, 2011, www.usatoday.com.

---

[6]

Managers as Leaders

A manager must demonstrate **leadership**, directing or inspiring people to attain certain goals. Great leaders do not all share the same qualities, but three traits are often mentioned: empathy (the ability to imagine yourself in someone else's position), self-awareness, and objectivity. While it might seem as though empathy and objectivity are opposite traits, they do balance each other. Many leaders share other traits—courage, passion, commitment, innovation, and flexibility to name a few.

Leadership involves the use of influence or power. This influence may come from one or more sources. One source of power is the leader's position in the company. A national sales manager has the authority to direct the activities of the sales force. Another source of power is a leader's expertise and experience. A first-line supervisor with expert machinist skills will most likely be respected by employees in the machining department. Some leaders derive power from their personalities. Employees may admire a leader because they recognize an exceptionally kind and fair, humorous, energetic, or enthusiastic person. Admiration, inspiration, and motivation are especially important during difficult economic times or when a leader has to make tough decisions for the company. Sometimes leaders who rise within the company are best able to make management transitions smooth, as was recently the case at IBM. See the accompanying "Hit & Miss" feature for an introduction to that company's first female CEO.

When Jim Skinner took over as CEO of McDonald's, the company had just lost two previous CEOs in a very short time and same-store sales were stagnant. Replacing CEOs

With more than 30 years of experience in various managerial positions at IBM, Ginni Rometty recently became the company's first female CEO.

Deepak G Pawar/The India Today Group/Getty Images, Inc.

leadership ability to direct or inspire people to attain certain goals.

LECTURE ENHANCER:
Are there additional traits that you feel should be listed here? Why?

LECTURE ENHANCER:
What might be the effects upon a leader's power if he or she lacks one of these factors?

LECTURE ENHANCER:
Provide a hypothetical example of a decision made with autocratic leadership.

empowerment giving employees shared authority, responsibility, and decision making with their managers.

LECTURE ENHANCER:
Provide a hypothetical example of a decision made with democratic leadership.

LECTURE ENHANCER:
Provide a hypothetical example of a decision made with free-rein leadership.

LECTURE ENHANCER:
Which leadership style would you prefer to work under? Why?

who died unexpectedly was a delicate situation, and the company's board looked to Skinner to right the ship. His ability to lead the company to record revenues and sales can be attributed to his confident, no-nonsense approach to management. Known as an operations whiz, he focuses on the performance of the 33,000 restaurants worldwide and the company infrastructure that supports them. His approach to leadership has recently led the company to an annual 5 percent growth with revenues of more than $24 billion. Same-store sales have increased every year since he took over the top job. Skinner requires McDonald's executives to train at least two potential successors—one for now and one for the future. This policy has recently come in handy, as Skinner announced his retirement, and Don Thompson, his successor, will take over CEO duties.[28]

Leadership Styles

The way a person uses power to lead others determines his or her leadership style. Leadership styles range along a continuum with autocratic leadership at one extreme end and free-rein leadership at the other. *Autocratic leadership* is centered on the boss. Autocratic leaders make decisions on their own without consulting employees. They reach decisions, communicate them to subordinates, and expect automatic implementation.

Democratic leadership includes subordinates in the decision-making process. This leadership style centers on employees' contributions. Democratic leaders delegate assignments, ask employees for suggestions, and encourage participation. An important outgrowth of democratic leadership in business is the concept of **empowerment**, in which employees share authority, responsibility, and decision making with their managers.

At the other end of the continuum from autocratic leadership is *free-rein leadership*. Free-rein leaders believe in minimal supervision. They allow subordinates to make most of their own decisions. Free-rein leaders communicate with employees frequently, as the situation warrants. For the first decade of its existence, Google was proud of its free-rein leadership style. Engineers were encouraged to pursue any and all ideas; teams formed or disbanded on their own; employees spent as much or as little time as they wanted to on any given project. But as the firm entered its second decade, it became apparent that not every innovation was worth pursuing—and some valuable ideas were getting lost in the chaos. Executive Chairman Eric Schmidt noted, "We were concerned that some of the biggest ideas were getting squashed." So the firm established a process for reviewing new project ideas in order to identify those most likely to succeed.[29]

Which Leadership Style Is Best?

No single leadership style is best for every firm in every situation. Sometimes leadership styles require change in order for a company to grow, as has been the case for Google. In a crisis, an autocratic leadership style might save the company—and sometimes the lives of customers and employees. This was the case when US Airways flight 1549 was forced to ditch into the Hudson River after hitting a wayward flock of Canada geese. Quick, autocratic decisions made by the pilot, Capt. Chesley Sullenberger, resulted in the survival of everyone on board the flight. But US Airways management on the ground demonstrated a democratic style of leadership in which managers at many levels were empowered to take actions to help the passengers and their families. For example, one executive arrived on the scene with a bag of emergency cash for passengers and credit cards for employees so they could purchase medicines, food, or anything else they needed.[30] A company that recognizes which leadership style works best for its employees, customers, and business conditions is most likely to choose the best leaders for its particular needs.

Assessment Check ☑

1. How is *leadership* defined?

2. Identify the styles of leadership as they appear along a continuum of greater or lesser employee participation.

7 Corporate Culture

An organization's **corporate culture** is its system of principles, beliefs, and values. The leadership style of its managers, the way it communicates, and the overall work environment influence a firm's corporate culture. A corporate culture is typically shaped by the leaders who founded and developed the company and by those who have succeeded them. Although Google has grown by leaps and bounds since its launch, the firm still tries to maintain the culture of innovation, creativity, and flexibility that its co-founders, Larry Page and Sergey Brin, promoted from the beginning. Google now has offices around the world, staffed by thousands of workers who speak a multitude of languages. "We are aggressively inclusive in our hiring, and we favor ability over experience," states the Web site. "The result is a team that reflects the global audience Google serves. When not at work, Googlers pursue interests from cross-country cycling to wine tasting, from flying to Frisbee."[31]

Although Google is no longer a start-up venture, the company still tries to maintain a culture of innovation, creativity, and flexibility that the founders promoted from the beginning. The recently opened Google office in Paris, France, features a photo booth for employees.

JACQUES BRINON/AFP/Getty Images, Inc.

Managers use symbols, rituals, ceremonies, and stories to reinforce corporate culture. The corporate culture at the Walt Disney Company is almost as famous as the original Disney characters themselves. In fact, Disney employees are known as cast members. All new employees attend training seminars in which they learn the language, customs, traditions, stories, product lines—everything there is to know about the Disney culture and its original founder, Walt Disney.[32]

Corporate cultures can be very strong and enduring, but sometimes they are forced to change to meet new demands in the business environment. A firm that is steeped in tradition and bureaucracy might have to shift to a leaner, more flexible culture in order to respond to shifts in technology or customer preferences. A firm that grows quickly—like Google—generally has to make some adjustments in its culture to accommodate more customers and employees.

In an organization with a strong culture, everyone knows and supports the same principles, beliefs, and values, as is the case at Southwest Airlines, described in the "Hit & Miss" feature. To achieve its goals, a business must also provide structure, which results from the management function of organizing.

corporate culture organization's system of principles, beliefs, and values.

LECTURE ENHANCER: Provide an example of a ceremony or ritual that a manager might use to strengthen corporate culture.

LECTURE ENHANCER: What are some possible effects upon employees if aspects of their corporate culture are discontinued?

Assessment Check ☑

1. What is the relationship between leadership style and corporate culture?

2. What is a strong corporate culture?

Hit & Miss

Southwest Airlines: "We Love Your Bags"

Southwest Airlines is well known for its reasonable fares, cheerful service, convenient schedules, and genuine interest in its passengers. When other airlines started charging customers for checked baggage, Southwest flatly refused. Instead, the airline poked fun at this change with an advertising campaign whose tagline was "We Love Your Bags."

Southwest's corporate culture—filled with a humor and energy that spills over to its customers—began with its founder, Herb Kelleher. The idea is that if the company's 32,000 employees are happy, they will be motivated to ensure their customers' happiness as well.

One of the characteristics that Southwest looks for in potential employees is a "servant's heart." Southwest managers conduct group interviews to see how flight-attendant candidates interact with one another—generally a good indicator of how they will respond to customers. Southwest empowers its middle managers, supervisors, and front-line employees with the authority to make decisions that strengthen relationships with customers. Ginger Hardage, Southwest's senior vice president for corporate communication, notes, "At Southwest, employees are encouraged to make decisions from the heart, and in turn, these proactive gestures provide positive benefits to the customers and the company."

Although a strong corporate culture is clearly part of an overall strategy, Southwest's employees and passengers frequently refer to Southwest as a company with "heart." That heart originated with Herb Kelleher. CEO Gary Kelly observes that at Southwest, "Our people are our single greatest strength and most enduring long-term competitive advantage."

Questions for Critical Thinking

1. How would you describe the principles, beliefs, and values at Southwest?
2. Herb Kelleher is no longer the CEO of Southwest, yet the company's original corporate culture seems to have survived. Why do you think this is?

Sources: Company Web site, http://www.southwest.com, accessed March 13, 2012; "Southwest's Secret to a Positive Corporate Culture: Its Employees," Business Civic Leadership Center, http://bclc2.uschamber.com, accessed March 13, 2012; Dan Oswald, "Corporate Culture Done Right: Southwest Airlines," HR Hero, http://blogs.hrhero.com, accessed March 13, 2012.

---

[8] Organizational Structures

organization structured group of people working together to achieve common goals.

An **organization** is a structured group of people working together to achieve common goals. An organization features three key elements: human interaction, goal-directed activities, and structure. The organizing process, much of which is led by managers, should result in an overall structure that permits interactions among individuals and departments needed to achieve company goals.

The steps involved in the organizing process are shown in Figure 7.5. Managers first determine the specific activities needed to implement plans and achieve goals. Next, they group these work activities into a logical structure. Then they assign work to specific employees and give the people the resources they need to complete it. Managers coordinate the work of different groups and employees within the firm. Finally, they evaluate the results

FIGURE 7.5 Steps in the Organizing Process

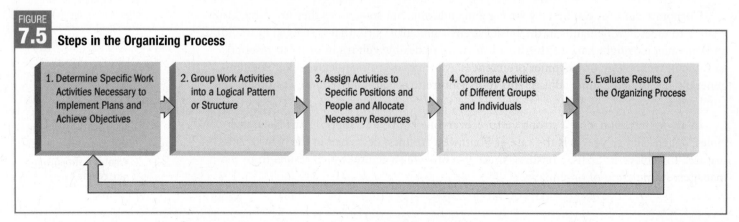

1. Determine Specific Work Activities Necessary to Implement Plans and Achieve Objectives
2. Group Work Activities into a Logical Pattern or Structure
3. Assign Activities to Specific Positions and People and Allocate Necessary Resources
4. Coordinate Activities of Different Groups and Individuals
5. Evaluate Results of the Organizing Process

of the organizing process to ensure effective and efficient progress toward planned goals. Evaluation sometimes results in changes to the way work is organized.

Many factors influence the results of organizing. The list includes a firm's goals and competitive strategy, the type of product it offers, the way it uses technology to accomplish work, and its size. Small firms typically create very simple structures. The owner of a dry-cleaning business generally is the top manager, who hires several employees to process orders, clean the clothing, and make deliveries. The owner handles the functions of purchasing supplies such as detergents and hangers, hiring and training employees and coordinating their work, preparing advertisements for the local newspaper, and keeping accounting records.

As a company grows, its structure increases in complexity. With increased size comes specialization and growing numbers of employees. A larger firm may employ many salespeople, along with a sales manager to direct and coordinate their work, or organize an accounting department.

LECTURE ENHANCER:
What are some potential negative results when a company increases its size?

An effective structure is one that is clear and easy to understand: Employees know what is expected of them and to whom they report. They also know how their jobs contribute to the company's mission and overall strategic plan. An *organization chart* can help clarify the structure of a firm. Figure 7.6 illustrates a sample organization chart.

Not-for-profit organizations also organize through formal structures so they can function efficiently and carry out their goals. These organizations, such as the Salvation Army and the American Society for Prevention of Cruelty to Animals (ASPCA), sometimes have a blend of paid staff and volunteers in their organizational structure.

LECTURE ENHANCER:
What are some potential drawbacks for a company with very rigid departmentalization?

Departmentalization

Departmentalization is the process of dividing work activities into units within the organization. In this arrangement, employees specialize in certain jobs—such as marketing, finance, or design. Depending on the size of the firm, usually an executive runs the department, followed by middle-level managers and supervisors. The five major forms of departmentalization subdivide work by product, geographical area, customer, function, and process.

departmentalization
process of dividing work activities into units within the organization.

- *Product departmentalization*. This approach organizes work units based on the goods and services a company offers. California's Activision Blizzard Inc. recently restructured

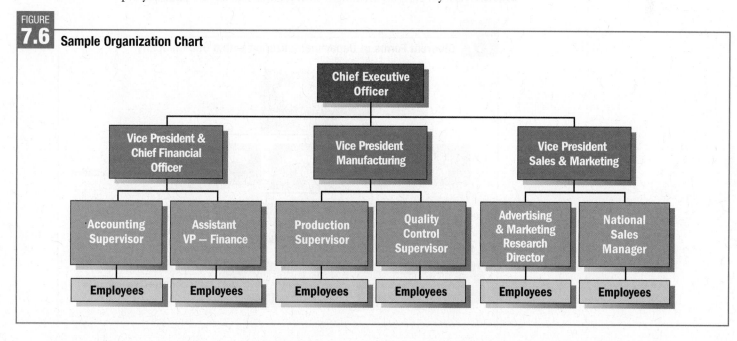

FIGURE 7.6 Sample Organization Chart

These familiar office products represent only one of 3M Corporation's many product lines. Because 3M serves such a broad spectrum of customers, it is organized on the basis of customer departmentalization.

LECTURE ENHANCER:
Discuss the pros and cons of each type of departmentalization.

its organization by product. The video game publisher is now divided into four divisions: "Call of Duty," a military game; internally owned games such as "Guitar Hero" and "Tony Hawk"; licensed properties; and Blizzard Entertainment, maker of the online game "World of Warcraft."[33]

- *Geographical departmentalization.* This form organizes units by geographical regions within a country or, for a multinational firm, by region throughout the world. The Web site Petswelcome.com makes it easy for traveling pet owners to locate hotel chains, rentals, amusement parks, and other recreational locations around the country that welcome pets. Users can search by type of lodging, route planned, and destination.[34]

- *Customer departmentalization.* A firm that offers a variety of goods and services targeted at different types of customers might structure itself based on customer departmentalization. Management of Procter & Gamble's wide array of products is divided between two major business units: Beauty and Grooming (Fusion, CoverGirl, Braun, Ivory) and Household Care (Pampers, Tide, Mr. Clean, Iams).[35]

- *Functional departmentalization.* Some firms organize work units according to business functions such as finance, marketing, human resources, and production. An advertising agency may create departments for creative personnel (say, copywriters), media buyers, and account executives.

- *Process departmentalization.* Some goods and services require multiple work processes to complete their production. A manufacturer may set up separate departments for cutting material, heat-treating it, forming it into its final shape, and painting it.

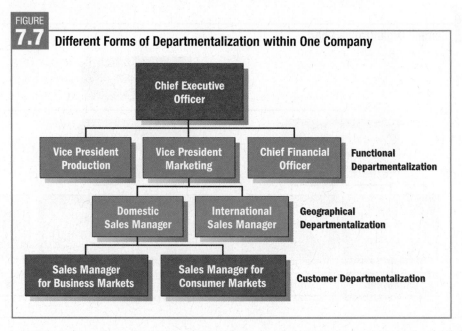

FIGURE 7.7 **Different Forms of Departmentalization within One Company**

Chief Executive Officer

Vice President Production — Vice President Marketing — Chief Financial Officer · **Functional Departmentalization**

Domestic Sales Manager — International Sales Manager · **Geographical Departmentalization**

Sales Manager for Business Markets — Sales Manager for Consumer Markets · **Customer Departmentalization**

As Figure 7.7 illustrates, a single company may implement several different departmentalization schemes. In deciding on a form of departmentalization, managers take into account the type of product they produce, the size of their company, their customer base, and the locations of their customers.

Delegating Work Assignments

Managers assign work to employees, a process called **delegation**. Employees might be responsible for answering customer calls, scooping ice cream, processing returns, making deliveries, opening or closing a store, cooking or serving food, contributing to new-product design, calculating a return on investment, or any of thousands of other tasks. Just as important, employees are given a certain amount of authority to make decisions.

Companies like Zappos, the online shoe retailer, that empower their workers to make decisions that could better serve their customers generally have happier employees and more satisfied customers.[36] As employees receive greater authority, they also must be accountable for their actions and decisions—they receive credit when things go well, and must accept responsibility when they don't. Managers also must figure out the best way to delegate responsibilities to employees who belong to different age groups, including Millennials, as discussed in the "Business Etiquette" feature.

Span of Management The *span of management*, or span of control, is the number of employees a manager supervises. These employees are often referred to as direct reports. First-line managers have wider spans of management, monitoring the work of many employees. The span of management varies depending on many factors, including the type of work performed and employees' training. In recent years, a growing trend has brought wider spans of control, as companies have reduced their layers of management to flatten their organizational structures, in the process increasing the decision-making responsibility they give employees.

Centralization and Decentralization How widely should managers disperse decision-making authority throughout an organization? A company that emphasizes *centralization* retains decision making at the top of the management hierarchy. A company that emphasizes *decentralization* locates decision making at lower levels.

Managing a Millennial Workforce

Today's firms include employees spanning a wide range of ages. One generation is known as the Millennials—people born between 1980 and 2000. Like every generation, Millennials are shaped by their experiences and relationships. They exhibit certain distinctive traits that knowledgeable managers can cultivate to win the best performance from them. For example, Millennials are accustomed to diversity, like to establish friendships at work, and are willing to work in teams. They tend to be positive and confident but also look for leadership and guidance from superiors.

Here are some tips from the experts for managing Millennial employees:

- Offer structure, leadership, and guidance. Provide feedback and as much information about the company and their job as they can handle.

- Make the most of Millennials' optimistic outlook. Especially when times look grim, Millennials' "I can do it" attitude can have a positive influence.

- Use Millennials comfort with teamwork and their desire to make friends on the job. Their belief in strength in numbers can be a powerful tool.

- Listen to Millennials' ideas and treat them with dignity. As a manager you still have the final say, but innovation can come from many different sources.

- Try to offer a work–life balance with flexibility when possible. You will get the most productivity from your Millennial employees and probably keep them on the job longer.

- Let Millennials know about career opportunities as they arise. Millennials want more than a job. They want to learn and grow throughout their careers.

Sources: Susan M. Heathfield, "Managing Millennials: Eleven Tips for Managing Millennials," About.com, http://humanresources.about.com, accessed March 13, 2012; Nancy Lublin, "Why Bashing Millennials Is Wrong," *Fast Company*, http://www.fastcompany.com, accessed March 13, 2012; Cara Newman, "Managing Millennials in the Workforce," *Young Money*, http://www.youngmoney.com, accessed March 13, 2012.

delegation managerial process of assigning work to employees.

LECTURE ENHANCER: What are the possible negative effects of increasing a manager's span of management?

A trend toward decentralization has pushed decision making down to operating employees in many cases. Firms that have decentralized believe that the change can improve their ability to serve customers. For example, the front-desk clerk at a hotel is much better equipped to fulfill a guest's request for a crib or a wake-up call than the hotel's general manager.

Types of Organization Structures

The four basic types of organization structures are line, line-and-staff, committee, and matrix. While some companies do follow one type of structure, most use a combination.

Line Organizations A *line organization*, the oldest and simplest organization structure, establishes a direct flow of authority from the chief executive to employees. The line organization defines a simple, clear *chain of command*—a hierarchy of managers and workers. With a clear chain of command, everyone knows who is in charge and decisions can be made quickly. This structure is particularly effective in a crisis situation. But a line organization has its drawbacks. Each manager has complete responsibility for a range of activities; in a medium-sized or large organization, however, this person can't possibly be expert in all of them. In a small organization such as a local hair salon or a dentist's office, a line organization is probably the most efficient way to run the business.

Line-and-Staff Organizations A *line-and-staff organization* combines the direct flow of authority of a line organization with staff departments that support the line departments. Line departments participate directly in decisions that affect the core operations of the organization. Staff departments lend specialized technical support. Figure 7.8 illustrates a line-and-staff organization. Accounting, engineering, and human resources are staff departments that support the line authority extending from the plant manager to the production manager and supervisors.

LECTURE ENHANCER:
Why do you think a line-and-staff structure might be the most effective structure in a crisis?

A line manager and a staff manager differ significantly in their authority relationships. A line manager forms part of the primary line of authority that flows throughout the organization. Line managers interact directly with the functions of production, financing, or marketing—the functions needed to produce and sell goods and services. A staff manager provides information, advice, or technical assistance to aid line managers. Staff managers do not have authority to give orders outside their own departments or to compel line managers to take action.

The line-and-staff organization is common in midsize and large organizations. It is an effective structure because it combines the line organization's capabilities for rapid decision making and direct communication with the expert knowledge of staff specialists.

Committee Organizations A *committee organization* is a structure that places authority and responsibility jointly in the hands of a group of individuals rather than a single manager. This model typically appears as part of a regular line-and-staff structure.

Committees also work in areas such as new-product development. A new-product committee may include managers from such areas as accounting, engineering, finance,

FIGURE
7.8 Line-and-Staff Organization

Plant Manager

Accounting · Engineering · Human Resources

Production Manager

Supervisor · Supervisor · Supervisor

— Line Relationships
▬ Staff Relationships

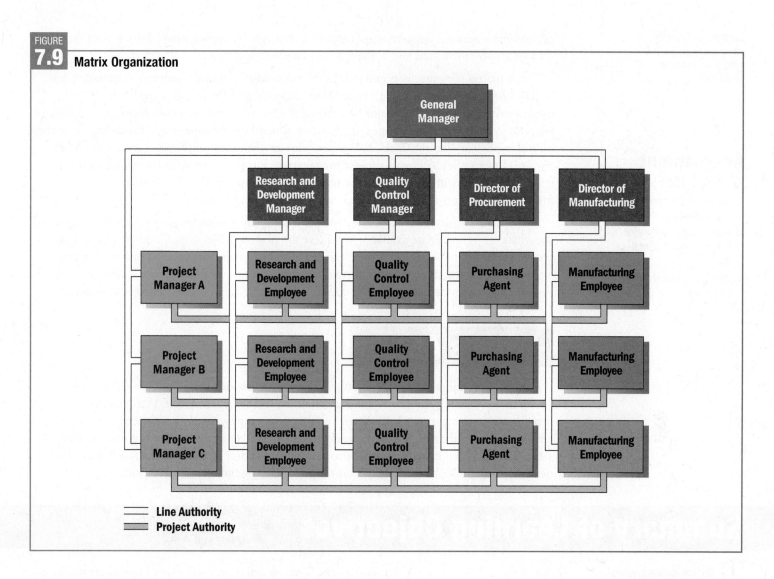

FIGURE 7.9 Matrix Organization

General Manager

Research and Development Manager | Quality Control Manager | Director of Procurement | Director of Manufacturing

Project Manager A | Research and Development Employee | Quality Control Employee | Purchasing Agent | Manufacturing Employee

Project Manager B | Research and Development Employee | Quality Control Employee | Purchasing Agent | Manufacturing Employee

Project Manager C | Research and Development Employee | Quality Control Employee | Purchasing Agent | Manufacturing Employee

— Line Authority
▬ Project Authority

manufacturing, marketing, and technical research. By including representatives from all areas involved in creating and marketing products, such a committee generally improves planning and employee morale because decisions reflect diverse perspectives.

Committees tend to act slowly and conservatively, however, and may make decisions by compromising conflicting interests rather than by choosing the best alternative. The definition of a camel as "a racehorse designed by committee" provides an apt description of some limitations of committee decisions.

Matrix Organizations Some organizations use a matrix or product management design to customize their structures. The *matrix structure* links employees from different parts of the organization to work together on specific projects. Figure 7.9 diagrams a matrix structure. A project manager assembles a group of employees from different functional areas. The employees keep their ties to the line-and-staff structure, as shown in the vertical white lines. As the horizontal gold lines show, employees are also members of project teams. When the project is completed, employees return to their regular jobs.

In the matrix structure, each employee reports to two managers: one line manager and one project manager. Employees who are chosen to work on a special project receive instructions from the project manager (horizontal authority), but they continue as employees in their

LECTURE ENHANCER:
What are some potential
pitfalls of a matrix
structure?

permanent functional departments (vertical authority). The term *matrix* comes from the intersecting grid of horizontal and vertical lines of authority.

The matrix structure is popular at high-technology and multinational corporations, as well as hospitals and consulting firms. Dow Chemical and Procter & Gamble have both used matrix structures. The major benefits of the matrix structure come from its flexibility in adapting quickly to rapid changes in the environment and its capability of focusing resources on major problems or products. It also provides an outlet for employees' creativity and initiative. However, it challenges project managers to integrate the skills of specialists from many departments into a coordinated team. It also means that team members' permanent functional managers must adjust their employees' regular workloads.

The matrix structure is most effective when company leaders empower project managers to use whatever resources are available to achieve the project's objectives. Good project managers know how to make the project goals clear and keep team members focused. A firm that truly embraces the matrix structure also nurtures a project culture by making sure staffing is adequate, the workload is reasonable, and other company resources are available to project managers.[37]

What's Ahead

In the next chapter, we sharpen our focus on the importance of people—the human resource—in shaping the growth and profitability of the organization. We examine how firms recruit, select, train, evaluate, and compensate employees in their attempts to attract, retain, and motivate a high-quality workforce. The concept of motivation is examined, and we will discuss how managers apply theories of motivation in the modern workplace. The next chapter also looks at the important topic of labor–management relations.

Assessment Check ✔

1. What is the purpose of an organization chart?
2. What are the five major forms of departmentalization?
3. What does *span of management* mean?

Summary of Learning Objectives

⌐1¬ Define *management*.

Management is the process of achieving organizational objectives through people and other resources. The management hierarchy is generally as follows: top managers provide overall direction for company activities, middle managers implement the strategies of top managers and direct the activities of supervisors, and supervisors interact directly with workers. The three basic managerial skills are: technical, human or interpersonal, and conceptual.

Assessment Check Answers ✔

1.1 What is management? Management is the process of achieving organizational objectives through people and other resources. The manager's job is to combine human and technical resources in the best way possible to achieve the company's goals.

1.2 How do the jobs of top managers, middle managers, and supervisory managers differ? Top managers develop long-range plans, set a direction for their organization, and inspire all employees to achieve the company's vision. Middle managers focus on specific operations, products, or

customers. They develop procedures to implement the firm's strategic plans. Supervisory managers interact directly with nonmanagerial employees who produce and sell the firm's goods and services. They are responsible for implementing the plans developed by middle managers and motivating workers to accomplish immediate goals.

1.3 What is the relationship between the manager's planning and controlling functions? Controlling is evaluating an organization's performance to determine whether it is accomplishing its objectives. The basic purpose of controlling is to assess the success of the planning function. Controlling also provides feedback for future rounds of planning.

⌐2¬ Explain the role of setting a vision and ethical standards for the firm.

Vision is the founder's perception of the marketplace needs and the firm's methods for meeting them. Vision helps clarify a firm's purpose and the actions it can take to make the most of opportunities. High ethical standards can help build success for a firm through job satisfaction and customer loyalty.

Assessment Check Answers ✓

2.1 What is meant by a vision for the firm? A vision is the target for a firm's actions, helping direct the company toward opportunities and differentiating it from its competitors.

2.2 Why is it important for a top executive to set high ethical standards? High ethical standards often result in a stable workforce, job satisfaction, and customer loyalty.

⌈3⌋ Summarize the importance of planning.

The planning process identifies organizational goals and develops the actions necessary to reach them. Planning helps a company turn vision into action, take advantage of opportunities, and avoid costly mistakes. Strategic planning is a far-reaching process. It views the world through a wide-angle lens to determine the long-range focus and activities of the organization. Tactical planning focuses on the current and short-range activities required to implement the organization's strategies. Operational planning sets standards and work targets for functional areas such as production, human resources, and marketing.

Assessment Check Answers ✓

3.1 Outline the planning process. Some plans are very broad and long range, focusing on key organizational objectives; others are more detailed and specify how particular objectives will be achieved. From the mission statement to objectives to specific plans, each phase must fit into a comprehensive planning framework.

3.2 Describe the purpose of tactical planning. The purpose of tactical planning is to determine which short-term activities should be implemented to accomplish the firm's overall strategy.

3.3 Compare the kinds of plans made by top managers and middle managers. How does their focus differ? Top managers focus on long-range, strategic plans. In contrast, middle-level managers and supervisors focus on short-term, tactical planning.

⌈4⌋ Describe the strategic planning process.

The first step of strategic planning is to translate the firm's vision into a mission statement that explains its overall intentions and aims. Next, planners must assess the firm's current competitive position using tools such as SWOT analysis. Managers then set specific objectives. The next step is to develop strategies for reaching objectives that will differentiate the firm from its competitors. Managers then develop an action plan that outlines the specific methods for implementing the strategy. Finally, the results achieved by the plan are evaluated, and the plan is adjusted as needed.

Assessment Check Answers ✓

4.1 What is the purpose of a mission statement? A mission statement is a public declaration of a firm's purpose, the reason it exists, the customers it will serve, and how it is different from competitors. A mission statement guides the actions of company managers and employees.

4.2 Which of the firm's characteristics does a SWOT analysis compare? A SWOT analysis determines a firm's strengths, weaknesses, opportunities, and threats relative to its competitors. A SWOT analysis helps determine a firm's competitive position in the marketplace.

4.3 How do managers use objectives? Objectives, which are derived from the firm's mission statement, are used to define desired performance levels in areas such as profitability, customer service, and employee satisfaction.

⌈5⌋ Discuss managers as decision makers.

A programmed decision applies a company rule or policy to solve a frequently occurring problem. A nonprogrammed decision forms a response to a complex and unique problem with important consequences for the organization. The five-step approach to decision making includes recognizing a problem or opportunity, developing alternative courses of action, evaluating the alternatives, selecting and implementing an alternative, and following up the decision to determine its effectiveness.

Assessment Check Answers ✓

5.1 Distinguish between programmed and nonprogrammed decisions. Programmed decisions, such as reordering office supplies, are simple and happen frequently, so procedures for them can streamline the process. Nonprogrammed decisions, such as the purchase of real estate or equipment, require more individual evaluation.

5.2 What are the steps in the decision-making process? The decision-making steps are recognition of a problem or opportunity, development of alternatives, evaluation of alternatives, selection and implementation of the chosen alternative, and follow-up to determine effectiveness of the decision.

⌈6⌋ Evaluate managers as leaders.

Leadership is the act of motivating others to achieve certain goals. The basic leadership styles are autocratic, democratic, and free-rein leadership. The best leadership style depends on three elements: the leader, the followers, and the situation.

Assessment Check Answers ✓

6.1 How is *leadership* defined? Leadership means directing or inspiring people to attain organizational goals. Effective leaders share several traits, such as empathy, self-awareness, and objectivity in dealing with others. Leaders also use the power of their jobs, expertise, and experience to influence others.

6.2 Identify the styles of leadership as they appear along a continuum of greater or lesser employee participation. At one end of the continuum, autocratic leaders make decisions without consulting employees. In the middle of the continuum, democratic leaders ask employees for suggestions and encourage participation. At the other end of the continuum, free-rein leaders leave most decisions to their employees.

[7] Discuss corporate culture.

Corporate culture refers to an organization's principles, beliefs, and values. It is typically shaped by a firm's founder and perpetuated through formal programs such as training, rituals, and ceremonies, as well as through informal discussions among employees. Corporate culture can influence a firm's success by giving it a competitive advantage.

Assessment Check Answers ✔

7.1 What is the relationship between leadership style and corporate culture? The best leadership style to adopt often depends on the organization's corporate culture and its system of principles, beliefs, and values. Managerial philosophies, communications networks, and workplace environments and practices all influence corporate culture.

7.2 What is a strong corporate culture? A corporate culture is an organization's system of principles, beliefs, and values. In an organization with a strong culture, everyone knows and supports the same principles, beliefs, and values.

[8] Identify organizational structures.

The subdivision of work activities into units within the organization is called *departmentalization*. It may be based on products, geographical locations, customers, functions, or processes. Most firms implement one or more of four structures: line, line-and-staff, committee, and matrix structures.

Assessment Check Answers ✔

8.1 What is the purpose of an organization chart? An organization chart is a visual representation of a firm's structure that illustrates job positions and functions.

8.2 What are the five major forms of departmentalization? Product departmentalization organizes units by the different goods and services a company offers. Geographical departmentalization organizes units by geographical regions. Customer departmentalization organizes units by different types of customers. Functional departmentalization organizes units by business activities such as finance, marketing, human resources, and production. Process departmentalization organizes units by the steps or work processes it takes to complete production or provide a service.

8.3 What does *span of management* mean? The span of management, or span of control, is the number of employees a manager supervises.

■ Business Terms You Need to Know

management 202
planning 204
organizing 205
directing 205
controlling 205
vision 205

mission statement 209
SWOT analysis 210
objectives 212
decision making 213
leadership 215
empowerment 216

corporate culture 217
organization 218
departmentalization 219
delegation 221

■ Review Questions

1. What are the three levels of management hierarchy? For each level, which management skills might be considered most important, and why?

2. Identify the four basic managerial functions. Suppose you were hired to be the manager of a local restaurant. Which managerial functions would likely be the biggest part of your job? In what ways?

3. Describe the link between a company's vision and its ethical standards. Why is it important for top management to put forth a clear vision and ethical standards for a company?

4. Identify the four types of planning, then think about the following scenario. Suppose you planned a large cookout with your friends, but when you woke up on the morning of the party, it was pouring rain. What type of planning would you use prior to the storm? What type of planning would allow you to cope with the rain? Specifically, what could you do?

5. What is the link between a firm's vision and its mission statement? Think about your own career as a start-up venture. What is your vision? What might be your mission statement?

6. Define *objectives*. Outline objectives you might have for your own college education and career. How might this outline help you implement your own career strategy?

7. Identify each of the following as a programmed or nonprogrammed decision:

   a. reordering printer cartridges

   b. selecting a cell-phone provider

   c. buying your favorite toothpaste or shampoo at the supermarket

   d. selecting a college to attend

   e. filling your car with gasoline

8. From what sources might a leader derive power? Which leadership style might work best for a manager whose firm is forced to make cost-cutting decisions? Why?

9. Why is a strong corporate culture important to a company's success? How might the corporate culture be linked to leadership style?

10. Which type of organization structure provides a firm with the most flexibility to respond to changes in the marketplace and engage in innovation? What might be the drawbacks of this structure?

■ Projects and Teamwork Applications

1. Imagine that you've been hired as a supervisor by a bakery shop called Clare's Cakes that is beginning to grow. Clare—the founder—is looking for ways to increase production capacity, expand its deliveries, and eventually open several more shops in the area. Create a job description for yourself, including the managerial functions you think you'll need and skills you believe you'll need for success.

2. On your own or with a classmate, create a mission statement for Clare's Cakes. Think about the type of company it is, the products it offers customers (cakes for special occasions or milestones), and the type of growth it is planning.

3. Contingency planning requires a combination of foresight and adaptability. Josh James, founder of Omniture, the Web analytics firm he recently sold to Adobe, recalls the importance of being able to adapt when his company seemed on the brink of disaster. "There were times when I lay down on the floor at night, close to crying. Then my wife would come over and kick me and say, 'Get up and figure it out.'"[38] Research the news headlines for situations that could (or did) require contingency planning. Report to the class what the challenge was, and how the managers involved handled it. Remark on whether the planning was effective or successful.

4. Identify someone who you think is a good leader—it can be someone you know personally or a public figure. Describe the traits that you think are most important in making this person an effective leader. Would this person's leadership style work in situations other than his or her current position? Why or why not?

5. Research a firm whose goods or services you purchase or admire. Learn what you can about the organization's culture. Do you think you would be an effective manager in this culture? Why or why not? Share your findings with the class.

■ Web Assignments

1. **Strategic planning**. Visit the Web site listed below, which summarizes Johnson & Johnson's strategic planning philosophy. Review several recent acquisitions by Johnson & Johnson and prepare a brief report discussing how the acquisitions resulted from the company's strategic planning process.

   http://www.investor.jnj.com/strategic.cfm

2. **Mission statements**. Go to the Web sites of two organizations, a for-profit firm and a not-for-profit organization. Print out both organizations' mission statements. Bring the material with you to class to participate in a discussion on mission statements.

3. **Management structure**. Visit the Web site listed below.

   http://investors.target.com/phoenix.zhtml?cv65828&pvirol-IRHome

   Click on "corporate governance" and answer the following questions:

   a. How would you characterize Target's organizational structure?

   b. What is the composition of Target's board of directors?

Note: Internet Web addresses change frequently. If you don't find the exact sites listed, you may need to access the organization's home page and search from there or use a search engine such as Bing or Google.

Ford Drives Out of the Financial Mud

When the other major U.S. automakers accepted federal funds in order to stay in business, Ford Motor Company—in the voice of CEO Alan R. Mulally—said no. The federal funds were to come in the form of short-term loans, which Ford determined it didn't need at the time. Several years earlier, the firm had restructured its debt so that when the economy slowed down, Ford didn't.

Mulally observes that this timing was a bit of luck and a bit of strategic planning. To implement this overall strategy, Ford sold off its luxury brands Aston Martin, Jaguar, and Land Rover and invested in the development of moderately priced, fuel-efficient cars and trucks. Ford took on some extra debt as a hedge against a recession—and had the cash on hand when other U.S. automakers didn't.

Decisions like these require strong leadership qualities that include a will to persevere during tough times. Mulally's first management position was at Boeing. He overmanaged his employees so closely that one engineer finally quit. Mulally says that this early experience taught him that his job as a manager was "to help connect people to a bigger goal, a bigger program and help them move forward to even bigger contributions. That experience stayed with me forever on what it really means to manage and lead."

Mulally believes that every employee has something to offer and that each worker must be clear about the firm's mission. He says that his job is to focus on four things:

(1) the process of connecting his firm to the outside world, (2) keeping track of the firm's identity in the marketplace, (3) balancing short-term objectives with long-term goals, and (4) the values and standards of the organization. When asked what career advice he would give to young recruits to the business world, Mulally answers without hesitation, "Don't manage your career. Follow your dream and contribute."

Questions for Critical Thinking

1. How does Alan Mulally's "focus on four things" help him with strategic planning for Ford? Do you believe it made a difference in the firm's decision to decline the federal loan?

2. Mulally emphasizes the importance of having every employee understand the firm's mission. How might this understanding help employees contribute to the company's performance?

Sources: Paul Ingrassia, "Ford's Renaissance Man," *Wall Street Journal*, http://www.marshallgoldsmithlibrary.com, accessed March 13, 2012; Keith Naughton and Ian King, "Mulally: Ford Marking 'Tremendous Progress,'" *BusinessWeek*, http://www.businessweek.com, accessed March 13, 2012; Adam Bryant, "Planes, Cars, and Cathedrals," *New York Times*, http://www.nytimes.com, accessed March 13, 2012; John Hockenberry, "Interview with Ford CEO Alan Mulally," PRI/WNYC, http://www.pri.org, accessed March 13, 2012; excerpt from "Interview with Ford CEO Alan Mulally," from The Takeaway, a co-production of Public Radio International and WNYC. Reprinted with permission.

Using Business Students as Consultants

Winning "Project Runway" and securing a contract with QVC might seem the complete recipe for retail success. But as Chloe Dao discovered, in the fashion world nothing is forever.

When publicity from her win faded and QVC's contract with Lot 8, her Houston boutique, ended, "I was stuck with all this overhead and a fraction of the revenue," said Dao. "I needed an outside view of my business to figure out what to do next."

That view came from an unexpected source: six business students from nearby Rice University. As part of their coursework and guided by their professors, the students scoured Lot 8's financial statements, interviewed employees, and designed and executed a customer survey. Their efforts uncovered waste and inefficiency that had pushed Dao's expenses 16 percent above industry average. The store was larger and its hours longer than necessary, for instance, and prices higher than customers (who were younger than Dao realized) could afford.

Regular meetings with the students were "like going to therapy every week," says Dao. Among the group's final recommendations were for Dao to rename her store after herself to leverage her local celebrity, position it as a destination boutique, cut unprofitable merchandise lines, shorten operating hours, and hire a part-timer. Dao received free consulting advice worth thousands of dollars, and the students received an A.

Questions for Critical Thinking

1. Find out more about Rice's program, the Action Learning Project, at the university's Web site. Is a program like this a good way to gain management experience early in your career? Why or why not?

2. How do you think the students' approach would have differed if Dao managed an e-business?

Sources: "Action Learning Project," Rice University Web site, http://rice.business.edu, accessed February 7, 2012; Francesca Di Meglio, "MBA Electives Offer Hands-On Learning," *Bloomberg BusinessWeek*, January 11, 2012, http://www.businessweek.com; Issie Lapowsky, "Need a Deal on Consulting? Hire B-School Students," *Inc.*, December 2011, http://www.inc.com.

Like many new businesses, Smart Design was founded by a collection of college classmates who wanted to change something. Dan Formosa, along with several college friends, had a background in design and ergonomics. The group believed that design should be about people, not things—and Smart Design was born. In the beginning, it was a hard sell—not the designs themselves, but the idea that the needs of individual *people* should be involved in the development of design. Formosa was interested in "how design can affect our quality of life, improve performance, and affect behavior." Based in San Francisco, the original Smart Design team "pulled together techniques in biomechanics and cognitive psychology," recalls Formosa. "This was a type of an approach that no other design group was undertaking in the U.S. at the time, so it was an early test of our beliefs about what and where design should be." Smart Design was successful throughout the 1980s, but Formosa admits that it was an uphill battle to convince clients that design was, indeed, for everyone.

Then came OXO. Around 1990, Smart Design acquired the manufacturing firm OXO as a client, giving Formosa's team a chance to re-invent the design of common household products ranging from can openers to scissors, resulting in the OXO Good Grips line of kitchen utensils. Because of the mundane nature of these products—consumers weren't accustomed to shopping for a potato peeler that actually felt comfortable in the hand—once they caught on, the idea that everyday design matters began to take hold in the marketplace. Smart Design's client base grew significantly, as did the company. Firms such as Ford, ESPN, Samsung, Nike, and Microsoft began to request Smart Design's services, and the number of employees increased.

No matter how much talent lies in the firm, though, managing a company of designers can be like trying to herd cats. Everyone has an idea, and everyone is running headlong in a different direction. So leadership is critical to the firm's success. Paulette Bluhm-Sauriol, director of brand communication, observes that while most designers are detail oriented, "Someone has to make sure that the team is keeping the big picture in mind, not just the details." That's part of her job as well as Formosa's: maintaining the overall vision. She also notes that, as a leader, Formosa has the natural gift of connecting and empathizing with people, whether it is employees or potential end-users of Smart Design's products. "Dan has the ability to make going into people's lives and becoming part of their lives comfortable," she observes.

This was particularly true during the development of a new type of pre-filled medical syringe that Smart Design undertook for UCB/OXO Cimzia. The medication Cimzia is a solution that alleviates chronic pain in patients with certain conditions. If patients could administer the solution themselves in a comfortable way, it would enhance their lives. When the pharmaceutical maker UCB and OXO partnered to develop the new product, they went to Smart Design for the design. Formosa asked his team to go straight to the patients themselves to ask them what they needed. Designers met and observed patients in their own environment, giving them a chance to express their wishes. "It can be uncomfortable, but it's amazing how you can get to the big ideas by approaching the project his way," says Bluhm-Sauriol.

The syringe has met with marketplace success, and has even won an International Design Excellence Award. Most important, patients are getting what they need, which is exactly what Formosa strives for in each product his firm designs. "If someone buys a product or signs up for a service, they expect it to work. If you actually encounter a product or service that exceeds expectations, that is the sign of a great design," he says. Formosa also contends that the same principles can be applied to the design of a delicate hospital instrument as are applied to a pizza cutter.

At Smart Design, the corporate culture supports the notion that the ideas of every employee are important. Regardless of job title, each person is considered a designer, with something valuable to contribute to the process. Formosa doesn't mind the potential chaos of this kind of organization—it's how he operates. "When we have everybody thinking everything, it's a positive sign," he says. It's a formula that works.

Questions for Critical Thinking

1. Describe Dan Formosa's vision for Smart Design. Why do you think it took so long to gain popularity in the marketplace?

2. Identify Smart Design's strategy for competitive differentiation.

3. How would you describe Dan Formosa's leadership style? Do you think it is the best style for Smart Design? Why or why not?

4. Discuss Smart Design's corporate culture. Do you think it is effective for the kind of business the company engages in? Why or why not?

Sources: Smart Design Web site, http://www.smartdesignworldwide. com, accessed March 13, 2012; "Smart Design," National Design Awards, http://www.nationaldesignawards.org/2010, accessed March 13, 2012; Ralph Goldsworthy, "Dan Formosa of Smart Design, Designer Q&A," *Design Droplets.com*, April 28, 2010, http://designdroplets.com.

Learning Objectives

[1] Explain the role of human resources: the people behind the people.

[2] Describe recruitment and selection.

[3] Discuss orientation, training, and evaluation.

[4] Describe compensation.

[5] Discuss employee separation.

[6] Explain the different methods for motivating employees.

[7] Discuss labor–management relations.

Chapter 8

Human Resource Management: From Recruitment to Labor Relations

Abel MitjaVarela/iStockphoto

Hiring Heroes Is Good Business

U. S. military veterans returning from wars in Afghanistan and Iraq have had a difficult time finding employment, making the transition from military to civilian life even more challenging. A recent government study reports that the unemployment rate among military vets is 4 percent *above* the national unemployment rate. And an estimated 30 percent of veterans under the age of 25 are jobless. With help from several well-known companies, veterans may see those unemployment numbers change dramatically for the better.

The Walt Disney Company recently announced a new initiative to hire 1,000 military veterans over the next several years. Dubbed "Heroes Work Here," the program will span across all segments of the company and will be implemented through career fairs designed to showcase opportunities for returning military personnel. In addition, the company will assist military families and veterans during their transition to civilian life and launch a national public awareness campaign to encourage other employers across the country to hire veterans. Announcing the new program, Disney CEO Robert Iger said, "It's a measure of our respect for how much they have sacrificed on our behalf, and our sincere gratitude for their extraordinary contributions to this country." Walmart has also made a commitment to hire military veterans returning home. Recently the company launched a five-year, $10 million program to promote job training among former armed forces personnel. Walmart CEO Bill Simon says the company "loves to hire veterans." Simon says military personnel not only know how to perform under pressure but they also are quick learners and team players. The company actively recruits veterans, offering them programs to help transition into civilian jobs. Walmart recently started a career Web site for former active-duty service members interested in building a career with the company.

Over the years, returning military veterans have played an important role in helping the U.S. economy get back on track by bringing their talents to the civilian workforce. NBC's Tom Brokaw observes, "there is a tradition of American business growing its leadership from military ranks."[1]

Overview

The importance of employees to the success of any organization is the very basis of management. In this chapter, we explore the important issues of human resource management and motivation. We begin with a discussion of the ways organizations attract, develop, and retain employees. Then we describe the concepts behind motivation and the way human resource managers apply them to increase employee satisfaction and organizational effectiveness.

We also discuss the reasons why labor unions exist and focus on legislation that affects labor–management relations. The process of collective bargaining is then discussed, along with tools used by unions and management in seeking their objectives.

human resource management function of attracting, developing, and retaining employees who can perform the activities necessary to accomplish organizational objectives.

Assessment Check ✔

1. What are the five main tasks of a human resource manager?

2. What are the three overall objectives of a human resource manager?

[1] Human Resources: The People Behind the People

A company is only as good as its workers. If people come to work each day eager to see each other, to do their very best on the job, to serve their customers, and to help their firm compete, then it's very likely that company will be a success. The best companies value their employees just as much as their customers—without workers, there would be no goods or services to offer customers. The Walt Disney Company and Walmart understand this. Management at these companies know that hiring good workers—including military veterans—is vital to their overall success. Achieving the highest level of job satisfaction and dedication among employees is the goal of **human resource management**, which attracts, develops, and retains the employees who can perform the activities necessary to accomplish organizational objectives.

Not every firm is large enough to have an entire human resources department. But whoever performs this function generally does the following: plan for staffing needs, recruit and hire workers, provide for training and evaluate performance, determine compensation and benefits, and oversee employee separation. In accomplishing these five tasks, shown in Figure 8.1, human resource managers achieve their objectives of

1. providing qualified, well-trained employees for the organization;

2. maximizing employee effectiveness in the organization; and

3. satisfying individual employee needs through monetary compensation, benefits, opportunities to advance, and job satisfaction.

Human resource plans must be based on an organization's overall competitive strategies. In conjunction with other managers, human resource managers predict how many employees a firm or department will need and what skills those workers should bring to the job—along with what skills they might learn on the job. Human resource managers are often consulted when a firm is considering reducing costs by laying off workers or increasing costs by hiring new ones. They may be involved in both long-term and short-term planning.

Anthony Behar/Sipa Press/AP/Wide World Photos

Hiring good workers—including military veterans—is the key to a company's overall success. Job fairs are popping up across the country, such as the U.S. Chamber of Commerce "Hire 500,000 Heroes" program, which aims to hire 500,000 military veterans and their spouses as a way of helping these heroes transition back to civilian life.

[2] Recruitment and Selection

Human resource managers recruit and help select the right workers for a company. To ensure that job candidates bring the necessary skills to the job or have the desire and ability to learn them, most firms implement the recruitment and selection process shown in Figure 8.2.

FIGURE 8.1 Human Resource Management Responsibilities

- Employee Recruitment and Selection
- Employee Training and Performance Evaluation
- Employee Compensation and Benefits
- Employee Separation
- Planning for Staffing Needs

Core Responsibilities of Human Resource Management

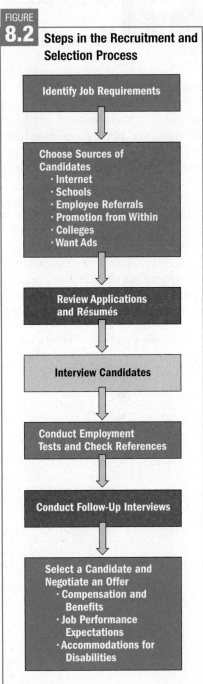

FIGURE 8.2 Steps in the Recruitment and Selection Process

Identify Job Requirements

↓

Choose Sources of Candidates
- Internet
- Schools
- Employee Referrals
- Promotion from Within
- Colleges
- Want Ads

↓

Review Applications and Résumés

↓

Interview Candidates

↓

Conduct Employment Tests and Check References

↓

Conduct Follow-Up Interviews

↓

Select a Candidate and Negotiate an Offer
- Compensation and Benefits
- Job Performance Expectations
- Accommodations for Disabilities

Finding Qualified Candidates

When the economy dips and jobs are lost, many people compete for a limited number of positions. When a company develops a great reputation for benefits or working conditions, it might be inundated with applications. But even with a large number of job candidates competing for a small number of openings, companies sometimes have trouble finding the right person for each position. According to a recent survey by the National Association of Colleges and Employers, firms are currently looking for candidates with these strengths: verbal communication skills, strong work ethic, teamwork skills, analytical skills, and initiative.[2]

In addition to traditional methods of recruiting, such as college job fairs, personal referrals, and want ads, most companies now rely on their Web sites. A firm's Web site might contain a career section with general employment information and a listing of open positions. Applicants are often able to submit a résumé and apply for an open position online. When applying for jobs online, it's helpful to use the key words in the job description as part of the application. Also, if a current résumé is required as part of the job application, tailor the wording of the résumé to reflect the key components of the job you are seeking.

Internet recruiting is such a quick, efficient, and inexpensive way to reach a large pool of job seekers that the vast majority of companies currently use the Internet, including social networking sites, to fill job openings. This is also the best way for firms to reach new graduates and workers in their 20s and even 30s. Using a social media site such as LinkedIn or Facebook allows firms to communicate directly with candidates and get feedback, as the "Hit & Miss" feature explains.

LECTURE ENHANCER: Which steps seem most important to this process?

Using Social Media for Recruitment

Companies use social networking for many purposes, but finding new employees has become the biggest and continues to grow. More than 7 in 10 executives at large U.S. firms use social media to recruit new talent, reveals one survey, and 89 percent of HR professionals in another survey plan to do so, up from 83 percent last year. Two in three firms using LinkedIn, Facebook, and Twitter report making successful hires through these sites. Job boards, in contrast, seem to be on the decline.

LinkedIn and Facebook are the networks recruiters use most heavily. Here employers maintain dedicated company pages, scour visitors for potential candidates, and join discussions and user groups to encourage applicants. Through firms like Jobvite they even use social networks to automate employee referrals.

A word of caution to potential job seekers: It is important to be careful about posting information in public places—even online. Once material is posted via social media, it is available for everyone to see.

Questions for Critical Thinking

1. One consultant says companies like social networking but don't know how to measure results. How should firms judge recruitment results from social networking?

2. Some job seekers like separate social and professional networks and find Facebook messages about job openings "invasive." How can recruiters overcome this bias?

Sources: Jessica Miller-Merrell, "Corporate Social Media Risk and Employment Law Concerns When Hiring," http://www.blogging4jobs.com, March 5, 2012; "Recruiting Tops List of Corporate Social Media Initiatives," Business Wire, October 5, 2011, www .businesswire.com; "$ Facebook Recruiting Tips Inspired by Sodexo," TalentMinded.com, September 15, 2011, http://talentminded.com; Christina DesMarais, "Facebook as a Recruiting Tool," *Inc.*, August 9, 2011, http://technology.com.com; Joe Light, "Recruiters Troll Facebook for Candidates They Like," *The Wall Street Journal,* August 8, 2011, http:// online.wsj.com; Susan Adams, "More Employers Using Social Media to Hunt for Talent," *Forbes,* July 13, 2011, www.forbes.com.

It's also important for job seekers to be as specific as possible when using the Internet to look for a job. For example, if possible, they should apply through the firm's Web site instead of one of the large, third-party job sites. "Employers see that the vast majority of applicants coming through these [third-party] sites have not done sufficient research, and often are questionable fits for the advertised positions," notes one human resource expert.[3]

Recruiting techniques continue to evolve as technology advances. JobsinPods.com is an online library of podcast interviews with hiring managers and employees at a variety of U.S. companies, including AT&T, Intel, and IBM. New podcasts, also called jobcasts, are posted in a blog format and older podcasts are archived. Some describe employers' hiring needs, while others talk about what it's like to work at a particular company. Job seekers can also download the podcasts to an iPod and listen to them at their leisure.[4]

Selecting and Hiring Employees

It's the human resource manager's job to select and hire employees, often in conjunction with department managers or supervisors. Every firm must follow state and federal employment laws. Title VII of the Civil Rights Act of 1964 prohibits employers from discriminating against applicants based on their race, religion, color, sex, or national origin. The Americans with Disabilities Act of 1990 prohibits employers from discriminating against disabled applicants. The Civil Rights Act created the *Equal Employment Opportunity Commission (EEOC)* to investigate discrimination complaints. The Uniform Employee Selection Guidelines were adopted by the EEOC in 1978 to further clarify ways in which employers must ensure that their employees will be hired and managed without discrimination.[5] The EEOC also helps employers set up *affirmative action programs* to increase job opportunities for women, minorities, people with disabilities, and other protected groups.

The Civil Rights Act of 1991 expanded the alternatives available to victims of employment discrimination by including the right to a jury trial, punitive damages, and damages for emotional distress. At the same time, opponents to such laws have launched initiatives to restrict affirmative action standards and protect employers against unnecessary litigation.

These laws have been the basis for thousands of legal cases over the years. Recently, Best Buy agreed to pay a $290,000 settlement to nine former employees who accused the retailer of discrimination against female, African American, and Latino employees. The employees claimed Best Buy had denied them promotions and more lucrative sales positions because of their gender and race.[6] Failure to comply with equal employment opportunity legislation can result in costly legal fees, expensive fines, bad publicity, and poor employee morale.

Because of the high cost of such lawsuits and settlements, human resource managers must understand the laws in order to prevent unintended violations. Even the process of interviewing a job candidate is covered by law. An interviewer may not ask any questions about marital status, children, race or nationality, religion, age, criminal records, mental illness, medical history, or alcohol and substance abuse problems. For more information about employment law, visit the Web sites of the Society for Human Resource Management (http://www.shrm.org) and the EEOC (http://www.eeoc.gov).

Navigating the maze of hiring restrictions is a challenge. Some firms try to screen out high-risk employees by requiring drug testing for job applicants, particularly in industries that deal with public safety—such as air travel or truck driving. But drug testing is controversial because of privacy issues. Also, positive test results may not be accurate. Another issue is whether employees can be required to speak a particular language—usually English—in the workplace. Although the EEOC views this as discrimination, one state recently legalized the practice. And some employers in other states are seeking guidance on whether they can lawfully require English to be spoken in the workplace.[7] Employers may legally establish requirements for specific jobs—a bona fide occupational qualification (BFOQ)—that may cut across EEOC protected classes. For example, a designer of women's clothes by necessity is permitted to hire only female models to show off new designs.

Recruitment and selection are expensive. There are costs for advertising, interviewing, administering employment tests and even medical exams. Once an applicant is hired, there are costs for training and perhaps equipment such as a computer. But a bad hiring decision is even more expensive, because the firm has to go through the whole process again to find the right person. One estimate states that the cost of hiring the wrong top-level manager amounts to 24 times the candidate's annual pay. To avoid bad hiring decisions, some companies require job candidates to perform tasks related to the job they're seeking as part of the job application process. For example, a company might ask job candidates for a sales position to work with a company salesperson in the local sales region before making a final decision on which candidate to hire.

To avoid these mistakes—and to get the right person for the job—many employers require applicants to complete employment tests. These tests may verify certain skills, including mechanical, technical, language, and computer skills. One example is the Wonderlic Basic Skills Test, which is a cognitive ability test that measures a person's abilities in understanding words, numbers, and logic. Cognitive ability tests accurately predict job performance on many types of jobs.

More and more companies are using the Internet to recruit potential employees. Posting job openings online (including social networking sites) is a quick, efficient, and inexpensive way for companies to reach a large pool of job seekers.

LECTURE ENHANCER:
What are some specific examples of these costs?

Assessment Check ✔

1. Describe several recruiting techniques used by human resource managers.

2. What is the function of the Equal Employment Opportunity Commission (EEOC)?

Orientation, Training, and Evaluation

Once hired, employees need to know what is expected of them and how well they are performing. Companies provide this information through orientation, training, and evaluation. A new hire may complete an orientation program administered jointly by the human resource personnel and the department in which the employee will work. During orientation, employees learn about company policies regarding their rights and benefits. They might receive an employee manual that includes the company's code of ethics and code of conduct. And they'll usually receive some form of training.

Training Programs

Training is a good investment for both employers and employees. Training provides workers with an opportunity to build their skills and knowledge, preparing them for new job opportunities within the company. It also provides employers with a better chance at retaining long-term, loyal, high-performing workers. Companies of all sizes take creative approaches to training. Nugget Market, a nine-store California supermarket chain named as one of *Fortune's* "100 Best Companies to Work For," rolls out continuous information about products, the company, and updates from executives, on a large, flat screen monitor in each store. Employees who watch—and absorb—the information are eligible for bonus rewards that range from $20 to $1,000.[8]

On-the-Job Training One popular teaching method is *on-the-job training*, which prepares employees for job duties by allowing them to perform tasks under the guidance of experienced employees. A variation of on-the-job training is apprenticeship training, in which an employee learns a job by serving for a time as an assistant to a trained worker. While American apprenticeships usually focus on blue-collar trades—such as plumbing and heating services—in Europe, many new entrants to white-collar professions complete apprenticeships. McDonald's sponsors apprenticeship-training programs in its U.K. restaurants as part of an economic stimulus plan launched by the British government. Offering 10,000 apprenticeships per year, the company says. "We're as serious about education as we are about burgers and fries."[9]

Classroom and Computer-Based Training Many firms offer some form of classroom instruction such as lectures, conferences, and workshops or seminars. Ernst & Young, a large tax-service firm, offers a training program called Ernst & Young and You (EYU), focusing on classroom learning, experiential learning, and coaching.[10]

Many firms are replacing classroom training with computer-based training programs, which can significantly reduce the cost of training. Computer-based training offers consistent presentations, along with videos that can simulate the work environment. Employees can learn at their own pace without having to sign up for a class. Through online training programs, employees can engage in interactive learning—they might conference with a mentor or instructor who is located elsewhere or they might participate in a simulation requiring them to make decisions related to their work. An extension of computer-based training is multimedia training, which may combine text with sound, 3-D animation, high-resolution graphics, games, simulations, and the like.

Management Development A *management development program* provides training designed to improve the skills and broaden the knowledge of current or future

LECTURE ENHANCER: Discuss the pros and cons of implementing apprenticeship training within a professional business environment.

LECTURE ENHANCER: Discuss the pros and cons of computer-based training versus classroom training.

managers and executives. Training may be aimed at increasing specific technical knowledge or more general knowledge in areas such as leadership and interpersonal skills. Glimmerglass Consulting Group, based in New Hampshire, provides management training in leadership, team development, and strategic implementation. After assessing a client's work environment as well as the strengths and weaknesses of its management team, Glimmerglass coaches design a program intended to strengthen management's leadership and team skills. The program may involve an outdoor learning experience such as rock climbing. Glimmerglass's client list includes such firms as American Express, Big Brothers/Big Sisters, Pfizer, and Shell International.[11]

Despite the importance of training talented employees for managerial jobs, many companies are searching for new hires to fill gaps in their executive ranks because they failed to develop future managers. In a move that surprised the international banking world, David de Rothschild appointed a successor from outside his family—the first in 200 years—to become CEO of the Rothschild banking empire. Nigel Higgins was no stranger to the firm; he had worked there for 27 years. But Rothschild chose Higgins because there was no family member ready to handle the job.[12]

LECTURE ENHANCER:
Why might some executives be hesitant to train and mentor potential future managers?

performance appraisal
evaluation of and feedback on an employee's job performance.

Performance Appraisals

Feedback about performance is the best way for a company—and its employees to improve. Most firms use annual **performance appraisals** to evaluate an employee's job performance and provide feedback about it. A performance appraisal can include assessments of everything from attendance to goals met. Based on this evaluation, a manager will make decisions about compensation, promotion, additional training needs, transfers, or even termination. While performance appraisals are common, not everyone agrees about their usefulness. See the "Solving an Ethical Controversy" feature for a discussion of their pros and cons.

Some management experts argue that a performance review is skewed in favor of a single manager's subjective opinion—whether it's positive or negative—and that most employees are afraid to speak honestly to their managers during a performance review. If a performance review is to be at all effective, it should meet the following criteria:

Employees value face-to-face feedback on their performance. Evaluations that are fair and consistent can improve an organization's productivity and profitability.

- be linked to organizational goals;
- be based on objective criteria;
- take place in the form of a two-way conversation.[13]

Some firms conduct peer reviews, in which employees assess the performance of their co-workers, while other firms ask employees to review their supervisors and managers. One such performance appraisal is the *360-degree performance review*, a process that gathers feedback

Who Needs Performance Appraisals?

Debate continues about the value of formal performance appraisals. Employers claim scheduled check-ins keep employees on their toes and aware of what they must achieve to win raises and promotions, and some workers agree. There's no question, however, that appraisals can be stressful, time-consuming, and, when bungled, even counterproductive.

Are performance appraisals a waste of time?

PRO

1. Performance appraisals require managers and employees to invest too much time and energy and often result only in reducing motivation and productivity.

2. Annual appraisals are the norm, but they are too infrequent to offer useful feedback for improved performance.

CON

1. Appraisals offer managers a formal, planned opportunity to help employees improve their performance through feedback and goal setting.

2. Employees can use the opportunity to ask questions, participate in goal setting, and promote recent accomplishments.

Summary

Some advocate shorter, quarterly appraisals to provide more frequent opportunities for feedback and improvement. Others say employees should take ownership of appraisals and be free to ask anyone in the company for feedback at any time. Meanwhile new software such as Rypple can create ongoing feedback loops to gather praise, thanks, and coaching into a single, continuous feed. "We think that real-time, ongoing feedback helps us move fast and avoid too much bureaucracy," says a Rypple executive.

Sources: Company Web site, Allonhill, www.allonhill.com, accessed January 31, 2012; John Reh, "Why Annual Performance Reviews Are a Waste of Time," About.com Management, accessed January 30, 2012, http://management.about.com; Thomas Goetz, "How Facebook Uses Feedback Loops: Meet Rypple," Wired.com, June 20, 2011, www.wired.com; "Should Performance Reviews Be Fired?" *Knowledge@Wharton*, April 27, 2011, http://www.knowledge.wharton.upenn.edu.

LECTURE ENHANCER:
Which of these types of performance reviews would you prefer as an employee? Why?

Assessment Check ☑

1. What are the benefits of computer-based training?
2. What is a management development program?
3. What are the four criteria of an effective performance appraisal?

compensation amount employees are paid in money and benefits.

from a review panel of 8 to 12 people, including co-workers, supervisors, team members, subordinates, and sometimes even customers. The idea is to get as much frank feedback from as many perspectives as possible. By its very nature, this kind of review involves a lot of work, but employees benefit from it because they are more involved with the process and ultimately better understand their own strengths, weaknesses, and roles in the company. Managers benefit because they get much more in-depth feedback from all parts of the organization. Companies such as Halogen Software offer computer programs to help firms gather and sift through this type of data. Organizations as diverse as Dole, Jelly Belly, Princess Cruises, and the San Diego Zoo use products from Canada-based Halogen. However, a potential weakness of this type of review is its anonymous nature.[14]

[4]
Compensation

Compensation—how much employees are paid in money and benefits—is one of the most highly charged issues faced by human resource managers. The amount employees are paid, along with whatever benefits they receive, has a tremendous influence on where they live, what they eat, and how they spend their leisure time. It also has an effect on job satisfaction. Balancing compensation for employees at all job levels can be a challenge for human

Stop Demotivating Employees—And They'll Be Motivated

What's the secret to nurturing high-performing employees? Some experts believe the answer lies not in motivating workers, but in *stopping their demotivation*.

Most new employees are highly motivated, but their enthusiasm drops off significantly after only six months and continues to decline, sometimes for years. The challenge for managers: staunch the outflow of the company's lifeblood.

What keeps employees engaged? Research shows it's rarely the extra two weeks' vacation or perks like an onsite gym. Actually, employees care about things that don't cost companies a dime: a sense of pride in achievement, having managers' respect, and building supportive relationships at work. Employees need to feel connected to their company's mission. It's up to the manager to convey that purpose. Managers must also acknowledge accomplishments. Sometimes a simple "thank you" or "good job" is enough. Managers also must communicate clearly and frequently, promoting teamwork whenever possible.

Savvy managers watch for sagging morale and move to repair it. They make sure to listen to their employees, involve them in decisions about their own jobs, and provide reinforcement and recognition for top performance.

Questions for Critical Thinking

1. How do employees lose their motivation to perform on the job?

2. What is the cost to a business when it loses a valued employee?

Sources: Gary M. Stern, "A Digital Pat on the Back from the Boss: What's It Worth?" http://management.fortune.cnn.com, January 26, 2012; Kishore Krishnan, "Stop Demotivating Employees," *Ezine Articles,* http://ezinearticles.com, accessed February 22, 2011; Dan Ariely, "(De)motivating Employees," February 5, 2011, http://danariely.com; David Sirota, Louis A. Mischkind, and Michael Irwin Seltzer, "Stop Demotivating Your Employees!" *Harvard Business Review,* Summer 2010, pp. 14–15.

---

resource managers. And while compensation certainly is a factor in job satisfaction, it isn't the only one, as discussed in the "Hit & Miss" feature.

Everyone likes to read about the companies that pay their employees the most in cash and benefits. *Fortune* magazine's annual "100 Best Companies to Work For" list includes cash and benefits information as well as other interesting facts. For example, even during a challenging economy, there are several companies on the list that have never laid off employees, including the Container Store chain and QuikTrip convenience stores.[15]

The terms *wages* and *salary* are often used interchangeably, but actually are different. Wages are based on an hourly pay rate or the amount of work accomplished. Typical wage earners are factory workers, construction workers, auto mechanics, retail salespeople, and restaurant wait staff. Salaries are calculated periodically, such as weekly or monthly. Salaried employees receive a set amount of pay that does not fluctuate with the number of hours worked. Whereas wage earners receive overtime pay, salaried workers do not. Office personnel, executives, and professional employees usually receive salaries.

An effective compensation system should attract well-qualified workers, keep them satisfied in their jobs, and inspire them to succeed. It's also important to note that certain laws, including minimum wage, must be taken into account. The Lilly Ledbetter Fair Pay Act of 2009 is one such law, which gives workers more time to file a complaint for pay discrimination.[16]

Most firms base their compensation policies on the following factors: (1) what competing companies are paying, (2) government regulation, (3) cost of living, (4) company profits, and (5) an employee's productivity. Many firms try to balance rewarding workers with maintaining profits by linking more of their pay to superior performance. Firms try to motivate employees to excel by offering some type of incentive compensation in addition to salaries or wages. These programs include the following:

- profit sharing, which awards bonuses based on company profits;

- gain sharing, when companies share the financial value of productivity gains, cost savings, or quality improvements with their workers;

CLASS ACTIVITY:
Lead a discussion on whether students think there should be a limit or ceiling on compensation for executives and the pros and cons of such a limit.

wage pay based on an hourly rate or the amount of work accomplished.

salary pay calculated on a periodic basis, such as weekly or monthly.

LECTURE ENHANCER:
Do you think these factors are appropriate? Are there any additional factors that you think should be considered?

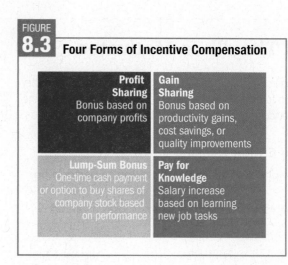

FIGURE 8.3 Four Forms of Incentive Compensation

Profit Sharing Bonus based on company profits	**Gain Sharing** Bonus based on productivity gains, cost savings, or quality improvements
Lump-Sum Bonus One-time cash payment or option to buy shares of company stock based on performance	**Pay for Knowledge** Salary increase based on learning new job tasks

employee benefits
additional compensation such as vacation, retirement plans, profit-sharing, health insurance, gym memberships, child and elder care, and tuition reimbursement, paid entirely or in part by the company.

LECTURE ENHANCER:
What are the pros and cons of each type of compensation?

- lump-sum bonuses and stock options, which reward one-time cash payments and the right to purchase stock in the company based on performance;
- pay for knowledge, which distributes wage or salary increases as employees learn new job tasks.

Figure 8.3 summarizes the four types of incentive compensation programs.

Employee Benefits

In addition to wages and salaries, firms provide benefits to employees and their families as part of their compensation. **Employee benefits**—such as vacation, retirement plans, profit-sharing, health insurance, gym memberships, child and elder care, and tuition reimbursement—are sometimes offered by the company. Benefits represent a large component of an employee's total compensation. Although wages and salaries account for around 70 percent of the typical employee's earnings, the other 30 percent takes the form of employee benefits.[17] Table 8.1 shows the breakdown of an average worker's benefits as compared to wages or salary.

Some benefits are required by law. U.S. firms are required to make Social Security and Medicare contributions, as well as payments to state unemployment insurance and workers' compensation programs, which protect workers in case of job-related injuries or illnesses. The Family and Medical Leave Act of 1993 requires covered employers to offer up to 12 weeks of unpaid, job-protected leave to eligible employees. Firms voluntarily provide other employee benefits, such as child care and health insurance, to help them attract and retain employees. Some states, such as California, New Jersey, and Washington, have laws mandating paid family leave.

TABLE 8.1 Average Costs for Employee Compensation

TYPE OF COMPENSATION	PERCENTAGE OF TOTAL COMPENSATION
Wages and salaries	68.3%
Benefits	31.6
Paid leave	7.0
Supplemental pay	2.0
Insurance	9.7
Health benefits	9.2
Retirement and savings	5.5
Legally required benefits	7.4

Source: Bureau of Labor Statistics, "Employer Costs for Employee Compensation," press release, http://www.bls.gov, accessed March 16, 2012.

In the past, companies have paid the greater share of the cost of health care benefits, with employees paying a much smaller share. However, as health care costs rise, employers are passing along premium increases to employees. Many companies now offer incentives for workers to live healthier lives. Gym memberships, nutrition programs, wellness visits to the doctor, and smoking-cessation classes are all examples of these incentives. At Qualcomm, a global mobile technologies firm, employee benefits include unlimited sick days, on-site gyms, tuition assistance, and work–life balance programs like job sharing, compressed workweeks, and telecommuting. In addition, Qualcomm provides a generous company match on its retirement savings plan and pays 100 percent of the monthly health insurance premium.[18]

Benefits like on-site fitness facilities improve both a company's health and that of its employees.

Retirement plans make up a chunk of employee benefits. Some companies have reduced the contributions they make to workers' *401(k) plans*—retirement savings plans to which employees can make pretax contributions. Some firms have cut back on cash contributions to the plans and contribute company stock instead. However, others provide a high level of funding. Raytheon Solipsys offers a 401(k) with company match of up to 200 percent on employee contributions.[19]

Flexible Benefits

In response to increasing diversity in the workplace, firms are developing creative ways to tailor their benefit plans to the needs of employees. One approach sets up *flexible benefit plans*, also called cafeteria plans. This system offers employees a choice of benefits, including different types of medical insurance, dental and vision plans, and life and disability insurance. This flexibility allows one working spouse to choose medical coverage for the entire family, while the other spouse uses benefit dollars to buy other types of coverage. Typically, each employee receives a set allowance (called flex dollars or credits) to pay for benefits depending on his or her needs. Contributions to cafeteria accounts can be made by both the employee and employer. Cafeteria plans also offer tax benefits to both employees and employers.

Another way of increasing the flexibility of employee benefits involves time off from work. Instead of establishing set numbers of holidays, vacation days, and sick days, some employers give each employee a bank of *paid time off (PTO)*. Employees use days from their PTO account without having to explain why they need the time. The greatest advantage of PTO is the freedom it gives workers to make their own choices; the greatest disadvantage is that it is an expensive benefit for employers.

Flexible Work

Some firms are moving toward the option of *flexible work plans*, which are benefits that allow employees to adjust their working hours or places of work according to their needs. Flexible work plan options include flextime, compressed workweeks, job sharing, and home-based work (telecommuting). These benefit programs have reduced employee turnover and absenteeism, and boosted productivity and job satisfaction. Flexible work has become critical in attracting and keeping talented human resources.

Rayn McVay/Photodisc/Alamy

A two-career couple heads for the daycare center and work. Many employees use flextime to mesh their work schedules with opening and closing times at schools and daycare programs.

Flextime allows employees to set their own work hours within certain parameters. Rather than mandating that all employees work, say, from 8:00 A.M. to 5:00 P.M., a manager might stipulate that everyone works between the core hours of 10:00 A.M. and 3:00 P.M. Outside the core hours, employees could choose to start and end early, or start and end late. Flextime works well in jobs that are independent, but not so well when teams or direct customer service are involved. Flextime has gained popularity in the accounting industry. Ernst & Young builds flexibility into its workplace, believing it fosters greater productivity in the long run.[20]

For workplaces that require continuous staffing, Web-based scheduling software can simplify scheduling and staffing tasks. One such software program, called ShiftSelect™, lets managers post schedules online; employees log in and request certain shifts or schedule changes.[21]

Some companies offer a *compressed workweek*, which allows employees to work longer hours on fewer days. Employees might work four 10-hour days and then have three days off each week. Such arrangements not only reduce the number of hours employees spend commuting each week, but can stretch out the company's overall workday, providing more availability to customers in other time zones. Hospitals, police and fire departments, and airlines often offer work schedules that allow several long days matched by several days off. Employees at AFLAC, an insurance company, have the option of a compressed workweek. In Utah, state government workers have observed a four-day workweek since 2008 under a plan called "Working 4 Utah." Reportedly, the schedule has yielded energy savings as well as employee satisfaction.[22]

A *job sharing program* allows two or more employees to divide the tasks of one job. This plan appeals to a growing number of people who prefer to work part-time rather than full-time—such as students, working parents, and people of all ages who want to devote time to personal interests or leisure. Job sharing requires a lot of cooperation and communication between the partners, but an employer can benefit from the talents of both people.

Home-based work programs allow employees to perform their jobs from home instead of at the workplace. These *telecommuters* are connected to their employers via the Internet, voice and video conferencing, and mobile devices. Working from home generally appeals to employees who want freedom, but also to persons with disabilities, older workers, and parents. Companies benefit from telework arrangements because they can expand their pool of talent and increase productivity without increasing costs.[23] Telecommuters need to be self-disciplined and reliable employees. They also need managers who are comfortable with setting goals and managing from afar. Researchers predict that telecommuting could grow to encompass 30 percent of the private sector in the next decade, helped by such annual events as Telework Week, which encourages businesses to embrace telecommuting for enhanced productivity and reduced environmental impact.[24]

More than 70 percent of Generation Y professionals—those just entering the workforce—are concerned with balancing career with personal life. Most simply reject the idea of sitting in an office cubicle for 8 to 10 hours a day. They want the flexibility to do their jobs anywhere, any time. This is placing increasing pressure on companies to offer options such as job sharing, compressed workweeks, and telecommuting.[25]

LECTURE ENHANCER:
Provide some examples of jobs that typically use a compressed workweek. What are the potential drawbacks to a compressed workweek?

LECTURE ENHANCER:
Discuss some possible drawbacks to job sharing.

LECTURE ENHANCER:
What are some specific drawbacks to telecommuting?

Assessment Check ✔

1. Explain the difference between *wage* and *salary*.

2. What are flexible benefit plans? How do they work?

5 | Employee Separation

Employee separation is a broad term covering the loss of an employee for any reason, voluntary or involuntary. Voluntary separation includes workers who resign to take a job at another firm or start a business. Involuntary separation includes downsizing and outsourcing.

Voluntary and Involuntary Turnover

Turnover occurs when an employee leaves a job. Voluntary turnover occurs when the employee resigns—perhaps to take another job, start a new business, or retire. The human resource manager might conduct an exit interview with the employee to learn why he or she is leaving; this conversation can provide valuable information to a firm. An employee might decide to resign because of lack of career opportunities. Learning this, the human resource manager might offer ongoing training. Sometimes employees choose to resign and accept jobs at other firms because they fear upcoming layoffs. In this case, the human resource manager might be able to allay fears about job security.

Occasionally, an employee resigns because of low pay. In some cases, to keep a high-performing employee, the human resource manager might offer a raise. The "Business Etiquette" feature offers some advice on how to ask for a raise.

Involuntary turnover occurs when employees are terminated because of poor job performance or unethical behavior. No matter how necessary a termination may be, it is never easy for the manager or the employee. The employee may react with anger or tears; co-workers may take sides. Managers should remain calm and professional, and must be educated in employment laws. Protests against wrongful dismissal are often involved in complaints filed by the EEOC or by lawsuits brought by fired employees. Involuntary turnover also occurs when firms are forced to eliminate jobs as a cost-cutting measure, as in the case of downsizing or outsourcing.

BusinessEtiquette

How to Ask for a Raise

Do you think you deserve a raise? If so, here are a few tips to guide your next steps.

- *Be prepared.* If your company uses pay ranges for positions, learn where your pay lies on the scale.

- *Gather important data.* Document your accomplishments, including special projects or tasks. Track any positive feedback from others—both clients and co-workers.

- *Know what you want.* A percentage increase? A set dollar amount? Expanded vacation time? Make your request reasonable and be as specific as possible.

- *Be confident, but not arrogant.* State your case clearly. Your goal is to get your supervisor to consider your request.

- *Ask for details.* If your supervisor turns down your request, ask for specifics about what you need to do in order to qualify for the raise—and when. If possible, ask for a follow-up meeting within a certain period of time, such as two months.

- *Express thanks.* Regardless of the outcome, promptly send an e-mail with thanks for the meeting and politely recap the conversation. If you got the raise, make sure you demonstrate you deserved it. No raise yet? Don't give up. Get back to work and keep on trying.

Sources: Lindsay Olson, "How to Ask for a Raise," http://www.money.usnews.com, accessed February 19, 2012; Samantha Maziarz Christmann, "Asking For More: Don't Be Afraid to Ask for a Raise," *Buffalo News,* March 15, 2010, http://www.buffalonews.com; "How to Negotiate for a Raise—Even in a Bad Economy," *EmploymentDigest.net,* March 4, 2010, http://www.employmentdigest .net; Mary Sevinsky, "Is a Raise in Your Future for 2010?" *CareerRealism.com,* January 15, 2010, http://www.careerealism.com.

employee separation
broad term covering the loss of an employee for any reason, voluntary or involuntary.

CLASS ACTIVITY:
Ask students to name some problems that might be created by extremely low employee turnover.

LECTURE ENHANCER:
What are some potential legal pitfalls that a manager must avoid during an involuntary separation?

Downsizing

downsizing process of reducing the number of employees within a firm by eliminating jobs.

As the economy tightens, companies are often faced with the hard choice of terminating employees in order to cut costs or streamline the organization. **Downsizing** is the process of reducing the number of employees within a firm by eliminating jobs. Downsizing can be accomplished through early retirement plans or voluntary severance programs.

Although some firms report improvements in profits, market share, employee productivity, quality, and customer service after downsizing, research shows that downsizing doesn't guarantee those improvements. And while in some cases downsizing is necessary and justified, it can have the following negative effects:

- Anxiety, health problems, low morale, and reduced productivity among remaining workers.

- Diminished trust in management.

- Expensive severance packages paid to laid-off workers.

- Loss of institutional memory and knowledge

- A domino effect on the local economy—unemployed workers have less money to spend, creating less demand for consumer goods and services, increasing the likelihood of more layoffs and other failing businesses.[26]

When downsizing is the only alternative for company survival, there are steps managers can take to make sure it is done the best way possible. A firm committed to its workforce as part of its mission will do everything it can to support the workers who must leave and those who will stay.

Sometimes firms downsize in the hope of attracting a buyer, as in the case of MySpace. The social network laid off about half of its employees in an effort to achieve a sale.[27]

Outsourcing

outsourcing transferring jobs from inside a firm to outside the firm.

LECTURE ENHANCER:
What are some drawbacks to outsourcing, from a managerial point of view?

Another way that firms shrink themselves into leaner organizations is by **outsourcing**. Outsourcing involves transferring jobs from inside a firm to outside the firm. Jobs that are typically outsourced include office maintenance, deliveries, food service, and security. However, other job functions can be outsourced as well, including manufacturing, design, information technology (IT), and accounting. In general, in order to save expenses and remain flexible, companies will try to outsource functions that are not part of their core business.

Although outsourcing might work on paper, often the reality is quite different. Industry observers claim aggressive outsourcing was the reason Boeing's highly touted 787 Dreamliner arrived three years behind schedule and billions of dollars over budget. Boeing outsourced the manufacture of 30 percent of the plane's parts; by contrast, it had outsourced only 5 percent of its iconic 747 aircraft. [28]

Assessment Check ☑

1. What is the difference between voluntary and involuntary turnover?

2. What is downsizing? How is it different from outsourcing?

[6] Motivating Employees

Everyone wants to enjoy going to work. Smart employers know that and look for ways to motivate workers to commit to their company's goals and perform their best. Motivation starts with high employee morale—a positive attitude towards the job. Each year, *Fortune* announces their rankings for the "100 Best Companies to Work For." The most recent top

TABLE
8.2 *Fortune's* Top 10 Companies to Work for

1. Google	6. NetApp
2. Boston Consulting Group	7. Camden Property Trust
3. SAS Institute	8. REI (Recreational Equipment, Inc.)
4. Wegmans Food Markets	9. CHG Healthcare Services
5. Edward Jones	10. Quicken Loans

Source: "100 Best Companies to Work For 2012," *Fortune*, February 6, 2012, http://money.cnn.com.

10 are listed in Table 8.2. Employees at these companies have high morale because they feel valued and empowered.

High morale generally results from good management, including an understanding of human needs and an effort to satisfy those needs in ways that move the company forward. Low employee morale, on the other hand, usually signals a poor relationship between managers and employees and often results in absenteeism, voluntary turnover, and a lack of motivation.

Generally speaking, managers use rewards and punishments to motivate employees. Extrinsic rewards are external to the work itself, such as pay, fringe benefits, and praise. Intrinsic rewards are feelings related to performing the job, such as feeling proud about meeting a deadline or achieving a sales goal. Punishment involves a negative consequence for such behavior as being late, skipping staff meetings, or treating a customer poorly.

There are several theories of motivation, all of which relate back to the basic process of motivation itself, which involves the recognition of a need, the move toward meeting that need, and the satisfaction of that need. For instance, if you are hungry you might be motivated to make yourself a peanut butter sandwich. Once you have eaten the sandwich, the need is satisfied and you are no longer hungry. Figure 8.4 illustrates the process of motivation.

FIGURE
8.4 **The Process of Motivation**

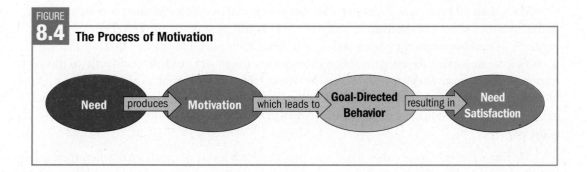

Maslow's Hierarchy of Needs Theory

Maslow's hierarchy of needs theory of motivation proposed by Abraham Maslow. According to the theory, people have five levels of needs that they seek to satisfy: physiological, safety, social, esteem, and self-actualization.

The studies of psychologist Abraham H. Maslow suggest how managers can motivate employees. **Maslow's hierarchy of needs** has become a widely accepted list of human needs based on these important assumptions:

- People's needs depend on what they already possess.

- A satisfied need is not a motivator; only needs that remain unsatisfied can influence behavior.

- People's needs are arranged in a hierarchy of importance; once they satisfy one need, at least partially, another emerges and demands satisfaction.

In his theory, Maslow proposed that all people have basic needs such as hunger and protection that they must satisfy before they can consider higher-order needs such as social relationships or self-worth. He identified five types of needs:

1. *Physiological needs.* These basic human needs include food, shelter, and clothing. On the job, employers satisfy these needs by paying salaries and wages and providing a temperature-controlled workspace.

2. *Safety needs.* These needs refer to desires for physical and economic protection. Companies satisfy these needs with benefits such as health insurance and meeting safety standards in the workplace.

3. *Social (belongingness) needs.* People want to be accepted by family, friends and co-workers. Managers might satisfy these needs through teamwork and group lunches.

4. *Esteem needs.* People like to feel valued and recognized by others. Managers can meet these needs through special awards or privileges.

5. *Self-actualization needs.* These needs drive people to seek fulfillment of their dreams and capabilities. Employers can satisfy these needs by offering challenging or creative projects, along with opportunities for education and advancement.[29]

CLASS ACTIVITY:
What techniques might a manager use to appeal to an employee with a primary need in each of the model's five categories?

According to Maslow, people must satisfy the lower-order needs in the hierarchy (physiological and safety needs) before they are motivated to satisfy higher-order needs (social, esteem, and self-actualization needs).

Herzberg's Two-Factor Model of Motivation

LECTURE ENHANCER:
Can you think of any exceptions? When might a hygiene factor be a major motivator?

More than 50 years ago, Frederick Herzberg—a social psychologist and consultant—came up with a theory of motivation and work that is still popular today. Herzberg surveyed workers to find out when they felt good or bad about their jobs. He learned that certain factors were important to job satisfaction though they might not contribute directly to motivation. These *hygiene factors* (or maintenance factors) refer to aspects of work that are not directly related to a task itself but instead related to the job environment, including pay, job security, working conditions, status, interpersonal relations, technical supervision, and company policies.

Motivator factors, on the other hand, can produce high levels of motivation when they are present. These relate directly to the specific aspects of a job, including job responsibilities, achievement and recognition, and opportunities for growth. Hygiene factors are extrinsic, while motivators are intrinsic. Managers should remember that hygiene factors, though not motivational, can result in satisfaction. But if managers want to motivate employees, they should emphasize recognition, achievement, and growth. Regardless of their size, companies that make the various lists of "best places to work" have managers who understand what it takes to motivate employees.

Expectancy Theory and Equity Theory

Victor Vroom's **expectancy theory** of motivation describes the process people use to evaluate the likelihood that their efforts will yield the results they want, along with the degree to which they want those results. Expectancy theory suggests that people use three factors to determine how much effort to put forth. First is a person's subjective prediction that a certain effort will lead to the desired result. This is the "can do" component of an employee's approach to work. Second is the value of the outcome (reward) to the person. Third is the person's assessment of how likely a successful performance will lead to a desirable reward. Vroom's expectancy theory is summarized in Figure 8.5. In short, an employee is motivated if he or she thinks he or she can complete a task. Next, the employee assesses the reward for accomplishing the task and is motivated if the reward is worth the effort.

Equity theory is concerned with an individual's perception of fair and equitable treatment. In their work, employees first consider their effort and then their rewards. Next, employees compare their results against those of their co-workers. As shown in Figure 8.6, if employees feel they are under-rewarded for their effort in comparison with others doing similar work, equity theory suggests they will decrease their effort to restore the balance. Conversely, if employees feel they are over-rewarded, they will feel guilty and put more effort into their job to restore equity and reduce guilt.

Many workers are willing to work hard as long as the burden is shared. Income inequality is higher in the United States than in any other developed society in the world. For example, today the CEO of a large company in America makes about 300 times more than

expectancy theory the process people use to evaluate the likelihood that their efforts will yield the results they want, along with the degree to which they want those results.

equity theory an individual's perception of fair and equitable treatment.

LECTURE ENHANCER
Do you think the principles of equity theory hold true for all personality types? Why or why not?

FIGURE
8.5 Vroom's Expectancy Theory

Can I perform the task? — YES → Is the reward worth the effort? — YES → Motivated

NO → Not Motivated

NO → Not Motivated

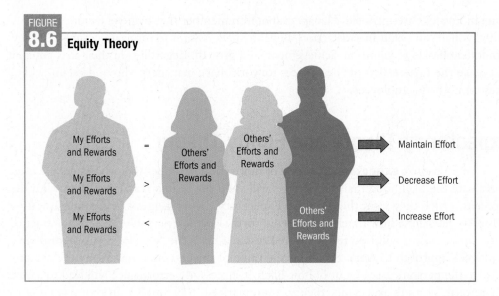

FIGURE
8.6 **Equity Theory**

My Efforts and Rewards = Others' Efforts and Rewards → Maintain Effort

My Efforts and Rewards > Others' Efforts and Rewards → Decrease Effort

My Efforts and Rewards < Others' Efforts and Rewards → Increase Effort

the average worker. Some believe this is unfair. Legislation has been introduced several times in Congress to cap CEO compensation but has been defeated.[30]

Goal-Setting Theory and Management by Objectives

Needs motivate people to direct their behavior toward something that will satisfy those needs. That something is a goal. A goal is a target, objective, or result that someone tries to accomplish. **Goal-setting theory** says that people will be motivated to the extent to which they accept specific, challenging goals and receive feedback that indicates their progress toward goal achievement. As shown in Figure 8.7, the basic components of goal-setting theory are goal specificity, goal difficulty, goal acceptance, and performance feedback.

Goal specificity is the extent to which goals are clear and concrete. A goal such as "we want to reduce our carbon footprint" is vague and hard to pin down. But, "we want to reduce our carbon footprint by 2 percent" gives employees a clear target. Goal difficulty outlines how hard the goal is to reach. A more difficult goal, such as "we want to reduce our carbon footprint by 5 percent in three years" is actually more motivating than the easier goal.

Goal acceptance is the extent to which people understand and agree to the goal. If a goal is too challenging—such as reducing the firm's carbon footprint by 20 percent in two years—people are likely to reject it. Finally, performance feedback is information about performance and how well the goal has been met. Goal setting typically won't work unless performance feedback is provided.

Goals help focus workers' attention on the important parts of their jobs. Goals also energize and motivate people. They create a positive tension between the current state of affairs and the desired state. This tension is satisfied by meeting the goal or abandoning it.

Fifty years ago, Peter Drucker introduced a goal-setting technique called **management by objectives (MBO)** in his book, *The Practice of Management*. MBO is a systematic approach that allows managers to focus on attainable goals and to achieve the best results based on the organization's resources. MBO helps motivate individuals by aligning their objectives with

goal-setting theory says that people will be motivated to the extent to which they accept specific, challenging goals and receive feedback that indicates their progress toward goal achievement.

CLASS ACTIVITY:
Ask students to provide examples of specific goals.

management by objectives systematic approach that allows managers to focus on attainable goals and to achieve the best results based on the organization's resources.

the goals of the organization, increasing overall organizational performance. MBO clearly outlines people's tasks, goals, and contributions to the company. MBO is a collaborative process between managers and employees. MBO principles include the following:

- a series of related organizational goals and objectives;
- specific objectives for each person;
- participative decision making;
- a set time period to accomplish goals; and
- performance evaluation and feedback.

Job Design and Motivation

Today's human resource managers constantly search for ways to motivate employees through their jobs. Three ways that jobs can be restructured to be more motivating are through job enlargement, job enrichment, and job rotation.

Job enlargement is a job design that expands an employee's responsibilities by increasing the number and variety of tasks. Redesigning the production process is one way to accomplish this. Instead of having an assembly line on which each worker repeatedly completes the same task, modular work areas allow employees to complete a variety of tasks, which may result in the construction of an entire product.

Job enrichment involves an expansion of job duties that empowers an employee to make decisions and learn new skills leading toward career growth. The Pampered Chef is a direct seller of kitchen tools and housewares that gives its managers and sales consultants the power to make decisions about many aspects of their work. Pampered Chef consultants, who organize home sales parties, can decide how much or how little they want to work and receive various incentive rewards for performance. The company's mission is to provide "opportunities for individuals to develop their talents and skills to their fullest potential for the benefit of themselves, their families, our customers, and the company."[31]

Job rotation involves systematically moving employees from one job to another. Job rotation increases the range of activities by introducing workers to more jobs and therefore more tasks. The goal is to increase employees' interest in their jobs and allow them to learn more about the company. Nurses might rotate from oncology to the ICU in a hospital. Job rotation is often part of a training program, as is the case at EMC, a global provider of business solutions for data backup, information security, risk and compliance, and many other products. EMC offers motivated employees the chance to participate in rotational training programs in business, leadership, finance, marketing, and other areas.[32]

Managers' Attitudes and Motivation

A manager's attitude toward his or her employees greatly influences their motivation. Maslow's theory, described earlier, has helped managers understand that employees have a range of needs beyond their paychecks. Psychologist Douglas McGregor, a student of Maslow, studied motivation from the perspective of how managers view employees. After

FIGURE 8.7 Components of Goal-Setting Theory

Goal Specificity

Goal Difficulty

Performance Feedback

Goal Acceptance

LECTURE ENHANCER: Why might MBO focus on the "contributions" an employee makes to the company rather than his or her job "responsibilities"?

LECTURE ENHANCER: Which of these methods of job design sounds the most appealing to you? Why?

CLASS ACTIVITY: Discuss the benefits of job rotation from the employer's perspective.

observing managers' interactions with employees, McGregor created two basic labels for the assumptions that different managers make about their workers' behavior, and how these assumptions affect management styles.

- *Theory X* assumes that employees dislike work and try to avoid it whenever possible, so management must coerce them to do their jobs. Theory X managers believe that the average worker prefers to receive instructions, avoid responsibility, take little initiative, and views money and job security as the only valid motivators—Maslow's lower order of needs.

- *Theory Y* assumes that the typical person actually likes work and will seek and accept greater responsibility. Theory Y managers assume that most people can think of creative ways to solve work-related problems, and should be given the opportunity to participate in decision making. Unlike the traditional management philosophy that relies on external control and constant supervision, Theory Y emphasizes self-control and self-direction—Maslow's higher order of needs.

Another perspective on management, proposed by management professor William Ouchi, has been labeled *Theory Z*. Organizations structured on Theory Z concepts attempt to blend the best of American and Japanese management practices. This approach views worker involvement as the key to increased productivity for the company and improved quality of work life for employees. Many U.S. firms have adopted the participative management style used in Japanese firms by asking workers for suggestions to improve their jobs and then giving them the authority to implement proposed changes.

⌐7⌐ Labor–Management Relations

The U.S. workplace is far different from what it was a century ago, when child labor, unsafe working conditions, and a 72-hour workweek were common. The development of labor unions, labor legislation, and the collective bargaining process have contributed to the changed environment. Today's human resource managers must be educated in labor–management relations, the settling of disputes, and the competitive tactics of unions and management.

Development of Labor Unions

A **labor union** is a group of workers who have banded together to achieve common goals in the areas of wages, hours, and working conditions. The organized efforts of Philadelphia printers in 1786 resulted in the first U.S. minimum wage—$1 a day. One hundred years later, New York City streetcar conductors were able to negotiate a reduction in their workday from 17 to 12 hours.

Labor unions can be found at the local, national, and international levels. A *local union* represents union members in a specific area, such as a single community, while a *national union* is a labor organization consisting of numerous local chapters. An *international union* is a national union with membership outside the United States, usually in Canada. About 14.8 million U.S. workers—just under 12 percent of the nation's full-time workforce—belong to labor unions.[33] Although only about 8 percent of workers in the private sector are unionized, more than one-third of government workers belong to unions. The largest union in the United States is the 3.2 million-member National Education Association (NEA), representing public school teachers and other support personnel. Other large unions include the

2.1 million members of the Service Employees International Union (SEIU), the 1.6 million members of the American Federation of State, County & Municipal Employees, the 1.4 million members of the International Brotherhood of Teamsters, the 1.3 million members of the United Food and Commercial Workers, and the 538,000 members of the United Automobile, Aerospace and Agricultural Implement Workers of America.[34]

LECTURE ENHANCER:
Why might unionization be more common in the public sector?

Labor Legislation

Over the past century, some major pieces of labor legislation have been enacted, including the following:

- *National Labor Relations Act of 1935 (Wagner Act)*. Legalized collective bargaining and required employers to negotiate with elected representatives of their employees. Established the National Labor Relations Board (NLRB) to supervise union elections and prohibit unfair labor practices such as firing workers for joining unions, refusing to hire union sympathizers, threatening to close if workers unionize, interfering with or dominating the administration of a union, and refusing to bargain with a union.

- *Fair Labor Standards Act of 1938*. Set the first federal minimum wage (25 cents an hour), and maximum basic workweek for certain industries. Also outlawed child labor.

- *Taft-Hartley Act of 1947 (Labor–Management Relations Act)*. Limited unions' power by banning such practices as coercing employees to join unions, coercing employers to discriminate against employees who are not union members, discrimination against nonunion employees, picketing or conducting secondary boycotts or strikes for illegal purposes, and excessive initiation fees.

- *Landrum-Griffin Act of 1959 (Labor–Management Reporting and Disclosure Act)*. Amended the Taft-Hartley Act to promote honesty and democracy in running unions' internal affairs. Required unions to set up a constitution and bylaws and to hold regularly scheduled elections of union officers by secret ballot. Set forth a bill of rights for members. Required unions to submit certain financial reports to the U.S. Secretary of Labor.

The Collective Bargaining Process

Labor unions work to increase job security for their members and to improve wages, hours, and working conditions. These goals are achieved primarily through **collective bargaining**, the process of negotiation between management and union representatives.

Union contracts, which typically cover a two- or three-year period, are often the result of weeks or months of discussion, disagreement, compromise, and eventual agreement. Once agreement is reached, union members must vote to accept or reject the contract. If the contract is rejected, union representatives may resume the bargaining process with management representatives, or union members may strike to obtain their demands.

collective bargaining
process of negotiation between management and union representatives.

LECTURE ENHANCER:
What are some potential drawbacks to working under a union contract?

Settling Labor–Management Disputes

Strikes make the headlines, but most labor–management negotiations result in a signed contract. If a dispute arises, it is usually settled through a mechanism such as a grievance procedure, mediation, or arbitration. Any of these alternatives is quicker and less expensive than a strike.

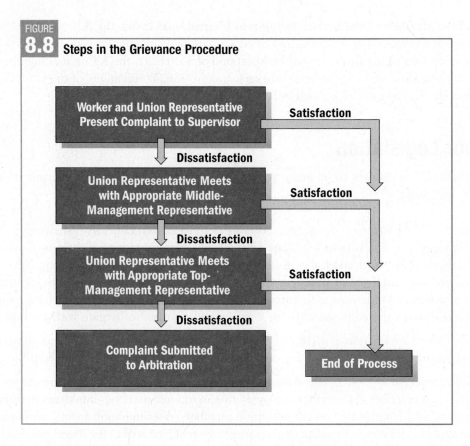

FIGURE 8.8 Steps in the Grievance Procedure

Worker and Union Representative Present Complaint to Supervisor

Satisfaction

Dissatisfaction

Union Representative Meets with Appropriate Middle-Management Representative

Satisfaction

Dissatisfaction

Union Representative Meets with Appropriate Top-Management Representative

Satisfaction

Dissatisfaction

Complaint Submitted to Arbitration

End of Process

The union contract serves as a guide to relations between the firm's management and its employees. The rights of each party are stated in the agreement. But no contract, regardless of how detailed, will eliminate the possibility of disagreement. Such differences can be the beginning of a *grievance*, a complaint—by a single employee or by the entire union—that management is violating some portion of the contract. Almost all union contracts require these complaints to be submitted through a formal grievance procedure similar to the one shown in Figure 8.8. A grievance might involve a dispute about pay, working hours, or the workplace itself. The grievance procedure usually begins with an employee's supervisor and then moves up the company's hierarchy. If the highest level of management can't settle the grievance, it is submitted to an outside party for mediation or arbitration.

Mediation is the process of settling labor–management disputes through an impartial third party. Although the mediator does not make the final decision, he or she can hear the whole story and make objective recommendations. If the dispute remains unresolved, the two parties can turn to *arbitration*—bringing in an outside arbitrator, who renders a legally binding decision. The arbitrator must be acceptable both to the union and to management, and his or her decision is final. Most union negotiations go to arbitration if union and management representatives fail to reach a contract agreement.

Competitive Tactics of Unions and Management

Both unions and management use tactics to make their views known and to win support.

LECTURE ENHANCER:
Discuss the pros and cons of each tactic.

Union Tactics The chief tactics of unions are strikes, picketing, and boycotts. The *strike*, or walkout, is one of the most effective tools of the labor union. It involves a temporary work stoppage by workers until a dispute has been settled or a contract signed. A strike generally seeks to disrupt business as usual, calling attention to workers' needs and union demands. Strikes can last for days or weeks and can be costly to both sides. Although a strike is powerful, it can also be damaging to the very people it is trying to help. Surrounding businesses may suffer too. If striking workers aren't eating at their usual lunch haunts, those businesses will lose profits. Strikes seem to be on the decline, however. During the past decade, there have been only 17 major work stoppages on average per year, half the number that took place in the 1990s.[35]

Picketing, which involves workers marching in a public protest against their employer, is another effective form of union pressure. As long as picketing does not involve violence or intimidation, it is protected under the U.S. Constitution as freedom of speech. Picketing may accompany a strike, or it may be a protest against alleged unfair labor practices. Recently Verizon union workers set up picket lines to show solidarity with other Verizon striking union members on the East Coast.[36]

Union workers demonstrate in front of a Verizon Wireless store on the West Coast to show solidarity with striking Verizon union workers on the East Coast. Strikes are a last-ditch tactic that can empty union coffers, injure an entire industry, and even damage the economy.

Justin Sullivan/Getty Images, Inc.

A *boycott* is an organized attempt to keep the public from purchasing the goods or services of a firm. Some unions have been quite successful in organizing boycotts, and some unions even fine members who defy a boycott.

Management Tactics Management also has tactics for competing with organized labor when negotiations break down. In the past, it has used the lockout—a management "strike" to put pressure on union members by closing the firm. However, companies more commonly try to recruit strikebreakers in highly visible fields such as professional sports, or transfer supervisors and other nonunion employees to continue operations during strikes. When union workers at British Airways went on strike, management leased aircraft from other airlines and used volunteer pilots and managers to take the place of the striking cabin crews.[37]

The Future of Labor Unions

Union membership and influence grew through most of the 20th century by giving industrial workers a voice in decisions about their wages, benefits, and working conditions. However, as the United States, western Europe, and Japan have shifted from manufacturing economies to information and service economies, union membership and influence has declined. Today, about 52 percent of all union members are government employees.[38]

How can labor unions change to maintain their relevance? They can be more flexible and adapt to a global economy and diverse workforce. They can respond to the growing need for environmentally responsible business and manufacturing processes, as the Operative Plasterers and Cement Masons International Association (OPCMIA) is doing, described in the "Going Green" feature. Unions can establish collaborative relationships with human resource managers and other managers. And they can recognize the potential for prosperity for all—management and union workers included.

Assessment Check ✓

1. What is a labor union? What is collective bargaining?

2. What are the three main tactics used by unions to win support for their demands?

Going Green

Labor Unions and Green Construction

The construction industry has nearly unlimited opportunities to make the world greener. One labor union, the Operative Plasterers and Cement Masons International Association (OPCMIA) has already recognized this and is training its members in the use of new green technologies and processes.

The OPCMIA training program, called Green Five, is being incorporated into existing training curricula to reach about 5,400 participants in 70 programs across local chapters, community colleges, vocational/technical schools, and OPCMIA Joint Apprenticeship and Training Centers. The Green Five program trains plasterers and cement masons in the sustainable use and application of concrete, exterior insulation finish systems, and American Clay. The Green Five program includes Green Awareness Training, which deals with energy-efficient building construction in general, addresses the process of energy assessment and retrofitting existing buildings, and provides an overview of environmentally sustainable products and manufacturing processes. Leadership training and "train-the-trainer" courses are offered as well.

Questions for Critical Thinking

1. How does a progressive stance toward green training help secure an important industry role for OPCMIA going forward?

2. Besides construction, what other industries might benefit from unions taking a leadership role in sustainability training? How might these steps benefit workers, unions, and management?

Sources: Marc Lifsher, "Unions Cry Foul Over Green Contracts," *ENR California*, http://california.construction.com, accessed March 16, 2012; David Bradley, "TR10: Green Concrete," *Technology Review*, May/June 2010, http://www.technologyreview.com, accessed March 16, 2012; "About OPCMIA," OPCMIA Web site, http://www.opcmia.org, accessed March 16, 2012; Gerry Ryan, "The Green Five Program," *Green Labor Journal*, http://green-laborjournal.com, accessed March 16, 2012.

What's Ahead

Treating employees well by enriching the work environment will continue to gain importance as a way to recruit and retain a highly motivated workforce. In addition, managers can tap the full potential of their employees by empowering them to make decisions, leading them to work effectively as teams, and fostering clear, positive communication. The next chapter covers these three means of improving performance. By involving employees more fully through empowerment, teamwork, and communication, companies can benefit from their knowledge while employees enjoy a more meaningful role in the company.

Summary of Learning Objectives

1 Explain the role of human resources: the people behind the people.

Human resource managers are responsible for attracting, developing, and retaining the employees who can perform the activities necessary to accomplish organizational objectives. They plan for staffing needs, recruit and hire workers, provide for training, evaluate performance, determine compensation and benefits, and oversee employee separation.

Assessment Check Answers

1.1 What are the five main tasks of a human resource manager? The five main tasks are planning for staffing needs, recruiting and hiring workers, providing for training

and evaluating performance, determining compensation and benefits, and overseeing employee separation.

1.2 What are the three overall objectives of a human resource manager? The three overall objectives are providing qualified, well-trained employees for the organization; maximizing employee effectiveness; and satisfying individual employee needs through monetary compensation.

2 Describe recruitment and selection.

Human resource managers use internal and external methods to recruit qualified employees. They may use college job fairs, personal referrals, want ads, and other resources. Internet recruiting is now the fastest, most efficient, and inexpensive way to reach a large pool of job seekers. Firms must abide by employment laws during selection. Before hiring candidates, human resource managers may require employment tests that evaluate certain skills or aptitudes. When all of this is complete, there is a better chance that the right person will be hired for the job.

Assessment Check Answers ☑

2.1 Describe several recruiting techniques used by human resource managers. Techniques include college job fairs, personal referrals, want ads, company Web sites, online job sites, and online interviews such as jobcasts.

2.2 What is the function of the Equal Employment Opportunity Commission (EEOC)? The EEOC investigates discrimination complaints and helps employers set up affirmative action programs.

⌐3⌐ Discuss orientation, training, and evaluation.

New employees often participate in an orientation where they learn about company policies and practices. Training programs provide opportunities for employees to build their skills and knowledge and prepare them for new job opportunities within the company. They also give employers a better chance of retaining employees. Performance appraisals give employees feedback about their strengths and weaknesses and how they can improve.

Assessment Check Answers ☑

3.1 What are the benefits of computer-based training? Computer-based training offers consistent presentations, interactive learning, and employees can learn at their own pace. It is also less expensive than other types of training.

3.2 What is a management development program? A management development program provides training designed to improve the skills and broaden the knowledge of current and potential executives.

3.3 What are the four criteria of an effective performance appraisal? A performance appraisal should take place several times a year, be linked to organizational goals, be based on objective criteria, and be a two-way conversation.

⌐4⌐ Describe compensation.

Firms compensate employees with wages, salaries, incentive pay systems, and benefits. Benefit programs vary among firms, but most companies offer health care programs, insurance, retirement plans, paid time off, and sick leave. A growing number of companies are offering flexible benefit plans and flexible work plans, such as flextime, compressed workweeks, job sharing, and home-based work.

Assessment Check Answers ☑

4.1 Explain the difference between *wage* and *salary*. Wages are based on an hourly pay rate or the amount of work

accomplished. Salaries are paid periodically, such as weekly or monthly. Salaries do not fluctuate with hours worked.

4.2 What are flexible benefit plans? How do they work? Flexible benefit plans offer a choice of benefits, including different types of medical insurance, dental and vision, and life and disability insurance. Typically, each employee receives a set allowance to pay for these benefits depending on his or her needs.

⌐5⌐ Discuss employee separation.

Employee separation occurs when a worker leaves his or her job, voluntarily or involuntarily. Sometimes an employee is terminated because of poor job performance or unethical behavior. Downsizing is the process of reducing the number of employees within a firm in order to cut costs and achieve a leaner organization. However, some negative effects include anxiety and lost productivity among remaining workers; expensive severance packages; and a domino effect in the local economy. Outsourcing involves transferring jobs from inside a firm to outside the firm. While some expenses may be cut, a firm may experience a backlash in performance and public image.

Assessment Check Answers ☑

5.1 What is the difference between voluntary and involuntary turnover? Voluntary turnover occurs when employees leave firms to start their own businesses, take jobs with other firms, move to another community, or retire. Involuntary turnover occurs because of poor job performance or unethical behavior in business practices or the workplace. It can also occur when a company is forced to eliminate jobs.

5.2 What is downsizing? How is it different from outsourcing? Downsizing is the process of reducing the number of employees within a firm by eliminating jobs. Downsizing is done to cut overhead costs and streamline the organizational structure. With outsourcing, companies contract with other firms to perform noncore jobs or business functions, such as housekeeping, maintenance, or relocation services. This allows companies to focus on what they do best, and can result in a downsized workforce.

⌐6⌐ Explain the different methods for motivating employees.

Employee motivation starts with high employee morale. According to Maslow's hierarchy of needs, people satisfy lower-order needs (such as food and safety) before moving to higher-order needs (such as esteem and fulfillment). Herzberg's two-factor model of motivation is based on the fulfillment of hygiene factors and motivation factors. Expectancy theory suggests that people use those factors to determine whether to put forth the effort to complete a task. Equity theory refers to a person's perception of fair and equitable treatment. Goal-setting theory says that people will be motivated to the extent to which they accept specific, challenging goals. Job design is also used by managers for motivation.

Assessment Check Answers ✔

6.1 What are the four steps in the process of motivation? The four steps are need, motivation, goal-directed behavior, and need satisfaction.

6.2 Explain how goal setting works. People will be motivated to the extent to which they accept specific, challenging goals and receive feedback that indicates their progress toward goal achievement.

6.3 Describe the three ways that managers structure jobs for increased motivation. Three ways that employers apply motivational theories to restructure jobs are job enlargement, job enrichment, and job rotation. Job enlargement is a job design that expands an employee's responsibilities by increasing the number and variety of tasks the person works on. Job enrichment is a change in job duties to increase employees' authority in planning their work, deciding how it should be done, and learning new skills that help them grow. Job rotation involves systematically moving employees from one job to another.

[7] Discuss labor–management relations.

Labor unions have resulted in the improvement of wages and working conditions for many workers over the past century, along with the passage of significant labor laws. Unions achieve these improvements through the collective bargaining process, resulting in an agreement. Most labor–management disputes are settled through the grievance process, in which mediation or arbitration sometimes is necessary.

Assessment Check Answers ✔

7.1 What is a labor union? What is collective bargaining? A labor union is a group of workers who have banded together to achieve common goals in the areas of wages, hours, and working conditions. Collective bargaining is the process of negotiation between management and union representatives.

7.2 What are the three main tactics used by unions to win support for their demands? Unions use strikes (walkouts), picketing, and boycotts.

■ Business Terms You Need to Know

human resource management 232	salary 239
performance appraisal 237	employee benefits 240
compensation 238	employee separation 243
wage 239	downsizing 244
	outsourcing 244

Maslow's hierarchy of needs 246	management by objectives (MBO) 249
expectancy theory 247	labor union 250
equity theory 247	collective bargaining 251
goal-setting theory 248	

■ Review Questions

1. Why has Internet recruiting become such an important tool for human resource managers?

2. Recruitment and selection are expensive. So, what precautions do human resource managers take to make sure they are hiring the right person for each job?

3. Give an example of a type of job that would be appropriate for on-the-job training. Then describe specifically how you think that type of training would work for your selected job, including types of tasks a new hire might learn this way.

4. On what five factors are compensation policies usually based? Name at least three employee benefits that are required by law and three more that are provided voluntarily by some firms.

5. Describe four types of flexible work plans. Identify an industry that would be well suited to each type of plan, and explain why.

6. Why do companies downsize? What are some of the drawbacks to downsizing? Why do companies outsource? What are some of the drawbacks to outsourcing?

7. Select three different theories of motivation, and explain how each can be used by managers to motivate employees.

8. Suppose a manager of a popular sandwich shop maintains a Theory X assumption about employees. At the beginning of each workweek, what types of things might the manager tell his or her employees? Now suppose the manager has a Theory Y assumption; then Theory Z. Describe what he or she might say to employees.

9. In what major ways has labor legislation changed the workplace over the past century? How might the workplace be different today without this legislation?

10. What are mediation and arbitration? Describe a situation that you think might result in arbitration.

■ Projects and Teamwork Applications

1. On your own or with a classmate, research consulting firms that provide management training programs, such as Glimmerglass Consulting Group, described in the chapter.

Prepare a presentation about one of these firms, describing the approach it takes as well as some of the specific elements of the program.

2. Choose one of the following companies, or one that you think you might like to work for sometime in the future. Using the firm's Web site and one of the job Web sites such as Monster.com (if applicable), research the company's benefits. Outline the firm's benefits and then determine if you still want to work for that company, and why. Suggested firms:

   a. Timberland

   b. SAS

   c. IBM

   d. Kraft Foods

   e. FedEx

3. With a classmate, choose an on-campus job and outline how you would share that job. Create a schedule and division of tasks.

4. Choose what you think would be your dream job five years from now. Then create a chart according to Maslow's hierarchy of needs, and identify the ways in which you envision this job fulfilling each level of need.

5. Research one of the major labor laws outlined in the text to learn more about the circumstances that led to its proposal and passage. In what ways do you believe this law has (or has not) affected the working world that you expect to enter when you graduate?

Web Assignments

1. **Human resources (HR) as a profession.** Go to the Web site listed here and review the material.

   http://www.bls.gov/oco/ocos021.htm

   Answer the following questions:

   a How many people are employed in HR?

   b What are the educational requirements to become an HR manager?

   c How rapidly is the occupation expected to grow over the next decade?

2. **Performance reviews.** Visit the Web sites listed here. Each lists some tips for conducting employee performance reviews. Print out the material and bring it to class to participate in a class discussion on performance reviews.

   http://www.squidoo.com/employeeperformancereview

   http://articles.techrepublic.com.com/5100-10878_11-1049853.html

   http://smallbusiness.dnb.com/human-resources/workforce-management/1385-1.html

3. **Teamsters.** The Teamsters is one of the nation's largest and oldest labor unions. Go to the union's Web site and review the material. When was the union founded? Originally, the union represented workers in what industry? How many members do the Teamsters currently have? Other than the United States, in what other country does the union represent workers?

   http://www.teamster.org

   Note: Internet Web addresses change frequently. If you don't find the exact sites listed, you may need to access the organization's home page and search from there or use a search engine such as Bing or Google.

The Coca-Cola Company: Training for the Future Right Now · CASE 8.1

One of the world's most recognizable brands, Coca-Cola has come a long way from its first fizzy drink; it is now a global empire with products sold in more than 200 countries. The key to its longevity, management says, isn't its secret recipe for the famous cola in the red can; it's the people behind the fizz. The company has become especially expert in wellness benefits and training, thus employing healthy, skilled, and knowledgeable workers.

Several years ago, The Coca-Cola Company integrated its health and wellness programs into the firm's overall strategy. Previously, the company did not communicate the important message that healthy workers are important to the organization.

Now, employees have employer-sponsored incentives to participate in wellness programs. In one recent year, management gave $120 to any worker who completed a wellness assessment. The following year, the company offered up to $180 to employees who participated in health coaching. Workers can earn and redeem points for healthy behaviors like getting enough sleep or eating fruits and vegetables. Most important, the effort is promoting the benefits of wellness through e-mail blasts and in-house ads on closed-circuit TV.

The Coca-Cola Company's training program prepares workers for future innovations and leadership roles. Coca-Cola University (CCU), founded a few years ago, is part of an overall strategy to develop the global workforce to reach its greatest potential.

Coca-Cola University operates on a 70-20-10 model of employee development. This means that 70 percent of learning takes place on the job, 20 percent occurs through coaching and mentoring, and 10 percent is acquired through formal, structured training. Within this model, human resource managers strive to match the right training to each worker's needs.

An important aspect of CCU's management training strategy is that it encompasses everyone. At their performance appraisal meetings, employees are encouraged to sign up for training sessions through CCU, ensuring that the company always has a deep pool from which to draw management talent that is already knowledgeable about the company's strategies and objectives, now and for the future.

Questions for Critical Thinking

1. Besides cash payments, what other incentives might motivate Coca-Cola Company employees to participate in its wellness programs?

2. The firm has developed a comprehensive, worldwide training program. In addition to increasing its leadership pool, what other positive effects do you predict this may have on the company's future success?

Sources: "Associate Training," The Coca-Cola Company, http://www.thecoca-colacompany.com, accessed March 16, 2012; "Behind the Fizz," HRM, http://wwwhrmasia.com, accessed March 16, 2012; Lydell C. Bridgeford, "Coca-Cola Retools Wellness Strategy," *SMB Human Resources*, http://smbhr.benefitnews.com, accessed March 16, 2012.

CASE 8.2 | Winning HR Practices at the Cheesecake Factory

There's more to a successful restaurant than good food and mouth-watering desserts. That's why the Cheesecake Factory's culture is built around employee strengths. Managers at the 170-store chain not only focus on improving skills through the employee development plan; they also develop employees' existing talents, such as analysis or collaboration, with enriched assignments and responsibilities. Cheesecake Factory job descriptions are standardized, but they're also flexible so managers can tweak the balance of, say, administrative and field work for individual employees.

While most firms conduct exit interviews to quiz departing employees, the Cheesecake Factory holds innovative "stay interviews." Says its senior vice president for HR, "You talk with them about how happy they are, how satisfied they are at work, and what would it take for somebody to take them away from us. And what is the one thing we could do to improve their work experience."

The chain's strategies show up in its bottom line as well. The Cheesecake Factory was recently voted consumers' favorite casual dining restaurant for two years running.

Questions for Critical Thinking

1. How can the Cheesecake Factory's "stay interviews" affect its bottom line?

2. Do you see any downside to managers' ability to tailor jobs to employees' strengths? Explain.

Sources: Company Web site, www.thecheesecakefactory.com, accessed March 16, 2012; Sherry Benjamin, "How (and Why) The Cheesecake Factory Builds a Strength-Based Culture," *Real Talent* newsletter, http://sbenjamin.virtualadminsplus.com, accessed February 9, 2012; Ron Ruggless, "Rewarding Excellence: People Report Recognizes HR Best Practices at Dallas Conference," *Nation's Restaurant News*, December 19, 2011, http://nrn.com; Mark Brandau, "Cheesecake Factory Consumers' Favorite Chain," *Nation's Restaurant News*, October 3, 2011, http://nrn.com

CASE 8.3 | Seventh Generation Promotes Company Ownership

Common sense dictates that companies that treat their employees well—from fair compensation to dignity in the workplace—will attract and retain the best workers. But from there, the picture becomes a bit murky. Traditional models of human resource management are being

re-evaluated and sometimes tossed out by firms whose goals and values these models do not fit. Seventh Generation is one such company. "When we win an award for being one of the best places to work in America, that to me is the most important award we can win because it's the hardest thing we do," says co-founder Jeffrey Hollender. Seventh Generation was founded on the premise of sustainability—that every product it manufactures, whether it is laundry detergent or paper towels, must be designed and produced in such a way that it leaves little or no impact on the environment. Sustainability includes its recruitment and development of human resources over the long term.

Most of the 100-plus employees at Seventh Generation have had at least some experience with another employer. Hollender points out that these employees arrive at Seventh Generation with all of the relationship patterns, values, and attitudes toward work they have learned elsewhere. "Most businesses teach us not to have a voice, not to speak up, not to challenge authority, not to unleash the maximum potential we have as individuals," he says. Because Seventh Generation incorporates a different set of values into its organizational culture, "the responsibility at Seventh Generation is to *unteach* people all of those habits and patterns, and unleash the potential that all of those other businesses have stifled," Hollender asserts.

Stephanie Lowe works in human resources at Seventh Generation. She notes that when she was hired, the company had only 30 employees—now there are more than 100. The increase in the number of employees has presented a challenge. Not only have people arrived from other firms with a variety of experience and expectations, the logistics of managing 100 employees are different from those of managing 30. "We can't do things as casually," says Lowe with some regret. "Things just wouldn't get done. It's a hard line to walk, and it's a challenge." In addition, the core value of sustainability is built into every decision the firm makes. "How do you do compensation in a socially responsible company?" asks Lowe. "How do you do that in a company that values different things, where people are asked to value themselves and bring more of themselves to work?"

Seventh Generation's answer to the compensation/social responsibility/sustainability question is ownership. Every person who works at Seventh Generation has a financial stake in the company. "The most significant way Seventh Generation's philosophy translates into HR is ownership," remarks Hollender. He points out that a firm can give employees health insurance, time off, grants for the purchase of hybrid vehicles, on-site fitness centers, and the like—but none of these benefits translates to ownership. "The most important thing is to let the people who are creating value by building the business participate in the value they create," Hollender asserts.

Stephanie Lowe echoes this philosophy. "We aren't trying to distinguish between the employees and the corporation," she explains. At Seventh Generation, the people are the company. Employees not only participate in company ownership, they are viewed as contributors

in ways that reach outside their job descriptions. "We are shifting away from traditional performance management to personal development plans," says Lowe. "We do look at what employees need to work on to hit company goals, but also what each person needs to grow personally—and we let them define that." Employees write personal initiatives that help the company recognize talents and potential that may not be readily evident during the performance of a particular job. "It's based on the concept that you measure what you value," explains Lowe. "We value volunteer time, making a difference in the world, raising more responsible global citizens." To that end, Seventh Generation encourages employees at every level to speak out with ideas for more sustainable products and processes.

When speaking about the Seventh Generation workforce, Hollender sounds more like a tribal elder than a business manager. Perhaps that's no coincidence, as Seventh Generation's mission is based on the Great Law of the Iroquois, which counsels each tribe member to consider the impact of all decisions on the next seven generations. "The thing I'm most proud of is the success of our employees at Seventh Generation," boasts Hollender, "their growth, the things they have thought of that I would never have dreamed of, the tough questions that they ask me that I wouldn't ask myself. Unleashing that potential—that is the most magical thing about running a business."

Questions for Critical Thinking

1. Visit the Seventh Generation Web site at http://www.seventhgeneration.com and view the current job listings there. What kinds of qualities in job candidates does the firm look for that might be different from those at other companies?

2. What might be the potential benefits and pitfalls of Seventh Generation's view of performance and compensation?

3. Choose one of the motivational theories described in the chapter and discuss how the theory would pertain to Seventh Generation's approach to motivating employees.

4. Do you predict that employees at Seventh Generation will attempt to unionize? Why or why not? If they did, how do you think the firm would respond?

Sources: Seventh Generation Web site, http://www.seventhgeneration.com, accessed March 16, 2012; "Sustainability Study," *Accenture*, http://microsite.accenture.com, accessed March 16, 2012; "Study Says Companies Should Train Managers in Sustainability," *7GenBlog*, http://www.seventhgeneration.com, accessed March 16, 2012; Danielle Sacks, "Jeffrey Hollender: Seventh Generation, Triple Bottom Line Entrepreneur," *Fast Company.com*, http://www.fastcompany.com, accessed March 16, 2012.

Learning Objectives

1. Discuss empowering employees.

2. Distinguish the five types of teams.

3. Identify team characteristics.

4. Evaluate team cohesiveness and norms.

5. Describe team conflict.

6. Explain the importance of effective communication.

7. Compare the basic forms of communication.

8. Explain external communication and crisis management.

Chapter 9

Top Performance through Empowerment, Teamwork, and Communication

Enterprise Rent-a-Car Thrives on Empowerment, Teamwork

What harried customer wouldn't love to hear a customer-service rep say, "You haven't described anything we can't solve"? That's exactly what happened to a couple of insurance executives racing to make the last plane home one evening. Frantic, they couldn't stop to fill the gas tank of their rental car, so the Enterprise Rent-a-Car employee who met them calmly drove them to their gate in a company van, filled out their paper-work, and e-mailed them copies so they could make their flight. Enterprise Holdings is a 55-year-old family-run business earning about $14 billion a year as the world's largest car rental firm and now includes Enterprise, Alamo, and National brands. The company was founded by Jack Taylor on a simple principle: "Take care of your customers and your employees first, and the profits will follow." Managed today by CEO Andy Taylor, son of the founder, the company honors employee empowerment and encourages teamwork. Andy started working for the company at the age of 16, washing cars during the holidays and summer vacations to learn the basics of the business.

Enterprise is the top recruiter at colleges, hiring thousands of graduates every year as management trainees if they have the right stuff: a passion for helping others, sales skills, a flexible approach toward work assignments, and lots of motivation to get things done right. To raise customer satisfaction, Taylor instituted better hiring practices to ensure employees have good communication skills. He insisted they know their customers' names, offer help without being asked, and never use industry jargon. Growth and profits increased dramatically, and Enterprise ranks number one among car rental companies in the JD Powers customer satisfaction survey.

The company's strong focus on customer service and employees' ability to make decisions on their own has been a major reason why Enterprise has built and maintained such a loyal group of customers. Its loyalty program, called Enterprise Plus, was recently upgraded to provide members with rewards and free rental days, as well as members-only check-in and special offers through the program's "Email Extras" e-newsletter. The company believes that upgrading its loyalty program is just one more way for the firm to demonstrate how much it appreciates its customers and their loyalty. Enterprise was recently recognized as the "Most Iconic Brand" in the car rental category.[1]

Overview

Top managers at organizations such as Enterprise Rent-a-Car recognize that team-work and communication are essential for empowering employees to perform their best. This chapter focuses on how organizations involve employees by sharing information and empowering them to make critical decisions, allowing them to work in teams, and fostering communication. We begin by discussing the ways managers can empower their employees' decision-making authority and responsibility. Then we explain why and how a growing number of firms rely on teams of workers rather than individuals to make decisions and carry out assignments. Finally, we discuss how effective communication allows workers to share information that improves the quality of decision making.

LECTURE ENHANCER: Ask if any students have ever had a job where teamwork was strongly emphasized, and have them describe their experience.

[1] Empowering Employees

An important component of effective management is the **empowerment** of employees. Managers promote this goal by giving employees the authority and responsibility to make decisions about their work. Empowerment seeks to tap the brainpower of all workers to find improved ways of doing their jobs, better serving customers, and achieving organizational goals. It also motivates workers by adding challenges to their jobs and giving them a feeling of ownership. Managers empower employees by sharing company information and decision-making authority and by rewarding them for their performance—as well as the company's.

Sharing Information and Decision-Making Authority

One of the most effective methods of empowering employees is to keep them informed about the company's financial performance. Companies such as Virginia-based engineering firm Anderson & Associates (A&A) provide regular reports to their employees on key financial information, such as profit-and-loss statements. A&A designs roads, water and sewer lines, and water treatment plants for municipalities, along with private construction projects such as Warm Hearth Village, a retirement community, in which residents were consulted during the planning process. The firm practices open-book management, giving every employee access to the same financial information about A&A. Like other companies that practice this strategy, A&A also trains its employees to interpret financial statements so that they can understand how their work contributes to company profits. Using information technology to empower employees does carry some risks. One is that information may reach competitors. Although A&A considered this problem, management decided that sharing information was essential to the company's strategy.[2]

The second way in which companies empower employees is to give them broad authority to make workplace decisions that implement a firm's vision and its competitive strategy. Even among non-management staff, empowerment extends to decisions and activities tradition- ally handled by managers. Employees might be responsible for such tasks as purchasing supplies, making hiring decisions, scheduling production or work hours, overseeing the safety program, and granting pay increases.

This can be an especially powerful tool in many health care environments. At Lebanon Valley Brethren Home, a long-term care facil- ity in Pennsylvania, workers at all levels are empowered to do whatever it takes to improve the quality of their elderly residents' lives. Each care worker attends to the same residents every day, so caregivers and residents form a strong personal bond. Caregivers are responsible for the overall management of their households, including meals and housekeeping. They make decisions for individual residents ranging from sleep schedules to room lighting. As a result, each Green House—or household within the larger community—feels like a home.[3]

Jacob Wackerhausen/iStockphoto

A way in which companies empower employees is to give them broad authority to make workplace decisions that implement a firm's vision and its competitive strategy without seeking managerial input. At Lebanon Valley Brethren Home, a long-term care facility in Pennsylvania, workers at all levels are empowered to do whatever it takes to improve the quality of their elderly residents' lives.

GM: Putting Workers in the Driver's Seat

Autoworkers at GM are used to doing many things as part of their jobs. But until recently, one thing they hadn't been asked to do very often is to drive the cars.

Workers at the GM assembly plant in Arlington, Texas, recently volunteered for a new program in which they could take a vehicle off the plant lot for a night or a weekend, and drive it just as they would their own car. The test drivers were asked for detailed feedback, for the first time giving them a powerful voice in the design and construction of the cars they build. "We had so much interest in [the program] we had to use a lottery to determine who would get to be a volunteer," reports Enrique Flores Jr., president of the United Auto Workers Local 276, the union representing 2,400 workers at the GM plant.

Executives and managers have participated in the test-drive program for years, but bringing it to rank-and-file workers marks an updated attitude toward empowering employees. "We want to engage employees to do underground marketing," explains Wendy Stachowicz, coordinator of the GM Vehicle Advocate Program.

In addition to a lottery, employees were chosen on the basis of their driving records. If they chose to purchase that vehicle or another one in the program, they qualified for steep discounts. "This is a tool to empower people, to get them really engaged with our products," explains Stachowicz.

Questions for Critical Thinking

1. In what ways does the GM test-drive program empower workers?

2. How might GM benefit from this type of empowerment of its assembly plant workers?

Sources: "GM Employees Getting Up-Close Look at New Line-up," GM News, http://media.gm.com, accessed March 17, 2012; "GM Launches Plant-City Tour to Showcase Line-up, Empower Employees to Promote New Vehicles," GM Web site, http://media.gm.com, accessed March 17, 2012; Terry Box, "Arlington GM Workers to Take Home New Cars to Try Out," *Dallas Morning News,* http://www.dallasnews.com, accessed March 17, 2012.

Empowerment can take other forms as well. GM recently announced an initiative in which GM workers could volunteer to take vehicles home and test drive them in real-life situations, as described in the "Hit & Miss" feature.

Linking Rewards to Company Performance

Perhaps the ultimate step in convincing employees of their stake in the prosperity of their firm is worker ownership. Two widely used ways that companies provide worker ownership are employee stock ownership plans and stock options. Table 9.1 compares these two methods of employee ownership.

LECTURE ENHANCER: Which of these rewards would you prefer? Why?

TABLE
9.1 Employee Stock Ownership Plans and Stock Options

EMPLOYEE STOCK OPTION PLANS	STOCK OPTIONS
Company-sponsored trust fund holds shares of stock for employees	Company gives employees the option to buy shares of its stock
Usually covers all full-time employees	Can be granted to one, a few, or all employees
Employer pays for the shares of stock	Employees pay a set price to exercise the option
Employees receive stock shares (or value of stock) upon retiring or leaving the company	Employees receive shares of stock when (and if) they exercise the option, usually during a set period

Sources: "Employee Stock Options and Ownership (ESOP)," Reference for Business, http://www.referenceforbusiness.com, accessed March 17, 2012; "Employee Stock Options Fact Sheet," National Center for Employee Ownership, http://www.nceo.org, accessed March 17, 2012.

Employee Stock Ownership Plans More than 10 million workers participate in 10,900 *employee stock ownership plans (ESOPs)* worth almost $870 billion.[4] These plans benefit employees by giving them ownership stakes in their companies, leading to potential profits as the value of their firm increases. Under ESOPs, the employer buys shares of the company stock on behalf of the employee as a retirement benefit. The accounts continue to grow in value tax-free, and when employees leave the company, they can cash in their stock shares. Employees are motivated to work harder and smarter than they would without ESOPs because as part owners, they share in their firm's financial success. More than 92 percent of companies surveyed that offer ESOPs report an increase in employee productivity.[5]

As retirement plans, ESOPs must comply with government regulations designed to protect pension benefits. Because ESOPs can be expensive to set up, they are more common in larger firms than in smaller ones. Public companies with ESOPs average around 14,000 employees, and private companies average about 1,500 employees.[6] One danger with ESOPs is that if the majority of an employee's retirement funds are in company stock and the value falls dramatically, the employee—like other investors—will be financially harmed.[7]

Stock Options Another popular way for companies to share ownership with their employees is through the use of *stock options*, or the right to buy a specified amount of company stock at a given price within a given time period. In contrast to an ESOP, in which the company holds stock for the benefit of employees, stock options give employees a chance to own the stock themselves if they exercise their options by completing the stock purchase. If an employee receives an option on 100 shares at $10 per share and the stock price goes up to $20, the employee can exercise the option to buy those 100 shares at $10 each, sell them at the market price of $20, and pocket the difference. If the stock price never goes above the option price, the employee isn't required to exercise the option.[8]

CLASS ACTIVITY:
Ask students to provide and discuss pros and cons of stock options.

Although options were once limited to senior executives and members of the board of directors, some companies now grant stock options to employees at all levels. Federal labor laws allow stock options to be granted to both hourly and salaried employees. It is estimated that 9 million employees in thousands of companies hold stock options.[9] About one-third of all stock options issued by U.S. corporations go to the top five executives at each firm. Much of the remainder goes to other executives and managers, who make up only about 2 percent of the U.S. workforce. Yet there is solid evidence that stock options motivate regular employees to perform better. Some argue that to be most effective as motivators, stock options need to be granted to a much broader base of employees.

Stock options have turned hundreds of employees at firms such as Home Depot, Microsoft, and Google into millionaires. But such success stories are no guarantee, especially when stock prices drop during economic downturns. As with ESOPs, employees face risks when they rely on a single company's stock to provide for them. In addition to stock options and ESOPs, many firms offer their executives other perks, or special privileges.

Assessment Check ☑

1. What is empowerment?

2. What kinds of information can companies provide employees to help them share decision-making responsibility?

3. How do employee stock ownership plans and stock options reward employees and encourage empowerment?

[2] ## Teams

A **team** is a group of people with certain skills who are committed to a common purpose, approach, and set of performance goals. All team members hold themselves mutually responsible and accountable for accomplishing their objectives. Teams are widely used in business and in many not-for-profit organizations such as hospitals and government agencies. Teams are one of the most frequently discussed topics in employee training programs, because teams require that people learn how to work effectively together. Many firms emphasize the

team group of people with certain skills who are committed to a common purpose, approach, and set of performance goals.

importance of teams during their hiring processes, asking job applicants about their previous experiences as team members. Why? Because companies want to hire people who can work well with other people and pool their talents and ideas to achieve more together than they could achieve working alone. Figure 9.1 outlines five basic types of teams: work teams, problem-solving teams, self-managed teams, cross-functional teams, and virtual teams.

About two-thirds of U.S. firms currently use **work teams**, which are relatively permanent groups of employees. In this approach, people with complementary skills perform the day-to-day work of the organization. A work team might include all the workers involved in assembling and packaging a product—it could be anything from cupcakes to cars. Most of Walmart's major vendors maintain offices near its headquarters in Bentonville, Arkansas. Typically, the vendor offices operate as work teams, and the heads of these vendor offices often have the title of "team leader."

In contrast to work teams, a **problem-solving team** is a temporary combination of workers who gather to solve a specific problem and then disband. They differ from work teams in important ways, though. Work teams are permanent units designed to handle any business problem that arises, but problem-solving teams pursue specific missions. When Toyota was faced with serious quality problems—unintended acceleration, faulty brakes, and then questions about tires—and was forced to recall thousands of vehicles, the company formed Rapid Response Swift Market Analysis Response Teams (SMART) to deal with the technical problems. SMART were made up of field technology specialists, engineers from manufacturing and design, and product engineers from the United States with specialists from Japan on call. Together, team members worked with dealers across the country to contact customers and arrange for on-site analyses of each problem vehicle to determine what went wrong and why. Teams were encouraged to "listen and react" to customers' descriptions of their experiences as part of their investigation.[10] Typically, when a problem is solved, the team disbands—but in some cases, the team may develop a more permanent role within the firm.

A work team empowered with the authority to decide how its members complete their daily tasks is called a **self-managed team**. A self-managed team works most effectively when it combines employees with a range of skills and functions. Members are cross-trained to perform each other's jobs as needed. Distributing decision-making authority in this way can free members to concentrate on satisfying customers. Whole Foods Market has a structure based on self-managed work teams. Company managers decided that Whole Foods could be most innovative if employees made decisions themselves. Every employee is part of a team, and each store has about ten teams handling separate functions, such as groceries, bakery, and customer service. Each team handles responsibilities related to setting goals, hiring and training employees, scheduling team members, and purchasing goods to stock. Teams meet at least monthly to review goals and performance, solve problems, and explore new ideas. Whole Foods awards bonuses based on the teams' performance relative to their goals.[11]

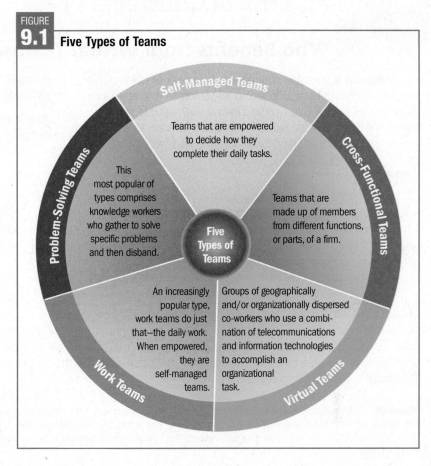

FIGURE 9.1 Five Types of Teams

Self-Managed Teams: Teams that are empowered to decide how they complete their daily tasks.

Problem-Solving Teams: This most popular of types comprises knowledge workers who gather to solve specific problems and then disband.

Cross-Functional Teams: Teams that are made up of members from different functions, or parts, of a firm.

Work Teams: An increasingly popular type, work teams do just that—the daily work. When empowered, they are self-managed teams.

Virtual Teams: Groups of geographically and/or organizationally dispersed co-workers who use a combination of telecommunications and information technologies to accomplish an organizational task.

Five Types of Teams

work team relatively permanent group of employees with complementary skills who perform the day-to-day work of organizations.

problem-solving team temporary combination of workers who gather to solve a specific problem and then disband.

self-managed team work team that has the authority to decide how its members complete their daily tasks.

LECTURE ENHANCER: Which type of team do you imagine would be the easiest to manage? Why?

Solving an Ethical Controversy

Who Benefits from Virtual Teamwork?

Virtual teams are teams of professionals, some or all of whose members work from home or in various off-site locations, to reach a common objective or goal. They work and keep in touch using technology including Web conferences, project management software, and voice-over-Internet services such as Skype. By reducing the need for office space and overhead, they can generate lower costs. But some companies fear that geographically dispersed employees pose greater management challenges.

Are virtual teams good for business and for employees?

PRO

1. Virtual teams let managers tap the most skilled and most diverse members regardless of their location.

2. Team members who don't commute can enjoy better work–life balance and flexible schedules with fewer interruptions.

CON

1. Communication among team members can be difficult across different cultures, time zones, and technologies, so misunderstandings and errors can occur.

2. Virtual teamwork calls for everyone to learn new skills and behaviors.

Summary

Virtual teams can't solve all problems, but with the right members, they can often achieve more than other teams and at lower cost. For best results, managers should hire people suited to working virtually, choose an experienced team leader, set clear goals, and make sure the right technology is in place. Occasional in-person team meetings help too.

Sources: "5 Tips to Establishing a Successful Virtual Team," Virtual Teams blog, http://virtualteamsblog.com, accessed February 2, 2012; "Virtual Teams: Pros, Cons, & Best Practices," Fast Fedora blog, http://blog.fastfedora.com, accessed February 2, 2012; Maan Laxa, "Pros & Cons of Working with Virtual Teams," Pepper Virtual Assistant, http://www.peppervirtualassistant.com, accessed February 2, 2012.

---

cross-functional team a team made up of members from different functions, such as production, marketing, and finance.

virtual team group of geographically or organizationally dispersed co-workers who use a combination of telecommunications and information technologies to accomplish an organizational task.

CLASS ACTIVITY:
Lead a discussion to identify work situations in which a team composed solely of members from the same function would be more effective than a cross-functional team.

A team made up of members from different functions, such as production, marketing, and finance, is called a **cross-functional team**. Most often, cross-functional teams work on specific problems or projects, but they can also serve as permanent work team arrangements. The value of cross-functional teams comes from their ability to bring different perspectives—as well as different types of expertise—to a work effort. Communication is key to the success of cross-functional teams. Chatter is a networking tool developed by Salesforce.com that allows internal information sharing across different business units and divisions of companies. Chatter "is an integrated view into your entire business," says Marc Benioff, Salesforce.com's founder.[12]

Virtual teams are groups of geographically or organizationally dispersed co-workers who use a combination of telecommunications and information technologies to accomplish an organizational task. Because of the availability of e-mail, videoconferencing, and group-communication software, members of virtual teams rarely meet face to face. The principal advantage of virtual teams is that they are very flexible. Employees can work with each other regardless of physical location, time zone, or organizational affiliation. Because of their very nature, virtual teams that are scattered across the globe can be difficult to manage. But firms that are committed to them believe that the benefits outweigh the drawbacks. See the "Solving an Ethical Controversy" feature for a discussion of both sides.

Although members of a virtual team rarely meet in person, they stay in touch through technologies such as videoconferencing. In today's global marketplace, the flexibility of virtual teams is a distinct advantage.

Assessment Check ☑
1. What is a team?
2. What are the five types of teams, and how are they different?

⌜3⌟ Team Characteristics

Effective teams share a number of characteristics. They must be an appropriate size to accomplish their work. In addition to size, teams also can be categorized according to the similarities and differences among team members, called *level* and *diversity*. We discuss these three characteristics next.

Team Size

Teams can range in number from as few as two people to as many as 150 people. In practice, however, most teams have fewer than 12 members. Although no ideal size limit applies to every team, research on team effectiveness indicates that they achieve their best results with about six or seven members. A group of this size is big enough to benefit from a variety of diverse skills, yet small enough to allow members to communicate easily and feel part of a close-knit group.

Certainly, groups smaller or larger than this can be effective, but they also create added challenges for team leaders. Participants in small teams of two to four members often show a desire to get along with each other. They tend to favor informal interactions marked by discussions of personal topics, and they make only limited demands on team leaders. A large team with more than 12 members poses a different challenge for team leaders because decision making may work slowly and participants may feel less committed to team goals. Larger teams also tend to foster disagreements, absenteeism, and membership turnover. Subgroups may form, leading to possible conflicts among various functions. As a general rule, a team of more than 20 people should be divided into subteams, each with its own members and goals.

LECTURE ENHANCER:
Why do you think larger groups might have lower participation rates?

Team Diversity at Ernst & Young

Ernst & Young provides tax, transaction, and advisory services. The firm has developed a new outlook on the business environment, especially how its 144,000 employees can contribute more fully to the company's future.

Ernst & Young is redefining the way it uses teams. A recent company survey revealed that companies operating in 25 or more countries base only 5 percent of their senior leadership in those countries—failing to make the most of the diverse cultures and ideas that could propel them forward. James S. Turley, chairman and CEO of Ernst & Young, observes, "Company leaders need to consider how a lack of diverse perspectives . . . might affect plans for global growth, new products, or mergers and acquisitions."

Ernst & Young has come up with a blueprint for its new team diversity. Managers who are planning or leading teams should consider:

- *The mindset.* Managers must think about how to achieve true cultural change within the organization.
- *The talent.* Managers should search the organization for true talent—including people in the cafeteria, at an assistant's desk, and in the human resources office.
- *Anticipation.* Creative managers need to use team members' diverse talents to identify new products and services.
- *Consensus.* Total agreement among team members isn't always necessary—or even the best thing. Disagreement can boost

a team's energy and force people to come up with new and better ideas and solutions.

CEO Jim Turley says, "Innovation comes from constructive clashes of different ideas, and from that, the sparks create some brilliance . . . It's getting all of our people to understand the direction of the world."

Questions for Critical Thinking

1. Why is team diversity so critical for a global firm such as Ernst & Young?

2. Based on the nature of its business, at what level would you expect Ernst & Young's teams to operate? Why?

Sources: Luke Visconti, "CEO Chat: E&Y's Leader Tells How Global Diversity Drives Revenue," *Diversity Inc.,* http://www.diversityinc.com, accessed March 19, 2012; "Ernst & Young LLP Diversity Award," *BAP Forums,* http://www.bap.org, accessed March 19, 2012; "Diversity Drives Innovation," Ernst & Young Web site, http://www.ey.com, accessed March 19, 2012; James S. Turley, "The New Global Mindset," *Bloomberg Businessweek,* http://www.businessweek.com, accessed March 19, 2012; "Ernst & Young LLP Starts 2010 with a Three-Day Event for Minority Students and a Faculty Roundtable Focused on Campus Diversity," *PR Newswire,* http://www.prnewswire.com, accessed March 19, 2012.

Team Level and Team Diversity

team level average level of ability, experience, personality, or any other factor on a team.

team diversity variances or differences in ability, experience, personality, or any other factor on a team.

Team level is the average level of ability, experience, personality, or any other factor on a team. Businesses consider team level when they need teams with a particular set of skills or capabilities to do their jobs well. For example, an environmental engineering firm might put together a team with a high level of experience to write a proposal for a large contract.

While team level represents the average level or capability on a team, **team diversity** represents the differences in ability, experience, personality, or any other factor on a team. Strong teams not only have talented members—as demonstrated by their team level—but also members who are different in terms of ability, experience, or personality. Team diversity is an important consideration for teams that must complete a wide range of different tasks or particularly complex tasks. For instance, the British Broadcasting Corporation (BBC) routinely creates teams for a variety of events such as golf's Masters Tournament or the Olympic Games. These teams involve production and broadcast groups larger than 100 people. Team members typically come from many different countries, with skills ranging from electrician to statistician or from scheduling to producing. And because an event at any of the sports venues takes place only once, the BBC teams have one chance to get it right. The BBC even created an additional temporary radio station to cover the 2012 London Summer Olympic Games.[13]

Team diversity is an important component of many successful companies. Read how Ernst & Young, a global firm that provides financial services, relies on diversity, as described in the "Hit & Miss" feature.

CLASS ACTIVITY:
Ask students to describe the possible challenges of working on a diverse team.

Strong teams not only have talented members but also members who are different in terms of ability, experience, or personality. Diversity is an important consideration for teams that must complete a wide range of different tasks or particularly complex tasks. For example, the BBC routinely creates teams for a variety of major events such as golf's Masters Tournament or the Olympic Games.

Stages of Team Development

Teams typically progress through five stages of development: forming, storming, norming, performing, and adjourning. Although not every team passes through each of these stages, those teams that do are usually better performers. These stages are summarized in Figure 9.2.

Stage 1: Forming Forming is an orientation period during which team members get to know each other and find out the behaviors that are acceptable to the group. Team members begin with curiosity about expectations of them and whether they will fit in with the group. An effective team leader provides time for members to become acquainted.

Stage 2: Storming The personalities of team members begin to emerge during the storming stage, as members clarify their roles and expectations. Conflicts may arise, as people disagree over the team's mission and jockey for position and control of the group. Subgroups may form based on common interests or concerns. At this stage, the team leader must encourage everyone to participate, allowing members to work through their uncertainties and conflicts. Teams must move beyond this stage to achieve real productivity.

Stage 3: Norming During the norming stage, members resolve differences, accept each other, and reach broad agreement about the roles of the team leader and other participants. This stage is usually brief, and the team leader should use it to emphasize the team's unity and the importance of its objectives.

Stage 4: Performing While performing, members focus on solving problems and accomplishing tasks. They interact frequently and handle conflicts in constructive ways. The team leader encourages contributions from all members. He or she should attempt to get any nonparticipating team members involved.

LECTURE ENHANCER:
During which stage is the manager's role most important? Why?

FIGURE
9.2 **Stages of Team Development**

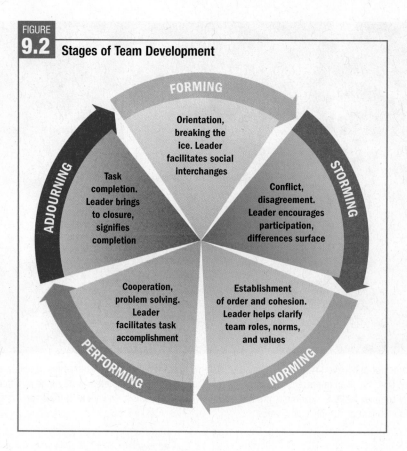

FORMING

Orientation, breaking the ice. Leader facilitates social interchanges

STORMING

Conflict, disagreement. Leader encourages participation, differences surface

NORMING

Establishment of order and cohesion. Leader helps clarify team roles, norms, and values

PERFORMING

Cooperation, problem solving. Leader facilitates task accomplishment

ADJOURNING

Task completion. Leader brings to closure, signifies completion

LECTURE ENHANCER:
What might be the effect on a team if a manager skips the adjourning stage?

Assessment Check ☑

1. Explain team level and team diversity.
2. Explain how teams progress through the stages of team development.

team cohesiveness
extent to which team members feel attracted to the team and motivated to remain part of it.

LECTURE ENHANCER:
What is likely to happen if team cohesiveness is low or nonexistent?

LECTURE ENHANCER:
Provide an example of a team norm you have experienced.

Stage 5: Adjourning The team adjourns after members have completed the assigned task or solved the problem. During this phase, the focus is on wrapping up and summarizing the team's experiences and accomplishments. The team leader may recognize the team's accomplishments with a celebration, perhaps handing out plaques or awards.

Team Cohesiveness and Norms

Teams tend to maximize productivity when they form into highly cohesive units. **Team cohesiveness** is the extent to which members feel attracted to the team and motivated to remain part of it. This cohesiveness typically increases when members interact frequently, share common attitudes and goals, and enjoy being together. Cohesive groups have a better chance of retaining their members than those that do not achieve cohesiveness. As a result, cohesive groups typically experience lower turnover. In addition, team cohesiveness promotes cooperative behavior, generosity, and a willingness on the part of team members to help each other. When team cohesiveness is high, team members are more motivated to contribute to the team, because they want the approval of other team members. Not surprisingly, studies have clearly established that cohesive teams quickly achieve high levels of performance and consistently perform better.

Team-building retreats are one way to encourage cohesiveness and improve satisfaction and retention. Firms that specialize in conducting these retreats offer a wide range of options. CEO Chef, based in California, offers the option of bringing its team-building program to its clients—which is typically less expensive than a traditional retreat. The culinary team from CEO Chef can travel to an off-site meeting location or to a company's own cafeteria for a team-building exercise in which participants work together to create a gourmet meal—then enjoy eating it.[14]

A **team norm** is a standard of conduct shared by team members that guides their behavior. Norms are not formal written guidelines; they are informal standards that identify key values and clarify team members' expectations. In highly productive teams, norms contribute to constructive work and the accomplishment of team goals. In Illinois, the Rockford Public Schools and Rock Valley College recently formed an alliance to create work teams of high school teachers and college faculty members to draft recommendations for the alignment of coursework so high school students would be better prepared to attend college.[15] In this case, team norms would include standards of conduct during meetings as well as a shared vision for the preparation of students.

⌐5⌐

Team Conflict

Conflict occurs when one person or group's needs do not match those of another, and attempts may be made to block the opposing side's intentions or goals. Conflict and disagreement are inevitable in most teams. But this shouldn't surprise anyone. People who work together are naturally going to disagree about what and how things are done. What causes conflict in teams? Although almost anything can lead to conflict—casual remarks that unintentionally offend a team member or fighting over scarce resources—the primary cause of team conflict is disagreement over goals and priorities. Other common causes of team conflict include disagreements over task-related issues, interpersonal incompatibilities, simple fatigue, and team diversity.

Earlier in this chapter we noted how teams can experience diversity among members. While diversity brings stimulation, challenge, and energy, it can also lead to conflict. The job of the manager is to create an environment in which differences are appreciated and in which a team of diverse individuals works productively together. Diversity awareness training programs can reduce conflict by bringing these differences out in the open and identifying the unique talents of diverse individuals.

Although most people think conflict should be avoided, management experts note that conflict can actually enhance team performance. The key to dealing with conflict is making sure that the team experiences the right kind of conflict. **Cognitive conflict** focuses on problem-related differences of opinion, and reconciling those differences strongly improves team performance. With cognitive conflict, team members disagree because their different experiences and expertise lead them to different views of the problem and its solutions. Cognitive conflict is also characterized by a willingness to examine, compare, and reconcile differences to produce the best possible solution. By contrast, **affective conflict** refers to the emotional reactions that can occur when disagreements become personal rather than professional, and these differences strongly decrease team performance. Because affective conflict often results in hostility, anger, resentment, distrust, cynicism, and apathy, it can make people uncomfortable, cause them to withdraw, decrease their commitment to a team, lower the satisfaction of team members, and decrease team cohesiveness. So, unlike cognitive conflict, affective conflict undermines team performance by preventing teams from engaging in activities that are critical to team effectiveness.

What can managers do to manage team conflict—and even make it work for them? Perhaps the team leader's most important contribution to conflict resolution can be facilitating good communication so that teammates respect each other and are free to disagree with each other. Ongoing, effective communication ensures that team members perceive each other accurately, understand what is expected of them, and obtain the information they need. Taking this a step further, organizations should evaluate situations or conditions in the workplace that might be causing conflict. Solving a single conflict isn't helpful if there are problems systemic to the team or to the company. Team-building exercises, listening exercises, and role-playing can help employees learn to become better team members.[16]

team norm standard of conduct shared by team members that guides their behavior.

Assessment Check ✔

1. How does cohesiveness affect teams?

2. Explain how team norms positively and negatively affect teams.

conflict situation in which one person or group's needs do not match those of another, and attempts may be made to block the opposing side's intentions or goals.

LECTURE ENHANCER: Share an instance of team conflict you have experienced within the workplace.

cognitive conflict disagreement that focuses on problem- and issue-related differences of opinion.

affective conflict disagreement that focuses on individuals or personal issues.

LECTURE ENHANCER: Which type of conflict would be the most difficult for a manager to resolve?

Assessment Check ✔

1. What is cognitive conflict, and how does it affect teams?

2. Explain affective conflict and its impact on teams.

┌ 6 ┐

The Importance of Effective Communication

Countries such as China, India, and Mexico are home to businesses that provide goods and services to companies or consumers in the United States. But the more parties involved in the production process, the harder it is to coordinate communication. Toyota Motor Corp. became embroiled in miscommunication when it tried to establish a clear timeline for the reporting of the number of its vehicles that were affected by unintended acceleration worldwide. While the National Highway Traffic Safety Administration (NHTSA) investigated the issue, Toyota continued the recalls over a period of several years, reaching a total of more than 8 million total vehicles recalled.[17]

communication meaningful exchange of information through messages.

Communication can be defined as a meaningful exchange of information through messages. Few businesses can succeed without effective communication. In fact, as illustrated by the Toyota example, miscommunication can result in damage to the company. By the time the NHTSA closed its investigation, Toyota had been ordered to pay more than $16.4 million in fines for miscommunication alone and suffered additional losses related to the recalls and repairs on its vehicles.[18]

Managers spend about 80 percent of their time—nearly six and a half hours of every eight-hour day—in direct communication with others, whether on the telephone, in meetings, via e-mail, or in individual conversations. Company recruiters consistently rate effective communication, such as listening, conversing, and giving feedback, as the most important skill they look for when hiring new employees. In the last half of this chapter, you'll learn about the communication process, the basic forms of communication, and ways to improve communication within organizations.

The Process of Communication

Every communication follows a step-by-step process that involves interactions among six elements: sender, message, channel, audience, feedback, and context. This process is illustrated in Figure 9.3.

In the first step, the *sender* composes the message and sends it through a communication carrier, or channel. Encoding a message means that the sender translates its meaning into understandable terms and a form that allows transmission through a chosen channel. The sender can communicate a particular message through many different channels, including face-to-face conversations, phone calls, and e-mail or texting. A promotional message to the firm's customers may be communicated through such forms as radio and television ads, billboards, magazines and newspapers, sales presentations, and social media such as Facebook and Twitter. The audience consists of the people who receive the message. In decoding, the receiver of the

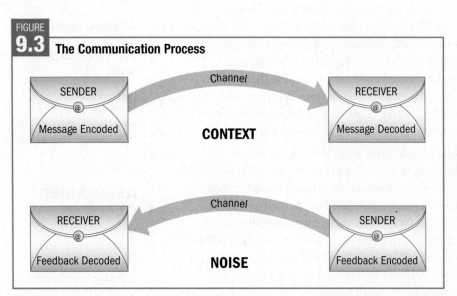

FIGURE 9.3 **The Communication Process**

message interprets its meaning. Feedback from the audience—in response to the sender's communication—helps the sender determine whether the audience has correctly interpreted the intended meaning of the message.

Every communication takes place in some sort of situational or cultural context. The *context* can exert a powerful influence on how well the process works. A conversation between two people in a quiet office, for example, may be a very different experience from the same conversation held at a noisy party. An American who orders chips in an English tavern will receive French fries.

Anthropologists classify cultures as low context and high context. Communication in *low-context cultures* tends to rely on explicit written and verbal messages. Examples include Switzerland, Austria, Germany, and the United States. In contrast, communication in *high-context cultures*—such as those of Japan, Latin America, and India—depends not only on the message itself but also on the conditions that surround it, including nonverbal cues, past and present experiences, and personal relationships among the parties. Westerners must carefully temper their low-context style to the expectations of colleagues and clients from high-context countries. Although Americans tend to favor direct interactions and want to "get down to business" soon after shaking hands or sitting down to a business dinner, business-people in Mexico and Asian countries prefer to become acquainted before discussing details. When conducting business in these cultures, wise visitors allow time for relaxed meals during which business-related topics are avoided.

Senders must pay attention to audience feedback, even requesting it if none is forthcoming, because this response clarifies whether the communication has conveyed the intended message. Feedback can indicate whether the receiver heard the message and was able to decode it accurately. Even when the receiver tries to understand, the communication may fail if the message contained jargon or ambiguous words.

Noise during the communication process is some type of interference that influences the transmission of messages and feedback. Noise can result from simple physical factors such as poor reception of a cell phone message or static that drowns out a radio commercial. It can also be caused by more complex differences in people's attitudes and perceptions. Consequently, even when people are exposed to the same communications, they can end up with very different perceptions and understandings because of communication noise.

Noise can be present at any point in the communication process. This is why managers must learn how to cut through noise when communicating with employees. Managers at London's i-level, a digital communications firm, found a creative way to cut through noise to communicate its plans to transition from a paper-based benefits

LECTURE ENHANCER:
What can happen to the communication process if this step is ignored?

CLASS ACTIVITY:
Ask students how noise in their households affects their ability to participate on a distance learning activity.

Don Bayley/iStockphoto

Noise during the communication process is some type of interference that influences the transmission of messages and feedback. It can result from simple physical factors such as poor reception of a cell phone message or it can be caused by complex differences in people's attitudes and perceptions. Consequently, even when people are exposed to the same communications, they may end up with very different levels of perception and understanding because of communication noise.

Assessment Check ☑️

1. What is the difference between communication in low-context and high-context cultures?

2. In the context of the communication process, what is noise?

process to an online system. First they distributed "i" character mugs to office staff. Then they sent messages to employees' mobile phones. Those with iPhones received animated messages. New hires and prospective employees without company phones received a portable disk drive containing the messages. "The communications felt really innovative and it was good using digital media because at the end of the day, that's what we're about as a company," says James Miller, the company's human resource director. "People have found it really good fun and I'm really, really pleased with the concept we have come up with."[19]

⌐7⌐ Basic Forms of Communication

Managers and co-workers communicate in many different ways—by making a phone call, sending an e-mail, holding a staff meeting, or chatting in the hallway. They also communicate with facial expressions, gestures, and other body language. Subtle variations can significantly influence the reception of a message. As Table 9.2 points out, communication takes various forms: oral and written, formal and informal, and nonverbal.

Oral Communication

Managers spend a lot of time engaged in oral communication, both in person and on the phone. Some people prefer to communicate this way, believing that oral channels convey messages more accurately. Face-to-face oral communication allows people to combine words with such cues as facial expressions and tone of voice. Oral communication over the telephone lacks visual cues, but it does allow people to hear the tone of voice and provide immediate feedback by asking questions or restating the message. Because of its immediacy, oral

TABLE

⌐**9.2**⌐ **Forms of Communication**

FORM	DESCRIPTION	EXAMPLES
Oral communication	Communication transmitted through speech	Personal conversations, speeches, meetings, voice mail, telephone conversations, videoconferences
Written communication	Communication transmitted through writing	e-mails, letters, memos, formal reports, news releases, online discussion groups, Internet messaging, faxes
Formal communication	Communication transmitted through the chain of command within an organization to other members or to people outside the organization	Internal—memos, reports, meetings, written proposals, oral presentations, meeting minutes; external—letters, written proposals, oral presentations, speeches, news releases, press conferences
Informal communication	Communication transmitted outside formal channels without regard for the organization's hierarchy of authority	Rumors spread informally among employees via the grapevine
Nonverbal communication	Communication transmitted through actions and behaviors rather than through words	Gestures, facial expressions, posture, body language, dress, makeup

communication has drawbacks. If one person is agitated or nervous during a conversation, noise enters the communication process. A hurried manager might brush off an employee who has an important message to deliver. A frustrated employee might feel compelled to fire a harsh retort at an unsupportive supervisor instead of thinking before responding.

In any medium, a vital component of oral communication is **listening**—receiving a message and interpreting its genuine meaning by accurately grasping the facts and feeling conveyed. Although listening may be the most important communication skill, most of us don't use it enough—or as well as we should.

Listening may seem easy, because the listener appears to make no effort. But the average person talks at a rate of roughly 150 words per minute, while the brain can handle up to 400 words per minute. This gap can lead to boredom, inattention, and misinterpretation. In fact, immediately after listening to a message, the average person can recall only half of it. After several days, the proportion of a message that a listener can recall falls to 25 percent or less.

Listening may seem easy, because the listener appears to make no effort. But the average person talks much slower than the amount of information the brain can handle at any given time. This gap may lead to boredom, inattention, and misinterpretation on the part of the listener.

Certain types of listening behaviors are common in both business and personal interactions:

- *Cynical or defensive listening.* This type of listening occurs when the receiver of a message feels that the sender is trying to gain some advantage from the communication.

- *Offensive listening.* In this type of listening, the receiver tries to catch the speaker in a mistake or contradiction.

- *Polite listening.* In this mechanical type of listening, the receiver listens to be polite rather than to contribute to communication. Polite listeners are usually inattentive and spend their time rehearsing what they want to say when the speaker finishes.

- *Active listening.* This form of listening requires involvement with the information and empathy with the speaker's situation. In both business and personal life, active listening is the basis for effective communication.

Learning how to be an active listener is an especially important goal for business leaders because effective communication is essential to their role. Listening is hard work, but it pays off with increased learning, better interpersonal relationships, and greater influence.[20] Both managers and employees can develop skills to make them better listeners, as described in the "Business Etiquette" feature.

Written Communication

Channels for written communication include reports, letters, memos, online discussion boards and social media, e-mails, and text messages. Many of these channels permit only delayed feedback and create a record of the message. So it is important for the sender of a written communication to prepare the message carefully and review it to avoid

listening receiving a message and interpreting its intended meaning by grasping the facts and feelings it conveys.

LECTURE ENHANCER:
Can you think of some additional drawbacks to oral communication?

LECTURE ENHANCER:
Are there specific body language cues for each type of listening behavior? What are they?

BusinessEtiquette

Tune Up Your Listening Skills

Smart managers know that good listening is an important key to business success. Tuning in to employees, customers, and competitors can provide a wealth of valuable insight and information. Listening means paying attention to verbal and nonverbal cues. It means turning off your cell phone during a face-to-face conversation or meeting. It involves strategies for understanding the message that is conveyed. Here are a few tips for enhancing your listening skills:

- *Be attentive.* If culturally appropriate, maintain eye contact with the speaker—without staring. Nod your head to convey that you are hearing the person. Screen out distractions such as background noise and irrelevant thoughts.

- *Keep an open mind.* Hear the other person all the way through, even if you are certain you will disagree. This not only shows respect for the speaker but also will result in your own informed reply.

- *Don't interrupt.* Even if you are absolutely certain of what the person is going to say—or convinced you have a solution or answer—wait until the speaker is finished. Then you can ask a question or make your point.

- *Ask questions.* Ask at least one question or paraphrase portions of the speaker's discussion to ensure that you understand the other person's point.

- *Be empathetic.* Laugh or be consoling where appropriate. You don't have to agree with the speaker, but even in the heat of disagreement, you can show empathy.

Sources: Norma Chew, "Are You a Good Listener?" Yahoo! Voices, http://voices.yahoo.com, accessed March 19, 2012; Rebecca Carswell, "Overcoming Barriers to Effective Listening," Women's Media, http://www.womensmedia.com, accessed March 19, 2012; "Are You an Active Listener?" New Horizons, http://blog.newhorizons123.com, accessed March 19, 2012.

LECTURE ENHANCER:
What are some possible drawbacks to written communication?

LECTURE ENHANCER:
Share some typical methods that companies use for downward formal communication.

misunderstandings—particularly before pressing that "send" button.

Effective written communication reflects its audience, the channel carrying the message, and the appropriate degree of formality. When writing a formal business document such as a complex marketing research report, a manager must plan in advance and carefully construct the document. The process of writing a formal document involves planning, research, organization, composition and design, and revision. Written communication via e-mail may call for a less-formal writing style, including short sentences, phrases, and lists.

E-mail is a very effective communication channel, especially for delivering straightforward messages and information. But e-mail's effectiveness also leads to its biggest problem: too much e-mail! Many workers find their valuable time being consumed with e-mail. To relieve this burden and leave more time for performing the most important aspects of the job, some companies are looking into ways to reduce the time employees spend sending and reading e-mail. To fulfill this need, there are now firms that provide e-mail management services. One such company is Tucson-based DakotaPro.biz, which provides customized e-mail solutions for firms that have been struggling to keep up with the volume of e-mail they receive and the time it takes to operate an in-house server.[21]

Other e-mail issues are security and retention. Because e-mail messages are often informal, senders occasionally forget that they are creating a written record. Even if the recipient deletes an e-mail message, other copies exist on company e-mail servers. E-mails on company servers can be used as evidence in a legal case or disciplinary action.

Formal Communication

A *formal communication channel* carries messages that flow within the chain of command structure defined by an organization. The most familiar channel, downward communication, carries messages from someone who holds a senior position in the organization to subordinates. Managers may communicate downward by sending employees e-mail messages, presiding at department meetings, giving employees policy manuals, posting notices on bulletin boards, and reporting news in company newsletters. The most important factor in formal communication is to be open and honest. "Spinning" bad news to make it look better almost always backfires. In a work environment characterized by open communication, employees feel free to express opinions, offer suggestions, and even voice complaints. Research has shown that open communication has the following seven characteristics:

1. *Employees are valued.* Employees are happier and more motivated when they feel they are valued and their opinions are heard.

2. *A high level of trust exists.* Telling the truth maintains a high level of trust; this forms the foundation for open communication and employee motivation and retention.

3. *Conflict is invited and resolved positively.* Without conflict, innovation and creativity are stifled.

4. *Creative dissent is welcomed.* By expressing unique ideas, employees feel they have contributed to the company and improved performance.

5. *Employee input is solicited.* The key to any company's success is input from employees, which establishes a sense of involvement and improves working relations.

6. *Employees are well informed.* Employees are kept informed about what is happening within the organization.

7. *Feedback is ongoing.* Both positive and negative feedback must be ongoing and provided in a manner that builds relationships rather than assigns blame.[22]

Many firms also define formal channels for upward communications. These channels encourage communication from employees to supervisors and upward to top management levels. Some examples of upward communication channels are employee surveys, suggestion boxes, and systems that allow employees to propose ideas for new products or voice complaints. Upward communication is also necessary for managers to evaluate the effectiveness of downward communication. Figure 9.4 illustrates the forms of organizational communication, both formal and informal.

Informal Communication

Informal communication channels carry messages outside formally authorized channels within an organization's hierarchy. A familiar example of an informal channel is the **grapevine**, an internal channel that passes information from unofficial sources. All organizations, large or small, have grapevines. Grapevines disseminate information with speed and economy and are surprisingly reliable. But company communications must be managed effectively so that the grapevine is not the main source of information. When properly nurtured, the grapevine can help managers get a feel for the morale of companies, understand the anxieties of the workforce, and evaluate the effectiveness of formal communications. Managers can improve the quality of information circulating through the company grapevine by sharing what they know, even if it is preliminary or partial information. By feeding information to selected people, smart leaders can harness the power of the grapevine.

Gossip—which usually travels along the grapevine—is the main drawback of this communication channel. Because gossip can spread misinformation quickly—particularly if it reaches the Internet—a manager should deal directly with the gossiper so the grapevine can become a legitimate source of information once again. Conversely, employees can nurture informal communication by taking the time to learn more about the communication needs of their managers.[23]

CLASS ACTIVITY:
Ask students how they would communicate with employees about an across-the-board 20 percent workforce reduction.

grapevine internal information channel that transmits information from unofficial sources.

LECTURE ENHANCER:
What are some other ways in which managers can use the grapevine?

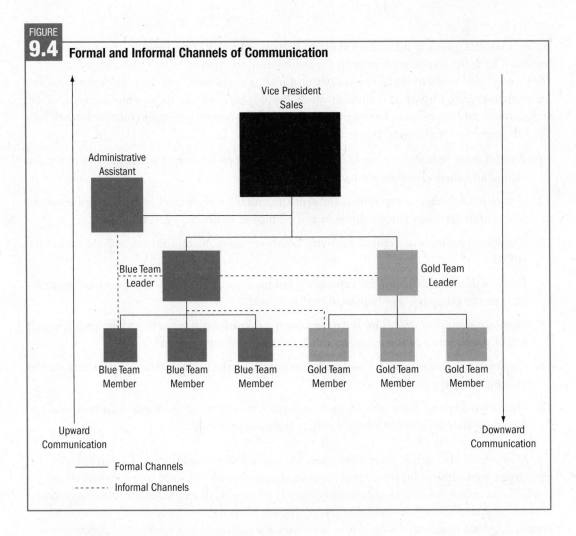

FIGURE 9.4 Formal and Informal Channels of Communication

Vice President Sales

Administrative Assistant

Blue Team Leader

Gold Team Leader

Blue Team Member

Blue Team Member

Blue Team Member

Gold Team Member

Gold Team Member

Gold Team Member

Upward Communication

Downward Communication

——— Formal Channels

----- Informal Channels

As organizations become more decentralized and more globally dispersed, informal communication—more than ever before—provides an important source of information, through e-mail, texting, and social media.

Nonverbal Communication

So far, this section has considered different forms of verbal communication, or communication that conveys meaning through words. Equally important is *nonverbal communication*, which transmits messages through actions and behaviors. Gestures, posture, eye contact, tone and volume of voice, and even clothing choices are all nonverbal actions that become communication cues. Nonverbal cues can have a far greater impact on communications than many people realize. In fact, it is estimated that 70 percent of interpersonal communication is conveyed through nonverbal cues. Top salespeople are particularly adept at reading and using these cues. For example, they practice "mirroring" a customer's gestures and body language in order to indicate agreement.[24]

Even personal space—the physical distance between people who are engaging in communication—can convey powerful messages. Figure 9.5 shows a continuum of personal space and social interaction with four zones: intimate, personal, social, and public. In the United States, most business conversations occur within the social zone, roughly between 4 and 12 feet apart. If one person tries to approach closer than that, the other individual will likely feel uncomfortable or even threatened.

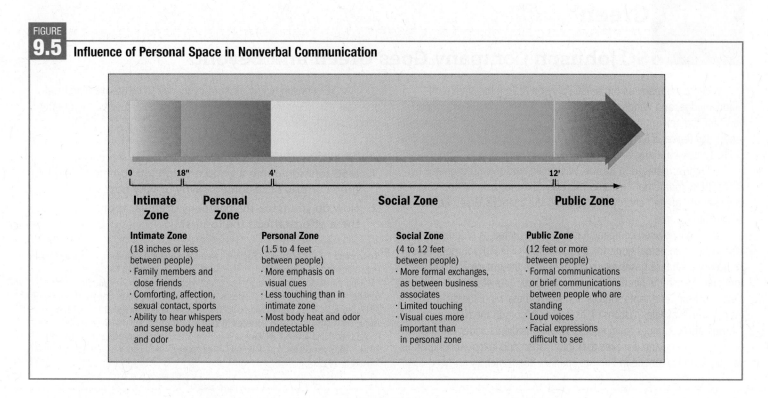

FIGURE
9.5 Influence of Personal Space in Nonverbal Communication

0	18"	4'	12'
Intimate Zone	**Personal Zone**	**Social Zone**	**Public Zone**

Intimate Zone
(18 inches or less between people)
· Family members and close friends
· Comforting, affection, sexual contact, sports
· Ability to hear whispers and sense body heat and odor

Personal Zone
(1.5 to 4 feet between people)
· More emphasis on visual cues
· Less touching than in intimate zone
· Most body heat and odor undetectable

Social Zone
(4 to 12 feet between people)
· More formal exchanges, as between business associates
· Limited touching
· Visual cues more important than in personal zone

Public Zone
(12 feet or more between people)
· Formal communications or brief communications between people who are standing
· Loud voices
· Facial expressions difficult to see

Interpreting nonverbal cues can be especially challenging for people with different cultural backgrounds. Concepts of appropriate personal space differ dramatically throughout most of the world. Latin Americans conduct business discussions in positions that most Americans and northern Europeans would find uncomfortably close. Americans often back away to preserve their personal space, a gesture that Latin Americans perceive as a sign of cold and unfriendly relations. To protect their personal space, some Americans separate themselves across desks or tables from their Latin American counterparts—at the risk of challenging their colleagues to maneuver around those obstacles to reduce the uncomfortable distance.

People send nonverbal messages even when they consciously try to avoid doing so. Sometimes nonverbal cues convey a person's true attitudes and thoughts, which may differ from spoken meanings. Generally, when verbal and nonverbal cues conflict, receivers of the communication tend to believe the nonverbal content. This is why firms seeking to hire people with good attitudes and a team orientation closely watch nonverbal behavior during job interviews in which job applicants participate in group sessions with other job candidates applying for the same job. If in those group interviews an applicant frowns or looks discouraged when a competing candidate gives a good answer, that nonverbal behavior suggests that this person may not be strongly team oriented.

[8]
External Communication and Crisis Management

External communication is a meaningful exchange of information through messages transmitted between an organization and its major audiences, such as customers, suppliers, other firms, the general public, and government officials. Businesses use external communication to keep their operations functioning, to maintain their positions in the

Assessment Check ✔

1. Define the four common listening behaviors.

2. What are the differences between formal and informal communication?

external communication meaningful exchange of information through messages transmitted between an organization and its major audiences.

SC Johnson Company Goes Green and Beyond

When a company as big as SC Johnson & Son, Inc., maker of Glade, Pledge, and Windex, reaches its sustainability goals, it's good news for the environment. SC Johnson recently announced, in its annual report *360 Degrees of Greener Choices,* that it met all its annual sustainability goals, surpassed many, and set new five-year targets.

SC Johnson, based in Racine, Wisconsin, was even recognized by the U.S. Environmental Protection Agency (EPA) for being a top voluntary user of "green" energy and received the agency's Green Power Leadership Award.

The family-owned company has publicly reported its progress in meeting environmental goals for 20 years. Says CEO Fisk Johnson, "We've reduced greenhouse gases nearly 32 percent in the last decade and we'll continue to push the needle." The company now gets 40 percent of its electricity from renewable sources and will harness wind energy at its largest plant (in Waxdale, Wisconsin), as it already does in the Netherlands. SC Johnson also continues to improve product ingredients under its patented Greenlist process, and it makes that information public too—online, on its packages, and by phone in English, Spanish, and French.

"At SC Johnson, we work hard every day to create winning products that use fewer resources, ensure less waste, and serve the greater good," said Johnson.

Questions for Critical Thinking

1. Is SC Johnson doing a good enough job communicating its green efforts to customers? Why or why not?

2. How do you think the company's regular reporting about these efforts affects the results?

Sources: "SC Johnson Helps Families Learn More about the Products They Use Every Day," company press release, http://www.scjohnson.com, accessed March 19, 2012; "Making the World a Better Place: New SC Johnson Report Examines 360 Degrees of Greener Choices," company press release, http://www.scjohnson.com, accessed March 19, 2012; David Schuyler, "Kohl's and SC Johnson Among Top Green Power Users," *Business Journal,* www.bizjournals.com, accessed March 19, 2012; "SC Johnson Receives EPA Green Power Leadership Award," *PR Newswire,* http://www.prnewswire.com, accessed March 19, 2012. "10 Green Giants: S. C. Johnson," *CNN Money,* http://money.cnn.com, accessed January 2, 2012.

marketplace, and to build customer relationships by supplying information about topics such as product modifications and price changes. Every communication with customers—including sales presentations and advertisements—should create goodwill and contribute to customer satisfaction. SC Johnson uses its annual report, its Web site, its product packaging, and even the phone to communicate good news about the company, as described in the "Going Green" feature. Letting the public know about new initiatives for environmentally friendly processes as well as community projects and other socially responsible activities in which the firm is involved is an important function of external communication.

However, all of this is threatened when companies experience a public relations crisis that threatens their reputation or goodwill, as in the case of the 2010 BP oil spill in the Gulf Coast. And, if bad publicity hits any of the social media sites, it can spread like wildfire. When the ambulance firm American Medical Response of Connecticut was accused of firing an employee because she had posted negative remarks about her boss on Facebook, not only was the company maligned by the workers, it was also investigated

Jacob Wackerhausen/iStockphoto

Businesses use external communication to keep their operations functioning, to maintain their positions in the marketplace, and to build customer relationships. Every communication with customers—including sales presentations and advertisements—should create goodwill and contribute to customer satisfaction.

by the National Labor Relations Board (NLRB). The NLRB alleged that the employee had a right to voice her opinion, whether in the company cafeteria or on Facebook. Eventually the firm agreed to a settlement of the case.[25]

How companies such as BP or Toyota handle such events can determine whether the company's reputation can be restored. Putting together a plan of action and dealing with facts and rumors immediately could be the difference between regaining trust and disaster. The following communication steps can help calm a public relations crisis:

1. When a crisis occurs, a firm should respond quickly. Executives should prepare a written statement—and stick to it. The statement should mention the time, place, initial description of what occurred (not the cause), and the number and status of the people involved.

2. As soon as possible, top company management should appear in public—if possible, to the press. Because the public will hold top management accountable, it's best to have top managers responding to reporters' questions.

3. When answering questions at an initial press conference or in an interview, the management representative must stick to the facts. It's likely that details about the event, the cause, and people's roles will not yet be known; the spokesperson shouldn't speculate. As information becomes available, the firm can provide accurate updates.

4. If a question is currently unanswerable, the executive can offer to find out the answer, which should be delivered in a timely manner. It's not advisable to answer a question by saying, "No comment." It's much better to say, "I don't know."

5. The firm should acknowledge problems, explain solutions, and welcome feedback. If a question or factual statement puts the organization in a negative light, the manager should acknowledge the problem, and then explain how the firm is correcting it.

6. The press conference or interview will be most effective if the executive speaks briefly, clearly and provides positive visual images.[26]

Crises faced by firms such as BP and American Medical Response are generally exacerbated by widespread criticism on social media sites. By the time they have a chance to reply, the damage to their reputations is significant. Although BP made good on its promise to clean up the Gulf, the company continues to deal with negative publicity. American Medical Response has tried to bolster its image with news releases that create a positive image, such as information for consumers on how to prepare for cold winter temperatures and the warning signs of a heart attack. Management experts warn that companies should take the proliferation of social media seriously.[27]

What's Ahead

Today's consumers expect the products they buy to be of the highest value for the price. Firms ensure this value by developing efficient systems for producing goods and services, as well as maintaining high quality. The next chapter examines the ways in which businesses produce world-class goods and services, efficiently organize their production facilities, purchase what they need to produce their goods and services, and manage large inventories to maximize efficiency and reduce costs.

LECTURE ENHANCER:
Share a recent example of a company that did not follow one or more of these steps. What were the consequences?

Assessment Check ☑

1. What is external communication?

2. What is the first thing a company should do when a public crisis occurs?

Summary of Learning Objectives

1 Discuss empowering employees.

Managers empower employees by giving them the authority and responsibility to make decisions about their work. Empowerment seeks to tap the brainpower of all workers to find improved ways of doing their jobs, better serving customers, and achieving organizational goals. Empowerment often includes linking rewards to company performance through employee stock ownership plans (ESOPs) and stock options.

Assessment Check Answers ✓

1.1 What is empowerment? Empowerment comes from giving employees authority and responsibility to make decisions about their work without traditional managerial approval and control.

1.2 What kinds of information can companies provide employees to help them share decision-making responsibility? Sharing information about company performance, particularly financial performance, is one of the best ways to share decision-making responsibility.

1.3 How do employee stock ownership plans and stock options reward employees and encourage empowerment? Employee stock ownership plans (ESOPs) benefit employees by giving them ownership stakes in their companies. Employees are motivated to work harder and smarter than they would without ESOPs, because they share in their firm's financial success. In contrast to an ESOP, in which the company holds stock for the benefit of employees (when employees leave the company, they cash in their stock), stock options give employees a chance to own the stock themselves if they exercise their options by completing the stock purchase.

2 Distinguish the five types of teams.

The five basic types of teams are work teams, problem-solving teams, self-managed teams, cross-functional teams, and virtual teams. Work teams are permanent groups of co-workers who perform the day-to-day tasks necessary to operate the organization. Problem-solving teams are temporary groups of employees who gather to solve specific problems and then disband. Self-managed teams have the authority to make decisions about how their members complete their daily tasks. Cross-functional teams are made up of members from different units, such as production, marketing, and finance. Virtual teams are groups of geographically or organizationally dispersed co-workers who use a combination of telecommunications and information technologies to accomplish an organizational task.

Assessment Check Answers ✓

2.1 What is a team? A team is a group of employees who are committed to a common purpose, approach, and set of performance goals.

2.2 What are the five types of teams, and how are they different? Work teams are permanent, while problem-solving teams are temporary. Unlike work teams, self-managed teams have the authority to change how they get

their work done. Cross-functional teams are composed of people from different backgrounds, while virtual teams are composed of people from different locations.

3 Identify team characteristics.

Three important characteristics of a team are its size, team level, and team diversity. The ideal team size is about six or seven members. Team level is the average level of ability, experience, personality, or any other factor on a team. Team diversity is the variances or differences in ability, experience, personality, or any other factor on a team. Team diversity is an important consideration for teams that must complete a wide range of different tasks or particularly complex tasks. Teams pass through five stages of development: (1) Forming is an orientation period during which members get to know each other and find out the behaviors that are acceptable to the group. (2) Storming is the stage during which individual personalities emerge as members clarify their roles and expectations. (3) Norming is the stage at which differences are resolved, members accept each other, and consensus emerges about the roles of the team leader and other participants. (4) Performing is characterized by problem solving and a focus on task accomplishment. (5) Adjourning is the final stage, with a focus on wrapping up and summarizing the team's experiences and accomplishments.

Assessment Check Answers ✓

3.1 Explain team level and team diversity. While team level is the average level or capability on a team, team diversity is the variances or differences in ability, experience, personality, or any other factor on a team.

3.2 Explain how teams progress through the stages of team development. Teams pass through five stages of development: forming, storming, norming, performing, and adjourning.

4 Evaluate team cohesiveness and norms.

Team cohesiveness is the extent to which team members feel attracted to the team and motivated to remain on it. Team norms are standards of conduct shared by team members that guide their behavior. Highly cohesive teams whose members share certain standards of conduct tend to be more productive and effective.

Assessment Check Answers ✓

4.1 How does cohesiveness affect teams? Members of cohesive teams interact more often, share common attitudes and goals, have higher morale, and are more likely to help each other. Cohesive teams also perform better.

4.2 Explain how team norms positively and negatively affect teams. Norms are informal standards that identify key values and clarify team members' expectations. But those norms can be positive or negative. Positive norms contribute to constructive work and the accomplishment of team goals. Negative norms can, for example, contribute to reduced work effort, reduced quality, and poor job attendance.

5. Describe team conflict.

Conflict and disagreement are inevitable in most teams. Conflict can stem from many sources: disagreements about goals and priorities, task-related issues, interpersonal incompatibilities, scarce resources, and simple fatigue. The key to dealing with team conflict is not avoiding it, but making sure that the team experiences the right kind of conflict. Cognitive conflict focuses on problem-related differences of opinion and, when reconciled, strongly improves team performance. By contrast, affective conflict refers to the emotional reactions that can occur when disagreements become personal rather than professional, and these differences strongly decrease team performance. A team leader can manage team conflict by fostering good communication so team members perceive each other accurately, understand what is expected of them, and obtain the information they need.

Assessment Check Answers ☑

5.1 What is cognitive conflict, and how does it affect teams? In cognitive conflict, team members disagree because their different experiences and expertise lead them to different views of the problem and its solutions. Cognitive conflict is characterized by a willingness to examine, compare, and reconcile differences to produce the best possible solution.

5.2 Explain affective conflict and its impact on teams. Because affective conflict often results in hostility, anger, resentment, distrust, cynicism, and apathy, it can make people uncomfortable, cause them to withdraw, decrease their commitment to a team, lower the satisfaction of team members, and decrease team cohesiveness.

6. Explain the importance of effective communication.

Managers spend about 80 percent of their time in direct communication with others. Company recruiters consistently rate effective communication—such as listening, conversing, and giving feedback—as the most important skill they look for when hiring new employees. The communication process follows a step-by-step process that involves interactions among six elements: sender, message, channel, audience, feedback, and context. The sender composes the message and sends it through the channel. The audience receives the message and interprets its meaning. The receiver gives feedback to the sender. The communication takes place in a situational or cultural context.

Assessment Check Answers ☑

6.1 What is the difference between communication in low-context and high-context cultures? Communication in low-context cultures tends to rely on explicit written and verbal messages. By contrast, communication in high-context cultures depends not only on the message itself but also on the conditions that surround it, including nonverbal cues, past and present experiences, and personal relationships between the parties.

6.2 In the context of the communication process, what is noise? Noise interferes with the transmission of messages and feedback. Noise can result from physical factors such as poor reception of a cell phone message or from differences in people's attitudes and perceptions.

7. Compare the basic forms of communication.

People exchange messages in many ways: oral and written, formal and informal, verbal and nonverbal communication. Effective written communication reflects its audience, its channel, and the appropriate degree of formality. Formal communication channels carry messages within the chain of command. Informal communication channels, such as the grapevine, carry messages outside the formal chain of command. Nonverbal communication plays a larger role than most people realize. Generally, when verbal and nonverbal cues conflict, the receiver of a message tends to believe the meaning conveyed by nonverbal cues.

Assessment Check Answers ☑

7.1 Define the four common listening behaviors. Cynical listening occurs when the receiver of a message feels that the sender is trying to gain some advantage from the communication. Offensive listening occurs when the receiver tries to catch the speaker in a mistake or contradiction. Polite listening occurs when the receiver is rehearsing what he or she wants to say when the speaker finishes. Active listening requires involvement with the information and empathy with the speaker's situation.

7.2 What are the differences between formal and informal communication? Formal communication occurs within the formal chain of command defined by an organization. Informal communication occurs outside the organization's hierarchy.

8. Explain external communication and crisis management.

External communication is a meaningful exchange of information through messages transmitted between an organization and its major audiences, such as customers, suppliers, other firms, the general public, and government officials. Every communication with customers should create goodwill and contribute to customer satisfaction. However, all of this is threatened when companies experience a public crisis that threatens their reputations or goodwill. To manage a public crisis, businesses should respond quickly and honestly, with a member of top management present.

Assessment Check Answers ☑

8.1 What is external communication? External communication is a meaningful exchange of information through messages transmitted between an organization and its major audiences.

8.2 What is the first thing a company should do when a public crisis occurs? The firm should respond quickly by preparing a written statement that includes the time, place, description of the event, and the number and status of people involved.

Business Terms You Need to Know

empowerment 262	cross-functional team 266	team norm 271	listening 275
team 264	virtual team 266	conflict 271	grapevine 277
work team 265	team level 268	cognitive conflict 271	external communication 279
problem-solving team 265	team diversity 268	affective conflict 271	
self-managed team 265	team cohesiveness 270	communication 272	

Review Questions

1. How do companies benefit from empowering their employees? How do employees benefit from empowerment?

2. How might a firm that manufactures shoes use teams to determine ways to improve its environmental standards in terms of products and processes? What type (or types) of teams would be best for this initiative? Why?

3. How do team level and team diversity affect team performance?

4. What are the characteristics of an effective team? Why are these features so significant?

5. At what stages of development might a team *not* be able to move forward? How might a team leader or manager resolve the situation?

6. Describe the norms associated with your business class. How do these norms influence the way students behave in class?

7. What steps can managers take to resolve team conflict?

8. In what ways is context a powerful influence on the effectiveness of communication? Describe an instance in which situational or cultural context has influenced one of your communication processes.

9. What are the benefits and drawbacks of oral and written communication?

10. What is the role of external communication? Why is it so important to companies?

Projects and Teamwork Applications

1. Having the power and authority to make decisions about work is the essence of empowerment. For this project, the instructor steps back and gives the class free rein to plan and implement a day of classwork. The class might appoint a leader, divide into teams (to plan a lecture, come up with an assignment, plan a field trip, and the like). It's completely up to the students how to organize and conduct the one-day class. After the class, discuss the experience—including the upside and downside (if any) of empowerment.

2. Divide the class into teams of relatively equal size. Each team may select one of the following problems to solve, or decide on one of its own: arranging for a guest speaker or expanding the menu in the school's coffee shop. Although it is not necessary to complete the entire problem-solving process, each team should go through the forming and norming stages of team development and outline a plan for accomplishing the group's task. Is each team cohesive? Why or why not?

3. Try this listening exercise with a partner. First, spend a few minutes writing a paragraph or two about the most

important thing that happened to you this week. Second, read your paragraph out loud to your partner. Next, have your partner read his or her paragraph. Finally, take turns summarizing the most important points in one another's stories. How well did you listen to one another?

4. On your own or with a classmate, visit the college library, a mall, or anywhere else people gather. For about 10 or 15 minutes, observe the nonverbal cues that people give each other: Does the librarian smile at students? What is the body language of students gathered in groups? When you leave the venue, jot down as many of your observations as you can. Notice things such as changes in nonverbal communication when someone joins a group or leaves it.

5. Choose a company with which you are familiar, or whose products you use. Research the company's offerings as well as some of its social responsibility and sustainability initiatives (e.g., the firm has set a goal to reduce its energy consumption by 20 percent). Create an advertisement that focuses on one of these initiatives as an example of positive external communication from the company.

Web Assignments

1. **Team-building exercises.** The Web site Team-Building-Bonanza.com calls itself "the motherlode of corporate team building ideas." You want to select a team-building exercise to help resolve conflicts. What are some of the suggested activities?
http://www.team-building-bonanza.com

2. **Writing better business letters.** Assume you'd like to improve your business letter–writing ability. Using a search engine such as Google or Bing, search the Web for sites with tips and suggestions to improve letter-writing skills. (An example site is listed below.) Select two of these sites and review the material. Prepare a brief summary.

http://www.askoxford.com/betterwriting/letterwriting/?viewvuk

Note: Internet Web addresses change frequently. If you don't find the exact sites listed, you may need to access the organization's home page and search from there or use a search engine such as Bing or Google.

3. **Employee stock ownership plans.** Visit the Web site of the ESOP Association. Click on "About ESOPs." Print out the materials (including the submenus) and bring them to class to participate in a discussion on employee stock ownership plans.

http://www.esopassociation.org

Southwest Airlines Thrives on Customer Service

CASE 9.1

For anyone doubting that customer service affects the bottom line, Southwest Airlines has an answer. The Dallas-based carrier has ranked number one in customer satisfaction for 18 straight years and is the only major airline that remains profitable. Its 37,000 employees also voted the low-fare leader into the top 50 best places to work in the annual Employee's Choice Awards, based on company culture, benefits and pay, and communication.

Sometimes Southwest's service is extraordinary, as when a pilot held a plane to allow a family member of a murdered child to make the flight. To the passenger's thanks the pilot responded, "They can't go anywhere without me and I wasn't going anywhere without you." On more routine trips, passengers appreciate Southwest's lack of extra fees and charges. And on the business-to-business side, Network Global Logistics, which arranges shipment of organ donations, named Southwest its Air Cargo Partner of the Year for its work ethic and commitment to customers.

Says the airline's executive vice president, "Here at Southwest, every ONE matters. We have the best workforce in the aviation industry and we are not afraid to show it. Our employees are filled with passion; we work hard and we learn from our mistakes. This makes us stronger as a company and the best place to work."

Questions for Critical Thinking

1. How does Southwest's customer service affect its bottom line?
2. Among 47 industries, airlines overall earn the lowest customer satisfaction score. What could they learn from Southwest?

Sources: "Next Flight Out: Pioneer Network Global Logistics Selects Southwest Airlines for Its Air Cargo Partner of the Year Award," StreetInsider.com, http://www.streetinsider.com, accessed March 20, 2012; "Southwest Posts Strong Profit Despite Rising Fuel Expenses," *New York Times,* http://www.nytimes.com, accessed March 20, 2012; Christopher Elliott, "Southwest Airlines Pilot Holds Plane for Murder Victim's Family," http://www.elliott.org/blog, accessed March 20, 2012; "Southwest Airlines Honored as One of the Top 50 Best Places to Work in 2012, a Glassdoor Employees' Choice Award," Nuts About Southwest blog, www.blogsouthwest.com, accessed March 20, 2012; "Commentary on Airlines, Express Delivery (Consumer Shipping), . . ." *ACSI Commentary,* http:// www.theacsi.org, accessed March 20, 2012; Rachel Saltz, "Even Less Love for Airlines," *The New York Times,* http://intransit.blogs.nytimes .com, accessed March 20, 2012.

Windy City Fieldhouse: It's All about Teams

CASE 9.2

Team building has become its own industry—as more managers understand the importance of fostering strong, effective teams—companies that specialize in creative ways to build teams. Chicago's Windy City Fieldhouse is one such firm. Even the name sounds like fun and games, and that's the intention.

Windy City Fieldhouse (WCF) develops and offers its corporate clients programs designed to bring people together in such a way that they don't even realize they are engaging in team-building and communication exercises. The WCF staff hosts outdoor corporate picnics, fun runs/walks, carnivals and block parties, even Grand Prix racing events. Of course, if a client wants a more traditional training program, WCF will do that, too—but most companies go for the fun. "Striving to provide programs that enhance meaningful relationships and add tremendous value, WCF continues to develop a variety of corporate event packages in order to respond to its clients' needs," states the Web site.

WCF is perhaps best known for its "Scavenger Hunts in Chicago" (SHIC) division, which custom designs "Mission Impossible" scavenger hunts around the Chicago area for client teams. SHIC creates, organizes, and leads the corporate event in such a way that team members must collaborate to solve clues used to reach a destination chosen by the client company. The destination can be anything from a cocktail party to dinner at a Chicago Cubs game—it's up to the client. A scavenger hunt facilitator is provided for each team, and once they reach their final destination, team members must complete certain missions such as taking funny photographs or finding special objects. With a facilitator acting as team leader, "Mission Impossible" team members learn how to set goals, establish norms, and make the most of diversity.

The response from participants is nearly always enthusiastic. "The feedback from my team was overwhelmingly positive," says one client. Another reports, "It has been a long time since this team has had a team gathering and when they did, we never had this much participation. Everyone really enjoyed the event." Windy City Fieldhouse is certainly on to something—the firm has been named "Best Teambuilding Company" in Chicago for three straight years.

Questions for Critical Thinking

1. Imagine that you had an opportunity to participate in one of SHIC's scavenger hunts. How do you think you would benefit from the experience as a team member?

2. Why is it important for SHIC to provide a facilitator for each team-building experience?

Sources: "Scavenger Hunts in Chicago" and "Client Testimonials," company Web site, http://www.scavengerhuntsinchicago.com, accessed March 20, 2012; "Scavenger Hunts in Chicago," Here's Chicago, http://www.hereschicago.com, accessed March 20, 2012; Toddi Gutner, "Applicants' Personalities Put to the Test," *The Wall Street Journal*, http://online.wsj.com, accessed March 20, 2012.

CASE 9.3

Kimpton Hotels: "Our Employees Are Our Brand"

The hotel and restaurant industry caters to its guests, but it has always had a reputation for being somewhat inhospitable to its employees. Traditionally, hotel and restaurant workers put in long hours for low pay and little or no recognition; they're the invisible hosts who fluff the pillows and sweep away crumbs. But Kimpton Hotels is setting a new example by treating its employees as something better than family: they are, in many ways, business partners.

Kimpton Hotels was founded in 1981 by Bill Kimpton, an investment banker with a vision for boutique hotels: small, luxurious hotels with impeccably intimate service and gourmet restaurants. Today, Kimpton operates 50 hotels and restaurants around the country, each beautifully designed and furnished. "But more than that," notes COO Niki Leondakis, "the people really separate us" from other hotels. As COO, Leondakis knows firsthand the difference at Kimpton. Leondakis talks about her company's full-blown commitment to empowering employees to make decisions, to take part in running the business, and to grow as professionals. "The employee of today wants more and expects more, and is not willing just to be a servant, loyal worker, or soldier," she says. Leondakis is proud of that fact and of the army of top-flight employees and managers who work at Kimpton's various locations.

One of those managers is Peggy Trott, the general manager of the Kimpton Hotel Palomar in Philadelphia. Trott explains how Kimpton empowers its employees.

"Kimpton wants each general manager to be an entrepreneur," she says. "They want you to operate your hotel as if it is your own business. So there's a lot of leeway." While some managers might argue that this puts undue pressure on them to perform as business owners, Trott views the challenge as an opportunity. She notes that the attitude toward empowerment travels from the top down in the organization. She says that each of her employees is charged with being a hero every day, especially when it comes to guest service. If an employee is acting on behalf of a guest, then he or she is free to make the decision on the spot.

"I have high expectations, but I think that when you give people high expectations, they rise to the occasion," says Trott. For example, if a housekeeper sees that one of her guest rooms is housing a family of two parents and two children, the housekeeper is expected to stock the room with extra towels instead of waiting for the guests to call the front desk requesting more towels. No matter how large or small the task might seem, "We expect people to be self-leaders," notes Leondakis. "We expect employees to use their heads."

Because each of the 50 Kimpton hotel and restaurant properties is unique to its location and local population, Kimpton actively recruits employees with diverse backgrounds and qualifications, then gives them the authority to serve their guests as they see best. Individuality is nurtured rather than squelched. Leondakis observes that, because her employees come with a wide range of experience at different locations in the hospitality industry, sometimes it is difficult to get them to leave behind their previous assumptions about their role as hotel workers. "The biggest challenge with employee empowerment and communication is that we're all products of our past," Leondakis says. New employees often have to be retrained to think outside the box, make decisions, and "rock the boat," as Leondakis puts it.

The results of this retraining toward empowerment have not gone unnoticed. Kimpton Hotels consistently win awards for service, and the group has received many accolades for its approach to human resource management, including a recent award from the Human Rights Campaign for "Workplace Equality Innovation." In addition, Kimpton is regularly named to *Fortune's* list of "100 Best Companies to Work For."

Recent praise from the industry publication *Hospitality Design* included a statement from Kimpton CEO Michael Depatie crediting Leondakis with much of the company's HR success. "Niki has an extraordinary ability to connect with people, from guests she meets on the road to each and every one of our employees," said Depatie. Leondakis, managers like Trott, and the entire staff embody their company's assertion that "Our employees are our brand."

Questions for Critical Thinking

1. Give three specific reasons why empowerment is key to the success of a firm like Kimpton Hotels. How might this distinguish it from other hotel companies?
2. Select the concept of either a problem-solving team or a self-managed team. How might this team function at a Kimpton hotel? Who might be on the team, and what role might it play in the running of the hotel?
3. Give an example of a situation in which informal communication would function well among empowered employees at a Kimpton hotel.
4. Currently all Kimpton hotels are located in the U.S., which is a low-context culture. If the firm decided to open a hotel in a high-context culture such as Japan, how might communication between staff and guests differ?

Sources: Kimpton Hotels & Restaurants Web site, http://www.kimptonhotels.com, accessed March 20, 2012; "Why Work for Kimpton?" http://www.imkimpton.com, accessed March 20, 2012; Sam Guidino, Mike Desimone, Jeff Jenssen, and Lynn Alley, "Kimpton Takes Philly," *Wine Spectator,* http://www.winespectator.com, accessed March 20, 2012; "Kimpton Hotels Aim for 100 Percent Green Seal Certification," GreenBiz.com, http://www.greenbiz.com, accessed March 20, 2012.

Learning Objectives

1 Explain the strategic importance of production.

2 Identify and describe the production processes.

3 Explain the role of technology in the production process.

4 Identify the factors involved in a location decision.

5 Explain the job of production managers.

6 Discuss controlling the production process.

7 Determine the importance of quality.

Production and Operations Management

sturti/iStockphoto

Intel's "Fab" New Manufacturing Facility

What's it like inside one of Intel's secure microprocessor chip-fabricating facilities? If you're lucky enough to visit a "fab" plant—and few people are—you'll enter dressed in a white jumpsuit, double-layered gloves, and special shoes, hair net, and goggles. All that gear is to protect the chips, by the way, not you.

Intel supplies chips for about 80 percent of all laptops, its core market, but with the rapid growth of smart phones and tablets, which require different, smaller microprocessors, the firm is investing $9 billion to increase its production capacity and stay ahead of demand for the new 22-nanometer technology. "By continuing to push our manufacturing leadership," says an industry observer, "Intel has a great opportunity to be a significant force in markets where it hasn't traditionally been a factor."

Intel's latest factory, the 1-million-square-foot Fab 42 now under construction in Arizona, will consume about $5 billion of the firm's production investment on its way to becoming the most advanced high-volume semiconductor manufacturing plant in the world. Fab 42 will require 11 million skilled-labor hours, the efforts of 2,000 to 3,000 construction workers, almost 600 miles of wiring, 86,000 cubic yards of concrete, more than 130 miles of mechanical piping, and 21,000 tons of structural steel. To lift 300-ton roof trusses into place, Intel also needed the largest land-based crane in the world, which was assembled on the site from pieces that filled 250 trucks. Building the new facility, set to employ about 1,000 people when it opens, is "a very large, complex construction process," says the company's head of manufacturing.

The rest of Intel's investment in production will help upgrade its existing facilities. At Fab 32, for instance, 30 quality-control specialists monitor the automated manufacturing processes 24/7, speedily shutting equipment down in the rare case of a defect. The facility can test for 1,500 different defects in silicon wafers the width of a human hair.

Fab 42 will doubtless do likewise and more. "We think Fab 42 will lead us into the future," says Intel's head of manufacturing.[1]

Overview

By producing and marketing the goods and services that people want, businesses satisfy their commitment to society as a whole. They create what economists call *utility*—the want-satisfying power of a good or service. Businesses can create or enhance four basic kinds of utility: time, place, ownership, and form. A firm's marketing operation generates time, place, and ownership utility by offering products to customers at a time and place that is convenient for purchase.

Production creates form utility by converting raw materials and other inputs into finished products, such as Intel's microprocessor chips. **Production** uses resources, including workers and machinery, to convert materials into finished goods and services. This conversion process may make major changes in raw materials or simply combine already finished parts into new products. The task of **production and operations management** in a firm is to oversee the production process by managing people and machinery in converting materials and resources into finished goods and services, which is illustrated by Figure 10.1.

People sometimes use the terms *production* and *manufacturing* interchangeably, but the two are actually different. Production spans both manufacturing and nonmanufacturing industries. For instance, companies that engage in fishing or mining engage in production, as do firms that provide package deliveries or lodging. Figure 10.2 lists five examples of production systems for a variety of goods and services.

production and operations management oversee the production process by managing people and machinery in converting materials and resources into finished goods and services.

LECTURE ENHANCER: Discuss the conversion process that occurs, and the resources needed, in a resort hotel.

production use of resources, such as workers and machinery, to convert materials into finished goods and services.

FIGURE
10.1 The Production Process: Converting Inputs to Outputs

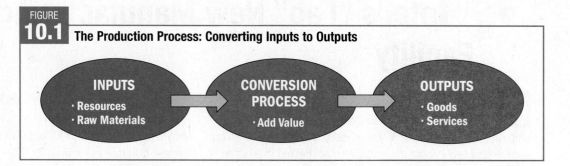

CLASS ACTIVITY:
Lead a class discussion on the inputs, transformation process, and outputs of a college.

But whether the production process results in a tangible good such as a car or an intangible service such as cable television, it always converts inputs into outputs. A cabinetmaker combines wood, tools, and skill to create finished kitchen cabinets for a new home. A transit system combines buses, trains, and employees to create its output: passenger transportation. Both of these production processes create utility.

This chapter describes the process of producing goods and services. It looks at the importance of production and operations management and discusses the new technologies that are transforming the production function. It then discusses the tasks of the production and operations manager, the importance of quality, and the methods businesses use to ensure high quality.

FIGURE
10.2 Typical Production Systems

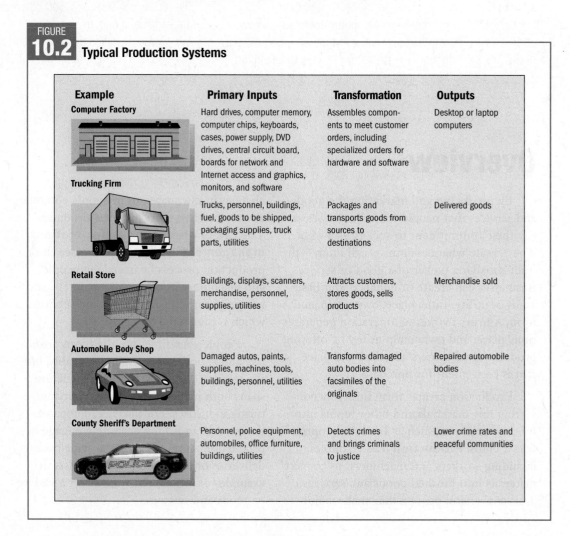

Example	Primary Inputs	Transformation	Outputs
Computer Factory	Hard drives, computer memory, computer chips, keyboards, cases, power supply, DVD drives, central circuit board, boards for network and Internet access and graphics, monitors, and software	Assembles components to meet customer orders, including specialized orders for hardware and software	Desktop or laptop computers
Trucking Firm	Trucks, personnel, buildings, fuel, goods to be shipped, packaging supplies, truck parts, utilities	Packages and transports goods from sources to destinations	Delivered goods
Retail Store	Buildings, displays, scanners, merchandise, personnel, supplies, utilities	Attracts customers, stores goods, sells products	Merchandise sold
Automobile Body Shop	Damaged autos, paints, supplies, machines, tools, buildings, personnel, utilities	Transforms damaged auto bodies into facsimiles of the originals	Repaired automobile bodies
County Sheriff's Department	Personnel, police equipment, automobiles, office furniture, buildings, utilities	Detects crimes and brings criminals to justice	Lower crime rates and peaceful communities

The Strategic Importance of Production

Along with marketing and finance, production is a vital business activity. Without products to sell, companies cannot generate money to pay their employees, lenders, and stockholders. And without the profits from products, firms quickly fail. The production process is just as crucial in nonprofit organizations such as St. Jude Children's Research Hospital or Goodwill Industries because the goods or services they offer justify their existence. Effective production and operations management can lower a firm's costs of production, boost the quality of its goods and services, allow it to respond dependably to customer demands, and enable it to renew itself by providing new products. Let's look at the differences among mass, flexible, and customer-driven production.

Mass Production

From its beginnings as a colonial supplier of raw materials to Europe, the United States has evolved into an industrial giant. Much of this change has resulted from **mass production**, a system for manufacturing products in large quantities through effective combinations of employees with specialized skills, mechanization, and standardization. Mass production makes outputs (goods and services) available in large quantities at lower prices than individually crafted items would cost. Mass production brought cars, computers, televisions, books, and even homes to the majority of the population. William Levitt made homes affordable to the average American from the 1940s to the 1960s by removing the most expensive item—the basement—and mass-producing them at the rate of one every 16 minutes. Levitt's first planned community, in Levittown, New York, brought his company a profit of about $5 million more than 60 years ago.[2]

Mass production begins with the specialization of labor, dividing work into its simplest components so that each worker can concentrate on performing one task. By separating jobs into small tasks, managers create conditions for high productivity through mechanization, in which machines perform much of the work previously done by people. Standardization, the third element of mass production, involves producing uniform, interchangeable goods and parts. Standardized parts simplify the replacement of defective or worn-out components. For instance, if your car's windshield wiper blades wear out, you can easily buy replacements at a local auto parts store such as AutoZone.

A logical extension of these principles of specialization, mechanization, and standardization led to development of the *assembly line*. This manufacturing method moves the product along a conveyor belt past a number of workstations, where workers perform specialized tasks such as welding, painting, installing individual parts, and tightening bolts. Henry Ford's application of this concept revolutionized auto assembly. Before the assembly line, it took Ford's workers 12 hours to assemble a Model T car. But with an assembly line, it took just 1.5 hours to make the same car. Not surprisingly, dozens of other industries soon adopted the assembly-line process.

Although mass production has important advantages, it has limitations, too. While mass production is highly efficient for producing large numbers of similar products, it is highly inefficient when producing small batches of different items. This trade-off might tempt some companies to focus on efficient production methods rather than on making what customers really want. In addition, the labor specialization associated with mass production can lead to

mass production a system for manufacturing products in large quantities through effective combinations of employees, with specialized skills, mechanization, and standardization.

This Honda auto plant uses flexible production techniques to turn out several different models. The auto industry, which developed mass-production methods, now finds flexible production to be more efficient.

boring jobs, because workers keep repeating the same task. To improve their competitive capabilities, many firms adopt flexible production and customer-driven production systems. These methods won't replace mass production in every case, but in many instances might lead to improved product quality and greater job satisfaction. It might also enhance the use of mass production.

Flexible Production

While mass production is effective for creating large quantities of one item, *flexible production* is usually more cost-effective for producing smaller runs. Flexible production can take many forms, but it generally involves using information technology to share the details of customer orders, programmable equipment to fulfill the orders, and skilled people to carry out whatever tasks are needed to fill a particular order. This system is even more beneficial when combined with lean production methods that use automation and information technology to reduce requirements for workers and inventory. Flexible production requires a lot of communication among everyone in the organization.

Flexible production is now widely used in the auto industry; whereas Henry Ford revolutionized auto production in the early 20th century, automakers such as Toyota and Honda are innovating with new methods of production. Changing from mass production to flexible production has enabled these companies to produce different kinds of cars at the same plant. Honda's flexible manufacturing plant in Marysville, Ohio, now builds more than 90 percent of all Honda sedans sold in the United States. The facility accomplishes this through team-based operations, relying on the expertise and knowledge of individual workers to innovate and improve manufacturing processes.[3]

Customer-Driven Production

A *customer-driven production* system evaluates customer demands in order to make the connection between products manufactured and products bought. Many firms use this approach with great success. One method is to establish computer links between factories and retailers' scanners, using data about sales as the basis for creating short-term forecasts and designing production schedules to meet those forecasts. Another approach to customer-driven production systems is simply not to make the product until a customer orders it—whether it's a taco or a computer. Massachusetts-based Shibui Designs creates custom-made dresses in high-end fabrics for female executives and other women over 40. Each item of clothing is custom cut and fit to a single customer's measurements. Founder Elizabeth Nill, who is over 60, started the business because she couldn't find clothing that fit well.[4]

LECTURE ENHANCER:
Do you think Chipotle is an example of customer-driven production? Can you provide other examples?

Assessment Check ☑

1. What is mass production?
2. What is the difference between flexible production and customer-driven production?

[2] Production Processes

Not surprisingly, the production processes and time required to make an Apple iPad and a gallon of gasoline are different. Production processes use either an analytic or synthetic system; time requirements call for either a continuous or an intermittent process.

An analytic production system reduces a raw material to its component parts in order to extract one or more marketable products. Petroleum refining breaks down crude oil into several marketable products, including gasoline, heating oil, and aviation fuel. When corn is processed, the resulting marketable food products include animal feed and corn sweetener.

A synthetic production system is the reverse of an analytic system. It combines a number of raw materials or parts or transforms raw materials to produce finished products. Canon's assembly line produces a camera by assembling various parts such as a shutter or a lens cap. Other synthetic production systems make drugs, chemicals, computer chips, and canned soup.

A continuous production process generates finished products over a lengthy period of time. The steel industry provides a classic example. Its blast furnaces never completely shut down except for malfunctions. Petroleum refineries, chemical plants, and nuclear power facilities also practice continuous production. A shutdown can damage sensitive equipment, with extremely costly results.

An intermittent production process generates products in short production runs, shutting down machines frequently or changing their configurations to produce different products. Most services result from intermittent production systems. For instance, accountants, plumbers, and dentists traditionally have not attempted to standardize their services because each service provider confronts different problems that require individual approaches. However, some companies, such as Jiffy Lube and H&R Block, offer standardized services as part of a strategy to operate more efficiently and compete with lower prices. McDonald's, well-known for its nearly continuous production of food, has moved toward a more intermittent production model. The fast-food chain invested millions in new cooking equipment to set up kitchens for preparing sandwiches quickly to order, rather than producing large batches ahead of time and keeping them warm under heat lamps.

3

Technology and the Production Process

Production continues to change rapidly as computer technologies develop. Many manufacturing plants are now "lights out" facilities that are completely automated—meaning no workers are required to build or make the products. While this signals a change in the types of jobs available in manufacturing, it also means that companies can design, produce, and adapt products more quickly to meet customers' changing needs.

Green Manufacturing Processes

More and more firms are pouring resources into the development of manufacturing processes that result in a reduction of waste, energy use, and pollution. Companies ranging in size from Walmart to the local café are finding ways to operate in a more sustainable manner—whether it is using biofuel to power a fleet of delivery trucks or eliminating unnecessary packaging, firms have begun to view the steps they take with pride. Chobani Greek Yogurt is manufactured in rural upstate New York with fresh ingredients from local dairy farms, reducing fuel consumption for refrigeration and transport. The yogurt contains no preservatives or artificial flavors, is made with milk free from synthetic growth hormones, and contains real fresh fruit.[5] Kraft Foods has achieved the goal of zero waste at 36 of its manufacturing plants around the world. See the "Going Green" feature for details.

LECTURE ENHANCER:
Is carbonated beverage production an analytic or synthetic production system?

LECTURE ENHANCER:
Is meat processing an analytic or synthetic production system?

CLASS ACTIVITY:
Ask students how the very high costs of a shutdown in a continuous production process might lead to poor or unethical decision-making by management.

Assessment Check ☑

1. What are the two main production systems?
2. What are the two time-related production processes?

Going Green

Kraft Foods' Recipe for Zero Waste

Kraft Foods, maker of Cadbury, Philadelphia Cream Cheese, Chips Ahoy, Cool Whip, Oreos, Maxwell House, and other brands, has achieved zero waste at 36 manufacturing plants in the United States and 12 other countries. "We're waging war on waste, one plant at a time," says its vice president for global sustainability.

Following employee suggestions, the company converts tons of food waste in California to animal feed, processes waste into energy for the local power grid in Wisconsin via an anaerobic digester, reuses shipping containers for coffee beans in Russia and turns coffee grounds into fertilizer, and recycles plastic packaging film into bags and buckets in Indonesia. In Vienna, tons of coffee bean husks are turned into power for local homes.

Waste management is only one of Kraft's sustainability drives, which include packaging, energy, water, and transportation and distribution. The company plans to reduce energy use, carbon dioxide emissions, water consumption, and manufacturing waste all by an additional 15 percent in the coming years. Judging by its achievements, which have placed it on the Dow Jones Sustainability Index seven years in a row, the company is well on its way.

Questions for Critical Thinking

1. Why does Kraft ask for employee suggestions on reducing waste?

2. Kraft switched a third of its snacks to foods with whole grains and lower sodium and calories. Should it continue shifting to healthier products? Why or why not?

Sources: Akhila Vijayaraghavan, "Kraft Uses Stakeholder Engagement to Achieve Zero Waste in 36 Plants," TriplePundit.com, February 6, 2012, www.triplepundit.com; Leslie Guevarra, "Kraft Achieves Zero Waste at 36 Food Plants Around the World," GreenBiz.com, February 2, 2012, www.greenbiz.com; Tilde Herrera, "Kraft's Recipe for Greener Mac-n-Cheese and Oreos," GreenBiz.com, May 16, 2011, www.greenbiz.com; "Kraft Foods on Dow Jones Sustainability Index Seventh Year in a Row," PR Newswire, September 9, 2011, www.prnewsire.com.

LEED (Leadership in Energy and Environmental Design) voluntary certification program administered by the U.S. Green Building Council, aimed at promoting the most sustainable construction processes available.

CLASS ACTIVITY: Ask students if a company's green efforts have positively affected their purchasing of that company's goods or services.

LECTURE ENHANCER: Name some industries where robots are used as part of the assembly line process.

Firms that are involved in construction—or are thinking of building new offices or manufacturing plants—are turning their attention to **LEED (Leadership in Energy and Environmental Design)** certification for their facilities. LEED is a voluntary certification program administered by the U.S. Green Building Council, aimed at promoting the most sustainable construction processes available. The LEED certification process is rigorous and involves meeting standards in energy savings, water efficiency, CO_2 emissions reduction, improved indoor environmental quality (including air and natural light), and other categories.[6]

Robots

A growing number of manufacturers have freed workers from boring, sometimes dangerous jobs by replacing them with robots. A *robot* is a reprogrammable machine capable of performing a variety of tasks that require the repeated manipulation of materials and tools. Robots can repeat the same tasks many times without varying their movements. Many factories use robots today to stack their products on pallets and shrink-wrap them for shipping. Boston Scientific, a firm that makes medical devices, uses robots made by Kiva in two of its distribution centers. The Gap also uses a Kiva robotic system for some of its warehousing operations.[7]

Historically, robots were most common in automotive and electronics manufacturing, but growing numbers of industries are adding robots to production lines as improvements in technology make them less expensive and more useful. Firms operate many different types of robots. The simplest kind, a pick-and-place robot, moves in only two or three directions as it picks up something from one spot and places it in another. So-called field robots assist people in nonmanufacturing, often hazardous, environments such as nuclear power plants, the international space station, and even battlefields. Police use robots to remotely dispose of suspected bombs. However, the same technology can be used in factories. Using vision systems, infrared sensors, and bumpers on mobile platforms, robots can automatically move parts or finished goods from one place to another, while either following or avoiding people, whichever is necessary to do the job. For instance, machine vision systems are being used more frequently for complex applications such as quality assurance in the manufacturing of medical devices. The advancements in machine vision components such as cameras, illumination systems, and processors have greatly improved their capabilities. Companies such as Texas-based National Instruments help customers around the work boost productivity, simplify development, and reduce time to market.[8]

Daniel Bringmann/iStockphoto

Remote-controlled robots are especially well suited for work in dangerous environments. This field robot, developed for use by bomb squads, can photograph suspicious-looking devices, move them to a safer location, and blow them up.

Computer-Aided Design and Manufacturing

A process called **computer-aided design (CAD)** allows engineers to design components as well as entire products on computer screens faster and with fewer mistakes than they could achieve working with traditional drafting systems. Using an electronic pen, an engineer can sketch three-dimensional (3-D) designs on an electronic drafting board or directly on the screen. The computer then provides tools to make major and minor design changes and to analyze the results for particular characteristics or problems. Engineers can put a new car design through a simulated road test to project its real-world performance. If they find a problem with weight distribution, for example, they can make the necessary changes virtually—without actually test-driving the car. With advanced CAD software, prototyping is as much "virtual" as it is "hands-on." Actual prototypes or parts aren't built until the engineers are satisfied that the required structural characteristics in their virtual designs have been met. Dentistry has benefited from CAD, which can design and create on-site such products as caps and crowns that fit a patient's mouth or jaw perfectly.[9]

The process of **computer-aided manufacturing (CAM)** picks up where the CAD system leaves off. Computer tools enable a manufacturer to analyze the steps that a machine must take to produce a needed product or part. Electronic signals transmitted to processing equipment provide instructions for performing the appropriate production steps in the correct order. Both CAD and CAM technologies are now used together at most modern production facilities. These so-called CAD/CAM systems are linked electronically to automatically transfer computerized designs into the production facilities, saving both time and effort. They also allow more precise manufacturing of parts.

Flexible Manufacturing Systems

A **flexible manufacturing system (FMS)** is a production facility that workers can quickly modify to manufacture different products. The typical system consists of computer-controlled machining centers to produce metal parts, robots to handle the parts, and remote-controlled carts to deliver materials. All components are linked by electronic controls that dictate activities at each stage of the manufacturing sequence, even automatically replacing broken or worn-out drill bits and other implements.

computer-aided design (CAD) process that allows engineers to design components as well as entire products on computer screens faster and with fewer mistakes than they could achieve working with traditional drafting systems.

computer-aided manufacturing (CAM) computer tools to analyze CAD output and enable a manufacturer to analyze the steps that a machine must take to produce a needed product or part.

LECTURE ENHANCER:
What are the advantages and disadvantages of robotic surgery in the medical field?

flexible manufacturing system (FMS) production facility that workers can quickly modify to manufacture different products.

LECTURE ENHANCER:
FMS is used by Toyota
Motors and Honda to
manufacture automobiles.
What do you see as the
benefits of using FMS in
this industry?

computer-integrated manufacturing (CIM) production system in which computers help workers design products, control machines, handle materials, and control the production function in an integrated fashion.

Assessment Check ✔

1. List some of the reasons businesses invest in robots.

2. What is a flexible manufacturing system (FMS)?

3. What are the major benefits of computer-integrated manufacturing (CIM)?

LECTURE ENHANCER:
What locations on streets
do you think are most
avoided by retailers and
why?

CLASS ACTIVITY:
Ask students what factors
were likely significant
causes for the automotive
industry to have been
located in Detroit during
that industry's first few
decades.

LECTURE ENHANCER:
In your state, what labor
skills might attract certain
businesses?

Flexible manufacturing systems have been enhanced by powerful new software that allows machine tools to be reprogrammed while they are running. This capability allows the same machine to make hundreds of different parts without the operator having to shut the machine down each time to load new programs. The software also connects to the Internet to receive updates or to control machine tools at other sites. And because the software resides on a company's computer network, engineers can use it to diagnose production problems any time, from anywhere they can access the network. Pharmaceutical companies are constantly looking for new ways to use flexible manufacturing. Asia—especially India, China, and Singapore—has become an important location for this and other innovations in manufacturing.[10]

Computer-Integrated Manufacturing

Companies integrate robots, CAD/CAM, FMS, computers, and other technologies to implement **computer-integrated manufacturing (CIM)**, a production system in which computers help workers design products, control machines, handle materials, and control the production function in an integrated fashion. This type of manufacturing does not necessarily imply more automation and fewer people than other alternatives. It does, however, involve a new type of automation organized around the computer. The key to CIM is a centralized computer system running software that integrates and controls separate processes and functions. The advantages of CIM include increased productivity, decreased design costs, increased equipment utilization, and improved quality.

CIM is widely used in the printing industry to coordinate thousands of printing jobs, some very small. CIM saves money by combining many small jobs into one larger one and by automating the printing process from design to delivery. [11]

4 | The Location Decision

The decision of where to locate a production facility hinges on transportation, human, and physical factors, as shown in Table 10.1. Transportation factors include proximity to markets and raw materials, along with availability of alternative modes for transporting both inputs and outputs. Automobile assembly plants are located near major rail lines. Inputs—such as engines, plastics, and metal parts—arrive by rail, and the finished vehicles are shipped out by rail. Shopping malls are often located next to major streets and freeways in suburban areas, because most customers arrive by car.

Physical variables involve such issues as weather, water supplies, available energy, and options for disposing of hazardous waste. Theme parks like Walt Disney World are often located in warm climates so they can be open and attract visitors year-round. A manufacturing business that wants to locate near a community must prepare an *environmental impact study* that analyzes how a proposed plant would affect the quality of life in the surrounding area. Regulatory agencies typically require these studies to cover topics such as the impact on transportation facilities; energy requirements; water and sewage treatment needs; natural plant life and wildlife; and water, air, and noise pollution.

Human factors in the location decision include an area's labor supply, local regulations, taxes, and living conditions. Management considers local labor costs, as well as the availability of workers with needed qualifications. Software makers and other computer-related firms concentrate in areas with the technical talent they need, including California's Silicon

10.1 Factors in the Location Decision

LOCATION FACTOR	EXAMPLES OF AFFECTED BUSINESSES
Transportation	
Proximity to markets	Baking companies and manufacturers of other perishable products, dry cleaners, hotels, other services
Proximity to raw materials	Paper mills
Availability of transportation alternatives	Brick manufacturers, retail stores
Physical Factors	
Water supply	Computer chip fabrication plants
Energy	Aluminum, chemical, and fertilizer manufacturers
Hazardous wastes	All businesses
Human Factors	
Labor supply	Auto manufacturers, software developers
Local zoning regulations	Manufacturing and distribution companies
Community living conditions	All businesses
Taxes	All businesses

Ian Dagnall/Alamy

Deciding where to locate a production facility can often depend on the weather. Some theme parks, such as Walt Disney World, are located in warm climates so they can be open and attract visitors year-round.

Hit & Miss

The Sun Is Shining Brighter in Senatobia

Mississippi is becoming a new hub of high-tech manufacturing. Two major manufacturers recently agreed to build facilities in the state. One of them, Twin Creeks Technologies, is locating its production facility in Senatobia. A manufacturer of solar panels, Twin Creeks is the state's first renewable solar technology producer, with manufacturing processes cleaner and greener than those used by other production plants. When completed, the plant will occupy 250,000 square feet and create more than 500 jobs.

Twin Creeks didn't go it alone. The State of Mississippi provided $50 million in loan assistance and partnered with the city of Senatobia to provide $4 million in infrastructure improvements. Twin Creeks considered 25 sites in seven states before deciding on Senatobia.

Twin Creeks is also working with Northwest Mississippi Community College and the University of Mississippi's Center for Manufacturing Excellence and School of Engineering to recruit engineers and other job candidates. Local residents hail the move: Unemployment in the area recently topped 13 percent.

Questions for Critical Thinking

1. Besides government incentives, what other factors did Twin Creeks likely consider in its decision to locate in Senotobia?

2. How does the community benefit from this decision? Could there be any drawbacks?

Sources: "Twin Creeks Technologies Introduces Hyperion: A Production System for Ultra-Thin Wafers," *Market Watch*, March 13, 2012, http://www.marketwatch.com; "Twin Creeks Officially Opens Solar Panel Manufacturing Plant," *Mississippi Business Journal*, http://www.msbusiness.com, accessed February 24, 2012; "Twin Creeks Technologies Breaks Ground on Solar Panel Manufacturing Facility in Senatobia, Miss.," press release, http://www.mississippi.org, accessed February 24, 2012; "Twin Creeks Technologies Locates Manufacturing Facility in Mississippi," Solarbuzz, http://www.solarbuzz.com, accessed February 24, 2012.

Valley, Boston, and Austin, Texas. By contrast, some labor-intensive industries have located plants in rural areas with readily available labor pools and limited high-wage alternatives. And some firms with headquarters in the United States and other industrialized countries have moved production off-shore in search of low wages. But no matter what type of industry a firm is in, a production and operations manager's facility location decision must consider the following factors:

- proximity to suppliers, warehouses, and service operations

- insurance and taxes

- availability of such employee needs as housing, schools, mass transportation, daycare, shopping, and recreational facilities

- size, skills, and costs of the labor force

- ample space for current and future needs of the firm

- distance to market for goods

- receptiveness of the community

- economical transportation for materials and supplies, as well as for finished goods

- climate and environment that matches the industry's needs and employees' lifestyle

- amount and cost of energy services

- government incentives.

A recent trend in location strategy is bringing production facilities closer to the final markets where the goods will be sold. One reason for this is reduced time and cost for shipping. Another reason is a closer cultural affinity between the parent company and supplier (in cases where production remains overseas). German automaker Volkswagen built a manufacturing plant near Chattanooga, Tennessee, to produce the newly redesigned Passat, a midsize sedan.

CLASS ACTIVITY:
Lead a discussion on the factors that exist in Silicon Valley that might explain why that area is attractive to so many technology companies.

Part 3 *Management: Empowering People to Achieve Business*

Engineered specifically for the U.S. market, the new design features a clean diesel fuel option and a larger interior than competing models. The Chattanooga plant recently became the first automobile production facility to earn LEED certification at the highest, platinum level.[12]

State and local governments may offer incentives to businesses that are willing to locate in their region. These incentives may take the form of tax breaks, agreements to improve infrastructure, and the like. The "Hit & Miss" feature describes how Twin Creeks Technologies teamed up with various agencies to bring a new solar panel plant to Senatobia, Mississippi.

Assessment Check ☑

1. How does an environmental impact study influence the location decision?

2. What human factors are relevant to the location decision?

LECTURE ENHANCER: What is most important—to plan, determine, implement, or control? Why?

CLASS ACTIVITY: Ask students which personality traits and skills they think would be needed to be an effective production manager.

5 The Job of Production Managers

Production and operations managers oversee the work of people and machinery to convert inputs (materials and resources) into finished goods and services. As Figure 10.3 shows, these managers perform four major tasks.

1. Plan the overall production process.

2. Determine the best layout for the firm's facilities.

3. Implement the production plan.

4. Control the manufacturing process to maintain the highest possible quality.

Part of the control process involves continuous evaluation of results. If problems occur, managers return to the first step and make adjustments.

Planning the Production Process

Production planning begins by choosing what goods or services to offer to customers. This decision is the essence of every company's reason for operating. Other decisions such as machinery purchases, pricing decisions, and selection of retail outlets all grow out of product planning. But with product planning, it's not enough to plan products that satisfy customers. Products must satisfy customers *and* be produced as efficiently and inexpensively as possible. So while marketing research studies determine consumer reactions to proposed products and estimate potential sales and profitability levels, production departments focus on planning the production process when they (1) convert original product ideas into final specifications and (2) design the most efficient facilities to produce those products.

FIGURE
10.3 Tasks of Production Managers

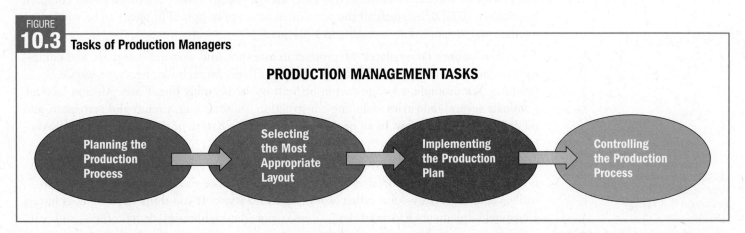

PRODUCTION MANAGEMENT TASKS

Planning the Production Process → Selecting the Most Appropriate Layout → Implementing the Production Plan → Controlling the Production Process

It is important for production managers to understand how a project fits into the company's structure because this will affect the success of the project. In a traditional manufacturing organization, each production manager is given a specific area of authority and responsibility such as purchasing or inventory control. One drawback to this structure is that it may actually pit the purchasing manager against the inventory control manager. As more organizations have moved toward team-oriented structures, some organizations assign team members to specific projects reporting to the production manager. Each team is responsible for the quality of its products and has the authority to make changes to improve performance and quality. The major difference between the two approaches is that all workers on teams are responsible for their output, and teamwork avoids the competitiveness between managers often found in traditional structures.

Determining the Facility Layout

The next production management task is determining the best layout for the facility. An efficient facility layout can reduce material handling, decrease costs, and improve product flow through the facility. This decision requires managers to consider all phases of production and the necessary inputs at each step. Figure 10.4 shows three common layout designs: process, product, and fixed-position layouts. It also shows a customer-oriented layout typical of service providers' production systems.

A *process layout* groups machinery and equipment according to their functions. The work in process moves around the plant to reach different workstations. A process layout often facilitates production of a variety of nonstandard items in relatively small batches. Its purpose is to process goods and services that have a variety of functions. For instance, a typical machine shop generally has separate departments where machines are grouped by functions such as grinding, drilling, pressing, and lathing. Process layouts accommodate a variety of production functions and use general-purpose equipment that can be less costly to purchase and maintain than specialized equipment.

A *product layout*, also referred to as an assembly line, sets up production equipment along a product-flow line, and the work in process moves along this line past workstations. This type of layout efficiently produces large numbers of similar items, but it may prove inflexible and able to accommodate only a few product variations. Although product layouts date back at least to the Model T assembly line, companies are refining this approach with modern touches. Many auto manufacturers continue to use a product layout, but robots perform many of the activities that humans once performed. Automation overcomes one of the major drawbacks of this system—unlike humans, robots don't get bored doing a dull, repetitive job. European automaker Holland Car PLC uses an assembly-line approach called complete knockdown (CKD), in which all the parts of an auto are imported in pieces to be welded, painted, and assembled at its facility in Ethiopia.[13]

A *fixed-position layout* places the product in one spot, and workers, materials, and equipment come to it. This approach suits production of very large, bulky, heavy, or fragile products. For example, a bridge cannot be built on an assembly line. Fixed-position layouts dominate several industries including construction, shipbuilding, aircraft and aerospace, and oil drilling, to name a few. In all of these industries, the nature of the product generally dictates a fixed-position layout.

Service organizations also must decide on appropriate layouts for their production processes. A service firm should arrange its facilities to enhance the interactions between customers and its services—also called *customer-oriented layout*. If you think of patients as inputs, a hospital implements a form of the process layout. Banks, libraries, dental offices, and hair

FIGURE
10.4 Basic Facility Layouts

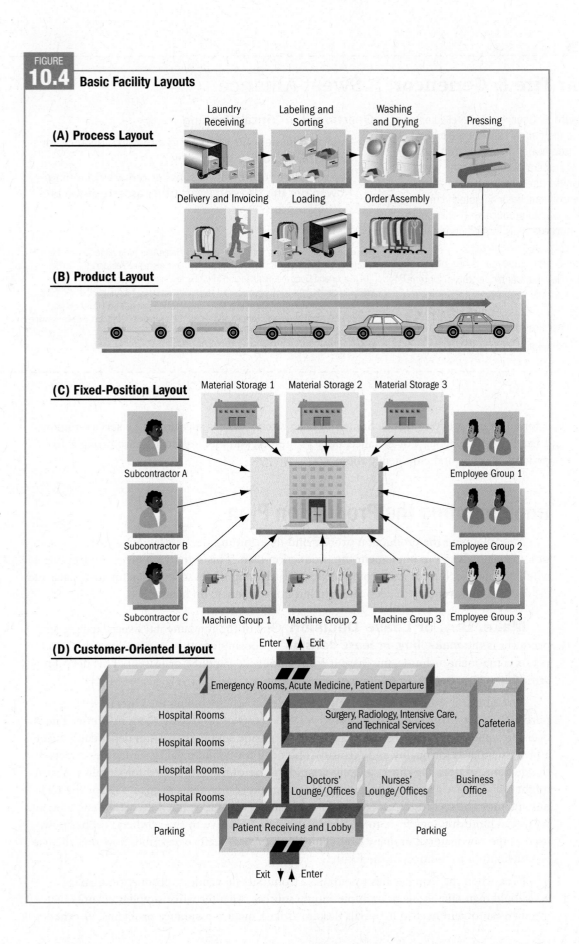

(A) Process Layout

Laundry Receiving → Labeling and Sorting → Washing and Drying → Pressing

Delivery and Invoicing ← Loading ← Order Assembly

(B) Product Layout

(C) Fixed-Position Layout

Material Storage 1   Material Storage 2   Material Storage 3

Subcontractor A

Subcontractor B

Subcontractor C   Machine Group 1   Machine Group 2   Machine Group 3

Employee Group 1

Employee Group 2

Employee Group 3

(D) Customer-Oriented Layout

Enter ▼ ▲ Exit

Emergency Rooms, Acute Medicine, Patient Departure

Hospital Rooms

Surgery, Radiology, Intensive Care, and Technical Services   Cafeteria

Hospital Rooms

Hospital Rooms

Doctors' Lounge/Offices   Nurses' Lounge/Offices   Business Office

Hospital Rooms

Parking   Patient Receiving and Lobby   Parking

Exit ▼ ▲ Enter

Goodyear Tire & Genencor: A Sweet Alliance

For years, tire manufacturers such as Goodyear have relied on synthetic rubber as a supplement to the natural rubber used in making tires. The basis of synthetic rubber, isoprene, is a volatile, toxic hydrocarbon produced during the refining of crude oil. While isoprene is bad for the environment, until recently, manufacturers had few alternatives.

However, researchers at Genencor, an industrial biotech firm in Rochester, New York, have devised a way to produce synthetic rubber from sugar. The product, called BioIsoprene™, is formed during the fermentation of sugar cane, corn, corncobs, and switch grass.

Manufacturing 200 million tires a year, Goodyear is one of the world's largest users of isoprene, so the eventual move to BioIsoprene™ will be significant. The company has already begun manufacturing "concept tires" using the substance. This collaboration of research and manufacturing entities to create greener tires from renewable materials promises to yield a win-win for everyone, particularly consumers.

Questions for Critical Thinking

1. Describe the benefits of creating a research alliance for future raw materials or supplies.

2. Investing in a future with a supplier requires planning. How might this decision affect other aspects of the production process?

Sources: "Revolutionary Technology Promises Green Tires for a More Sustainable Future," *Clean Technology*, http://www.azocleantech.com, accessed February 24, 2012; "Genencor and Goodyear Partnering on Process to Develop BioIsoprene from Sugars," *Green Car Congress*, http://www.greencarcongress.com, accessed February 24, 2012; "On the Road to Sweet Tires Made with a More Sustainable Process," *Physorg.com*, http://www.physorg.com, accessed February 24, 2012; "BioIsoprene™ Product Begins Flowing from Genencor to Goodyear," *The Auto Channel*, http://www.theautochannel.com, accessed February 24, 2012.

CLASS ACTIVITY:
Ask students what type of a layout the Apple stores utilize.

salons also use process layouts. Sometimes the circumstances surrounding a service require a fixed-position layout. For instance, doctors, nurses, and medical devices are brought to patients in a hospital emergency room.

Implementing the Production Plan

After planning the production process and determining the best layout, a firm's production managers begin to implement the production plan. This activity involves (1) deciding whether to make, buy, or lease components; (2) selecting the best suppliers for materials; and (3) controlling inventory to keep enough, but not too much, on hand.

make, buy, or lease decision choosing whether to manufacture a product or component in-house, purchase it from an outside supplier, or lease it.

Make, Buy, or Lease Decision One of the fundamental issues facing every producer is the **make, buy, or lease decision**—choosing whether to manufacture a product or component in-house, purchase it from an outside supplier, or lease it. This decision is critical in many contemporary business situations.

Several factors affect the make, buy, or lease decision, including the costs of leasing or purchasing parts from vendors compared with the costs of producing them in-house. The decision sometimes hinges on the availability of outside suppliers that can dependably meet a firm's standards for quality and quantity. The need for confidentiality sometimes affects the decision, as does the short- or long-term duration of the firm's need for supplies. A firm might not yet have the technology to produce certain components or materials, or the technology might be too costly. Goodyear Tire & Rubber Co. has teamed up with Genencor, an industrial biotechnology firm, to develop a cleaner alternative to the synthetic rubber now used as the raw material in many tires. The "Hit & Miss" feature describes how this alliance is contributing to the tires of the future.

Even when the firm decides to purchase from outside vendors, production managers should maintain access to multiple supply sources. An alternative supplier ensures that the firm can obtain needed materials despite strikes, quality-assurance problems, or other situations that may affect inputs. Outsourcing has its disadvantages. The main reasons companies say they use outsourcing is to reduce costs and focus on their core business activities, but outsourcing also may trigger layoffs and compromise quality.

In an industry where outsourcing is common, American Apparel chooses to keep all of its clothing production in the metropolitan Los Angeles area. Though the firm pays higher wages than rivals who outsource to other countries, American Apparel is able to offer quicker response times and maintain higher quality and better inventory control.[14]

Selection of Suppliers Once a company decides what inputs to purchase, it must choose the best vendors for its needs. To make this choice, production managers compare the quality, prices, dependability of delivery, and services offered by competing companies. Different suppliers may offer virtually identical quality levels and prices, so the final decision often rests on factors such as the firm's experience with each supplier, speed of delivery, warranties on purchases, and other services.

For a major purchase, negotiations between the purchaser and potential vendors may stretch over several weeks or even months, and the buying decision may rest with a number of colleagues who must say yes before the final decision is made. The choice of a supplier for an industrial drill press, for example, may require a joint decision by the production, engineering, purchasing, and quality-control departments. These departments often must reconcile their different views to settle on a purchasing decision.

The Internet has given buyers powerful tools for finding and comparing suppliers. Buyers can log on to business exchanges to compare specifications, prices, and availability. Ariba, with headquarters in California, offers organizations online software and other tools that allow them to source from a worldwide network of suppliers, buying an estimated $548 million in goods and services daily.[15]

Firms often purchase raw materials and component parts on long-term contracts. If a manufacturer requires a continuous supply of materials, a one-year or two-year contract with a vendor helps ensure availability. Today, many firms are building long-term relationships with suppliers and slashing the number of companies with which they do business. At the same time, they are asking their vendors to expand their roles in the production process.

Networking provides a way for production managers to learn about suppliers and get to know them personally. Trade shows, conferences, seminars, and other meetings enable managers to meet vendors, competitors, and colleagues.

Inventory Control Production and operations managers' responsibility for **inventory control** requires them to balance the need to keep stock on hand to meet demand against the costs of carrying inventory. Among the expenses involved in storing inventory are warehousing costs, taxes, insurance, and maintenance. Firms waste money if they hold more inventory than they need. On the other hand, having too little inventory on hand may result in a shortage of raw materials, parts, or goods for sale that could lead to delays and unhappy customers.

Firms stand to lose business when they miss promised delivery dates or turn away orders. Having an efficient inventory control system can save customers and money. Many firms maintain *perpetual inventory* systems to continuously monitor the amounts and locations of their stock. Such inventory control systems typically rely on computers, and many automatically generate orders at the appropriate times. Many supermarkets link their scanning devices to perpetual inventory systems that reorder needed merchandise without human interaction. As the system records a shopper's purchase, it reduces the inventory count stored in the computer. Once inventory on hand drops to a predetermined level, the system automatically reorders the merchandise. Roundy's Supermarkets, headquartered in Wisconsin, uses a software system called SoftGrocer Inventory Management throughout its 159-store chain to manage its stock. The system is responsible for ordering and receiving inventory as well as counting and picking inventory in stockrooms. In addition, the software updates and verifies perpetual inventory balances. The software helps Roundy's avoid running out of items and keeps inventory at optimal levels. [16]

Some companies go further and hand over their inventory control functions to suppliers. This concept is known as *vendor-managed inventory*. Chicago-based Elkay, the nation's leading manufacturer of stainless-steel sinks, uses a software program created by Datalliance, an independent VMI service provider, to better serve its distributor customers.[17]

Just-in-Time Systems

A **just-in-time (JIT) system** implements a broad management philosophy that reaches beyond the narrow activity of inventory control to influence the entire system of production and operations management. A JIT system seeks to eliminate anything that does not add value in operations activities by providing the right part at the right place at just the right time—right before it is needed in production.

JIT systems are being used in a wide range of industries, including medical supplies. Seattle Children's Hospital uses a two bin system called Demand Flow to manage the distribution of its supplies, equipment, and clinical materials. The Demand Flow system distributes supplies in a two bin, low unit of measure (LUM) system, where supplies are delivered in the right quantity and at the right time, removing the clinician from the ordering process. Unlike other distribution systems, Demand Flow monitors inventory turns of the supply bins at the point of use, where a more traditional distribution system monitors usage at the warehouse. Demand Flow enables Seattle Children's to monitor performance of the supplies within the bins so the bins can be right sized at the point of use, eliminating supply stock-outs and stale inventory. The hospital partners with its key distributors to deploy the system. While the hospital does keep an inventory of certain emergency supplies on hand, the rest are distributed on a JIT basis, saving the hospital more than $2.5 million in its first year.[18]

Production using JIT shifts much of the responsibility for carrying inventory to vendors, which operate on forecasts and keep stock on hand to respond to manufacturers' needs. Suppliers that cannot keep enough high-quality parts on hand may be assessed steep penalties by purchasers. Another risk of using JIT systems is what happens if manufacturers underestimate demand for a product. Strong demand will begin to overtax JIT systems, as suppliers and their customers struggle to keep up with orders with no inventory cushion to tide them over.

Materials Requirement Planning

Besides efficiency, effective inventory control requires careful planning to ensure the firm has all the inputs it needs to make its products. How do production and operations managers coordinate all of this information? They rely on **materials requirement planning (MRP)**, a computer-based

Courtesy Seattle Children's Hospital

JIT inventory systems are used in a wide range of industries, including the healthcare field. Seattle Children's Hospital uses a JIT system to manage distribution of its supplies and other materials.

production planning system that lets a firm ensure that it has all the parts and materials it needs to produce its output at the right time and place and in the right amounts.

Production managers use MRP programs to create schedules that identify the specific parts and materials required to produce an item. These schedules specify the exact quantities needed and the dates on which to order those quantities from suppliers so that they are delivered at the correct time in the production cycle. A small company might get by without an MRP system. If a firm makes a simple product with few components, a telephone call may ensure overnight delivery of crucial parts. For a complex product, however, such as a high-definition TV or an aircraft, longer lead times are necessary.

Turtle Wax Ltd., an Illinois manufacturer of car care products including Turtle Wax, Color Magic, and Clear Vue, uses MRP software for a better picture of its operations. The software provides immediate production summaries, inventory levels, and sales and stock forecasts.[19]

[6] Controlling the Production Process

The final task of production and operations managers is controlling the production process to maintain the highest possible quality. **Production control** creates a well-defined set of procedures for coordinating people, materials, and machinery to provide maximum production efficiency. Suppose that a watch factory must produce 80,000 watches during October. Production control managers break down this total into a daily production assignment of 4,000 watches for each of the month's 20 working days. Next, they determine the number of workers, raw materials, parts, and machines the plant needs to meet the production schedule. Similarly, a manager in a service business such as a restaurant must estimate how many dinners the outlet will serve each day and then determine how many people are needed to prepare and serve the food, as well as what food to purchase.

Figure 10.5 illustrates production control as a five-step process composed of planning, routing, scheduling, dispatching, and follow-up. These steps are part of the firm's overall emphasis on total quality management.

Production Planning

The phase of production control called *production planning* determines the amount of resources (including raw materials and other components) an organization needs to produce a certain output. The production planning process develops a bill of materials that lists all needed parts and materials. By comparing information about needed parts and materials with the firm's perpetual inventory data, purchasing staff can identify necessary purchases. Employees or automated systems establish delivery schedules to provide needed parts and materials when required during the production process. Production planning also ensures

Assessment Check ✔

1. List the four major tasks of production and operations managers.
2. What is the difference between a traditional manufacturing structure and a team-based structure?
3. What factors affect the make, buy, or lease decision?

production control creates a well-defined set of procedures for coordinating people, materials, and machinery to provide maximum production efficiency.

LECTURE ENHANCER: What control steps can you see that McDonald's takes to provide uniform quality and control costs?

FIGURE 10.5 Steps in Production Control

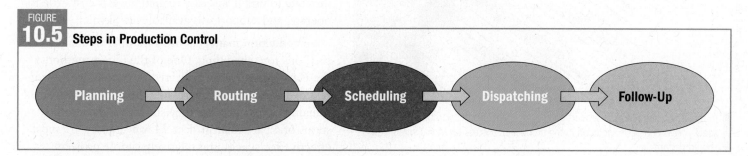

Planning → Routing → Scheduling → Dispatching → Follow-Up

LECTURE ENHANCER: How would an unexpected spike in product demand affect human resources?

the availability of needed machines and personnel. Workers at a Wilson Sporting Goods Company factory in Ohio have made every football ever used in a Super Bowl game. Each January, production begins; the footballs are about 70 percent complete before the final playoff games are decided. Once the Super Bowl teams emerge and workers know which two team names will be printed on the balls, production goes into overdrive. The plant makes 228 official game balls and around 15,000 replicas for sale to fans.[20]

Although material inputs contribute to service-production systems, production planning for services tends to emphasize human resources more than materials.

Routing

Another phase of production control, called *routing*, determines the sequence of work throughout the facility and specifies who will perform each aspect of the work at what location. Routing choices depend on two factors: the nature of the good or service and the facility layouts discussed earlier in the chapter—product, process, fixed position, or customer oriented. JETCAM is a firm headquartered in Monaco that provides routing software to the aerospace composite industry, in which quality and accuracy is absolutely critical. One feature of the software is that it allows instructions for processes to be provided automatically instead of keyed in by workers—thus avoiding errors.[21]

Scheduling

In the *scheduling* phase of production control, managers develop timetables that specify how long each operation in the production process takes and when workers should perform it. Efficient scheduling ensures that production will meet delivery schedules and make efficient use of resources.

Scheduling is important whether the product is complex or simple to produce and whether it is a tangible good or a service. A pencil is simpler to produce than a computer, but each production process has scheduling requirements. A stylist may take 25 minutes to complete each haircut with just one or two tools, whereas every day a hospital has to schedule procedures and treatments ranging from X-rays to surgery to follow-up appointments. Sleepmaster is an Australian-based manufacturer of bedding products that recently moved some of its production offshore to China. Although the Chinese factory is completely owned and managed by Sleepmaster, the firm's MRP system did not have adequate scheduling capacity, and Chinese workers were not familiar with the technology. So Sleepmaster's operations manager implemented a new scheduling program called Resource Manager because it was more intuitive to use; it was easy to configure; it cost little to operate; and support was available via Skype.[22]

Production managers use a number of analytical methods for scheduling. One of the oldest methods, the *Gantt chart*, tracks projected and actual work progress over time. Gantt charts like the one in Figure 10.6 remain popular because they show at a glance the status of a particular project. However, they are most effective for scheduling relatively simple projects.

Andrew Houghton/iStockphoto

In the scheduling phase of production control, managers develop timetables that specify how long each operation in the production process takes and when workers should perform it.

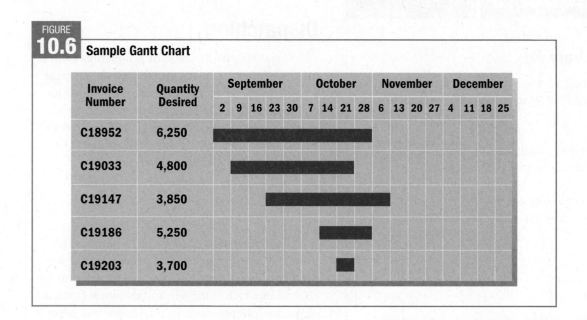

FIGURE 10.6 Sample Gantt Chart

Invoice Number	Quantity Desired	September					October				November				December			
		2	9	16	23	30	7	14	21	28	6	13	20	27	4	11	18	25
C18952	6,250	▬	▬	▬	▬	▬												
C19033	4,800		▬	▬	▬	▬	▬											
C19147	3,850			▬	▬	▬	▬	▬	▬									
C19186	5,250						▬	▬										
C19203	3,700							▬										

A complex project might require a *PERT (program evaluation and review technique)* chart, which seeks to minimize delays by coordinating all aspects of the production process. First developed for the military, PERT has been modified for industry. The simplified PERT diagram in Figure 10.7 summarizes the schedule for purchasing and installing a new robot in a factory. The heavy gold line indicates the *critical path*—the sequence of operations that requires the longest time for completion. In this case, the project cannot be completed in fewer than 17 weeks.

In practice, a PERT network may consist of thousands of events and cover months of time. Complex computer programs help production managers develop such a network and find the critical path among the maze of events and activities. The construction of a huge office building requires complex production planning of this nature.

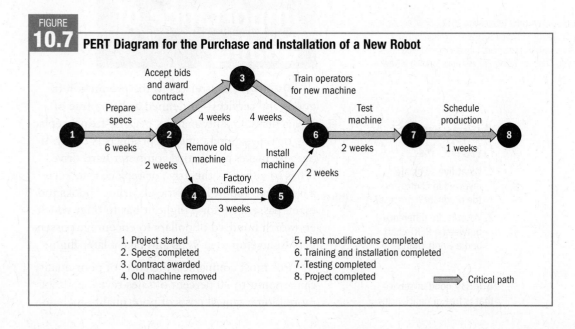

FIGURE 10.7 PERT Diagram for the Purchase and Installation of a New Robot

1. Project started
2. Specs completed
3. Contract awarded
4. Old machine removed
5. Plant modifications completed
6. Training and installation completed
7. Testing completed
8. Project completed

→ Critical path

BusinessEtiquette

Tips for Starting That New Job

It's natural to be a little nervous about starting a new job. But nerves shouldn't hamper your performance. Here are some tips to build your confidence on the first day.

1 *Look professional.* Be a little overdressed rather than underdressed in the beginning, to make a good first impression.

2 *Ask lots of questions.* Be sure you know what your boss expects you to do, both long-term and day-to-day. Check in periodically to confirm your understanding.

3 *Be innovative and creative.* But listen, too, and know when to offer your opinion and when not to.

4 *Build relationships from day one, and don't restrict yourself to co-workers at your own level or in your own department.* Network in every direction and nurture connections with people you click with.

5 *Don't know how to build relationships?* Start by offering to help someone.

6 *Show your confidence.* Don't be cocky or smug, but be positive and smile.

7 *Keep work and home separate.* Avoid personal phone calls and e-mails while on the job.

8 *Continue the company research you started before your interview.* You can never know enough about the organization you work for, its history, its culture, and its goals.

Good luck!

Sources: "Welcome to Your New Job," First 30 Days.com, February 6, 2012, www.first30days.com; William Donckets, "Starting a New Job: Some Tips for Early Success," Technorati.com, November 12, 2011, www.technorati.com; Michelle Tillis Lederman, Jobs@aol.com, September 18, 2011, http://jobs@aol.com; Jacquelyn Smith, "Tips for Young Professionals Starting a New Job," *Forbes,* January 14, 2011, www.forbes.com.

LECTURE ENHANCER:
How could a restaurant use follow-up meetings to improve its service and profitability?

LECTURE ENHANCER:
Can you think of any examples of companies that incurred additional costs because of product quality issues?

Assessment Check ✔

1. What five steps are involved in controlling the production process?
2. What is the difference between a PERT chart and a Gantt chart?

quality good or service that is free of deficiencies.

Dispatching

Dispatching is the phase of production control in which management instructs each department on what work to do and the time allowed for its completion. The dispatcher authorizes performance, provides instructions, and lists job priorities. Dispatching may be the responsibility of a manager or a self-managed work team.

Follow-Up

Because even the best plans sometimes fail, production managers need to be aware of any problems. *Follow-up* is the phase of production control in which managers and employees or team members spot problems in the production process and come up with solutions. Problems take many forms: machinery malfunctions, delayed shipments, and employee absenteeism can all affect production. The production control system must detect and report these delays to managers or work teams so they can adjust schedules and correct the underlying problems.

If your interest in any of the production planning and control functions has been piqued, you might be thinking about possible jobs in these areas. See the "Business Etiquette" feature for some tips about handling the first day on a new job.

7

Importance of Quality

Quality—as it relates to the production of goods and services—is defined as being free of deficiencies. Quality matters because fixing, replacing, or redesigning deficient products is costly. If Seagate makes a defective computer hard drive, it has to either fix the drive or replace it to keep a customer happy. If American Airlines books too many passengers for a flight, it has to offer vouchers worth hundred of dollars to encourage passengers to give up their seats and take a later flight.

For most companies, the costs of poor quality can amount to 20 percent of sales revenue, if not more. Some typical costs of poor quality include downtime, repair costs, rework, and employee turnover. Poor quality can also result in lost sales and a tarnished image. In an ironic twist, candymaker Candy Dynamics was forced to recall certain lots of its super sour candy bars called Toxic Waste Nuclear Sludge because it was discovered that they contained more than double the amount of lead considered allowable by law. It is possible that the candy, which is manufactured in Pakistan, was contaminated when ingredients were not correctly processed.[23]

One process that companies use to ensure that they produce high-quality products from the start is **benchmarking**—determining how well other companies perform business functions or tasks. In other words, benchmarking is the process of determining other firms' standards and best practices. Automobile companies routinely purchase each other's cars and take them apart to examine and compare the design, components, and materials used to make even the smallest part. They then make improvements to match or exceed the quality found in their competitors' cars. Companies may use many different benchmarks, depending on their objectives. For instance, organizations that want to make more money may compare their operating profits or expenses to those of other firms. Retailers concerned with productivity may benchmark sales per square foot.

It's important when benchmarking for a firm to establish what it wants to accomplish, what it wants to measure, and which company can provide the most useful benchmarking information. A firm might choose a direct competitor for benchmarking, or it might select a company in an entirely different industry—but one that has processes the firm wants to study and emulate.

benchmarking process of determining how well other companies perform business functions or tasks.

CLASS ACTIVITY: Ask students how the types of companies that a hospital might benchmark could improve the patient check-in process.

Quality Control

Quality control involves measuring output against established quality standards. Firms need such checks to spot defective products and to avoid delivering inferior shipments to customers. Standards should be set high enough to meet customer expectations. A 90 or 95 percent success rate might seem to be a good number, but consider what your phone service or ATM network would be like if it worked only 90 percent of the time. You would feel frustrated and inconvenienced, and would probably switch your account to another service provider or bank.

Manufacturing firms can monitor quality levels through visual inspections, electronic sensors, robots, and X-rays. Surveys can provide quality-control information to services. Negative feedback from customers or a high rejection rate on a product or component sends a signal that production is not achieving quality standards. Firms that outsource operations may face a greater challenge in monitoring quality and assuring customers of the quality of their goods or services, especially if they are highly visible companies such as airlines. The "Solving an Ethical Controversy" feature discusses recent concerns over the quality of multivitamins manufactured for U.S. companies in China.

Because the typical factory can spend up to half its operating budget identifying and fixing mistakes, a company cannot rely solely on inspections to achieve its quality goals. Instead, quality-driven production managers identify all processes involved in producing goods and services and work to maximize their efficiency. The causes of problems in the processes must be found and eliminated. If a company concentrates its efforts on better designs of products and processes with clear quality targets, it can ensure virtually defect-free production.

General Electric, Heinz, 3M, Sears, and the U.S. military are among the organizations that use the Six Sigma concept to achieve quality goals. *Six Sigma* means a company tries to make error-free products 99.9997 percent of the time—a tiny 3.4 errors per million opportunities. The goal of Six Sigma programs is for companies to eliminate virtually all defects in output, processes, and transactions. Motorola—also a Six Sigma firm—recently completed

quality control measuring output against established quality standards.

LECTURE ENHANCER: How might the standards for cake quality vary between a traditional bakery and a bakery that specializes in wedding cakes?

LECTURE ENHANCER: Have you ever participated in a customer survey on quality?

Solving an Ethical Controversy

Multivitamins Produced in China: Are Stricter Quality Controls Necessary?

Chinese-made multivitamins reportedly contain dangerous levels of lead and toxic bacteria—and are showing up in U.S. stores. Some people have called for stricter quality standards.

Should tighter quality controls be placed on Chinese-made goods?

PRO

1. According to the Chinese Ministry of Commerce, 85 percent of Chinese citizens rank quality concerns high for food and drugs made in their own country. Tighter controls would also benefit Chinese consumers.

2. Vitamins stamped "Made in Germany" or "Made in the USA" might still contain ingredients from China. Because it has already been demonstrated that these products contain high levels of toxic substances, tighter quality controls must be put into place.

CON

1. Many vitamins contain ingredients from multiple sources, so it is impossible to target China as the sole source of contamination.

2. Chinese production offers companies good value. With lower-cost labor and other services, savings can be passed along to the consumer.

Summary

Despite ongoing concerns, Swiss manufacturer Lonza recently announced it would locate its vitamin B3 manufacturing in China. Meanwhile, China is considering new production regulations on vitamin C—but with an emphasis on pricing power.

Sources: Steve Kelman, "Secret Chinese Vitamins," *Federal Computer Week*, http://www.fcw.com/blogs, accessed February 24, 2012; "China VC Industry to be Regulated in 2011," *Free Press Release*, January 26, 2011, http://www.free-press-release.com; "Lonza to Build Vitamin B3 Plant in China," *All About Feed*, May 4, 2010, http://www.allaboutfeed.net; "New Multivitamins Target Concern Over China's Quality Problems," *EIN*, April 27, 2010, http://www.einpresswire.com; "China Outsourcing: A Benefit to Companies Worldwide," *New Articles*, April 27, 2010, http://newarticles.co.tv.

an initiative to redesign and simplify much of its software architecture in order to improve operational efficiencies and cut costs by reducing redundant IT applications.[24]

ISO Standards

International Organization for Standardization, ISO organization whose mission is to develop and promote international standards for business, government, and society to facilitate global trade and cooperation.

For many goods and services, an important measure of quality is to meet the standards of the **International Organization for Standardization**, known as ISO for short—not an acronym but a shorter name derived from the Greek word *isos*, meaning "equal." Operating since 1947, ISO is a network of national standards bodies from 162 countries. Its mission is to develop and promote international standards for business, government, and society to facilitate global trade and cooperation. ISO has developed voluntary standards for everything from the format of banking and telephone cards to freight containers to paper sizes to metric screw threads. The U.S. member body of ISO is the American National Standards Institute.

The ISO 9000 family of standards gives requirements and guidance for quality management to help organizations ensure that their goods and services achieve customer satisfaction and also provide a framework for continual improvement. The ISO 14000 family of standards for environmental management helps organizations to ensure that their operations cause minimal harm to the environment and to achieve continual improvement of their environmental performance.

ISO 9001:2008 and ISO 14001:2004 respectively give the requirements for a quality management system and an environmental management system. Both can be used for certification, which means that the organization's management system (the way it manages its processes) is independently audited by a certification body (also known in North American as a registration body, or registrar) and confirmed as conforming to the requirements of the standard. The organization is then issued with an ISO 9001:2008 or an ISO 14001:2004 certificate.

It should be noted that certification is not a requirement of either standard, which can be implemented solely for the benefits it provides the organization and its customers. However, many organizations opt to seek certification because of the perception that an independent audit adds confidence in its abilities. Business partners, customers, suppliers, and consumers may prefer to deal with or buy products from a certified organization. Certifications have to be periodically renewed through accompanying audits.

A second point is that ISO itself develops standards but does not itself carry out auditing and certification. This is done independently of ISO by hundreds of certification bodies around the world. The certificates they issue carry their own logo, but not ISO's because the latter does not approve or control their activities.

Whether or not an organization decides to seek certification of its management system, many have reported significant benefits from implementing ISO's management system standards, such as increased efficiency, better teamwork, improved customer satisfaction, and reduced consumption of resources.[25]

Olivier Le Moal/iStockphoto

Many consumers prefer to buy from companies that are ISO-certified.

Assessment Check ✅

1. What are some ways in which a company can monitor the quality level of its output?

2. List some of the benefits of acquiring ISO 9000 certification.

LECTURE ENHANCER: What types of benefits would a global manufacturer obtain from using ISO-certified suppliers?

What's Ahead

Maintaining high quality is an important part of satisfying customers. Product quality and customer satisfaction are also objectives of the business function of marketing. The next part consists of three chapters that explore the many activities involved in customer-driven marketing. These activities include product development, distribution, promotion, and pricing.

Summary of Learning Objectives

1 Explain the strategic importance of production.

Production and operations management is a vital business function. Without a quality good or service, a company cannot create profits, and it soon fails. The production process is also crucial in a not-for-profit organization, because the good or service it produces justifies the organization's existence. Production and operations management plays an important strategic role by lowering the costs of production, boosting output quality, and allowing the firm to respond flexibly and dependably to customers' demands.

Assessment Check Answers ✅

1.1 What is mass production? Mass production is a system for manufacturing products in large quantities through effective combinations of employees with specialized skills, mechanization, and standardization.

1.2 What is the difference between flexible production and customer-driven production? Flexible production generally involves using technology to receive and fulfill orders and skilled people to carry out tasks needed to fill a particular order. Customer-driven production evaluates buyer demands in order to make the connection between products manufactured and products bought.

2. Identify and describe the production processes.

The four main categories of production processes are the analytic production system, which reduces a raw material to its component parts in order to extract one or more marketable products; the synthetic production system, which combines a number of raw materials or parts to produce finished products; the continuous production process, which generates finished items over a lengthy period of time; and the intermittent production process, which generates products in short production runs.

Assessment Check Answers ☑

2.1 What are the two main production systems? The two systems are analytic production and synthetic production.

2.2 What are the two time-related production processes? The two time-related production processes are the continuous production process and the intermittent production process.

3. Explain the role of technology in the production process.

Computer-driven automation allows companies to design, create, and modify products rapidly and produce them in ways that effectively meet customers' changing needs. Important design and production technologies include robots, computer-aided design (CAD), computer-aided manufacturing (CAM), and computer-integrated manufacturing (CIM). Many firms are pouring resources into the development of manufacturing processes that result in a reduction of waste, energy use, and pollution.

Assessment Check Answers ☑

3.1 List some of the reasons businesses invest in robots. Businesses use robots to free people from sometimes dangerous assignments and to move heavy items from one place to another in a factory.

3.2 What is a flexible manufacturing system (FMS)? An FMS is a production facility that workers can quickly modify to manufacture different products.

3.3 What are the major benefits of computer-integrated manufacturing (CIM)? The main benefits are increased productivity, decreased design costs, increased equipment utilization, and improved quality.

4. Identify the factors involved in a location decision.

Criteria for choosing the best site for a production facility fall into three categories: transportation, physical, and human factors. Transportation factors include proximity to markets and raw materials, along with availability of transportation alternatives. Physical variables involve such issues as water supply, available energy, and options for disposing

of hazardous wastes. Human factors include the area's labor supply, local regulations, taxes, and living conditions.

Assessment Check Answers ☑

4.1 How does an environmental impact study influence the location decision? An environmental impact study influences the location decision because it outlines how transportation, energy use, water and sewer treatment needs, and other factors will affect plants, wildlife, water, air, and other features of the natural environment.

4.2 What human factors are relevant to the location decision? Human factors include an area's labor supply, labor costs, local regulations, taxes, and living conditions.

5. Explain the job of production managers.

Production and operations managers use people and machinery to convert inputs (materials and resources) into finished goods and services. Four major tasks are involved. First, the managers must plan the overall production process. Next, they must pick the best layout for their facilities. Then they implement their production plans. Finally, they control the production process and evaluate results to maintain the highest possible quality.

Implementation involves deciding whether to make, buy, or lease components; selecting the best suppliers for materials; and controlling inventory to keep enough, but not too much, on hand.

Assessment Check Answers ☑

5.1 List the four major tasks of production and operations managers. The four tasks are planning overall production, laying out the firm's facilities, implementing the production plan, and controlling manufacturing to achieve high quality.

5.2 What is the difference between a traditional manufacturing structure and a team-based structure? In the traditional structure, each manager is given a specific area of authority. In a team-based structure, all workers are responsible for their output.

5.3 What factors affect the make, buy, or lease decision? The costs of leasing or purchasing parts from vendors, versus producing them in-house, the availability of dependable outside suppliers, and the need for confidentiality impact this decision.

6. Discuss controlling the production process.

The production control process consists of five steps: planning, routing, scheduling, dispatching, and follow-up. Quality control is an important consideration throughout this process. Coordination of each of these phases should result in high production efficiency and low production costs.

Assessment Check Answers ☑

6.1 What five steps are involved in controlling the production process? The five steps are planning, routing, scheduling, dispatching, and follow-up.

6.2 What is the difference between a PERT chart and a Gantt chart? PERT charts, which seek to minimize delays by coordinating all aspects of the production process, are used for more complex projects; Gantt charts, which track projected and actual work progress over time, are used for scheduling relatively simple projects.

⌐7⌐ Determine the importance of quality.

Quality control involves evaluating goods and services against established quality standards. Such checks are necessary to spot defective products and to see that they are not shipped to customers. Devices for monitoring quality levels of the firm's output include visual inspection, electronic sensors, robots, and X-rays. Companies are increasing the quality of their goods and services by using Six Sigma techniques and by becoming ISO 9000 and 14000 certified.

Assessment Check Answers ✓

7.1 What are some ways in which a company can monitor the quality level of its output? Benchmarking, quality control, Six Sigma, and ISO standards are ways of monitoring quality.

7.2 List some of the benefits of acquiring ISO 9000 certification. These standards define how a company should ensure that its products meet customers' requirements. Studies show that customers prefer to buy from companies that are ISO 9000 certified.

■ Business Terms You Need to Know

production 289	computer-aided design (CAD) 295
production and operations management 289	computer-aided manufacturing (CAM) 295
mass production 291	flexible manufacturing system (FMS) 295
LEED (Leadership in Energy and Environmental Design) 294	

computer-integrated manufacturing (CIM) 296	production control 305
make, buy, or lease decision 302	quality 308
inventory control 303	benchmarking 309
just-in-time (JIT) system 304	quality control 309
materials requirement planning (MRP) 304	International Organization for Standardization, ISO 310

■ Review Questions

1. What is utility? How does production create utility?

2. Why is production such an important business activity? In what ways does it create value for the company and its customers?

3. Why are firms now moving more toward flexible production and customer-driven production instead of mass production? Describe a product that you think would be better suited to flexible production or customer-driven production than mass production. Explain your choice.

4. Identify which production system—analytic or synthetic—applies to each of the following products:
   a. logging
   b. medical care
   c. soybean farming
   d. fishing
   e. microchips

5. Industries such as home construction and dentistry benefit from the use of CAD. In both of these, CAM could be used as well—in the manufacture of home components as well as dental implants, crowns, and the like. Choose another industry that seems like a candidate for the use of both CAD and CAM systems. Explain how the industry could use both.

6. SeaWorld has facilities in Florida, Texas, and California. What specific factors might have contributed to those choices?

7. What would be the best facility layout for each of the following?
   a. movie rental shop
   b. nail salon
   c. car wash
   d. sandwich shop

8. What might be the factors involved in the selection of suppliers for a steakhouse restaurant?

9. What is inventory control? Why is the management of inventory crucial to a company's success?

10. What is benchmarking? How can it help a firm improve the quality of its goods and services?

■ Projects and Teamwork Applications

1. Imagine that you recently became the owner of a popular ice cream shop. You want to attract more customers and ultimately expand the business. Choose the type of production process—continuous or intermittent—you think would best fit your business. Then create a plan outlining specifically how you would use this process and why it would help you achieve your goal as a business owner.

2. On your own or with a classmate, imagine that you've been hired to help a business group design a shopping mall. Taking into account the factors listed in the chapter, come

up with recommendations for where the mall should be located—and why. Present your plan to the class.

3. On your own or with a classmate, select one of the following businesses and sketch or describe the layout that you think would be best for attracting and serving customers:

   a. Mexican restaurant
   b. home furnishings store
   c. pet store
   d. motorcycle dealership
   e. attorney's office

4. Suppose you and your best friend decided to operate a house-painting service. Draft a production plan for your business, including the following decisions: (a) make, buy, or lease; (b) suppliers; and (c) inventory control.

5. Choose two firms for comparison (one firm should provide a good benchmarking opportunity for its production processes). Keep in mind that the benchmarking firm doesn't necessarily have to be in the same industry as the other selected firm. Present your decisions to the class and explain why you made both choices.

■ Web Assignments

1. **Just-in-time inventory management systems**. Go to the Web sites listed here to learn more about just-in-time inventory management systems. Make some notes on what you learn and bring them to class to participate in a class discussion.

   http://www.wisegeek.com/what-is-a-just-in-time-inventory.htm

   http://smallbusiness.dnb.com/manage/finances/12375503-1.html

   http://www.smcdata.com/software-choices/just-in-time-inventory-control-systems-1.html

2. **Plant location decision**. Using an Internet news service, such as Google news (http://news.google.com) or Yahoo! news (http://news.yahoo.com), search for information on a recent plant location decision. An example is Volkswagen's Chattanooga plant. Research the decision and then prepare a brief report outlining the factors that went into the firm's decision to locate the plant where it did.

   http://www.vw.com/vwbuzz/browse/en/us/detail/Volkswagen_Group_of_America_announces_it_will_produce_cars_in_Chattanooga/219

3. **ISO certification**. Visit the Web site of the International Organization for Standardization (http://www.iso.org). Click on "standards development" and then "processes and procedures." What are some of the products for which ISO standards are currently being developed?

Note: Internet Web addresses change frequently. If you don't find the exact sites listed, you may need to access the organization's home page and search from there or use a search engine such as Bing or Google.

CASE 10.1 — Macedonia: New Apparel Manufacturing Hub?

Tiny Macedonia, with its population of about 2 million, is becoming a hotbed of apparel manufacturing. Although textiles and clothing already make up one of the country's largest industries, Macedonian manufacturers are pushing for more, claiming their factories are working at only half-capacity.

Macedonia's 500 factories currently fulfill cut-make and cut-make-trim orders, but the goal is to offer full-package production, including design and domestic fabric procurement. Macedonian factories already supply major European brands and retailers with everything from jackets and coats to skirts, pants, and shirts. They're small by international standards—most employ from 30 to 500 workers—but what they can't provide in volume they offer in flexibility. While their competitors focus on high volume at the lowest cost, Macedonian manufacturers focus on short production runs and high quality. Unlike the competitive

environment in other countries, many of Macedonia's firms work together to serve the same customers. For example, Germany-based Okitex, a women's wear company, works with 20 factories in Macedonia to produce a complete collection of coats, blazers, and blouses. Location also works in Macedonia's favor. Deliveries to the United Kingdom arrive in three days; to Germany, about two days. With Macedonia located near the high-end fabric producers in Turkey and Italy, the average lead time from receipt of fabric to delivery of finished product is around three weeks. The small, flexible Macedonian factories can easily produce minimum orders of just 100 pieces per style and color—and have them at a customer's doorstep anywhere in western Europe in less than a month.

But Macedonia still faces some obstacles. Not all of its workers have the technical skills, and Macedonia is not yet a member of the European Union. But some factories are sending workers to Germany and other countries for training, and the country recently held an international business event sponsored by USAID (the U.S. Agency for International Development) and the Macedonian Competitiveness Project. During the event, 29 manufacturers showcased their capabilities to buyers that included such popular European brands as Topshop, Monsoon, Whistles, and BMB Clothing. Buyers were surprised—and impressed—by Macedonia's facilities, quality, flexibility, and location. So the next time you shop for clothing, check the label; it might read, "Made in Macedonia."

Questions for Critical Thinking

1. Do you think Macedonia's strategy will be successful in the long run? Why?
2. How might Macedonian apparel manufacturers attract U.S. buyers?

Sources: "Macedonian Apparel on Buyers' Radar," *Carana Corporation,* http://www.carana.com, accessed February 24, 2012; "Macedonia: Stip on Radar of UK Apparel Retailers," *Fibre2Fashion,* http://www.fibre2fashion.com, accessed February 24, 2012; Leonie Barrie, "Analysis: Macedonian Makers Eye Fast Fashion Partnerships," *Just-Style,* http://www.just-style.com, accessed February 24, 2012.

The F-35 Fighter Jet Flies Over Budget

CASE 10.2

What would you think if a product you ordered was delivered late, at twice the estimated cost, with testing only 20 percent complete and the necessary software delayed four years? What if it also proved to have structural flaws?

That's what happened to the U.S. government when it started taking delivery of F-35 fighter planes built by Lockheed Martin, using thousands of parts sourced from nine different countries and 48 states. The $133 million F-35 uses sophisticated stealth technology and is intended to serve the Air Force, the Marine Corps, the Navy, and several U.S. allies. However, many believe production delays, cost overruns, and quality problems have made it a prime candidate for Congressional budget cuts, which could further delay production and damage Lockheed Martin's revenue projections. The $45 billion manufacturer has been expecting to earn about 20 percent of its revenues from the F-35.

Some military administrators of the F-35 program are recommending production delays while testing continues, since the planes already manufactured are known to require costly repairs. The $400 billion program has been delayed twice so far, and the Pentagon recently decreased its original order of nearly 2,500 jets.

Questions for Critical Thinking

1. Why did Lockheed Martin choose a concurrent production strategy, building planes while testing was still ongoing?
2. What can Lockheed Martin do to compensate for government-mandated production delays that hamper its efforts to achieve cost-saving economies of scale?

Sources: Andrea Shalai-Esa, "Government Sees Lifetime Cost of F-35 Fighter at $1.51 Trillion," *Reuters,* http://www.reuters.com, accessed April 9, 2012; "F-35 Airplane Joint Strike Fighter," *The New York Times,* http://www.nytimes.com, accessed April 6, 2012; "Exclusive: Parachute Issue Grounds Some Lockheed F-35 Jets," *Reuters,* January 30, 2012, http://www.reuters.com; "Lockheed Martin Delivers First Two Marine Corps F-35s to Eglin," company press release, January 11, 2012, www.lockheedmartin.com; Walter Pincus, "F-35 Production a Troubling Example of Pentagon Spending," *The Washington Post,* December 26, 2011, http://www.washington-post.com; "Pentagon: Slow F-35 Production," DefenseTech.org, December 2, 2011, http://defensetech.org; Jim Wolf, "Lockheed F-35 Output Should Slow: Program Chief," *Reuters,* December 2, 2011, http://www.reuters.com; David Alexander, "F-35 Makes Headway Amid Criticism, U.S. Budget Crunch," *Reuters,* November 26, 2011, http://www.reuters.com; "Robert Levinson, "The F-35's Global Supply Chain," *Bloomberg Government Insider,* Fall 2011.

Kimpton Hotels Puts Green Initiatives to Work

CASE 10.3

It's one thing for a company to talk about green initiatives; it's quite another for the firm to put those initiatives into practice. Kimpton Hotels & Restaurants began putting green initiatives to work in its hotels and restaurants nearly 30 years ago, long before these practices became popular. Of course, it's the operations function of the business that implements this type of plan; it's the hotel manager, the dishwasher in the restaurant, the housekeeping staff, the front desk clerk. "*How* we do what we do defines us," observes Niki Leondakis, COO of Kimpton Hotels & Restaurants, which runs 50 boutique-style luxury hotels and restaurants across the U.S.

Although Kimpton began its green practices long ago, in 2005 the company launched a company-wide program called EarthCare in order to standardize these practices across all of its hotels and restaurants. Frank Kawecki, director of operations for Kimpton Restaurants in the Northeast, recalls that Kimpton's green efforts started first in the restaurants with the chefs, then spread. When the EarthCare program began, the company asked for volunteers from each property who were devoted to the green effort because they were already committed to the idea and could communicate best between management and staff. Volunteers ranged from bartenders to general managers who were willing to meet once a month. One of the first initiatives—which came from restaurant servers—was to eliminate imported bottled water, shifting instead to locally bottled water and the use of recycled water bottles.

As EarthCare has expanded throughout the company, standard guidelines have been set for nearly every facet of the firm's operation. Home office materials and procedures include shifting to online publication of many documents; using post-consumer recycled paper and eco-friendly inks for those documents that are printed; making hotel key-cards from recycled plastic; offering continuous education in green initiatives for staff, and more. At the hotels themselves, all in-room materials and bills are printed on recycled paper; phone books are offered by request only; all plumbing is water-efficient; lighting is LED or CFL, and subject to motion sensors; rooms are stocked with green-certified linens and towels; guest room soaps are made of natural ingredients, and carpet cleaning is done with non-toxic products. If the list seems endless, it nearly is—and the complexity of the operations management required to implement standards such as these is daunting.

Waste management is a category unto itself, with hotel and restaurant-wide recycling and reuse of everything from cardboard and paper to batteries and computers. Restaurants in particular present a huge challenge. "There's an enormous amount of waste from a lot of restaurants," observes Kawecki. "A lot of it can be composted, recycled, or reused. There can be a 40-percent savings in waste removal. Waste removal was traditionally a fixed expense that we have manipulated," through EarthCare. In addition to reducing waste and energy use, Kimpton restaurants purchase and serve as many certified organic products as possible, ranging from local produce and seafood to coffee, tea, and wine.

Saving the planet can be expensive. Running a business incurs costs as well. One of the challenges of implementing the EarthCare program is monitoring costs. "Green efforts can't compromise the experience for our guests and it can't cost our shareholders more money. If we go out of business, saving the planet as hoteliers goes away," notes Leondakis. "So that premise was very good in helping us decide what we would tackle first—water savings, energy savings." Whatever is good for the planet has to be good for the bottom line. One way that Kimpton Hotels meets this goal is by looking at ways for certain costs to offset each other. If purchasing recycled paper costs more, there might be a way to find savings in another area. "We put measurements on all of our efforts to see what impact they have on the bottom line," says Leondakis. "We've still been able to say that it saves us money."

Recently Kimpton Hotels announced its plan to seek third-party Green Seal certification on all 50 of its properties; 10 properties have already been certified. Green Seal certification involves an application process and evaluation similar to LEED certification, which the company is also seeking for its new or renovated properties. "It will be an ongoing work in progress forever," predicts Leondakis. But Kimpton Hotels has a head start.

Questions for Critical Thinking

1. Location is certainly a production factor for Kimpton Hotels & Restaurants, which are located in cities such as New York, Los Angeles, Boston, Chicago, and Seattle. What location factors might Kimpton managers consider when thinking about whether to acquire or build a new Kimpton hotel and restaurant?

2. According to the EarthCare program, what factors might a Kimpton restaurant chef or manager consider when selecting suppliers?

3. A daily staff meeting at a Kimpton hotel can be considered part of production control, contributing to the smooth running of the hotel. Who might attend such a meeting? What kinds of topics might they discuss?

4. Quality is top priority at Kimpton Hotels & Restaurants. What steps can a Kimpton hotel manager take to balance quality and the initiatives of the EarthCare program?

Sources: Kimpton Hotels Web site, http://www.kimptonhotels. com, accessed February 24, 2012; Matt Courtland, "Environmental Mission Statements: A List of Hotel Sustainability Policies," *Environmental Leader*, http://www.environmentalleader.com, accessed February 24, 2012; "Kimpton Hotels Aim for 100 Percent Green Seal Certification," *GreenerBuildings*, http://www.greenbiz.com, accessed February 24, 2012.

GREENSBURG, KS

No Time to Micromanage

"This is a stepping stone for me," thought Greensburg's town administrator, Steve Hewitt. Hewitt, who had grown up in Greensburg, had moved back home and taken a position in the tiny rural town of 1,500. Standing in what was left of his kitchen on the night of Friday, May 4, 2007, he realized he had gotten more than he bargained for.

Across town, Mayor Lonnie McCollum and his wife had survived by clinging to a mattress as the storm ravaged their home. A write-in candidate in the past election, McCollum had accepted the job and set out to revive the dying town. Among his many ideas, the most innovative had been green building. McCollum was no tree-hugger; he was simply looking for a way to save money on fuel and utilities, to conserve the town's resources.

Like many people in town, Hewitt and McCollum had no idea of the extent of the damage. They would later learn that the two-mile-wide F5 tornado drove right through the two-mile-wide town. By the end of the weekend, though, they knew that Greensburg was gone. At a press conference, McCollum announced that the town would rebuild, and would do it using green technology.

By May 2008, the town was on its third mayor since the disaster, but Hewitt was still the town administrator. He had expanded his staff from 20 to 35 people, establishing a full-time fire department, a planning department, and a community development department. Each week Hewitt spent hours giving interviews to reporters from all over the world. "He's very open as far as information," said Recovery Coordinator and Assistant Town Administrator Kim Alderfer. "He's very good about delegating authority. He gives you the authority to do your job. He doesn't have time to micromanage."

Meanwhile, residents Janice and John Haney had rebuilt their family farm on the outskirts of town. Although their new home, an earth berm structure, was full of energy-efficient features, Janice wasn't convinced that the plan to rebuild Greensburg using green technology was the right one. "I do worry that it will be a T-shirt slogan," said Haney. "I personally don't think the persons that are living in Greensburg right now are really committed to it. We didn't have a choice. You MUST go green. That's really not everybody's option." She added that many people feared higher taxes would force some families out of town.

Questions

After viewing the video, answer the following questions:

1. What kind of leader is Steve Hewitt?
2. How would you describe Greensburg's culture?
3. Do you believe that as town administrator, Hewitt had the right to impose green building codes on residents and businesses?
4. Perform a SWOT analysis of Greensburg's green initiative.

LAUNCHING YOUR
[Management Career]

3

Part 3, "Management: Empowering People to Achieve Business Objectives," covers Chapters 7 through 10, which discuss management, leadership, and the internal organization; human resource management, motivation, and labor–management relations; improving performance through empowerment, teamwork, and communication; and production and operations management. In those chapters, you read about top executives and company founders who not only direct their companies' strategy but lead others in their day-to-day tasks to keep them on track, middle managers who devise plans to turn the strategies into realities, and supervisors who work directly with employees to create strong teams that satisfy customers. An incredible variety of jobs is available to those choosing management careers. And the demand for managers will continue to grow. The U.S. Department of Labor estimates that managerial jobs will grow by about 7 percent over the next decade.[1]

So what kinds of jobs might you be able to choose from if you launch a management career? As you learned in Chapter 7, three types of management jobs exist: supervisory managers, middle managers, and top managers. Supervisory management, or first-line management, includes positions such as supervisor, office manager, department manager, section chief, and team leader. Managers at this level work directly with the employees who produce and sell a firm's goods and services.

Middle management includes positions such as general managers, plant managers, division managers, and regional or branch managers. They are responsible for setting objectives consistent with top management's goals and planning and implementing strategies for achieving those objectives.

Top managers include such positions as chief executive officer (CEO), chief operating officer (COO), chief financial officer (CFO), chief information officer (CIO), and executive vice president. Top managers devote most of their time to developing long-range plans, setting a direction for their organization, and inspiring a company's executives and employees to achieve their vision for the company's future. Top managers travel frequently between local, national, and global offices as they meet and work with customers, vendors, and company managers and employees.

Most managers start their careers in areas such as sales, production, or finance, so you likely will start in a similar entry-level job. If you do that job and other jobs well, you may be considered for a supervisory position. Then, if you are interested and have the technical, human, and conceptual skills to succeed, you'll begin your management career path. But what kinds of supervisory management jobs are typically available? Let's review the exciting possibilities.

Administrative services managers manage basic services—such as clerical work, payroll, travel, printing and copying, data records,

telecommunications, security, parking, and supplies—without which no organization could operate. On average, administrative service managers earn $84,000 a year.[2]

Construction managers plan, schedule, and coordinate the building of homes, commercial buildings such as offices and stores, and industrial facilities such as manufacturing plants and distribution centers. Unlike administrative service managers, who work in offices, construction managers typically work on building sites with architects, engineers, construction workers, and suppliers. On average, construction managers earn $94,000 a year.[3]

Food service managers run restaurants and services that prepare and offer meals to customers. They coordinate workers and suppliers in kitchens, dining areas, and banquet operations; are responsible for those who order and purchase food inventories; maintain kitchen equipment; and recruit, hire, and train new workers. Food service managers can work for chains such as Ruby Tuesday or Olive Garden, for local restaurants, and for corporate food service departments in organizations. On average, food service managers earn more than $52,000 a year.[4]

Human resource managers help organizations follow federal and local labor laws; effectively recruit, hire, train, and retain talented workers; administer corporate pay and benefits plans; develop and administer organizational human resource policies; and, when necessary, participate in contract negotiations or handle disputes. Human resource management jobs vary widely, depending on how specialized the requirements are. On average, human resource managers earn $108,000 a year.[5]

Lodging managers work in hotels and motels but also help run camps, ranches, and recreational resorts. They may oversee guest services, front desk, kitchen, restaurant, banquet, house cleaning, and maintenance workers. Because they are expected to help satisfy customers around the clock, they often work long hours and may be on call when not at work. On average, lodging managers earn about $54,000 a year.[6]

Medical and health services managers work in hospitals, nursing homes, doctors' offices, and corporate and university settings. They run departments that offer clinical services; ensure that state and federal laws are followed; and handle decisions related to the management of patient care, nursing, surgery, therapy, medical records, and financial payments. On average, medical and health service managers earn $93,000 a year.[7]

Purchasing managers lead and control organizational supply chains that ensure that companies have needed materials to produce the goods and services they sell, purchase materials at reasonable prices, and oversee deliveries when and where they are needed. Purchasing managers work with wholesale and retail buyers, buying goods that are then resold to others; purchasing agents, who buy supplies and raw materials for their organizations; and contract specialists, who negotiate and supervise purchasing contracts with key suppliers and vendors. On average, purchasing managers earn nearly $100,000 a year.[8]

Production managers direct and coordinate operations that manufacture goods. They work with employees who produce parts and assemble products, help determine which new machines should be purchased and when existing machines need maintenance, and are responsible for achieving production goals that specify the quality, cost, schedule, and quantity of units to be produced. On average, production managers earn almost $95,000 a year.[9]

Career Assessment Exercises in Management

1. The American Management Association is a global, not-for-profit professional organization that provides a range of management development and educational services to individuals, companies, and government agencies. Access the AMA's Web site at http://www.amanet.org. Explore the "Free Resources" link there (you will have to register). Pick an article or research area that interests you. Provide a one-page summary of the management issues discussed in the feature.

2. Go online to a business news service, such as Yahoo! News or Google News, or look at the business section of your local newspaper. Find a story relating to a first-line supervisor, middle manager, or top executive. Summarize that person's duties. What decisions does that person make and how do those decisions impact his or her organization?

3. Pick a supervisory management position from the descriptions provided here that interests you. Research the career field. What skills do you possess that would make you a good candidate for a management position in that field? What work and other experience do you need to help you get started? Create a list of both your strengths and weaknesses and formulate a plan to add to your strengths.

Chapter 11

Learning Objectives

1. Define marketing.
2. Discuss the evolution of the marketing concept.
3. Describe not-for-profit marketing and nontraditional marketing.
4. Outline the basic steps in developing a marketing strategy.
5. Describe marketing research.
6. Discuss market segmentation.
7. Summarize consumer behavior.
8. Discuss relationship marketing.

Customer-Driven Marketing

Fuse/Getty Images, Inc.

Walmart Introduces "Great for You"

Even in an economic downturn, research shows, customers want more from retailers than just low prices. So Walmart, already the undisputed leader in low-price retail, is identifying healthier, low-cost food choices for consumers by adding a bright green-and-white "Great for You" label to foods that meet the store's new set of nutritional quality standards. Fresh fruits and vegetables make the cut; sugary cereals don't. "There are no candy bars," said the company's senior vice president of sustainability. Lean cuts of meat, brown rice, and skim milk also qualify, and, after a long debate about their protein value versus their cholesterol content, so do eggs. About 20 percent of packaged food products sold in Walmart's nearly 3,600 stores—both its own brands and those of its suppliers— will eventually carry the "Great for You" label. The U.S. Food and Drug Administration (FDA) has yet to unveil an official food quality designation of its own. When it does, says Walmart's sustainability officer, "we'll be happy to make a switch. At this point we feel like our customers need help right now."

Walmart is also lowering the prices of about 350 healthier foods, such as low-fat peanut butter and fat-free salad dressings, making them as affordable as regular products to encourage customers to purchase them. The company has worked with suppliers to reduce the sugar, trans fats, and sodium in many of the prepared products it carries. And it reduced prices on fresh fruits and vegetables enough to save consumers more than $1 billion a year over the prices charged at competing stores.

Many observers give the company credit for establishing pretty strict criteria for its "Great for You" label, though some question whether it is just a green "buy me" scheme. But the CEO of Partnership for a Healthier America, which focuses on addressing childhood obesity, says the organization is pleased that Walmart continues to be a critical leader among a growing number of private sector companies looking to help end the obesity crisis.

Ever cost-conscious, Walmart will use up all its label-free packaging before it prints new boxes marked "Great for You."[1]

Overview

Business success in the 21st century is directly tied to a company's ability to identify and serve its target markets. In fact, all organizations—profit-oriented and not-for-profit, manufacturing and retailing—*must* serve customer needs to succeed, just as Walmart does by offering multiple choices to its shoppers. Marketing is the link between the organization and the people who buy and use its goods and services. It is the way organizations determine buyer needs and inform potential customers that their firms can meet those needs by supplying a quality product at a reasonable price. And it is the path to developing loyal, long-term customers.

Consumers who purchase goods for their own use and business purchasers seeking products to use in their firm's operation may seem to fall in the same category, but marketers see distinct wants and needs for each group. To understand buyers—from manufacturers to Web surfers to shoppers in the grocery aisles—companies gather mountains of data on every aspect of consumer lifestyles and buying behaviors. Marketers use the data to understand the needs and wants of both final customers and business buyers. Satisfying customers goes a long way toward building relationships with them. It's not always easy.

This chapter begins with an examination of the marketing concept and the way businesspeople develop a marketing strategy. We then turn to marketing research techniques and how businesses apply data to market segmentation and understanding customer behavior. The chapter closes with a detailed look at the important role customer relationships play in today's highly competitive business world.

What Is Marketing?

Every organization—from profit-seeking firms such as Jimmy John's and Zappos.com to such not-for-profits as the Make-a-Wish Foundation and the American Cancer Society—must serve customer needs to succeed. Perhaps the retail pioneer J. C. Penney best expressed this priority when he told his store managers, "Either you or your replacement will greet the customer within the first 60 seconds."

According to the American Marketing Association Board of Directors, **marketing** is an organizational function and set of processes for creating, communicating, and delivering value to customers, and for managing customer relationships in ways that benefit the organization and its stakeholders.[2] In addition to selling goods and services, marketing techniques help people advocate ideas or viewpoints and educate others. The American Heart Association mails out questionnaires that ask, "Are you at risk for a heart attack?" The documents help educate the general public about this widespread condition by listing its risk factors and common symptoms and describing the work of the association.

Department store founder Marshall Field explained marketing quite clearly when he advised one employee to "give the lady what she wants." The phrase became the company motto, and it remains a business truism today. The best marketers not only give consumers what they want but even anticipate consumers' needs before those needs surface. Ideally, they can get a jump on the competition by creating a link in consumers' minds between the new need and the fulfillment of that need by the marketers' products. Principal Financial Group, with headquarters in Iowa, markets employee retirement plans to other firms that then custom tailor those plans to retain key employees. NetJets offers fractional jet ownership to executives who want the luxury and flexibility of private ownership without the cost of owning their own plane. Samsung offers its next generation of high-definition TV with its SMART TVs. Owners can connect their televisions to their home Internet connection, then add widgets to track the weather, use Skype, stream video content, and check for Twitter updates—all in real time. In addition, they can get video-on-demand service and other apps through the company's Web site. "Get the best of the Web right on your TV," one of Samsung's promotions says.

As these examples illustrate, marketing is more than just selling. It is a process that begins with discovering unmet customer needs and continues with researching the potential market; producing a good or service capable of satisfying the targeted customers; and promoting, pricing, and distributing that good or service. Throughout the entire marketing process, a successful organization focuses on building customer relationships.

When two or more parties benefit from trading things of value, they have entered into an **exchange process**. When you purchase a cup of coffee, the other party may be a convenience store clerk, a vending machine, or a Seattle's Best server. The exchange seems simple—some money changes hands, and you receive your cup of coffee. But the exchange process is more complex than that. It could not occur if you didn't feel the need for a cup of coffee or if the

The best marketers give consumers what they want and anticipate their needs. Samsung's SMART TVs allow consumers to interact, connect, and multi-task without leaving their homes.

ThomasPeter/Reuters/NewsCom

& Miss

Ethnic Cuisine Goes Mobile

In restaurant-rich cities like New York and Los Angeles and smaller communities with fewer dining choices, food trucks are a thriving trend bringing novel and often exotic cuisines to the streets. About 3 million trucks and 5 million carts are going where diners are, bringing tantalizing flavors and aromas.

With chefs serving their native cuisines, quality can be high, and variety ranges from Korean and Thai to Salvadoran and Jamaican. "Food trucks have changed the conversation," says one restaurant trend–watching agency.

Customers tend to be Millennials who enjoy experimentation. Nearly half of those between 18 and 30 say they visit food trucks weekly for unique meals that fast-food chains can't match. An even higher percentage of Facebook and Twitter users patronize mobile eateries. "If you take a look at what [food truck operators] have been able to do with Twitter and Facebook from a marketing standpoint," said one food industry expert, "having people follow them around . . . it's brilliant."

Questions for Critical Thinking

1. One big growth area for food trucks is converting people reluctant to buy food from a truck. How can operators overcome this reluctance?

2. Some truck operators are only test-marketing before expanding to brick-and-mortar eateries or supermarket distribution. List some pros and cons of this strategy.

Sources: Maureen Morrison, "Food Trucks Spread 'New' Cuisine, Shake up Restaurant Model," *Ad Age,* http://adage.com, accessed March 21, 2012; Entrepreneur Press and Rich Mintzer, "Beyond the Food Truck: Six Ideas for Mobile Food Businesses," *Entrepreneur,* http://www.entrepreneur.com, accessed March 21, 2012; Marc Brandau, "Technomic: Open Road for Food Trucks," *Nation's Restaurant News,* http://nrn.com, accessed March 21, 2012.

---

convenience store or vending machine were not available. You wouldn't choose Seattle's Best Coffee unless you were aware of the brand. Because of marketing, your desire for a flavored blend, plain black coffee, or decaf is identified, and the coffee manufacturer's business is successful.

How Marketing Creates Utility

Marketing affects many aspects of an organization and its dealings with customers. The ability of a good or service to satisfy the wants and needs of customers is called **utility**. A company's production function creates *form utility* by converting raw materials, component parts, and other inputs into finished goods and services. But the marketing function creates time, place, and ownership utility. *Time utility* is created by making a good or service available when customers want to purchase it. *Place utility* is created by making a product available in a location convenient for customers. *Ownership utility* refers to an orderly transfer of goods and services from the seller to the buyer. Firms may be able to create all three forms of utility. Target is the first nationwide retailer to offer bar-coded, scannable mobile coupons direct to cell phones. Guests can sign on to the program either on their personal computers or on their cell phones. Each month, they receive a text message with a link to a mobile Web site page where they will find offers for various products. They can use the mobile coupons at any Target store nationwide because Target is the first retailer to have point-of-sale scanning technology for the coupons in all of its stores. Steve Eastman, the president of Target.com, says, "At Target, we know that mobile phones are an integral part of our guests' lives, and mobile coupons are just another way we're providing convenient, on-the-go shopping solutions."[3] Even food is going mobile, creating place utility as described in the "Hit & Miss" feature.

utility power of a good or service to satisfy a want or need.

Assessment Check ☑

1. What is utility?
2. Identify ways in which marketing creates utility.

Evolution of the Marketing Concept

Marketing has always been a part of business, from the earliest village traders to large 21st-century organizations producing and selling complex goods and services. Over time, however, marketing activities evolved through the five eras shown in Figure 11.1: the production, sales, marketing, and relationship eras, and now the social era. Note that these eras parallel some of the time periods discussed in Chapter 1.

For centuries, organizations of the *production era* stressed efficiency in producing quality products. Their philosophy could be summed up by the remark, "A good product will sell itself." Although this production orientation continued into the 20th century, it gradually gave way to the *sales era*, in which businesses assumed that consumers would buy as a result of energetic sales efforts. Organizations didn't fully recognize the importance of their customers until the *marketing era* of the 1950s, when they began to adopt a consumer orientation. This focus intensified, leading to the emergence of the *relationship era* in the 1990s. In the relationship era, companies emphasized customer satisfaction and building long-term business relationships. As the second decade of the new century gets underway, the *social era* of marketing is in full swing, thanks to the Internet and the creation of social media sites such as Twitter and Facebook. Companies now routinely use the Web and social media sites to connect to consumers as a way of marketing their goods and services.

Emergence of the Marketing Concept

marketing concept
companywide consumer orientation to promote long-run success.

The term **marketing concept** refers to a companywide customer orientation with the objective of achieving long-run success. The basic idea of the marketing concept is that marketplace success begins with the customer. A firm should analyze each customer's needs

FIGURE
11.1 Five Eras in the History of Marketing

DEGREE OF EMPHASIS

High   Low

RELATIONSHIP
"Long-term relationships lead to success."

SOCIAL
"Connecting to consumers via Internet and social media sites is an effective tool."

MARKETING
"The consumer is king! Find a need and fill it."

SALES
"Creative advertising and selling will overcome consumers' resistance and convince them to buy."

PRODUCTION
"A good product will sell itself."

1900   1950   2015

and then work backward to offer products that fulfill them. The emergence of the marketing concept can be explained best by the shift from a *seller's market*, one with a shortage of goods and services, to a *buyer's market*, one with an abundance of goods and services. During the 1950s, the United States became a strong buyer's market, forcing companies to satisfy customers rather than just producing and selling goods and services.

Today, much competition among firms centers on the effort to satisfy customers. Amazon and Barnes & Noble have been battling for consumer preference for their e-readers, the Kindle and Nook. The two firms are continually adding features, making price adjustments, and offering new models of their products in order to satisfy consumers. Kindle's price has dropped dramatically, and Amazon recently released Kindle software for Android users and introduced a tablet version called the Kindle Fire. Barnes & Noble followed its original Nook with Nook Color, touting its superiority at displaying magazines and children's books. Now both are facing competition from the Sony Reader and Apple's iPad.[4]

3

Not-for-Profit and Nontraditional Marketing

The marketing concept has traditionally been associated with products of profit-seeking organizations. Today, however, it is also being applied to not-for-profit sectors and other nontraditional areas ranging from religious organizations to political campaigns.

Not-for-Profit Marketing

Residents of every continent benefit in various ways from the approximately 20 million not-for-profit organizations currently operating around the globe. Nearly 1.9 million of them are located in the United States, where they employ 13.5 million workers and benefit from volunteers representing the equivalent of 9 million full-time employees.[5] Women tend to volunteer at a higher rate than men, and 35- to 44-year-olds and 45- to 54-year-olds are also the most likely to volunteer.[6] The largest not-for-profit organization in the world is the Red Cross/Red Crescent. Other not-for-profits range from Habitat for Humanity to the Boys & Girls Clubs of America to the Juvenile Diabetes Research Foundation. These organizations all benefit by applying many of the strategies and business concepts used by profit-seeking firms. They apply marketing tools to reach audiences, secure funding, and accomplish their overall missions. Marketing strategies are important for not-for-profit organizations because they are all competing for dollars—from individuals, foundations, and corporations—just as commercial businesses are.

Not-for-profit organizations operate in both public and private sectors. Public groups include federal, state, and local government units as well as agencies that receive tax funding. A state's department of natural resources, for instance, regulates land conservation and environmental programs; the local animal control officer enforces ordinances protecting people and animals; a city's public health board ensures safe drinking water for its citizens. The private not-for-profit sector comprises many different types of organizations, including the Philadelphia Zoo, the United States Olympic Committee, and the American Academy of Orthopaedic Surgeons. Although some private not-for-profits generate surplus revenue, their primary goals are not earning profits. If they earn funds beyond their expenses, they invest the excess in their organizational missions.

In some cases, not-for-profit organizations form a partnership with a profit-seeking company to promote the firm's message or distribute its goods and services. This partnership

LECTURE ENHANCER:
Can you think of an example where a firm created a need for its product?

Assessment Check ✔

1. What is the marketing concept?
2. How is the marketing concept tied to the relationship and social eras of marketing?

CLASS ACTIVITY:
Discuss how the success of e-book readers (such as the iPad, Nook, and Kindle) and iTunes has affected Barnes & Noble and Sony Records.

CLASS ACTIVITY:
Ask students to name not-for-profit organizations in the local community that they think have used effective marketing.

KevinMazur/WireImage/GettyImages, Inc.

Some not-for-profit organizations enlist the help of celebrities to spread the word about their charitable causes. To mark its 125th anniversary, Avon presented grants to women's domestic shelters and other agencies in the United States as well as in countries around the world. Here actress Reese Witherspoon and Avon's Executive Chairman Andrea Jung present a grant to Partnership Against Domestic Violence in Atlanta, Georgia.

usually benefits both organizations. The National Football League and the United Way joined to form one of the longest-running public-service partnerships in the United States. NFL athletes and other personalities appear in public-service advertisements and in person to promote community service and fundraising. Since 1999, the "Hometown Huddle" has been an NFL-wide day of service when team members, their families, coaches, and staff members participate in local community service activities.[7]

Celebrities are particularly visible campaigning for not-for-profit organizations—their own as well as others. The actress Reese Witherspoon is the Avon Global Ambassador and Honorary Chairperson of the Avon Foundation for Women. Witherspoon recently helped announce and present ten $60,000 grants to women's domestic-violence shelters and other agencies in countries around the world. The grants are from the $2 million Avon Global Believe Fund, which Avon Products, Inc. established in 2011 to mark its 125th anniversary and to maintain the commitment to ending violence against women everywhere.[8]

Nontraditional Marketing

Not-for-profit organizations often engage in one or more of five major categories of nontraditional marketing: person marketing, place marketing, event marketing, cause marketing, and organization marketing. Figure 11.2 provides examples of these types of marketing. As described in the "Going Green" feature, through each of these types of marketing, an organization seeks to connect with the audience that is most likely to offer time, money, or other resources. In some cases, the effort may reach the market the organization intends to serve.

LECTURE ENHANCER:
Choose one of the categories and think of goods or services that might be marketed by using the selected method.

FIGURE 11.2 Categories of Nontraditional Marketing

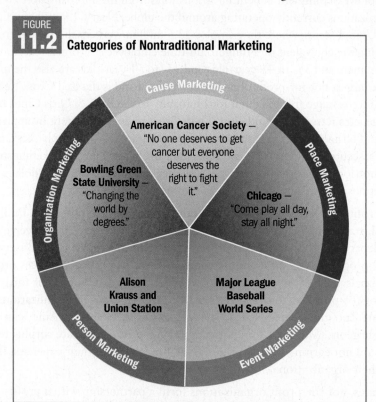

Cause Marketing

Organization Marketing

Place Marketing

American Cancer Society — "No one deserves to get cancer but everyone deserves the right to fight it."

Bowling Green State University — "Changing the world by degrees."

Chicago — "Come play all day, stay all night."

Alison Krauss and Union Station

Major League Baseball World Series

Person Marketing

Event Marketing

The Tap Project

Esquire magazine challenged David Droga, the founder of the Droga5 advertising firm, to prove that his creative thinking deserved the magazine's "Best and Brightest" award. After seeing a documentary about New Orleans after Hurricane Katrina, Droga started thinking about how many people don't have access to clean, safe drinking water—which most Americans take for granted. When he was served the typical free glass of tap water at a New York City restaurant, he got the inspiration for his next advertising campaign. He presented his idea to UNICEF, and the Tap Project was born.

Approximately 900 million people around the world—about half of them children—lack safe, accessible drinking water. Over the past two decades, UNICEF has brought improved sources of drinking water to more than 2 billion people.

During the UN's World Water Week, top restaurants in New York City asked their patrons to donate $1 or more for a glass of tap water. Since its inception, the Tap Project has raised almost $3 million in the United States. One dollar allows UNICEF to provide safe drinking water to one child for 40 days.

Leading advertising agencies in the United States have participated in the Tap Project. In succeeding years, the Tap Project spread to other U.S. cities and advertising agencies.

The Tap Project's very success has spawned other water charities, all vying for donations and volunteers. The earthquake in Haiti also had an impact. However, UNICEF continues to grow the campaign and announced that funds for the coming year would be targeted for Togo, Vietnam, Mauritania, and Cameroon.

Questions for Critical Thinking

1. What types of nontraditional marketing does the Tap Project engage in?

2. As the story mentions, the Tap Project now faces competition from other water charities. What would you suggest to help the Tap Project "stand out from the crowd"?

Sources: Tap Project Web site, http://www.tapproject.org, accessed March 21, 2012; Droga5 Web site, http://www.droga5.com, accessed March 21, 2012; Karyn McCormack, "UNICEF: Tapping the Power of Water," *BusinessWeek,* http://www.businessweek.com, accessed March 21, 2012; Alessandra Bulow, "UNICEF Tap Project," *Food & Wine,* http://www.foodandwine.com, accessed March 21, 2012; Helena Bottemiller, "Restaurants Join in Clean Water Project," Food Safety News, http://www.foodsafetynews.com, accessed March 21, 2012; United States Fund for UNICEF, "2010 UNICEF Tap Project Launches to Help Provide Safe Water to Children Worldwide," http://www.unicefusa.org, accessed March 21, 2012; Water Conferences Web site, http://water-conferences.com, accessed March 21, 2012; World Water Week Web site, http://www.worldwaterweek.org, accessed March 21, 2012.

Person Marketing Efforts designed to attract the attention, interest, and preference of a target market toward a person are called **person marketing**. Campaign managers for a political candidate conduct marketing research, identify groups of voters and financial supporters, and then design advertising campaigns, fund-raising events, and political rallies to reach them. Person marketing gained a lot of attention during a recent broadcast of the Academy Awards, during which commercials featured Ellen DeGeneres for JCP (retailer JC Penney).[9]

Many successful job seekers apply the tools of person marketing. They research the wants and needs of prospective employers, and they identify ways they can meet them. They seek employers through a variety of channels, sending messages that emphasize how they can benefit the employer.

person marketing use of efforts designed to attract the attention, interest, and preference of a target market toward a person.

Place Marketing As the term suggests, **place marketing** attempts to attract people to a particular area, such as a city, state, or nation. It may involve appealing to consumers as a tourist destination or to businesses as a desirable business location. A strategy for place marketing often includes advertising.

Place marketing may be combined with event marketing, such as the Olympics. The official Web site for the Rio de Janeiro 2016 Summer Games features images of the various athletic venues around Rio, ticket sales, and videos capturing the energy and spirit of the upcoming competition starting more than four years before the games—all in an effort to get people to visit Brazil.[10]

place marketing attempt to attract people to a particular area, such as a city, state, or nation.

Event Marketing Marketing or sponsoring short-term events such as athletic competitions and cultural and charitable performances is known as **event marketing**.

event marketing marketing or sponsoring short-term events such as athletic competitions and cultural and charitable performances.

The American Diabetes Association sponsors the "Tour de Cure," a series of fund-raising cycling events held across the United States to raise funds to support its mission to prevent and cure diabetes.[11]

Event marketing often forges partnerships between not-for-profit and profit-seeking organizations. Many businesses sponsor events such as 10K runs to raise funds for health-related charities. These occasions require a marketing effort to plan the event and attract participants and sponsors. Events may be intended to raise money or awareness, or both.

Cause Marketing Marketing that promotes awareness of, or raises money for, a cause or social issue, such as drug abuse prevention or childhood hunger is **cause marketing**. Cause marketing seeks to educate the public and may or may not attempt to directly raise funds. An advertisement often contains a phone number or Web site address through which people can obtain more information about the organization or issue. Then they can either donate money or take other actions of support. The international accounting firm Deloitte sponsors the United Way's Alternative Spring Break program. Instead of heading for the beach, young adults and student volunteers participate in community service activities such as rebuilding communities devastated by hurricanes or tornadoes and helping low-income families with tax preparation.[12]

Profit-seeking companies look for ways to contribute to their communities by joining forces with charities and causes, providing financial, marketing, and human resources. For-profit firms can also combine their goods and services with a cause. In an effort to reduce energy use and pollution, entrepreneurs Jonathan Shriftman and Jake Medwell founded Solé Bicycles in California, which builds hand-made, affordable bicycles from recycled parts. The bikes are popular among students and commuters.[13]

Organization Marketing The final category of nontraditional marketing, **organization marketing**, influences consumers to accept the goals of, receive the services of, or contribute in some way to an organization. The U.S. Postal Service, the ALS Association, and the National Basketball Association (NBA) are all examples of organizations that engage in marketing. Recently the NBA has turned to social media for much of its marketing. The NBA claims more than 6.7 million followers on Facebook and Twitter. "Sports are communal experiences," says Melissa Rosenthal Brenner, NBA's vice president of marketing, explaining why the organization now focuses on social media marketing. NBA teams with the greatest presence in social media include the Los Angeles Lakers, the Miami Heat, and the Boston Celtics.[14]

4 Developing a Marketing Strategy

Decision makers in any successful organization, for-profit or not-for-profit, follow a two-step process to develop a *marketing strategy*. First, they study and analyze potential target markets and choose among them. Second, they create a marketing mix to satisfy the chosen market. Figure 11.3 shows the relationships among the target market, the marketing mix variables, and the marketing environment. Later discussions refer back to this figure as they cover each topic. This section describes the development of a marketing strategy designed to attract and build relationships with customers. Sometimes, in an effort to do this, marketers use questionable methods, as described in the "Solving an Ethical Controversy" feature.

Earlier chapters of this book introduced many of the environmental factors that affect the success or failure of a firm's business strategy, including today's rapidly changing and highly competitive world of business, a vast array of social and cultural factors, economic

cause marketing
marketing that promotes a cause or social issue, such as preventing child abuse, anti-littering efforts, and stop-smoking campaigns.

organization marketing marketing strategy that influences consumers to accept the goals of, receive the services of, or contribute in some way to an organization.

Assessment Check ✔

1. Why do not-for-profit organizations engage in marketing?

2. What are the five types of nontraditional marketing used by not-for-profit organizations?

challenges, political and legal factors, and technological innovations. Although these external forces frequently operate outside managers' control, marketers must still consider the impact of environmental factors on their decisions.

A marketing plan is a key component of a firm's overall business plan. The marketing plan outlines its marketing strategy and includes information about the target market, sales and revenue goals, the marketing budget, and the timing for implementing the elements of the marketing mix.

Selecting a Target Market

The expression "find a need and fill it" is perhaps the simplest explanation of the two elements of a marketing strategy. A firm's marketers find a need through careful and continuing study of the individuals and business decision makers in its potential market. A market consists of people with purchasing power, willingness to buy, and authority to make purchase decisions.

Markets can be classified by type of product. **Consumer products**—often known as business-to-consumer (B2C) products—are goods and services, such as GPS systems, tomato sauce, and a haircut, that are purchased by end users. **Business products**—or business-to-business (B2B) products—are goods and services purchased to be used, either directly or

consumer (B2C) product good or service that is purchased by end users.

business (B2B) product good or service purchased to be used, either directly or indirectly, in the production of other goods for resale.

Solving an Ethical Controversy

When Free Credit Reports Aren't Free

When times are tough and credit is tight, consumers are more likely to search for and monitor their credit scores. The Fair Credit Reporting Act (FCRA) requires the three major consumer reporting companies—Equifax, Experian, and TransUnion—to provide consumers a free copy of their credit reports once a year. Consumers must request the report through the official Annual Credit Report Request Service by phone or mail, or online at AnnualCreditReport.com. Credit report companies claim to offer free credit reports—but many offers contain hidden charges. Also, Experian has profited because consumers confuse its FreeCreditReport.com division with the federal government's AnnualCreditReport.com, the only truly free Web site.

Should firms be allowed to use the word "free" in advertising for credit reports if the service contains hidden charges?

PRO

1. If the credit score itself is free, but related services are not, then the advertising is truthful.

2. Some promotional offers contain free credit scores, with a tie-in to additional services for a fee.

CON

1. Some companies provide "free" reports, then bill consumers for services they have to cancel.

2. Consumer advocates say firms exploit people's fears.

Summary

The Federal Trade Commission's Free Credit Reports Rule requires credit report Web sites to carry the following across the top of each page: "THIS NOTICE IS REQUIRED BY LAW. Read more at FTC.GOV. You have the right to a free credit report from AnnualCreditReport.com or 877-322-8228, the ONLY authorized source under federal law." Very recently, rather than including this disclosure, Experian began charging $1 for a credit report and donating the fee to charity.

Sources: "FREE Annual Credit Reports," Federal Trade Commission, http://www.ftc.gov, accessed March 21, 2012; Ron Lieber, "Free Credit on Credit? No Longer," *New York Times,* http://www.nytimes.com, accessed March 21, 2012; Joe Taylor Jr., "New Laws Crack Down on Free Credit Report Marketing," *CardRatings,* http://www.cardratings.com, accessed March 21, 2012; Michelle Singletary, "Free Credit Reports Get Easier to Find," *Washington Post,* http://www.boston.com, accessed March 21, 2012.

---

target market group of people toward whom an organization markets its goods, services, or ideas with a strategy designed to satisfy their specific needs and preferences.

marketing mix blending of the four elements of marketing strategy—product, distribution, promotion, and pricing—to fit the needs and preferences of a specific target market.

indirectly, in the production of other goods for resale. Some products can fit either classification depending on who buys them and why. A computer or credit card can be used by a business or a consumer.

An organization's **target market** is the group of potential customers toward whom it directs its marketing efforts. Customer needs and wants vary considerably, and no single organization has the resources to satisfy everyone. *Popular Science* is geared toward readers who are interested in science and technology, whereas *Bon Appétit* is aimed at readers who are interested in fine food and cooking.

Decisions about marketing involve strategies for four areas of marketing activity: product, distribution, promotion, and pricing. A firm's **marketing mix** blends the four strategies to fit the needs and preferences of a specific target market. Marketing success depends not on the four individual strategies but on their unique combination.

Product strategy involves more than just designing a good or service with needed attributes. It also includes decisions about package design, brand names, trademarks, warranties, product image, new-product development, and customer service. Think about your favorite pair of jeans. Do you like them because they fit the best, or do other attributes—such as styling and overall image—also contribute to your brand preference? *Distribution strategy*, the second marketing mix variable, ensures that customers receive their purchases in the proper quantities at the right times and locations. *Promotional strategy*, another marketing mix element, effectively blends advertising, personal selling, sales promotion, and public relations to achieve its goals of informing, persuading, and influencing purchase decisions.

Pricing strategy, the final mix element, is also one of the most difficult areas of marketing decision making in setting profitable and justifiable prices for the firm's product offerings. Such actions are sometimes subject to government regulation and considerable public scrutiny. They also represent a powerful competitive weapon and frequently produce responses by the other firms in the industry, who match price changes to avoid losing customers. Think about your jeans again. Would you continue to purchase them if they were priced either much higher or much lower?

LECTURE ENHANCER:
Which of these strategies seems to be the most crucial? What might happen if a firm were to ignore one of these strategies?

Retail clinics are low-cost, walk-in medical facilities usually found in supermarkets, chain drugstores, and big-box stores. Patients typically see nurse practitioners or physician assistants, who can diagnose and treat minor medical conditions and prescribe some medications. The clinics are open late in the evenings and on weekends and also offer appropriate vaccinations and inexpensive sports and summer-camp physicals for children. They have proved to be a popular alternative to primary care in areas where primary-care physicians are scarce and because of their low cost, usually about $80 per visit. A recent survey found that there were about 1,100 retail clinics throughout the United States, and that number appears to be growing. One important problem with walk-in clinics is that often the patients don't tell their primary-care doctors about the visits—or about any medications they were prescribed. In an attempt to solve these problems, drugstore chain CVS has been marketing its Minute Clinics with some nationwide health-care organizations. Other challenges include the seasonality of such products as flu shots and summer-camp physicals, oversaturation of the market in some areas, and difficulty in reaching potential patients who don't shop at the particular store. Retail clinics are evolving with the changing economic landscape, and how the operators of the clinics will solve these marketing problems remains to be seen.[15]

Developing a Marketing Mix for International Markets

Marketing a good or service in foreign markets means deciding whether to offer the same marketing mix in every market (*standardization*) or to develop a unique mix to fit each market (*adaptation*). The advantages of standardizing the marketing mix include reliable marketing performance and low costs. This approach works best with B2B goods, such as steel, chemicals, and aircraft, which require little sensitivity to a nation's culture.

LECTURE ENHANCER:
Provide an example of a good or service that has used standardization.

Adaptation, on the other hand, lets marketers vary their marketing mix to suit local competitive conditions, consumer preferences, and government regulations. Consumer tastes are often shaped by local cultures. Because consumer products generally tend to be more culture dependent than business products, they more often require adaptation. SUBWAY already has almost 300 stores in China, with more than 70 in Beijing alone. In the next few years, the company plans to have 180 stores in Beijing and more than 600 throughout China. It has already surpassed McDonald's in the number of stores worldwide. As SUBWAY opens stores in different regions, it plans to adapt its menu to local tastes with such offerings as Beijing roast duck sandwiches and "hot spicy Szechuan sauce." Why do these firms go out of their way to adapt to Chinese preferences? China is a market with 1.3 billion potential consumers.[16]

LECTURE ENHANCER:
Provide an example of a good or service that has used adaptation.

CLASS ACTIVITY:
What challenges does Starbucks face in entering and successfully selling coffee in China? Ask students their ideas for tactics to overcome these challenges.

Karen Cowled/Alamy

Adaptation allows marketers to vary their marketing mix to suit local competitive conditions, consumer preferences, and government regulations. Because consumer products generally tend to be more culture dependent than business products, they more often require adaptation. SUBWAY has almost 300 stores in China now, and plans to have over 600 stores there in the next few years.

Assessment Check ✓

1. Distinguish between consumer products and business products.
2. What are the steps in developing a marketing strategy?

marketing research collecting and evaluating information to help marketers make effective decisions.

Marketers also try to build adaptability into the designs of standardized goods and services for international and domestic markets. *Mass customization* allows a firm to mass produce goods and services while adding unique features to individual or small groups of orders. For example, the online firm Blank Label specializes in custom men's dress shirts and allows customers to choose their own fabric, style, individual features, and size. Spreadshirt, with U.S. headquarters in Boston, specializes in customized casual wear, accessories, and even personalized underwear.[17]

5 | Marketing Research

Marketing research involves more than just collecting data. Researchers must decide how to collect data, interpret the results, convert the data into decision-oriented information, and communicate those results to managers for use in decision making. **Marketing research** is the process of collecting and evaluating information to help marketers make effective decisions. It links business decision makers to the marketplace by providing data about potential target markets that help them design effective marketing mixes.

Obtaining Marketing Research Data

Marketing researchers need both internal and external data. Firms generate *internal data* within their organizations. Financial records provide a tremendous amount of useful information, such as changes in unpaid bills; inventory levels; sales generated by different categories of customers or product lines; profitability of particular divisions; or comparisons of sales by territories, salespeople, customers, or product lines.

Researchers gather *external data* from outside sources, including previously published data. Trade associations publish reports on activities in particular industries. Advertising agencies collect information on the audiences reached by various media. National marketing research firms offer information through subscription services. Some of these professional research firms specialize in specific markets, such as teens or ethnic groups. This information helps companies make decisions about developing or modifying products.

A recent report by the marketing research firm comScore on smart phone and tablet purchases indicates that consumers now use these devices as well as personal computers in a process of cross-platform consumption that was unheard of a few years ago. The report revealed that in a recent year, noncomputer devices accounted for almost 7 percent of all digital traffic. Most of that was due to smart phone use, with tablet use making up the rest. More than 37 percent of mobile phone use was through WiFi connections; mobile broadband access is increasingly supporting tablet use. And almost half of the owners of those tablets have completed at least one purchase using that device. Mark Donovan, comScore's senior vice president of mobile, says the popularity of smart phones and the introduction of tablets and other Web-enabled devices has contributed to the explosion in digital media consumption. Such data can give indirect but very clear indications of what consumers are looking for in a product.[18]

The largest consumer-goods manufacturer in the world, Procter & Gamble, has excelled in marketing research for a long time; it created its own marketing research department in 1923 and began conducting its research online in 2001. To help the company recover from the global recession, Bob McDonald, P&G's chief executive officer, has set the goal of reaching 1 billion new customers worldwide over the next few years. This expansion involves reaching customers in developing regions. As part of this strategy, he traveled undercover to 30 countries, posing as a marketing researcher.[19]

Secondary data, or previously published data, are low cost and easy to obtain. Federal, state, and local government publications are excellent data sources, and most are available online. The most frequently used government statistics include census data, which contain the population's age, gender, education level, household size and composition, occupation, employment status, and income. Even private research firms such as TRU (formerly Teenage Research Unlimited), which studies the purchasing habits of teens, provide some free information on their Web sites. This information helps firms evaluate consumers' buying behavior, anticipate possible changes in the marketplace, and identify new markets.

Even though secondary data are a quick and inexpensive resource, marketing researchers sometimes discover that this information isn't specific or current enough for their needs. If so, researchers may conclude that they must collect *primary data*—data collected firsthand through such methods as observation and surveys.

Observational studies view the actions of consumers either directly or through mechanical devices. As more retailers watch their customers via video cameras, they can solve problems such as widening a too-narrow aisle to allow shoppers easier access, but such close monitoring has also raised privacy concerns.[20] Procter & Gamble spends about $200 million on consumer observation each year, citing it as the firm's most important type of marketing research. CEO McDonald says, "If we can continue to innovate and continue to mind consumer needs and delight consumers, that ability outweighs any macroeconomic force."[21]

Simply observing customers cannot provide some types of information. A researcher might observe a customer buying a red sweater, but have no idea why the purchase was

LECTURE ENHANCER:
Which type of data do you think is more reliable? Why?

CLASS ACTIVITY:
Lead a class discussion on how students might collect primary and secondary data to research a potential pet grooming service in the community.

made—or for whom. When researchers need information about consumers' attitudes, opinions, and motives, they need to ask the consumers themselves. They may conduct surveys by telephone, in person, online, or in focus groups.

A *focus group* gathers 8 to 12 people in a room or over the Internet to discuss a particular topic. A focus group can generate new ideas, address consumers' needs, and even point out flaws in existing products. Pottery Barn Kids, a division of Pottery Barn, developed its Learning Toys Collection through observation, reading, and focus groups. Focus groups that included both parents and children were gathered and observed as they played with and talked about the new toys. Marketing researchers have also begun to take advantage of social media outlets such as Facebook, Twitter, and blogs as well as mobile marketing.[22]

Applying Marketing Research Data

<aside>
LECTURE ENHANCER:
What are some potential problems with data obtained through a focus group?
</aside>

<aside>
business intelligence activities and technologies for gathering, storing, and analyzing data to make better competitive decisions.
</aside>

As the accuracy of information collected by researchers increases, so does the effectiveness of resulting marketing strategies. One field of research is known as **business intelligence**, which uses various activities and technologies to gather, store, and analyze data to make better competitive decisions. Dell established its IdeaStorm Web site to gather information, criticism, compliments, and ideas for developing new computer products and improving existing ones. New users must register at the site and follow guidelines in order to post their ideas and reactions. Submitted ideas receive scores for their popularity, which helps Dell sort through material and decide which ideas to pursue. Recently, Dell added "Storm Sessions," where the company posts a topic and asks visitors to contribute their ideas. To make the discussions specific and relevant to the topic, each session is open only for a limited time. "Dream It. Share It. Make an Impact," says the IdeaStorm Web site, which recently logged over 16,000 submitted ideas.[23]

Data Mining

<aside>
LECTURE ENHANCER:
Provide some examples of typical methods used to mine data from consumers.
</aside>

<aside>
data mining the task of using computer-based technology to evaluate data in a database and identify useful trends.
</aside>

Once a company has built a database, marketers must be able to analyze the data and use the information it provides. **Data mining**, part of the broader field of business intelligence, is the task of using computer-based technology to evaluate data in a database and identify useful trends. These trends or patterns may suggest predictive models of real-world business activities. Accurate data mining can help researchers forecast recessions and pinpoint sales prospects.

<aside>
data warehouse customer database that allows managers to combine data from several different organizational functions.
</aside>

Data mining uses **data warehouses**, which are sophisticated customer databases that allow managers to combine data from several different organizational functions. Companies such as the San Francisco–based RapLeaf Inc. collect publicly available personal information from social-networking sites such as Facebook, Twitter, and other forums. They then sell this information to entities such as airlines and credit card companies that regard those individuals as potential customers. Such information can include everything from your blogging or posting habits to your credit rating. Among the issues arising from data mining are ownership of Web user data, the targeting capabilities of the Web, government supervision—and, of course, privacy.

<aside>
LECTURE ENHANCER:
What are some potential dangers presented by data warehouses?
</aside>

Google intended its social network Google Buzz to compete with Twitter, with members sharing status updates, photos and videos, and links with "friends" via Gmail. The platform also mined users' Gmail contacts, automatically letting users follow the people with whom they had the most contact. But this meant that lists of followers had to be public. Also, there was no way to block anyone—even someone who did *not* have a Gmail public profile—from following any user. After numerous complaints, Google agreed to sweeping privacy-protection measures. Despite these fixes, Google Buzz never really took off and is no longer operating, largely because it didn't differentiate itself from other more popular social media sites such as Facebook and Twitter. Some observers feel that privacy norms are changing, with confidentiality giving way to increasing openness.[24]

Playnomics' segmentation technology and predictive analysis mine and analyze the behavior of online game players by tracking the number of hours they spend on which games and creating behavioral profiles. Game publishers pay a monthly fee for the resulting data. The company's CEO says providing scores for game players gives marketers a way to find the right player for their specific games. They send messages to those players with personal promotions while the games are still in progress. Scores also ultimately give players a way to see their play personality.[25]

Assessment Check ✔

1. What is the difference between primary data and secondary data?

2. What is data mining?

6   Market Segmentation

Market segmentation is the process of dividing a market into several relatively homogeneous groups. Both profit-seeking and not-for-profit organizations use segmentation to help them reach desirable target markets. Market segmentation is often based on the results of research, which attempts to identify trends among certain groups of people. For instance, one recent survey revealed that social media use among Internet-using Baby Boomers—those Americans between 50 and 64 years old—grew from 20 to 32 percent. Younger adults—those under age 30—are still the heaviest users, with 61 percent visiting a social networking site on any given day. Overall, 65 percent of adult Internet users visit social networking sites, but the rise in use by older consumers is important information for businesses.[26] This kind of information can help marketers decide what types of products to develop and to whom they should be marketed.

Market segmentation attempts to isolate the traits that distinguish a certain group of customers from the overall market. However, segmentation doesn't automatically produce marketing success. Table 11.1 lists several criteria that marketers should consider. The effectiveness of a segmentation strategy depends on how well the market meets these criteria. Once marketers identify a market segment to target, they can create an appropriate marketing strategy.

Companies that can identify trends in consumer preferences before their rivals do can benefit greatly; those that miss the boat generally suffer the consequences. Blockbuster

market segmentation process of dividing a total market into several relatively homogeneous groups.

LECTURE ENHANCER: Name some market segments that have newly emerged within the past 10 years.

TABLE

11.1   Criteria for Market Segmentation

CRITERION	EXAMPLE
A segment must be a measurable group.	Data can be collected on the dollar amount and number of purchases by college students.
A segment must be accessible for communication.	A growing number of seniors are going online, so they can be reached through Internet channels.
A segment must be large enough to offer profit potential.	In a small community, a store carrying only large-size shoes might not be profitable. Similarly, a specialty retail chain may not locate in a small market.

lagged behind Netflix in capturing the segment of movie watchers who preferred traveling only as far as the mailbox to retrieve a DVD and wanted to keep it for an unspecified time period without paying a late fee. Netflix is now surging ahead with its online streaming option and recently signed a streaming deal with DreamWorks Animation.[27]

How Market Segmentation Works

An immediate segmentation distinction involves whether the firm is offering goods and services to customers for their own use or to purchasers who will use them directly or indirectly in providing other products for resale (the so-called B2B market). Depending on whether their firms offer consumer or business products, marketers segment their target markets differently. Four common bases for segmenting consumer markets are geographical segmentation, demographic segmentation, psychographic segmentation, and product-related segmentation. By contrast, business markets can segment on three criteria: customer-based segmentation, end-use segmentation, and geographical segmentation. Figure 11.4 illustrates the segmentation methods for these two types of markets.

Segmenting Consumer Markets

Market segmentation has been around since people first began selling products. Tailors made some clothing items for men and others for women. Tea was imported from India for tea drinkers in England and other European countries. In addition to demographic and geographical segmentation, today's marketers also define customer groups based on psychographic—lifestyle and values—criteria as well as product-related distinctions.

Geographical Segmentation The oldest segmentation method is **geographical segmentation**—dividing a market into homogeneous groups on the basis of their locations. Geographical location does not guarantee that consumers in a certain region will all

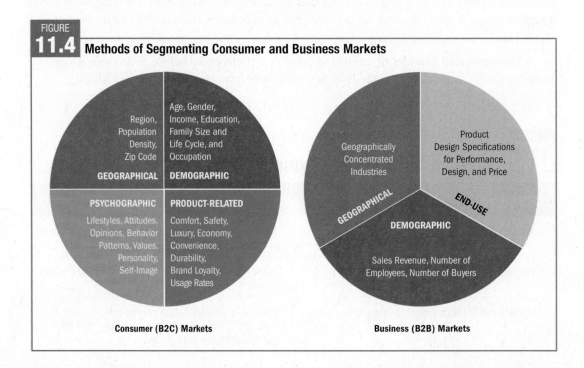

FIGURE 11.4 Methods of Segmenting Consumer and Business Markets

Consumer (B2C) Markets

- GEOGRAPHICAL: Region, Population Density, Zip Code
- DEMOGRAPHIC: Age, Gender, Income, Education, Family Size and Life Cycle, and Occupation
- PSYCHOGRAPHIC: Lifestyles, Attitudes, Opinions, Behavior Patterns, Values, Personality, Self-Image
- PRODUCT-RELATED: Comfort, Safety, Luxury, Economy, Convenience, Durability, Brand Loyalty, Usage Rates

Business (B2B) Markets

- GEOGRAPHICAL: Geographically Concentrated Industries
- END-USE: Product Design Specifications for Performance, Design, and Price
- DEMOGRAPHIC: Sales Revenue, Number of Employees, Number of Buyers

buy the same kinds of products, but it does provide some indication of needs. For instance, suburbanites buy more lawn-care products than central-city dwellers. However, many suburbanites choose instead to purchase the services of a lawn maintenance firm. Consumers who live in northern states, where winter is more severe, are more likely to buy ice scrapers, snow shovels, and snow blowers than those who live in warmer climates. They are also more likely to contract with firms who remove the snow from driveways. Marketers also look at the size of the population of an area, as well as who lives there—are residents old or young? Do they reflect an ethnic background? What is the level of their income?

CLASS ACTIVITY: Discuss food preferences by geographic region of the United States.

Job growth and migration patterns are important considerations as well. Some businesses combine areas or even entire countries that share similar population and product-use patterns instead of treating each as an independent segment.

Demographic Segmentation By far the most common method of market segmentation, **demographic segmentation** distinguishes markets on the basis of various demographic or socioeconomic characteristics. Common demographic measures include gender, income, age, occupation, household size, stage in the family life cycle, education, and racial or ethnic group. The U.S. Census Bureau is one of the best sources of demographic information for the domestic market. Figure 11.5 lists some of the measures used in demographic segmentation.

demographic segmentation distinguishes markets on the basis of various demographic or socioeconomic characteristics.

Police departments around the United States constitute a highly specialized occupational demographic group. Popular for its durability, the Ford Crown Victoria has long held 75 percent of the patrol-car market share. Ford plans to phase out the "Crown Vic," replacing it with the Police Interceptor, modeled on the Taurus sedan but modified for the extreme circumstances of police work. The Interceptor's fuel efficiency is 25 percent better than the Crown Vic's. Its 365-horsepower engine outguns the Crown Vic's by 115 horsepower. Ford's police advisory board helped develop the Interceptor, but the Interceptor faces competition from General Motors and Chrysler, which produce police vehicles of their own. Several police departments around the United States have adopted the Interceptor.[28]

CLASS ACTIVITY: Ask students what type of businesses might segment goods or services using religion as a key segmentation criterion.

Gender used to be a simple way to define markets for certain products—jewelry and skin care products for women; tools and motorcycles for men. Much of that has changed—dramatically. Men now buy jewelry and skin care products, and women buy tools and motorcycles. But

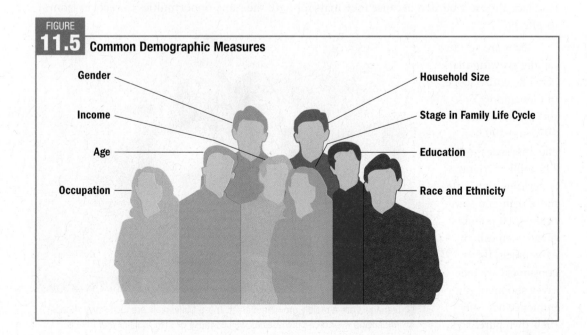

FIGURE **11.5** Common Demographic Measures

Gender

Income

Age

Occupation

Household Size

Stage in Family Life Cycle

Education

Race and Ethnicity

Digital Vision/GettyImages, Inc.

Gender used to be a simple way to define markets for certain products. Marketers know that there are still differences in the way men and women shop. A recent study revealed that more men than women use a mobile device to compare prices while shopping in a brick-and-mortar store.

marketers have also found that even though these shifts have blurred the lines between products, there are still differences in the *way* that women and men shop.

A recent study revealed that more than 57 percent of men research products on deal Web sites, while only 40 percent of women do. More men (63 percent) than women (52 percent) use shopping Web sites. More men (62 percent) than women (50 percent) use a mobile device to compare prices while in a brick-and-mortar store. Seventy-one percent of men visit company or brand-name social-networking pages, while only 64 percent of women do. However, women outnumber men (78 percent versus 72 percent) in "liking" a Web page after visiting it.[29]

Another shift involves purchasing power. Women now control an estimated 80 percent of consumer spending, or about $5 trillion per year.[30] With this knowledge in hand, Amazon purchased online retailer Zappos.com and launched a program called Amazon Mom.[31]

With our rapidly aging population, age is perhaps the most volatile factor in demographic segmentation in the United States. Of the 325-plus million people estimated to be living in the United States in the year 2015, almost 87 million will be age 55 or older.[32] Working from these statistics, marketers for travel and leisure products, as well as retirement and business investments, are working hard to attract the attention of this age group, the aging Baby Boomers—those born between 1946 and 1964. Active-adult housing communities are one result of these efforts. Some developers have built communities with a resort-style atmosphere in desirable locations such as Colorado ski country or the outskirts of a large cities such as Chicago and San Francisco. However, because of the recent recession, many older Americans will have to work longer, and many others have been forced to take early retirement. A recent report by the Government Accountability Office states, "While the recession has affected all age groups, older adults—particularly those close to or in retirement—may face a greater burden because they may not have the same opportunities to recover from its effects."[33]

Teens are another rapidly growing market. The entire scope of Generation Y— those born between 1976 and 1997— encompasses about 113 million young Americans, or a little more than one-third of the total population. Often called Millennials, these consumers are tech-savvy shoppers who influence not only their own purchases

MatthewEnnis/iStockphoto

Teenagers are a rapidly growing market. These Millennials are tech-savvy shoppers influencing their own purchases as well as those of their families and friends.

Redbox Teams with Verizon to Offer Streaming

Even as competitor Netflix deemphasizes DVD rentals in favor of streaming content over the Internet, Redbox's new video streaming partnership with Verizon will retain all the firm's 35,400 rental kiosks for customers who still want DVDs rather than downloading videos over the Internet. "We have to stay focused on giving the customers what they want," said the CFO of Redbox parent, Coinstar.

Redbox kiosks currently serve about 30 million DVD and game renters, compared to almost 25 million Netflix users. Its new combination of physical and digital video will be competitively priced and customer focused. Streaming will be available nationwide, not just to Verizon broadband and wireless customers, who number about 110 million combined.

None of Netflix's streaming competitors—Amazon, Hulu, or Walmart—offer DVD rentals. But Redbox and Verizon do have their eyes on the future. Their hope is that the nearly 60 million U.S. homes that will have Internet-enabled televisions will become Redbox streaming customers in the near future.

Questions for Critical Thinking

1. Coinstar recently acquired Blockbuster assets including 9,000 additional rental kiosks because the company thinks there is still a bright future in renting DVDs to consumers. Do you agree? Why or why not?

2. Redbox counts on Verizon to negotiate successfully with Hollywood for more video content. How will Verizon profit from the partnership?

Sources: Amy Chozick, "Verizon Teaming with Redbox for DVD and Streaming Service," *The New York Times,* February 7, 2012, www.nytimes.com; Austin Carr, "New Details on Redbox-Verizon Streaming Service, Netflix Competition," *Fast Company,* February 7, 2012, www.fastcompany.com; "Coinstar's 4Q Earnings Nearly Triple as Redbox DVD Kiosks Pick up Customers from Netflix," *The Washington Post,* February 6, 2012, www.washingtonpost.com; Stacey Higginbotham, "Verizon Teams up with Redbox to Cash in on Video," Gigaom.com, February 6, 2012, http://gigaom.com.

---

but also those of their families and friends. They are educated consumers who comparison shop and usually avoid impulse purchases, partly because of the recession and partly because they are spending their own money. According to a Nielsen survey, compared with older generations, such as the so-called Greatest Generation (those who lived through World War II) and the Baby Boomers, Generation Y consumers shop less often but buy more when they do, preferring megastores and big box-retailers.[34]

Statistics can be helpful, but they don't tell the whole story. Marketers must also learn where people live, how old they are, what language or languages they speak, and how much income they have in order to serve them well. They learn cultural tastes and preferences, too. Smart marketers also follow technology trends, as Redbox has done to cater to consumers' changing video-viewing habits and buying preferences with new offerings. See the "Hit & Miss" feature for the story.

Above all, companies must avoid stereotyping if they are going to market successfully to a diverse group of consumers. One way to do this is to break a large group into smaller segments. For instance, the Hispanic market is made up of many smaller segments, based on country of origin, language, lifestyle, and cultural values. In an attempt to target a younger Hispanic audience, three television networks have begun to offer bilingual, Spanish, and English-language programming with Hispanic themes. Because many Hispanic American teens and young adults are bilingual, the networks are trying to capture their attention while their parents and grandparents continue to watch Spanish-only programming. The Spanish-language network Telemundo recently launched an app for downloading its wildly popular *telenovelas* (nightly soap operas) onto a user's iPhone, iPad, or iPod Touch. The app also features interviews, news, and the chance to rate episodes. Another Spanish-language network, Univision, recently launched a radio app that lets users search for local Univision stations by name, location, or genre. The Univision Radio App has a bilingual interface in Spanish and English. Users can buy songs they hear on the app via iTunes. The president of Univision says the Radio App provides Hispanic audiences with high-quality content across all media platforms.[35]

Entrepreneurs who are members of minority groups may start their own businesses out of frustration at not being able to find food, clothing, entertainment, or other goods and services that fit their tastes and needs. In fact, almost 10 percent of all business owners in the United States are immigrants. Mexicans are the largest group, with 6.5 percent of immigrant-owned businesses. Motivated by the American dream that hard work will bring success and the good life, extended families often work in these businesses, which also support their ethnic communities. This localization makes them particularly vulnerable during hard times, but many immigrant entrepreneurs remain optimistic. In fact, during the recent economic downturn, immigrants started businesses at more than twice the rate of citizens born in America.[36]

Psychographic Segmentation Lifestyle is the sum of a person's needs, preferences, motives, attitudes, social habits, and cultural background. In recent years, marketing researchers have tried to formulate lifestyle portraits of consumers. This effort has led to another strategy for segmenting target markets, **psychographic segmentation**, which divides consumer markets into groups with similar psychological characteristics, values, and lifestyles.

Psychographic studies have evaluated motivations for purchases of hundreds of goods and services, ranging from soft drinks to health care services. Using the resulting data, firms tailor their marketing strategies to carefully chosen market segments. A frequently used method of developing psychographic profiles involves the use of *AIO statements*—people's verbal descriptions of various attitudes, interests, and opinions. Researchers survey a sample of consumers, asking them whether they agree or disagree with each statement. The answers are then tabulated and analyzed for use in identifying various lifestyle categories.

Another way to get current information from consumers about their lifestyles is to create *blogs* to which consumers can respond. Companies including Stonyfield Farm, Verizon, and Microsoft have hired bloggers to run online Web journals as a way to connect with and receive information from consumers. Other firms encourage employees at all levels to use blogs to communicate with consumers. General Motors has several blogs at its GMblogs. com site, each tailored to a specific brand or consumer interest. The FastLane blog discusses GM cars and trucks, inviting consumers to offer their thoughts and ideas. Chevrolet Voltage is aimed at fans of the Volt and other electric vehicles. The Lab is where GM's advanced design team talks about its work and invites feedback from community members.[37]

Although demographic classifications such as age, gender, and income are relatively easy to identify and measure, researchers also need to define psychographic categories. Often marketing research firms conduct extensive studies of consumers and then share their psychographic data with clients. In addition, businesses look to studies done by sociologists and psychologists to help them understand their customers. For instance, while children may fall into one age group and their parents in another, they also live certain lifestyles together. Recent marketing research reveals that today's parents are willing and able to spend more on goods and services for their children than parents were a generation or two ago. Spending on toys and video games for children topped $41 billion for a recent year in the United States.[38] These are just a few trends identified by the researchers, but they provide valuable information to firms that may be considering developing games, designing the interiors of family vehicles, or implementing new wireless plans.

Product-Related Segmentation Using **product-related segmentation**, sellers can divide a consumer market into groups based on buyers' relationships to the good or service. The three most popular approaches to product-related segmentation are based on benefits sought, usage rates, and brand-loyalty levels.

Segmenting by *benefits sought* focuses on the attributes that people seek in a good or service and the benefits they expect to receive from it. As more firms shift toward consumer demand for products that are eco-friendly, marketers find ways to emphasize the benefits of these products. The Swedish home-goods retailer IKEA follows strict guidelines for sourcing its solid-wood furniture products. For example, the worldwide company does not accept any illegally felled wood. IKEA's own forest specialists trace batches of timber to their origins to ensure that the lumber is properly documented and certified by the Forest Stewardship Council (FSC). In addition, these specialists work with suppliers to promote more sustainably managed forests worldwide. IKEA uses its Web site and signage in its stores to educate consumers about its wood-source policies.[39]

Consumer markets can also be segmented according to the amounts of a product that people buy and use. Segmentation by *product usage rate* usually defines such categories as heavy users, medium users, and light users. The 80/20 principle states that roughly 80 percent of a product's revenues come from only 20 percent of its buyers. Companies can now pinpoint which of their customers are the heaviest users—and even the most profitable customers—and direct their heaviest marketing efforts to those customers.

The third technique for product-related segmentation divides customers by *brand loyalty*— the degree to which consumers recognize, prefer, and insist on a particular brand. Marketers define groups of consumers with similar degrees of brand loyalty. They then attempt to tie loyal customers to a good or service by giving away premiums, which can be anything from a logo-emblazoned T-shirt to a pair of free tickets to a concert or sports event.

LECTURE ENHANCER:
What methods might companies use to obtain information about customer purchasing habits?

Segmenting Business Markets

In many ways, the segmentation process for business markets resembles that for consumer markets. However, some specific methods differ. Business markets can be divided through geographical segmentation; demographic, or customer-based, segmentation; and end-use segmentation.

Geographical segmentation methods for business markets resemble those for consumer markets. Many B2B marketers target geographically concentrated industries, such as aircraft manufacturing, automobiles, and oil field equipment. Especially on an international scale, customer needs, languages, and other variables may require differences in the marketing mix from one location to another.

Demographic, or *customer-based*, *segmentation* begins with a good or service design intended to suit a specific organizational market. Sodexo is the largest provider of food services in North America. Its customers include health care institutions, business and government offices, schools, and colleges and universities. Within these broad business segments, Sodexo identifies more specific segments, which might include colleges in the South or universities with culturally diverse populations—and differing food preferences or dining styles. Sodexo uses data obtained from surveys that cover students' lifestyles, attitudes, preferences for consumer products in general, services, and media categories. In addition, it uses targeted surveys that identify preferences for restaurant brands or certain foods, meal habits, amount of spending, and the like. Marketers evaluate the data, which sometime reveal surprising trends. Noting the rise of food trucks across the country, Sodexo recently started a food-truck program at a university. The truck visits the campus several times a month, offering lunch items such as grilled-cheese sandwiches and a Korean-style sandwich wrap with pulled pork.[40]

CLASS ACTIVITY:
Lead a discussion of why fast-food restaurants and medical offices would likely be treated as two distinct segments by furniture manufacturers.

To simplify the process of focusing on a particular type of business customer, the federal government has developed a system for subdividing the business marketplace into detailed segments. The six-digit *North American Industry Classification System (NAICS)* provides a common classification system used by the member nations of NAFTA (the United States, Canada, and Mexico). It divides industries into broad categories such as agriculture, forestry, and fishing; manufacturing; transportation; and retail and wholesale trade. Each major category is further

end-use segmentation
marketing strategy that
focuses on the precise way
a B2B purchaser will use a
product.

Assessment Check ✔

1. What is the most common form of segmentation for consumer markets?

2. What are the three approaches to product-related segmentation?

3. What is end-use segmentation in the B2B market?

consumer behavior
actions of ultimate con-
sumers directly involved in
obtaining, consuming, and
disposing of products
and the decision processes
that precede and follow
these actions.

CLASS ACTIVITY:
Ask students how the
recent recession altered
their shopping habits.

subdivided into smaller segments—such as gas stations with convenience food and warehouse clubs—for more detailed information and to facilitate comparison among the member nations.

Another way to group firms by their demographics is to segment them by size based on their sales revenues or numbers of employees. Some firms collect data from visitors to its Web site and use the data to segment customers by size. Modern information processing also enables companies to segment business markets based on how much they buy, not just how big they are. **End-use segmentation** focuses on the precise way a B2B purchaser will use a product. Resembling benefits-sought segmentation for consumer markets, this method helps small and mid-size companies target specific end-user markets rather than competing directly with large firms for wider customer groups. A company might also design a marketing mix based on certain criteria for making a purchase.

⌐7⌐ Consumer Behavior

A fundamental marketing task is to find out why people buy one product and not another. The answer requires an understanding of consumer behavior, the actions of ultimate consumers directly involved in obtaining, consuming, and disposing of products and the decision processes that precede and follow these actions.

Determinants of Consumer Behavior

By studying people's purchasing behavior, businesses can identify consumers' attitudes toward and uses of their products. This information also helps marketers reach their targeted customers. Both personal and interpersonal factors influence the way buyers behave. Personal influences on **consumer behavior** include individual needs and motives, perceptions, attitudes, learned experiences, and self-concept. For instance, today people are constantly looking for ways to save time, so firms do everything they can to provide goods and services designed for convenience. However, when it comes to products such as dinner foods, consumers want convenience, but they also want to enjoy the flavor of a home-cooked meal and spend quality time with their families. So companies such as Stouffer's offer frozen lasagna or manicotti in family sizes, and supermarkets have entire sections devoted to freshly prepared take-out meals that range from roast turkey to filet mignon.

McDonald's is betting that consumers who drink premium coffee beverages also like to buy them at bargain prices. In many U.S. locations, McDonald's has placed McCafé coffee bars—serving cappuccinos, lattes, and mochas—near the cash register. The company also offers fruit smoothies, which, added to the McCafé beverages, resulted in an uptick in sales.[41]

The interpersonal determinants of consumer behavior include cultural, social, and family influences. In the area of convenience foods, cultural, social, and family influences come into play as much as an individual's need to save time. Understanding that many consumers value the time they spend with their families and want to care for them by providing good nutrition, marketers often emphasize these values in advertisements for convenience food products.

Sometimes external events influence consumer behavior. One study suggests that as a result of the recent recession, consumers may have permanently altered their buying and spending behavior. The survey found that 72 percent of consumers said that they had significantly or somewhat changed their shopping habits; only 7 percent said they had made no change. Manufacturers and retailers—and especially small businesses—will need to create new marketing strategies in response to these challenges.[42]

Determinants of Business Buying Behavior

Because a number of people can influence purchases of B2B products, business buyers face a variety of organizational influences in addition to their own preferences. A design engineer may help set the specifications that potential vendors must satisfy. A procurement manager may invite selected companies to bid on a purchase. A production supervisor may evaluate the operational aspects of the proposals that the firm receives, and the vice president of manufacturing may head a committee making the final decision.

Steps in the Consumer Behavior Process

Consumer decision making follows the sequential process outlined in Figure 11.6, with interpersonal and personal influences affecting every step. The process begins when the consumer recognizes a problem or opportunity. If someone needs a new pair of shoes, that need becomes a problem to solve. If you receive a promotion at work and a 20 percent salary increase, that change may also become a purchase opportunity.

To solve the problem or take advantage of the opportunity, the consumer seeks information about his or her intended purchase and evaluates alternatives, such as available brands. The goal is to find the best response to the problem or opportunity.

Eventually, the consumer reaches a decision and completes the transaction. Later, he or she evaluates the experience by making a postpurchase evaluation. Feelings about the experience serve as feedback that will influence future purchase decisions. The various steps in the sequence are affected by both interpersonal and personal factors.

LECTURE ENHANCER:
Can you think of a situation in which a consumer might skip one or more of these steps? Why?

Assessment Check ✔

1. Define *consumer behavior*.

2. What are some determinants of consumer behavior?

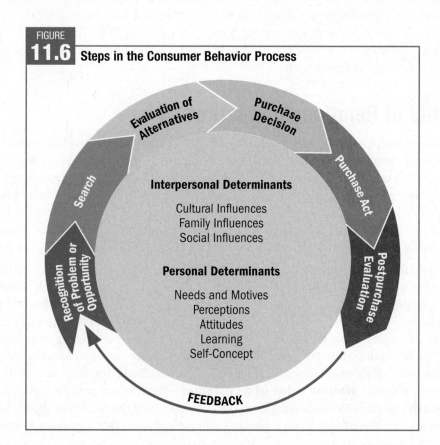

FIGURE
11.6 Steps in the Consumer Behavior Process

Relationship Marketing

The past decade has brought rapid change to most industries, as customers have become better-informed and more-demanding purchasers through closely comparing competing goods and services. They expect, even demand, new benefits from the companies that supply them, making it harder for firms to gain a competitive advantage based on product features alone.

In today's hypercompetitive era, businesses need to find new ways of relating to customers if they hope to maintain long-term success. Businesses are developing strategies and tactics that draw them into tighter connections with their customers, suppliers, and even employees. As a result, many firms are turning their attention to the issues of relationship marketing. **Relationship marketing** goes beyond an effort toward making the sale. Instead, it develops and maintains long-term, cost-effective exchange relationships with partners. These partners include individual customers, suppliers, and employees. As its ultimate goal, relationship marketing seeks to achieve customer satisfaction.

Managing relationships instead of simply completing transactions often leads to creative partnerships. However, customers enter into relationships with firms only if they are assured that the relationship will somehow benefit them. As the intensity of commitment increases, so does the likelihood of a business continuing a long-term relationship with its customers. Businesses are building relationships by partnering with customers, suppliers, and other businesses. Timberland, maker of footwear and clothing, creates many partnerships that foster long-term relationships. The firm partners with not-for-profit organizations such as City Year and the Planet Water Foundation to complete service projects for communities and the environment. Through its Serv-a-Palooza, hundreds of Timberland employees engage in volunteer tasks in their communities. Those opportunities even extend to customers who have expressed an interest in participating in programs in their own regions. If you want to volunteer for a food drive or to help restore a marsh, just log on to the Timberland Web site to see what's available. All of these activities help build relationships with customers, communities, and other organizations.[43]

Benefits of Relationship Marketing

Relationship marketing helps all parties involved. In addition to providing mutual protection against competitors, businesses that forge solid links with vendors and customers are often rewarded with lower costs and higher profits than they would generate on their own. Long-term agreements with a few high-quality suppliers frequently reduce a firm's production costs. Unlike one-time sales, ongoing relationships encourage suppliers to offer customers preferential treatment, quickly adjusting shipments to accommodate changes in orders and correcting any quality problems that might arise.

Good relationships with customers can be vital strategic weapons for a firm. By identifying current purchasers and maintaining positive relationships with them, organizations can efficiently target their best customers. Studying current customers' buying habits and preferences can help marketers identify potential new customers and establish ongoing contact with them. Attracting a new customer can cost five times as much as keeping an existing one. Not only do marketing costs go down, but long-term customers usually buy more, require less service, refer other customers, and provide valuable feedback. Together, these elements contribute to a higher **lifetime value of a customer**—the revenues and intangible benefits (referrals and customer feedback) from the customer over the life of the relationship, minus the amount the company must spend to acquire and serve that customer. Keeping

relationship marketing developing and maintaining long-term, cost-effective exchange relationships with partners.

LECTURE ENHANCER:
Provide examples of how modern banking uses relationship marketing to gain customers.

lifetime value of a customer revenues and intangible benefits (referrals and customer feedback) from a customer over the life of the relationship, minus the amount the company must spend to acquire and serve that customer.

that customer may occasionally require some extra effort, especially if the customer has become upset or dissatisfied with a good or service. But good marketers can overcome this particular challenge, as described in the "Business Etiquette" feature.

Businesses also benefit from strong relationships with other companies. Purchasers who repeatedly buy from one business may find that they save time and gain service quality as the business learns their specific needs. Some relationship-oriented companies also customize items based on customer preferences. Because many businesses reward loyal customers with discounts or bonuses, some buyers may even find that they save money by developing long-term relationships. Alliances with other firms to serve the same customers also can be rewarding. The partners combine their capabilities and resources to accomplish goals that they could not reach on their own. In addition, alliances with other firms may help businesses develop the skills and experience they need to successfully enter new markets or improve service to current customers.

Tools for Nurturing Customer Relationships

Although relationship marketing has important benefits for both customers and businesses, most relationship-oriented businesses quickly discover that some customers generate more profitable business than others. If 20 percent of a firm's customers account for 80 percent of its sales and profits—the 80/20 principle mentioned earlier in the chapter—a customer in that category undoubtedly has a higher lifetime value than a customer who buys only once or twice or who makes small purchases.

While businesses shouldn't ignore any customer, they need to allocate their marketing resources wisely. A firm may choose to customize goods or services for high-value customers while working to increase repeat sales of stock products to less-valuable customers. Differentiating between these two groups also helps marketers focus on each in an effort to increase their commitment.

Frequency Marketing and Affinity Marketing Programs Popular techniques through which firms try to build and protect customer relationships include

Calming the Angry Customer

An angry customer is a challenge representing not only an immediate problem but also a potential loss of future business. You, the businessperson, should view this customer not as a disruption but as an opportunity to see your company from the outside. With common sense, good personal skills, and knowledge of your company and its products, you can very likely turn the customer's dissatisfaction into satisfaction.

- *Remain calm and professional.* The customer isn't angry with you personally. Let the customer speak first, and listen carefully. Make written notes. Acknowledge the customer's anger, then assure him or her that you will correct the situation.

- *Repeat the customer's stated problem.* Using your own words assures the customer that you have been listening. For example, you might say, "The shoes you received were the right color but the wrong size." Make sure you understand the problem before offering a solution.

- *Focus on the solution.* Having procedures in place can help you resolve a problem quickly. If you can't solve the problem yourself, immediately refer it to someone who can.

- *Thank the customer for his or her patience.* By bringing the problem to your attention, the customer is actually giving you an opportunity to improve service to all your clients.

- *Follow up.* If appropriate, send an e-mail or make a phone call to make sure the correct pair of shoes arrived. Your professionalism will strengthen the customer's relationship with your firm—and positive word of mouth may even bring you new customers.

Sources: Lynne McClure, "Handling Angry Customers," Impact Publications, http://www.impactpublications.com, accessed March 23, 2012; Katy Tynan, "Conflict Management Part 2—Calming an Irate Customer," Ezinearticles.com, http://ezinearticles.com, accessed March 23, 2012; "How to Calm an Angry Customer," BusinessKnowledgeSource.com, http://www.businessknowledgesource.com, accessed March 23, 2012.

Assessment Check ☑

1. What is the lifetime value of a customer?
2. Discuss the increasing importance of one-on-one marketing efforts.

frequent-buyer or -user programs. These so-called **frequency marketing** programs reward purchasers with cash, rebates, merchandise, or other premiums. Frequency programs have grown more sophisticated over the years. They offer more personalization and customization than in the past. Airlines, hotel groups, restaurants, and many retailers including supermarkets offer frequency programs. For example, vacationers who book a certain number of nights at the Atlantis resort in the Bahamas may earn airfare credit for their trip.[44]

Affinity programs are another tool for building emotional links with customers. An affinity program is a marketing effort sponsored by an organization that solicits involvement by individuals who share common interests and activities. Affinity programs are common in the credit-card industry. For instance, a person can sign up for a credit card emblazoned with the logo of a favorite charity, a sports or entertainment celebrity, or a photograph of his or her college. Bank of America offers credit cards featuring the logos of all the 30 Major League Baseball clubs.

Many businesses also use comarketing and cobranding. In a **comarketing** deal, two businesses jointly market each other's products. When two or more businesses link their names to a single product, **cobranding** occurs. When two seemingly unlikely businesses team up, the marketing sparks fly—and two very different groups of consumers may come together to buy the same product. Nike and iPod have marketed the Nike+ iPod Sport kit, which allows a runner to insert a special sensor into a built-in pocket in a Nike+ shoe, which synchronizes the runner's activity with workout data and music that plays through the iPod. Enthusiasts can also purchase specially designed Nike workout apparel that has pockets designed to hold an iPod nano itself.[45]

One-on-One Marketing The ability to customize products and rapidly deliver goods and services has become increasingly dependent on technology such as computer-aided design and manufacturing (CAD/CAM). The Internet offers a way for businesses to connect with customers in a direct and intimate manner. Companies can take orders for customized products, gather data about buyers, and predict what items a customer might want in the future. Computer databases provide strong support for effective relationship marketing. Marketers can maintain databases on customer tastes, price-range preferences, and lifestyles, and they can quickly obtain names and other information about promising prospects. Amazon.com greets each online customer with a list of suggested books he or she might like to purchase. Many online retailers send their customers e-mails about upcoming sales, new products, and special events.

Small and large companies often rely on *customer relationship management (CRM)* software technology that helps them gather, sort, and interpret data about customers. Software firms develop this software in order to help businesses build and manage their relationships with customers. QueueBuster is one such product. The software offers callers the choice of receiving an automated return call at a convenient time instead of waiting on hold for the next available representative. After implementing the software to support its central reservations team, the Apex Hotel chain minimized the number of dropped customer calls and increased the level of service to its guests. This simple solution to customers' frustration not only helped build customer loyalty and improve employee morale but also helped save Apex Hotels from losing business as well.[46]

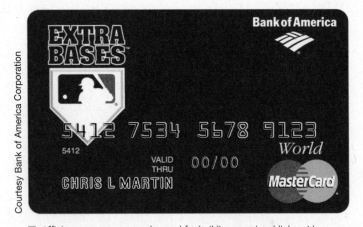

Courtesy Bank of America Corporation

Affinity programs are another tool for building emotional links with customers and are common in the credit-card industry. For instance, Bank of America offers credit cards featuring Major League Baseball logos, like the one pictured here, as well as the logos of all 30 MLB clubs.

The next two chapters examine each of the four elements of the marketing mix that marketers use to satisfy their selected target markets. Chapter 12 focuses on products and their distribution through various channels to different outlets. Chapter 13 covers promotion and the various methods marketers use to communicate with their target customers, along with strategies for setting prices for different products.

Summary of Learning Objectives

1 Define marketing.

Utility is the ability of a good or service to satisfy the wants and needs of customers. The production function creates form utility by converting inputs to finished goods and services. Marketing creates time, place, and ownership utility by making the product available when and where consumers want to buy and by arranging for orderly transfers of ownership.

Assessment Check Answers ✅

1.1 What is utility? Utility is the ability of a good or service to satisfy the wants and needs of customers.

1.2 Identify ways in which marketing creates utility. Marketing creates time utility by making a good or service available when customers want to purchase it, place utility by making the product available in a convenient location, and ownership utility by transferring the product from the buyer to the seller.

2 Discuss the evolution of the marketing concept.

The marketing concept refers to a companywide customer orientation with the objective of achieving long-run success. This concept is essential in today's marketplace, which is primarily a buyer's market, meaning buyers can choose from an abundance of goods and services. Marketing now centers on the satisfaction of customers and building long-term relationships with those customers.

Assessment Check Answers ✅

2.1 What is the marketing concept? The marketing concept is a companywide customer orientation with the objective of achieving long-run success. According to the marketing concept, success begins with the customer.

2.2 How is the marketing concept tied to the relationship era of marketing? Most marketing now centers on the satisfaction of customers and building long-term relationships with them, rather than simply producing and selling goods and services.

3 Describe not-for-profit marketing and nontraditional marketing.

Not-for-profit organizations must engage in marketing just as for-profit firms do. Not-for-profit organizations operate in both the public and private sectors, and use marketing to obtain volunteers and donations, make people aware of their existence, achieve certain goals for society, and so on. Not-for-profit organizations may engage in several types of nontraditional marketing—person, place, event, cause, or organization marketing. They may rely on one type or a combination.

Assessment Check Answers ✅

3.1 Why do not-for-profit organizations engage in marketing? Not-for-profit organizations use marketing to attract volunteers and donors, communicate their message, and achieve their organizational goals.

3.2 What are the five types of nontraditional marketing used by not-for-profit organizations? The five types of nontraditional marketing are person, place, event, cause, and organization marketing.

4 Outline the basic steps in developing a marketing strategy.

All organizations develop marketing strategies to reach customers. This process involves analyzing the overall market, selecting a target market, and developing a marketing mix that blends elements related to product, distribution, promotion, and pricing decisions.

Assessment Check Answers ✅

4.1 Distinguish between consumer products and business products. Business products are goods and services purchased to be used, either directly or indirectly, in the production of other goods for resale. Consumer products are purchased by end users.

4.2 What are the steps in developing a marketing strategy? The steps in developing a marketing strategy are analyzing the overall market, selecting a target market, and developing a marketing mix.

⌜5⌟ Describe marketing research.

Marketing research is the information-gathering function that links marketers to the marketplace. It provides valuable information about potential target markets. Firms may generate internal data or gather external data. They may use secondary data or conduct research to obtain primary data. Data mining, which involves computer searches through customer data to detect patterns or relationships, is one helpful tool in forecasting various trends such as sales revenues and consumer behavior.

Assessment Check Answers ☑

5.1 What is the difference between primary data and secondary data? Secondary data are previously published facts that are inexpensive to retrieve and easy to obtain. Primary data are collected firsthand through observation or surveys.

5.2 What is data mining? Data mining involves computer searches through customer data in order to evaluate the data and spot useful trends.

⌜6⌟ Discuss market segmentation.

Consumer markets can be divided according to four criteria: geographical factors; demographic characteristics, such as age and family size; psychographic variables, which involve behavioral and lifestyle profiles; and product-related variables, such as the benefits consumers seek when buying a product or the degree of brand loyalty they feel toward it. Business markets are segmented according to three criteria: geographical characteristics, customer-based specifications for products, and end-user applications.

Assessment Check Answers ☑

6.1 What is the most common form of segmentation for consumer markets? Demographics is the most commonly used consumer market segmentation method.

6.2 What are the three approaches to product-related segmentation? The three approaches to product-related segmentation are by benefits sought, product usage rate, and brand loyalty.

6.3 What is end-use segmentation in the B2B market? End-use segmentation focuses on the precise way a B2B purchaser will use a product.

⌜7⌟ Summarize consumer behavior.

Consumer behavior refers to the actions of ultimate consumers with direct effects on obtaining, consuming, and disposing of products, as well as the decision processes that precede and follow these actions. Personal influences on consumer behavior include an individual's needs and motives, perceptions, attitudes, learned experiences, and self-concept. The interpersonal determinants include cultural influences, social influences, and family influences. A number of people within a firm may participate in business purchase decisions, so business buyers must consider a variety of organizational influences in addition to their own preferences.

Assessment Check Answers ☑

7.1 Define *consumer behavior*. Consumer behavior refers to the actions of ultimate consumers directly involved in obtaining, consuming, and disposing of products, along with the decision processes surrounding these actions.

7.2 What are some determinants of consumer behavior? Determinants of consumer behavior include both personal influences and interpersonal influences. Personal influences include an individual's needs and motives; perceptions, attitudes, and experiences; and self-concept. Interpersonal influences include cultural, social and family influences.

⌜8⌟ Discuss relationship marketing.

Relationship marketing is an organization's attempt to develop long-term, cost-effective links with individual customers for mutual benefit. Good relationships with customers can be a vital strategic weapon for a firm. By identifying current purchasers and maintaining a positive relationship with them, an organization can efficiently target its best customers, fulfill their needs, and create loyalty. Information technologies, frequency and affinity programs, and one-on-one efforts all help build relationships with customers.

Assessment Check Answers ☑

8.1 What is the lifetime value of a customer? The lifetime value of a customer incorporates the revenues and intangible benefits from the customer over the life of the relationship with a firm, minus the amount the company must spend to acquire and serve the customer.

8.2 Discuss the increasing importance of one-on-one marketing efforts. One-on-one marketing is increasing in importance as consumers demand more customization in goods and services. It is also increasingly dependent on technology such as computer-aided design and manufacturing (CAD/CAM). The Internet also offers a way for businesses to connect with customers in a direct and personal manner.

Business Terms You Need to Know

marketing 322
exchange process 322
utility 323
marketing concept 324
person marketing 327
place marketing 327
event marketing 327
cause marketing 328
organization marketing 328

consumer (B2C) product 329
business (B2B) product 329
target market 330
marketing mix 330
marketing research 332
business intelligence 334
data mining 334
data warehouse 334
market segmentation 335

geographical
 segmentation 336
demographic
 segmentation 337
psychographic
 segmentation 340
product-related
 segmentation 340
end-use segmentation 342

consumer behavior 342
relationship marketing 344
lifetime value of a
 customer 344
frequency marketing 346
affinity program 346
comarketing 346
cobranding 346

Review Questions

1. Define the four different types of utility and explain how marketing contributes to the creation of utility. Then choose one of the following companies and describe how it creates each type of utility with its goods or services:

   a. Taco Bell

   b. Polo Ralph Lauren

   c. Miami Dolphins

   d. Supercuts hair salons

   e. Adobe Systems

2. Describe the shift from a seller's market to a buyer's market. Why was this move important to marketers?

3. Describe how an organization might combine person marketing and event marketing. Give an example.

4. Describe how an organization might combine cause marketing and organization marketing. Give an example.

5. Identify each of the following as a consumer product or a business product, or classify it as both:

   a. cup of coffee

   b. iPad

   c. gasoline

   d. boat trailer

   e. hand sanitizer

   f. Post-its

6. Identify and describe the four strategies that blend to create a marketing mix.

7. What is a target market? Why is target-market selection usually the first step in the development of a marketing strategy?

8. Identify the two strategies that a firm could use to develop a marketing mix for international markets. What are the advantages and disadvantages of each?

9. Describe the types of data that someone who is thinking of starting an accounting practice might choose to gather. How might this businessperson use the data in making the start-up decision?

10. Explain each of the methods used to segment consumer and business markets. Which methods do you think would be most effective for each of the following? Why? (Note that a combination of methods might be applicable.)

    a. supermarket featuring organic foods

    b. hair-care products

    c. tour bus company

    d. line of baby food

    e. pet insurance

    f. dry cleaner

11. What are the three major determinants of consumer behavior? Give an example of how each one might influence a person's purchasing decision.

12. What are the benefits of relationship marketing? Describe how frequency and affinity programs work toward building relationships.

Projects and Teamwork Applications

1. On your own or with a classmate, choose one of the following products and create an advertisement that illustrates how your firm creates time, place, and form utility in its delivery of the product to the customer.

   a. auto-repair service

   b. hiking tours

   c. craft supply store

   d. pet-sitting service

2. Choose one of the following nonprofit organizations or find one on your own. Research the organization online to learn more about it. Outline your proposed contents for a fund-raising event based on the chapter discussion of

nontraditional marketing, such as cause marketing or organization marketing.

   a. ASPCA

   b. Arthritis Foundation

   c. Red Cross

   d. Salvation Army

3. As a marketer, if you can find ways to classify your firm's goods and services as both business and consumer products, most likely your company's sales will increase as you build relationships with a new category of customers. On your own or with a classmate, choose one of the following products and outline a marketing strategy for attracting the classification of customer that is *opposite* the one listed in parentheses.

   a. hybrid car (consumer)

   b. LCD TV (consumer)

   c. limousine service (business)

   d. office furniture (business)

4. Think of two situations in which you have been a customer: one in which you were satisfied with the merchandise you received and one in which you were not. Make a list of the reasons you were satisfied in the first case and a list of the reasons you were not satisfied in the second case. Would you say that the failure was the result of the seller's not understanding your needs?

5. Comarketing and cobranding are techniques that organizations often use to market their own and each other's products, such as Nike running shoes and the Apple iPod. On your own or with a classmate, choose two firms with products you think would work well together for comarketing separate products or cobranding a single product. Then create an advertisement for your comarketing or cobranding effort.

▊ Web Assignments

1. **Demographic trends**. *The Statistical Abstract of the United States* is an excellent source of demographic and economic data about the United States. Visit the Web site listed here and click on "population." In terms of age and race, what does the U.S. population currently look like? What will the U.S. population look like in the decades to come?

   http://www.census.gov/compendia/statab/

2. **Market segmentation**. Go to the Web site of Canon USA and review the company's array of product offerings. Prepare a brief report on how Canon segments its markets.

   http://www.usa.canon.com/home

3. **Customer loyalty programs**. Airlines and hotel chains have extensive customer loyalty programs. Pick an airline and hotel chain and print out information on the firm's customer loyalty program. (Two examples can be found at the Web sites listed below.) Bring the material to class to participate in a discussion on this topic.

   http://www.southwest.com/rapid_rewards/

   http://www.marriott.com/rewards/rewards-program.mi

Note: Internet Web addresses change frequently. If you don't find the exact sites listed, you may need to access the organization's home page and search from there or use a search engine such as Bing or Google.

CASE 11.1   Advertising on Facebook: Unlimited Potential?

With 800 million active members, Facebook is a global social network of unprecedented size—and untold potential revenue. Users are familiar with the advertisements in the right-hand margins. Big names, such as Walmart and PepsiCo, post ads, as do smaller companies. What users may not realize is that advertisers can use personal information and connections within Facebook to refine the targeting of ads. For example, women who change their relationship status to "engaged" will suddenly start seeing ads from local caterers, planners, wedding-gown stores, photographers, and so on.

Facebook recently surpassed Google as the most visited site in the United States. Facebook's "self-service" ads consist of a small photo and some text. An advertiser establishes a daily budget—there is no minimum—using Facebook's ad-creation tool. When the advertiser has spent the day's entire budget, Facebook stops running the ad. If money is left over, the advertiser can roll it over to the next day's budget. Advertisers pay either every time a user views the ad or every time a user actually clicks on the link in the ad to open the company's Web site.

Facebook members can become "fans" of an advertiser's Facebook page or can reply to an invitation to a company-sponsored event through Facebook. But as with other media, consumers have a deep mistrust of Web advertising as a credible source of information. With ads on Facebook becoming omnipresent, click-through rates (CTRs) have fallen to about 0.3 percent from close to 3 percent. Some Facebook users find the ads off-putting—or worse—because advertisers can target them so precisely. But Dan Rose, the vice president for business development at Facebook, predicted that the quality of the ads would improve as more companies use the system.

Facebook requires the text and photo in an ad to be relevant to what is being advertised. However, Facebook does not review ads before they are posted. The only review system is user feedback. If a user reports an ad as misleading, offensive, uninteresting, irrelevant, repetitive, or "other," Facebook deletes the ad from that user's page. The more people ask for an ad to be removed, the less likely Facebook is to allow it be posted on other people's pages.

Some observers predict that Facebook will transform Web advertising and even the advertising industry itself. And just as in the real world, in the virtual world people are much more likely to value the opinions of their friends more than those of people—or advertisers—they don't know.

Questions for Critical Thinking

1. Why do advertisers continue to post ads on Facebook, even though the click-through response rate is so low?
2. How does Web advertising affect consumer behavior? Does it help build customer relationships or not?

Sources: Christy Hunter, "Number of Facebook Users Could Reach 1 Billion by 2012," *The Exponent Online,* http://www.purdueexponent.org, accessed March 24, 2012; Claire Cain Miller, "Twitter Unveils Plan to Draw Money from Ads," *The New York Times,* http://www.nytimes.com, accessed March 24, 2012; Courtney Rubin, "Should You Advertise on Facebook?" Inc.com, http://www.inc.com, accessed March 24, 2012; Carmen Nobel, "Facebook Ad Model Is Friend to Small Business," *The Street,* http://www.thestreet.com, accessed March 24, 2012; Steve Rubal, "Facebook Will Rule the Web During the Next Decade," *Advertising Age,* http://www.adage.com, accessed March 24, 2012; Jonathan L. Yarmis, "How Facebook Will Upend Advertising," *BusinessWeek,* http://www.businessweek.com, accessed March 24, 2012; Brad Stone, "Ads Posted on Facebook Strike Some as Off-Key," *The New York Times,* http://www.nytimes.com, accessed March 24, 2012; Kunur Patel, "Will E-Commerce Help Facebook's Ad Sales?" *Ad Age Digital,* http://www.adage.com, accessed March 24, 2012.

Arthritis Foundation Takes Aim at Pain

CASE 11.2

If you believe medication is the best way to alleviate arthritis pain, the Arthritis Foundation and the Ad Council have a message for you: Exercise.

New ads in a continuing print, television, and online campaign created pro bono by New York's Young & Rubicam Agency feature former tennis star Billie Jean King, who promotes pain relievers such as swimming, walking, running, biking, and of course tennis. After the campaign's light-hearted introduction, "We want it to be more urgent and hard hitting, to aim at Baby Boomers 55 and older, to have them take action today to prevent the progression of arthritis," says a vice president for the Arthritis Foundation.

Arthritis affects one in five adults and is the leading cause of disability in the United States. "We're really proud of our work with the Arthritis Foundation," says Y&R's president. "Helping raise awareness for such a prevalent disease and empowering those with arthritis to take action is incredibly important." King was chosen for the campaign because she suffers from osteoarthritis, and because tennis is a sport for all ages.

Questions for Critical Thinking

1. King says of her spokesperson role, "I'm a little chubby, I think people are going to relate." Do you agree? Why or why not?

2. One critic called the campaign "too rational. Most effective ads are emotional." Do you agree? Why or why not?

Sources: U.S. Open corporate Web site, "Billie Jean King in New Arthritis Campaign," http://www.usopen.org, accessed March 24, 2012; Arthritis Foundation, "Billie Jean King, Arthritis Foundation, Ad Council and USTA Launch Arthritis Campaign," press release, http://www.arthritis.org, accessed March 24, 2012; Jane L. Levere, "On the Move, Athletically, Against Arthritis," *The New York Times*, www.nytimes.com, accessed March 24, 2012.

CASE 11.3 — Zipcar and UNH: Customer-Driven Marketing

When you're a college student, getting around campus (or off campus) can sometimes be a challenge. You can walk. You can ride your bike or your skateboard. But when rain is pummeling your backpack or when you have to carry that heavy box of marketing flyers across campus, you wish you had a car—not to mention if you want to head off campus for a weekend road trip. So you decide to bring a car to campus, but discover that you're forking over several hundred dollars for a parking permit and you can't find a place to park anyway. Then there's the expense of gas and insurance, and the nattering of friends who want a ride or who want to borrow your car—just for an hour or an evening. Depending on where you go to school, Zipcar has got you covered. If you happen to attend the University of New Hampshire, you're in luck.

Zipcar is a car-sharing network based in Cambridge, Massachusetts, that operates in metropolitan areas and on university campuses around the United States, Canada, and the United Kingdom. Car-sharing was already popular in Europe 10 years ago when Zipcar founders decided to see if the idea would fly in the U.S. Shortly after its introduction to urban dwellers and U.S. students, Zipcar's message had wheels.

At the University of New Hampshire (UNH), students and faculty already had several transportation options, including an Amtrak station nearby and several bus services. But Brett Pasinella, who works for the University Office of Sustainability, wanted to find a way to link the different transportation options and expand them in a sustainable fashion. His research told him that Zipcar fit UNH's existing options. "We went through a bidding process to get the right company," Pasinella says. The firm had to meet UNH's requirement that membership include insurance and fuel. "Zipcar really stood out because of their technology and understanding of the services and what we were looking for," explains Pasinella. But UNH still had to sell the idea to budget-conscious students in order to make it work.

The Zipcar system is simple: for a $35 annual fee, UNH students or faculty get round-the-clock access to Zipcars that are parked in designated parking spots around campus. When they join, members receive their own Zipcard (like a key card) that unlocks any Zipcar. Members reserve a car online, then use their Zipcard to access it. Gas and insurance are included with membership, as well as an average of 180 miles per day.

To sell the concept to UNH students, Brett Pasinella engaged a senior class of marketing students to develop a marketing plan for all the transportation systems available on campus. The class split into teams, one of which chose the Zipcar project. The marketing students created presentations designed to answer questions and help classmates overcome the hurdle of a $35 fee. Once they realized that an annual parking permit at UNH is $400—and that gas and insurance are included with Zipcar membership—they began to recognize the benefits. In addition, they saw Zipcars parked around the campus so they became familiar with the brand.

Pasinella notes that UNH is also a sustainable campus, and that most of his job is focused on finding ways to reduce waste and energy use—including throughout the university's transportation system. Zipcar's entire fleet is EPA Smart Way certified and includes hybrids as well as other zero-emission vehicles. But Pasinella and UNH marketing student Erin Badger point out the realities of college life. "A lot of students will focus on the fact that Zipcar is easier for them and saves them money," concedes Erin Badger. "We have to promote Zipcar toward what students are looking for, and those are the two biggest factors."

After the first year in operation at UNH, Zipcar membership is growing. Pasinella plans to market the service proactively in coming years—sending Zipcar information to incoming students and faculty before they arrive on campus with their own vehicles. UNH conducted a survey of members and discovered that users like the convenience and visibility of the cars as well as the low cost. Badger might be the Zipcar's best spokesperson at UNH. "I wish I'd figured it out a lot sooner," she admits. She accrued a lot of parking tickets around campus before she joined Zipcar. "I'd have saved myself a lot of money if I'd joined sooner," she says.

Questions for Critical Thinking

1. Who is Zipcar's target market? How might Zipcar's market be further segmented?

2. Describe how Zipcar might create a marketing mix for colleges and universities.

3. Just as Zipcar must market to UNH, UNH in turn must market the Zipcar concept to its customers—students and faculty. Describe how studying consumer behavior could help select a strategy for UNH's marketing effort.

4. What steps can Zipcar take to manage its relationship with UNH?

Sources: Zipcar Web site, http://www.zipcar.com, accessed March 24, 2012; University of New Hampshire Transportation Services, http://www.unh.edu/transportation, accessed March 24, 2012; "Zipcar, Inc.," Bloomberg Businessweek, http://investingbusinessweek.com, accessed March 24, 2012.

Learning Objectives

1. Explain product strategy.

2. Briefly describe the four stages of the product life cycle.

3. Discuss product identification.

4. Outline the major components of an effective distribution strategy.

5. Explain wholesaling.

6. Describe retailing.

7. Identify distribution channel decisions and logistics.

Chapter 12

Product and Distribution Strategies

Steve Cole/iStockphoto

Panama Canal's Expansion Is a Game Changer

Life has changed in many ways since the 1960s, but here's one way you might not have thought about. Back then, every commercial ship afloat could pass through the Panama Canal. Today, about 15 percent of shipping must travel a different route than through the 100-year-old passage between the Atlantic and Pacific Oceans because the ships are too wide or too deep to navigate the canal.

Rising fuel prices have driven shipping companies to build ever-larger ships that can carry more cargo in fewer trips. When ships can't travel through the canal, goods from Asia must travel over land by truck and rail, which is more expensive, to reach consumers on the East Coast where about two-thirds of the U.S. population lives.

A $5.25 billion expansion project is underway to widen and deepen the canal, allowing larger, post-Panama-sized ships to pass through the all-water route from Asia to the U.S. Atlantic coast. The expansion doubles the amount of freight that can go through the canal and will have a significant impact on distribution.

By reducing shipping costs, the canal's expansion will reward shipping companies, manufacturers, and retailers with higher profit margins and consumers with lower prices, although goods will take a bit longer to arrive. Still, the trade-off is considered worthwhile. The largest ships passing through the canal today can carry about 4,000 20-foot containers; after the expansion is complete in 2014, ships carrying 12,600—triple the amount—will sail through.

Exactly where these ships will dock is still an open question. Currently they can put in only at Norfolk, Virginia, but ports in New York, New Jersey, Maryland, and Florida are among those racing to prepare for the arrival of the larger ships. "The Panama Canal . . . is stimulating a great deal of infrastructure investment and attention into the port systems, particularly along the East Coast of the U.S., the mid-Atlantic coast, and certain areas of the Gulf Coast as well," says one report. With new access to and from Asia through the canal, even railroads expect things in the transportation and distribution business to change. Whenever new capacity is built in a global transportation system, people find a way to use it.[1]

Overview

In this chapter we examine ways in which organizations design and implement marketing strategies that address customers' needs and wants. Two of the most powerful such tools are strategies that relate to products, which include both goods and services, and those that relate to the distribution of those products.

As the story of the Panama Canal illustrates, successful organizations stay ahead of changes in their business environment and anticipate their customers' needs. Widening the Panama Canal assures that it remains the route of choice for today's commercial vessels, saving fuel and minimizing shipping costs.

This chapter focuses on the first two elements of the marketing mix: product and distribution. Our discussion of product strategy begins by describing the classifications of goods and services, customer service, product lines and the product mix, and the product life cycle. Companies often shape their marketing strategies differently when they are introducing a new product, when the product has established itself in the marketplace, and when it is declining in popularity. We also discuss product identification through brand name and distinctive packaging, and the ways in which companies foster loyalty to their brands to keep customers coming back for more.

Distribution, the second mix variable discussed, focuses on moving goods and services from producer to wholesaler to retailer to buyers. Managing the distribution process includes making decisions such as what kind of wholesaler to use and where to offer products for sale. Retailers can range from specialty stores to factory outlets and everything in between, and they must choose appropriate customer service, pricing, and location strategies in order to succeed. The chapter concludes with a look at logistics, the process of coordinating the flow of information, goods, and services among suppliers and on to final consumers.

`1` Product Strategy

product bundle of physical, service, and symbolic characteristics designed to satisfy consumer wants.

Most people respond to the question "What is a product?" by listing its physical features. By contrast, marketers take a broader view. To them, a **product** is a bundle of physical, service, and symbolic characteristics designed to satisfy consumer wants. The chief executive officer of a major tool manufacturer once startled his stockholders with this statement: "Last year our customers bought over 1 million quarter-inch drill bits, and none of them wanted to buy the product. They all wanted quarter-inch holes." Product strategy involves considerably more than just producing a good or service; instead, it focuses on benefits. The marketing conception of a product includes decisions about package design, brand name, trademarks, warranties, product image, new-product development, and customer service. Think, for instance, about your favorite soft drink. Do you like it for its taste alone? Or do other attributes, such as clever ads, attractive packaging, ease of purchase from vending machines and other convenient locations, and overall image, also attract you? These other attributes may influence your choice more than you realize.

Classifying Goods and Services

LECTURE ENHANCER:
In your opinion, is it more difficult to market products and services for B2B or B2C? Why?

Marketers have found it useful to classify goods and services as either B2C or B2B, depending on whether the purchasers of the particular item are consumers or businesses. These classifications can be subdivided further, and each type requires a different competitive strategy.

Classifying Consumer Goods and Services

The classification typically used for ultimate consumers who purchase products for their own use and enjoyment and not for resale is based on consumer buying habits. *Convenience products* are items the consumer seeks to purchase frequently, immediately, and with little effort. Items stocked in gas-station markets, vending machines, and local newsstands are usually convenience products—for example, newspapers, snacks, candy, coffee, and bread.

LECTURE ENHANCER:
Which of these B2C classifications do you think would be the most difficult to market? Why?

Shopping products are those typically purchased only after the buyer has compared competing products in competing stores. A person intent on buying a new sofa or dining room table may visit many stores, examine perhaps dozens of pieces of furniture, and spend days making the final decision. *Specialty products*, the third category of consumer products, are those that a purchaser is willing to make a special effort to obtain. The purchaser is already familiar with the item and considers it to have no reasonable substitute. The nearest Lexus dealer may be 75 miles away, but if you have decided you want one, you will make the trip.

Note that a shopping product for one person may be a convenience item for someone else. Each item's product classification is based on buying patterns of the majority of people who purchase it.

The interrelationship of the marketing mix factors is shown in Figure 12.1. By knowing the appropriate classification for a specific product, the marketing decision maker knows quite a bit about how the other mix variables will adapt to create a profitable, customer-driven marketing strategy.

Classifying Business Goods *Business products* are goods and services such as paycheck services and huge multifunction copying machines used in operating an organization; they also include machinery, tools, raw materials, components, and buildings used to produce other items for resale. While consumer products are classified by buying habits, business products are classified based on how they are used and by their basic characteristics. Products that are long-lived and relatively expensive are called *capital items*. Less costly products that are consumed within a year are referred to as *expense items*.

Buying a *specialty product* takes extra effort. The Fiat 500 is sold in a limited number of places.

FIGURE 12.1 — Marketing Impacts of Consumer Product Classification

Marketing Strategy Factor	Convenience Product	Shopping Product	Specialty Product
· Purchase Frequency	· Frequent	· Relatively infrequent	· Infrequent
· Store Image	· Unimportant	· Very important	· Important
· Price	· Low	· Relatively high	· High
· Promotion	· By manufacturer	· By manufacturer and retailers	· By manufacturer and retailers
· Distribution Channel	· Many wholesalers and retailers	· Relatively few wholesalers and retailers	· Very few wholesalers and retailers
· Number of Retail Outlets	· Many	· Few	· Very small number; often one per market area

LECTURE ENHANCER:
Which of these B2B
classifications do you think
would be the most difficult
to market? Why?

CLASS ACTIVITY:
Ask students what product
attributes an apple orchard
might emphasize in
marketing the apples to a
pie filling processor.

LECTURE ENHANCER:
Discuss the pros and cons of
marketing products versus
services.

CLASS ACTIVITY:
Ask students what ideas
they might have for a hotel
cleaning service company
to market their intangible
service.

LECTURE ENHANCER:
Why might it be a good
idea for producers of
installations to include
customer input in the
development of new
products?

Five basic categories of B2B products exist: installations, accessory equipment, component parts and materials, raw materials, and supplies. *Installations* are major capital items, such as new factories, heavy equipment and machinery, and custom-made equipment. Installations are expensive and often involve buyer and seller negotiations that may last for more than a year before a purchase actually is made. Purchase approval frequently involves a number of different people—production specialists, representatives from the purchasing department, and members of top management—who must agree on the final choice.

Although *accessory equipment* also includes capital items, they are usually less expensive and shorter lived than installations and involve fewer decision makers. Examples include hand tools and fax machines. *Component parts and materials* are finished business goods that become part of a final product, such as disk drives that are sold to computer manufacturers or batteries purchased by automakers. *Raw materials* are farm and natural products used in producing other final products. Examples include milk, wood, leather, and soybeans. *Supplies* are expense items used in a firm's daily operation that do not become part of the final product. Often referred to as MRO (maintenance, repair, and operating supplies), they include paper clips, light bulbs, and copy paper.

Classifying Services Services can be classified as either B2C or B2B. Child and elder care centers and auto detail shops provide services for consumers, while the Pinkerton security patrol at a local factory and Kelly Services' temporary office workers are examples of business services. In some cases, a service can accommodate both consumer and business markets. For example, when ServiceMaster cleans the upholstery in a home, it is a B2C service, but when it spruces up the painting system and robots in a manufacturing plant, it is a B2B service.

Like tangible goods, services can also be convenience, shopping, or specialty products depending on the buying patterns of customers. However, they are distinguished from goods in several ways. First, services, unlike goods, are intangible. In addition, they are perishable because firms cannot stockpile them in inventory. They are also difficult to standardize, because they must meet individual customers' needs. Finally, from a buyer's perspective, the service provider is the service; the two are inseparable in the buyer's mind.

Marketing Strategy Implications

The consumer product classification system is a useful tool in marketing strategy. As described in Figure 12.1, because a new refrigerator is classified as a shopping good, its marketers have a better idea of its promotion, pricing, and distribution needs.

Each group of business products, however, requires a different marketing strategy. Because most installations and many component parts are frequently marketed directly from manufacturer to business buyer, the promotional emphasis is on personal selling rather than on advertising. By contrast, marketers of supplies and accessory equipment rely more on advertising, because their products are often sold through an intermediary, such as a wholesaler. Producers of installations and component parts may involve their customers in new-product development, especially when the business product is custom made. Finally, firms selling supplies and accessory equipment place greater emphasis on competitive pricing strategies than do other B2B marketers, who tend to concentrate more on product quality and customer service.

Product Lines and Product Mix

Few firms operate with a single product. If their initial entry is successful, they tend to increase their profit and growth chances by adding new offerings. The iPhone and iPad, with their touchscreen technology and App Stores, are harbingers of things to come. Although most mainstream knowledge workers will probably continue to use conventional computers for some time, touchscreen technology is fast becoming a standard feature in consumer electronics.[2]

A company's **product line** is a group of related products marked by physical similarities or intended for a similar market. A **product mix** is the assortment of product lines and individual goods and services that a firm offers to consumers and business users. The Coca-Cola Company and PepsiCo both have product lines that include old standards—Coke Classic and Diet Coke, Pepsi and Diet Pepsi. But recently, PepsiCo announced it would start distributing Tampico Plus in selected states. Unlike other products from Tampico Beverages, Tampico Plus drinks contain vitamins A, C, and E. They also have half as much sugar as regular Tampico drinks. Thus, they meet the guidelines for beverages that can be sold in U.S. high schools, which want to limit the amount of sugar in drinks available to students.[3]

Marketers must assess their product mix continually to ensure company growth, to satisfy changing consumer needs and wants, and to adjust to competitors' offerings. To remain competitive, marketers look for gaps in their product lines and fill them with new offerings or modified versions of existing ones. A helpful tool that is frequently used in making product decisions is the product life cycle.

Teri Stratford

A *product line* includes several related products designed to have the same appearance, like these PepsiCo products.

2 Product Life Cycle

Once a product is on the market, it usually goes through four stages known as the **product life cycle**: introduction, growth, maturity, and decline. As Figure 12.2 shows, industry sales and profits vary depending on the life cycle stage of an item.

Product life cycles are not set in stone; not all products follow this pattern precisely, and different products may spend different periods of time in each stage. The concept, however, helps the marketing planner anticipate developments throughout the various stages of a product's life. Profits assume a predictable pattern through the stages, and promotional emphasis shifts from dispensing product information in the early stages to heavy brand promotion in the later ones.

Stages of the Product Life Cycle

In the *introduction stage*, the firm tries to promote demand for its new offering; inform the market about it; give free samples to entice consumers to make a trial purchase; and explain its features, uses, and benefits. Sometimes companies partner at this stage to promote new products. Others launch product offerings that enhance the use of products made by other companies, thus granting the start-up nearly immediate name recognition. Loopt is one such firm. Created by three college students, California-based Loopt transforms users'

product line group of related products marked by physical similarities or intended for a similar market.

product mix the assortment of product lines and individual goods and services that a firm offers to consumers and business users.

Assessment Check ✓

1. How do consumer products differ from business products?

2. Differentiate among convenience, shopping, and specialty products.

product life cycle four basic stages—introduction, growth, maturity, and decline—through which a successful product progresses.

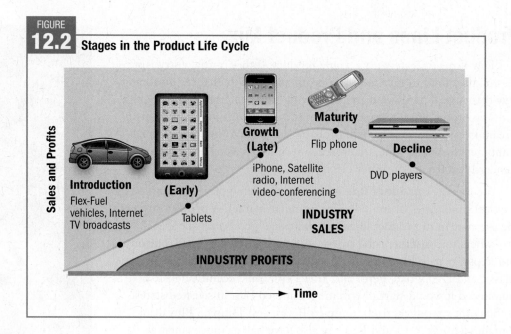

FIGURE 12.2 Stages in the Product Life Cycle

Sales and Profits

Introduction
Flex-Fuel vehicles, Internet TV broadcasts

(Early)
Tablets

Growth (Late)
iPhone, Satellite radio, Internet video-conferencing

Maturity
Flip phone

Decline
DVD players

INDUSTRY SALES

INDUSTRY PROFITS

Time

cell phones into a GPS-sharing system that alerts them when friends are nearby. In addition, Loopt uses integrated content from Facebook, Citysearch, Bing, and other Web services to provide more geographic search data to users, and offers iPad and BlackBerry apps.[4]

New-product development costs and extensive introductory promotional campaigns to acquaint prospective buyers with the merits of the innovation, though essential to later success, are expensive and commonly lead to losses in the introductory stage. Some firms are seeking to lower these costs through ultra-low-cost product development, which involves meeting customer needs with the lowest-cost innovations possible, designing from scratch with a stripped-down budget, and the simplest engineering possible. But all these expenditures are necessary if the firm is to profit later.

During the *growth stage*, sales climb quickly as new customers join early users who now are repurchasing the item. Word-of-mouth referrals and continued advertising and other special promotions by the firm induce others to make trial purchases. At this point, the company begins to earn profits on the new product. This success encourages competitors to enter the field with similar offerings, and price competition develops. After its initial success with the Kindle, Amazon faced competition from Barnes & Noble's Nook. Amazon rushed to launch its Kindle for the iPad, then Barnes & Noble countered with its popular NOOK Color. The two competitors continue to release new models with additional features.[5]

In the *maturity stage*, industry sales at first increase, but they eventually reach a saturation level at which further expansion is difficult. Competition also intensifies, increasing the availability of the product. Firms concentrate on capturing competitors' customers, often dropping prices to further the appeal. Cell phones are in the maturity stage: competitors compete not only on price but also on features such as calendars, e-mail and attachments, messaging capability, full-color screens, keyboards, and fax and word-processing functions. When flat-screen TVs reached the maturity stage, companies tried to entice consumers to buy new ones by offering even bigger TVs than they had before, topping the 90-inch mark. As worldwide production of high-definition TVs increased dramatically, makers of TVs with the old LED backlight display lowered their prices dramatically to stay competitive with TVs featuring newer technology.[6]

LECTURE ENHANCER:
Think of a product introduced in recent years. How did it pass from introduction to growth cycle?

CLASS ACTIVITY:
Ask students to identify examples of products that are in each stage of the product life cycle.

LECTURE ENHANCER:
In what stage of the product life cycle is a latte from Starbucks?

Hit & Miss

Kodak Ignores the Digital Picture

When Eastman Kodak entered a restructuring bankruptcy recently, it had become a victim of its own success. The 131-year-old Rochester, New York, company virtually invented the film industry, made Hollywood possible, and later dominated the market with iconic brands such as Brownie, Instamatic, and Kodachrome. But it acted years too late to adapt to the digital technology that replaced its most innovative product—film. "Clearly they could have made some changes faster," said one former employee, "but there just weren't a lot of options to replace the film business."

One option, ironically, was the digital camera, which Kodak also invented but failed to pursue aggressively for fear of hurting its profitable film products. Kodak's focus on film while other technologies were created caused the company to lose focus on its future and caused a severe decline in its business. Instead of capitalizing on its digital technology, Kodak's storied film products became a liability. The restructured, smaller firm will focus on photo printing and desktop inkjet printers.

Questions for Critical Thinking

1. In what way did Kodak let its history become a liability?

2. Kodak's CEO says the company was better at inventing products than at commercializing them. What does that statement mean?

Sources: "Kodak to Stop Making Cameras, Digital Frames," *The Wall Street Journal,* February 9, 2012, http://online.wsj.com; Dawn McCarty and Beth Jinks, "Kodak Files for Bankruptcy as Digital Era Spells End to Film," *Bloomberg Businessweek,* January 25, 2012, www .businessweek.com; Michael J. De La Merced, "Eastman Kodak Files for Bankruptcy," *The New York Times,* January 19, 2012, www.nytimes.com; Michael Kraten, "Sears, Kodak, and the Product Life Cycle," AQPQ, January 3, 2012, http://aqpq.org.

Sales volume fades late in the maturity stage, and some of the weaker competitors leave the market. During this stage, firms promote mature products aggressively to protect their market share and to distinguish their products from those of competitors.

Sales continue to fall in the *decline stage,* the fourth phase of the product life cycle. Profits decline and may become losses as further price-cutting occurs in the reduced overall market for the item. Competitors gradually exit, making some profits possible for the remaining firms in the shrinking market. The decline stage usually is caused by a product innovation or a shift in consumer preferences. Sometimes technology change can hasten the decline stage for a product. For example, more than 90 percent of U.S. homes contain at least one DVD player. Once touted as the ultimate in DVD technology, high-definition DVDs have now been superseded by Blu-ray technology and online streaming sites. Online sites where consumers can simply download movies or television shows are becoming another major competitor for entertainment as the link between computer and television is becoming faster and more reliable.[7]

LECTURE ENHANCER: When does a popular movie enter the decline stage? Why?

Marketing Strategy Implications of the Product Life Cycle

Like the product classification system, the product life cycle is a useful concept for designing a marketing strategy that will be flexible enough to accommodate changing marketplace characteristics. These competitive moves may involve developing new products, lowering prices, increasing distribution coverage, creating new promotional campaigns, or any combination of these approaches. In general, the marketer's objective is to extend the product life cycle as long as the item is profitable. Some products can be highly profitable during the later stages of their life cycle, because all the initial development costs have already been recovered. Others, like conventional film, can drag down a company that can't let go even as the product dies, as Eastman Kodak found. See the "Hit & Miss" feature.

A commonly used strategy for extending the life cycle is to increase customers' frequency of use. Walmart and Target offer grocery sections in many of their stores to increase the frequency of shopper visits. Another strategy is to add new users. Despite the recent lending crunch, credit-card issuers are actively advertising for new—and viable—customers. Chase has been pushing its new line of credit cards designed for small businesses, called Ink. Each Ink card program has its own benefits and rewards, such as no interest (Ink Bold) and cash back (Ink Cash).[8]

A third product life cycle extension strategy is to find new uses for products. Post-it has made successful use of this strategy. One recent blog posting lists 20 innovative ways students can use Post-it Notes, including wrapping the sticky edge around a cable to identify it and using the sticky edge to clean between the keys of a computer keyboard.[9] Finally, a firm may decide to change package sizes, labels, and product designs. Mattel has done this several times with its iconic Barbie doll.

Stages in New-Product Development

New-product development is expensive, time consuming, and risky, because only about one-third of new products become success stories. Products can fail for many reasons. Some are not properly developed and tested, some are poorly packaged, and others lack adequate promotional support or distribution or do not satisfy a consumer need or want. Even successful products eventually reach the end of the decline stage and must be replaced with new-product offerings.

Most of today's newly developed items are aimed at satisfying specific consumer demands. New-product development is becoming increasingly efficient and cost-effective because marketers use a systematic approach in developing new products. As Figure 12.3 shows, the new-product development process has six stages. Each stage requires a "go/no-go" decision by management before moving on to subsequent stages. Because items that go through each development stage only to be rejected at one of the final stages involve significant investments in both time and money, the sooner decision makers can identify a marginal product and drop it from further consideration, the less time and money will be wasted.

The starting point in the new-product development process is generating ideas for new offerings. Ideas come from many sources, including customer suggestions, suppliers, employees, research scientists, marketing research, inventors outside the firm, and competitive products. The most successful ideas are directly related to satisfying customer needs. Procter & Gamble's Febreze eliminates odors in the home and leaves a fresh scent. When P&G researchers discovered that cars often need freshening up, too—from transporting well-used athletic equipment, small children, and carryout meals—the company added Febreze CAR Vent Clips to the product line. The clip attaches to a car's air vent and comes in five scents.[10]

In the second stage, screening eliminates ideas that do not mesh with overall company objectives or that cannot be developed given the company's resources. Some firms hold

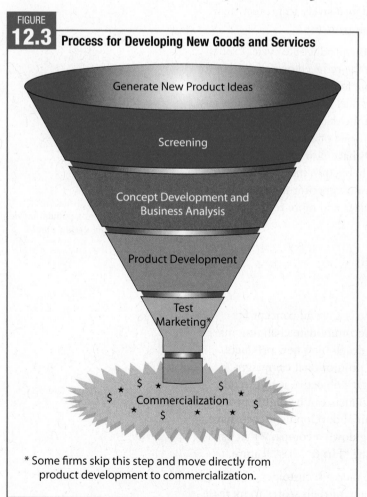

FIGURE 12.3 Process for Developing New Goods and Services

Generate New Product Ideas

Screening

Concept Development and Business Analysis

Product Development

Test Marketing*

Commercialization

* Some firms skip this step and move directly from product development to commercialization.

open discussions of new-product ideas with specialists who work in different functional areas in the organization.

During the concept development and business analysis phase, further screening occurs. The analysis involves assessing the new product's potential sales, profits, growth rate, and competitive strengths and determining whether it fits with the company's product, distribution, and promotional resources. *Concept testing*—marketing research designed to solicit initial consumer reaction to new-product ideas—may be used at this stage. For example, potential consumers might be asked about proposed brand names and other methods of product identification. *Focus groups* are sessions in which consumers meet with marketers to discuss what they like or dislike about current products and perhaps test or sample a new offering to provide some immediate feedback.

Next, an actual product is developed, subjected to a series of tests, and revised. Functioning prototypes or detailed descriptions of the product may be created. These designs are the joint responsibility of the firm's development staff and its marketers, who provide feedback on consumer reactions to the proposed product design, color, and other physical features. Sometimes prototypes do not meet the stated requirements. When the U.S. military began looking for an improved helmet, it asked four companies to submit prototypes for helmets that would be 35 percent more effective against fragmentation as well as handgun and small-arms bullets. But all four prototypes failed. Then, a couple of years later, one firm submitted a prototype so strong that military engineers didn't have equipment powerful enough to penetrate the shell. "We don't know exactly [how strong] it is, but it's better than we've ever seen before," said one U.S. Army spokesman. The military then had to build stronger testing equipment.[11]

Test marketing introduces a new product supported by a complete marketing campaign to a selected city or TV coverage area. Marketers look for a location with a manageable size, where residents match their target market's demographic profile, to test their product. During the test marketing stage, the item is sold in a limited area while the company examines both consumer responses to the new offering and the marketing effort used to support it. Test market results can help managers determine the product's likely performance in a full-scale introduction. Some firms skip test marketing, however, because of concerns that the test could reveal their strategies to the competition. Also, the expense of doing limited production runs of complex products such as a new auto or refrigerator is sometimes so high that the test marketing stage is skipped and the development process moves directly to the next stage.

In the final stage, commercialization, the product is made available in the marketplace. Sometimes this stage is referred to as a product launch. Considerable planning goes into this stage, because the firm's distribution, promotion, and pricing strategies must all be geared to support the new product offering. The video game maker Electronic Arts (EA) announced a new distribution strategy for future products. The company will release premium downloadable content (PLDC) for a game before releasing the complete, packaged version. The PLDC will be moderately priced and include three to four hours of playing time. The company will invite comments from reviewers and players and make changes to the final version prior to release.[12]

The need for a steady stream of new products to offer the firm's customers, the chances of product failure, and the tens of millions of dollars needed to complete a successful new-product launch make new-product development a vital process for 21st-century firms. However, as Table 12.1 illustrates, success is not guaranteed until the new-product offering achieves customer acceptance. Microsoft introduced a new operating system, Windows Vista, but it just never caught on. The next version of Windows, Windows 7, fared better. Sony's sock case for cameras is cute—but doesn't protect cameras from bumps and scrapes. And who

test marketing introduction of a new product supported by a complete marketing campaign to a selected city or TV coverage area.

LECTURE ENHANCER: What outside factors might affect the popularity or failure of a new product?

⌐12.1⌐ The Worst-Made Cars on the Road

RANK	AUTO	TYPICAL OWNER COMMENT
1	Yugo	"I once test drove a Yugo, during which the radio fell out, the gear shift knob came off in my hand, and I saw daylight through the strip around the windshield."
2	Chevy Vega	"As near as I could tell, the car was built from compressed rust."
3	Ford Pinto	"The barbecue that seats four."
4	AMC Gremlin	"It was entirely possible to read a Russian novel during the pause between stepping on the gas and feeling any semblance of forward motion."
5	Chevy Chevette	"The ad didn't show the car going anywhere fast . . . because it couldn't."

Source: Claire Martin, "The Worst Cars Ever," *MSN Autos,* January 11, 2012, http://editorial.autos.msn.com; *Car Talk,* http://www.cartalk.com, accessed March 1, 2012.

Assessment Check ☑

1. What are the stages of the product life cycle?

2. What are the marketing implications of each stage?

LECTURE ENHANCER: Choose a popular product. What is the brand, brand name, and trademark of the product?

brand name, term, sign, symbol, design, or some combination that identifies the products of one firm and differentiates them from competitors' offerings.

brand name part of the brand consisting of words or letters included in a name used to identify and distinguish the firm's offerings from those of competitors.

trademark brand that has been given legal protection.

CLASS ACTIVITY: Ask students which trademarks they think are most recognizable.

needs a heated mouse pad? Yet a firm recently introduced one. Sometimes a name is enough to doom a product from the start—consider Chicken Poop lip gloss.[13]

3 Product Identification

A major aspect of developing a successful new product involves methods used for identifying a product and distinguishing it from competing offerings. Both tangible goods and intangible services are identified by brands, brand names, and trademarks. A **brand** is a name, term, sign, symbol, design, or some combination that identifies the products of one firm and differentiates them from competitors' offerings. Tropicana, Pepsi, and Gatorade are all made by PepsiCo, but a unique combination of name, symbol, and package design distinguishes each brand from the others.

A **brand name** is that part of the brand consisting of words or letters included in a name used to identify and distinguish the firm's offerings from those of competitors. The brand name is the part of the brand that can be vocalized. Many brand names, such as Coca-Cola, McDonald's, American Express, Google, and Nike, are famous around the world. Likewise, the golden arches brand mark of McDonald's also is widely recognized.

A **trademark** is a brand that has been given legal protection. The protection is granted solely to the brand's owner. Trademark protection includes not only the brand name but also design logos, slogans, packaging elements, and product features such as color and shape. A well-designed trademark, such as the Nike swoosh, can make a difference in how positively consumers perceive a brand.

Selecting an Effective Brand Name

Good brands are easy to pronounce, recognize, and remember: Crest, Visa, and Dell are examples. Global firms face a real problem in selecting brand names, because an excellent brand name in one country may prove disastrous in another. Most languages have a short *a,* so Coca-Cola is pronounceable almost anywhere. But an advertising campaign for E-Z washing machines failed in the United Kingdom because the British pronounce z as "zed."

Brand names should also convey the right image to the buyer. One effective technique is to create a name that links the product with its positioning strategy. The name Purell reinforces the concept of sanitizing hands to protect against germs, Dove soap and beauty products give an impression of mildness, and Taster's Choice instant coffee supports the promotional claim "Tastes and smells like ground roast coffee."

Brand names also must be legally protectable. Trademark law specifies that brand names cannot contain words in general use, such as *television* or *automobile*. Generic words—words that describe a type of product—cannot be used exclusively by any organization. On the other hand, if a brand name becomes so popular that it passes into common language and turns into a generic word, the company can no longer use it as a brand name. Once upon a time, aspirin, linoleum, and zipper were exclusive brand names, but today they have become generic terms and are no longer legally protectable.

Brand Categories

A brand offered and promoted by a manufacturer is known as a *manufacturer's* (or *national* *brand*. Examples are Tide, Cheerios, Windex, Fossil, and Nike. But not all brand names belong to manufacturers; some are the property of retailers or distributors. A *private* (or *store*) *brand* identifies a product that is not linked to the manufacturer but instead carries a wholesaler's or retailer's label. Sears's Craftsman tools and Walmart's Ol' Roy dog food are examples.

Another branding decision marketers must make is whether to use a family branding strategy or an individual branding strategy. A *family brand* is a single brand name used for several related products. KitchenAid, Johnson & Johnson, Hewlett-Packard, and Arm & Hammer use a family name for their entire line of products. When a firm using family branding introduces a new product, both customers and retailers recognize the familiar brand name. The promotion of individual products within a line benefits all the items because the family brand is well known.

Other firms use an *individual branding* strategy by giving each product within a line a different name. For example, Procter & Gamble has individual brand names for its different laundry detergents, including Tide, Cheer, and Dash. Each brand targets a unique market segment. Consumers who want a cold-water detergent can choose Cheer over Tide or Dash, instead of purchasing a competitor's brand. Individual branding also builds competition within a firm and enables the company to increase overall sales.

Brand Loyalty and Brand Equity

Brands achieve varying consumer familiarity and acceptance. While a homeowner may insist on Anderson windows when renovating, the consumer buying a loaf of bread may not prefer any brand. Consumer loyalty increases a brand's value, so marketers try to strengthen brand loyalty. When a brand image suffers, marketers try to recreate a positive image.

Brand Loyalty Marketers measure brand loyalty in three stages: brand recognition, brand preference, and brand insistence. *Brand recognition* is brand acceptance strong enough that the consumer is aware of the brand, but not strong enough to cause a preference over other brands. A consumer might have heard of L'Oréal hair care products, for instance, without necessarily preferring them to Redken. Advertising, free samples, and discount coupons are among the most common ways to increase brand recognition.

Helen Sessions/Alamy

To be effective, *brand names* must be easy for consumers to pronounce, recognize, and remember.

LECTURE ENHANCER: Share an example of a brand name you have encountered that is not easy to pronounce. How does this affect the marketing of the good or service?

LECTURE ENHANCER: Discuss which brands of tissues students typically purchase. What factors influence their choices?

CLASS ACTIVITY: Lead a discussion regarding which store brand products are equal to or better than their brand name competitive counterparts.

Brian Besone/Feature Photo Service/NewsCom

Good design can make the everyday a little better.

IKEA

Everyday Fabulous Exhibit

IKEA installed this clever showpiece, meant to look like a bus stop, in New York City during Design Week. The retailer of affordable, well-designed contemporary furniture enjoys *brand insistence*—the ultimate expression of brand loyalty. For devoted IKEA fans, no other brand will do.

Brand preference occurs when a consumer chooses one firm's brand over a competitor's. At this stage, the consumer usually relies on previous experience in selecting the product. Furniture and other home furnishings fall into this category. A shopper who purchased an IKEA dining room table and chairs and was satisfied with them is likely to return to purchase a bedroom set. While there, this shopper might pick up a set of mixing bowls for the kitchen or a lamp for the family room—because he or she knows and likes the IKEA brand.

Brand insistence is the ultimate degree of brand loyalty, in which the consumer will look for it at another outlet, special-order it from a dealer, order by mail, or search the Internet. Shoppers who insist on IKEA products for their homes may drive an hour or two—making a day excursion of the venture—to visit an IKEA store. The combination of value for the money and the concept of IKEA as a shopping destination have given the brand a unique allure for shoppers.[14]

Brand-building strategies were once limited to the consumer realm, but now they are becoming more important for B2B brands as well. Intel, Xerox, IBM, and service providers such as Krystal Klean and Cisco are among the suppliers who have built brand names among business customers.

Brand Equity Brand loyalty is at the heart of **brand equity**, the added value that a respected and successful name gives to a product. This value results from a combination of factors, including awareness, loyalty, and perceived quality, as well as any feelings or images the customer associates with the brand. High brand equity offers financial advantages to a firm, because the product commands a relatively large market share and sometimes reduces price sensitivity, generating higher profits. Figure 12.4 shows the world's 10 most valuable brands and their estimated worth.

Brand awareness means the product is the first one that comes to mind when a product category is mentioned. If someone says "coffee," do you think of Starbucks, Dunkin' Donuts, or Folgers? Brand association is the link between a brand and other favorable images. A recent survey by American City Business Journals revealed that Apple, Southwest Airlines, UPS, Holiday Inn Express, and FedEx were the most recognizable brands in a field of 25.[15]

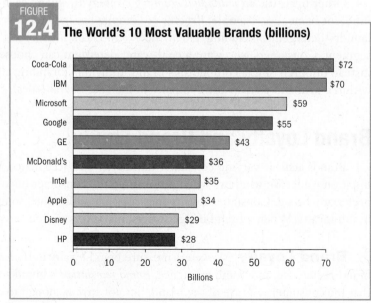

FIGURE 12.4 **The World's 10 Most Valuable Brands (billions)**

Brand	Billions
Coca-Cola	$72
IBM	$70
Microsoft	$59
Google	$55
GE	$43
McDonald's	$36
Intel	$35
Apple	$34
Disney	$29
HP	$28

Source: Interbrand, "Best Global Brands 2011," http://www.interbrand.com, accessed March 1, 2012.

Large companies have typically assigned the task of managing a brand's marketing strategies to a *brand manager*, who may also be called a *product manager* at some firms. This marketer plans and implements the balance of promotional, pricing, distribution, and product arrangements that leads to strong brand equity. A *category manager*, a newer type of marketer, oversees an entire group of products. Unlike traditional brand or product managers, category managers have profit responsibility for their product group. These managers are assisted by associates, usually called *analysts*. Part of the shift to category management was initiated by large retailers, when they realized there could be a benefit from the marketing muscle of large grocery and household goods producers such as Kraft and Procter & Gamble. As a result, producers began to focus their attention on in-store merchandising instead of mass-market advertising. A few years ago, Kraft reorganized its sales force so that each representative was responsible for a retailer's needs instead of pushing a single brand.

A **category advisor** functions in the B2B context. This vendor is the major supplier designated by a business customer to assume responsibility for dealing with all the other vendors for a project and presenting the entire package to the business buyer.

LECTURE ENHANCER:
How does global distribution affect a brand?

category advisor vendor that is designated by the business customer as the major supplier to assume responsibility for dealing with all the other vendors for a project and presenting the entire package to the business buyer.

Packages and Labels

Packaging and labels are important in product identification. They also play an important role in a firm's overall product strategy. Packaging affects the durability, image, and convenience of an item and is responsible for one of the biggest costs in many consumer products. Due to a growing demand to produce smaller, more environmentally friendly packages, box manufacturers and chemical companies are now working harder to create more compact packaging that is made from renewable sources and is recyclable. One-third of America's waste consists of containers and packaging, much of it from fast-food chains. Quiznos' "Eat Toasty, Be Green" campaign introduced environmentally friendly packaging. Among the changes to reduce the chain's environmental impact are 100 percent compostable, wax-coated paper cups; salad containers made of renewable sugarcane; napkins made from 100 percent recycled materials; and plastic lids made from 30 percent recycled PET bottles. Even the employees' uniforms were changed, with hats and aprons made from 100 percent recycled soda bottles.[16] PortionPac, maker of commercial cleaning solutions, has taken similar steps, as described in the "Hit & Miss" feature.

Choosing the right package is especially crucial in international marketing because marketers must be aware of such factors as language variations and cultural preferences. Consumers in African nations often prefer bold colors, but use of the country's flag colors may be problematic. Some countries frown on other uses of their flag. Also, in Africa red is often associated with death or witchcraft. Package size can vary according to the purchasing patterns and market conditions of a country. In countries with small refrigerators, people may want to buy their beverages one at a time rather than in six-packs. Package weight is another important issue, because shipping costs are often based on weight.

Labeling is an integral part of the packaging process as well. In the United States, labeling must meet federal laws requiring companies to provide enough information to allow consumers to make value comparisons among competitive

WORLD'S FIRST 100% COMPOSTABLE CHIP PACKAGE
Sun Chips Original

Teri Stratford

Due to a growing demand to produce more environmentally friendly packages, box manufacturers and chemical companies are now working harder to create more compact packaging that is made from renewable sources and is recyclable.

Hit & Miss

PortionPac Makes More By Selling Less

Founded in 1964, Chicago-based PortionPac is committed to its business model of selling less. PortionPac manufactures cleaning products for commercial use. It sells its cleaning systems of environmentally friendly cleaning solutions in concentrated premeasured "doses" to ensure accurate and controlled use. Instead of producing cleaning solutions in large bottles that contain water as an ingredient, PortionPac delivers concentrated solutions in smaller bottles with instructions for dilution. Customers reuse the original bottle, refilling it each time with a packet of cleaning solution.

The company believes using less of a product is akin to recycling, and it has won several green business awards for its business practices, and sustainability awards for 13 of its 22 products. PortionPac customers—school districts, office managers, health care facilities, and state agencies—like the company's philosophy. They save money and minimize the health hazards associated with cleaning products. While PortionPac currently sells only to organizations, the firm's long-term strategy includes a plan for retail sales.

Questions for Critical Thinking

1. How does PortionPac's practice of selling a product in small, premeasured doses contribute to its product strategy?
2. What issues should PortionPac consider before making the decision to sell in the retail market?

Sources: Company Web site, http://www.portionpaccorp.com, accessed March 1, 2012; Hosea Sanders, "Less Is More For Green Business," *ABC News*, http://abclocal.go.com, accessed March 1, 2012; Leigh Buchanan, "The Un-Factory," *Inc.*, http://www.inc.com, accessed March 1, 2012.

products and, in the case of food packaging, provide nutrition information on the label. Marketers who ship products to other countries have to comply with labeling requirements in those nations. This means knowing the answers to such questions as the following:

- Should the labels be in more than one language?
- Should ingredients be specified?
- Do the labels give enough information about the product to meet government standards?

CLASS ACTIVITY: Survey students for the labels they read most carefully and the reasons why.

The U.S. Food and Drug Administration (FDA) regulates the labeling of food and drug products, investigates violations, and enforces compliance with the Food, Drug, and Cosmetic Act. Typical violations include unauthorized health claims, unauthorized nutrient content claims, and unauthorized use of such terms as "healthy" and others that have strict regulatory definitions.[17]

Another important aspect of packaging and labeling is the *universal product code (UPC)*, the bar code read by optical scanners that print the name of the item and the price on a receipt. For many stores, these identifiers are useful not just for packaging and labeling but also for simplifying and speeding retail transactions and for evaluating customer purchases and controlling inventory. Radio-frequency identification (RFID) technology—embedded chips that can broadcast their product information to receivers—may replace UPC bar codes, however, as we'll discuss later in this chapter.

Assessment Check

1. Differentiate among a brand, a brand name, and a trademark.
2. Define *brand equity*.

4 Distribution Strategy

distribution strategy deals with the marketing activities and institutions involved in getting the right good or service to the firm's customers.

The next element of the marketing mix, **distribution strategy**, deals with the marketing activities and institutions involved in getting the right good or service to the firm's customers. Distribution decisions involve modes of transportation, warehousing, inventory control, order processing, and selection of marketing channels. Marketing channels typically

Going Green

Ava Anderson Non-Toxic: Makeup via Direct Distribution

Ava Anderson's cosmetics company, Ava Anderson Non-Toxic, grew from a teenager's alarm at discovering that most personal care products contain harmful ingredients, including carcinogens and endocrine disrupters. Then just 14, Anderson set out to find manufacturers who could develop and manufacture cosmetics to her own green standards. Only a few years later, the privately held company she founded with her mother was a finalist in *Entrepreneur* magazine's "Entrepreneur of the Year" competition, selected for its innovation, impact, and community.

The firm produces cosmetics, sunscreen, and skin, hair, and body care products without harmful chemicals. The products are sold by independent part- and full-time consultants who host parties and seminars and schedule individual customer appointments, providing direct distribution. The company offers ongoing training and rewards consultants with a percentage of their total sales, plus a percentage of the sales of any new consultants they recruit.

Anderson says she is thrilled to watch the company's consultants be successful, really enjoy their jobs, and share her passion to provide safer alternatives to consumers.

Questions for Critical Thinking

1. Is direct distribution appropriate for a product like Non-Toxic's cosmetics? Why or why not?

2. The company offers consultants their own personal online office and Web site. How would a consultant make the best use of these tools?

Sources: Company Web site, Ava Anderson Non-Toxic, www.acaandersonnontoxic.com, accessed February 9, 2012; Sara Bagwell, "Ava Anderson Non-Toxic Is a Finalist in Entrepreneur 2011 Contest," Bristol-Warren Patch, http://bristol-warren.patch.com, accessed February 9, 2012; Sarah Cook, "It's Not Kids Business: Interview with Ava Anderson, Founder of Ava Anderson Non-Toxic," Raising CEO Kids, http://www.raisingceokids.com, accessed February 9, 2012.

---

are made up of intermediaries such as retailers and wholesalers that move a product from producer to final purchaser.

The two major components of an organization's distribution strategy are distribution channels and physical distribution. **Distribution channels** are the paths that products—and legal ownership of them—follow from producer to consumer or business user. They are the means by which all organizations distribute their goods and services. **Physical distribution** is the actual movement of products from producer to consumers or business users. Physical distribution covers a broad range of activities, including customer service, transportation, inventory control, materials handling, order processing, and warehousing. Ava Anderson's Non-Toxic, a cosmetics company, uses direct distribution to market its products, as the "Going Green" feature describes.

distribution channels
path that products—and legal ownership of them—follow from producer to consumers or business user.

physical distribution
actual movement of products from producer to consumers or business users.

Distribution Channels

In their first decision for distribution channel selection, marketers choose which type of channel will best meet both their firm's marketing objectives and the needs of their customers. As shown in Figure 12.5, marketers can choose either a *direct distribution channel*, which carries goods directly from producer to consumer or business user, or distribution channels that involve several different marketing intermediaries. A *marketing intermediary* (also called a *middleman*) is a business firm that moves goods between producers and consumers or business users. Marketing intermediaries perform various functions that help the distribution channel operate smoothly, such as buying, selling, storing, and transporting products; sorting and grading bulky items; and providing information to other channel members. The two main categories of marketing intermediaries are wholesalers and retailers.

No one channel suits every product. The best choice depends on the circumstances of the market and on customer needs. The most appropriate channel choice may also change over time as new opportunities arise and marketers strive to maintain their competitiveness.

LECTURE ENHANCER:
Choose one of the channels and identify products that might be moved by this intermediary.

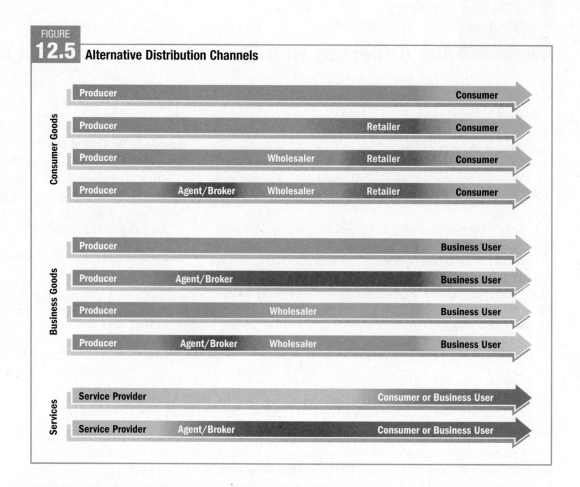

FIGURE 12.5 Alternative Distribution Channels

Consumer Goods

Producer				Consumer
Producer			Retailer	Consumer
Producer		Wholesaler	Retailer	Consumer
Producer	Agent/Broker	Wholesaler	Retailer	Consumer

Business Goods

Producer			Business User
Producer	Agent/Broker		Business User
Producer		Wholesaler	Business User
Producer	Agent/Broker	Wholesaler	Business User

Services

| Service Provider | | Consumer or Business User |
| Service Provider | Agent/Broker | Consumer or Business User |

Currently, most smart phones sold in the United States are tied to a specific wireless carrier that controls all distribution of its particular phone. Consumers can choose a smart phone but can't choose the carrier. Recently, Google offered its Nexus One smart phone for sale. Google's long-range goal is to change the distribution channels for smart phones. Buyers have the option of buying a conventional version of the Nexus One that is locked to T-Mobile's service plan and therefore controlled by T-Mobile, or an unlocked version—that is, one that can be used with any wireless service plan. By offering an unlocked smart phone, Google is gambling that consumers will choose a distribution channel that isn't tied to a wireless carrier and that Google itself will be able to create software that can compete with that available for the iPhone. In this type of business model, buyers would be able to select a phone first and then sign up with a carrier, much as they can now buy any brand of computer regardless of their Internet service provider.[18]

Direct Distribution The shortest and simplest means of connecting producers and customers is direct contact between the two parties. This approach is most common in the B2B market. Consumers who buy fresh fruits and vegetables at rural roadside stands or farmers markets use direct distribution, as do services ranging from banking and 10-minute oil changes to ear piercing and Mary Kay Cosmetics.

Direct distribution is commonly found in the marketing of relatively expensive, complex products that may require demonstrations. Most major B2B products such as installations, accessory equipment, component parts, business services, and even raw materials are typically marketed through direct contacts between producers and business buyers. The Internet

LECTURE ENHANCER:
How do intermediaries reduce the number of contacts needed to deliver goods?

has also made direct distribution an attractive option for many retail companies and service providers. FedEx customers have long used online tools to track conventional shipments. FedEx's new International Priority Direct Distribution service allows users to ship more than one package from a single country of origin to different recipients in a single destination country. The packages are cleared through customs as a single shipment. In addition, multiple shipments to multiple recipients in multiple European Union countries can be cleared through customs as a single shipment through Charles de Gaulle Airport near Paris.[19]

Distribution Channels Using Marketing Intermediaries Although direct channels allow simple and straightforward connections between producers and their customers, the list of channel alternatives in Figure 12.5 suggests that direct distribution is not the best choice in every instance. Some products sell in small quantities for relatively low prices to thousands of widely scattered consumers. Makers of such products cannot cost effectively contact each of their customers, so they distribute products through specialized intermediaries called *wholesalers* and *retailers*.

Although you might think that adding intermediaries to the distribution process would increase the final cost of products, more often than not this choice actually lowers consumer prices. Intermediaries such as wholesalers and retailers often add significant value to a product as it moves through the distribution channel. They do so by creating utility, providing additional services, and reducing costs.

Marketing utility is created when intermediaries help ensure that products are available for sale when and where customers want to purchase them. If you want something warm to eat on a cold winter night, you don't call up Campbell's Soup and ask them to ship a can of chicken noodle soup. Instead, you go to the nearest grocery store, where you find utility in the form of product availability. In addition, intermediaries perform such important services as transporting merchandise to convenient locations. Finally, by representing numerous producers, a marketing intermediary can cut the costs of buying and selling. As Figure 12.6 shows, if four manufacturers each sold directly to four consumers, this would require 16 separate transactions. Adding a marketing intermediary, such as a retailer, to the exchange cuts the number of necessary transactions to eight.

5

Wholesaling

A **wholesaler** is a distribution channel member that sells primarily to retailers, other wholesalers, or business users. For instance, Sysco is a wholesaler that buys food products from producers and then resells them to restaurants, hotels, and other institutions in the United States and Canada.

Wholesaling is a crucial part of the distribution channel for many products, particularly consumer goods and business supplies. Wholesaling intermediaries can

Assessment Check ✓

1. Define *distribution channels*.
2. What is a marketing intermediary?

wholesaler distribution channel member that sells primarily to retailers, other wholesalers, or business users.

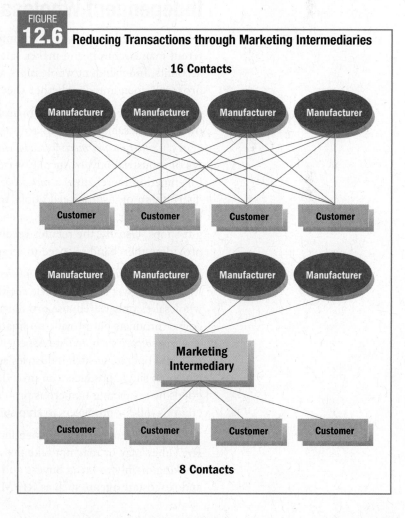

FIGURE **12.6** Reducing Transactions through Marketing Intermediaries

be classified on the basis of ownership; some are owned by manufacturers, some are owned by retailers, and others are independently owned. The United States has about 486,000 wholesalers, two-thirds of which have fewer than 20 employees.[20]

Manufacturer-Owned Wholesaling Intermediaries

A manufacturer's marketing manager may decide to distribute goods directly through company-owned facilities to control distribution or customer service. Firms operate two main types of manufacturer-owned wholesaling intermediaries: sales branches and sales offices.

Sales branches stock the products they distribute and fill orders from their inventories. They also provide offices for sales representatives. Sales branches are common in the chemical, petroleum products, motor vehicle, and machine and equipment industries.

A *sales office* is exactly what its name implies: an office for a producer's salespeople. Manufacturers set up sales offices in various regions to support local selling efforts and improve customer service. Some kitchen and bath fixture manufacturers maintain showrooms to display their products. Builders and decorators can visit these showrooms to see how the items would look in place. Unlike sales branches, however, sales offices do not store any inventory. When a customer orders from a showroom or other sales office, the merchandise is delivered from a separate warehouse.

Independent Wholesaling Intermediaries

An independent wholesaling intermediary is a business that represents a number of different manufacturers and makes sales calls on retailers, manufacturers, and other business accounts. Independent wholesalers are classified as either merchant wholesalers or agents and brokers, depending on whether they take title to the products they handle.

Merchant wholesalers, like apparel wholesaler WholesaleSarong.com, are independently owned wholesaling intermediaries that take title to the goods they handle. Within this category, a *full-function merchant wholesaler* provides a complete assortment of services for retailers or industrial buyers, such as warehousing, shipping, and even financing. A subtype of full-function merchant is a *rack jobber*, such as Virginia-based Choice Books, which handles distribution of inspirational books to retail stores. This type of firm stocks, displays, and services particular retail products, such as calendars, books, and note cards, in drug stores and gift shops. Usually, the retailer receives a commission based on actual sales as payment for providing merchandise space to a rack jobber.

A *limited-function merchant wholesaler* also takes legal title to the products it handles, but it provides fewer services to the retailers to which it sells. Some limited-function merchant wholesalers only warehouse products but do not offer delivery service. Others warehouse and deliver products but provide no financing. One type of limited-function merchant wholesaler is a *drop shipper* such as Kate Aspen, an Atlanta-based wholesaler of wedding favors. Drop shippers also operate in such industries as coal and lumber, characterized by bulky products for which no single producer can provide a complete assortment. They give access to many related goods by contacting numerous producers and negotiating the best possible prices. Cost considerations call for producers to ship such products directly to the drop shipper's customers.

Another category of independent wholesaling intermediaries consists of *agents* and *brokers*. They may or may not take possession of the goods they handle, but they never take title, working mainly to bring buyers and sellers together. Stockbrokers such as Charles Schwab and real estate agents such as RE/MAX perform functions similar to those of agents and brokers, but at the retail level. They do not take title to the sellers' property; instead, they create time and ownership utility for both buyer and seller by helping carry out transactions.

Manufacturers' reps act as independent sales forces by representing the manufacturers of related but noncompeting products. These agent intermediaries, sometimes referred to as *manufacturers' agents*, receive commissions based on a percentage of the sales they make.

Retailer-Owned Cooperatives and Buying Offices

Retailers sometimes band together to form their own wholesaling organizations. Such organizations can take the form of either a buying group or a cooperative. The participating retailers set up the new operation to reduce costs or to provide some special service that is not readily available in the marketplace. To achieve cost savings through quantity purchases, independent retailers may form a buying group that negotiates bulk sales with manufacturers. Ace Hardware is a retailer-owned cooperative. The independent owners of its 4,400 stores have access to bulk merchandise purchases that save them—and their customers— money.[21] In a cooperative, an independent group of retailers may decide to band together to share functions such as shipping or warehousing.

₆

Retailing

Retailers, in contrast to wholesalers, are distribution channel members that sell goods and services to individuals for their own use rather than for resale. Consumers usually buy their food, clothing, shampoo, furniture, and appliances from some type of retailer. The supermarket where you buy your groceries may have bought some of its items from a wholesaler such as Unified Grocers and then resold them to you.

Retailers are the final link—the so-called last three feet—of the distribution channel. Because they are often the only channel members that deal directly with consumers, it is essential that retailers remain alert to changing shopper needs. For instance, soaring gas prices affect consumers' budgets, so they may make fewer trips to the mall or cut back on nonessential purchases. As a result, retailers may need to offer special sales or events to lure customers to their outlets. It is also important for retailers to keep pace with developments in the fast-changing business environment, such as the disruption in delivery of supplies from widespread wildfires or storms.

Nonstore Retailers

Two categories of retailers exist: store and nonstore. As Figure 12.7 shows, nonstore retailing includes four forms: direct-response retailing, Internet retailing, automatic merchandising, and direct selling. *Direct-response retailing* reaches prospective customers through catalogs; telemarketing; and even magazine, newspaper, and television ads. Shoppers order merchandise by mail, telephone, computer, and fax machine and then receive home delivery or pick the merchandise up

This Zoom Shop kiosk dispenses Proactiv acne treatments automatically, just as an ATM dispenses cash. Automatic merchandising is a form of nonstore retailing.

©Jae C. Hong/AP/Wide World Photos

Assessment Check ✔
1. Define *wholesaling*.
2. Differentiate between a merchant wholesaler and an agent or broker in terms of title to the goods.

retailer distribution channel members that sell goods and services to individuals for their own use rather than for resale.

FIGURE
12.7 Types of Nonstore Retailing

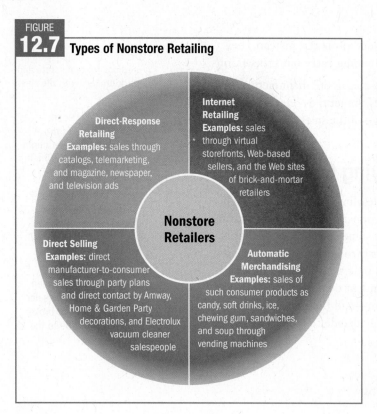

at a local store. Lands' End has long stood out as a highly successful direct-response retailer; its well-known clothing catalog and stellar customer service have set the standard for this type of distribution channel. With the retailer's purchase by Sears, however, customers can now see, feel, and try on its clothing at Lands' End Shops in Sears locations around the country.

Internet retailing, the second form of nonstore retailing, has grown rapidly. Tens of thousands of retailers have set up shop online, with sales growing at a rate of about 5 percent a year (as compared with declines in total retail sales). Today, online sales account for about 4.6 percent of total retail sales.[22] A severe shakeout saw hundreds of Internet enterprises shut down during the first decade of the 21st century, but firms that survived have stronger business models than those that failed. Two examples of successful pure dot-coms are Amazon and eBay. A major shift in retailing has seen traditional brick-and-mortar retailers competing with pure dot-com start-ups by setting up their own Web sites as an option for shoppers. Nordstrom, JCPenney, and Walmart report strong online sales. Shopping sites are among the most popular Internet destinations, and sales of clothing and DVDs in particular have risen.

The last two forms of nonstore retailing are automatic merchandising and direct selling. *Automatic merchandising* provides convenience through the use of vending machines. ATMs may soon join the ranks of vending machines as banks find new ways to compete for customers. Some ATMs offer extra services such as check cashing and stamps, as well as concert tickets and road maps. Future ATMs will be able to connect wirelessly to cell phones to allow customers to download and pay for games and music. *Direct selling* includes direct-to-consumer sales by Pampered Chef kitchen consultants and salespeople for Silpada sterling silver jewelry through party-plan selling methods. Both are forms of direct selling.

Companies that previously relied heavily on telemarketing in generating new customers have encountered consumer resistance to intrusive phone calls. Among the growing barriers are caller ID, call-blocking devices such as the TeleZapper, and the National Do Not Call list, which made it illegal for most companies to call people who are registered. As a result, dozens of companies, including telecommunications and regional utilities, have sent direct-mail pieces to promote such services as phones, cable television, and natural gas distributors.

Store Retailers

In-store sales still outpace nonstore retailing methods such as direct-response retailing and Internet selling. Store retailers range in size from tiny newsstands to multistory department stores and multiacre warehouse-like retailers such as Sam's Club. Table 12.2 lists the different types of store retailers, with examples of each type. Clearly, there are many approaches to retailing and a variety of services, prices, and product lines offered by each retail outlet.

12.2 Types of Retail Stores

STORE TYPE	DESCRIPTION	EXAMPLE
Specialty store	Offers complete selection in a narrow line of merchandise	Bass Pro Shops, Dick's Sporting Goods, Williams-Sonoma
Convenience store	Offers staple convenience goods, easily accessible locations, extended store hours, and rapid checkouts	7-Eleven, Mobil Mart, QuikTrip
Discount store	Offers wide selection of merchandise at low prices; off-price discounters offer designer or brand-name merchandise	Target, Walmart, Nordstrom Rack, Marshalls
Warehouse club	Large, warehouse-style store selling food and general merchandise at discount prices to membership cardholders	Costco, Sam's Club, BJ's
Factory outlet	Manufacturer-owned store selling seconds, production overruns, or discontinued lines	Adidas, Coach, Pottery Barn, Ralph Lauren
Supermarket	Large, self-service retailer offering a wide selection of food and nonfood merchandise	Safeway, Whole Foods Market, Kroger
Supercenter	Giant store offering food and general merchandise at discount prices	Walmart Supercenter, Super Target, Meijer
Department store	Offers a wide variety of merchandise selections (furniture, cosmetics, housewares, clothing) and many customer services	Macy's, Nordstrom, Neiman Marcus

The Wheel of Retailing Retailers are subject to constant change as new stores replace older establishments. In a process called the *wheel of retailing*, new retailers enter the market by offering lower prices made possible through reductions in service. Supermarkets and discount houses, for example, gained their initial market footholds through low-price, limited-service appeals. These new entries gradually add services as they grow and ultimately become targets for new retailers.

As Figure 12.8 shows, most major developments in retailing appear to fit the wheel pattern. The low-price, limited-service strategy characterized supermarkets, catalog retailers, discount stores, and, most recently, Internet retailers and giant big-box stores, such as PetSmart, Lowe's, and Office Depot. Corner grocery stores gave way to supermarkets and then to warehouse clubs such as Costco or BJ's. Department stores lost market share to discount clothing retailers such as Target and Marshalls. Independent bookstores have lost business to giant chains such as Barnes & Noble and such online-only sellers such as Amazon.com and Buy.com.

Even though the wheel of retailing does not fit every pattern of retail evolution—for example, automatic merchandising

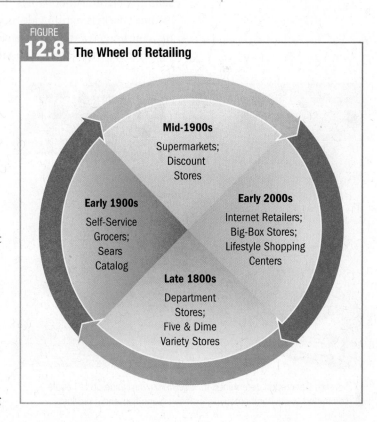

FIGURE

12.8 **The Wheel of Retailing**

has always been a relatively high-priced method of retailing—it does give retail managers a general idea of what is likely to occur during the evolution of retailing. It also shows that business success involves the "survival of the fittest." Retailers that fail to change fail to survive.

How Retailers Compete

Retailers compete with each other in many ways. Nonstore retailers focus on making the shopping experience as convenient as possible. Shoppers at stores such as Saks Fifth Avenue enjoy a luxurious atmosphere and personal service. In fact, those who visit the new shoe department at the flagship store in New York have the run of the entire eighth floor, devoted entirely to shoes—with its own zip code. The elite shopping experience includes a private VIP room, a repair service, and a chocolate café.[23]

Like manufacturers, retailers must develop marketing strategies based on goals and strategic plans. Successful retailers convey images that alert consumers to the stores' identities and the shopping experiences they provide. To create that image, all components of a retailer's strategy must complement each other. After identifying their target markets, retailers must choose merchandising, customer service, pricing, and location strategies that will attract customers in those market segments.

Identifying a Target Market The first step in developing a competitive retailing strategy is to select a target market. This choice requires careful evaluation of the size and profit potential of the chosen market segment and the current level of competition for the segment's business. Bargain stores such as Family Dollar target the price-conscious consumer, for example, while convenience stores like 7-Eleven target consumers who want an easy way to purchase items they buy frequently. Seventh Generation, the Vermont-based manufacturer of green household and personal-care items, began as a mail-order company in 1988, started selling at natural-food stores, then grew into a major business whose products are featured at supermarkets nationwide as well as at Target and at Amazon.com. Committed to increasing consumer awareness of environmentally safe cleaning and household products, Seventh Generation articulates its mission: "To inspire a revolution that nurtures the health of the next seven generations."[24]

Selecting a Product Strategy Next, the retailer must develop a product strategy to determine the best mix of merchandise to carry to satisfy that market. Retail strategists must decide on the general product categories, product lines, and variety to offer. Sometimes that involves expanding the product mix and sometime it involves contracting it. Under Polaroid's five-year licensing agreement with Starlight, a leading consumer electronics manufacturer and distributor, Starlight develops a range of Polaroid-brand consumer electronics equipment, including Blu-ray players, stand-alone and portable DVD players, e-readers, iPod docking stations, and home theater systems.[25]

Shaping a Customer Service Strategy A retailer's customer service strategy focuses on attracting and retaining target customers to maximize sales and profits. Some stores offer a wide variety of services, such as gift wrapping, alterations, returns, interior design services, and delivery.

Teri Stratford

Seventh Generation determined its *target market* was made up of people committed to environmentally safe cleaning and household products.

Other stores offer bare-bones customer service, stressing low price instead. Some grocery shoppers, for instance, find convenience online through a service such as Peapod, which handles product selection, packing, and delivery. Other shoppers choose to visit a supermarket and make their own selections. Or they can go to a discount supermarket like Iowa-based ALDI, where they not only assemble their orders but also bag their purchases.

Selecting a Pricing Strategy Retailers base their pricing decisions on the costs of purchasing products from other channel members and offering services to customers. Pricing can play a major role in consumers' perceptions of a retailer, and not just because they appreciate low prices. The grocery retailer Trader Joe's offers organic and gourmet foods under its own private labels at rock-bottom prices. Customers enjoy shopping for Trader Jose's Mexican specialties and Trader Darwin's nutritional supplements at prices lower than other gourmet or organic markets.[26] Pricing strategy is covered in more detail in Chapter 13.

Choosing a Location A good location often marks the difference between success and failure in retailing. The location decision depends on the retailer's size, financial resources, product offerings, competition, and, of course, its target market. Traffic patterns, the visibility of the store's signage, parking, and the location of complementary stores also influence the choice of a retail location.

A *planned shopping center* is a group of retail stores planned, coordinated, and marketed as a unit to shoppers in a geographical trade area. By providing convenient locations with free parking, shopping centers have replaced downtown shopping in many urban areas. But time-pressed consumers are increasingly looking for more efficient ways to shop, including catalogs, Internet retailers, and one-stop shopping at large free-standing stores such as Walmart Supercenters. To lure more customers, shopping centers are recasting themselves as entertainment destinations, with movie theaters, art displays, carousel rides, and musical entertainment. The giant Mall of America in Bloomington, Minnesota, features a seven-acre amusement park and an aquarium.

Shopping malls are well-known magnets for teens, who often meet there to socialize with friends. Businesses want to welcome their teen customers, but sometimes the cluster of teens hanging around the mall causes difficulties for other customers and some retailers, as described in the "Solving an Ethical Controversy" feature.

Large regional malls have witnessed a shift in shopping center traffic to smaller strip centers, name-brand outlet centers, and *lifestyle centers*, open-air complexes containing retailers that often focus on specific shopper segments and product interests. In recent years, lifestyle centers grew at a rate of more than 30 percent.[27]

Building a Promotional Strategy A retailer designs advertisements and develops other promotions to stimulate demand and to provide information such as the store's location, merchandise offerings, prices, and hours. When a recent year proved to be difficult, Starbucks turned to social media for a new promotional strategy. The chain launched MyStarbucksIdea.com, a forum where customers could ask questions, offer suggestions, and even voice their dislikes. The site's more than 180,000 registered users have offered more than 100,000 ideas, of which 130 have been implemented. The Starbucks Facebook page has a staggering 27.6 million fans; the chain also has 2 million Twitter followers.[28]

Nonstore retailers provide their phone numbers and Web site addresses. More recently, online retailers have scaled back their big advertising campaigns and worked to build traffic through word of mouth and clever promotions. Promotional strategy is also discussed in depth in Chapter 13.

LECTURE ENHANCER: Discuss a retailer that is particularly adept at shaping its customer service strategy.

CLASS ACTIVITY: Ask students if they can think of products for which high prices increase consumer attraction.

CLASS ACTIVITY: What retail stores seem always to be clustered together in strip malls, and why?

Solving an Ethical Controversy

Teens at the Mall: Good or Bad for Business?

Some shopping malls have banned unsupervised minors on weekend evenings. Others are considering a total ban on unaccompanied teens. However, teenagers also spend money at malls. Some merchants who once complained about groups of unsupervised teens have now pinned their revenue hopes on these young spenders.

Should malls lift curfews on teenagers to boost business?

PRO

1. Some studies suggest teenage spending has increased, contrary to expectations after several years of declining figures.

2. Most teenagers are well behaved and should not be banned as a group because of the bad behavior of a few.

CON

1. Some merchants are still wary because some parents ignore their children's bad behavior.

2. The attractiveness of teenage spending has to be weighed against the reality of crowd behavior. Malls provide a venue for teen fights and other disturbances.

Summary

Just as adults spent much less during the recent recession, so did their children. Teenagers have now returned in some measure to previous spending habits, particularly if they are carrying credit cards. Mall owners and civic leaders will need to find a balance between maintaining order and encouraging tomorrow's consumers.

Sources: Pattie Kate, "What Are the Characteristics of Teenage Spending?" *wiseGEEK*, http://www.wisegeek.com, accessed March 1, 2012; Andrea Chang, "Free-Spending Teens Return to Malls," *Los Angeles Times*, http://articles.latimes.com, accessed March 1, 2012; Erica Shaffer, "City Leaders Recommend Total Ban of Unsupervised Teens at Mall," WTOL, http://www.wtol.com, accessed March 1, 2012; Fran Daniel, "Mall May Limit Teens: Policy Expected to Require Parental Supervision on Friday, Saturday Evenings," *Winston-Salem Journal*, http://www2.journalnow.com, accessed March 1, 2012.

Assessment Check ✓

1. Define *retailer*.
2. What are the elements of a retailer's marketing strategy?

CLASS ACTIVITY:
Can students think of any examples of store music being integral to a store's atmosphere?

Creating a Store Atmosphere A successful retailer closely aligns its merchandising, pricing, and promotion strategies with *store atmospherics*, the physical characteristics of a store and its amenities, to influence consumers' perceptions of the shopping experience. Atmospherics begin with the store's exterior, which may use eye-catching architectural elements and signage to attract customer attention and interest. Interior atmospheric elements include store layout, merchandise presentation, lighting, color, sound, and cleanliness. A high-end store such as Nordstrom, for instance, features high ceilings in selling areas that spotlight tasteful and meticulously cared-for displays of carefully chosen items of obvious quality. Dick's Sporting Goods, on the other hand, carries an ever-changing array of moderately priced clothing and gear in its warehouse-like settings furnished with industrial-style display hardware.

7 Distribution Channel Decisions and Logistics

Every firm faces two major decisions when choosing how to distribute its goods or services: selecting a specific distribution channel and deciding on the level of distribution intensity. In deciding which distribution channel is most efficient, business managers need to consider four factors: the market, the product, the producer, and the competition. These factors are often interrelated and may change over time. In today's global business environment, strong relationships with customers and suppliers are important for survival. One way to help cement such relationships online is to practice proper social media manners, as the "Business Etiquette" feature explains.

Selecting Distribution Channels

Market factors may be the most important consideration in choosing a distribution channel. To reach a target market with a small number of buyers or buyers concentrated in a geographical area, the most feasible alternative may be a direct channel. In contrast, if the firm must reach customers who are dispersed or who make frequent small purchases, then the channel may need to incorporate marketing intermediaries to make goods available when and where customers want them.

In general, standardized products or items with low unit values usually pass through relatively long distribution channels. On the other hand, products that are complex, expensive, custom made, or perishable move through shorter distribution channels involving few—or no—intermediaries. The increasing prevalence of e-commerce is resulting in changes in traditional distribution practices. The European Commission recently issued a set of rules, effective until 2022, that permit makers of goods with less than a 30 percent market share—usually high-end manufacturers—to block Internet-only retailers from carrying their products The European Alliance—representing such luxury goods manufacturers as LVMH (Louis Vuitton Moët Hennessey), Gucci, and Burberry—lobbied for and welcomed the new rules as a way to protect the quality image of their products. Online-only retailers, such as Amazon, eBay, and their European counterparts, called for repeal of the bricks-and-mortar requirement and warned that some manufacturers would use the new rules to "restrict the availability" of their products online and thus keep prices high.[29]

Producers that offer a broad product line, with the financial and marketing resources to distribute and promote it, are more likely to choose a shorter

BusinessEtiquette

Minding Your Social Media Manners

Entrepreneurs are increasingly using social media to promote their businesses. In a recent survey, 70 percent of small businesses planned to increase their use of social media. Seventy-nine percent did not plan to run TV commercials, and 70 percent didn't use radio.

Good manners, common courtesy, and common sense will take you far in cyberspace. Here are some tips:

1 *Although you join social networks to promote your business*, don't make it too obvious. Don't promote your business nonstop, instead, use selected posts to show you have something of value to offer.

2 *Realize that you're in it for the long haul.* Group members are real people with real interests and ideas. Get to know the members of your forums and learn how the community works. Just like real networks, virtual networks have unwritten rules.

3 *It's not the numbers that count.* Getting your brand known or achieving other marketing goals doesn't necessarily depend on how many Twitter followers you have but on how you engage with them.

4 *Watch your language.* Avoid off-color jokes and racial or gender bias. Don't bring up religion or politics, and leave strong opinions out of your marketing profile.

Sources: Mickie Kennedy, "Do You Have Good Social Media Manners?" *eReleases*, accessed http://www.ereleases.com, accessed March 1, 2012; Michelle Bowles, "5 Social Media Tips for eCommerce Marketing," *Online Marketing Blog*, http://www.toprankblog.com, accessed March 1, 2012; Kim States, "Five Social Media Tips to Connect Small Businesses," *AzBiz.com*, http://www.azbiz.com, accessed March 1, 2012.

channel. Instead of depending on marketing intermediaries, financially strong manufacturers with broad product lines typically use their own sales representatives, warehouses, and credit departments to serve both retailers and consumers.

In many cases, start-up manufacturers turn to direct channels because they can't persuade intermediaries to carry their products or because they want to extend their sales reach. Some companies employ direct channels to carry intangible goods as well. Based in New York City, Art Meets Commerce uses the Internet and social networking to promote small Broadway and off-Broadway shows with tight marketing budgets. The company posts short videos of its client shows on YouTube and takes advantage of Facebook and Twitter to amplify traditional word-of-mouth publicity. When celebrities see the shows and post favorable tweets, their followers may feel encouraged to see the shows too.[30]

Competitive performance is the fourth key consideration when choosing a distribution channel. A producer loses customers when an intermediary fails to achieve promotion or product delivery. Channels used by established competitors as well as new market entries also can influence decisions. Sometimes a joint venture between competitors can work well. Best Buy and Apple have teamed up to sell their products under the same roof. Under the agreement, Apple controls its own retail space within Best Buy stores. Best Buy benefits by generating more traffic from customers who want to see and buy Apple's innovative products in convenient locations. The strategy has worked well, as the sales of Macs in particular have increased. Consumers can log on to the Best Buy Web site for product information, store locator, or to purchase the latest Apple items, ranging from the iPad2 to AppleTV.[31]

Selecting Distribution Intensity

A second key distribution decision involves *distribution intensity*—the number of intermediaries or outlets through which a manufacturer distributes its goods. Only one BMW dealership may be operating in your immediate area, but you can find Coca-Cola everywhere—in supermarkets, convenience stores, gas stations, vending machines, and restaurants. BMW has chosen a different level of distribution intensity than that used for Coca-Cola. In general, market coverage varies along a continuum with three different intensity levels:

1. *Intensive distribution* involves placing a firm's products in nearly every available outlet. Generally, intensive distribution suits low-priced convenience goods such as milk, newspapers, and soft drinks. This kind of market saturation requires cooperation by many intermediaries, including wholesalers and retailers, to achieve maximum coverage.

2. *Selective distribution* is a market-coverage strategy in which a manufacturer selects only a limited number of retailers to distribute its product lines. Selective distribution can reduce total marketing costs and establish strong working relationships within the channel.

3. *Exclusive distribution*, at the other end of the continuum from intensive distribution, limits market coverage in a specific geographical region. The approach suits relatively expensive specialty products such as Omega watches. Retailers are carefully selected to enhance the product's image to the market and to ensure that well-trained personnel will contribute to customer satisfaction. Although producers may sacrifice some market coverage by granting an exclusive territory to a single intermediary, the decision usually pays off in developing and maintaining an image of quality and prestige.

When companies are offloading excess inventory, even high-priced retailers may look to discounters to help them clear the merchandise from their warehouses. To satisfy consumers' taste for luxury goods, designer outlet malls offer shoppers a chance to buy status items at lower prices. Chicago Premium Outlets features 120 stores carrying such upscale brands as Michael Kors, Juicy Couture, and Diesel. Similar centers include Desert Hills Premium Outlets in California, Las Vegas Premium Outlets, and Seattle Premium Outlets.[32]

Selective distribution is a market-coverage strategy in which a manufacturer selects only a limited number of retailers to distribute its product lines. This strategy is used by Honda to distribute its ATVs.

Logistics and Physical Distribution

A firm's choice of distribution channels creates the final link in the **supply chain**, the complete sequence of suppliers that contribute to creating a good or service and delivering it to business users and final consumers. The supply chain begins when the raw materials used in production are delivered to the producer and continues with the actual production activities that create finished goods. Finally, the finished goods move through the producer's distribution channels to end customers.

The process of coordinating the flow of goods, services, and information among members of the supply chain is called **logistics**. The term originally referred to strategic movements of military troops and supplies. Today, however, it describes all of the business activities involved in the supply chain with the ultimate goal of getting finished goods to customers.

Physical Distribution A major focus of logistics management—identified earlier in the chapter as one of the two basic dimensions of distribution strategy—is *physical distribution*, the activities aimed at efficiently moving finished goods from the production line to the consumer or business buyer. As Figure 12.9 shows, physical distribution is a broad concept that includes transportation and numerous other elements that help link buyers and sellers.

supply chain complete sequence of suppliers that contribute to creating a good or service and delivering it to business users and final consumers.

logistics process of coordinating the flow of goods, services, and information among members of the supply chain.

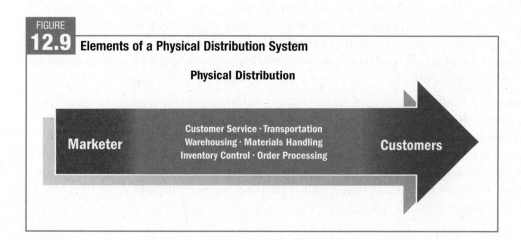

FIGURE 12.9 **Elements of a Physical Distribution System**

Physical Distribution

Marketer → Customer Service · Transportation · Warehousing · Materials Handling · Inventory Control · Order Processing → Customers

An effectively managed physical distribution system can increase customer satisfaction by ensuring reliable movements of products through the supply chain. For instance, Walmart studies the speed with which goods can be shelved once they arrive at the store because strategies that look efficient at the warehouse, such as completely filling pallets with goods, can actually be time-consuming or costly in the aisles.

Radio-frequency identification (RFID) technology relies on a computer chip implanted somewhere on a product or its packaging that emits a low-frequency radio signal identifying the item. The radio signal doesn't require a line of sight to register on the store's computers the way a bar code does, so a hand-held RFID reader can scan crates and cartons before they are unloaded. Because the chip can store information about the product's progress through the distribution channel, retailers can efficiently manage inventories, maintain stock levels, reduce loss, track stolen goods, and cut costs. The technology is similar to that already used to identify lost pets and speed vehicles through toll booths. Walmart, Target, the U.S. Department of Defense, and the German retailer Metro Group already require their suppliers to use RFID technology. The U.S. Army is now using solar power to activate battery-powered RFIDs, which are particularly useful in remote areas. Automakers are also using RFID technology to improve their production processes by tracking parts and other supplies. A new version of the RFID chip can be printed on paper or plastic. RFID technology brings with it privacy and counterfeiting concerns. However, one company has developed a process that uses unique silicon "fingerprints" to generate unclonable RFID chips.[33]

Warehousing is the physical distribution activity that involves the storage of products. *Materials handling* is moving items within factories, warehouses, transportation terminals, and stores. Inventory control involves managing inventory costs, such as storage facilities, insurance, taxes, and handling. The physical distribution activity of *order processing* includes preparing orders for shipment and receiving orders when shipments arrive.

The wide use of electronic data interchange (EDI) and the constant pressure on suppliers to improve their response time have led to **vendor-managed inventory**, in which the producer and the retailer agree that the producer (or the wholesaler) will determine how much of a product a buyer needs and automatically ship new supplies when needed.

The form of transportation used to ship products depends primarily on the kind of product, the distance involved, and the cost. The logistics manager can choose from a number of companies and modes of transportation. As Table 12.3 shows, the five major transport modes are—in order of total expenditures—trucks (with about 75 percent of total expenditures), railroads (approximately 12 percent), water carriers (6 percent), air freight (4 percent), and pipelines (3 percent). The faster methods typically cost more than the slower ones. Speed, reliable delivery, shipment frequency, location availability, handling flexibility, and cost are all important considerations when choosing the most appropriate mode of transportation.

About 15.5 million trucks operate in the United States, carrying most finished goods all or part of the way to the consumer. Nearly 2 million of these are tractor trailers.[34] But railroads, which compete with many truck routes despite their recent loss of market share, are a major mode of transportation. The 565 freight railroads in the United States operate across nearly 162,000 miles of track and earned more than $56 billion in revenues. A freight train needs only 1 gallon of diesel fuel to transport 1 ton of cargo almost 484 miles.[35]

vendor-managed inventory process in which the producer and the retailer agree that the producer (or the wholesaler) will determine how much of a product a buyer needs and automatically ship new supplies when needed.

12.3 Comparison of Transportation Modes

MODE	SPEED	DEPENDABILITY IN MEETING SCHEDULES	FREQUENCY OF SHIPMENTS	AVAILABILITY IN DIFFERENT LOCATIONS	FLEXIBILITY IN HANDLING	COST
Truck	Fast	High	High	Very extensive	Average	High
Rail	Average	Average	Low	Low	High	Average
Water	Very slow	Average	Very low	Limited	Very high	Very low
Air	Very fast	High	Average	Average	Low	Very high
Pipeline	Slow	High	High	Very limited	Very Low	Low

Customer Service Customer service is a vital component of both product and distribution strategies. *Customer service standards* measure the quality of service a firm provides for its customers. Managers frequently set quantitative guidelines—for example, that all orders be processed within 24 hours after they are received or that salespeople approach shoppers within two minutes after they enter the store. Sometimes customers set their own service standards and choose suppliers that meet or exceed them.

The customer service components of product strategy include warranty and repair service programs. *Warranties* are firms' promises to repair a defective product, refund money paid, or replace a product if it proves unsatisfactory. Repair services are also important. Consumers want to know that help is available if something goes wrong. Those who shop for home computers, for example, often choose retailers that not only feature low prices but also offer repair services and tech support centers. Products with inadequate service backing quickly disappear from the market as a result of word-of-mouth criticism.

Consumers' complaints of the impersonal service they received at Web sites led dot-coms to take a number of steps to "humanize" their customer interactions and deal with complaints. Many Web sites contain button help icons that link the visitor to a representative.

CLASS ACTIVITY:
Ask students for examples of businesses with excellent and inferior customer service quality.

Assessment Check ✓

1. What is distribution intensity?
2. Define *supply chain*.
3. What do customer service standards measure?

What's Ahead

This chapter covered two of the elements of the marketing mix: product and distribution. It introduced the key marketing tasks of developing, marketing, and packaging want-satisfying goods and services. It also focused on the three major components of an organization's distribution strategy: the design of efficient distribution channels; wholesalers and retailers who make up many distribution channels; and logistics and physical distribution. We now turn to the remaining two—promotion and pricing—in Chapter 13.

Summary of Learning Objectives

1 **Explain product strategy.**

A product is a bundle of physical, service, and symbolic attributes designed to satisfy consumer wants. The marketing conception of a product includes the brand, product image, warranty, service attributes, packaging, and labeling, in addition to the physical or functional characteristics of the good or service.

Goods and services can be classified as consumer (B2C) or business (B2B) products. Consumer products are those purchased by ultimate consumers for their own use. They can be convenience products, shopping products, or specialty products, depending on consumer habits in buying them. Business products are those purchased for use either directly or indirectly in the production of other goods and services for resale. They can be classified as installations, accessory equipment, component parts and materials, raw materials, and supplies. This classification is based on how the items are used and product characteristics. Services can be classified as either consumer or business services.

A product mix is the assortment of goods and services a firm offers to individual consumers and B2B users. A product line is a series of related products.

Assessment Check Answers ✔

1.1 How do consumer products differ from business products? Business products, such as drill presses, are sold to firms or organizations. Consumer products, such as personal-care items, are sold to final users.

1.2 Differentiate among convenience, shopping, and specialty products. Convenience products are items the consumer seeks to purchase frequently, immediately, and with little effort. Shopping products are typically purchased after the buyer has compared competing products in competing stores. Specialty products are those a purchaser is willing to make a special effort to obtain.

2 **Briefly describe the four stages of the product life cycle.**

Every successful new product passes through four stages in its product life cycle: introduction, growth, maturity, and decline. In the introduction stage, the firm attempts to elicit demand for the new product. In the product's growth stage, sales climb, and the company earns its initial profits. In the maturity stage, sales reach a saturation level. In the decline stage, both sales and profits decline. Marketers sometimes employ strategies to extend the product life cycle, including increasing the frequency of use, adding new users, finding new uses for the product, and changing package size, labeling, or product quality.

The new-product development process for most products has six stages: idea generation, screening, concept development and business analysis, product development, test marketing, and commercialization. At each stage, marketers must decide whether to continue to the next stage, modify the new product, or discontinue the development process. Some new products skip the test marketing stage due to the desire to quickly introduce a new product with excellent potential, a desire not to reveal new-product strategies to competitors, and the high costs involved in limited production runs.

Assessment Check Answers ✔

2.1 What are the stages of the product life cycle? In the introduction stage, the firm attempts to elicit demand for the new product. In the product's growth stage, sales climb, and the company earns its initial profits. In the maturity stage, sales reach a saturation level. In the decline stage, both sales and profits decline.

2.2 What are the marketing implications of each stage? Marketers sometimes employ strategies to extend the product life cycle, including increasing frequency of use, adding new users, finding new uses for the product, and changing package size, labeling, or product quality.

3 **Discuss product identification.**

Products are identified by brands, brand names, and trademarks, which are important elements of product images. Effective brand names are easy to pronounce, recognize, and remember, and they project the right images to buyers. Brand names cannot contain generic words. Under certain circumstances, companies lose exclusive rights to their brand names if common use makes them generic terms for product categories. Some brand names belong to retailers or distributors rather than to manufacturers. Brand loyalty is measured in three degrees: brand recognition, brand preference, and brand insistence. Some marketers use family brands to identify several related items in a product line. Others employ individual branding strategies by giving each product within a line a different brand name.

Assessment Check Answers ✔

3.1 Differentiate among a brand, a brand name, and a trademark. A brand is a name, term, sign, symbol, design, or some combination thereof used to identify the products of one firm and differentiate them from competitive offerings. A brand name is that part of the brand consisting of words or letters used to identify and distinguish the firm's offerings from those of competitors. A trademark is a brand that has been given legal protection.

3.2 Define *brand equity*. Brand equity is the added value that a respected and successful brand name gives to a product.

4 **Outline the major components of an effective distribution strategy.**

A firm must consider whether to move products through direct or indirect distribution. Once the decision is made, the company needs to identify the types of marketing intermediaries, if any, through which it will distribute its goods and services. The Internet has made direct distribution an attractive option for many retail companies. Another component is distribution intensity. The business must decide on the amount of market coverage—intensive, selective, or exclusive—needed to achieve its marketing strategies. Finally, attention must be paid to managing the distribution channel. It is vital to minimize conflict between channel members.

Assessment Check Answers ✔

4.1 Define *distribution channels*. Distribution channels are the paths that products, and title to them, follow from producer to consumer or business user.

4.2 What is a marketing intermediary? A marketing intermediary (also called a middleman) is a business firm that moves goods between producers and consumers or business users.

⌐5⌐ Explain wholesaling.

Wholesaling is a crucial part of the distribution channel for many products, particularly consumer goods and business supplies. Wholesaling intermediaries can be classified on the basis of ownership; some are owned by manufacturers, some are owned by retailers, and others are independently owned. Firms operate two main types of manufacturer-owned wholesaling intermediaries: sales branches and sales offices.

An independent wholesaling intermediary is a business that represents a number of different manufacturers and makes sales calls on retailers, manufacturers, and other business accounts. Independent wholesalers are classified as either merchant wholesalers or agents and brokers, depending on whether they take title to the products they handle.

Retailers sometimes band together to form their own wholesaling organizations. Such organizations can take the form of either a buying group or a cooperative.

Assessment Check Answers ✔

5.1 Define *wholesaling*. Wholesaling is a crucial part of the distribution channel for many products, particularly consumer goods and business supplies.

5.2 Differentiate between a merchant wholesaler and an agent or broker in terms of title to the goods. Merchant wholesalers are independently owned wholesaling intermediaries that take title to the goods they handle. Agents and brokers may or may not take possession of the goods they handle, but they never take title, working mainly to bring buyers and sellers together.

⌐6⌐ Describe retailing.

Retailers, in contrast to wholesalers, are distribution channel members that sell goods and services to individuals for their own use rather than for resale. Nonstore retailing includes four forms: direct-response retailing, Internet retailing, automatic merchandising, and direct selling. Store retailers range in size from tiny newsstands to multistory department stores and warehouse-like retailers such as Sam's Club.

The first step in developing a competitive retailing strategy is to select a target market. Next, the retailer must develop a product strategy to determine the best mix of merchandise to carry to satisfy that market. A retailer's customer service strategy focuses on attracting and retaining target customers to maximize sales and profits. Retailers base their pricing decisions on the costs of purchasing products from other channel members and offering services to customers. A good location often marks the difference between success and failure in retailing. A retailer designs advertisements and develops other promotions to stimulate demand and to provide information such as the store's location, merchandise offerings, prices, and hours. A successful retailer closely aligns its merchandising, pricing, and promotion strategies with store atmospherics, the physical characteristics of a store and its amenities, to influence consumers' perceptions of the shopping experience.

Assessment Check Answers ✔

6.1 Define *retailer*. Retailers are distribution channel members that sell goods and services to individuals for their own use rather than for resale.

6.2 What are the elements of a retailer's marketing strategy? After identifying their target markets, retailers must choose merchandising, customer service, pricing, and location strategies that will attract customers in those market segments.

⌐7⌐ Identify distribution channel decisions and logistics.

Marketers can choose either a direct distribution channel, which moves goods directly from the producer to the consumer, or indirect distribution channels, which involve marketing intermediaries in the paths through which products—and legal ownership of them—flow from producer to the final customer. Ideally, the choice of a distribution channel should support a firm's overall marketing strategy. Before selecting distribution channels, firms must consider their target markets, the types of goods being distributed, their own internal systems and concerns, and competitive factors.

Assessment Check Answers ✔

7.1 What is distribution intensity? Distribution intensity is the number of intermediaries or outlets through which a manufacturer distributes its goods.

7.2 Define *supply chain*. A supply chain is the sequence of suppliers that contribute to creating a good or service and delivering it to business users and final consumers.

7.3 What do customer service standards measure? Customer service standards measure the quality of service a firm provides for its customers.

Business Terms You Need to Know

product 356	brand 364	distribution strategy 368	supply chain 381
product line 359	brand name 364	distribution channels 369	logistics 381
product mix 359	trademark 364	physical distribution 369	vendor-managed
product life cycle 359	brand equity 366	wholesaler 371	inventory 382
test marketing 363	category advisor 367	retailer 373	

Review Questions

1. Classify each of the following business-to-consumer (B2C) and business-to-business (B2B) goods and services. Then choose one and describe how it could be classified as both.

   a. *Runner's World* or *Esquire* magazine

   b. six-pack of apple juice

   c. limousine service

   d. tech support for a communications system

   e. golf course

   f. Thai restaurant

2. What is the relationship between a product line and a product mix? Give an example of each.

3. Identify and briefly describe the six stages of new-product development.

4. What is the difference between a manufacturer's brand and a private brand? What is the difference between a family brand and an individual brand?

5. What are the three stages of brand loyalty? Why is the progression to the last stage so important to marketers?

6. What are the advantages of direct distribution? When is a producer most likely to use direct distribution?

7. What is the wheel of retailing? How has the Internet affected the wheel of retailing?

8. Identify and briefly describe the four different types of nonstore retailers. Give an example of at least one type of good or service that would be suited to each type of nonstore retailer.

9. What are the three intensity levels of distribution? Give an example of two products for each level.

10. Define *logistics*. How does it relate to physical distribution?

Projects and Teamwork Applications

1. On your own or with a classmate, choose one of the following goods or services. Decide whether you want to market it as a consumer product or a business product. Now create a brand name and marketing strategy for your product.

   a. lawnmower repair service

   b. health foods store

   c. soft drink

   d. English-language class

   e. accounting firm

2. Choose one of the following products that is either in the maturity or decline stage of its life cycle (or select one of your own), and develop a marketing strategy for extending its life cycle.

   a. popcorn

   b. fast-food restaurant chain

   c. newspaper

   d. music CDs

   e. paper stationery or notecards

3. Where do you do most of your shopping—in stores or online? Choose your favorite retailer and analyze why you like it. Outline your reasons for shopping there, then add two or three suggestions for improvement.

4. Choose one of the following products and select a distribution intensity for the product. Describe specifically where and how your product would be sold. Then describe the reasons for your strategy.

   a. line of furniture manufactured from recycled or reclaimed materials

   b. custom-designed jewelry

   c. house-painting service

   d. handicraft supplies

   e. talk radio show

Web Assignments

1. **Product classification**. Visit the Web site of Johnson & Johnson (http://www.jnj.com) and click on "Our Products." Review the material in the chapter on product classification and then classify Johnson & Johnson's vast array of products.

2. **Shopping centers**. The Mall of America in Minnesota is the nation's largest shopping center. Go to the Mall's Web site (http://www.mallofamerica.com) to learn more about it. Make a list of five interesting facts you learned about the Mall of America.

3. Railroad statistics. Visit the Web site of the American Association of Railroads (http://www.aar.org). Click on "Statistics and Publication" and then "Railroad Statistics." Review the material and answer the following questions:

   a. What is a so-called Class I railroad? How many are there?

   b. How many workers do these railroads employ?

   c. How much freight did Class I railroads carry during the most recent year for which data are available?

Note: Internet Web addresses change frequently. If you don't find the exact sites listed, you may need to access the organization's home page and search from there or use a search engine such as Bing or Google.

Marketing Luxury Brands in China

CASE 12.1

If, as currently projected, 55 percent of purchases of luxury brands worldwide are made by Chinese consumers in 2020, it won't surprise Prada. The company already collects 43 percent of its global earnings from China.

As newly wealthy young Chinese consumers embrace a culture of spending, observers see China becoming the world's largest market for high-end watches, leather goods, designer clothing, cosmetics, and perfume. Recently, Chinese luxury-goods shoppers spent more than $16 billion, an increase of about 25 percent over the preceding year, and they often bought abroad, citing lower prices, better selection, and better service in France, Italy, Great Britain, and Switzerland than they find at home.

The spending trend is expected to continue, even if at a slower pace. "People will have more and more cash to spend on discretionary items, including luxury goods," said the head of Asia-Pacific investment banking at Citigroup. Of course that description doesn't include every Chinese consumer. Unlike their older Western counterparts, who spend big on homes, cars, and vacations, nearly half of Chinese luxury-goods buyers are between 18 and 34.

But "if you have a population of 1.4 billion," says the Citigroup executive, "even 1 percent of that is a very large number."

Questions for Critical Thinking

1. What advice would you give Western luxury brands such as Prada, Burberry, Ferragamo, and Hugo Boss as they focus on Chinese luxury shoppers?

2. What does the luxury-buying trend suggest for Western manufacturers of ordinary consumer goods that want to do business in China?

Sources: Yang Lina, "Chinese Tourists Spend Record Amounts on Luxury Goods Overseas," Brunei fm, February 8, 2012, http://news.brunei .fm; Wang Zhuoqiong, "Chinese Snap Up Luxury Products," ChinaDaily. com, February 7, 2012, www.chinadaily.com; Bettina Wassener, "Across Asia, an Engine of Growth for Luxury Firms," *The New York Times,* December 8, 2011, www.nytimes.com; Kayla Hutzler, "China Offers Quickest Growth in Emerging Markets for Luxury Brands: Luxury Briefing Wealth Summit," LuxuryDaily.com, October 28, 2011, www.luxurydaily.com.

The Convergence of TV and the Internet

CASE 12.2

Industry observers say consumers someday will watch television programming on any device—TV, computer, or smart phone. Already, they can watch selected broadcast shows on the Web. One survey reported more than 178 million Americans watched 33 billion TV shows online.

Revenues from advertising fees bring $70 billion to broadcast and cable television networks. Cable and satellite providers pay broadcast networks billions more

in retransmission fees and make billions in fees from subscribers.

But when broadcast television networks upload shows to the Internet, viewers don't pay cable and satellite providers, and networks lose the revenue from cable and satellite licensing fees. Advertisers pay networks for the right to embed their ads within the video content, but advertisers are leery of online TV because they have no clear way to measure the effectiveness of their commercials. Online TV has another drawback: most of it is not live. Live broadcasts of shows such as *American Idol* and the Super Bowl charge the highest advertising fees. But online licensing problems and technical issues make TV networks wary of live online broadcasting.

As viewers exercise their increasing options to watch what they want when they want it, some analysts predict that the only programming audiences will view at the same time will be sports and news. Some viewers have discontinued their cable subscriptions and watch TV exclusively online via downloads from Netflix, iTunes, and Amazon.

Subscription TV may be the way of the future, although some generic shows, such as news, cooking shows, and how-to programs will remain free just because they are not unique. Microsoft's recently unveiled Mediaroom 2.0 combines client software with cloud-based services, allowing consumers to watch shows on flat-screen TVs, personal computers, or compatible smart phones.

Questions for Critical Thinking

1. Where is broadcast television in the product life cycle? What steps have broadcast networks taken to prolong their product's life cycle?
2. At this time, broadcast and cable television, Internet programming, and advertisers all have different distribution strategies. How might they bring these strategies closer together?

Sources: David Goldman, "Get Ready to Pay for Online TV," *CNN Money*, http://money.cnn.com, accessed March 1, 2012; "Microsoft Mediaroom 2.0 Delivers the Future of TV," press release, http://www.microsoft.com, accessed March 1, 2012; Holman W. Jenkins, Jr., "The Future on TV," *The Wall Street Journal*, http://online.wsj.com, accessed March 1, 2012.

CASE 12.3

Secret Acres: Getting the Word Out

No matter how powerful they are, comic book heroes can't get themselves into bookstores—and readers' hands—without a little help. Leon Avelino and Barry Matthews, co-founders of Secret Acres, know that one of the greatest challenges of publishing is getting books onto the shelves and into readers' shopping carts. The task is even more difficult for small publishers—in this case, small publishers of comic books and graphic novels—because they don't have the wide distribution network of major publishers. But Avelino and Matthews, whose authors consider them the superheroes of comicbook publishing, are undaunted. They know what they are trying to achieve and work doggedly to make it happen.

"Distribution is a difficult thing right now," admits Matthews. "The publishing industry is changing and comic books themselves have a different distribution methodology and wholesale methodology than traditional books do." Unlike conventional book shops, comic book shops do not operate on a return basis. Conventional bookstores receive a small discount when they purchase books from a publisher, but then have the option to return any unsold books to the publisher. Comic book shops take a deeper discount but make no returns. Matthews also notes that currently there is only one major distributor of comic books—Diamond Distributors—which has the leverage to dictate much of what happens in the business of comic book distribution.

In addition, Matthews observes that Secret Acres' graphic novels could easily be sold to the general book market, but many general book distributors prefer not to deal with smaller publishers because they simply don't produce enough books to be profitable.

All of that said, Matthews explains that they are learning alternative ways to distribute their books. "Amazon is great," he says. "They make it very easy for smaller publishers. They treat your books as if they are Amazon books, giving them the sheen of being part of a larger retail channel." Amazon does take a significant cut of sales, but Matthews says it's worth it to broaden the distribution of Secret Acres products. Of course, Secret Acres also sells its entire line directly through its Web site, along with some books from other independent authors and publishers. This sales method is the most profitable for Secret Acres. More importantly, it allows Matthews and Avelino to keep closer tabs on their readers.

Matthews explains that because orders are filled on an individual basis, he can slip promotional materials, notices of upcoming events or new books, and tie-ins right into the package of a customer whose preferences he knows. This one-on-one interaction helps in the management of customer relationships.

Matthews and Avelino also enjoy one other form of distribution—attending comic book conventions around the country, such as the Stumptown Comics Fest in Portland, Oregon. There, they have the opportunity to interact with readers, other publishers, comic book authors and artists, and even some smaller distributors who have begun to attend these events. They note that readers in particular love to meet the authors and artists. "It feeds the interest in what we're doing," says Matthews. While at an event, Matthews and Avelino try to carve out some time to meet with other small publishers. "A lot of small publishers are in the same position" with regard to distribution, Matthews explains. "So we have been talking with them to see if we can band together to share resources."

For the future, Matthews admits that he and Avelino have no idea how some of the new technologies, including e-readers, will ultimately affect distribution, but they plan to research the possibility of digitizing some of Secret Acres' titles for online distribution.

Despite its small size, Secret Acres' authors consider the firm a mighty one. Theo Ellsworth, author of such titles as *Capacity* and *Sleeper Car*, praises Secret Acres for its personal attention and efforts to market and distribute his books. "It feels good to have the distribution part in someone else's hands," says Ellsworth. He explains that having

someone else take care of that aspect of publishing frees him up to concentrate on his art, producing more posters and books—which is, after all, the author's job.

Questions for Critical Thinking

1. Visit Secret Acres' web site at http://www .secretacres.com to learn more about the firm's product line. Write a marketing blurb describing the line to a potential distributor.

2. What steps can Secret Acres take to develop brand loyalty and ultimately brand equity for its products?

3. How might Secret Acres expand its Internet retailing presence?

4. Secret Acres is a tiny firm with limited distribution. How can the company use customer service to create a competitive advantage, increase distribution, and help it grow?

Sources: Secret Acres Web site, http://www.secretacres.com, accessed March 1, 2012; Stumptown Comics Fest, http://www.stumptowncomics .com, accessed March 1, 2012; "Great Graphic Novels for Teens," Young Adult Library Services Association, http://www.ala.org/yalsa, accessed March 1, 2012; Harry McCracken, "E-Readers May Be Dead, But They're Not Going Away Yet," PC World, http://www.pcworld.com, accessed March 1, 2012.

Learning Objectives

1. Discuss integrated marketing communications (IMC).
2. Summarize the different types of advertising.
3. Outline sales promotion.
4. Describe pushing and pulling strategies.
5. Discuss the pricing objectives in the marketing mix.
6. Outline pricing strategies.
7. Discuss consumer perceptions of prices.

Chapter 13

Promotion and Pricing Strategies

Alexander Gatsenko/iStockphoto

Pfizer Faces the Impact of Generic Drug Pricing

What product has earned as much revenue in a year as Major League Baseball, or all the commercial films released in the United States?

The answer is Lipitor, the cholesterol-reducing drug taken by almost 9 million Americans. The most successful and widely prescribed drug in the United States, Lipitor was protected from competition for years by its patent, which gave Pfizer the exclusive right to market it and earn almost $11 billion a year from its sales. In the past 10 years Lipitor has accounted for about 25 percent of Pfizer's total revenue, bringing in more than $100 billion since its introduction in the late 1990s.

Recently, however, Pfizer's patent on Lipitor expired, and competitors could sell inexpensive generic versions of the drug, called atorvastatin, for the first time. During the first six months, generic competition was limited by law to the first few companies that applied to the FDA, but after that any approved company could sell the generic drug. At this point in a prescription drug's life, prices typically plummet. Atoravastatin was expected to sell for only pennies a day.

Pfizer, however, had carefully planned to protect the market share of its blockbuster brand-name drug. First, it created its own mail-order operation (mail orders account for about 30 percent of Lipitor sales). It signed deals with many prescription drug and benefit plans, persuading them to provide Lipitor at discounted or even generic prices. Finally, it began manufacturing its own generic version of the drug, marketed by Watson Pharmaceuticals (which gave Pfizer 70 percent of the profits). While lower prices of generic drugs directly benefit the patients who take them, they may have a down side. So many drugs are coming off patent in the next few years that some manufacturers have reduced their research and development budgets in anticipation of lower revenues. And with 8 of 10 prescriptions calling for generics, drug companies will probably be focusing their remaining R&D efforts on specialty drugs that benefit fewer people.[1]

Overview

This chapter focuses on the different types of promotional activities and the way prices are established for goods and services. **Promotion** is the function of informing, persuading, and influencing a purchase decision. This activity is as important to not-for-profit organizations as it is to profit-seeking companies.

Some promotional strategies try to develop *primary demand*, or consumer desire for a general product category. The objective of such a campaign is to stimulate sales for an entire industry so that individual firms benefit from this market growth. A popular example is the dairy industry's "Got Milk?" campaign. Print and television messages about the nutritional benefits of milk show various celebrities. Other promotional campaigns aimed at increasing per-capita consumption have been commissioned by the California Strawberry Commission and the National Cattlemen's Beef Association.

Most promotional strategies, in contrast, seek to stimulate *selective demand*—desire for a specific brand. The San Francisco Giants try to stimulate loyalty with promotions like ballpark tours and their Annual Slumber Party. Country-western star Toby Keith promotes Ford F-150 trucks, which encourages his fans to choose that brand over competitors.

promotion function of informing, persuading, and influencing a purchase decision.

Mike Cassese/Reuters/Landov LLC

Most promotional strategies seek to stimulate *selective demand*—a desire for a specific brand. Country-western star Toby Keith encourages his fans to buy Ford F-150 trucks.

integrated marketing communications (IMC) coordination of all promotional activities—media advertising, direct mail, personal selling, sales promotion, and public relations—to produce a unified, customer-focused promotional strategy.

Marketers choose from among many promotional options to communicate with potential customers. Each marketing message a buyer receives—through a television or radio commercial, newspaper or magazine ad, Web site, direct-mail flyer, or sales call—reflects the product, place, person, cause, or organization promoted in the content. Through **integrated marketing communications (IMC)**, marketers coordinate all promotional activities—media advertising, direct mail, personal selling, sales promotion, and public relations—to produce a unified, customer-focused promotional strategy. This coordination is designed to avoid confusing the consumer and to focus positive attention on the promotional message.

This chapter begins by explaining the role of IMC and then discusses the objectives of promotion and the importance of promotional planning. Next, it examines the components of the promotional mix: advertising, sales promotion, personal selling, and public relations. Finally, the chapter addresses pricing strategies for goods and services, as described in the chapter opener about Lipitor.

1 Integrated Marketing Communications

An integrated marketing communications strategy focuses on customer needs to create a unified promotional message in the firm's ads, in-store displays, product samples, and presentations by company sales representatives. To gain a competitive advantage, marketers that implement IMC need a broad view of promotion. Media options continue to multiply, and marketers cannot simply rely on traditional broadcast and print media and direct mail. Plans must include all forms of customer contact. Packaging, store displays, sales promotions, sales presentations, and online and interactive media also communicate information about a brand or organization. With IMC, marketers create a unified personality and message for the good, brand, or service they promote. Coordinated activities also enhance the effectiveness of reaching and serving target markets.

Marketing managers set the goals and objectives for the firm's promotional strategy with overall organizational objectives and marketing goals in mind. Using these objectives, marketers weave the various elements of the strategy—personal selling, advertising, sales promotion, publicity, and public relations—into an integrated communications plan. This document becomes a central part of the firm's total marketing strategy to reach its selected target market. Feedback, including marketing research and sales reports, completes the system by identifying any deviations from the plan and suggesting improvements.

One of the most successful IMC campaigns recently was the Old Spice Guy. The campaign primarily focused on actor Isaiah Mustafa's six-pack abs, and the rest is advertising history. Marketing communications included commercials for traditional broadcast TV; ads cued up on Old Spice's You Tube channel, which then spread to other social media channels; communication with the Old Spice Guy via Twitter; media buys on Google and Facebook; and interactive digital treasure hunts.[2]

The Promotional Mix

Just as every organization creates a marketing mix combining product, distribution, promotion, and pricing strategies, each also requires a similar mix to blend the many facets of promotion into a cohesive plan. The **promotional mix** consists of two components—personal and nonpersonal selling—that marketers combine to meet the needs of their firm's target customers and effectively and efficiently communicate its message to them. **Personal selling** is the most basic form of promotion: a direct person-to-person promotional presentation to a potential buyer. The buyer–seller communication can occur during a face-to-face meeting or via telephone, videoconference, or interactive computer link. Salespeople represent their company and should demonstrate high standards of ethical behavior. See the "Business Etiquette" feature for a few helpful do's and don'ts for personal selling situations.

promotional mix combination of personal and nonpersonal selling components designed to meet the needs of a firm's target customers and effectively and efficiently communicate its message to them.

LECTURE ENHANCER:
What challenges do companies face in trying to reach consumers?

LECTURE ENHANCER:
How do you prefer that advertisers reach you? TV? Online? Other?

personal selling the most basic form of promotion: a direct person-to-person promotional presentation to a potential buyer.

Nonpersonal selling consists of advertising, sales promotion, direct marketing, and public relations. Advertising is the best-known form of nonpersonal selling, but sales promotion accounts for about half of these marketing expenditures. Spending for sponsorships, which involves marketing messages delivered in association with another activity such as a golf tournament or a benefit concert, is on the rise as well. Marketers need to be careful about the types of promotion they choose or risk alienating the very people they are trying to reach.

Each component in the promotional mix offers its own advantages and disadvantages, as Table 13.1 demonstrates. By selecting the most effective combination of promotional mix elements, a firm may reach its promotional objectives. Spending within the promotional mix varies by industry. Manufacturers of many business-to-business (B2B) products typically spend more on personal selling than on advertising because those products—such as a new telecommunications system—may require a significant investment. Consumer-goods marketers may focus more on advertising and sponsorships. Later sections of this chapter discuss how the parts of the mix contribute to effective promotion.

Objectives of Promotional Strategy

Promotional strategy objectives vary among organizations. Some use promotion to expand their markets, and others use it to defend their current positions. As Figure 13.1 illustrates, common objectives include providing information, differentiating a product, increasing sales, stabilizing sales, and accentuating a product's value.

Marketers often pursue multiple promotional objectives at the same time. To promote its Microsoft Office software, Microsoft has to convince business owners, who buy the software, and their employees, who use the software, that the product is a worthwhile investment.

TABLE

13.1 Comparing the Components of the Promotional Mix

COMPONENT	ADVANTAGES	DISADVANTAGES
Advertising	Reaches large consumer audience at low cost per contact Allows strong control of the message Message can be modified to match different audiences	Difficult to measure effectiveness Limited value for closing sales
Personal selling	Message can be tailored for each customer Produces immediate buyer response Effectiveness is easily measured	High cost per contact High expense and difficulty of attracting and retaining effective salespeople
Sales promotion	Attracts attention and creates awareness Effectiveness is easily measured Produces short-term sales increases	Difficult to differentiate from similar programs of competitors Nonpersonal appeal
Public relations	Enhances product or firm credibility Creates a positive attitude about the product or company	Difficult to measure effectiveness Often devoted to nonmarketing activities
Sponsorships	Viewed positively by consumers Enhances brand awareness	Difficult to control message

Marketers need to keep their firm's promotional objectives in mind at all times. Sometimes the objectives are obscured by a fast-paced, creative ad campaign. In this case, the message—or worse, the brand name or image—is lost. The series of comic Geico ads that featured grumpy Neanderthals and the tag line "So easy a caveman could do it" were an instant hit. They were widely viewed on YouTube and even inspired a short-lived TV sitcom. But despite their quirky originality, the ads allowed humor to overtake the message; few viewers remembered the product—car insurance.

Providing Information A major portion of U.S. advertising is information oriented. Credit-card ads provide information about benefits and rates. Ads for hair-care products include information about benefits such as shine and volume. Ads for breakfast cereals often contain nutritional information. Television ads for prescription drugs, a nearly $2 billion industry, are sometimes criticized for relying on emotional appeals rather than providing information about the causes, risk factors, and especially the prevention of disease.[3] But print advertisements for drugs often contain an entire page of warnings, side-effects, and usage guidelines.

FIGURE
13.1 **Five Major Promotional Objectives**

DIFFERENTIATE PRODUCT
Example: Television ad comparing performance of two leading laundry detergents

PROVIDE INFORMATION
Example: Print ad describing features and availability of a new breakfast cereal

STABILIZE SALES
Example: Even out sales patterns by promoting low weekend rates for hotels, holding contests during slow sales periods, or advertising cold fruit soups during summer months

INCREASE SALES
Example: End-of-aisle (end caps) grocery displays, to encourage impulse purchases

ACCENTUATE PRODUCT VALUE
Example: Warranty programs and guarantees that make a product more attractive than its major competitors

Differentiating a Product Promotion can also be used to differentiate a firm's offerings from the competition. Applying a concept called **positioning**, marketers attempt to establish their products in the minds of customers. The idea is to communicate to buyers meaningful distinctions about the attributes, price, quality, or use of a good or service.

Marketers of luxury goods position their products as upscale, expensive, high quality, and exclusive. But how do they position goods that are intended for the vast number of "ordinary" consumers? Zappos recently met this challenge by using staff members in its marketing videos—wearing shoes, clothing, and handbags from the Zappos site. The message that real people can wear Zappos products was received positively by the firm's customers.[4]

Increasing Sales Increasing sales volume is the most common objective of a promotional strategy. Naturalizer became the third-largest seller of women's dress shoes by appealing to Baby Boomers. But as these women have grown older, they have bought fewer pairs of shoes each year. Naturalizer wants to keep those customers but also attract the younger generation. So the firm developed a new line of trendy shoes. The promotional strategy included ads in magazines read by younger women—such as *Elle* and *Marie Claire*—featuring young women in beach attire and Naturalizer shoes. The response to this strategy was a substantial increase in Naturalizer's sales through department stores.

Stabilizing Sales Sales stabilization is another goal of promotional strategy. Firms often use sales contests during slack periods, motivating salespeople by offering prizes such as vacations, TVs, smart phones, and cash to those who meet certain goals. Companies distribute sales promotion materials—such as calendars, pens, and notepads—to customers

positioning form of promotion in which marketers attempt to establish their products in the minds of customers by communicating to buyers meaningful distinctions about the attributes, price, quality, or use of a good or service.

CLASS ACTIVITY:
In viewing pharmaceutical television product ads, do students perceive the information provided regarding benefits and risks of the medicine as fair or biased?

CLASS ACTIVITY:
Ask students for their ideas on how a local CPA firm might attract more summer business.

to stimulate sales during the off-season. Jiffy Lube puts that little sticker on your windshield to remind you when to schedule your car's next oil change—the regular visits help stabilize sales. A stable sales pattern brings several advantages. It evens out the production cycle, reduces some management and production costs, and simplifies financial, purchasing, and marketing planning. An effective promotional strategy can contribute to these goals.

Dunkin' Donuts came up with a marketing campaign via Twitter for a recent holiday season. On Black Friday—the day after Thanksgiving and the biggest shopping day of the year—anyone who tweeted how Dunkin' Donuts K-Cup packs (individual coffee servings) kept them going through the holidays got a chance to win a Keurig coffee machine and a box of K-Cup packs. This special promotion was in addition to the company's holiday-themed gift cards.[5]

Accentuating the Product's Value Some promotional strategies enhance product values by explaining hidden benefits of ownership. Carmakers offer long-term warranty programs; life insurance companies promote certain policies as investments. The creation of brand awareness and brand loyalty also enhances a product's image and increases its desirability. Advertising with luxurious images supports the reputation of premium brands such as Jaguar, Tiffany, and Rolex.

Promotional Planning

Today's marketers can promote their products in many ways, and the lines between the different elements of the promotional mix are blurring. Consider the practice of **product placement**. A growing number of marketers pay placement fees to have their products showcased in various media, ranging from newspapers and magazines to television and movies. Coca-Cola gets prominent placement on *American Idol*, which features as many as 102 product placements in a single month. However, Chevrolet recently beat out Coca-Cola for its number of television placements in a month at 57; Coca-Cola grabbed second with 53, and Microsoft was third with 38 placements.[6] The top three shows for product placement were *American Idol* (Fox), *The Biggest Loser* (NBC), and *Gossip Girl* (CW).[7]

Another type of promotional planning must be considered by firms with small budgets. **Guerrilla marketing** involves innovative, low-cost marketing efforts designed to get consumers' attention in unusual ways. Guerrilla marketing is an increasingly popular tactic for marketers, especially those with limited promotional budgets. The Coca-Cola Company recently maximized a humorous guerrilla marketing effort by combining it with social media marketing. How many times have you tried to get a snack or a drink from a vending machine, only to have the machine keep your change, or worse, not give you your requested item? A vending machine at St. John's University in Queens, New York, was apparently broken. It gave the student customer a Coke—and then another, and another, and another. The pleased student handed out the unexpected bonus drinks, getting huge smiles from other students. The whole incident was filmed, guerrilla style, and posted on YouTube. It quickly went viral as viewers tweeted and blogged about it and sent the link to their friends.[8]

Marketers for larger companies have caught on and are using guerrilla approaches as well. Video game maker Electronic Arts (EA) took an unusual approach to promoting its new multiplayer online role-playing game, Star Wars: The Old Republic. In a live, flash-mob promotion in New York's Times Square, Jedi and Sith warriors, in full costume and wielding light sabers, entered the area from all directions and began a freeze-tag duel. While amazed and delighted fans watched, more warriors—men and women in ordinary street clothes—stepped out of the crowd and joined the action. After a few exciting moments, the Jedi, Sith, and "plainclothes" fighters quickly disappeared as mysteriously as they had arrived.[9]

product placement
form of promotion in which marketers pay placement fees to have their products showcased in various media, ranging from newspapers and magazines to television and movies.

guerrilla marketing
innovative, low-cost marketing efforts designed to get consumers' attention in unusual ways.

LECTURE ENHANCER:
Provide an example of a company or product that uses this promotional strategy as its primary promotional method.

©Jason DeCrow/AP/Wide World Photos

Electronic Arts used guerrilla marketing to promote a new game, Star Wars: The Old Republic, in a live flash-mob promotion in New York's Times Square. Clearly gaining consumers' attention, the promotion has received almost 3 million views on YouTube.

From this overview of the promotional mix, we now turn to discussions of each of its elements. The following sections detail the major components of advertising, sales promotion, personal selling, and public relations.

[2]

Advertising

According to one survey, consumers receive from 3,000 to 20,000 marketing messages each day, many of them in the form of advertising.[10] Advertising is the most visible form of nonpersonal promotion—and the most effective for many firms. **Advertising** is paid nonpersonal communication usually targeted at large numbers of potential buyers. Although U.S. citizens often think of advertising as a typically American function, it is a global activity. In a recent year, Procter & Gamble led the list of global advertisers, with measured media spending of $11.43 billion. Earlier, the firm devoted two-thirds of its total advertising budget to international markets. Unilever, P&G's European competitor and the world's second largest global advertiser, recently allocated 86 percent of its advertising budget to non-U.S. markets. These two firms, along with other top global advertisers such as L'Oreal, Colgate-Palmolive, the Coca-Cola Company, and PepsiCo, aimed more than 10 percent of their spending at China, which accounts for 20 percent of the world's population.[11]

Advertising expenditures vary among industries, companies, and media. The top five categories for global advertisers are personal care, automotive, food, pharmaceuticals, and entertainment. But in the United States, pharmaceuticals take top honors, followed by entertainment, automotive, food, and personal care. Because advertising expenditures are so great, and because consumers around the world are bombarded with messages, advertisers need to be increasingly creative and efficient at attracting consumers' attention.[12]

Assessment Check ☑

1. What is the objective of an integrated marketing communications program?

2. Why do firms pursue multiple promotional objectives at the same time?

3. What are product placement and guerrilla marketing?

advertising paid nonpersonal communication, usually targeted at large numbers of potential buyers.

LECTURE ENHANCER: Does the number of marketing messages received on a daily basis surprise you? Why or why not? As a consumer, are you conscious of this bombardment of marketing messages?

LECTURE ENHANCER: For each category, think of a good or service that uses that method of advertising and discuss why.

Business Wire/Getty Images, Inc.

Product advertising consists of messages designed to sell a particular good or service.

product advertising consists of messages designed to sell a particular good or service.

institutional advertising involves messages that promote concepts, ideas, philosophies, or goodwill for industries, companies, organizations, or government entities.

cause advertising form of institutional advertising that promotes a specific viewpoint on a public issue as a way to influence public opinion and the legislative process.

Types of Advertising

The two basic types of ads are product and institutional advertisements. **Product advertising** consists of messages designed to sell a particular good or service. Advertisements for Nantucket Nectars juices, iPods, and Capital One credit cards are examples of product advertising. **Institutional advertising** involves messages that promote concepts, ideas, philosophies, or goodwill for industries, companies, organizations, or government entities. Each year, the Juvenile Diabetes Research Foundation promotes its Walk for the Cure fund-raising event, and your college may place advertisements in local papers or news shows to promote its activities.

A form of institutional advertising that is growing in importance, **cause advertising**, promotes a specific viewpoint on a public issue as a way to influence public opinion and the legislative process about issues such as literacy, hunger and poverty, and alternative energy sources. Both not-for-profit organizations and businesses use cause advertising, sometimes called *advocacy advertising*. As part of Avon's corporate responsibility, the Avon Foundation promotes its Speak Out Against Domestic Violence program with endorsements from celebrities such as Reese Witherspoon in its advertising.[13]

The Bill & Melinda Gates Foundation is a not-for-profit organization dedicated to raising public awareness and generating legislation and other efforts in the fight against poverty, lack of education, and disease. Funded through grants from the Gates family and investment guru Warren Buffett, the foundation operates in all 50 states, the District of Columbia, and more than 100 countries. Through well-publicized grants of $1.37 billion to the United Negro College fund for its Millennium Scholars Program and tours abroad by Bill and Melinda Gates to oversee vaccination programs, the Gates Foundation generates interest in their causes. For their efforts they received a recent *Time* Person of the Year award.[14]

Advertising and the Product Life Cycle

Both product and institutional advertising fall into one of three categories based on whether the ads are intended to inform, persuade, or remind. A firm uses *informative advertising* to build initial demand for a product in the introductory phase of the product life cycle. Highly publicized new-product entries attract the interest of potential buyers who seek information about the advantages of the new products over existing ones, warranties provided, prices, and places that offer the new products. Ads for new smart phones boast of new features, colors, designs, and pricing options to attract new customers.

Persuasive advertising attempts to improve the competitive status of a product, institution, or concept, usually in the growth and maturity stages of the product life cycle. One of the most popular types of persuasive product advertising, *comparative advertising*, compares products directly with their competitors—either by name or by inference. Tylenol advertisements mention the possible stomach problems that the generic drug aspirin could cause, stating that its own pain reliever does not irritate the stomach. But advertisers need to be careful when they name competing brands in comparison ads because they might leave themselves open to controversy or even legal action by competitors. Notice that Tylenol does not mention a specific aspirin brand in its promotions.

Reminder-oriented advertising often appears in the late maturity or decline stages of the product life cycle to maintain awareness of the importance and usefulness of a product, concept, or institution. Triscuits have been around for a long time, but Nabisco attempts to enhance sales with up-to-date advertising that appeals to health and fitness–conscious consumers. The advertising mentions its new no-trans-fat formulations.

CLASS ACTIVITY:
Lead a discussion regarding which comparative advertising campaigns have been most memorable with students.

Advertising Media

Marketers must choose how to allocate their advertising budgets among various media. All media offer advantages and disadvantages. Cost is an important consideration in media selection, but marketers must also choose the media best suited for communicating their message. As Figure 13.2 indicates, the three leading media outlets for advertising are television, the Internet, and newspapers.

Advertising executives agree that firms need to rethink traditional ad campaigns to incorporate new media as well as updated uses of traditional media. Google is looking for ways to combine the targeting capabilities of Internet advertising and the richness of the television medium. Working with television manufacturer Sony, Google launched Google TV, which allows viewers to turn their sets into smart TVs—for downloading apps as well as TV programs and movies from Netflix, browsing the entire Web, searching every cable and satellite channel, and more. Users can create a homepage for their TVs. Working with Logitech, Google now offers the capability for viewers to use their phone as a remote control.[15] The project has advanced to the point where Google is now offering the capability to search and record programs from the Dish Network Corp. Google is far from alone in the effort to bring the television and the Web together, however. It faces stiff competition from Microsoft and Apple, among others.[16]

Television Television is still one of America's leading national advertising media. Television advertising can be classified as network, national, local, and cable ads. The four major national networks—ABC, CBS, NBC, and Fox—broadcast almost one-fifth of all television ads. Despite a decline in audience share and growing competition from cable, network television remains the easiest way for advertisers to reach large numbers of viewers—10 million to 20 million with a single commercial. Automakers, fast-food restaurants, and food manufacturers are heavy users of network TV advertising.

About 58 percent of U.S. households with TVs now subscribe to cable and broadband Internet connections. These viewers are drawn to the more than 800 channels available through cable or satellite services. But the cable and satellite networks are facing new competition. One survey indicates that 60 percent of American homes have one or more video game consoles. People are using the consoles to download apps and video-on-demand offerings. And a small but growing number of viewers are discontinuing their cable service and opting for online services such as Netflix, Hulu, Apple's iTunes, and the networks' own Web sites. One recent survey found that about half of the total U.S. population now watches at least some TV programming online. People still prefer free, advertising-supported downloads, although online network advertising made up only 2.5 percent of the yearly $62 billion in advertising revenues. However, the number of homes with digital video recorders

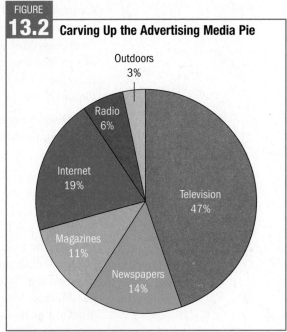

FIGURE 13.2 Carving Up the Advertising Media Pie

- Television 47%
- Internet 19%
- Newspapers 14%
- Magazines 11%
- Radio 6%
- Outdoors 3%

Note: Percentages do not total to 100% due to rounding. Direct mail was not measured in these data.

Sources: Data from "100 Leading National Advertisers Index," *Advertising Age*, http://adage.com, accessed April 2, 2012; "US Online Ad Spend to Close in on $40 billion," *eMarketer*, January 19, 2012, http://www.emarketer.com.

LECTURE ENHANCER:
Discuss the qualities that
set TV ads apart from other
media.

CLASS ACTIVITY:
Ask students which
television ads they think
have been most effective
during the Super Bowl.

LECTURE ENHANCER:
What are the most common
drawbacks to Internet ads,
particularly pop-ups?

(DVRs) and high-definition (HD) televisions is increasing steadily. Recent research suggests that even people who can use their DVRs to skip TV ads don't always do so. According to the Nielsen Company, many DVR users still watch shows at their scheduled times, when they must watch the ads, and even those who record shows for later viewing watch almost half the ads they could skip. With more people watching playbacks of their favorite shows, the networks' ratings—and commercial watching—increase too.[17]

Although—or perhaps because—television reaches the greatest number of consumers at once, it is the most expensive advertising medium. The Super Bowl is widely known for its hefty advertising price tag. Firms such as Skechers, Toyota, GoDaddy, Kia, and M&Ms paid as much as $3.5 million for a 30-second spot during one recent game—although about half the advertisers posted their ads on line in the days leading up to the game. But the most expensive TV commercial of all time—so far—was the $6.5 million that Honda paid for an ad about its Accord.[18] Marketers want to be certain that their commercials reach the greatest number of viewers. Because of the high cost, advertisers may demand guarantees of audience size and receive compensation if a show fails to deliver the promised number of viewers.

Internet Advertising
Although online and interactive advertising revenues have already hit $21.7 billion annually—surpassing print media—they are expected to reach $42.5 billion by 2015. The rising number of smart phones and tablets is affecting this increase, as is the rapid multiplication of social media.[19]

Online and interactive media have already changed the nature of advertising. Starting with simple banner ads, Internet advertising has become much more complex and sophisticated. Miniature television screen images, called *widgets* or *gadgets*, can carry marketing messages only a few inches high on a Web site, blog, or desktop display. And they contain embedded links to their home sites. Online advertising can take other forms as well. The Century Council, a nonprofit organization that combats drunk driving and underage drinking, recently launched a public-service campaign called "Ask, Listen, Learn" for Alcohol Awareness Month. Each state attorney general recorded a version—animated or for radio— of the announcement that promoted "saying yes to a healthy lifestyle and no to underage drinking." The campaign proved highly successful, with millions of hits on the Century Council's YouTube Channel.[20]

Discount coupons are another form of Internet advertising, and one that has grown rapidly in popularity. See the "Hit & Miss" feature for more about daily deal sites such as Groupon.

Another example is *viral advertising*, which creates a message that is novel or entertaining enough for consumers to forward it to others, spreading it like a virus. The great advantage is that spreading the word online, which often relies on social networking sites such as Facebook, YouTube, and Twitter, costs the advertiser nothing. Although viral marketing can be risky, the best campaigns are edgy or funny. Among the most popular viral videos of late are the Volkswagen commercial in which a small boy, in full Darth Vader costume, thinks he has used the "force" to start his dad's car; Doug, a sock puppet, selling Ford cars; and rapper Method Man promoting Sour Patch Kids candy. Salesforce.com recently decided to use YouTube as its video delivery platform because marketing surveys revealed that the site was "one of the most trusted" by users.[21]

Some viral campaigns rely on personal word-of-mouth promotions, and when ordinary consumers are recruited as "brand ambassadors" or "buzz agents" for pay, questions can arise about ethics. One company, BzzAgent, gives its members products instead of money. But these ambassadors are not required to tell others that they're being paid or receiving free gifts to discuss products, which some view as problematic.[22]

Daily Deal Sites Crowd a Brand-New Market

The spectacular rise of Groupon, which *Forbes* called the fastest-growing company of all time, led to a multi-million dollar IPO, millions of subscribers, and a new industry. The daily deal market is growing fast. New entrants focus on ever-narrower niches, such as Facebook users living in or near specific major cities, singles, entrepreneurs and small-business owners, suburban mothers, and even coupon buyers who want to resell unused discounts before they expire.

Breaking into the daily deal market has become challenging because this type of business is very expensive to operate. One owner observes, "the biggest challenge in this new space is that there's not an existing talent pool to pull [employees] from." And by tapping a dormant resource—local search ads—daily deal sites are raising their own cost of doing business. Still, those looking to leverage customer data and work with local businesses are finding daily deals an effective product to offer.

Questions for Critical Thinking

1. Some daily deal sites publicize subscribers' deal sign-ups on Facebook. Do you think a discount or freebie is worth a loss of privacy? Why or why not?

2. What factors might motivate small businesses to sign up with daily deal sites?

Sources: "Some Like It Hot: Daily Deal Industry Continues to Be 'on Fire' in 2012," PR Newswire, http://www.prnewswire.com, accessed March 19, 2012; "Daily Deal Frenzy Jolts Local Online Ad Market," Reuters.com, http://www.reuters.com, accessed March 19, 2012; Catherine New, "Don't Let Groupons Go to Waste: Secondary Websites Do a Brisk Resale Business," Daily Finance.com, http://www.dailyfinance.com, accessed March 19, 2012; Stu Woo and Geoffrey A. Fowler, "Daily Deals Rescue Local-Ad Market," *The Wall Street Journal*, http://online.wsj.com, accessed March 19, 2012.

Newspapers Daily and weekly newspapers continue to dominate local advertising. Marketers can easily tailor newspaper advertising to local tastes and preferences. Advertisers can also coordinate advertisements with other promotional efforts such as discount coupons from supermarkets and one-day sales at department stores. One disadvantage is the relatively short lifespan of daily newspapers; people usually discard them soon after reading. Retailers and automobile dealers rank first among newspaper advertisers. Most newspapers now maintain Web sites, some of which offer separate material and features, to complement their print editions.

Radio Despite the proliferation of other media, the average U.S. household owns five radios—including those in cars—a market penetration that makes radio an important advertising medium. Advertisers like the captive audience of listeners as they commute to and from work. As a result, morning and evening drive-time shows command top ad rates. In major markets, many stations serve different demographic groups with targeted programming. Internet radio programming also offers opportunities for yet more focused targeting.

Satellite stations offer great potential for advertisers. Sirius and XM both offer commercial-free music, with advertising on news and talk shows. A recent study predicts that Internet radio will have 200 million listeners by 2020, although 250 million will still listen to AM/FM (sometimes referred to as terrestrial) radio. In a recent year, Internet radio advertising revenues reached $260 million in a year, with an additional $28 million from podcasting.[23] Google recently updated its AdWords application to include ads that can be broadcast by traditional radio stations. An advertiser fills out a questionnaire indicating the target audience and where and how often the ad should be run. The advertiser pays a fee each time the ad is aired and can have the ad tracked to find the best possible time to reach the desired audience.[24]

Magazines Magazines include consumer publications and business trade journals. *Time*, *Reader's Digest*, and *Sports Illustrated* are consumer magazines, whereas *Advertising Age* and *Oil & Gas Journal* fall into the trade category.

LECTURE ENHANCER:
What are some possible threats to the continued effectiveness of magazine sales?

Magazines can customize their publications and target advertising messages to different regions of the country. One method places local advertising in regional editions of the magazines. Other magazines attach wraparounds—half-size covers on top of full-size covers—to highlight articles inside that relate to particular regions; different wraparounds appear in different parts of the country.

Magazines are a natural choice for targeted advertising. Media buyers study the demographics of subscribers and select magazines that attract the desired readers. American Express advertises in *Fortune* and *Bloomberg Businessweek* to reach businesspeople, while PacSun clothes and Clearasil skin medications are advertised in *Teen Vogue*.

Direct Mail The average U.S. household receives about 550 pieces of direct mail each year, including 100 catalogs. The huge growth in the variety of direct-mail offerings combined with the convenience they offer today's busy, time-pressed shoppers has made direct-mail advertising a multi-billion-dollar business. Even consumers who like to shop online often page through a catalog before placing an online order. Although direct mail is expensive per person, a small business can afford a limited direct-mail campaign but not a television or radio ad. For businesses with a small advertising budget, a carefully targeted direct-mail effort can be highly effective. E-mail is a low-cost form of direct marketing. Marketers can target the most interested Internet users by offering Web site visitors an option to register to receive e-mail. Amazon.com, Gardener's Supply, and Abercrombie & Fitch routinely send e-mails to regular customers.

LECTURE ENHANCER:
Discuss how accurate direct-mail profiles may be. Have you ever received direct mail that drastically differed from your interests?

Address lists are at the heart of direct-mail advertising. Using data-mining techniques to segment markets, direct-mail marketers create profiles that show the traits of consumers who are likely to buy their products or donate to their organizations. Catalog retailers sometimes experiment by sending direct-mail pieces randomly to people who subscribe to particular magazines. Next, they analyze the orders received from the mailings and develop profiles of purchasers. Finally, they rent lists of additional subscriber names that match the profiles they have developed.

Studies have shown that most U.S. consumers are annoyed by the amount of so-called junk mail they receive every day, including catalogs, advertising postcards, and flyers. Among Internet users, a major pet peeve is *spam*, or junk e-mail. Many states have outlawed such practices as sending e-mail promotions without legitimate return addresses, although it is difficult to track down and catch offenders.

The Direct Marketing Association (DMA; www.the-dma.org) helps marketers combat negative attitudes by offering its members guidelines on ethical business practices. The DMA also provides consumer information at its Web site, as well as services that enable consumers to opt out of receiving unsolicited offers. In addition, Federal Trade Commission regulations have taken effect for direct mail in certain industries. With the passage of the CARD Act of 2009, credit-card issuers must follow stricter regulations in their direct mail practices. Unsolicited, preapproved applications sent to consumers must be accompanied by a prominent notice explaining how to get off the issuer's mailing list. Some issuers initially cut back on the number of mailings they sent, but recent figures show an increase in offers from 575 million to 1.4 billion, indicating an upswing in confidence.[25]

CLASS ACTIVITY:
Discuss goods or services in the local community for which outdoor advertising might be most effective.

Outdoor Advertising In one recent year, outdoor advertising accounted for almost $6.4 billion in advertising revenues.[26] The majority of spending on outdoor advertising is for billboards, but spending for other types of outdoor advertising, such as signs in transit stations, stores, airports, and sports stadiums, is growing fast. Advertisers are exploring new forms of outdoor media, many of which involve technology: computerized paintings;

digital billboards; "trivision," which displays three revolving images on a single billboard; and moving billboards mounted on trucks. Other innovations include ads displayed on the Goodyear blimp, using an electronic system that offers animation and video.

Digital advertising is now available on taxi tops. With more than 13,000 yellow medallion taxis in New York City, the potential visibility is enormous. Clear Channel Outdoor Advertising offers its Digital Outdoor Networks, a complete line of electronic advertising.[27] CBS Outdoor unveiled the first-ever high-definition, 3D projection display in New York City's Grand Central Station. And the Coca-Cola Company inaugurated its Digital Network, 28 electronic billboards that it owns in 27 locations. (The company leases the space from outdoor advertising firms such as Clear Channel Outdoor and Boardworks but owns the boards themselves.) The Coca-Cola Company's Digital Network recently featured advertisements by CardioSmart, the patient education and support program of the American College of Cardiology Foundation. The Outdoor Advertising Association of America predicts that several hundred digital billboards will be introduced each year, with a total of about 3,200 so far.[28]

Sponsorship   One of the hottest trends in promotion offers marketers the ability to integrate several elements of the promotional mix. <u>Sponsorship</u> involves providing funds for a sporting or cultural event in exchange for a direct association with the event. Sports sponsorships attract two-thirds of total sponsorship dollars in the United States alone. Entertainment, festivals, causes, and the arts divide up the remaining third of sponsorship dollars.

Technology plays an important role in advertising, especially for outdoor media. This electronic billboard promotes the movie *The Hunger Games*.

NASCAR, the biggest spectator sport in the United States, thrives on sponsorships. Sponsorships can run in the tens of millions. Hendricks Motorsports, based in North Carolina, is the wealthiest and most successful NASCAR team to date, with more than $115 million in sponsorships from firms such as PepsiCo, DuPont, Lowes, and Farmers Insurance Group.[29] Firms may also sponsor charitable or other not-for-profit awards or events. In conjunction with sports network ESPN, Gatorade sponsors its High School Athlete of the Year award, presented to the top male and female high school athletes who "strive for their best on and off the field."

Sponsors benefit in two major ways: exposure to the event's audience and association with the image of the activity. If a celebrity is involved, sponsors usually earn the right to use his or her name along with the name of the event in advertisements. They can set up signs at the event, offer sales promotions, and the like. Sponsorships play an important role in relationship marketing, bringing together the event, its participants, and the sponsoring firms.

Other Media Options   As consumers filter out familiar advertising messages, marketers look for novel ways to catch their attention. In addition to the major media, firms promote through many other vehicles such as infomercials and specialized media.

<u>Infomercials</u> are a form of broadcast direct marketing, also called *direct-response television (DRTV)*. These 30-minute programs resemble regular television programs but are devoted to selling goods or services such as exercise equipment, skin-care products, or kitchenware. The long format allows an advertiser to thoroughly present product benefits, increase awareness, and make an impact on consumers. Advertisers also receive immediate responses in the form of sales or inquiries because most infomercials feature toll-free phone numbers. Infomercial stars may become celebrities in their own right, attracting more customers wherever they go. The most effective infomercials tend to be for auto-care products,

Assessment Check ✓

1. What are the two basic types of advertising? Into what three categories do they fall?

2. What is the leading advertising medium in the United States?

3. In what two major ways do firms benefit from sponsorship?

beauty and personal-care items, investing and business opportunities, collectibles, fitness and self-improvement products, and housewares and electronics.[30]

Advertisers use just about any medium they can find. They place messages on New York City MetroCard transit cards and toll receipts on the Massachusetts Turnpike. A more recent development is the use of ATMs for advertising. Some ATMs can play 15-second commercials on their screens, and many can print advertising messages on receipts. An ATM screen has a captive audience because the user must watch the screen to complete a transaction. Directory advertising includes the familiar Yellow Pages listings in telephone books and thousands of other types of directories, most presenting business-related promotions. Besides local and regional directories, publishers also have produced special printed and online versions of the Yellow Pages that target ethnic groups.

[3] Sales Promotion

Traditionally viewed as a supplement to a firm's sales or advertising efforts, sales promotion has emerged as an integral part of the promotional mix. Promotion now accounts for more than half as many marketing dollars as are spent on advertising, and promotion spending is rising faster than ad spending. **Sales promotion** consists of forms of promotion such as coupons, product samples, and rebates that support advertising and personal selling.

sales promotion consists of forms of promotion such as coupons, product samples, and rebates that support advertising and personal selling.

Both retailers and manufacturers use sales promotions to offer consumers extra incentives to buy. Beyond the short-term advantage of increased sales, sales promotions can also help marketers build brand equity and enhance customer relationships. Examples include samples, coupons, contests, displays, trade shows, and dealer incentives.

FIGURE 13.3 Spending on Consumer-Oriented Promotions

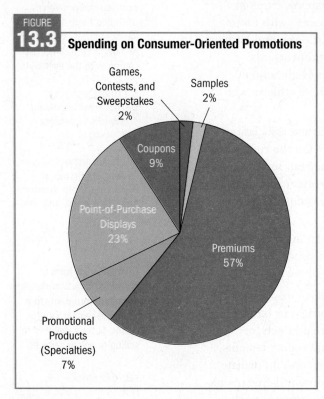

Source: Data from Kathleen M. Joyce, "Higher Gear," *Promo Magazine,* http://chiefmarketer.com, accessed March 30, 2012.

Consumer-Oriented Promotions

The goal of a consumer-oriented sales promotion is to get new and existing customers to try or buy products. In addition, marketers want to encourage repeat purchases by rewarding current users, increase sales of complimentary products, and boost impulse purchases. Figure 13.3 shows how marketers allocate their consumer-oriented spending among the categories of promotions.

Promotions can also popularize an idea, such as the growing awareness of how much eco-friendly business processes can help the environment. See the "Going Green" feature for information about how green certification is catching on in the hotel industry.

Premiums, Coupons, Rebates, and Samples

Nearly six of every ten sales promotion dollars are spent on *premiums*—items given free or at a reduced price with the purchase of another product. Cosmetics companies such as Clinique offer sample kits with purchases of their products. Fast-food restaurants are also big users of premiums. McDonald's and Burger King include a toy with every children's meal—the toys often tie in with new movies or popular cartoon shows. In general, marketers choose premiums that are likely to get consumers thinking about and caring about the brand

What do you look for in a hotel—speedy check-in, free Wi Fi, good security? What about indoor air quality?

More travelers than ever look for evidence their hotel is "green." In a recent survey of Expedia customers, 75 percent agreed that sustainability in the hospitality industry should be defined as building, furnishing, and operating hotels in ways that are better for the guest, better for the community, and better for the planet.

Many forms of green certification exist, but perhaps the most respected is Green Seal certification. Green Seal, a nonprofit organization, began in 1989 as the first tool for U.S. shoppers looking for reliably sustainable products. It now certifies 40 categories of goods and services, and since 1995 it has applied its rigorous science-based criteria to assess eco-friendly practices in the hotel industry.

"Green Seal is a trustworthy label guests are much more likely to be familiar with in the products they have in their homes," says its vice president. Most Kimpton Hotels will soon be certified. "We are extremely proud to be associated with Green Seal," says the chain's CEO.

Questions for Critical Thinking

1. **What advantages can a hotel chain expect from green certification?**
2. **How might Kimpton Hotels promote its Green Seal certification to prospective guests?**

Sources: Scott Parisi and Ray Burger, "Green Hotel Certification Programs Snowball, Sparks Confusion," *Eco Green Hotel*, http://www.ecogreenhotel.com, accessed February 13, 2012; "Survey of Expedia Consumers Reveals that Hotels Can Drive Growth Through Sustainability But Consumer Benefits Are Critical," PR Web, http://www.prweb.com, accessed February 13, 2012; Green Seal corporate Web site, http://www.greenseal.org, accessed February 13, 2012, "Green Seal," Natural Resources Defense Council, http://www.nrdc.org, accessed February 13, 2012.

---

and the product. People who purchase health foods at a grocery store may find an offer for a free personal training session at a local health club printed on the back of their sales receipt.

Customers redeem *coupons* for small price discounts when they purchase the promoted products. Such offers may persuade a customer to try a new or different product. Some large supermarket chains double the face value of manufacturers' coupons. Coupons have the disadvantage of focusing customers on price rather than brand loyalty. While some consumers complain that clipping or printing out coupons is too time consuming, others relish the savings, particularly when money is tight and prices seem to be high.

American consumers' use of coupons has increased more than 25 percent, using 3.3 billion coupons to redeem $3.5 billion. Internet coupon use skyrocketed a whopping 360 percent. Marketers issued 367 billion coupons with a face value averaging $1.44, but shortened the expiration periods by some 10 percent. Some analysts predict that the growing use of paperless mobile coupons, which consumers can access on their Web-enabled cell phones while shopping and pioneered by such retailers as Target, could soon make clippable or even printed-out coupons obsolete.[31]

Rebates offer cash back to consumers who mail in required proofs of purchase. Rebates help packaged-goods manufacturers increase purchase rates, promote multiple purchases, and reward product users. Other types of companies also offer rebates, especially for electronics, computers and their accessories, and automobiles. Processing rebates gives marketers a way to collect data about their customers, but many shoppers find it inconvenient to collect the required receipts, forms, and UPC codes and then wait several weeks for their refund. Services such as RebateRemedy can cut the waiting time to days instead of weeks but take a 20 to 30 percent cut of the rebate, plus a processing fee. Recently, Verizon Wireless and LG Mobile launched the new Lucid smart phone, offering a $50 mail-in rebate when customers sign a two-year agreement. Instead of receiving a check for that amount, customers will get a debit card that can be used at any store that accepts them.[32]

A *sample* is a gift of a product distributed by mail, door to door, in a demonstration, or inside packages of another product. On any given day you might receive a sample

LECTURE ENHANCER: Which is the most commonly used form of consumer-oriented promotion?

moisturizer, a bar of soap, or a packet of laundry detergent. Three of every four consumers who receive samples will try them.

Games, Contests, and Sweepstakes Games, contests, and sweepstakes offer cash, merchandise, or travel as prizes to participating winners. Firms often sponsor these activities to introduce new goods and services and to attract additional customers. Games and contests require entrants to solve problems or write essays and sometimes provide proof of purchase. Sweepstakes choose winners by chance and require no product purchase. Consumers typically prefer them because games and contests require more effort. Companies like sweepstakes, too, because they are inexpensive to run and determine the number of winners from the beginning. With games and contests, the company cannot predict the number of people who will correctly complete a puzzle or gather the right number of symbols from scratch-off cards. Sweepstakes, games, contests, and sweepstakes can reinforce a company's image and advertising message, but consumer attention may focus on the promotion rather than the product.

In recent years, court rulings and legal restrictions have limited the use of games and contests. Companies must proceed carefully in advertising their contests and games and the prizes they award. Marketers must indicate the chances of winning and avoid false promises such as implying that a person has already won.

Specialty Advertising Do you have any pens, t-shirts, or refrigerator magnets imprinted with a business name that you received for free? These offers are examples of **specialty advertising** or *advertising specialties*. This type of sales promotion involves the gift of useful merchandise carrying the name, logo, or slogan of a profit-seeking business or a not-for-profit organization. Because those products are useful and sometimes personalized with recipients' names, people tend to keep and use them, giving advertisers repeated exposure. Originally designed to identify and create goodwill for advertisers, advertising specialties now generate sales leads and develop traffic for stores and trade show exhibitors. Like premiums, these promotions should reinforce the brand's image and its relationship with the recipient.

Trade-Oriented Promotions

Sales promotion techniques can also contribute to campaigns directed to retailers and wholesalers. **Trade promotion** is sales promotion geared to marketing intermediaries rather than to consumers. Marketers use trade promotion to encourage retailers to stock new products, continue carrying existing ones, and promote both new and existing products effectively to consumers. Successful trade promotions offer financial incentives. They require careful timing, attention to costs, and easy implementation for intermediaries. These promotions should bring quick results and improve retail sales. Major trade promotions include point-of-purchase advertising and trade shows.

Point-of-purchase (POP) advertising consists of displays or demonstrations that promote products when and where consumers buy them, such as in retail stores. When the Swiffer floor cleaner was being introduced, Procter & Gamble used in-store demonstrations to show consumers how it worked. Marketing research has shown that consumers are more likely to purchase certain products when such displays are present. Sunscreen, painting supplies, and snacks are typically displayed this way. A high-tech version of POP advertising is digital advertising consoles mounted on grocery carts. With impulse purchases making up 53 percent of total buying, POP has already begun to evolve into what is being called "mobile advertising." Although privacy is still an issue, more and more Web sites and other services are now able to locate Internet users, and location-based mobile spending is expected to increase from a current $1.6 million to $4 billion in 2015. About one third of the 750 million Facebook members visit the site via mobile electronic devices. Location-based advertising will not be directed primarily to stationary computers but to smart phones, iPads, Kindles, game consoles, and even automobiles.[33]

Manufacturers and other sellers often exhibit at *trade shows* to promote goods or services to members of their distribution channels. These shows are often organized by industry trade associations. Each year, thousands of trade shows attract millions of exhibitors and hundreds of millions of attendees. Such shows are particularly important in fast-changing industries like those for computers, toys, furniture, and fashions. The annual Consumer Electronics Show, which is held in Las Vegas and attracts more than 100,000 visitors, is the nation's largest. But shows in the medical and health care, RV and camping, and even woodworking machinery fields remain well attended. These shows are especially effective for introducing new products and generating sales leads.

Personal Selling

Many companies consider personal selling—a person-to-person promotional presentation to a potential buyer—the key to marketing effectiveness. Unless a seller matches a firm's goods or services to the needs of a particular client or customer, none of the firm's other activities produces any benefits. Today, sales and sales-related jobs employ about 15 million U.S. workers.[34] Businesses often spend five to ten times as much on personal selling as on advertising. Given the significant cost of hiring, training, benefits, and salaries, businesses are very concerned with the effectiveness of their sales personnel. One of their continuing concerns is with the way representatives communicate with others.

How do marketers decide whether to make personal selling the primary component of their firm's marketing mix? In general, firms are likely to emphasize personal selling rather than advertising or sales promotion under four conditions:

1. Customers are relatively few in number and geographically concentrated.

2. The product is technically complex, involves trade-ins, or requires special handling.

3. The product carries a relatively high price.

4. The product moves through direct-distribution channels.

Selling luxury items such as the Porsche 918 Spyder hybrid ($630,000) or a John Lennon– themed Steinway piano ($90,000) would require a personal touch. Then there's the $20,000 home theater device offered by California-based Prima Cinema, which automatically sends Hollywood films to customers' home systems the same day they premiere. Installation, including instructions on how to use the system, would require personal selling.[35]

The sales functions of most companies are experiencing rapid change. Today's salespeople are more concerned with establishing long-term buyer–seller relationships and acting as consultants to their customers than in the past. In the aftermath of the recession, salespeople face a new challenge—consumers who haggle over prices, even on retail items. One survey found that 88 percent of those questioned had haggled over at least one price in the preceding six months. Unlike in the Great Depression of the 1930s, the last time Americans engaged in serious amounts of haggling, today's consumers have advantages that would astound their predecessors. Anyone with a Web-enabled cell phone can Google competing prices of merchandise while standing in front of it in a retail store. Many have learned to bargain via Web sites such as eBay or have used Priceline to negotiate deals on travel. The survey found that hagglers had better than a 75 percent success rate in making deals on clothing, appliances, and jewelry. Consumers who negotiated medical bills were successful 58 percent of the time.[36]

Personal selling can occur in several environments, each of which can involve business-to-business or business-to-consumer selling. Sales representatives who make sales calls on prospective customers at their businesses are involved in *field selling*. Companies that sell major industrial equipment typically rely heavily on field selling. *Over-the-counter selling* describes sales activities in retailing and some wholesale locations, where customers visit the seller's facility to purchase items. *Telemarketing* sales representatives make their presentations over the phone. A later section reviews telemarketing in more detail.

Sales Tasks All sales activities involve assisting customers in some manner. Although a salesperson's work can vary significantly from one company or situation to another, it usually includes a mix of three basic tasks: order processing, creative selling, and missionary selling.

Order Processing Although both field selling and telemarketing involve this activity, **order processing** is most often related to retail and wholesale firms. The salesperson identifies customer needs, points out merchandise to meet them, and processes the order. Route sales personnel process orders for such consumer goods as bread, milk, soft drinks, and snack foods. They check each store's stock, report inventory needs to the store manager, and complete the sale. Most of these jobs include at least minor order-processing functions.

order processing form of selling, mostly at the wholesale and retail levels, that involves identifying customer needs, pointing them out to customers, and completing orders.

Creative Selling Sales representatives for most business products and some consumer items perform **creative selling**, a persuasive type of promotional presentation. Creative selling promotes a good or service whose benefits are not readily apparent or whose purchase decision requires a close analysis of alternatives. Sales of intangible products such as insurance rely heavily on creative selling, but sales of tangible goods benefit as well.

creative selling persuasive type of promotional presentation.

Many retail salespeople just process orders, but many consumers are looking for more in the form of customer service, which is where creative selling comes in. Personal shoppers at Topshop—located in London and New York City—help customers create entire looks from three floors of clothing. They also offer customers refreshments and the option to ring up purchases at a special cash register without waiting in line.

Missionary Selling Sales work also includes an indirect form of selling in which the representative promotes goodwill for a company or provides technical or operational assistance to the customer; this practice is called **missionary selling**. Many businesses that sell technical equipment, such as Oracle and Fujitsu, provide systems specialists who act as consultants to customers. These salespeople work to solve problems and sometimes help their clients with questions not directly related to their employers' products. Other industries also use missionary selling techniques. Pharmaceutical company representatives—called *detailers*—visit physicians to introduce the firm's latest offerings, although some firms are finding success with more subtle methods, including Web-based sales calls outside office hours. Drug companies are turning to e-detailing, including Web sites, iPad apps, and other digital devices that are increasingly replacing office visits by human sales reps. The pharmaceutical giant Astra Zeneca recently inaugurated a digital marketing group whose target audience is health care providers. This marketing group set up a Web site called AZ

missionary selling indirect form of selling in which the representative promotes goodwill for a company or provides technical or operational assistance to the customer.

Touchpoints, where doctors can post questions, request free samples of drugs, and inquire about health insurance coverage. They can also download and print brochures and other literature. If a doctor wants to speak with a sales rep, the site lists a phone number. A company official says that Touchpoints has helped the company "redirect our sales force to new products that need more of a scientific discussion."[37]

Telemarketing <u>Telemarketing</u>, personal selling conducted by telephone, provides a firm's marketers with a high return on their expenditures, an immediate response, and an opportunity for personalized two-way conversation. Many firms use telemarketing because expense or other obstacles prevent salespeople from meeting many potential customers in person. Telemarketers can use databases to target prospects based on demographic data. Telemarketing takes two forms. A sales representative who calls you is practicing *outbound telemarketing*. On the other hand, *inbound telemarketing* occurs when you call a toll-free phone number to get product information or place an order.

Outbound telemarketers must abide by the Federal Trade Commission's 1996 Telemarketing Sales Rule. Telemarketers must disclose that they are selling something and on whose behalf they are calling before they make their presentations. The rule also limits calls to between 8 a.m. and 9 p.m., requires sellers to disclose details on exchange policies, and requires them to keep lists of people who do not want to receive calls. In some states, it is also against the law for telemarketers to leave messages on consumers' answering machines. Congress enacted another law in 2003 that created the National Do Not Call registry, intended to help consumers block unwanted telemarketing calls. Consumers who want to be on the list must call a special number or visit a Web site to register. Telemarketers must stop calling registered numbers within 31 days or face stiff fines of up to $16,000 for each violation.[38] Charities, surveys, and political campaign calls are exempt from these restrictions. Businesses with which consumers already have a relationship, such as the bank where they have accounts or the dealership where they buy their cars, may conduct telemarketing calls under the guidelines of the Telemarketing Sales Rule.

The Sales Process The sales process typically follows the seven-step sequence shown in Figure 13.4: prospecting and qualifying, the approach, presentation, the demonstration, handling objections, closing, and the follow-up. Remember the importance of flexibility, though; a good salesperson is not afraid to vary the sales process based on a customer's responses and needs. The process of selling to a potential customer who is unfamiliar with a company's products differs from the process of serving a long-time customer.

Prospecting, Qualifying, and Approaching At the prospecting stage, salespeople identify potential customers. They may seek leads for prospective sales from such sources as existing

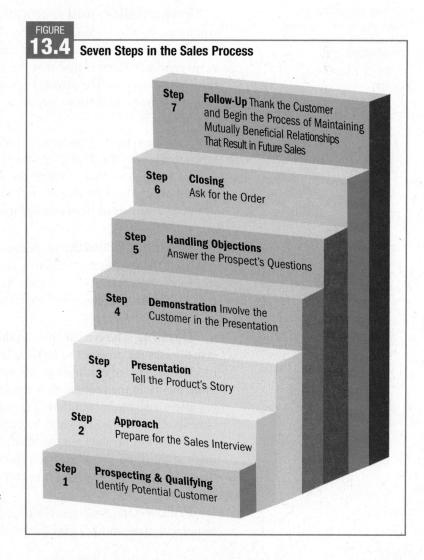

FIGURE 13.4 **Seven Steps in the Sales Process**

Step 7 **Follow-Up** Thank the Customer and Begin the Process of Maintaining Mutually Beneficial Relationships That Result in Future Sales

Step 6 **Closing** Ask for the Order

Step 5 **Handling Objections** Answer the Prospect's Questions

Step 4 **Demonstration** Involve the Customer in the Presentation

Step 3 **Presentation** Tell the Product's Story

Step 2 **Approach** Prepare for the Sales Interview

Step 1 **Prospecting & Qualifying** Identify Potential Customer

telemarketing personal selling conducted entirely by telephone, which provides a firm's marketers with a high return on their expenditures, an immediate response, and an opportunity for personalized two-way conversation.

At the makeup counter, salespeople provide a free makeup demonstration to reinforce the message of how their cosmetic products can enhance a person's look.

customers, friends and family, and business associates. The qualifying process identifies potential customers who have the financial ability and authority to buy.

Companies use different tactics to identify and qualify prospects. Some companies rely on business development teams, passing responses from direct mail along to their sales reps. Others believe in personal visits. Many firms are now using electronic social media, which cost little or nothing, to boost sales. Online newsletters, virtual trade shows, podcasts, Webinars, and blogs are good examples. Experts advise developing a clear strategy in order to be successful with social media.[39]

Successful salespeople make careful preparations, analyzing available data about a prospective customer's product lines and other pertinent information before making the initial contact. They realize the importance of a first impression in influencing a customer's future attitudes toward the seller and its products.

LECTURE ENHANCER:
Which step in the sequence do you feel is the most crucial? Why?

Presentation and Demonstration

At the presentation stage, salespeople communicate promotional messages. They may describe the major features of their products, highlight the advantages, and cite examples of satisfied consumers. A demonstration helps reinforce the message that the salesperson has been communicating—a critical step in the sales process. Department-store shoppers can get a free makeover at the cosmetics counter. Anyone looking to buy a car will take it for a test drive before deciding whether to purchase it.

Some products are too large to transport to prospective buyers or require special installation to demonstrate. Using laptop computers, multimedia presentations, graphic programs such as SmartDraw, Web conferences, and even podcasts, sales representatives can demonstrate these products for customers.[40] Others, such as services, are intangible. So a presentation including testimonials from satisfied customers or graphs illustrating results may be helpful.

Handling Objections

Some salespeople fear potential customers' objections because they view the questions as criticism. But a good salesperson can use objections as an opportunity to answer questions and explain how the product will benefit the customer. As a general rule, the key is to sell benefits, not features: How will this product help the customer?

Closing

The critical point in the sales process—the time at which the salesperson actually asks the prospect to buy—is the closing. If the presentation effectively matches product benefits to customer needs, the closing should be a natural conclusion. If there are more bumps in the process, the salesperson can try some different techniques, such as offering alternative products, offering a special incentive for purchase, or restating the product benefits. Closing the sale—and beginning a relationship in which the customer builds loyalty to the brand or product—is the ideal outcome of this interaction. But even if the sale is not made at this time, the salesperson should regard the interaction as the beginning of a potential relationship anyway. The prospect might very well become a customer in the future.

Follow-Up

A salesperson's actions after the sale may determine whether the customer will make another purchase. Follow-up is an important part of building a long-lasting relationship. After closing, the salesperson should process the order efficiently. By calling soon after a purchase, the salesperson provides reassurance about the customer's decision to buy and creates an opportunity to correct any problems.

CLASS ACTIVITY: Ask students how a salesperson might follow up after selling a car to a customer.

Public Relations

A final element of the promotional mix, public relations (PR)—including publicity—supports advertising, personal selling, and sales promotion, usually by pursuing broader objectives. Through PR, companies attempt to improve their prestige and image with the public by distributing specific messages or ideas to target audiences. Cause-related promotional activities are often supported by public relations and publicity campaigns. In addition, PR helps a firm establish awareness of goods and services and then builds a positive image of them.

Public relations refers to an organization's communications and relationships with its various public audiences, such as customers, vendors, news media, employees, stockholders, the government, and the general public. Many of these communication efforts serve marketing purposes. Public relations is an efficient, indirect communications channel for promoting products. It can publicize items and help create and maintain a positive image of the company.

The public relations department links a firm with the media. It provides the media with news releases and video and audio clips and holds news conferences to announce new products, the formation of strategic alliances, management changes, financial results, and similar developments. Publications issued by the department include newsletters, brochures, and reports.

Publicity The type of public relations that is tied most closely to promoting a company's products is **publicity**—nonpersonal stimulation of demand for a good, service, place, idea, event, person, or organization by unpaid placement of information in print or broadcast media. Press releases generate publicity, as does news coverage. Publicity can even help save a struggling business. Fred Daley, owner of Fresh Fish Daley, faced the fact that he might have to close his New Hampshire business when state regulations governing the transportation of fish changed; he could not afford the upgrades to his van. When local news reported Daley's plight, his loyal customers came forward with donations; one man found an affordable van on eBay and helped Daley complete the purchase. "It's a story of goodwill," said Daley with gratitude.[41]

Not-for-profit organizations benefit from publicity when they receive coverage of events such as the Susan G. Komen Race for the Cure, which raises money for breast cancer research.[42] When a for-profit firm teams up with a not-for-profit firm in a fund-raising effort, the move usually generates good publicity for both organizations.

public relations organization's communications and relationships with its various public audiences.

publicity nonpersonal stimulation of demand for a good, service, place, idea, event, person, or organization by unpaid placement of information in print or broadcast media.

Assessment Check ☑

1. Why do retailers and manufacturers use sales promotions?

2. When does a firm use personal selling instead of nonpersonal selling?

3. How does public relations serve a marketing purpose?

4 Pushing and Pulling Strategies

Marketers can choose between two general promotional strategies: a pushing strategy or a pulling strategy. A **pushing strategy** relies on personal selling to market an item to wholesalers and retailers in a company's distribution channels. So companies promote the product to members of the marketing channel, not to end users. Sales personnel explain to marketing intermediaries why they should carry particular merchandise, usually supported by offers of special discounts and promotional materials. Marketers also provide **cooperative advertising** allowances, in which they share the cost of local advertising of their firm's product or

pushing strategy personal selling to market an item to wholesalers and retailers in a company's distribution channels.

cooperative advertising allowances provided by marketers in which they share the cost of local advertising of their firm's product or product line with channel partners.

Assessment Check ✓

1. Give an example of a pushing strategy.
2. Give an example of a pulling strategy.

LECTURE ENHANCER:
Which of these two strategies do you believe is the most powerful? Why?

LECTURE ENHANCER:
When should a company cut the price of a new product?

price exchange value of a good or service.

profitability objectives common objectives included in the strategic plans of most firms.

line with channel partners. All of these strategies are designed to motivate wholesalers and retailers to push the good or service to their own customers.

A **pulling strategy** attempts to promote a product by generating consumer demand for it, primarily through advertising and sales promotion appeals. Potential buyers will then request that their suppliers—retailers or local distributors—carry the product, thereby pulling it through the distribution channel. Dove used this strategy when it launched its new Men + Care line of men's personal-care products during a recent Super Bowl. The 30-second commercial, with its tagline "Be comfortable in your own skin," generated significant online response, with consumers searching such terms as "Super Bowl," "ad," and "men" to find retailers that stocked the products.[43]

Most marketing situations require combinations of pushing and pulling strategies, although the primary emphasis can vary. Consumer products usually depend more heavily on pulling strategies than do B2B products, which favor pushing strategies.

⌐5⌐

Pricing Objectives in the Marketing Mix

Products offer utility, or want-satisfying power. However, we as consumers determine how much value we associate with each one. In the aftermath of a major storm, we may value electricity and food and water above everything else. If we commute a long distance or are planning a driving vacation, fuel may be of greater concern. But all consumers have limited amounts of money and a variety of possible uses for it. So the **price**—the exchange value of a good or service—becomes a major factor in consumer buying decisions.

Businesspeople attempt to accomplish certain objectives through their pricing decisions. Pricing objectives vary from firm to firm, and many companies pursue multiple pricing objectives. Some try to improve profits by setting high prices; others set low prices to attract new business. As Figure 13.5 shows, the four basic categories of pricing objectives are (1) profitability, (2) volume, (3) meeting competition, and (4) prestige.

Profitability Objectives

Profitability objectives are the most common objectives included in the strategic plans of most firms. Marketers know that profits are the revenue the company brings in, minus its expenses. Usually a big difference exists between revenue and profit. Automakers try to produce at least one luxury vehicle for which they can charge $50,000 or more instead of relying entirely on the sale of $15,000 to $25,000 models.

Some firms maximize profits by reducing costs rather than through higher prices. Companies can maintain prices and increase profitability by operating more efficiently or by modifying the product to make it less costly to produce. One strategy is to maintain a steady price while reducing the size or amount of the product in the package—something that manufacturers of candy, coffee, and cereal have done over the years.

FIGURE 13.5 Pricing Objectives

Profitability
"We want profits to increase by 10 percent a year through 2015."

Volume
"By 2015, we plan to achieve a 28 percent share of the personal watercraft market."

Pricing Objectives

Meeting Competition
"We will meet their prices and achieve profit and volume growth by offering better customer service."

Prestige
"The new perfume has an exquisite package, a beautiful label, and one of the highest retail prices."

Volume Objectives

A second approach to pricing strategy—**volume objectives**—bases pricing decisions on market share, the percentage of a market controlled by a certain company or product. One firm may seek to achieve a 25 percent market share in a certain product category, and another may want to maintain or expand its market share for particular products. Family Dollar Stores relies on volume sales to make a profit. The nationwide chain of stores, which sells everything from ice cube trays to holiday decorations—for a dollar each—must find ways to attract as much traffic and sell as many products as possible on given day. Recently the North Carolina–based firm announced a strategy to increase the number of consumables, such as grocery, health, and beauty products offered in its stores. Family Dollar plans to add more than 350 new items that consumers need to re-purchase on a regular basis, "leveraging slightly higher shelf heights and reducing space in some underperforming categories," according to Howard R. Levine, the company's chairman and CEO.[44]

Pricing to Meet Competition

A third set of pricing objectives seeks simply to meet competitors' prices so that price essentially becomes a nonissue. In many lines of business, firms set their own prices to match those of established industry leaders. However, companies may not legally work together to agree on prices.

Because price is such a highly visible component of a firm's marketing mix, businesses may be tempted to use it to obtain an advantage over competitors. But sometimes the race to match competitors' prices results in a *price war*, which has happened periodically in the airline and fast-food industries. The ability of competitors to match a price cut leads many marketers to try to avoid price wars by favoring other strategies, such as adding value, improving quality, educating consumers, and establishing relationships.

Although price is a major component of the marketing mix, it is not the only one. Electronic readers such as the Kindle and the iPad are in a fierce pricing competition for digital books, as the "Solving an Ethical Controversy" feature explains.

Prestige Objectives

The final category of objectives encompasses the effect of prices on prestige. **Prestige pricing** establishes a relatively high price to develop and maintain an image of quality and exclusiveness. Marketers set such objectives because they recognize the role of price in communicating an overall image for the firm and its products. People expect to pay more for a Mercedes, Christian Louboutin shoes, or a vacation on St. Barts in the Caribbean. Despite the recession, Mercedes-Benz sold more cars in one month than it had during the same month over several years.[45]

Scarcity can create prestige. Products that are limited in distribution or so popular that they become scarce generate their own prestige—allowing businesses to charge more for them. Unfortunately, scarcity can also invite crime. Recently, federal prosecutors charged four men with hacking into the computer systems of Ticketmaster, Major League Baseball, Telecharge, and Live Nation

Thomas Kienzle/AFP/Getty Images, Inc.

Prestige pricing sets a relatively high price to develop and maintain an image of quality and exclusiveness. People expect to pay more for cars adorned with the Mercedes hood ornament known as "the star."

Solving an Ethical Controversy

Free E-Books: Good or Bad for Business?

When Amazon's Kindle electronic reader first became available, Amazon charged consumers $9.99 for each e-book they purchased. Publishers insisted that that price was too low to keep their business profitable. But Amazon actually gave some e-books away for free, including those of living authors who earn an income from their writing.

Amazon explained that the free e-books were a way to get consumers to check out unfamiliar writers. The hope was that they would then buy other works by those writers. But some publishers delay publication of electronic editions for several months after the hardcover books were issued, much as they delay paperback editions.

Should e-books be given away for free?

PRO

1. Some publishers regard free e-books as promotion to generate buzz about new or unknown authors.

2. Some publishers that give away e-books on a regular basis have noticed an increase in sales that's "all found money," as one executive says.

CON

1. "It is illogical to give books away for free," said David Young of Hachette Book Group, which publishes Stephanie Meyer's Twilight series.

2. The relatively low price of e-books may discourage consumers from buying actual books with suggested retail prices of $25 or more.

Summary

Both Amazon's Kindle and Barnes & Noble's Nook continue to offer free e-books. In addition, both offer the capability for customers to lend e-books to friends and family for 14 days by simply inputting a name and e-mail address. Although some publishers might cringe at these practices, it is likely that the trend will continue.

Sources: Alec Liu, "Kindle, Nook, Whatever: Here's How to Get Free E-Books," FoxNews.com, http://www.foxnews.com, accessed March 31, 2012; Stan Schroeder, "The E-Book Price War Isn't Over Yet," *Mashable Business*, http://mashable.com, accessed March 31, 2012; Motoko Rich, "Apple's Prices for E-Books May Be Lower Than Expected," *The New York Times*, http://www.nytimes .com, accessed March 31, 2012; Motoko Rich, "With Kindle, the Best Sellers Don't Need to Sell," *The New York Times*, http://www .nytimes.com, accessed March 31, 2012; "The Kindle Pricing Strategy & the Kindle Pricing History," askDeb.com, http://www .askdeb.com, accessed March 31, 2012.

Assessment Check ✓

1. Define *price*.
2. What is a second approach to pricing strategy?

Entertainment to highjack 1.5 million tickets to concerts by Bruce Springsteen and Miley Cyrus, baseball playoff games at Yankee Stadium, and other events. The men or their agents posed as individual online buyers, electronically bypassed the vendors' security systems, and bought blocks of tickets that they resold at hugely inflated prices. The scam had been in operation for more than a decade and had generated almost $29 million in illegal profits.[46]

6 Pricing Strategies

People from different areas of a company contribute their expertise to set the most strategic price for a product. Accountants, financial managers, and marketers provide relevant sales and cost data, along with customer feedback. Designers, engineers, and systems analysts all contribute important data as well.

Prices are determined in two basic ways: by applying the concepts of supply and demand discussed in Chapter 3 and by completing cost-oriented analyses. Economic theory assumes that a market price will be set at the point at which the amount of a product desired at a given price equals the amount that suppliers will offer for sale at that price. In other words, this price occurs at the point at which the amount demanded and the amount supplied are equal. Online auctions, such as those conducted on eBay, are a popular application of the demand-and-supply approach.

Price Determination in Practice

Economic theory might lead to the best pricing decisions, but most businesses do not have all the information they need to make those decisions, so they adopt **cost-based pricing** formulas. These formulas calculate total costs per unit and then add markups to cover overhead costs and generate profits.

Cost-based pricing totals all costs associated with offering a product in the market, including research and development, production, transportation, and marketing expenses. An added amount, the markup, then covers any unexpected or overlooked expenses and provides a profit. The total becomes the price. Although the actual markup used varies by such factors as brand image and type of store, the typical markup for clothing is determined by doubling the wholesale price (the cost to the merchant) to arrive at the retail price for the item.

cost-based pricing formulas that calculate total costs per unit and then add markups to cover overhead costs and generate profits.

LECTURE ENHANCER: Provide an example of cost-based pricing for a fast-food cheeseburger.

Breakeven Analysis

Businesses often conduct a **breakeven analysis** to determine the minimum sales volume a product must generate at a certain price level to cover all costs. This method involves a consideration of various costs and total revenues. *Total cost* is the sum of total variable costs and total fixed costs. *Variable costs* change with the level of production, as labor and raw materials do, while *fixed costs* such as insurance premiums and utility rates charged by water, natural gas, and electric power suppliers are constants regardless of the production level. *Total revenue* is determined by multiplying price by the number of units sold.

breakeven analysis pricing-related technique used to determine the minimum sales volume a product must generate at a certain price level to cover all costs.

LECTURE ENHANCER: Consider a lemonade stand. What are the fixed and variable costs?

Finding the Breakeven Point The level of sales that will generate enough revenue to cover all of the company's fixed and variable costs is called the *breakeven point*. It is the point at which total revenue just equals total costs. Sales beyond the breakeven point will generate profits; sales volume below the breakeven point will result in losses. The following formulas give the breakeven point in units and dollars:

$$\text{Breakeven Point (in units)} = \frac{\text{Total fixed costs}}{\text{Contribution to fixed costs per units}}$$

$$\text{Breakeven Point (in dollars)} = \frac{\text{Total fixed costs}}{1 - \text{Variable cost per unit/Price}}$$

A product selling for $20 with a variable cost of $14 per unit produces a $6 per-unit contribution to fixed costs. If the firm has total fixed costs of $42,000, then it must sell 7,000 units to break even on the product as shown in Figure 13.6. The calculation of the breakeven point in units and dollars is as follows:

$$\text{Breakeven Point (in units)} = \frac{\$42,000}{\$20 - \$14} = \frac{\$42,000}{\$6} = 7,000 \; units$$

$$\text{Breakeven Point (in dollars)} = \frac{\$42,000}{1 - \$14/\$20} = \frac{\$42,000}{1 - 0.7} = \frac{\$42,000}{0.3} = \$140,000$$

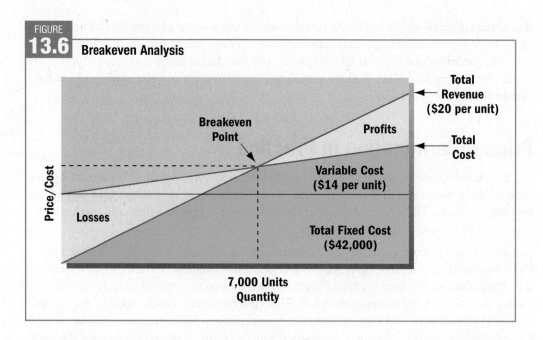

FIGURE 13.6 Breakeven Analysis

Total Revenue ($20 per unit)

Total Cost

Breakeven Point

Profits

Variable Cost ($14 per unit)

Price/Cost

Losses

Total Fixed Cost ($42,000)

7,000 Units Quantity

CLASS ACTIVITY:
Discuss ways in which a company can lower the breakeven point.

LECTURE ENHANCER:
Can you think of a recent product that used skimming pricing?

LECTURE ENHANCER:
Identify retailers that use EDLP and those that primarily use discount pricing. What are some differences within the retail shopping environment of each?

skimming pricing strategy that sets an intentionally high price relative to the prices of competing products.

penetration pricing strategy that sets a low price as a major marketing weapon.

Marketers use breakeven analysis to determine the profits or losses that would result from several different proposed prices. Because different prices produce different breakeven points, marketers could compare their calculations of required sales to break even with sales estimates from marketing research studies. This comparison can identify the best price—one that would attract enough customers to exceed the breakeven point and earn profits for the firm.

Most firms add consumer demand—determining whether enough customers will buy the number of units the firm must sell at a particular price to break even—by developing estimates through surveys of likely customers, interviews with retailers that would be handling the product, and assessments of prices charged by competitors. Then the breakeven points for several possible prices are calculated and compared with sales estimates for each price. This practice is referred to as *modified breakeven analysis*.

Alternative Pricing Strategies

The strategy a company uses to set its prices should grow out of the firm's overall marketing strategy. In general, firms can choose from four alternative pricing strategies: skimming, penetration, discount or everyday low pricing, and competitive pricing.

Skimming Pricing A **skimming pricing** strategy sets an intentionally high price relative to the prices of competing products. The term comes from the expression "skimming the cream." This pricing strategy often works for the introduction of a distinctive good or service with little or no competition, although it can be used at other stages of the product life cycle as well. A skimming strategy can help marketers set a price that distinguishes a firm's high-end product from those of competitors. It can also help a firm recover its product development costs before competitors enter the field. This is often the case with prescription drugs.

Penetration Pricing By contrast, a **penetration pricing** strategy sets a low price as a major marketing weapon. Businesses may price new products noticeably lower than competing offerings when they enter new industries characterized by dozens of competing brands. Once the new product achieves some market recognition through consumer trial purchases stimulated by its low price, marketers may increase the price to the level of competing products. However, stiff competition might prevent the price increase.

Everyday Low Pricing and Discount Pricing
Everyday low pricing (EDLP) is a strategy devoted to maintaining continuous low prices rather than relying on short-term price-cutting tactics such as cents-off coupons, rebates, and special sales. This strategy has been used successfully by retailers such as Walmart and Lowe's to consistently offer low prices to consumers; manufacturers also use EDLP to set stable prices for retailers.

everyday low pricing (EDLP) is a strategy devoted to maintaining continuous low prices rather than relying on short-term price-cutting tactics such as cents-off coupons, rebates, and special sales.

Some retailers such as Lowe's use an everyday low pricing strategy that maintains continuous low prices rather than relying on short-term price-cutting tactics such as cents-off coupons, rebates, and special sales.

With *discount pricing*, businesses hope to attract customers by dropping prices for a set period of time. Automakers usually offer consumers special discounts on most or all of their vehicles during the holiday shopping season. After the holidays, prices usually rebound. But experts warn that discounting must be done carefully, or profits can disappear. Businesses should offer discounts only for a specified period of time and with a clear understanding of what they are trying to accomplish with the strategy. They should advertise the discount, so customers know it is a special deal. When the time period has elapsed, so should the discount. JC Penney has taken these lessons about discounting to heart. See the "Hit & Miss" feature for the story of how its new "every day" pricing strategy has done away with sales and discounts altogether, in favor of predictable pricing.

Competitive Pricing
Although many organizations rely heavily on price as a competitive weapon, even more implement **competitive pricing** strategies. They try to reduce the emphasis on price competition by matching other firms' prices and concentrating their own marketing efforts on the product, distribution, and promotional elements of the marketing mix. In fact, in industries with relatively homogeneous products, competitors must match one another's price reductions to maintain market share and remain competitive. By pricing their products at the levels of competing offerings, marketers largely negate the price variable in their marketing strategies.

competitive pricing strategy that tries to reduce the emphasis on price competition by matching other firms' prices and concentrating their own marketing efforts on the product, distribution, and promotional elements of the marketing mix.

Assessment Check

1. What is a cost-based pricing formula?
2. Why do companies implement competitive pricing strategies?

Hit & Miss

JC Penney Eliminates Sales

Like most retailers, 110-year-old JC Penney held numerous sale events every year, taking a whopping 75 percent of its revenue from items reduced in price by half or more. Now, to draw more shoppers and boost lackluster profits, Penney is trying a radical innovation: permanently slashing all prices by 40 percent, using "every day" pricing to entice bargain hunters without forcing them to wait for sales. So an item priced at $14.99 before a sale will now be $7 from the start. That's $7, not $6.99, because Penney is also adopting whole numbers on its price tags. "We are not going to make customers jump through hoops," said the manager of one North Carolina store.

Penney will still have a few seasonal sales, such as jewelry at Valentine's Day and holiday ornaments in November, and slow-selling items will go on clearance twice each month. But recently appointed CEO Ron Johnson, whose resume includes retail successes with Apple Stores and Target, says, "pricing is actually a pretty simple and straightforward thing. Customers will not pay literally a penny more than the true value of the product."

Questions for Critical Thinking

1. Do you agree that pricing is "a pretty simple and straight-forward thing"? Why or why not?
2. Do you think shoppers prefer "every day" pricing to sales? Why or why not?

Sources: Brad Tuttle, "The Price Is Righter," *Time*, February 13, 2012, http://www.time.com; Emily Ford, "New Strategy, Pricing on Display at JC Penney," *Salisbury Post*, February 2, 2012, http://www.salisburypost.com; Susanna Kim, "What to Expect: J.C. Penney's New Pricing Strategy," *ABC News*, January 31, 2012, http://abcnews.go.com/blogs; Marianne Bickle, "JC Penney's Consumers Voice Opinions Regarding Sales," *Forbes*, January 30, 2012, http://www.forbes.com; Anne d'Innocenzio, "J.C. Penney Gets Rid of Hundreds of Sales," Yahoo! Finance, January 25, 2012, http://finance.yahoo.com.

7 Consumer Perceptions of Prices

How do you perceive prices for certain products? Marketers must consider this. If large numbers of potential buyers consider a price too high or too low, businesses must correct the situation. Price–quality relationships and the use of odd pricing are important considerations in setting prices.

Price–Quality Relationships

Research shows that a consumer's perception of product quality is closely related to an item's price. Most marketers believe that this perceived price–quality relationship remains steady over a relatively wide range of prices, although extremely high or low prices have less credibility. The price–quality relationship can critically affect a firm's pricing strategy.

Many consumers associate prestige, quality, and high price together—believing that paying a high price for an item such as a BMW or a Chanel bag not only conveys prestige but also ensures quality. Others believe that eating at an expensive restaurant automatically means the food will be better than food served at a modestly priced eating establishment. Conversely, consumers may view an extremely low price as an indication that corners have been cut and quality will suffer. But what about the perception associated with a sale? If a line of designer boots goes on sale for 50 percent off the original price, a bargain hunter will snap them up with a sense of victory—high quality at a rock bottom price.

Marketing researchers also know that the verbal sound of a price influences consumers' perceptions of price, quality, and resulting value. The vowel sound "oo" (as in "two") makes people think of larger sizes and prices, while the vowel sound "ee" (as in "three") evokes a smaller size and price. These perceptions can influence consumers' perception of the quality of the products they are considering buying.[47]

Odd Pricing

Have you ever wondered why retailers set prices at $1.99 instead of $2 or $9.95 instead of $10? Before the age of cash registers and sales taxes, retailers reportedly followed this practice of **odd pricing**—pricing method using uneven amounts, which appear less than they really are to consumers—to force clerks to make correct change as part of their cash control efforts. But now odd pricing is commonly used because many retailers believe that consumers favor uneven amounts or amounts that sound less than they really are. However, some retailers also use this method to identify items that have been marked down. The odd price suggests the item is on sale.

What's Ahead

The chapters in Part 4 have explained the main principles underlying marketing management and described how each fits a firm's overall business strategy. The next few chapters will help you understand how companies manage the technology and information that are available to businesses to create value for their customers and enhance their competitiveness in the marketplace. You'll also learn how firms manage their financial resources.

odd pricing pricing method using uneven amounts, which sometimes appear smaller than they really are to consumers.

Assessment Check ✔

1. How does the price–quality relationship affect a firm's pricing strategy?
2. Why is odd pricing used?

Summary of Learning Objectives

⌜1⌟ Discuss integrated marketing communications (IMC).
In practicing IMC, a firm coordinates promotional activities to produce a unified, customer-focused message. IMC identifies consumer needs and shows how a company's products meet them. Marketers select the promotional media that best target and reach customers. Teamwork and careful promotional planning to coordinate IMC strategy components are important elements of these programs.

A company's promotional mix integrates two components: personal selling and nonpersonal selling, which includes advertising, sales promotion, and public relations. By selecting the appropriate combination of promotional mix elements, marketers attempt to achieve the firm's five major promotional objectives: provide information, differentiate a product, increase demand, stabilize sales, and accentuate the product's value.

Assessment Check Answers ✔

1.1 What is the objective of an integrated marketing communications program? An IMC strategy focuses on customer needs to create a unified promotional message about a firm's goods or services.

1.2 Why do firms pursue multiple promotional objectives at the same time? Firms pursue multiple promotional objectives because they may need to convey different messages to different audiences.

1.3 What are product placement and guerrilla marketing? Product placement involves paying a fee to have a product showcased in certain media. Guerrilla marketing consists of innovative, low-cost marketing efforts designed to get consumers' attention in unusual ways.

⌜2⌟ Summarize the different types of advertising.
Advertising, the most visible form of nonpersonal promotion, is designed to inform, persuade, or remind. Product advertising promotes a good or service, while institutional advertising promotes a concept, idea, organization, or philosophy. Television, newspapers, and magazines are the largest advertising media categories. Others include direct

mail, radio, and outdoor advertising. Interactive advertising directly involves the consumer, who controls the flow of information.

Assessment Check Answers ✓

2.1 What are the two basic types of advertising? Into what three categories do they fall? The two basic types of advertising are product and institutional. They fall into the categories of informative, persuasive, and reminder-oriented advertising.

2.2 What is the leading advertising medium in the United States? According to the most recent statistics listed in Figure 13.2, television is the leading advertising medium in the U.S.

2.3 In what two major ways do firms benefit from sponsorship? Firms benefit from sponsorship in two ways: they gain exposure to the event's audience, and they become associated with the activity's image.

⌐3⌐ Outline sales promotion.

Sales promotion accounts for greater expenditures than advertising. Consumer-oriented sales promotions such as coupons, games, rebates, samples, premiums, contests, sweepstakes, and promotional products offer an extra incentive to buy a product. Point-of-purchase advertising displays and trade shows are sales promotions directed to the trade markets. Personal selling involves face-to-face interactions between seller and buyer. The primary sales tasks are order processing, creative selling, and missionary selling. Public relations is nonpaid promotion that seeks to enhance a company's public image.

Assessment Check Answers ✓

3.1 Why do retailers and manufacturers use sales promotions? Retailers and manufacturers use sales promotions to offer consumers extra incentives to buy their products.

3.2 When does a firm use personal selling instead of nonpersonal selling? Firms generally use personal selling when customers are few and geographically concentrated, the product is technically complex or requires special handling, the price is high, or the product moves through direct-distribution channels.

3.3 How does public relations serve a marketing purpose? Public relations can be an efficient, indirect communications channel for promoting products. It can publicize products and help create and maintain a positive image of the company.

⌐4⌐ Describe pushing and pulling strategies.

A pushing strategy relies on personal selling to market a product to wholesalers and retailers in a company's distribution channels. A pulling strategy promotes the product by generating consumer demand for it, through advertising and sales promotion.

Assessment Check Answers ✓

4.1 Give an example of a pushing strategy. An example of a pushing strategy is one used by drug manufacturers, which used to market solely to physicians and hospitals. Today, they also use a pulling strategy by marketing directly to patients through advertising, which encourages patients to ask their doctors about medications.

4.2 Give an example of a pulling strategy. Pulling strategies are used by retailers and by manufacturers of consumer goods such as cosmetics, automobiles, and clothing.

⌐5⌐ Discuss the pricing objectives in the marketing mix.

Pricing objectives can be classified as profitability, volume, meeting competition, and prestige. Profitability objectives are the most common. Volume objectives base pricing decisions on market share. Meeting competitors' prices makes price a nonissue in competition. Prestige pricing establishes a high price to develop and maintain an image of quality or exclusiveness.

Assessment Check Answers ✓

5.1 Define *price*. Price is the exchange value of a good or service.

5.2 What is a second approach to pricing strategy? A second approach to pricing strategy is *volume objectives*, which bases pricing decisions on market share.

⌐6⌐ Outline pricing strategies.

Although economic theory determines prices by the law of demand and supply, most firms use cost-based pricing, which adds a markup after costs. They usually conduct a break-even analysis to determine the minimum sales volume a product must generate at a certain price to cover costs. The four alternative pricing strategies are skimming, penetration, everyday low pricing and discounting, and competitive pricing. A skimming strategy sets a high price initially to recover costs and then lowers it; a penetration strategy sets a lower price and then raises it later. Everyday low pricing and discounting offers a lower price for a period of time. Competitive pricing matches other firms' prices and emphasizes nonprice benefits of an item.

Assessment Check Answers ✓

6.1 What is a cost-based pricing formula? A cost-based pricing formula calculates the total costs per unit and then adds markups to cover overhead costs and generate profits.

6.2 Why do companies implement competitive pricing strategies? Companies use competitive pricing strategies to reduce the emphasis on price competition by matching other firms' prices and concentrating their own marketing efforts on the product, distribution, and promotional elements of the marketing mix.

7 Discuss consumer perceptions of prices.

Marketers must consider how consumers perceive the price–quality relationship of their products. Consumers may be willing to pay a higher price if they perceive a product to be of superior quality. Marketers often use odd pricing to convey a message to consumers.

Assessment Check Answers ✔

7.1 How does the price–quality relationship affect a firm's pricing strategy? Consumers must believe that the price of an item reflects its quality, except in extreme cases. So a firm must try to set its prices accordingly.

7.2 Why is odd pricing used? Retailers believe that consumers favor uneven amounts or amounts that sound like less than they really are. Odd pricing may also be used to suggest a sale item.

Business Terms You Need to Know

promotion 391	sponsorship 403	cooperative advertising 411
integrated marketing communications (IMC) 392	infomercial 403	pulling strategy 412
	sales promotion 404	price 412
promotional mix 393	specialty advertising 406	profitability objectives 412
personal selling 393	trade promotion 406	volume objectives 413
nonpersonal selling 394	point-of-purchase (POP) advertising 406	prestige pricing 413
positioning 395	order processing 408	cost-based pricing 415
product placement 396	creative selling 408	breakeven analysis 415
guerrilla marketing 396	missionary selling 408	skimming pricing 416
advertising 397	telemarketing 409	penetration pricing 416
product advertising 398	public relations 411	everyday low pricing (EDLP) 417
institutional advertising 398	publicity 411	competitive pricing 417
cause advertising 398	pushing strategy 411	odd pricing 419

Review Questions

1. What is the purpose of integrated marketing communications?

2. What are the five major objectives of a promotional strategy?

3. Identify and define each of the three categories of advertising based on their purpose. Which type of advertising might marketers use for the following products?
   a. cars
   b. e-reader
   c. organic produce
   d. health care insurance

4. What are the benefits of online and interactive advertising? What might be some drawbacks?

5. For each of the following, describe potential benefits and drawbacks of a sponsorship relationship:
   a. LG and the Snowboard FIS World Cup
   b. ING Bank and the New York City Marathon
   c. Mattel Corporation and the Special Olympics

6. If you were a marketer for Rolex, what kind of sales promotion might you use for your watches?

7. Under what circumstances are firms likely to emphasize personal selling?

8. Describe the seven-step sales process.

9. Define the four basic categories of pricing objectives.

10. What are the four alternative pricing strategies that marketers use? Give an example of the circumstances under which each might be selected.

Projects and Teamwork Applications

1. Choose a product that you purchased recently. Identify the various media that were used to promote the product and analyze the promotional mix. Do you agree with the company's marketing strategy? Or would you recommend changes to the mix? Why? Create your own print ad for the product you chose, using any business strategies or knowledge you have learned in this course so far.

2. Evaluate the price of the product you selected in the preceding exercise. What appears to be the pricing strategy that its manufacturer used? Do you think the price is fair? Why or why not? Choose a different strategy and develop a new price for the product based on your strategy. Poll your classmates to learn whether they would purchase the product at the new price—and why.

3. Some schools have received financial benefits by allowing companies to promote their goods and services to students. Others have decided against this practice, and some states have laws banning this type of promotion. Find some examples of corporate sponsors in public elementary and high schools and on college campuses. With your class, discuss the pros and cons of promotion in public schools and on college campuses. In your view, is there a distinction between a public elementary or high school and a college campus? Why or why not?

4. On your own or with a classmate, research a recent situation that has caused a business, a not-for-profit organization, or a government agency to suffer from bad publicity. Evaluate the situation, then create a program outlining steps the organization might take to build better public relations.

5. You are the marketing manager for a company that is introducing a new line of video games. What approach would you take for establishing prices?

Web Assignments

Top advertisers. *Advertising Age* compiles data annually on the top national advertisers. Visit the Web site listed here and access the most recent year. Answer the following questions:

 a Which were the top ten advertisers in that year?

 b How much did they spend on advertising?

 c What was the most advertised brand that year?

 http://adage.com/datacenter/article?article_idv106348

2. **Online coupon fraud.** Go to the Web sites listed here to learn about online coupon fraud. Prepare a brief report. Make sure to answer the following questions: How big a problem is online coupon fraud? What are some changes marketers have made in an attempt to reduce online coupon fraud?

 http://www.newser.com/story/35962/hackers-spread-coupon-scam.html

 http://online.wsj.com/article/SB10001424052748703862704575099971939458554.html

 http://multichannelmerchant.com/retail/news/0308-curtailing-online-coupon-fraud/

3. **Yield management.** Assume you're interested in flying between Baltimore and Chicago. Visit some travel sites. Search for fares, varying such factors as advance purchase, day, time of departure, and so forth. What did this exercise teach you about yield management?

 http://www.expedia.com

 http://www.kayak.com

 http://www.travelocity.com

Note: Internet Web addresses change frequently. If you don't find the exact sites listed, you may need to access the organization's home page and search from there or use a search engine such as Bing or Google.

CASE 13.1   Brand Names versus Store Brands

Shoppers who buy brand-name products usually cite quality as a reason. Shoppers who buy store-brand products usually cite price. Is it possible to have the best of both worlds?

Retailers such as Target, CVS, and Walgreens have found they had too many of the same products under different brand names. They saw that shoppers were buying less and looking for bigger bargains than usual. Items that weren't selling well were replaced by more popular brands or by in-house generics. This was particularly true of such basic items as household and personal products and food staples. As one observer said, "People don't want to have to choose among 15 or 20 different brands of toilet paper or paper towels or even basic food stuff." The retailers were confident that shoppers would be eager to snap up these bargains.

Target guessed that consumers would buy their in-house brands, and it looks like they were correct. The in-store brands up & up, Archer Farms, and Market Pantry account for more than 20 percent of all food products sold at Target.

To some extent, this overall strategy has worked. The market share of store brands has grown between 2 and 6 percent. And 77 percent of consumers who bought less expensive store-brand items were satisfied with their choice.

Questions for Critical Thinking

1. Why do you think chain stores carry brand-name items alongside their own in-house brands?

2. What are some of the ways that stores such as Target are able to keep their prices low?

Sources: "Target's Comeback Plan on Track," *Store Brands Decisions*, http://www.storebrandsdecisions.com, accessed April 2, 2012; "Target Elevates Store Brands to Front Page Status," *Store Brands Decisions*, http://www.storebrandsdecisions.com, accessed April 2, 2012; Parija Kavilanz, "Dumped! Brand Names Fight to Stay in Stores," CNN Money.com, http://money.cnn.com, accessed April 2, 2012; Kevin Cokeley, "Retailers Replacing Big Names with House Brands," *NBC Dallas–Fort Worth*, http://www.nbcdfw.com, accessed April 2, 2012; Sara Zucker, "Wal-Mart Reintroduces Brands after Customer Complaints," Brandchannel.com, http://www.brandchannel.com, accessed April 2, 2012.

Marketing to the Teenage Crowd

CASE 13.2

Today's teenagers were born at the turn of the 21st century. They represent billions of dollars in buying power, but the big question for marketers is how to reach them.

These teens have grown up in the electronic age and take it for granted. They like to communicate with each other—and can do so almost constantly. One study estimates that teenagers spend more than seven hours a day using media of various kinds, mostly electronic. How do they log this astonishing amount of time? By sacrificing sleep and by multitasking. Parents often find their teens listening to music, watching TV, doing homework, playing a videogame, and text messaging.

Which media do teenagers neglect or ignore? They hardly ever read newspapers. Jeffrey Cole, the director of the Center for the Digital Future at the University of Southern California, predicts that printed newspapers will eventually become extinct as social media steadily increase in power. Teens want news, he explains, but only about the narrowly focused community of their peers.

Teenagers don't contact their peers through e-mail. One survey indicates that although 73 percent of teens visit social-networking sites, only about 8 percent use Twitter. They do like smart phones, especially those with apps for constant status updates, but don't make many phone calls. Instead, they text message, sometimes sending up to 10 messages an hour.

Marketers will need to learn how to reach teenagers by inviting their input, listening to them with genuine respect, adopting their suggestions, and continuing to ask for feedback. Morgan Stewart of ExactTarget conducted a survey asking teens which brand they thought did the best job of communicating with them. To his surprise, Amazon got more write-in votes than any other brand, including Facebook. He says of Amazon, "Teens can read reviews, they can submit their own, and they can get recommendations based on what they like." Stewart believes that "managing your Amazon presence is more important than building out a Facebook strategy."

Of course, even Amazon is only one component of an integrated marketing plan. Teenagers are highly suspicious of anything that even remotely resembles advertising. When shopping, they depend heavily on the opinions of their peers. They also enjoy fun sites such as Sporcle.com, FunnyOrDie.com, and FailBlog.org. YouTube is another important—and free—tool for viral marketing.

Jeffrey Cole thinks that as today's teens mature, the allure of knowing everything about their friends will fade. What will endure will be what every generation wants: they will still want to have "total control over their media" as a way of having "real control over their lives."

Questions for Critical Thinking

1. Do you think marketers can reach teens with specially tailored promotional campaigns for such goods and services as video games, smartphone apps, concert tickets, and so on? Why or why not?

2. How can marketers best target teens so as to appeal to them but without making them feel talked down to? Suggest a marketing or promotional theme for one product that you think would appeal to a teen.

Sources: Carol Phillips, "Where Teens Hang Out Digitally," *Millennial Marketing*, http://millennialmarketing.com, accessed April 2, 2012; Tim Loc, "Teens Love Social Media, Detest Newspapers," *iMedia Connection*, http://www.imediaconnection.com, accessed April 2, 2012; Steve McClellan, "Teens Into Social Media, Not Newspapers," *Adweek*, http://www.adweek.com, accessed April 2, 2012; Tamar Lewin, "If Your Kids Are Awake, They're Probably Online," *The New York Times*, http://www.nytimes.com, accessed April 2, 2012; Seth Lieberman, "Teen Marketing: A Look Ahead," *Mind Maps ZA*, http://mindmapsza.com, accessed April 2, 2012.

Pet owners want the best for their dogs and cats, as evidenced by the $50 billion pet industry in the U.S., including everything from grooming services to squeaky toys. One area that has received little attention is travel. Although owners can find lodging that allows pets and they can purchase travel carriers and gear, until recently there was little choice when it came to transport. If the animal had to travel long distance, it was relegated to the cargo hold of a plane. A couple of years ago, that changed when Dan Wiesel and Alysa Binder wanted to be able to transport their Jack Russell terrier safely and comfortably. So they started a pet transport business called Pet Airways.

"There are 80 million pets traveling around the U.S.," says Binder. "There's definitely a market for this. We're part of the pet community—we understand." Wiesel and Binder contracted with a firm that flies Beechcraft 1900 aircraft, selecting this plane for its versatility and safety record. They had the planes retrofitted to accommodate pet carriers in the main cabin. They launched their reservation system online and spread the word via social media. When traditional media heard of the new company, Wiesel and Binder appeared on such television shows as *Good Morning America* and *The Today Show*, as well as in magazines and newspapers. Because of this publicity, Pet Airways has spent nothing on advertising. Its greatest marketing challenge has been educating the public about their service. "Because we're the first to market, we have to tell people what we're all about," explains Binder.

Pet owners who want to book their animals on a Pet Airways flight make a reservation on the airline's Web site, http://www.petairways.com. One hour before departure, owners check in at the Pet Lounge. Pet passengers are boarded in their carriers, attended to by professional pet attendants who accompany the animals on the flight, checking on them every 15 minutes to make sure they are secure and comfortable. Once the plane has landed, owners (or designated recipients) collect their pets in the Pet Lounge.

Pet Airways currently operates flights to nine cities around the United States. Binder says the firm's goal is to reach 20 cities in the near future. She notes that customers are willing and eager to pay for the service, considering it reasonable compared to traditional airlines.

Pet Airways fares start at $149. By comparison, American Airlines charges $100 for a pet to travel beneath a seat and $150 as baggage, and Delta charges $150 and $275 respectively. Binder remarks that her customers don't usually consider price anyway because "we aren't the same as general carriers. It's a completely different service. People know that."

Pet Airways customers can register to receive the company's newsletter, which includes insider news on special flight deals and other promotions. They can join the MyPAWS Club, which offers a 40 percent discount on pet supplies at the Pet Airways online store, a 10 percent discount at pet-friendly hotels, 10 percent off at 1-800-PetMeds, 5 percent off on pet health insurance from Pets Best Insurance, and discounts and free samples from other Pet Airways partners.

Wiesel and Binder saw an opportunity in the marketplace and jumped at the chance to offer a safe, reliable solution for pet owners to transport their pets. "On Pet Airways, your pets aren't packages, they're passengers."

Questions for Critical Thinking

1. At this stage of Pet Airway's life cycle, what should be the company's primary promotional objectives? Why?

2. Pet Airways has not yet engaged in major advertising efforts. Which media would probably be most effective at reaching the firm's intended market? Why?

3. Pet Airways already offers some consumer-oriented promotions. Describe or outline an idea for a new promotion and explain your choice.

4. Outline Pet Airways' pricing objectives. How might these change over the next five years? Ten years? What do you think the best pricing strategy for Pet Airways should be? Why?

Sources: Pet Airways Web site, http://www.petairways.com, accessed April 2, 2012; "Pet Airways Combines with a Public Company Through Share Exchange with American Antiquities," *PR Newswire*, http://www.prnewswire.com, accessed April 2, 2012; "Doctors Call for Airline Pet Ban," *The Independent*, http://license.icopyright.net, accessed April 2, 2012; "Bone Voyage as Pets Get Airline," *BBC News*, http://news.bbc.co.uk, accessed April 2, 2012.

GREENSBURG, KS

Think Green, Go Green, Save Green

Not long ago, the phrase "hybrid SUV" would have seemed an oxymoron. But in just a few short years, fuel-efficient hybrids of all shapes and sizes have appeared in showrooms. This new generation of vehicles combines fuel-efficient gas engines, natural gas engines, and hydrogen fuel cells. As gas prices soar and concern over the environment grows, consumers will become more and more interested in them.

Enter Lee Lindquist, alternative fuels specialist at Scholfield Honda in Wichita, Kansas. A passionate environmentalist, Lee was researching alternative-fuel vehicles when he learned that Honda had been selling a natural gas Civic GX in New York and California since 1998. Originally marketed to municipalities and corporations as a way of addressing air quality issues, the Civic GX seemed the perfect way for cost-conscious Kansans to combat rising fuel prices. It was also a way to promote local resources, since Kansas is a major producer of natural gas.

Lee took the idea of the Civic GX to his boss, owner Roger Scholfield, who was skeptical of it at first. Scholfield had long promoted the Honda as a fuel-efficient vehicle and didn't want to muddy the waters with this new vehicle. But eventually he warmed to the idea and began offering the car to his corporate customers.

When the tornado hit Greensburg, the idea of going green took on a whole new life at Scholfield Honda. One of the problems with offering the Civic GX had been the lack of natural gas fueling stations, as well as the high cost

of constructing one. Well aware of the media attention surrounding Greensburg, Scholfield decided to donate a natural gas Civic to the town, along with a fueling station.

Scholfield was up-front about the decision to donate the car. The investment was a costly one, and there were many less expensive ways of reaching his customers in Wichita. Scholfield admits he questioned his decision even as he drove into Greensburg for the presentation. But the bottom line was that it was the right thing to do. Today, when customers come into Scholfield's dealership, they are more interested in alternative-fuel and high-efficiency vehicles.

If you want to buy a Civic GX from Scholfield Honda today, get in line, because the staff can't keep them in stock. While you wait, enjoy a nice cup of coffee served in a compostable, corn-based disposable cup. Toss those old soda cans rattling around in your back seat into Scholfield's recycling bins. And on your way out, don't forget to take your complimentary Scholfield Honda reusable green shopping bag and water bottle.

Questions

After viewing the video, answer the following questions:

1. Do you think Scholfield's green marketing campaign will change consumers' opinions of hybrid and alternative-fuel cars?

2. Do you think Scholfield's donation of a natural gas Civic to the town of Greensburg will drive business to his dealership in Wichita? Why or why not?

LAUNCHING YOUR
[Marketing Career]

In Part 4, "Marketing Management," you learned about the goals and functions of marketing. The chapters in this part emphasized the central role of customer satisfaction in defining value and developing a marketing strategy in traditional and nontraditional marketing settings. You learned about the part played by marketing research and the need for relationship marketing in today's competitive environment. You discovered how new products are developed and how they evolve through the four stages of the product life cycle, from introduction through growth and maturity to decline. You also learned about the role of different channels in creating effective distribution strategies. Finally, you saw the impact of integrated marketing communications on the firm's promotional strategy, the role of advertising, and the way pricing influences consumer behavior. Perhaps you came across some marketing tasks and functions that sounded especially appealing to you. Here are a few ideas about careers in marketing that you may want to pursue.

The first thing to remember is that, as the chapters in this part made clear, marketing is about a great deal more than personal selling and advertising. For instance, are you curious about why people behave the way they do? Are you good at spotting trends? *Marketing research analysts* seek answers to a wide range of questions about business competition, customer preferences, market trends, and past and future sales. They often design and conduct their own consumer surveys, using the telephone, mail, the Internet, or personal interviews and focus groups. After they analyze the data they've collected, their recommendations form input for managerial decisions about whether to introduce new products, revamp current ones, enter new markets, or abandon products or markets where profitability is low. As members of a new-product development team, marketing researchers often work directly with members of other business departments such as scientists, production and manufacturing personnel, and finance employees. Also, marketing researchers are increasingly asked to help clients implement their recommendations. With today's highly competitive economy, jobs in this area are expected to grow. Annual earnings for marketing research analysts average about $61,000.[1]

Another career path in marketing is sales. Do you work well with others and read their feelings accurately? Are you a self-starter? Being a *sales representative* might be for you. Selling jobs exist in every industry, and because many use a combination of salary and performance-based commissions, they can pay handsomely. Sales jobs are often a first step on the ladder to upper-management positions as well. Sales representatives work for wholesalers and manufacturing companies (and even for publishers such as the one that produces this book). They sell automobiles, computer systems and technology, pharmaceuticals, advertising, insurance, real estate, commodities and financial services, and all kinds of consumer goods and services.

If you're interested in mass communications, note that print and online magazines, newspapers, and broadcast companies such as ESPN and MTV generate most of their revenue from advertising, so sales representatives who sell space and time slots in the media contribute a great deal to the success of these firms.[2] And if you like to travel, consider that many sales jobs involve travel.

Advertising, marketing management, and *public relations* are other categories of marketing. In large companies, marketing managers, product managers, promotion managers, and public relations managers often work long hours under pressure; they may travel frequently or transfer between jobs at headquarters and positions in regional offices. Their responsibilities include directing promotional programs, overseeing advertising campaigns and budgets, and creating communications such as press releases for the firm's customers. Thousands of new positions for public relations managers and specialists are expected to open up in the next several years; the field is expected to grow 20 percent over the next decade. Growth of the Internet and new media has especially increased demand for advertising and public relations specialists.[3]

Advertising and public relations firms together employed about 480,000 people in a recent year.[4] About one in five U.S. advertising employees work in New York, and about a quarter in California. Most advertising firms develop specialties; many of the largest are international in scope and earn a major proportion of their revenue abroad. Online advertising is just one area in which new jobs will be opening in the future, as more and more client firms expand their online sales operations.

Career Assessment Exercises in Marketing

1. Select a field that interests you. Use the Internet to research types of sales positions available in that field. Locate a few entry-level job openings and see the career steps that the positions can lead to. (You might start with a popular job-posting site such as Monster. com.) Note the job requirements, the starting salary, and the form of compensation—straight salary? salary plus commission?—and write a one-page summary of your findings.

2. Use the Internet to identify and investigate two or three of the leading advertising agencies in the United States, such as Young & Rubicam or J. Walter Thompson. What are some of their recent ad campaigns, or who are their best-known clients? Where do the agencies have offices? What job openings do they currently list, and what qualifications should applicants for these positions have? Write a brief report comparing the agencies you selected, decide which one you would prefer to work for, and give your reasons.

3. Test your research skills. Choose an ordinary product, such as toothpaste or soft drinks, and conduct a survey to find out why people chose the brand they most recently purchased. For instance, suppose you wanted to find out how people choose their shampoo. List as many decision criteria as you can think of, such as availability, scent, price, packaging, benefits from use (conditioning, dandruff-reducing, and so on), brand name, and ad campaign. Ask eight to ten friends to rank these decision factors, and note some simple demographics about your research subjects such as their age, gender, and occupation. Tabulate your results. What did you find out about how your subjects made their purchase decision? Did any of your findings surprise you? Can you think of any ways in which you might have improved your survey?

Chapter 14

Learning Objectives

[1] Distinguish between data and information and discuss information systems.

[2] List the components and types of information systems.

[3] Discuss computer hardware and software.

[4] Describe computer networks.

[5] Discuss the security and ethical issues affecting information systems.

[6] Explain disaster recovery and backup.

[7] Review information systems trends.

Using Technology to Manage Information

Masterfile

Evernote Raises Notetaking to a Profitable Art

If you've ever forgotten something—a deadline, the name of a restaurant, an idea—and worse, couldn't remember how to retrieve it, a software startup called Evernote has a solution for you.

Evernote is a software app for desktops, laptops, and smart phones that lets users store "notes"— typed or handwritten jottings, Web clips, voice memos, receipts, photos, and other data and images—and easily find them. Evernote stores each user's data in the cloud, but in searchable (and rigorously backed-up) storage that lets you find whatever you've forgotten, using any Internet-connected device, by looking up information associated with it, such as when and where you were when you recorded it, who you were with, what you were eating, or any other tag you've attached to it. You can create separate "notebooks" to file your data, and—although the platform isn't intended as a social network—you can also share your notes with others.

"It's the electronic version of having something on the tip of your tongue," says CEO Phil Libin. With marketing depending largely on word of mouth, the company's base has quickly grown to 15 million users, about three-quarters of whom download the full-featured free version of the software. The $5-per-month version, which brings in Evernote's revenue, offers more storage space.

Libin's somewhat unconventional business model and pricing structure seem to be working. With 80 employees in Mountain View, California, Moscow, and Tokyo, the company continues to grow, buying other companies, seeking new investors, attracting third-party developers, and adding new users at a steady rate. Its success is even more notable because Evernote almost shut its doors at one point when it ran out of cash to pay the bills. But an unexpected offer of investment money from an entrepreneur in Sweden—an early Evernote fan—gave the company a new lease on life, and it hasn't looked back. Its second product, Evernote Peek, turns an iPad into a flash-card system and already has huge appeal in classrooms from kindergarten through high school.

Libin would like Evernote eventually to recognize faces and even smells. When that happens, he says, "your own brain might end up being the last place you search for information." Evernote was recently named company of the year by *Inc.* magazine.[1]

Overview

This chapter explores how businesses manage information as a resource, particularly how they use technology to do so. Today, virtually all business functions—from human resources to production to supply chain management—rely on information systems. The chapter begins by differentiating between information and data and then defines an information system. The components of information systems are presented, and two major types of information systems are described. Because of their importance to organizations, the chapter discusses databases, the heart of all information systems. Then the chapter looks at the computer hardware and software that drive information systems. Today, specialized networks make information access and transmission function smoothly, so the chapter examines different types of telecommunications and computer networks to see how start-ups like Evernote are applying them for competitive advantage. The chapter then turns to a discussion of the ethical and security issues affecting information systems, followed by a description of how organizations plan for, and recover from, information system disasters. A review of the current trends in information systems concludes the chapter.

LECTURE ENHANCER:
Think of a recent situation in which you needed to gather data on a subject. What method(s) did you use to do so?

Data, Information, and Information Systems

Every day, businesspeople ask themselves questions such as the following:

- How well is our product selling in Boston compared with Phoenix? Have sales among consumers aged 25 to 45 increased or decreased within the past year?

- How will rising energy prices affect production and distribution costs?

- If employees can access the benefits system through our network, will this increase or decrease benefit costs?

- Can we communicate more efficiently and effectively with our increasingly dispersed workforce?

An effective information system can help answer these and many other questions. **Data** consist of raw facts and figures that may or may not be relevant to a business decision. **Information** is knowledge gained from processing those facts and figures. So although businesspeople need to gather data about the demographics of a target market or the specifications of a certain product, the data are useless unless they are transformed into relevant information that can be used to make a competitive decision. For instance, data might be the sizes of various demographic groups. Information drawn from those data could be how many of those individuals are potential customers for a firm's products. Technology has advanced so quickly that all businesses, regardless of size or location, now have access to data and information that can make them competitive in a global arena.

An **information system** is an organized method for collecting, storing, and communicating past, present, and projected information on internal operations and external intelligence. Most information systems today use computer and telecommunications technology. A large organization typically assigns responsibility for directing its information systems and related operations to an executive called the **chief information officer (CIO)**. Often, the CIO reports directly to the firm's chief executive officer (CEO). An effective CIO will understand and harness technology so that the company can communicate internally and externally in one seamless operation. But small companies rely just as much on information systems as do large ones, even if they do not employ a manager assigned to this area on a full-time basis.

The role of the CIO is expanding and growing in importance as technology becomes increasingly critical to business operations. Ten years ago, the role of a CIO was primarily technical; now, the CIO is an essential business partner who exerts strong influence over organizational strategy. Their expertise makes CIOs and former CIOs good candidates for corporate boards.[2]

Information systems can be tailored to assist many business functions and departments— from marketing and manufacturing to finance and accounting. They can manage the overwhelming flood of information by organizing data in a logical and accessible manner. Through the system, a company can monitor all components of its operations and business strategy, identifying problems and opportunities. Information systems gather data from inside and outside the organization; they then process the data to produce information that is relevant to all aspects of the organization. Processing steps could involve storing data for later use, classifying and analyzing it, and retrieving it easily when needed.

LECTURE ENHANCER:
Continuing with the example from above, consider what process you used in order to transform your data into useful information.

data raw facts and figures that may or may not be relevant to a business decision.

information knowledge gained from processing data.

information system organized method for collecting, storing, and communicating past, present, and projected information on internal operations and external intelligence.

chief information officer (CIO) executive responsible for managing a firm's information system and related computer technologies.

LECTURE ENHANCER:
What recent changes in the business environment might account for this change in a CIO's role?

Many companies—and nations—combine high-tech and low-tech solutions to manage the flow of information. E-mail, wireless communications, and videoconferencing haven't totally replaced paper memos, phone conversations, and face-to-face meetings, but they are increasingly common. Information can make the difference between staying in business and going bankrupt. Keeping on top of changing consumer demands, competitors' actions, and the latest government regulations will help a firm fine-tune existing products, develop new winners, and maintain effective marketing.

Components and Types of Information Systems

The definition of *information system* in the previous section does not specifically mention the use of computers or technology. In fact, information systems have been around since the beginning of civilization but were, by today's standards, very low tech. Think about your college or university's library. At one time the library probably had card catalog files to help you find information. Those files were information systems because they stored data about books and periodicals on 3-by-5-inch index cards.

Today, however, when businesspeople think about information systems, they are most likely thinking about **computer-based information systems**. These systems rely on computer and related technologies to store information electronically in an organized, accessible manner. So, instead of card catalogs, your college library probably uses a computerized information system that allows users to search through library holdings much faster and easier.

Computer-based information systems consist of four components and technologies:

- computer hardware
- computer software
- telecommunications and computer networks
- data resource management

Computer hardware consists of machines that range from supercomputers to smart phones. It also includes the input, output, and storage devices needed to support computing machines. Software includes operating systems, such as Microsoft's Windows 8 or Linux, and applications programs, such as Adobe Acrobat or Oracle's PeopleSoft Enterprise applications. Telecommunications and computer networks encompass the hardware and software needed to provide wired or wireless voice and data communications. This includes support for external networks such as the Internet and private internal networks. Data resource management involves developing and maintaining an organization's databases so that decision makers are able to access the information they need in a timely manner.

In the case of your institution's library, the computer-based information system is generally made up of computer hardware, such as monitors

Assessment Check ✓

1. Distinguish between data and information.

2. What is an information system?

LECTURE ENHANCER: Can you think of an example of an information system that is not computer-based?

computer-based information systems information systems that rely on computer and related technologies to store information electronically in an organized, accessible manner.

Libraries typically use a computer-based information system, made up of computer hardware linked to the library's network and a database containing information on the books in the library. Specialized software allows users to access the database.

Purestock/Getty Images, Inc.

and keyboards, which are linked to the library's network and a database containing information on the library's holdings. Specialized software allows users to access the database. In addition, the library's network is likely also connected to a larger private network and the Internet. This connection gives users remote access to the library's database, as well as access to other computerized databases such as LexisNexis.

Databases

database centralized integrated collection of data resources.

The heart of any information system is its **database**, a centralized integrated collection of data resources. A company designs its databases to meet particular information processing and retrieval needs of its workforce. Businesses obtain databases in many ways. They can hire a staff person to build them on site, hire an outside source to do so, or buy packaged database programs from specialized vendors, such as Oracle. A database serves as an electronic filing cabinet, capable of storing massive amounts of data and retrieving it within seconds. A database should be continually updated; otherwise, a firm may find itself with data that are outdated and possibly useless. One problem with databases is that they can contribute to information overload—too much data for people to absorb or data that are not relevant to decision making. Because both computer processing speed and storage capacity are increasing rapidly, and because data have become more abundant, businesspeople need to be careful that their databases contain only the facts they need. If they don't, they can waste time wading through unnecessary data. Another challenge with databases is keeping them safe, as the "Hit & Miss" feature describes.

Decision makers can also look up online data. Online systems give access to enormous amounts of government data, such as economic data from the Bureau of Labor Statistics and the Department of Commerce. One of the largest online databases is that of the U.S. Census Bureau. The census of population, conducted every ten years, collects data on more than 120 million households across the United States. After attempting to count everyone in the country, the Census Bureau has selected participants fill out forms containing questions about marital status, place of birth, ethnic background, citizenship, workplaces, commuting time, income, occupation, type of housing, number of telephones and vehicles, even grandparents as caregivers. Households receiving the most recent questionnaire can respond in English as well as a variety of other languages including Spanish, Chinese, Vietnamese, and Korean. Not surprisingly, sifting through all the collected data takes time. Although certain restrictions limit how businesspeople can access and use specific census data, the general public may access the data via the American FactFinder on the Census Bureau's Web site (http://factfinder.census.gov), as well as at state data centers and public libraries.

Another source of free information is company Web sites. Interested parties can visit firms' home pages to look for information about customers, suppliers, and competitors. Trade associations and academic institutions also maintain Web sites with information on topics of interest.

Types of Information Systems

Many different types of information systems exist. In general, however, information systems fall into two broad categories: operational support systems or management support systems.

Operational Support Systems <u>**Operational support systems**</u> are designed to produce a variety of information on an organization's activities for both internal and external users. Examples of operational support systems include transaction processing systems and process control systems. <u>**Transaction processing systems**</u> record

LECTURE ENHANCER: Does the availability of so many different types of data surprise you? Why or why not?

LECTURE ENHANCER: Identify an example of a company in which the operational support system is the most vital information system.

operational support systems information systems designed to produce a variety of information on an organization's activities for both internal and external users.

transaction processing systems operational support system to record and process data from business transactions.

Cyber Attack Trips Up Zappos

No one likes hearing their personal information has been compromised, but that's what recently happened to 24 million customers of Zappos, the popular online shoe store owned by Amazon. Hackers broke into Zappos' database and accessed users' names, addresses, e-mails, and phone numbers.

Zappos e-mailed customers immediately, advising them to change their passwords. "We've spent over 12 years building our reputation, brand, and trust with customers," CEO Tony Hsieh told shoppers. "It's painful to see us take so many steps back due to a single incident." Credit card and password information was encrypted and still secure, but no one was taking chances.

The hackers could attempt identify theft or credit card fraud, or sell the information to spammers, fraudsters, and perpetrators of phishing attacks. Despite Zappos' industry-standard encryption policies, the last four digits of customers' credit cards were still vulnerable, giving crooks a means of convincing customers that phishing attacks were real e-mails.

Some observers conclude that no online data can ever be truly secure. The attack is a timely reminder that Internet shoppers should use a different password on every site, something 30 percent fail to do.

Questions for Critical Thinking

1. Do you think Zappos reacted appropriately by e-mailing customers? Why or why not?
2. Do you use a different password for every shopping site you visit?

Sources: Matt Brownell, "What Zappos Customers Should Be Worried About," Main Street.com, January 17, 2012, http://www.mainstreet.com; Byron Acohido, "Hackers Swipe Zappos Data; Customers Should Change Password," *USA Today*, January 17, 2012, http://www.usatoday.com; Nicole Perlroth, "Even Big Companies Cannot Protect Their Data," *The New York Times*, January 17, 2012, http://bits.blogs.nytimes.com; Geoff Duncan, "Zappos Breach: 24 Million Customer Accounts Compromised," *Yahoo! News*, January 16, 2012, http://news.yahoo.com.

---

and process data from business transactions. For example, major retailers use point-of-sale systems, which link electronic cash registers to the retailer's computer centers. Sales data are transmitted from cash registers to the computer center either immediately or at regular intervals. **Process control systems** monitor and control physical processes. A steel mill, for instance, may have electronic sensors linked to a computer system monitoring the entire production process. The system makes necessary changes and alerts operators to potential problems.

Walmart quickly adopted an information system based on RFID (radio-frequency identification) technology to track supply chain activities. Today, many retailers use RFID. The RFID software developed by Truecount Corporation helps retailers monitor shipping and receiving of goods, with the goal of achieving up-to-the-minute knowledge of inventory status—a significant competitive advantage.[3]

Management Support Systems Information systems that are designed to provide support for effective decision making are classified as **management support systems**. Several different types of management support systems are available. A **management information system (MIS)** is designed to produce reports for managers and other personnel.

A **decision support system (DSS)** gives direct support to businesspeople during the decision-making process. For instance, a marketing manager might use a decision support system to analyze the impact on sales and profits of a product price change.

An **executive support system (ESS)** lets senior executives access the firm's primary databases, often by touching the computer screen, pointing and clicking a mouse, or using voice recognition. The typical ESS allows users to choose from many kinds of data, such as

process control systems operational support system to monitor and control physical processes.

management support systems information systems that are designed to provide support for effective decision making.

management information system (MIS) information system that is designed to produce reports for managers and other personnel.

decision support system (DSS) gives direct support to businesspeople during the decision-making process.

executive support system (ESS) lets senior executives access the firm's primary databases, often by touching the computer screen, pointing and clicking a mouse, or using voice recognition.

The complex process of airline maintenance is critical to passenger safety. To track parts, schedule inspections, and manage inventory levels, many airlines use an operational support system. In this ad, American Airlines reports that improved business processes have turned costly maintenance operations into a source of profit.

expert system computer program that imitates human thinking through complicated sets of if-then rules.

Assessment Check ✔

1. List the four components of a computer-based information system.

2. What is a database?

3. What are the two general types of information systems? Give examples of each.

hardware all tangible elements of a computer system.

the firm's financial statements and sales figures, as well as stock market trends for the company and for the industry as a whole. Managers can start by looking at summaries and then access more detailed information when needed.

Finally, an **expert system** is a computer program that imitates human thinking through complicated sets of if-then rules. The system applies human knowledge in a specific subject area to solve a problem. Expert systems are used for a variety of business purposes: determining credit limits for credit card applicants, monitoring machinery in a plant to predict potential problems or breakdowns, making mortgage loans, and determining optimal plant layouts. They are typically developed by capturing the knowledge of recognized experts in a field whether within a business itself or outside it.

[3] Computer Hardware and Software

Only a few decades ago computers were considered exotic curiosities, used only for very specialized applications and understood by only a few people. The first commercial computer, UNIVAC I, was sold to the U.S. Census Bureau in the early 1950s. It cost $1 million, took up most of a room, and could perform about 2,000 calculations per second.[4] The invention of transistors and then integrated circuits (microchips) quickly led to smaller and more powerful devices. By the 1980s, computers could routinely perform several million calculations per second. Now, computers perform billions of calculations per second, and some fit in the palm of your hand.

When the first personal computers were introduced in the late 1970s and early 1980s, the idea of a computer on every desk, or in every home, seemed far-fetched. Today they have become indispensable to both businesses and households. Not only have computers become much more powerful and faster over the past 25 years, but they are less expensive as well. IBM's first personal computer (PC), introduced in 1981, cost well over $5,000 fully configured. Today, the typical PC sells for under $800.

Types of Computer Hardware

Hardware consists of all tangible elements of a computer system—the input devices, the components that store and process data and perform required calculations, and the output devices that present the results to information users. Input devices allow users to enter data and commands for processing, storage, and output. The most common input devices are the keyboard and mouse. Storage and processing components consist of the hard drive as well as various other storage components, including DVD drives and flash memory devices. Flash memory devices are becoming increasingly popular because they are small and can hold large amounts of data. Some, called thumb drives, can even fit on a keychain. To gain access to the data they hold, users just plug them into an unused USB (universal serial bus) port, standard on today's computers. Output devices, such as monitors and printers, are the hardware elements that transmit or display documents and other results of a computer system's work.

Different types of computers incorporate widely varying memory capacities and processing speeds. These differences define four broad classifications: mainframe computers, midrange systems, personal computers, and hand-held devices. A mainframe computer is the largest type of computer system with the most extensive storage capacity and the fastest processing speeds. Especially powerful mainframes called *supercomputers* can handle extremely rapid, complex calculations involving thousands of variables, such as weather modeling and forecasting. Today's supercomputers can perform a trillion or more calculations per second.

Midrange systems consist of high-end network servers and other types of computers that can handle large-scale processing needs. They are less powerful than mainframe computers but more powerful than most personal computers. A **server** is the heart of a midrange computer network, supporting applications and allowing the sharing of output devices, software, and databases among networked users. Many Internet-related functions at organizations are handled by midrange systems. Midrange systems are also commonly employed in process control systems, computer-aided manufacturing (CAM), and computer-aided design (CAD).

Personal computers are everywhere today—in homes, businesses, schools, nonprofit organizations, and government agencies. Recent estimates of PC ownership say that more than two-thirds of American households have at least one personal computer. They have earned increasing popularity because of their ever-expanding capability to handle many of the functions that large mainframes performed only a few decades ago. Most desktop computers are linked to networks, such as the Internet.

Desktop computers used to be the standard PC seen in offices and homes. While millions of desktop computers remain on the job, laptops—including notebooks and netbooks—now account for more than half of all PCs sold. The increasing popularity of these computers can be explained by their improved displays, faster processing speeds, ability to handle more intense graphics, larger storage capacities, and more durable designs. Last but not least is the most obvious advantage—they are portable. They are thinner and lighter than ever before. Business owners, managers, salespeople, and students all benefit from the constant innovation of the laptop.

While prices for full-size laptops, notebooks, and netbooks vary greatly—you can purchase a netbook for $300 or a MacBook Pro for $2,200—they still generally run less than a comparable desktop. A netbook doesn't have the computing capacity of a larger, more expensive notebook, but for a few hundred dollars it can perform basic tasks such as e-mail, word processing, and spreadsheet calculations.

Hand-held devices such as smart phones are even smaller. Smart phones, such as the iPhone, Android, and BlackJack, essentially combine a phone with the Internet. Because of their ever-increasing capacity to surf the

| Because of their ever-increasing capacity, smart phones are rapidly outpacing traditional cell phones.

Jacob Wackerhausen/iStockphoto

LECTURE ENHANCER:
What specific details must a company take into consideration when deciding on hardware purchases?

LECTURE ENHANCER:
What are some drawbacks to using mainframe computer systems?

server the heart of a midrange computer network.

LECTURE ENHANCER:
Consider and discuss the advantages and disadvantages of each type of PC.

CLASS ACTIVITY:
Survey students to see how many have smart phones; ask if any use the phone more for Internet access than to talk to someone.

BusinessEtiquette

Courteous Communications via Wireless Devices

Cell phone use in America has skyrocketed in a decade from about 3.5 million subscribers to about 285 million. With so much cell phone use, it's more important than ever to communicate courteously. Consider these tips:

1 *Be aware of your surroundings and your neighbors.* If you're someplace where a phone conversation would be disruptive, turn off your ringtone. If the call or e-mail simply can't wait, excuse yourself and leave the room to respond.

2 *Lower your voice.* If you're in a room that's quieter than your speaking voice, go somewhere else.

3 *When e-mailing or texting, don't overabbreviate.* Business messages can be concise without being cute or unintelligible. For example, say "See you at 3," not "cu@3."

4 *Before sending a text message or e-mail, reread it carefully.* Typos and grammatical errors have no place in a business message.

5 *Be careful with Facebook photos.* Now that smart phones let users link all their contact information, your photo will appear on the other person's phone when you call. And people beyond those on your Facebook friends list will see it. Be sure your photo is appropriate for both friends and business callers.

Sources: Christopher Elliott, "E-Mail Etiquette for Wireless Devices: 7 Tips," Microsoft Small Business Center, http://www.microsoft.com, accessed March 9, 2012; Taya Flores, "Cell Phone Etiquette Is Important," *JC Online.com,* http://www.jconline.com, accessed March 9, 2012; Mike Elgan, "Here Comes the New Cell Phone Etiquette," *IT World,* http://www.itworld.com, accessed March 9, 2012.

software all the programs, routines, and computer languages that control a computer and tell it how to operate.

Internet, open and edit documents, send and receive messages, make calls, and more, sales of smart phones are rapidly outpacing traditional cell phones.

Two other devices—tablets and e-readers—are also making inroads in business. In addition to the Apple iPad, there are now more than 100 tablet models on the market. Dell, Hewlett Packard, Motorola, and Samsung have all entered the tablet market with serious intentions and constant innovations designed to make them standard business tools. E-readers such as Amazon's Kindle and Barnes & Noble's Nook continue to expand their capacities as well—and will likely find their way into the business market before long.[5]

While smart phones can be terrific tools that boost productivity, some people overuse or even misuse them. The "Business Etiquette" feature describes some do's and don'ts of smart phone use in a business environment.

In addition to smart phones, specialized hand-held devices are used in a variety of businesses for different applications. Some restaurants, for example, have small wireless devices that allow servers to swipe a credit card and print out a receipt right at the customer's table. Drivers for UPS and FedEx use special hand-held scanning devices to track package deliveries and accept delivery signatures. The driver scans each package as it is delivered, and the information is transmitted to the delivery firm's network. Within a few seconds, the sender, using an Internet connection, can obtain the delivery information and even see a facsimile of the recipient's signature.

Computer Software

Software includes all of the programs, routines, and computer languages that control a computer and tell it how to operate. The software that controls the basic workings of a computer system is its *operating system*. More than 80 percent of personal computers use a version of Microsoft's popular Windows operating system. Personal computers made by Apple use the Mac operating system. Most hand-held devices use other operating systems, such as Garnet or Windows Phone. The Droid and iPhone models have their own operating systems. Other operating systems include Unix, which runs on many midrange computer systems, and Linux, which runs on both PCs and midrange systems.

14.1 Common Types of Applications Software

TYPE	DESCRIPTION	EXAMPLES
Word processing	Programs that input, store, retrieve, edit, and print various types of documents.	Microsoft Word, Pages (Apple)
Spreadsheets	Programs that prepare and analyze financial statements, sales forecasts, budgets, and similar numerical and statistical data.	Microsoft Excel, Numbers (Apple)
Presentation software	Programs that create presentations. Users can create bulleted lists, charts, graphs, pictures, audio, and even short video clips.	Microsoft PowerPoint, Keynote (Apple)
Desktop publishing	Software that combines high-quality type, graphics, and layout tools to create output that can look as attractive as documents produced by professional publishers and printers.	Adobe Acrobat, Microsoft Publisher
Financial software	Programs that compile accounting and financial data to create financial statements, reports, and budgets; they perform basic financial management tasks such as balancing a checkbook.	Quicken, QuickBooks
Database programs	Software that searches and retrieves data from a database; it can sort data based on various criteria.	Microsoft Access, Approach
Personal information managers	Specialized database programs that allow people to track communications with personal and business contacts; some combine e-mail capability.	Microsoft Outlook, Lotus Organizer
Enterprise resource planning	Integrated cross-functional software that controls many business activities, including distribution, finance, and human resources.	SAP Enterprise Resource Planning

A program that performs the specific tasks that the user wants to carry out—such as writing a letter or looking up data—is called *application software*. Examples of application software include Adobe Acrobat, Microsoft PowerPoint, and Quicken. Table 14.1 lists the major categories of application software. Most application programs are currently stored on individual computers. As the chapter's opening vignette discussed, the future of applications software is constantly changing. Some believe much of it will eventually become Web based, with the programs themselves stored in the so-called cloud, on Internet-connected servers. Others disagree, arguing that most computer users will not want to rely on an Internet connection to perform tasks such as preparing a spreadsheet using Microsoft Excel.

4 Computer Networks

As mentioned earlier, virtually all computers today are linked to networks. In fact, if your PC has Internet access, you're linked to a network. Local area networks and wide area networks allow businesses to communicate, transmit and print documents, and share data. These networks, however, require businesses to install special equipment and connections between office sites. But Internet technology has also been applied to internal company communications and business tasks, tapping a ready-made network. Among these new Internet-based applications are intranets, virtual private networks (VPNs), and voice over Internet protocol (VoIP). Each has contributed to the effectiveness and speed of business processes, so we discuss them next.

Assessment Check ✓

1. List two input and output devices.

2. What accounts for the increasing popularity of notebook computers?

3. What is software? List the two categories of software.

local area networks (LANs) computer networks that connect machines within limited areas, such as a building or several nearby buildings.

wide area networks (WANs) tie larger geographical regions together by using telephone lines and microwave and satellite transmission.

WiFi wireless network that connects various devices and allows them to communicate with one another through radio waves.

intranet computer network that is similar to the Internet but limits access to authorized users.

LECTURE ENHANCER:
What are some drawbacks to a wireless local network?

Local Area Networks and Wide Area Networks

Most organizations connect their offices and buildings by creating **local area networks (LANs)**, computer networks that connect machines within limited areas, such as a building or several nearby buildings. LANs are useful because they link computers and allow them to share printers, documents, and information, as well as provide access to the Internet. Figure 14.1 shows what a small business computer network might look like.

Wide area networks (WANs) tie larger geographical regions together by using telephone lines and microwave and satellite transmission. One familiar WAN is long-distance telephone service. Companies such as AT&T and Verizon provide WAN services to businesses and consumers. Firms also use WANs to conduct their own operations. Typically, companies link their own network systems to outside communications equipment and services for transmission across long distances.

Wireless Local Networks

A wireless network allows computers, printers, and other devices to be connected without the hassle of stringing cables in traditional office settings. The current standard for wireless networks is called WiFi. **WiFi**—short for *wireless fidelity*—is a wireless network that connects various devices and allows them to communicate with one another through radio waves. Any PC with a WiFi receptor can connect with the Internet at so-called hot spots—locations with a wireless router and a high-speed Internet modem. There are almost hundreds of thousands of hot spots worldwide today. They are found in a variety of places, including airports, libraries, and coffee shops. Examples include Panera Bread's 1,500 bakery-cafes in the United States and Kansai International Airport in Osaka, Japan. Some locations provide free access, while others charge a fee.

Many believe that the successor to WiFi will be *Wi-Max*. Unlike WiFi's relatively limited geographic coverage area—generally around 300 feet—a single Wi-Max access point can provide coverage over many miles. In addition, cell phone service providers, such as Sprint Nextel and AT&T, offer broadband network cards for notebook PCs. These devices allow users to access the provider's mobile broadband network from virtually any location where cell phone reception is available.

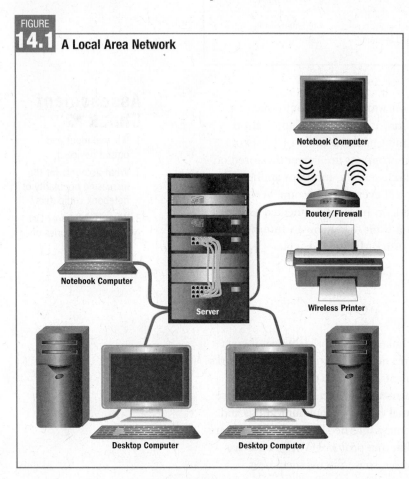

FIGURE 14.1 A Local Area Network

Notebook Computer

Router/Firewall

Notebook Computer

Server

Wireless Printer

Desktop Computer

Desktop Computer

Intranets

A broad approach to sharing information in an organization is to establish a company network patterned after the Internet. Such a network is called an **intranet**. Intranets are similar to the Internet, but they limit access to employees or other authorized users. An intranet blocks outsiders without valid passwords from entering its network by incorporating both software and hardware known as a **firewall**. Firewalls limit data transfers to certain locations and log system use so that managers can identify attempts to log on with invalid passwords and other threats to a system's security. Highly sophisticated packages immediately alert system administrators about suspicious activities and permit authorized personnel to use smart cards to connect from remote terminals.

Intranets solve the problem of linking different types of computers. Like the Internet, intranets can integrate computers running all kinds of operating systems. In addition, intranets are relatively easy and inexpensive to set up because most businesses already have some of the required hardware and software. For instance, a small business can simply purchase a DSL router and a few cables and create an intranet using phone jacks and internal phone lines. All the business's computers will be linked with each other and with the Internet.

WiFi connections are often called hot spots—locations with a wireless router and a high-speed Internet modem. There are almost hundreds of thousands of hot spots worldwide today found in a variety of places, including airports, libraries, and coffee shops.

Intranets can support teamwork among employees who are traveling or telecommuting. They can nurture innovation when designated for the development of creative ideas. They can be used to share marketing and brand information worldwide. Mobile intranets—with access from smart phones—are becoming increasingly popular for companies with employees who are often on the go. Mota-Engil, a leading construction firm based in Portugal, recently won an award for its intranet called InnovCenter, which operates solely for the purpose of generating and capturing ideas for improving the firm's performance and services. InnovCenter receives employees' ideas via their mobile phones much like an old-fashioned suggestion box—even when workers are on the job at a faraway site.[6]

Virtual Private Networks

To gain increased security for Internet communications, companies often turn to **virtual private networks (VPNs)**, secure connections between two points on the Internet. These VPNs use firewalls and programs that encapsulate data to make them more secure during transit. Loosely defined, a VPN can include a range of networking technologies, from secure Internet connections to private networks from service providers such as IBM. A VPN is cheaper for a company to use than leasing several of its own lines. It can also take months to install a leased line in some parts of the world, but a new user can be added to a VPN in a day. Because a VPN uses the Internet, it can be wired, wireless, or a combination of the two.

Colorado-based Advanced Systems Group (ASG) provides data storage and management services to other companies. As the company expanded and opened branch offices, its own security became a concern. ASG turned to Check Point, which created a secure VPN connecting ASG's home office and five branch offices. The VPN allows ASG to add new sites and new remote users automatically.[7]

firewalls limit data transfers to certain locations and log system use so that managers can identify attempts to log on with invalid passwords and other threats to a system's security.

LECTURE ENHANCER:
What are some drawbacks to accessing the Internet via a WiFi hotspot?

virtual private networks (VPNs) secure connections between two points on the Internet.

LECTURE ENHANCER:
Describe a situation in which a VPN would be particularly useful for two firms.

VoIP

VoIP alternative to traditional telecommunication services provided by companies such as Verizon and Qwest.

VoIP—which stands for *voice over Internet Protocol*—is an alternative to traditional telecommunication services provided by companies such as Verizon and Qwest. The VoIP telephone is connected to a personal computer with any type of broadband connection instead of a traditional phone jack. Special software transmits phone conversations over the Internet, rather than through telephone lines. A VoIP user dials the phone as usual. The person can make and receive calls to and from those with traditional telephone connections (landline or wireless).

A growing number of consumers and businesses have embraced VoIP, mainly due to its cost savings and extra features. As technology continues to advance, demand for the service has increased. Several wireless companies, including AT&T, Verizon, and Vonage, permit VoIP on smart phones. Google integrates its Google Voice over VoIP. The various VoIP providers are working together with the goal of creating a single VoIP standard that would permit seamless roaming worldwide.[8]

In spite of VoIP's apparent advantages, there are several potential drawbacks to replacing traditional telephony with Internet telephony. For one thing, your Internet phone service will be only as reliable as your broadband connection. If your broadband connection goes out, so will your phone service. Also, without extensive safeguards, VoIP can expose a phone system to the havoc that can affect the rest of the Internet, such as worms and viruses.

LECTURE ENHANCER:
Share examples of current VoIP providers.

Assessment Check ☑

1. What is a LAN?
2. What are the differences between an intranet and a VPN?
3. Briefly explain how VoIP works.

⌐5⌐ Security and Ethical Issues Affecting Information Systems

Numerous security and ethical issues affect information systems. As information systems become increasingly important business assets, they also become progressively harder and more expensive to replace. Damage to information systems or theft of data can have disastrous consequences. When computers are connected to a network, a problem at any individual computer can affect the entire network. Two of the major security threats are e-crime and so-called malware.

E-Crime

LECTURE ENHANCER:
Discuss a recent film or television show that featured an act of e-crime. What were the effects of the crime for the firms or individuals involved?

Computers provide efficient ways for employees to share information. But they may also allow people with more malicious intentions to access information. Or they may allow pranksters—who have no motive other than to see whether they can hack into a system—to gain access to private information. Common e-crimes involve stealing or altering data in several ways:

- Employees or outsiders may change or invent data to produce inaccurate or misleading information.

- Employees or outsiders may modify computer programs to create false information or illegal transactions or to insert viruses.

- Unauthorized people can access computer systems for their own benefit or knowledge or just to see if they can get in.

LECTURE ENHANCER:
Why might an employee want to produce inaccurate or misleading company information?

Individuals, businesses, and government agencies are all vulnerable to computer crime. Computer hackers—unauthorized users—sometimes work alone and sometimes work in groups. Hackers can break into computer systems just to show that they can do it; other times they have more sinister motives. A recent survey reported that although computer crime decreased slightly recently, the majority of such attacks may go undetected because many firms have concentrated on foiling hackers and blocking pornography while leaving themselves open to cybercriminals who are developing increasingly sophisticated weapons. Even Apple computers, usually immune to cybercrime, are becoming vulnerable as more and more Mac users store data in the cloud—that is, on the Internet itself—rather than on hard drives. Until now there has been no single uniform system for reporting cybercrime, but the Internet Engineering Task Force (IETF) is proposing a common format able to analyze massive amounts of data much faster than human analysts can.[9]

Information system administrators implement two basic protections against computer crime: They try to prevent access to their systems by unauthorized users and the viewing of data by unauthorized system users. The simplest method of preventing access requires authorized users to enter passwords. The company may also install firewalls, described earlier. To prevent system users from reading sensitive information, the company may use encryption software, which encodes, or scrambles, messages. To read encrypted messages, users must use an electronic key to convert them to regular text. But as fast as software developers invent new and more elaborate protective measures, hackers seem to break through their defenses. Thus, security is an ongoing battle.

Consumers with credit cards are particularly at risk from hackers. Recently Global Payments, a payments processing company used by major credit card companies, announced that consumer credit and debit card information may have been compromised.[10] When a customer swipes a credit or debit card, the data is sent to a payment processor such as Global Payments, which then forwards the transaction information to credit card companies such as Visa and MasterCard.

As the size of computer hardware diminishes, it becomes increasingly vulnerable to theft. Hand-held devices, for instance, can easily vanish with a pickpocket or purse snatcher. Many notebook computers and hand-held devices contain special security software or passwords that makes it difficult for a thief or any unauthorized person to access the data stored in the computer's memory. If you have a notebook computer that contains sensitive personal information, you should consider having such safeguards.

Computer Viruses, Worms, Trojan Horses, and Spyware

Viruses, worms, Trojan horses, and spyware, collectively referred to as **malware**, are malicious software programs designed to infect computer systems. These programs can destroy data, steal sensitive information, and even render information systems inoperable. Recently, malware has been discovered in advertisements on major sites such as Yahoo, Fox, and Google as well as *The New York Times* and WhitePages.com. Malware attacks cost consumers and businesses billions of dollars annually. And malware is proliferating: according to a recent estimate, malware occurrences exceeded 75 million.[11]

Computer **viruses** are programs that secretly attach themselves to other programs (called *hosts*) and change them or destroy data. Viruses can be programmed to become active immediately or to remain dormant for a period of time, after which the infections suddenly activate themselves and cause problems. A virus can reproduce by copying itself onto other programs stored in the same drive. It spreads as users install infected software on their systems or exchange files with others, usually by exchanging e-mail, accessing electronic bulletin boards, trading disks, or downloading programs or data from unknown sources on the Internet.

A **worm** is a small piece of software that exploits a security hole in a network to replicate itself. A copy of the worm scans the network for another machine that has a specific security hole. It copies itself to the new machine using the security hole and then starts replicating from there as well. Unlike viruses, worms don't need host programs to damage computer systems.

A **botnet** is a network of PCs that have been infected with one or more data-stealing viruses. Computer criminals tie the infected computers into a network, often without the owners being aware of it, and sell the botnet on the black market. They or others use the botnet to commit identity theft, sell fake pharmaceuticals, buy blocks of concert tickets for scalping, and attack the Internet itself. Thousands of botnets are active today. Grum, thought to be the largest botnet currently operating, sends more than 18 billion spam emails daily. Computer-security experts say Grum is responsible for more than one-third of the world's junk email.[12]

A **Trojan horse** is a program that claims to do one thing but in reality does something else, usually something malicious. For example, a Trojan horse might claim, and even appear, to be a game. When an unsuspecting user clicks on the Trojan horse to launch it, the program might erase the hard drive or steal any personal data stored on the computer.

Spyware is software that secretly gathers user information through the user's Internet connection without his or her knowledge, usually for advertising purposes. Spyware applications are typically bundled with other programs downloaded from the Internet. Once installed, the spyware monitors user activity on the Internet and transmits that information in the background to someone else.

Attacks by malware are not limited to computers and computer networks. Users of smart phones have reported a sharp increase in viruses, worms, and other forms of malware. Recently, a Trojan horse known as Nickispy, masquerading as a Google+ app, managed to infiltrate smart phones. By reverse-engineering the malware, technology experts were able to unravel how it ended up on smart phones, and eliminate the threat.[13]

As viruses, worms, botnets, and Trojan horses become more complex, the technology to fight them must increase in sophistication as well. The simplest way to protect against computer viruses is to install one of the many available antivirus software programs, such as Norton AntiVirus and McAfee VirusScan. These programs, which also protect against worms and some Trojan horses, continuously monitor systems for viruses and automatically eliminate any they spot. Users should regularly update them by downloading the latest virus definitions. In addition, computer users should also install and regularly update antispyware programs because many Trojan horses are forms of spyware.

But management must begin to emphasize security at a deeper level: during software design, in corporate servers, at Web gateways, and through Internet service providers. Because the vast majority of the world's computers run on Microsoft operating systems, a single virus, worm, or Trojan horse can spread among them quickly. Individual computer users should carefully choose the files they load onto their systems, scan their systems regularly, make sure their antivirus software is up to date, and install software only from known sources. They should also be very careful when opening attachments to e-mails because many viruses, worms, and Trojan horses are spread that way.

worm small piece of software that exploits a security hole in a network to replicate itself.

botnet a network of PCs that have been infected with one or more data-stealing viruses.

Trojan horse program that claims to do one thing but in reality does something else, usually something malicious.

spyware software that secretly gathers user information through the user's Internet connection without his or her knowledge, usually for advertising purposes.

LECTURE ENHANCER: Have students discuss additional antivirus software programs with which they are familiar.

Solving an Ethical Controversy

Should Employers Monitor Employees' Internet Use?

A recent survey says two-thirds of employers monitor their employees' Internet use. Technology enables them to check the sites employees visit, the amount of time spent online—even keystrokes on individual computers. But most employees need e-mail capability and access to the Internet, so a certain amount of Internet surfing may be necessary as well. And while a company's Facebook page can be a powerful marketing tool, it can also be a liability if employees use Facebook to complain about the company.

Should employers monitor employees' Web use?

PRO

1. Employees spend an estimated one to two hours daily online for personal use. Regardless of the purpose, this is lost time for employers.

2. Employees' inappropriate use of office technology could leave a company vulnerable to security breaches.

CON

1. Some employers say monitoring erodes employees' trust and commitment.

2. Without notification of monitoring, employees have a legitimate privacy concern.

Summary

Federal law permits employers' monitoring of computer activity. However, to avoid privacy issues, employers should establish clear policies on personal use of the organization's technology.

Sources: "How Do Employers Monitor Internet Usage at Work," *wiseGEEK*, http://www.wisegeek.com, accessed March 9, 2012; Susan M. Heathfield, "Electronic Surveillance of Employees," *About.com* Human Resources, http://humanresources.about .com, accessed March 9, 2012; Karen Codere, "Managing Social Media in the Workplace," *The Business Ledger*, http://www .thebusinessledger.com, accessed March 9, 2012; Laura Petrecca, "More Employers Use Tech to Track Workers," *USA Today*, http://www.usatoday.com, accessed March 9, 2012.

Information Systems and Ethics

The scope and power of today's information systems not surprisingly raise a number of ethical issues and concerns. These affect both employees and organizations. For instance, it is not uncommon for organizations to have specific ethical standards and policies regarding the use of information systems by employees and vendors. These standards include obligations to protect system security and the privacy and confidentiality of data. Policies also may cover the personal use of computers and related technologies, both hardware and software, by employees.

Ethical issues also involve organizational use of information systems. Organizations have an obligation to protect the privacy and confidentiality of data about employees and customers. Employment records contain sensitive personal information, such as bank account numbers, which, if not protected, could lead to identity theft. Another ethical issue is the use of computer technology to monitor employees while they are working. The "Solving an Ethical Controversy" feature debates the issue of employee monitoring further.

LECTURE ENHANCER:
Have you ever worked for a company that had policies regarding the use of its information system? If so, how did the policy affect your use of the system and its components?

Assessment Check ☑

1. Explain computer hacking.
2. What is malware?
3. How does a computer virus work?

Disaster Recovery and Backup

Natural disasters, power failures, equipment malfunctions, software glitches, human error, and terrorist attacks can disrupt even the most sophisticated computer information systems. These problems can cost businesses and other organizations billions of dollars. Even more serious consequences can occur. For example, one study found that 93 percent of firms that lost their data centers for ten days or more went bankrupt within one year.[14]

FalconStor, a global firm headquartered in Melville, New York, provides data back-up applications and sophisticated disaster recovery solutions for businesses. The firm's services go way beyond simply replicating data because organizations that have suffered a major loss have needs well beyond replicating their data. FalconStor's software solutions permit them to access their applications, restart operations, and return to serving customers.[15]

Disaster recovery planning—deciding how to prevent system failures and continue operations if computer systems fail—is a critical function of all organizations. Disaster prevention programs can avoid some of these costly problems. The most basic precaution is routinely backing up software and data—at the organizational and individual levels. However, the organization's data center cannot be the sole repository of critical data because a single location is vulnerable to threats from both natural and human-caused disasters. Consequently, off-site data backup is a necessity, whether in a separate physical location or online. Companies that perform online backups store the encrypted data in secure facilities that in turn have their own backups. The initial backup may take a day or more, but subsequent ones take far less time because they involve only new or modified files. Cloud computing services can greatly simplify off-site backup; see the accompanying "Going Green" feature for a profile of Box.net, a market leader.

According to security experts, there are five important tasks regarding off-site data storage. First is planning. The organization needs to decide what data need to be protected. Priority should be given to data having severe legal or business consequences should they be lost. Second, a backup schedule must be established and closely adhered to. Third, when data are transmitted off site, they must be protected by the highest level of security possible. Fourth, care should be taken in selecting the right security vendor. There are dozens of vendors offering different services and having different areas of expertise. Finally, the backup system should be continually tested and evaluated.

Assessment Check ☑

1. What are the types of disasters to which information systems are vulnerable?

2. List the tasks regarding off-site data storage.

Information System Trends

Computer information systems are constantly—and rapidly—evolving. To keep their information systems up-to-date, firms must continually keep abreast of changes in technology. Some of the most significant trends in information systems today include the growing demands of the so-called distributed workforce, the increased use of application service providers, on-demand computing, and cloud and grid computing.

The Distributed Workforce

As discussed in earlier chapters, many companies rely more and more on a *distributed workforce*—employees who no longer work in traditional offices but rather in what are called *virtual offices*, including at home. Information technology makes a distributed workforce possible. Computers, networks, and other components of information systems allow workers

Going Green

Box.net Serving in the Cloud

Procter & Gamble, Pandora, and Six Flags are among the 7 million customers of Box.net, a six-year-old cloud storage company whose 20-something founder, Aaron Levie, started developing the service while still in college. Now the company has 165 employees in its Palo Alto, California, offices and is worth about $11 million.

Box.net serves two customer segments, businesses and individuals. The business version of its cloud-based storage system, used by about 100,000 firms (including three-quarters of the Fortune 500), offers applications for PCs, Macs, and mobile platforms and can provide highly secure shared access for groups of multiple users. Security for the personal version is a bit more limited and works for only one user at a time. But both versions earn high marks for ease of use (Box.net is Web based so no downloading of software is required) and simplicity, even for users who aren't tech-savvy.

Competing services include Microsoft's SharePoint, with 100 million users, and Dropbox, which is targeted to consumers but plans to break into the business market. Box.net has big plans, too. It has raised millions of dollars in investment capital and is looking to expand its staff and introduce new products for larger businesses.

Questions for Critical Thinking

1. Do you think business users of cloud services such as Box.net will ever set up cloud storage as part of their IT departments? Explain.

2. Should Box.net provide the same degree of security for individual users as for business customers? Why or why not?

Sources: "Box.net Review: A Close Up Look at the #1 Online Storage Site," Don't Lose Your Data.com, http://www.dontloseyourdata.com, accessed February 14, 2012; "Box.net," Top Ten Reviews.com, http://online-storage-service-review.toptenreviews.com, accessed February 14, 2012; Stephen Lawson, "Box.net Boosts Sync, Security Features," *Computer World,* September 28, 2011, http://www.computerworld.com; Ari Levy, "Getting Business to Think Inside the Box.net," *Bloomberg Businessweek,* September 22, 2011, http://www.businessweek.com.

---

to do their jobs effectively almost anywhere. For instance, none of JetBlue's reservations agents work in offices; they all work at home, connected to the airline's information system. JetBlue is hardly alone in its use of home-based workers. Boeing, Starbucks, Agilent Technologies, Sun Microsystems, and most other companies have policies and options that permit at least some employees to work outside the organization's offices exclusively in a virtual setting. Virtual offices can range from a mailing address, mail forwarding, and a phone answering service to a full office, usually leased by the month. The increasing demands of the distributed workforce will likely lead to more innovative and increasingly powerful information systems.

Cavan Images/Getty Images, Inc.

Recent technological advances in data storage and cloud computing allow businesspeople to work on their laptops, tablets, or smart phones from anywhere in the world.

Application Service Providers

As with other business functions, many firms find that outsourcing at least some of their information technology function makes sense. Because of the increasing cost and complexity of obtaining and maintaining information systems, many firms hire an **application service provider (ASP)**, an outside supplier that provides both the computers and the application support for managing an information system. An ASP can simplify complex software for its customers so that it is easier for them to manage and use. When an ASP relationship is successful, the buyer can then devote more time and resources to its core businesses instead of struggling to manage its information systems. Other benefits include stretching

application service provider (ASP) outside supplier that provides both the computers and the application support for managing an information system.

Hit & Miss

Cisco Systems Tackles Cloud Security

Businesses increasingly find themselves managing greater amounts of e-mail and data. Many save money and physical space by turning to cloud computing and storage, including software as a service (SaaS). Rather than installing software on site, with SaaS a business gains access to software over the Internet either by subscription or by a pay-as-you-go plan. However, businesses must also protect their data from computer crime. It's relatively easy to secure a traditional local area network, but significantly more challenging to do so in a borderless environment.

Cisco Systems has developed security applications for cloud-based computing. One application directs a business's Web traffic to security towers in 100 countries worldwide, using layers of antivirus and anti-malware utilities to keep traffic secure.

Other apps support security for off-site workers using computers and smart phones. Features permit an administrator to disable former employees' access and enable access for new employees.

Although it's challenging to secure the cloud, it's a top priority for the IT industry.

Questions for Critical Thinking

1. What are the advantages and disadvantage of storing data "in the cloud"?

2. Why is it important to block former employees' access to company data?

Sources: "New Security Architecture Enables Context-Aware Capabilities in the Cisco ASA Firewall," press release, Cisco Systems Web site, http://newsroom .cisco.com, accessed March 9, 2012; James Urquhart, "Cloud Computing and the Economy," *CNET News,* http://news.cnet.com, accessed March 9, 2012; Margaret Steen, "Cloud Services and SaaS: A Smarter Way to Do Business," *Cisco News,* http:// newsroom.cisco.com, accessed March 9, 2012; Stuart Young, Andy Taylor, and James Macaulay, "Small Businesses Ride the Cloud: SMB Cloud Watch—U.S. Survey Results," Cisco Internet Business Solutions Group, http://www.cisco.com, accessed March 9, 2012; Mike Kirkwood, "Rulers of the Cloud: Will Cloud Computing Be the Second Coming of Cisco?" *ReadWriteWe,* http://www.readwriteweb.com, accessed March 9, 2012.

LECTURE ENHANCER:
Can you think of an example of an ASP?

the firm's technology dollar farther and giving smaller companies more competitive information power. Even large companies turn to ASPs to manage some or all of their information systems. Microsoft outsourced much of its internal information technology services to Infosys Technology to save money and streamline, simplify, and support its services. "Think Microsoft Dynamics. Think Infosys," says the Infosys Web site about the partnership.[16]

Companies that decide to use ASPs should check the backgrounds and references of these firms before hiring them to manage critical systems. In addition, customers should try to ensure that the service provider has strong security measures to block computer hackers or other unauthorized access to the data, that its data centers are running reliably, and that adequate data and applications backups are maintained.

On-Demand, Cloud, and Grid Computing

on-demand computing firms essentially rent the software time from application providers and pay only for their usage of the software.

Another recent trend is **on-demand computing**, also called *utility computing*. Instead of purchasing and maintaining expensive software, firms essentially rent the software time from application providers and pay only for their usage of the software, similar to purchasing electricity from a utility. On-demand computing is particularly useful for firms that experience annual peaks in demand or seasonal spikes in customer usage of their applications. By renting the service they need only when they need it, they can avoid buying the software that is not routinely required. On-demand computing can also help companies remain current with the most efficient software on the market without purchasing huge upgrades.

cloud computing powerful servers store applications software and databases for users to access the software and databases via the Web using anything from a PC to a smart phone.

Cloud computing uses powerful servers to store applications software and databases. Users access the software and databases via the Web using anything from a PC to a smart phone. The software as a service (SaaS) movement is an example of cloud computing. The "Hit & Miss" feature describes how Cisco Systems provides security for cloud-based applications.

Small and medium-sized companies occasionally find themselves with jobs that require more computing power than their current systems offer. A cost-effective solution for these firms may be something called **grid computing**, which consists of a network of smaller computers running special software. The software breaks down a large, complex job into smaller tasks and then distributes them to the networked computers. The software then reassembles the individual task results into the finished job. By combining multiple small computers, grid computing creates a virtual mainframe or even a supercomputer.

grid computing consists of a network of smaller computers running special software.

Assessment Check ☑

1. What is an application service provider?

2. Explain on-demand computing.

What's Ahead

This is the first of two chapters devoted to managing technology and information. The next chapter, "Understanding Accounting and Financial Statements," focuses on accounting, financial information, and financing reporting. Accounting is the process of measuring, interpreting, and communicating financial information to enable people inside and outside the firm to make informed decisions. The chapter describes the functions of accounting and role of accountants; the steps in the accounting cycle; the types, functions, and components of financial statements; and the role of budgets in an organization.

Summary of Learning Objectives

1 **Distinguish between data and information and discuss information systems.**

It is important for businesspeople to know the difference between data and information. Data are raw facts and figures that may or may not be relevant to a business decision. Information is knowledge gained from processing those facts and figures. An information system is an organized method for collecting, storing, and communicating past, present, and projected information on internal operations and external intelligence. Most information systems today use computer and telecommunications technology.

Assessment Check Answers ☑

1.1 Distinguish between data and information. Data consist of raw facts and figures that may or may not be relevant to a decision. Information is the knowledge gained from processing data.

1.2 What is an information system? An information system is an organized method for collecting, storing, and communicating past, present, and projected information on internal operations and external intelligence.

2 **List the components and types of information systems.**

When people think about information systems today, they're generally thinking about computer-based systems, those that

rely on computers and related technologies. Computer-based information systems rely on four components: computer hardware, software, telecommunications and computer networks, and data resource management. The heart of an information system is its database, a centralized integrated collection of data resources. Information systems fall into two broad categories: operational support systems and management support systems. Operational support systems are designed to produce a variety of information for users. Examples include transaction processing systems and process control systems. Management support systems are those designed to support effective decision making. They include management information systems, decision support systems, executive support systems, and expert systems.

Assessment Check Answers ☑

2.1 List the four components of a computer-based information system. The four components of a computer-based information system are computer hardware, software, telecommunications and computer networks, and data resource management.

2.2 What is a database? A database is a centralized, integrated collection of data resources.

2.3 What are the two general types of information systems? Give examples of each. The two categories of information systems are operational support systems (such as transactions processing and process control systems) and management support systems (such as management information, decision support, executive support, and expert systems).

3 Discuss computer hardware and software.

Hardware consists of all tangible elements of a computer system, including input and output devices. Major categories of computers include mainframes, supercomputers, midrange systems, personal computers (PCs), and hand-held devices. Computer software provides the instructions that tell the hardware what to do. The software that controls the basic workings of the computer is its operating system. Other programs, called application software, perform specific tasks that users want to complete.

Assessment Check Answers

3.1 List two input and output devices. Input devices include the keyboard and mouse. Output devices include the monitor and printer.

3.2 What accounts for the increasing popularity of notebook computers? Notebook computers account for more than half of all new personal computers sold. Their increased popularity is due to better displays, lower prices, more rugged designs, increasing computing power, and slimmer designs.

3.3 What is software? List the two categories of software. Computer software provides the instructions that tell the hardware what to do. The software that controls the basic workings of the computer is its operating system. Other programs, called application software, perform specific tasks that users want to complete.

4 Describe computer networks.

Local area networks connect computers within a limited area. Wide area networks tie together larger geographical regions by using telephone lines, microwave, or satellite transmission. A wireless network allows computers to communicate through radio waves. Intranets allow employees to share information on a ready-made company network. Access to an intranet is restricted to authorized users and is protected by a firewall. Virtual private networks (VPNs) provide a secure Internet connection between two or more points. VoIP—voice over Internet protocol—uses a personal computer running special software and a broadband Internet connection to make and receive telephone calls over the Internet rather than over traditional telephone networks.

Assessment Check Answers

4.1 What is a LAN? A local area network (LAN) is a computer network that connects machines within a limited area, such as a building or several nearby buildings.

4.2 What are the differences between an intranet and a VPN? An intranet is a computer network patterned after the Internet. Unlike the Internet, access to an intranet is limited to employees and other authorized users. A virtual private network (VPN) is a way of gaining increased security for Internet connections.

4.3 Briefly explain how VoIP works. The VoIP phone is connected to a personal computer with any type of broadband connection. Special software transmits phone conversations over the Internet. A VoIP user can make and receive calls to and from those with traditional telephone connections (either landline or wireless).

5 Discuss the security and ethical issues affecting information systems.

Numerous security and ethical issues affect information systems. Two of the main security threats are e-crime and malware. E-crimes range from hacking—unauthorized penetration of an information system—to the theft of hardware. Malware is any malicious software program designed to infect computer systems. Examples include viruses, worms, botnets, Trojan horses, and spyware. Ethical issues affecting information systems include the proper use of the systems by authorized users. Organizations also have an obligation to employees, vendors, and customers to protect the security and confidentiality of the data stored in information systems.

Assessment Check Answers

5.1 Explain computer hacking. Computer hacking is a breach of a computer system by unauthorized people. Sometimes the hackers' motive is just to see if they can get in. Other times, hackers have more sinister motives, including stealing or altering data.

5.2 What is malware? Malware is any malicious software program designed to infect computer systems.

5.3 How does a computer virus work? A virus is a program that secretly attaches itself to another program (called a host). The virus then changes the host, destroys data, or even makes the computer system inoperable.

6 Explain disaster recovery and backup.

Information system disasters, whether human caused or due to natural causes, can cost businesses billions of dollars. The consequences of a disaster can be minimized by routinely backing up software and data, both at an organizational level and at an individual level. Organizations should back up critical data at an off-site location. Some firms may also want to invest in extra hardware and software sites, which can be accessed during emergencies.

Assessment Check Answers

6.1 What are the types of disasters to which information systems are vulnerable? Natural disasters, power failures, equipment malfunctions, software glitches, human error, and even terrorist attacks can disrupt even the most powerful, sophisticated computer information systems.

6.2 List the tasks regarding off-site data storage. The five tasks are planning and deciding which data to back up, establishing and following a backup schedule, protecting data when they are transmitted off site, choosing the right vendor, and continually testing and refining the backup system.

⌐7⌐ **Review information systems trends.**

Information systems are continually and rapidly evolving. Some of the most significant trends are the increasing demands of the distributed workforce, the increased use of application service providers, on-demand computing, and grid computing. Many people now work in virtual offices, including at home. Information technology makes this possible. Application service providers allow organizations to outsource most of their IT functions. Rather than buying

and maintaining expensive software, on-demand computing offers users the option of renting software time from outside vendors and paying only for their usage. Grid computing consists of a network of smaller computers running special software creating a virtual mainframe or even supercomputer.

Assessment Check Answers ✔

7.1 What is an application service provider? An application service provider (ASP) is an outside vendor that provides both the computers and application support for managing an information system. By using an ASP, the organization effectively outsources some, or all, of its IT function.

7.2 Explain on-demand computing. Instead of purchasing and maintaining expensive software, some organizations use on-demand computing. In this arrangement, software is rented from a vendor and the organization only pays for its actual usage.

■ Business Terms You Need to Know

data 430	decision support system (DSS) 434	malware 441
information 430	executive support system (ESS) 434	viruses 441
information system 430	expert system 434	worm 442
chief information officer (CIO) 430	hardware 434	botnet 442
computer-based information systems 431	server 435	Trojan horse 442
	software 436	spyware 442
database 432	local area networks (LANs) 438	application service provider (ASP) 445
operational support systems 432	wide area networks (WAN) 438	on-demand computing 446
transaction processing systems 433	WiFi 438	cloud computing 446
process control systems 433	intranet 438	grid computing 447
management support systems 434	firewall 439	
management information system (MIS) 434	virtual private networks (VPNs) 439	
	VoIP 440	

■ Review Questions

1. Distinguish between data and information. Why is the distinction important to businesspeople in their management of information?

2. What are the four components of an information system?

3. Describe the two different types of information systems, and give an example of how each might help a particular business.

4. Explain decision support systems, executive support systems, and expert systems.

5. What are the major categories of computers? What is a smart phone?

6. What is an intranet? Give specific examples of benefits for firms that set up their own intranets.

7. What steps can organizations and individuals take to prevent computer crime?

8. How does a computer virus work? What can individuals and organizational computer users do to reduce the likelihood of acquiring a computer virus?

9. Why is disaster recovery important for businesses? Relate your answer to a natural disaster such as a hurricane, tornado, or fire.

10. Describe four information system trends.

Projects and Teamwork Applications

1. Suppose you've been hired to design an information system for a midsized retailer. Describe what that information system might look like, including the necessary components. Would the system be an operational support system, a management support system, or both?

2. Select a local company and contact the person in charge of its information system for a brief interview. Ask that individual to outline his or her company's information system. Also, ask the person what he or she likes most about the job. Did this interview make you more or less interested in a career in information systems?

3. Working with a partner, research the current status of Wi-Max. Prepare a short report on its growth, its current uses, and its future for business computing.

4. Your supervisor has asked your advice. She isn't sure the company's information system needs any elaborate safeguards because the company has little Web presence beyond a simple home page. However, employees use e-mail extensively to contact suppliers and customers. Make a list of the threats to which the company's information system is vulnerable. What types of safeguards would you suggest?

5. Has your computer ever been hacked or attacked by a virus? What steps did you take to recover lost files and data? How would you prevent something similar from happening again?

Web Assignments

1. **Enterprise resource planning (ERP).** SAP is one of the world's largest enterprise resource planning software companies. Go to the firm's Web site (http://www.sap .com) and click on "Customer Testimonials." Choose one of the customers listed and read its testimonial. Prepare a brief summary and explain how this exercise improved your understanding of the business applications of ERP software.

2. **Computer security.** Visit the Web site listed below. Review the material and answer the following questions:

   a. What are two current malware threats? How serious are they?

   b. What is a potentially unwanted program (PUP)? What are two recent PUPs?

   http://www.mcafee.com/us/threat center/default.asp

3. **Cloud computing.** IBM is one of the largest providers of so-called cloud computing. Visit the IBM Web site (http:// www.ibm.com) and click on "solutions" and then "cloud computing." Print out the material and bring it to class to participate in a class discussion on the subject.

Note: Internet Web addresses change frequently. If you don't find the exact sites listed, you may need to access the organization's home page and search from there or use a search engine such as Bing or Google.

CASE 14.1 **MICROS Systems Works on a Large Scale**

Major venues like resorts or sports stadiums have larger technology requirements than smaller businesses. They must be able to provide a safe and secure environment for events involving thousands, or even tens of thousands, of guests or fans. They need to keep track of reservations or ticket sales and ensure well-stocked dining facilities or concession stands. Certain companies have made a specialty of meeting the information-technology needs of such immense venues.

Maryland-based MICROS Systems develops information technology systems for the hospitality industry. With ninety distributors in fifth countries, MICROS provides hardware and software solutions for more than 335,000 restaurants, hotels, and retailers worldwide. One MICROS client, the four-star M Resort Spa Casino in Las Vegas, has almost 400 hotel rooms and suites, a 92,000-square-foot casino, nine restaurants and five bars, meeting and conference space, a full spa, and a large plaza for special events. MICROS installed a single-system with 120 point-of-sale workstations that linked the restaurants, bars, wine cellar, room service, and many other services. The system's hosted environment has lower emissions and electricity use. MICROS's disaster recovery helps the resort come back online from outages in less time and using fewer resources. As it plans a large retail center and a fourteen-screen movie complex, the resort will rely on MICROS's scalable technology.

For the Atlantis, Paradise Island resort in the Bahamas, MICROS created a cashless environment. Guests receive a magnetic-striped key card at check-in, which they can use for purchases throughout the resort. New Jersey's MetLife Stadium (formerly known as the Meadowlands) seats 82,500 and is a showcase for the New York Giants and New York Jets football teams, as well as for big-name concerts, college football, and international soccer. MICROS Systems hardware and software meets the stadium's large-scale requirements, with

workstations, terminals, and hand-held devices. The system manages the stadium's inventory and purchasing, luxury suites, catering, and dining facilities. Customer-relations software tracks sales, recognizes season-ticket holders and other core clientele, and cultivates new customers.

Questions for Critical Thinking

1. Visit the MICROS Systems Web site to learn more about its products for the global market. In what ways do you think the company can increase sales in Africa, Asia, and Latin America? How might the company have to adapt to conditions in these countries?
2. Imagine you are the manager of a sports arena. What sorts of hardware and software would help you manage such a large facility?

Sources: Company Web site, http://www.micros.com, accessed March 9, 2012; Diane Snyder, "At Atlantis, Cashless = Control," http://www.micros.com, accessed March 9, 2012; "The Revolutionary New Meadowlands Stadium to Open with MICROS," press release, http://www.micros.com, accessed March 9, 2012; "MICROS Systems, Inc. Announces Deployment of MICROS 9700 HMS at M Resort Spa Casino in Las Vegas," press release, http://www.prnewswire.com, accessed March 9, 2012.

Skype Enters a New Era

CASE 14.2

On any given Sunday morning, about 30 million people log onto Skype and begin using its free VoIP (voice over Internet protocol) service. About half a million of those users are making video phone calls with family and friends despite being in different cities.

Skype, which Microsoft recently purchased from eBay for $8.5 billion, popularized the use of the computer as a phone and still offers its basic service and software for free. About 145 million users sign on to the system at least monthly, and almost 9 million pay for premium services that allow them to call mobile phones and landlines and also to do videoconferencing, an option business customers find attractive.

Microsoft, headquartered in Redmond, Washington, plans to allow the Silicon Valley company to operate independently, but it has big plans for integrating Skype's services with its popular online gaming system, Xbox

Live, allowing its 50 million members to video chat while gaming.

Questions for Critical Thinking

1. Microsoft is considering charging business users for some Skype services. Do you think this is a good strategy? Why or why not?
2. What might be motivating Microsoft to let Skype operate independently?

Sources: Julie Scelfo, "Video Chat Reshapes Domestic Rituals," *The New York Times,* http://www.nytimes.com, accessed March 9, 2012; Trefis Team, "Microsoft Preps to Get Paid for Skype, Stock Worth $32," *Forbes,* December 21, 2011, http://www.forbes.com; Bill Rigby, "Analysis: Microsoft Works Out How to Play Skype," Reuters.com, October 28, 2011, http://www.reuters.com; Robert Hof, "Steve Ballmer: Skype Is Microsoft's Big Social Play," *Forbes,* October 18, 2011, www.forbes.com.

Zipcar: Technology Fuels Its Business

When you need a car, you want one. When you don't need a car, you don't want to be bothered with the hassle or the expense. That's what makes Zipcar so great. Zipcar is a car-sharing network based in Cambridge, Massachusetts, that operates in urban and metropolitan areas and on university campuses around the United States, Canada, and the United Kingdom. Currently, Zipcar serves more than 200 colleges and universities, and the number is growing steadily. "The service provides a new level of freedom for students, faculty, and staff," says Matthew Malloy, vice president of international university operations for Zipcar. "Members can use Zipcars to run errands, attend meetings, or get away for the weekend on a pay-as-you-go basis. You no longer need to own to be free."

Once members sign up for the program, they receive a Zipcard that gives them access to any Zipcar parked around campus (or around town). The annual fee for the service is $35, and it includes fuel, insurance, and 180 travel miles per day. A member who wants to use a Zipcar simply goes online to reserve it, then picks up the designated car at the reserved time. "It's easy," says Erin Badger, a senior marketing student at the University of New Hampshire, where the Zipcar program is now in full swing. "You swipe your Zipcard [over a sensor] on the windshield and it unlocks the car. You get in, turn the key, and go." Each Zipcar comes equipped with an individually numbered Zipcard gas card that the driver uses to fill the tank with fuel. So members—especially budget-conscious students—don't need cash or their own credit cards when the gas gauge runs low. Members are asked to return each car with at least one-quarter of a tank of gas in it, so no one picks up a car with an empty tank.

Technology plays a huge role in the success of the Zipcar system. "When you think about the member experience, what makes it a seamless and enjoyable experience for the consumer is the technology infrastructure," observes Rob Weisberg, chief marketing officer at Zipcar. When marketing and setting up the system at colleges and universities, Zipcar looks at how students use cars on campus, asking such questions as: Are there places on campus where use is more frequent, or do students want hybrids? "Any time you understand your consumers better, you are able to cater to them more effectively," says Weisberg. He notes that Zipcar puts a lot of effort into understanding

demographic and psychographic (lifestyle) trends on and around a campus.

Badger likes the fact that she can use her iPhone app to reserve a Zipcar or extend the reservation if she is driving a car and isn't ready to return it. "The iPhone app relates to the student age group," she says. "They care about us." The Zipcar app was named to *Time* magazine's annual list of "Best Travel Gadgets" in one recent issue. "Beyond helping you manage reservations, find nearby pickup locations and browse car models available, the app offers clever capabilities like remote locking and unlocking and honking your car's horn from your phone when you inevitably forget what it looks like in a crowded lot," praises the *Time* review.

Zipcar is always looking toward the future and ways to better serve its customers. Weisberg predicts that Zipcar technology eventually will allow for customized seat settings and even pre-set radio station settings that automatically click into place when a member reserves a car. Still, Weisberg emphasizes the importance of the personal touch. He recalls that when a student member posted a note on Twitter joking that he loved everything about Zipcar except the fact that there wasn't a package of Skittles waiting for him when he unlocked the car, a Zipcar employee left a package of Skittles on the dashboard the next time the student reserved a car.

"Technology will never replace human interaction," warns Weisberg. "You'd never take the recommendation of a computer over the recommendation of a friend or family member or colleague. So our laser focus on the customer experience and ensuring that it is second to none is really where we need to play. Technology enables that, but it's never going to replace the human touch."

Questions for Critical Thinking

1. Through member surveys and social media postings, Zipcar collects information about members and their lifestyles in order to design the best system for a community. Write ten questions that you think might elicit useful information for Zipcar about students at your own collegiate institution.

2. What kind of data would Zipcar's operational support systems likely collect? What kind of information might they provide?

3. The ZipcariPhone app already takes care of several tasks. If you were a Zipcar member, what new task would you add to the app?

4. Do you think your campus would be a good candidate for the Zipcar system? Why or why not? If your college or university already has Zipcar, are you a member? Why or why not?

Sources: Zipcar Web site, http://www.zipcar.com, accessed March 9, 2012; "Zipcar and SCVNGR, East Cambridge Neighbors, Partner on New Rewards Program," *Boston.com,* http://www.boston.com, accessed March 9, 2012; "Zipcar, Inc.," *Bloomberg Businessweek,* http://investing.businessweek.com, accessed March 9, 2012; University of New Hampshire Transportation Services, http://www.unh.edu/transportation, accessed March 9, 2012; Peter Ha, "The Best Travel Gadgets of 2009," *Time,* http://www.time.com, accessed March 9, 2012.

KANSAS

GREENSBURG, KS
The Dog Ate My Laptop

The night of the tornado, Superintendent of Schools Darin Headrick heard the storm sirens go off on his way home from work. He stopped at the home of High School Principal Randy Fulton and the two men headed for the basement, just in case. The next thing they knew, the entire school system was gone. Textbooks were scattered everywhere, computers destroyed.

For the first three months after the storm, no one could live in town. People stayed in shelters or with friends and family outside of town. No one had a home phone anymore, but people were eager to connect with each other and find out what was happening. Although the Federal Emergency Management Agency (FEMA) was distributing information at checkpoints on the edges of town, people had to go to town to get it.

Like 95 percent of the town's 1,500 residents, Headrick himself was homeless. With just four months to rebuild an entire school system, all he had were his laptop and cell phone, so he got into his truck and began searching for a wireless signal. Taking a lesson from his students, he used text messaging to distribute information. Although very few people still had computers, almost everyone had a cell phone. Residents who subscribed to the text service could receive updates and instant messages over the phone, wherever they were.

Rebuilding the schools was a bigger task. Headrick secured temporary trailers for grades K–12 and received generous donations of desks and school supplies. By August 15,

he had the basics needed to start the school year, but he still lacked textbooks. Technology would have to fill in the gaps so the students wouldn't fall behind.

One of the school system's existing programs was ITV, for Interactive Distance Learning Network. ITV allowed Greensburg's rural schools to log in to classrooms around the state via Web cam. This type of real-time distance learning is referred to as *synchronous learning*, as opposed to the asynchronous online courses given on college campuses. After the tornado, all that was needed to get the program up and running again were a computer, an Internet connection, and a Web cam.

Early in the winter each of Greensburg High's students got an unexpected gift: a laptop computer containing e-books, handwriting recognition software, and a tablet screen for note taking. The new laptops replaced their tattered textbooks. Students would hand in their assignments via e-mail and receive feedback from their teachers via instant messaging.

Questions

After viewing the video, answer the following questions:

1. Was Greensburg Public Schools' investment in technology a smart move?

2. Would you consider enrolling in an asynchronous online course? What might be the benefits and drawbacks?

3. Do you think hand-held devices and text messaging improve productivity and communication or distract their users?

LAUNCHING YOUR
[Information Technology Career]

Part 5, "Managing Technology and Information," includes Chapter 14, which discusses using computers and related technology to manage information. In Chapter 14, we discussed well-known technology companies such as Google as well as smaller organizations that use computer technology to manage information. These examples illustrate that all organizations need to manage technology and information. And with the complexity and scope of technology and information likely to increase in the years ahead, the demand for information systems professionals is expected to grow.

According to the U.S. Department of Labor, employment in such information technology occupations as computer systems design, the manufacture of computers, electronic components and peripheral equipment, and information services is expected to grow faster than the average for all occupations in the next decade.[1] In *U.S. News & World Report*'s recent study of occupations, software developer, database administrator, Web developer, computer systems analyst, and computer programmer all made the magazine's "Best 25 Jobs" list, based on salary, projected growth, and job satisfaction.[2]

What types of jobs are available in information systems? What are the working conditions like? What are the career paths? Information technology is a fairly broad occupation

and encompasses a wide variety of jobs. In some cases you'll work in the IT department of a business such as Procter & Gamble or Shell. In other cases, you'll work for a specialized information systems firm, such as PricewaterhouseCoopers or IBM, which provides the services to governments, not-for-profit organizations, and businesses.

Information technology and information systems are popular business majors, and many entry-level positions are available each year. Many IT graduates spend their entire careers in the field, while others move into other areas. People who began their careers in information systems are well represented in the ranks of senior management today. Let's look briefly at some of the specific jobs you might find after earning an IT degree.

Technical support specialists are troubleshooters who monitor the performance of computer systems; provide technical support and solve problems for computer users; install, modify, clean, and repair computer hardware and software; and write training manuals and train computer users.

Network administrators design, install, and support an organization's computer networks, including its local area network, wide area network, Internet, and intranet systems. They provide administrative support for software and hardware users and

ensure that the design of an organization's computer networks and all of the components fit together efficiently and effectively.

Computer security specialists plan, coordinate, and implement an organization's information security. They educate users about how to protect computer systems, install antivirus and similar software, and monitor the networks for security breaches. In recent years, the role and importance of computer security specialists have increased in response to the growing number of attacks on networks and data.

Career Assessment Exercises in Information Systems

1. Assume you're interested in a career as a systems administrator. Go to http://www.usenix.org and click on the "Jobs" tab. Prepare a brief report outlining the responsibilities of a systems administrator, who hires for these positions, and what kind of educational background you need to become one.

2. Identify a person working in your local area in information technology and arrange an interview with that person (your college career center may be able to help you). Ask that person about his or her job responsibilities, educational background, and the best and worst aspects of his or her job.

Learning Objectives

[1] Discuss the users of accounting information.

[2] Describe accounting professionals.

[3] Identify the foundation of the accounting system.

[4] Outline the steps in the accounting cycle.

[5] Explain financial statements.

[6] Discuss financial ratio analysis.

[7] Describe the role of budgeting.

[8] Outline international accounting practices.

Chapter 15

Understanding Accounting and Financial Statements

©NuStock/iStockphoto

BKD LLP: A 21st Century Accounting Firm

BKD LLP, one of the top ten U.S. CPA and advisory firms, takes its commitment to its clients and its community seriously. The 90-year-old firm, headquartered in Springfield, Missouri, earns more than $400 million a year serving businesses and individuals in 30 offices in the South and Southwest.

BKD provides a wide range of accounting and audit services. It helps its corporate clients with mergers and acquisitions, sales, risk management, employee benefit plans, management buyouts, IPOs, and other financing operations. It advises individual clients on wealth planning, investments, and estate planning, and it also operates the BKD Foundation, a non-profit arm offering volunteer hours and millions in financial support to charitable organizations in local communities from Arkansas to Texas. According to the firm's Web site, "Accounting for numbers—accurately, objectively and with integrity—is at the heart of our business. But we are also professional, prepared, attentive, and ready to deliver our services with PRIDE: passion, respect, integrity, discipline and excellence." Each year one of BKD's partners and one employee receive the annual PRIDE award after being nominated by their peers.

As a member of Praxity, a global alliance of independent firms, BKD can also serve multinational customers. It is at the forefront of business technology, too. It recently launched an Android app version of the Web site for its health care consulting practice, making it easier for health practitioners to contact about 200 experts listed on the site.

BKD also makes time for social responsibility issues. Recent winner of a corporate citizenship award, the firm has "really taken corporate sponsorship to a new level," says the president of the Envision Foundation, an international non-profit group that, among other goals, helps thousands of blind and vision-impaired children. BKD recently made a substantial gift to Envision and also sponsors its pediatric services each year.[1]

Overview

Accounting professionals prepare the financial information that organizations present in their annual reports. Whether you begin your career by working for a company or by starting your own firm, you need to understand what accountants do and why their work is so important in contemporary business.

Accounting is the process of measuring, interpreting, and communicating financial information to enable people inside and outside the firm to make informed decisions. In many ways, accounting is the language of business. Accountants gather, record, report, and interpret financial information in a way that describes the status and operation of an organization and aids in decision making.

Millions of men and women throughout the world describe their occupation as an accountant. In the United States alone, more than 1.2 million people work as accountants. According to the Bureau of Labor Statistics, the number of accounting-related jobs is expected to increase by around 16 percent between now and 2020.[2] The availability of jobs and relatively high starting salaries for talented graduates have made accounting one of the most in-demand majors on college campuses. After the recent recession, hiring levels fell, but the most recent report estimates that firms will hire more accounting graduates in the near future.[3]

This chapter begins by describing who uses accounting information. It discusses business activities involving accounting statements: financing, investing, and operations. It explains the accounting process, defines double-entry bookkeeping, and presents the accounting equation. We then discuss the development of financial statements from information about financial transactions, the methods of interpreting these statements, and the roles of budgeting in planning and controlling a business. The chapter concludes with a discussion of the development and implementation schedule of a uniform set of accounting rules for global business.

accounting process of measuring, interpreting, and communicating financial information to enable people inside and outside the firm to make informed decisions.

Users of Accounting Information

FIGURE 15.1 Users of Accounting Information

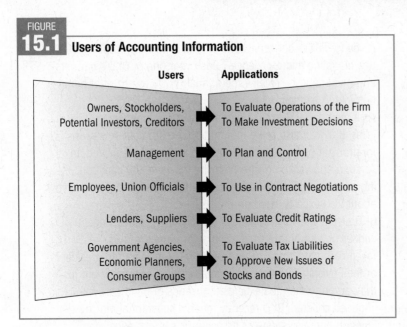

Users		Applications
Owners, Stockholders, Potential Investors, Creditors	➤	To Evaluate Operations of the Firm To Make Investment Decisions
Management	➤	To Plan and Control
Employees, Union Officials	➤	To Use in Contract Negotiations
Lenders, Suppliers	➤	To Evaluate Credit Ratings
Government Agencies, Economic Planners, Consumer Groups	➤	To Evaluate Tax Liabilities To Approve New Issues of Stocks and Bonds

LECTURE ENHANCER:
Why would accounting information be useful to a union in its negotiations?

LECTURE ENHANCER:
How might managers use accounting information to help control daily operations?

LECTURE ENHANCER:
What are some possible drawbacks to practicing open book management?

People both inside and outside an organization rely on accounting information to help them make business decisions. Figure 15.1 lists the users of accounting information and the applications they find for that information. Firms such as Deloitte Consulting provide such information and help their customers make the best use of it.

Managers with a business, government agency, or not-for-profit organization are the major users of accounting information, because it helps them plan and control daily and long-range operations. Business owners and boards of directors of not-for-profit groups also rely on accounting data to determine how well managers are operating the organizations. Union officials use accounting data in contract negotiations, and employees refer to it as they monitor their firms' productivity and profitability performance.

To help employees understand how their work affects the bottom line, many companies share sensitive financial information with their employees and teach them how to understand and use financial statements. Proponents of what is often referred to as *open book management* believe that allowing employees to view financial information helps them better understand how their work contributes to the company's success, which, in turn, benefits them.

Outside a firm, potential investors evaluate accounting information to help them decide whether to buy a firm's stock. As we'll discuss in more detail later in the chapter, any company whose stock is traded publicly is required to report its financial results on a regular basis. So anyone, for example, can find out what Costco's sales were last year or how much money Intel made during the last quarter. Bankers and other lenders use accounting information to evaluate a potential borrower's financial soundness. The Internal Revenue Service (IRS) and state tax officials use it to determine a company's tax liability. Citizens' groups and government agencies use such information in assessing the efficiency of operations such as Massachusetts General Hospital; the Topeka, Kansas, school system; Community College of Denver; and the Art Institute of Chicago.

Accountants play fundamental roles not only in business but also in other aspects of society. Their work influences each of the business environments discussed earlier in this book. They clearly contribute important information to help managers deal with the competitive and economic environments.

Less obvious contributions help others understand, predict, and react to the technological, regulatory, and social and cultural environments. For instance, thousands of people volunteer each year to help people with their taxes.

Sawayasu Tsuji/iStockphoto

Accountants play a key role in organizations by providing services to businesses, individuals, government agencies, and not-for-profit organizations.

One of the largest organized programs is Tax-Aide, sponsored by AARP (formally known as the American Association of Retired Persons). For more than 40 years this volunteer program has assisted about 50 million low- and middle-income Americans—especially people 60 and older—with their income tax preparation.[4]

Business Activities Involving Accounting

The natural progression of a business begins with financing. Subsequent steps, including investing, lead to operating the business. All organizations, profit oriented and not-for-profit, perform these three basic activities, and accounting plays a key role in each one:

1. Financing activities provide necessary funds to start a business and expand it after it begins operating.

2. Investing activities provide valuable assets required to run a business.

3. Operating activities focus on selling goods and services, but they also consider expenses as important elements of sound financial management.

Assessment Check ☑

1. Define *accounting*.
2. Who uses accounting information?
3. What are the three business activities that involve accounting?

Accounting Professionals

Accounting professionals work in a variety of areas in and for business firms, government agencies, and not-for-profit organizations. They can be classified as public, management, government, and not-for-profit accountants.

Public Accountants

A **public accountant** provides accounting services to individuals or business firms for a fee. Most public accounting firms provide three basic services to clients: (1) auditing, or examining, financial records; (2) tax preparation, planning, and related services; and (3) management consulting. Because public accountants are not employees of a client firm, they can provide unbiased advice about the firm's financial condition.

Although there are hundreds of public accounting firms in the United States, a handful of firms dominate the industry. The four largest public accounting firms—Deloitte & Touche, PricewaterhouseCoopers (PwC), Ernst & Young, and KPMG—collect well over $36 billion annually from U.S. clients alone. In contrast, the Minneapolis-based McGladrey & Pullen, the nation's fifth-largest accounting firm, has annual revenues of approximately $1.4 billion.[5]

One challenge these firms face is attracting and hiring the best talent. Ernst & Young recently adopted a new approach to reaching accounting students as well as new grads: inviting them to meet on Facebook. "We want to find the best and brightest, for internships and for full-time jobs," says Dan Black, director of the firm's campus recruiting effort. E&Y also reaches out to students via LinkedIn and Twitter. "This is just another way for people to meet us and learn about us and what we do," explains Black.[6]

Some years ago, public accounting firms came under sharp criticism for providing management consulting services to many of the same firms they audited. Critics argued

public accountant accountant who provides accounting services to individuals or business firms for a fee.

Hit & Miss

Forensic Accountants: Fraud Busters

When most people think of accountants, they usually don't think of crime fighters. But the rapidly growing field of forensic accounting involves investigating such white-collar crimes as business fraud, improper financial reporting, and illegal investment schemes.

Forensic accounting is accounting performed in preparation for legal review. Forensic accountants investigate below the surface of an organization's accounting system to find out what actually happened. They also testify as expert witnesses if a case goes to trial. The job requires a bachelor's degree in accounting and CPA certification, with further training in investigative techniques for certification as a certified fraud examiner (CFE) or a certified forensic accountant (CrFA).

When the energy giant Enron Corporation collapsed, forensic accounting investigations revealed that for several years the firm had issued false financial statements that exaggerated the company's earnings and thereby increased the firm's stock prices. The statements painted a rosy picture of steady profits that met earnings expectations. In reality, Enron's own investments were doing badly. As for profits, the company was actually losing money. Even after the truth leaked out and the company's stock prices tumbled, top management kept issuing false financial statements, hoping to slow the fall. In a federal trial, two former executives were convicted of conspiracy, wire fraud, and securities fraud.

Annual national conferences focus on issues faced by forensic accountants. RGL Forensics recently posted 10 percent growth during one year and was named the fastest-growing U.S. forensic accounting firm. "Growth in accounting is dependent on changing with the market," notes RGL Forensics CFO Angie McPhee.

Questions for Critical Thinking

1. Describe how a shift in the economy has created a new career path for accounting students.

2. How might forensic accounting change the world of business?

Sources: "Marking a 10-Percent Growth, Forensic Accounting Firm Named Fastest Growing in U.S.," *PRNewswire*, http://www.prnewswire.com, accessed April 3, 2012; Caleb Newquist, "What Are Your Questions for a Forensic Accounting Partner?" *Going Concern*, http://goingconcern.com, accessed April 3, 2012; "Risk Management," PricewaterhouseCoopers New Zealand, http://www.pwc.com/nz, accessed April 3, 2012; Tracy L. Coenen, "Enron: The Good, the Bad, and the Ugly," *Wisconsin Law Journal*, http://wislawjournal.com, accessed April 3, 2012; James A. DiGabriele, "Applying Forensic Skepticism to Lost Profits Valuations," *Journal of Accountancy*, http://www.journalofaccountancy.com, accessed April 3, 2012; Rick Romell, "Accountants Who Focus on Fraud," *Milwaukee Journal Sentinel*, http://www.sequenceinc.com, accessed April 3, 2012.

---

that when a public accounting firm does both—auditing and management consulting—an inherent conflict of interest is created. In addition, this conflict of interest may undermine confidence in the quality of the financial statements that accounting firms audit. The bankruptcies of some high-profile firms increased pressure on public accounting firms to end this practice. Legislation also established strict limits on the types of consulting services auditors can provide. For example, an accounting firm that audits a company's books cannot provide any other services to that company, including tax services. As a result, three of the four largest public accounting firms either sold large portions of their consulting practices or spun them off into separate companies, and they now concentrate on providing auditing and tax services. PwC, for instance, sold much of its consulting business to IBM.

As the "Hit & Miss" feature outlines, a growing number of public accountants are also certified as *forensic accountants*, and some smaller public accounting firms actually specialize in forensic accounting. These professionals, and the firms that employ them, focus on uncovering potential fraud in a variety of organizations.

Certified public accountants (CPAs) demonstrate their accounting knowledge by meeting state requirements for education and experience and successfully completing a number of rigorous tests in accounting theory and practice, auditing, law, and taxes. Other accountants who meet specified educational and experience requirements and pass certification exams carry the title *certified management accountant, certified fraud examiner,* or *certified internal auditor*.

LECTURE ENHANCER:
What situation could result when an accounting firm also provides consulting services to a client?

LECTURE ENHANCER:
In what way might providing consulting services affect the auditing services of a public accounting firm?

LECTURE ENHANCER:
Compare and contrast the role of a management accountant with that of a public accountant.

Management Accountants

An accountant employed by a business other than a public accounting firm is called a *management accountant*. Such a person collects and records financial transactions and prepares financial statements used by the firm's managers in decision making. Management accountants provide timely, relevant, accurate, and concise information that executives can use to operate their firms more effectively and more profitably than they could without this input. In addition to preparing financial statements, a management accountant plays a major role in interpreting them. A management accountant should provide answers to many important questions:

- Where is the company going?

- What opportunities await it?

- Do certain situations expose the company to excessive risk?

- Does the firm's information system provide detailed and timely information to all levels of management?

Management accountants frequently specialize in different aspects of accounting. A cost accountant, for example, determines the cost of goods and services and helps set their prices. An internal auditor examines the firm's financial practices to ensure that its records include accurate data and that its operations comply with federal, state, and local laws and regulations. A tax accountant works to minimize a firm's tax bill and assumes responsibility for its federal, state, county, and city tax returns. Some management accountants achieve a *certified management accountant (CMA)* designation through experience and passing a comprehensive examination.

Management accountants are usually involved in the development and enforcement of organizational policies on such items as employee travel. As part of their job, many employees travel and accumulate airline frequent flyer miles and hotel reward points. Although some organizations have strict policies over the personal use of travel perks, many do not.

Changing federal regulations affecting accounting and public reporting have increased the demand for management accountants in recent years. As a result, salaries for these professionals are rising.

CLASS ACTIVITY:
Discuss how students could pursue a career in cost accounting, including the types of courses they might take to acquire needed skills.

Government and Not-for-Profit Accountants

Federal, state, and local governments also require accounting services. Government accountants and those who work for not-for-profit organizations perform professional services similar to those of management accountants. Accountants in these sectors concern themselves primarily with determining how efficiently the organizations accomplish their objectives. Among the many government agencies that employ accountants are the National Aeronautics and Space Administration, the Federal Bureau of Investigation, the Internal Revenue Service, the Commonwealth of Pennsylvania, and the City of Fresno, California. The federal government alone employs thousands of accountants.

Not-for-profit organizations, such as churches, labor unions, charities, schools, hospitals, and universities, also hire accountants. In fact, the not-for-profit sector is one of the fastest growing segments of accounting practice. An increasing number of not-for-profits publish financial information because contributors want more accountability from these organizations and are interested in knowing how the groups spend the money that they raise.

LECTURE ENHANCER:
Why might financial information be particularly important to a not-for-profit as opposed to a for-profit firm?

Assessment Check ☑

1. List the three services offered by public accounting firms.

2. What tasks do management accountants perform?

The Foundation of the Accounting System

To provide reliable, consistent, and unbiased information to decision makers, accountants follow guidelines, or standards, known as **generally accepted accounting principles (GAAP)**. These principles encompass the conventions, rules, and procedures for determining acceptable accounting and financial reporting practices at a particular time.

All GAAP standards are based on four basic principles: consistency, relevance, reliability, and comparability. Consistency means that all data should be collected and presented in the same manner across all periods. Any change in the way in which specific data are collected or presented must be noted and explained. Relevance states that all information being reported should be appropriate and assist users in evaluating that information. Reliability implies that the accounting data presented in financial statements are reliable and can be verified by an independent party such as an outside auditor. Finally, comparability ensures that one firm's financial statements can be compared with those of similar businesses.

In the United States, the **Financial Accounting Standards Board (FASB)** is primarily responsible for evaluating, setting, or modifying GAAP. The U.S. Securities and Exchange Commission (SEC), the chief federal regulator of the financial markets and accounting industry, actually has the statutory authority to establish financial accounting and reporting standards for publicly held companies. (A publicly held company is one whose stock is publicly traded in a market such as the New York Stock Exchange.) However, the SEC's policy has been to rely on the accounting industry for this function, as long as the SEC believes the private sector is operating in the public interest. Consequently, the Financial Accounting Foundation—an organization made up of members of many different professional groups—actually appoints the members (currently seven) of the FASB, although the SEC does have some input. Board members are all experienced accounting professionals and serve five-year terms. They may be reappointed for a second five-year term. Board members must sever all connections with the firms they served prior to joining the board. The board is supported by a professional staff of more than 60 individuals.[7]

The FASB carefully monitors changing business conditions, enacting new rules and modifying existing rules when necessary. It also considers input and requests from all segments of its diverse constituency, including corporations and the SEC. One major change in accounting rules recently dealt with executive and employee stock options. Stock options give the holder the right to buy stock at a fixed price. The FASB now requires firms that give employees stock options to calculate the cost of the options and treat the cost as an expense, similar to salaries.

In response to well-known cases of accounting fraud, and questions about the independence of auditors, the Sarbanes-Oxley Act—commonly known as SOX—created the Public Accounting Oversight Board. The five-member board has the power to set audit standards and to investigate and sanction accounting firms that certify the books of publicly traded firms. Members of the Public Accounting Oversight Board are appointed by the SEC. No more than two of the five members of the board can be certified public accountants.

In addition to creating the Public Accounting Oversight Board, SOX also added to the reporting requirements for publicly traded companies. Senior executives including the CEO and chief financial officer (CFO), for example, must personally certify that the financial information reported by the company is correct. As noted earlier, these requirements have increased the demand for accounting professionals, especially managerial accountants. One result of this increased demand has been higher salaries.

It is expensive for firms to adhere to GAAP standards and SOX requirements. Audits, for instance, can cost millions of dollars each year. These expenses can be especially burdensome for small businesses. Consequently, some have proposed modifications to GAAP and SOX for smaller firms, arguing that some accounting rules were really designed for larger companies. Others disagree.

The **Foreign Corrupt Practices Act** is a federal law that prohibits U.S. citizens and companies from bribing foreign officials in order to win or continue business. This law was later extended to make foreign officials subject to penalties if they in any way cause similar corrupt practices to occur within the United States or its territories.

[4] The Accounting Cycle

Accounting deals with financial transactions between a firm and its employees, customers, suppliers, and owners; bankers; and various government agencies. For example, payroll checks result in a cash outflow to compensate employees. A payment to a vendor results in receipt of needed materials for the production process. Cash, check, and credit purchases by customers generate funds to cover the costs of operations and to earn a profit. Prompt payment of bills preserves the firm's credit rating and its future ability to earn a profit. The procedure by which accountants convert data about individual transactions to financial statements is called the **accounting cycle**

Figure 15.2 illustrates the activities involved in the accounting cycle: recording, classifying, and summarizing transactions. Initially, any transaction that has a financial impact on the business, such as wages or payments to suppliers, should be documented. All these transactions are recorded in journals, which list transactions in chronological order. Journal listings are then posted to ledgers. A ledger shows increases or decreases in specific accounts such as cash or wages. Ledgers are used to prepare the financial statements, which summarize financial transactions. Management and other interested parties use the resulting financial statements for a variety of purposes.

Foreign Corrupt Practices Act federal law that prohibits U.S. citizens and companies from bribing foreign officials in order to win or continue business.

Assessment Check ✓

1. Define *GAAP*.
2. What are the four basic requirements to which all accounting rules must adhere?
3. What is the role played by the FASB?

accounting cycle set of activities involved in converting information and individual transactions into financial statements.

LECTURE ENHANCER: Think about your everyday financial transactions. Can you record, classify, and summarize them?

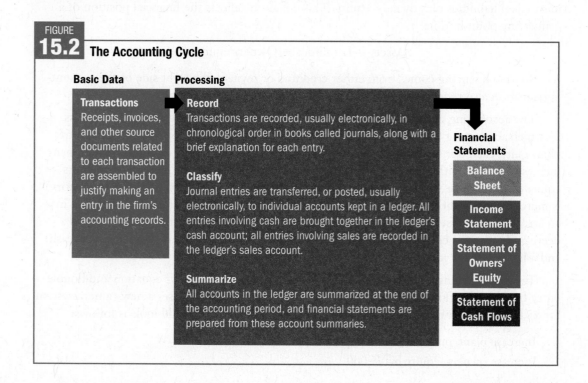

FIGURE 15.2 The Accounting Cycle

Basic Data

Transactions
Receipts, invoices, and other source documents related to each transaction are assembled to justify making an entry in the firm's accounting records.

Processing

Record
Transactions are recorded, usually electronically, in chronological order in books called journals, along with a brief explanation for each entry.

Classify
Journal entries are transferred, or posted, usually electronically, to individual accounts kept in a ledger. All entries involving cash are brought together in the ledger's cash account; all entries involving sales are recorded in the ledger's sales account.

Summarize
All accounts in the ledger are summarized at the end of the accounting period, and financial statements are prepared from these account summaries.

Financial Statements

Balance Sheet

Income Statement

Statement of Owners' Equity

Statement of Cash Flows

The Accounting Equation

Three fundamental terms appear in the accounting equation: assets, liabilities, and owners' equity. An **asset** is anything of value owned or leased by a business. Assets include land, buildings, supplies, cash, accounts receivable (amounts owed to the business as payment for credit sales), and marketable securities.

Although most assets are tangible assets, such as equipment, buildings, and inventories, intangible possessions such as patents and trademarks are often some of a firm's most important assets. This kind of asset is especially essential for many companies, including computer software firms, biotechnology companies, and pharmaceutical companies. For instance, Johnson & Johnson—which has both biotechnology and pharmaceutical operations—reported more than $18 billion in intangible assets (including goodwill) in one recent year, out of a total of almost $114 billion in assets.[8]

Although tangible assets such as buildings, equipment, and inventories may look impressive, they are sometimes less important to a company than intangible assets, such as patents and trademarks.

Nikada/iStockphoto

asset anything of value owned or leased by a business.

liability anything owed to creditors—the claims of a firm's creditors.

owners' equity the owner's initial investment in the business plus profits that were not paid out to owners over time in the form of cash dividends.

accounting equation formula that states that assets must equal liabilities plus owners' equity.

double-entry bookkeeping process by which accounting transactions are recorded; each transaction must have an offsetting transaction.

LECTURE ENHANCER:
What are some additional examples of intangible assets?

Two groups have claims against the assets of a firm: creditors and owners. A **liability** of a business is anything owed to creditors—that is, the claims of a firm's creditors. When a firm borrows money to purchase inventory, land, or machinery, the claims of creditors are shown as accounts payable, notes payable, or long-term debt. Wages and salaries owed to employees also are liabilities (known as *wages payable* or *accrued wages*).

Owners' equity is the owner's initial investment in the business plus profits that were not paid out to owners over time in the form of cash dividends. A strong owners' equity position often is used as evidence of a firm's financial strength and stability.

The **accounting equation** (also referred to as the *accounting identity*) states that assets must equal liabilities plus owners' equity. This equation reflects the financial position of a firm at any point in time:

$$\text{Assets} = \text{Liabilities} + \text{Owners'equity}$$

Because financing comes from either creditors or owners, the right side of the accounting equation also represents the business's financial structure.

The accounting equation also illustrates **double-entry bookkeeping**—the process by which accounting transactions are recorded. Because assets must always equal liabilities plus equity, each transaction must have an offsetting transaction. For example, if a company increases an asset, either another asset must decrease, a liability must increase, or owners' equity must increase. So if a company uses cash to purchase inventory, one asset (inventory) is increased while another (cash) is decreased by the same amount. Similarly, a decrease in an asset must be offset by either an increase in another asset, a decrease in a liability, or a decrease in owners' equity. If a company uses cash to repay a bank loan, both an asset (cash) and a liability (bank loans) decrease, and by the same amount.

Two simple numerical examples will help illustrate the accounting equation and double-entry bookkeeping. First, assume the owner of a photo studio purchases a new camera system for $5,000 using her personal funds. The accounting transaction would look as follows:

Increase plant, property, and equipment (an asset) by $5,000

Increase owners' equity by $5,000

So, the left side of the accounting equation would increase by $5,000 and be offset by a $5,000 increase on the right side.

Second, assume a firm has a $100,000 loan from a bank and decides to pay it off using some of its cash. The transaction would be recorded as:

Decrease bank loan (liability) by $100,000

Decrease cash (asset) by $100,000

In this second example, the left side and right side of the accounting equation would both decrease by $100,000.

The relationship expressed by the accounting equation underlies development of the firm's financial statements. Three financial statements form the foundation: the balance sheet, the income statement, and the statement of owners' equity. The information found in these statements is calculated using the double-entry bookkeeping system and reflects the basic accounting equation. A fourth statement, the statement of cash flows, is also prepared to focus specifically on the sources and uses of cash for a firm from its operating, investing, and financing activities.

The Impact of Computers and the Internet on the Accounting Process

For hundreds of years, bookkeepers recorded, or posted, accounting transactions as manual entries in journals. They then transferred the information, or posted it, to individual accounts listed in ledgers. Computers have streamlined the process, making it both faster and easier. For instance, point-of-sale terminals in retail stores perform a number of functions each time they record sales. These terminals not only recall prices from computer system memory and maintain constant inventory counts of individual items in stock but also automatically perform accounting data entry functions.

LECTURE ENHANCER:
In what ways have computers simplified your tax preparation, filing, and paperwork?

Accounting software programs are used widely in both large and small businesses today. They allow a do-it-once approach, in which a single input leads to automatic conversion of a sale into a journal entry, which then is stored until needed. Decision makers can then request up-to-date financial statements and financial ratios instantly. Improvements in accounting software continue to make the process even faster and easier. In addition, accounting firms have begun to use mobile computing to better serve their clients. Smart phones provide connections between employees and their company's network, which means they can access current, vital information from anywhere. Accounting firms may also provide mobile computing to clients with branded applications allowing clients to access their financial information and services via their phones. As they increase their Internet capabilities, tablet computers are also emerging as important business tools for accounting firms.[9]

Because the accounting needs of entrepreneurs and small businesses differ from those of larger firms, accounting software makers have designed programs that meet specific user needs. Some examples of accounting software programs designed for entrepreneurs and small businesses, and designed to run on personal computers, include QuickBooks, Peachtree, and BusinessWorks. Software programs designed for larger firms, often requiring more sophisticated computer systems, include products from Oracle and SAP.

For firms that conduct business worldwide, software producers have introduced new accounting programs that handle all of a company's accounting information for every country

KPMG's Award-Winning Green IT

If you think of accountants as "paper pushers," the New York–based audit, tax, and consulting firm KPMG wants you to think again. Since 2007 the Big Four company has reduced paper consumption 33 percent. In fact, it was recently singled out by *Computerworld* for outstanding performance in reducing its energy consumption in IT and other operations.

KPMG has reduced carbon use by almost 25 percent and non-recycled waste by more than 50 percent in the past few years. Using IT to almost double its use of videoconferencing technology, it eliminated more than $2 million a year in travel costs in a single year. Under its aggressive new five-year goals for reducing its carbon footprint, KPMG will move more operations to cloud computing systems, purchase greener forms of energy by installing solar panels, and seek Leadership in Energy and Environment Design (LEED) certification for any new construction it undertakes.

Says the firm's head of operations services, "We're committed to affecting change in our business operations to minimize the firm's environmental profile."

Questions for Critical Thinking

1. KPMG says it will continue "to focus on environmental stewardship in the communities where we operate." What impact on its communities can KPMG's actions have?

2. KPMG's green planning includes implementing flexible work arrangements. What is the environmental payoff of this step?

Sources: Danielle Lee, "KPMG Ranks High in Green IT," *Accounting Tomorrow*, http://www.accountingtoday.com, accessed April 3, 2012; Bob Biolino, "KPMG: Aims to Reduce Its Carbon Footprint by 25% through Environmental Stewardship," *Computerworld*, http://www.computerworld.com, accessed April 3, 2012; Ellen Fanning, "The Top Green-IT Organizations: Hard-wired To Be Green," *Computerworld*, http://www.computerworld.com, accessed April 3, 2012.

Assessment Check ✓

1. List the steps in the accounting cycle.
2. What is the accounting equation?
3. Briefly explain double-entry bookkeeping.

CLASS ACTIVITY: Discuss the aspects of payroll accounting that allowed this area to be outsourced earlier than most other accounting applications.

in which it operates. The software handles different languages and currencies, as well as the financial, legal, and tax requirements of each nation in which the firm conducts business.

The Internet also influences the accounting process. Several software producers offer Web-based accounting products designed for small and medium-sized businesses. Among other benefits, these products allow users to access their complete accounting systems from anywhere using a standard Web browser. The "Going Green" feature explains how KPMG is relying on IT to help reduce its carbon footprint.

5 Financial Statements

Financial statements provide managers with essential information they need to evaluate the liquidity position of an organization—its ability to meet current obligations and needs by converting assets into cash; the firm's profitability; and its overall financial health. The balance sheet, income statement, statement of owners' equity, and statement of cash flows provide a foundation on which managers can base their decisions. By interpreting the data provided in these statements, managers can communicate the appropriate information to internal decision makers and to interested parties outside the organization.

Of the four financial statements, only the balance sheet is considered to be a permanent statement; its amounts are carried over from year to year. The income statement, statement of owners' equity, and statement of cash flows are considered temporary because they are closed out at the end of each year.

Public companies are required to report their financial statements at the end of each three-month period, as well as

The balance sheet, the only permanent statement of the four financial statements, shows the firm's financial position on a particular date.

Solving an Ethical Controversy

Should Whistle-Blowers Be Rewarded?

The Sarbanes-Oxley Act of 2002 (SOX) was intended to reduce fraud, partly by requiring CEOs and CFOs to sign off on the accuracy of their companies' financial statements. However, the largest percentage of reported fraud is revealed by anonymous whistle-blowers or by journalists or others.

The U.S. False Claims Act allows citizens to file lawsuits alleging fraud against the federal government. The biggest settlements have involved hospital chains and drug manufacturers; the largest fine was $1 billion. Some whistle-blowers have collected almost $47 million in rewards. Provisions of the Foreign Corrupt Practices Act (FCPA) can also potentially result in huge rewards. The Dodd-Frank Wall Street Reform and Consumer Protection Act requires the Securities and Exchange Commission (SEC) to award whistle-blowers up to 30 percent of fines the government collects on the basis of "original information." However, in some cases, some whistle-blowers have been fired, forced to quit, or demoted.

Should whistle-blowers be rewarded for reporting financial fraud?

PRO

1. A recent survey found that "a strong monetary incentive to blow the whistle does motivate people with information to come forward."

2. Despite the strict penalties for fraud under SOX and the FCPA, one survey reported that 83 percent of fraud examiners believe that internal corporate controls over fraud will actually decline.

CON

1. Some observers feel that certain whistle-blower-friendly provisions of the FCPA may discourage accused firms from simply settling with the federal government and paying a fine to avoid costly legal procedures.

2. Not all whistle-blowers are innocent. A former UBS banker exposed tax evasion at the firm but was sentenced to prison because he did not reveal at first that he had participated in the fraud himself.

Summary

Nearly a decade after co-writing SOX, former congressman Michael Oxley registered as a lobbyist for the Financial Industry Regulatory Authority (FINRA), which promotes self-regulation of investment advisors. Currently, more than 1,000 whistle-blower cases are pending.

Sources: "Oxley of Sarbanes-Oxley to Lobby for Financial Self-Regulator," Bloomberg.com, http://www.bloomberg.com, accessed April 3, 2012; "Sarbanes-Oxley Can Help Curb Company Fraud," McGladrey, http://mcgladrey.com, accessed April 3, 2012; Deloitte Webcast Poll, "Poll: More Financial Statement Fraud Expected to Be Uncovered in 2010, 2011," *Corporate Compliance Insights*, http://www.corporate complianceinsights.com, accessed April 3, 2012; James Hyatt, "Who Detects Corporate Fraud? (Tip: It's Not Usually the SEC . . .)," *Business Ethics*, http://business-ethics.com, accessed April 3, 2012; Michael Rubinkam, "UBS Tax Evasion Whistle-Blower Reports to Federal Prison," *USA Today*, http://www.usatoday.com, accessed April 3, 2012; Ben Kerschberg, "The Dodd-Frank Act's Robust Whistleblowing Incentives," Forbes.com, http://www.forbes.com, accessed April 3, 2012.

---

at the end of each fiscal year. Annual statements must be examined and verified by the firm's outside auditors. These financial statements are public information available to anyone. The "Solving an Ethical Controversy" feature discusses the problem of financial fraud.

A fiscal year does not have to coincide with the calendar year, and companies set different fiscal years. For instance, Starbucks's fiscal year runs from October 1 to September 30 of the following year. Nike's fiscal year consists of the 12 months between June 1 and May 31. By contrast, GE's fiscal year is the same as the calendar year, running from January 1 to December 31.

CLASS ACTIVITY:
Discuss Bernie Madoff's Ponzi scheme and the SEC whistle-blower's attempts to expose it, which were ignored.

The Balance Sheet

A firm's **balance sheet** shows its financial position on a particular date. It is similar to a photograph of the firm's assets together with its liabilities and owners' equity at a specific moment in time. Balance sheets must be prepared at regular intervals, because a firm's managers and other internal parties often request this information every day, every week, or at least every month. On the other hand, external users, such as stockholders or industry analysts, may use this information less frequently, perhaps every quarter or once a year.

The balance sheet follows the accounting equation. On the left side of the balance sheet are the firm's assets—what it owns. These assets, shown in descending order of liquidity (in other words, convertibility to cash), represent the uses that management has made of available funds. Cash is always listed first on the asset side of the balance sheet.

On the right side of the equation are the claims against the firm's assets. Liabilities and owners' equity indicate the sources of the firm's assets and are listed in the order in which they are due. Liabilities reflect the claims of creditors—financial institutions or bondholders that have loaned the firm money; suppliers that have provided goods and services on credit; and others to be paid, such as federal, state, and local tax authorities. Owners' equity represents the owners' claims (those of stockholders, in the case of a corporation) against the firm's assets. It also amounts to the excess of all assets over liabilities.

Figure 15.3 shows the balance sheet for Belle's Fine Coffees, a small California-based coffee wholesaler. The accounting equation is illustrated by the three classifications of assets, liabilities, and owners' equity on the company's balance sheet. Remember, total assets must always equal the sum of liabilities and owners' equity. In other words, the balance sheet must always balance.

The Income Statement

Whereas the balance sheet reflects a firm's financial situation at a specific point in time, the **income statement** indicates the flow of resources that reveals the performance of the organization over a specific time period. Resembling a video rather than a photograph, the income statement is a financial record summarizing a firm's financial performance in terms of revenues, expenses, and profits over a given time period, say, a quarter or a year.

In addition to reporting the firm's profit or loss results, the income statement helps decision makers focus on overall revenues and the costs involved in generating these revenues. Managers of a not-for-profit organization use this statement to determine whether its revenues from contributions, grants, and investments will cover its operating costs. Finally, the income statement provides much of the basic data needed to calculate the financial ratios managers use in planning and controlling activities. Figure 15.4 shows the income statement for Belle's Fine Coffees.

An income statement (some times called *a profit-and-loss,* or *P&L, statement*) begins with total sales or revenues generated during a year, quarter, or month. Subsequent lines then deduct all of the costs related to producing the revenues. Typical categories of costs include those involved in producing the firm's goods or services, operating expenses, interest, and taxes. After all of them have been subtracted, the remaining net income may be distributed to the firm's owners (stockholders, proprietors, or partners) or reinvested in the company as retained earnings. The final figure on the income statement—net income after taxes—is literally the *bottom line.*

Keeping costs under control is an important part of running a business. Too often, however, companies concentrate more on increasing revenue than on controlling costs. Regardless of how much money a company collects in revenues, it won't stay in business for long unless it eventually earns a profit.

1 Current Assets:
Cash and other liquid assets that can or will be converted to cash within one year.

2 Plant, Property, and Equipment (net):
Physical assets expected to last for more than one year; shown net of accumulated depreciation—the cumulative value that plant, property, and equipment have been expensed (depreciated).

3 Value of assets such as patents and trademarks.

4 Current Liabilities:
Claims of creditors that are to be repaid within one year; accruals are expenses, such as wages, that have been incurred but not yet paid.

5 Long-Term Debt:
Debts that come due one year or longer after the date on the balance sheet.

6 Owners' (or shareholders') Equity:
Claims of the owners against the assets of the firm; the difference between total assets and total liabilities.

Belle's Fine Coffees

Balance Sheet

($ thousands)	2014	2013
Assets		
1 Current Assets		
Cash	$ 800	$ 600
Short-term investments	1,250	940
Accounts receivable	990	775
Inventory	2,200	1,850
Total current assets	5,240	4,165
2 Plant, property, and equipment (net)	3,300	2,890
3 Goodwill and other intangible assets	250	250
Total Assets	8,790	7,305
Liabilities and Shareholders' Equity		
4 Current Liabilities		
Accruals	$ 350	$ 450
Accounts payable	980	900
Notes payable	700	500
Total current liabilities	2,030	1,850
5 Long-term debt	1,100	1,000
Total liabilities	3,130	2,850
6 Shareholders' equity	5,660	4,455
Total Liabilities and Equity	8,790	7,305

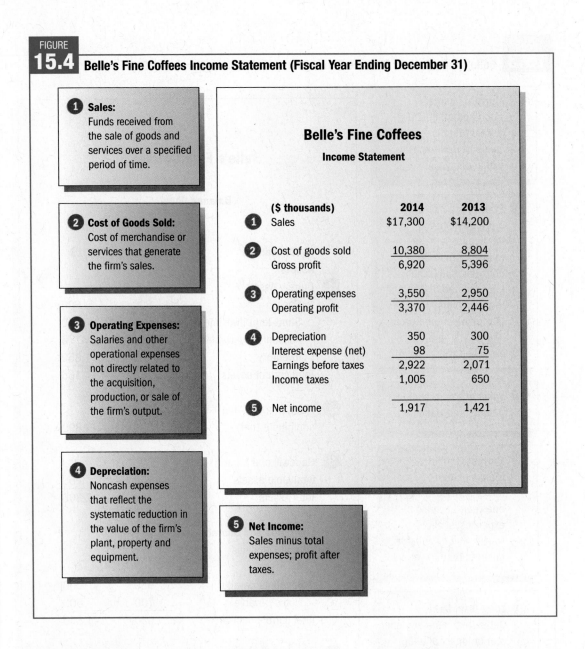

FIGURE 15.4 Belle's Fine Coffees Income Statement (Fiscal Year Ending December 31)

1 Sales:
Funds received from the sale of goods and services over a specified period of time.

2 Cost of Goods Sold:
Cost of merchandise or services that generate the firm's sales.

3 Operating Expenses:
Salaries and other operational expenses not directly related to the acquisition, production, or sale of the firm's output.

4 Depreciation:
Noncash expenses that reflect the systematic reduction in the value of the firm's plant, property and equipment.

5 Net Income:
Sales minus total expenses; profit after taxes.

Belle's Fine Coffees

Income Statement

($ thousands)	2014	2013
1 Sales	$17,300	$14,200
2 Cost of goods sold	10,380	8,804
Gross profit	6,920	5,396
3 Operating expenses	3,550	2,950
Operating profit	3,370	2,446
4 Depreciation	350	300
Interest expense (net)	98	75
Earnings before taxes	2,922	2,071
Income taxes	1,005	650
5 Net income	1,917	1,421

Statement of Owners' Equity

statement of owners' equity record of the change in owners' equity from the end of one fiscal period to the end of the next.

The **statement of owners', or shareholders', equity** is designed to show the components of the change in equity from the end of one fiscal year to the end of the next. It uses information from both the balance sheet and income statement. A somewhat simplified example is shown in Figure 15.5 for Belle's Fine Coffees.

Note that the statement begins with the amount of equity shown on the balance sheet at the end of the prior year. Net income is added, and cash dividends paid to owners are subtracted (both are found on the income statement for the current year). If owners contributed any additional capital, say, through the sale of new shares, this amount is added to equity. On the other hand, if owners withdrew capital, for example, through the repurchase of existing shares, equity declines. All of the additions and subtractions, taken together, equal the change in owners' equity from the end of the last fiscal year to the end of the current one. The new amount of owners' equity is then reported on the balance sheet for the current year.

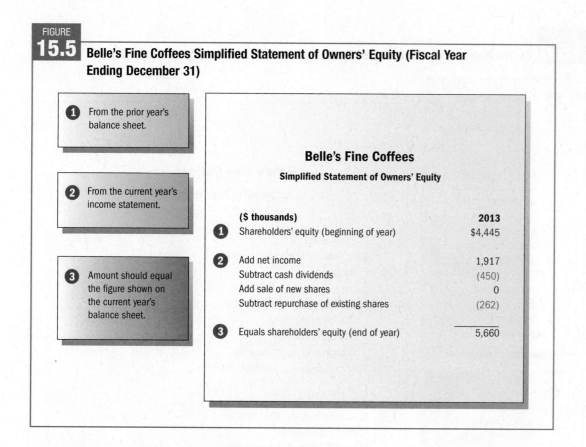

FIGURE 15.5 Belle's Fine Coffees Simplified Statement of Owners' Equity (Fiscal Year Ending December 31)

1 From the prior year's balance sheet.

2 From the current year's income statement.

3 Amount should equal the figure shown on the current year's balance sheet.

Belle's Fine Coffees

Simplified Statement of Owners' Equity

($ thousands)	2013
1 Shareholders' equity (beginning of year)	$4,445
2 Add net income	1,917
Subtract cash dividends	(450)
Add sale of new shares	0
Subtract repurchase of existing shares	(262)
3 Equals shareholders' equity (end of year)	5,660

The Statement of Cash Flows

In addition to the statement of owners' equity, the income statement, and the balance sheet, most firms prepare a fourth accounting statement—the **statement of cash flows**. Public companies are required to prepare and publish a statement of cash flows. In addition, commercial lenders often require a borrower to submit a statement of cash flows. The statement of cash flows provides investors and creditors with relevant information about a firm's cash receipts and cash payments for its operations, investments, and financing during an accounting period. Figure 15.6 shows the statement of cash flows for Belle's Fine Coffees.

Companies prepare a statement of cash flows due to the widespread use of accrual accounting. **Accrual accounting** recognizes revenues and costs when they occur, not when actual cash changes hands. As a result, there can be differences between what is reported as sales, expenses, and profits, and the amount of cash that actually flows into and out of the business during a period of time. An example is depreciation. Companies depreciate fixed assets—such as machinery and buildings—over a specified period of time, meaning that they systematically reduce the value of the asset. Depreciation is reported as an expense on the firm's income statement (see Figure 15.4) but does not involve any actual cash. The fact that depreciation is a noncash expense means that what a firm reports as net income (profits after tax) for a particular period actually understates the amount of cash the firm took in, less expenses, during that period of time. Consequently, depreciation is added back to net income when calculating cash flow.

The fact that *cash flow* is the lifeblood of every organization is evidenced by the business failure rate. Many former owners of failed firms blame inadequate cash flow for their companies' demise. Those who value the statement of cash flow maintain that its preparation and

statement of cash flows statement showing the sources and uses of cash during a period of time.

accrual accounting accounting method that records revenues and expenses when they occur, not necessarily when cash actually changes hands.

① Operating Activities:
The nuts and bolts of day-to-day activities of a company carrying out its regular business; Increases in accounts receivable and inventory are uses of cash, while increases in accruals and accounts payables are sources of cash; in financially healthy firms, net cash flow from operating activities should be positive.

② Investing Activities:
Transactions to accumulate or use cash in ways that affect operating activities in the future; often a use of cash.

③ Financing Activities:
Ways to transfer cash to or from creditors and to or from owners; can be either positive or negative.

④ Net Cash Flow:
The sum of cash flow from operating, investing, and financing activities, a reconcilement of cash from the beginning to the end of the accounting period (one year in this example).

Belle's Fine Coffees
Statement of Cash Flows

($ thousands)	2013
Cash Flow from Operating Activities	
① Net income	$1,917
Depreciation	350
Change in accounts receivable	(215)
Change in inventory	(350)
Change in accruals	(100)
Change in accounts payable	80
Total cash flow from operating activities	1,682
② Cash Flow from Investing Activities	
Capital expenditures	(760)
Change in short-term investments	(310)
Total cash flow from investing activities	(1,070)
③ Cash Flow from Financing Activities	
Cash dividends	(450)
Sale/repurchase of shares	(262)
Change in notes payable	200
Change in long-term debt	100
Total cash flow from financing activities	(412)
④ Net Cash Flow	200
Cash (beginning of year)	600
Cash (end of year)	800

scrutiny by various parties can prevent financial distress for otherwise profitable firms, too many of which are forced into bankruptcy due to a lack of cash needed to continue day-to-day operations.

Even for firms for which bankruptcy is not an issue, the statement of cash flows can provide investors and other interested parties with vital information. For instance, assume that a firm's income statement reports rising earnings. At the same time, however, the statement of cash flows shows that the firm's inventory is rising faster than sales—often a signal that demand for the firm's products is softening, which may in turn be a sign of impending financial trouble.

Assessment Check ✅

1. List the four financial statements.

2. How is the balance sheet organized?

3. Define *accrual accounting*.

Financial Ratio Analysis

Accounting professionals fulfill important responsibilities beyond preparing financial statements. In a more critical role, they help managers interpret the statements by comparing data about the firm's current activities to those for previous periods and to results posted by other companies in the industry. *Ratio analysis* is one of the most commonly used tools for measuring a firm's liquidity, profitability, and reliance on debt financing, as well as the effectiveness of management's resource utilization. This analysis also allows comparisons with other firms and with the firm's own past performance.

Ratios assist managers in interpreting actual performance and making comparisons to what should have happened. Comparisons with ratios of similar companies help managers understand their firm's performance relative to competitors' results. These industry standards are important yardsticks and help pinpoint problem areas, as well as areas of excellence. Ratios for the current accounting period also may be compared with similar calculations for previous periods to spot developing trends. Ratios can be classified according to their specific purposes.

CLASS ACTIVITY:
Why would a decline in inventory turnover ratio several years in a row raise concern?

Liquidity Ratios

A firm's ability to meet its short-term obligations when they must be paid is measured by *liquidity ratios*. Increasing liquidity reduces the likelihood that a firm will face emergencies caused by the need to raise funds to repay loans. On the other hand, firms with low liquidity may be forced to choose between default or borrowing from high-cost lending sources to meet their maturing obligations.

Two commonly used liquidity ratios are the current ratio and the acid-test, or quick, ratio. The current ratio compares current assets to current liabilities, giving executives information about the firm's ability to pay its current debts as they mature. The current ratio of Belle's Fine Coffees can be computed as follows (unless indicated, all amounts from the balance sheet or income statement are in thousands of dollars):

$$\text{Liquidity ratio} = \frac{\text{Current assests}}{\text{Current liabilities}} = \frac{5,240}{2,030} = 2.58$$

In other words, Belle's Fine Coffees has $2.58 of current assets for every $1.00 of current liabilities. In general, a current ratio of 2:1 is considered satisfactory liquidity. This rule of thumb must be considered along with other factors, such as the nature of the business, the season, and the quality of the company's management team. Belle's Fine Coffees' management and other interested parties are likely to evaluate this ratio of 2.58:1 by comparing it with ratios for previous operating periods and with industry averages.

The acid-test (or quick) ratio measures the ability of a firm to meet its debt payments on short notice. This ratio compares quick assets—the most liquid current assets—against current liabilities. Quick assets generally consist of cash and equivalents, short-term investments, and accounts receivable. So, generally quick assets equal total current assets minus inventory.

Belle's Fine Coffees' current balance sheet lists total current assets of $5.24 million and inventory of $2.2 million. Therefore, its quick ratio is as follows:

$$\text{Acid-test ratio} = \frac{\text{Current assets} - \text{Inventory}}{\text{Current liabilities}} = \frac{(5{,}240 - 2{,}200)}{2{,}030} = 1.50$$

Because the traditional rule of thumb for an adequate acid-test ratio is around 1:1, Belle's Fine Coffees appears to have a strong level of liquidity. However, the same cautions apply here as for the current ratio. The ratio should be compared with industry averages and data from previous operating periods to determine whether it is adequate for the firm.

Activity Ratios

Activity ratios measure the effectiveness of management's use of the firm's resources. One of the most frequently used activity ratios, the inventory turnover ratio, indicates the number of times merchandise moves through a business:

$$\text{Inventory turnover} = \frac{\text{Cost of goods sold}}{\text{Average inventory}} = \frac{10{,}380}{[(2{,}200 + 1{,}850)/2]} = 5.13$$

Average inventory for Belle's Fine Coffees is determined by adding the inventory as of December 31, 2014 ($2.2 million) with the inventory as of December 31, 2013 ($1.85 million) and dividing it by 2. Comparing the 5.13 inventory turnover ratio with industry standards gives a measure of efficiency. It is important to note, however, that inventory turnover can vary substantially, depending on the products a company sells and the industry in which it operates.

If a company makes a substantial portion of its sales on credit, measuring receivables turnover can provide useful information. Receivables turnover can be calculated as follows:

$$\text{Receivables turnover} = \frac{\text{Credit sales}}{\text{Average accounts receivable}}$$

Because Belle's Fine Coffees is a wholesaler, let's assume that all of its sales are credit sales. Average receivables equals the simple average of 2014's receivables and 2013's receivables. The ratio for the company is:

$$\text{Receivables turnover} = \frac{17{,}300}{[(990 + 775)/2]} = 19.60$$

Dividing 365 by the figure for receivables turnover, 19.6, equals the average age of receivables, 18.62 days. Assume Belle's Fine Coffees expects its retail customers to pay outstanding bills within 30 days of the date of purchase. Given that the average age of its

LECTURE ENHANCER:
Provide examples of industries with low and high inventory turnover.

receivables is less than 30 days, Belle's Fine Coffees appears to be doing a good job collecting its credit sales.

Another measure of efficiency is total asset turnover. It measures how much in sales each dollar invested in assets generates:

$$\text{Total asset turnover} = \frac{\text{Sales}}{\text{Average total assets}}$$

$$= \frac{17,300}{[(8,790 + 7,305)/2]} = 2.15$$

Average total assets for Belle's Fine Coffees equals total assets as of December 31, 2014 ($8.79 million) plus total assets as of December 31, 2013 ($7.305 million) divided by 2.

Belle's Fine Coffees generates about $2.15 in sales for each dollar invested in assets. Although a higher ratio generally indicates that a firm is operating more efficiently, care must be taken when comparing firms that operate in different industries. Some industries simply require higher investment in assets than do other industries.

Profitability Ratios

Some ratios measure the organization's overall financial performance by evaluating its ability to generate revenues in excess of operating costs and other expenses. These measures are called *profitability ratios*. To compute these ratios, accountants compare the firm's earnings with total sales or investments. Over a period of time, profitability ratios may reveal the effectiveness of management in operating the business. Three important profitability ratios are gross profit margin, net profit margin, and return on equity:

$$\text{Gross profit margin} = \frac{\text{Gross profit}}{\text{Sales}} = \frac{6,920}{17,300} = 40.0\%$$

$$\text{Net profit margin} = \frac{\text{Net income}}{\text{Sales}} = \frac{1,917}{17,300} = 11.1\%$$

$$\text{Return one quity} = \frac{\text{Net income}}{\text{Average equity}} = \frac{1,1917}{[(5,660 + 4,455)/2]} = 37.9\%$$

All of these ratios indicate positive evaluations of the current operations of Belle's Fine Coffees. For example, the net profit margin indicates that the firm realizes a profit of slightly more than 11 cents on each dollar of merchandise it sells. Although this ratio varies widely among business firms, Belle's Fine Coffees compares favorably with wholesalers in general, which have an average net profit margin of around 5 percent. However, this ratio, like the other profitability ratios, should be evaluated in relation to profit forecasts, past performance, or more specific industry averages to enhance the interpretation of results. Similarly, although the firm's return on equity of almost 38 percent appears outstanding, the degree of risk in the industry also must be considered.

Starbucks chairman and CEO Howard Schultz walks on stage to address Starbucks shareholders at a recent meeting and to discuss various topics, including return on equity. Return on equity is one measure of a company's profitability.

CLASS ACTIVITY:
What types of companies might have very slow receivables turnover?

Leverage Ratios

Leverage ratios measure the extent to which a firm relies on debt financing. They provide particularly interesting information to potential investors and lenders. If management has assumed too much debt in financing the firm's operations, problems may arise in meeting future interest payments and repaying outstanding loans. As we discuss in Chapter 17, borrowing money does have advantages. However, relying too heavily on debt financing may lead to bankruptcy. More generally, both investors and lenders may prefer to deal with firms whose owners have invested enough of their own money to avoid overreliance on borrowing. The debt ratio and long-term debt to equity ratio help interested parties evaluate a firm's leverage:

$$\text{Debt ratio} = \frac{\text{Total liabilities}}{\text{Total assets}} = \frac{3,130}{8,790} = 35.6\%$$

$$\text{Long-term debt to equity} = \frac{\text{Long-term debt}}{\text{Owners' equity}} = \frac{1,100}{5,660} = 19.64\%$$

A total liabilities to total assets ratio greater than 50 percent indicates that a firm is relying more on borrowed money than owners' equity. Because Belle's Fine Coffees' total liabilities to total assets ratio is 35.6 percent, the firm's owners have invested considerably more than the total amount of liabilities shown on the firm's balance sheet. Moreover, the firm's long-term debt to equity ratio is only 19.64 percent, indicating that Belle's Fine Coffees has only about 19.6 cents in long-term debt to every dollar in equity. The long-term debt to equity ratio also indicates that Belle's Fine Coffees hasn't relied very heavily on borrowed money.

The four categories of financial ratios relate balance sheet and income statement data to one another, help management pinpoint a firm's strengths and weaknesses, and indicate areas in need of further investigation. Large, multiproduct firms that operate in diverse markets use their information systems to update their financial ratios every day or even every hour. Each company's management must decide on an appropriate review schedule to avoid the costly and time-consuming mistake of overmonitoring.

In addition to calculating financial ratios, managers, investors, and lenders should pay close attention to how accountants apply a number of accounting rules when preparing financial statements. GAAP gives accountants leeway in reporting certain revenues and expenses. Public companies are required to disclose, in footnotes to the financial statements, how the various accounting rules were applied.

[7]

Budgeting

Although the financial statements discussed in this chapter focus on past business activities, they also provide the basis for planning in the future. A **budget** is a planning and controlling tool that reflects the firm's expected sales revenues, operating expenses, and cash receipts and outlays. It quantifies the firm's plans for a specified future period. Because it reflects management estimates of expected sales, cash inflows and outflows, and costs, the budget is a financial blueprint and can be thought of as a short-term financial plan. It becomes the standard for comparison against actual performance.

LECTURE ENHANCER:
Is a company with no debt leverage better than one with some leverage? Why or why not?

Assessment Check ✓

1. List the four categories of financial ratios.

2. Define the following ratios: *current ratio, inventory turnover, net profit margin,* and *debt ratio.*

budget a planning and controlling tool that reflects the firm's expected sales revenues, operating expenses, and cash receipts and outlays.

Budget preparation is frequently a time-consuming task that involves many people from various departments within the organization. The complexity of the budgeting process varies with the size and complexity of the organization. Large corporations such as United Technologies, Paramount Pictures, and Verizon maintain complex and sophisticated budgeting systems. Besides being planning and controlling tools, their budgets help managers integrate their numerous divisions. But budgeting in both large and small firms is similar to household budgeting in its purpose: to match income and expenses in a way that accomplishes objectives and correctly times cash inflows and outflows.

Because the accounting department is an organization's financial nerve center, it provides many of the data for budget development. The overall master, or operating, budget is actually a composite of many individual budgets for separate units of the firm. These individual budgets typically include the production budget, cash budget, capital expenditures budget, advertising budget, sales budget, and travel budget. When you travel for business, you are responsible for keeping track of and recording your own financial transactions for the purpose of compiling your expense report, as the "Business Etiquette" feature describes.

Technology has improved the efficiency of the budgeting process. The accounting software products discussed earlier—such as QuickBooks—all include budgeting features. Moreover, modules designed for specific businesses are often available from third parties. Many banks now offer their customers personal financial management tools (PFMs) developed by software companies. One such tool is FinanceWorks, an online finance program from Intuit's Digital Insight division. BBVA, a multinational Spanish banking group, offers Tu Cuentas ("you count"), based on a PFM program from Strands, a California software developer.[10]

One of the most important budgets prepared by firms is the *cash budget*. The cash budget, usually prepared monthly, tracks the firm's cash inflows and outflows. Figure 15.7 illustrates a sample cash budget for Birchwood Paper, a small Maine-based paper products company. The company has set a $150,000 target cash balance. The cash budget indicates months in which the firm

BusinessEtiquette

Managing Travel Expenses

Business travel is an exciting aspect of many jobs. It also carries a higher level of responsibility, since you must carefully manage and track legitimate travel expenses your company will reimburse. Here are some tips for managing the task.

1 Whenever possible, book travel in advance for the best prices. Avoid deals that include penalties for changing your plans.

2 Save receipts for all expenditures in a single safe place, like a folder or envelope.

3 Use credit cards as much as possible, yours or the company's. This guarantees you a receipt of your expenses, or at least a record on your monthly statement.

4 When paying in cash, always ask for a receipt.

5 For small purchases that don't generate a receipt, make a note of the amount, the date, and the purpose of the expenditure. Write it down or use your smart phone.

6 Avoid expensive options such as room service, the minibar in your hotel room, and pricey restaurants (unless you are entertaining clients).

7 For prompt reimbursement and to avoid memory lapses, complete your expense report within a few days of your return.

Sources: "5 Tips for Tracking Expenses While Traveling," Mind Your Decisions blog, http://mindyourdecisions.com/blog, accessed April 3, 2012; Michael Valkevich, "Twenty Tips for Managing Travel Expenses," *Fast Company,* http://www.fastcompany.com, accessed April 3, 2012; "How to Track Expenses when Traveling," Traveling Mom blog, http://travelingmom.com/blogs, accessed April 3, 2012.

LECTURE ENHANCER:
What are some items that you could include in your personal budget?

FIGURE
15.7 Four-Month Cash Budget for Birchwood Paper Company

Birchwood Paper Company
Four-Month Cash Budget

($ thousands)	May	June	July	August
Gross sales	$1,200.0	$3,200.0	$5,500.0	$4,500.0
Cash sales	300.0	800.0	1,375.0	1,125.0
One month prior	600.0	600.0	1,600.0	2,750.0
Two months prior	300.0	300.0	300.0	800.0
Total cash inflows	1,200.0	1,700.0	3,275.0	4,675.0
Purchases				
Cash purchases	1,040.0	1,787.5	1,462.5	390.0
One month prior	390.0	1,040.0	1,787.5	1,462.5
Wages and salaries	250.0	250.0	250.0	250.0
Office rent	75.0	75.0	75.0	75.0
Marketing and other expenses	150.0	150.0	150.0	150.0
Taxes		300.0		
Total cash outflows	1,905.0	3,602.5	3,725.0	2,327.5
Net cash flow				
(Inflows – Outflows)	(705.0)	(1,902.5)	(450.0)	2,347.5
Beginnning cash balance	250.0	150.0	150.0	150.0
Net cash flow	(705.0)	(1,902.5)	(450.0)	2,347.5
Ending cash balance	(455.0)	(1,752.5)	(300.0)	2,497.5
Target cash balance	150.0	150.0	150.0	150.0
Surplus (deficit)	(605.0)	(1,902.5)	(450.0)	2,347.5
Cumulative surplus (deficit)	(605.0)	(2,507.5)	(2,957.5)	610.0

will need temporary loans—May, June, and July—and how much it will need (close to $3 million). The document also indicates that Birchwood will generate a cash surplus in August and can begin repaying the short-term loan. Finally, the cash budget produces a tangible standard against which to compare actual cash inflows and outflows.

8 International Accounting

Today, accounting procedures and practices must be adapted to accommodate an international business environment. The Coca-Cola Company and McDonald's both generate more than half their annual revenues from sales outside the United States. Nestlé, the giant chocolate and food products firm, operates throughout the world. It derives 98 percent of its revenues from outside Switzerland, its home country. International accounting practices for global firms must reliably translate the financial statements of the firm's international affiliates, branches, and subsidiaries and convert data about foreign currency transactions to

Behind the Olympus Accounting Scandal

To conceal investment losses of almost $2 billion, top executives at Olympus, the Japanese camera and medical equipment maker, created dubious financial transactions and misled auditors for years. When Michael C. Woodford became CEO and grew suspicious, he arranged a new audit by PricewaterhouseCoopers that called Olympus's management "rotten to the core." In October 2011, Woodford was fired and left Japan.

The global media covered the accounting story extensively. Olympus's share values dropped by half, board members and executives were forced to resign, and the company stood in danger of being delisted by the Tokyo Stock Exchange, which fined it $1.27 million for "falsifying financial records to conceal losses." Those responsible face possible criminal charges.

Company funds remain missing. "We still don't know what they were actually doing," says Woodford. "There has never been any explanation that makes sense."

Questions for Critical Thinking

1. Olympus's auditors, KPMG AZSA and Ernst & Young Nippon, questioned the shady transactions but were told a third party had found all in order. Were they correct not to act?

2. Olympus's new president said, "We deeply regret that we have given a very negative impression to Japan and possibly the world." What should Olympus do now?

Sources: Kari Taro Greenfield, "The Story Behind the Olympus Scandal," *Bloomberg Businessweek,* February 16, 2012, http://www.businessweek.com; Hiroko Tabushi, "Former Chief Ends His Bid to Overhaul Olympus," *The New York Times,* January 6, 2012, http://www.nytimes.com; Hiroko Tabushi, "Olympus Restates Earnings, Showing Losses," *The New York Times,* December 14, 2011, http://www.nytimes.com; "Olympus Board Signals Intent to Resign," *The New York Times,* December 7, 2011, http://www.nytimes.com; Hiroko Tabushi, "Executives Organized Olympus Cover-Up, Panel Finds," *The New York Times,* December 6, 2011, http://www.nytimes.com.

---

dollars. Also, foreign currencies and exchange rates influence the accounting and financial reporting processes of firms operating internationally.

As market economies in countries such as Poland and China have developed, the demand for accountants has increased. As the "Hit & Miss" feature explains in describing the recent Olympus accounting scandal, however, ethical standards can be violated anywhere in the world.

Exchange Rates

As defined in Chapter 4, an exchange rate is the ratio at which a country's currency can be exchanged for other currencies. Currencies can be treated as goods to be bought and sold. Like the price of any product, currency prices change daily according to supply and demand. So exchange rate fluctuations complicate accounting entries and accounting practices.

Accountants who deal with international transactions must appropriately record their firms' foreign sales and purchases. Today's sophisticated accounting software helps firms handle all of their international transactions within a single program. An international firm's consolidated financial statements must reflect any gains or losses due to changes in exchange rates during specific periods of time. Financial statements that cover operations in two or more countries also need to treat fluctuations consistently to allow for comparison.

In the United States, GAAP requires firms to make adjustments to their earnings that reflect changes in exchange rates. In general, a weakening dollar increases the earnings of a U.S. firm that has international operations because the same units of a foreign currency will translate into more U.S. dollars. By the same token, a strengthening dollar will have the opposite effect on earnings—the same number of units of a foreign currency will translate into fewer dollars. Recently the Mexican peso increased in value as the United States started

LECTURE ENHANCER:
What problems face American accounting firms doing business abroad?

CLASS ACTIVITY:
How could a decrease in the exchange rate of the U.S. dollar relative to the euro be positive for the export business of an American company?

Nelson Ching/Bloomberg/Getty Images, Inc.

Nestlé's Nescafe coffee is packaged for shipment at a Chinese production plant. Because this Swiss corporation operates around the world, its profits and its financial statements are affected by foreign exchange rates.

to climb out of its recession. The U.S. recovery actually helped boost Mexican exports to nearly $300 billion in a year.[11]

International Accounting Standards

The International Accounting Standards Committee (IASC) was established in 1973 to promote worldwide consistency in financial reporting practices and soon developed its first set of accounting standards and interpretations. In 2001, the IASC became the **International Accounting Standards Board (IASB)**. **International Financial Reporting Standards (IFRS)** are the standards and interpretations adopted by the IASB. The IASB operates in much the same manner as the FASB does in the United States, interpreting and modifying IFRS.

International Accounting Standards Board (IASB) organization established in 1973 to promote worldwide consistency in financial reporting practices.

International Financial Reporting Standards (IFRS) standards and interpretations adopted by the IASB.

Because of the boom in worldwide trade, there is a real need for comparability of and uniformity in international accounting rules. Trade agreements such as NAFTA and the expansion of the European Union have only heightened interest in creating a uniform set of global accounting rules. In addition, an increasing number of investors are buying shares in foreign multinational corporations, and they need a practical way to evaluate firms in other countries. To assist global investors, more and more firms are beginning to report their financial information according to international accounting standards. This practice helps investors make informed decisions.

Nearly 100 other countries currently require, permit the use of, or have a policy of convergence with IFRS. These nations and other entities include members of the European Union, India, Australia, Canada, and Hong Kong. At first, the United States was skeptical of IFRS, even though major American accounting organizations have been involved with the IASB since its inception. In fact, the SEC used to require all firms whose shares were publicly traded in the United States to report financial results using GAAP. This rule applied regardless of where firms were located.

This requirement started to change some years back, when the FASB and the IASB met and committed to the eventual convergence of IFRS with GAAP. This agreement was further clarified in 2005. Around the same time, the SEC began to loosen its rules on the use of IFRS by foreign firms whose shares trade in the United States. Today, many foreign companies can report results using IFRS as long as they reconcile these results to GAAP in a footnote. Some large U.S. companies were allowed to use international accounting standards beginning in 2009. By 2016, all U.S. firms will be required to do so. Almost half the companies polled in a recent survey said they wanted an option for early adoption of the standards. Meanwhile, the IASB and the FASB continue to develop convergence standards.[12]

How does IFRS differ from GAAP? Although many similarities between IFRS and GAAP exist, there are some important differences. For example, under GAAP, plant, property, and equipment is reported on the balance sheet at the historical cost minus depreciation. Under IFRS, on the other hand, plant, property, and equipment is shown on the balance sheet at current market value. This gives a better picture of the real value of a firm's assets. Many accounting experts believe that IFRS is overall less complicated than GAAP and more transparent.[13]

Assessment Check ✓

1. How are financial statements adjusted for exchange rates?

2. What is the purpose of the IASB?

What's Ahead

This chapter describes the role of accounting in an organization. Accounting is the process of measuring, interpreting, and communicating financial information to interested parties both inside and outside the firm. The next two chapters discuss the finance function of an organization. Finance deals with planning, obtaining, and managing the organization's funds to accomplish its objectives in the most efficient and effective manner possible. Chapter 16 outlines the financial system, the system by which funds are transferred from savers to borrowers. Organizations rely on the financial system to raise funds for expansion or operations. The chapter includes a description of financial institutions, such as banks; financial markets, such as the New York Stock Exchange; financial instruments, such as stocks and bonds; and the role of the Federal Reserve System. Chapter 17 discusses the role of finance and the financial manager in an organization.

Summary of Learning Objectives

1 Discuss the users of accounting information.

Accountants measure, interpret, and communicate financial information to parties inside and outside the firm to support improved decision making. Accountants gather, record, and interpret financial information for management. They also provide financial information on the status and operations of the firm for evaluation by outside parties, such as government agencies, stockholders, potential investors, and lenders. Accounting plays key roles in financing activities, which help start and expand an organization; investing activities, which provide the assets it needs to continue operating; and operating activities, which focus on selling goods and services and paying expenses incurred in regular operations.

Assessment Check Answers ✔

1.1 Define *accounting*. Accounting is the process of measuring, interpreting, and communicating financial information in a way that describes the status and operation of an organization and aids in decision making.

1.2 Who uses accounting information? Managers of all types of organizations use accounting information to help them plan, assess performance, and control daily and long-term operations. Outside users of accounting information include government officials, investors, creditors, and donors.

1.3 What are the three business activities that involve accounting? The three activities involving accounting are financing, investing, and operating activities.

2 Describe accounting professionals.

Public accountants provide accounting services to other firms or individuals for a fee. They are involved in such activities as auditing, tax return preparation, management consulting, and accounting system design. Management accountants collect and record financial transactions, prepare financial statements, and interpret them for managers in their own firms. Government and not-for-profit accountants perform many of the same functions as management accountants, but they analyze how effectively the organization or agency is operating, rather than its profits and losses.

Assessment Check Answers ✔

2.1 List the three services offered by public accounting firms. The three services offered by public accounting firms are auditing, management consulting, and tax services.

2.2 What tasks do management accountants perform? Management accountants work for the organization and are responsible for collecting and recording financial transactions, and preparing and interpreting financial statements.

3 Identify the foundation of the accounting system.

The foundation of the accounting system in the United States is GAAP (generally accepted accounting principles), a set of guidelines or standards that accountants follow. There are four basic requirements to which all accounting rules should adhere: consistency, relevance, reliability, and comparability. The Financial Accounting Standards Board (FASB), an independent body made up of accounting professionals, is primarily responsible for evaluating, setting, and modifying GAAP. The U.S. Securities and Exchange Commission (SEC) also plays a role in establishing and modifying accounting standards for public companies, firms whose shares are traded in the financial markets.

Assessment Check Answers ☑

3.1 Define GAAP. GAAP stands for generally accepted accounting principles and is a set of standards or guidelines that accountants follow in recording and reporting financial transactions.

3.2 What are the four basic requirements to which all accounting rules must adhere? The four basic requirements to which all accounting rules must adhere are consistency, relevance, reliability, and comparability.

3.3 What is the role played by the FASB? The Financial Accounting Standards Board (FASB) is an independent body made up of accounting professionals and is primarily responsible for evaluating, setting, and modifying GAAP.

4 **Outline the steps in the accounting cycle.**

The accounting process involves recording, classifying, and summarizing data about transactions and then using this information to produce financial statements for the firm's managers and other interested parties. Transactions are recorded chronologically in journals, posted in ledgers, and then summarized in accounting statements. Today, much of this activity takes place electronically. The basic accounting equation states that assets (what a firm owns) must always equal liabilities (what a firm owes creditors) plus owners' equity. This equation also illustrates double-entry bookkeeping, the process by which accounting transactions are recorded. Under double-entry bookkeeping, each individual transaction must have an offsetting transaction.

Assessment Check Answers ☑

4.1 List the steps in the accounting cycle. The accounting cycle involves the following steps: recording transactions, classifying the transactions, summarizing transactions, and using the summaries to produce financial statements.

4.2 What is the accounting equation? The accounting equation states that assets (what a firm owns) must always equal liabilities (what a firm owes) plus owners' equity. Therefore, if assets increase or decrease, there must be an offsetting increase or decrease in liabilities, owners' equity, or both.

4.3 Briefly explain double-entry bookkeeping. Double-entry bookkeeping is an accounting method in which every transaction must have an offsetting transaction.

5 **Explain financial statements.**

The balance sheet shows the financial position of a company on a particular date. The three major classifications of balance sheet data are the components of the accounting equation: assets, liabilities, and owners' equity. The income statement shows the results of a firm's operations over a specific period. It focuses on the firm's activities—its revenues and expenditures—and the resulting profit or loss during the period. The major components of the income statement

are revenues, cost of goods sold, expenses, and profit or loss. The statement of owners' equity shows the components of the change in owners' equity from the end of the prior year to the end of the current year. Finally, the statement of cash flows records a firm's cash receipts and cash payments during an accounting period. It outlines the sources and uses of cash in the basic business activities of operating, investing, and financing.

Assessment Check Answers ☑

5.1 List the four financial statements. The four financial statements are the balance sheet, the income statement, the statement of owners' equity, and the cash flow statement.

5.2 How is the balance sheet organized? Assets (what a firm owns) are shown on one side of the balance sheet and are listed in order of convertibility into cash. On the other side of the balance sheet are claims to assets, liabilities (what a firm owes), and owners' equity. Claims are listed in the order in which they are due, so liabilities are listed before owners' equity. Assets always equal liabilities plus owners' equity.

5.3 Define accrual accounting. Accrual accounting recognizes revenues and expenses when they occur, not when cash actually changes hands. Most companies use accrual accounting to prepare their financial statements.

6 **Discuss financial ratio analysis.**

Liquidity ratios measure a firm's ability to meet short-term obligations. Examples are the current ratio and the quick, or acid-test, ratio. Activity ratios—such as the inventory turnover ratio, accounts receivable turnover ratio, and the total asset turnover ratio—measure how effectively a firm uses its resources. Profitability ratios assess the overall financial performance of the business. The gross profit margin, net profit margin, and return on owners' equity are examples of profitability ratios. Leverage ratios, such as the total liabilities to total assets ratio and the long-term debt to equity ratio, measure the extent to which the firm relies on debt to finance its operations. Financial ratios help managers and outside evaluators compare a firm's current financial information with that of previous years and with results for other firms in the same industry.

Assessment Check Answers ☑

6.1 List the four categories of financial ratios. The four categories of ratios are liquidity, activity, profitability, and leverage.

6.2 Define the following ratios: current ratio, inventory turnover, net profit margin, and debt ratio. The current ratio equals current assets divided by current liabilities. Inventory turnover equals cost of goods sold divided by average inventory. Net profit margin equals net income divided by sales. The debt ratio equals total liabilities divided by total assets.

7 Describe the role of budgeting.

Budgets are financial guidelines for future periods and reflect expected sales revenues, operating expenses, and cash receipts and outlays. They reflect management expectations for future occurrences and are based on plans that have been made. Budgets are important planning and controlling tools because they provide standards against which actual performance can be measured. One important type of budget is the cash budget, which estimates cash inflows and outflows over a period of time.

Assessment Check Answers ✓

7.1 What is a budget? A budget is a planning and control tool that reflects the firm's expected sales revenues, operating expenses, cash receipts, and cash outlays.

7.2 How is a cash budget organized? Cash budgets are generally prepared monthly. Cash receipts are listed first. They include cash sales as well as the collection of past credit sales. Cash outlays are listed next. These include cash purchases, payment of past credit purchases, and operating expenses. The difference between cash receipts and cash outlays is net cash flow.

8 Outline international accounting practices.

One accounting issue that affects global business is exchange rates. An exchange rate is the ratio at which a country's currency can be exchanged for other currencies. Daily changes in exchange rates affect the accounting entries for sales and purchases of firms involved in international markets. These fluctuations create either losses or gains for particular companies. The International Accounting Standards Board (IASB) was established to provide worldwide consistency in financial reporting practices and comparability of and uniformity in international accounting standards. It has developed International Financial Reporting Standards (IFRS). Many countries have already adopted IFRS, and the United States is in the process of making the transition to it.

Assessment Check Answers ✓

8.1 How are financial statements adjusted for exchange rates? An exchange rate is the ratio at which a country's currency can be exchanged for other currencies. Fluctuations of exchange rates create either gains or losses for particular companies because data about international financial transactions must be translated into the currency of the country in which the parent company is based.

8.2 What is the purpose of the IASB? The International Accounting Standards Board (IASB) was established to provide worldwide consistency in financial reporting practices and comparability and uniformity of international accounting rules. The IASB has developed the International Financial Reporting Standards (IFRS).

■ Business Terms You Need to Know

accounting 457	asset 464	statement of cash flows 471
public accountant 459	liability 464	accrual accounting 471
generally accepted accounting principles (GAAP) 462	owners' equity 464	budget 476
	accounting equation 464	International Accounting Standards Board (IASB) 480
Financial Accounting Standards Board (FASB) 462	double-entry bookkeeping 464	International Financial Reporting Standards (IFRS) 480
	balance sheet 468	
Foreign Corrupt Practices Act 463	income statement 468	
accounting cycle 463	statement of owners' equity 470	

■ Review Questions

1. Define *accounting*. Who are the major users of accounting information?

2. What are the three major business activities in which accountants play a major role? Give an example of each.

3. What does the term *GAAP* mean? Briefly explain the roles of the Financial Accounting Standards Board and the Securities and Exchange Commission.

4. What is double-entry bookkeeping? Give a brief example.

5. List the four major financial statements. Which financial statements are permanent and which are temporary?

6. What is the difference between a current asset and a long-term asset? Why is cash typically listed first on a balance sheet?

7. List and explain the major items found on an income statement.

8. What is accrual accounting? Give an example of how accrual accounting affects a firm's financial statement.

9. List the four categories of financial ratios and give an example of each. What is the purpose of ratio analysis?

10. What is a cash budget? Briefly outline what a simple cash budget might look like.

■ Projects and Teamwork Applications

1. Contact a local public accounting firm and set up an interview with one of the accountants. Ask the individual what his or her educational background is, what attracted the individual to the accounting profession, and what he or she does during a typical day. Prepare a brief report on your interview. Do you now want to learn more about the accounting profession? Are you more interested in possibly pursuing a career in accounting?

2. Suppose you work for a U.S. firm that has extensive European operations. You need to restate data from the various European currencies in U.S. dollars in order to prepare your firm's financial statements. Which financial statements and which components of these statements will be affected?

3. Identify two public companies operating in different industries. Collect at least three years' worth of financial statements for the firms. Calculate the financial ratios discussed in the chapter. Prepare an oral report summarizing your findings.

4. You've been appointed treasurer of a local not-for-profit organization. You would like to improve the quality of the organization's financial reporting to current and potential donors. Describe the kinds of financial statements you would like to see the organization's accountant prepare.

5. Adapting the format of Figure 15.7, prepare on a sheet of paper your personal cash budget for next month. Keep in mind the following suggestions as you prepare your budget:

   a. *Cash inflows*. Your sources of cash would include your payroll earnings, if any; gifts; scholarship monies; tax refunds; dividends and interest; and income from self-employment.

   b. *Cash outflows*. When estimating next month's cash outflows, include any of the following that may apply to your situation:

      i. Household expenses (rent or mortgage, utilities, maintenance, home furnishings, telephone/cell phone, cable TV, household supplies, groceries)
      ii. Education (tuition, fees, textbooks, supplies)
      iii. Work (lunches, clothing)
      iv. Clothing (purchases, cleaning, laundry)
      v. Automobile (auto payments, repairs) or other transportation (bus, train)
      vi. Gasoline expenses
      vii. Insurance premiums
         • Renters (or homeowners)
         • Auto
         • Health
         • Life
      viii. Taxes (income, Social Security, Medicare, real estate)
      ix. Savings and investments
      x. Entertainment/recreation (dining, movies, health club, vacation/travel)
      xi. Debt (credit cards, installment loans)
      xii. Miscellaneous (charitable contributions, child care, gifts, medical expenses)

   c. *Beginning cash balance*. This amount could be based on a minimum cash balance you keep in your checking account and should include only the cash available for your use; therefore, money such as that invested in retirement plans should not be included.

■ Web Assignments

1. **International Accounting Standards Board (IASB).** The IASB is responsible for setting and modifying international accounting rules. Go to the IASB's Web site at http://www.iasb.org and click on "about us." Print out the material and bring it to class to participate in a class discussion on the IASB.

2. **Certified management accountant (CMA).** As noted in the chapter, managerial accountants often seek CMA certifications. Visit the Web site of the Institute of Management Accountants at http://www.imanet.org. Click on "CMA Certification" and then "Become a CMA." Once on the Become a CMA page, click on the subsection, "How to Get Started." What are the educational and experiential requirements for obtaining a CMA? How many exams does a CMA candidate have to pass? What do these exams cover?

3. **Financial reporting requirements.** This chapter discussed the financial reporting requirements of public companies in the United States. Public companies are those whose shares are traded on a stock exchange. Go to http://www.google.com/finance and type in the name of a public company and then click on "financials" to view the firm's current financial statements. Prepare a brief report comparing those statements to the ones shown in the chapter.

Note: Internet Web addresses change frequently. If you don't find the exact sites listed, you may need to access the organization's home page and search from there or use a search engine such as Bing or Google.

Shoeboxed to the Rescue

CASE 15.1

There's no lack of great software to help you with your accounting, your recordkeeping, and your tax preparation. If only you could easily get your collection of little paper receipts into one of those programs.

But now you can. Shoeboxed Inc., a small North Carolina company, will extract data from your receipts, business cards, e-mails, and paper documents, and organize them into an online account ready for feeding into your favorite financial-management program. Users can e-mail, upload, photograph, or scan their information; Shoeboxed even provides prepaid envelopes for those who prefer snail mail.

"Shoeboxed set out to be (and has become) the bridge between the pile of physical receipts on your desk and an organized and online IRS-accepted archive of your financial information that is accessible at your fingers anytime, anywhere," said the company's marketing manager.

With 100,000 customers in 100 countries, Shoeboxed is committed to growth and is cementing partnerships with companies such as Hewlett Packard to use Web-enabled printers for scanning information directly to their Shoeboxed accounts.

"We want to be in every small business, that's our goal," says founder Taylor Mingos. "We are partnering aggressively."

Questions for Critical Thinking

1. Shoeboxed users can decide whether to get their receipts back or have the firm shred them. What do you recommend?
2. Are there any disadvantages of a service such as Shoeboxed? If so, what are they?

Sources: Laura Oleniacz, "Shoeboxed Scores Scanning Partnership with HP," *The Herald Sun,* February 6, 2012, http://www.heraldsun.com; Nicole Fende, "5 Easy Ways to Stay on Top of Your Accounting," Small Biz Trends.com, January 26, 2012, http://smallbixtrends.com; "Shoeboxed Finds a Better Place for Your Receipts," *Geekpreneur,* December 27, 2011, http://www.geekpreneur.com.

BDO Seidman: Growing with the 20th Century and Beyond

CASE 15.2

In 1910, Maximillian Leonard Seidman (1888–1963), the son of Russian immigrants, founded the accounting firm of Seidman & Seidman in New York City. The profession of accounting was also brand new.

When the income tax on individuals was established in 1913 by the Sixteenth Amendment to the U.S. Constitution, Seidman recognized the potential for growth as accountants took on a new role in tax planning for individuals. And when Congress enacted legislation in 1917, instituting corporate income taxes, Seidman—now joined by two brothers—expanded the business to include corporations. The firm opened a second office in Michigan, just when the federal government converted furniture and woodworking factories to airplane manufacturing for World War I. Seidman & Seidman quickly became known

for serving this industry when it developed a successful system for keeping track of furniture-plant costs.

Maximillian Seidman ran the firm for 45 years. He wrote many articles and served in many industry organizations. He advocated "Total Involvement" of his firm's employees in the business of their clients. In 1944 he declared, "It is the manner in which we serve our clients today that will determine whether we shall have them to serve as clients in the future."

Seidman & Seidman became a truly national firm by the 1960s. In 1963, it joined other accounting companies from Canada, Britain, the Netherlands and (then West) Germany in an international organization. In 1973, these firms formed a new group called BDO (Binder Dijker Otte & Co.). This group, now called BDO International, is the seventh largest accounting firm in the world, with 1,118 branches in 135 countries. The U.S. member, BDO Seidman LLP, has 41 branches and more than 400 independent locations.

BDO has received a number of industry honors. The company recently announced that 34 of its U.S. offices had won the Alfred P. Sloan Award for Business Excellence in Workplace Flexibility. This award acknowledges the personal and workplace advantages of flexibility programs when a firm uses them to improve its effectiveness and to benefit its employees. *Accounting Today* magazine and Best Companies Group named BDO one of the "best accounting firms." The Best Accounting Firms program identifies the best employers in the accounting industry and their benefits to the U.S. economy, workforce, and businesses. And the American Society of Women Accountants (ASWA) and the American Woman's Society of CPAs (AWSCPA) both named BDO one of the "best 2010 CPA firms for women."

Questions for Critical Thinking

1. What historic and economic factors do you think might have contributed to the growth and expansion of the accounting industry, and Seidman's firm, from the early 20th century to today?

2. What advantages does BDO Seidman LLP enjoy in belonging to a large, international group?

Sources: Company Web site, http://www.bdo.com, accessed April 5, 2012; Big 4 Accounting Firms, "The Top Accounting Firms in the World," http://www.big4accountingfirms.org, accessed April 5, 2012; "BDO Named a Best CPA Firm for Women by American Society of Women Accountants and American Woman's Society of CPAs," press release, http://www.bdo.com, accessed April 5, 2012; "BDO USA, LLP Recognized for Exemplary Workplace Practices with the Alfred P. Sloan Award," press release, http://www.bdo.com, accessed April 5, 2012.

CASE 15.3 — Pet Airways Is a "Feel-Good" Business

It's great to love the business you're in, as do Alysa Binder and Dan Wiesel, co-founders of Pet Airways. They not only love their business, they also care for their customers, who happen to be furry and four-legged. But Pet Airways, the only service devoted entirely to transporting cats and dogs around the country by air, is also a business—which means that Binder and Wiesel must pay attention to the financial aspects of their company. "We're doing something that's a feel-good, do-good service and it's absolutely rewarding," says Wiesel. But Wiesel knows that, without a thorough accounting of finances, any small business is likely to crash shortly after takeoff.

Binder and Wiesel started Pet Airways based on personal experience—they wanted a better, safer travel option for their Jack Russell terrier than being stashed in the cargo hold. With fluctuating temperatures and dark, cramped quarters, a trip aboard a commercial airline can be unsafe and traumatic for many animals. Binder and Wiesel, who both have backgrounds in business, decided they could do a better job than the passenger airlines by offering pet owners a choice.

As soon as they agreed on their business idea, Wiesel jumped into the financial questions. "I had to ask, 'Is this a viable financial enterprise? What would people pay for a service like this?'" recalls Wiesel. He researched such issues as how much it would cost to retrofit the climate-controlled cabin of a plane to carry animals; how much it would cost to fly a plane from one location to another;

and how much it would cost to staff the company. He also researched how much demand there would really be for a pet airline, and how many pets would have to be booked on each flight in order for the trip to be profitable. He put all of these variables—and more—onto a spreadsheet so he could see what he and Binder would need to do for Pet Airways to take off.

Wiesel says that financial modeling, financial spreadsheets, and good research on costs and pricing can make or break the launch of any small business. "Accounting itself is an absolute full-time, big job," he admits. He wants to "know how much money is coming in, how much is going out, and what's the bottom line." In addition there are taxes, payroll, benefits, and other financial documentation. Wiesel advises that in many cases it's a good idea for small businesses to contract out their accounting to professionals. He prefers this because outsourcing actually contains the cost of accounting.

Running a business is a balancing act, observes Wiesel. "You have to be able to reconcile how much cash you have with how you are going to spend it." For example, as Pet Airways looks to expand to more cities, the firm has to consider the cost of adding more flights and more staff as compared to how many more customers it might attract. Binder points out that, while it's exciting to think about growing, they have to factor in the expenditures of everything from additional hiring to developing a more sophisticated Web site and online reservation system.

All of this comes back to a sound financial plan, says Wiesel. "The financial plan is really the core of it because you can play the what-if game. You can look at the implications of certain decisions." For example, if Binder and Wiesel want to fly to a certain city, they can research which passenger airlines already serve that city. If it's United Airlines, they know that pet owners will be charged $175 for an animal to fly beneath a passenger's seat, or $250 to fly in the cargo hold. They can look at how many flights a day these airlines fly to the city, and probably learn how many pets are booked. And they can find out which terminal Pet Airways would use in addition to any airport taxes and fees. They can plug all this data into the financial plan and see if it works before making the final decision.

Binder and Wiesel usually agree on their company's goals and objectives. Wiesel says it all boils down to one question: "What's it going to cost you to achieve your plan?" Recently, Pet Airways announced its merger with the firm American Antiquities in a share-exchange agreement, a major step toward expansion. "We are delighted to complete this transaction . . . and believe this event represents a significant step in implementing our business plan and continued expansion," stated Wiesel.

Questions for Critical Thinking

1. In Pet Airways' accounting equation, what might be some of the firm's liabilities? What might be considered its assets?
2. Identify the types of costs that Pet Airways might list on its income statement.
3. Why is it important for a small company like Pet Airways to prepare a regular budget?
4. If Pet Airways decides to expand its operations overseas, what kinds of accounting issues would the firm have to take into consideration?

Sources: Pet Airways Web site, http://www.petairways.com, accessed April 3, 2012; "Pet Airways Combines with a Public Company Through Share Exchange with American Antiquities," *PR Newswire*, http://www.prnewswire.com, accessed April 3, 2012; "Doctors Call for Airline Pet Ban," *The Independent*, http://license.icopyright.net, accessed April 3, 2012.

Learning Objectives

[1] Understand the financial system.

[2] List the various types of securities.

[3] Discuss financial markets.

[4] Understand the stock markets.

[5] Evaluate financial institutions.

[6] Explain the role of the Federal Reserve System.

[7] Describe the regulation of the financial system.

[8] Discuss the global perspective of the financial system.

Chapter
16

The Financial System

Community Banks Team up to Fight the Megabanks

Here's what one customer recently had to say about her relationship with a major U.S. bank: "I'm sick of their fees. I'm sick of not knowing where my money goes."

Does that sound familiar? Millions of bank customers who feel the same are finding smaller community banks and credit unions more appealing alternatives than megabanks, with their multiplying fees and impersonal service. But smaller institutions have been woefully lacking in competitive clout and product offerings compared to major banks like Bank of America and Citibank—until now.

Almost 130 banks and credit unions in 35 states have joined forces under a new national brand called Kasasa, pooling their resources to offer banking products that compete with the big names. BancVue is the parent company of Kasasa; it provides staff training to member institutions and does their marketing and promotion. Member banks pay Kasasa a fee based on their size and contribute some marketing funds. In return they're reporting increases in checking and savings deposits between 15 percent and 25 percent.

Customers benefit from the alliance's scope. They still bank locally with no minimum-balance requirement, and they can sign up for online banking, higher-yield accounts, and refunds of ATM fees. They can also make automatic charitable donations, automatically deposit interest into savings accounts, and earn free iTunes downloads. Requirements are few and include using a debit card for 10 transactions in any amount per month.

The more banks that join Kasasa, the more it can do. With seven Ohio banks on board, for instance, Kasasa achieved a powerful marketing milestone none could achieve alone by winning sponsorship of the Cleveland Cavaliers NBA basketball team. The small-bank alliance expects to double its membership soon, raise its advertising budget to $13.5 million, and reach 1,000 members within a few years.

Some current members are doing their part to help Kasasa achieve that goal, including the veteran CEO of one Minnesota bank who persuaded two neighboring banks to join. "Over the past couple years," he said, "I've realized that other banks like us that serve their communities shouldn't be the ones we're competing with." Another CEO in Missouri who reached out to rivals said they were skeptical about Kasasa at first, but "once they see the results we've had, I think they'll be coming back around."[1]

Overview

Businesses, governments, and individuals often need to raise capital. Assume the owner of a small business either forecasts a sharp increase or drop in sales; one might require more inventory and the other reduced production in order to survive. The owner might turn to a major bank or a nontraditional lender like a Kasasa member bank for a loan that would provide the needed cash for either situation. On the other hand, some individuals and businesses have incomes that are greater than their current expenditures and wish to earn a rate of return on the excess funds. For instance, say your income this month is $3,000 but your expenditures are only $2,500. You can take the extra $500 and deposit it in your bank savings account, which pays you a rate of interest.

The two transactions just described are small parts of what is known as the **financial system**, the process by which money flows from savers to users. Virtually all businesses, governments, and individuals participate in the financial system, and a well-functioning one is vital to a nation's economic well-being. The financial system is the topic of this chapter.

We begin by describing the financial system and its components in more detail. Then, the major types of financial instruments, such as stocks and bonds, are outlined. Next we discuss financial markets, where financial instruments are bought and sold. We then describe the world's major stock markets, such as the New York Stock Exchange.

financial system process by which money flows from savers to users.

Next, banks and other financial institutions are described in depth. The structure and responsibilities of the U.S. Federal Reserve System, along with the tools the Fed uses to control the supply of money and credit, are detailed. The chapter concludes with an overview of the major laws and regulations affecting the financial system and a discussion of today's global financial system.

[1]

Understanding the Financial System

LECTURE ENHANCER:
How are savers served by the components of the financial system? How do users benefit?

CLASS ACTIVITY:
Ask students why it is difficult for them to save money as compared to older people.

LECTURE ENHANCER:
What expenses typically decrease as you get older? Which ones might rise?

Households, businesses, government, financial institutions, and financial markets together form what is known as the financial system. A simple diagram of the financial system is shown in Figure 16.1.

On the left are savers—those with excess funds. For a variety of reasons, savers choose not to spend all of their current income, so they have a surplus of funds. Users are the opposite of savers; their spending needs exceed their current income, so they have a deficit. They need to obtain additional funds to make up the difference. Savings are provided by some households, businesses, and the government, but other households, businesses, and the government are also borrowers. Households may need money to buy automobiles or homes. Businesses may need money to purchase inventory or build new production facilities. Governments may need money to build highways and courthouses.

Generally, in the United States, households are net savers—meaning that as a whole they save more funds than they use—whereas businesses and governments are net users—meaning that they use more funds than they save. The fact that most of the net savings in the U.S. financial system are provided by households may be a bit of a surprise initially, because Americans do not have a reputation for being thrifty. Yet even though the savings rate of American households is low compared with those of other countries, American households still save hundreds of billions of dollars each year.

How much an individual saves is a function of many variables. One of the most important is the person's age. People often transition from net borrowers to net savers as they get older. When you graduate from college and begin a career, you likely have little in the way of savings. In fact, you may be deeply in debt. In the early years of your career, you may spend more than you make as you acquire major assets, such as a home. So in these early years your *net worth*—the difference between what you own and what you owe—is very low and may even be negative. However, as your career progresses and your income rises, you will begin to build a financial nest egg to fund retirement and other needs. Your net worth will also increase. It will continue to increase until you retire and begin drawing on your retirement savings.

FIGURE 16.1 Overview of the Financial Systems and Its Components

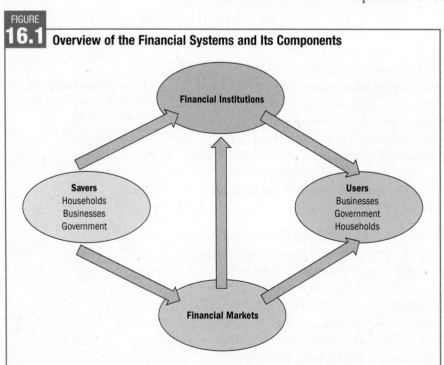

Going Green

Green Banking at New Resource Bank

Would you drive 25 miles to move your money to a "green" bank? One couple in Illinois recently did. The trend toward small banks with personalized service and Earth-friendly profiles has gained steam in the wake of recent protests and gaffes like Bank of America's quickly withdrawn debit card fee.

New Resource Bank is a popular green-bank alternative for many San Francisco customers. "Our business has tripled this month," its CEO said recently after New Resource gained $1.5 million in deposits from 150 new accounts. "We have had nonstop, all day long, people moving their money."

New Resource earns part of its appeal from its sustainability focus. It is a Certified B Corporation and San Francisco-certified Green Business, its headquarters are LEED Gold certified, and it won a regional Outstanding Achievement award from the U.S. Environmental Protection Agency. The bank reuses and recycles to keep 95 percent of its waste from entering local landfills, it purchases Green-e certified wind power certificates to offset electricity use, and it uses remanufactured toner cartridges and recycled paper. It is also a leading local lender to communities and businesses installing solar panels in California. The loans are funded by certificate of deposit (CD) accounts dedicated exclusively to financing solar panels.

Questions for Critical Thinking

1. One bank's COO calls the popularity of green banks "a broader cultural shift in what people expect from their bank." Do you agree? Why or why not?

2. How important to bank customers is community involvement like New Resource's solar lending program and dedicated solar CDs?

Sources: Company website, New Resource Bank, http://www.newresourcebank.com, accessed February 21, 2012; Constance Gustke, "5 Green Banking Tips to Save the Planet," Bankrate.com, http://www.bankrate.com, accessed February 21, 2012; Kevin Roose, "Amid Wall Street Protests, Smaller Banks Gain Favor," *The New York Times*, http://dealbook.nytimes.com, accessed February 21, 2012.

Funds can be transferred between savers and users in two ways: directly and indirectly. A direct transfer means that the user raises the needed funds directly from savers. While direct transfers occur, the vast majority of funds flow through either financial markets or financial institutions. For example, assume a local school district needs to build a new high school. The district doesn't have enough cash on hand to pay for the school construction costs, so it sells bonds to investors (savers) in the financial market. The district uses the proceeds from the sale to pay for the new school and in return pays bond investors interest each year for the use of their money.

The other way in which funds can be transferred indirectly is through financial institutions—for example, a commercial bank such as Cincinnati-based Fifth Third Bank or Alabama-based Regions Bank. The bank pools customer deposits and uses the funds to make loans to businesses and households. These borrowers pay the bank interest, and it, in turn, pays depositors interest for the use of their money.

The accompanying "Going Green" feature describes the growing appeal of "green" banking.

2 Types of Securities

For the funds they borrow from savers, businesses and governments provide different types of guarantees for repayment. **Securities**, also called financial instruments, represent obligations on the part of the issuers—businesses and governments—to provide the purchasers with expected or stated returns on the funds invested or loaned. Securities can be grouped into three categories: money market instruments, bonds, and stock. Money market instruments and bonds are both debt securities. Stocks are units of ownership in corporations like General Electric, McDonald's, Apple, and PepsiCo.

Assessment Check ✅

1. What is the financial system?

2. In the financial system, who are the borrowers and who are the savers?

3. List the two most common ways in which funds are transferred between borrowers and savers.

securities financial instruments that represent obligations on the part of the issuers to provide the purchasers with expected stated returns on the funds invested or loaned.

Money Market Instruments

Money market instruments are short-term debt securities issued by governments, financial institutions, and corporations. All money market instruments mature within one year from the date of issue. The issuer pays interest to the investors for the use of their funds. Money market instruments are generally low-risk securities and are purchased by investors when they have surplus cash. Examples of money market instruments include U.S. Treasury bills, commercial paper, and bank certificates of deposit.

Treasury bills are short-term securities issued by the U.S. Treasury and backed by the full faith and credit of the U.S. government. Treasury bills are sold with a maturity of 30, 90, 180, or 360 days and have a minimum denomination of $1,000. They are considered virtually risk free and easy to resell. Commercial paper is securities sold by corporations, such as Raytheon, that mature in from 1 to 270 days from the date of issue. Although slightly riskier than Treasury bills, commercial paper is still generally considered a very low-risk security.

A certificate of deposit (CD) is a time deposit at a financial institution, such as a commercial bank, savings bank, or credit union. The sizes and maturity dates of CDs vary considerably and can often be tailored to meet the needs of purchasers. CDs in denominations of $250,000 or less per depositor are federally insured. CDs in larger denominations are not federally insured but can be sold more easily before they mature.

Bonds

Bondholders are creditors of a corporation or government body. By selling bonds, a firm obtains long-term debt capital. Federal, state, and local governments also acquire funds through bonds. Bonds are issued in various denominations, or face values, usually between $1,000 and $25,000. Each issue indicates a rate of interest to be paid to the bondholder—stated as a percentage of the bond's face value—as well as a maturity date on which the bondholder is paid the bond's full face value. Because bondholders are creditors, they have a claim on the firm's assets that must be satisfied before any claims of stockholders in the event of the firm's bankruptcy, reorganization, or liquidation.

Types of Bonds A prospective bond investor can choose among a variety of bonds. The major types of bonds are summarized in Table 16.1. *Government bonds* are bonds sold by the U.S. Department of the Treasury. Because government bonds are backed by the full faith and credit of the U.S. government, they are considered the least risky of all bonds. The Treasury sells bonds that mature in 2, 5, 10, and 30 years from the date of issue.

Municipal bonds are bonds issued by state or local governments. Two types of municipal bonds are available. A *revenue bond* is a bond issue whose proceeds will be used to pay for a project that will produce revenue, such as a toll road or bridge. The Oklahoma Turnpike Authority has issued such bonds. A *general obligation bond* is a bond whose proceeds are to be used to pay for a project that will not produce any revenue, such as a new Indiana State Police Post. General obligation bonds can be sold only by states or local governmental units—such as Grand Rapids, Michigan, or Bergen County, New Jersey—that have the power to levy taxes. An important feature of municipal bonds is that their interest payments are exempt from federal income tax. Because of this attractive feature, municipal bonds generally carry lower interest rates than either corporate or government bonds.

LECTURE ENHANCER:
What type of person would be more likely to invest in low-risk securities?

LECTURE ENHANCER:
Compare the risks and features of each type of bond. Why would a firm choose a certain type as an investment?

16.1 Types of Bonds

ISSUER	TYPES OF SECURITIES	RISK	SPECIAL FEATURES
U.S. Treasury (government bonds)	Notes: Mature in 10 years or fewer from date of issue.	Treasury bonds and notes carry virtually no risk.	Interest is exempt from state income taxes.
	Bonds: Mature in 30 years from date of issue.		
State and local governments (municipal bonds)	General obligation: Issued by state or local governmental units with taxing authority; backed by the full faith and credit of the state where issued.	Risk varies, depending on the financial health of the issuer.	Interest is exempt from federal income taxes and may be exempt from state income taxes.
	Revenue: Issued to pay for projects that generate revenue, such as water systems or toll roads; revenue from project used to pay principal and interest.	Most large municipal bond issues are rated in terms of credit risk (AAA or Aaa is the highest rating).	
Corporations	Secured bonds: Bonds are backed by specific assets.	Risk varies depending on the financial health of the issuer.	A few corporate bonds are convertible into shares of common stock of the issuing company.
	Unsecured bonds (debentures): Backed by the financial health and reputation of the issuer.	Most corporate bond issues are rated in terms of credit risk (AAA or Aaa is the highest rating).	
Financial institutions	Mortgage pass-through securities.	Generally very low risk.	They pay monthly income consisting of both interest and principal.

Corporate bonds are a diverse group and often vary based on the collateral—the property pledged by the borrower—that backs the bond. For example, a *secured bond* is backed by a specific pledge of company assets. These assets are collateral, just like a home is collateral for a mortgage. However, many firms also issue unsecured bonds, called *debentures*. These bonds are backed only by the financial reputation of the issuing corporation.

Another popular type of bond is the *mortgage pass-through security*. These securities are backed by a pool of mortgage loans purchased from lenders, such as savings banks. As borrowers make their monthly mortgage payments, these payments are "passed through" to the holders of the securities. Most mortgage pass-through securities are relatively safe because all mortgages in the pool are insured. However, in recent years, mortgage pass-through securities consisting of pools of so-called *subprime mortgages*, loans made to borrowers with poor credit ratings, were issued. Many of these securities turned out to be quite risky and, in part, triggered what became known as the *credit crisis*. The extent of the crisis forced the federal government to undertake a massive bailout of the financial system. The Office of Financial Stability—part of the U.S. Treasury department—was created to purchase poor-quality mortgage-backed and other securities from financial institutions.

LECTURE ENHANCER:
Do you think unsecured bonds would pay higher or lower interest? Why?

LECTURE ENHANCER:
How did subprime mortgage loans lead to the $700 billion government bailout?

16.2   Standard & Poor's Bond Ratings

Highest	AAA	Investment grade
	AA	
	A	
	BBB	
	BB	Speculative grade
	B	
	CCC	
	CC	
Lowest	C	

Note: Standard & Poor's occasionally assigns a plus or minus following the letter rating. For instance, AA+ means that the bond is higher quality than most AA bonds but hasn't quite met AAA standards. Ratings below C indicate that the bond is currently not paying interest.

Quality Ratings for Bonds Two factors determine the price of a bond: its risk and its interest rate. Bonds vary considerably in terms of risk. One tool bond investors use to assess the risk of a bond is its *bond rating*. Several investment firms rate corporate and municipal bonds, the best known of which are Standard & Poor's (S&P), Moody's, and Fitch. Table 16.2 lists the S&P bond ratings. Moody's and Fitch use similar rating systems. Bonds with the lowest level of risk are rated AAA. As ratings descend, risk increases. Bonds with ratings of BBB and above are classified as *investment-grade bonds*. By contrast, bonds with ratings of BB and below are classified as *speculative* or *junk bonds*. Junk bonds attract investors by offering high interest rates in exchange for greater risk. Today, junk bonds pay about 50 percent more in interest than do investment-grade corporate bonds. The credit crisis of recent years generated a great deal of criticism of the ratings companies.

The second factor affecting the price of a bond is its interest rate. Other things being equal, the higher the interest rate, the higher the price of a bond. However, everything else often is not equal; the bonds may not be equally risky, or one may have a longer maturity. Investors must evaluate the trade-offs involved.

Another important influence on bond prices is the *market interest rate*. Because bonds pay fixed rates of interest, as market interest rates rise, bond prices fall, and vice versa. For instance, the price of a ten-year bond, paying 5 percent per year, would fall by about 8 percent if market interest rates rose from 5 percent to 6 percent.

Most corporate and municipal bonds, and some government bonds, are callable. A *call provision* allows the issuer to redeem the bond before its maturity at a specified price. Not surprisingly, issuers tend to call bonds when market interest rates are declining. For example, if York County, Pennsylvania, had $50 million in bonds outstanding with a 5 percent annual interest rate, it would pay $2.5 million annually in interest. If interest rates decline to 3 percent, the county may decide to call the 5 percent bonds, repaying the principal from the proceeds of newly issued 3 percent bonds. Calling the 5 percent bonds and issuing 3 percent bonds will save the county $1 million a year in interest payments. The savings in annual interest expense should more than offset the cost of retiring the old bonds and issuing new ones.

Stock

The basic form of corporate ownership is embodied in **common stock**. Purchasers of common stock are the true owners of a corporation. Holders of common stock vote on major company decisions, such as purchasing another company or electing a board of directors. In return for the money they invest, they expect to receive some sort of return. This return can come in the form of cash dividend payments, expected price appreciation, or both. Dividends vary widely from firm to firm. As a general rule, faster-growing companies pay less in dividends because they need more funds to finance their growth. Consequently, investors expect stocks paying little or no cash dividends to show greater price appreciation compared with stocks paying more generous cash dividends.

common stock basic form of corporate ownership.

Sometimes unforeseen events can have a profound effect on dividends. The 2010 explosion and fire on the oil-drilling rig *Deepwater Horizon* killed 11 oil workers and injured others. Leased by British oil firm BP, the oil well began leaking millions of gallons of crude oil and methane into the Gulf of Mexico, endangering countless fish, birds, and other marine animals. The first oil rig disaster of this magnitude to occur in the United States, it threatened the livelihoods of fishermen and others who made their living on the gulf. The oil polluted the wetlands and beaches of Louisiana, Mississippi, Alabama, and Florida, harming wildlife and damaging the tourist industry. Local residents, the media, and government figures condemned BP for its mishandling of the event and its aftereffects.

LECTURE ENHANCER: How might a fast-growing company need and use more money than a slower growing company?

Amid intense public and political scrutiny, BP launched a television and print campaign promising to "make this right." Many called on BP to suspend its dividends, stop the ad campaign, and instead use that money to clean up the oil spill. BP's stock fell and Standard & Poor's downgraded BP's debt rating from AA-minus to A. BP then announced it would cancel dividend payments to shareholders for the first quarter of the fiscal year and suspend dividend payments to shareholders for the second and third quarters.

CLASS ACTIVITY: Discuss the BP oil spill and how damage estimates might be developed for such an incident.

Before the disaster, BP had been Britain's largest company, but in the following months its value fell by half. Although the dividend suspension is not likely to have a severe effect on American shareholders, many investors and retirees in Britain rely on those dividends for income. In fact, BP's stock is the source of roughly 12 percent of all dividends paid on the London Stock Exchange. A year after the disaster, 43 percent of shareholders voted not to support Sir William Castell, the firm's safety committee chairman.

BP also agreed to create a fund to pay damages to fishermen, small-business owners, and others with financial losses caused by the oil spill. The fund, which will eventually total $20 billion and represents approximately one year's profit, will be administered by a neutral third party. Anyone whose claim is turned down will have the right of appeal. Scientists estimated the well leaked more than 2.5 million gallons a day, making it the largest oil-related disaster in U.S. history.[2]

Common stockholders benefit from company success, and they risk the loss of their investments if the company fails. If a firm dissolves, claims of creditors must be satisfied before stockholders receive anything. Because creditors have the first (or senior) claim to assets, holders of common stock are said to have a residual claim on company assets.

LECTURE ENHANCER: In a corporate bankruptcy, would you rather hold preferred stock or common stock? Why?

The market value of a stock is the price at which the stock is currently selling. For example, Johnson & Johnson's stock price fluctuated between $59 and $69 per share during a recent year. What determines this market value is complicated; many variables cause stock prices to move up or down. However, in the long run stock prices tend to follow a company's profits.

Preferred Stock   In addition to common stock, a few companies also issue preferred stock—stock whose holders receive preference in the payment of dividends. General Motors and Ford are examples of firms with preferred stock outstanding. Also, if a company is dissolved, holders of preferred stock have claims on the firm's assets that are ahead of the claims of common stockholders. On the other hand, preferred stockholders rarely have any voting rights, and the dividend they are paid is fixed, regardless of how profitable the firm becomes. Therefore, although preferred stock is legally classified as equity, many investors consider it to be more like a bond than common stock.

Convertible Securities   Companies may issue bonds or preferred stock that contains a conversion feature. Such bonds or stock are called *convertible securities*. This feature gives the bondholder or preferred stockholder the right to exchange the bond or preferred stock for a fixed number of shares of common stock. Convertible bonds pay lower interest rates than those lacking conversion features, helping to reduce the interest expense of the issuing firms. Investors are willing to accept these lower interest rates because they value the potential for additional gains if the price of the firm's stock increases. For instance, at a price of $61 per share, Peabody Energy's convertible bond would have a common stock value of at least $1,043 ($61 × 17.1). Should the price of Peabody's common stock increase by $10 per share, the value of the convertible will increase by at least $171.

⌈3⌉ Financial Markets

Securities are issued and traded in **financial markets**. While there are many different types of financial markets, one of the most important distinctions is between primary and secondary markets. In the **primary markets**, firms and governments issue securities and sell them initially to the general public. When a company needs capital to purchase inventory, expand a plant, make major investments, acquire another firm, or pursue other business goals, it may sell a bond or stock issue to the investing public. For example, the European Financial Stability Facility recently issued a bond whose proceeds are designed to support the financial stability of Ireland.[3]

A stock offering gives investors the opportunity to purchase ownership shares in a firm and to participate in its future growth, in exchange for providing current capital. When a company offers stock for sale to the general public for the first time, it is called an *initial public offering (IPO)*. Analysts predicted IPOs from a number of American companies during one recent year, including Caesars Entertainment, LivingSocial, and Rovio (the creator of the Angry Birds video game).[4] The "Hit & Miss" feature describes Facebook's upcoming IPO.

Both profit-seeking corporations and government agencies also rely on primary markets to raise funds by issuing bonds. For example, the federal government sells Treasury bonds to finance part of federal outlays such as interest on outstanding federal debt. State and local governments sell bonds to finance capital projects such as the construction of sewer systems, streets, and fire stations.

Announcements of new stock and bond offerings appear daily in business publications such as *The Wall Street Journal*. These announcements are often in the form of a simple black-and-white ad called a *tombstone*.

Securities are sold to the investing public in two ways: in open auctions and through investment bankers. Virtually all securities sold through open auctions consist of U.S.

Assessment Check ✔

1. What are the major types of securities?
2. What is a government bond? A municipal bond?
3. Why do investors purchase common stock?

financial markets market in which securities are issued and traded.

primary markets financial market in which firms and governments issue securities and sell them initially to the general public.

CLASS ACTIVITY:
Review the academic courses that an investment banker might take.

Facebook at the IPO Crossroads

Because privately held companies with assets over $10 million and 500 shareholders must file financial statements with the Securities and Exchange Commission (SEC), Facebook, valued at $75 to $100 billion, recently announced its IPO, seeking $5 billion in funding. The eagerly awaited stock offering could disappoint investors, however, since trades among company insiders may have generated all the early profits possible from shares.

But the IPO nevertheless represents a crossroads. Despite having 850 million members worldwide, Facebook earns only $4.39 a year from each active user. Once it goes public, it must find new ways to capitalize on its biggest asset—an unmatched store of members' personal data—or stop growing. Some believe Facebook's targeted ads, which bring 84 percent of its revenues, are an outmoded model that "doesn't work very well." Making deeper use of members' data, such as to further fine-tune ads without running afoul of privacy laws worldwide—or raising users' ire—will be a difficult challenge.

To battle Google, Amazon, Apple, and Microsoft, tech giants "competing to become the operating systems of our lives," Facebook must make savvy use of its new store of IPO cash.

Questions for Critical Thinking

1. What impact on Facebook's mission do you think the IPO will have?

2. Would you invest in Facebook stock? Why or why not?

Sources: Laura Hoffmans, "Facebook's IPO . . . Like?" *Forbes,* February 7, 2012, http://www.forbes.com; Damon Poeter, "Facebook IPO: What They're Saying," PC Mag.com, February 2, 2012, http://www.pcmag.com; John Swartz, Scott Martin, and Matt Krantz, "Facebook IPO Puts High Value on Social Network," *USA Today,* February 2, 2012, http://www.usatoday.com; Tom Carmody and Mike Isaac, "Facebook's $5 Billion IPO: The Next Google? Or the Next Groupon?" Wired.com, February 1, 2012, http://www.wired.com.

Treasury securities. A week before an upcoming auction, the Department of the Treasury announces the type and number of securities it will be auctioning. Treasury bills are auctioned weekly, but longer-term Treasury securities are auctioned once a month or once a quarter. Sales of most corporate and municipal securities are made via financial institutions such as Morgan Stanley. These institutions purchase the issue from the firm or government and then resell the issue to investors. This process is known as *underwriting*.

Financial institutions underwrite stock and bond issues at a discount, meaning that they pay the issuing firm or government less than the price the financial institutions charge investors. This discount is compensation for services rendered, including the risk financial institutions incur whenever they underwrite a new security issue. Although the size of the discount is often negotiable, it usually averages around 5 percent for all types of securities. The size of the underwriting discount, however, is generally higher for stock issues than it is for bond issues. For instance, underwriting discounts for IPOs are generally between 7 and 10 percent.

Corporations and governments are willing to pay for the services provided by financial institutions because they are financial market experts. In addition to locating buyers for the issue, the underwriter typically advises the issuer on such details as the general characteristics of the issue, its pricing, and the timing of the offering. Several financial institutions commonly participate in the underwriting process. The issuer selects a lead, or primary, financial institution, which in turn forms a syndicate consisting of other financial institutions. Each member of the syndicate purchases a portion of the security issue, which it resells to investors.

Media reports of stock and bond trading are most likely to refer to trading in the **secondary market**, a collection of financial markets in which previously issued securities are traded among investors. The corporations or governments that originally issued the securities being traded are not directly involved in the secondary market. They make no

LECTURE ENHANCER: Do you think investment banking would be an interesting career opportunity?

secondary market collection of financial markets in which previously issued securities are traded among investors.

Assessment Check ✅

1. What is a financial market?

2. Distinguish between a primary and a secondary financial market.

3. Briefly explain the role of financial institutions in the sale of securities.

stock markets (exchanges) market in which shares of stock are bought and sold by investors.

payments when securities are sold nor receive any of the proceeds when securities are purchased. The New York Stock Exchange (NYSE), for example, is a secondary market. In terms of the dollar value of securities bought and sold, the secondary market is four to five times as large as the primary market. Each day, more than 1.5 billion shares worth about $73 billion are traded on the NYSE.[5] The characteristics of the world's major stock exchanges are discussed in the next section.

[4] Understanding Stock Markets

Stock markets, or **exchanges**, are probably the best-known of the world's financial markets. In these markets, shares of stock are bought and sold by investors. The two largest stock markets in the world, the New York Stock Exchange (NYSE) and the NASDAQ stock market, are located in the United States. The Dow Jones Industrial Average (often referred to as the Dow) is a price-weighted average of the 30 most significant stocks traded on the NYSE and the NASDAQ.

The New York Stock Exchange

The New York Stock Exchange—sometimes referred to as the Big Board—is the most famous and one of the oldest stock markets in the world, having been founded in 1792. Today, the stock of about 2,300 companies are listed on the NYSE. These stocks represent most of the largest, best-known companies in the United States and have a total market value exceeding $12 trillion. In terms of the total value of stock traded, the NYSE is the world's largest stock market.

For a company's stock to be traded on the NYSE, the firm must apply to the exchange for listing and meet certain listing requirements. In addition, the firm must continue to meet requirements each year to remain listed on the NYSE. Corporate bonds are also traded on the NYSE, but bond trading makes up less than 1 percent of the total value of securities traded there during a typical year.

Trading on the NYSE takes place face-to-face on a trading floor. Buy and sell orders are transmitted to a specific post on the floor of the exchange. Buyers and sellers then bid against one another in an open auction. Only investment firms that are designated members of the NYSE and that own at least one trading license are allowed to trade on the floor of the exchange. The NYSE issues up to 1,366 trading licenses at a cost of about $40,000 each.[6]

Each NYSE stock is assigned to a specialist firm. Specialists are unique investment firms that maintain an orderly and liquid market in the stocks assigned to them. Specialists must be willing to buy when there are no other buyers and sell when there are no other sellers. Specialists also act as auctioneers and catalysts, bringing buyers and sellers together.

Some observers portray the NYSE and its trading practices as somewhat old fashioned, especially in this technological age. Most markets, they note, have abandoned their trading floors in favor of electronic trading. However, even though the NYSE still retains a trading floor, the exchange has become highly automated in recent years. Its computer systems automatically match and route most orders, which are typically filled within a few seconds.

The NASDAQ Stock Market

The world's second-largest stock market, NASDAQ, is very different from the NYSE. NASDAQ—which stands for National Association of Securities Dealers Automated Quotation—is actually a computerized communications network that links member investment firms. It is the world's largest intranet. All trading on NASDAQ takes place through its intranet, rather than on a trading floor. Buy and sell orders are entered into the network and executed electronically. All NASDAQ-listed stocks have two or more market makers— investment firms that perform essentially the same functions as NYSE specialists.

More than 3,600 companies have their stocks listed on NASDAQ. Generally, NASDAQ-listed corporations tend to be smaller firms and less well-known than NYSE-listed ones. Some are relatively new businesses and cannot meet NYSE listing requirements. Many NASDAQ firms eventually transfer the trading of their stocks to the NYSE. However, NASDAQ is also home to some of the largest U.S. companies and iconic brands—for example, Amgen, Cisco Systems, Dell, Intel, and Microsoft. These firms would easily meet NYSE listing requirements but, for a variety of reasons, decided to remain listed on NASDAQ.

Other U.S. Stock Markets

In addition to the NYSE and NASDAQ, several other stock markets operate in the United States. The American Stock Exchange, or AMEX, focuses on the stocks of smaller firms, as well as other financial instruments such as options. In comparison with the NYSE and NASDAQ, the AMEX is tiny. Daily trading volume is generally less than 100 million shares compared with the more than 1 billion shares on each of the larger two exchanges.

Often referred to as the Dow, the Dow Jones Industrial Average is a price-weighted average of the 30 most significant stocks traded on the NYSE and the NASDAQ.

Established in the 1700s, the London Stock Exchange is one of the largest stock markets outside of the United States. The Exchange uses a trading communications network similar to the one used at the NASDAQ in New York.

Several regional stock exchanges also operate throughout the United States. They include the Chicago, Pacific (San Francisco), Boston, Cincinnati, and Philadelphia stock exchanges. Originally established to trade the shares of small, regional companies, the regional exchanges now list securities of many large corporations as well. In fact, more than half of the companies listed on the NYSE are also listed on one or more regional exchanges.

Foreign Stock Markets

Stock markets exist throughout the world. Virtually all developed countries and many developing countries have stock exchanges. Examples include Mumbai, Helsinki, Hong Kong, Mexico City, Paris, and Toronto. One of the largest stock exchanges outside the United States is the London Stock Exchange. Founded in the early 17th century, the London Stock Exchange lists approximately 3,000 stock and bond issues by companies from more than 70 countries around the world. Trading on the London Stock Exchange takes place using a NASDAQ-type computerized communications network.

The London Stock Exchange is the most international of all stock markets. Approximately two-thirds of all cross-border trading in the world—for example, the trading of stocks of American companies outside the United States—takes place in London. It is not uncommon for institutional investors in the United States to trade NYSE- or NASDAQ-listed stocks in London.

Because stock markets around the world are so closely interconnected, changes in one country's economy can affect other countries too, as the "Hit & Miss" feature explains.

ECNs and the Future of Stock Markets

For years a so-called *fourth market* has existed—the direct trading of exchange-listed stocks off the floor of the exchange (in the case of NYSE-listed stocks) or outside the network (in the case of NASDAQ-listed stocks). Originally, trading in the fourth market was limited to institutional investors buying or selling large blocks of stock.

Now, however, the fourth market is open to smaller, individual investors through markets called *electronic communications networks* (ECNs). In ECNs, buyers and sellers meet in a virtual stock market and trade directly with one another. No specialist or market maker is involved. ECNs are a significant force in the stock market--around half of all trades involving NASDAQ-listed stocks take place on INET or Archipelago—the two largest ECNs—rather than directly through the NASDAQ system. Some suggest that ECNs represent the future for stock markets, given that INET is owned by NASDAQ and Archipelago, by the NYSE.

Hit & Miss

How News Lifts—or Sinks—World Stocks

The growth of computerized trading has closely connected world markets. Here's a snapshot of how events in one country influence markets everywhere.

In a recent year, Americans hoped that the country was starting to climb out of the worst financial crisis since the Great Depression. The economy was slowly improving and companies were beginning to notice an uptick in consumer demand.

At the same time, as America was emerging from its credit crisis, Europe was facing tough times across the continent, especially in Greece. Because it is part of the European Union, Greece had to be rescued by the EU, and Standard & Poor's reduced the country's bond rating.

Despite public outrage, the Greek government enforced an austerity policy that reduced government spending on social programs. Nearly a year later and despite several bailouts from the European Union and International Monetary Fund, economists predicted that the only way Greece could get back on its feet would be to restructure its debt.

Questions for Critical Thinking

1. Why would a financial crisis on the other side of the world affect the U.S. economy?

2. Greece continues to struggle with its debt crisis. In what ways do its investors share the cost?

Sources: Tony Czuczka, "Greece Debt Buybacks Raised by Merkel's Economic Adviser Field," *Bloomberg Businessweek,* http://www.businessweek.com, accessed March 16, 2012; Mark Rohner, "Greece Ahead of Targets, Will Not Default, Papandreou Says," *Bloomberg Businessweek*, http://www.businessweek.com, accessed March 16, 2012; European Union Web site, http://europa.eu, accessed March 16, 2012; Will Swarts, "Stocks Surge as Earnings Stay Robust," *SmartMoney*, http://www.smartmoney.com, accessed March 16, 2012; Christine Hauser, "Stocks Higher as Earnings Lift Sentiment," *The New York Times,* http://www.nytimes.com, accessed March 16, 2012.

Investor Participation in the Stock Markets

Because most investors aren't members of the NYSE or any other stock market, they need to use the services of a brokerage firm to buy or sell stocks. Examples of brokerage firms include Edward Jones and TD Ameritrade. Investors establish an account with the brokerage firm and then enter orders to trade stocks. The brokerage firm executes the trade on behalf of the investor, charging the investor a fee for the service. While some investors phone in orders or visit the brokerage firm in person, many today use their PCs and trade stocks online. The requirements for setting up an account vary from broker to broker. Selecting the right brokerage firm is one of the most important decisions investors make.

The most common type of order is called a *market order*. It instructs the broker to obtain the best possible price—the highest price when selling and the lowest price when buying. If the stock market is open, market orders are filled within seconds. Another popular type of order is called a *limit order*. It sets a price ceiling when buying or a price floor when selling. If the order cannot be executed when it is placed, the order is left with the exchange's market maker. It may be filed later if the price limits are met.

LECTURE ENHANCER: How might you find a broker if you wanted to begin investing?

Assessment Check ☑

1. What are the world's two largest stock markets?

2. Why is the London Stock Exchange unique?

3. Explain the difference between a market order and a limit order.

5 Financial Institutions

One of the most important components of the financial system is **financial institutions**. They are an intermediary between savers and borrowers, collecting funds from savers and then lending the funds to individuals, businesses, and governments. Financial institutions greatly increase the efficiency and effectiveness of the transfer of funds from savers to users. Because of financial institutions, savers earn more, and users pay less, than

financial institutions intermediary between savers and borrowers, collecting funds from savers and then lending the funds to individuals, businesses, and governments.

they would without them. In fact, it is difficult to imagine how any modern economy could function without well-developed financial institutions. Think about how difficult it would be for a businessperson to obtain inventory financing or an individual to purchase a new home without financial institutions. Prospective borrowers would have to identify and negotiate terms with each saver individually.

Traditionally, financial institutions have been classified into depository institutions—institutions that accept deposits that customers can withdraw on demand—and nondepository institutions. Examples of depository institutions include commercial banks, such as US Bancorp and Sun Trust; savings banks, such as Acacia Federal Savings Bank and Ohio Savings Bank; and credit unions, such as the State Employees' Credit Union of North Carolina. Nondepository institutions include life insurance companies, such as Northwestern Mutual; pension funds, such as the Florida state employee pension fund; and mutual funds. In total, financial institutions have trillions of dollars in assets. Figure 16.2 illustrates the size of the most prominent financial institutions.

LECTURE ENHANCER:
Which type of institution has the largest assets? The second largest?

Commercial Banks

Commercial banks are the largest and probably most important financial institution in the United States, and in most other countries as well. In the United States, the approximately 6,300 commercial banks hold total assets of more than $19 trillion. Commercial banks offer the most services of any financial institution. These services include a wide range of checking and savings deposit accounts, consumer loans, credit cards, home mortgage loans, business loans, and trust services. Commercial banks also sell other financial products, including securities and insurance.

Although 6,300 may sound like a lot of banks, the number of banks has actually declined dramatically in recent years; just 20 years ago there were 12,000 commercial banks. At the same time, banks have grown larger: today, the typical commercial bank is about five times as large as it was ten years ago. Both changes can be explained by the fact that bank mergers are commonplace.

Although the overall trend in the banking industry has been toward fewer, larger banks, a countertrend has also emerged: the growth of small community banks. It is not uncommon for several dozen of these banks to begin operation in any one year. Community banks typically serve a single city or county and have millions, rather than billions, of dollars in assets and deposits. Many consumers and small-business owners prefer smaller banks because they believe they offer a higher level of personal service and often charge lower fees.

FIGURE 16.2 Assets of Major Financial Institutions

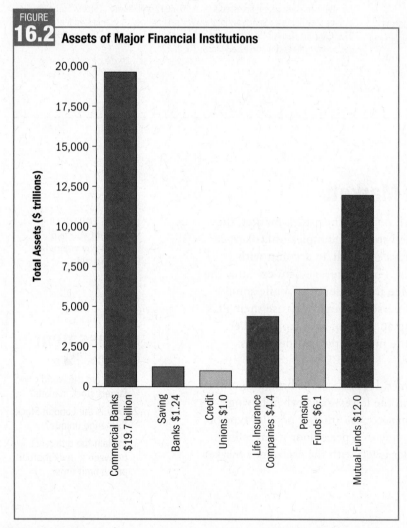

Sources: Organization Web site, "Assets of Private Pension Funds by Type of Asset, 2008-2010," Insurance Information Institute, http://www.iii.org, accessed March 18, 2012; Federal Deposit Insurance Corporation, "Quarterly Banking Profile: Table III-B. Full-Year 2011, FDIC-Insured Savings Institutions," http://www2.fdic.gov, accessed March 17, 2012; Board of Governors of the Federal Reserve System, "Federal Reserve Statistical Release, Z.1, Flow of Funds Accounts of the United States," http://www.federalreserve.gov, accessed March 8, 2012; Matz: "Credit Unions Ended 2011 in a Safer Position," National Credit Union Administration, press release, March 1, 2012, http://www.ncua.gov; Investment Company Institute, "Trends in Mutual Fund Investing January 2012," press release, February 28, 2012, http://www.ici.org.

How Banks Operate Banks raise funds by offering a variety of checking and savings deposits to customers. The banks then pool these deposits and lend most of them out in the form of consumer and business loans. Recently, banks held over $7.8 trillion in deposits and had about $6.7 trillion in outstanding loans.[7] The distribution of outstanding loans is shown in Figure 16.3. As the figure shows, banks lend a great deal of money to both households and businesses for a variety of purposes. Commercial banks are an especially important source of funds for small businesses. When evaluating loan applications, banks consider the borrower's ability and willingness to repay the loan. Occasionally, banks reject applications.

Banks make money primarily because the interest rate they charge borrowers is higher than the rate of interest they pay depositors. Banks also make money from other sources, such as fees they charge customers for checking accounts and using automated teller machines.

In the aftermath of the recent credit crisis, many small business owners have suffered because banks have begun pulling their lines of credit. The "Business Etiquette" feature offers some suggestions if this happens to you.

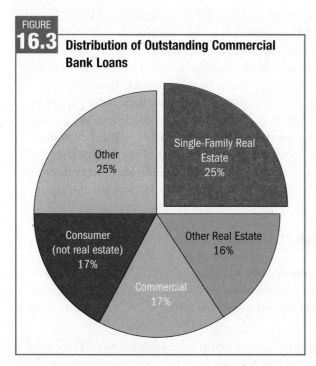

FIGURE 16.3

Distribution of Outstanding Commercial Bank Loans

- Single-Family Real Estate 25%
- Other 25%
- Consumer (not real estate) 17%
- Commercial 17%
- Other Real Estate 16%

Source: Federal Deposit Insurance Corporation (FDIC), "Statistics on Depository Institutions Report," http://www2.fdic.gov, accessed March 16, 2012.

BusinessEtiquette

What to Do When Your Credit Gets Pulled

For years, banks have issued business credit cards to small business owners. The cards include a line of credit—usually several thousand dollars or more—that provides a safety net. After the credit crisis hit, millions of small business owners found themselves working without a net as banks began to call in loans or cap credit lines at the amount outstanding. Thousands of small business owners reported that their credit lines had been decreased or loan extensions rejected. Whereas losing a line of credit was once considered a crisis, today it occurs frequently. Here are some tips if it happens to you.

1 Avoid maxing out your remaining credit or it may impact your credit score.

2 Make monthly payments as quickly as possible, either online or by phone.

3 Apply for a new credit card immediately. By acting quickly, you may receive a new card before your credit score is lowered.

4 If possible, pay down existing credit card debt—but weigh any short-term money need against your credit score before writing the check.

5 Track your credit score. AnnualCreditReport.com is the only government-authorized source for free annual credit reports.

Sources: Federal Trade Commission, "Credit and Your Consumer Rights," http://www.ftc.gov, accessed March 16, 2012; Sam Thacker, "Steps to Take When Your Credit Line Is Pulled," *All-Business*, http://www.allbusiness.com, accessed March 16, 2012; Jeffrey Weber, "What to Do When Your Credit Limit Is Decreased," *SmartBalanceTransfers.com*, http://www.smartbalancetransfers.com, accessed March 16, 2012; Julie Bennett, "What to Do When the Bank Pulls Your Line of Credit," *Entrepreneur*, http://www.entrepreneur.com, accessed March 16, 2012.

LECTURE ENHANCER:
What would make your finances more attractive to a lender?

Electronic Banking More and more funds each year move through electronic funds transfer systems (EFTSs), computerized systems for conducting financial transactions over electronic links. Millions of businesses and consumers now pay bills and receive payments electronically. Most employers, for example, directly deposit employee paychecks in their bank accounts, rather than issuing employees paper checks. Today nearly all Social Security checks and other federal payments made each year arrive as electronic data rather than paper documents.

One of the original forms of electronic banking, the automated teller machine (ATM) continues to grow in popularity. ATMs allow customers to make banking transactions at any time by inserting an electronic card into the machine and entering a personal identification number (PIN). Networked systems enable ATM users to access their bank accounts in distant states and even throughout the world. Most banks now offer customers debit cards—also called *check cards*—that allow customers to pay for purchases directly from their checking or savings account. A debit card looks like a credit card but acts like a check and replaces the customer's ATM card. Many large retailers—including Home Depot, Supervalu, Target, Walmart, and Walgreens—have installed special terminals that allow customers to use their ATM or debit cards to make purchases. Customers are required to enter their personal identification numbers and can often get cash back. Consumers enjoy the convenience of this feature; at the same time, it eliminates the problem of bad checks for retailers. The number of annual ATM and debit card transactions is expected to exceed 52 billion soon.[8]

Online Banking Today, many consumers do some or all of their banking on the Internet. According to a survey by the American Bankers Association, 62 percent of U.S. consumers prefer online banking.[9] Two types of online banks exist: Internet-only banks, such as ING Direct, and traditional brick-and-mortar banks with Web sites, such as JPMorgan Chase and PNC. A major reason people are attracted to online banking is convenience. Customers can transfer money, check account balances, and pay bills at any time.

Federal Deposit Insurance Most commercial bank deposits are insured by the **Federal Deposit Insurance Corporation (FDIC)**, a federal agency. Deposit insurance means that, in the event the bank fails, insured depositors are paid in full by the FDIC, up to $250,000. Federal deposit insurance was enacted by the Banking Act of 1933 as one of the measures designed to restore public confidence in the banking system. Before deposit insurance, so-called *runs* were common as people rushed to withdraw their money from a bank, often just on a rumor that the bank was in precarious financial condition. With more and more withdrawals in a short period, the bank was eventually unable to meet customer demands and closed its doors. Remaining depositors often lost most of the money they had in the bank. Deposit insurance shifts the risk of bank failures from individual depositors to the FDIC. Although banks still fail today, no insured depositor has ever lost any money.

Savings Banks and Credit Unions

Commercial banks are by far the largest depository financial institution in the United States, but savings banks and credit unions also serve a significant segment of the financial community. Today savings banks and credit unions offer many of the same services as commercial banks.

Savings banks used to be called *savings and loan associations* or *thrift institutions*. They were originally established in the early 1800s to make home mortgage loans. Savings and loans originally raised funds by accepting only savings deposits and then lent these funds to consumers to buy homes. Today, there are around 1,070 savings banks with total assets of about $1.24

LECTURE ENHANCER:
Does having a debit card increase the likelihood that you will spend more?

Federal Deposit Insurance Corporation (FDIC) federal agency that insures deposits at commercial and savings banks.

trillion.[10] Although savings banks offer many of the same services as commercial banks, including checking accounts, they are not major lenders to businesses. About 78 percent of their outstanding loans are real estate loans.[11] Deposits in savings banks are now FDIC insured.

Credit unions are cooperative financial institutions that are owned by their depositors, all of whom are members. Around 92 million Americans belong to one of the nation's approximately 7,100 credit unions. Combined, credit unions have more than $962 billion in assets. By law, credit union members must share similar occupations, employers, or membership in certain organizations. This law effectively caps the size of credit unions. In fact, the nation's largest bank—Bank of America—holds more deposits than all the country's credit unions combined.[12]

Credit unions are designed to serve consumers, not businesses. Credit unions raise funds by offering members a number of demand and saving deposits—checking accounts at credit unions are referred to as share draft accounts—and then, in turn, lend these funds to members. Because credit unions are not-for-profit institutions, they often pay savers higher rates of interest, charge lower rates of interest on loans, and have fewer fees than other financial institutions. Credit unions can have either state or federal charters, and deposits are insured by a federal agency, the National Credit Union Administration (NCUA), which functions essentially the same way that the FDIC does.

Nondepository Financial Institutions

Nondepository financial institutions accept funds from businesses and households, much of which they then invest. Generally, these institutions do not offer checking accounts (demand deposits). Three examples of nondepository financial institutions are insurance companies, pension funds, and finance companies.

Insurance Companies Households and businesses buy insurance to transfer risk from themselves to the insurance company. The insurance company accepts the risk in return for a series of payments, called *premiums*. Underwriting is the process insurance companies use to determine whom to insure and what to charge. During a typical year, insurance companies collect more in premiums than they pay in claims. After they pay operating expenses, they invest this difference. Insurance companies are a major source of short- and long-term financing for businesses. Life insurance companies alone have total assets of more than $4.4 trillion invested in everything from bonds and stocks to real estate.[13] Examples of life insurers include Prudential and New York Life.

Pension Funds Pension funds provide retirement benefits to workers and their families. They are set up by employers and are funded by regular contributions made by employers and employees. Because pension funds have predictable long-term cash inflows and very predictable cash outflows, they invest heavily in assets, such as common stocks and real estate. At one time,

John Crowe/Alamy Limited

Life insurance companies such as New York Life are a major source of financing for businesses. Considered a *nondepository financial institution,* insurance companies accept funds from consumers and businesses and invest most of the money.

pension funds owned more than 25 percent of all common stocks. One study that compared U.S. pension funds and those in other countries found that even after the financial crisis, U.S. pension funds had more than 61 percent of their assets invested in stocks but only about 23 percent in less risky bonds; Germany, which was second, had only 34.5 percent in stocks and more than 61 percent in bonds. Recently, U.S. companies have begun quietly moving their pension assets out of stocks and have begun buying more long-term bonds. In contrast, some states and other government agencies, wanting to make up for funds lost in the crisis, have begun investing in higher-risk categories. In total, pension funds have more than $6.1 trillion in assets.[14]

Finance Companies Consumer and commercial finance companies, such as Ford Credit, John Deere Capital Corporation, and the Pennsylvania-based Dollar Financial, offer short-term loans to borrowers. A commercial finance company supplies short-term funds to businesses that pledge tangible assets such as inventory, accounts receivable, machinery, or property as collateral for the loan. A consumer finance company plays a similar role for consumers. Finance companies raise funds by selling securities or borrowing funds from commercial banks. Many finance companies, such as GMAC, are actually subsidiaries of a manufacturer. GMAC finances dealer inventories of new cars and trucks, and provides loans to consumers and other buyers of General Motors products.

Mutual Funds

One of the most significant types of financial institutions today is the mutual fund. *Mutual funds* are financial intermediaries that raise money from investors by selling shares. They then use the money to invest in securities that are consistent with the mutual fund's objectives. For example, a stock mutual fund invests mainly in shares of common stocks. Mutual funds have become extremely popular over the last few decades. The United States' nearly 7,600 mutual funds have about $12 trillion in assets and more than 292 million share-holder accounts. Just 20 years ago, only about 3,400 funds were in existence, with nearly 69 million shareholder accounts and about $1.4 trillion in assets. One reason for this growth is the increased popularity of 401(k) and similar types of retirement plans.[15]

Mutual fund investors are indirect owners of a portfolio of securities. As the value of the securities owned by the mutual fund changes, so too will the value of the mutual fund's shares. Moreover, investment income, such as bond interest and stock dividends, is passed through to fund shareholders.

Slightly less than half of mutual fund assets, around $5.5 trillion, are invested in stock funds. Taxable bond mutual funds—funds that invest in bonds issued by governments or corporations—are also popular. These funds have total assets of nearly $2.5 trillion.[16]

[6]

The Role of the Federal Reserve System

Created in 1913, the **Federal Reserve System, or Fed**, or is the central bank of the United States and is an important part of the nation's financial system. The Fed has four basic responsibilities: regulating commercial banks, performing banking-related activities for the U.S. Department of the Treasury, providing services for banks, and setting monetary

Assessment Check ✔

1. What are the two main types of financial institutions?
2. What are the primary differences between commercial banks and savings banks?
3. What is a mutual fund?

Federal Reserve System (Fed) central bank of the United States.

policy. Not all banks belong to the Fed. Banks with federal charters are required to belong to the Fed, but membership is optional for state-chartered banks. Because the largest banks in the country are all federally chartered, the bulk of banking assets is controlled by Fed members. The Fed acts as the bankers' bank for members. It provides wire transfer facilities, clears checks, replaces worn-out currency, and lends banks money.

Organization of the Federal Reserve System

The nation is divided into 12 federal reserve districts, each with its own federal reserve bank. Each district bank supplies banks within its district with currency and facilitates the clearing of checks. District banks are run by a nine-member board of directors, headed by a president.

The governing body of the Fed is the board of governors. The board consists of seven members, including a chair and vice chair, appointed by the president and confirmed by the Senate. A full term for a Fed governor is 14 years. If a governor serves a full term, he or she cannot be reappointed. A governor can be reappointed if he or she was initially appointed to an unexpired term. The chair and vice chair serve in those capacities for four years and can be reappointed. The chair of the board of governors is a very important position. Some have commented, only half jokingly, that the Fed chair is the second most powerful person in the nation.

The Fed is designed to be politically independent. Terms for Fed governors are staggered in such a way that a president cannot appoint a majority of members, assuming that all members serve their entire terms. The Fed also has its own sources of revenue and does not depend on congressional appropriations.

An important part of the Fed is the *Federal Open Markets Committee (FOMC)*. The FOMC sets most policies concerning monetary policy and interest rates. It consists of 12 members—the seven Fed board governors plus five representatives of the district banks, who serve on a rotating basis. The Fed chair is also chair of the FOMC.

Check Clearing and the Fed

As mentioned earlier, one of the Fed's responsibilities is to help facilitate the clearing of checks. Even in this age of electronic and online banking, Americans still write billions of paper checks each year. The clearing of a check is the process by which funds are transferred from the check writer to the recipient.

Assume the owner of Gulf View Townhouses of Tampa buys a $600 carpet cleaner from the local Home Depot and writes a check. If Home Depot has an account at the same bank as Gulf View, the bank will clear the check in house. It will decrease the balance in the owner's account by $600 and increase the balance in Home Depot's account by $600. If Home Depot has an account at another bank in Tampa, the two banks may still clear the check directly with one another. This process is cumbersome, however, so it is more likely that the banks will use the services of a local check clearinghouse.

But if Home Depot has its account with a bank in another state—perhaps in Atlanta, where Home Depot is based—the check will likely be cleared through the Federal Reserve System. Home Depot will deposit the check in its Atlanta bank account. That bank, in turn, will deposit the check in the Federal Reserve Bank of Atlanta. The Atlanta Federal Reserve bank will present the check to Gulf View's bank for payment, which pays the check by deducting $600 from Gulf View's account. Regardless of the method used, the Check Clearing for the 21st Century Act allows banks and the Fed to use electronic images of checks—rather than the paper documents themselves—during the clearing process. Because these images are transferred electronically, the time it takes to clear a check has been reduced substantially, often to less than 48 hours.

Monetary Policy

LECTURE ENHANCER: How do higher interest rates affect consumer spending?

The Fed's most important function is controlling the supply of money and credit, or monetary policy. The Fed's job is to make sure that the money supply grows at an appropriate rate, allowing the economy to expand and inflation to remain in check. If the money supply grows too slowly, economic growth will slow, unemployment will increase, and the risk of a recession will increase. If the money supply grows too rapidly, inflationary pressures will build. The Fed uses its policy tools to push interest rates up or down. If the Fed pushes interest rates up, the growth rate in the money supply will slow, economic growth will slow, and inflationary pressures will ease. If the Fed pushes interest rates down, the growth rate in the money supply will increase, economic growth will pick up, and unemployment will fall.

The two common measures of the money supply are called M1 and M2. M1 consists of currency in circulation and balances in bank checking accounts. M2 equals M1 plus balances in some savings accounts and money market mutual funds. Figure 16.4 shows the approximate breakdowns of M1 and M2. The Fed has three major policy tools for controlling the growth in the supply of money and credit: reserve requirements, the discount rate, and open market operations.

The Fed requires banks to maintain reserves—defined as cash in their vaults plus deposits at district Federal Reserve banks or other banks—equal to a certain percentage of what the banks hold in deposits. For example, if the Fed sets the reserve requirement at 5 percent, a bank that receives a $500 deposit must reserve $25, so it has only $475 to invest or lend to individuals or businesses. By changing the reserve requirement, the Fed can affect the

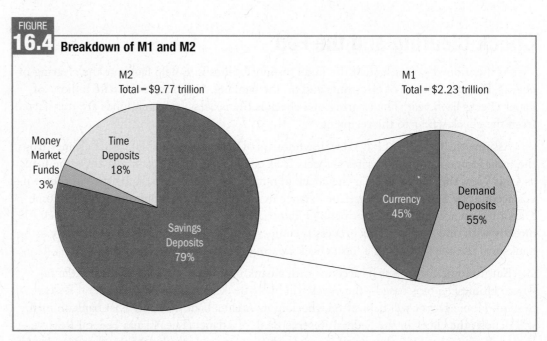

FIGURE 16.4 Breakdown of M1 and M2

M2
Total = $9.77 trillion

M1
Total = $2.23 trillion

Money Market Funds 3%
Time Deposits 18%
Savings Deposits 79%

Currency 45%
Demand Deposits 55%

Source: Board of Governors of the Federal Reserve System, Federal Reserve Statistical Release, March 15, 2012, http://www.federalreserve.gov, accessed March 19, 2012.

TABLE 16.3 Tools Used by the Federal Reserve to Regulate the Growth in the Money Supply

TOOL	BRIEF DESCRIPTION	IMPACT ON THE GROWTH RATE OF THE MONEY SUPPLY	IMPACT ON INTEREST RATES AND THE ECONOMY	FREQUENCY OF USE
1. Reserve requirements	Change in the percentage of deposits held as reserves.	Increases in reserve requirements slow the growth rate in the money supply.	Increases in reserve requirements push interest rates up and slow economic growth.	Rarely used.
2. Discount rate	Change in the rate the Fed charges banks for loans.	An increase in the discount rate slows the growth rate in the money supply.	An increase in the discount rate pushes interest rates up and slows economic growth.	Used only in conjunction with open market operations.
3. Open market operations	Buying and selling government securities to increase or decrease bank reserves.	Selling government securities reduces bank reserves and slows the growth rate in the money supply.	Selling government securities pushes interest rates up and slows economic growth.	Used frequently.

amount of money available for making loans. The higher the reserve requirement, the less banks can lend out to consumers and businesses. The lower the reserve requirement, the more banks can lend out. Because any change in the reserve requirement can have a sudden and dramatic impact on the money supply, the Fed rarely uses this tool. Reserve requirements range from 0 to 10 percent, depending on the type of account.

Another policy tool is the so-called *discount rate*, the interest rate at which Federal Reserve banks make short-term loans to member banks. A bank might need a short-term loan if transactions leave it short of reserves. If the Fed wants to slow the growth rate in the money supply, it increases the discount rate. This increase makes it more expensive for banks to borrow funds. Banks, in turn, raise the interest rates they charge on loans to consumers and businesses. The end result is a slowdown in economic activity. Lowering the discount rate has the opposite effect.

The third policy tool, and the one used most often, is *open market operations*, the technique of controlling the money supply growth rate by buying or selling U.S. Treasury securities. If the Fed buys Treasury securities, the money it pays enters circulation, increasing the money supply and lowering interest rates. When the Fed sells Treasury securities, money is taken out of circulation and interest rates rise. When the Fed uses open market operations it employs the so-called *federal funds rate*—the rate at which banks lend money to each other overnight—as its benchmark.

Table 16.3 illustrates how the tools used by the Federal Reserve can stimulate or slow the economy.

The Federal Reserve has the authority to exercise selective credit controls when it thinks the economy is growing too rapidly or too slowly. These credit controls include the power to set margin requirements—the percentage of the purchase price of a security that an investor must pay in cash on credit purchases of stocks or bonds.

Assessment Check ✔

1. What is the Federal Reserve System?

2. How is the Fed organized?

3. List the four tools the Fed uses to control the supply of money and credit.

The Fed can also inject capital into the financial system in response to a financial crisis. During the recent credit crisis, the Fed pumped hundreds of billions of dollars into the financial system. The Fed even came to the rescue of AIG, a major insurance company, by purchasing some of the firm's stock.

Transactions in the foreign exchange markets also affect the U.S. money supply and interest rates. The Fed can lower the exchange value of the dollar by selling dollars and buying foreign currencies, and it can raise the dollar's exchange value by doing the opposite—buying dollars and selling foreign currencies. When the Fed buys foreign currencies, the effect is the same as buying securities because it increases the U.S. banking system's reserves. Selling foreign currencies, on the other hand, is like selling securities, in that it reduces bank reserves.

⌐7⌐ Regulation of the Financial System

Given the importance of the financial system, it is probably not surprising that many components are subject to government regulation and oversight. In addition, industry self-regulation is commonplace.

Bank Regulation

Banks are among the nation's most heavily regulated businesses. The main purpose of bank regulation is to ensure public confidence in the safety and security of the banking system. Banks are critical to the overall functioning of the economy, and a collapse of the banking system can have disastrous results. Many believe that one of the major causes of the Great Depression was the collapse of the banking system that started in the late 1920s.

All banks, whether commercial or savings, and credit unions have either state or federal charters. Most commercial banks are state chartered; however, federally chartered banks control more than half of all banking assets. State-chartered banks are regulated by the appropriate state banking authorities; federally chartered commercial banks are regulated by the Federal Reserve, the Federal Deposit Insurance Corporation, and the Comptroller of the Currency. Furthermore, state-chartered commercial banks that are federally insured—and virtually all are—are also subject to FDIC regulation.

At the federal level, savings banks are regulated by the Office of Thrift Supervision and the FDIC. Federal credit unions are subject to NCUA regulation. State-chartered savings banks and credit unions are also regulated by state authorities.

Banks and credit unions are subject to periodic examination by state or federal regulators. Examinations ensure that the institution is following sound banking practices and is complying with all applicable regulations. These examinations include the review of detailed reports on the bank's operating and financial condition, as well as on-site inspections. Regulators can impose various penalties on institutions deemed not in compliance with sound banking practices, including forcing the delinquent financial institution into a merger with a healthier one.

Government Regulation of the Financial Markets

Regulation of U.S. financial markets is primarily a function of the federal government, although states also regulate them. Federal regulation grew out of various trading abuses during the 1920s. To restore confidence and stability in the financial markets after the 1929 stock market crash, Congress passed a series of landmark legislative acts that have formed

Solving an Ethical Controversy

Are Debit Card Fees Too High?

Recent financial reform legislation capped the fees that banks are allowed to charge retailers when customers make purchases with debit cards. Down from an average of 44 cents per transaction, the top "swipe" fee is now 21 cents. Retailers, who either pass the fee on to consumers or absorb it, think the cap is still too high. Banks, claiming the reduction is costing them billions, tried making up the difference with new charges to customers, including Bank of America's ill-fated $5 monthly debit card fee.

Should debit card swipe fees be capped?

PRO

1. Debit card fees should be capped, says a credit union executive, because "paying a fee to access your own money is . . . unacceptable."

2. High fees impose a burden on retailers, who must pass it on to consumers in higher prices.

CON

1. Banks need swipe fees to fund anti-fraud activities. Consumers, who directly benefit, should help bear the cost.

2. If banks lose money on low fees, they must compensate with more aggressive marketing and new charges for other services.

Summary

Expect bank fees to continue rising. Whatever happens, says one financial analyst, "the consumer is getting stuck with the costs."

Sources: Andrew Dunn, "Bank Fees 2.0: What Financial Reform Is Costing Banks—and Consumers," TwinCities.com, February 18, 2012, http://www.twincities.com; Hadley Malcolm, "Retailers Sue Fed, Say Debit Card Fees Are Still Too High," *USA Today*, http://www.usatoday.com, accessed March 16, 2012; Jennifer Waters, "High Fees? Here's How to Fire Your Bank," *Market Watch*, http://www.marketwatch.com, accessed March 16, 2012; "The Durbin Amendment Explained," *Nerd Wallet*, http://www.nerdwallet .com/blog, accessed March 16, 2012.

the basis of federal securities regulation ever since. Many other regulations have followed. One of the most recent, the Dodd-Frank Wall Street Reform and Consumer Protection Act, is having some effects on the banking business and its customers, as the "Solving an Ethical Controversy" feature explains.

As noted in Chapter 15, the U.S. Securities and Exchange Commission, created in 1934, is the principal federal regulatory overseer of the securities markets. The SEC's mission is to administer securities laws and protect investors in public securities transactions. The SEC has broad enforcement power. It can pursue civil actions against individuals and corporations, but actions requiring criminal proceedings are referred to the U.S. Justice Department.

The SEC requires virtually all new public issues of corporate securities to be registered. As part of the registration process for a new security issue, the issuer must prepare a prospectus. The typical prospectus gives a detailed description of the company issuing the securities, including financial data, products, research and development projects, and pending litigation. It also describes the stock or bond issue and underwriting agreement in detail. The registration process seeks to guarantee full and fair disclosure. The SEC does not rule on the investment merits of a registered security. It is concerned only that an issuer gives investors enough information to make their own informed decisions.

The Securities and Exchange Commission is charged with regulating financial markets. Its Web site, featured here, is a good source of information for would-be investors.

Besides primary market registration requirements, SEC regulation extends to the secondary markets as well, keeping tabs on trading activity to make sure it is fair to all participants. Every securities exchange must by law follow a set of trading rules that have been approved by the SEC. In addition, the Market Reform Act of 1990 gave the SEC emergency authority to halt trading and restrict practices such as program trading—whereby computer systems are programmed to buy or sell securities if certain conditions arise—during periods of extreme volatility.

One area to which the SEC pays particular attention is insider trading. **Insider trading** is defined as the use of material nonpublic information about a company to make investment profits. Examples of material nonpublic information include a pending merger or a major oil discovery, which could affect the firm's stock price. The SEC's definition of insider trading goes beyond corporate insiders—people such as the company's officers and directors. It includes lawyers, accountants, investment bankers, and even reporters—anyone who uses nonpublic information to profit in the stock market at the expense of ordinary investors. Although some actions or communications are clearly insider trading, others are more ambiguous. Consequently, all employees of public companies have to be mindful of what is and isn't permitted.

Securities laws also require every public corporation to file several reports each year with the SEC; the contents of these reports become public information. The best known, of course, is the annual report. Public corporations prepare annual reports for their shareholders, and they file another report containing essentially the same information, Form 10-K, with the SEC. The SEC requires additional reports each time certain company officers and directors buy or sell a company's stock for their own accounts (Form 4) or anytime an investor accumulates more than 5 percent of a company's outstanding stock (Form 13-d). All of these reports are available for viewing and download at the Edgar Online Web site (http://www.freeedgar.com).

Industry Self-Regulation

The securities markets are also heavily self-regulated by professional associations and the major financial markets. The securities industry recognizes that rules and regulations designed to ensure fair and orderly markets promote investor confidence and benefit all participants. Two examples of self-regulation are the rules of conduct established by the various professional organizations and the market surveillance techniques used by the major securities markets.

Professional Rules of Conduct Prodded initially by federal legislation, the National Association of Securities Dealers (NASD) established and periodically updates rules of conduct for members—both individuals and firms. These rules are intended to ensure that brokers perform their basic functions honestly and fairly, under constant supervision. Failure

insider trading use of material nonpublic information about a company to make investment profits.

to adhere to rules of conduct can result in disciplinary action. The NASD also established a formal arbitration procedure through which investors can attempt to resolve disputes with brokers without litigation.

Market Surveillance All securities markets use a variety of methods to spot possible violations of trading rules or securities laws. For example, the NYSE continuously monitors trading activity throughout the trading day. A key technical tool used by the NYSE is called Stock Watch, an electronic monitoring system that flags unusual price and volume activity. The NYSE then seeks explanations for unusual activity from the member firms and companies involved. In addition, all market participants must keep detailed records of every aspect of every trade (called an *audit trail*). The NYSE's enforcement division may impose a variety of penalties on members for rule violations. In addition, the exchange turns over evidence to the SEC for further action if it believes that violations of federal securities laws may have occurred.

Although self-regulation by the financial industry has been an important component of securities market regulation, some contend that the industry can never truly regulate itself effectively in today's market environment.

Assessment Check ☑

1. Who regulates banks?
2. Define *insider trading*.
3. List two ways in which the securities markets are self-regulated.

[8]

The Financial System: A Global Perspective

Assessment Check ☑

1. Where do U.S. banks rank compared with international banks?
2. Do other countries have organizations that play roles similar to those played by the Federal Reserve?

Not surprisingly, the global financial system is becoming more and more integrated each year. As we've noted, financial markets exist throughout the world. Shares of U.S. firms trade in other countries, and shares of international companies trade in the United States. In fact, investors in China and Japan own more U.S. Treasury securities than do domestic investors.

Financial institutions have also become a global industry. Major U.S. banks—such as JPMorgan Chase and Bank of America—have extensive international operations. They have offices, lend money, and accept deposits from customers throughout the world.

Although most Americans recognize large U.S. banks such as Citibank among the global financial giants, only two of the world's twenty largest banks (measured by total assets) are U.S. institutions—JPMorgan Chase (ranked tenth) and Bank of America (ranked seventeenth). The other eighteen are based in continental Europe, Great Britain, and Asia. The world's largest bank is BNP Paribas SA, based in Paris, with $2.7 trillion in assets. These international banks operate worldwide, including locations in the United States.[17]

Virtually all nations have some sort of a central bank, similar to the U.S. Federal Reserve. Examples include the Banks of Canada, England, and Japan and the European Central Bank. These central banks play roles much like that of the Fed, such as controlling the money supply and regulating banks. Policymakers at other nations' central banks often respond to changes in the U.S. financial system by making similar changes in their own systems. For example, if the Fed pushes U.S. interest rates lower, central banks in Japan and Europe may also push their interest rates lower. These changes can influence events in countries around the world. Lower U.S. and European interest rates not only decrease the cost of borrowing for U.S. and European firms but also increase the amount of money available for loans to borrowers in other countries such as Chile and India.

In Frankfurt, Germany, a sculpture of the euro—the symbol for the European Union's currency—stands outside the headquarters of Europe's central bank. The 12 gold stars represent all the peoples of Europe.

Alex Grimm/Reuters/Landov

What's Ahead

This chapter explored the financial system, a key component of the U.S. economy and something that affects many aspects of contemporary business. The financial system is the process by which funds are transferred between savers and borrowers and includes securities, financial markets, and financial institutions. The chapter also described the role of the Federal Reserve and discussed the global financial system. In the next chapter, we discuss the finance function of a business including the role of the financial managers, financial planning, asset management, and sources of short- and long-term funds.

Summary of Learning Objectives

⌐1⌐ Understand the financial system.

The financial system is the process by which funds are transferred between those having excess funds (savers) and those needing additional funds (users). Savers and users are individuals, businesses, and governments. Savers expect to earn a rate of return in exchange for the use of their funds. Financial markets, financial institutions, and financial instruments (securities) make up the financial system. Although direct transfers are possible, most funds flow from savers to users through the financial markets or financial institutions, such as commercial banks. A well-functioning financial system is critical to the overall health of a nation's economy.

Assessment Check Answers ✅

1.1 What is the financial system? The financial system is the process by which funds are transferred between those having excess funds (savers) and those needing additional funds (users).

1.2 In the financial system, who are the borrowers and who are the savers? Savers and borrowers are individuals, businesses, and governments. Generally, individuals are net savers, meaning they spend less than they make, whereas businesses and governments are net borrowers.

1.3 List the two most common ways in which funds are transferred between borrowers and savers. The two most common ways funds are transferred are through the financial markets and through financial institutions.

⌐2⌐ List the various types of securities.

Securities, also called *financial instruments*, represent obligations on the part of issuers—businesses and governments—to provide purchasers with expected or stated returns on the funds invested or loaned. Securities can be classified into three categories: money market instruments, bonds, and stock. Money market instruments and bonds are debt instruments. Money market instruments are short-term debt securities and tend to be low-risk securities. Bonds are longer-term debt

securities and pay a fixed amount of interest each year. Bonds are sold by the U.S. Department of the Treasury (government bonds), state and local governments (municipal bonds), and corporations. Mortgage pass-through securities are bonds backed by a pool of mortgage loans. Most municipal and corporate bonds have risk ratings. Common stock represents ownership in corporations. Common stockholders have voting rights and a residual claim on the firm's assets.

Assessment Check Answers ✅

2.1 What are the major types of securities? The major types of securities are money market instruments, bonds, and stock.

2.2 What is a government bond? A municipal bond? A government bond is one issued by the U.S. Treasury. Municipal bonds are issued by state and local governments.

2.3 Why do investors purchase common stock? There are two primary motives for purchasing common stock. One is to receive dividends, cash payments to shareholders by the firm. The other is potential price appreciation of the shares.

⌐3⌐ Discuss financial markets.

A financial market is a market where securities are bought and sold. The primary market for securities serves businesses and governments that want to sell new security issues to raise funds. Securities are sold in the primary market either through an open auction or via a process called *underwriting*. The secondary market handles transactions of previously issued securities between investors. The New York Stock Exchange is a secondary market. The business or government that issued the security is not directly involved in secondary market transactions. In terms of the dollar value of trading volume, the secondary market is about four to five times larger than the primary market.

Assessment Check Answers ✅

3.1 What is a financial market? A financial market is a market in which securities are bought and sold.

3.2 Distinguish between a primary and a secondary financial market. The primary market for securities serves businesses and governments that want to sell new security issues to raise funds. The secondary market handles transactions of previously issued securities between investors.

3.3 Briefly explain the role of financial institutions in the sale of securities. Financial institutions purchase new securities issues from corporations or state and local governments and then resell the securities to investors. The institutions charge a fee for their services.

4 **Understand the stock markets.**

The best-known financial markets are the stock exchanges. They exist throughout the world. The two largest—the New York Stock Exchange and NASDAQ—are located in the United States. The NYSE is bigger, measured in terms of the total value of stock traded. Larger and better-known companies dominate the NYSE. Buy and sell orders are transmitted to the trading floor for execution. The NASDAQ stock market is an electronic market in which buy and sell orders are entered into a computerized communication system for execution. Most of the world's major stock markets today use similar electronic trading systems.

Assessment Check Answers ✔

4.1 What are the world's two largest stock markets? The world's two largest stock markets are the New York Stock Exchange and the NASDAQ.

4.2 Why is the London Stock Exchange unique? The London Stock Exchange is probably the most international of the world's stock markets because a large percentage of the shares traded are not those of British firms.

4.3 Explain the difference between a market order and a limit order. A market order instructs the investor's broker to obtain the best possible price when buying or selling securities. A limit order sets a maximum price (if the investor wants to buy) or a minimum price (if the investor wants to sell).

5 **Evaluate financial institutions.**

Financial institutions act as intermediaries between savers and users of funds. Depository institutions—commercial banks, savings banks, and credit unions—accept deposits from customers that can be redeemed on demand. Commercial banks are the largest and most important of the depository institutions and offer the widest range of services. Savings banks are a major source of home mortgage loans. Credit unions are not-for-profit institutions offering financial services to consumers. Government agencies, most notably the Federal Deposit Insurance Corporation, insure deposits at these institutions. Nondepository institutions include pension funds and insurance companies. Nondepository institutions invest a large portion of their funds in stocks, bonds, and real estate. Mutual funds are

another important financial institution. These companies sell shares to investors and, in turn, invest the proceeds in securities. Many individuals today invest a large portion of their retirement savings in mutual fund shares.

Assessment Check Answers ✔

5.1 What are the two main types of financial institutions? The two major types of financial institutions are depository institutions (those that accept checking and similar accounts) and nondepository institutions.

5.2 What are the primary differences between commercial banks and savings banks? Today commercial and savings banks offer many of the same services. However, commercial banks lend money to businesses as well as to individuals. Savings banks lend money primarily to individuals, principally in the form of home mortgage loans.

5.3 What is a mutual fund? A mutual fund is an intermediary that raises money by selling shares to investors. It then pools investor funds and purchases securities that are consistent with the fund's objectives.

6 **Explain the role of the Federal Reserve System.**

The Federal Reserve System is the central bank of the United States. The Federal Reserve regulates banks, performs banking functions for the U.S. Department of the Treasury, and acts as the bankers' bank (clearing checks, lending money to banks, and replacing worn-out currency). It controls the supply of credit and money in the economy to promote growth and control inflation. The Federal Reserve's tools include reserve requirements, the discount rate, and open market operations. Selective credit controls and purchases and sales of foreign currencies also help the Federal Reserve manage the economy.

Assessment Check Answers ✔

6.1 What is the Federal Reserve System? The Federal Reserve System is the U.S. central bank. It is responsible for regulating banks, providing banking-related services for the federal government, acting as the banker's bank, and setting monetary policy.

6.2 How is the Fed organized? The country is divided into 12 districts, each of which has a Federal Reserve Bank. The Fed is run by a seven-member board of governors headed by a chair and vice chair. An important part of the Fed is the Federal Open Markets Committee, which sets monetary and interest rate policy. The Fed is designed to be politically independent.

6.3 List the three tools the Fed uses to control the supply of money and credit. The four tools are reserve requirements, the discount rate, and open market operations.

7 **Describe the regulation of the financial system.**

Commercial banks, savings banks, and credit unions in the United States are heavily regulated by federal or state banking authorities. Banking regulators require institutions to follow sound banking practices and have the power to close noncompliant ones. In the United States, financial markets are regulated at both the federal and state levels. Markets are also heavily self-regulated by the financial markets and professional organizations. The chief regulatory body is the Securities and Exchange Commission. It sets the requirements for both primary and secondary market activity, prohibiting a number of practices, including insider trading. The SEC also requires public companies to disclose financial information regularly. Professional organizations and the securities markets also have rules and procedures that all members must follow.

Assessment Check Answers ✔

7.1 Who regulates banks? All banks have either state or federal charters. Federally chartered banks are regulated by the Federal Reserve, the FDIC, and the Comptroller of the Currency. State-chartered banks are regulated by state banking authorities and the FDIC.

7.2 Define _insider trading_. Insider trading is defined as the use of material nonpublic information to make an investment profit.

7.3 List two ways in which the securities markets are self-regulated. Professional organizations such as the National Association of Securities Dealers have codes of conduct that members are expected to follow. Major

financial markets have trading rules and procedures to identify suspicious trading activity.

⌐8⌐ Discuss the global perspective of the financial system.

Financial markets exist throughout the world and are increasingly interconnected. Investors in other countries purchase U.S. securities, and U.S. investors purchase foreign securities. Large U.S. banks and other financial institutions have a global presence. They accept deposits, make loans, and have branches throughout the world. Foreign banks also operate worldwide. The average European or Japanese bank is much larger than the average American bank. Virtually all nations have central banks that perform the same roles as the U.S. Federal Reserve System. Central bankers often act together, raising and lowering interest rates as economic conditions warrant.

Assessment Check Answers ✔

8.1 Where do U.S. banks rank compared with international banks? Banks in Asia and Europe are generally much larger than U.S. banks. In fact, only 3 out of the world's 30 largest banks are based in the United States.

8.2 Do other countries have organizations that play roles similar to those played by the Federal Reserve? Yes, virtually all nations have central banks that perform many of the same functions that the U.S. Federal Reserve System does.

■ Business Terms You Need to Know

financial system 489
securities 491
common stock 495
financial markets 496
primary markets 496
secondary market 497

stock markets (exchanges) 498
financial institutions 501
Federal Deposit Insurance Corporation (FDIC) 504
Federal Reserve System (Fed) 506
insider trading 512

■ Review Questions

1. What is the financial system? Why is the direct transfer of funds from savers to users rare?

2. What is a security? Give several examples.

3. List the major types of bonds. Explain a mortgage pass-through.

4. What are the differences between common stock and preferred stock?

5. Explain the difference between a primary financial market and a secondary financial market.

6. Why are commercial banks, savings banks, and credit unions classified as depository financial institutions? How do the three differ?

7. Why are life insurance companies, pension funds, and mutual funds considered financial institutions?

8. Briefly explain the role of the Federal Reserve and list the tools it uses to control the supply of money and credit.

9. What methods are used to regulate banks? Why are state-chartered banks also regulated by the FDIC?

10. Explain how the Federal Reserve, acting in conjunction with other central banks, could affect exchange rates.

■ Projects and Teamwork Applications

1. Collect current interest rates on the following types of bonds: U.S. Treasury bonds, AAA-rated municipal bonds, AAA-rated corporate bonds, and BBB-rated corporate bonds. Arrange the interest rates from lowest to highest. Explain the reasons for the ranking.

2. You've probably heard of U.S. savings bonds—you may even have received some bonds as a gift. What you may not know is that two different types of savings bonds exist. Do some research and compare and contrast the two types of savings bonds. What are their features? Their pros and cons? Assuming you were interested in buying savings bonds, which of the two do you find more attractive?

3. Working with a partner, assume you are considering buying shares of Lowe's or Home Depot. Describe how you would go about analyzing the two companies' stocks and deciding which, if either, you would buy.

4. Working in a small team, identify a large bank. Visit that bank's Web site and obtain its most recent financial statements. Compare the bank's financial statements to those of a nonfinancial company, such as a manufacturer or retailer. Report on your findings.

5. Assume you're investing money for retirement. Specify several investment criteria you believe are most important. Go to the MSN Money Web Site (http://moneycentral.msn.com). Click "Fund Research" (under "Investing"), then choose either "Find top performers by category" or "Find using Easy Screener." Identify at least three mutual funds that most closely meet your criteria. Choose one of the funds and research it. Answer the following questions:

   a. What was the fund's average annual return for the past five years?

   b. How well did the fund perform relative to its peer group and relative to an index such as the Standard & Poor's 500?

   c. What are the fund's ten largest holdings?

■ Web Assignments

1. **Online stock trading**. Visit the Web site of a brokerage firm that offers online trading, such as E*Trade (www.etrade.com) or Charles Schwab (www.schwab.com), to learn more about online trading. Most electronic brokerage firms also offer a trading demonstration. Use the demonstration to see how you obtain price information, company news, place buy or sell orders, and check account balances. Make some notes about your experience and bring them to class to participate in a class discussion.

2. **Banking statistics**. Visit the Web site listed here. Access the most recent year you can find and answer the following questions:

   a. How many commercial banks were in operation at the end of the year? How many savings banks (institutions) were in operation?

   b. What were the total assets of commercial banks and savings banks at the end of the year?

   c. How many commercial banks had assets in excess of $5 billion at the end of the year? How many commercial banks had assets of less than $500 million at the end of the year?

   http://www2.fdic.gov/sdi/sob/

3. **Federal reserve system**. Go to the Web site of the Board of Governors of the Federal Reserve System (www.federalreserve.gov). Prepare a short report on the seven-member board. Who are the current members? What are their backgrounds? When were they appointed? When do their terms expire?

Note: Internet Web addresses change frequently. If you don't find the exact sites listed, you may need to access the organization's home page and search from there or use a search engine such as Bing or Google.

Silicon Valley's Banker

CASE 16.1

In his past job at Credit Suisse First Boston (CSFB), Frank Quattrone brokered some of the biggest tech sales and mergers in Silicon Valley's early days, including taking Cisco and Amazon public. Once he sent a beleaguered prospect a live mule bearing a note: "Stop feeling like a mule and pick CSFB." Quattrone won the business.

Recently, after being sidelined for several years overturning an obstruction-of-justice conviction from that period,

he returned to banking and to Silicon Valley in less flamboyant mode with Qatalyst Partners, a new "boutique" advisory firm he founded with just 30 employees. Qatalyst Partners has worked with some of Quattrone's old clients and new ones to achieve an impressive track record, advising several tech-company acquisitions worth more than $1 billion each and two worth more than $10 billion. In dollar volume of sales, Qatalyst beat out all competing firms except Goldman Sachs and Morgan Stanley.

Observers credit Quattrone's successful comeback and continued ability to negotiate high-priced deals to a combination of luck, financial savvy, and strong industry relationships. One prominent client says Quattrone's appeal is simple: "Frank's a very likeable guy who knows what he's talking about."

Questions for Critical Thinking

1. Do you agree with observers' explanations for Quattrone's success? Why or why not?

2. Why are banker–client relationships important in billion-dollar deals?

Sources: Robert Cyran and John Foley, "Frank Quattrone's Golden Touch," *The New York Times,* September 14, 2011, www.nytimes.com; Anupreeta Das and Randall Smih, "Quattrone Revisits 'Friends,'" *The Wall Street Journal,* September 12, 2011, http://online.wsj.com; "Brainstorm Tech Video: Frank Quattrone on Bubble 2.0—Or Is It?" an interview by Adam Lashinsky, CNN Money, July 21, 2011, http://tech.fortune.cnn.com; Andrew Ross Sorkin, "The Valley's Banker Returns to the Top," *The New York Times,* April 7, 2011, pp. F1, F9.

CASE 16.2 — Credit Unions Find a Silver Lining in the Financial Crisis

Like most Americans, the residents of Meigs County, Tennessee, suffered during the recent recession. As the county's largest employers had often heard, the timing was bad to launch a credit union. Yet, the Middle Tennessee Federal Credit Union, now worth $3 million, has recently celebrated its first birthday.

Credit union founders had begun seeking a charter before the recession. They knew employees were turning in desperation to high-interest payday loans to meet their financial needs, and they wanted to help people secure small, short-term loans on more reasonable terms. Thus, the credit union opened for business in the midst of the recession. Whereas a bank is a for-profit institution beholden to its board members and shareholders, a credit union is a nonprofit cooperative owned by its members. Credit unions emphasize the basic finances of everyday life: savings and checking accounts, credit cards, and relatively small loans for homes or cars. Credit unions generally pay more interest on savings accounts and charge less interest on loans. Any excess funds are channeled back to members. Deposits are insured up to $250,000 by the federal government's National Credit Union Administration.

Credit unions are chartered to serve particular groups and, originally, most were affiliated with employers. However, credit unions began to ease their membership requirements about ten years ago. Now, to join the Middle Tennessee Federal Credit Union, a person must simply work, worship, live, or go to school in the local area.

With big banks tightening credit, consumers and small-business owners have had trouble getting even the most routine loans. Credit unions have filled the gap. But credit unions don't perform all the services of traditional banks: for example, only 59 percent issue ATM cards and only 22 percent offer safe-deposit boxes. Few credit unions are likely to have any branches.

To learn more about credit unions, go online to the Credit Union National Association (CUNA) or the National Credit Union Administration (NCUA). Both organizations offer online tools to help consumers find a credit union nearby.

Questions for Critical Thinking

1. Why is an organization like the Credit Union National Association important to the credit union industry?

2. Go online to either the CUNA or the NCUA Web site to find a credit union near you. If you are eligible to join, compare the credit union with your current bank. What are the advantages of joining the credit union or staying with your bank?

Sources: "Credit Union vs. Bank," Star Community Credit Union, http://www.starcreditunion.com, accessed March 16, 2012; Middle Tennessee Federal Credit Union Web site, http://www.midtenfcu.com, accessed March 16, 2012; National Credit Union Administration Web site, http://www.ncua.gov, accessed March 16, 2012; Credit Union National Association Web site, http://www.cuna.org, accessed March 16, 2012; David Morrison, "Year-Old Tenn. Credit Union Finds Success Despite Great Recession," *Credit Union Times,* http://www.cutimes.com, accessed March 16, 2012; Bob Trebilcock, "Bye, Banks: Time to Join a Credit Union," *MoneyWatch/CBS News,* http://www.cbsnews.com, accessed March 16, 2012; James Briggs, "Credit Unions Thrive as Big Banks Cut Back on Lending," *Oakland Press,* http://www.theoaklandpress.com, accessed March 16, 2012.

"Fair Trade has always been part of my legacy in coffee," says Rik Kleinfeldt, president and co-founder of Rhode Island-based New Harvest Coffee Roasters. "That's where I started with New Harvest." But in less than a decade, New Harvest's business model has evolved beyond Fair Trade to something different.

New Harvest is a small-batch coffee roaster specializing in certified organic coffee that is grown and harvested by farms with sustainable practices. Rik Kleinfeldt notes that he built his company on two pillars: 1) the highest quality coffee, and 2) sustainable sourcing practices. "But these two weren't really gelling at first," he admits. At the beginning, Kleinfeldt tried to source from Fair Trade cooperatives, but this wasn't really fulfilling his objective. "Fair Trade is based on the commodity system," Kleinfeldt explains, "which creates a floor price at which coffee can't drop below. But it doesn't really address the issue of quality." The groups that work with Fair Trade are large cooperatives, sometimes encompassing several thousand small farms. All the coffee is blended together as a commodity, so it is impossible for a roaster like New Harvest to deal directly with each farm, selecting the specific harvest that it wants to buy.

Kleinfeldt is quick to point out that when Fair Trade began around a decade ago, it was a lifeline to small farmers because coffee prices were at an all-time low—these growers were selling their crops for less than it cost to produce them. Without Fair Trade, many of these farms would have gone out of business. With the coffee market somewhat stabilized though, commodity pricing brings its own set of problems. "The commodity pricing usually has nothing to do with the coffee itself," says Kleinfeldt. Prices are set at the New York Stock Exchange, not in the growing fields of Costa Rica or Colombia. He notes that roasters, retailers, and consumers may end up paying way too much or way too little for a particular year's crop.

So Kleinfeldt has become part of what he calls the Artisan Coffee movement—growers, roasters, and retailers who prefer to deal directly with each other as individual businesses. "We connect directly with our growers and determine price based on quality," he explains. Kleinfeldt and his staff, along with some of his retailers such as the owner of Blue State Coffee and the owner of Pejamajo Café, travel to the farms in Costa Rica and Colombia where they actually taste the coffee before purchasing a crop. Kleinfeldt believes this is the only way to get the best coffee on the market. These visits help develop strong relationships, find solutions to problems, and develop strategies for surviving and thriving as businesses. Through visiting, he says, "we can understand their challenges." One farm in particular is located in Colombia. The farmer decided he didn't want to participate in a large Fair Trade cooperative—instead, he wanted to develop a market for his own coffee. So he approached New Harvest with the idea, and the match was ideal. He is now one of New Harvest's premier growers.

Sourcing the coffee beans directly from individual farms also helps New Harvest keep close track of organic and sustainability practices. Gerra Harrigan, director of business development for New Harvest Coffee Roasters, notes that this is an important part of the firm's business. The owners of local coffee shops—and their customers—like the reassurance that New Harvest stands behind all of its claims. Harrigan takes the hands-on approach. "When we deal direct-trade coffee, the coffee has to be cared for a little more," she explains. Harrigan grades the coffee on several factors before pricing it for New Harvest.

Kleinfeldt wants consumers to know they are getting a great deal when they ask for New Harvest at their local shop. He points out that the price differentiation isn't as much as people might think. A visit to the supermarket reveals that Starbucks and Green Mountain sell for about $9 to $11 per pound, whereas most New Harvest coffee sells for about $11 to $13 a pound. Because of the richness of New Harvest, most customers actually get more cups of coffee from a pound of New Harvest than they do from the other premium brands.

Kleinfeldt hopes that the Artisan Coffee movement, as he refers to his company's practices, will flourish and grow. He believes that if you're going to drink a cup of coffee, it should be really fresh and of the highest quality—with beans preferably roasted by New Harvest.

Questions for Critical Thinking

1. What are the benefits and drawbacks of treating coffee as a commodity in the marketplace? What do you predict will be the future of Fair Trade?

2. Should the entire coffee market be regulated in any way? Why or why not? If so, how?

3. How would New Harvest change as a business if it made an initial public offering (IPO)?

4. What is your opinion of the so-called Artisan Coffee movement as a business model? Do you think it will be successful in the long run? Why or why not?

Sources: New Harvest Coffee Roasters Web site, http://www.newharvestcoffee.com, accessed March 16, 2012; "New Harvest Coffee Roasters," *GreenPeople*, http://www.greenpeople.org, accessed March 16, 2012; Richard Garcia, "Pejamajo Café & New Harvest Coffee Roasters," *Chefs Daily Food Bank*, http://www.chefsdailyfoodbank.com, accessed March 16, 2012.

Learning Objectives

[1] Define the role of the financial manager.

[2] Describe financial planning.

[3] Outline how organizations manage their assets.

[4] Discuss the sources of funds and capital structure.

[5] Identify short-term funding options.

[6] Discuss sources of long-term financing.

[7] Describe mergers, acquisitions, buyouts, and divestitures.

Chapter 17

Financial Management

Andreessen Horowitz: Silicon Valley's Venture Capital Firm

Venture capitalist funds invest in promising but cash-strapped startups in return for a share in ownership of the company and a say in its strategic decision making. One such fund that's attracting much attention of late is Andreessen Horowitz, which raised a staggering total of $2.7 billion in venture capital for technology startups in under three years.

Founded in 2009 by Marc Andreessen (who also cofounded Netscape) and Ben Horowitz, the fast-growing firm deliberately set out to be different. Understanding that entrepreneurs want to become CEOs of their firms but often lack the skills and support networks to succeed, Andreessen and Horowitz decided to provide company founders with mentoring, to offer expert help with business operations like marketing and recruiting, and to pull together a huge network of engineers, designers, product managers, and other partners that entrepreneurs can call upon—and to make it easy for them to do so. Horowitz included a full description of the network in his blog, saying, "One reason we published the data is because the question I always get is, 'Are you guys really different?' It really is a firm network. There's proof of that—we can count on that." And so can the many tech entrepreneurs who seek out the fund for financial and other support. Their interest is one reason Andreessen Horowitz has been able to raise so much money, even in a slow economy, and why it has been able to invest in such innovative firms as Airbnb, Box.net, Foursquare, Skype, Zynga, Twitter, and Facebook.

With so much cash to invest, Andreessen Horowitz can afford to make huge transactions that are likely to shake up the venture capital market. Its founders aren't afraid to make waves. "Innovation cascades," says Andreessen, "and we keep finding new layers to invest it." [1]

Overview

Previous chapters discuss two essential functions that a business must perform. First, the company must produce a good or service or contract with suppliers to produce it. Second, the firm must market its good or service to prospective customers. This chapter introduces a third, equally important, function: a company's managers must ensure that it has enough money to perform its other tasks successfully, in both the present and the future, and that these funds are invested properly. Adequate funds must be available to buy materials, equipment, and other assets; pay bills; and compensate employees. This third business function is **finance**—planning, obtaining, and managing the company's funds in order to accomplish its objectives as effectively and efficiently as possible.

An organization's financial objectives include not only meeting expenses and investing in assets but also maximizing its overall worth, often determined by the value of the firm's common stock. Financial managers are responsible for meeting expenses, investing in assets, and increasing profits to shareholders. Solid financial management is critical to the success of a business. The successful acquisition of Android by Google could take place with only carefully planned financial management.

This chapter focuses on the finance function of organizations. It begins by describing the role of financial managers, their place in the organizational hierarchy, and the increasing importance of finance. Next, the financial planning process and the components of a financial plan are outlined. Then the discussion focuses on how organizations manage assets as efficiently and effectively as possible. The two major sources of funds—debt and equity—are then compared, and the concept of leverage is introduced. The major sources of short-term and long-term funding are described in the following sections. A description of mergers, acquisitions, buyouts, and divestitures concludes the chapter.

finance planning, obtaining, and managing a company's funds to accomplish its objectives as effectively and efficiently as possible.

LECTURE ENHANCER: How does finance differ from accounting?

The Role of the Financial Manager

Because of the intense pressures they face today, organizations are increasingly measuring and reducing the costs of business operations, as well as maximizing revenues and profits. As a result, **financial managers**—executives who develop and implement their firm's financial plan and determine the most appropriate sources and uses of funds—are among the most vital people on the corporate payroll.

Figure 17.1 shows what the finance function of a typical company might look like. At the top is the chief financial officer (CFO). The CFO usually reports directly to the company's chief executive officer (CEO) or chief operating officer (COO). In some companies, the CFO is also a member of the board of directors. In the case of the software maker Oracle, both the current CFO and the former CFO serve on that company's board, the latter as its chairman. Moreover, it's not uncommon for CFOs to serve as independent directors on other firms' boards, such as HP, Microsoft, and Target. As noted in Chapter 15, the CFO, along with the firm's CEO, must certify the accuracy of the firm's financial statements.

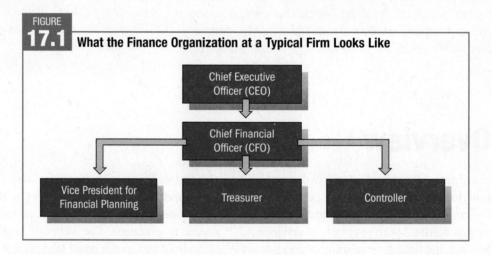

FIGURE 17.1 **What the Finance Organization at a Typical Firm Looks Like**

Reporting directly to the CFO are often three senior managers. Although titles can vary, these three executives are commonly called the *vice president for financial management* (or *planning*), the *treasurer*, and the *controller*. The vice president for financial management or planning is responsible for preparing financial forecasts and analyzing major investment decisions, such as new products, new production facilities, and acquisitions. The treasurer is responsible for all of the company's financing activities, including cash management, tax planning and preparation, and shareholder relations. The treasurer also works on the sale of new security issues to investors. The controller is the chief accounting manager. The controller's functions include keeping the company's books, preparing financial statements, and conducting internal audits. The "Hit & Miss" feature explains the increasing importance of financially sound IT management.

The growing importance of financial professionals is reflected in the growing number of CEOs who have been promoted from financial positions. Indra Nooyi, CEO of PepsiCo, and Jim Marsh, CEO of the British telecommunications company Cable and Wireless, both served as their firm's CFO prior to assuming the top job. The importance of finance professionals is also reflected in how much CFOs earn today. According to a survey by the executive compensation consulting firm Equilar, the median annual salary for CFOs is almost

Hit & Miss

Apptio Calculates Financial Costs for Technology

Apptio, located in Bellevue, Washington, provides hosted Internet technology solutions. Recently, Apptio introduced its new Cost Transparency Template. This template generates the formulas necessary for a company to calculate how much more—or less—it would cost the company to invest in cloud computing as opposed to other options, including traditional in-house hardware and storage. Among Apptio's clients are BNP Paribas, Starbucks, Hallmark, and Facebook. Jeff Day, Apptio's director of marketing, says, "We see that cloud computing is going to change the way IT leaders think about how they manage IT."

St. Luke's Health System of Kansas City has 1,200 doctors among 9,000 total employees in 11 hospitals. The chief information officer, Debe Gash, wanted to eliminate nonessential IT-related costs. A spending-analytics tool from Apptio allowed Gash and her team to save millions of dollars by highlighting unnecessary or redundant spending. For example, St. Luke's had too many desktop software licenses, two full-time employees dealt only with spam management, and the hospital spent a lot of money on electronic storage. Those expenses were reduced or eliminated, and funds are being redirected toward such needed programs as electronic health records. "We were surprised at the efficiencies we were able to derive from getting those insights," Gash said.

Future IT managers will need to understand how the cloud works and whether it will be financially more cost effective to businesses than other in-house or external systems. Day says, "The greatest inhibitor of the cloud is a lack of understanding. IT leaders need better systems and tools to perform accurate analysis."

Questions for Critical Thinking

1. Why have companies recently become so concerned with cost management?
2. Why might it be difficult for very large companies to keep accurate account of spending on such items as computer hardware and software licenses?

Sources: Company Web site, http://www.apptio.com, accessed April 5, 2012; Denise Dubie, "IT Cost Management and the Cloud," Network World, http://www.networkworld.com, accessed April 5, 2012; Bob Evans, "Global CIO: St. Luke's CIO Saves Millions with Apptio's Help," InformationWeek, http://www.informationweek.com, accessed April 5, 2012.

$925,000, up from over $769,000 the previous year. [2] The median bonus is over $200,000, up from over $136,000 the previous year. [3]

In performing their jobs, financial professionals continually seek to balance risks with expected financial returns. Risk is the uncertainty of gain or loss; return is the gain or loss that results from an investment over a specified period of time. Financial managers strive to maximize the wealth of their firm's shareholders by striking the optimal balance between risk and return. This balance is called the **risk-return trade-off**. For example, relying heavily on borrowed funds may increase the return (in the form of cash) to shareholders, but the more money a firm borrows, the greater the risks to shareholders. An increase in a firm's cash on hand reduces the risk of being unable to meet unexpected cash needs. However, because cash in and of itself does not earn much, if any, return, failure to invest surplus funds in an income-earning asset—such as in securities—reduces a firm's potential return or profitability. Many illustrations of the risk-return trade-off are provided throughout this chapter.

Every financial manager must perform this risk-return balancing act. For example, in the late 1990s, Airbus wrestled with a major decision: whether to begin development and production of the giant A380 jetliner. The development costs for the aircraft—the world's largest jetliner—were initially estimated at more than $10 billion. Before committing to such a huge investment, financial managers had to weigh the potential profits of the A380 with the risk that the profits would not materialize. With its future on the line, Airbus decided to go ahead with the development of the A380, spending more than $15 billion on research and development. The A380 entered commercial service a few years ago. Airbus currently has 253 confirmed orders for the A380 and so far has delivered 71 planes to such carriers as Emirates, China Southern Airlines, and Singapore Airlines. [4]

risk-return trade-off process of maximizing the wealth of a firm's shareholders by striking the optimal balance between risk and return.

LECTURE ENHANCER: If you were asked to invest by lending money to a friend for his or her business, would you do so? If so, what interest rate would you charge and why?

Charly Diaz Azcue/LatinContent/Getty Images

Before committing to building the A380 jetliner, financial managers at Airbus had to weigh the potential profits for the company against the risk that the financial investment would not be a success. The plane entered commercial service a few years ago, and the company currently has more than 250 confirmed orders.

Assessment Check ✔

1. What is the structure of the finance function at the typical firm?

2. Explain the risk-return trade-off.

financial plan document that specifies the funds needed by a firm for a period of time, the timing of inflows and outflows, and the most appropriate sources and uses of funds.

Financial managers must also learn to adapt to changes in the financial system. The recent credit crisis has made it more difficult for some companies to borrow money from traditional lenders such as banks. This, in turn, has forced firms to scale back expansion plans or seek funding from other sources such as commercial financing companies. In addition, financial managers must adapt to internal changes as well.

2 Financial Planning

Financial managers develop their organization's **financial plan**, a document that specifies the funds needed by a firm for a given period of time, the timing of inflows and outflows, and the most appropriate sources and uses of funds. Some financial plans, often called *operating plans*, are short-term in nature, focusing on projections no more than a year or two in the future. Other financial plans, sometimes referred to as *strategic plans*, have a much longer time horizon, perhaps up to five or ten years. For colleges selling so-called century bonds, the time period is unusually long, as the "Hit & Miss" feature describes.

Regardless of the time period, a financial plan is based on forecasts of production costs, purchasing needs, plant and equipment expenditures, and expected sales activities for the period covered. Financial managers use forecasts to determine the specific amounts and timing of expenditures and receipts. They build a financial plan based on the answers to three questions:

1. What funds will the firm require during the planning period?

2. When will it need additional funds?

3. Where will it obtain the necessary funds?

Colleges Sell Century Bonds

Would you lend your money out for 100 years? That's what pension funds, hedge funds, and life insurance companies are doing when they participate in the University of California's recent $860 million taxable "century bond" offering. In fact, demand for these bonds was so high that the university increased the size of the AA-rated issue, which was originally set for $500 million.

What makes these bonds so attractive? It's partly their higher-than-average return of 4.85 percent, substantially higher than 30-year Treasury bonds. Adding to the appeal is the stability of the university compared to other bond issuers. "Universities are among the longest-living institutions in the world," said a managing director from Moody's. "The top universities can be expected to be around 100 years from now, whereas many corporations and forms of government may not be."

The University of California is not alone. Massachusetts Institute of Technology, the University Southern California, and the California Institute of Technology have all issued multimillion-dollar bond offerings and plan to apply the proceeds to various projects at their campuses.

Of the bonds' popularity California's state treasurer said, "This deal was extremely well received by the market. We like the outcome."

Questions for Critical Thinking

1. One analyst called century bonds debt "that won't mature until well after everyone involved in the sale is dead." Why are they popular?

2. Do you agree that universities will outlive today's corporations? Why or why not?

Sources: Laura Mandaro, "California's 22ⁿᵈ Century Bond Sale," MarketWatch.com, February 22, 2012, http://blogs.marketwatch.com; Kelly Nolan and Patrick McGee, "2112: A Rush for Bonds from University of California System," *The Wall Street Journal*, February 22, 2012, http://online.wsj.com; Michael Aneiro, "California Sells 100-Year 'Century' Bonds," *Barron's*, February 22, 2012, http://blogs.barrons.com.

Some funds flow into the firm when it sells its goods or services, but funding needs vary. The financial plan must reflect both the amounts and timing of inflows and outflows of funds. Even a profitable firm may face a financial squeeze as a result of its need for funds when sales lag, when the volume of its credit sales increases, or when customers are slow in making payments.

In general, preparing a financial plan consists of three steps. The first is a forecast of sales or revenue over some future time period. This projection is, in fact, the key variable in any financial plan because without an accurate sales forecast, the firm will have difficulty accurately estimating other variables, such as production costs and purchasing needs. The best method of forecasting sales depends on the nature of the business. For instance, a retailer's CFO might begin with the current sales-per-store figure. Then he or she would look toward the near future, factoring in expected same-store sales growth, along with any planned store openings or closings, to come up with a forecast of sales for the next period. If the company sells merchandise through other channels, such as online, the forecast is adjusted to reflect those additional channels.

Next, the CFO uses the sales forecast to determine the expected level of profits for future periods. This longer-term projection involves estimating expenses such as purchases, employee compensation, and taxes. Many expenses are themselves functions of sales. For instance, the more a firm sells, generally the greater its purchases. Along with estimating future profits, the CFO should also determine what portion of these profits will likely be paid to shareholders in the form of cash dividends.

After coming up with the sales and profit forecast, the CFO needs to estimate how many additional assets the firm will need to support projected sales. Increased sales, for example, might mean the company needs additional inventory, stepped-up collections for accounts receivable, or even new plant and equipment. Depending on the nature of the industry, some businesses need more assets than do other companies to support the same amount of sales.

CLASS ACTIVITY:
Discuss why a skilled financial manager needs to not only have strong skills in accounting and finance, but also a keen understanding of the other business functions.

■ Costco has a lower *asset intensity* than a typical manufacturing business might have.

The technical term for this requirement is *asset intensity*. For instance, the chemical manufacturer DuPont has approximately $0.68 in assets for every dollar in sales. So for every $100 increase in sales, the firm would need about $68 of additional assets. The warehouse retailer Costco, by contrast, has only roughly $0.34 in assets for every dollar in sales. It would require an additional $34 of assets for every $100 of additional sales. This difference is not surprising; manufacturing is a more asset-intensive business than retailing.

A simplified financial plan illustrates these steps. Assume a growing company is forecasting that sales next year will increase by $40 million to $140 million. After estimating expenses, the CFO believes that after-tax profits next year will be $12 million and the firm will pay nothing in dividends. The projected increase in sales next year will require the firm to invest another $20 million in assets, and because increases in assets are uses of funds, the company will need an additional $20 million in funds. The company's after-tax earnings will contribute $12 million, meaning that the other $8 million must come from outside sources. So the financial plan tells the CFO how much money will be needed and when it will be needed. Armed with this knowledge, and given that the firm has decided to borrow the needed funds, the CFO can then begin negotiations with banks and other lenders.

The cash inflows and outflows of a business are similar to those of a household. The members of a household depend on weekly or monthly paychecks for funds, but their expenditures vary greatly from one pay period to the next. The financial plan should indicate when the flows of funds entering and leaving the organization will occur and in what amounts. One of the most significant business expenses is employee compensation.

A good financial plan also includes financial control, a process of comparing actual revenues, costs, and expenses with forecasts. This comparison may reveal significant differences between projected and actual figures, so it is important to discover them early to take quick action.

LECTURE ENHANCER:
Why does having strong skills in software like Excel strengthen your chances of obtaining an accounting or finance position?

Bill Morrison is the CFO of Pittsburgh-based Genco Marketplace, which liquidates, or sells off, other companies' excess inventory. Genco buys inventory that is not selling well, then resells it to wholesalers. In turn, the wholesalers sell the inventory to discount retailers. Always vigilant about the cost of freight, including fuel, Genco pays the transportation costs of taking the goods from their current location to where they will be liquidated. Some excess inventory is seasonal. When a retailer has winter coats left over in June, Genco will buy those coats, hold them in inventory, and sell them to a wholesaler in the fall, when demand rises again. But the longer a product remains unsold, the harder it will be to liquidate, even at a deep discount. In all cases, Morrison or members of his team have to prepare a financial plan that takes into account not only the benefits of buying the merchandise but the risks as well. [5]

3 Managing Assets

As we noted in Chapter 15, assets consist of what a firm owns. But assets also represent uses of funds. To grow and prosper, companies need to obtain additional assets. Sound financial management requires assets to be acquired and managed as effectively and efficiently as possible. The "Business Etiquette" feature offers tips for managing assets.

Short-Term Assets

Short-term, or current, assets consist of cash and assets that can be, or are expected to be, converted into cash within a year. The major current assets are cash, marketable securities, accounts receivable, and inventory.

Cash and Marketable Securities

The major purpose of cash is to pay day-to-day expenses, much as when individuals maintain balances in checking accounts to pay bills or buy food and clothing. In addition, most organizations strive to maintain a minimum cash balance in order to have

BusinessEtiquette

Tips from LearnVest

Sometimes it's tough to figure out how to manage your own assets—controlling expenses and understanding how to save and plan for the future. Alexa von Tobel had the same problem. So she founded LearnVest, a Web site designed to help young women improve their financial literacy. Following are a few tips from the LearnVest team:

- Do open a retirement account and establish a relationship with a reputable financial planner.
- Set a realistic goal and back it up with a realistic strategy, then design your daily and weekly spending accordingly. Three strategies could be "eat at home," "avoid the dry cleaners," and "carpool to work."
- Online shopping makes it too easy to run up credit-card debt with the click of a mouse, especially late at night. If you use a browser such as Firefox, you can add its LeechBlock tool to block any sites that you are likely to drift to between certain hours.
- Don't count on your tax refund, holiday gifts, or bonuses for any of your regular expenses. Instead, build an emergency fund slowly and steadily. You can always deposit any cash windfalls in that fund.
- Coupons are great money savers, but use them wisely. Limit the amount of time you spend searching and clipping. Make sure that the coupon saves you more money than the generic or store brand. Edit your coupons regularly, throwing away expired ones.

Sources: LearnVest Web site, http://www.learnvest.com, accessed April 6, 2012; Tara Siegel Bernard, "LearnVest: A Money-Management Site for Women," *The New York Times*, http://bucks.blogs.nytimes.com, accessed April 6, 2012; Sophie Moura, "Alexa von Tobel," *Marie Claire*, http://www.marieclaire.com, accessed April 6, 2012.

Assessment Check ☑

1. What three questions does a financial plan address?

2. Explain the steps involved in preparing a financial plan.

Mark Peterson/Redux Pictures

At Bed Bath & Beyond, inventory is the most valuable asset. Managing inventory can be a costly and highly complicated undertaking, especially for retailers.

funds available in the event of unexpected expenses. As noted earlier, because cash earns little, if any, return, most firms invest excess cash in so-called *marketable securities*—low-risk securities that either have short maturities or can be easily sold in secondary markets. Money market instruments—described in Chapter 16—are popular choices for firms with excess cash. The cash budget, which we discussed in Chapter 15, is one tool for managing cash and marketable securities because it shows expected cash inflows and outflows for a period of time. The cash budget indicates months when the firm will have surplus cash and can invest in marketable securities and months when it will need additional cash.

Critics of some companies' budgeting practices contend that occasionally firms hoard cash. Recently, Apple had more than $98 billion in cash and marketable securities. Yet firms may have good reasons for holding large amounts of cash and marketable securities. They may plan on using these funds shortly to make a large investment, pay dividends to shareholders, or repurchase outstanding bonds.

Accounts Receivable Accounts receivable are uncollected credit sales and can be a significant asset. The financial manager's job is to collect the funds owed the firm as quickly as possible while still offering sufficient credit to customers to generate increased sales. In general, a more liberal credit policy means higher sales but also increased collection expenses, higher levels of bad debt, and a higher investment in accounts receivable.

Management of accounts receivable is composed of two functions: determining an overall credit policy and deciding which customers will be offered credit. Formulating a credit policy involves deciding whether the firm will offer credit and, if so, on what terms. Will a discount be offered to customers who pay in cash? Often, the overall credit policy is dictated by competitive pressures or general industry practices. If all your competitors offer customers credit, your firm will likely have to as well. The other aspect of a credit policy is deciding which customers will be offered credit. Managers must consider the importance of the customer as well as its financial health and repayment history.

One simple tool for assessing how well receivables are being managed is calculating accounts receivable turnover over successive time periods. We showed how this ratio is calculated in Chapter 15. If receivables turnover shows signs of slowing, it means that the average credit customer is paying later. This trend warrants further investigation.

Inventory Management For many firms, such as retailers, inventory represents the largest single asset. At the home furnishings retailer Bed Bath & Beyond, inventory makes up about 49 percent of total assets. Even for nonretailers, inventory is an important asset. At the heavy-equipment manufacturer Caterpillar, inventory is almost 12 percent of total assets. On the other hand, some types of firms, such as electric utilities and transportation companies, have no inventory. For the majority of firms, which do carry inventory, proper management of it is vital.

Managing inventory can be complicated. The cost of inventory includes more than just the acquisition cost. It also includes the cost of ordering, storing, insuring, and financing inventory, as well as the cost of stockouts, lost sales due to insufficient inventory. Financial managers try to minimize the cost of inventory. But production, marketing, and logistics also play important roles in determining proper inventory levels. The production considerations of inventory management were discussed in Chapter 10. In Chapter 12, we outlined the marketing and logistics issues surrounding inventory.

Trends in the inventory turnover ratio—described in Chapter 15—can be early warning signs of impending trouble. For instance, if inventory turnover has been slowing for several consecutive quarters, it indicates that inventory is rising faster than sales. In turn, this may suggest that customer demand is softening and the firm needs to take action, such as reducing production or increasing promotional efforts.

CLASS ACTIVITY:
Discuss the impact of style changes, spoilage, and obsolescence on inventory values.

Capital Investment Analysis

In addition to current assets, firms also invest in long-lived assets. Unlike current assets, long-lived assets are expected to produce economic benefits for more than one year. These investments often involve substantial amounts of money. For example, as noted earlier in the chapter, Airbus invested more than $15 billion in development of the A380. In another example, a few years ago, auto manufacturer BMW spent $750 million to expand its production facility in Spartanburg, South Carolina, bringing its total investment in the state to $4.6 billion. Then the firm unveiled its first Super Bowl ad in many years—with scenes shot around South Carolina. [6]

The process by which decisions are made regarding investments in long-lived assets is called *capital investment analysis*. Firms make two basic types of capital investment decisions: expansion and replacement. The A380 and the BMW South Carolina plant investments are examples of expansion decisions. Replacement decisions involve upgrading assets by substituting new ones. A retailer might decide to replace an old store with a new Supercenter, as Walmart did in Oxford, Ohio.

Financial managers must estimate all of the costs and benefits of a proposed investment, which can be quite difficult, especially for very long-lived investments. Only those investments that offer an acceptable return—measured by the difference between benefits and costs—should be undertaken. BMW's financial managers believed that the benefits of expanding the South Carolina production facility outweighed the high cost. The expansion will allow BMW to produce three new models designed mainly for the North American market, so the expected profit from the sale of these models would be considered in the decision. Some other benefits cited by BMW include lower production costs, improved logistics, and expanded use of renewable energy. The Spartanburg facility recently produced its 1 millionth BMW X5 and continues to emphasize its commitment to the U.S. market. [7]

Managing International Assets

Today, firms often have assets worldwide. Both McDonald's and The Coca-Cola Company generate more than half of their annual sales outside the United States. The vast majority of sales for Unilever and Nestlé occur outside their home countries (the Netherlands and Switzerland, respectively). Managing international assets creates several challenges for the financial manager, one of the most important of which is the problem of exchange rates.

LECTURE ENHANCER:
Can a change in exchange rates ever benefit a company?

As we discussed in several other chapters, an exchange rate is the rate at which one currency can be exchanged for another. Exchange rates can vary substantially from year to year, creating a problem for any company with international assets. As an example, assume a U.S. firm has a major subsidiary in the United Kingdom. Assume that the U.K. subsidiary earns an annual profit of £750 million (stated in British pounds). Over the past five years, the exchange rate between the U.S. dollar and the British pound has varied between 1.82 (dollars per pound) and 1.56. [8] This means the dollar value of the U.K. profits ranged from $1.37 billion to $1.17 billion.

Consequently, many global firms engage in activities that reduce the risks associated with exchange rate fluctuations. Some are quite complicated. However, one of the simplest and most widely used is called a *balance sheet hedge*. Essentially, a balance sheet hedge creates an offsetting liability to the non-dollar-denominated asset, one that is denominated in the same currency as the asset. In our example, the U.K. subsidiary is a pound-denominated asset. To create an offsetting liability, the firm could take out a loan, denominated in British pounds, creating a pound-denominated liability. If done correctly, this hedge will reduce or even eliminate the risk associated with changes in the value of the dollar relative to the pound. This will improve the financial performance of the firm, which can have a positive impact on its stock price.

[4] Sources of Funds and Capital Structure

The use of debt for financing can increase the potential for return as well as increase loss potential. Recall the accounting equation introduced in Chapter 15:

$$\text{Assets} = \text{Liabilities} + \text{Owners' equity}$$

If you view this equation from a financial management perspective, it reveals that there are only two types of funding: debt and equity. *Debt capital* consists of funds obtained through borrowing. *Equity capital* consists of funds provided by the firm's owners when they reinvest earnings, make additional contributions, liquidate assets, issue stock to the general public, or raise capital from outside investors. The mix of a firm's debt and equity capital is known as its **capital structure**.

Companies often take very different approaches to choosing a capital structure. As more debt is used, the risk to the company increases since the firm is now obligated to make the interest payments on the money borrowed, regardless of the cash flows coming into the company. Choosing more debt increases the fixed costs a company must pay, which in turn makes a company more sensitive to changing sales revenues. Debt is frequently the least costly method of raising additional financing dollars, one of the reasons it is so frequently used.

Differing industries choose varying amounts of debt and equity to use when financing. Using the information provided by Datamonitor, we find that the automotive industry has debt ratios (the ratio of liabilities to assets) of over 60 percent for both Toyota and Honda and over 90 percent for Ford. These companies are primarily using debt to finance their asset expenditures. Food-service companies such as McDonald's and Starbucks use only 49 percent debt and 27 percent debt, respectively. The mixture of debt and equity a company uses is a major management decision.

Assessment Check ☑

1. Why do firms often choose to invest excess cash in marketable securities?

2. What are the two aspects of accounts receivable management?

3. Explain the difference between an expansion decision and a replacement decision.

capital structure mix of a firm's debt and equity capital.

LECTURE ENHANCER:
Which type of funds (debt or equity) offers a firm a more flexible pay arrangement? Which offers more control?

Leverage and Capital Structure Decisions

Raising needed cash by borrowing allows a firm to benefit from the principle of **leverage**, increasing the rate of return on funds invested by borrowing funds. The key to managing leverage is to ensure that a company's earnings remain larger than its interest payments, which increases the leverage on the rate of return on shareholders' investment. Of course, if the company earns less than its interest payments, shareholders lose money on their original investments.

Figure 17.2 shows the relationship between earnings and shareholder returns for two identical hypothetical firms that choose to raise funds in different ways. Leverage Company obtains 50 percent of its funds from lenders who purchase company bonds. Leverage Company pays 10 percent interest on its bonds. Equity Company raises all of its funds through sales of company stock.

Notice that if earnings double, from, say, $10 million to $20 million, returns to shareholders of Equity Company also double—from 10 percent to 20 percent. But returns to shareholders of Leverage Company more than double—from 10 percent to 30 percent. However, leverage works in the opposite direction as well. If earnings fall from $10 million to $5 million, a decline of 50 percent, returns to shareholders of Equity Company also fall by 50 percent—from 10 percent to 5 percent. By contrast, returns to shareholders of Leverage Company fall from 10 percent to zero. Thus, leverage increases potential returns to shareholders but also increases risk.

Another problem with borrowing money is that an overreliance on borrowed funds may reduce management's flexibility in future financing decisions. If a company raises equity capital this year and needs to raise funds next year, it will probably be able to raise either debt or equity capital. But if it raises debt capital this year, it may be forced to raise equity capital next year.

Equity capital has drawbacks as well. Because shareholders are owners of the company, they usually have the right to vote on major company issues and elect the board of directors. Whenever new equity is sold, the control of existing shareholders is diluted, and the outcome of these votes could potentially change. One contentious subject today between companies and shareholders is whether shareholders should be able to vote on executive pay packages.

Another disadvantage of equity capital is that it is more expensive than debt capital. First, creditors have a senior claim to the assets of a firm relative to shareholders. Because of this advantage, creditors are willing to accept a lower rate of return than shareholders are. Second, the firm can deduct interest payments on debt, reducing its taxable income and tax bill. Dividends paid to shareholders, on the other hand, are not tax deductible. A key component of the financial manager's job is to weigh the advantages and disadvantages of debt capital and equity capital, creating the most appropriate capital structure for his or her firm.

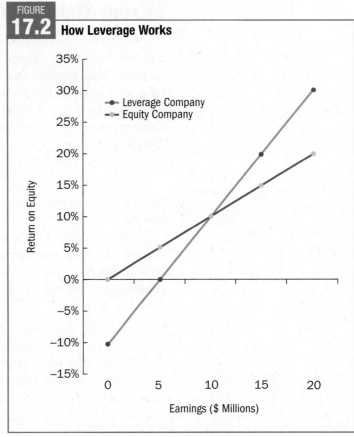

FIGURE 17.2 How Leverage Works

Note: The example assumes that both companies have $100 million in capital. Leverage Company consists of $50 million in equity and $50 million in bonds (with an interest rate of 10 percent). Equity Company consists of $100 million in equity and no bonds. This example also assumes no corporate taxes.

leverage increasing the rate of return on funds invested by borrowing funds.

LECTURE ENHANCER: Provide an example of a company that recently failed because of excessive leverage.

Mixing Short-Term and Long-Term Funds

Another decision financial managers face is determining the appropriate mix of short- and long-term funds. Short-term funds consist of current liabilities, and long-term funds consist of long-term debt and equity. Short-term funds are generally less expensive than long-term funds, but they also expose the firm to more risk. This is because short-term funds have to be renewed, or rolled over, frequently. Short-term interest rates can be volatile. During a recent 12-month period, for example, rates on commercial paper, a popular short-term financing option, ranged from a high of 17 percent (for 90-day loans) to a low of 9 percent (for 1-day loans). [9]

Because short-term rates move up and down frequently, interest expense on short-term funds can change substantially from year to year. For instance, if a firm borrows $50 million for ten years at 5 percent interest, its annual interest expense is fixed at $2.5 million for the entire ten years. On the other hand, if it borrows $50 million for one year at a rate of 4 percent, its annual interest expense of $2 million is only fixed for that year. If interest rates increase the following year to 6 percent, $1 million will be added to the interest expense bill. Another potential risk of relying on short-term funds is availability. Even financially healthy firms can occasionally find it difficult to borrow money.

Because of the added risk of short-term funding, most firms choose to finance all of their long-term assets, and even a portion of their short-term assets, with long-term funds. Johnson & Johnson is typical of this choice. Figure 17.3 shows a recent balance sheet broken down between short- and long-term assets, and short- and long-term funds.

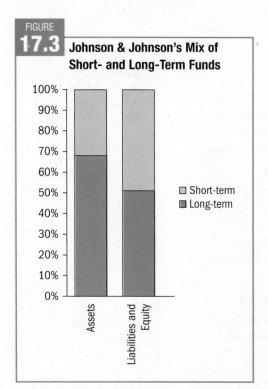

FIGURE 17.3 Johnson & Johnson's Mix of Short- and Long-Term Funds

Source: Johnson & Johnson balance sheet, Yahoo! Finance, http://finance.yahoo.com, accessed April 6, 2012.

Dividend Policy

Along with decisions regarding capital structure and the mix of short- and long-term funds, financial managers also make decisions regarding a firm's dividend policy. *Dividends* are periodic cash payments to shareholders. The most common type of dividend is paid quarterly and is often labeled as a *regular dividend*. Occasionally, firms make one-time special or extra dividend payments, as Microsoft did some years ago. Earnings that are paid in dividends are not reinvested in the firm and don't contribute additional equity capital.

Firms are under no legal obligation to pay dividends to shareholders. Although some companies pay generous dividends, others pay nothing. Until 2010, Starbucks never paid a dividend to its shareholders, and Apple recently announced it would pay its first dividend in nearly 20 years. See the "Solving an Ethical Controversy" feature for some pros and cons of such decisions for investors. In contrast, 3M has paid dividends for 30-plus consecutive years, during which time the amount has more than quadrupled. Companies that pay dividends try to increase them or at the very least hold them steady from year to year. However, in rare cases firms must cut or eliminate dividends. After spending heavily to launch and market its Nook e-reader, Barnes & Noble experienced a drop in profits despite the Nook's success. So the firm decided temporarily to suspend dividends to its shareholders, allowing it to continue pumping money into the business rather than increase its debt. [10]

Solving an Ethical Controversy

Are Dividends Necessary?

Although Apple's CEO Steve Jobs made tens of millions from dividends paid by Disney stock he owned, Apple itself hadn't paid a dividend in almost 20 years, dismaying some shareholders. The company's shares have appreciated more than 25 percent in value, and it held more than $30 billion in cash, which the late founder believed allowed the company to take necessary risks. Others argue that companies should share their profits, and more generously than at the current 27 percent average payout ratio, down from a historic average of 50 percent.

Should successful corporations pay or increase dividends to shareholders?

PRO

1. Shareholders expect a return on their investments, making dividends only fair to the company's real owners.

2. Nearly 75 percent of Standard & Poor's 500 companies pay dividends. The remaining 25 percent should do likewise.

CON

1. Companies should hold their cash in reserve for contingencies so they can respond quickly and flexibly.

2. Earnings reinvested in R&D, for instance, make the company stronger and increase the value of its shares.

Summary

Dividend payouts today are increasing at a growing rate, and more companies are paying investors dividends, even tech companies that have historically held on to their cash. Recently, Apple announced that it would pay dividends to shareholders in the near future—at a cost of more than $10 billion a year for the next three years.

Sources: Nick Wingfield, "Flush with Cash, Apple Plans Buyback and Dividend," *The New York Times,* March 19, 2012, http://www.nytimes.com; Jeff Reeves, "7 Skinflint Blue Chips That Owe Shareholders a Dividend Hike," *Investor Place,* February 17, 2012, www.investorplace.com; Nancy Zambell, "Are Dividend Players the New Growth Stocks?" *Investor Place,* January 23, 2012, www.investorplace.com; Kevin Kelleher, "An Apple Dividend in 2012? Keep Praying," *Investor Place,* January 6, 2012, www.investorplace.com; Paul Sullivan, "Assessing the Value of Owning Dividend-Paying Stocks," *The New York Times,* http://www.nytimes.com, accessed January 6, 2012.

Kevork Djansezian/Getty Images, Inc.

Companies are under no legal obligation to pay dividends to their shareholders. However, some companies pay dividends every year, while others pay dividends on a not-so-regular basis. Apple recently announced that it would pay its first dividend in nearly 20 years.

LECTURE ENHANCER:
Why do you think older
investors prefer stock in
companies that provide
dividend payments?

Assessment Check ✔

1. Explain the concept of leverage.

2. Why do firms generally rely more on long-term funds than short-term funds?

3. What is an important determinant of a firm's dividend policy?

Many factors determine a company's dividend policy, one of which is its investment opportunities. If a firm has numerous investment opportunities and wishes to finance some or all of them with equity funding, it will likely pay little, if any, of its earnings in dividends. Shareholders may actually want the company to retain earnings, because if they are reinvested, the firm's future profits, and the value of its shares, will increase faster. By contrast, a firm with more limited investment opportunities generally pays more of its earnings in dividends.

In addition to dividends, some firms buy back a portion of their outstanding stock. Home Depot, for instance, has repurchased more than $1 billion of stock over the past few years. Generally, shares are purchased on the secondary markets. The main purpose of share buy-backs is to raise the market value of the remaining shares, thus benefiting shareholders.

5 Short-Term Funding Options

Many times throughout a year, an organization may discover that its cash needs exceed its available funds. Retailers generate surplus cash for most of the year, but they need to build up inventory during the late summer and fall to get ready for the holiday shopping season. Consequently, they often need funds to pay for merchandise until holiday sales generate revenue. Then they use the incoming funds to repay the amount they borrowed. In these instances, financial managers evaluate short-term sources of funds. By definition, short-term sources of funds are repaid within one year. Three major sources of short-term funds exist: trade credit, short-term loans, and commercial paper. Large firms often rely on a combination of all three sources of short-term financing.

Trade Credit

CLASS ACTIVITY:
Ask students why large
companies might be more
likely to obtain favorable
trade credit as compared to
smaller companies.

Trade credit is extended by suppliers when a firm receives goods or services, agreeing to pay for them at a later date. Trade credit is common in many industries such as retailing and manufacturing. Suppliers routinely ship billions of dollars of merchandise to retailers each day and are paid at a later date. Without trade credit, the retailing sector would probably look much different—with fewer selections. Under this system, the supplier records the transactions as an account receivable, and the retailer records it as an account payable. Target alone currently has more than $6.5 billion of accounts payable on its books. The main advantage of trade credit is its easy availability because credit sales are common in many industries. The main drawback to trade credit is that the amount a company can borrow is limited to the amount it purchases.

LECTURE ENHANCER:
Why would trade credit
be limited to the amount
of goods or services a
company purchases?

What is the cost of trade credit? If suppliers do not offer a cash discount, trade credit is effectively free. For example, assume a supplier offers trade credit under the terms net 30—meaning that the buyer has 30 days to pay. This is similar to borrowing $100 and repaying $100 in 30 days. The effective rate of interest is zero. However, some suppliers offer a discount if they are paid in cash. If a discount is offered, trade credit can get quite expensive. Now assume that a 2 percent discount is offered to cash buyers. If they do not take the discount, they have 30 days to pay. Essentially, then, if the buyer doesn't pay cash, it is borrowing $98 today and repaying $100 30 days from today. The annual interest rate on such a loan exceeds 24 percent.

Short-Term Loans

Loans from commercial banks are a significant source of short-term financing for businesses. Often businesses use these loans to finance inventory and accounts receivable. For example, late fall and early winter is the period of highest sales for a small manufacturer of ski equipment. To meet this demand, it has to begin building inventory during the summer. The manufacturer also has to finance accounts receivable (credit sales to customers) during the fall and winter. So it takes out a bank loan during the summer. As the inventory is sold and accounts receivable collected, the firm repays the loan.

There are two types of short-term bank loans: lines of credit and revolving credit agreements. A line of credit specifies the maximum amount the firm can borrow over a period of time, usually a year. The bank is under no obligation actually to lend the money, however. It does so only if funds are available. Most lines of credit require the borrower to repay the original amount, plus interest, within one year. By contrast, a revolving credit agreement is essentially a guaranteed line of credit—the bank guarantees that the funds will be available when needed. Banks typically charge a fee, on top of interest, for revolving credit agreements.

The cash budget is an important tool for determining the size of a line of credit because it shows the months when additional financing will be needed or when borrowed funds can be repaid. For instance, assume the ski manufacturer's cash budget indicates that it will need $2.5 million for the June through November period. The financial manager might set up a line of credit with the bank for $2.8 million. The extra $300,000 is for any unexpected cash outflows.

In addition to commercial banks, commercial finance companies also make short-term loans to businesses. Although most bank loans are unsecured, meaning that no specific assets are pledged as collateral, loans from commercial finance companies are often secured with accounts receivable or inventory.

Another form of short-term financing backed by accounts receivable is called *factoring*. The business sells its accounts receivable to either a bank or finance company—called a *factor*—at a discount. The size of the discount determines the cost of the transaction. Factoring allows the firm to convert its receivables into cash quickly without worrying about collections.

The cost of short-term loans depends not only on the interest rate but also on the fees charged by the lender. In addition to fees, some lenders require the borrower to keep so-called *compensating balances*—5 to 20 percent of the outstanding loan amount—in a checking account. Compensating balances increase the effective cost of a loan, because the borrower doesn't have full use of the amount borrowed.

Say, for example, that a firm borrows $100,000 for one year at 5 percent interest. The borrower will pay $5,000 in interest (5 percent × $100,000). If the lender requires that 10 percent of the loan amount be kept as a compensating balance, the firm has use of only $90,000. However, because it still will pay $5,000 in interest, the effective rate on the loan is actually 5.56 percent ($5,000 divided by $90,000).

Commercial Paper

Commercial paper is a short-term IOU sold by a company; this concept was briefly described in Chapter 16. Commercial paper is typically sold in multiples of $100,000 to $1 million and has a maturity that ranges from 1 to 270 days. Most commercial paper is unsecured. It is an attractive source of financing because large amounts of money can be raised at rates that are typically 1 to 2 percent less that those charged by banks. At the end of a recent

CLASS ACTIVITY:
Lead a class discussion on the risks in lending to a ski manufacturer.

year, almost $1.04 trillion in commercial paper was outstanding. [11] Although commercial paper is an attractive short-term financing alternative, only a small percentage of businesses can issue it. That is because access to the commercial paper market has traditionally been restricted to large, financially strong corporations.

Assessment Check ✓

1. What are the three sources of short-term funding?

2. Explain trade credit.

3. Why is commercial paper an attractive short-term financing option?

6 Sources of Long-Term Financing

Funds from short-term sources can help a firm meet current needs for cash or inventory. A larger project or plan, however, such as acquiring another company or making a major investment in real estate or equipment, usually requires funds for a much longer period of time. Unlike short-term sources, long-term sources are repaid over many years.

Organizations acquire long-term funds from three sources. One is long-term loans obtained from financial institutions such as commercial banks, life insurance companies, and pension funds. A second source is bonds—certificates of indebtedness—sold to investors. A third source is equity financing that is acquired by selling stock in the firm or reinvesting company profits.

Public Sale of Stocks and Bonds

Public sales of securities such as stocks and bonds are a major source of funds for corporations. Such sales provide cash inflows for the issuing firm and either a share in its ownership (for a stock purchaser) or a specified rate of interest and repayment at a stated time (for a bond purchaser). Because stock and bond issues of many corporations are traded in the secondary markets, stockholders and bondholders can easily sell these securities. Recently, when a European debt crisis seemed likely, it caused a massive slowdown in bond sales. But as fears of a crisis eased later in the year, bond sales reached their highest level since the same time the previous year. As of the first quarter, companies had sold about $1 *trillion* in U.S. corporate bonds. [12] Public sales of securities, however, can vary substantially from year to year depending on conditions in the financial markets. Bond sales, for instance, tend to be higher when interest rates are lower.

In Chapter 16, we discussed the process by which most companies sell securities publicly—through investment bankers via a process called *underwriting*. Investment bankers purchase the securities from the issuer and then resell them to investors. The issuer pays a fee to the investment banker, called an *underwriting discount*.

Private Placements

Some new stock or bond issues are not sold publicly but instead to a small group of major investors such as pension funds and insurance companies. These sales are referred to as *private placements*. Most private placements involve corporate debt issues. More than $376 billion in corporate bonds were sold privately in a recent year in the United States. [13]

It is often cheaper for a company to sell a security privately than publicly, and there is less government regulation with which to contend because SEC registration is not required. Institutional investors such as insurance companies and pension funds buy private placements because they typically carry slightly higher interest rates than publicly issued bonds. In addition, the terms of the issue can be tailored to meet the specific needs of both the issuer and the institutional investors. Of course, the institutional investor gives up liquidity because privately placed securities do not trade in secondary markets.

Venture Capitalists

Venture capitalists are an important source of long-term financing, especially to new companies. **Venture capitalists** raise money from wealthy individuals and institutional investors and invest these funds in promising firms. Venture capitalists also provide management consulting advice as well as funds. In exchange for their investment, venture capitalists become part owners of the business. If the business succeeds, venture capitalists can earn substantial profits.

Draper Fisher Jurvetson, one of the largest venture capital firms in the country, has invested in many small start-up companies, including Twitter.

One of the largest venture capital firms is Draper Fisher Jurvetson, based in Menlo Park, California. During the past 20 years, DFJ has invested in hundreds of small start-ups including Hotmail (acquired by Microsoft) and Twitter. Other firms in its $7 billion portfolio are Bright Source Energy, SpaceX, and Tumbleweed. [14]

Private Equity Funds

Similar to venture capitalists, *private equity funds* are investment companies that raise funds from wealthy individuals and institutional investors and use those funds to make large investments in both public and privately held companies. Unlike venture capital funds, which tend to focus on small, start-up companies, private equity funds invest in all types of businesses, including mature ones. For example, Cerberus Capital Management, a private equity fund, recently bought 53 percent of AT&T's Yellow Pages business for $950 million. [15] Another private equity fund, Kohlberg Kravis Roberts & Co. (KKR), helps firms such as Dollar General reduce the size of their environmental footprint; see the "Going Green" feature for the story. Often, private equity funds invest in transactions that take public companies private, or leveraged buyouts (LBOs). In these transactions, discussed in more detail in the next section, a public company reverts to private status.

A variation of the private equity fund is the so-called *sovereign wealth fund*. These companies are owned by governments and invest in a variety of financial and real assets, such as real estate. Although sovereign wealth funds generally make investments based on the best risk-return trade-off, political, social, and strategic considerations also play roles in their investment decisions.

Recently, several sovereign wealth funds made large investments in major U.S. financial firms, including Morgan Stanley and Citigroup. For instance, the Abu Dhabi Investment Authority (ADIA) invested in Citigroup, buying $7.5 billion in "equity shares" and becoming the giant bank's largest single shareholder in the process. Subsequently, ADIA filed suit against Citigroup, claiming that the bank had misled ADIA about its financial health, which Citigroup denied. A year later, Citigroup announced the reinstatement of dividend payments and a reverse stock split, whereupon the billionaire Prince Alwaleed of neighboring Saudi Arabia declared his support. [16] The assets of the ten largest sovereign wealth funds are shown in Figure 17.4. Together, these ten funds have almost $4 trillion in assets.

venture capitalist
person or entity that raises money from wealthy individuals and institutional investors and invests the funds in promising firms.

LECTURE ENHANCER:
What are some possible risks for a firm owner if he or she seeks advice from a venture capitalist company?

LECTURE ENHANCER:
What are the risks of private equity funds?

Going Green

KKR's Smart Investments Yield Greener Profits at Dollar General

Kohlberg Kravis Roberts & Co. (KKR), a private equity fund, uses its Green Portfolio program to decrease the environmental impact of 14 of its portfolio firms. In three years the program has saved the firms almost $400 million in operating costs and prevented 810,000 metric tons of greenhouse gas emissions.

One participant, the discount chain Dollar General, reduced waste about 75 percent by reducing and reusing cardboard at its nearly 10,000 U.S. stores, while increasing profits about $80 million through cost savings and earnings from recycling. Since joining the program in 2008, Dollar General has saved $155 million in fuel and energy costs, even as its operations increased over the same period. It has installed more efficient lighting in its stores and support center, and its improved shipping and routing practices are increasing cartons per mile and reducing miles driven.

In partnership with the Environmental Defense Fund, KKR's Green Portfolio program offers participating firms tools to measure and improve their environmental performance. "KKR's Green Portfolio program is a great model for investors who wants to see rigorous and transparent environmental results," says a spokesperson for the Fund.

Questions for Critical Thinking

1. "Today's institutional investors want their dollars to create both financial returns and environmental and social value," says the Fund. Why is this so?

2. A KKR manager was "encouraged by the enthusiasm which our portfolio companies have shown for the Green Portfolio Program." What accounts for their enthusiasm?

Sources: Company website, KKK Green Portfolio, http://green.kkr.com, accessed April 9, 2012; Zach Goldman and Andrew Malk, "Sustainability Boosts Returns for Private Equity Funds," http://www.environmentalleader.com, accessed April 9, 2012; Audrey Davenport, "Smart Investments See Green: KKR Reports Savings and Growth in Third Year of the Green Portfolio Program," Environmental Defense Fund, http://blogs.edf.org, accessed April 9, 2012; "KKR & Co. L.P.: KKR's Green Portfolio Program Delivers Solid Financial and Environmental Results for Third Year," 4-Traders.com, www.4-traders.com, accessed April 9, 2012.

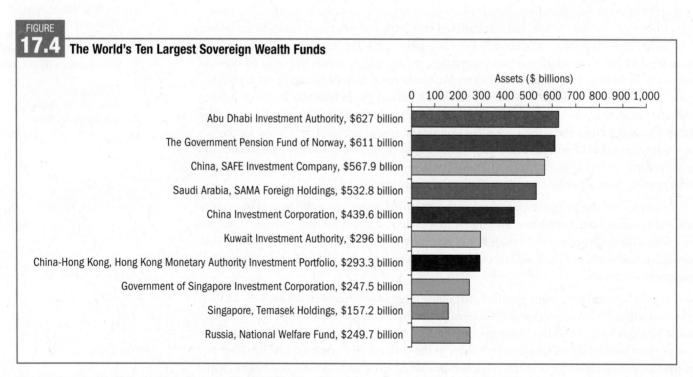

FIGURE 17.4 The World's Ten Largest Sovereign Wealth Funds

Source: Sovereign Wealth Fund Institute, "Sovereign Wealth Fund Rankings," http://www.swfinstitute.org, accessed April 9, 2012.

Hedge Funds

Hedge funds are private investment companies open only to qualified large investors. In recent years, hedge funds have become a significant presence in U.S. financial markets. Before the recent recession, some analysts estimated that hedge funds accounted for about 60 percent of all secondary bond market trading and around one-third of all activity on stock exchanges. In a recent year, the European debt crisis, the slow U.S. economic recovery, and unpredictable events such as the earthquake and tsunami in Japan all contributed to an average 4.8 percent drop in hedge fund prices. [17] They are also significant investors in noninvestment grade, or junk, bonds. Hedge funds are estimated to have total assets that exceed $1.7 trillion. [18] Unlike mutual funds, hedge funds are not regulated by the SEC.

Traditionally, hedge funds, unlike venture capitalists and private equity funds, did not make direct investments in companies, preferring instead to purchase existing stock and bond issues.

Assessment Check ✔

1. What is the most common type of security sold privately?
2. Explain venture capital.
3. What is a sovereign wealth fund?

7 Mergers, Acquisitions, Buyouts, and Divestitures

Chapter 5 briefly described mergers and acquisitions. A merger is a transaction in which two or more firms combine into one company. In an acquisition, one firm buys the assets and assumes the obligations of another firm. Chapter 5 also listed the classifications of mergers and acquisitions—vertical, horizontal, and conglomerate—and noted that many of these transactions involve large sums of money. A recent example is Facebook's acquisition of Instagram, a photo-sharing app for smartphones, for $1 billion dollars. In this section, we focus on the financial implications of not only mergers and acquisitions but also buyouts and divestitures.

Note that even in a merger, there is a buyer and seller. The seller is often referred to as the *target*. Financial managers evaluate a proposed merger or acquisition in much the same way they would evaluate any large investment—by comparing the costs and benefits. To acquire a company, a firm typically offers a higher price than the current market price for the target's shares. The action usually triggers a fluctuation in the stock prices of both firms. When Intel purchased Internet security firm McAfee, Intel's share price dropped 3.5 percent to $18.90, while McAfee's price rose 57 percent to $47. [19]

When the buyer makes what is known as a **tender offer** for the target's shares, it specifies a price and the form of payment. The buyer can offer cash, securities, or a combination of the two. The Intel offer to buy McAfee was a combination of cash and short-term investments totaling $7.68 billion. The tender offer can be friendly, meaning it is endorsed by the target firm's board of directors, or unfriendly. Shareholders of both the buyer and target must vote to approve a merger.

Justifying such a premium requires the financial manager also to estimate the benefits of a proposed merger. These benefits could take the form of cost savings from economies of scale or reduced workforces or the buyer getting a bargain price for the target's assets. Sometimes, a buyer finds that the most cost-effective method of entering a new market is simply to buy an existing company that serves the market. Johnson & Johnson has a long history of making such acquisitions. When it decided to enter the contact lens market several years ago, Johnson & Johnson bought Vistakon, the firm that invented disposable contact

LECTURE ENHANCER:
Give an example of a recent merger and discuss the potential benefits to both companies.

tender offer offer made by a firm to the target firm's shareholders specifying a price and the form of payment.

lenses under the brand name Acuvue. Whatever the reasons, the term used to describe the benefits produced by a merger or acquisition is *synergy*—the notion that the combined firm is worth more than the buyer and the target are individually.

Leveraged buyouts, or LBOs, were briefly introduced in the preceding section. In an LBO, public shareholders are bought out, and the firm reverts to private status. The term *leverage* comes from the fact that many of these transactions are financed with high degrees of debt—often in excess of 75 percent. Private equity companies and hedge funds provide equity and debt financing for many LBOs. The firm's incumbent senior management is often part of the buyout group. LBO activity decreased sharply with the recent economic downturn. As the economy began to recover, LBO activity increased again. But with the European debt crisis and the weak U.S. economy, LBO financing costs rose once more. According to Standard & Poor's, LBO financing recently grew to almost $14 billion. Average monthly interest rates rose to the equivalent of an additional $11.3 million annually for every $1 billion that buyers borrowed. More recently, private equity firms sold $16.6 billion in bonds to finance LBOs, four times the amount spent in a previous year. [20]

Why do so many LBOs occur? One reason is that private companies enjoy benefits that public companies do not. Private companies are not required to publish financial results, are subject to less SEC oversight, and are not pressured to produce the short-term profits often demanded by Wall Street. Some argue that LBOs, because of the high degree of debt, enforce more discipline on management to control costs. Although LBOs do have advantages, history has shown that many companies that go private reemerge as public companies several years later.

In a sense, a **divestiture** is the reverse of a merger. That is, a company sells assets such as subsidiaries, product lines, or production facilities. Two types of divestitures exist: sell-offs and spin-offs. In a *sell-off*, assets are sold by one firm to another. Verizon Wireless, an affiliate of Verizon Communications Inc., sold some of its wireless assets to AT&T. AT&T then announced plans to roll out its 3G wireless service to about 1.6 million former Verizon subscribers in rural areas across 18 states.

The other type of divestiture is a *spin-off*. In this transaction, the assets sold form a new firm. Shareholders of the divesting firm become shareholders of the new firm as well. For example, Motorola announced that it would split into two publicly traded firms. The parent company will handle its core business of mobile converged devices, digital home-entertainment devices, and video voice and data solutions. The spin-off firm will handle heavy-duty two-way radios, mobile computers, public security systems, wireless network infrastructure, and other business-oriented goods and services. Both entities will continue to use the Motorola brand name, with the parent company now named Motorola Mobile Devices and Home. Motorola shareholders will receive shares of the new company, Motorola Enterprise Mobility and Networks.

Firms divest assets for several reasons. Sometimes divestitures result from prior acquisitions that didn't work out as well as expected. In early 2001, America Online and Time Warner merged to create AOL Time Warner, Inc. Nine years later, Time Warner announced it would spin off AOL. The merger—now considered one of the worst mistakes in corporate history—failed to generate the much-heralded synergies between the two companies. Shortly after the merger, AOL had 27 million subscribers; more recently, that number had shrunk to about 3.4 million.

In other cases, a firm makes a strategic decision to concentrate on its core businesses and decides to divest anything that falls outside this core. That was the explanation that Motorola gave in response to criticism that the company had become too large and had seen its mobile-device business overtaken first by Nokia, then Samsung, and then Apple. Still another explanation

leveraged buyout (LBO) transaction in which public shareholders are bought out and the firm reverts to private status.

divestiture sale of assets by a firm.

LECTURE ENHANCER:
Can you provide an example of a recent divestiture that resulted from an unsuccessful acquisition?

relates to antitrust issues. Verizon originally wanted to buy Alltel. The U.S. Department of Justice required Verizon to divest itself of assets in markets where Alltel was already operating—mainly rural areas in many central states—before it would approve the purchase.

What's Ahead

Contemporary Business concludes with five appendixes. Appendix A, "Business Law," outlines the main legal issues concerning business. It reviews the types of laws, the regulatory environment of business, and the core of business law, including discussions of contract law and property law. Appendix B examines risk management and insurance. It describes the concept of risk, alternative ways of dealing with risk, and the various kinds of insurance available to business and individuals. Appendix C discusses some of the important components of personal financial planning, such as budgeting, credit, and retirement planning. Appendix D describes how to write an effective business plan, and Appendix E discusses career searches and options to help you prepare for your future in business.

Summary of Learning Objectives

1 Define the role of the financial manager.

Finance deals with planning, obtaining, and managing a company's funds to accomplish its objectives efficiently and effectively. The major responsibilities of financial managers are to develop and implement financial plans and determine the most appropriate sources and uses of funds. The chief financial officer (CFO) heads a firm's finance organization. Three senior executives reporting to the CFO are the vice president for financial management, the treasurer, and the controller. When making decisions, financial professionals continually seek to balance risks with expected financial returns.

Assessment Check Answers ✓

1.1 What is the structure of the finance function at the typical firm? The person in charge of the finance function of a firm has the title of chief financial officer (CFO) and generally reports directly to the firm's chief executive officer. Reporting to the CFO are the treasurer, the controller, and the vice president for financial management.

1.2 Explain the risk-return trade-off. Financial managers strive to maximize the wealth of their firm's shareholders by striking the optimal balance between risk and return. Often, decisions involving the highest potential returns expose the firm to the greatest risks.

2 Describe financial planning.

A financial plan is a document that specifies the funds needed by a firm for a given period of time, the timing of inflows and outflows, and the most appropriate sources and uses of

funds. The financial plan addresses three questions: What funds will be required during the planning period? When will funds be needed? Where will funds be obtained? Three steps are involved in the financial planning process: forecasting sales over a future period of time, estimating the expected level of profits over the planning period, and determining the additional assets needed to support additional sales.

Assessment Check Answers ✓

2.1 What three questions does a financial plan address? The financial plan addresses three questions: What funds will be required during the planning period? When will funds be needed? Where will funds be obtained?

2.2 Explain the steps involved in preparing a financial plan. The first step is to forecast sales over a future period of time. Second, the financial manager must estimate the expected level of profits over the planning period. The final step is to determine the additional assets needed to support additional sales.

3 Outline how organizations manage their assets.

Assets consist of what a firm owns and also comprise the uses of its funds. Sound financial management requires assets to be acquired and managed as effectively and efficiently as possible. The major current assets are cash, marketable securities, accounts receivable, and inventory. The goal of cash management is to have sufficient funds on hand to meet day-to-day transactions and pay any unexpected expenses. Excess cash should be invested in marketable securities, which are low-risk securities with short maturities. Managing accounts receivable, which are uncollected credit sales, involves securing funds owed the firm as quickly as possible while offering sufficient credit to customers to generate increased sales. The main goal of inventory management is to minimize the overall cost of inventory. Production, marketing, and logistics also play roles in determining proper inventory levels. Capital investment analysis is the process by which financial managers make decisions on long-lived assets. This involves comparing the benefits and costs of a proposed investment. Managing international assets poses additional challenges for the financial manager, including the problem of fluctuating exchange rates.

Assessment Check Answers ✓

3.1 Why do firms often choose to invest excess cash in marketable securities? Cash earns no rate of return, which is why excess cash should be invested in marketable securities. These are low-risk securities that have short maturities and can be sold easily in the secondary markets. As a result, they are easily converted back into cash, when needed.

3.2 What are the two aspects of accounts receivable management? The two aspects of accounts receivable management are deciding on an overall credit policy (whether to offer credit and, if so, on what terms) and determining which customers will be offered credit.

3.3 Explain the difference between an expansion decision and a replacement decision. An expansion decision involves choosing between offering new products or building or acquiring new production facilities. A replacement decision is one that considers whether to replace an existing asset with a new one.

⌐4⌐ Discuss the sources of funds and capital structure.
Businesses have two sources of funds: debt capital and equity capital. Debt capital consists of funds obtained through borrowing, and equity capital consists of funds provided by the firm's owners. The mix of debt and equity capital is known as the firm's capital structure, and the financial manager's job is to find the proper mix. Leverage is a technique of increasing the rate of return on funds invested by borrowing. However, leverage increases risk. Also, overreliance on borrowed funds may reduce management's flexibility in future financing decisions. Equity capital also has drawbacks. When additional equity capital is sold, the control of existing shareholders is diluted. In addition, equity capital is more expensive than debt capital. Financial managers are also faced with decisions concerning the appropriate mix of short- and long-term funds. Short-term funds are generally less expensive than long-term funds but expose firms to more risk. Another decision involving financial managers is determining the firm's dividend policy.

Assessment Check Answers ✓

4.1 Explain the concept of leverage. Leverage is a technique of increasing the rate of return by borrowing funds. However, leverage also increases risk.

4.2 Why do firms generally rely more on long-term funds rather than short-term funds? Although short-term funds are generally less expensive than long-term funds, short-term funds expose the firm to additional risks. The cost of short-term funds can vary substantially from year to year. In addition, at times short-term funds can be difficult to obtain.

4.3 What is an important determinant of a firm's dividend policy? The main determinant of a firm's dividend policy is its investment opportunities. Firms with more profitable investment opportunities often pay less in dividends than do firms with fewer such opportunities.

⌐5⌐ Identify short-term funding options.
The three major short-term funding options are trade credit, short-term loans from banks and other financial institutions, and commercial paper. Trade credit is extended by suppliers when a firm receives goods or services, agreeing to pay for them at a later date. Trade credit is relatively easy to obtain and costs nothing unless a supplier offers a cash discount. Loans from commercial banks are a significant source of short-term financing and are often used to finance accounts receivable and inventory. Loans can be either unsecured or secured, with accounts receivable or inventory pledged as collateral. Commercial paper is a short-term IOU sold by a company. Although large amounts of money can be raised through the sale of commercial paper, usually at rates below those charged by banks, access to the commercial-paper market is limited to large, financially strong corporations.

Assessment Check Answers ✓

5.1 What are the three sources of short-term funding? The three sources of short-term funding are trade credit, short-term loans from banks and other financial institutions, and commercial paper.

5.2 Explain trade credit. Trade credit is extended by suppliers when a buyer agrees to pay for goods and services at a later date. Trade credit is relatively easy to obtain and costs nothing unless a cash discount is offered.

5.3 Why is commercial paper an attractive short-term financing option? Commercial paper is an attractive financing option because companies can raise large amounts by selling commercial paper at rates that are generally lower than those charged by banks.

⌐6⌐ Discuss sources of long-term financing.
Long-term funds are repaid over many years. There are three sources: long-term loans obtained from financial institutions, bonds sold to investors, and equity financing. Public sales of securities represent a major source of funds for corporations. These securities can generally be traded in secondary markets. Public sales can vary substantially from year to year depending on the conditions in the financial markets. Private placements are securities sold to a small number of institutional investors. Most private placements

involve debt securities. Venture capitalists are an important source of financing for new companies. If the business succeeds, venture capitalists stand to earn large profits. Private equity funds are investment companies that raise funds from wealthy individuals and institutional investors and use the funds to make investments in both public and private companies. Unlike venture capitalists, private equity funds invest in all types of businesses. Sovereign wealth funds are investment companies owned by governments.

Assessment Check Answers ✅

6.1 What is the most common type of security sold privately? Corporate debt securities are the most common type of security sold privately.

6.2 Explain venture capital. Venture capitalists are important sources of funding, especially for new companies. Venture capitalists invest in these companies by taking an ownership position. If the business succeeds, venture capitalists can earn substantial profits.

6.3 What is a sovereign wealth fund? A sovereign wealth fund is a government-owned investment company. These companies make investments in a variety of financial and real assets, such as real estate. Although most investments are based on the best risk-return trade-off, political, social, and strategic considerations play roles as well.

⌐7⌐ Describe mergers, acquisitions, buyouts, and divestitures.

A merger is a combination of two or more firms into one company. An acquisition is a transaction in which one company buys another. Even in a merger, there is a buyer and a seller (called the *target*). The buyer offers cash, secu-

rities, or a combination of the two in return for the target's shares. Mergers and acquisitions should be evaluated as any large investment is, by comparing the costs with the benefits. Synergy is the term used to describe the benefits a merger or acquisition is expected to produce. A leveraged buyout (LBO) is a transaction in which shares are purchased from public shareholders, and the company reverts to private status. Usually LBOs are financed with substantial amounts of borrowed funds. Private equity companies are often major financers of LBOs. Divestitures are the opposite of mergers, in which companies sell assets such as subsidiaries, product lines, or production facilities. A sell-off is a divestiture in which assets are sold to another firm. In a spin-off, a new firm is created from the assets divested. Shareholders of the divesting firm become shareholders of the new firm as well.

Assessment Check Answers ✅

7.1 Define *synergy*. Synergy is the term used to describe the benefits produced by a merger or acquisition. It is the notion that the combined firm is worth more than the buyer and the target are individually.

7.2 What is an LBO? An LBO—a leveraged buyout—is a transaction whereby public shareholders are bought out, and the firm reverts to private status. LBOs are usually financed with large amounts of borrowed money.

7.3 What are the two types of divestitures? A sell-off is a divestiture in which assets are sold to another firm. In a spin-off, a new firm is created from the assets divested. Shareholders of the divesting firm become shareholders of the new firm as well.

▪ Business Terms You Need to Know

finance 521	capital structure 530	leveraged buyout (LBO) 540
financial manager 522	leverage 531	divestiture 540
risk-return trade-off 523	venture capitalist 537	
financial plan 524	tender offer 539	

▪ Review Questions

1. Explain the risk-return trade-off and give two examples.

2. Describe the financial planning process. How does asset intensity affect a financial plan?

3. What are the principal considerations in determining an overall credit policy? How do the actions of competitors affect a firm's credit policy?

4. Why do exchange rates pose a challenge for financial managers of companies with international operations?

5. Discuss the concept of leverage. Use a numerical example to illustrate the effect of leverage.

6. What are the advantages and disadvantages of both debt and equity financing?

7. Compare and contrast the three sources of short-term financing.

8. Define *venture capitalist*, *private equity fund*, *sovereign wealth fund*, and *hedge fund*. Which of these four sources of funds invests the most money in start-up companies?

9. Briefly describe the mechanics of a merger or acquisition.

10. Why do firms divest assets?

Projects and Teamwork Applications

1. Assume you are about to start a business. Put together a rough financial plan that addresses the three financial planning questions listed in the textbook.

2. Working with a partner, assume that a firm needs $10 million in additional long-term capital. It currently has no debt and $40 million in equity. The options are issuing a ten-year bond (with an interest rate of 7 percent) or selling $10 million in new equity. You expect next year's earnings before interest and taxes to be $5 million. (The firm's tax rate is 35 percent.) Prepare a memo outlining the advantages and disadvantages of debt and equity financing. Using the numbers provided, prepare a numerical illustration of leverage similar to the one shown in Figure 17.2.

3. Your new small business has really grown, but now it needs a substantial infusion of capital. A venture capital firm has agreed to invest the money you need. In return, the venture capital firm will own 75 percent of the business, and you will be replaced as CEO by someone whom the venture capitalist chooses. You will retain the titles of founder and chairman of the board. Would you be willing to take the money but lose control over your business? Why or why not?

4. Working in a small team, select three publicly traded companies. Visit each firm's Web site. Most have a section devoted to information for investors. Review each firm's dividend policy. Does the company pay dividends? If so, when did it begin paying dividends? Have dividends increased each year? Or have they fluctuated from year to year? Is the company currently repurchasing shares? Has it done so in the past? Prepare a report summarizing your findings.

5. As noted in the chapter, one of the most unfortunate mergers in corporate history involved Time Warner and America Online. Research this merger. Why did analysts expect it to be successful? Why did it fail? What has happened to AOL since then?

Web Assignments

1. **Jobs in financial management.** Visit the Web site listed here to explore careers in finance. How many people currently work as financial managers? What is the projected increase in employment over the next 10 to 20 years? What is the average level of compensation?

   http://www.bls.gov/oco/ocos010.htm

2. **Capital structure.** Go to the Web site listed here to access recent financial statements for the retailer Costco Wholesale Corporation. Click on "balance sheet." What is the firm's current capital structure (the breakdown between debt and equity)? Has it changed significantly over the past five years? Why would a firm such as Costco choose to become more or less levered?

   http://moneycentral.msn.com/investor/invsub/results/statemnt.aspx?symbolcost

3. **Mergers and acquisitions.** Using a news source, such as Google News (http://news.google.com) or Yahoo! News (http://news.yahoo.com), search for a recent merger or acquisition announcement. An example would be Facebook's acquisition of Instagram. (A link is shown here.) Print out the articles and bring them to class.

   http://newsroom.fb.com/Announcements/Facebook-to-Acquire-Instagram-141.aspx

   Note: Internet Web addresses change frequently. If you don't find the exact sites listed, you may need to access the organization's home page and search from there or use a search engine such as Bing or Google.

CASE 17.1 ConocoPhillips Divests to Return to Its Core

ConocoPhillips, with headquarters in Houston, Texas, is the third largest American oil company. It has nearly 30,000 employees in offices in more than 30 countries around the world. But for two years running, Conoco did poorly in the New York Stock Exchange, with its shares losing 40 percent of their value. Conoco more than doubled its debt when it bought Burlington Resources Inc., a natural-gas producer, for $36 billion. At the end of a recent year, Conoco's debt was three times that of the largest U.S. oil company, ExxonMobil, even though ExxonMobil was almost twice Conoco's size in terms of revenue. How could Conoco turn itself around?

At its annual analyst meeting, the company announced plans to enhance its value to its shareholders by increasing dividends by 10 percent and buying back some shares of its stock. Another goal was to raise $10 billion.

ConocoPhillips decided to raise these funds through divestiture, selling off some of its noncore assets. The company said that these assets did not fit well strategically with its core operations, they had high operation costs, and they were marketable. Although the company acknowledged that it would lose oil production and oil equivalent in reserve, it hoped to emerge leaner and stronger, with a renewed focus on core projects that would bring in a higher return on investment.

Jim Mulva, the chairman and CEO, said, "We are focused on creating and delivering value to our shareholders. We are taking decisive action to sell assets, reduce debt, build on our record of shareholder distributions, and improve returns while growing production and reserves per share."

Conoco announced that it had sold its stake in Syncrude, located in Alberta, Canada, to China's Sinopec for $4.65 billion. The company also began selling its stake in the Russian oil company Lukoil, a stake reportedly worth $10 billion.

ConocoPhillips split into two companies in April 2012. The refining and marketing branch of the company will retake the firm's original name, Phillips 66. The exploration and production (E&P) side will keep the name ConocoPhillips. The company hopes this move will increase E&P operations. The Phillips 66 side will give company shareholders one share of Phillips 66 stock for every two ConocoPhillips shares.

Questions for Critical Thinking

1. Why is it important for ConocoPhillips to increase the value of its shares for its investors?

2. Research ConocoPhillips. How close has it come to raising the desired $10 billion?

Sources: Company Web site, ConocoPhillips, http://www.conocophillips.com, accessed April 10, 2012; "ConocoPhillips Sells Syncrude Stake to Sinopec," press release, *Rigzone,* http://www.rigzone.com, accessed April 10, 2012; Steve Gelsi, "ConocoPhillips Sells Syncrude Stake for $4.65 Billion," *MarketWatch,* http://articles.marketwatch.com, accessed April 10, 2012; Eric Fox, "ConocoPhillips Aims to Boost Returns," *Investopedia,* http://www.investopedia.com, accessed April 10, 2012; "Conoco Phillips Ups Ante for Shareholders," *Rigzone,* http://www.rigzone.com, accessed April 10, 2012; Edward Klump, "Conoco's Divestiture Plan Seen Hinging on Syncrude (Update 2)," Bloomberg Businessweek, http://www.bloomberg.com, accessed April 10, 2012; Ry Frank, "ConocoPhillips Has High Upside Potential in 2012," *Seeking Alpha,* http://www.seekingalpha.com, accessed April 10, 2012; "ConocoPhillips' Exit from Lukoil Makes Sense Now," *Emerging Money,* http://emergingmoney.com, accessed April 10, 2012.

Hewlett-Packard Still Sailing into Financial Headwinds

CASE 17.2

Meg Whitman, Hewlett-Packard's (HP) new CEO, says the tech giant, the world's largest PC maker, faces a rough few years as it struggles to rebound after weak consumer demand, supply shortages, and management missteps brought profits to a new low. "I feel very good that we know the challenges," she said. "We know what we're going to do about them, and we're headed in the right direction."

By bringing a new tablet computer to market, reducing costs, and resolving operational problems, Whitman hopes to help HP weather a transition that will free up cash to invest in new markets and capitalize on emerging countries' hunger for PCs (even as consumers in industrialized countries flock to Macs instead). HP also wants to dominate in the burgeoning cloud computing market, as well as in tech security and data management.

So rather than spend the company's resources on any more large acquisitions, like its recent $10 billion purchase of Autonomy Corp., which sells server systems, Whitman foresees investing in research and development for the next few years. "Let's optimize what we have before we go off and do something else," she says.

Questions for Critical Thinking

1. Can Whitman's financial strategy to reinvest in R&D achieve the company's goals? Why or why not?

2. Whitman says, "We've been late to market too often. We have to lead again." How did HP's underinvestment in its PC division contribute to this problem?

Sources: Ben Worthen, "Defending H-P in Age of Tablets," The Wall Street Journal, June 5, 2012, http://online.wsj.com; Ben Worthen, "Meg Whitman: H-P at Beginning of Multi-Year Transformation," *The Wall Street Journal,* February 23, 2012, http://blogs.wsj.com; Nilay Patel, "Meg Whitman Says HP Is 'Too Complex and Too Slow,' Underinvested in PC Division," The Verge.com, February 22, 2012, www.theverge.com; "HP CEO Please Patience as Earnings Fall 44 Pct," The Wall Street Journal, February 22, 2012, http://online.wsj.com.

Comet Skateboards Rides the Triple Bottom Line

Jason Salfi, co-founder and president of Comet Skateboards, is the first to admit he can let the wheels get away from him. Since the inception of Comet Skateboards, he estimates that he has personally "tanked the company four times. I started the company with a friend and we would sacrifice everything for quality," Salfi admits. It's easy to see how this could happen. Salfi loves skateboarding and he's a fanatic about building the best skateboards on the market with the most sustainable materials available.

During the first years of production—when Comet moved from California to Ithaca, New York in order to source bio-composite materials—Salfi and his partner paid top dollar for all the materials they used in building the boards. "We weren't really watching how much money we were making," Salfi says sheepishly. They were so wrapped up in the excitement of developing and manufacturing an entirely new class of skateboard, they forgot to watch the bank account balance. Salfi recalls that they did all the stereotypical things that small start-ups do to obtain financing—maxed out their credit cards, got friends and family to co-sign for loans, found angel investors. But Comet Skateboards just seemed to roll through the money without enough return to ensure its survival.

Then the firm hired a manager to specialize in financial details. With a professional in place, Salfi began to understand the real and potential impacts certain buying decisions would have on the bottom line, and the way cash flow would affect getting products to the marketplace. Now, Comet can forecast better how a product release will affect cash flow, and how that in turn will affect the way they as a business can reach customers. "Ultimately we're trying to create a sustainable business platform to get our sustainable business vision out there in the marketplace," explains Salfi. But they couldn't do this without managing the company's financial resources.

Comet Skateboards is considered a triple bottom line company, carrying the B Corporation logo. This means that Comet strives to create benefit for the company owners (profit), the community (people), and the environment (planet). Currently there are more than two hundred B Corporations in thirty industries around the nation. Each company has submitted to rigorous evaluation and has put written standards in place addressing social and environmental responsibility. Everything that Comet does, from its closed-loop manufacturing process to its community involvement, refers to its triple bottom line commitment.

Jason Salfi insists that managing the finances for a triple bottom line company is pretty much the same as managing the finances for a traditional company. But there are some differences, particularly in the procurement of raw materials, energy use, and waste disposal. Also, triple bottom line companies are held accountable for the way they treat employees and how they are involved in the community. "The 'magic' is making sure we can afford all that," observes Salfi. "It's just a matter of prioritization. We're not going on $50,000 golf retreats. We're reinvesting the capital we have in the materials we use and the way we interact with people."

Despite the fact that he says he didn't pay attention to finances in the company's early days, Salfi has a good grasp on Comet's role in the larger economic picture. He likes the idea of projecting the impact Comet has on consumers' buying decisions, particularly young people. Teenagers who choose Comet skateboards are choosing products that are made by a triple bottom line firm. "If you look at the way a 14-year-old decides to buy things for the rest of his or her life, and you look at the number of decisions that young person is going to make over the span of 50 or 60 years, you could extrapolate that we have impacted 1,000 people in a certain way that could eventually transfer billions of dollars toward socially responsible businesses," explains Salfi. "We're influencing the buying decisions of youth."

Salfi believes that, decades ago, "commerce used to be about improving the quality of life, but somewhere along the line, profits skewed motivations." He likes the idea of the triple bottom line rebalancing the priorities of business. "We like to think that as a B Corporation, we are part of a group that wants to bring back the original motivation for business, which was all about creating an improved quality of life for everyone, not just a select few." It might actually be possible for a few well-engineered skateboards to change the world.

Questions for Critical Thinking

1. Hiring a financial manager was a major step for Comet Skateboards. Identify some of the factors the manager would have to consider when creating a plan for risk-return trade-off.

2. What might be some short-term funding options for Comet? Some long-term options? Which would be best for this company, and why?

3. Suppose a larger firm approached Comet with an offer of acquisition. Create a chart outlining the major pros and cons of such an offer.

4. How might Comet's designation as a B Corporation affect the way it answers the three essential questions for building a financial plan?

Sources: Comet Skateboards Web site, http://cometskateboards.com, accessed April 10, 2012; "GOOD Products," Halogen TV, http://www.halogentv.com/shows/good-products/, accessed April 10, 2012; Nadia Hosni, "Triple Bottom Line: Comet Skateboards," *Tonic*, http://www.tonic.com, accessed April 10, 2012.

KANSAS

Saline River

Kansas City

70

Smoky Hill River

Salina

335

Greensburg

135

en City

36

Wichita

PART 6

GREENSBURG, KS

So Much to Do, So Little Cash

When Dan Wallach started Greensburg GreenTown, he knew it wouldn't be easy. A self-proclaimed idea guy, he admits that the details of high finance elude him. What he is good at is rallying people around a cause and getting them to write a few big checks. This time, though, Wallach decided to involve the largest number of people possible. Greensburg GreenTown's One Million $5.00 Donations campaign was the result.

The money that is raised will be used to cover GreenTown's operating expenses, as well as to fund gaps in municipal projects, build model green homes, and educate residents about green building practices. Another aspect of GreenTown's work is to provide information and access to media organizations. Shortly after the tornado, the Planet Green cable channel began production on a television series that would chronicle the town's rebuilding. Wallach thought the exposure created by that show and others like it would be valuable in his fund-raising efforts.

As a not-for-profit organization, Greensburg GreenTown is heavily regulated by the IRS, because the donations it receives are fully tax deductible. It falls into the same category as religious organizations and educational institutions, which are exempt from federal income taxes but must pay other federal taxes, such as employment taxes. Because working through the red tape required to obtain this IRS status can take time, many organizations, GreenTown included, work through an approved intermediary while their applications are processed.

Although Greensburg GreenTown supports and educates Greensburg's residents, the town itself must rely on other sources of funding. All towns have budgets for repairs and improvements, but no one expected to have to rebuild the entire town. After the tornado, Greensburg had no roads, no hospital, no school system, no utilities, or any of the other services one might expect to find in a town. Money was tight even before the tornado, so rebuilding seemed an impossible task.

Luckily, various government and corporate organizations chipped in. The Federal Emergency Management Agency (FEMA) and the U.S. Department of Agriculture (USDA) provided aid in the form of grants. Corporations like Frito-Lay donated significant amounts of money to support the town's innovative business incubator. With millions of dollars at stake and hundreds of projects under way at once, Assistant Town Administrator and Recovery Coordinator Kim Alderfer says the hardest part is keeping track of it all.

Questions

After viewing the video, answer the following questions:

1. What are the key legal and financial distinctions of Greensburg GreenTown?

2. If you were in Kim Alderfer's shoes, what kind of financial contingency plan would you put in place for Greensburg's future?

3. Should not-for-profit organizations be required to open their books to donors? Why or why not?

LAUNCHING YOUR
[Finance Career]

6

Part 6, "Managing Financial Resources," describes the finance function in organizations. Finance deals with planning, obtaining, and managing an organization's funds to accomplish its objectives in the most effective way possible. In Chapter 15, we covered accounting principles and various financial statements. In Chapter 16, we discussed the financial system, including the various types of securities, financial markets and institutions, the Federal Reserve System, financial regulators, and global financial markets. In Chapter 17, we examined the role financial managers play in an organization; financial planning; short- and long-term financing options; and mergers, acquisitions, buyouts, and divestitures. Throughout both chapters, we described the finance functions of a variety of businesses, governments, and not-for-profit organizations. As Part 6 illustrates, finance is a very diverse profession and encompasses many different occupations. According to the U.S. Department of Labor, over the next decade most finance-related occupations are expected to experience 9 percent employment growth. Employment in the financial investment industry should be strong because of the number of Baby Boomers in their peak earning years with funds to invest and the globalization of securities markets. [1]

In most business schools, finance is one of the most popular majors among undergraduates. Combining finance with accounting is a common double major. Those with degrees in finance also enjoy relatively high starting salaries. A recent survey found that the average starting salary for a person with an undergraduate degree in finance was nearly $68,000 per year. [2]

All organizations need to obtain and manage funds, so they employ finance professionals. Financial institutions and other financial services firms employ a large percentage of finance graduates. These businesses provide important finance-related services to businesses, governments, and not-for-profit organizations. Some graduates with finance degrees take jobs with financial services firms such as Bank of America and JP Morgan Chase, while others begin their careers working in the finance departments of businesses in other industries such as Caterpillar and Boeing, governments, or not-for-profit organizations. You may begin your career evaluating commercial loan applications for a bank, analyzing capital investments for a business, or helping a not-for-profit organization decide how to invest its endowment. Often finance professionals work as members of a team, advising top management. Some individuals spend their entire careers working in finance-related occupations; others use their finance experience to move into other areas of the firm. Today, the chief financial officer—the senior finance executive—holds one of the most critical jobs in any organization. In addition, the number of CEOs who began their careers in finance is growing.

Finance is a diverse, exciting profession. Here are a few of the specific occupations you might find after earning a degree in finance.

Financial managers prepare financial reports, direct investment activities, raise funds, and implement cash management strategies. Computer technology has significantly reduced the time needed to produce financial reports. Many financial managers spend less time preparing reports and more time analyzing financial data. All organizations employ financial managers, although roughly 30 percent of all financial managers work for financial services firms such as commercial banks and insurance companies. [3] Specific responsibilities vary with titles. For instance, credit managers oversee the firm's issuance of credit, establish standards, and monitor the collection of accounts. Cash managers control the flow of cash receipts and disbursements to meet the needs of the organization.

Most *loan officers* work for commercial banks and other financial institutions. They find potential clients and help them apply for loans. Loan officers typically specialize in commercial, consumer, or mortgage loans. In many cases, loan officers act in a sales capacity, contacting individuals and organizations about their need for funds and trying to persuade them to borrow the funds from the loan officer's institution. Thus, loan officers often need marketing as well as finance skills.

Security analysts generally work for financial services firms such as Fidelity or Raymond James & Associates. Security analysts review economic data, financial statements, and other information to determine the outlook for securities such as common stocks and bonds. They make investment recommendations to individual and institutional investors. Many senior security analysts hold a chartered financial analyst (CFA) designation. Obtaining a CFA requires a specific educational background, several years of related experience, and a passing grade on a comprehensive, three-stage examination.

Portfolio managers manage money for an individual or institutional client. Many portfolio managers work for pension funds or mutual funds for which they make investment decisions to benefit the funds' beneficiaries. Portfolio managers generally have extensive experience as financial managers or security analysts, and many are CFAs.

Personal financial planners help individuals make decisions in areas such as insurance, investments, and retirement planning. Personal financial planners meet with their clients, assess their needs and goals, and make recommendations. Approximately 30 percent of personal financial planners are self-employed, and many hold certified financial planner (CFP) designations. Like the CFA, obtaining a CFP requires a specific educational background, related experience, and passing a comprehensive examination.

Career Assessment Exercises in Finance

1. Assume you're interested in pursuing a career as a security analyst. You've heard that the CFA is an important designation and can help enhance your career. Visit the CFA's Web site (http://www .cfainstitute.org) to learn more about the CFA. Specifically, what are the requirements to obtain a CFA, and what are the professional benefits of having a CFA?

2. Arrange for an interview with a commercial loan officer at a local bank. Ask the loan officer about his or her educational background, what a typical day is like, and what the loan officer likes and doesn't like about his or her job.

3. Ameriprise Financial offers financial planning services to individuals and organizations. Visit the firm's careers Web site (http:/// www.ameriprise.com/careers). Review the material and write a brief summary of what you learned about being a personal financial planner. Does such a career interest you? Why or why not?

Business Law

Rocket Lawyer's Online Legal Services

A recent Gallup poll found that over a one-year period 65 percent of small-business owners had consulted a lawyer. In fact, for many small-business owners legal issues are a top concern, including contract negotiations, real estate transactions, corporate compliance and debt collection, and the incorporation process. Now these owners can find legal advice online. Cash-short entrepreneurs who are concerned about compliance with tax or contract law, for instance, can get help from a new online legal service called Rocket Lawyer, and much of it is free.

Rocket Lawyer's Web site offers free interactive legal templates that small-business owners can adapt, draft, save, and share, as well as other handy tools and features. For a small subscription fee, entrepreneurs can also sign up for more individualized attention for themselves or their business that includes document review and phone consultations, as well as discounted hourly fees and flat-rate charges for filing legal papers, such as for corporate restructuring. Rocket Lawyer will also refer clients to real-life lawyers in their area.

"We want to empower business owners to keep their businesses legally healthy through every stage of their company's lifespan," says Rocket Lawyer's founder Charley Moore. To achieve that goal, the company offers a personalized "Legal Health Score" with its subscription fee, which helps identify all relevant areas for the business, including compliance issues the owners might not even know about. Sole proprietors are the most vulnerable, according to Moore, who has also taped a one-hour webinar for SCORE, the small-business resource staffed by volunteer executives.

Seven "bulletproofing" guidelines Moore offers are to "build on the right foundation, comply with the law, protect what's yours, be a smart employer, maintain enough insurance, record everything in writing, [and] keep good counsel." While he stresses that there's no such thing as "one size fits all" when it comes to the law, some more specific strategies the firm suggests are to avoid tax issues by hiring a trustworthy accountant and a business attorney, to learn how to negotiate contracts and get a lawyer's advice about anything that's not clear, and to rely on written rather than verbal agreements to safeguard entrepreneurial dreams.[1]

Appendix

Overview

A

Legal issues affect every aspect of business. Despite the best efforts of most businesspeople, legal cases do arise. A dispute may arise over a contract, an employee may protest being passed over for a promotion, or a town may challenge the environmental impact of a new gas station. Unfortunately, the United States has the dubious distinction of being the world's most litigious society. Lawsuits are as common as business deals. Consider Walmart, which is involved in as many as 7,000 legal cases at any one time.

Even if you are never involved in a lawsuit, the cost still affects you. The average U.S. family pays a hidden "litigation tax" of 5 percent each year because of the costs of lawsuits that force businesses to increase their prices. Small businesses, such as dentists' offices, doctors' offices, and daycare providers are often the hardest hit and may cut back on their services or close. The total cost of frivolous lawsuits—those brought for petty reasons—runs about $865 billion a year. Rule 11 of the Federal Rules of Civil Procedure was designed in 1993 to prevent frivolous lawsuits, but has been weakened by loopholes. A bill pending in Congress would tighten the regulations again.[2]

On the lighter side, every day brings news reports of proposed laws intended to protect businesses, consumers, and the general public—but somehow miss the mark. In addition, old laws are still on the books that no longer serve a purpose and are all but forgotten. For instance, in Alaska, it's illegal to wake a bear to take its picture, but it is perfectly legal to shoot a bear while it is sleeping. In Hawaii, it is against the law to insert pennies in your ear. In Louisiana, it is illegal to gargle in public. In Montana, it is against the law to operate a vehicle with ice picks attached to the wheels. In North Carolina, it is illegal to use elephants to plow cotton fields. And in Arizona, it's illegal to hunt camels.[3] The origins of these laws raise about as many questions as the laws themselves.

Legislation that specifically affects how business functions is analyzed in each chapter of this book. Chapter 2 presents an overview of the legal environment, and legislation affecting international operations is covered in Chapter 4. Chapter 5 discusses laws related to small businesses. Laws regarding human resource management and labor unions are examined in Chapter 8. Laws affecting other business operations, such as environmental regulations and product safety, are one of the topics in Chapter 12, and marketing-related legislation is examined in Chapter 13. Finally, legislation pertaining to banking and the securities markets is discussed in Chapters 16 and 17.

In this appendix, we provide a general perspective of legislation at the federal, state, and local levels, and point out that, although business executives may not be legal experts, they do need to be knowledgeable in their specific area of responsibility. A good dose of common sense also helps avoid potential legal problems. This appendix looks at the general nature of business law, the court system, basic legal concepts, and the changing regulatory environment for U.S. business. Let's start with some initial definitions and related examples.

Legal System and Administrative Agencies

judiciary court system, or branch of government that is responsible for settling disputes by applying laws.

The **judiciary**, or court system, is the branch of government responsible for settling disputes among parties by applying laws. This branch consists of several types and levels of courts, each with a specific jurisdiction. Court systems are organized at the federal, state, and local levels. Administrative agencies also perform some limited judicial functions, but these agencies are more properly regarded as belonging to the executive or legislative branches of government.

At both the federal and state levels, *trial courts*—courts of general jurisdiction—hear a wide range of cases. Unless a case is assigned by law to another court or to an administrative agency, a court of general jurisdiction will hear it. The majority of cases, both criminal and civil, pass through these courts. Within the federal system, trial courts are known as U.S. district courts, and at least one such court operates in each state. In state court systems, the general jurisdiction courts are often called circuit courts, and states typically provide one for each county. Other names for general jurisdiction courts are superior courts, common pleas courts, or district courts.

State judiciary systems also include many courts with lower, or more specific, jurisdictions. In most states, parties can appeal the decisions of the lower courts to the general jurisdiction courts. Examples of lower courts are probate courts—which settle the estates of people who have died—and small-claims courts—where people can represent themselves in suits involving limited amounts of money. For example, a landlord might go to small-claims court to settle a dispute with a tenant over a security deposit.

Decisions made at the general trial court level may be appealed *in appellate courts*. Both the federal and state systems have appellate courts. For instance, the U.S. Court of Appeals for the Fourth Circuit, which is based in Richmond, Virginia, covers the states of Maryland, Virginia, West Virginia, North Carolina, and South Carolina.[4] The appeals process allows a higher court to review the case and correct any lower court error indicated by the appellant, the party making the appeal.

Appeals from decisions of the U.S. circuit courts of appeals can go all the way to the nation's highest court, the U.S. Supreme Court. Appeals from state courts of appeal are heard by the highest court in each state, usually called the state supreme court. In a state without intermediate appellate courts, the state supreme court hears appeals directly from the trial courts. Parties who are not satisfied by the verdict of a state supreme court can appeal to the U.S. Supreme Court and may be granted a hearing if they can cite grounds for such an appeal, and if the Supreme Court considers the case significant enough to be heard. The Supreme Court typically has more than 10,000 cases on the docket per year. However, only about 100 are granted review with oral arguments by attorneys. Formal written decisions are delivered for 80 to 90 of those cases.[5]

While most cases are resolved by the system of courts described here, certain highly specialized cases require particular expertise. Examples of specialized federal courts are the U.S. Tax Court for tax cases and the U.S. Court of Claims, which hears claims against the U.S. government itself. Similar specialized courts operate at the state level.

Administrative agencies, also known as bureaus, commissions, or boards, decide a variety of cases at all levels of government. These agencies usually derive their powers and responsibilities from state or federal statutes. Technically, they conduct hearings or inquiries rather than trials. Examples of federal administrative agencies are the Federal Trade Commission (FTC), the National Labor Relations Board (NLRB), and the Federal Energy Regulatory Commission (FERC). The FTC has the broadest power of any of the federal regulatory agencies. It enforces laws regulating unfair business practices, and it can stop false and deceptive advertising practices. Examples at the state level include public utility commissions and boards that govern the licensing of various trades and professions. Zoning boards, planning commissions, and boards of appeal operate at the city or county level.

Types of Law

Law consists of the standards set by government and society in the form of either legislation or custom. This broad body of principles, regulations, rules, and customs that govern the actions of all members of society, including businesspeople, is derived from several sources. **Common law** refers to the body of law arising out of judicial decisions, some of

law standards set by government and society in the form of either legislation or custom.

common law body of law arising out of judicial decisions, some of which can be traced back to early England.

which can be traced back to early England. For example, in some states, an unmarried couple that has lived together for a certain period of time is said to be legally husband and wife by common law.

Statutory law, or written law, includes state and federal constitutions, legislative enactments, treaties of the federal government, and ordinances of local governments. Statutes must be drawn precisely and reasonably to be constitutional, and thus enforceable. Still, courts frequently must interpret their intentions and meanings.

With the growth of the global economy, knowledge of international law has become crucial. **International law** refers to the numerous regulations that govern international commerce. Companies must be aware of the domestic laws of trading partners, trade agreements such as NAFTA, and the rulings of such organizations as the World Trade Organization. International law affects trade in all kinds of industries. When a range of defective or tainted products manufactured in China—but sold in the United States—was recalled, companies discovered that although the goods came from China, the liability for their defects lay squarely within the United States. Tainted or defective toothpaste, pet food, toys, tires, and shrimp all fell under the scrutiny of the Food and Drug Administration (FDA), the Consumer Product Safety Commission (CPSC), and other agencies, which hold U.S. manufacturers responsible for the quality of their foreign-made products. Recently, the United States, the World Trade Organization (WTO), and Japan joined forces to bring a lawsuit against China for its restrictions on exports of rare-earth metals, which are used in making electronic goods such as smart phones, flat-screen TVs, compact fluorescent light bulbs, and electric cars. Currently, China mines 95 to 97 percent of these metals, which include scandium, lanthanum, and fifteen other elements.[6]

In a broad sense, all law is business law because all firms are subject to the entire body of law, just as individuals are. In a narrower sense, however, **business law** consists of those

statutory law written law, including state and federal constitutions, legislative enactments, treaties of the federal government, and ordinances of local governments.

international law the numerous regulations that govern international commerce.

business law aspects of law that most directly influence and regulate the management of business activity.

With the explosive growth of the global economy, expertise in international law has become crucial. In a recent case, the United States, Japan, and the WTO joined forces to bring a lawsuit against China for its restrictions on exports of rare metals used to make various electronic goods. Currently China mines more than 95 percent of the world's rare metals.

aspects of law that most directly influence and regulate the management of various types of business activity. Specific laws vary widely in their intent from business to business and from industry to industry. The legal interests of airlines, for example, differ from those of oil companies.

State and local statutes also have varying applications. Some state laws affect all businesses that operate in a particular state. Workers' compensation laws, which govern payments to workers for injuries incurred on the job, are an example. Other state laws apply only to certain firms or business activities. States have specific licensing requirements for businesses, such as law firms, funeral directors, and hair salons. Many local ordinances also deal with specific business activities. Local regulations on the sizes and types of business signs are commonplace. Some communities even restrict the sizes of stores, including height and square footage.

Regulatory Environment for Business

Government regulation of business has changed over time. Depending on public sentiment, the economy, and the political climate, we see the pendulum swing back and forth between increased regulation and deregulation. But the goal of both types of legislation is protection of healthy competition. One industry that has experienced some deregulation in the past is still subject to relatively tight regulations: banking. Despite the relaxation of banking regulations across state lines and the advent of online banking, laws governing everything from stock trading to retirement investing remain strict. In response to a crisis in which lending institutions granted mortgages to home buyers who were then unable to meet payments that later increased—precipitating record numbers of foreclosures—a new bill was introduced in Congress. The Mortgage Reform and Anti-Predatory Lending Act of 2007 modifies the Truth in Lending Act. The intent of this legislation is to protect consumers by establishing fair lending practices. In addition, after the near-collapse of Wall Street, the Dodd-Frank Act was signed into law in 2010. This law created the Bureau of Consumer Financial Protection and tightened regulations on all firms involved in the financial industry. Under the Dodd-Frank Act, taxpayers can no longer be asked to bail out failing financial firms.[7]

Let's look at the issues surrounding regulation and deregulation and the legislation that has characterized them.

Antitrust and Business Regulation

John D. Rockefeller's Standard Oil monopoly launched antitrust legislation. Breaking up monopolies and restraints of trade was a popular issue in the late 1800s and early 1900s. In fact, President Theodore Roosevelt always promoted himself as a "trust-buster." The highly publicized Microsoft case of the 1990s is another example of antitrust litigation.

During the 1930s, several laws designed to regulate business were passed. The basis for many of these laws was protecting employment. The world was in the midst of the Great Depression, so the government focused on keeping its citizens employed. Recently, government officials became concerned with the security aspects of international business transactions, Internet usage, the sources of funds, and their effects on U.S. business practices. New regulatory legislation in the form of the USA Patriot Act was enacted in 2001. Congress has voted to reauthorize this law several times. The law includes a provision that allows the federal government, with approval from a federal judge, to seize business records in investigations involving national security.[8]

The major federal antitrust and business regulation legislation includes the following:

LAW	WHAT IT DID
Sherman Act (1890)	Set a competitive business system as a national policy goal. The act specifically banned monopolies and restraints of trade.
Clayton Act (1914)	Put restrictions on price discrimination, exclusive dealing, tying contracts, and interlocking boards of directors that lessened competition or might lead to a monopoly.
Federal Trade Commission Act (1914)	Established the FTC with the authority to investigate business practices. The act also prohibited unfair methods of competition.
Robinson-Patman Act (1936)	Outlawed price discrimination in sales to wholesalers, retailers, or other producers. The act also banned pricing designed to eliminate competition.
Wheeler-Lea Act (1938)	Banned deceptive advertising. The act gave the FTC jurisdiction in such cases.
USA Patriot Act (2001)	Limited interactions between U.S. and foreign banks to those with "know your customer" policies; allowed the U.S. Treasury Department to freeze assets and bar a country, government, or institution from doing business in the United States; gave federal authorities broad powers to monitor Internet usage and expanded the way data is shared among different agencies. Reauthorization (2005) created a new Assistant Attorney General for Security, enhanced penalties for terrorism financing, and provided clear standards and penalties for attacks on mass transit systems.

The protection of fair competition remains an issue in industries today. According to the Federal Trade Commission (FCC), 78 percent of U.S. households have access to two land-based broadband Internet providers, and 13 percent have access to one. But when the FCC cracked down on Comcast for interfering with customers' access to competing Internet services, the U.S. Court of Appeals ruled that the FCC had exceeded its authority.[9]

Business Deregulation

Deregulation was a concept started in the 1970s whose influence continues today. Many formerly regulated industries were freed to pick the markets they wanted to serve. The deregulated industries, such as utilities and airlines, were also allowed to price their products without the guidance of federal regulations. For the most part, deregulation led to lower consumer prices. In some cases, it also led to a loss of service. Many smaller cities and airports lost airline service because of deregulation.

Following are several major laws related to deregulation:

LAW	WHAT IT DID
Airline Deregulation Act (1978)	Allowed airlines to set fares and pick their routes.
Motor Carrier Act and Staggers Rail Act (1980)	Permitted the trucking and railroad industries to negotiate rates and services.
Telecommunications Act (1996)	Cut barriers to competition in local and long-distance phone, cable, and television markets.
Gramm-Leach-Bliley Act (1999)	Permitted banks, securities firms, and insurance companies to affiliate within a new financial organizational structure; required them to disclose to customers their policies and practices for protecting the privacy of personal information.

Consumer Protection

Numerous laws designed to protect consumers have been passed in the past 100 years. In many ways, business itself has evolved to reflect this focus on consumer safety and satisfaction. Recently, Congress passed the broadest changes in the country's consumer protection system in decades, including stricter regulations governing toy manufacturing, public access to complaints about products, and a major overhaul of the Consumer Product Safety Commission (CPSC) designed to improve communication and efficiency. One provision includes stricter limits on the amount of lead in children's toys, and another requires mandatory safety standards for nursery items such as cribs and playpens. The Dodd-Frank Act covers consumer financial protection.[10] The Food and Drug Administration Amendments Act (FDAA) of 2007 reauthorizes existing laws and includes new provisions designed to enhance drug safety, encourage the development of pediatric medical devices, and enhance food safety.[11]

The major federal laws related to consumer protection include the following:

LAW	WHAT IT DID
Federal Food and Drug Act (1906)	Banned adulteration and misbranding of foods and drugs involved in interstate commerce.
Consumer Credit Protection Act (1968)	Required disclosure of annual interest rates on loans and credit purchases.
National Environmental Policy Act (1970)	Established the Environmental Protection Agency to deal with various types of pollution and organizations that create pollution.
Public Health Cigarette Smoking Act (1970)	Prohibited tobacco advertising on radio and television.
Consumer Product Safety Act (1972)	Established the Consumer Product Safety Commission with authority to specify safety standards for most products.
Nutrition Labeling and Education Act (1990)	Stipulated detailed information on the labeling of most foods.
Dietary Supplement Health and Education Act (1994)	Established standards with respect to dietary supplements including vitamins, minerals, herbs, amino acids, and the like.
Food and Drug Administration Amendments Act of 2007	Reauthorized several laws dealing with prescription drugs and added new ones enhancing food safety, drug safety, development of pediatric medical devices, and clinical trial registries.

Employee Protection

Chapters 2 and 8 cover many of the issues employers face in protecting their employees from injury and harm while on the job. But employees must also be protected from unfair practices by employers. Recently, Congress passed the Lilly Ledbetter Fair Pay Act. This law helps protect workers from wage discrimination.[12]

Some of the relevant laws related to employee protection include the following:

LAW	WHAT IT DID
Fair Labor Standards Act (1938)	For hourly workers, provided payment of the minimum wage, overtime pay for time worked over 40 hours in a workweek, restricted the employment of children, and required employers to keep records of wages and hours.
OSHA Act (1970)	Required employers to provide workers with workplaces free of recognized hazards that could cause serious injury or death and required employees to abide by all safety and health standards that apply to their jobs.
Americans with Disabilities Act (1991)	Banned discrimination against the disabled in public accommodations, transportation, and telecommunications.
Family and Medical Leave Act (1993)	Required covered employers to grant eligible employees up to 12 workweeks of unpaid leave during any 12-month period for the birth and care of a newborn child of the employee, placement with the employee of a son or daughter for adoption or foster care, care of an immediate family member with a serious health condition, or medical leave for the employee if unable to work because of a serious health condition.
Uniformed Services Employment and Reemployment Rights Act (1994)	Protects the job rights of individuals who voluntarily or involuntarily leave their jobs to perform military service. Also prohibits employment discrimination in such cases.
American Jobs Creation Act (2004)	Reduced taxes for manufacturing in the United States, provided temporary tax breaks for income repatriated to the United States, and encouraged domestic job growth.
Pension Protection Act (2006)	Required companies with underfunded pension plans to pay extra premiums; made it easier for companies to automatically enroll employees in defined contribution plans; provided greater access to professional advice about investing.
Patient Protection and Affordable Care Act (2010) and the Health Care and Education Reconciliation Act (2010)	Health-related provisions to expand Medicaid eligibility, subsidize insurance premiums, provide businesses with incentives to provide health care benefits, prohibit claims denied for preexisting conditions.

Investor Protection

Chapters 15, 16, and 17 describe the institutions subject to investor protection laws and some of the events that brought the Sarbanes-Oxley law into being. (See the entry in the following table for specific provisions of Sarbanes-Oxley.) Following is a summary of legislation to protect investors:

LAW	WHAT IT DID
Securities Exchange Act (1934)	Created the Securities and Exchange Commission with the authority to register, regulate, and oversee brokerage firms, transfer agents, clearing agencies, and stock exchanges; the SEC also has the power to enforce securities laws and protect investors in public transactions.
Bank Secrecy Act (1970)	Deterred laundering and use of secret foreign bank accounts; created an investigative paper trail for large currency transactions; imposed civil and criminal penalties for noncompliance with reporting requirements; improved detection and investigation of criminal, tax, and regulatory violations.

LAW	WHAT IT DID
Sarbanes-Oxley Act (2002)	Required top corporate executives to attest to the validity of the company's financial statements; increased the documentation and monitoring of internal controls; prohibited CPA firms from providing some types of consulting services for their clients; established a five-member accounting oversight board.
Dodd-Frank Wall Street Reform and Consumer Protection Act (2010)	Established the Bureau of Consumer Financial Protection and the Financial Stability Oversight Council; instituted stringent new regulations for transparency and accountability, designed to protect investors.

Cyberspace and Telecommunications Protection

Computers and widespread use of the Internet and telecommunications have dramatically expanded the reach of businesses. They have also raised some thorny issues such as computer fraud and abuse, online privacy, cyberbullying, and cyberterrorism. Under a Supreme Court ruling, Internet file-sharing services are now held accountable if their intention is for consumers to use software to exchange songs and videos illegally. This ruling helps protect copyrights, which are covered later in this appendix. Recently Viacom—the parent company of MTV and Comedy Central—sued YouTube and its parent company, Google, for $1 billion in federal court, claiming "massive intentional copyright infringement." Viacom argued that YouTube's success was partly built on the unlicensed use of video taken from Viacom cable channels. Google and YouTube denied the claim, but later Google unveiled a copyright filter designed to catch unauthorized use of copyrighted videos and other materials. The judge dismissed the case finding that YouTube was protected by the Digital Millennium Copyright Act's safe harbor clause. This states that companies can be protected if their services host content without review as long as infringing content is removed quickly.[13]

Following are some of the major laws enacted to regulate cyberspace and telecommunications:

LAW	WHAT IT DID
Computer Fraud and Abuse Act (1986)	Clarified definitions of criminal fraud and abuse for federal computer crimes and removed legal ambiguities and obstacles to prosecuting these crimes; established felony offenses for unauthorized access of "federal interest" computers and made it a misdemeanor to engage in unauthorized trafficking in computer passwords.
Children's Online Privacy Protection Act (1998)	Authorized the FTC to set rules regarding how and when firms must obtain parental permission before asking children marketing research questions.
Identity Theft and Assumption Deterrence Act (1998)	Made it a federal crime to knowingly transfer or use, without lawful authority, a means of identification of another person with intent to commit, aid, or abet any violation of federal, state, or local law.
Anticybersquatting Consumer Protection Act (1999)	Prohibited people from registering Internet domain names similar to company or celebrity names and then offering them for sale to these same parties.

LAW	WHAT IT DID
Homeland Security Act (2002)	Established the Department of Homeland Security; gave government wide new powers to collect and mine data on individuals and groups, including databases that combine personal, governmental, and corporate records including e-mails and Web sites viewed; limited information citizens can obtain under the Freedom of Information Act; gave government committees more latitude for meeting in secret.
Amendments to the Telemarketing Sales Rule (2003), extended by the Do-Not-Call Improvement Act of 2007 and the Do-Not-Call Fee Extension Act of 2007	Created a national do-not-call registry, which prohibits telemarketing calls to registered telephone numbers; restricted the number and duration of telemarketing calls generating dead air space with use of automatic dialers; cracked down on unauthorized billing; and required telemarketers to transmit their caller ID information. Telemarketers must check the do-not-call list quarterly, and violators could be fined for each occurrence. Excluded from the registry's restrictions are charities, opinion pollsters, and political candidates. The 2007 DNC Improvement Act allowed registered numbers to remain on the list permanently, unless consumers call to remove them themselves; the FTC will remove disconnected and reassigned numbers from the list. The Fee Extension Act of 2007 set annual fees telemarketers must pay to access the registry.
Check Clearing for the 21st Century Act (2003)	Created the substitute check, allowing banks to process check information electronically and to deliver substitute checks to banks that want to continue receiving paper checks. A substitute check is the legal equivalent of the original check.

The Core of Business Law

Contract law and the law of agency; the Uniform Commercial Code, sales law, and negotiable instruments law; property law and the law of bailment; trademark, patent, and copyright law; tort law; bankruptcy law; and tax law are the cornerstones of U.S. business law. The sections that follow set out the key provisions of each of these legal concepts.

Contract Law and Law of Agency

Contract law is important because it is the legal foundation on which business dealings are conducted. A **contract** is a legally enforceable agreement between two or more parties regarding a specified act or thing.

Contract Requirements As Figure A.1 points out, the four elements of an enforceable contract are agreement, consideration, legal and serious purpose, and capacity. The parties must reach agreement about the act or thing specified. For such an agreement, or contract, to be valid and legally enforceable, each party must furnish consideration—the value or benefit that a party provides to the others with whom the contract is made. Assume that a builder hires an electrician to install wiring in a new house. The wiring job and the resulting payment are the considerations in this instance. In addition to consideration, an enforceable contract must involve a legal and serious purpose. Agreements made as a joke or involving the commission of crimes are not enforceable as legal contracts. An agreement between two competitors to fix the prices for their products is not enforceable as a contract because the subject matter is illegal.

contract legally enforceable agreement between two or more parties regarding a specified act or thing.

The last element of a legally enforceable contract is capacity, the legal ability of a party to enter into agreements. The law does not permit certain people, such as those judged to be insane, to enter into legally enforceable contracts. Contracts govern almost all types of business activities. You might sign a contract to purchase a car or cell phone service, or to lease an apartment.

Breach of Contract A violation of a valid contract is called a *breach of contract*. The injured party can go to court to enforce the contract provisions and, in some cases, collect *damages*—financial payments to compensate for a loss and related suffering.

Law of Agency All types of firms conduct business affairs through a variety of agents, such as partners, directors, corporate officers, and sales personnel. An agency relationship exists when one party, called the principal, appoints another party, called the agent, to enter into contracts with third parties on the principal's behalf.

The law of agency is based on common-law principles and case law decisions of state and federal courts. Relatively little agency law has been enacted into statute. The law of agency is important because the principal is generally bound by the actions of the agent.

The legal basis for holding the principal liable for acts of the agent is the Latin maxim *respondeat superior* ("let the master answer"). In a case involving agency law, the court must decide the rights and obligations of the various parties. Generally, the principal is held liable if an agency relationship exists and the agent has some type of authority to do the wrongful act. The agent in such cases is liable to the principal for any damages.

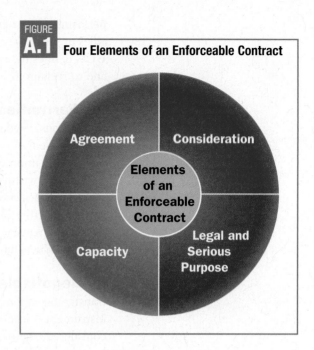

FIGURE A.1 Four Elements of an Enforceable Contract

Agreement — Consideration — Elements of an Enforceable Contract — Capacity — Legal and Serious Purpose

Uniform Commercial Code

Most U.S. business law is based on the *Uniform Commercial Code*—usually referred to simply as the UCC. The UCC covers topics such as sales law, warranties, and negotiable instruments. All 50 states have adopted the UCC, although Louisiana also relies on elements of civil law based on French, German, and Spanish codes, in addition to Roman law. While the other U.S. states rely on the tenets of English common law, which is also known as judge-based law, Louisiana's civil law system is found in most European nations. The UCC is actually a "model law" first written by the National Conference of Commissioners on Uniform State Laws, which states can then review and adopt, adopt with amendments, or replace with their own laws. The idea of the UCC is to create at least some degree of uniformity among the states.[14]

<u>Sales law</u> governs sales of goods or services for money or on credit. Article 2 of the UCC specifies the circumstances under which a buyer and a seller enter into a sales contract. Such agreements are based on the express conduct of the parties. The UCC generally requires written agreements for enforceable sales contracts for products worth more than $500. The formation of a sales contract is quite flexible because certain missing terms in a written contract or other ambiguities do not prevent the contract from being legally enforceable. A court will look to past dealings, commercial customs, and other standards of reasonableness to evaluate whether a legal contract exists.

Courts also consider these variables when either the buyer or the seller seeks to enforce his or her rights in cases in which the other party fails to perform as specified in the contract,

sales law law governing the sale of goods or services for money or on credit.

performs only partially, or performs in a defective or unsatisfactory way. The UCC's remedies in such cases usually involve the award of monetary damages to injured parties. The UCC defines the rights of the parties to have the contract performed, to have it terminated, and to reclaim the goods or place a lien—a legal claim—against them.

Warranties Article 2 of the UCC also sets forth the law of warranties for sales transactions. Products carry two basic types of warranties: an express warranty is a specific representation made by the seller regarding the product, and an implied warranty is only legally imposed on the seller. Generally, unless implied warranties are disclaimed by the seller in writing, they are automatically in effect. Other provisions govern the rights of acceptance, rejection, and inspection of products by the buyer; the rights of the parties during manufacture, shipment, delivery, and passing of title to products; the legal significance of sales documents; and the placement of the risk of loss in the event of destruction or damage to the products during manufacture, shipment, or delivery.

Negotiable Instruments A *negotiable instrument* is commercial paper that is transferable among individuals and businesses. The most common example of a negotiable instrument is a check. Drafts, certificates of deposit (CDs), and notes are also sometimes considered negotiable instruments.

Article 3 of the UCC specifies that a negotiable instrument must be written and must meet the following conditions:

1. It must be signed by the maker or drawer.

2. It must contain an unconditional promise or order to pay a certain sum of money.

3. It must be payable on demand or at a definite time.

4. It must be payable to order or to bearer.

Checks and other forms of commercial paper are transferred when the payee signs the back of the instrument, a procedure known as endorsement.

Property Law and Law of Bailment

Property law is a key feature of the private enterprise system. *Property* is something for which a person or firm has the unrestricted right of possession or use. Property rights are guaranteed and protected by the U.S. Constitution. However, under certain circumstances property may be legally seized under the law of eminent domain. In a U.S. Supreme Court ruling, the city of New London, Connecticut, was granted permission to seize a distressed area of real estate—owned by individual citizens—for future economic development by private business. In fact, this development was never completed. In response, 43 states have since passed legislation limiting the use of eminent domain. Although an appellate court in New York ruled that the state could not seize a tract of land by eminent domain in order for Columbia University to expand its campus, the higher court of appeals overturned the ruling, paving the way for the university's $6.3 billion expansion.[15] And in an unusual twist of the law, Utah passed two bills allowing the state to take some of the U.S. government's vast federal land holdings by eminent domain.[16]

As Figure A.2 shows, property can be divided into three basic categories. Tangible personal property consists of physical items such as equipment, supplies, and delivery vehicles. Intangible personal property is nonphysical property such as mortgages, stocks, and checks that are most often represented by a document or other written instrument, although it may be as vague and remote as a computer entry. You are probably familiar with certain types of intangible personal property such as checks or money orders. But other examples include bonds, notes, letters of credit, and receipts.

A third category of property is real property, or real estate. Most firms have some interaction with real estate law because of the need to buy or lease the space in which they operate. Some companies are created to serve these real estate needs. Real estate developers, builders, contractors, brokers, appraisers, mortgage companies, escrow companies, title companies, and architects all deal with various aspects of real property law.

The law of bailment deals with the surrender of personal property by one person to another when the property is to be returned at a later date. The person delivering the property is known as the bailor, and the person receiving the property is the bailee. Some bailments benefit bailees, others benefit bailors, and still others provide mutual benefits. Most courts now require that all parties practice reasonable care in all bailment situations. The degree of benefit received from the bailment is a factor in court decisions about whether parties have met the reasonable-care standards.

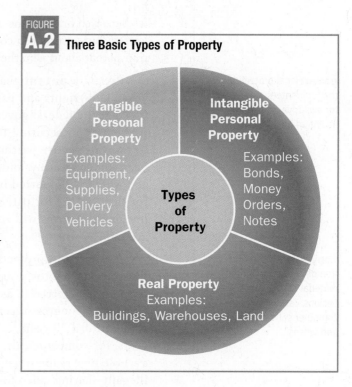

FIGURE A.2 Three Basic Types of Property

Bailment disputes are most likely to arise in business settings such as hotels, restaurants, banks, and parking lots. A series of rules have been established to govern settlement of these disagreements. The law focuses on actual delivery of an item. For instance, a restaurant owner is not liable if a customer's coat or purse is stolen from the back of his or her chair. This is because the customer has not given the item to the restaurant for safekeeping. However, if the customer delivers the coat or purse to the restaurant checkroom, receives a claim check, and the item is stolen, then the restaurant is liable.

Trademarks, Patents, and Copyrights

Trademarks, patents, and copyrights provide legal protection for key business assets by giving a firm the exclusive right to use these assets. A **trademark** consists of words, symbols, or other designations used by firms to identify their offerings. The Lanham Act (1946) provides for federal registration of trademarks. Trademarks are a valuable commercial property. Coca-Cola and McDonald's are two of the world's most widely recognized trademarks, so they are very valuable to the companies that own them.

If a product becomes too well known, its fame can create problems. Once a trademark becomes a part of everyday usage, it loses its protection as a legal trademark. Consider the words *aspirin, cola, nylon, kerosene,* and *linoleum.* All these product names were once the exclusive property of their manufacturers, but they have passed into common language, and now anyone can use them. More recent examples are *Xerox, Kleenex,* and *Velcro.* Although legally these are trademarked names, people often use them in everyday language instead of the correct generic terms *photocopy, facial tissue,* and *hook-and-loop.*

Companies understand the value of their trademarks and fight hard to protect them. Louis Vuitton sued Google for allowing other companies to bid for and use the firm's

trademark words, symbols, or other designations used by firms to identify their offerings.

trademarked brand names as keywords to trigger ads on Google's site. Louis Vuitton lost the lawsuit, but a European court ruled that companies borrowing such keywords must be more transparent about who they are and what they are actually selling.[17]

By law, a **patent** guarantees an inventor exclusive rights to an invention for 17 years. Copyrights and patents have a constitutional basis; the U.S. Constitution specifies that the federal government has the power "to promote the progress of science and useful arts, by securing for limited times to authors and inventors the exclusive rights to their respective writings or discoveries." Recently, the patent process and laws have been under scrutiny, and the Patent Reform Act was introduced in 2011. Under the act, which is supported by the information technology industry, it is now more difficult for firms to sue for patent infringement. Instead of filing for a patent on a first-to-invent basis, firms will receive patents on a first-to-file basis, which is more common around the world.[18]

A **copyright** protects written or printed material such as books, designs, cartoon illustrations, photos, computer software, music, and videos. This class of business property is referred to as *intellectual property*. Copyrights are filed with the Library of Congress. Congress recently extended copyright protection for creative material by an additional 20 years, covering artistic works for the lifetime of the creator plus 70 years; for companies, the time is 95 years. Not surprisingly, the Internet has opened up a whole new realm of copyright infringement, ranging from downloading music files to illegally sharing video footage.

Google faces a challenge both here and abroad as it compiles a massive digital library in an effort to create the world's largest online library. Already Google has put nearly 10 million books from around the world online. The firm has been challenged by authors and publishers on potential copyright infringement. Despite an agreement reached among Google, authors, and publishers, a district court judge in New York recently rejected the settlement, saying that Google had gone "too far" in its ambitious project. In its current form, the online library would "give Google a significant advantage over competitors, rewarding it for engaging in wholesale copying of copyrighted works without permission," the judge wrote.[19]

Despite publicity about Internet copyright infringement, many people engage in this practice unintentionally. Some schools are now making an effort to educate students about the practice so they can make better and more informed choices about downloading material from the Internet.

Law of Torts

A **tort** (French for "wrong") refers to a civil wrong inflicted on another person or the person's property. The law of torts is closely related to the law of agency because a business entity, or principal, can be held liable for torts committed by its agents in the course of business dealings. Tort law differs from both criminal and contract law. While criminal law is concerned with crimes against the state or society, tort law deals with compensation for injured people who are the victims of noncriminal wrongs.

Tort cases are often extremely complex and may result in large monetary awards. Because these awards have skyrocketed, some states have taken steps to limit them. Wisconsin recently limited the amount of any compensatory damages recovered by a plaintiff in a tort litigation dealing with injury or health problems resulting from exposure to toxins to $200,000.[20]

patent legal protection that guarantees an inventor exclusive rights to an invention for 17 years.

copyright legal protection of written or printed material such as books, designs, cartoons, photos, computer software, music, and videos.

tort civil wrong inflicted on one person or the person's property by another person.

Types of Torts A tort may be intentional, or it may be caused by negligence. Assault, slander, libel, and fraud are all examples of intentional torts. Businesses can become involved in such cases through the actions of both owners and employees. A security guard who uses excessive force to apprehend an alleged shoplifter may have committed a tort. Under agency law, the guard's employers, such as a shopping mall or retailer, can be also held liable for any damages or injury caused by the security guard.

The other major group of torts results from negligence. This type of tort is based on carelessness rather than intentional behavior that causes injury to another person. Under agency law, businesses can also be held liable for the negligence of their employees or agents. A delivery truck driver who injures a pedestrian while transporting goods creates a tort liability for his or her employer if the accident results from negligence.

Product Liability An area of tort law known as *product liability* has been developed by both statutory and case law to hold businesses liable for negligence in the design, manufacture, sale, or use of products. Some states have extended the theory of tort law to cover injuries caused by products, regardless of whether the manufacturer is proven negligent. This legal concept is known as strict product liability.

The business response to product liability has been mixed. To avoid lawsuits and fines, some recall defective products voluntarily; others decide to fight recall mandates if they believe the recall is not justified. Auto manufacturers and toy makers typically issue voluntary recalls, as do drug manufacturers.

Class-Action Fairness

A *class-action suit* groups a number of individual plaintiffs, such as consumers with adverse reactions to medications, to allow for efficient processing under one lawsuit. Congress passed the Class-Action Fairness Act of 2005, which imposes certain restrictions on class-action lawsuits. First, it automatically moves most large, multistate class actions—those with potential damages exceeding $5 million and in which more than two-thirds of the plaintiffs are geographically dispersed—from state courts into federal courts. This restriction prevents "shopping around" for sympathetic locations but lets cases that belong within a particular state remain there. Second, judges must consider the actual monetary value of any damage done so that plaintiffs receive true compensation for injury instead of large, arbitrary awards. Third, attorneys now receive payment differently. Under the old system, attorneys would receive a percentage of the gross settlement amount, regardless of whether all plaintiffs collected. Now judges can require uncollected awards to go to charity or government agencies, instead of into the pockets of lawyers. If the attorneys' fees are not based on a percentage, then they must charge based on the time they spent on the case.

Effects of the act are already being felt. In many states, the tide has already begun to turn away from huge, long, expensive lawsuits. Some states have passed their own laws restricting the types of suits that can be filed. Michigan has virtually eliminated class-action suits against drug manufacturers, and New York threw out a case accusing investment firms of manipulating the price of certain initial stock offerings. Twenty-three states have instituted statutes prohibiting suits against fast-food restaurants for causing obesity. And damage limits in many states have restricted medical malpractice suits.

Bankruptcy Law

bankruptcy legal nonpayment of financial obligations.

Bankruptcy, legal nonpayment of financial obligations, is a common occurrence in contemporary society. Federal legislation passed in 1918 and revised several times since then provides a system for handling bankruptcies. Bankruptcy has two purposes. One is to protect creditors by providing a way to obtain compensation through debtors' assets. The second goal, which is almost unique to the United States, is to also protect debtors, allowing them to get a fresh financial start.

Federal law recognizes two types of bankruptcy. Under voluntary bankruptcy, a person or firm asks to be judged bankrupt because of inability to repay creditors. Under involuntary bankruptcy, creditors may request that a party be judged bankrupt.

Personal Bankruptcies

With a growing number of individuals amassing large personal debt—often through credit cards—Congress recently revised personal bankruptcy law to make it more difficult for people to erase their debt instead of being held accountable for it. Under the Bankruptcy Abuse Prevention and Consumer Protection Act of 2005, it is harder for individuals to file Chapter 7 bankruptcy, which traditionally has wiped out most debt. If their earnings exceed their state's median income, they will instead be required to file Chapter 13 bankruptcy, which sets up a repayment plan as designed by the court. A few years after the law's passage, personal bankruptcies still hovered at the high mark, likely because of a slow economy. Reports revealed that more homeowners were walking away from large mortgages that they were unable to pay instead of reorganizing their debt and trying to hang onto their homes. As the economy began to recover, the rate of personal bankruptcies declined.[21]

Business Bankruptcies

Businesses can also go bankrupt for a variety of reasons—mismanagement, plunging sales, an inability to keep up with changes in the marketplace. Under Chapter 11, a firm may reorganize and develop a plan to repay its debts. Chapter 11 also permits prepackaged bankruptcies, in which companies enter bankruptcy proceedings after obtaining approval of most—but not necessarily all—of their creditors. Often companies can emerge from prepackaged bankruptcies sooner than those that opt for conventional Chapter 11 filings. Airlines have managed to accomplish this, as well as some large retailers.

Tax Law

tax assessment by a governmental unit.

A branch of law that affects every business, employee, and consumer in the United States is tax law. A **tax** is an assessment by a governmental unit. Federal, state, and local governments and special taxing authorities all levy taxes. Appendix C, "Personal Financial Planning," also covers tax law.

Some taxes are paid by individuals and some by businesses. Both have a decided impact on contemporary business. Business taxes reduce profits, and personal taxes cut the disposable incomes that individuals can spend on the products of industry. Governments spend the revenue from taxes to buy goods and services produced by businesses. Governments also act as transfer agents, moving tax revenue to other consumers and transferring Social Security taxes from the working population to retired or disabled people.

Governments can levy taxes on several different bases: income, sales, business receipts, property, and assets. The type of tax varies from one taxing authority to the other. The individual income tax is the biggest source of revenue for the federal government. Many states also rely heavily on income taxes as well as sales taxes, which vary widely. Cities and towns may collect property taxes in order to operate schools and improve roads. So-called luxury taxes are levied on items such as yachts and expensive sports cars, while so-called sin taxes are levied on items such as cigarettes and alcohol. In addition, the issue of whether to tax different types of Internet services and use has been hotly debated.

Business Terms You Need to Know

judiciary A-2	business law A-4	copyright A-14
law A-3	contract A-10	tort A-14
common law A-3	sales law A-11	bankruptcy A-16
statutory law A-4	trademark A-13	tax A-16
international law A-4	patent A-14	

Projects and Teamwork Applications

1. Consumer protection is an idea that took root in the early 1900s and continues today. Choose an industry that you think should—or will—be the next area of concern for the Consumer Product Safety Commission. It might be travel, organic foods, health care, or anything else that interests you. Research the consumer protections that may already exist in this industry and then outline a plan for future protections.

2. To be effective, laws must be practical and enforceable; they must also be changed periodically to reflect changes in societal views and values. You've already learned about some of the wacky laws enacted by states. Go online and research your home state or community to find other outdated, unenforceable, or strange laws that affect business. Present them in class and discuss how they might be revised so that they could actually work.

3. The business world is filled with tort cases, particularly those involving product liability. One of the most famous cases is probably the one in which a customer sued McDonald's because a cup of hot McDonald's coffee spilled in her lap, causing burns and scalding. A jury awarded her $2.7 million in punitive damages, an amount that was later reduced by a judge to less than $500,000. On your own or with a classmate, go online to research other famous product liability cases. Choose a case and learn as much as you can about it, including the effect the outcome had on the firm or firms involved. Present your findings in class.

4. Go online and research more about the Bankruptcy Abuse Prevention and Consumer Protection Act of 2005, and the implications it has in today's economy. Do you think the law is fair? Why or why not? How does filing for personal bankruptcy affect a person's standing in the marketplace? Present your thoughts to the class.

| Appendix B |

Insurance and Risk Management

Pay-as-You-Drive Insurance Plans

What would you do to save up to 30 percent on your auto insurance? Would you allow your insurance company to track your driving habits, including how far you drive, how fast, and how aggressively?

Several U.S. insurance companies, including Allstate, State Farm, Travelers, Progressive, and GMAC, are offering new pay-as-you-drive auto insurance policies in many states. The programs differ in details, but they generally rely on telematic tracking devices that plug into onboard diagnostic computers such as OnStar and measure statistics about usage that help create a unique driver risk profile. For the first time, those whose profiles put them in lower-risk categories can qualify for individualized lower rates based on their actual driving habits.

For instance, says a Progressive executive, "If you drive a lot compared to average, you are a higher risk. And if you drive aggressively, odds are you're higher risk as well … you're probably in closer proximity to other vehicles and trying to get around them, and so you have more braking events." Your rates would likely not go down.

But if you're a particularly safe and cautious driver, you might pay less for insurance even if you fit into a normally higher-risk group, such as teenage males. "This capability has really redefined the way we think about pricing auto," said an executive of Hartford Financial Services Group, which is launching a pilot program.

Some critics say cheaper rates are available through other means, like combining discounts. But the biggest obstacle many drivers see isn't price but the potential loss of privacy. Insurers insist they don't need to and won't track *where* the car is driven, or even who is driving it, but GPS devices can already do that, and insurers use them to offer roadside assistance. Some fear insurance companies won't be able to resist drawing on location data to further identify individual drivers and adjust coverage based on destination.[1]

Appendix

B   Overview

Risk is a daily fact of life for both individuals and businesses. Sometimes it arrives in the form of a serious illness or injury. In other instances, it takes the form of property loss, such as the extensive damage to homes and businesses due to the tornadoes that swept across midwestern and southern states. Risk can also occur as the result of the actions of others—such as a driver who is busy texting and runs a stop sign. In still other cases, risk may occur as a result of our own actions—we might venture out in a boat during a thunderstorm or fail to heed warnings about high blood pressure.

Businesspeople must understand the types of risk they face and develop methods for dealing with them. One approach to risk is to shift it to the specialized expertise of insurance companies. This appendix discusses the concept of insurance in a business setting. It begins with a definition of risk. We then describe the various ways in which risk can be managed. Next, we list some of the major insurance concepts, such as what constitutes an insurable risk. The appendix concludes with an overview of the major types of insurance.

The Concept of Risk

Risk is uncertainty about loss or injury. Consider the risks faced by a typical business. A factory or warehouse faces the risk of fire and smoke, burglary, and storm damage. Data loss, injuries to workers, and loss of facilities are some of the risks faced by businesses. Risks can be divided into two major categories: speculative risk and pure risk.

Speculative risk gives the firm or individual the chance of either a profit or a loss. A firm that expands operations into a new market may experience higher profits or the loss of invested funds. A contractor who builds a house without a specific buyer may sell the house at a profit or lose money if the house sits unsold for months.

Pure risk, on the other hand, involves only the chance of loss. Motorists, for example, always face the risk of accidents. If they occur, both financial and physical losses may result. If they do not occur, however, drivers do not profit. Insurance often helps individuals and businesses protect against financial loss resulting from some types of pure risk.

> **risk** uncertainty about loss or injury.

Risk Management

Because risk is an unavoidable part of business, managers must find ways to deal with it. The first step in any **risk management** plan is to recognize what's at risk and why it's at risk. After that, the manager must decide how to handle the risk. In general, businesses have four alternatives in handling risk: avoid it, minimize it, assume it, or transfer it.

Executives must consider many factors when evaluating risks, both at home and abroad. These factors include a nation's economic stability; social and cultural factors, such as language; available technologies; distribution systems; and government regulations. International businesses are typically exposed to less risk in countries with stable economic, social and cultural, and political and legal environments.

> **risk management** calculations and actions a firm takes to recognize and deal with real or potential risks to its survival.

Avoiding Risk

Some of the pure risks facing people can be avoided by living a healthful life. Not smoking and not swimming alone are two ways of avoiding personal risk. By the same token, businesses can also avoid some of the pure risks they face. A manufacturer can locate a new production facility away from an area that is prone to tornadoes, hurricanes, or earthquakes.

Reducing Risk

Managers can reduce or even eliminate many types of risk by removing hazards or taking preventive measures. Many companies develop safety programs to educate employees

Businesses can reduce some of the pure risks they encounter. For example, a company can locate a new production facility away from areas that are prone to tornadoes.

about potential hazards and the proper methods of performing certain dangerous tasks. Any employee who works at a hazardous waste site is required to have training and medical monitoring that meet the federal Occupational Safety and Health Administration (OSHA) standards. The training and monitoring not only reduce risk but pay off on the bottom line. Aside from the human tragedy, accidents cost companies time and money.

Although many actions can reduce the risk involved in business operations, they cannot eliminate risk entirely. Most major insurers help their clients avoid or minimize risk by offering the services of loss-prevention experts to conduct thorough reviews of their operations. These health and safety professionals evaluate customers' work environments and recommend procedures and equipment to help firms minimize worker injuries and property losses.

By the same token, people can take actions to reduce risk. For instance, obeying the rules of the road and doing regular maintenance on a car can reduce the risks associated with driving. Boarding up windows in preparation for a hurricane can reduce the risk of wind damage. Taking these actions, however, can't entirely eliminate risk.

Self-Insuring Against Risk

Instead of purchasing insurance against certain types of pure risk, some companies accumulate funds to cover potential losses. These self-insurance funds are special funds created by periodically setting aside cash reserves that the firm can draw on in the event of a financial loss resulting from a pure risk. A firm makes regular payments to the fund, and it charges losses to the fund. Such a fund typically accompanies a risk-reduction program aimed at minimizing losses.

One of the most common forms of self-insurance is employee health insurance. Most employers provide health insurance coverage to employees as a component of their fringe benefit programs. Some, especially larger ones, find it more economical to create a self-insurance fund covering projected employee health care expenses, as opposed to purchasing a health insurance policy from a health insurance company. Self-insured employers, however, almost always contract with a health insurer to administer their employee health plans.

Shifting Risk to an Insurance Company

insurance contract by which the insurer, for a fee, agrees to reimburse the insured a sum of money if a loss occurs.

Although organizations and individuals can take steps to avoid or reduce risk, the most common method of dealing with it is to shift it to others in the form of **insurance**—a contract by which an insurer, for a fee, agrees to reimburse another firm or individual a sum of money if a loss occurs. The insured party's fee to the insurance company for coverage against losses is called a *premium*. Insurance substitutes a small, known loss—the insurance premium—for a larger, unknown loss that may or may not occur. In the case of life insurance, the loss—death—is a certainty; the main uncertainty is the date when it will occur.

It is important for the insurer to understand the customer's business, risk exposure, and insurance needs. Firms that operate in several countries usually do business with insurance companies that maintain global networks of offices.

Basic Insurance Concepts

Figure B.1 illustrates how an insurance company operates. The insurer collects premiums from policyholders in exchange for insurance coverage. The insurance company uses some of these funds to pay current claims and operating expenses. What's left over is held in the form of reserves, which are in turn invested. Reserves can be used to pay for unexpected losses. The returns from insurance company reserves may allow the insurer to reduce premiums, generate profits, or both. By investing reserves, the insurance industry represents a major source of long-term financing for other businesses.

An insurance company is a professional risk taker. For a fee, it accepts risks of loss or damage to businesses and individuals. Four basic principles underlie insurance: the concept of insurable interest, the concept of insurable risk, the rule of indemnity, and the law of large numbers.

Insurable Interest

To purchase insurance, an applicant must demonstrate an *insurable interest* in the property or life of the insured. In other words, the policyholder must stand to suffer a loss, financial or otherwise, due to fire, storm damage, accident, theft, illness, death, or lawsuit. A homeowner has an insurable interest in his or her home and its contents. In the case of life insurance coverage purchased for the main income provider in a household, the policyholder's spouse and children have a clear insurable interest.

A firm can purchase property and liability insurance on physical assets—such as an office or warehouse—to cover losses due to such hazards as fire and theft because the company can demonstrate an obvious insurable interest. Because top executives are important assets to a company, a business often purchases key-person life insurance, which compensates the business should an important individual die.

Insurable Risk

Insurable risk refers to the requirements that a risk must meet in order for the insurer to provide protection. Only some pure risks, and no speculative ones, are insurable. There are four basic requirements for a pure risk to be considered an insurable risk:

1. The likelihood of loss should be reasonably predictable. If an insurance company cannot reasonably predict losses, it has no basis for setting affordable premiums.

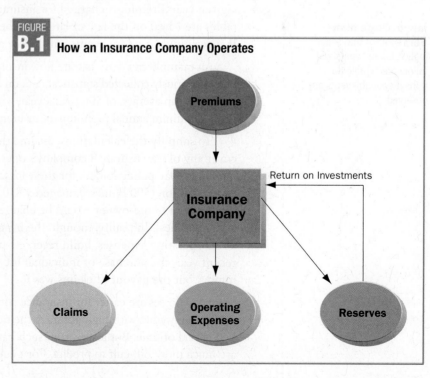

FIGURE B.1 **How an Insurance Company Operates**

Premiums → Insurance Company → Claims, Operating Expenses, Reserves; Return on Investments

2. The loss should be financially measurable.

3. The loss should be accidental, or fortuitous.

4. The risk should be spread over a certain geographic area.

The insurance company has the right to set standards for accepting risk. This process of setting these standards, and deciding what to charge, is known as *underwriting*.

Rule of Indemnity

The **rule of indemnity** states that the insured cannot collect more than the amount of the loss. Nor can the insured collect for that loss more than once. Assume that a florist's delivery van is damaged in an accident. If the total damage amounts to $2,500, then that is the maximum amount the business can collect from the insurance company.

Occasionally a loss may be covered by more than one policy. For instance, assume that a $5,000 loss is covered by two different policies. The rule of indemnity means that the insured individual or business can only collect a total of $5,000 from both insurance companies. It is up to the insurers to decide which pays how much based on policy specifics.

The Law of Large Numbers

Insurance is based on the law of averages, or statistical probability. Insurance companies simply cannot afford to sell insurance policies unless they can reasonably predict losses. As a result, insurance companies have studied the chances of occurrences of deaths, injuries, property damage, lawsuits, and other types of hazards. Table B.1 is an example of the kind of data insurance companies examine. It shows the automobile accident rate, by the age of the driver, for a recent year. From their investigations, insurance companies have developed *actuarial tables*, which predict the number of fires, automobile accidents, or deaths that will occur in a given year. Premiums charged for insurance coverage are based on these tables. Actuarial tables are based on the law of large numbers. In essence, the **law of large numbers** states that seemingly random events will follow a predictable pattern if enough events are observed.

An example can demonstrate how insurers use the law of large numbers to calculate premiums. Previously collected statistical data on a city with 50,000 homes indicates that the city will experience an average of 500 fires a year, with damages averaging $30,000 per occurrence. What is the minimum annual premium an insurance company would charge to insure one residence?

To simplify the calculations, assume that the premiums would not produce profits or cover any of the insurance company's operating expenses—they would just produce enough income to pay policyholders for their losses. In total, fires in the city would generate claims of $15 million (500 homes damaged x $30,000). If these losses were spread over all 50,000 homes, each home-owner would be charged an annual premium of $300 ($15 million x 50,000 homes). In reality, though, the insurer would set the premium at a higher figure to cover operating expenses, build reserves, and earn a reasonable profit. For instance, during a recent year, the purchase of individual life insurance policies totaled over $27 trillion in premiums, but the payout of claims was less.[2]

Some losses are easier for insurance companies to predict than others. Life insurance companies can predict with high accuracy the number of policyholders who will die within a specified period of time. But losses from such hazards as automobile accidents and weather events are much more difficult to predict. For example, the number of damage claims on homeowners'

TABLE B.1 Relationship between the Age of the Driver and the Number of Motor Vehicle Accidents

AGE GROUP	ACCIDENT RATE (PER 100 DRIVERS)
19 years old and under	**20**
16 years old	23
17 years old	20
18 years old	19
19 years old	15
20 to 24 years old	**14**
20 years old	15
21 years old	14
22 years old	14
23 years old	17
24 years old	11
25 to 34 years old	**9**
35 to 44 years old	**8**
45 to 54 years old	**7**
55 to 64 years old	**5**
65 to 74 years old	**4**
75 years old and over	**4**

Source: National Safety Council, *Injury Facts*, 2011 edition, Licensed Drivers and Number in Accidents by Age of Driver, 2009, http://www.nsc.org, accessed April 12, 2012.

policies due to lightning has increased dramatically, costing insurers more than $1 billion in claims one year. Still, the homeowners insurance industry realized $34.7 billion in profits.[3]

Sources of Insurance Coverage

The insurance industry includes both for-profit companies—such as Prudential, State Farm, and Liberty Mutual—and a number of public agencies that provide insurance coverage for business firms, not-for-profit organizations, and individuals.

Public Insurance Agencies

A *public insurance agency* is a state or federal government unit established to provide specialized insurance protection for individuals and organizations. It provides protection in such areas as job loss (unemployment insurance) and work-related injuries (workers' compensation). Public insurance agencies also sponsor specialized programs, such as deposit, flood, and crop insurance.

Unemployment Insurance Every state in the United States has an unemployment insurance program that assists unemployed workers by providing financial benefits, job counseling, and placement services. Compensation amounts vary depending on workers' previous incomes and the states in which they file claims. These insurance programs are funded by payroll taxes paid by employers.

Workers' Compensation Under state laws, employers must provide workers' compensation insurance to guarantee payment of wages and salaries, medical care costs, and such rehabilitation services as retraining, job placement, and vocational rehabilitation to employees who are injured on the job. In addition, workers' compensation provides benefits in the form of weekly payments or single, lump-sum payments to survivors of workers who die as a result of work-related injuries. Premiums are based on the company's payroll, the on-the-job hazards to which it exposes workers, and its safety record.

Social Security The federal government is the nation's largest insurer. The Social Security program, established in 1935, provides retirement, survivor, and disability benefits to millions of Americans. *Medicare* was added to the Social Security program in 1965 to provide health insurance for people age 65 and older and certain other Social Security recipients. More than nine out of ten workers in the United States and their dependents are eligible for Social Security program benefits. The program is funded through a payroll tax, half of which is paid by employers and half by workers. Self-employed people pay the full tax.

Private Insurance Companies

Much of the insurance in force is provided by private firms. These companies provide protection in exchange for the payment of premiums. Some private insurers are stockholder owned, and therefore are run like any other business, and others are so-called mutual associations. Most, though not all, mutual insurance companies specialize in life insurance. Technically, mutual insurance companies are owned by their policyholders, who may receive premium rebates in the form of dividends. In spite of this, however, there is no evidence that an insurance policy from a mutual company costs any less than a comparable policy from a stockholder-owned insurer. In recent years some mutual insurance companies have reorganized as stockholder-owned companies, including Prudential, one of the nation's largest insurers.

Types of Insurance

Individuals and businesses spend hundreds of billions of dollars each year on insurance coverage. Figure B.2 shows how much insurance companies collected in premiums for selected types of insurance in a recent year. Unfortunately, both business firms and consumers make poor decisions when buying insurance. Here are four common sense tips to remember when buying insurance:

1. Insure against large losses, not small ones. It is generally much more cost effective to self-insure against small losses.

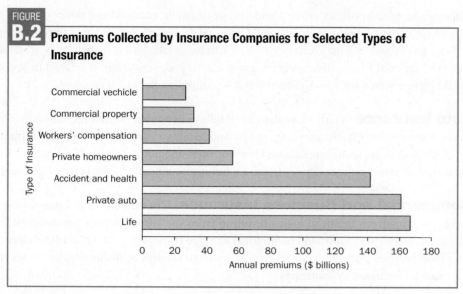

FIGURE B.2 Premiums Collected by Insurance Companies for Selected Types of Insurance

Note: Accident and health includes long-term care and disability insurance.
Source: Insurance Information Institute, *Insurance Fact Book*, http://www.iii.org.

2. Buy insurance with broad coverage, not narrow coverage. For example, it is much less expensive generally to buy a homeowners policy that protects you from multiple events (perils such as fire and theft) than to buy several policies that cover individual events.

3. Shop around. Premiums for similar policies can vary widely from company to company.

4. Buy insurance only from financially strong companies. Insurance companies occasionally go bankrupt. If that happens, the insured is left with no coverage and little hope of getting premiums back.

Although insurers offer hundreds of different policies, they all fall into three broad categories: property and liability insurance, health and disability insurance, and life insurance.

Property and Liability Insurance

Insurance that protects against fire, accident, theft, or other destructive events or perils, is called **property and liability insurance**. Examples of this insurance category include homeowners' insurance, auto insurance, business or commercial insurance, and liability insurance. Most property and liability policies are subject to deductibles. A deductible is the amount of the loss the insured pays out of pocket.

property and liability insurance general category of insurance that protects against losses due to a number of perils.

Homeowners' Insurance Homeowners' insurance protects homeowners from damage to their residences due to various perils. If a home is destroyed by fire, for example, the homeowners' policy will pay to replace the home and its contents. Virtually all homeowners carry coverage of this nature.

Homeowners' insurance premiums have risen sharply in recent years. Moreover, homeowners in coastal areas are finding it increasingly difficult to obtain insurance because of the rising number of claims related to erosion, hurricanes, and floods. If homeowners can obtain private coverage, those plans may be very expensive. In some cases they may be able to purchase insurance through a state-run program instead.[4]

Although standard policies cover a wide range of perils, most do not cover damage from widespread catastrophes such as floods and earthquakes. Homeowners must purchase separate policies to protect against damage caused by these perils. Flood insurance is available through the National Flood Insurance Program. Earthquake coverage is offered in several earthquake-prone states such as California and Washington but is very expensive.

Auto Insurance With more than $150 billion in annual premiums, automobile insurance is the country's largest category of property and liability insurance. Automobile insurance policies cover losses due to automobile accidents or theft, including personal and property claims. Almost all states require drivers to have a minimum amount of auto insurance coverage.

Commercial and Business Insurance Commercial and business insurance protects firms from financial losses resulting from the suspension of business operations (*business interruption insurance*) or physical damage to property as a result of destructive events. These policies may also protect employers from employee dishonesty or losses resulting from nonperformance of contracts.

Liability Insurance *Liability insurance* protects an individual or business against financial losses to others for which the individual or business was responsible. If a business sells a defective product, the firm's liability insurance would pay for financial losses sustained by customers. A standard amount of liability coverage is usually attached to auto, homeowners', and commercial insurance policies. Additional amounts of liability insurance can be purchased if needed. Adequate liability insurance is critically important today for both businesses and individuals. Walmart, for example, requires its suppliers to have at least $2 million in liability coverage for their products; some products considered to be high risk can require a minimum of $10 million.[5]

Health and Disability Insurance

health insurance category of insurance that pays for losses due to illness or injury.

Each of us faces the risk of getting sick or being injured in some way. Even a relatively minor illness can result in substantial health care bills. To guard against this risk, most Americans have some form of **health insurance**—insurance that provides coverage for expenses due to sickness or accidents. With soaring costs in health care, this type of insurance has become an important consideration for both businesses and individuals.

Sources of health insurance include private individual policies, private group policies, and the federal government, through Medicare and Medicaid (health insurance for lower-income people). More than 60 percent of Americans are covered by private group health insurance provided by their employer as an employee benefit. Four of every five U.S. employees work for businesses and not-for-profits that offer some form of group health insurance. Group policies resemble individual health insurance policies but are offered at lower premiums. Individual health insurance policies are simply too expensive for most people. Health insurance costs have soared in recent years,

©Catherine Yeulet/iStockphoto

Some providers offer low-cost health plans to companies. The goal for all health insurance is to provide coverage for expenses due to sickness or accidents that require medical care.

and employers have responded by cutting back on benefits, requiring employees to pay more of the premium, charging higher deductibles, or even dropping coverage altogether. In response to the growing cost and increasing numbers of individuals without adequate coverage, Congress passed a pair of health care reform bills entitled the Patient Protection and Affordable Care Act and the Health Care and Education Reconciliation Act. Although the bills were the subject of heated debate among legislators, businesspeople, and consumers, they were signed into law.[6]

Private health insurance plans fall into one of two general categories: fee-for-service plans and managed care plans. In a *fee-for-service plan*, the insured picks his or her doctor and has almost unlimited access to specialists. Fee-for-service plans charge an annual deductible and copayments. By contrast, a *managed care plan* pays most of the insured's health care bills. In return, the program has a great deal of say over the conditions of health care provided for the insured. Most managed care plans, for example, restrict the use of specialists and may specify which hospitals and pharmacies can be used. Some employers offer employees a choice between a fee-for-service and a managed care plan. Multiple managed care plans are sometimes available.

Managed care plans have become extremely popular in recent years. More than 150 million Americans are enrolled in some form of managed care plan, and many fee-for-service plans have adopted some elements of managed care. A primary reason for the popularity of managed care is simply cost: managed care plans generally cost employers and employees less than fee-for-service plans. Managed care, however, is not without its critics. The effort to control costs has caused a backlash because of restrictions placed on doctors and patients. Legislation at both the federal and state levels has forced managed care plans to give patients and physicians more control over medical decisions.

Types of Managed Care Plans
Two types of managed care plans can be found in the United States: health maintenance organizations and preferred provider organizations. Although both manage health care, important differences exist between the two.

Health maintenance organizations (HMOs) do not provide health insurance, they provide health care. An HMO supplies all of the individual's health care needs, including prescription drugs and hospitalization. The individual must use the HMO's own doctors and approved treatment facilities in order to receive benefits. Doctors and other health care professionals are actually employees of the HMO. Individuals pick a primary care physician and cannot see a specialist without a referral. An HMO charges no deductibles and only a low, fixed-dollar copayment.

The second type of managed care plan is the preferred provider organization (PPO). In the United States, more individuals are covered by PPOs than by HMOs. In a PPO, an employer negotiates a contract between local health care providers (physicians, hospitals, and pharmacies) to provide medical care to its employees at a discount. These plans have low fixed-dollar copayments. They are generally much more flexible than HMOs. Members can choose their primary care physician from a list of doctors. If a referral is given or hospitalization is required, the member again chooses from a list of approved health care providers. A member who obtains treatment from a health care provider outside the PPO network may be reimbursed for only part of the cost.

Disability Income Insurance
Not only is *disability income insurance* one of the most overlooked forms of insurance, but many workers also don't have enough coverage. The odds that a person will develop a disability are considerably higher than most people realize. Take a group of five randomly selected 45-year-olds. There is approximately a 95

percent chance that one of the five will develop some form of disability during the next 20 years. Disability income insurance is designed to replace lost income when a wage earner cannot work due to an accident or illness.

Two sources of disability income insurance exist: Social Security and private disability insurance policies. Social Security disability benefits are available to virtually all workers, but they have very strict requirements. Private disability insurance is available on either an individual or group basis. As with health insurance, a group policy is much cheaper than an individual policy. Many employers provide at least some disability coverage as an employee benefit. Employees often have the option of obtaining additional coverage by paying more.

Life Insurance

life insurance protects people against the financial losses that occur with premature death.

Life insurance protects people against the financial losses that occur with premature death. Three of every four Americans have some form of life insurance. The main reason people buy life insurance is to provide financial security for their families in the event of their death. With assets totaling $4.8 trillion, the life insurance industry is one of the nation's largest businesses.

Types of Life Insurance As with health and disability insurance, both individual and group life insurance policies are available. Many employers offer life insurance to employees as a component of the firm's benefit program. However, unlike health and disability insurance, an individual life insurance policy is usually cheaper than a group policy for younger people.

The different types of life insurance fall neatly into two categories: term policies and cash value policies. Term policies provide a death benefit if the policyholder dies within a specified period of time. It has no value at the end of that period. Cash value policies—sometimes called whole life and universal life—combine life insurance protection with a savings or investment feature. The cash value represents the amount of the savings or investment portion of the policy. Although there are arguments in favor of cash value policies, many experts believe that term life insurance is a better choice for most consumers. For one thing, a term policy is much cheaper than a cash value policy.

How Much Life Insurance Should You Have? People can purchase life insurance policies for almost any amount. Life insurance purchases are limited only by the amount of premiums people can afford and their ability to meet medical qualifications. The amount of life insurance a person needs, however, is a very personal decision. The general rule of thumb is that a person needs life insurance if he or she has family members who financially depend on that individual. A young parent with three small children could easily need $500,000 or more of life insurance. A single person with no dependents would reasonably see little or no need for a life insurance policy.

Businesses, as well as individual consumers, buy life insurance. The death of a partner or a key executive is likely to result in a financial loss to an

Steve Debenport/iStockphoto

Do you need life insurance? The general rule is that a person should have life insurance if he or she has family members who depend financially on that individual. For example, a young parent with several children could easily need $500,000 or more of life insurance. A single person with no dependents may see little or no need for life insurance coverage.

organization. Key person insurance reimburses the organization for the loss of the services of an essential senior executive and to cover the executive search expenses needed to find a replacement. In addition, life insurance policies may be purchased for each member of a partnership to be able to repay the deceased partner's survivors for his or her share of the firm and permit the business to continue.

■ Business Terms You Need to Know

risk A-19

risk management A-19

insurance A-20

rule of indemnity A-22

law of large numbers A-22

property and liability insurance A-25

health insurance A-26

life insurance A-28

■ Projects and Teamwork Applications

1. Choose one of the following companies, or select another one that interests you. Research the company online, learning what you can about the firm's goods and services, work processes, and facilities. Then create a chart identifying risks you believe the company faces—and ways the firm can avoid those risks or reduce the risks. Suggested firms:

   a. Carnival Cruises

   b. Tampa Bay Rays

   c. Whole Food Markets

   d. Hershey's chocolate

2. Assess your own personal insurance needs. What types of coverage do you currently have? How do you see your insurance needs changing in the next five to ten years?

3. Go online and research one of these human-made disasters: the BP oil spill in the Gulf of Mexico or the explosion in the Massie mine in West Virginia. Learn what you can about the role of insurance companies. Did they meet or exceed their obligations? Or did they fall short? Report your findings in class.

4. Table B.1 illustrates the relationship between the age of a driver and the number of motor vehicle accidents. The greatest number of accidents occurs between the ages of 16 and 19, and the fewest occur starting at age 65. Research the causes of these accidents, noting similarities and differences. Then create a report outlining your research as well as steps you think the younger group of drivers might take to reduce their risks.

| Appendix C |

Personal Financial Planning

Personal Saving Strategies for the Millennial Generation

Do you know how to have $90,000 in the bank in just 30 years? By saving only $250 a month, beginning now. That's about what most workers today spend on coffee and lunch each month.

Unfortunately, saving isn't as easy for the Millennial generation as it sounds. Burdened with tuition and credit-card debt, many young people view saving for retirement as a job for someone else, despite their declining faith in Social Security. And in the wake of the recent economic recession, many U.S. consumers are focusing on paying down personal debt rather than on saving for the long term.

At the same time, however, many financial advisors believe younger workers need to save for retirement even more carefully than earlier generations, because they'll need much more money in reserve than today's retirees to see them through their later years. Most advisors agree that because nothing is certain, including the future of the Social Security system, today's younger workers should be aiming to set aside between $2 and $3 million for themselves and their families.

That's a daunting number for most people when viewed as a lump sum. The only way to approach it realistically is to save as much as possible on a regular basis, beginning as early as you can. For instance, back to that $250 a month: some advisors suggest simple strategies such as eating breakfast at home and packing a lunch, including a container of home-brewed coffee, instead of stopping at Starbucks on the way to work.

Other advice includes acknowledging that you'll have competing financial priorities, and that their relative importance will change as you get older. Also try thinking of your financial health as being just as important as your physical health. You exercise, so why not save too? If you find it easier to stick with an exercise program when you have a buddy, include your spouse or a friend in your savings plan. A little reinforcement can go a long way.

Finally, even if you start small, be sure you start. As one financial advisor says, "It's the pennies that add up."[1]

Appendix

C   Overview

You are studying business, but much of what you learn in this course will also apply to your personal life. For instance, you learn about each of the important functions of a business—from accounting to marketing, from finance to management. Learning about each business function will help you choose a career, and a career choice is one of the most important personal financial decisions you will make. You will learn why firms prepare budgets and financial statements. But budgets and financial statements are also important tools for individuals and households.

Everyone, regardless of age or income, can probably do a better job of managing his or her finances. As a group, Americans are much better at making money than they are at managing money. This appendix introduces you to personal financial management. **Personal financial management** deals with a variety of issues and decisions that affect a person's financial well-being. It includes basic money management, credit, tax planning, major consumer purchases, insurance, investing, and retirement planning.

The appendix will draw from many of the topics you will learn while studying business, but it introduces you to some new concepts as well. It is hoped that after completing the appendix, you will be a better informed financial consumer and personal money manager and that you will be motivated to learn more about personal finance. The rewards, in both monetary and nonmonetary terms, can be tremendous.

personal financial management study of the economic factors and personal decisions that affect a person's financial well-being.

The Meaning and Importance of Personal Finance

Personal finance affects, and is affected by, many things we do and many decisions we make throughout our lives.

On one level, personal finance involves money know-how. It is essential to know how to earn money, as well as how to save, spend, invest, and control it in order to achieve goals. The reward of sound money management is an improvement in a person's standard of living. **Standard of living** consists of the necessities, comforts, or luxuries a person seeks to attain or maintain.

On another level, personal finance is intertwined with each person's lifestyle—the way we live our daily lives. Our choice of careers, friends, hobbies, communities, and possessions is determined by personal finances, and yet our personal finances can also be determined by our lifestyles. If you're a college student living on a shoestring budget, you may have to make serious financial sacrifices to achieve your educational goals. Where you live is determined by the school you attend and how much you can afford to pay for room and board; your vacation is set by your academic schedule and your savings account; your clothing depends on the climate and your budget. All these lifestyle decisions are largely determined by your personal finances.

standard of living necessities, comforts, and luxuries one seeks to obtain or to maintain.

Ryan McVay/The Image Bank/Getty Images, Inc.

The Importance of Personal Finance Today

Good money management has always been important, but major changes in the economic environment over the past few years have made personal finance even more important

Your lifestyle affects your finances. Skiing at expensive resorts won't leave much money in your savings account.

today. And this is true whether you're a 20-year-old college student with hefty tuition bills, a 40-year-old parent with a mortgage to pay, or a 60-year-old thinking about retirement. Let's look at three reasons personal financial planning is so important in today's environment.

Sluggish Growth in Personal Income Personal income in the United States has grown very slowly in recent years. For example, median household income actually fell 6.7 percent since the recent recession.[2] During this time, financial institutions faltered and unemployment soared. While the U.S. economy is now moving forward slowly, most predict that annual increases in wages and salaries will barely keep pace with the rate of inflation in the coming years.

The sluggish growth in personal income makes sound money management very important. You cannot count on rising personal income by itself to improve your standard of living. Rather, you need to save and invest more money, stick to a budget, and make major purchases wisely.

Changes in the Labor Market Job security and the notion of work have changed in recent years. People rarely work for the same company throughout an entire career; in fact, most people change jobs every five years. And a recent poll revealed that nearly half of Americans age 50 and older say they plan to postpone retirement due to the sluggish economy, the current value of their 401(k) retirement plans and other investments, and insufficient savings.[3]

The fact is that you and your classmates will likely change jobs and even employers several times during your careers. Some will end up working part-time or on a contract basis, with little job security and fewer benefits. Others will take time off to care for small children or elderly parents. And a goal many people have today is to start their own business and work for themselves.

Furthermore, it is estimated that one in four workers today will be unemployed at some point during their working lives. You never know when your employer will downsize, taking your job with it, or outsource your job elsewhere. Just review today's headlines and you will see that announcements of prominent companies downsizing and outsourcing are common.

These changes make sound personal financial management even more important. You must keep your career skills up-to-date and accumulate sufficient financial resources to weather an unexpected crisis.

More Options The number of choices today in such areas as banking, credit, investments, and retirement planning can be bewildering. Today you can do most of your banking with a brokerage firm and then buy mutual fund shares at a bank. Even the simple checking account has become more complicated. The typical bank offers several different types of checking accounts, each with its own features and fees. Choosing the wrong account could easily cost you $100 or more in unnecessary fees each year.

Twenty years ago, few college students carried credit cards, and those who did typically had cards tied to their parents' accounts. Banks and other credit card issuers didn't consider college students to be reasonable risks. Then the situation changed, resulting in a credit card debt crisis among students. The CARD Act however, contains reforms aimed at reversing this trend so that students will become more educated about their use of money.

One of the first things you'll do when you start a full-time job is make decisions about employee benefits. The typical employer may offer lots of choices in such areas as health insurance, disability insurance, group life insurance, and retirement plans. Selecting the right health insurance plan can save you thousands of dollars each year; by the same token, choosing the right retirement plan will enhance your economic security many years from now.

Personal Financial Planning—A Lifelong Activity

Personal financial planning is as important an activity whether you're 20, 40, or 60; whether you're single or married with children; and whether your annual income is $20,000 or $200,000. Many experts say that if you can't stick to a budget and control your spending when you're making $25,000 a year, you'll find it difficult to live within your means even if your income doubles or triples.

The fact that sound planning is a lifelong activity, of course, doesn't mean your financial goals and plans remain the same throughout your life—they won't. The major goal when you're young may be to buy your first condominium or pay off your college loans. For older people, the major goal is to pay off their home mortgage and stockpile as much in retirement funds as possible.

A Personal Financial Management Model

A **financial plan** is a guide to help you reach targeted goals in the future, closing the gap between where you are currently and where you'd like to be in the future. Goals might include buying a home, starting your own business, traveling extensively, sending children to college, or retiring early. Developing a personal financial plan consists of several steps, as illustrated in Figure C.1.

financial plan guide to help a person reach desired financial goals.

The first step in the process is to establish a clear picture of where you currently stand financially. Next, develop a series of short- and long-term goals. These goals should be influenced by your values, as well as an assessment of your current financial situation. The next step is to establish a set of financial strategies—in each of the personal planning areas—designed to help close the gap between where you are now and where you want to be in the future. Next, put your plan into action and closely monitor its performance. Periodically evaluate the effectiveness of your financial plan and make adjustments when necessary.

Financial plans cannot be developed in a vacuum. They should reflect your available resources—especially salary and fringe benefits, such as health insurance and retirement plans. For example, your goals and financial strategies should be based on a realistic estimate of your future income. If you cannot reach your financial goals through your present career path, you will have to scale back your goals or consider switching careers.

In addition, external factors—such as economic conditions and employment prospects—will influence

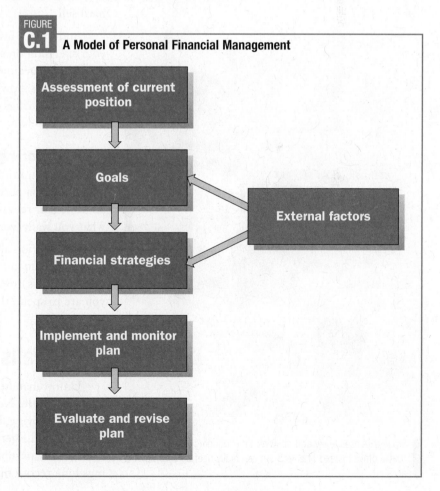

FIGURE **C.1** A Model of Personal Financial Management

- Assessment of current position
- Goals
- Financial strategies
- Implement and monitor plan
- Evaluate and revise plan
- External factors

your financial plan and decisions. For instance, assume you currently rent an apartment but have a goal of buying a duplex. While you can afford to buy right now, you believe there is a good chance you'll be offered a much better job in a new city within the next year. A wise financial move might be to postpone buying until your employment future becomes clearer.

General Themes Common to All Financial Plans

Regardless of the specifics, all financial plans revolve around three general themes: (1) maximizing income and wealth, (2) using money more effectively, and (3) monitoring expenditures.

Maximizing Income and Wealth Maximizing your income and wealth means getting more money. Work smarter; seek retraining for a better, higher-paying job; take career risks that may pay off in the long run; make sound investment decisions—all these are examples of the implementation of the first step. The amount of money you earn is a vital part of any financial plan, and it is up to you to make the most of your opportunities.

Using Money More Effectively Money has two basic uses: consumption and savings. Even if you are a regular saver, you'll still spend most of your income, probably more than 90 percent. You must try to spend every dollar wisely and make every major buying decision part of your overall financial plan. Avoid impulsive spending or giving in to a hard sell.

And it's not just big expenditures you need to watch. Cutting back your spending on small items can make a difference. Little purchases do add up. Packing your own lunch a few times a week rather than buying your sandwiches at the local deli could save about $15 a week. Invest that savings at 3 percent interest (per year) and you'll have almost $38,000 in 30 years.

Monitoring Expenditures Budgeting is the key to controlling expenditures. A budget focuses on where the money is going and whether a person's goals are being met. It also suggests appropriate times for reevaluating priorities. If your budget doesn't reflect what you want from life both now and in the future, change it.

Information also helps you keep your expenditures under control. The more you know about real estate, consumer loans, credit-card rates and laws, insurance, taxes, and major purchases, the more likely you are to spend the least money to purchase the greatest value.

Small expenses really add up. Over time, bringing your own lunch to the office instead of eating out can really beef up your bank account.

The Pitfalls of Poor Financial Planning

Unfortunately, too many people fail to plan effectively for their financial future. Not only do many find it difficult to improve their standard of living, but quite a few also find themselves with mounting debts and a general inability to make ends meet. According to the American Bankruptcy Institute, the number of personal bankruptcy filings hit a record number of more than 1.5 million in a recent year, but has since begun to recede.[4] Related to these bankruptcies is foreclosure, which results when homeowners are unable to pay their mortgage loans.

Although there are laws in effect that generally favor consumers who run into difficulty, and although there are credit consolidation and counseling bureaus that help people organize and pay their debt, foreclosure and bankruptcy are generally actions of last resort and it's best to avoid taking these steps.

Setting Personal Goals

Whatever your personal financial goals, they should reflect your values. Values are a set of fundamental beliefs of what is important, desirable, and worthwhile in your life. Your values will influence how you spend your money and, therefore, should be the foundation of your financial plan. Each person's financial goals will be determined by the individual's values because every individual considers some things more desirable or important than others. Start by asking yourself some questions about your values, the things that are most important to you, and what you would like to accomplish in your life.

Your goals are also influenced by your current financial situation. Prepare a set of current financial statements for yourself and update them at least once a year. Just like a business, a personal income statement reflects income and expenditures during a year. A balance sheet is a statement of what you own (assets) and what you owe (liabilities) at a specific point in time. For an individual or household, the difference between assets and liabilities is called **net worth**. As shown in Figure C.2, as you accumulate assets over your life, your net worth increases.

net worth difference between an individual or household's assets and liabilities.

After reviewing your current financial statements, you should prepare a budget. It is an excellent tool for monitoring your expenditures and cash flow and permits you to track past and current expenditures and plan future ones. Budgets are usually prepared on a monthly basis, but you can make a weekly budget if that works better for you. Most budgets divide expenditures into fixed expenses (those that don't change much from month to month) and variable expenses (those that vary). Your monthly apartment rent or your meal plan at school is probably a fixed expense, but the amount you spend on gas for your car or on entertainment is a variable expense. One key to effective budgeting is to make sure that the budgeted amounts are realistic.

Next, establish a series of financial goals based on your values and current financial situation. Separate your goals into short-term goals (those you want to achieve within the next six months or year) and long-term goals (those you plan to achieve over the next five or ten years). A short-term goal might be to pay off your credit-card balances by the end of this year, or to save enough money to take a vacation next summer. A long-term goal might be to buy a house by age 30. Your goals are reinforced if they support each other—if you pay off your credit cards, you'll likely have enough money saved to take that vacation or eventually buy your house. Some goals are monetary—such as paying off your credit cards. Others are nonmonetary, such as planning to retire by age 55. Whether short-term or long-term, monetary or nonmonetary, the best financial goals are defined specifically and focused on results. Goals also need to be realistic. You might not be able to pay off all of your credit cards by the end of this year, but you might pay off one. You might not buy the house by age 30, but maybe by 35. So be sure to set goals that you can actually attain. Keep in mind

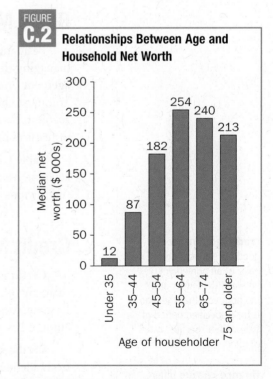

FIGURE C.2 Relationships Between Age and Household Net Worth

Median net worth ($ 000s) by Age of householder:
- Under 35: 12
- 35–44: 87
- 45–54: 182
- 55–64: 254
- 65–74: 240
- 75 and older: 213

Source: U.S. Census Bureau, "Table 721. Family Net Worth—Mean and Median Net Worth in Constant Dollars by Selected Family Characteristics: 1998 to 2007," *Statistical Abstract of the United States, 2012,* accessed March 27, 2012.

also that your financial goals will change over your lifetime. It's a good idea to review them periodically and adjust them when necessary, such as when you lose or get a job, relocate to another area of the country, or have children.

Your Personal Financial Decisions

You can use financial strategies in such areas as career choice, credit management, and tax planning to help you chart your economic future. These strategies should reflect your goals and be designed to close the gap between where you are and where you want to be.

Career Choice

No factor exerts as strong an influence on your personal finances as your career choice. Virtually all of your income, especially when you're just starting out, will come from wages and salaries. It is through work that all of us acquire the income needed to build a lifestyle; to buy goods and services, including insurance protection; to save and invest; and to plan for retirement. Your job is also the source of many important fringe benefits, such as health insurance and retirement savings plans, that are important components of your financial future. Throughout *Contemporary Business*, we've discussed ways to select a career that fits your skills and interests, find a job, and perform in that job.

Basic Money Management

Basic money management involves managing checking and savings accounts. Properly managing these relatively simple financial assets is an important first step toward propermanagement of more complicated financial assets such as investment and retirement accounts. You must choose a bank or other financial institution and then select the right checking account. Banks today offer several different types of checking accounts, each with its own set of features and fees.

Table C.1 lists several common sense tips for selecting and managing a checking/debit account. Managing a savings account involves understanding the importance of savings, setting savings goals, and picking the best savings option.

Credit Management

credit receiving money, goods, or services on the basis of an agreement between the lender and the borrower that the loan is for a specified period of time with a specified rate of interest.

finance charge difference between the amount borrowed and the amount repaid on a loan.

Credit is the area of personal finance that gets more people into financial difficulties than any other area. And Americans love credit. According to recent data from the Federal Reserve, Americans now owe in excess of $2.5 trillion, excluding home mortgage loans. This amount has almost doubled over the past 15 years.[5]

Credit allows a person to purchase goods and services by borrowing the necessary funds from a lender, such as a bank. The borrower agrees to repay the loan over a specified period of time, paying a specified rate of interest. The **finance charge** is the difference between the amount borrowed and the amount repaid. Credit is available from many sources today, but rates vary, so it pays to shop around.

TABLE C.1 Some Common Sense Tips for Choosing and Managing a Checking Account

• Shop around. There are lots of financial institutions that offer checking accounts. Fees and services vary considerably.
• Choose the best account for the way you bank. Consider how often you write checks, if at all; how often you use ATMs; when and where you use your debit card; and your average monthly balance.
• Keep good records and balance your account regularly. If there is no fee, sign up for online banking to monitor your account and pay bills electronically.
• Watch how you use your ATM card. Know which ATMs are owned by your bank and how much you're charged to use another bank's ATM. Be careful when using an ATM to check your current balance.
• Notify your bank immediately if your ATM card is lost or stolen.
• Sign up for overdraft protection.
• Understand how your bank computes minimum monthly balance.
• Read the fine print in your monthly statement.

There are two broad types of consumer credit: revolving (or open-end) credit and installment credit. Revolving credit is a type of credit arrangement that enables consumers to make a number of different purchases up to a credit limit, specified by the lender. The consumer has the option of repaying some or all of the outstanding balance each month. If the consumer carries a balance from month to month, finance charges (interest) are levied. An example of revolving credit is a credit card, such as Visa or MasterCard.

An installment loan is a credit arrangement in which the borrower takes out a loan for a specified amount, agreeing to repay the loan in regular installments over a specified period of time. Part of each payment is interest and part goes to repay principal (the amount borrowed). Generally, installment loan payments are made monthly and are for the same amount. Most student loans, auto loans, and home mortgage loans are examples of installment loans.

People have good reasons for borrowing money. They include purchasing large, important goods and services (cars, homes, or a college education), dealing with financial emergencies, taking advantage of opportunities, and establishing or improving your credit rating. All of these reasons are appropriate uses of credit if you can repay the loans in a timely manner.

However, a wrong reason for borrowing money is using credit to live beyond your means. For instance, you may want to go to Cancun for vacation but really cannot afford to, so you charge the trip. Using credit to live beyond your means often leads to credit problems. Watch for these warning signs of potential credit problems:

- You use credit to meet basic living expenses.

- You use credit to make impulse purchases.

- You take a cash advance on one credit card to repay another.

- The unpaid balance on your credit cards increases month after month.

Consumers who think of credit purchases as a series of small monthly payments are fooling themselves. As we noted earlier, most college students today have at least one credit card, and more than half carry balances from month to month. The average student has $3,200 in credit-card debt for college expenses, including books, meals, and activities fees (and separate from student loans). Although the CARD Act is aimed at curbing this debt, college students—and consumers in general—must also curb their credit spending.[6] How long would it take you to become debt-free if you had $3,200 on your credit card, if you paid only $50 each month? The answer is more than 18 years—and you would have paid more than $7,600 in interest.

If you feel as though you have a problem with credit, or may be developing one, you should seek help as soon as possible. Your college or university may offer credit counseling services. If not, contact a local not-for-profit credit counseling service or the National Foundation for Credit Counseling (http://www.nfcc.org). According to the experts, one of the keys to the wise use of credit is education. Learning about the pros and cons of borrowing money, as well as learning about responsible spending, can help people avoid problems with credit.

Tax Planning

Everyone pays a variety of taxes to federal, state, and local governments. The major taxes paid by individuals include federal and state income taxes, Social Security and Medicare taxes, real estate taxes, and sales taxes. The median-income family paid almost 38 percent of its income in taxes during a recent year. Think about your own situation and the taxes you pay. You have federal income taxes withheld from each paycheck. In addition, if you live in one of the 41 states with a state income tax, you have state income tax withheld also. Social Security and Medicare taxes amount to a percentage of your wages split between you and your employer (you pay the entire amount if you're self-employed). If you rent an apartment, part of your monthly rent goes to pay the landlord's real estate tax bill. In most states, every time you buy something, you pay sales tax to your state or local government.

By law, you must pay your taxes. You can use some of the popular software such as TurboTax to calculate your federal and state income taxes, or have a professional handle them—these two options are likely to find you any legal deductions you can take. If you do the tax return yourself—even with the aid of software—you will learn more about your personal finances. The Internal Revenue Service (IRS) has several excellent publications to help you prepare a federal income tax return. One of the best is IRS Publication #17 (*You and Your Federal Income Tax*). This and all other IRS publications are available free of charge from local IRS offices or the IRS Web site (http://www.irs.gov).

Major Purchases

Even if you follow a strict budget and manage to save money regularly, you will still spend most of your income each year. Effective buying is an important part of your financial plan. Within personal budget limits, an individual exercises his or her rights as a consumer to select or reject the wide range of goods and services that are available. As you purchase an automobile, a home, or any other major item, you need to carefully evaluate alternatives, separate needs from wants, and determine how you are going to finance the purchase. Your goal is to make every dollar you spend count.

Americans spend more than $900 billion annually on transportation, most of which goes to purchasing and maintaining automobiles. Given that new vehicles average more than $20,000 today, and even good used cars can cost in excess of $14,000, buying an automobile is a substantial purchase. On top of that, most car purchases are financed. Buying a car involves weighing many factors, including whether you want a new or used car, what makes and models appeal to you, and how much you can afford to pay. Many consumers today choose not to buy a new car but rather to lease one. While leasing has advantages, it also has drawbacks and, overall, is often more expensive than buying.

For most people, housing consumes a large share of their monthly budgets, whether in rent or mortgage payments. Home ownership is a goal of most people. Owning a home has a number of advantages, both financial and nonfinancial. Some of the financial benefits include tax savings (home mortgage interest and property taxes are both tax deductible) and the potential increase in the home's value. Nonfinancial benefits include pride of ownership and the freedom to improve or change the home however you want. The major barrier to home ownership is the money required for a down payment, along with the income required to obtain a mortgage loan.

The other major housing option is renting. Renting also offers a number of advantages, including cost savings (the landlord takes care of maintenance and repairs) and mobility. It is much easier to move if you rent than if you own a home. People who plan on staying in an area for a short period of time are usually better off renting even if they can afford to buy a home. The choice between buying and renting is obviously a major financial decision that needs to be approached rationally, not emotionally.

Although leasing a car has some advantages, over the long run it may cost more than buying the same car.

Insurance

Another important personal planning area is insurance. Insurance is an admittedly expensive but necessary purchase. Americans spend approximately $100 billion each year on auto insurance alone.[7] Some of the basic principles and the various types of insurance are described in Appendix B. Although the focus of that appendix is business insurance, much of what is discussed applies to your personal insurance needs as well.

Your goal is to have adequate and appropriate coverage in each of the major insurance types—life, health, disability, and property and liability. Insurance needs can vary substantially from individual to individual. As noted earlier in *Contemporary Business*, some types of insurance are provided to employees as fringe benefits. They typically include health insurance, disability insurance, and life insurance. In the standard arrangement, employers pay a portion of the premium. A few employers contract with insurance companies to offer employees auto and homeowners' insurance at discounts.

Investment Planning

Investing is a process by which money acquired through work, inheritance, or other sources is preserved and increased. Sound investment management is an important component of the financial plan and can make it easier to attain other personal goals, such as buying a home, sending children to college, starting a business, or retiring comfortably. Furthermore, it is very difficult today to substantially increase wealth without investing. And, given the changes to the external environment—such as employer-sponsored retirement plans—it is likely that you will have to make investment decisions at some point during your life.

The investment process consists of four steps. The first step is to complete some preliminary tasks, including setting overall personal goals, having a regular savings program, and managing credit properly. The second step is to establish a set of investment goals—why you want to invest, what you want to accomplish, and what kind of time frame you have. Obviously, your investment goals should be closely related to your overall personal goals. Next, you need to assess risk and return. You invest because you expect to earn some future rate of return. At the same time, however, all investing exposes you to a variety of risks. You need to find the proper balance between risk and return because investments offering the highest potential returns also expose you to more risk. Your age, income, and short- and long-term investment time frames all have an impact on the risk-return trade-off.

The final step is to select the appropriate investments. As discussed in Chapter 16 of *Contemporary Business*, there are three general types of investments: money market instruments, bonds, and common stock. The proper mix of these three investments depends on such factors as your investment goals and investment time horizon. For instance, a 25-year-old investing for retirement should have close to 100 percent of his or her funds invested in common stocks because growth in capital is the overriding investment objective. Stocks have generally outperformed all other investment alternatives over longer periods of time. On the other hand, if the 25-year-old is investing to have sufficient funds for a down payment on a house within the next couple of years, the investor should have a proportion of his or her funds invested in money market instruments or bonds given the short time horizon. Even after selecting the appropriate investments, the investor must monitor their performance and be prepared to make changes when necessary.

Financial Planning for Tomorrow

The last major personal planning area deals with future financial issues, such as sending children to college and retirement and estate planning. As you know, college is expensive and college costs are rising at a rate that exceeds the overall rate of inflation. By beginning a college savings program early, parents will have a better chance of offering their children a choice of colleges when the time comes. While they probably won't have enough to cover tuition entirely, they (and their children) will likely have to borrow less and accrue less debt for a college education. A variety of college savings programs exist, some of which provide parents with tax benefits.

Most people want to retire with sufficient funds to ensure a degree of financial security. Social Security will provide only a fraction of what you will need; you will be responsible for the rest. Depending on the standard of living you hope to maintain, you will probably need a savings nest egg of at least $1.5 million by the time you retire. Four important principles apply when it comes to saving for retirement: start early, save as much as you can each month, take advantage of all tax-deferred retirement savings plans to which you are entitled, and invest your retirement savings appropriately.

Two major sources of retirement income exist: employer-sponsored retirement plans and individual retirement plans. Most employers offer their workers a retirement plan; some offer more than one plan. For most people, employer-sponsored retirement plans will likely provide the bulk of their retirement income. Essentially, two types of employer-sponsored retirement plans exist. A defined benefit plan guarantees a worker a certain retirement benefit each year. The size depends on a number of factors, including the worker's income and the length of time he or she worked for the employer. Pension plans are classified as defined benefit plans.

The other type of employer-sponsored retirement plan is the defined contribution plan. In this type of retirement plan, you contribute to your retirement account and so does your employer. You are given some choice of where your retirement funds can be invested. Often you are given a list of mutual funds in which to invest your money. A so-called 401(k) is an example of a defined contribution plan. Defined contribution plans are widely used and are in many cases replacing defined benefit plans.

Millions of Americans have some sort of individual retirement plan not tied to any employer. These workers may be self-employed or may merely want to supplement their employer-sponsored retirement savings. Examples of individual retirement plans include regular IRAs (individual retirement accounts), Roth IRAs, Keogh plans, and simplified employee pension (SEP) plans. To set up one of these retirement plans, you must meet certain eligibility requirements.

Another element of financial planning for tomorrow is estate planning. Of all the personal planning areas, estate planning is probably the least relevant for you, although your parents and grandparents probably face some estate-planning issues. However, all adults, regardless of age, need to have two documents: a valid will (naming a guardian if you have any minor children) and a durable power of attorney (the name varies from state to state, but it is a document that gives someone else the power to make financial and medical decisions if you are incapacitated).

This appendix has just scratched the surface of personal financial planning. We hope it has encouraged you to learn more. Consider taking a class in personal financial planning if your institution offers one. It may be one of the most helpful classes you take while you're in college.

■ Business Terms You Need to Know

personal financial management A-31	net worth A-35
standard of living A-31	credit A-36
financial plan A-33	finance charge A-36

Projects and Teamwork Applications

1. Prepare a chart outlining your current standard of living, the standard of living you had while growing up, and the standard of living you expect or hope to achieve once you have completed your education.

2. Create a chart detailing how you think you could use your money most effectively. What are your pitfalls—late-night pizza, downloading music, trips to the city? In what areas do you already use your money well?

3. Create a weekly budget and a monthly budget. Keep a daily journal of your expenses for the next month to see how well you stick to the budget. Compare your results in class. In what areas did you do well? In what areas do you need improvement? For additional help, you can go to the Web site http://www.nelliemae.com/calculators to fill out the budget worksheet.

4. Even though you are still in school, you face a number of important financial issues, everything from paying college expenses to dealing with credit cards. Visit the Web site: http://getcollegefunds.org and click on "10 Steps to Financial Fitness" for more suggestions on managing your money while in college.

5. Analyze your current credit situation. What are your existing debts? How much are you paying each month? Did you borrow for the right reasons? List some steps you think you should take to improve your management of credit. Go to the Web site http://getcollegefunds.org and click on "There Is Life After Debt!" for more advice on managing your credit.

Developing a Business Plan

Road ID Will Speak for You

When Edward Wimmer was a college student training for a marathon, his father's advice to "wear some form of ID" while running didn't impress him until he suddenly had to jump into a ditch to avoid an oncoming truck. Then the wisdom of his father's words struck him. "I was almost hit by a truck and nobody knew where I was," he recalls.

After graduating, Wimmer came up with engravable Velcro-equipped tags that attach to wrists, ankles, running shoes, and even dog collars. Partnering with his dad, he created a company called Road ID, whose products have become popular among athletes who travel light while training, often leaving identifying items such as cell phones and wallets at home. Some loyal customers are simply proud of their sport. "Every cyclist wears one of these," says the owner of one Georgia triathlon shop. "I wear mine all the time. It shows who you are. It is like you are saying, 'I am a cyclist.'"

On the practical side, the identification and vital statistics engraved on Road ID products have proven invaluable for athletes who have suffered an illness or accident that left them unable to communicate while competing or training. Testimonials on its Web site attest to the benefits of wearing "some form of ID." Says Greg Friese, an emergency medical services educator who works with the firm, "There is nothing worse than having a John or Jane Doe as a patient."

Started as an online business, Road ID has updated its business plan several times, not only because it keeps outgrowing its headquarters and has seen its sales increase about 50 percent a year since 2002. First it expanded from the Web site to small kiosks in sporting goods stores. Then it began sponsoring thousands of running and cycling events and set up promotions on Facebook and Twitter. Currently it's reaching out to first responders with Friese's help. That fits well with Road ID's two-part mission statement: "One, to educate outdoor enthusiasts … about the importance of wearing ID. Two, to provide these athletes with innovative identification products that they will want to include as part of their gear."

Wimmer hopes to make ID as common as seatbelts and sees continued growth ahead, so more changes in the company's business model are probably likely. [1]

Overview

Appendix D

Many entrepreneurs and small-business owners have written business plans to help them organize their businesses, get them up and running, and raise money for expansion. In this appendix, we cover the basics of business planning: what business plans are, why they're important, and who needs them. We also explain the steps involved in writing a good plan and the major elements it should contain. Finally, we cover additional resources to get you started with your own business plan—to help you bring your unique ideas to reality with a business of your own.

What Is a Business Plan?

You may wonder how the millions of different businesses operating in the United States and throughout the world today got their start. Often it is with a formal business plan. A *business plan* is a written document that defines what a company's objectives are, how those objectives will be achieved, how the business will be financed, and how much money the company expects to bring in. In short, it describes where a company is, where it wants to go, and how it intends to get there.

Why a Business Plan Is So Important

A well-written business plan serves two key functions:

1. It organizes the business and validates its central idea.

2. It summarizes the business and its strategy to obtain funding from lenders and investors.

First, a business plan gives a business formal direction, whether it is just starting, going through a phase of growth, or struggling. The business plan forces the principals—the owners—through rigorous planning, to think through the realities of running and financing a business. In their planning, they consider many details. How will inventory be stored, shipped, and stocked? Where should the business be located? How will the business use the Internet? And most important, how will the business make enough money to make it all worthwhile?

A business plan also gives the owners a well-reasoned blueprint to refer to when daily challenges arise, and it acts as a benchmark by which successes and disappointments can be measured. Additionally, a solid business plan will sell the potential owner on the validity of the idea. In some cases, the by-product of developing the plan is demonstrating to a starry-eyed person that he or she is trying to start a bad business. In other words, the process of writing a plan benefits a would-be businessperson as much as the final plan benefits potential investors.

Finally, a business plan articulates the business's strategy to financiers who may fund the business, and it is usually required to obtain a bank loan. Lenders and venture capitalists need to see that the business owner has thought through the critical issues and presented a promising idea before they will consider investing in it. They are, after all, interested in whether it will bring them significant returns.

Who Needs a Business Plan?

Every business owner who expects to be successful needs a business plan. Some people mistakenly believe that they need a business plan only if it will land on the desk of a venture capitalist or the loan committee of a bank. Others think that writing a plan is unnecessary if their bank or lending institution doesn't require it. Such assumptions miss the point of planning, because a business plan acts as a map to guide the way through the often tangled roads of running a business. Every small-business owner should develop a business plan because it empowers that person to take control.

How Do I Write a Business Plan?

Developing a business plan should mean something different to everyone. Think of a business plan as a clear statement of a business's identity. A construction company has a different identity from a newly launched magazine, which has yet a different identity from a restaurant hoping to expand its share of the market. Each business has unique objectives and processes, and each faces different obstacles.

At the same time, good business plans contain some similar elements no matter who the business owner is, what he or she sells, or how far the owner is into the venture. A savvy business owner molds the elements of a business plan into a professional and personal representation of the firm's needs and goals. The plan should also realistically assess the risks and obstacles specific to the business and present solutions for overcoming them.

Because the document is important, it takes time to collect needed information and organize it. Don't be misled into believing that you will simply sit down and begin writing. Before any writing begins, the business owner must become an expert in his or her field. Readying important information about the company and the market will make the writing easier and faster. Some critical pieces of information to have on hand are the following items:

- The company's name, legal form of organization, location, financial highlights, and owners or shareholders (if any).

- Organization charts, list of top managers, consultants or directors, and employee agreements.

- Marketing research, customer surveys, and information about the company's major competitors.

- Product information, including goods and services offered; brochures; patents, licenses, and trademarks; and research and development plans.

- Marketing plans and materials.

- Financial statements (both current and forecasted).

The business owner also must do a lot of soul searching and brainstorming to answer important questions necessary to build the backbone of a healthy business. Figure D.1 lists some critical questions to ask yourself.

Once equipped with these answers, you can begin writing the document, which can be anywhere between 10 and 50 pages long. The length of the plan depends on the complexity of the company, whether the company is a start-up (established companies have longer histories to detail), and what the plan will be used for. Regardless of size, the document should be well organized and easy to use, especially if the business plan is intended for external uses, such as to secure financing. Number all pages, include a table of contents, and make sure the format is attractive and professional. Include two or three illustrative charts or graphs and highlight the sections and important points with headings and bulleted lists. Figure D.2 outlines the major sections of a business plan.

The following paragraphs discuss the most common elements of an effective business plan. When you need additional instruction or information as you write, refer to the "Resources" section at the end of the appendix.

**Take a few minutes to read and answer these questions.
Don't worry about answering in too much detail at this point.
The questions are preliminary and
intended to help you think through your venture.**

1. In general terms, how would you explain your idea to a friend?

2. What is the purpose or objective of your venture?

3. What service are you going to provide, or what goods are you going to manufacture?

4. Is there any significant difference between what you are planning and what already exists?

5. How will the quality of your product compare with competitive offerings?

6. What is the overview of the industry or service sector you are going to enter? Write it out.

7. What is the history, current status, and future of the industry?

8. Who is your customer or client base?

9. Where and by whom will your good or service be marketed?

10. How much will you charge for the product you are planning?

11. Where is the financing going to come from to initiate your venture?

12. What training and experience do you have that qualifies you for this venture?

13. Does such training or experience give you a significant edge?

14. If you lack specific experience, how do you plan to gain it?

Executive Summary

The primary purpose of an executive summary is to entice readers to read more about the business. An *executive summary* is a one- to two-page snapshot of what the overall business plan explains in detail. Consider it a business plan within a business plan. Through its enthusiasm and quick momentum, the summary should capture the reader's imagination. Describe your strategy for succeeding in a positive, intriguing, and realistic way and briefly yet thoroughly answer the first questions anyone would have about your business: who, what, why, when, where, and how. Financiers always turn to the executive summary first. If it isn't well presented or lacks the proper information, they will quickly move on to the next business plan in the stack. The executive summary is just as important to people funding the business with personal resources, however, because it channels their motivations into an

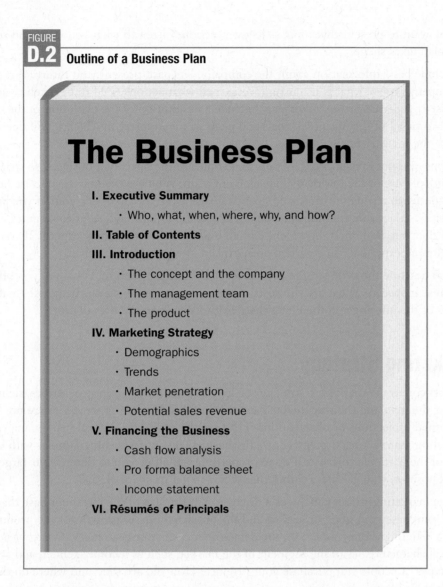

FIGURE D.2 Outline of a Business Plan

The Business Plan

I. Executive Summary
- Who, what, when, where, why, and how?

II. Table of Contents

III. Introduction
- The concept and the company
- The management team
- The product

IV. Marketing Strategy
- Demographics
- Trends
- Market penetration
- Potential sales revenue

V. Financing the Business
- Cash flow analysis
- Pro forma balance sheet
- Income statement

VI. Résumés of Principals

articulate mission statement. It is a good idea to write the summary last, because it will inevitably be revised once the business plan takes final shape.

To write an effective executive summary, focus on the issues that are most important to your business's success and save the supporting matters for the text. The executive summary should describe the firm's strategy and goals, the good or service it is selling, and the advantages it has over the competition. It should also give a snapshot of how much money will be required to launch the business, how it will be used, and how the lenders or investors will recoup their funds.

Introduction

The introduction follows the executive summary. After the executive summary has offered an attractive synopsis, the introduction should begin to discuss the fine details of the business. It should be crafted to include any material the upcoming marketing and financing sections do not cover. The introduction should describe the company, the management team, and the product in detail. If one of these topics is particularly noteworthy for your business, you may want to present that topic as its own section. Listen to what you write and respond as the plan takes shape.

Include basic information about the company—its past, present, and future. What are the company's roots, what is its current status, and what actions need to be taken to achieve its goals? If you are starting a company, include a description of the evolution of the concept. Be sure to tie all of the business's goals and plans to the industry in which it will operate, and describe the industry itself.

A business doesn't run itself, of course. People are the heart of a business, so write an appealing picture of the business's management team. Who are the key players and how does their experience resonate with the company's goals? Describe their—or your, if you are a sole proprietor—education, training, and experience, and highlight and refer to résumés included later in the plan. Be honest, however—not all businesses are started by experts. If you lack demonstrated experience in a certain area, explain how you plan to get it.

Also describe the product, the driving force behind the venture. What are you offering, and why is it special? What are the costs of the service or price tag on the good? Analyze the features of the offering and the effect these features have on the overall cost.

Marketing Strategy

Next comes the marketing strategy section. The *marketing strategy* describes the market's need for the item and the way the business will fulfill it. Marketing strategies are not based on informal projections or observations. They are the result of a careful market analysis. So formulating a marketing strategy allows the business owner to become familiar with every aspect of the particular market. If done properly, it will allow you to define your target market and position your business within that sector to get its share of sales.

The marketing strategy includes a discussion of the size of the customer base that will want to purchase your good or service and the projected rate of growth for the product or category. Highlight information on the demographics of your customers. *Demographics* are statistical characteristics of the segment of the market, such as income, gender, and age. What types of people will purchase your product? How old are they, and where do they live? What is their lifestyle like? For example, someone starting an interior design business will want to report how many homeowners live within a certain radius of the firm, as well as their median income. Of course, this section of the marketing analysis will be quite different for a company that conducts all of its business online. In that case, you will want to know the types of people who will shop at your Web site, but your discussion won't be limited to one geographic area. It is also a good idea to describe the trends in your product category. Trends are consumer and business tendencies or patterns that business owners can exploit to gain market share in an industry.

The marketing strategy should also detail your distribution, pricing, and promotional goals. Discuss the average price of your offering and the reasons behind the price you have chosen. How do you intend to let your potential customers know that you have a product to sell? How will you sell it—through a catalog, in a retail location, online, or perhaps a combination of all three? The effectiveness of your distribution, pricing, and promotional goals determines the extent to which you will be able to garner market share.

Competitors are another important part of your marketing strategy. What companies are already selling products similar to yours? Include a list of your competitors to show that you know exactly who they are and what you are up against. Describe what you think are their major strengths and weaknesses and how successful they have been within your market.

Also include the *market penetration*, which is the percentage of total customers who have purchased a company's product. If there are 10,000 people in your market, and 5,000 have purchased your product, your market penetration is 50 percent. The *potential sales revenue*, also an important figure to include, is the total revenue of a company if it captured 100 percent market penetration. In other words, this figure represents the total dollar value of sales you would bring in if everyone who is a potential customer purchased your product.

Financing the Business

The goal of a business is to make money. Everything in the business plan lays the foundation for the *financing section*. Business owners should not skip this section even if they are not seeking outside money. While it is crucial to have an accurate financial analysis to get financing, it also is a necessary exercise for business owners funding the venture themselves. The financing section demonstrates the cost of the product, operating expenses, expected sales revenue and profit, and the amount of the business owner's personal funds that will be invested to get the business up and running. The financial projections should be compelling but accurate and based on realistic assumptions. The owner should be able to defend them.

Any assumptions made in the body of the business plan should be tied into the financial section. For instance, if you think you will need a staff of five, your cash flow analysis should explain how you are going to pay them. A cash flow analysis, a mandatory component of a financial analysis, shows how much money will flow through your business throughout the year. It helps you plan for staggered purchasing, high-volume months, and slow periods. Your business may be cyclical or seasonal, so the cash flow projection lets you know if you need to arrange a line of credit to cover periodic shortfalls. In addition, an income statement is a critical component. The income statement is a statement of income and expenses your company has accrued over a period of time.

Remember that leaving out important details can undercut your credibility, so be thorough. The plan must include your assumptions about the conditions under which your business will operate. It should cover details such as market strength; date of start-up; sales buildup; gross profit margin; equipment, furniture, and fixtures required; and payroll and other key expenses that will affect the financial plan. In addition, a banker will want a pro forma balance sheet, which provides an estimate of what the business owns (assets), what it owes (liabilities), and what it is worth (owner's equity). Refer to Chapters 15, 16, and 17 of *Contemporary Business* for additional details on accounting, financial statements, and financial management.

Résumés of Principals

The final element of the business plan is the inclusion of the résumés of the principals behind the business: the management team. Each résumé should include detailed employment information and accomplishments. If applicable to your business, consider expanding on the traditional résumé by including business affiliations, professional memberships, hobbies, and leisure activities.

However you choose to develop a business plan, make sure that *you* develop the plan. It should sound as though it was written by the entrepreneur, not by some outside "expert."

Resources

A tremendous amount of material is available to help business owners—whether existing or prospective—write effective business plans. The biggest task is narrowing down which resources are right for you. The Internet delivers an abundance of sound business-planning tools and advice, much of which are free. It allows you to seek diverse examples and opinions, which is important because no one source will match your situation exactly. Your library and career center also have a wealth of resources. Following are some helpful resources for business planning.

Books

Dozens of books exist on how to write a business plan. Examples include the following:

- Colin Barrow, *Business Plans Kit for Dummies* (Wiley Publishing, 2012).
- Edward Blackwell, *How to Prepare a Business Plan*, 7th ed. (London: Kogan Page Ltd., 2011).
- Mike McKeever, *How to Write a Business Plan*, 10th ed. (Berkeley, CA: Nolo Press, 2010).
- John W. Mullins, *The New Business Road Test: What Entrepreneurs and Executives Should Do Before Writing a Business Plan*, 3rd ed. (*Prentice Hall Financial Times*, 2010).
- Michael Gerber, *The E-Myth Enterprise: How to Turn a Great Idea into a Thriving Business* (New York: Harper Collins, 2009); paperback edition 2010.

Web Sites

Useful Web sites include the following:

- *Entrepreneur, Inc.*, and *Bloomberg Businessweek* magazines offer knowledgeable guides to writing a business plan. *Entrepreneur*'s Web site also contains sample business plans.
  http://www.entrepreneur.com
  http://www.inc.com
  http://www.businessweek.com
- If you are hoping to obtain funding with your business plan, you should familiarize yourself with what investors are looking for. Two professional associations for the venture capital industry are the following:
  http://www.nvca.org (National Venture Capital Association)
  http://www.nasbic.org (Small Business Investor Alliance—formerly the National Association of Small Business Investment Companies)

Software

Business-planning software can give an initial shape to your business plan. However, a word of caution is in order if you write a business plan using the software's template. Bankers and potential investors, such as venture capitalists, read so many business plans that those based on templates may sink to the bottom of the pile. Also, if you aren't looking for funding, using software can undercut a chief purpose of writing a plan—learning about your unique idea. So think twice before you deprive yourself of that experience. Remember, software is a tool. It can help you get started, stay organized, and build a professional-looking business plan, but it can't actually write the plan for you.

Associations and Organizations

Many government and professional organizations provide assistance to would-be business owners. Here is a partial list:

- The U.S. Small Business Administration offers planning materials, along with other resources.

  http://www.sba.gov

- Women's Business Centers represent a national network, sponsored by the SBA, that helps female entrepreneurs.

  http://www.sba.gov/content/women-s-business-centers

- One of the missions of the Ewing Marion Kauffman Foundation is to encourage entrepreneurship across the United States. The foundation's Web sites offer online resources for new and growing businesses.

  http://www.kauffman.org

Courtesy Ewing Marion Kauffman Foundation

The Ewing Marion Kauffman Foundation's Web site, www.kauffman.org, offers a wealth of information about starting, managing, and expanding small businesses.

Projects and Teamwork Applications

1. Visit the Web site for Road ID at http://www.roadid.com to learn more about the company's innovative product line. Now think of another business that caters to athletes such as runners or cyclists. Write a brief plan for adding safety-related items to the company's product line. Why do you think this would be successful? What might be the drawbacks?

2. Do you dream of starting your own business? Take your idea and answer as many of the self-evaluation questions in Figure D.1 as you can. Share your answers with the class. Then file your answers away to read at a future date—either when you have graduated from college or when you think you are ready to pursue your own business.

3. Write the executive summary portion of the business plan for your potential business. You may use the answers to the questions in Figure D.1 as a springboard.

| Appendix E |

Careers in Contemporary Business

You'll be hitting the job market soon—if you haven't already. Regardless of what industry you want to work in—financial services, advertising, travel, construction, hospitality, manufacturing, wireless communications—you need an education. Attending college and taking a business course like this one gives you an edge because business skills and knowledge are needed in many different fields. But education comes in many forms. In addition to taking classes, you should try to gain related real-life experience. A summer job, an internship, or even a volunteer opportunity can give you excellent experience that you can build on once you graduate. Cooperative education programs and work-study programs can also give you hands-on experience while you pursue your education. While many students across the country will be doing the same thing, you can set yourself apart through your work ethic and initiative.

You will be responsible for earning a living once you leave school—if you aren't already doing so. Your level of education will probably influence your earnings. Table E.1 shows some hard facts about earnings as reported by the U.S. Census Bureau. Not only is there a wide discrepancy between earnings for high-school graduates and college graduates, but there is still a gap between earnings for men and women.[1]

Keep in mind that while a degree may help you get in the door for certain job interviews and may put you on a path for advancement, it doesn't guarantee success; you have to achieve that yourself.

Companies plan their hiring strategies carefully in order to attract and keep the most productive, creative employees and avoid the cost of rehiring. So, soon-to-be graduates still need to be on their toes. But creativity has never been in short supply among business students, and by the time you finish this class—and college—you will be well equipped to take on the challenge. You'll be able to think of your hunt for employment as a course in itself, at the end of which you will have a job. And you will be on your way toward a rewarding business career.

TABLE E.1 | Average Annual Earnings of Workers by Educational Level

GENDER & AGE	HIGH SCHOOL	COLLEGE
Men: 18 to 24 years	$27,822	$42,299
Men: 25 to 34 years	$38,037	$67,555
Men: 35 to 44 years	$43,518	$98,045
Women: 18 to 24 years	$22,620	$32,103
Women: 25 to 34 years	$27,993	$52,102
Women: 35 to 44 years	$32,947	$65,881

Source: U.S. Census Bureau, "Average Earnings of Year-Round, Full-Time Workers by Educational Attainment," *Current Population Reports*, http://www.census.gov, accessed March 28, 2012.

During this course, you are exposed to all the functional areas of business. You learn how firms are organized and operated. You find out who does what in a company. Gradually, you identify industries and disciplines—such as sales, finance, or product design—that interest you. And you learn about many organizations, large and small—who founded them, what products they offer, how they serve their customers, and what types of decisions they make. In short, you gain knowledge about business that you can apply to your career search and life.

Choosing a career is an important life decision. It sets you on a path that will influence where you live, how much money you earn, what type of people you meet, and what you do every day. And whether your goal is to operate an organic farm or to rise high in the ranks of a major corporation, you'll need to understand the principles of business. Even if you think you're headed down a different path, business skills may prove to be important. In addition, many fields are beginning to recognize the importance of a broader base of knowledge than specialized technical skills, and business knowledge is part of that base.

For example, engineers used to rely almost solely on a foundation of technical skill and expertise. But experts in the industry now report a trend toward a more well-rounded education. While engineers still need a strong technical foundation, they need additional skills as well. Engineers who survived the economic downturn without being laid off claim that having capabilities across several areas made them more valuable to their employer than, say, a colleague whose knowledge was concentrated in one or two areas. That's why this appendix discusses the best way to approach career decisions and to prepare for an *entry-level job*—your first permanent employment after leaving school. We then look at a range of business careers and discuss employment opportunities in a variety of fields.

It's important to remember that you'll be looking for a job regardless of the state of the overall economy, whether it's sluggish or booming. You'll read about job cuts and unemployment rates, hiring freezes and wage increases. But if you stay flexible and are ready to work—just about anytime and anywhere—you'll succeed.

Internships—A Great Way to Acquire Real-World Experience

Many business students complete one or more *internships* prior to completing their academic careers. Some arrange internships during the summer, while others work at them during a semester away from college. An internship gives you hands-on experience in a real business environment, whether it's in banking, the hotel industry, or retailing. Not only does an internship teach you how a business runs, but it can also help you decide whether you want to pursue a career in a particular industry. You might spend a summer interning in the admissions department of a hospital and then graduate with your job search focused on hospital administration. Or you might decide you'd much rather work for a magazine publisher or a retailer.

When you apply for an internship, don't expect to be paid much, if at all. The true value of an internship lies in its hands-on experience. An internship bridges the theory–practice educational gap. It will help carry you from your academic experience to your professional future. Also keep in mind that, as an intern, you will not be running a department. People may not ask for your input or ideas. You may work in the warehouse or copy center. You might be answering phones or entering data. But it is important to make the most of your internship. Because many companies make permanent

TheGift777/iStockphoto

Internships provide college students with critical hands-on business experience. It is important for students to make the most of the opportunities that internships provide both in terms of experience and a future job hunt once they have completed their schooling.

job offers—or offers to enter paid training programs—to the best interns, you'll want to stand out.

Internships can serve as critical networking and job-hunting tools. In many instances, they lead to future employment opportunities, allowing students to demonstrate technical proficiency while providing cost-effective employee training for the company. Even if you don't end up being hired by the company for which you interned, the experience is extremely valuable to your job hunt because you include it on your résumé. During one recent year, accounting firm Deloitte made job offers to 75 percent of its interns.[2]

With this information in mind, start thinking the way a professional does now. Here are some tips for a successful internship experience. These guidelines are also helpful for your first job.

- **Dress like a professional.** Dress appropriately for your future career. During an interview visit, look around to see what employees are wearing. If you have any questions, ask your supervisor.

- **Act like a professional.** Arrive on time to work. Be punctual for any meetings or assignments. Ask questions and listen to the answers carefully. Complete your work thoroughly and on time. Maintain good etiquette on the phone, in meetings, and in all interactions with other people.

- **Stand out.** Work hard and show initiative, but behave appropriately. Don't try to use authority that you do not have. Show that you are willing to learn.

- **Be evaluated.** Even if your internship does not include a formal evaluation, ask your employer how you are doing to learn about your strengths and weaknesses.

- **Keep in touch.** Once you complete your internship, stay in touch periodically with the firm so that people know what you are currently doing.

An excellent source of information about the nation's outstanding internships can be found at your local bookstore—*The Best 109 Internships*, 9th edition, published by The Princeton Review. The same organization also publishes *The Internship Bible*, 10th edition, which is also helpful.

In addition to an internship, you can build your résumé with work and life experience through volunteer opportunities, extracurricular activities, and summer or off-campus study programs. *Cooperative education* also provides valuable experience. Cooperative education programs are similar to internships, but the jobs themselves usually pay more. These programs may take place during the summer or during the school year—typically, students might take classes one semester and hold jobs the next semester. Most cooperative programs are specific to a major field of study, such as retailing or information technology. At your cooperative job, you'll be treated like a real full-time employee, meaning you'll work long hours and probably have more responsibility that you would as an intern. And depending on how these programs are scheduled, you might add a semester or two to your college education. But in the long run, you will gain knowledge and work experience that will serve you well as you build your career.[3]

Self-Assessment For Career Development

You are going to spend a lot of time during your life working, so why not find a job—or at least an industry—that interests you? To choose the line of work that suits you best, you must first understand yourself. Self-assessment involves looking in the mirror and seeing the real you—with all your strengths and weaknesses. It means answering some tough questions. But being honest with yourself pays off because it will help you find a career that is challenging, rewarding, and meaningful to you. You may realize that to feel secure, you need to earn enough to put away substantial savings. Or you might learn that you are drawn to risks and the unknown, characteristics that might point you toward owning your own business someday. Each of these discoveries provides you with valuable information in choosing a career.

Many resources are available to help you in selecting a career. They include school libraries, career guidance and placement offices, counseling centers, and online job-search services. They include alumni from your college, as well as friends, family, and neighbors. Don't forget the contacts you make during an internship—they can help you in many ways. Ask questions of anyone you know—a local accountant, banker, or restaurant owner. Most people will be happy to speak with you or arrange a time to do so.

If you are interested in a particular industry or company, you might be able to arrange an informational interview—an appointment with someone who can provide you with more knowledge about an industry or career path. This type of interview is different from one that follows your application for a specific job, although it may ultimately lead to that. The informational interview can help you decide whether you want to pursue a particular avenue of employment. It also gives you some added experience in the interview process—without the pressure. To arrange an interview, tap anyone you know—friends of your parents, local businesspeople, or coordinators of not-for-profit organizations. Colleges often have databases of graduates who are working in various fields who are willing to talk with students on an informational basis, so be sure to start your search right at your own school.

To help you get started asking and answering the questions that will help you begin looking in the right direction, you can visit a number of Web sites that offer online career assessment tests. Career Explorer, at http://www.careerexplorer.net is one such site; LiveCareer at http://www.livecareer.com is another. These and other sites, such as Monster.com, help you identify your interests, strengths, and weaknesses—including some that may surprise you.[4] In addition, follow the self-assessment process outlined in the next section to learn more about yourself.

The Self-Assessment Process

For a thorough assessment of your goals and interests, follow these steps:

1. **Outline your career interests.** What field or work activities interest you? What rewards do you want to gain from work?

2. **Outline your career goals.** What do you want to achieve through your career? What type of job can you see yourself doing? Where do you see yourself in a year? In five years? Do you have an ultimate dream job? How long are you willing to work to reach it? Write your goals down so that you can refer to them later.

3. **Make plans to reach your goal.** Do you need more education? Does the career require an apprenticeship or a certain number of years on the job? Outline the requirements you'll need to meet in order to reach your goal.

4. **List your skills and specific talents.** Write down your strengths—job skills you already have, as well as skills you have developed in life. For instance, you might know how to use financial software, and you might have strong interpersonal skills. In addition, your school's career development office probably has standardized tests that can help determine your aptitude for specific careers. However, take these only as a guideline. If you really want to pursue a certain career, go for it.

5. **List your weaknesses.** This can be tough, but it can also be fun. If you are shy about meeting new people, put shyness on your list. If you are quick to argue, admit it. If you aren't the best business-letter writer or think you're terrible at math, confess to yourself. This list gives you an opportunity to see where you need improvement—and take steps to turn weaknesses into strengths.

6. **Briefly sketch out your educational background.** Write down the schools, colleges, and special training programs you have attended, along with any courses you plan to complete before starting full-time employment. Make a candid assessment of how your background matches up with the current job market. Then make plans to complete any further education you may need.

7. **List the jobs you have held.** Include paid jobs, internships, and volunteer opportunities. They all gave you valuable experience. As you make your list, think about what you liked and disliked about each. Maybe you liked working with the general public as a supermarket cashier. Perhaps you enjoyed caring for animals at a local shelter.

8. **Consider your hobbies and personal interests.** Many people have turned hobbies and personal pursuits into rewarding careers. Mick Jagger, lead singer of the Rolling Stones, has a master's degree from the London School of Economics. This fact probably helped him manage his rock group's vast business dealings. Jake Burton Carpenter earned a bachelor's degree in economics, but he loved winter sports. So he started a snowboard manufacturing company—and revolutionized the way people get from the top of a snowy mountain to the bottom. Celebrity chef Paula Deen needed to support her young family. She loved the cooking from her own region—the South—so she opened a small business in which she and her boys delivered freshly made bag lunches to local businesses. Today she has her own television show, cookbooks, Web site, retail products, and more.[5] Turning a hobby into a career doesn't happen overnight, though, nor is it easy. It requires the same amount of research and hard work as any other business. But for many people, it is a labor of love—and ultimately succeeds because they refuse to give up.

Job Search Guidelines

Once you have narrowed your choice of career possibilities to two or three that seem right for you, get your job search under way. The characteristics that made these career choices attractive to you are also likely to catch the attention of other job seekers, so you must expect competition. Locate available positions that interest you; then be resourceful! Your success depends on gathering as much information as possible.

Register at Your Career Center

Register at your school's career center. Establish an applicant file, including letters of recommendation and supporting personal information. Most placement offices send out periodic lists of new job vacancies by e-mail, so be sure to get your name and e-mail address on the list. Visit the office regularly, and become a familiar face. Find out how the office arranges interviews with company representatives who visit campus. If your school has a career event, be sure to attend.

Preparing Your Job Credentials

Most placement or credential files include the following information:

1. letters of reference from people who know you well—instructors and employers

2. transcripts of course work to date

3. personal data form to report factual information

4. statement of career goals.

The career center will provide you with special forms to help you to develop your file. Often, these forms can be completed online. Prepare the forms carefully, since employers are always interested in your written communication skills. Keep a copy of the final file for later use in preparing similar information for other employment sources. Check back with the career center to make sure your file is in order, and update it whenever necessary to reflect additional academic accomplishments and added work experiences.

Letters of reference are very important, because they give prospective employers both personal and professional insights about you. They can influence a hiring decision. So, make a careful list of people who might be willing to write letters of reference. Your references should not be family members or close friends. Instead, choose a coach, an instructor, a former employer, or someone else whose knowledge could contribute to your job application. A soccer coach could vouch for your hard work and determination. A teacher might be able to detail how well you accept instruction. A former employer might describe your solid work ethic and ability to get along with others. If possible, include one or more references from your school's business faculty.

Always ask people personally for letters of reference. Be prepared to give them brief outlines of your academic preparation, along with information about your job interests and career goals. This information will help them prepare their letters quickly and efficiently. It also shows that you are serious about the task and respect their time. Remember, however, that these people are very busy. Allow them at least a couple of weeks to prepare their reference letters; then follow up politely on missing ones. Always call or write to thank them for writing the letters and, once you've landed that job, let them know.

Finding Employment through the Internet

The Internet plays an important role in connecting employers and job seekers. Companies of all sizes post their job opportunities on the Web, both on their own sites and on job sites such as Monster.com, Yahoo!HotJobs.com, and CareerBuilder.com. Specialized or niche sites such as Accounting.com and TechCareers.com are also gaining popularity. Some sites are free to applicants, while others charge a subscription fee. Figure E.1 provides a sampling of general and more-focused career sites.

FIGURE E.1 Helpful Internet Job Sites

General Sites
- CareerBuilder.com
- Indeed.com
- Monster.com
- SimplyHired.com
- Yahoo!HotJobs.com

Government Sites
- Careersingovernment.com
- Federaljobs.net
- Todaymilitary.com

Industry and Specialized Sites

Business and Finance
- Accounting.com
- Careerfinance.com
- Efinancialcareers.com

Communication
- iABC.com

Healthcare
- Cdc.gov/employment
- jobs.nih.gov
- Medicalworkers.com

Marketing
- Marketingjobs.com
- Marketingpower.com

Nonprofits/Social Entrepreneurship
- Idealist.org
- Socialedge.org

Sales
- Salescareersonline.com
- Salesjobs.com

Technology
- Dice.com
- Techcareers.com

Women/Minorities
- Hirediversity.com
- iHispano.com
- Womensjoblist.com

Career Web sites typically offer job postings, tips on creating an effective résumé, a place to post your résumé, and advice on interviews and careers. If this sounds easy, keep in mind that these sites may receive hundreds of thousands of hits each day from job hunters, which means you have plenty of competition. This doesn't mean you shouldn't use one of these sites as part of your job search; just don't make it your sole source. Savvy job seekers often find that their time is better spent zeroing in on niche boards offering more focused listings. Naturally, if a particular company interests you, go to that firm's Web site, where available positions will be posted. For example, if you are interested in working at the accounting firm Ernst & Young, visit the Ernst & Young Web site, http://www.ey.com. If you are looking for a job with Whole Foods Market, visit http://www.wholefoods.com. And if you fancy yourself working for an outdoor retailer, go to Recreational Equipment Inc. (REI) at http://www.rei.com.

Newspapers, the source for traditional classified want ads, also post their ads on the Web. Job seekers can even visit sites that merge ads from many different newspapers into one searchable database, such as CareerBuilder (http://www.careerbuilder.com). Some sites go a step farther and create separate sections for each career area. For example, entire sections may be devoted to accounting, marketing, and other business professions. Searches can then be narrowed according to geographic location, entry level, company name, job title, job description, and other categories.

As mentioned earlier, you can connect with potential employers by posting your résumé on job sites. Employers search the résumé database for prospects with the right qualifications. One commonly used approach is for an employer to list one or more *keywords* to select candidates for personal interviews—for example, "retail sales experience," "network architecture," or "spa management"—and then browse the résumés that contain all the required keywords. Employers also scan résumés into their human resource database, and then when a manager requests, say, 10 candidates, the database is searched by keywords that have been specified as part of the request. Job seekers are responding to this computer screening of applicants by making sure that relevant keywords appear on their résumés.

The *Contemporary Business* Web site hosts a comprehensive job and career assistance section. The site is updated frequently to include the best job and career sites for identifying and landing the career you want, as well as current strategies for getting the best results from your Web-based career-search activities.

Finding Employment through Other Sources

The importance of registering at your college's career planning or placement office was noted earlier. If you have completed formal academic coursework at more than one institution, you may be able to set up a placement file at each. In addition, you may want to contact private and public employment services available in your location or in the area where you would like to live.

Private Employment Agencies These firms often specialize in certain types of jobs—such as marketing, finance, sales, or engineering—offering services for both employers and job candidates that are not available elsewhere. Many private agencies interview, test, and screen job applicants so that potential employers do not have to do so. Job candidates benefit from the service by being accepted by the agency and because the agency makes the first contact with the potential employer.

A private employment agency usually charges the prospective employer a fee for finding a suitable employee. Other firms charge job seekers a fee for helping find them a job. Be sure that you understand the terms of any agreement you sign with a private employment agency.

State Employment Offices Don't forget to check the employment office of your state government. Remember that in many states, these public agencies process unemployment compensation applications along with other related work. Because of the mix of duties, some people view state employment agencies as providing services for semiskilled or unskilled workers. However, these agencies *do* list jobs in many professional categories and are often intimately involved with identifying job finalists for major new facilities moving to your state. In addition, many of the jobs listed at state employment offices may be with state or federal agencies and may include professionals such as accountants, attorneys, health care professionals, and scientists.

Learning More About Job Opportunities

Carefully study the various employment opportunities you have identified. Obviously, you will like some more than others, but you can examine a variety of factors when assessing each job possibility:

- actual job responsibilities
- industry characteristics
- nature of the company
- geographic location
- salary and opportunities for advancement
- contribution of the job to your long-range career objectives.

Too many job applicants consider only the most striking features of a job, perhaps its location or the salary offer. However, a comprehensive review of job openings should provide a balanced perspective of the overall employment opportunity, including both long-run and short-run factors.

Building a Résumé

Regardless of how you locate job openings, you must learn how to prepare and submit a *résumé*, a written summary of your personal, educational, and professional achievements. The résumé is a personal document covering your educational background, work experience, career preferences and goals, and major interests that may be relevant. It also includes such basic contact information as your home and e-mail addresses, as well as your telephone number. It should *not* include information on your age, marital status, race, or ethnic background.

Your résumé is usually your formal introduction to an employer, so it should present you in the best light, accentuating your strengths and potential to contribute to a firm as an employee. However, it should *never* contain embellishments or inaccuracies. You don't want to begin your career with unethical behavior, and an employer is bound to discover any discrepancies in fact—either immediately or during the months following your employment. Either event typically results in short-circuiting your career path.

Organizing Your Résumé

The primary purpose of a résumé is to highlight your qualifications for a job, usually on a single page. An attractive layout facilitates the employer's review of your qualifications. You can prepare your résumé in several ways. You may use narrative sentences to explain job duties and career goals, or you may present information in outline form. A résumé included as part of your credentials file at the career center on campus should be quite short. Remember to design it around your specific career objectives.

Figures E.2, E.3, and E.4 illustrate different ways to organize your résumé—by *reverse chronology*, or time; by *function*; and by *results*. Regardless of which format you select, you will

---

FIGURE E.2 Chronological Résumé

FELICIA SMITH-WHITEHEAD
4265 Popular Lane
Cleveland, Ohio 44120
216-555-3296
FeliciaSW@gmail.com

Experienced office manager with excellent organizational and interpersonal skills. Conscientious team player; creative problem solver.

WORK EXPERIENCE

ADM Distribution Enterprises, Cleveland, Ohio   2012–Present
Office Manager of leading regional soft-drink bottler. Coordinate all bookkeeping, correspondence, scheduling of 12-truck fleet to serve 300 customers, promotional mailings, and personnel records, including payroll. Install computerized systems.

Merriweather, Hicks & Bradshaw Attorneys, Columbus, Ohio   2010–2012
Office Supervisor and Executive Assistant for Douglas H. Bradshaw, Managing Partner. Supervised four clerical workers and two paraprofessionals, automated legal research and correspondence functions, and assisted in coordinating outside services and relations with other firms and agencies. Promoted three times from Secretary to Office Supervisor.

Conner & Sons Custom Coverings, Cleveland, Ohio   2006–2010
Secretary in father's upholstery and awning company. Performed all office functions over the years, running the office when the owner was on vacation.

EDUCATION

McBundy Community College, Associate's Degree in Business   2010

Mill Valley High School, Honors   2006

COMPUTER SKILLS

Familiar with Microsoft Office and Adobe Acrobat

LANGUAGE SKILLS

Fluent in Spanish (speaking and writing)
Adequate speaking and writing skills in Portuguese

PERSONAL

Member of various community associations; avid reader; enjoy sports such as camping and cycling; enjoy volunteering in community projects.

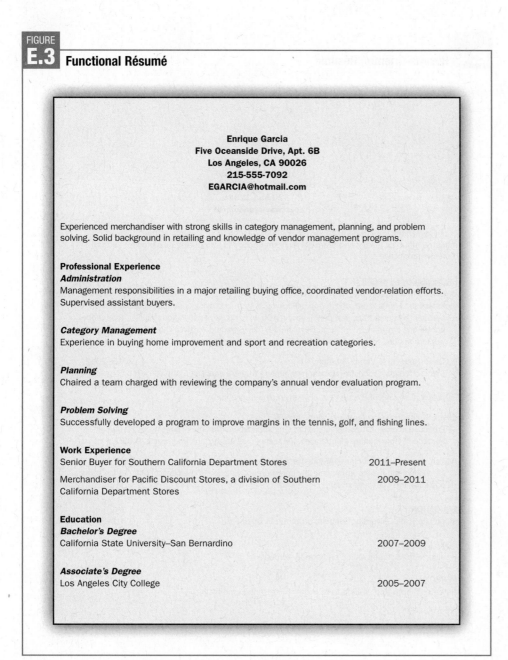

Enrique Garcia
Five Oceanside Drive, Apt. 6B
Los Angeles, CA 90026
215-555-7092
EGARCIA@hotmail.com

Experienced merchandiser with strong skills in category management, planning, and problem solving. Solid background in retailing and knowledge of vendor management programs.

Professional Experience
Administration
Management responsibilities in a major retailing buying office, coordinated vendor-relation efforts. Supervised assistant buyers.

Category Management
Experience in buying home improvement and sport and recreation categories.

Planning
Chaired a team charged with reviewing the company's annual vendor evaluation program.

Problem Solving
Successfully developed a program to improve margins in the tennis, golf, and fishing lines.

Work Experience
Senior Buyer for Southern California Department Stores	2011–Present
Merchandiser for Pacific Discount Stores, a division of Southern California Department Stores	2009–2011

Education
Bachelor's Degree
California State University–San Bernardino	2007–2009

Associate's Degree
Los Angeles City College	2005–2007

want to include the following: a career "snapshot" highlighting some of your key skills; your work or professional experience; your education; your personal interests such as sports or music; and your volunteer work. While all three formats are acceptable, recruiters and prospective employers generally prefer the reverse chronological format—with the most recent experience listed first—because it is easiest to follow.[6]

Tips for Creating a Strong Résumé

Your résumé should help you stand out from the crowd, just as your college admissions application did. A company may receive hundreds or even thousands of résumés, so you want yours to be on the top of the stack. Here are some do's and don'ts:

ANTONIO PETTWAY
101 Beverly Road
Upper Montclair, NJ 07043
820-555-1234
apettway@yahoo.com

Highly motivated construction supervisor with knowledge in all aspects of the construction industry. Affirming leader and team player; experienced in introducing new processes that increase productivity.

PROFESSIONAL EXPERIENCE
DAL Construction Company, Orange, NJ   2012–Present
   Established automated, on-site recordkeeping system improving communications and morale between field and office personnel, saving 400 work hours per year, and reducing the number of accounting errors by 20 percent. Developed a crew selected as "first choice crew" by most workers wanting transfers. Completed five housing projects ahead of deadline and under budget.

NJ State Housing Authority, Trenton, NJ   2010–2012
   Created friendly, productive atmosphere among workers enabling first on-time job completion in 4 years and one-half of usual materials waste. Initiated pilot materials delivery program with potential savings of 3.5 percent of yearly maintenance budget.

Essex County Housing Authority, Montclair, NJ   2010
   Produced information pamphlets increasing applications for county housing by 22 percent. Introduced labor-management discussion techniques saving jobs and over $29,000 in lost time.

Payton, Durnbell & Associates Architects, Glen Ridge, NJ   2007–2010
   Developed and monitored productivity improvements, saving 60 percent on information transfer costs for firm's 12 largest jobs.

EDUCATION
Montclair State University, Bachelor's Degree in Business   2001–2007

COMPUTER SKILLS
Familiar with Microsoft Office and Adobe Acrobat

PERSONAL
Highly self-motivated. Willing to relocate. Enjoy tennis and hiking.

Do:

- Begin the résumé with a few descriptive phrases that give the reader an immediate "snapshot" of who you are and help set the tone for the reader to review your document.

- Use terms related to your field, so that a human resource manager can locate them quickly. If you are submitting your résumé online, use words that will create an automatic "match" with a job description or field. If you are applying for an entry-level job in marketing, the phrase "communication skills" is likely to generate a match. You can identify such words and phrases by reading job descriptions online.

- Provide facts about previous jobs, internships, cooperative education programs, or volunteer work, including results or specific achievements. Include any projects or tasks you undertook through your own initiative.

- Emphasize your education if you are a recent graduate. Place it closer to the top of your résumé instead of the bottom.

- Highlight your strengths and skills, such as research, writing, or organizing.

- Write clearly and concisely.

- Proofread your résumé carefully for grammar, usage, and typographical errors. Refer to a dictionary or style manual.

- Keep your résumé to a single page.

- Avoid including personal information unless it has a direct bearing on the job for which you're applying (for example, playing intramural basketball and volleyball during school might be relevant details if you were applying for a job as a recreation director at a community center).

Don't:

- Offer any misleading or inaccurate information.

- Make vague statements, such as "I work well with others," or "I want a position in business."

- State your objective as, "to run this company" or to "advance as quickly as possible."

- Include a salary request.

- Make demands about vacation time, work hours, or excessive benefits.

- Highlight your weaknesses.

- Submit a résumé with typos or grammatical errors.

- Use slang or other inappropriate phrases or comments.

- Include pictures or graphics, or use fancy type fonts.[7]

Take your time with your résumé; it is one of the most important documents you'll create during your career. If you need help, go to your school's career center. If you are dealing with an employment agency, a counselor there should be able to help as well.

Keep in mind that you will probably have to modify your résumé at times to tailor it to a particular company or job. Again, take the time to do this; it may mean the difference between standing out and being lost in a sea of other applicants.

Preparing Your Cover Letter

In most cases, your résumé will be accompanied by a *cover letter*. This letter should introduce you, explain why you are submitting a résumé (cite the specific job opening if possible), call out some specific point in your résumé that qualifies you for the position, and ask for an interview. An effective cover letter will make the recipient want to take the next step and read your résumé. Here are a few tips for preparing an outstanding letter:

- Write the letter to a specific person, if possible. A letter addressed to "To whom it may concern" may never reach the right person. Call the company or check its Web site for the name of the person to whom you should send your letter. It might be someone in human resources or a person in the department where you'd actually be working. Be sure to obtain the person's title if possible (such as general manager or director), and spell the person's name correctly.

- Introduce yourself and explain the purpose of your letter—to apply for a job.

- Describe briefly an example of your best work or most ambitious project.

- Keep it short—a page is acceptable, half a page even better.

- Request an interview.

- Thank the person for his or her time and consideration.

- Make sure all your contact information is in the letter—name, address, home phone number, cell phone number, and e-mail address.

- Proofread your letter carefully.[8]

Submitting Your Online Résumé

You may write a sparkling cover letter and stellar résumé, but if your online submission is blocked or tossed aside by an automated processing system, it won't have a chance to impress the person for whom it was intended. Here are a few tips for making certain your letter and résumé reach their mark.

- Review the formatting of your résumé to make sure it will appear the same to the recipient as it does to you. Delete any unusual symbols or fonts.

- Use keywords that create a match and allow your résumé through the company's filter. This applies to the subject line of your e-mail as well, which should be specific and contain keywords such as "application for sales trainee job."

- Include your cover letter in the e-mail.

- Send your résumé in the body of the e-mail—not as an attachment. This is more convenient for the recipient, and it also avoids the disaster of having your attachment automatically deleted by an antivirus system.

- Do not send graphics, because they may be blocked or deleted as well.

- If you are answering an ad, read the instructions for application and follow them exactly.[9]

The Job Interview

Congratulations! You've prepared an effective résumé, and you've been contacted for an interview. An interview is more than a casual conversation. During an interview, at least one manager will learn about you, and you'll learn more about the company and the job. Although you may feel nervous about the interview, you can control some of its outcome by doing your homework: planning and preparing for this important encounter with your potential employer. Before you meet with an interviewer, learn everything you can about the firm. The simplest way to do this is to visit the company's Web site. You can also check with your school's career center. If you know anyone who works for the company, you may ask the person about the firm. Try to learn the answers to the following questions about the organization:

- What does the firm do—manufacture clothing, market snack foods, produce films, sell cars? If you are applying for a job at a large corporation, zero in on the division for which you would be working.

- What is the company's mission? Many firms include a statement about their purpose in the business world—to supply affordable energy to communities, to serve fresh food, to make communication easier. Understanding why the company exists will help you grasp where it is headed and why.

- Where, when, and by whom was the company founded? Learn a little about the history of the firm.

- What is its position in the marketplace? Is it a leader or is it trying to gain a competitive advantage? Who are its main competitors?

- Where is the firm based? Does it have facilities located around the country and the world, or is it purely local?

- How is the company organized? Are there multiple divisions and products?

- Learning about the firm indicates to the interviewer that you have initiative and motivation, as well as an interest in the firm's culture and history. You have taken the time and effort to find out more about the organization, and your enthusiasm shows.

Tips for Successful Interviewing

An interview is your personal introduction to the company. You want to make a good impression, but you also want to find out whether you and the firm are a good fit. Although the interviewer will be asking most of the questions, you will want to ask some, as well. People who conduct interviews say that the most important qualities candidates can exhibit are self-confidence, preparedness, and an ability to communicate clearly.

When you are contacted for an interview, find out the name(s) of the person or people who will be interviewing you. It's also appropriate to ask whether the initial interview will be with a human resource manager or with the person to whom you would be reporting on the job, or both. Many people who conduct initial job interviews work in their firms' human resource divisions. These interviewers act as gatekeepers and can make recommendations to managers and supervisors about which individuals to interview further or hire. Managers who head the units in which an applicant will be employed may get involved later in the hiring process. Some hiring decisions come from human resource personnel together with the immediate supervisor of the prospective employee. In other cases, immediate supervisors make the decision alone. At your interview, keep in mind the following tips.

Do:

- **Dress appropriately.** Dress as if it is your first day of work at the firm. Conceal any tattoos or body piercings and, if you wear jewelry, keep it simple.

- **Arrive a few minutes early.** This gives you time to relax and take in the surroundings. It also shows that you are punctual and care about other people's time.

- **Introduce yourself with a smile and a handshake.** Be friendly, but not overly familiar.

- **Be yourself—at your best.** Don't suddenly adopt a new personality. But try to be confident, polite, respectful, and interested in the people who are spending time with you. Be sure to thank each person who interviews you.

- **Listen.** Pay attention to what the interviewer is saying. If something is unclear to you, ask for clarification. Turn off your cell phone and put it away. Your full attention should be on the conversation you are having in the interview.

- **Use appropriate language.** As in your résumé and cover letter, be sure to use correct English. You don't need to be stiff or formal, but avoid slang or phrases that you know are inappropriate for the situation.

- **Be positive in your outlook.** Be enthusiastic about the firm and the job, but don't go overboard.

Don't:

- **Talk too much.** Avoid telling the interviewer a lot about your personal life, or why you left a particular job. Answer questions honestly and thoroughly, but don't dip into irrelevant details.

- **Be arrogant or aggressive.** Self-confidence is a good trait, but don't miss the mark by behaving in an arrogant or condescending manner. Certainly don't become aggressive, demanding that the interviewer offer you the job or even another interview.

- **Act indifferent or bored.** This may not be the job you ultimately want, but treat the interview and the interviewer with respect and attention. If you make a good impression, the firm is likely to keep your name on file—and that dream job may appear after all.

- **Don't get ahead of yourself.** This is not the time to discuss salary, vacation, or benefits.[10]

Answering and Asking Questions

In a typical format, the interviewer gives you ample opportunity to talk about yourself and your goals. Prepare in advance for this opportunity. You want to present your thoughts clearly and concisely, in an organized fashion, without rambling or bringing up unrelated topics. The interviewer may wait until you are finished or prompt you to talk about certain subjects by asking questions. Be as specific as possible when answering questions. The questions that interviewers ask often include the following:

- "Why do you want this job?"
- "Why do you want to work in this field?"
- "What are your short-term goals? Long-term objectives?"
- "Where do you see yourself in five years? In ten years?"
- "What are your strengths? What are your weaknesses?"
- "What motivates you?"
- "Describe a situation in which you made a tough decision or solved a problem."
- "What did you like best about your last job? What did you like least?"
- "Why did you leave your last job?"
- "Why should my firm hire you?"
- "Are you considering other jobs or companies?"

Some of these questions may seem tougher than others, but you can reduce your anxiety by preparing for them. First, figure out which questions you fear the most. Then think about possible answers that are both truthful and positive. Rehearse your delivery in front of a mirror or with a friend.[11]

At some point, the interviewer will probably ask you whether you have any questions of your own. It's a good idea to come prepared with some questions, but others may arise during the interview. Try to keep your list concise, say, three or four of your most important questions. The questions you ask reflect just as much about you as the answers you give to the interviewer's questions. Here is a sample of appropriate questions for the initial interview:

- "Could you clarify a certain aspect of the job responsibilities for me?"
- "Do people who start in entry-level jobs at this company tend to develop their careers here?"
- "In what ways could I perform above and beyond the job requirements?"

At some point during your conversation, the interviewer may give you an idea of the salary range for the job. If not, he or she will do so during a subsequent interview. You may ask about the range, but do not ask exactly how much you will be paid if you get the job. Keep in mind that usually there is little or no negotiation of an entry-level salary. However, you may ask if there is a probationary period with a review at the end of the period. Here are a few other questions *not* to ask:

- "When will I be promoted?"
- "How much time off do I get?"
- "When will I get my first raise?"
- "How many people are applying for this job?"
- "What are my chances of getting this job?"

At the end of the interview, be sure to thank the interviewer with a smile and a handshake, even if you both know the job is not for you. Again, another opportunity may come along in the future and you want to leave the door open. Be sure to ask for a business card from each person who interviewed. When you get home, write a note or e-mail to each person separately, thanking him or her for time spent with you. Thank-you notes really do make a lasting impression on a person, and it gives you another chance to reinforce your interest.

A successful first interview often leads to a second. The purpose of a second interview is to better determine your specific qualifications and fit with the company. You may be introduced to more people—potential co-workers, people in other divisions, or sales staff. You may have another meeting with human resource staff members in which you'll learn more about salary, employee benefits, the firm's code of ethics, and the like. Depending on the type of job, you might be asked to take some skills tests. If you are entering a training program for a bank, you might be required to take some math-oriented tests. If you are going to work for a publisher, you might be asked to take an editing test or do some proofreading. If you are applying for a job as a sales representative, you may be given a test that assesses your personality traits. Don't be intimidated by these tests; you are not expected to know everything or be perfect. Just do your best.

Making the Employment Decision

After receiving your résumé, conducting one or two interviews, and administering a skills test, a potential employer knows a lot about you. You should also know a lot about the company. If the experience has been positive on both sides, you may be offered a job. If you have interviewed at several companies and are offered more than one job, congratulations! Often, an employer will phone you to make the job offer, saying that the formal offer will follow in the mail. Whether you receive one offer or several, thank the person making the offer. If you choose to accept immediately, feel free to do so. However, employers commonly expect that candidate will want to review the offer letter before formally accepting. If you have doubts about the job or need to decide between two, it is appropriate to ask for 24 hours to respond. If you must decline an offer, do so promptly and politely. After all, you may end up working for that firm sometime in the future. If you get a few rejections before you receive an offer, don't give up. Every application and interview adds to your experience.

As you think about an offer, consider the aspects that are most important. You'll want to choose a job that comes closest to your career interests and objectives. But don't rule out the element of surprise—you might wind up with a job you like in an industry you'd never considered before. Don't worry too much about the salary. The point of an entry-level job is to set you on a forward path. And keep in mind that your first job won't be your last. Once you have accepted an offer, you'll be given a start date as well as the name of the person to whom you should report on arrival.

Congratulations! You've accepted an offer for your first job. You are now a member of the workforce.

Nontraditional Students

Take a quick glance around your class. You'll likely see classmates of all ages. Some will fall into the traditional college age group of 18 to 22, but many don't. Perhaps you are a veteran returning from military duty overseas. Maybe you have been engaged in a full-time career but want to broaden your education. Students who fall outside the 18- to 22-year-old age group are often referred to as *nontraditional students*, but these students have become the norm on many campuses. Homemakers returning to school to freshen up their résumés before returning to the workforce and workers who have been laid off due to an economic downturn are other examples of nontraditional students. As diverse as this group is, they share one thing in common: they are older than traditional students. This means that they face different challenges—but also enjoy some advantages over their younger classmates.

One major challenge faced by nontraditional students is scheduling. Often they are juggling the responsibilities of work, school, and family. They may have to study at odd times—during meals, while commuting, or after putting the kids to bed. If they are switching careers, they may be learning an entirely new set of skills, as well. But nontraditional students have an important advantage: experience. Even experience in an unrelated field is a plus. Older students know how organizations operate. Often, they have developed useful skills in human relations, management, budgeting, and communications. Even a former stay-at-home parent has skills in all of these areas. Through observing other people's successes and failures—as well as living through their own—they have developed an inventory of what to do and what not to do. So, in some ways, these students have a head start on their younger counterparts. But they also face the reality that they have fewer years in which to develop a career.

The Job Market: Where Do You Fit In?

The industry you choose, and the career you follow within it, are part of a bigger picture. They reflect the needs of society, changing populations, developing technology, and the overall economy. For instance, the U.S. population is expected to increase at a slower rate of growth for the foreseeable future than during the previous two decades. The U.S. workforce will continue to become more diverse, with Hispanics accounting for both the largest share of jobs among minorities by the year 2020 as well as the fastest-growing. The size of the Hispanic workforce is expected to increase more than 3 percent per year to nearly 19 percent of the U.S. workforce. White, non-Hispanic workers will make up a declining share of the workforce, falling from approximately 68 percent to about 62 percent.[12]

The number of women in the workforce is growing at a slightly faster rate than that of men. The male labor force is expected to grow by 6.3 percent by the year 2020, compared with 7.4 percent for women. So the men's share of the labor force will likely continue to decrease, while the women's share will increase.[13]

All of these facts combine to shape a picture of the needs of U.S. society and the workforce available to serve it. As the Baby Boom generation ages, the age group between 55 and 64 will increase by more than one third. Thus, the United States will need more health care services as well as other services for an aging population, such as assisted living facilities and leisure and hospitality. The group between the ages 25 and 54 will rise a mere 1.6 percent, while the youth population between 16 and 24 will decline by more than 12 percent. But today's younger workers are receiving more education and training to fill the need for professional and business service workers. These projections affect both the workforce and the types of goods and services needed to satisfy consumers. So jobs in health care are estimated to increase by more than 5.6 million and in professional and business services by 3.8 million.[14]

Careers in service-providing industries continue a long-term rise. Service jobs in educational services will increase by about 23 percent by the year 2020, while manufacturing jobs will continue to shrink. But industries that produce certain types of goods, such as those related to the needs of an aging population and those related to green technologies or products, will probably increase.[15]

The good news is that even in a weaker job market, employers are looking to hire recent college graduates. Continuing to hire entry-level employees makes good business sense. The National Associate of Colleges and Employers (NACE) reports that college hiring is actually on the rise.[16] Some of the hot jobs can be found in accounting, sales, management training, engineering, and business services. So celebrate your graduation, and keep your résumé current and your outlook positive: a job is out there for you.

A Long-Range View of Your Career

Choosing a career is an important life decision. A career is a professional journey—regardless of whether you want to run a small restaurant or a branch bank, whether you are fascinated by language or math, whether you prefer to work with animals or people. In the end, you hope to contribute something good to society while enjoying what you do—and make a reasonable living at it.

Throughout your career, it is important to stay flexible and continue learning. Challenging new skills will be required of managers and other businesspeople during these first decades of the 21st century. Remain open to unexpected changes and opportunities that can help you learn and develop new skills. Keep in mind that your first job will not be your last. But tackle that first job with the same enthusiasm you'd have if someone asked you to run the company itself, because everything you learn on that job will be valuable at some point during your career—and someday you may actually run the company.

Finally, if you haven't already started your career search, begin now. Do this by talking with various resources, lining up an internship, looking for a part-time job on or off campus, or volunteering for an organization. Register with the campus career center long before you graduate. Then, when you reach your final semester, you'll be well on your way to finding the job you want.

This textbook presents a panorama of career options for you. Whatever you decide, be sure it is right for you—not your friends, your instructors, or your parents. As the old saying goes, "You pass this way just once." Enjoy the journey!

More Career Information on the *Contemporary Business* Web Site

More career information is available to students using *Contemporary Business* at the book's Web site.

The "Management Careers" section on the Web site enables you to learn more about business careers and to locate currently posted job opportunities. The site provides a vast number of career resources such as links to job sites, career guidance sites, and the like. Also, many links include extensive career information and guidance, such as interviewing techniques and tips for résumé writing.

◼ Projects and Teamwork Applications

1. Visit one of the job Web sites such as CareerBuilder or Monster and research an industry in which you think you might be interested. Prepare a report on what you learned about the field. Was the site helpful? What types of jobs were available in the field? Based on your report, do you plan to pursue this industry or select another field?

2. Prepare your résumé following the procedures outlined earlier in this section. Exchange your résumé with a classmate so you can critique each other's work. Then revise and proofread your résumé.

3. Go online to the Web site for a specific company for which you might be interested in working. Click on the "Careers" or "Job Opportunities" section of the site, and read carefully the job descriptions for any entry-level positions and the procedure for applying for them. Also review any general information about career development at the firm. Write a cover letter as if you were actually applying for one of the jobs.

4. With a classmate, practice interviewing for the job you selected in the previous question. Prepare questions for each other and take turns interviewing and being interviewed. What parts of the interview did you handle well? What could you improve?

5. Think about where you would like to be in your career in five years and write about your plans. Share your plans with the class, then seal them in an envelope. Keep the envelope and open it in five years to see how close you came to your predictions.

360-degree performance review employee performance review that gathers feedback from co-workers, supervisors, managers, and sometimes customers.

401(k) plan retirement savings plan to which employees can make pretax contributions; employers often make additional contributions to the plan.

accounting process of measuring, interpreting, and communicating financial information to support internal and external business decision making.

accounting cycle set of activities involved in converting information and individual transactions into financial statements.

accounting equation formula that states that assets must always equal the sum of liabilities and owners' equity.

accrual accounting accounting method that records revenues and expenses when they occur, not necessarily when cash actually changes hands.

acquisition agreement in which one firm purchases another.

activity ratios measures of how efficiently a firm utilizes its assets.

actuarial table probability of the number of events that are expected to occur within a given year.

advertising paid nonpersonal communication usually targeted at large numbers of potential buyers.

affective conflict disagreement that focuses on individuals or personal issues.

affinity program marketing effort sponsored by an organization that solicits involvement by individuals who share common interests and activities.

affirmative action programs programs designed by employers to increase job opportunities for women, minorities, disabled people, and other protected groups.

agency legal relationship whereby one party, called a *principal*, appoints another party, called an *agent*, to enter into contracts with third parties on the principal's behalf.

alien corporation firm incorporated in one nation and operating in another nation.

angel investors wealthy individuals who invest directly in a new venture in exchange for an equity stake.

appellate courts courts that hear appeals of decisions made at the general trial court level; both the federal and state systems have appellate courts.

application service provider (ASP) outside supplier that provides both the computers and the application support for managing an information system.

arbitration bringing in an impartial third party called an arbitrator to render a binding decision in a dispute.

assembly line manufacturing technique that carries the product on a conveyor system past several workstations where workers perform specialized tasks.

asset anything of value owned by a firm.

asset intensity amount of assets needed to generate a given level of sales.

autocratic leadership management approach whereby leaders make decisions on their own without consulting employees.

balance of payments overall money flows into and out of a country.

balance of trade difference between a nation's exports and imports.

balance sheet statement of a firm's financial position—what it owns and claims against its assets—at a particular point in time.

balanced budget situation in which total revenues raised by taxes and fees equal total proposed government spending for the year.

bankruptcy legal nonpayment of financial obligations.

banner ad advertisement placed by an organization on another organization's Web site; interested parties click on the ad for more information.

benchmarking process of determining how well other companies perform business functions or tasks.

blog online journal written by a blogger.

board of directors governing body of a corporation.

bot short for *robot*—a program that allows online shoppers to compare prices for a specific product at several e-tailers.

botnet a network of PCs that have been infected with one or more data-stealing viruses.

boycott effort to prevent people from purchasing a firm's goods or services.

brand name, term, sign, symbol, design, or some combination that identifies the products of one firm and differentiates them from competitors' offerings.

brand equity added value that a respected and successful name gives to a product.

brand name part of a brand consisting of words or letters that form a name that identifies and distinguishes an offering from those of competitors.

branding process of creating an identity in consumers' minds for a good, service, or company; a major marketing tool in contemporary business.

breach of contract violation of a valid contract.

breakeven analysis pricing-related technique used to determine the minimum sales volume a product must generate at a certain price level to cover all costs.

budget organization's plan for how it will raise and spend money during a given period of time.

budget deficit situation in which the government spends more than the amount of money it raises through taxes.

budget surplus excess funding that occurs when government spends less than the amount of funds raised through taxes and fees.

business all profit-seeking activities and enterprises that provide goods and services necessary to an economic system.

business (B2B) product good or service purchased to be used, either directly or indirectly, in the production of other goods for resale.

business ethics standards of conduct and moral values regarding right and wrong actions in the work environment.

business incubator local programs designed to provide low-cost shared business facilities to small start-up ventures.

business intelligence activities and technologies for gathering, storing, and analyzing data to make better competitive decisions.

business interruption insurance type of insurance that protects firms from financial losses resulting from the suspension of business operations.

business law aspects of law that most directly influence and regulate the management of business activity.

business plan written document that provides an orderly statement of a company's goals, methods, and standards.

business-to-business (B2B) e-business electronic business transactions between organizations using the Internet.

business-to-consumer (B2C) e-business selling directly to consumers over the Internet.

call provision right of the issuer to buy a bond back from the investor before maturity at a specified price.

capital production inputs consisting of technology, tools, information, and physical facilities.

capital investment analysis process of comparing the costs and benefits of a long-term asset investment.

capital structure mix of a firm's debt and equity capital.

capitalism economic system that rewards firms for their ability to perceive and serve the needs and demands of consumers; also called the private enterprise system.

cash budget budget that shows cash inflows and outflows during a period of time.

cash flow sources of cash minus uses of cash during a specified period of time.

cash value policy type of life insurance that combines insurance protection with a savings feature.

category advisor vendor that is designated by the business customer as the major supplier to assume responsibility for dealing with all the other vendors for a project and presenting the entire package to the business buyer.

category manager person who oversees an entire group of products and assumes profit responsibility for the product group.

cause advertising form of institutional advertising that promotes a specific viewpoint on a public issue as a way to influence public opinion and the legislative process.

cause marketing marketing that promotes a cause or social issue, such as preventing child abuse, anti-littering efforts, and stop-smoking campaigns.

Central America–Dominican Republic Free Trade Agreement (CAFTA-DR) agreement among the United States, Costa Rica, the Dominican Republic, El Salvador, Guatemala, Honduras, and Nicaragua to reduce tariffs and trade restrictions.

centralization decision making based at the top of the management hierarchy.

certified management accountant (CMA) management accountant who meets specified educational and experience requirements and has passed an examination covering management accounting topics.

certified public accountant (CPA) public accountant who meets specified educational and experiential requirements and has passed a comprehensive examination on accounting theory and practice.

chain of command set of relationships that indicates who directs which activities and who reports to whom.

channel conflict conflict between two or more members of a supply chain, such as a manufacturer, wholesaler, or retailer.

chief information officer (CIO) executive responsible for managing a firm's information system and related computer technologies.

Class-Action Fairness Act of 2005 law that moves most large, multistate class-action lawsuits to federal courts, ensures judicial oversight of plaintiffs' compensation, bases lawyers' compensation on awards actually distributed or actual time spent, and ensures plaintiffs' interests are protected equally with those of their lawyers.

classic entrepreneur person who identifies a business opportunity and allocates available resources to tap that market.

click-through rate number of visitors who click on a Web banner ad.

cloud computing powerful servers store applications software and databases for users to access the software and databases via the Web using anything from a PC to a smart phone.

cobranding cooperative arrangement in which two or more businesses team up to closely link their names on a single product.

code of conduct formal statement that defines how an organization expects its employees to resolve ethical issues.

cognitive ability tests tests that measure job candidates' abilities in perceptual speed, verbal comprehension, numerical aptitude, general reasoning, and spatial aptitude.

cognitive conflict disagreement that focuses on problem- and issue-related differences of opinion.

collective bargaining process of negotiation between management and union representatives.

comarketing cooperative arrangement in which two businesses jointly market each other's products.

committee organization organizational structure that places authority and responsibility jointly in the hands of a group of individuals rather than a single manager.

common law body of law arising out of judicial decisions, some of which can be traced back to early England.

common stock shares that give owners voting rights but only residual claims to the firm's assets and income distributions.

communication meaningful exchange of information through messages.

communism economic system in which all property would be shared equally by the people of a community under the direction of a strong central government.

compensation amount employees are paid in money and benefits.

competition battle among businesses for consumer acceptance.

competitive differentiation unique combination of organizational abilities, products, and approaches that sets a company apart from competitors in the minds of customers.

competitive pricing strategy that tries to reduce the emphasis on price competition by matching other firms' prices and concentrating their own marketing efforts on the product, distribution, and promotional elements of the marketing mix.

compressed workweek scheduling option that allows employees to work the regular number of hours per week in fewer than the typical five days.

computer-aided design (CAD) process that allows engineers to design components as well as entire products on computer screens faster and with fewer mistakes than they could achieve working with traditional drafting systems.

computer-aided manufacturing (CAM) computer tools to analyze CAD output and enable a manufacturer to analyze the steps that a machine must take to produce a needed product or part.

computer-based information systems information systems that rely on computer and related technologies to store information electronically in an organized, accessible manner.

computer-integrated manufacturing (CIM) production system in which computers help workers design products, control machines, handle materials, and control the production function in an integrated fashion.

conceptual skills ability to see the organization as a unified whole and to understand how each part interacts with others.

conflict situation in which one person or group's needs do not match those of another, and attempts may be made to block the opposing side's intentions or goals.

conflict of interest situation in which an employee must choose between a business's welfare and personal gain.

conglomerate merger merger that combines unrelated firms, usually with the goal of diversification, spurring sales growth, or spending a cash surplus in order to avoid a takeover attempt.

consumer (B2C) product good or service that is purchased by end users.

consumer behavior actions of ultimate consumers directly involved in obtaining, consuming, and disposing of products and the decision processes that precede and follow these actions.

consumer orientation business philosophy that focuses first on determining unmet consumer wants and needs and then designing products to satisfy those needs.

Consumer Price Index (CPI) measurement of the monthly average change in prices of goods and services.

consumerism public demand that a business consider the wants and needs of its customers in making decisions.

contingency planning plans that allow a firm to resume operations as quickly and as smoothly as possible after a crisis while openly communicating with the public about what happened.

contract legally enforceable agreement between two or more parties regarding a specified act or thing.

controlling function of evaluating an organization's performance against its objectives.

convenience product item the consumer seeks to purchase frequently, immediately, and with little effort.

conversion rate percentage of visitors to a Web site who actually make a purchase.

convertible securities bonds or preferred stock issues that are convertible into a set number of shares of the issuing company's common stock.

cooperative organization whose owners join forces to collectively operate all or part of the functions in their business.

cooperative advertising allowances provided by marketers in which they share the cost of local advertising of their firm's product or product line with channel partners.

copyright protection of written material such as textbooks, designs, cartoon illustrations, photos, and computer software.

core inflation rate inflation rate of an economy after energy and food prices are removed.

corporate charter legal document that formally establishes a corporation.

corporate culture organization's system of principles, beliefs, and values.

corporate philanthropy effort of an organization to make a contribution to the communities in which it earns profits.

corporate Web site Web site designed to increase a firm's visibility, promote its offerings, and provide information to interested parties.

corporation legal organization with assets and liabilities separate from those of its owner(s).

cost-based pricing formulas that calculate total costs per unit and then add markups to cover overhead costs and generate profits.

countertrade barter agreement whereby trade between two or more nations involves payment made in the form of local products instead of currency.

creative selling persuasive type of promotional presentation.

creativity capacity to develop novel solutions to perceived organizational problems.

credit receiving money, goods, or services on the basis of an agreement between the lender and the borrower that the loan is for a specified period of time with a specified rate of interest.

critical path sequence of operations that requires the longest time for completion.

critical thinking ability to analyze and assess information to pinpoint problems or opportunities.

cross-functional team a team made up of members from different functions, such as production, marketing, and finance.

cyclical unemployment people who are out of work because of a cyclical contraction in the economy.

damages financial payments to compensate for a loss and related suffering.

data raw facts and figures that may or may not be relevant to a business decision.

data mining computer searches of customer data to detect patterns and relationships.

data warehouse customer database that allows managers to combine data from several different organizational functions.

database centralized integrated collection of data resources.

debenture unsecured corporate bond.

debt capital funds obtained from borrowing.

debt financing borrowed funds that entrepreneurs must repay.

decentralization decision makeup based at lower levels of the organization.

decision making process of recognizing a problem or opportunity, evaluating alternative solutions, selecting and implementing an alternative, and assessing the results.

decision support system (DSS) gives direct support to businesspeople during the decision-making process.

deflation opposite of inflation, occurs when prices continue to fall.

delegation managerial process of assigning work to employees.

demand willingness and ability of buyers to purchase goods and services.

demand curve graph of the amount of a product that buyers will purchase at different prices.

democratic leadership management approach whereby leaders delegate assignments, ask employees for suggestions, and encourage their participation.

demographic segmentation dividing markets on the basis of various demographic or socioeconomic characteristics such as gender, age, income, occupation, household size, stage in family life cycle, education, or ethnic group.

demographics statistical characteristics of the segment of the market that might purchase a product.

departmentalization process of dividing work activities into units within the organization.

deregulation regulatory trend toward elimination of legal restraints on competition in industries previously served by a single firm in an attempt to improve customer service and lower prices through increased competition.

devaluation reduction in a currency's value relative to other currencies or to a fixed standard.

direct distribution channel marketing channel that moves goods directly from producer to ultimate user.

directing guiding and motivating employees to accomplish organizational objectives.

disability income insurance type of insurance that pays benefits to those who cannot work due to some sort of disability.

discrimination biased treatment of a job candidate or employee.

dispatching phase of production control in which the manager instructs each department on what work to do and the time allowed for its completion.

display ad glossy-looking online ad often targeted at a specific user.

distribution channel path through which products—and legal ownership of them—flow from producer to consumers or business users.

diversity blending individuals of different genders, ethnic backgrounds, cultures, religions, and ages to enhance a firm's chances of success.

divestiture sale of assets by a firm.

domestic corporation firm that operates in the state where it is incorporated.

double-entry bookkeeping process by which accounting transactions are entered; each individual transaction always has an offsetting transaction.

downsizing process of reducing the number of employees within a firm by eliminating jobs.

dumping selling products abroad at prices below production costs or below typical prices in the home market to capture market share from domestic competitors.

economics social science that analyzes the choices people and governments make in allocating scarce resources.

electronic bulletin board Internet chat room that allows users to post and read messages on a specific topic.

electronic business (e-business) conducting business via the Internet.

electronic data interchange (EDI) computer-to-computer exchanges of invoices, purchase orders, price quotations, and other information between buyers and sellers.

electronic exchange online marketplace that caters to an industry's specific needs.

electronic shopping cart file that holds items that the online shopper has chosen to buy.

electronic storefront company Web site that sells products to customers.

electronic wallet secure computer data file set up by an online shopper at an e-business site that contains credit card and personal identification information.

embargo total ban on importing specific products or a total halt to trading with a particular country.

employee benefits additional compensation such as vacation, retirement plans, profit-sharing, health insurance, gym membership, child and elder care, and tuition reimbursement, paid entirely or in part by the company.

employee ownership business ownership in which workers buy shares of stock in the company that employs them.

employee stock-ownership plan (ESOP) plan that benefits employees by giving them ownership stakes in the companies for which they work.

empowerment giving employees shared authority, responsibility, and decision making with their managers.

employee separation broad term covering the loss of an employee for any reason, voluntary or involuntary.

encryption process of encoding data for security purposes, using software that encodes and scrambles messages.

end-use segmentation marketing strategy that focuses on the precise way a B2B purchaser will use a product.

enterprise zones specific geographic areas designated for economic revitalization.

entrepreneur person who seeks a profitable opportunity and takes the necessary risks to set up and operate a business.

entrepreneurship willingness to take risks to create and operate a business.

environmental impact study analyzes how a proposed plant would affect the quality of life in the surrounding area.

e-procurement use of the Internet by business and government agencies to solicit bids and purchase goods and services from suppliers.

Equal Employment Opportunity Commission (EEOC) this commission created to increase job opportunities for women and minorities and to help end discrimination based on race, color, religion, disability, gender, or national origin in any personnel action.

equilibrium price prevailing market price at which you can buy an item.

equity capital funds obtained from owners.

equity financing funds invested in new ventures in exchange for part ownership.

equity theory an individual's perception of fair and equitable treatment.

European Union (EU) 27-nation European economic alliance.

event marketing marketing or sponsoring short-term events such as athletic competitions and cultural and charitable performances.

everyday low pricing (EDLP) is a strategy devoted to maintaining continuous low prices rather than relying on short-term price cuts such as cents-off coupons, rebates, and special sales.

exchange control restriction on importation of certain products or against certain companies to reduce trade and expenditures of foreign currency.

exchange process activity in which two or more parties give something of value to each other to satisfy perceived needs.

exchange rate value of one nation's currency relative to the currencies of other countries.

exclusive distribution distribution strategy involving limited market coverage by a single retailer or wholesaler in a specific geographical territory.

executive summary one- to two-page snapshot of what the overall business plan explains in detail.

executive support system (ESS) lets senior executives access the firm's primary databases, often by touching the computer screen, pointing and clicking a mouse, or using voice recognition.

expansionary monetary policy government actions to increase the money supply in an effort to cut the cost of borrowing, which encourages business decision makers to make new investments, in turn stimulating employment and economic growth.

expectancy theory the process people use to evaluate the likelihood that their efforts will yield the results they want, along with the degree to which they want those results.

expert system computer program that imitates human thinking through complicated sets of "if-then" rules.

exports domestically produced goods and services sold in other countries.

external communication meaningful exchange of information through messages transmitted between an organization and its major audiences.

extranet secure network used for e-business and accessible through an organization's Web site; available to external customers, suppliers, and other authorized users.

factoring selling receivables to another party, called a factor, for cash.

factors of production four basic inputs for effective operation: natural resources, capital, human resources, and entrepreneurship.

fair trade a market-based approach to pay higher prices to producers on exports from developing countries to developed countries in order for the developing countries to obtain better trading conditions and promote sustainability.

family brand brand name used to identify several different, but related, products.

family leave the Family and Medical Leave Act of 1993 states that employers with 50 or more employees must provide unpaid leave up to 12 weeks annually for any employee who wants time off for the birth or adoption of a child, to become a foster parent, or to care for a seriously ill relative, spouse, or self if he or she has a serious health condition or injury.

Federal Deposit Insurance Corporation (FDIC) federal agency that insures deposits at commercial and savings banks.

Federal Open Markets Committee Fed body that has primary responsibility for money policy.

Federal Reserve System (Fed) central bank of the United States.

fee-for-service plan traditional form of health insurance in which the insured chooses his or her healthcare provider, pays for treatment, and is reimbursed by the insurance company; also called an indemnity plan.

finance planning, obtaining, and managing a company's funds to accomplish its objectives as effectively and efficiently as possible.

finance charge the difference between the amount borrowed and the amount repaid on a loan.

Financial Accounting Standards Board (FASB) organization that interprets and modifies GAAP in the United States.

financial institutions intermediary between savers and borrowers, collecting funds from savers and then lending the funds to individuals, businesses, and governments.

financial manager executive who develops and implements the firm's financial plan and determines the most appropriate sources and uses of funds.

financial markets market in which securities are bought and sold.

financial plan document that specifies the funds needed by a firm for a period of time, the timing of inflows and outflows, and the most appropriate sources and uses of funds.

financial system process by which money flows from savers to users.

financing section section of a business plan that demonstrates the cost of the product, operating expenses, expected sales revenue and profit, and the amount of the business owner's own funds that will be invested to get the business up and running.

firewall limit data transfers to certain locations and log system use so that managers can identify attempts to log on with invalid passwords and other threats to a system's security.

fiscal policy government spending and taxation decisions designed to control inflation, reduce unemployment, improve the general welfare of citizens, and encourage economic growth.

flexible benefit plan benefit system that offers employees a range of options from which they may choose the types of benefits they receive.

flexible manufacturing system (FMS) production facility that workers can quickly modify to manufacture different products.

flexible work plan employment that allows personnel to adjust their working hours and places of work to accommodate their personal needs.

flextime scheduling system that allows employees to set their own work hours within constraints specified by the firm.

follow-up phase of production control in which employees and their supervisors spot problems in the production process and determine needed adjustments.

foreign corporation firm that operates in states where it is not incorporated.

Foreign Corrupt Practices Act federal law that prohibits U.S. citizens and companies from bribing foreign officials to win or continue business.

foreign licensing agreement international agreement in which one firm allows another to produce or sell its product, or use its trademark, patent, or manufacturing processes, in a specific geographical area in return for royalties or other compensation.

formal communication channel messages that flow within the chain of command defined by an organization.

franchise contractual agreement in which a franchisee gains the right to produce and/or sell the franchisor's products under that company's brand name if they agree to certain operating requirements.

franchisee individual or business firm purchasing a franchise.

franchising contractual business arrangement between a manufacturer or other supplier, and a dealer such as a restaurant operator or retailer.

franchisor firm whose products are sold to customers by the franchisee.

free-rein leadership management style of leaders who believe in minimal supervision and leave most decisions to their subordinates.

frequency marketing marketing initiative that rewards frequent purchases with cash, rebates, merchandise, or other premiums.

frictional unemployment applies to members of the workforce who are temporarily not working but are looking for jobs.

General Agreement on Tariffs and Trade (GATT) international trade accord that substantially reduced worldwide tariffs and other trade barriers.

generally accepted accounting principles (GAAP) principles that encompass the conventions, rules, and procedures for determining acceptable accounting practices at a particular time.

geographical segmentation dividing an overall market into homogeneous groups on the basis of their locations.

global business strategy offering a standardized, worldwide product and selling it in essentially the same manner throughout a firm's domestic and foreign markets.

goal target, objective, or result that someone tries to accomplish.

goal-setting theory says that people will be motivated to the extent to which they accept specific, challenging goals and receive feedback that indicates their progress toward goal achievement.

government bonds bonds issued by the U.S. Department of the Treasury.

grapevine internal information channel that transmits information from unofficial sources.

green marketing a marketing strategy that promotes environmentally safe products and production methods.

grid computing consists of a network of smaller computers running special software.

grievance formal complaint filed by an employee or a union that management is violating some provision of a union contract.

gross domestic product (GDP) sum of all goods and services produced within a country's boundaries during a specific time period, such as a year.

guerrilla marketing innovative, low-cost marketing effort designed to get consumers' attention in unusual ways.

hardware all tangible elements of a computer system.

health insurance category of insurance that pays for losses due to illness or injury.

high-context culture society in which communication depends not only on the message itself but also on nonverbal cues, past and present experiences, and personal relationships between the parties.

home-based businesses firm operated from the residence of the business owner.

horizontal merger merger that joins firms in the same industry for the purpose of diversification, increasing customer bases, cutting costs, or expanding product lines.

human resource management function of attracting, developing, and retaining employees who can perform the activities necessary to accomplish organizational objectives.

human resources production inputs consisting of anyone who works, including both the physical labor and the intellectual inputs contributed by workers.

human skills interpersonal skills that enable a manager to work effectively with and through people; the ability to communicate with, motivate, and lead employees to accomplish assigned activities.

hygiene factors factors that if present are essential to job satisfaction, although they cannot motivate an employee.

hyperinflation economic situation characterized by soaring prices.

imports foreign goods and services purchased by domestic customers.

income statement financial record of a company's revenues, expenses, and profits over a period of time.

individual brand different brand names given to each product within a line.

inflation economic situation characterized by rising prices caused by a combination of excess consumer demand and increases in the costs of raw materials, component parts, human resources, and other factors of production.

infomercial form of broadcast direct marketing; 30-minute programs that resemble regular TV programs, but are devoted to selling goods or services.

informal communication channel messages outside formally authorized channels within an organization's hierarchy.

information knowledge gained from processing data.

information system organized method for collecting, storing, and communicating past, present, and projected information on internal operations and external intelligence.

infrastructure basic systems of communication, transportation, and energy facilities in a country.

initial public offering (IPO) sale of stock to the public for the first time.

insider trading use of material nonpublic information about a company to make investment profits.

institutional advertising involves messages that promote of concepts, ideas, philosophies, or goodwill for industries, companies, organizations, or government entities.

insurable interest demonstration that a direct financial loss will result if some event occurs.

insurable risk requirement that a pure risk must meet for an insurer to agree to provide coverage.

insurance contract by which the insurer for a fee agrees to reimburse the insured a sum of money if a loss occurs.

integrated marketing communications (IMC) coordination of all promotional activities—media advertising, direct mail, personal selling, sales promotion, and public relations—to produce a unified customer-focused message.

integrity adhering to deeply felt ethical principles in business situations.

intensive distribution distribution strategy that involves placing a firm's products in nearly every available outlet.

International Accounting Standards Board (IASB) organization established in 1973 to promote worldwide consistency in financial reporting practices.

International Financial Reporting Standards (IFRS) standards and interpretations adopted by the IASB.

international law regulations that govern international commerce.

International Monetary Fund (IMF) organization created to promote trade, eliminate barriers, and make short-term loans to member nations that are unable to meet their budgets.

International Organization for Standardization (ISO) organization whose mission is to develop and promote International Standards for business, government and society to facilitate global trade and cooperation.

intranet computer network that is similar to the Internet but limits access to authorized users.

intrapreneurship process of promoting innovation within the structure of an existing organization.

introduction section of a business plan that describes the company, the management team, and the product in detail.

inventory control function requiring production and operations managers to balance the need to keep stock on hand to meet demand against the costs of carrying inventory.

investment-grade bond bond with a rating of BBB or above.

job enlargement job design that expands an employee's responsibilities by increasing the number and variety of tasks assigned to the worker.

job enrichment change in job duties to increase employees' authority in planning their work, deciding how it should be done, and learning new skills.

job rotation systematically moving employees from one job to another.

job sharing program management decision that allows two or more employees to divide the tasks of one job.

joint venture partnership between companies formed for a specific undertaking.

judiciary court system, or branch of government that is responsible for settling disputes by applying laws.

just-in-time (JIT) system broad management philosophy that reaches beyond the narrow activity of inventory control to influence the entire system of production and operations management.

labor union group of workers who have banded together to achieve common goals in the areas of wages, hours, and working conditions.

law standards set by government and society in the form of either legislation or custom.

law of large numbers concept that seemingly random events will follow predictable patterns if enough events are observed.

leadership ability to direct or inspire people to attain certain goals.

leverage increasing the rate of return on funds invested by borrowing funds.

leverage ratios measures of the extent to which a company relies on borrowed funds.

leveraged buyout (LBO) transaction in which public shareholders are bought out and the firm reverts to private status.

LEED (Leadership in Energy and Environmental Design) voluntary certification program administered by the U.S. Green Building Council, aimed at promoting the most sustainable construction processes available.

liability claims against assets by creditors.

liability insurance a type of insurance that protects people against financial losses to others for acts for which the insured was responsible.

life insurance a type of insurance that protects people against the financial losses that occur with premature death.

lifestyle entrepreneur person who starts a business to reduce work hours and create a more relaxed lifestyle.

lifetime value of a customer revenues and intangible benefits (referrals and customer feedback) from a customer over the life of the relationship, minus the amount the company must spend to acquire and serve that customer.

limit order order that puts a ceiling or floor on a security purchase or sale.

limited-liability company (LLC) corporation that secures the corporate advantage of limited liability while avoiding the double taxation characteristic of corporations.

line manager executive involved with the functions of production, financing, or marketing.

line organization organizational structure that establishes a direct flow of authority from the chief executive to subordinates.

line-and-staff organization structure that combines the direct flow of authority of a line organization with staff departments that support the line departments.

liquidity ratios measures of a firm's ability to meet its short-term obligations.

listening receiving a message and interpreting its intended meaning by grasping the facts and feelings it conveys.

local area networks (LANs) computer networks that connect machines within limited areas, such as a building or several nearby buildings.

lockout management decision to put pressure on union members by closing the firm.

logistics process of coordinating flow of goods, services, and information among members of the supply chain.

low-context culture society in which communication tends to rely on explicit written and verbal messages.

macroeconomics study of a nation's overall economic issues, such as how an economy maintains and allocates resources and how a government's policies affect the standards of living of its citizens.

make, buy, or lease decision choosing whether to manufacture a needed product or component in house, purchase it from an outside supplier, or lease it.

malware any malicious software program designed to infect computer systems.

managed care plan health care plan in which most, if not all, of the insured's health care bills are paid by the insurance company; in exchange, the insured has much less say over his or her treatment.

management process of achieving organizational objectives through people and other resources.

management accountant accountant who works for a firm and provides accounting services to that firm.

management by objectives systematic approach that allows managers to focus on attainable goals and to achieve the best results based on the organization's resources.

management development program training designed to improve the skills and broaden the knowledge of current and potential executives.

management information system (MIS) information system designed to produce reports for managers and other personnel.

management support systems information systems that are designed to provide support for effective decision making.

manufacturer's (national) brand brand offered and promoted by a manufacturer or producer.

market order order that instructs the investor's broker to obtain the best possible price.

market penetration percentage of the market that has purchased your product.

market segmentation process of dividing a total market into several relatively homogeneous groups.

marketable securities low-risk securities with short maturities.

marketing organizational function and set of processes for creating, communicating, and delivering value to customers and for managing customer relationships in ways that benefit the organization and its stakeholders.

marketing concept companywide consumer orientation to promote long-run success.

marketing mix blending the four elements of marketing strategy—product, distribution, promotion, and pricing—to satisfy chosen customer segments.

marketing research collecting and evaluating information to support marketing decision making.

marketing strategy section of a business plan that presents information describing the market's need for a product and how the business will satisfy it.

marketing Web site Web site whose main purpose is to increase purchases by visitors.

Maslow's hierarchy of needs theory of motivation proposed by Abraham Maslow. According to the theory, people have five levels of needs that they seek to satisfy: physiological, safety, social, esteem, and self-actualization.

mass production system for manufacturing products in large quantities through effective combinations of employees with specialized skills, mechanization, and standardization.

materials requirement planning (MRP) computer-based production planning system that lets a firm ensure that it has all the parts and materials it needs to produce its output at the right time and place and in the right amounts.

matrix structure project management structure that links employees from different parts of the organization to work together on specific projects.

mediation dispute resolution process that uses a third party, called a mediator, to make recommendations for settling labor–management differences.

Medicare public health insurance program for those 65 or older.

merger agreement in which two or more firms combine to form one company.

microeconomics study of small economic units, such as individual consumers, families, and businesses.

microloans small-business loans often used to buy equipment or operate a business.

middle management second tier in the management pyramid that focuses on specific operations within the organizations.

mission statement written explanation of an organization's business intentions and aims.

missionary selling indirect form of selling in which the representative promotes goodwill for a company or provides technical or operational assistance to the customer.

mixed market economy economic system that draws from both types of economies, to different degrees.

monetary policy government actions to increase or decrease the money supply and change banking requirements and interest rates to influence bankers' willingness to make loans.

money market instruments short-term debt securities issued by financial institutions, companies, and governments.

monopolistic competition market structure in which large numbers of buyers and sellers exchange heterogeneous products so each participant has some control over price.

monopoly market situation in which a single seller dominates trade in a good or service for which buyers can find no close substitutes.

morale mental attitude of employees toward their employer and jobs.

motivator factors factors that can produce high levels of motivation when they are present.

multidomestic business strategy developing and marketing products to serve different needs and tastes of separate national markets.

multinational corporation (MNC) firm with significant operations and marketing activities outside its home country.

municipal bonds bonds issued by state and local governments.

mutual fund financial intermediary that pools funds from investors by selling shares of itself and uses the funds to purchase securities.

national debt money owed by government to individuals, businesses, and government agencies

who purchase Treasury bills, Treasury notes, and Treasury bonds sold to cover expenditures.

natural resources all production inputs that are useful in their natural states, including agricultural land, building sites, forests, and mineral deposits.

nearshoring outsourcing production or services to locations near a firm's home base.

negotiable instrument commercial paper that is transferable among individuals and businesses.

net worth the difference between an individual or household's assets and liabilities.

newsgroup noncommercial online forum.

nonpersonal selling consists of advertising, sales promotion, direct marketing, and public relations.

nonprogrammed decision complex and unique problem or opportunity with important consequences for the organization.

nonverbal communication transmission of messages through actions and behaviors.

North American Free Trade Agreement (NAFTA) agreement among the United States, Canada, and Mexico to break down tariffs and trade restrictions.

not-for-profit corporation organization whose goals do not include pursuing a profit.

not-for-profit organizations organization that has primary objectives such as public service rather than returning a profit to its owners.

objectives guideposts by which managers define the organization's desired performance in such areas as new-product development, sales, customer service, growth, environmental and social responsibility, and employee satisfaction.

odd pricing pricing method using uneven amounts, which sometimes appear smaller than they really are to consumers.

offshoring relocation of business processes to lower-cost locations overseas.

oligopoly market structure in which relatively few sellers compete and high start-up costs form barriers to keep out new competitors.

on-demand computing firms essentially rent the software time from application providers and pay only for their usage of the software.

on-the-job training training method that teaches an employee to complete new tasks by performing them under the guidance of an experienced employee.

open book management practice of sharing financial information with employees and teaching them how to understand and use financial statements.

open market operations technique in which the Fed buys or sells government bonds to affect the supply of money and credit.

operational planning detailed standards that guide implementation of tactical plans.

operational support systems information systems designed to produce a variety of information on an organization's activities for both internal and external users.

order processing form of selling, mostly at the wholesale and retail levels, that involves identifying customer needs, pointing them out to customers, and completing orders.

organization structured group of people working together to achieve common goals.

organization chart visual representation of a firm's structure that illustrates job positions and functions.

organization marketing marketing strategy that influences consumers to accept the goals of, receive the services of, or contribute in some way to an organization.

organizing process of blending human and material resources through a formal structure of tasks and authority; arranging work, dividing tasks among employees, and coordinating them to ensure implementation of plans and accomplishment of objectives.

outsourcing using outside vendors to produce goods or fulfill services and functions that were previously handled in-house or in-country.

owners' equity funds contributed by owners plus profits not distributed to owners in the form of cash dividends.

ownership utility orderly transfer of goods and services from the seller to the buyer; also called possession utility.

pacing program company-initiated and financed program to develop new products.

paid time off (PTO) bank of time that employees can use for holidays, vacation, and sick days.

partnership association of two or more persons who operate a business as co-owners by voluntary legal agreement.

patent guarantee to an inventor exclusive rights to an invention for 17 years.

penetration pricing strategy that sets a low price as a major marketing tactic.

performance appraisal evaluation of and feedback on an employee's job performance.

perpetual inventory system that continuously monitors the amount and location of a company's stocks.

person marketing use of efforts designed to attract the attention, interest, and preference of a target market toward a person.

personal financial management study of the economic factors and personal decisions that affect a person's financial well-being.

personal selling the most basic form of promotion: a direct person-to-person promotional presentation to a potential buyer.

PERT (Program Evaluation and Review Technique) chart that seeks to minimize delays by coordinating all aspects of the production process.

phishing high-tech scam that uses authentic looking e-mail or pop-up ads to get unsuspecting victims to reveal personal information.

physical distribution actual movement of products from producer to consumers or business users.

picketing workers marching at a plant entrance to protest some management practice.

place marketing attempt to attract people to a particular area, such as a city, state, or nation.

place utility availability of a product in a location convenient for customers.

planned economy economic system in which government controls determine business ownership, profits, and resource allocation to accomplish government goals rather than those set by individual firms.

planning process of anticipating future events and conditions and determining courses of action for achieving organizational objectives.

podcast audio or video blog.

point-of-purchase (POP) advertising displays or demonstrations that promote products when and where consumers buy them, such as in retail stores.

pollution environmental damage caused by a company's products or operating processes.

pop-up ad Internet ad that pops-up in a new window; interested parties can click on the ad for more information.

positioning form of promotion in which marketers attempt to establish their products in the minds of customers by communicating to buyers meaningful distinctions about the attributes, price, quality, or use of a good or service.

potential sales revenue amount of revenue the business would collect if its market penetration were 100 percent.

preferred stock shares that give owners limited voting rights, and the right to receive dividends or assets before owners of common stock.

premium amount paid by the insured to the insurer to exchange for insurance coverage.

pre-roll video ad a short advertising video clip that begins automatically whenever a user visits a particular Web site.

prestige pricing strategies that establish relatively high prices to develop and maintain an image of quality and exclusiveness.

price exchange value of a good or service.

primary market financial market in which firms and governments issue securities and sell them initially to the general public.

private enterprise system economic system that rewards firms for their ability to identify and serve the needs and demands of customers.

private equity funds investment companies that raise funds from individuals and institutional investors and use the funds to take large stakes in a wide range of public and private companies.

private exchange secure Web site at which a company and its suppliers share all types of data related to e-business, from product design through order delivery.

private placements sale of securities to a small number of investors.

private property most basic freedom under the private enterprise system; the right to own, use, buy, sell, and bequeath land, buildings, machinery, equipment, patents, individual possessions, and various intangible kinds of property.

private (store) brand product that is not linked to the manufacturer, but instead carries the label of a retailer or wholesaler.

privatization conversion of government-owned and operated companies into privately held businesses.

problem-solving team temporary combination of workers who gather to solve a specific problem and then disband.

process control systems operational support system to monitor and control physical processes.

product bundle of physical, service, and symbolic attributes designed to satisfy buyers' wants.

product advertising consists of messages designed to sell a particular good or service.

product liability the responsibility of manufacturers for injuries and damages caused by their products.

product life cycle four basic stages—introduction, growth, maturity, and decline—through which a successful product progresses.

product line group of related products marked by physical similarities or intended for the same market.

product mix the assortment of product lines and individual goods and services that a firm offers to consumers and business users.

product placement form of promotion in which marketers pay fees to have their products showcased in various media, ranging from newspapers and magazines to television and movies.

production use of resources, such as people and machinery, to convert materials into finished goods and services.

production and operations management oversee the production process by managing people and machinery in converting materials and resources into finished goods and services.

production control creates a well-defined set of procedures for coordinating people, materials, and machinery to provide maximum production efficiency.

production planning phase of production control that determines the amount of resources (including raw materials and other components) a firm needs in order to produce a certain output.

productivity relationship between the number of units produced and the number of human and other production inputs necessary to produce them.

product-related segmentation dividing consumer markets into groups based on benefits sought by buyers, usage rates and loyalty levels.

profitability objectives common objectives included in the strategic plans of most firms.

profitability ratios measures of a company's overall financial performance by evaluating its ability to generate revenues in excess of expenses.

profits rewards earned by businesspeople who take the risks involved to offer goods and services to customers.

programmed decision simple, common, and frequently occurring problem for which a solution has already been determined.

promotion function of informing, persuading, and influencing a purchase decision.

promotional mix combination of personal and nonpersonal selling components designed to meet the needs of a firm's target customers and effectively and efficiently communicate its message to them.

property and liability insurance general category of insurance that protects against losses due to a number of perils.

psychographic segmentation dividing consumer markets into groups with similar attitudes, values, and lifestyles.

public accountant accountant who provides accounting services to other organizations.

public insurance agency public agency that provides certain types of insurance coverage.

public ownership organization owned and operated by a unit or agency of government.

public relations organization's communications and relationships with its various public audiences.

publicity nonpersonal stimulation of demand for a good, service, place, idea, event, person, or organization by unpaid placement of information in print or broadcast media.

pulling strategy promoting a product by generating consumer demand for it, primarily through advertising and sales promotion appeals.

pure competition market structure, in which large numbers of buyers and sellers exchange homogeneous products and no single participant has a significant influence on price.

pure risk type of risk where there is only the possibility of loss.

pushing strategy personal selling to market an item to wholesalers and retailers in a company's distribution channels.

quality control measuring output against established quality standards.

quality good or service that is free of deficiencies.

quota limit set on the amounts of particular products that can be imported.

ratio analysis commonly used tool for measuring the financial strength of a firm.

recession cyclical economic contraction that lasts for six months or longer.

recycling reprocessing of used materials for reuse.

regulated monopoly market situation in which local, state, or federal government grants exclusive rights in a certain market to a single firm.

relationship era business era in which firms seek ways to actively nurture customer loyalty by carefully managing every interaction.

relationship management collection of activities that build and maintain ongoing, mutually beneficial ties with customers and other parties.

relationship marketing developing and maintaining long-term, cost-effective exchange relationships with partners.

restrictive monetary policy government actions to reduce the money supply to curb rising prices, overexpansion, and concerns about overly rapid economic growth.

retailer distribution channel members that sell goods and services to individuals for their own use rather than for resale.

risk uncertainty about loss or injury.

risk-return trade-off process of maximizing the wealth of a firm's shareholders by striking the optimal balance between risk and return.

robot reprogrammable machine capable of performing numerous tasks that require manipulation of materials and tools.

routing phase of production control that determines the sequence of work throughout the facility and specifies who will perform each aspect of production at what location.

rule of indemnity requirement that the insured cannot collect more than the amount of the loss and cannot collect for the same loss more than once.

S corporation corporations that do not pay corporate taxes on profits; instead, profits are distributed to shareholders, who pay individual income taxes.

salary pay calculated on a periodic basis, such as weekly or monthly.

sales law law governing the sale of goods or services for money or on credit.

sales promotion consists of forms of promotion such as coupons, product samples, and rebates that support advertising and personal selling.

Sarbanes-Oxley Act federal legislation designed to deter and punish corporate and accounting fraud and corruption and to protect the interests of workers and shareholders through enhanced financial disclosures, criminal penalties on CEOs and CFOs who defraud investors, safeguards for whistle-blowers, and establishment of a new regulatory body for public accounting firms.

scheduling development of timetables that specify how long each operation in the production process takes and when workers should perform it.

search marketing paying search engines, such as Google, a fee to make sure that the company's listing appears toward the top of the search results.

seasonal unemployment joblessness of workers in a seasonal industry.

secondary market collection of financial markets in which previously issued securities are traded among investors.

Secure Sockets Layer (SSL) technology that secures a Web site by encrypting information and providing authentication.

securities financial instruments that represent obligations on the part of the issuers to provide the purchasers with expected stated returns in the funds invested or loaned.

seed capital initial funding needed to launch a new venture.

selective distribution distribution strategy in which a manufacturer selects only a limited number of retailers to distribute its product lines.

self-managed team work team that has the authority to decide how its members complete their daily tasks.

sell-off transaction in which assets are sold by one firm to another.

serial entrepreneur person who starts one business, runs it, and then starts and runs additional businesses in succession.

server the heart of a midrange computer network

set-aside program component of a government contract specifying that certain government contracts (or portions of those contracts) are restricted to small businesses and/or to women- or minority-owned companies.

sexism discrimination against members of either sex, but primarily affecting women.

sexual harassment unwelcome and inappropriate actions of a sexual nature in the workplace.

shopping product item typically purchased only after the buyer has compared competing products in competing stores.

skimming pricing strategy that sets an intentionally high price relative to the prices of competing products.

skunkworks project initiated by a company employee who conceives the idea, convinces top management of its potential, and then recruits human and other resources from within the firm to turn it into a commercial project.

small business independent business with fewer than 500 employees, not dominant in its market.

Small Business Administration (SBA) principal government agency concerned with helping small U.S. firms.

Small Business Investment Company (SBIC) business licensed by the Small Business Administration to provide loans to small businesses.

social audits formal procedure that identifies and evaluates all company activities that relate to social issues such as conservation, employment practices, environmental protection, and philanthropy.

social entrepreneur person who recognizes societal problems and uses business principles to develop innovative solutions.

social responsibility business's consideration of society's well-being and consumer satisfaction, in addition to profits.

socialism economic system characterized by government ownership and operation of major industries such as communications.

software all the programs, routines, and computer languages that control a computer and tell it how to operate.

sole proprietorship business ownership in which there is no legal distinction between the sole proprietor's status as an individual and his or her status as a business owner.

sovereign wealth funds government-owned investment companies

spam popular name for junk e-mail.

span of management number of subordinates a manager can supervise effectively.

specialty advertising promotional items that prominently display a firm's name, logo, or business slogan.

specialty product item that a purchaser is willing to make a special effort to obtain.

speculative (junk) bond a bond with a rating below BB.

speculative risk type of risk where the possibility of gain and loss both exist.

spin-off transaction in which divested assets form a new company.

sponsorship involves providing funds for a sporting or cultural event in exchange for a direct association with the event.

spyware software that secretly gathers user information through the user's Internet connections without his or her knowledge, usually for advertising purposes.

staff manager executive who provides information, advice, or technical assistance to aid line managers; does not have the authority to give orders outside his or her own department or to compel line managers to take action.

stakeholders customers, investors, employees, and public affected by or with an interest in a company.

standard of living necessities, comforts, and luxuries one seeks to obtain or to maintain.

statement of cash flows statement showing the sources and uses of cash during a period of time.

statement of owners' equity record of the change in owners' equity from the end of one fiscal period to the end of the next.

statutory law written law, including state and federal constitutions, legislative enactments, treaties of the federal government, and ordinances of local governments.

stock market (exchanges) market in which shares of stock are bought and sold by investors.

stock options rights to buy a specified amount of company stock at a given price within a given time period.

stockholders owners of a corporation due to their purchase of stock in the corporation.

strategic alliance partnership formed to create a competitive advantage for the businesses involved; in international business, a business strategy in which a company finds a partner in the country where it wants to do business.

strategic planning process of determining the primary objectives of an organization and then acting and allocating resources to achieve those objectives.

strike temporary work stoppage by employees until a dispute is settled or a contract signed.

structural unemployment people who remain unemployed for long periods of time, often with little hope of finding new jobs like their old ones.

subcontracting international agreement that involves hiring local companies to produce, distribute, or sell goods or services in a specific country or geographical region.

subprime mortgage loan made to a borrower with a poor credit rating.

supervisory management first-line management; includes positions such as supervisor, line manager, and group leader; responsible for assigning non-managerial employees to specific jobs and evaluating their performance every day.

supply willingness and ability of sellers to provide goods and services.

supply chain complete sequence of suppliers that contribute to creating a good or service and delivering it to business users and final consumers.

supply curve graph that shows the relationship between different prices and the quantities that sellers will offer for sale, regardless of demand.

sustainable the capacity to endure in ecology.

SWOT analysis SWOT is an acronym for *strengths, weaknesses, opportunities,* and *threats.* By systematically evaluating all four of these factors, a firm can then develop the best strategies for gaining a competitive advantage.

synergy notion that a combined firm is worth more than the two firms are individually.

tactical planning implementing the activities specified by strategic plans.

target market group of people toward whom an organization markets its goods, services, or ideas with a strategy designed to satisfy their specific needs and preferences.

tariff tax imposed on imported goods.

tax assessment by a governmental unit.

team group of people with certain skills who are committed to a common purpose, approach, and set of performance goals.

team cohesiveness extent to which team members feel attracted to the team and motivated to remain part of it.

team diversity variances or differences in ability, experience, personality, or any other factor on a team.

team level average level of ability, experience, personality, or any other factor on a team.

team norm standard of conduct shared by team members that guides their behavior.

technical skills manager's ability to understand and use techniques, knowledge, and tools and equipment of a specific discipline or department.

technology business application of knowledge based on scientific discoveries, inventions, and innovations.

telecommuter home-based employee.

telemarketing personal selling conducted entirely by telephone, which provides a firm's marketers with a high return on their expenditures, an immediate response, and an opportunity for personalized two-way conversation.

tender offer offer made by a firm to the target firm's shareholders specifying a price and the form of payment.

term policy pure type of life insurance policy providing only a death benefit.

test marketing introduction of a new product supported by a complete marketing campaign to a selected city or TV coverage area.

Theory X assumption that employees dislike work and will try to avoid it.

Theory Y assumption that employees enjoy work and seek social, esteem, and self-actualization fulfillment.

Theory Z assumption that employee involvement is key to productivity and quality of work life.

time utility availability of a good or service when customers want to purchase it.

top management managers at the highest level of the management pyramid who devote most of their time to developing long-range plans for their organizations.

tort civil wrong inflicted on another person or the person's property.

trade credit credit extended by suppliers in which the buyer agrees to pay for goods and services received now at a later date.

trade promotion sales promotion geared to marketing intermediaries rather than to final consumers.

trademark brand a legal protection that has been given.

transaction management building and promoting products in the hope that enough customers will buy them to cover costs and earn profits.

transaction processing systems operational support system to record and process data from business transactions.

trends consumer and business tendencies or patterns that firms can exploit to gain market share in an industry.

trial courts federal and state courts of general jurisdiction.

Trojan horse program that claims to do one thing but in reality does something else, usually something malicious.

underwriting process used by an insurance company to determine who, or what, to insure and how much to charge.

unemployment rate percentage of the total workforce actively seeking work but are currently unemployed.

Uniform Commercial Code The basis of U.S. business law; referred to as UCC.

utility power of a good or service to satisfy a want or need.

vendor-managed inventory process in which the producer and the retailer agree that the producer (or the wholesaler) will determine how much of a product a buyer needs and automatically ship new supplies when needed.

venture capital money invested in a business by another business firm or group of individuals in exchange for an ownership share.

venture capitalists business firms or groups of individuals that invest in new and growing firms in exchange for an ownership share.

vertical merger merger that combines firms operating at different levels in the production and marketing process.

virtual private networks (VPNs) secure connections between two points on the Internet.

virtual team group of geographically or organizationally dispersed coworkers who use a combination of telecommunications and information technologies to accomplish an organizational task.

viruses programs that secretly attach themselves to other programs (called *hosts*) and change them or destroy data.

vishing variation on phishing that involves a voice system in which the intended victim receives a voice message directing him or her to reveal personal financial information.

VoIP alternative to traditional telecommunication services provided by companies such as Verizon and AT&T.

volume objectives objects based on pricing decisions on market share, the percentage of a market controlled by a certain company or product.

wage pay based on an hourly rate or the amount of work accomplished.

Web-to-store use of the Web to aid shoppers at brick-and-mortar retailers.

wheel of retailing theory of retailing in which new retailers gain a competitive foothold by offering low prices and limited services and then add services and raise prices, creating opportunities for new low-price competitors.

whistle-blowing employee's disclosure to company officials, government authorities, or the media of illegal, immoral, or unethical practices committed by an organization.

wholesaler distribution channel member that sells primarily to retailers, other wholesalers, or business users.

wide area networks (WANs) tie larger geographical regions together by using telephone lines and microwave and satellite transmission.

WiFi wireless network that connects various devices and allows them to communicate with one another through radio waves.

wiki Web page that can be edited by users.

work team relatively permanent group of employees with complementary skills who perform the day-to-day work of organizations.

World Bank organization established by industrialized nations to lend money to less developed countries.

World Trade Organization (WTO) 153-member international institution that monitors GATT agreements and mediates international trade disputes.

worm small piece of software that exploits a security hole in a network to replicate itself.

Chapter 1

1. Katie Marsal, "Former Apple Product Manager Recounts How Jobs Motivated First iPhone Team," *Apple Insider*, February 3, 2012, www.appleinsider.com; Brian Caulfield, "The Steve Jobs Economy," *Forbes*, November 7, 2011, p. 16; Gianpiero Petriglieri, "How Steve Jobs Reinvented Leadership," *Forbes*, October 10, 2011, www.forbes.com; John Baldoni, "Learning from Steve Jobs: How to Lead with Purpose," *CNN Opinion*, October 14, 2011, www.cnn.com; John Markoff, "Apple's Visionary Redefined Digital Age," *The New York Times*, October 5, 2011, www.nytimes.com; Joe Nocera, "What Makes Steve Jobs Great," *The New York Times*, August 26, 2011, www.nytimes.com; David Pogue, "Steve Jobs Reshaped Industries," *The New York Times*, blog post, August 25, 2011, www.nytimes.com.

2. "Quick Facts About Nonprofits," National Center for Charitable Statistics, http://nccs.urban.org/statistics, accessed February 8, 2012.

3. "Quick Facts About Nonprofits," National Center for Charitable Statistics, http://nccs.urban.org/statistics, accessed February 8, 2012; Foundation Center, Grant Space, http://grantspace.org/, accessed February 8, 2012; Bureau of Labor Statistics, Career Guide to Industries, 2010–11 Edition, http://www.bls.gov/oco/cg/cgs042.htm, accessed February 8, 2012.

4. Organization Web site, http://www.stjude.org, accessed February 8, 2012.

5. "American Red Cross Contributes an Initial $10 Million to Assist Japan's Earthquake and Tsunami Survivors," *American Red Cross*, March 15, 2011, http://www.redcross.org.

6. LiveStrong, http://www.livestrong.org, accessed February 8, 2012.

7. "Amazon Announces Increased Prime Instant Video Selection for Kindle Fire and Prime Customers via Digital Video License Agreement with Viacom," *Yahoo! Finance*, February 8, 2012, http://finance.yahoo.com.

8. "UPS Partners with Red Cross," *Atlanta Business Chronicle*, January 11, 2011, http://www.bizjournals.com.

9. "100 Best Companies to Work For (2012): #1 Google," CNNMoney.com, http://money.cnn.com, accessed February 8, 2012.

10. Max Chafkin, in "Entrepreneurs We Love," *Inc.*, December 2010/January 2011, p. 96.

11. Brad Reed, "Apple Loses Latest Round in Android Patent Fight," *Network World*, January 24, 2012, http://www.networkworld.com; Wayne Rash, "Apple, Microsoft, Oracle Lead Unholy Patent Alliance Against Android," July 11, 2011, http:www.eweek.com.

12. Rick Barrett, "Antitrust Hearing Planned for Verizon–Time Warner Deals," *Milwaukee Journal Sentinel*, February 6, 2012, http://www.jsonline.com.

13. Office of Advocacy, Small Business Administration, "Frequently Asked Questions," http://www.sba.gov/sites/default/files/sbfaq.pdf, accessed February 9, 2012; U.S. Census Bureau, Statistics about Business Size, Employment Size of Firms, Table 2a, Employment Size of Employer and Nonemployer Firms, 2008, http://www.census.gov/econ/smallbus.html, accessed February 9, 2012.

14. Company Web site, http://stockboxgrocers.com/, accessed February 10, 2012; Kevin Roose, "Sheep Lawn Mowers, and Other Go-Getters," *The New York Times*, November 2, 2011.

15. Dan Macsai, "eBay Dials M for Makeover," *Fast Company*, December 2010/January 2011, pp. 42–44.

16. Company Web site, "History," http://www.steinway.com, accessed February 8, 2012.

17. "Best Global Brands 2011," *Interbrand*, http://www.interbrand.com, accessed February 8, 2012.

18. Mark W. Schaefer, "The 10 Best Corporate Blogs in the World," business grow.com, January 5, 2011, http://www.businessesgrow.com.

19. Company Web site, http://www.amazon.com/Careers-Homepage/b?ie=UTF8&node=239364011, accessed February 10, 2012; http://investing.businessweek.com, accessed February 10, 2012; John Grgurich, "Amazon Makes Two Brilliant Business Moves," DailyFinance, February 9, 2012, http://www.dailyfinance.com; Katherine Field Boccaccio, "NRF: Amazon.com Tops in Customer Service," *Chain Store Age*, January 17, 2012, http://www.chainstoreage.com.

20. "King & King Architects LLP Receives High-Performance Energy Efficiency Award from NYSERDA," press release, November 21, 2011, http://www.nyserda.ny.gov, accessed February 10, 2012.

21. Christine Lagoria, in "Entrepreneurs We Love," *Inc.*, December 2010/January 2011, p. 104.

22. Company Web site, http://www.solarcity.com, accessed February 10, 2012.

23. Jacqueline Palank, "Attorney: Solyndra Still Open to Turnkey Bids," *The Wall Street Journal*, January 31, 2012, http://blogs.wsj.com; ABC News Investigation of the Year: The Solyndra Scandal, December 29, 2011, http://abcnews.go.com; Joe Nocera, "The Phony Solyndra Scandal," *The New York Times*, September 23, 2011, http://www.nytimes.com.

24. "Census: More Diversity, Slower Growth in U.S.A. 2050," U.S. Census Bureau Press Release, in *IMDiversity.com*, http://www.imdiversity.com, accessed February 11, 2012.

25. "The 2011 Diversity Inc. Top 50 Companies for Diversity List," *DiversityInc*, n.d., http://www.diversityinc.com, accessed February 11, 2012.

26. Diane Stafford, "EEOC Received Record Job Discrimination Complaints in 2011," *Kansas City Star*, January 25, 2012, http://www.kansascity.com.

27. Company Web site, http://www.nobisengineering.com, accessed February 24, 2012; Matthew J. Mowry, "Celebrating Business Excellence," *Business NH Magazine*, May 2011, p. 54.

28. 2011 Commencement Address at Purdue University by Chesley Sullenberger, May 15, 2011, http://www.sweetspeeches.com, accessed February 19, 2012; Mitch Weiss and Samantha Bomkamp, "Sully Retires: Chelsey Sullenberger, 'Miracle on the Hudson' Pilot, Retiring," *Huffington Post*, March 3, 2010, http://www.huffingtonpost.com.

29. "World's Most Admired Companies 2011," *Fortune*, http://money.cnn.com, accessed February 11, 2012.

Chapter 2

1. PepsiCo Company Web site, "Reducing Malnutrition in Emerging Countries," http://www.pepsico.com, accessed March 6, 2012; Pepsi and Chickpeas: An Interview with Derek Yach," *USAID Frontlines*, November/December 2011, http://www.usaid.gov; "PepsiCo, World Food Programme and USAID Partner to Increase Food Production and Address Malnutrition in Ethiopia," PepsiCo press release, September 21, 2011, http://www.pepsi.com; Stephanie Strom, "PepsiCo to Foster Chickpeas in Ethiopia," *The New York Times*, September 20, 2011, www.nytimes.com.

2. "Home Depot Expands Supply Chain Gains, Tabs Fidelitone," *Journal of Commerce Online,* September 23, 2011, http://www.joc.com.

3. Company Web site, http://www.jnj.com, accessed March 6, 2012; "Recall of Tylenol, Benadryl, Sudafed, Sinutab Issued over Sanitary Problems," *AboutLawsuits.com,* January 17, 2011, http://www.aboutlaws.com.

4. Company Web site, "Sustainability," http://www.walmartstores.com, accessed January 17, 2012.

5. Ethics Resource Center, "NBES Key Findings," http://www.ethics.org, accessed February 3, 2012; Samuel Rubenfeld, "Survey Sees Less Misconduct But More Reporting and Retaliation," *Wall Street Journal,* January 5, 2012, http://blogs.wsj.com.

6. Daniel Franklin, "Just Good Business," *The Economist,* http://www.economist.com, accessed January 17, 2012.

7. Samuel Rubenfeld, "Survey Sees Less Misconduct But More Reporting and Retaliation," *Wall Street Journal,* January 5, 2012, http://blogs.wsj.com.

8. "2011 Breach List," *Identity Theft Resource Center,* accessed January 11, 2012, http://www.idtheftcenter.org.

9. Gina-Marie Cheeseman, "H&M Creates Clothing Line Made Out of Unsold Merchandise," *Triple Pundit,* January 28, 2011, http://www.triplepundit.com.

10. "Zimbabwe Diamond Miner Gets 'Watchdog Approval'," http://www.news.yahoo.com, accessed March 6, 2012; "Kimberley Process: Zimbabwe Diamond Exports Approved," *BBC,* November 2, 2011, http://www.bbc.co.uk; Damon van der Linde, "Blood Diamond Trade Resuming in Zimbabwe?" *International Business Times,* January 12, 2011, http://www.ibtimes.com.

11. Jim Fuller, "Yale Football Coach Tom Williams Resigns Following Rhodes Scholarship Flap," *New Haven Register,* December 21, 2011, http://www.nhregister.com.

12. "Internet Abuse at Work," *Memory Spy,* January 15, 2012, http://memoryspy.com.

13. "Virgin America Is Investigated by FAA & OSHA for 'Cooking Maintenance Log Books'," *PR Log,* January 11, 2011, http://www.prlog.org.

14. Company Web site, http://www.lockheedmartin.com, accessed February 3, 2012.

15. Company Web site, http://www.saiglobal.com, accessed February 3, 2012.

16. Natalie Peace, "How Kindness and Generosity Made by Businesses More Profitable," *Forbes,* March 3, 2012, http://www.forbes.com.

17. "The Mercadien Group Donates Toys for Children in Need to Toys for Tots Foundation," Mercadien Group press release, December 20, 2011, http://www.mercadien.com.

18. Marisa Novello, "Couple's Business Venture Comes Full Circle," *Exeter Newsletter,* January 18, 2011, p. A8.

19. "Many U.S. Kids Still Exposed to Smoke in Cars: Study," February 6, 2012, http://www.reuters.com.

20. Company Web site, http://www.subway.com/, accessed February 3, 2012; Jared Foundation, http://www.jaredfoundation.org, accessed February 3, 2012.

21. "Milwaukee Brewers Ryan Braun Has Positive Drug-Test Ruling Overturned," *RBI Magazine,* February 28, 2012, http://www.rbimagazine.com.

22. Akhila Vijayaraghavan, "Kaiser Permanente Greens Its Supply Chain by Switching to Safer IV Equipment," *Triple Pundit,* January 20, 2012, http://www.triplepundit.com; Simon Pitman, "P&G Declares Its Suppliers Sustainability Supplier Assessment Program a Success," *Cosmetics Design,* April 7, 2011, http://www.cosmeticsdesign.com.

23. Company Web site, http://www.chevrolet.com/volt, accessed March 6, 2012; Jonathan Welsh, "Chevy Volt: Why Isn't It Selling Well?" *The Wall Street Journal,* March 3, 2012, http://blogs.wsj.com.

24. Dana Capiello and Matthew Daly, "Spill Report Rekindles Democratic Push for Reform," *Associated Press,* January 11, 2011, http://news.yahoo.com; "Gulf Oil Spill Findings: Prison Time Unlikely," *CBS News,* January 6, 2011, http://www.cbsnews.com.

25. Institute of Scrap Recycling Industries, http://www.isri.org, accessed March 6, 2012.

26. Company Web site, "E-Cycle," http://www.bestbuy.com, accessed February 4, 2012; "Dell Reconnect Expands Computer Recycling Program to 319 Additional Goodwill Donation Sites," press release, December 14, 2011, http://content.dell.com.

27. "Betting on Green," *The Economist,* March 10, 2011, http://www.economist.com.

28. "Dove® Brand Chocolate Is First Mainstream U.S. Chocolate Brand to Bear Rainforest Alliance™ Certified Seal," press release, August 9, 2011, http://www.mars.com.

29. U.S. Bureau of Labor Statistics, "Table 5. Quartiles and Selected Deciles of Usual Weekly Earnings of Full-Time Wage and Salary Workers by Selected Characteristics, Fourth Quarter 2011 Averages, Not Seasonally Adjusted," http://data.bls.gov, accessed February 4, 2012.

30. Company Web site, "Cheerios Spoonfuls of Stories," http://pages.simonandschuter.com, accessed February 4, 2012.

31. Barbara Frankel, "Is Walmart's Women's Initiative for Real?" *DiversityInc,* September 22, 2011, http://diversityinc.com.

32. Company Web site, "Brand Partnerships," http://www.generalmills.com, accessed February 4, 2012.

33. Company Web site, "FedEx Pledges $1 Million to Support Japan Disaster Relief," press release, March 22, 2011, http://news.van.fedex.com.

34. U.S. Food & Drug Administration, "Nestlé Purina Recalls Limited Number of Dry Cat Food Bags Due to a Potential Health Risk," press release, June 27, 2011, http://www.fda.gov.

35. "PowerBalance Admits Their Wristbands Are a Scam," Gizmodo, February 4, 2012, http://gizmodo.com; "PowerBalance Files for Bankruptcy After Retracting Health Claims," Los Angeles Times, November 22, 2011, http://latimesblogs.com; "PowerBalance Bracelets Lawsuit – Forced to Pay $57 Million, Expected to Close Shop," TMZ, November 21, 2011, http://www.tmz.com; Truman Lewis, "PowerBalance Bracelet Faces More Class Actions," ConsumerAffairs.com, February 7, 2011, http://www.consumeraffairs.com.

36. Company Web site, "Rules and Policies," http://pages.ebay.com, accessed February 4, 2012.

37. Organization Web site, "Teen Workers," http://www.osha.gov, accessed February 4, 2012; organization Web site, "Youth Rules!", http://youthrules.dol.gov, accessed February 4, 2012.

38. "2011 Working Mother 100 Best Companies," *Working Mother,* http://www.workingmother.com, accessed February 4, 2012.

39. Shelley DuBois, "Flexible Vacation Policies Are Here to Stay," http://www.money.cnn.com, accessed March 6, 2012.

40. Organization Web site, "Human Rights Campaign Applauds Introduction of Domestic Partnership Benefits and Obligations Act," press release, November 18, 2011, http://www.hrc.org.

41. EEOC Web site, http://www.eeoc.gov, accessed February 4, 2012.

42. "Recent Case Law Threatens Older Workers' Rights Against Age Discrimination," http://www.wrongfulterminationlaws.com, accessed

March 6, 2012; Warren Richey, "Supreme Court Sets High Bar For Age-Bias Suits," *Christian Science Monitor*, http://www.csmonitor.com, accessed March 6, 2012.

43. "Conference Board Job Satisfaction Survey Finds Older Workers as Dissatisfied as Others," *Aging Workforce News*, http://www.agingworkforcenews.com, accessed March 6, 2012.

44. "Civilian Noninstitutional Population, by Age, Gender, Race, and Ethnicity, 1990, 2000, 2010, and Projected 2020," *Monthly Labor Review*, January 2012, http://www.bls.gov, p. 47.

45. U.S. Equal Employment Opportunity Commission, "Sexual Harassment Charges EEOC & FEPAs Combined: FY 1997-FY 2011," http://www.eeoc.gov, accessed February 4, 2012.

46. David Dayen, "Lilly Ledbetter Did Not Alter Pay Equity Gap Whatsoever," http://news.firedoglake.com, accessed March 6, 2012; Russell Cawyer, "Bill to Add Lilly Ledbetter Act Provisions to Texas Labor Code Enrolled," *Texas Employment Law Update*, January 6, 2011, http://www.texasemploymentlawupdate.com.

47. National Committee on Pay Equity, "Wage Gap Statistically Unchanged," http://www.pay-equity.org, accessed March 7, 2012.

Chapter 3

1. Rebecca Trounson, "Boomerang Babies Don't Mind Return," *Chicago Tribune*, March 20, 2012; Derek Sankey, "Boomer's Adult 'Kids' Affect Life Decisions," *Calgary Herald*, November 20, 2011, www.calgaryherald.com; Joann S. Lublin, "The Toll on Parents When Kids Return Home," *The Wall Street Journal*, November 10, 2011, http://onlinewsj.com; Erica Ho, "Survey: 85% of New College Grads Move Back in with Mom and Dad," *Time*, May 10, 2011, http://newsfeed.time.com; "Adult Children Moving Back Home: Don't Let 'Boomerang Kids' Derail Your Goals," New York Life, December 2, 2010, www.newyorklife.com.

2. "Global Top Sellers," *VGChartz.com*, February 21, 2012, http://www.vgchartz.com.

3. Chloe Albanesius, "Hulu Plus Added to Nintendo Wii," PC Magazine Digital Edition, http://www.pcmag.com, February 16, 2012.

4. Chris Kahn, "Oil Price Climbs on Fear Iran May Stop More Oil," Associated Press, February 21, 2012.

5. Susan Reda, "Predictions 2012: What's in Store for Retail in 2012," *Stores*, http://www.stores.org, accessed February 23, 2012; "Top 100 Retailers," *Stores*, July 2011.

6. "USDA's Florida Orange Crop Estimate Increases," *Orlando Business Journal*, http://www.biz.journals, accessed February 24, 2012; Florida Citrus Mutual, "2011–2012 Florida Citrus Crop Outlook Positive," Growing Produce, http://www.growingproduce.com, accessed February 24, 2012.

7. Benjamin Alexander-Bloch, "Gulf Shrimp Harvest Numbers Are Eagerly Awaited," *Times Picayune*, January 30, 2012, http://www.nola.com; "Vietnam's Shrimp Industry Booming," *Associated Press*, January 4, 2011, http://www.oregonlive.com.

8. Myra P. Saefong, "Gold Drops over $77, Down 1.7% on month," *MarketWatch*, February 29, 2012; Ross Tucker, "Gold Prices Spike on Greek Rescue Plan," The Street, February 21, 2012, http://www.thestreet.com.

9. Ann Cates and Steve Potisk, "Unemployment Eats into the Fast Food Bottom Line," *MarketWatch*, September 27, 2011, http://www.marketwatch.com.

10. Erick Schonfeld, "Microsoft 365 Rolls Out Its Online Productivity Suite," TechCrunch, June 28, 2011, http://techcrunch.com; Doug Henschen, "Microsoft Office 365 vs. Google Apps," Information Week, June 27, 2011, http://www.informationweek.com.

11. David Rosen, "Media Current: End to Cross-Ownership Rules?" http://www.filmmakermagazine.com, accessed February 24, 2012; Brent Lang, "Broadcasters Want Ownership Rules Overturned," Reuters, December 5, 2011, http://www.reuters.com.

12. Air Canada Web site, http://www.aircanada.com, accessed February 22, 2012.

13. *World Factbook*, Central Intelligence Agency, http://www.cia.gov, accessed February 23, 2012.

14. Aaron Smith, "Millionaires on the Rebound," CNNMoney, March 16, 2011, http://money.cnn.com.

15. *Occupational Outlook Handbook 2012–2013 Edition*, U.S. Bureau of Labor Statistics, http://www.bls.gov, accessed February 23, 2012.

16. World Bank Web site, http://web.worldbank.org, accessed February 23, 2012; "World Bank Group Support for Haiti Reconstruction," December 2011, http://siteresources.worldbank.org.; Pascal Fletcher, "World Bank Grants $255 Million for Haiti's Recovery," Reuters, December 1, 2011, http://www.reuters.com.

17. U.S. National Debt Clock, http://www.brillig.com, accessed February 23, 2012.

18. "U.S. and World Population Clocks," U.S. Census Bureau, http://www.census.gov, accessed February 23, 2012.

19. U. S. Consumer Product Safety Commission, "CPSC Regional Product Safety Office, Beijing," http://cpsc.gov, accessed February 23, 2012; Jonathan Carr, "CPSC Opens Office in China," Weil, Gotshal & Manges LLP, January 13, 2011, http://product-liability.weil.com.

20. "Asian Soft Drinks Consumption Continues to Drive Future Closure Demand," Market Publishers, March 29, 2011, http://marketpublishers.com.

Chapter 4

1. Bill Vlasic, "Chrysler Ends Quarter with a $225 Million Profit," February 1, 2012, www.nytimes.com; Larry P. Vellequette, "CEO: We'll Fix Fiat Launch," *Automotive News*, January 16, 2012, www.autonews.com; Dan Neil, "Detroit Show's Soundtrack: America the Beautiful," *The Wall Street Journal*, January 14, 2012, http://online.wsj.com; Brent Snavely, "Marchionne denies Peugeot report, confirms Maserati production for Detroit," *Detroit Free Press*, January 10, 2012, www.freep.com; Bill Vlasic, "A Merger Once Scoffed At Bears Fruit in Detroit," *The New York Times*, January 9, 2012, www.nytimes.com.

2. *World Factbook*, "United States," https://www.cia.gov, accessed February 13, 2012.

3. U.S. Census Bureau, "International Data Base," www.census.gov, accessed February 24, 2012; "You Think! But Do You Know?" World Bank, http://youthink.worldbank.org, accessed February 13, 2012.

4. World Bank, http://data.worldbank.org, accessed February 15, 2012.

5. Company Web site, http://walmartstores.com, "International," accessed February 15, 2012.

6. "Top Ten Countries with Which the U.S. Trades, for the Month of December 2011," http://www.census.gov, accessed February 15, 2012.

7. U.S. Census, "Origin of Movement of U.S. Exports of Goods by State by NAICS-Based Product Code Groupings, Not Seasonally Adjusted, 2010," http://www.census.gov, accessed February 15, 2012.

8. Company Web site, http://www.penzeys.com, accessed February 15, 2012; company Web site, http://www.royalsaffron.com, accessed February 15, 2012;. company Web site, http://www.saffron-spain.com, accessed February 15, 2012; company Web site, http://www.tarvandsaffron.com, accessed February 15, 2012.

9. Company Web site, "IBM Opens Research and Development Laboratory in Australia," press release, October 14, 2011, http://www-03.ibm.com.

10. U.S. Bureau of Economic Analysis, "U.S. International Trade in Goods and Services," press release, February 10, 2012, http://www.bea.gov.

11. David Barboza and Brooks Barnes, "Disney Plans Lavish Park in Shanghai," *New York Times*, http://www.nytimes.com, accessed February 15, 2012.

12. Bank for International Settlements, http://www.bis.org, accessed February 17, 2012.

13. "Sweet Business," *AsiaOne*, http://www.asiaone.com, accessed February 17, 2012.

14. Tanya Mohn, "Going Global, Stateside," *The New York Times*, http://www.nytimes.com, accessed February 17, 2012.

15. "Doing Business in Libya after the 2011 Revolution," *Out-Law.com*, http://www.out-law.com, accessed February 17, 2012.

16. Joe Ayling, "'Made in Italy' Thrives Without EU Label Law," *Just-Style*, http://www.just-style.com, accessed February 17, 2012.

17. Jessica Anne D. Hermosa, "Electronics Boost Seen with Removal of EU Tariffs," *GMA News.TV*, http://www.gmanews.tv, accessed February 17, 2012.

18. "U.S. Sugar Import Program," The U.S. Department of Agriculture Foreign Agricultural Service, http://www.fas.usda.gov, accessed February 17 2012.

19. "Lucky If Doha Talks Concluded by 2014: Khullar," *Economic Times*, http://economictimes.com, accessed February 17, 2012.

20. Pascal Fletcher, "World Bank Grants $255 Million for Haiti's Recovery," *Reuters*, http://www.reuters.com, accessed February 17, 2012; "G7 to Forgive Haiti Foreign Debt," *ABC News*, http://www.abc.net.au, accessed February 17, 2012; press release, "World Bank Statement on Haiti Debt," The World Bank, http://www.worldbank.org, accessed February 17, 2012.

21. *World Factbook*, "North America," https://www.cia.gov, accessed February 18, 2012.

22. Ibid.

23. Ibid.

24. Office of the United States Trade Representative, "CAFTA-DR," http://www.ustr.gov, accessed February 18, 2012.

25. European Union Web site, "Countries," http://europa.eu, accessed February 18, 2012; *World Factbook*, www.cia.gov, accessed February 18, 2012.

26. Company Web site, http://www.dlush.com, accessed February 18, 2012.

27. Company Web site, http://www.zazzle.com, accessed February 18, 2012.

28. Company Web site, http://www.dominosbiz.com, accessed February 18, 2012.

29. Company Web site, Morinaga Co., http://www.morinagamilk.co.jp, accessed February 18, 2012.

30. Kate O'Sullivan, "Best Buys in Offshore Manufacturing," CFO.com, http://www.cfo.com, accessed February 18, 2012.

31. "Polaris Acquires Engine Developer Swissauto," *Motorcycle-USA*, http://www.motorcycle-usa.com, accessed February 18, 2012.

32. Company Web site, "Alcoa Best in Class in Covalence Ethical Reputation Ranking," press release, http://www.alcoa.com, accessed February 18, 2012.

End of Part 1: Launching Your Global Business and Economics Career

1. C. Brett Lockard and Michael Wolf, "Occupational Employment Projections to 2020," *Monthly Labor Review Online*, January 2012, http://www.bls.gov.

2. U.S. Bureau of Labor Statistics, "Economists," *Occupational Outlook Handbook, 2010–2011*, http://www.bls.gov, accessed February 18, 2012.

3. Adapted from Michael R. Czinkota, Ilkka A. Ronkainen, and Michael H. Moffett, "Criteria for Selecting Managers for Overseas Assignments," in International Business, 7th ed. (Mason, OH: SouthWestern, 2005), Table 19.2, p. 634.

4. Organization Web site, "MBA Compensation Heads Up as Recession Wanes, GMAC Survey Finds," press release, http://gmac.mediaroom.com, accessed February 18, 2012.

Chapter 5

1. Jacob Geiger, "Snagajob Keeps Employees Happy with Perks, Relaxed Atmosphere," *Richmond Times-Dispatch*, January 16, 2012, www2.timesdispatch.com; company Web site, www.snagajob.com, accessed January 16, 2012; John Reid Blackwell, "SnagAJob Gets $27 Million Investment," *Richmond Times-Dispatch*, March 10, 2011, www2.timesdispatch.com.

2. "Advocacy Small Business Statistics and Research," U.S. Small Business Administration, http://web.sba.gov/faqs, accessed March 2, 2012.

3. Ibid.

4. "Guide to SBA's Definitions of Small Business," http://archive.sba.gov, "Table of Small Business Size Standards Matched to North American Industry Classification System Codes," http://www.sba.gov, accessed March 2, 2012.

5. Arizona Pro DJs Web site, http://www.azprodjs.com, accessed March 5, 2012; "America's Coolest College Start-ups 2012," http://www.inc.com, accessed March 5, 2012.

6. ModCloth Web site, http://www.modcloth.com, accessed March 2, 2012.

7. U.S. Department of Agriculture, *Agricultural Fact Book*, pp. 12–23, http://www.usda.gov/factbook, accessed March 2, 2012.

8. Cider Hill Farm Web site, http://www.ciderhill.com, accessed March 2, 2012.

9. "Advocacy Small Business Statistics and Research."

10. EBeanstalk Web site, http://www.ebeanstalk.com, accessed March 2, 2012; "Toy Testers to the Rescue," *ABC News*, http://abcnews.com, accessed March 2, 2012.

11. Ned Smith, "Small Business Exports Receive Boon from Jobs Act," BusinessNewsDaily, http://www.businessnewsdaily.com, accessed March 6, 2012; "Advocacy Small Business Statistics and Research."

12. Gwen Moran, "10 Hot Export Markets for Small Businesses," *Entrepreneur*, February 22, 2012, http://www.entrepreneur.com.

13. U.S. Small Business Administration, Frequently Asked Questions, http://archive.sba.gov/advo/stats/sbfaq.pdf, accessed March 2, 2012.

14. *U.S. Small Business Administration*, "Small Business Jobs Act of 2010," http://www.sba.gov, accessed March 2, 2012; David Ferris, "Law Can Have Big Impact on Small Businesses," http://www.workforce.com, January 25, 2012.

15. Facebook Web site, http://www.facebook.com, accessed March 3, 2012.

16. Stephanie Clifford, "Men Step Out of the Recession, Bag on Hip, Bracelet on Wrist," *The New York Times*, February 19, 2012, http://www.nytimes.com.

17. Nina Boccia, "Generation Green," AzureMagazine.com, January/February 2012, pp. 98–99, http://thinkecoinc.com; Katie Fehrenbacher, "ClearEdge Power Lands World's Largest Utility Fuel Cell Deal," GigaOM, January 10, 2012, http://gigaom.com.

18. U.S. Small Business Administration, "Frequently Asked Questions"; BOCNetwork, Facts, http://www.bocnet.org, accessed March 3, 2012.

19. U.S. Small Business Administration, "Frequently Asked Questions."

20. Krispy Kreme Web site, http://www.krispykreme.com, accessed March 3, 2012.

21. Patricia Schaefer, "How to Avoid the Pitfalls of Business Failure," http://www.bizaims.com, accessed March 3, 2012.

22. Ibid.

23. "Advocacy Small Business Statistics and Research."

24. Legends of the Game Cookie Company Web site, http://legendscookies.com/, accessed March 3, 2012; Emily Crisman, "'Legends of the Game' Reflects Interests of Owners, Customers," *Chattanooga Times Free Press*, December 15, 2011, http://community.timesfreepress.com.

25. W. Mark Crain, "The Impact of Regulatory Costs on Small Firms," Office of Advocacy, U.S. Small Business Administration, accessed March 3, 2012, http://archive.sba.gov/advo/research/rs264tot.pdf.

26. U.S. Department of Labor, e-laws, Family and Medical Leave Act Advisor, http://webapps.dol.gov, accessed March 3, 2012.

27. "Business Tax Credits," IRS, http://www.irs.gov/businesses/small, accessed March 3, 2012.

28. TOMS Shoes Web site, http://www.toms.com/our-movement/movement-one-for-one, accessed March 3, 2012.

29. "Top 10 Tips for Writing Your Business Plan," *AllBusiness*, http://www.allbusiness.com, accessed March 3, 2012.

30. U.S. Small Business Administration, What We Do, http://www.sba.gov/about-sba-services/what-we-do, accessed March 3, 2012.

31. U.S. Small Business Administration, Mission Statement, http://www.sba.gov/content/mission-statement, accessed March 3, 2012.

32. U.S. Small Business Administration, Loans and Grants, http://www.sba.gov/category/navigation-structure/loans-grants, accessed March 3, 2012.

33. U.S. Small Business Administration, "2009 Recovery Act: Q&A For Small Business Owners," http://www.sbaonline.sba.gov, accessed March 3, 2012.

34. U.S. Small Business Administration, "Small Business Jobs Act of 2010," http://www.sba.gov, accessed March 3, 2012.

35. U.S. Small Business Administration, Microloan Program, http://www.sba.gov/content/microloan-program, accessed March 3, 2012.

36. U.S. Small Business Administration, Local Resources, http://www.sba.gov/localresources/index.html, accessed March 3, 2012.

37. Thurston County Economic Development Council, "Mission," http://www.thurstonedc.com, accessed March 3, 2012.

38. Ibid.

39. National Business Incubator Association, http://www.nbia.org, accessed March 3, 2012.

40. National Venture Capital Association, http://www.nvca.org, accessed March 5, 2012.

41. "Key Facts About Women-Owned Businesses," Center for Women's Business Research, http://www.womensbusinessresearchcenter.org/research/keyfacts, accessed March 5, 2012.

42. Lexicon Consulting Web site, http://www.LexiconInc.com, accessed March 5, 2012; "The 2010 Inc. 5000: The Top 10 Women Entrepreneurs," http://www.inc.com, accessed March 5, 2012.

43. "Mentor-Protégé Program," Small Business Administration, http://www.sba.gov, accessed March 5, 2012.

44. International Franchise Association, "The Economic Impact of Franchised Businesses," http://www.franchise.org, accessed March 5, 2012.

45. Baskin-Robbins Web site, http://www.baskinrobbins.com, accessed March 5, 2012.

46. SUBWAY Web site, http://www.subway.com, accessed March 5, 2012.

47. Edward N. Levitt, "What's So Great About Franchising?" *Franchise Know How*, http://www.franchiseknowhow.com, accessed March 5, 2012.

48. Ibid.

49. "Franchise 101: Why People Are Drawn to Franchising," http://www.businessfranchiseworld.com, accessed March 5, 2012.

50. Levitt, "What's So Great About Franchising?"

51. "How Much Does a Franchise Cost?" *AllBusiness.com*, http://www.allbusiness.com, accessed March 5, 2012.

52. Levitt, "What's So Great About Franchising?"

53. "Top Franchises By Investment Level," *Franchise Business Review*, 2012 Franchisee Satisfaction Awards, http://topfranchises.franchisebusinessreview.com, accessed March 5, 2012.

54. Janean Chun, "Burger King Franchisees Dismiss Lawsuit over $1 Cheeseburger," http://www.smallbusiness.aol.com, accessed March 5, 2012; Chris Morran, "Judge Dismisses Burger King Franchisee Suit Over Pricing Limits," *The Consumerist*, http://consumerist.com, accessed March 5, 2012.

55. John Schwartz, "Accord Reached Settling Lawsuit over BP Oil Spill," *The New York Times*, March 2, 2012, http://www.nytimes.com.

56. Internal Revenue Service, "IRS Launches Study of S Corporation Reporting Compliance," http://www.irs.gov, accessed March 5, 2012.

57. "The World of Employee Ownership," National Center for Employee Ownership, http://www.nceo.org, accessed March 5, 2012.

58. Michael J. Conway and Stephen J. Baumgartner, "The Family-Owned Business," *Graziadio Business Report*, Pepperdine University, http://gbr.pepperdine.edu, accessed March 5, 2012.

59. Squamscot Beverages Web site, http://www.nhsoda.com, accessed March 5, 2012; Lara Bricker, "Soda Sparkles on West Coast," *Seacoast Sunday*, http://www.seascoastonline.com, accessed March 5, 2012.

60. "About City Year," http://www.cityyear.org, accessed March 5, 2012.

61. "Company Directory by Business Classification," Hoover's, http://www.hoovers.com, accessed March 5, 2012.

62. "Amtrak," Federal Railroad Administration, http://www.fra.dot.gov, accessed March 5, 2012.

63. "Cabot's Cooperative Heritage," Cabot Creamery, http://www.cabotcheese.coop, accessed March 5, 2012.

64. Ibid.

65. Jason Gallagher, "United and Continental to Officially Become United Airlines in March," Yahoo! News, February 21, 2012, http://news.yahoo.com.

66. Elizabeth Woyke, "With Deal Dead, Attention Turns to A&T/T-Mobile Roaming Agreement," Forbes.com, accessed March 5, 2012; Tom Schoenberg, Sara Forden, and Jeff Bliss, "T-Mobile Antitrust Challenge Leaves AT&T with Little Recourse on Takeover," Bloomberg.com, September 1, 2011, http://www.bloomberg.com.

67. Brookes Barnes, "DreamWorks Animation Forms Studio with Chinese Partners," *The New York Times*, February 17, 2012, http://mediadecoder.blogs.nytimes.com; Brent Lang, "DreamWorks Animation Announces China Joint Venture," *The Wrap*, February 17, 2012, http://www.thewrap.com.

68. "About City Year" and "City Year Tumblr," http://www.cityyear.org, accessed March 5, 2012; "Volunteers Repair War Veteran's West Kendall Home in Appreciation for His Service," http://rebuildingtogethermiami.org, accessed March 5, 2012; "Starbucks Service Day: Operation Rebuild for Heroes at Home," http://cityyearmiami.wordpress.com, accessed March 5, 2012.

Chapter 6

1. Company Web site, www.marketingzen.com, accessed January 13, 2012; Matt Vilano, "From Grad Student to Social Media Millionaire," Entrepreneur.com, September 5, 2011, www.emtrepreneur.com; Shama Kabani, "26 Lessons from a 26 Year Old CEO," Forbes.com, July 25, 2011, www.forbes.com.

2. Company Web site, http://investors.walmartstores.com, accessed February 5, 2012.

3. Company Web site, http://www.bobbieweiner.com, accessed February 5, 2012; Michele Meyer, "The Other Makeup Mogul," *More*, January 3, 2011, http://www.more.com.

4. Company Web site, http://www.fortheloveofdog.com, accessed February 5, 2012; David Port, "Earn Your Bones with a Doggie Daycare," *Entrepreneur's StartUps*, March 2010, http://www.entrepreneur.com.

5. Company Web site, http://www.stelladot.com, accessed February 5, 2012; video, *Forbes.com Video Network*, on Stella & Dot Web site, http://home.stelladot.com, accessed February 9, 2012; Tricia Duryee, "Sequoia Bets $37 Million on Stella & Dot, a Next-Gen Mary Kay," *All Things Digital*, January 10, 2011, http://allthinsgd.com.

6. Meg Cadoux Hirshberg, "The Full Story," http://www.stonyfield.com/about-us, accessed February 5, 2012.

7. "Kauffman Index of Entrepreneurial Activity," http://www.kauffman.org, accessed February 5, 2012.

8. Company Web site, http://www.craigtechinc.com, accessed February 5, 2012; "Craig Technologies Names Chief Operating Officer," *Space Coast Business*, January 6, 2012, http://www.spacecoastbusiness.com; Janet Steele Holloway, "Disabled Vet Designs the Perfect Tech Job," *Women Entrepreneur*, February 4, 2010, http://www.womenentrepreneur.com.

9. Company Web site, http://www.snapfitness.com, accessed February 5, 2012; David Port, "Fitness Franchise Flexes Its Muscle," *Entrepreneur's StartUps*, March 2010, http://www.entrepreneur.com.

10. Liana B. Baker, "Electronic Arts Buying PopCap Games for up to $1.3 Billion," *Reuters*, July 13, 2011, http://www.reuters.com; company Web site, "EA to Acquire PopCap Games," press release, July 12, 2011, http://popcap.mediaroom.com; Liz Welch, "John Vechey: PopCap, Making Big Bucks out of Little Games," *Inc.*, October 2010, pp. 101–102.

11. Office of Advocacy, U.S. Small Business Administration, "The Facts About Small Businesses," http://www.sba.gov, accessed February 5, 2012.

12. Hannah Seligson, "Nine Young Chinese Entrepreneurs to Watch," http://www.forbes.com, accessed February 7, 2012.

13. Company Web site, http://www.flylowgear.com, accessed February 7, 2012; Mike Kessler, "The Outdoorsman," in "Dream Companies," *Inc.*, October 2010, pp. 71–72.

14. Organization Web site, "'Jobless Entrepreneurship' Tarnishes Steady Rate of U.S. Startup Activity, Kauffman Study Shows," press release, March 7, 2011, http://www.kauffman.org.

15. Company Web site, http://www.bhatibeads.com, accessed February 7, 2012.

16. Niels Bosma, Sander Wennekers, and José Ernesto Amorós, "2011 Extended Report: Entrepreneurs and Entrepreneurial Employees Across the Globe," *Global Entrepreneurship Monitor*, 2011, p. 20.

17. Organization Web site, Boston Entrepreneurs Take Top Honors in Global Startup Open Competition," press release, November 14, 2011, http://www.unleashingideas.org.

18. "Entrepreneurship and Innovation Group," Northeastern University, http://www.cba.neu.edu, accessed February 7, 2012.

19. Organization Web site, http://www.entreprep.org, accessed February 7, 2012; "Leadership and Career Connections," Students in Free Enterprise, http://www.sife.org, accessed February 7, 2012.

20. Mark Henricks, "Honor Roll," *Entrepreneur*, http://www.entrepreneur.com, accessed March 4, 2012.

21. Max Chafkin, "Ge Wang: For Turning the App into an Art Form," in "Entrepreneurs We Love," *Inc.*, December 2010/January 2011, p. 114.

22. Company Web site, http://4food.com, accessed February 7, 2012.

23. "Kauffman Index of Entrepreneurial Activity."

24. Company Web site, http://www.railtronix.com, accessed February 7, 2012.

25. "From Curbing Racism to Feeding the Homeless: The Philanthropic Journey of Restaurateur Bobby Flam," *The American Entrepreneur*, radio program, April 28, 2011, http://taeradio.com.

26. "Whoops! The 10 Greatest (Accidental) Inventions of All Time," *Popular Science.com*, http://www.popsci.com, accessed February 11, 2012.

27. "A Day in the Life of an Entrepreneur," *Princeton Review*, http://www.princetonreview.com, accessed February 8, 2012.

28. "Oprah Winfrey—About.com Readers' Most Admired Entrepreneur," http://www.entrepreneurs.about.com, accessed March 4, 2012.

29. Company Web site, http://www.nakedpizza.com, accessed February 8, 2012; Christine Champagne, "The Little Shop That Could," *OMMA*, April 29, 2011.

30. Company Web site, http://www.bobbibrown.co.uk, accessed February 8, 2012; Bobbi Brown and Athena Schindelheim, "How I Did It," *Inc.*, http://www.inc.com, accessed March 4, 2012.

31. Company Web site, http://www.lubbersfarm.com, accessed February 8, 2012.

32. Company Web site, http://www.funeralrecording.com, accessed February 8, 2012; "Cool College Start-ups 2010," *Inc.*, http://www.inc.com, accessed February 12, 2012.

33. Company Web site, http://www.mitnicksecurity.com, accessed February 8, 2012; "Kevin Mitnick," *Living Internet*, http://www.livinginternet.com, accessed February 12, 2012.

34. Company Web site, http://www.braunability.com, accessed February 8, 2012; "Braun Corporation," *InsideView*, http://www.insideview.com, accessed February 8, 2012.

35. Company Web site, http://shopdeen.com, accessed February 8, 2012; Robert Tuchman, "The Passion's Only as Good As the Plan," *Entrepreneur*, March 5, 2010, http://www.entrepreneur.com.

36. Company Web site, http://www.ableplanet.com, accessed February 10, 2012.

37. Ibid.

38. Company Web site, http://www.offshoreodysseys.com, accessed February 10, 2012.

39. Darren Dahl, "How to Read a Term Sheet," http://www.inc.com, accessed February 10, 2012.

40. Government Web site, "Immigration Act of 1990 (IMMACT 90)," http://www.labor.state.ny.us, accessed February 10, 2012.

41. Michael Goldman, Inc., http://www.michaelgoldman.com, accessed February 12, 2011.

42. Steve Strauss, "Intrapreneurship: 5 Ways to Get Employees to Be More Entrepreneurial," *OpenForum*, February 22, 2011, http://www.openforum.com.

43. Company Web site, http://www.3m.com, accessed February 10, 2012.

End of Part 2: Launching Your Entrepreneurial Career

1. Small Business Association Web site, http://www.sba.gov, accessed February 11, 2012.

2. U.S. Bureau of Labor Statistics, "Employment Projections: 2010-2020 Summary," press release, February 1, 2012, http://www.bls.gov.

3. Alex Salkever, "The Furniture Company Wanted to Sell Him Its Buildings—and Close Down. Should He Buy the Company, Too?" http://www.inc.com, *accessed February 11, 2012.*

4. U.S. Bureau of Labor Statistics, "Industries with the Fastest Growing and Most Rapidly Declining Wage and Salary Employment," http://data.bls.gov, accessed February 11, 2012.

Chapter 7

1. "100 Best Companies to Work For," *CNNMoney,* accessed February 7, 2012, http://money.cnn.com; FMI Presents Robert B. Wegman Award to Danny Wegman," *Progressive Grocer,* January 30, 2012, http://www.progressivegrocer.com; "Wegmans Again Near Top of 'Best Companies' List," (tweet) January 19, 2012; Samantha Maziarz Christmann, "Wegman's Remains One of the 'Best Places to Work,' Ranking No. 4 on the Fortune List," *Buffalo News,* January 19, 2012, http://www.buffalonews.com; "Wegmans CEO Shares 'Counterintuitive' Advice on Success at University of Rochester Commencement Ceremony," University of Rochester Web site, http:// www.rochester.edu, accessed January 19, 2012.

2. "The Stop and Shop Supermarket Company," *Hoovers.com,* http://www.hoovers.com, accessed March 12, 2012.

3. David Lidsky, "Who's Next: Laura Ipsen," *Fast Company,* http://www.fastcompany.com, accessed March 12, 2012.

4. Jon Swartz, "Amazon.com Tops Customer-Service Rankings," USA Today.com, http://content.usatoday.com, accessed March 12, 2012.

5. Cold Stone Creamery Web site, http://www.coldstonecreamery.com, accessed March 12, 2012.

6. Zappos Web site, http://about.zappos.com, accessed March 12, 2012.

7. Chris Carmon, "Succession Planning Starts Yesterday," *Smart Business,* February 1, 2012, http://www.sbnonline.com.

8. Steve Schaefer, "Buffett Says Berkshire Has Picked Next CEO, Won't Name Names," *Forbes,* February 25, 2012, http://www.forbes.com.

9. Catherine Carlock, "How to Lower Workplace Energy Costs," *The Business Journals,* January 25, 2012, http://www.bizjournals.com.

10. "10 Leadership Tips from Eileen Fisher," *Inc.,* http://www.inc.com, accessed March 12, 2012.

11. Peter Cohan, "PoverUp Kick-Starts Microfinance One $200 Ice Cream Outing at a Time," http://www.forbes.com, accessed March 12, 2012.

12. Eric Markowitz, "Uniting Students in Sustainable Microfinance," *Inc.,* http://www.inc.com, accessed March 12, 2012.

13. Eleanor Bloxham, "How Can We Address Excessive CEO Pay?" *CNNMoney,* http://management.fortune.cnn.com, accessed March 12, 2012.

14. Best Buy Web site, http://www.bestbuy.com, accessed March 12, 2012; Jacquelyn Smith, "The World's Most Ethical Companies," http://www.forbes.com, accessed March 12, 2012.

15. Alexei Oreskovic and Jennifer Saba, "Facebook Looks at China, Zuckerberg Packs Bags," *Reuters,* http://www.reuters.com, accessed March 12, 2012; Mark Lee, "Facebook Says China Is Biggest App Developer Source in Asia," *Bloomberg Businessweek,* March 6, 2012, http://www.businessweek.com.

16. "University of Cincinnati Team Wins $25,000 Grand Prize in Staples Global EcoEasy Challenge," *press release,* http://investor.staples.com, accessed March 12, 2012.

17. Staples Web site, http://www.staples.com, accessed March 12, 2012.

18. James R. Healey, "GM has Crisis Ads Ready if Volt Fire Controversy Worsens," USA Today, January 11, 2012, http://content.usatoday.com.

19. Starbucks Web site, http://www.starbucks.com, accessed March 13, 2012.

20. Ibid.

21. Piperlime Web site, http://piperlime.gap.com, accessed March 13, 2012.

22. Sarah Duxbury, "Gap Brand Closing 34% of U.S. Stores; Piperlime Test Store Coming," *Pacific Business News,* http://www.bizjournals.com, accessed March 13, 2012.

23. "Coolest College Start-ups 2011," *Inc.,* http://www.inc.com, accessed March 13, 2012.

24. Retail Institute, "Key to Success in Retail—Developing the Skills of Frontline Managers," http://www.pharmacy-today.co.nz, accessed March 13, 2012.

25. Peter Cohan, "What Start-Ups Can Teach Big Companies about Service," *Forbes,* February 23, 2012, http://www.forbes.com.

26. Company Web site, http://www.apple.com, accessed March 13, 2012.

27. "CR's 100 Best Corporate Citizens 2011," *CR Magazine,* http://www.thecro.org, accessed March 13, 2012.

28. Shaila Dewan, "McDonald's Says Its Chief Will Retire This Summer," *The New York Times,* March 21, 2012; Beth Kowitt, "Why McDonald's Wins in Any Economy," *Fortune,* September 5, 2011.

29. Scott D. Anthony, "Google's Management Style Grows Up," http://www.businessweek.com, accessed March 13, 2012.

30. Dean Foust, "US Airways: After the Miracle on the Hudson," http://www.businessweek.com, accessed March 13, 2012.

31. "Corporate Information," Google Web site, http://www.google.com/corporate/culture.html, accessed March 13, 2012.

32. Bruce I. Jones, "People Management Lessons from Disney," http://www.trainingindustry.com, accessed March 13, 2012.

33. Ben Fritz, "Activision Quietly Restructures Senior Management and Internal Organization," *Los Angeles Times,* http://latimesblogs.latimes.com, accessed March 13, 2012.

34. Petswelcome.com Web site, http://www.petswelcome.com, accessed March 13, 2012.

35. Procter & Gamble Web site, http://www.pg.com, accessed March 13, 2012.

36. Brandon Gutman, "Zappos' Marketing Chief: 'Customer Service Is the New Marketing!'" *Fast Company,* http://www.fastcompany.com, accessed March 13, 2012.

37. Mike Gordon, Chris Musso, Eric Rebentisch, and Nisheeth Gupta, "The Path to Successful New Products," *McKinsey Quarterly,* http://www.mckinseyquarterly.com, accessed March 13, 2012.

38. Jason Del Rey, "How I Did It: Omniture's Josh James," *Inc.com,* http://www.inc.com, accessed March 13, 2012.

Chapter 8

1. "Disney to Hire 1,000 Vets, Launches PR Campaign," *West Orlando News,* http://westorlandonews.com, accessed March 26, 2012; Company Web site, "Walmart U.S. CEO Bill Simon Calls on Veterans to Help Lead an

'American Renewal,'" http://walmartstores.com, accessed March 26, 2012; Bureau of Labor Statistics, "Employment Situation of Veterans Summary," http://www.bls.gov, accessed March 26, 2012; Halimah Abdullah, "Hiring Our Heroes: McChrystal on Hiring Veterans: We Need to Understand Where Soldiers Come From," *MSNBC*, http://hiringourheroes .today.msnbc.msn.com, accessed March 26, 2012.

2. Heather R. Huhman, "5 Job Skills in Demand 2011," http://www .careerealism.com, accessed February 19, 2012.

3. Mark Kolakowski, "Find a Job Online," *About.com*, http://financecareers .about.com, accessed February 19, 2012; Susan Adams, "How to Make Them Respond When You Apply for a Job Online," *Forbes*, January 24, 2012, http://www.forbes.com; Lauren Weber, "Your Resume vs. Oblivion," *The Wall Street Journal*, January 24, 2012, http://online.wsj.com.

4. Company Web site, http://www.jobsinpods.com, accessed February 19, 2012.

5. Government Web site, "Fact Sheet on Employment Tests and Selection Procedures," http://eeoc.gov, accessed February 19, 2012.

6. "Best Buy Settles Discrimination Lawsuit," *Market Watch*, June 17, 2011, http://articles.marketwatch.com.

7. Faith Alejandro, "Only English in the Workplace?" *Virginia Workplace Law*, January 5, 2012, http://virginiaworkplacelaw.com; Chasity Goddard, "Tennessee Passes English Only Bill," *Knoxville Examiner*, June 3, 2010, http://www.examiner.com.

8. "100 Best Companies to Work For," *CNN Money.com*, February 6, 2012, http://money.cnn.com; company Web site, "Nugget Markets Ranked in FORTUNE Magazine's '100 Best Companies to Work For' List for Seventh Consecutive Year," press release, January 20, 2012, http://www .nuggetmarket.com; "Nugget Market" in "100 Best Companies to Work For," *CNN Money.com*, January 2011, http://money.cnn.com.

9. Company Web site, "McDonald's Puts Apprenticeships on the Menu," http://www.aboutmcdonalds.com, accessed February 19, 2012; Linda Fort, "McDonald's Apprentices Learn While They Earn," *Get Reading*, September 14, 2011, http://www.getreading.co.uk.

10. Company Web site, "Welcome to EYU," http://www.ey.com, accessed February 19, 2012.

11. Company Web site, http://www.glimmerglassgroup.com, accessed February 19, 2012.

12. Company Web site, http://www.rothschild.com, accessed February 19, 2012; Julia Werdigier, "Rothschilds Bring in an Outsider to Run the Show," *The New York Times*, March 29, 2010, http://www.nytimes.com.

13. "Turn Your Performance Review System into One That Works," *Quality Digest Magazine*, http://www.qualitydigest.com, accessed March 4, 2011.

14. Company Web site, http://www.halogensoftware.com, accessed February 19, 2012.

15. "100 Best Companies to Work For," *Fortune*, February 6, 2012, http://money.cnn.com.

16. "S.181 Lilly Ledbetter Fair Pay Act of 2009," *Open Congress*, http://www .opencongress.org, accessed February 19, 2012.

17. Bureau of Labor Statistics, "Employer Costs for Employee Compensation," press release, http://www.bls.gov, accessed February 19, 2012.

18. Company Web site, http://www.qualcomm.com, accessed February 20, 2012; "100 Best Companies to Work For 2012: Best Benefits," *Fortune*, February 6, 2012, http://money.cnn.com.

19. Company Web site, http://www.solipsys.com, accessed February 20, 2012.

20. Steven Greenhouse, "Flex Time Flourishes in Accounting Industry," *The New York Times*, January 7, 2011, http://www.nytimes.com.

21. Company Web site, http://www.concerro.com, accessed February 20, 2012; "Concerro Acquired by Francisco Partners," *SocalTech.com*, February 9, 2012, http://www.socaltech.com.

22. "Employers Offering Better Schedules for Hourly Workers," *Careerbuilder. com*, November 30, 2011, http://msn.careerbuilder.com; Eve Tahmincioglu, "Employer Rethinking Five-Day Workweek," *MSNBC.com*, May 8, 2011, http://www.msnbc.com.

23. Dave Johnson, "Study Shows Significant Benefits for Telework Programs," *CBS News*, November 21, 2011, http://www.cbsnews.com.

24. Organization Web site, "Telework Week 2012," http://teleworkexchange .com, accessed February 20, 2012; Daniel Walsh, "How Telecommuting Lets Workers Mobilize for Sustainability," *Greenbiz.com*, February 17, 2011, http://www.greenbiz.com.

25. Jeff Mariola, "Bridging Generational Workplace Chasms: Setting the Stage for Gen Y Leaders," http://www.jobs.aol.com, February 2, 2012; Lisa Orrell, "5 Tips to Retain Gen Y Talent," *Women Entrepreneur*, April 12, 2010, http://www.womenentrepreneur.com.

26. Ken Eisold, "The American Way of Unemployment," *Psychology Today*, August 8, 2011, http://www.psychologytoday.com.

27. Emily Steel, "MySpace CEO Announces Deal, Layoffs in Memo to Staff," http://www.blogs.wsj.com, accessed February 19, 2012; "MySpace Prepares Downsizing, Layoffs Ahead of Possible Sale," *Fox Business*, January 4, 2011, http://www.foxbusiness.com.

28. Kim Peterson, "Boeing's Billion-Dollar Outsourcing Problem," *Money*, February 18, 2011, http://money.msn.com.

29. "Maslow's Hierarchy of Needs," *Accel-Team.com*, http://www.accel-team. com, accessed February 20, 2012.

30. Jon Talton, "Income Inequality Grows as CEO Pay Climbs Above Historic Levels," *Seattle Times*, June 27, 2011, http://seattletimes.com.

31. Company Web site, "Our Company," http://www.pamperedchef.com, accessed February 20, 2012.

32. Company Web site, http://www.emc.com, accessed February 20, 2012.

33. Bureau of Labor Statistics, "Union Membership (Annual) News Release," January 27, 2012, http://www.bls.gov.

34. Company Web sites: http://www.afscme.org; http://www.seiu.org; http://www.teamster.org; http://www.ufcw.org, accessed March 16, 2012; John C. Henry, "Largest Unions Pay Leaders Well, Give Extensively to Democrats," *Milwaukee Journal Sentinel*, March 3, 2011, http://www .jsonline.com.

35. Bureau of Labor Statistics, "Major Work Stoppages in 2011," press release, February 8, 2012, http://www.bls.gov.

36. Scott Woolley, "Both Sides Could Lose in Verizon Strike," http://www. tech.fortune.cnn.com, accessed March 16, 2012.

37. "BA: United We Stand Campaign," http://www.unitetheunion.org/ba, accessed March 16, 2012; "BA Strike: Airline and Union Agree to End Dispute," *BBC*, May 12, 2011, http://www.bbc.co.uk.

38. Organization Web site, "About the American Postal Workers Union," http://www.apwu.org, accessed February 21, 2012; Bureau of Labor Statistics, "Union Members – 2011," press release, January 27, 2012, http://www.bls.gov.

Chapter 9

1. "Enterprise Rent-a-Car Ranked One of the 'Most Iconic Brands' of 2012," *KMOX News*, March 30, 2012, http://stlouis.cbslocal.com; "New Enterprise Plus Program Rewards Loyal Enterprise Rent-a-Car Customers," press release, http://www.finance.yahoo.com, accessed

March 30, 2012; Company Web site, "Culture of Customer Service," http://www.aboutus.enterprise.com, accessed March 17, 2012; Scott S. Smith, "The Car-Rental Enterprise of CEO Andy Taylor," *Investor's Business Daily,* January 24, 2012, http://news.investors.com; Christine M. Riordan, "Give the Holiday Gift of a Remarkable Customer Experience," *Forbes,* December 21, 2011, www.forbes.com; "Campaign Highlights Customer Service, Employee Empowerment, Family Heritage," *MarketWire,* February 28, 2011, www.marketwire.com.

2. Anderson & Associates Web site, http://www.andassoc.com, accessed March 17, 2012; Su Clauson-Wicker, "Warm Hearth CEO Ferne Moschella: Seeing the Trees & the Forest," *Ampersand 24, no. 1,* http://www.andassoc.com, accessed March 17, 2012.

3. Lebanon Valley Brethren Home, http://www.lvbh.org, accessed March 17, 2012; Becka Livesay, "The Culture Change Way: Empowering Direct Care Workers to Improve Care," *Direct Care Alliance,* http://blog.directcarealliance.org, accessed March 17, 2012.

4. National Center for Employee Ownership, "A Statistical Profile of Employee Ownership," http://www.nceo.org, accessed March 17, 2012.

5. ESOP Association, "Corporate Performance," http://www.esopassociation.org, accessed March 17, 2012.

6. National Center for Employee Ownership, "A Statistical Profile of Employee Ownership," http://www.nceo.org, accessed March 17, 2012.

7. National Center for Employee Ownership, "Employee Ownership as a Retirement Plan," http://www.nceo.org, accessed March 17, 2012.

8. National Center for Employee Ownership, "Employee Stock Options Fact Sheet," http://www.nceo.org, accessed March 17, 2012.

9. Ibid.

10. Toyota Web site, http://www.toyota.com/safety/smart-team, accessed March 17, 2012.

11. "Whole Foods Market's Core Values," Whole Foods Market Web site, http://www.wholefoodsmarket.com, accessed March 17, 2012.

12. Salesforce Web site, http://www.salesforce.com, accessed March 17, 2012; Victoria Barret, "Salesforce.com's Marc Benioff on Why Chatter Matters," Forbes, http://www.forbes.com, accessed March 17, 2012.

13. BBC Web site, http://www.bbc.co.uk, accessed March 17, 2012; Matt Cutler, "BBC Trust Approves London 2012 Olympics Coverage Plans," *Sport Business,* http://www.sportbusiness.com, accessed March 17, 2012.

14. CEO Chef Web site, http://ceochef.com, accessed March 19, 2012.

15. Rockford Public Schools, "Sessions Help Parents Prepare Teens for College and Careers," http://www2.rps205.com, accessed March 19, 2012.

16. Michiel Kruyt, Judy Malan, and Rachel Tuffield, "Three Steps to Building a Better Top Team," Forbes.com, accessed March 19, 2012; Tara Duggan, "Leadership vs. Conflict Resolution," Chron.com, http://smallbusiness.chron.com, accessed March 19, 2012.

17. Mike Ramsey, "U.S. Ends Toyota Probe," *The Wall Street Journal,* http://online.wsj.com, accessed March 19, 2012.

18. Christopher Jensen, "Toyota Recalls Nearly 700,000 Vehicles for Potential Brake Light and Air-Bag Failures," *The New York Times,* http://www.nytimes, March 9, 2012; Associated Press, "Toyota to Pay $16.4 Million for Delay in Reporting Defective Pedals," WITN, http://www.witn.com, accessed March 19, 2012.

19. David Woods, "i-level Redesigns Its Employee Reward Communication Strategy," *HR Magazine,* http://www.humanresourcesmagazine.co.uk, accessed March 19, 2012.

20. Norma Chew, "Are You a Good Listener?" Yahoo! Voices, February 5, 2010, http://voices.yahoo.com, accessed March 19, 2012.

21. "Why Outsource Email?" DakotaPro.biz Web site, http://www.dakotapro.biz, accessed March 19, 2012.

22. "Expand Trust in Your Organization," *Peter Stark.com,* http://www.peterstark.com, accessed March 19, 2012.

23. Susan Adams, "Ten Questions You'd Better Ask Your Boss," *Forbes.com,* January 4, 2011, http://www.forbes.com.

24. John Boe, "How to Read Your Prospect Like a Book!" John Boe International, http://johnboe.com, accessed March 19, 2012.

25. Toni Bowers, "Company Settles Facebook/NLRB Case of Employee Firing," *Tech Republic,* http://techrepublic.com, accessed March 19, 2012; Steven Greenhouse, "Company Accused of Firing over Facebook Post," *The New York Times,* http://www.nytimes.com, accessed March 19, 2012.

26. American Medical Response Web site, http://www.amr.net, accessed March 19, 2012; Bowers, "Company Settles Facebook/NLRB Case of Employee Firing."

27. "Keep Current with Latest AMR News," AMR Web site, http://www.amr.net, accessed March 19, 2012; Mike Ramsey, "U.S. Ends Toyota Probe"; Toni Bowers, "Company Settles Facebook/NLRB Case of Employee Firing."

Chapter 10

1. Esther Andrews, "What's Behind the Products You Love?" Technology@Intel, January 22, 2012, http://blogs.intel.com; Chris Nuttall, "Intel's Chip Plans Bloom in Arizona Desert," *Financial Times,* January 22, 2012, http://www.ft.com; Jon Swartz, "Intel Bets Big on Manufacturing," *USA Today,* March 29, 2011, pp. 1B, 2B.

2. "William Levitt," *Anwers.com,* http://www.answers.com, accessed February 23, 2012.

3. Company Web site, "Operations Facilities," http://corporate.honda.com, accessed February 23, 2012.

4. Company Web site, http://www.shibuidesignsltd.com, accessed February 23, 2012.

5. Company Web site, http://www.chobani.com, accessed February 23, 2012.

6. Organization Web site, http://www.usgbc.org, accessed February 23, 2012.

7. Adam Ryan, "Robots in Disguise," *Supply Chain Digital,* February 14, 2012, http://www.supplychaindigital.com.

8. Company Web site, http://www.ni.com, accessed February 24, 2012.

9. "Shaping Dentistry with CAD/CAM Technology," *Your Dentistry Guide,* March 23, 2011, http://www.yourdentistryguide.com.

10. Event Web site, "World Drug Manufacturing Summit 2012," http://www.wdmsummit.com, accessed February 24, 2012.

11. "On the Open Road to CIM with JDF: An EFI White Paper on Computer Integrated Manufacturing," *Office Product News,* August 8, 2011, http://www.officeproductnews.net.

12. Dave Flessner, "VW Contractor Hiring More Workers in Chattanooga," *Chattanooga Times Free Press,* April 4, 2012, http://www.timesfreepress.com; "Volkswagen Chattanooga Earns LEED Platinum," press release, December 1, 2011, http://www.volkswagengroupamerica.com; Mike Ramsey, "VW Chops Labor Costs in U.S.," *The Wall Street Journal,* May 23, 2011, http://online.wsj.com.

13. Company Web site, http://www.holland-car.com, accessed February 24, 2012.

14. Company Web site, http://www.americanapparel.net, accessed February 24, 2012.

15. Company Web site, http://www.ariba.com, accessed February 24, 2012.

16. Company Web site, http://phx.corporate-ir.net, accessed February 24, 2012; "Roundy's Implements Inventory Management System," *Supermarket News,* January 6, 2010, http://www.supermarketnews.com.

17. "Elkay Manufacturing Company Selects Datalliance VMI for Plumbia Industry Vendor Managed Inventory Program," press release, February 10, 2011, http://www.datalliance.com.

18. Corporate Web site, "Continuous Performance Improvement," http://www.seattlechildrens.org, accessed February 24, 2012; "Seattle Children's Hospital Saves $2.5 Million in First Year with Streamlined Inventory Distribution," *Healthcare Financial Management Association,* http://www.hfma.org, accessed February 24, 2012.

19. Company Web site, "Turtle Wax Ltd.," http://www.solarsoft.com, accessed February 24, 2012.

20. "The Road to the Super Bowl Runs Through Ada, Ohio," press release, January 19, 2012, http://www.wilson.com.

21. Company Web site, http://www.jetcam.com, accessed February 24, 2012.

22. Company Web site, http://www.sleepmaster.co.uk, accessed February 24, 2012; "Success Stories: Sleepmaster, Ltd.," *Usersolutions.com,* http://www.usersolutions.com, accessed March 9, 2011.

23. Linda Doell, "Toxic Waste Nuclear Sludge Candy Recalled Over Lead Levels," *Wallet Pop,* January 14, 2011, http://www.walletpop.com.

24. Organization Web site, "What Is Six Sigma?" http://www.isixsigma.com, accessed February 24, 2012.

25. Organization Web site, http://www.iso.org, accessed February 24, 2012.

Part 3 Launching Your Management Career

1. U.S. Bureau of Labor Statistics, "Employment Projections – 2010-20," press release, February 1, 2012, http://www.bls.gov.

2. U.S. Bureau of Labor Statistics, "Occupational Employment Statistics," *Occupational Outlook Handbook, 2010–2011 edition,* http://www.bls.gov, accessed February 25, 2012.

3. U.S. Bureau of Labor Statistics, "Occupational Employment Statistics," *Occupational Outlook Handbook, 2010–2011 Edition,* http://www.bls.gov, accessed February 25, 2012.

4. U.S. Bureau of Labor Statistics, "Occupational Employment Statistics," *Occupational Outlook Handbook, 2010–2011 Edition,* http://www.bls.gov, accessed February 25, 2012.

5. U.S. Bureau of Labor Statistics, "Occupational Employment Statistics," *Occupational Outlook Handbook, 2010–2011 Edition,* http://www.bls.gov, accessed February 25, 2012.

6. U.S. Bureau of Labor Statistics, "Occupational Employment Statistics," *Occupational Outlook Handbook, 2010–2011 Edition,* http://www.bls.gov, accessed February 25, 2012.

7. U.S. Bureau of Labor Statistics, "Occupational Employment Statistics," *Occupational Outlook Handbook, 2010–2011 edition,* http://www.bls.gov, accessed February 25, 2012.

8. U.S. Bureau of Labor Statistics, "Occupational Employment Statistics," *Occupational Outlook Handbook, 2010–2011 edition,* http://www.bls.gov, accessed February 25, 2012.

9. U.S. Bureau of Labor Statistics, "Occupational Employment Statistics," *Occupational Outlook Handbook, 2010–2011 edition,* http://www.bls.gov, accessed February 25, 2012.

Chapter 11

1. Stephanie Strom, "Walmart to Label Healthy Foods," *The New York Times,* February 7, 2012, http://www.nytimes.com; Jessica Wohl, "Walmart to Label Healthier Food as "Great for You," *Reuters,* February 7, 2012, http://www.reuters.com; Christine Moorman, "What Customers Want," *CMO Survey,* December 20, 2011, www.cmosurvey.com; Geoff Colvin, "Wal-Mart's Makeover," CNNMoney.com, December 19, 2011, http://money.cnn.com.

2. American Marketing Association, "Definition of Marketing," http://www.marketingpower.com, accessed March 21, 2012.

3. Company Web site, http://www.target.com, accessed March 21, 2012; Brad Gilligan, "Target Starts Mobile Coupon Program," *All Tech Considered,* http://www.npr.org, accessed March 21, 2012; Business Wire, "Target Launches First-Ever Scannable Mobile Coupon Program," http://www.businesswire.com, accessed March 21, 2012; Marguerite Reardon, "Attention Shoppers: Target Offers Mobile Coupons," *CNET News,* http://news.cnet.com, accessed March 21, 2012.

4. "Kindle Puts Readers and Friends on Same Page," *Physorg,* http://www.physorg.com, accessed March 21, 2012; KL Tech Muse, "Barnes & Noble Nook Color," *Geek News Central,* http://www.geeknewscentral.com, accessed March 21, 2012; Rachel Metz, "Amazon Releasing Kindle Software for Android," *Physorg,* http://www.physorg.com, accessed March 21, 2012.

5. "Scope of the Sector," *Independent Sector,* http://independentsector.org, accessed March 21, 2012.

6. "Volunteering in the United States, 2011," *Bureau of Labor Statistics,* February 22, 2012, http://www.bls.gov.

7. Live United, "Hometown Huddle," United Way, http://www.unitedway .org, *accessed March 21, 2012.*

8. Company Web site, http://www.avoncompany.com, accessed March 21, 2012; "Avon Foundation for Women and Reese Witherspoon Announce New Domestic Violence Grants on International Women's Day," press release, http://www.multivu.com, accessed March 21, 2012.

9. Karlene Lukovitz, "Oscar Ads: Samsung, Other Tech Brands Ruled," *Marketing Daily,* http://www.mediapost.com, accessed March 21, 2012; Barbara Farfan, "Ellen Commercials Seen by 39 Million Oscar Viewers and One Million Mad Moms—Why Protests Against JC Penney and Ellen DeGeneres Didn't Work," http://retailindustry.about.com, accessed March 21, 2012; "And the Winner for Best Oscar Ad Goes to ... Samsung," http://acemetrix.com, accessed March 21, 2012.

10. Olympics 2016 Web site, http://www.rio2016.org, accessed March 21, 2012.

11. "Tour de Cure 2012," American Diabetes Association, http://tour .diabetes.org, accessed March 21, 2012.

12. "2011 United Way Alternative Spring Break Kicks-Off!" http://liveunited .org, accessed March 21, 2012.

13. Donna Fenn, "Ten College Startups That Want to Change the World," *CBS News,* http://www.cbsnews.com, accessed March 21, 2012.

14. Patrick J. Sauer, "NBA Effectively Utilizes Social Media to Connect with Fans," *Fast Company,* http://www.fastcompany.com, accessed March 21, 2012.

15. Take Care Clinic Web site, http://www.takecarehealth.com, accessed March 21, 2012; "Take Care Clinics at Select Walgreens Offer Families Convenient and Affordable Option for Camp and Sports Physicals," press release, http://news.walgreens.com, accessed March 22, 2012; Pamela Lewis Dolan, "Retail Clinics: Struggling to Find Their Place," *American Medical News,* http://www.ama-assn.org/amednews, accessed March 22, 2012; Sarah Kliff, "Retail Clinics Make Their Pitch," Washington Post,

http://www.washingtonpost.com, accessed March 22, 2012; Donna Fuscaldo, "Health Care in the Express Lane: Retail Clinics Popping Up All Over the Place," *Fox Business,* http://www.foxbusiness.com, accessed March 22, 2012.

16. Marco Lui, "Subway Plans to Open 500 Stores across China in Next Five Years," *Bloomberg,* http://www.bloomberg.com, accessed March 22, 2012; Farah Master, "Subway Eyes Matching McDonalds in China in 10 Years," *Reuters,* http://www.reuters.com, accessed March 22, 2012; Subway Restaurants International Web site, http://world.subway.com, accessed March 22, 2012; Ben Yue, "Subway Eyes Further China Expansion," *China Daily USA,* http://usa.chinadaily.com.cn, accessed March 22, 2012.

17. Blank Label Web site, http://www.blanklabel.com, accessed March 22, 2012; Spreadshirt Web site, http://www.spreadshirt.com, accessed March 22, 2012.

18. comScore, "Smartphones and Tablets Drive Nearly 7 Percent of Total U.S. Digital Traffic," press release, http://www.comscore.com, accessed March 22, 2012.

19. Christopher T. Heun, "Procter & Gamble Readies Online Market-Research Push," *InformationWeek,* http://www.informationweek.com, accessed March 22, 2012; Mark Clothier, "P&G's McDonald Pins Growth on Closer Shave than Mumbai Barber," *BusinessWeek,* http://www.businessweek.com, accessed March 22, 2012.

20. Stephanie Rosenbloom, "In Bid to Sway Sales, Cameras Track Shoppers," *The New York Times,* http://www.nytimes.com, accessed March 22, 2012; Science Nation, "Science of Shopping: Cameras and Software That Track Our Buying Behavior," Mother Nature Network, http://www.mnn.com, accessed March 22, 2012.

21. Clothier, "P&G's McDonald Pins Growth on Closer Shave."

22. Pottery Barn Kids Web site, http://www.potterybarnkids.com, accessed March 22, 2012; Timothy Lorang, "The State of Social Media for Your Small Business," Image Media Partners, http://www.imagemediapartners.com, accessed March 22, 2012.

23. IdeaStorm Web site, http://www.ideastorm.com, accessed March 22, 2012.

24. Declan McCullagh, "Why No One Cares about Privacy Anymore," *CNET News,* March 12, 2010, http://news.cnet.com, accessed March 22, 2012; Leah Betancourt, "How Companies Are Using Your Social Media Data," *Mashable,* http://mashable.com, accessed March 22, 2012; Jim Cooper, "Yahoo's Carol Bartz Touts Data," *Mediaweek,* http://www.mediaweek.com, accessed March 22, 2012; Jared Newman, "Google Buzz Bites the Dust," *PCWorld,* http://www.pcworld.com, accessed March 22, 2012.

25. Company Web site, http://www.playnomics.com, accessed March 22, 2012; PR Newswire, "Playnomics Releases a Free Player Scoring Dashboard for Game Platforms and Publishers," press release, http://www.marketwatch.com, accessed March 22, 2012.

26. Mary Madden and Kathryn Zickuhr, "65% of Online Adults Use Social Networking Sites," Pew Internet Organization Web site, http://pewinternet.org, accessed March 22, 2012.

27. Damon Darlin, "Always Pushing Beyond the Envelope," *The New York Times,* http://www.nytimes.com, accessed March 22, 2012; Brooks Barnes and Brian Stelter, "Netflix Secures Streaming Deal with DreamWorks," *The New York Times,* http://www.nytimes.com, accessed March 22, 2012.

28. Nelson Ireson, "2012 Ford Police Interceptor: Taurus Does Law and Order," *Motor Authority,* http://www.motorauthority.com, accessed March 22, 2012; Brent Snavely, "Ford to Unveil Police Interceptor," *Detroit Free Press,* http://www.managemylife.com, *accessed March 22, 2012;* Chris Woodyard, "Ford Unveils Next-Generation, V-6-Only Taurus Police Car," *USA Today,* http://content.usatoday.com, accessed March 22, 2012; Fran Spielman, "Chicago Police Department to Buy 500 Police Cars from South Side Ford Plant," *Chicago Sun Times,* http://www.suntimes.com, accessed March 22, 2012; Owen Ray, "San Francisco Police: Ford Police Interceptor to Replace Crown Victoria," *Examiner,* http://www.examiner.com, accessed March 22, 2012.

29. Helen Leggatt, "The Surprising Social Shopping Habits of Men," *Biz Report,* http://www.bizreport.com, accessed March 22, 2012.

30. Aileen Lee, "Why Women Rule the Internet," *TechCrunch,* http://techcrunch.com, accessed March 22, 2012.

31. Lee, "Why Women Rule the Internet."

32. U.S. Census Bureau, *2012 Statistical Abstract,* Resident Population Projections by Sex and Age: 2010 to 2050, http://www.census.gov, accessed March 22, 2012.

33. Emily Brandon, "The Recession's Impact on Baby Boomer Retirement," USNews Money, http://money.usnews.com, accessed March 22, 2012.

34. "Nielsen: Shopping Habits by Generation," *Convenience Store News,* http://www.csnews.com, accessed March 23, 2012.

35. "Telemundo Novelas for iPhone," CNET ownload.com, http://download.cnet.com, accessed March 23, 2012; Leila Cobo, "Univision Launches Radio App for iPhone," Billboard.biz, http://www.billboard.biz, accessed March 23, 2012.

36. Emily Maltby, "Immigrant Entrepreneurs Top List," *Wall Street Journal Blogs,* http://blogs.wsj.com, accessed March 23, 2012; Robert W. Fairlie, "Estimating the Contribution of Immigrant Business Owners to the U.S. Economy," Office of Advocacy, U.S. Small Business Administration, http://archive.sba.gov, accessed March 23, 2012.

37. Company Web site, http://www.gmblogs.com, accessed March 23, 2012.

38. "Where Does the Money Go?" *Visual Economics,* http://visualeconomics.creditloan.com, accessed March 23, 2012; Ruth Mantell, "Despite Tough Times, Parents Spend Big on Kids," *MarketWatch,* http://www.marketwatch.com, accessed March 23, 2012.

39. IKEA Web site, "People and the Environment: Forestry and Wood," http://www.ikea.com, accessed March 23, 2012.

40. Company Web site, http://www.sodexousa.com, accessed March 23, 2012; "Sodexo Introduces Food Truck at Assumption College," *Food Service Director,* http://www.foodservicedirector.com, accessed March 23, 2012.

41. "McDonald's February Global Comparable Sales Rise 7.5%," press release, *PRNewswire,* March 8, 2012; Jennifer Booton, "McDonald's July Sales Climb on Popular Beverages," *Fox Business,* http://www.foxbusiness.com, accessed March 8, 2012.

42. Resources for Entrepreneurs staff, "Consumer Habits Could Be Permanently Changed by Recession," *Resources for Entrepreneurs,* http://www.gaebler.com, accessed March 23, 2012.

43. Company Web site, http://www.timberland.com, accessed March 23, 2012.

44. Company Web site, http://www.atlantis.com, accessed March 23, 2012.

45. Company Web site, http://www.apple.com/ipod/nike, accessed March 23, 2012.

46. Company Web site, http://www.netcall.com, accessed March 23, 2012.

Chapter 12

1. Mark Thomton, "Panama Canal Expansion Could Bring Shift in Distribution Patterns," RE Journals.com, http://www.rejournals.com, accessed March 1, 2012; Robert Wright, "Panama Canal Upgrade

Sparks US Ports Battle," *Financial Times,* http://www.ft.com, accessed March 1, 2012; Alex Leff, "Panama Canal Expansion a 'Game Changer,'" TicoTimes.net, http://www.ticotimes.net, accessed March 1, 2012.

2. E. D. Kain, "The Future of Touchscreen Technology," *Forbes,* February 19, 2012, http://www.forbes.com.

3. Associated Press, "Pepsi to Distribute New Line of Tampico Drinks," *msn.com,* http://news.moneycentral.msn.com, accessed March 1, 2012.

4. Company Web site, http://www.loopt.com, accessed February 29, 2012.

5. "Kindle vs. Nook vs. iPad2 Video Comparison," *DeafTechNews,* February 17, 2012, http://www.deaftechnews.com; Kathy Erickson, "Nook or Kindle? New Developments in 2011 Creating a Stir," *Ezine Articles,* January 28, 2011, http://ezinearticles.com; "Barnes & Noble NOOKcolor Wins Last Gadget Standing 2011," *citybizlist,* January 10, 2011, http://nework.citybizlist.com.

6. Pete Putnam, "HDTV Expert—What Do You Do After You Realize LCD's Glory Days Are Gone?" *HDTV Magazine,* http://www.ldtvmagazine.com, accessed March 1, 2012; Alfred Poor, "HDTV Almanac—LED Backlight Prices Falling," *HDTV Magazine,* http://www.hdtvmagazine.com, accessed March 1, 2012.

7. "A Gadget's Life: From Gee-Whiz to Junk," *Washington Post,* http://www.washingtonpost.com, accessed March 1, 2012; "Blu-ray & DVD Player Buying Guide," *Consumer Reports,* February 2012, http://www.consumerreports.org.

8. Company Web site, http://www.chase.com, accessed March 1, 2012.

9. "Twenty-Eight Uses for Everyday Items," *Real Simple,* http://www.realsimple.com, accessed March 1, 2012.

10. "Drive Away Odors and Experience Freshness with Febreze CAR Vent Clips," press release, January 10, 2012, http://news.febreze.com.

11. "New Helmet Blocks Rifle Shots," *Military.com,* http://www.military.com, accessed March 1, 2012.

12. Zacks Equity Research, "EA to Release Amalur's Second DLC," *Yahoo Finance,* http://www.finance.yahoo.com, accessed April 12, 2012; company Web site, http://www.ea.com, accessed March 2, 2012; Ben Gilbert, "Report: EA Planning Premium, Pre-Launch DLC for Retail Games at $10–$15," *Joystiq,* http://www.joystiq.com, accessed March 2, 2012.

13. "Top 10 Worst Beauty Products Ever," *Beauty High,* http://www.beautyhigh.com, accessed March 2, 2012; "Worst Products of CES 2011," *Huffington Post,* http://www.huffingtonpost.com, accessed March 2, 2012.

14. Company Web site, http://www.ikea.com, accessed March 1, 2012.

15. "2011 Power Brands," *Portfolio.com,* http://www.portfolio.com, accessed March 2, 2012; "Survey: FedEx in Top 10 for Brand Awareness," *Memphis Business Journal,* http://memphis.bizjournals.com, accessed March 2, 2012.

16. Company Web site, http://www.quiznos.com, accessed March 2, 2012; "Quiznos Rolls Out Green Packaging," http://www.chainleader.com, accessed March 2, 2012.

17. Government Web site, "Nutrition Labeling Information," http://www.fsis.usda.gov, accessed March 2, 2012.

18. Phil Goldstein, "Google's Nexus One Promises New Distribution Channel for Smartphones," *FierceWireless,* http://www.fiercewireless.com, accessed March 1, 2012; Tom Krazit, "Google's Mobile Hopes Go Beyond Nexus One," *CNET News,* http://new.cnet.com, accessed March 1, 2012; "What Are Unlocked Cell Phones?" *wiseGEEK,* February 22, 2012, http://www.wisegeek.com.

19. Company Web site, "FedEx International," http://www.fedex.com, accessed March 2, 2012.

20. Bureau of Labor Statistics, "Occupational Outlook Handbook, 2012-2013 Edition," http://www.bls.gov, accessed March 29, 2012; U.S. Census

Bureau, "County Business Patterns," http://www.census.gov, accessed March 2, 2012.

21. Company Web site, http://www.acehardware.com, accessed March 2, 2012.

22. U.S. Census Bureau, "Quarterly Retail E-Commerce Sales, 4th Quarter 2011," February 16, 2012, http://www.census.gov.

23. Company Web site, http://saksfifthavenue.com, accessed March 2, 2012.

24. Company Web site, http://www.seventhgeneration.com, accessed March 2, 2012.

25. "Starlight Electronics USA Selects SED International Holdings as Exclusive US Distributor for Polaroid-Branded Imaging and Printing Products," *Enhanced Online News,* http://eon.businesswire.com, accessed March 2, 2012; Company Web site, "Starlight to Expand Digital Entertainment Product Category under the Polaroid Brand," press release, http://www.polaroid.com, accessed March 2, 2012.

26. Company Web site, http://www.traderjoes.com, accessed March 2, 2012.

27. Eric Schwartzberg, "Lifestyle Centers Draw Retailers, Shoppers," *Middletown Journal,* http://www.middletownjournal.com, accessed March 2, 2012.

28. Robert Gembarski, "How Starbucks Built an Engaging Brand on Social Media," *Branding Personality,* February 6, 2012, http://www.brandingpersonality.com; "Happy Third Anniversary My Starbucks Idea," *Ideas in Action Blog,* March 18, 2011, http://blogs.starbucks.com.

29. James Kanter, "Luxury Goods May Pick and Choose Venues for Sales," *The New York Times,* http://www.nytimes.com, accessed March 3, 2012.

30. "Broadway's Serino Coyne and Art Meets Commerce Join Forces," *BroadwayWorld.com,* http://broadwayworld.com, accessed March 3, 2012.

31. Company Web site, http://www.bestbuy.com, accessed March 3, 2012.

32. Company Web site, http://www.premiumoutlets.com, accessed March 3, 2012.

33. Company Web site, http://www.verayo.com, accessed March 3, 2012; company Web site, "METRO GROUP Future Store Initiative," press release, March 24, 2011, http://www.metrogroup.com.

34. Association Web site, "Trucking Statistics," http://www.truckinfo.net, accessed March 3, 2012.

35. Association Web site, "Freight Railroads in United States," http://www.aar.org, accessed March 3, 2012; "Class I Railroad Statistics," November 8, 2011, http://www.aar.org.

Chapter 13

1. Larry Huston, "Generic Atorvastatin Hits the Market," *Forbes,* http://www.forbes.com, accessed March 29, 2012; Matthew Herper, "Why There Will Never Be Another Drug Like Lipitor," *Forbes,* http://www.forbes.com, accessed March 29, 2012; Jonathan D. Rockoff and Timothy W. Martin, "Generic Lipitor Goes on Sale: A User's Guide," *The Wall Street Journal,* November 29, 2011, http://online.wsj.com; Duff Wilson, "Facing Generic Lipitor Rivals, Pfizer Battles to Protect Its Cash Cow," *The New York Times,* November 29, 2011, www.nytimes.com; Heidi Ledford, "Blockbuster Drug Bows Out," *Nature,* November 29, 2011, www.nature.com.

2. Aaron Perlut, "CMOs Must Ask Whether Campaigns Triangulate," Forbes.com, http://www.blogs.forbes.com, accessed March 29, 2012.

3. Rebecca Ruiz, "Ten Misleading Drug Ads," Forbes.com, http://www.forbes.com, accessed March 29, 2012.

4. Sarah Nassauer, "A New Sales Model: Employees," *The Wall Street Journal,* http://onlinewsj.com, accessed March 29, 2012.

5. "Dunkin' Donuts Twitter Promotion Kicks Off Holiday Season," *QSR Web*, http://www.qsrweb.com, accessed March 29, 2012.

6. Nat Ives, "American Idol Returns to Dominance in Product Placement," *AdAge Mediaworks*, http://www.adage.com, accessed March 29, 2012.

7. Ibid.

8. Mark Wyatt, "Guerilla [sic] Marketing Meets Social Media," *Articlesbase*, http://www.articlesbase.com, accessed March 29, 2012.

9. Courtney Boyd Myers, "Check Out This Star Wars Flash Mob in Times Square," The Next Web.com, http://thenextweb.com, accessed March 29, 2012.

10. David Lamoureux, "How Many Marketiong Messages Do We See in a Day?" *Fluid Drive Media*, February 23, 2012, http://www.fluiddrive media.com.

11. Bradley Johnson, "Where's the Growth in Marketing? Follow the BRIC Road," *AdAgeGlobal*, http://adage.com, accessed March 29, 2012; Bradley Johnson, "Top 100 Global Advertisers See World of Opportunity," *AdAgeGlobal*, http://adage.com, accessed March 29, 2012.

12. Johnson, "Top 100 Global Advertisers See World of Opportunity."

13. Avon Foundation for Women Web site, http://www.avonfoundation.org, accessed March 29, 2012.

14. "Foundation Fact Sheet," Bill & Melinda Gates Foundation, http://www.gatesfoundation.org, accessed March 29, 2012.

15. Google Web site, http://www.google.com/tv, accessed March 29, 2012.

16. Ibid.

17. Rachel King, "Nielsen: Number of Homes Subscribing to Cable Decreasing," http://www.zdnet.com, accessed March 29, 2012; Erick Schonfeld, "How People Watch TV Online and Off," TechCrunch, http://techcrunch.com, accessed March 29, 2012; "Web TV Evolution: Insights and Statistics," *Online Marketing Trends*, http://www.onlinemarketing-trends.com, accessed March 29, 2012; Erick Schonfeld, "Estimate: 800,000 U.S. Households Abandoned Their TVs for the Web," *TechCrunch*, http://techcrunch.com, accessed March 29, 2012; John Latchem, "More U.S. Homes Have Game Consoles than Cable Boxes," Home Media Magazine, http://www.homemediamagazine.com, accessed March 29, 2012.

18. Associated Press, "Super Bowl Ads Cost Average of $3.5M," ESPN, February 6, 2012, http://espn.go.com, accessed March 29, 2012; "Most Expensive Television Commercial of All Time," Hole in the Hull, http://www.holeinthehull.com, accessed March 29, 2012.

19. Mike Sachoff, "Local Online Ad Revenue to Top $42 Billion," Web Pro News, http://www.webpronews.com, accessed March 30, 2012.

20. Erica Swallow, "6 New & Innovative Social Media Campaigns to Learn From," *Mashable Business*, http://mashable.com, accessed March 30, 2012; Century Council Web site, http://www.centurycouncil.org, accessed March 30, 2012.

21. Jimm Fox, "Web Video Practices? Salesforce.com Chooses YouTube," *One Market Media*, http://onemarketmedia.com, accessed March 30, 2012; Josh Warner, "The 10 Most Innovative Viral Video Ads of 2011," *Mashable Entertainment*, http://mashable.com, accessed March 30, 2012.

22. BzzAgent Web site, http://www.bzzagent.com, accessed March 30, 2012; Andrew M. Kaikati, "Let's Make a Deal," *The Wall Street Journal*, http://online.wsj.com, accessed March 30, 2012.

23. "Internet Radio—Traditional Radio's Future?" *Bridge Ratings Consumer Update*, http://www.bridgeratings.com, accessed March 30, 2012.

24. "The Future of Radio Advertising?—Google Audio Ads," Benton Group, http://www.savemyadbudget.com, accessed March 30, 2012.

25. Larry Riggs, "Credit Card Mailings Expected to Rebound," *Chief Marketer*, http://chiefmarketer.com, accessed March 30, 2012.

26. "Facts and Figures," *Outdoor Advertising Association of America*, http://www.oaaa.org, accessed March 30, 2012.

27. Clear Channel Outdoor Advertising, "Reach the Mobile Consumer," http://www.clearchanneloutdoor.com, accessed March 30, 2012; Schaller Consulting, *The New York City Taxicab Factbook*, 2006, http://www.schallerconsult.com, accessed March 30, 2012; "Taxi Top Digital Advertising," *Shining Ltd's Advertising Products*, http://shiningltd.blog.com, accessed March 30, 2012.

28. Natalie Zmuda, "Coca-Cola Gets Hands-on with Its Own Digital Billboards," *Advertising Age*, http://adage.com, accessed March 30, 2012; "A Summertime Greeting from Coca-Cola and CardioSmart," CardioSmart, http://www.cardiosmart.org, accessed March 30, 2012; "CBS Outdoor Brings 3D Outdoor Advertising to New York's Grand Central Station," press release, http://www.marketwatch.com; Outdoor Advertising Association of America, "Digital Billboards Today," http://www.oaaa.org, accessed March 30, 2012.

29. "Top NASCAR Team Helps Marketing for Lowes, Pepsi, DuPont and GoDaddy," *Quarterly Retail Review*, http://www.quarterlyretailreview.com, accessed March 30, 2012; Hendrick Motorsports Web site, http://www.hendrickmotorsports.com, accessed March 30, 2012.

30. "Effective Infomercials," *Infomercial DRTV*, http://www.infomercialdrtv.com, accessed March 30, 2012.

31. Edward C. Baig, "Target Puts Mobile Coupons on Customers' Cellphones," *USA Today*, http://www.usatoday.com, accessed March 30, 2012; Phil Wahba, "Coupon Use Up 27 Pct Last Year—Inmar," *Shop Talk*, http://blogs.reuters.com, accessed March 30, 2012.

32. PR Newswire, "Step Up to the Verizon Wireless 4G LTE Nework with Lucid by LG," Sys-Con Media, http://www.sys-con.com, accessed March 31, 2012.

33. Lahle Wolfe, "How Many People Use Facebook?" About.com Women in Business, http://womeninbusiness.about.com, accessed March 31, 2012; Jack Marshall, "Location-Based Mobile Ad Spend to Quadruple by 2015," *ClickZ*, http://www.clickz.com, accessed March 31, 2012.

34. U.S. Department of Labor, Economic News Release, Table 5. Employment by Major Occupational Group, 2010 and Projected 2020, http://www.bls.gov, accessed March 31, 2012.

35. Gary Strauss, "For the Wealthy, a Return to Luxury Spending," *USA Today*, http://www.usatoday.com, accessed March 31, 2012.

36. Matthew Hathaway, "Recession-Weary Consumers Find Haggling Can Cut Costs," *Chicago Tribune*, http://articles.chicagotribune.com, accessed March 31, 2012; Michael S. Rosenwald, "In Tough Economic Times, Shoppers Take Haggling to New Heights," *Washington Post*, http://www.washingtonpost.com, accessed March 31, 2012.

37. Jeanne Whalen, "Drug Makers Replace Reps with Digital Tools," *The Wall Street Journal*, http://online.wsj.com, accessed March 31, 2012.

38. Federal Trade Commission, "Q&A for Telemarketers and Sellers About the Do Not Call Provisions of the FTC's Telemarketing Sales Rule," http://www.business.ftc.gov, accessed March 31, 2012.

39. Barbara Weaver Smith, "Ten Tactics to Drive B2B Sales with Social Media," *Blog World*, http://www.blogworld.com, accessed March 31, 2012.

40. Nat Robinson, "SlideRocket Presentation Tip—4 Ways For Using MultiMedia Strategically," *SlideRocket*, http://www.sliderocket.com, accessed March 31, 2012.

41. Marisa Novello, "Outpouring of Support for Local Merchant," *Seacoastonline.com*, http://www.seacoastonline.com, accessed March 31, 2012.

42. Susan G. Komen Race for the Cure Web site, http://ww5.komen.org, accessed March 31, 2012.

43. Elaine Wong, "Dove Super Bowl Spot Scores Initial Points with Men," *Adweek,* http://www.adweek.com, accessed March 31, 2012; Jack Neff and Rupal Parekh, "Dove Takes Its New Men's Line to the Super Bowl," *Advertising Age,* http://adage.com, accessed March 31, 2012.

44. Elliot Zwiebach, "Family Dollar Plans Consumables Promotions," *Supermarket News,* http://supermarketnews.com, accessed March 31, 2012.

45. Stephanie Clifford, "Even Marked Up, Luxury Goods Fly off Shelves," *The New York Times,* http://www.nytimes.com, accessed March 31, 2012.

46. Richard Esposito, "'Wise Guys' Accused of Scalping $29 Million in Springsteen, Yankees, Miley Cyrus Tickets," *ABC News,* http://abcnews .go.com, accessed March 31, 2012.

47. Alex Mindlin, "Vowel Sounds Influence Consumers' Price Perceptions," The New York Times, http://www.cnbc.com, accessed March 31, 2012.

Part 4: Launching Your Marketing Career

1. U.S. Department of Labor, "Market and Survey Researchers," *Occupational Outlook Handbook, 2012–2013,* Bureau of Labor Statistics, http://www.bls .gov, accessed April 2, 2012.

2. U.S. Department of Labor, "Advertising Sales Agents," *Occupational Outlook Handbook, 2012–2013,* Bureau of Labor Statistics, http://www.bls.gov, accessed April 2, 2012.

3. U.S. Department of Labor, "Occupational Employment and Wages, May 2011: 11-2121 Marketing Managers"; "Public Relations Managers and Specialists," *Occupational Outlook Handbook, 2012–2013,* http://www.bls.gov, accessed April 2, 2012.

4. Ibid.

Chapter 14

1. Company Web site, http://evernote.com, accessed March 9, 2012; Neil McIntosh, "At Le Web, Visions of Not-So-Social Future," TechEurope blog, http://blogs.wsj.com, accessed March 9, 2012; David H. Freedman, "Evernote: Company of the Year," *Inc.,* December 8, 2011, http://www .inc.com; David H. Freedman, "How Evernote, the Company of the Year, Works," *Inc.,* December 7, 2011, http://www.inc.com; Peter Cohan, "The Job Creators: Evernote Asks Why Seven Billion People Don't Yet Use Its Service," *Forbes,* September 26, 2011, http://www.forbes.com; Jennifer Van Grove, "Why Evernote Bet the Company on Mobile and Social Media," Mashable, August 11, 2011, http://mashable.com; Gary Little, "Why Evernote Is Winning with the Soft Stuff," *Forbes,* July 13, 2011, http://www.forbes.com.

2. Martha Heller, "A Modest Proposal," *CFO.com,* http://www3.cfo.com, accessed March 9, 2012.

3. Company Web site, http://www.truecount.com, accessed March 9, 2012.

4. Museum Web site, "Timeline of Computer History," http://www.computer history.org, accessed March 9, 2012.

5. Eric Lai, "How Many Tablets on the Market Today? North of 100," *ZDNet. com,* http://webcache.googleusercontent.com, accessed March 9, 2012.

6. Rob Howard, "How a Platform Makes Innovation Possible," *Telligent Blog,* February 22, 2012, http://telligent.com.

7. Company Web site, http://www.virtual.com, accessed March 9, 2012.

8. Leena Rao, "Google Voice Founder Sets His Sights on VoIP Once Again," *Techcrunch,* March 7, 2012, http://techcrunch.com; Charles Schelle,

"Update: Verizon VoIP Phone Outage Resolved." *SarasotaPatch,* February 25, 2012, http://sarasota.patch.com; Bryan M. Wolfe, "AT&T Offering VoIP International Calls for Anyone with a Smartphone," *Appadvice,* http://appadvice.com, accessed March 9, 2012.

9. Internet Engineering Task Force, "Recommendations for the Remediation of Bots in ISP Networks," January 9, 2012, http://tools.ietf.org.

10. Julianne Pepitone and Leigh Remizowski, "'Massive' Credit Card Data Breach Involves All Major Brands," *CNNMoney,* March 31, 2012, http: money.cnn.com.

11. Kelly Jackson Higgins, "Mobile Malware on the Move, McAfee Report Says," *Dark Reading,* February 21, 2012, http://www.darkreading.com.

12. Brian Krebs, "Who's Behind the World's Largest Spam Botnet?" *Krebs on Security,* February 1, 2012, http://krebsonsecurity.com.

13. Ken Dilanian, "Chinese Nickispy Malware Targets Smartphones," *Sydney Morning Herald,* February 26, 2012, http://www.smh.com.au.

14. Company Web site, "Data Loss Statistics," http://www.bostoncomputing .net, accessed March 10, 2012.

15. Company Web site, "FalconStor Provides Data Migration Technology for Dell Services Offering," press release, March 6, 2012, http://www.falconstor.com.

16. Company Web site, http://www.infosys.com, accessed March 12, 2012.

Part 5: Launching Your Information Technology

1. Kathryn J. Byun and Christopher Frey, "The U.S. Economy in 2020: Recovery in Uncertain Times," *Monthly Labor Review,* January 2012, www.bls .gov.

2. "The Best 25 Jobs of 2012 Rankings," *U.S. News & World Report,* February 27, 2012, http://money.usnews.com.

Chapter 15

1. Company Web site, www.bkd.com, accessed February 17, 2012; Chris Moon, "Giving Back to the Community Part of the Mission at BKD," *Wichita Business Journal,* November 11, 2011, www.bizjournals.com; Michael Cohn, "BKD Acquires Parrish, Moody & Fikes," *Accounting Today,* July 8, 2011, www.accountingtoday.com; Jeff Bounds, "BKD Buys Waco's Parrish, Moody & Fikes," *Dallas Business Journal,* July 8, 2011, www.bizjournals.com; Michael Cohn, "BKD Launches Android App for Health Care Practice," *Accounting Today,* June 22, 2011, www.accountingtoday.com.

2. Bureau of Labor Statistics, *Occupational Outlook Handbook, 2012–2013,* http:// data.bls.gov, accessed April 3, 2012.

3. NACE Research, *Job Outlook 2012,* Fig. 8, National Association of Colleges and Employers, http://www.unco.edu, accessed April 3, 2012.

4. AARP Foundation Tax-Aide Locator, http://www.aarp.org, accessed April 3, 2012.

5. "The 2012 *Accounting Today* Top 100 Firms," http://digital.accountingtoday .com, accessed April 3, 2012.

6. "A New Way to Attract Accounting Talent? E&Y Might Be Onto Something Big," *Accounting WEB,* http://www.accountingweb.com, accessed April 3, 2012.

7. FASB Web site, http://www.fasb.org, accessed April 3, 2012.

8. Johnson & Johnson Annual Report 2011, Consolidated Balance Sheets, http://files.shareholder.com/downloads/JNJ, accessed April 3, 2012.

9. Matt Jagst, "Mobile Computing Takes Accountants to a New Level of Productivity," Accounting WEB, http://www.accountingweb.com, accessed April 3, 2012.

10. John Adams, "Success Story," *US Banker,* http://www.americanbanker.com, accessed April 4, 2012.

11. "Bullish Peso Bets Jump 35% to $5 Billion As Exports Climb: Mexico Credit," *Bloomberg.com,* http://www.bloomberg.com, accessed April 4, 2012.

12. "Despite Uncertainty, Initial Response to SEC's IFRS Announcement Finds Executives Won't Delay Their Own IFRS Planning," *PRNewswire,* http://www.prnewswire.com, accessed April 4, 2012; PwC, "IFRS and US GAAP: Similarities and Differences," PricewaterhouseCoopers, http://www.pwc.com, accessed April 4, 2012.

13. Ernst & Young, "SEC Reaffirms Its Commitment to IFRS," *Hot Topic,* http://www.ey.com, accessed April 4, 2012; Ra'id Marie, "IFRS vs. GAAP—What Does This Have to Do with the Financial Crisis?" Meirc Training and Consulting, http://www.meirc.com, accessed April 4, 2012.

Chapter 16

1. "The Top Five Reasons to Have a Kasasa Banking Account," ListMyFive. com, http://www.listmyfive.com, accessed February 21, 2012; Blake Ellis, "Community Banks Team Up to Fight the Megabanks," *CNN Money,* February 17, 2012, http://money.cnn.com; Jim Bruene, "Is BancVue's Kasasa to Checking What 'Intel Inside' Was to PCs?" *Net Banker,* January 11, 2012, http://www.netbanker.com; Eric Wilkinson, "Americans Urged to 'Break Up' with Big Banks Saturday," King5.com, November 4, 2011, http://www.king5.com.

2. Company Web site, "Gulf Coast Economic Restoration Update, http://www.bpgulfupdate.com, accessed March 16, 2012; Rowena Mason, "A Bloody Nose for Sir William Castell at BP's AGM," *The Telegraph,* http://www.telegraph.co.uk, accessed March 16, 2012; Anya Kamanetz, "Not So Slick," *Fast Company,* http://fastcompany.com, accessed March 16, 2012; Andrew Ross Sorkin, "S&P Cuts BP Ratings, Citing Liabilities and Politics," *The New York Times,* http://dealbook.blogs.nytimes.com, accessed March 16, 2012; "BP Suspends Dividend after Deepwater Horizon Spill," *MarketWatch,* http://www.marketwatch.com, accessed March 16, 2012; Peter Nicholas, "BP Will Create Fund to Pay Claims," *Los Angeles Times,* http://articles.latimes.com, accessed March 16, 2012; Ben Baden, "The Case for (and against) BP Cutting Its Dividend," *U.S. News & World Report,* http://www.usnews.com, accessed March 16, 2012.

3. "EFSF Places €3 Billion Benchmark Bond in Support of Ireland and Portugal," press release, January 5, 2012, http://www.efsf.europa.eu.

4. "The 10 Most Important IPOs to Watch in 2012," *24/7 Wall Street,* January 17, 2012, http://www.dailyfinance.com.

5. "New York Stock Exchange," *Money-Zine,* http://www.money-zine.com, accessed March 16, 2012; "Program Trading Averaged 29.4 Percent of NYSE Volume During Mar. 5-9," press release, March 15, 2012, http://www.nyse.com.

6. Organization Web site, "Rule 300. Trading Licenses," http://rules.nyse.com, accessed March 16, 2012; "Fee Changes Effective January 1, 2012," *Trader Update,* December 30, 2011, http://www.nyse.com.

7. Federal Deposit Insurance Corporation, "Statistics at a Glance," http://www.fdic.gov, accessed March 16, 2012.

8. "Debit Cards—Holders, Number, Transactions, and Volume, 2000 and 2008, and Projections, 2012," U.S. Census Bureau, http://www.census.gov, accessed March 17, 2012.

9. "ABA Survey: Popularity of Online Banking Explodes," American Bankers Association, press release, September 8, 2011, http://www.aba.com.

10. Federal Deposit Insurance Corporation, "Quarterly Banking Profile: Table III-B. Full-Year 2011, FDIC-Insured Savings Institutions," http://www2.fdic.gov, accessed March 17, 2012.

11. Federal Deposit Insurance Corporation, "Quarterly Banking Profile: Table II-B. Aggregate Condition and Income Data, FDIC-Insured Savings Institutions," http://www2.fdic.gov, accessed March 17, 2012.

12. "Matz: 'Credit Unions Ended 2011 in a Safer Position,'" National Credit Union Administration, press release, March 1, 2012, http://www.ncua.gov; Stephen Grocer, "Ranking the 50 Biggest U.S. Banks: From BofA to Commerce Bancshares," *The Wall Street Journal,* http://blogs.wsj.com, accessed March 16, 2012.

13. Board of Governors of the Federal Reserve System, "Federal Reserve Statistical Release, Z.1, Flow of Funds Accounts of the United States," http://www.federalreserve.gov, accessed March 8, 2012

14. Organization Web site, "Assets of Private Pension Funds by Type of Asset, 2008-2010," Insurance Information Institute, http://www.iii.org, accessed March 18, 2012.

15. *2011 Investment Company Fact Book,* "Table 1 Total Net Assets, Number of Funds, Number of Share Classes, and Number of Shareholder Accounts of the U.S. Mutual Fund Industry," p. 128, http://www.icifactbook.org; Investment Company Institute, "Trends in Mutual Fund Investing January 2012," press release, February 28, 2012, http://www.ici.org.

16. Investment Company Institute, "Trends in Mutual Fund Investing January 2012."

17. "Top Banks in the World," *Bankers Almanac,* February 14, 2012, http://www.bankersalmanac.com.

Chapter 17

1. Pui-Wang Tam, "Andreessen's Firm Raises $1.5 Billion," *The Wall Street Journal,* February 1, 2012, http://online.wsj.com; Ben Horowitz, "Why Has Andreessen Horowitz Raised $2.7B in 3 Years?", Ben's Blog, January 31, 2012, http://bhorowitz.com; Peter Delevett, "Andreessen Horowitz Raises $1.5 Billion Venture Fund, One of Industry's Largest in Years," Mercury News.com, January 31, 2012, http://www.mercurynews.com; Tomio Geron, "Andreesse Horowitz Closes $1.5 Billion Third Fund," *Forbes,* January 31, 2012, http://www.forbes.com; Ari Levy, "Venture Funding Rises 10% in 2011 as Consumer Web Attracts Cash," *Bloomberg Businessweek,* January 20, 2012, http://www.businessweek.com.

2. "2011 CFO Pay Strategies Report for S&P 600 Companies," *Equilar,* http://www.equilar.com, accessed April 6, 2012.

3. Ibid.

4. "Orders and Deliveries," Airbus Web site, http://www.airbus.com, accessed April 5, 2012.

5. Genco Marketplace Web site, https://www.gencomarketplace.com, accessed April 6, 2012.

6. Horatiu Boerlu, "BMW Super Bowl Ad Shot Around Spartanburg," BMW Blog, http://www.bmwblog.com, accessed April 6, 2012.

7. "BMW Manufacturing Reaches Another Milestone," press release, BMW Factory Web site, http://www.bmwusfactory.com, accessed April 6, 2012.

8. Federal Reserve Bank of St. Louis, Series: AEXUSUK, U.S./U.K. Foreign Exchange Rate, http://research.stlouisfed.org, accessed April 6, 2012.

9. Federal Reserve Board, "Commercial Paper," Federal Reserve release, http://federalreserve.gov, accessed April 5, 2012.

10. Jeffrey A. Trachtenberg, "Barnes & Noble Profit Slides," *The Wall Street Journal,* http://online.wsj.com, accessed April 9, 2012.

11. Federal Reserve Board, Commercial Paper Outstanding, Federal Reserve Release, http://federalreserve.gov, accessed April 9, 2012.

12. Sridhar Natarajan, "Bond Sales Top $1 Trillion on Record-Low Yields," Bloomberg.com, http://www.bloomberg.com, accessed April 9, 2012; Sridhar Natarajan, "U.S. Corporate Bond Sales Hit Record $427 Billion This Quarter," *Bloomberg Businessweek*, http://www.businessweek.com, accessed April 9, 2012.

13. Board of Governors of the Federal Reserve System, "Federal Reserve Statistical Release Z.1, Flow of Funds Accounts of the United States: Flows and Outstandings, Fourth Quarter 2011," http://www.federalreserve.gov, accessed April 9, 2012.

14. DFJ Web site, Portfolio, http://www.dfj.com, accessed April 9, 2012.

15. "UPDATE 1—AT&T to Sell Yellow Pages Stake to Cerberus," *Reuters*, http://www.reuters.com, accessed April 9, 2012.

16. "Saudi Alwaleed Backs Citigroup Reverse Stock Split," *Reuters*, http://www.reuters.com, accessed April 9, 2012.

17. Hibah Yousuf, "Hedge Funds Suffer Worst Quarter since 2008," CNNMoney, http://money.cnn.com, accessed April 9, 2012; Svea Herbst and Katya Wachtel, "The Great Hedge Fund Humbling of 2011," Reuters, http://www.reuters.com, accessed April 9, 2012.

18. Herbst and Wachtel, "The Great Hedge Fund Humbling of 2011."

19. "2011 Mergers & Acquisitions Outlook and 2010 Summary," *The Investment Blog*, http://investmentblog.wordpress.com, accessed April 9, 2011; Ashlee Vance, "With McAfee Deal, Intel Looks for Edge," *The New York Times*, http://www.nytimes.com, accessed April 9, 2011.

20. Christine Idzelis, "LBO Loan Costs Soar to Highest of 2011 on Crisis: Credit Markets," PBN.com, http://www.pbn.com, accessed April 10, 2012; Kate Mackenzie, "Buy-Out Bond Deals at Europe High," *Financial Times*, http://ftalphaville.ft.com, accessed April 10, 2012.

Part 6 Launching Your Finance Career

1. U.S. Department of Labor, "Projections Overview," *Occupational Outlook Handbook, 2012–2013*, Bureau of Labor Statistics, http://www.bls.gov, accessed April 10, 2012.

2. Andrea Koncz, "Class of 2011: Top Pay for Finance Grads in Financial Manager Positions," National Association of Colleges and Employers, http://www.naceweb.org, accessed April 10, 2012.

3. U.S. Department of Labor, "Financial Managers," *Occupational Outlook Handbook, 2012–2013*, Bureau of Labor Statistics, http://www.bls.gov, accessed April 10, 2012.

Chapter 18

1. "Was Acquiring OMGPOP a Smart Move for Zynga?" *Forbes*, April 5, 2012, http://www.forbes.com; "Zynga," Business Insider.com, www.businessinsider.com, accessed February 28, 2012; Douglas MacMillan and Adam Satariano, "Zynga Said to Plan Game Promotions to Curb Facebook Reliance," *Bloomberg Businessweek*, February 27, 2012, www.businessweek.com; Pascal-Emmanuel Gobry, "The Social Gaming Market Will Explode to $5+ Billion by 2015," Business Insider.com, February 21, 2012, www.businessinsider.com; Peter Paschal, "Zynga: We Want to Teach the World to Play," *Mashable*, February 14, 2012, http://mashable.com; "Flat Growth, Booming Revenue: 11 Facts from the Zynga IPO Filing," *Mashable*, July 1, 2011, http://mashable.com.

2. "World Internet Usage and Population Statistics," *Internet World Stats*, http://www.internetworldstats.com, accessed February 27, 2012.

3. U.S. Census Bureau, "E-Stats," http://www.census.gov, accessed March 21, 2012.

4. Allison Enright, "E-commerce Sales Jump 16% in 2011," *Internet Retailer*, February 2012, http://www.internetretailer.com.

5. Sam Gustin, "Will Google's Insanely-Fast Kansas City Network Shame U.S. ISPs?" *Time*, February 7, 2012, http://business.time.com; Bob Biddlebock, "Cities Rush into High Speed Internet," *Time*, June 17, 2011, http://www.time.com.

6. Company Web site, http://www.kasasa.com, accessed March 21, 2012.

7. Company Web site, http://www262.americanexpress.com, accessed March 21, 2012; organization Web site, http://www.teachforamerica.org, accessed March 21, 2012.

8. Company Web site, http://www.vrbo.com, accessed March 21, 2012.

9. Company Web site, http://www.udemy.com, accessed March 21, 2012.

10. Company Web site, http://www.qvc.com, accessed March 21, 2012.

11. Company Web site, http://quickbooksonline.intuit.com, accessed March 21, 2012.

12. David Moth, "IAB Study Reveals 44% of Those Surveyed Use Mobile to Respond to TV Ads," *Econsultancy*, January 31, 2012, http://econsultancy.com.

13. Susan J. Aluise, "Brick-and-Mortar Retailers Should Read the Writing on the Wall," *Investor Place*, December 9, 2011, http://www.investorplace.com.

14. Company Web site, http://www.cannondale.com, accessed March 21, 2012.

15. Company Web site, http://www.overstock.com, accessed March 21, 2012.

16. U.S. Census Bureau, "E-Stats," http://www.census.gov, accessed March 21, 2012.

17. Company Web site, http://www.aetna.com, accessed March 23, 2012.

18. "CBOE Holdings' SPXpm to Launch on C2 on October 4," press release, September 13, 2011, http://ir.cboe.com.

19. Aluise, Brick-and-Mortar Retailers Should Read the Writing on the Wall."

20. Michael Wolf, "Why 2012 Will Be Year of the Artist-Entrepreneur," *GigaOM*, December 29, 2011, http://gigaom.com.

21. "Report: Broadband Access Up Slightly in U.S. Homes," *Government Technology*, November 9, 2011, http://www.govtech.com; Cecilia Kang, "Internet Service Map Data Show No Broadband Access for up to 10% in U.S.," *Washington Post*, February 17, 2011, http://voices.washingtonpost.com.

22. "Media Usage and Shopping Habits of Teens," *eMarketer*, http://www.emarketer.com, accessed March 21, 2012.

23. "Broadband Online Shopping Continues to Grow," *WildBruce Satellite Internet*, http://www.mybluedish.com, accessed March 25, 2012.

24. "Usage of Arabic for Websites," *W3Techs*, http://w3techs.com, accessed March 25, 2012.

25. Company Web site, http://www.symantec.com, accessed March 25, 2012.

26. Company Web site, http://www.paypal.com, accessed March 25, 2012.

27. "Global Payments Data Breach Exposes Card Payments to Vulnerability," *Forbes*, April 3, 2012, http://www.forbes.com.

28. Company Web site, http://www.oracle.com, accessed March 26, 2012.

29. Ric Romero, "Craigslist Illegal Drug Trade Exposed," *ABC7.com*, http://abclocal.go.com, accessed March 26, 2012.

30. Organization Web site, http://www.ic3.gov, accessed March 26, 2012.

31. "Online Music Hub Vevo Eyes New Ad Deal with YouTube (Report)," *Hollywood Reporter,* http://www.hollywoodreporter.com, accessed March 26, 2012.

32. Company Web site, "About Google Instant," http://www.google.com, accessed March 26, 2012.

33. Matt McGee, "Bing, Yahoo Now Neck and Neck in U.S. Search Market Share," Search Engineland, http://searchengineland.com, accessed March 26, 2012.

34. Eric Eldon, "Facebook Started Saturating the U.S. Market in 2011," *Tech Crunch,* December 29, 2011, http://techcrunch.com.

35. "Top 15 Most Popular Social Networking Sites – March 2012," *Ebizmba. com,* March 20, 2012, http://www.ebizmba.com.

36. "Mobile Passes Print in Time Spent Among U.S. Adults," *eMartketer,* press release, December 12, 2011, http://www.emarketer.com; Sarah Kessler, "Americans Spend 23% of Internet Time on Social Networks," *Mashable,* September 12, 2011, http://mashable.com; Mary Madden and Kathryn Zickuhr, "65% of Online Adults Use Social Networking Sites," *Pew Internet,* August 26, 2011, http://pewinternet.org.

37. Company Web site, http://press.linkedin.com, accessed March 26, 2012.

38. "Internet Usage Statistics," *Internet World Stats,* http://www.internetworldstats .com, accessed March 26, 2012.

39. "Internet World Users by Language," *Internet World Stats,* http://www .internetworldstats.com, accessed March 26, 2012.

40. "Web Do's & Don'ts," *Web Do's & Don'ts,* http://webdosanddonts.com, accessed March 26, 2012.

41. Company Web site, http://www.stopandshop.com, accessed March 26, 2012.

42. Company Web site, "Cross-Platform Measurement," http://www.nielsen. com, accessed March 26, 2012.

43. "Friday Night at the Movies – March 23, 2012," *The Digital Americana Blog,* http://thedigitalamericana.com, accessed March 26, 2012.

44. Roger Yu, "Consumers Ignore Most Apps on Their Smartphones," *USA Today,* January 30, 2012, http://www.usatoday.com.

45. "Next New Networks," *CrunchBase,* http://www.crunchbase.com, accessed March 27, 2012; Danny Goodwin, "YouTube Buys Video Producer Next New Networks," *Search Engine Watch,* http://searchenginewatch.com, accessed March 26, 2012.

Appendix A

1. Jessica Stillman, "7 Ways to Bulletproof Your Business," *Inc.,* February 23, 2012, http://www.inc.com; company press release, "Rocket Lawyer™ Survey Reveals Top Issues for Small Business Are Legal and Financial," February 1, 2012, http://www.rocketlawyer.com; Jonathan Blum, "Rocket Lawyer: Cutting Out Small Business Attorneys' Fees," *Entrepreneur,* http://www.entrepreneur.com, accessed February 1, 2012; company press release, "New NFIB Partnership with Rocket Lawyer™ to Provide Legal Resources for Small Businesses," http://www.rocketlawyer.com, accessed February 1, 2012.

2. National Federation of Independent Business, "Frivolous Lawsuits," http://www.nfib.com, accessed April 12, 2012.

3. "All States Have Silly Laws, http://foodstamp.aphsa.org/01wkshps/ AllStatesHaveSillyLaws.pdf, accessed April 12, 2012.

4. United States Court of Appeals for the Fourth Circuit, http://www.ca4 .uscourts.gov, accessed April 12, 2012.

5. "The Justices' Caseload," Supreme Court of the United States, http://www.supremecourt.gov, accessed April 12, 2012.

6. Keith Bradsher, "Trade Issues with China Flare Anew," *The New York Times,* http://www.nytimes.com, accessed April 12, 2012; Stephanie Ginter, "WTO Lawsuit over China's Rare Earth," *Energy & Capital,* http://www .energyandcapital.com, accessed April 12, 2012.

7. U.S. Senate Committee on Banking, House, and Urban Affairs, "Brief Summary of the Dodd-Frank Wall Street Reform and Consumer Protection Act," http://www.banking.senate.gov, accessed April 12, 2012; Beverly Blair Harzog, "New Credit Card Rules' Double Standard," *CNN U.S.,* http://articles.cnn.com, accessed April 12, 2012.

8. Charlie Savage, "Deal Reached on Extension of Patriot Act," *The New York Times,* http://www.nytimes.com, accessed April 12, 2012; Gail Russell Chaddock, "Patriot Act: Three Controversial Provisions That Congress Voted to Keep," *Christian Science Monitor,* http://www.csmonitor.com, accessed April 12, 2012.

9. Rob Pegoraro, "Court Cuts FCC's Net-Neutrality Power; Now What?" *Washington Post,* http://voices.washingtonpost.com, accessed April 12, 2012.

10. U.S. Senate Committee on Banking, House, and Urban Affairs, "Brief Summary of the Dodd-Frank Wall Street Reform and Consumer Protection Act."

11. "Food and Drug Administration Amendments Act (FDAAA) of 2007," U.S. Food and Drug Administration, http://www.fda.gov, accessed April 12, 2012.

12. U.S. Equal Employment Opportunity Commission, "Notice Concerning the Lilly Ledbetter Fair Pay Act of 2009," http://www.eeoc.gov/laws/ statutes, accessed April 12, 2012.

13. Miguel Helft, "Judge Sides With Google in Viacom Video Suit," *The New York Times,* http://www.nytimes.com, accessed April 12, 2012.

14. Kelly Kunsch, "Commercial Law and the Uniform Code," Seattle University School of Law, http://lawlibguides.seattleu.edu, accessed April 12, 2012.

15. Charles V. Bagli, "Court Upholds Columbia Campus Expansion Plan," *The New York Times,* http://www.nytimes.com, accessed April 12, 2012.

16. Scott Streater, "Utah Eminent Domain Law More Than a 'Message Bill,'" *The New York Times,* http://www.nytimes.com, accessed April 12, 2012.

17. Mark Sweney, "Google Wins Louis Vuitton Trademark Case," *The Guardian,* http://www.guardian.co.uk, accessed April 12, 2012.

18. "Patent Reform Act of 2011: An Overview," *Patently-O,* http://www .patentlyo.com, accessed April 12, 2012.

19. Dominic Rushe, "US Judge Writes Unhappy Ending for Google's Online Library Plans," *The Guardian,* http://www.guardian.co.uk, accessed April 12, 2012.

20. Melissa J. Lauritch, "New Wisconsin Law in Toxic Tort Litigation," Martindale.com, http://www.martindale.com, accessed April 12, 2012.

21. Duff Wilson, "Sharp Increase in March in Personal Bankruptcies," *The New York Times,* http://www.nytimes.com, accessed April 12, 2012; Tiffany Hsu, "Personal Bankruptcies Fall in 2011 to One Out of 175 Americans," *Los Angeles Times,* http://articles.latimes.com, accessed April 12, 2012.

Appendix B

1. Erik Holm, "Hartford to Enter Pay-as-You-Drive Arena," Market Watch. com, http://www.marketwatch.com, accessed April 6, 2012; Jamie Reno, "'Pay-as-You-Drive' Auto Insurance Raises Privacy Concerns," Newsmax. com, http://www.newsmax.com, accessed April 6, 2012; Ameet Sachdev, "Insurers Try Basing Rates on Individual Cars' Data," *Los Angeles Times,* http://articles.latimes.com, accessed April 6, 2012; Tara Baukus Melio,

"Save with Pay-as-You-Drive Car Insurance?" Bankrate.com, http://www.bankrate.com, accessed April 6, 2012; Ina Fried, "Progressive Insurance Taps AT&T to Get a Snapshot of Customers' Driving Habits," *All Things Digital,* http://www.allthingsd.com, accessed April 6, 2012; Carol Lachnit, "Pay-as-You-Drive Insurance Goes into High Gear," Edmunds.com, http://www.edmunds.com, accessed April 6, 2012.

2. *ACLI Life Insurers Fact Book 2011,* Table 10.3, "Life Insurance in Force, by State," http://www.acli.com, accessed April 13, 2012.

3. "Claim Costs from Lightning Continue to Rise: The Culprit Is Often Expensive Electronics," *Insurance Information Institute,* http://www.iii.org, accessed April 13, 2012; Robert P. Hartwig, "2010—Year End Results," Insurance Information Institute, http://www.iii.org, accessed April 13, 2012.

4. "Home Buyers Insurance Checklist," *Insurance Information Institute,* http://www.iii.org, accessed April 13, 2012.

5. "Insurance Requirements," Walmart Web site, http://walmartstores.com, accessed April 13, 2012.

6. "Patient Protection and Affordable Care Act (PPACA) Guidelines Effective September 23rd, 2010," *JLBH Health,* August 17, 2010, http://www.jlbghealth.com, accessed April 13, 2012.

Appendix C

1. Ruth Mantell, "How You Can Get a Raise This Year," *The Wall Street Journal,* February 12, 2012, http://online.wsj.com; press release, "American Workers Focused on Personal Financial Recovery for 2012," *Accounting Principals,* January 30, 2012, http://www.accountingprincipals.com; Jen Wieczner, "Will Peer Pressure Make Americans Save More?" Smart Money.com, http://www.smartmoney.com, accessed January 30, 2012; Lisa V. Gillespie, "Getting Retirement Plan Buy-In from 'Gen Me' Employees," *Employee Benefit Adviser,* http://eba.benefitnews.com, accessed January 30, 2012; Danielle Andrus, "Millennials See Social Security as Doomed, Aren't Saving, Either," *Advisor One,* http://www.advisorone.com, accessed January 30, 2012.

2. Robert Pear, "Recession Officially Over, U.S. Incomes Kept Falling," *The New York Times,* http://www.nytimes.com, accessed March 7, 2012.

3. Emily Brandon, "Poll: More Americans Postpone Retirement," *SecondAct,* February 16, 2012, http://www.secondact.com.

4. American Bankruptcy Institute, "November Consumer Bankruptcy Filings Drop 12 Percent from Last Year," press release, http://www.abiworld.org, accessed March 7, 2012; "U.S. Personal Bankruptcies Below 2010 Pace," *The Wall Street Journal,* http://blogs.wsj.com, accessed March 7, 2012.

5. "Consumer Credit," *Federal Reserve Statistical Release,* March 7, 2012, http://federalreserve.gov.

6. Ryan Yates, "How Not to Be Average When It Comes to Credit Card Debt," *Deliver Away Debt,* http://deliverawaydebt.com, accessed March 7, 2012.

7. National Bureau of Economic Research, "Auto Insurance and Traffic Fatalities," http://www.nber.org, accessed March 27, 2012.

Appendix D

1. Company Web site, http://www.roadid.com, accessed February 26, 2012; Margaret Littman, "A Dad's Cautionary Advice Led to a Growing Family Business," *Entrepreneur,* February 25, 2012, http://www.entrepreneur.com; Greg Friese, "First Responder Outreach Campaign by Road ID," Everyday EMS Tips.com, www.everydayemstips.com, accessed February 25, 2012.

Appendix E

1. U.S. Census Bureau, "Table 708. Average Earnings of Year-Round, Full-Time Workers by Educational Attainment: 2009," *Current Population Reports,* http://www.census.gov, accessed March 28, 2012.

2. "College Internships," *College View,* http://www.collegeview.com, accessed March 28, 2012; Susan Adams, "The Best Internships for 2011," *Forbes,* http://www.forbes.com, accessed March 28, 2012.

3. "The Cooperative Education Model," National Commission for Cooperative Education, http://www.co-op.edu, accessed March 28, 2012.

4. "Take Our Career Aptitude Test!" *Career Explorer,* http://www.careerexplorer.net, accessed March 28, 2012; "Free Career Test!" *Live Career,* http://www.livecareer.com, accessed March 28, 2012; "Assessing Your Skills," *Monster,* http://career-advice.monster.com, accessed March 28, 2012.

5. "Paula's Story," *Paula Deen.com,* http://www.pauladeen.com, accessed March 29, 2012.

6. "Chronological Resume: The Preferred Resume Layout," *Top Sales Jobs,* http://www.top-sales-jobs.com, accessed March 29, 2012.

7. Kim Isaacs, "Five Resume Tips for College Students," *Monster.com,* accessed March 29, 2012; Michael Murray, "Five Resume Tips for College Students," *The Student Development Company,* December 14, 2011, http://www.thestudentdevelopment.com.

8. Eugene Volokh, "How to Write a Great Cover Letter: Top 7 Tips," *Opposing Views,* February 22, 2012, http://www.opposingviews.com; "Here's an Example of a Great Cover Letter," *Ask a Manager,* September 14, 2011, http://www.askamanager.com.

9. Debra Wheatman, "5 Tricks to Get Noticed When Submitting a Resume Online," *GlassDoor.com,* February 9, 2011, http://www.glassdoor.com; Pattie Hunt Sinacole, "Tips on Sending a Resume via Email," *Boston.com,* January 31, 2011, http://www.boston.com.

10. Carole Martin, "Ten Tips to Boost Your Interview IQ," docstoc.com, July 4, 2011, http://www.docstoc.com.

11. Rob Taub, "How to Answer Tough Interview Questions Correctly," *Career Realism,* January 19, 2012, http://www.careerrealism.com.

12. U.S. Bureau of Labor Statistics, "Overview of Projections to 2020," *Monthly Labor Review,* January 2012, http://www.bls.gov.

13. Ibid.

14. Ibid.

15. Ibid.

16. Organization Web site, "Job Outlook 2012," http://www.nace.org, accessed March 29, 2012.

Name Index

Entries in **bold** refer to the "Business Terms You Need to Know," which are listed at the end of each chapter.

Subject Index

*Entries in **bold** refer to the "Business Terms You Need to Know," which are listed at the end of each chapter.*

C

Cable television, 387–388, 399
CAD (computer-aided design), 295
Cafeteria benefit plans, 241
CAFTA-DR (Central America-Dominican Republic Free Trade Agreement), 414
Call provisions, 494
CAM (computer-aided manufacturing), 295
Camera industry, 361
Canada
  IFRS standards compliance, 480
  international unions in, 250
  NAFTA participation, 113, 114
  Nordstrom expansion in, 28
  trade with U.S., 100
  uranium mining, 92
Candle market, 194
Capital, 6–7
Capital investment analysis, 529
Capital items, 357
Capital structure, 530–534
Capitalism, 8, 72–75, 77. *See also* **Private enterprise system**
CARD Act of 2009, 402, A-32, A-38
Career assessment exercises
  economics and global business, 131
  entrepreneurship and business ownership, 199
  finance, 549
  information technology, 455
  management, 319
  marketing, 427
  self-assessment, A-55–A-56
Career centers, A-57
Careers. *See also* Job search; Jobs
  accepting a job, A-67–A-68
  in accounting, 457
  basic considerations, A-52–A-53
  in finance, 548–549
  in global business and economics, 130–131
  in information technology, 455
  internships and, A-53–A-54
  job interviews, A-64–A-67
  job market and, A-68–A-69
  job search guidelines, A-56–A-59

long-range view of, A-69–A-70
  in management, 318–319
  in marketing, 426–427
  personal finance and, A-36
  résumé preparation, A-59–A-64
  self-assessment for, A-55–A-56
  small business and entrepreneurial, 198–199
Carpooling, 20
Car-sharing, 352–353, 452–453
Cash, as short-term asset, 527–528
Cash budgets, 477–478, 528, 535
Cash flow, 471, 473, 526
Cash value life insurance, A-28
Category advisors, 367
Category managers, 367
Cause advertising, 398
Cause marketing, 328
Celebrities
  advertising by, 391, 392
  campaigns for nonprofits, 326
Cell phones. *See* Mobile phones
Central America-Dominican Republic Free Trade Agreement (CAFTA-DR), 114
Centralization, 221–222
Century bonds, 525
CEOs. *See* Chief executive officers (CEOs)
Certificates of deposit (CDs), 492
Certified financial planners (CFPs), 549
Certified fraud examiners, 460
Certified internal auditors, 460
Certified management accountants (CMAs), 460, 461
Certified public accountants (CPAs), 460
CFOs. *See* Chief financial officers (CFOs)
Chain of command, 222
Change, leadership for, 22
Change in demand, 67
Change in quantity demanded, 67
Channels, in communication process, 272, 273

Charitable participation, 43. *See also* **Corporate philanthropy; Social responsibility**
Chartered financial analysts (CFAs), 549
Chartering a corporation, 157–158
Check cards, 504
Check clearing, 507–508
Check Clearing for the 21st Century Act, 507–508
Checking accounts, 505, A-37
Chickpea program, Ethiopia, 31
Chief executive officers (CEOs)
  compensation for, 159, 247–248
  defined, 159
  financial management role, 522
Chief financial officers (CFOs)
  defined, 159
  financial plan preparation, 525–526
  overview of role, 522–523
Chief information officers (CIOs), 430
Chief operating officers (COOs), 159, 522
Children's Online Privacy Protection Act, A-9
Chile, customs union in, 113
China
  advertising in, 397
  Apple suppliers in, 126–127
  bedding products factory, 306
  beverage industry, 88
  censorship in, 206
  defective goods from, A-4
  economic growth of, 87
  entrepreneurs in, 174
  fast-food market in, 331, 332
  financial markets in, 102
  flexible manufacturing systems, 296
  GDP growth, 99
  globalization and, 99
  Groupon company and, 120
  guanxi, 122
  huilui practice, 108
  luxury goods market, 387
  multinational corporations in, 120
  multivitamin production, 310
  offshoring in, 19, 119
  potential Facebook presence, 206
  rare-earth metal export restrictions, A-4

recalls in, 88
  shift toward market-oriented economy, 76
  textile production in, 100, 101
  trade with U.S., 100, 102, 109
Chip manufacturing, 289
Chronological résumés, A-60
CIM (computer-integrated manufacturing), 296
CIOs (chief information officers), 430
Circuit courts, A-3
Civil Rights Act of 1964, 53, 56, 234
Civil Rights Act of 1991, 53, 54, 235
Class-Action Fairness Act of 2005, A-15
Class-action suits, A-15
Classic entrepreneurs, 171
Classroom training, 236
Clayton Act, 74, A-6
Clean energy. *See* Renewable energy
Cleaning products, sustainability and, 62, 368
Click-through rates, 351
Closed/closely held corporations, 158
Closing the sale, 410
Clothing industry. *See* Apparel manufacturing
Cloud computing, 444, 445, 446, 523
Cobranding, 346
Cocoa, sustainable, 47
Code of conduct, 32, 40–41
Code of ethics
  for entrepreneurs, 181
  Sarbanes-Oxley Act requirements, 34
Coffee industry
  fair trade practices, 28–29, 519
  freshness of coffee, 28–29
  McCafé coffee bars, 342
  social networking for, 29, 377
  Starbucks sustainability programs, 43
Cognitive ability tests, 235
Cognitive conflict, 271
Collaboration, innovation through, 19–20
Collective (cooperative) ownership, 156
Collective bargaining, 251
College savings programs, A-40–A-41

International Index

*Entries in **bold** refer to the "Business Terms You Need to Know," which are listed at the end of each chapter.*